JOHN BRANDES

Philosophic Problems

Edited by

MAURICE MANDELBAUM
The Johns Hopkins University

FRANCIS W. GRAMLICH
Dartmouth College

ALAN ROSS ANDERSON
University of Pittsburgh

JEROME B. SCHNEEWIND
University of Pittsburgh

Philosophic Problems

An Introductory Book of Readings

SECOND EDITION

The Macmillan Company, New York

Collier-Macmillan Limited, London

Preface

This volume, like its predecessor, is designed to furnish material for a one-term introductory course in philosophy. Primary emphasis has been placed on perennial problems in philosophy rather than on particular schools of thought, ancient or modern. We have accordingly tried to provide readings that will help students find out for themselves that philosophical questions, in spite of their antiquity, remain fascinating.

More is included here than can be conveniently covered in a one-term course. The reason for this is obvious: competent teachers of diverse philosophical persuasions like to organize courses differently. Custom requires that pages of a book be numbered consecutively, but the organization of this book need not be followed by any reader; indeed, some of us have begun introductory courses with the last section.

This second edition contains two innovations, in addition to changes in contents: (1) annotated lists of readings designed to help those students who want to follow a topic more closely are appended to each section; (2) some readings of a more specialized nature are given under the heading "Current Issues." These issues are "current" only in the sense that they are currently under vigorous discussion. We do not mean to suggest that they are novel; their roots lie in earlier discussions, which prepare the reader to understand what is at stake.

We should like to extend our thanks to Mr. Louis Goble, who has helped us in a variety of ways, and to Mr. John D. Moore of The Macmillan Company, for his kind, patient (and persistent) assistance in preparing this volume for the press.

M. M. / F. W. G. / A. R. A. / J. B. S.

Contents

III   KNOWLEDGE AND BELIEF

IV ✒ MIND, BODY, AND FREEDOM

V   THE NATURE AND STRUCTURE OF MORALITY

VI ✍ RELIGION AND NATURALISM

Philosophic Problems

I ❧ WHAT IS PHILOSOPHY?

Philosophy has been described in a number of ways, but no single characterization has won universal assent among philosophers. There is a sense, of course, in which we all know what philosophy is; we all discuss topics traditionally placed under the heading "philosophy." For example, we have implicit or explicit beliefs about human freedom, about right and wrong, about the existence of God. But the philosophical views that we acquire uncritically (and in large part unconsciously) from our culture are usually quite different from those we arrive at after a detailed and disciplined study of the issues involved. We take it for granted that the tables and chairs around us *really* are (in some sense) as they *appear* to be; that they are made of hard *substances* such as wood or metal; that they have *properties,* such as color, which can be *changed* while leaving the underlying substance unchanged, or *permanent;* that we come to *know* about all these things by seeing, hearing, feeling, and so on. But when we come to think about these concepts—*appearance* and *reality, substance* and *property, permanence* and *change, knowledge*—it becomes clear that they are not so transparent as we may unreflectingly believe. To choose a single example, current physical theories may lead us to believe that a table is (or perhaps, *really* is) a swarm of energy-packets, in constant motion, which are organized into atoms and molecules, which in turn manifest the familiar property of color as a result of action of light waves on the retina.

How do physicists find out these things? What relations hold between the common-sense table and the physicist's account? For that matter, we might ask similar questions simply about our common-sense views. A table we believe to be *really* square, sometimes *looks* diamond-shaped. We invoke theories of perspective to explain these "distortions"—but which is the distortion and which is the truth?

Parallel problems arise when we think of the persons who populate our environment. Each of our lives is marked by great changes in the size and shape of our bodies and by equally great changes in personality traits, intellectual abilities, sensitivity to various experiences, and the like. Yet we feel that a person remains *one thing* throughout the vast variety of changes he undergoes. We also notice that some of these changes may involve moral character. Othello was in one way *the same man* before and after Iago aroused his jealousy, but we describe him in a different way—as a murderer—when he failed to curb his jealousy and killed Desdemona.

Is it possible to take concepts like *same, different, permanence, change, cause,* which are not the special property of any of the particular sciences or arts, and put them together, or *synthesize* them, in such a way as to provide a coherent picture of the whole? Or could some similar picture be drawn concerning the relations of men to nature and to each other which would clarify our understanding of mankind, society, and morality? Finally, can we further generalize so as to give a comprehensive account dealing with both of these broad syntheses, so as to give us one big synoptic picture of the universe?

One mainstream in the Western philosophical tradition contends that the job of philosophy is to answer just such questions. This point of view is espoused by SIDGWICK: philosophy should lead to a synthesis of the most general concepts and principles involved in other areas of knowledge, including the results both of the sciences, and of a general theory of value.

BROAD agrees with Sidgwick in taking the results of scientific investigations as a starting point for one important branch of philosophical inquiry, but he places a different emphasis on the importance of synthetic speculation. While granting the value of an attempt to view the universe synoptically, he holds that such *speculative philosophy* must necessarily rest on *critical philosophy,* which is more likely to reach well-grounded results. The critical branch of philosophy deals with the analysis of concepts and the critical appraisal of fundamental assumptions; it is only *after* this task has been accomplished that we can begin to attempt a synthesis of the kind Sidgwick envisaged. Even then speculative philosophy is more likely to be purely suggestive of interesting ideas, than it is to lead to the solid conclusions that mark the results of its critical counterpart.

Both Sidgwick and Broad tend to think of philosophy as a body of knowledge, like other particular disciplines except that it is more general. COLLINGWOOD rejects this idea and argues rather that philosophy should be viewed as an *activity.* It is not the task of philosophy to provide us with a body of results, such as Broad requires of critical philosophy. We do not learn new facts of which we were formerly ignorant; we simply come to understand better some things we already knew, vaguely, all along. The critical function of philosophy lies largely in finding errors and the inadequacies in the writings of our predecessors, in the light of the continuing expansion of our knowledge and experience. The principal value of philosophical activity is to be found in the increased comprehension it gives us of the world in which we live, and for this reason it must be both constructive and speculative.

WARNOCK gives an account of the views of Ludwig Wittgenstein, who agreed with Collingwood that philosophy should be thought of as an activity. But in contrast with Collingwood, he thought of this activity as primarily critical and to some extent even destructive. Still, this kind of activity was supposed to lead to a new understanding, because careful and detailed analysis of the errors and confusions to be found in much of philosophy in a sense "takes off our conceptual blinders" and enables us to see how we have been victimized by inadequate, confused, and inaccurate ways of talking and thinking about the problems.

Unlike any of the foregoing philosophers, JASPERS finds the principal source of problems in our awareness of, and wonder and doubt concerning, fundamental human situations: love, birth, suffering, struggle, death. He agrees with Wittgenstein that every man must try to be his own philosopher, and he agrees with both Wittgenstein and Collingwood that philosophy is not the possession of truth but the search for it. On the other hand, he disagrees with the view of both Broad and Sidgwick that philosophy springs from science. Science is relevant, but the basic concern is with problems of human beings in society and in particular with their desperate need to communicate with one another about fundamental aspects of human existence. This communication leads to a heightened consciousness of one's own being and that of others. In short, the aim of philosophy is to find one's Self and to attain peace of soul with the aid of love as rooted in communication with the Other.

As was remarked at the outset, philosophers are not in general agreement about the nature and methods of philosophy; what philosophy and its method is, or should be, is itself an important philosophical question. But in spite of the variety of interests and approaches among philosophers, all agree on one important point: competent philosophical investigations proceed by the examination of a problem in the light of all available relevant evidence, without limitation to special disciplines or restricted areas of experience. It is for this reason that philosophy has perhaps most appropriately been described as "an unusually persistent attempt to think things through."

Philosophy as Synthesis[*]

Henry Sidgwick [1838–1900] was educated at Cambridge University, taught there, and helped found its first college for women. He is best known for his *Methods of Ethics,* a careful and comprehensive study of alternative ways of synthesizing our moral beliefs. He also wrote an excellent short *History of Ethics.*

I wish to give to the term 'Philosophy' a meaning which will be (1) clear, (2) useful—*i.e.* which will denote something that wants a separate name—and (3) *as far as possible* in conformity with common usage. Note that the last aim cannot be attained completely, so far as common usage is confused and varying: *e.g.* so far as Philosophy is confounded with Science. Still I think that here and in other cases we may find distinctions, vaguely and imperfectly recognised in ordinary discourse, which when made clear and explicit will furnish the required definition. So far as usage is vague and varying, it would be futile to aim at complete uniformity with it: but in my view there is a distinction between 'Philosophy' and the subjects otherwise named which I seek to distinguish from it precisely—Science, Psychology, Epistemology, Logic, etc.—which is more or less recognised in the ordinary thought of educated persons and may be made clear by careful reflection.

I will first endeavour to distinguish Philosophy from Science. Science is certainly a kind of knowledge: no one doubts that the geometer, physicist, botanist, has attained important knowledge that other men lack who have not studied geometry, physics, botany.

It will be convenient to begin by getting a definition of Science. In the first place scientific knowledge is clearly systematic knowledge, or knowledge arranged and grasped in a certain order; a number of cognitions of particular facts, however accurately observed, do not constitute science so long as they remain loose and unconnected. Still knowledge may be systematised otherwise than in Science: thus History systematises our knowledge of past events by arranging them in order of time, and Geography systematises our knowledge of states, cities, rivers, mountains, etc. by giving a connected view of their positions on the surface of the globe. But neither of these arrangements is as such scientific, though scientific method may be required to work it out with accuracy and completeness. Shall we say then that Science systematises by ascertaining the causal relations of facts; that scientific

[*] From Sidgwick: *Philosophy, Its Scope and Relations: An Introductory Course of Lectures,* Macmillan & Co., Ltd., 1902.

knowledge is "knowledge of effects as dependent on their causes." This is largely true; still it seems too narrow a conception for the ordinary denotation of the term. 'Science,' as ordinarily used, is applied to the abstract studies of relations of quantity which we class together as pure mathematics, where causation is altogether ignored: it is applied also to such studies as Botany and Zoology, where the investigation of causes, though it certainly forms a part of these studies, is not the sole ground of their claim to be called 'sciences.' It is, partly at least, as systematising the matter studied, by arranging objects according to relations of resemblance, that Botany and Zoology have been regarded as scientific. They have been called Sciences of Classification, and it was *primarily* as classificatory that they assumed the character of sciences: though all would agree that they reach a higher stage of development, so far as they become Sciences of Causation also.

To get a definition of Science applicable to all the instances named we must, I think, take the characteristic of 'generality' as the essential distinction between scientific knowledge and merely 'historical' knowledge of particular facts. The mathematical sciences deal with objects essentially general; the study of causes is a study of general laws or uniformities—for a cause is a kind of thing which tends *generally*, and not merely in one particular case, to be followed by the kind of thing which we call its effect. The classificatory sciences are concerned, as their name imports, with classes—'genera' and 'species'—or general types. It is true that we largely regard knowledge of particular facts—*e.g.* of a new planet—as scientific knowledge; but only, I think, in view of its relation to general knowledge. Thus an uninstructed person might conceivably discover a new planet by accidentally looking through a telescope at the right time; but this observation would be unscientific, though of great value to science.

I regard 'Philosophy' then—if the term is used without qualification—as the study which 'takes all knowledge for its province.' To such a study the human mind would be palpably incompetent if it attempted to deal with all the facts: it therefore selects the most important. Thus if we conceive the sciences as sets of connected knowledge, and imagine them as rising from the particular to the general, we may consider these sets in their turn as connected by Philosophy at the higher end. Philosophy, therefore, deals not with the whole matter of any science, but with the most important of its special notions, its fundamental principles, its distinctive method, its main conclusions. Philosophy examines these with the view of co-ordinating them with the fundamental notions and principles, methods and conclusions of other sciences. It may be called in this sense 'scientia scientiarum.'

The important distinction is that the Sciences concentrate attention on particular parts or aspects while it is, in contrast, the essential characteristic of Philosophy that it aims at putting together the parts of knowledge thus attained into a systematic whole; so that all methods of attaining truth may be grasped as parts of one method; and all the conclusions attained may be presented, so far as possible, as harmonious and consistent.

Perhaps some devotee of a special science may ask, "Is it worth while to do this till we have gone further in our knowledge of the parts?"

To this there is more than one answer. The most important answer I will give more fully later. Here I will say that in fact we cannot help doing it somehow. We grow up with ideas of the whole, which are continually modified as our knowledge extends: and no student of any special science ever acquiesces in having no idea of the relation of his part of knowledge to the rest. He may avoid philosophy in the sense of avoiding the attempt to make his conception of the universe as clear, precise, and systematic as possible, but that only means that he will be content with a vague, obscure, and altogether inadequate conception.

In fact, when a writer speaks of another's arguments as 'unphilosophical,' he often seems to mean no more than that he profoundly disagrees with him. It would, however, be a pity to allow the word to be used in this sense: and perhaps the different schools would agree that there is an instructed and an uninstructed way of reasoning on behalf of what each school regards as sound conclusions; the characteristic of an instructed way of reasoning being that it shows an adequate knowledge of the arguments used on the other side, some apprehension of their force, and that it endeavours either to meet or to avoid those arguments. Philosophical knowledge in this sense—on points on which experts are disagreed—would be knowledge of the confusions of thought to which the human intellect is liable when it begins to speculate on the questions of Philosophy: knowledge of how to state these questions so as to avoid to some extent confusions of thought: and knowledge of considerations that have some force, though not necessarily decisive force, for or against conclusions on disputed questions of Philosophy. And if Philosophy is regarded as a subject of academic teaching and study, this, I conceive, is the kind of knowledge which the teacher ought mainly to seek to convey, on subjects of controversy.

But it is evident that this acquaintance with arguments is not the kind of knowledge at which Philosophy *aims*, although it may be all the knowledge for which a consensus of experts can be claimed at present. So long as this is so, the notion of philosophy being a *pursuit* rather than a system of knowledge will maintain itself, as it has maintained itself throughout two thousand years in which dogmatic systems have succeeded each other. This lack of a 'consensus of experts' as to the method and main conclusions of Philosophy, is, I fear, strong evidence that study of it is still—after so many centuries—in a rudimentary condition as compared with the more special studies of the branches of systematised knowledge that we call Sciences. As philosophers we aim at knowledge of the whole, and therefore at knowledge of the underlying reality.

The complete unification at which Philosophy aims must enable us to view every portion of knowledge—and every object known—as a part of a coherent whole: and in comprehending the relation of diverse parts of a whole to the whole, and to each other, systematic difference—difference essentially belonging to the nature of the whole—is as important a feature as resemblance.

This statement is perhaps hardly clear without illustration. What, it may be asked, is exactly meant by comprehending differences as 'rational' and 'systematic' and 'following from the nature of the whole'? The best way to make this clear will be to take some case in which sciences have been—as Mr. Spencer says—'unified' by the comprehension of narrower in wider generalisations. I will take the most famous case, the identification, worked out mathematically by Newton, of the fundamental laws of terrestrial with the fundamental laws of celestial motion. When men began to observe and reflect on physical phenomena, the movements of falling bodies to the earth seemed as unlike as possible to the movements of the starry heavens: the former moved in a straight line, and the latter—apart from the problem presented by the planets—were, it seemed, circular and uniform. In each case the true view of the matter was impeded by erroneous inferences from observation—in the case of terrestrial motion by the erroneous idea that heavy bodies fall quicker than light bodies, and in the case of celestial motions by the simple and inevitable geocentric hypothesis.

Well, we all know vaguely how the erroneous view of terrestrial motions was cleared away—chiefly by Galileo; and the heliocentric substituted for the geocentric hypothesis—chiefly through the work of Copernicus—and how the marvellous industry and genius of Kepler working on the observations of Tycho Brahe had ascertained the empirical laws of the movements of planets round the sun—i.e. that they moved not in circles but in ellipses with the sun in one focus, and that each moved at such a rate as to describe equal areas of the orbit in equal times. When the knowledge of the two kinds of motion had come to this point, matters were ripe for the great identification which comprehended planetary motions as a case of the operation of the law of universal gravitation.

But, you will observe, this identification or unification did not merely point out the similarity between the two kinds of motion, but it at the same time explained the differences—explained, that is, why bodies fall to the earth approximately in a straight line, while planets go round the sun in ellipses: these *prima facie* diverse kinds of motion being both viewed as different applications of the same general laws of matter in motion.

Now take, by contrast, Mr. Spencer's great generalisation—the doctrine of Evolution. Mr. Spencer claims to comprehend the chief laws of the changes through which the world of inorganic matter has passed in time, the laws of the world of organic life, and the laws of mental development, by comprehending them under the same great law of Evolution or 'progress from indefinite, incoherent homogeneity to definite, coherent heterogeneity.' I shall have occasion to criticise this doctrine later on: but what I now wish to point out is that however completely we may grant that certain resemblances have been made out between (1) the laws of change in inorganic and organic matter and (2) the laws of change and development of mind, the resemblance does not in the least help us to explain the differences between the world of living things and the inorganic world. The differences between mind and matter still remain unexplained by the generalisation, and present unsolved problems for philosophy, just as obstinate and perplexing, *after* we have admitted the evolutional doctrine, as they were before.

The knowledge at which the sciences aim, and which they claim to have partially attained, is knowledge of what exists or has existed or will exist.

If so, it seems clear that the matter presented by Science so defined cannot be regarded as the whole of the matter on which Philosophy has to work. For Philosophy must deal with the principles and methods of rationally determining 'what ought to be,' as distinct from the principles and methods of ascertaining what is, has been, and will be. The current use of the terms 'Moral' and 'Political' Philosophy clearly implies this department of the work of Philosophy. We cannot say that there is no such thing as Moral or Political Philosophy, without violent divergence from common thought and common usage of terms: and on the other hand we cannot say that Moral or Political Philosophy has for its business the co-ordination of the co-existences and sequences of phenomena, without neglecting the fundamental distinction between 'what ought to be' and what actually is or appears. We must therefore, I think, give a wider scope to the term 'Philosophy' than we have hitherto given, and regard it as including in the range of its 'unifying' function not only the systems of knowledge commonly called 'sciences' or 'positive sciences,' but also the systems of knowledge or reasoned thought distinguished as Ethics, Politics, and Jurisprudence.

I have spoken of Ethics, Politics, and Jurisprudence. The last mentioned is clearly distinguished in ordinary thought from Philosophy. There are, no doubt, philosophical jurists; but all jurists are not as such philosophers: it is recognised that a man may have a sound knowledge of law—even of the conceptions and rules of law in general, as distinct from the law of a particular state—without being at all a philosopher. The distinction between Ethics or Politics and Philosophy is not so clear: still I think that some distinction is vaguely made in ordinary thought, and might with advantage be made somewhat more explicit. It is vaguely recognised that it is the business of *Ethics* to supply an answer to questions as to details of duty or right conduct—so far as they are questions which it is held legitimate, and not idle, to ask—but that this is not the business of Moral or Ethical *Philosophy,* which is primarily concerned with the general principles and methods of moral reasoning, and only with details of conduct so far as the discussion of them affords instructive examples of general principles and method. It is commonly felt that an attempt to work out a complete system of duties would inevitably lead us out of Philosophy into Casuistry: and that whether Casuistry is a good thing or a bad thing, it certainly is not Philosophy.

A similar distinction may, I think, be applied to Politics:—accordingly when I had to select a title for a bulky volume in which I have attempted to treat systematically the chief questions for which the statesman has to find answers, I called the book 'Elements of Politics,' not 'Political Philosophy' or 'Political Science.' I did not call it Political Philosophy, since it aims at determining the rules for governmental action, and for the construction of governmental organs with more fulness of detail than it belongs to Philosophy to do: nor, again, did I call it Political Science, since it is primarily concerned with polity as it ought to be, and not with polities as they are, have been, and—so far as we can foresee—will be.

I think, then, that we have to recognise it as part of the business of Philosophy, to 'unify' the principles and methods of reasoning directed to practical conclusions, which we call 'political' when they refer to the constitution and action of government, and 'ethical' when they refer to private conduct. We may call this part or function of Philosophy 'practical,' as distinct from the Philosophy that seeks to unify those sciences, which we may suitably call 'theoretical' or 'positive,'—according as we wish to imply that the objects of scientific knowledge are *real* or merely *phenomenal.* Taking science as conversant with real existence, I shall provisionally use the term 'theoretical.'

In insisting on the recognition of the two departments of Philosophy as fundamental and important, I do not wish to imply that there is an absolute separation between them: and that there are in reality two quite separate studies, one systematising the different sciences, and the other systematising the different ends of human action and the different sets of rules for practice, or ideals of what ought to be. On the contrary, I wish to emphasize, as the final and most important task of Philosophy, the problem of coordinating these two divisions of its subject-matter, and connecting fact and ideal in some rational and satisfactory manner. The problem, however, must be recognised as a very difficult one. For its solution should enable us to answer the question 'How comes it that what ought to be is not and yet ought to be?': or, negatively, 'Whence comes the existence of what ought not to be?' And any one who knows anything of the history of human thought may well despair of attaining a satisfactory answer to this question;—unless he holds firmly to the conviction that such despair, at any rate, is one of the things that ought not to be.

Let us pass on to contemplate the admitted common ground of Philosophy and Psychology—Thoughts, Judgments, Beliefs. I shall try to show that there are important differences between the methods and aims of the two studies in treating this common subject-matter. These differences chiefly spring from or are connected with an essential characteristic of thoughts or beliefs as investigated by Philosophy, which we have not yet noticed: *viz.* that they are assumed to be true and valid. This is obviously involved in the view of Theoretical Philosophy as systematising the sciences; since a science is a system of true beliefs: so far as any actual science as taught is not this, it is imperfect or spurious science. So again Practical Philosophy is in intention a theory of the principles of what 'really' ought to be; *i.e.* not of what men merely think or judge ought to be, but of what they truly so think or judge. Philosophy therefore is concerned primarily with truth, and only secondarily with error in order to distinguish it from truth, or to elicit the element of truth contained in it. Psychology on the other hand has for its function to discriminate, analyse into elements, classify, and ascertain the laws of all such beliefs or thoughts as are found among the phenomena of the particular minds observed; of the false no less than the true. For instance, in studying laws of association of ideas, the associations that lead the mind to wrong judgment and expectation are just as interesting as those that lead to right judgment and expectation; and may even sometimes be more interesting and more instructive examples of the laws of association. Indeed the characteristic of being true or untrue is not one which necessarily claims our attention —so far at least as the true or untrue beliefs are not psychological beliefs—so long as we are merely concerned with mind as the object of a special science, abstracted as far as possible from the objects of other sciences.

But further: even so far as Philosophy and Psychology are both concerned with true beliefs, still from the point of view of either study respectively these beliefs are connected and systematised in ways *prima facie* different. The general aim of Psychology, in the systematisation that it attempts of mental facts, is—besides classifying them,—to discover the laws of coexistence and sequence among them: accordingly, so far as it is concerned with knowledge or true beliefs, it aims at ascertaining the order in which and the processes by which the particular minds observed actually pass from one part of knowledge to another. On the other hand, the aim of Philosophy, in dealing with the same beliefs, is to arrange them in such order as may make manifest the important permanent relations among them,—*e.g.* the relations of the simple to the complex, of the more general to the less general, of the fundamental principles of any science to their applications or the deductions founded on them. Relations of this latter kind are, speaking broadly, the same for all minds that think and judge truly respecting them; whereas the former may and do vary from one mind to another, and include sequences of thought other than valid or cogent inference.

In connexion with this I may observe that in my view Philosophy—so far as it does not construct its system, or aim at constructing it completely *a priori*—uses primarily what I may call the Dialectical Method, *i.e.* the method of reflection on the thought which we all share, by the aid of the symbolism which we all share, language: whereas Psychology uses primarily the introspective method of observation by each of his own thoughts and feelings as his own—a group of objects of which he alone can have first-hand knowledge. I do not mean that Philosophy may not use the introspective method, or that Psychology may not use the dialectical, or that the two can be completely separated. But so far as the Philosopher observes the relations of thought in his own individual mind, it is as a means to the end of ascertaining the relations of thought in a normal mind, free from the peculiarities and limitations of his own individual mind. On the other hand, so far as the Psychologist adopts the method of reflecting on the common thought of the society to which he belongs, through the symbolism of its common language, it is as a means to the end of generalisations applicable to the particular experiences of an indefinite number of particular minds. Hence we may put the difference in another form, and say that Psychology is primarily concerned with knowledge and its attainment as processes of thought belonging to particular human minds; but that Philosophy is primarily concerned with the relations of true or valid beliefs as they may be conceived to exist for an ideal mind independent—not only of the errors but—of the particularities of growth and development of particular finite minds.

Philosophy and Science[*]

C H A R L I E D U N B A R B R O A D [1887–   ] studied at Cambridge University and (with the exception of seven years at Dundee and Bristol) has taught at Cambridge since he took his degree. He has written extensively on metaphysics, ethics, the philosophy of science, and the history of philosophy. In 1953 he retired from the Knightsbridge Professorship of Moral Philosophy at Cambridge. The following year he was a Visiting Professor at the University of Michigan and at the University of California at Los Angeles.

Common sense constantly makes use of a number of concepts, in terms of which it interprets its experience. It talks of *things* of various kinds; it says that they have *places* and *dates,* that they *change,* and that *changes* in one *cause* changes in others, and so on. Thus it makes constant use of such concepts or categories as thinghood, space, time, change, cause, etc. Science takes over these concepts from common-sense with but slight modification, and uses them in its work. Now we can and do *use* concepts without having any very clear idea of their meaning or their mutual relations. I do not of course suggest that to the ordinary man the words *substance, cause, change,* etc., are mere meaningless noises, like *Jabberwock* or *Snark.* It is clear that we mean something, and something different in each case, by such words. If we did not we could not use them consistently, and it is obvious that on the whole we do consistently apply and withhold such names. But it is possible to apply concepts more or less successfully when one has only a very confused idea as to their meaning. No man confuses place with date, and for practical purposes any two men agree as a rule in the places that they assign to a given object. Nevertheless, if you ask them what exactly they mean by *place* and *date,* they will be puzzled to tell you.

Now the most fundamental task of Philosophy is to take the concepts that we daily use in common life and science, to analyse them, and thus to determine their precise meanings and their mutual relations. Evidently this is an important duty. In the first place, clear and accurate knowledge of anything is an advance on a mere hazy general familiarity with it. Moreover, in the absence of clear knowledge of the meanings and relations of the concepts

[*] From Broad: *Scientific Thought,* Chapter 1. Copyright, 1923; Kegan Paul, Trench, Trubner and Co., Ltd., London; Harcourt Brace and Co., New York. Reprinted by permission of Routledge and Kegan Paul, Ltd., London, and Humanities Press, New York.

that we use, we are certain sooner or later to apply them wrongly or to meet with exceptional cases where we are puzzled as to how to apply them at all. For instance, we all agree pretty well as to the place of a certain pin which we are looking at. But suppose we go on to ask: "Where is the image of that pin in a certain mirror; and is it in this place (whatever it may be) in precisely the sense in which the pin itself is in *its* place?" We shall find the question a very puzzling one, and there will be no hope of answering it until we have carefully analysed what we mean by *being in a place*.

Again, this task of clearing up the meanings and determining the relations of fundamental concepts is not performed to any extent by any other science. Chemistry *uses* the notion of substance, geometry that of space, and mechanics that of motion. But they assume that you already know what is meant by *substance* and *space* and *motion*. So you do in a vague way; and it is not their business to enter, more than is necessary for their own special purposes, into the meaning and relations of these concepts as such. Of course the special sciences do in some measure clear up the meanings of the concepts that they use. A chemist, with his distinction between elements and compounds and his laws of combination, has a clearer idea of substance than an ordinary layman. But the special sciences only discuss the meanings of their concepts so far as this is needful for their own special purposes. Such discussion is incidental to them, whilst it is of the essence of Philosophy, which deals with such questions for their own sake. Whenever a scientist begins to discuss the concepts of his science in this thorough and disinterested way we begin to say that he is studying, not so much Chemistry or Physics, as the *Philosophy* of Chemistry or Physics. It will therefore perhaps be agreed that, in the above sense of Philosophy, there is both room and need for such a study, and that there is no special reason to fear that it will be beyond the compass of human faculties.

At this point a criticism may be made which had better be met at once. It may be said: "By your own admission the task of Philosophy is purely verbal; it consists entirely of discussions about the meanings of words." This criticism is of course absolutely wide of the mark. When we say that Philosophy tries to clear up the meanings of concepts we do not mean that it is simply concerned to substitute some long phrase for some familiar word. Any analysis, when once it has been made, is naturally *expressed* in words; but so too is any other discovery. When Cantor gave his definition of Continuity, the final result of his work was expressed by saying that you can substitute for the word "continuous" such and such a verbal phrase. But the essential part of the work was to find out exactly what properties are present in objects when we predicate continuity of them, and what properties are absent when we refuse to predicate continuity. This was evidently not a question of words but of things and their properties.

Philosophy has another and closely connected task. We not only make continual use of vague and unanalysed concepts. We have also a number of uncriticised beliefs, which we constantly assume in ordinary life and in the sciences. We constantly assume, *e.g.* that every event has a cause, that nature obeys uniform laws, that we live in a world of objects whose existence and behaviour are independent of our knowledge of them, and so on. Now science takes over these beliefs without criticism from common-sense, and simply works with them. We know by experience, however, that beliefs which are very strongly held may be mere prejudices. . . . Is it not possible that we believe that nature as a whole will always act uniformly simply because the part of nature in which the human race has lived has happened to act so up to the present? All such beliefs then, however deeply rooted, call for criticism. The first duty of Philosophy is to state them clearly; and this can only be done when we have analysed and defined the concepts that they involve. Until you know exactly what you mean by *change* and *cause* you cannot know what is meant by the statement that *every change has a cause*. And not much weight can be attached to a person's most passionate beliefs if he does not know what precisely he is passionately believing. The next duty of Philosophy is to test such beliefs; and this can only be done by resolutely and honestly exposing them to every objection that one can think of oneself or find in the writings of others. We ought only to go on believing a proposition if, at the end of this process, we still find it impossible to doubt it. Even then of course it may not be true, but we have at least done our best.

These two branches of Philosophy—the analysis and definition of our fundamental concepts, and the clear statement and resolute criticism of our fundamental beliefs—I call *Critical Philosophy*. It is obviously a necessary and a possible task, and it is not performed by any other science. The other sciences *use* the concepts and *assume* the beliefs; Critical Philosophy tries to analyse the former and to criticise the latter. Thus, so long as science and Critical Philosophy keep to their own spheres, there is no possibility of conflict between them, since their subject-matter is quite different. Philosophy claims to analyse the general concepts of substance and cause; *e.g.*, it does not claim to tell us about particular substances, like gold, or about particular laws of causation, as that *aqua regia* dissolves gold. Chemistry, on the other hand, tells us a great deal about the various kinds of substances in the world, and how changes in one cause changes in another. But it does not profess to analyse the general concepts of substance or causation, or to consider what right we have to assume that every event has a cause.

It should now be clear why the method of Philosophy is so different from that of the natural sciences. Experiments are not made, because they would be utterly useless. If you want to find out how one substance behaves in the presence of another you naturally put the two together, vary the conditions, and note the results. But no experiment will clear up your ideas as to the meaning of *cause* in general or of *substance* in general. Again, all conclusions from experiments rest on some of those very assumptions which it is the business of Philosophy to state clearly and to criticise. The experimenter assumes that nature obeys uniform laws, and that similar results will follow always and everywhere from sufficiently similar conditions. This is one of the assumptions that Philosophy wants to consider critically. The method of Philosophy thus resembles that of pure mathematics, at least in the respect that neither has any use for experiment.

There is, however, a very important difference. In pure mathematics we start either from axioms which no one questions, or from premises which are quite explicitly assumed merely as hypotheses; and our main interest is to deduce remote consequences. Now most of the tacit assumptions of ordinary life and of natural science claim to be true and not merely to be hypotheses, and at the same time they are found to be neither clear nor self-evident when critically reflected upon. Most mathematical axioms are very simple and clear, whilst most other propositions which men strongly believe are highly complex and confused. Philosophy is mainly concerned, not with remote conclusions, but with the analysis and appraisement of the original premises. For this purpose analytical power and a certain kind of insight are necessary, and the mathematical method is not of much use.

Now there is another kind of Philosophy; and, as this is more exciting, it is what laymen generally understand by the name. This is what I call *Speculative Philosophy*. It has a different object, is pursued by a different method, and leads to results of a different degree of certainty from Critical Philosophy. Its object is to take over the results of the various sciences, to add to them the results of the religious and ethical experiences of mankind, and then to reflect upon the whole. The hope is that, by this means, we may be able to reach some general conclusions as to the nature of the Universe, and as to our position and prospects in it.

There are several points to be noted about Speculative Philosophy. (i) If it is to be of the slightest use it must presuppose Critical Philosophy. It is useless to take over masses of uncriticised detail from the sciences and from the ethical and religious experiences of men. We do not know what they mean, or what degree of certainty they possess till they have been clarified and appraised by Critical Philosophy. It is thus quite possible that the time for Speculative Philosophy has not yet come; for Critical Philosophy may not have advanced far enough to supply it with a firm basis. In the past people have tended to rush on to Speculative Philosophy, because of its greater practical interest. The result has been the production of elaborate systems which may quite fairly be described as moonshine. The discredit which the general public quite rightly attaches to those hasty attempts at Speculative Philosophy is reflected back on Critical Philosophy, and Philosophy as a whole thus falls into undeserved disrepute.

(ii) At the best Speculative Philosophy can only consist of more or less happy guesses, made on a very slender basis. There is no hope of its reaching the certainty which some parts of Critical Philosophy might quite well attain. Now speculative philosophers as a class have been the most dogmatic of men. They have been more certain of everything than they had a right to be of anything.

(iii) A man's final view of the Universe as a whole, and of the position and prospects of himself and his fellows, is peculiarly liable to be biased by his hopes and fears, his likes and dislikes, and his judgments of value. One's Speculative Philosophy tends to be influenced to an altogether undue extent by the state of one's liver and the amount of one's bank-balance. No doubt livers and bank-balances have their place in the Universe, and no view of it which fails to give them their due weight is ultimately satisfactory. But their due weight is considerably less than their influence on Speculative Philosophy might lead one to suspect. But, if we bear this in mind and try our hardest to be "ethically neutral," we are rather liable to go to the other extreme and entertain a theory of the Universe which renders the existence of our judgments of value unintelligible.

A large part of Critical Philosophy is almost exempt from this source of error. Our analysis of truth and falsehood, or of the nature of judgment, is not very likely to be influenced by our hopes and fears. Yet even here there is a slight danger of intellectual dishonesty. We sometimes do our Critical Philosophy with half an eye on our Speculative Philosophy, and accept or reject beliefs, or analyse concepts in a certain way, because we feel that this will fit in better than any alternative with the view of Reality as a whole that we happen to like.

(iv) Nevertheless, if Speculative Philosophy remembers its limitations, it is of value to scientists, in its methods, if not in its results. The reason is this. In all the sciences except Psychology we deal with objects and their changes, and leave out of account as far as possible the mind which observes them. In Psychology, on the other hand, we deal with minds and their processes, and leave out of account as far as possible the objects that we get to know by means of them. A man who confines himself to either of these subjects is likely therefore to get a very one-sided view of the world. The pure natural scientist is liable to forget that minds exist, and that if it were not for them he could neither know nor act on physical objects. The pure psychologist is inclined to forget that the main business of minds is to know and act upon objects; that they are most intimately connected with certain portions of matter; and that they have apparently arisen gradually in a world which at one time contained nothing but matter. . . . The truth is that both these doctrines commit the fallacy of over-simplification; and we can hardly avoid falling into some form of this unless at some time we make a resolute attempt to think *synoptically* of all the facts. Our *results* may be trivial; but the *process* will at least remind us of the extreme complexity of the world, and teach us to reject any cheap and easy philosophical theory.

Refutation and Discovery in Philosophy*

R. G. COLLINGWOOD [1889–1943] was Professor of Metaphysics at Oxford. He was trained as an archeologist and produced a standard work on the history of Britain at the time of the Roman domination. He also published widely in major branches of philosophy and is best known for his work on aesthetics and the philosophy of history.

There are some things which we can do without understanding what we are doing; not only things which we do with our bodies, like locomotion and digestion, but even things which we do with our minds, like making a poem or recognizing a face. But when that which we do is in the nature of thinking, it begins to be desirable, if we are to do it well, that we should understand what we are trying to do. Scientific and historical thought could never go very far unless scientists and historians reflected on their own work, tried to understand what they were aiming at, and asked themselves how best to attain it. Most of all, this is true of philosophy. It is possible to raise and solve philosophical problems with no very clear idea of what philosophy is, what it is trying to do, and how it can best do it; but no great progress can be made until these questions have been asked and some answer to them given.

* From Collingwood: *An Essay on Philosophical Method*, Oxford: at The Clarendon Press, 1933. Reprinted by permission of The Clarendon Press, Oxford.

Philosophy, moreover, has this peculiarity, that reflection upon it is part of itself. The theory of poetry may or may not be of service to a poet—opinions on that question have differed—but it is no part of poetry. The theory of science and the theory of history are not parts of science and of history; if scientists and historians study these things, they study them not in their capacity as scientists or historians, but in their capacity as philosophers. But the theory of philosophy is itself a problem for philosophy; and not only a possible problem, but an inevitable problem, one which sooner or later it is bound to raise.

For these two reasons, both because it is among his proper subjects of study and because without it his chance of success in his other subjects is diminished, the philosopher is under an obligation to study the nature of philosophy itself. Towards that study the present essay is intended as a contribution; its primary purpose being to consider the question what philosophy is.

There are various lines by which that question might be approached. One of these would depend upon the relation between an object and the thought of it. Any special science, we might argue, must have something special to study, and whatever peculiarities it presents in aim and method must be due to peculiarities in its object; from this point of view it would appear that the most hopeful way of approaching our question is first to define the proper object of philosophical thought, and then to deduce from this definition the proper methods it should follow. But this line of approach would offer no hope of success except to a person convinced that he already possessed an adequate conception of this object; convinced that is, that his philosophical thought had already reached its goal. To me at least, therefore, this path is closed; for though I believe that certain ways of philosophizing are more fruitful than others, I know of no philosophy that is not a voyage of exploration whose end, the adequate knowledge of its proper object, remains as yet unreached.

A second way, which might be open even if the first were closed, depends on the relation between means and end. We might ask what kind of results philosophy hopes or desires to achieve; and, having thus laid down its programme, consider what means can be found of realizing it. But although every philosopher has some idea of what he hopes to achieve, this idea varies from person to person and in the same person from time to time; nor could it be otherwise, for any progress in thought must bring with it a certain change in the conception of its own end, the goal of one stage being the starting-point of the next. If I followed this method, therefore, I could not hope or even desire to command the assent of my readers, or even my own assent hereafter.

There remains a third line of approach. Philosophy never with any of us reaches its ultimate goal; and with its temporary gains it never rests content; *e pur si muove*: it is an activity which goes on in our minds, and we are able to distinguish it from among others, and to recognize it by certain peculiar marks. These marks characterize it as an activity or process; they are, therefore, peculiarities of procedure; and accordingly it is possible to answer the question what philosophy is by giving an account of philosophical method.

This suggests taking philosophical thought as a special kind of fact, scrutinizing it, and describing the procedure which it is found to exhibit. But that would not be enough. The question what philosophy is, cannot be separated from the question what philosophy ought to be. When we distinguish philosophy from the other activities of our minds, we do not think of it as something that merely happens in us like the circulation of the blood; we think of it as something we try to do, an activity which we are trying to bring into conformity with an idea of what it ought to be. Consequently, when we set out to give an account of philosophical method, what we are trying to describe is not so much a method actually followed by ourselves or any one else, as a method which in our philosophical work we are trying to follow, even if we never entirely succeed. Hence an account of philosophical method must attempt to satisfy two conditions. First, to avoid a kind of philosophical utopianism, it must keep in touch with facts, and never lose sight of the question what methods have actually been used by philosophers of the past. Secondly, to avoid replacing a philosophical question by an historical one, it must treat all such precedents as mere preliminaries to the main question: the final appeal must be to our own experience of philosophical work, and to our consciousness that when we are engaged in it these are the principles which we are trying to follow. . . .

As in science and in history, so in philosophy the ideal of thought demands that no proposition be admitted into the body of knowledge except for sufficient reason, or, in logical terms, as the conclusion of an inference. The question must therefore be raised: by what special kind of reasoning or inference are the propositions of philosophy established?

There are persons who think that this question admits of no answer; who believe, that is, that no such thing as constructive philosophical reasoning is possible. Like most sceptics, they do not adopt this belief lightly; they are driven to it after serious thought, and their doubts deserve serious consideration. They agree in disclaiming, whether for themselves merely, or for their own generations, or for the entire body of human thinkers everywhere and always, any philosophical doctrine supported by constructive philosophical argument; but beyond this they differ. Some deny that they have any philosophical doctrine at all, and hold that philosophical reasoning is not constructive but critical, its function being solely to destroy false philosophies. Others claim to have a philosophical position, but think that the judgements that go to make it up are based not on philosophical arguments but on science or common sense.

'I do not know,' say the first of these, 'what the right answer to any philosophical question is; but I think there is work to be done in showing that the answers usually given are wrong. And I can prove that one answer is wrong without claiming to know that another is right; for my method is to examine the answers given by other people, and to show that they are self-contradictory. What is self-contradictory is, properly speaking, meaningless; what is meaningless cannot mean the truth; and therefore by this method I can preserve a purely critical attitude towards the philosophy of others, without having any philosophy of my own. As to that, I neither assert nor deny its possibility; I merely, for the present, suspend judgement and continue my work of criticism.'

A philosophy which defines its task in this way I propose to call a critical philosophy, meaning by that a philosophy which sets out to be critical as opposed to constructive. A critical attitude, in this sense, differs from [an] attitude of abstract negation: . . . to negate a view is simply to assert its falsity, to criticize it is to give reasons for this assertion. In using the term critical here I am inevitably suggesting a comparision with the Critical Philosophy of Kant; but what I have to say on this subject must not be understood as directed to Kant's address; for criticism, in his view, was not the whole of his philosophy; it is directed rather at one of the various schools of thought which have divided Kant's inheritance.

The merits of such an attitude need no emphasis. But it has defects of two kinds. First, it betrays a defect of temper. It is characteristic of acute and accomplished thinkers, used to studying closely the work of great writers, who have become disheartened and inclined to dismiss all philosophical thought as futile. This failure of heart is bound up with a failure of sympathy towards the writers whom they criticize. To study a philosophy with the avowed intention, not of asking how adequately it deals with its subject-matter, but solely of looking for inconsistencies in its logical form, implies a withdrawal of interest from that which most interested the author, the subject-matter, and a consequent alienation of sympathy from him which makes it impossible to estimate his work fairly. Criticism of this kind will bear most hardly on writers who are genuinely grappling with the intricacies of a difficult problem, and since the critic claims no knowledge of the subject-matter, they will get from him no credit for the insight which they have shown; it will be most lenient to those who, abandoning all attempt at profound or close study of the matter in hand, content themselves with a one-sided account of some partial aspect of it. Consequently criticism of this kind is not only based on a defective scale of values, but its judgments run grave risk of being inversely related to the merits of the authors judged; and even if that danger is averted its general temper, instead of being sympathetic, as good criticism should be, can hardly escape being superficial and to some extent frivolous.

Defects of temper, I may be told, are irrelevant in philosophy, which, as the pursuit of truth, cares only for logical values, not moral. So be it. The philosopher I am criticizing is no less open to criticism in his logic. He asserts that he has no philosophical doctrine of his own; but this assertion is belied by his practice, which implies two things, each in effect a constructive philosophical position.

He has condemned the philosophies of other people for showing certain characteristics which, he thinks, are faults. This implies a conception of what a constructive philosophy should be, and the use of this conception as a standard by which to condemn existing philosophies. Now, the idea of a philosophy is itself a philosophical idea; and the critic who uses such an idea as a standard is under an obligation to state it and defend it against criticism.

He has also a conception of what philosophical criticism should be; and this is a standard whose claims he thinks he can and does satisfy in his own philosophical practice. But this again is a philosophical conception; and hence a philosophical critic is bound to give us his theory of philosophical criticism, and satisfy us by positive or constructive argument that his principles are sound and that his practice faithfully follows them.

Scepticism in this form, as in all its forms, is in reality a convert dogmatism; it contains positive theories of the nature, method, and limitations of philosophical thought, but disclaims their possession and conceals them from criticism. Hence it is both inconsistent, or false to its own professed principles, and—intentionally or unintentionally—dishonest, because applying to others a form of criticism which in its own case it will not admit.

A second form of scepticism agrees with the first in holding that philosophy cannot establish positive or constructive positions; but holds that we are not on that account necessarily ignorant of the right answers to philosophical questions. These answers are supplied, it maintains, not by philosophical argument but by science and common sense.

For example: is there a material world? are there other minds beside my own? Yes; common sense tells me that these things are so; philosophical thinking is neither needed to convince me of them, nor able to demonstrate them, if I am so foolish as to doubt them or so disingenuous as to profess a doubt I cannot feel.

On the other hand, there are many questions, traditionally referred to philosophy for decision, which, because they cannot be decided by science or common sense, cannot be decided at all. Is there a God; shall we have a future life; what is the general nature of the universe as a whole? Because we do not know the answers to these questions independently of philosophizing, philosophy cannot give them.

What, then, is left for philosophy to do? It has no longer, as on the critical view, the function of controverting error; for example, it does not demolish the false view that duty is merely expediency and leave us ignorant indeed but free from delusions; for, according to this view, we know what duty is, and always did know; if any one asks what it is, we can reply 'it is what you and I and every one know it to be.' Nothing is left for philosophy except the task of analysing the knowledge we already possess: taking the propositions which are given by science and common sense, and revealing their logical structure or 'showing what exactly we mean when we say,' for example, that there is a material world.

Like the other, this form of scepticism is the fruit of much philosophical learning and labour; . . . both are worthy of respect and, as we shall see, within limits true. But the analytic view is hardly more defensible than the critical.

If a person holding a view of this type were asked to state his philosophical position, he would probably begin by stating a series of propositions belonging to the sphere of common sense, which some philosophers have, wrongly as he thinks, questioned or denied. But the task of philosophy, on this view, is to analyse such propositions as these; and consequently a philosopher holding this view would presumably describe as part of his philosophical position not only the data of analysis, the propositions of common sense, such as 'this is a human hand,' but the results of analysis, such propositions as 'there is a thing, and only one thing, of which it is true both that it is a human hand and that this surface is a part of its surface.' But the analytic view of philosophy implies a third class of propositions: neither the data of analysis (the common-sense propositions to be analysed), nor its results (the propositions into which these are resolved), but the principles according to which it proceeds; some of them logical, such as that a complex proposition can be divided up into two or more simple ones, some metaphysical, such as (to take one involved in the above instance) that sense-data are not mental entities which somehow represent physical objects, but are actually parts of physical objects.

The analytic philosopher, invited to state his philosophical position, would perhaps include in the statement propositions of all these three classes. But, on such a view of philosophy, it is not quite clear that data, results, and principles have an equal right to be included. The data of analysis are only the subject-matter upon which philosophical thought exercises itself, as logic may exercise itself on propositions made (for example) by a botanist. That all oaks are dicotyledonous is not a part of logical theory; the logician is not, as a logician, called upon either to assert it or deny it. He merely studies its logical structure. Hence, if the philosopher's task is neither to attack nor to defend the statements of common sense, but only to analyse them, such a statement as 'there are other human beings with experiences like my own' cannot be a part of his philosophical position; it is only an example of the things about which he philosophizes; and to think of it as an element in his philosophical position is to relapse into that very view of philosophy as criticizing or corroborating common sense against which this theory is expressly in revolt.

The results of analysis would seem to be in the same case. For the analysis of a common-sense proposition states what exactly that proposition means; and if the datum of analysis is a common-sense proposition, its result, being identical with it in meaning, is a common-sense proposition also.

The one class of propositions which beyond any doubt ought to be included in the analytic philosopher's statement of his position is that which comprises the principles on which analysis proceeds. These principles constitute a theory concerning the nature and method of philosophy; this is a philosophical theory, and a constructive one; and, therefore, whatever else the analytical philosopher ought to tell us when asked to state his philosophical position, it is clear that his first duty is to expound these. Yet he, like the critical philosopher, not only neglects this duty but makes a merit of neglecting it and asserting that he has no constructive or systematic theory of his own. . . .

Both these sceptical theories, therefore, break down under examination, and both for the same reason. Each disclaims a constructive philosophy; each claims to possess, not a body of doctrine, but only a method: not a method of reaching positive philosophical conclusions, but a method of doing something else—in the one case, of demolishing false philosophies, in the other, of deciding what exactly we mean when we make a statement. They both fail to recognize that methods imply principles, and systematic methods, systematic principles; and that their professed scepticism is merely a veiled claim to exempt these principles from criticism or even from explicit statement, while assuming their truth and sufficiency. While this state of things continues, it cannot be allowed that the critical or analytic philosopher, however much we may value him as a commentator or critic of the philosophy of others, has even begun the task of formulating a philosophical position or programme of his own. . . .

When . . . Kant laid it down that philosophy could contain no axioms, and that its first principles required proof, but proof of a special kind; when he attacked in principle and in detail the use of mathematical methods in philosophy, and concluded that they could lead to nothing but 'houses of cards'; when Hegel, following Kant's lead, pointed out that philosophy was in the peculiar position of being obliged to justify its own starting-point; those contentions were not new: they were familiar to the great mathematical philosophers of the seventeenth century, as they have always been to all competent philosophers. . . .

But what can be meant by saying that philosophy must justify its own starting-point? Plainly it cannot mean that, before the work of substantive philosophy can begin, there must be a preliminary philosophy charged with the task of justifying its principles. That would be to support the world on an elephant, and the elephant on a tortoise: a procedure which, as Kant came to see, is not adequately explained by calling the elephant Metaphysics and the tortoise a Critical or Transcendental Propaedeutic. If the first principles of philosophy are to be justified, they must be justified by that philosophy itself.

This can be done only if the arguments of philosophy, instead of having an irreversible direction from principles to conclusions, have a reversible one, the principles establishing the conclusions and the conclusions reciprocally establishing the principles. But an argument of this kind, in which A rests on B and B rests reciprocally on A, is a vicious circle. Are we to conclude that philosophy is in the dilemma of either renouncing this characteristic function and conforming to the irreversible pattern of exact science, or else losing all cogency in a circular argument?

The solution of the dilemma lies in a feature of philosophical thought to which I have already referred more than once: the Socratic principle that philosophical reasoning leads to no conclusions which we did not in some sense know already. Every school of philosophical thought has accepted this principle, recognizing that philosophy does not, like exact or empirical science, bring us to know things of which we were simply ignorant, but brings us to know in a different way things which we already knew in some way; and indeed it follows from our own hypothesis; for if the species of a philosophical genus overlap, the distinction between the known and the unknown, which in a nonphilosophical subject-matter involves a difference between two mutually exclusive classes of truths, in a philosophical subject-matter implies that we may both know and not know the same thing; a paradox which disappears in the light of the notion of a scale of forms of knowledge, where coming to know means coming to know in a different and better way.

Establishing a proposition in philosophy, then, means not transferring it from the class of things unknown to the class of things known, but making it known in a different and better way. For example, it is a relatively bad way of knowing a thing if we merely observe that it is so but do not understand why it is so; a better way of knowing it would be by observation and understanding together; and if by seeing certain facts in the light of certain principles we come to understand the facts and at the same time to have visible confirmation of the principles, this is a gain to our knowledge both of the principles and of the facts.

Here philosophical thought shows a contrast with that of the exact sciences. Our knowledge that the square on the hypotenuse is equal to the sum of the squares on the other two sides depends (I speak for myself) on the proof. There are cases, as I have already remarked, in which we intuitively apprehend the conclusion without any proof; but normally the proof is our only source of assurance that the conclusion is true. In philosophy this is not so; we know this normally without any proof at all; and the service which the proof does for us is not to assure us that it is so, but to show us why it is so, and thus enable us to know it better. . . .

At every stage in the scale, there is a datum or body of experience, the stage that has actually been reached; and there is a problem, the task of explaining this experience by constructing a theory of it, which is nothing but the same experience raised by intenser thought to a higher level of rationality. The accomplishment of this task is only the continuation of a process already begun; it was only by thinking that we reached the point at which we stand, for the experience upon which we philosophize is already a rational experience; so our reason for going on is that we already stand committed to the task. But the new and intenser thinking must be thinking of a new kind; new principles are appearing in it, and these give a criterion by which the principles involved in the last step are superseded. Thus the stage last reached, regarded as a theory, is now a theory criticized and refuted; what stands firm is not its truth as theory, but the fact that it has actually been reached, the fact that we have experienced it; and in criticizing and demolishing it as a theory we are confirming and explaining it as an experience.

This, then, is the general nature of philosophical inference. The critical view of it was so far right, that it consists always and essentially in refutation; whatever positive doctrine has been propounded, the next step for philosophy is to demolish it, to destroy it as a theory, and leave it standing only as an experience. But this view only apprehends the negative side of the process; it misses the positive side, the necessity of explaining that experience by reference to the new principles implied in the critical process itself.

The analytic view was so far right, that every movement of philosophical thought begins with a datum which is already knowledge, and goes on to explain what this knowledge means. It is only wrong because it forgets that, in explaining our knowledge, we come to know it in a different way; the datum does not remain a fixed point, it undergoes development in undergoing analysis, and therefore vanishes in its original form, to reappear in a new.

It is right to describe philosophical thought as deductive, because at every phase in its development it is, ideally at least, a complete system based on principles and connected throughout its texture by strict logical bonds; but this system is more than a deductive system, because the principles are open to criticism and must be defended by their success in explaining our experience.

For this reason, because philosophy is always an attempt to discern the principles which run through experience and make it a rational whole, it is right to call it inductive; but it differs from an inductive science because the experience on which its theories are based is itself an experience of rational living, theorizing, philosophizing. Consequently, because the data from which it begins and which it has to explain are homogeneous with its conclusions, the theories by which it seeks to explain them, the activity of philosophizing is a datum to philosophy, and among its tasks is the task of accounting for itself; and this, which is true even at a quite low level of philosophical development, is more and more so as it becomes more and more philosophical; so that the maturity of a philosophy may be judged by the clearness with which it apprehends the principle laid down at the beginning of this essay, that the theory of philosophy is an essential part of philosophy.

Philosophy and Language*

G E O F F R E Y J. W A R N O C K [1923–   ] was educated at Oxford and now teaches there as a fellow of Magdalen College. He has published a book on Berkeley (1953) and a number of articles in professional journals. In collaboration with J. O. Urmson, he edited some of the philosophical papers of J. L. Austin (who is also represented in this anthology).

There can be no serious doubt that the most powerful and pervasive influence upon the practice of philosophy in this country today has been that of Ludwig Wittgenstein. An account of his work and its effect presents peculiar

* From Warnock, *English Philosophy Since 1900*, Home University Library, Oxford University Press, 1958. Reprinted by permission of the Oxford University Press.

difficulties; but an attempt to provide one, provisional no doubt and very imperfect, must be made.

The causes of difficulty at this point are various. In the first place, chronology becomes somewhat confusing. Wittgenstein's *Tractatus* was published in 1919. For a few years thereafter he lived near Vienna, being at that time in fairly close touch with, though never one of, the philosophers of the Vienna Circle; and he had been in England from 1912 to 1914, spending part of that period in Cambridge as a pupil of Russell's. He returned to Cambridge in 1929, and from about that date onwards his philosophical work began to take on a radically different character. However, for one reason or another, it was several years before anything much was generally known of these new developments. Not only did Wittgenstein publish nothing himself; he seems also to have been strongly opposed to any publication by those to whom his ideas were imparted. Several years passed before even articles bearing the new character were generally available, and even these were, to say the least, unauthorized by Wittgenstein himself. At the same time interest in his work was so strong in many quarters that reports of it did in fact achieve a considerable though half-clandestine currency. These could not be regarded, of course, as final or authoritative; but by 1953, when his *Philosophical Investigations* was posthumously published, a good many philosophers had been for several years more or less familiar with the trend of his work. . . .

[Logical Atomism.] Fundamental to the change in his philosophical views which occurred quite soon after his *Tractatus* was published was a radically altered conception of language. In order to see what this change was, we must consider very briefly the position from which he began. This was in fact closely related to Russell's Logical Atomism; it could be called perhaps a more consistent, more thorough, and therefore more extreme working out of some of Russell's principles and ideas. Wittgenstein in a sense took these ideas more seriously; he saw more deeply into their consequences. . . . [He] paid more attention than Russell had done to the ways in which language must be supposed to be related to the world of which we wish to speak, and to the character of the 'logical atoms' of which, according to the doctrine, reality was composed. On both points his views were ruthlessly peculiar.

Like Russell, he located the real link between language and reality in the relation of atomic propositions to atomic facts. His general conception of this relation is well suggested in his own comparison with *pictures*. In a picture of an object or scene, there is a kind of correspondence between the parts of or elements in the picture, and the parts of or elements in the object or scene. But these elements must not only be present; their structure, form, or arrangement must be the same—according of course to some system of projection, whether simple perspective or something more elaborate. Now 'an atomic fact is a combination of objects (entities, things). . . . The configuration of objects forms the atomic fact.' But the 'sentential sign' is itself also a fact; it too is a combination of elements, namely *words*. This sort of fact is therefore capable of 'picturing' those other, non-verbal facts; and it is thus that language can refer to the world, can *mean* something other than itself. What were the elements of these facts taken to be? On the side of language they were said to be, in a queer sense, names, simple demonstrative symbols; on the side of reality they were objects, 'particulars.' But a particular cannot be, as Russell had supposed, such a thing as a white dot or a red patch. For that a particular is white or red is merely a fact about it; it *itself* is merely what *can* be white or red, and can be said (misleadingly perhaps) to be really colourless. And since an object is what *can* enter into a 'configuration,' it must not itself *be* a configuration; it must be simple. . . .

[ABANDONMENT OF LOGICAL ATOMISM.] It is remarkable that, in his *Investigations*, Wittgenstein did not deploy any set, systematic attack on his own earlier views; he did not attempt to say just what mistakes were made, what bad arguments used, what distinctions missed. Now his refusal to proceed in this way, though it might seem to add to his readers' difficulties, was deliberate. For he believed that what lay behind the old way of thinking was not a mistake of fact or logic, nor even a cluster of such mistakes, but something better called a *superstition*. And how is one to deal with a superstitious man? Suppose he believes that natural events are the work of demons. It would not help him to say, for example, 'But look, it is only the match that makes the paper catch fire; it really isn't true that there is a demon at work'—for until one has somehow shaken or removed his entire system of queer ideas, he can only see the phenomena you show him in the light of them, still as the work of demons. What we need is not to point out this mistake or that, but 'to turn our whole examination round.' It is not, to put the point rather differently, that Russell and Wittgenstein were not intelligent enough to detect mistakes and flaws in their reasoning; it was as if their intelligence was 'bewitched'; they did not simply overlook the true facts of the case, but in some way were *unable* to see those facts in the natural way. We have, then, not to detect mistakes, but to dethrone a superstition, defeat a bewitchment; it is the *source* of the trouble that is to be exposed, not the errors which were simply its natural manifestations.

What then was the source, or were the sources, of the superstition? Here we find a curious position. The source of the superstitious beliefs about language is, as Wittgenstein argues, language itself. We have to resist 'the bewitchment of our intelligence by means of language,' superstitions 'produced by grammatical illusions,' 'through a misinterpretation of our forms of language'; therefore, we must look 'into the workings of our language, and that in such a way as to make us recognize those workings: *in despite of* an urge to misunderstand them.' We must make it our aim to 'command a clear view,' in spite of the fact that 'our forms of expression prevent us in all sorts of ways' from seeing clearly what lies before us.

What is meant by 'the bewitchment of our intelligence by means of language'? Something like this: there are in our language certain forms of question, for example, which suggest—perhaps because most questions of that form would receive—a certain form of answer; or there are, in general, forms of expression which suggest—perhaps because they often have—a certain kind of interpretation. Yet, in some cases, it may be that the form of answer which a question suggests is not really appropriate to just that question; or that, more generally, a certain expression cannot rightly be interpreted in the kind of way that its form seems to require. But it may be extremely difficult, and particularly so in the practice of philosophy, to recognize such cases for what they are; we may be unable to resist the suggestion of our forms of language, and hence persist in the attempt to find answers to questions, or to interpret expressions, in ways that are quite inappropriate to the cases at issue. It is, one might say, as if the surface of our language were thickly covered with well-trodden paths, and we were constantly tempted to follow these paths even when they did not lead in the direction we were trying to go.

Consider, for example, what became in the hands of the Atomists of the question 'What is a name?' What came to mind first, it seems, was a certain simple procedure of naming—the object is before us and we give it its name, as Adam did with the animals. But to be named in *this* way an object must both exist and be present to the namer. But can I not say, of a ship that has been blown up and of which the pieces are at the bottom of the sea, 'The *Britannia* struck a mine and sank'? And in saying this do I not use the name of an object not present, which indeed no longer exists? Russell's answer would have been that 'Britannia' is not a real name; no doubt I can *describe* what is absent or no longer exists, but I cannot (as Adam did with the animals) *name* it; so 'Britannia' must really be a description in disguise, and so indeed must be everything we commonly think of as a name. 'The whole business of proper names,' Russell said, 'is rather curious'—so curious indeed that he came to the conclusion that 'the only words one does use as names in the logical sense are words like "this" or "that",' words certainly which it would never enter one's head, in the ordinary way, to classify as names.

But what was it that led him into this curious view? What indeed made

Wittgenstein at one time inclined to agree with him? In this case, as in others, 'a *picture* held us captive'—the simple picture of names as assigned by Adam to the animals, as thus confined to the case of what exists and is present before us. This picture is, undoubtedly, a picture of naming—'and we could not get outside it, for it lay in our language and language seemed to repeat it to us inexorably.' It is true that the actual uses of actual names are in most cases nothing like that which the picture suggested. But two forces combined to push that fact into the background. First—and this was another case of 'grammatical illusion'—the fact that the question 'What is a name?' seemed difficult to answer was assumed to be due to the fact that the answer was somehow *hidden*—that the *real* nature of names was in some way concealed *behind* the plain facts as to actual uses of names, so that these actual uses should be kept out of the way, should be not looked *at* but rather seen *through*. Second, in the course of the philosophical discussion names were considered without a context, not in use, but as if taken out of use for more careful inspection. But words out of use are apt to get out of control. Thus 'naming appears as a *queer* connexion of a word with an object.—And you really get such a queer connexion when the philosopher tries to bring out *the* relation between name and thing by staring at an object in front of him and repeating a name or even the word "this" innumerable times. . . . And we can also say the word "this" *to* the object, as it were *address* the object as "this"—a queer use of this word, which doubtless only occurs in doing philosophy.' Words thus inspected, repeated, thought about in abstraction from any actual use are liable to pose as having most peculiar uses which perhaps none actually has 'in the language-game which is its original home.' The harder one thinks in such a contextless vacuum, the more hopelessly 'bewitched' one is liable to become; 'one thinks that one is tracing the outline of the thing's nature over and over again, and one is merely tracing round the frame through which we look at it.'

More generally: The Atomists had been ostensibly concerned with such questions as 'What is a language? How do sentences *mean* something? What is a name, and what sorts of things can be named?' The answers to these questions were not obvious; and here the first 'picture' began to operate. If the answers were not obvious, then obvious phenomena surely could not be relevant to the problem; the answer must surely be something quite different, something which the things we all see merely conceal. What then? And here countless other pictures, 'preconceived ideas,' came into play—the picture of a calculus with clear and fixed rules, the picture of naming, the picture of dismantling something composite in order to discover its basic components, the picture indeed of a picture and what it portrays. All these and many others combined to produce the conviction that language *must* be, could *only* be, like this or like that—and at the same time to keep out of sight the actual facts, too obvious to be noticed or to seem important. All these pictures, so Wittgenstein suggests, are embodied in the forms of language itself. It is language itself which works to prevent the realization of its own character. To see how this is so is to have defeated the superstition. It is comparable rather with conversion than with the detection of error.

PHILOSOPHICAL PROBLEMS. So far, we have sketched the way in which Wittgenstein came to see the problems of Logical Atomism. These problems he explained as due primarily to an attempt to impose upon language a 'preconceived,' artificial view which was, when once one came to look at language with open eyes, startlingly inadequate to its actual variousness, complexity, flexibility; and the urge to make this attempt he attributed to an 'illusion,' a superstition arising in some way out of language itself. From this point he came, even jumped, to the bold conclusion that *all* philosophical problems are of this type.

This conclusion was certainly not reached by induction. At no time, I believe, did Wittgenstein make any wide historical survey of philosophy in order to test his opinion against actual evidence. He believed no doubt that it was in fact true of his own problems, those with which he had himself been engaged in his earlier years. He perhaps thought also that his view *must* be true, if there were to be a distinct class of 'philosophical' problems at all. And perhaps he was also half-unconsciously inclined to make his view generally true by definition—that is, to classify a problem as philosophical only if it could be interpreted in the light of his views. Let us consider again, more generally, what those views were.

First, then, what is a philosophical problem like? Or what sort of problem is it to which we are inclined to give the name 'philosophical'? In Wittgenstein's view what marks off such a problem is a characteristic *unclarity*, a certain power to baffle and confuse. 'A philosophical problem has the form: "I don't know my way about." ' This sort of problem arises typically in cases where certainly it is not ignorance that defeats us. What is more thoroughly familiar to us, for example, than perception, the use of our senses? Yet here there has repeatedly arisen a most formidable cluster of baffling problems. Conversely, if it *is* ignorance that defeats us, we do not feel ourselves to be faced by a philosophical problem. Questions about the structure of the remoter galaxies, the causes of cancer, the properties of the human nervous system, are questions to which perhaps we do not know the answers; but we see pretty well what sorts of questions they are, more or less how their answers are to be looked for, and whose specialized business it is to look for those answers. Nor do we feel that a philosophical problem arises where a question is clearly to be answered by some sort of calculation—we see it as a question in mathematics, for instance, or in logic, not in philosophy. A philosophical problem typically gives us the impression that, although we know all that might be relevant to it, yet we cannot see clearly; it is as if we were lost and did not know which way to turn; or as if we had become entangled and could not see how to extricate ourselves. We see all the pieces of the puzzle, but not how they fit together to form a picture. Very often, this shows itself in the baffling fact that the only answer to our question which seems to us possible is also an answer which we cannot believe to be true— 'But *this* isn't how it is!'—we say. 'Yet *this* is how it has to be!' It is not that we do not know what is the case, but that we also seem to be driven to deny it.

In Wittgenstein's account of the ways in which such typical predicaments arise two elements can be roughly distinguished. There is, first of all, the plain but extremely important fact that the verbal or grammatical forms of our language are incomparably less various than are the actual uses of words. Such grammatical categories as *noun, adjective, verb,* are no doubt not absolutely straightforward—no doubt one could think of marginal cases that would present difficulties even of grammatical classification; but still, it is clear in the vast majority of cases how words should be grammatically classified, how sentences should be parsed; and the complexity required for these purposes is not very great. But the ways in which words are actually used are enormously more diverse and complex than this. 'Pink,' 'past,' 'ambitious' are all adjectives; 'believe,' 'walk,' 'see,' are all verbs; 'consciousness,' 'table,' 'cause' are all nouns. But cutting across these grammatical resemblances it is clear that there are immense divergences of use. But it is not, of course, clear at a glance what these divergences are; 'our grammar is lacking in this sort of perspicuity'; and therefore it is always possible that the very visible, grammatical resemblance will lead us to think that there are other resemblances, and even prevent us from noticing that there are not.

It should not be supposed that this possible way of being misled is surely too simple and obvious to be a philosophical danger. It would be possible to illustrate its workings in many hundreds of actual cases. But let us take one to serve as a specimen. Moore, in examining the old Idealist contention that time is not real, was once led to raise the question, what the word 'real' means. But he considers this question in a very peculiar way. We apply the word 'real' to many things, to things of all kinds—we speak of a real (as opposed to an illusory) advantage, of a real (as opposed to a false) beard, of a real (as opposed to a toy) pistol, of real (as opposed to hallucinatory) pink rats; we employ the word, that is, to exclude a wide variety of oddities, defects, or deviations, it being as a rule quite clear from the context what exactly we mean to exclude in a particular case. Moore, however, raises his question in this way: what *property* is it that we mean to assert that all those things which we call 'real' have in common? Now there is, fairly clearly, no such property at all. When I say that the juvenile delinquent had a real pistol in his pocket, and that a long spell in a reformatory would be of real benefit to him, I do not in the least mean to assert that the benefit and his pistol have a property in common; but rather to make clear that the pistol was not a toy, and that the benefit would not be negligible. Why then did Moore assume, as the form of his question shows that he did, that there *must* be *one* property of 'reality'? Was it not because he thought of the *typical adjective* as being used to ascribe a property common to all those things to which it applies, and assumed that the word 'real' must be used in this way because it too is grammatically an adjective? That is, the very visible adjectival grammar of the word produced an 'illusion' as to its actual use. Moore in fact fell victim to a similar but more notorious illusion in his discussion of 'good' in *Principia Ethica;* this word too, he thought, must connote an 'indefinable' *quality.*

Rather different from but closely connected with this first point is our liability to be swayed, or even 'enslaved,' by what Wittgenstein often calls 'pictures,' or what could also be called *models* or *standard cases.* In a sense this point includes the first, since it may sometimes occur that a grammatical resemblance induces us to try to assimilate the use of a word to that of some other word of the same grammatical type, which we think of as exhibiting *the,* or the *standard,* use of words of that type. But the issues involved here may go far beyond grammar. Consider, as a simplified example, the notion of *proof.* Now there are proofs of many sorts—geometrical proofs, scientific proofs, police-court proofs, proofs of the pudding in the eating, and many others. But it may be that a philosopher becomes obsessed with *one* kind of proof, a particular 'picture' or model or standard of what it is to prove something; and so long as this picture retains its exclusive hold, he may feel obliged to maintain in the teeth of paradox that nothing else is really a proof at all, perhaps even that we do not really *know* anything but what can be proved in his ideal or standard way. Or it may be simply that he feels perplexed by proofs of any other sort—they may seem to him, however familiar, to be puzzling, because they do not fit in with his picture of a proof. There is, Wittgenstein thought, a characteristic way in which such puzzlement as this may arise and then become chronic: there is a certain temptation to suppose that such a question as 'What is a proof?' is a question to be answered just by *thinking,* as it were by inwardly surveying the idea of a proof—by attempting to discern, as Moore often put it, 'what comes before our minds,' when we say 'a *proof.*' It is against this notion that Wittgenstein directs the injunction 'Don't think, but look!' For 'does the whole *use* of the word come before my mind, when I *understand* it in this way?' No—the same picture, whatever it may be, simply presents itself over and over again; I repeatedly 'trace round the frame through which I look at it'; constantly seem to confirm my preconceived idea; and never think of *looking to see* what in fact proofs are, how many kinds of procedures are all called 'proofs,' and how familiar really these various procedures are.

What then is the remedy for this predicament? The actual uses of the word must be identified and described. It is not, of course, that we do not know what the word in question means; no doubt we are well able to use it correctly. But we do not 'command a clear view' of its use. It is not that there is anything obscure or hidden to be discovered; what we need already 'lies open to view' in the actual uses we make of the word. So we need to describe these, in order to remind ourselves of them—'the work of the philosopher consists in assembling reminders for a particular purpose.' And the purpose here is not only to make clear the use of the word, but also to oppose the powerful temptations that there may be to misrepresent it. It is true that there is nothing to be revealed, discovered, or explained—'we must do away with all *explanation,* and description alone must take its place.' But this description must not be haphazard and undirected; it 'gets its light—i.e. its purpose—from the philosophical problems. These are, of course, not empirical problems; they are solved, rather, by looking into the workings of our language, and that in such a way as to make us recognize those workings: *in despite of* an urge to misunderstand them. The problems are solved, not by giving new information, but by arranging what we have always known. Philosophy is a battle against the bewitchment of our intelligence by means of language.'

[PHILOSOPHICAL PARADOX.] Part of the explanation of the notoriety of the Logical Positivists lay, as was mentioned earlier, in their highly polemical and even abusive characterization of the efforts of very many other philosophers—in their zeal to attach the label 'meaningless' to many venerable doctrines, theses, and counter-theses. Now in a good many passages Wittgenstein says things which would quite naturally give the impression that he too took this view. It is worth inquiring how far he actually did so.

Certainly one does get the impression that, according to Wittgenstein, the philosopher's task today is to dispel confusion. 'What *we* do is to bring words back from their metaphysical to their everyday usage'—and to do this, it seems, is to substitute sense for nonsense. Indeed he does actually say that 'the results of philosophy are the uncovering of one or another piece of plain nonsense'; this may seem purely and painfully destructive, but 'what we are destroying is nothing but houses of cards and we are clearing up the ground of language on which they stand.' Again, 'when we do philosophy [i.e.

when it is done in the old, unenlightened way, we are like savages, primitive
people, who hear the expressions of civilized men, put a false interpretation
on them, and then draw the queerest conclusions from it.' He asks himself
'What is your aim in philosophy?'; and he answers 'To show the fly the way
out of the fly-bottle.' And where is he when he has made his escape? He is, it
appears, exactly where he started; for philosophy 'leaves everything as it is.'

I believe that, in fact, these and a few other passages tend to misrepresent
Wittgenstein's real position. He did not really believe that philosophical doctrines were *plain* nonsense, *nothing but* houses of cards, that a philosopher
was *merely* a fly in a fly-bottle. Why then did he say these things? They are,
in the first place, here detached from their context—they do not stand in his
book absolutely unqualified. Moreover they have, like so much of his writing, the character of aphorisms; and the aphorist is not required to go to the
stake for the literal truth of everything he says. It should also always be remembered that the philosophical 'illusions' which concerned Wittgenstein
most deeply and constantly were those to which he had himself been at one
time subject;· and it is natural to repudiate one's own illusions with a
vehemence and even rudeness that one would probably withhold from the
illusions of others. When Wittgenstein thought of philosophy in the old style,
he tended always to think first of philosophy in his old style; and certainly
much of his more sweeping condemnation is primarily addressed to himself.

If for these reasons the remarks quoted above ought to be in some way
discounted, how exactly ought they to be qualified or explained? In two
ways, I think, both fairly obvious. In the first place though Wittgenstein
speaks of philosophical doctrines as 'houses of cards,' he does not think of
the business of constructing them as in any way silly or trivial. No doubt very
many of the sayings of philosophers really are 'plain nonsense,' no more and
no less; no doubt they are sometimes the outcome of sheer confusion and
nothing else. But these are merely the uninteresting cases. The interesting
ones, although they too find expression in queer and distorted uses of language, 'have the character of *depth*. They are deep disquietudes; their roots
are as deep in us as the forms of our language and their significance is as
great as the importance of our language.' If there is a prejudice which, arising from some pervasive feature of our thought or language, from some 'picture' which our way of speaking imposes upon us, prevents us from recognizing the actual 'workings of our language,' this 'is not a *stupid* prejudice.' Its
source may lie so deep in our way of thinking that both it, and its removal,
may be of the greatest importance to us; for of course the removal of a prejudice must be an affair of no less significance than was the prejudice itself. It
may even be that some philosophical tangles are due to 'bumps that the

understanding has got by running its head up against the limits of language'—and this makes us at least see where those limits lie. It is true that the ordered description of the workings of language gets its importance only 'from the problems'; but the importance it thus gets is as great as that of the problems themselves. In the end they are simply removed, cleared away; but that they existed was never a *trivial* matter. They had after all the power to 'bewitch our intelligence.' Should treatment by psychoanalysis be regarded as trivial on the ground that it leaves a man nothing more exciting than sane?

The second point can be conveniently made with the help of some words of Wittgenstein's own. A philosophical problem, he said, has the form: 'I don't know my way about.' If so, then its successful treatment may indeed 'leave everything as it is,' in the sense that it leaves me still in the same place. But it has not made no difference either; for now I *do* know my way about. The point that Wittgenstein had in mind was that it was not the business of philosophy to add to our information, nor yet to alter our language; it makes no difference of this sort. But it does make a difference in that by it we may achieve a clear view, a grasp, a command of what was indeed always there to be seen, but had not before been seen in all its bearings and connexions. We *leave* things as they are; but perhaps for the first time we come to *see* them as they are.

Is it necessary here to add that Wittgenstein of course does *not* suggest that philosophical problems are all 'about language'? Of course they are not; they are about knowledge, memory, truth, space and time, perception, and innumerable other things. What he suggests is that, though thus not *about* language, they spring *from* language; they show themselves in distorted uses of language; they reveal confusion as to the uses of language; they are to be solved (or removed) by our coming to see and to employ our language properly. It would make no difference of substance here if one referred, instead of to 'language,' to 'concepts.' This may sound more important; but the problems were never thought to be *trivial*.

Philosophy and the Personal*

KARL JASPERS [1883–   ], after switching from jurisprudence to medicine, worked as a psychiatric assistant and taught psychology and philosophy at Heidelberg. Deprived of his professorship there by the National Socialists in 1937, he was reinstated by the Allies in 1945. Since 1948 he has lived in Switzerland. Many of his books are now available in English; among them are *The European Spirit, The Future of Mankind, The Great Philosophers, The Origin and Goal of History,* and *Man in the Modern Age.*

I

What philosophy is and how much it is worth are matters of controversy. One may expect it to yield extraordinary revelations or one may view it with indifference as a thinking in the void. One may look upon it with awe as the meaningful endeavour of exceptional men or despise it as the superfluous broodings of dreamers. One may take the attitude that it is the concern of all men, and hence must be basically simple and intelligible, or one may think of it as hopelessly difficult. And indeed, what goes by the name of philosophy provides examples to warrant all these conflicting judgments.

For the scientific-minded, the worst aspect of philosophy is that it produces no universally valid results; it provides nothing that we can know and thus possess. Whereas the sciences in their fields have gained compellingly certain and universally recognized insights, philosophy, despite thousands of years of endeavour, has done nothing of the sort. This is undeniable: in philosophy there is no generally accepted, definitive knowledge. Any insight which for cogent reasons is recognized by all has ipso facto become scientific knowledge and ceased to be philosophy; its relevance is limited to a special sphere of the knowable.

Nor is philosophical thought, like the sciences, characterized by progressive development. Beyond any doubt, we are far more advanced than Hippocrates, the Greek physician. But we are scarcely entitled to say that we have progressed beyond Plato. We have only advanced beyond his materials, beyond the scientific findings of which he made use. In philosophy itself we have scarcely regained his level.

It lies in the very nature of philosophy, as distinguished from the sciences, that in any of its forms it must dispense with the unanimous recognition of

* From Jaspers: *Way to Wisdom,* translated by Ralph Manheim, Yale University Press, 1951. Reprinted by permission of the Yale University Press.

all. The certainty to which it aspires is not of the objective, scientific sort, which is the same for every mind; it is an inner certainty in which a man's whole being participates. Whereas science always pertains to particular objects, the knowledge of which is by no means indispensable to all men, philosophy deals with the whole of being, which concerns man as man, with a truth which, wherever it is manifested, moves us more deeply than any scientific knowledge.

Systematic philosophy is indeed bound up with the sciences. It always reckons with the most advanced scientific findings of its time. But essentially philosophy springs from a different source. It emerges before any science, wherever men achieve awareness.

The existence of such a *philosophy without science* is revealed in several striking ways:

First: In philosophical matters almost everyone believes himself capable of judgment. Whereas it is recognized that in the sciences study, training, method are indispensable to understanding, in philosophy men generally assume that they are competent to form an opinion without preliminary study. Our own humanity, our own destiny, our own experience strike us as a sufficient basis for philosophical opinions.

This notion that philosophy must be accessible to all is justified. The circuitous paths travelled by specialists in philosophy have meaning only if they lead man to an awareness of being and of his place in it.

Second: Philosophical thought must always spring from free creation. Every man must accomplish it for himself.

A marvellous indication of man's innate disposition to philosophy is to be found in the questions asked by children. It is not uncommon to hear from the mouths of children words which penetrate to the very depths of philosophy. A few examples:

A child cries out in wonderment, "I keep trying to think that I am somebody else, but I'm always myself." This boy has touched on one of the universal sources of certainty, awareness of being through awareness of self. He is perplexed at the mystery of his I, this mystery that can be apprehended through nothing else. Questioningly, he stands before this ultimate reality.

Another boy hears the story of the Creation: In the beginning God made heaven and earth . . . and immediately asks, "What was before the beginning?" This child has sensed that there is no end to questioning, that there is no stopping place for the mind, that no conclusive answer is possible.

A little girl out walking in the woods with her father listens to his stories about the elves that dance in the clearings at night . . . "But there are no elves . . ." Her father shifts over to realities, describes the motion of the sun, discusses the question of whether it is the sun or the earth that revolves, and explains the reasons for supposing that the earth is round and rotates on its axis . . . "Oh, that isn't so," says the little girl and stamps her foot. "The earth stands still. I only believe what I see." "Then," says her father, "you don't believe in God, you can't see Him either." The little girl is puzzled for a moment, but then says with great assurance, "If there weren't any God, we wouldn't be here at all." This child was seized with the wonder of existence: things do not exist through themselves. And she understood that there is a difference between questions bearing on particular objects in the world and those bearing on our existence as a whole.

Another little girl is climbing the stairs on her way to visit her aunt. She begins to reflect on how everything changes, flows, passes, as though it had never been. "But there must be something that always stays the same . . . I'm climbing these stairs on my way to see my aunt—that's something I'll never forget." Wonderment and terror at the universal transience of things here seek a forlorn evasion.

Anyone who chose to collect these stories might compile a rich store of children's philosophy. It is sometimes said that the children must have heard all this from their parents or someone else, but such an objection obviously does not apply to the child's really serious questions. To argue that these children do not continue to philosophize and that consequently such utterances must be accidental is to overlook the fact that children often possess gifts which they lose as they grow up. With the years we seem to enter into a prison of conventions and opinions, concealments and unquestioned acceptance, and there we lose the candour of childhood. The child still reacts spontaneously to the spontaneity of life; the child feels and sees and inquires into things which soon disappear from his vision. He forgets what for a moment was revealed to him and is surprised when grownups later tell him what he said and what questions he asked.

Third: Spontaneous philosophy is found not only in children but also in the insane. Sometimes—rarely—the veils of universal occlusion seem to part and penetrating truths are manifested. The beginning of certain mental disorders is often distinguished by shattering metaphysical revelations, though they are usually formulated in terms that cannot achieve significance: exceptions are such cases as Hölderlin and Van Gogh. But anyone witnessing these revelations cannot help feeling that the mists in which we ordinarily live our lives have been torn asunder. And many sane people have, in awaking from sleep, experienced strangely revealing insights which vanish with full wakefulness, leaving behind them only the impression that they can never be recaptured. There is profound meaning in the saying that children and fools tell the truth. But the creative originality to which we owe great philosophical ideas is not to be sought here but among those great minds—and in all history there have been only a few of them—who preserve their candour and independence.

Fourth: Since man cannot avoid philosophy, it is always present: in the proverbs handed down by tradition, in popular philosophical phrases, in dominant convictions such as are embodied in the idiom of the "emancipated," in political opinions, but most of all, since the very beginnings of history, in myths. There is no escape from philosophy. The question is only whether a philosophy is conscious or not, whether it is good or bad, muddled or clear. Anyone who rejects philosophy is himself unconsciously practising a philosophy.

What then is this philosophy, which manifests itself so universally and in such strange forms?

The Greek word for philosopher (*philosophos*) connotes a distinction from *sophos*. It signifies the lover of wisdom (knowledge) as distinguished from him who considers himself wise in the possession of knowledge. This meaning of the word still endures: the essence of philosophy is not the possession of truth but the search for truth, regardless of how many philosophers may belie it with their dogmatism, that is, with a body of didactic principles purporting to be definitive and complete. Philosophy means to be on the way. Its questions are more essential than its answers, and every answer becomes a new question.

But this on-the-wayness—man's destiny in time—contains within it the possibility of deep satisfaction, and indeed, in exalted moments, of perfection. This perfection never resides in formulable knowledge, in dogmas and articles of faith, but in a historical consummation of man's essence in which being itself is revealed. To apprehend this reality in man's actual situation is the aim of philosophical endeavour.

To be searchingly on the way, or to find peace and the fulfilment of the moment—these are no definitions of philosophy. There is nothing above or beside philosophy. It cannot be derived from something else. Every philosophy defines itself by its realization. We can determine the nature of philosophy only by actually experiencing it. Philosophy then becomes the realization of the living idea and the reflection upon this idea, action and discourse on action in one. Only by thus experiencing philosophy for ourselves can we understand previously formulated philosophical thought.

But we can define the nature of philosophy in other ways. No formula can exhaust its meaning and none can be exclusive. In antiquity philosophy was defined (by its object) as the knowledge of things divine and human, the knowledge of being as being, or it was defined (by its aim) as learning how to die, as the striving for happiness by the exercise of thought; as an endeavour to resemble the divine; and finally (in the broadest sense) as the knowledge of all knowledge, the art of all arts, as *the* science—confined to no particular field.

Today perhaps we may speak of philosophy in the following terms; its aim is

to find reality in the primal source;

to apprehend reality in my thinking attitude toward myself, in my inner acts;

to open man to the Comprehensive in all its scope;

to attempt the communication of every aspect of truth from man to man, in loving contest;

patiently and unremittingly to sustain the vigilance of reason in the presence of failure and in the presence of that which seems alien to it.

Philosophy is the principle of concentration through which man becomes himself, by partaking of reality.

Although philosophy, in the form of simple, stirring ideas, can move every man and even children, its conscious elaboration is never complete, must forever be undertaken anew and must at all times be approached as a living whole—it is manifested in the works of the great philosophers and echoed in the lesser philosophers. It is a task which man will face in one form or another as long as he remains man.

Today, and not for the first time, philosophy is radically attacked and totally rejected as superfluous or harmful. What is the good of it? It does not help us in affliction.

Authoritarian church thought has condemned independent philosophy on the ground that it is a worldly temptation which leads man away from God, destroys his soul with vain preoccupations. Political totalitarianism has attacked it on the ground that philosophers have merely interpreted the world in various ways, when the important thing was to change it. Both these schools of thought regarded philosophy as dangerous, for it undermined order, promoted a spirit of independence, hence of revolt, deluded man and distracted him from his practical tasks. Those who uphold another world illumined by a revealed God and those who stand for the exclusive power of a godless here and now would equally wish to extinguish philosophy.

And everyday common sense clamours for the simple yardstick of utility, measured by which philosophy again fails. Thales, who is regarded as the first of Greek philosophers, was ridiculed by a slave girl who saw him fall into a well while observing the sky. Why does he search the remote heavens when he is so awkward in his dealings with the things of this world?

Must philosophy then justify itself? That is impossible. It cannot justify itself on the basis of a something else for which it is useful. It can only appeal to the forces in every man which drive him toward philosophical thought. It is a disinterested pursuit, to which questions of utility or injuriousness have no relevance, an endeavour proper to man as man, and it will continue to fulfil this striving as long as there are men alive. Even those groups which are hostile to it cannot help harbouring their own peculiar ideas and bringing forth pragmatic systems which are a substitute for philosophy, though subservient to a desired end—such as Marxism or fascism. The existence of even these systems shows how indispensable philosophy is to man. Philosophy is always with us.

Philosophy cannot fight, it cannot prove its truth, but it can communicate itself. It offers no resistance where it is rejected, it does not triumph where it gains a hearing. It is a living expression of the basic universality of man, of the bond between all men.

Great systematic philosophies have existed for two and one-half millennia in the West, in China, and in India. A great tradition beckons to us. Despite the wide variety of philosophical thought, despite all the contradictions and mutually exclusive claims to truth, there is in all philosophy a One, which no man possesses but about which all serious efforts have at all times gravitated: the one eternal philosophy, the *philosophia perennis*. We must seek this historical foundation of our thinking if we would think clearly and meaningfully.

II

The history of philosophy as methodical thinking began twenty-five hundred years ago, but as mythical thought much earlier.

The beginning however is something quite different from the source. The beginning is historical and provides those who follow with a mounting accumulation of insights. But it is always from the source that the impulsion to philosophize springs. The source alone lends meaning to present philosophy and through it alone is past philosophy understood.

This source is of many kinds. Wonderment gives rise to question and insight; man's doubt in the knowledge he has attained gives rise to critical examination and clear certainty; his awe and sense of forsakenness lead him to inquire into himself. And now let us examine these three drives.

First: Plato said that the source of philosophy was wonder. Our eyes gave us "the sight of the stars, the sun and the firmament." This "impelled us to examine the universe, whence grew philosophy, the greatest good conferred upon mortals by the gods." And Aristotle: "For it is owing to their wonder that men both now begin and at first began to philosophize: they wondered originally at the obvious difficulties, then advanced little by little and stated difficulties about the greater matters, e.g., about the phenomena of the moon, and those of the sun, and of the stars, and about the genesis of the universe."

Wonder impels man to seek knowledge. In my wonderment I become aware of my lack of knowledge. I seek knowledge, but for its own sake and not "to satisfy any common need."

In philosophical thought man awakens from his bondage to practical needs. Without ulterior purpose he contemplates things, the heavens, the world, and asks, what is all this? Where does it come from? From the answers to his questions he expects no profit but an intrinsic satisfaction.

Second: Once I have satisfied my wonderment and admiration by knowledge of what is, *doubt* arises. I have heaped up insights, but upon critical examination nothing is certain. Sensory perceptions are conditioned by our sense organs and hence deceptive; in any event they do not coincide with what exists in itself outside me, independently of my perception. Our categories are those of our human understanding. They become entangled in hopeless contradictions. Everywhere proposition stands against proposition. In my philosophical progress I seize upon doubt and attempt to apply it radically to everything, either taking pleasure in the sceptical negation which recognizes nothing but by itself cannot take a single step forward, or inquiring: Where then is there a certainty that rises above all doubt and withstands all critique?

Descartes' famous proposition, "I think, therefore I am," was for him a solid certainty, though he doubted everything else. For even a total fallacy in my thinking, a fallacy which may be beyond my understanding, cannot blind me to the realization that in order to be deluded in my thinking I must *be*.

Methodical doubt gives rise to a critical examination of all knowledge, and without radical doubt there can be no true philosophical thought. But the crucial question is: How and where has a foundation for certainty been gained through doubt itself?

And third: While I concentrate my energies upon the knowledge of things in the world, while I am engaged in doubt as a road to certainty, I am immersed in things; I do not think of myself, of my aims, my happiness, my salvation. In forgetfulness of myself I am content with the attainment of this knowledge.

This changes when I become aware of myself in my situation.

The Stoic Epictetus said, "Philosophy arises when we become *aware of our own weakness and helplessness*." How shall I help myself in my weakness? His answer was: By looking upon everything that is not within my power as necessary and indifferent to me, but by raising what does depend on me, namely the mode and content of my ideas, to clarity and freedom by thought.

And now let us take a look at our human state. We are always in situations. Situations change, opportunities arise. If they are missed they never return. I myself can work to change the situation. But there are situations which remain essentially the same even if their momentary aspect changes and their shattering force is obscured: I must die, I must suffer, I must struggle, I am subject to chance, I involve myself inexorably in guilt. We call these fundamental situations of our existence ultimate situations. That is to say, they are situations which we cannot evade or change. Along with wonder and doubt, awareness of these ultimate situations is the most profound source of philosophy. In our day-to-day lives we often evade them, by closing our eyes and living as if they did not exist. We forget that we must die, forget our guilt, and forget that we are at the mercy of chance. We face only concrete situations and master them to our profit, we react to them by planning and acting in the world, under the impulsion of our practical interests. But to ultimate situations we react either by obfuscation or, if we really apprehend them, by despair and rebirth: we become ourselves by a change in our consciousness of being.

Or we may define our human situation by saying that *no reliance can be placed in worldly existence.*

Ingenuously we mistake the world for being as such. In happy situations we rejoice at our strength, we are thoughtlessly confident, we know nothing but our actuality. In pain and weakness we despair. But if we come out of this situation alive we let ourselves slip back into forgetfulness of self and a life of happiness.

Such experience however has sharpened man's wits. The menace beneath which he lives drives him to seek security. He expects his mastery of nature and his community with other men to guarantee his existence.

Man gains power over nature in order to make it serve him; through science and technology he seeks to make it reliable.

But in man's domination of nature there remains an element of the incalculable which represents a constant threat, and the end is always failure: hard labour, old age, sickness and death cannot be done away with. Our dominated nature is reliable only in isolated cases; in the whole we can place no reliance.

Men band together in a community in order to limit and ultimately abolish the endless struggle of all against all; they seek to achieve security through mutual aid.

But here again there is a limit. Only if there were states in which every citizen stood to every other in a relation of absolute solidarity could justice and freedom be secure. For only then, if a citizen suffered injustice, would all others oppose it as one man. Such a state has never been seen. Those who have stood by one another in extremity and weakness have never been more than limited groups, and sometimes no more than a few individuals. No state, no church, no society offers absolute security. Such security has been a pleasing delusion of quiet times, in which the ultimate situations were veiled.

But there is a counterweight to the general unreliability of the world: there are in the world things worthy of faith, things that arouse confidence; there is a foundation which sustains us: home and country, parents and ancestors, brothers and sisters and friends, husbands and wives. There is a foundation of historical tradition, in native language, in faith, in the work of thinkers, poets, and artists. However, this tradition also gives no security, it is not absolutely reliable. For we encounter it always as the work of man; God is nowhere in the world. Tradition always implies a question. Keeping sight of the tradition, man must always derive what for him is certainty, being, the reliable, from his own primal source. But the precariousness of all worldly existence is a warning to us, it forbids us to content ourselves with the world; it points to something else.

The ultimate situations—death, chance, guilt, and the uncertainty of the world—confront me with the reality of failure. What do I do in the face of this absolute failure, which if I am honest I cannot fail to recognize?

The advice of the Stoic, to withdraw to our own freedom in the independence of the mind, is not adequate. The Stoic's perception of man's weakness was not radical enough. He failed to see that the mind in itself is empty, dependent on what is put into it, and he failed to consider the possibility of madness. The Stoic leaves us without consolation; the independent mind is barren, lacking all content. He leaves us without hope, because his doctrine affords us no opportunity of inner transformation, no fulfilment through self-conquest in love, no hopeful expectation of the possible.

And yet the Stoics' striving is toward true philosophy. Their thought, because its source is in ultimate situations, expresses the basic drive to find a revelation of true being in human failure.

Crucial for man is his attitude toward failure: whether it remains hidden from him and overwhelms him only objectively at the end or whether he perceives it unobscured as the constant limit of his existence; whether he snatches at fantastic solutions and consolations or faces it honestly, in silence before the unfathomable. The way in which man approaches his failure determines what he will become.

In ultimate situations man either perceives nothingness or senses true being in spite of and above all ephemeral worldly existence. Even despair, by the very fact that it is possible in the world, points beyond the world.

Or, differently formulated, man seeks redemption. Redemption is offered by the great, universal religions of redemption. They are characterized by an objective guarantee of the truth and reality of redemption. Their road leads to an act of individual conversion. This philosophy cannot provide. And yet all philosophy is a transcending of the world, analogous to redemption.

To sum up: The source of philosophy is to be sought in wonder, in doubt, in a sense of forsakenness. In any case it begins with an inner upheaval, which determines its goal.

Plato and Aristotle were moved by wonder to seek the nature of being.

Amid infinite uncertainty Descartes sought compelling certainty.

Amid the sufferings of life the Stoics sought the repose of the mind.

Each of these experiences has its own truth, clothed always in historical conceptions and language. In making these philosophies our own we penetrate the historical husk to the primal sources that are alive within us.

The inner drive is toward firm foundations, depth of being, eternity.

But for us perhaps none of these is the most fundamental, absolute source. The discovery that being can be revealed to wonder is a source of inspiration, but beguiles us into withdrawing from the world and succumbing to a pure, magical metaphysic. Compelling certainty is limited to the scientific knowledge by which we orient ourselves in the world. Stoic imperturbability serves us only as a makeshift in distress, as a refuge from total ruin, but in itself remains without content and life.

These three motives—wonder leading to knowledge, doubt leading to certainty, forsakenness leading to the self—cannot by themselves account for our present philosophical thought.

In this crucial turning point in history, in this age of unprecedented ruin and of potentialities that can only be darkly surmised, the three motives we have thus far considered remain in force, but they are not adequate. They can operate only if there is *communication* among men.

In all past history there was a self-evident bond between man and man, in stable communities, in institutions, and in universal ideas. Even the isolated individual was in a sense sustained in his isolation. The most visible sign of today's disintegration is that more and more men do not understand one another, that they meet and scatter, that they are indifferent to one another, that there is no longer any reliable community or loyalty.

Today a universal situation that has always existed in fact assumes crucial importance: That I can, and cannot, become one with the Other in truth;

that my faith, precisely when I am certain, clashes with other men's faith; that there is always somewhere a limit beyond which there appears to be nothing but battle without hope of unity, ending inevitably in subjugation or annihilation; that softness and complaisance cause men without faith either to band blindly together or stubbornly to attack one another.

All this is not incidental or unimportant. It might be, if there were a truth that might satisfy me in my isolation. I should not suffer so deeply from lack of communication or find such unique pleasure in authentic communication if I for myself, in absolute solitude, could be certain of the truth. But I am only in conjunction with the Other, alone I am nothing.

Communication from understanding to understanding, from mind to mind, and also from existence to existence, is only a medium for impersonal meanings and values. Defence and attack then become means not by which men gain power but by which they approach one another. The contest is a loving contest in which each man surrenders his weapons to the other. The certainty of authentic being resides only in unreserved communication between men who live together and vie with one another in a free community, who regard their association with one another as but a preliminary stage, who take nothing for granted and question everything. Only in communication is all other truth fulfilled, only in communication am I myself not merely living but fulfilling life. God manifests Himself only indirectly, and only through man's love of man; compelling certainty is particular and relative, subordinated to the Whole. The Stoical attitude is in fact empty and rigid.

The basic philosophical attitude of which I am speaking is rooted in distress at the absence of communication, in the drive to authentic communication, and in the possibility of the loving contest which profoundly unites self and self.

And this philosophical endeavour is at the same time rooted in the three philosophical experiences we have mentioned, which must all be considered in the light of their meaning, whether favourable or hostile, for communication from man to man.

And so we may say that wonder, doubt, the experience of ultimate situations, are indeed sources of philosophy, but the ultimate source is the will to authentic communication, which embraces all the rest. This becomes apparent at the very outset, for does not all philosophy strive for communication, express itself, demand a hearing? And is not its very essence communicability, which is in turn inseparable from truth?

Communication then is the aim of philosophy, and in communication all its other aims are ultimately rooted: awareness of being, illumination through love, attainment of peace.

SUGGESTED READINGS

Practically every great philosopher has expounded his conception of the nature of philosophy, but these discussions are often hard to follow without substantial acquaintance with the other aspects of the philosopher's view. This is true of Plato's discussion of philosophy in the *Republic*, Book V, and of Aristotle's in *Metaphysics*, Book I, Chapters 1 and 2, and Book III, Chapter 1. Only in comparatively recent years have examinations of the nature of philosophy constituted a large part of the philosophical enterprise. A useful volume of short excerpts from representatives of various positions, entitled *What Is Philosophy?*, has been edited by Henry W. Johnstone, Jr. For a comprehensive bibliography of writings by analytically oriented philosophers and well-chosen selections from their work the reader should consult *The Linguistic Turn: Recent Essays in Philosophical Method*, edited by Richard M. Rorty. In the collection entitled *Logical Positivism* A. J. Ayer has included essays by F. P. Ramsey, Gilbert Ryle, and F. Waismann which give an excellent idea of a variety of analytic approaches to the nature of philosophy. John Passmore discusses in *Philosophical Reasoning* the types of argument that he thinks are typically used by philosophers. John Wisdom's brilliant and challenging essays on the nature of philosophy are available in *Philosophy and Psycho-analysis* and *Paradox and Discovery*. For further acquaintance with Continental European views the reader should consult E. Husserl, "Philosophy as Rigorous Science," available in a translation by Q. Lauer in *Phenomenology and the Crisis of Philosophy*, and M. Merleau-Ponty, *In Praise of Philosophy*, translated by Wild and Edie. Alan Donagan has written an excellent study of Collingwood, *The Later Philosophy of R. G. Collingwood*.

II ❧ THE NATURE
AND LIMITS OF SCIENTIFIC
EXPLANATION

Introduction

It is generally agreed that the pursuit of knowledge is one of our most distinctively human characteristics. Some philosophers believe that our desire for knowledge stems ultimately from its practical importance in the concerns of life. Others, while not denying the value of knowledge as a practical instrument, believe that a principal motive in our search for knowledge is an interest in truth for its own sake. All agree, however, that the importance of knowledge in human affairs justifies a special concern with its nature and problems.

Many of these problems spring from the intimate connection between knowledge and the *method* by which knowledge is acquired. A question such as "How do you know?" reflects our everyday concern with problems of method. In daily life, of course, we do not always ask this question. But when we are told something strange or hard to believe, we are frequently led to ask *how* our informant knows what he claims to know. If, for example, we are told that a world of physical objects does not exist, or that our feeling of freedom is an illusion, we may very naturally react by asking how, or by what method, this conclusion was reached. And the method used may very well influence our acceptance or rejection of the conclusion. Most of us would agree that dreams, guesses, hunches, are on the whole not very reliable ways of acquiring dependable beliefs. We would probably be sceptical if someone insisted that strange animals had inhabited the earth at an early period of history, *simply* because he had dreamed that it was so. If on the other hand, he arrived at his belief by some more acceptable method (by the methods paleontologists use, for example), we would be much more likely to credit his claim. To put the matter in other words, it is clear that we don't regard a person as having real knowledge, or even a dependable belief or opinion, unless he has acquired the knowledge or belief by some method that we endorse as sound.

51

The intimate connection between knowledge and method leads to a host of questions. How much can we hope to know? Are there limits beyond which our knowledge can never penetrate? Can we know anything for certain? If so, what can be known for certain, and how do we discover it? If not, what kind of warrant do we have for such beliefs as we hold?

In the history of thought a number of ways for acquiring knowledge have been recommended. Each of these methods makes special claims, emphasizing the extent of its application, or the certainty of its conclusions, or the importance of the questions with which it can deal. Some of these methods have been unalterably opposed to each other; others have sometimes been held to be complementary. This situation leads us to ask if there is any one method that is superior to all others, and if so, of what it consists. If, on the other hand, we believe that there are alternative, complementary methods, we must ask when we can rely on one and when on another. Such questions are important in their own right and have implications for a vast range of philosophical problems.

The Method of Science

The investigations of biologists, chemists, and astronomers are, at first glance, not much alike; they study different aspects of the universe and use distinctive tools and techniques. In spite of obvious differences such studies have much in common. As scientific inquiries they pursue common aims by a common method, and it is with this method that the following selections are concerned.

One general feature of scientific method is of sufficient importance to have suggested the term "the empirical method" as a comprehensive label for scientific procedures. In calling science "empirical," we are drawing attention to its reliance on experience (Greek: *empeiria*). Scientists depend on experience in two important ways: (1) they search for data as a basis on which to found beliefs and theories, and (2) they seek to confirm or refute theories by a further appeal to experience.

In these respects, scientific method is similar to the procedures of everyday life. Given a problem, we search for data to help us solve it; if a belief is questioned, we look for data to confirm or refute it. In everyday life, however, we rarely sift or scrutinize the data on which our beliefs are based, and we rarely make further conscious, explicit tests to see if our beliefs are actually confirmed or justified. In science no theory is regarded as acceptable unless these conditions have been satisfied.

This conscious and deliberate search for data, characteristic of science, has led to the formulation of certain ideals that scientists attempt to satisfy. *All* data directly relevant to a problem must be investigated; hypotheses and theories must be precisely and explicitly formulated; alternative hypotheses are to be tested with reference to the consequences that follow from them; and an attempt must be made to find a consistent set of hypotheses that take into account as many facts as possible. The special procedures of science reflect these demands. Scientists stress the repeatability and public verifiability of their observations; they employ mathematical formulations wherever possible; they use experimental methods to test alternative hypotheses; and they attempt to extend the range of applicability of any hypothesis to include as much data as they can. It is evident that the procedures of science represent a refinement of those of everyday life and a more rigorous application of them.

BLACK discusses the important role of observation and experiment in science. The selection from COPI considers the relation between data and hypotheses and the criteria that we apply in evaluating hypotheses. These readings are complementary: science consists neither of observations alone nor of inferences alone; its aim is to formulate general explanatory hypotheses that are based upon, and confirmed by, the facts that observations and experiments establish. DUHEM emphasizes an aspect of scientific methodology which has recently received much discussion, namely, the *interdependence* of scientific disciplines. Our results in astronomy, for example, depend heavily on our theories of the propagation of light, on theories of optics used in the construction of telescopes, and so on. He suggests a more holistic interpretation of the scientific enterprise in which the coherence of the "whole story" plays an important role in accepting or rejecting particular scientific doctrines.

Observation and Experiment[*]

M A X   B L A C K [1909–   ] studied at Cambridge, Göttingen, and London Universities. He came to the United States in 1940 and taught at the University of Illinois; he is now Professor of Philosophy at Cornell University. He has written widely on logic, the philosophy of science, and related topics.

INTRODUCTION. Thoughtful men have long realized that the decisive respect in which contemporary societies differ from earlier civilizations is in changes due to mastery and application of science. Men alive today are not noticeably more gifted in intelligence, moral insight, or artistic imagination, than the Athenians. Yet hardly more than a hundred years of intense scientific activity has given modern man almost godlike powers to remake the very stuff of the universe itself. The invention of the atomic bomb was hardly needed to demonstrate that understanding and control of science are cardinal conditions for survival of civilization; and understanding is a necessary preliminary to control.

Hundreds of books and many thousands of pages have been written about scientific method; and it might be supposed that the nature of the scientific activity would by this time be generally agreed upon. Yet, in spite of renewed efforts at clarification (often brilliant in their insight) by distinguished scientists and philosophers, universal agreement concerning the nature of scientific method is still lacking. The subject upon which we are now embarking is, in some important respects, controversial.

There are several reasons for such lack of agreement concerning the nature of scientific method.

(1) The ever-increasing complexity of science makes it difficult to perceive clearly the *general* features of the entire scientific enterprise. This is the ancient and proverbial difficulty of "seeing the wood for the trees." The practicing scientist, who is a specialist in some subdivision of the enormous range of collective human knowledge, is often too absorbed in his specialty to be a safe guide to questions concerning the *general* features of scientific investigation. The man who has exceptionally detailed information concerning Entomology, Organic Chemistry, or Topology, is not necessarily clearly aware of the pattern of investigation common to all scientific subjects.

(2) In the last paragraphs we have talked of "scientific method" in the singular, as if it could be safely assumed that all scientific inquiry displays a *single* pattern of investigation. The assumption is to some extent justified, and scientific inquiries, as we shall see, do show many interesting and uniform common features. Yet sciences also *differ* significantly among each other, and the variety of scientific methods is no less important than the unity of scientific method as a whole.

(3) It is a matter of historical record that the sophisticated scientific techniques in use today have evolved from simpler procedures at the "common-sense level." Physics and chemistry arose from the practical concerns of mining, pottery, medicine, and other crafts, and are still largely directed to the improvement of technology. This would hardly concern us here, but for the fact that the earlier and cruder methods of "common-sense" are still in use today, side by side with other methods which show scarcely a trace of their humble origins. Only a small part of science requires the manipulation of machines as elaborate as the cyclotron (or "atom-smasher"). The spectacular "miracles" of scientific experimentation are made possible by an enormous mass of prosaic, even routine, observations.

This continuity of scientific method with common-sense procedures makes all accurate description of scientific method necessarily an affair of differences of degree. We should not expect to find in science some entirely new and "revolutionary" methods in use; there will be sufficient cause for wonder and admiration in noting the remarkable results which follow from the elaboration of methods already used in rough form at the familiar common-sense level. . . .

THE IMPORTANCE OF EXPERIENCE. If one trait, more than any other, is characteristic of the scientific attitude, it is *reliance upon the data of experience.* As musical aptitude requires exceptional sensitivity to tones and rhythms, so scientific aptitude correspondingly demands an exceptional flair for the *objective aspect* of experience: the stubborn capacity of objects to reveal themselves as they are, independent of human desires, hopes, and expectations. The characters of the great scientists (say Faraday, Newton, Darwin, or Pasteur) show clearly to any reader of their lives and work, unusual capacity to put speculation to the test of observation and experiment.

The history of science should disabuse us of any notion that respect for experience comes naturally to men or is achieved without persistent struggle and self-discipline. It is easy to smile today at the "glorious folly" of those opponents of Galileo who preferred to rely upon Aristotle's authority rather than look through the newly invented telescope, and labored "with logical arguments, as if with magical incantations, to charm the new planets out of the sky." Since astronomy, no longer thought relevant to controversial questions of theology, has ceased to be literally a burning subject, it has become easier to be objective about it. But where the testimony of observation still impinges upon jingoism or sectarian prejudice, the investigator must still tread delicately or bury his results in the obscurity of learned journals. Economists are sometimes treated like witches in otherwise civilized communities; and there are parts of the world where inquiry into racial differences ranks among the dangerous occupations.

The position of those who resist an appeal to experience in controversial subjects would be weaker than it is but for two circumstances: The unwarranted claims often made in behalf of science in fields of inquiry where science is still a hope rather than an achievement; and the difficulties which arise in determining what exactly *is* "shown by experience." It is easy to advise "recourse to the facts"; often enough it proves difficult to determine what kind of evidence shall be recognized as a "fact."

If we are to get a reasonable understanding of the aims and values of science (avoiding the philistinism of those who ignore its importance and the dogmatism of those who use it as a prop for unexamined prejudices) we need familiarity with the procedures employed in the *scientific* use of experience. The implied distinction between "scientific" and non-scientific appeal to experience is intended to emphasize the point, now sufficiently obvious, that a scientist does not accept experience *uncritically* or *passively*. He exercises the privilege of *discriminating* between experiences, carefully preserving one result but promptly rejecting another, recorded when he was "too tired to notice what he was doing." In arranging an experiment . . . the scientist takes elaborate steps to *ensure* that "things shall happen." We shall therefore pay special attention to the principles used by scientists in the criticism and manipulation of experience, with particular reference to the possible influence such intervention might have upon the resulting data. Since critical and active scientific recourse to experience tends to take the form of an *experiment,* we shall be particularly interested to establish the difference between experiment and "mere" observation.

The Nature of Scientific Observation

The use of the senses. The simplest conceivable use of experience consists in noticing something seen, heard, felt, or smelled. Not all such experiences are of equal value to science, yet without them no knowledge can be acquired through experience. In modern scientific procedure, elaborate use is often made of cameras, and other instruments for the automatic recording of observations; but those recordings must, in their turn, be *seen* by the human observer if they are to be of any use. Steps are often taken to eliminate the use of the senses of hearing, touch, and smell, and vision may be confined to the observation of a number on a dial; yet the scientist must still use his eyes if any observations are to be made. Scientific observation begins with the use of the senses, though it does not end there.

Choice of significant material. Some important scientific observations have been made accidentally. Thus, Becquerel's famous discovery of the radio-activity of uranium compounds arose through leaving a photographic plate in the neighborhood of the radio-active material. It has even been said that "a great science has *in many cases* risen from an accidental observation."

Such cases are, however, exceptional, and have always been followed by long series of deliberate, intentional, and directed observations. Very seldom does haphazard garnering of observations have much contribution to make to the discovery of the generalizations, theories and principles sought by scientists. And it is only in the light of accepted generalization that the scientist knows where to look for *significant* data.

Examples of scientific method . . . contain reference to many hundreds of individual observations—observations of the presence of moss or pebbles, of the color of light emitted by fluorescent stuffs, readings of rulers, thermometers, spectroscopes, and other instruments, and many more. The vast majority of them were undertaken deliberately in order to test, support, or modify some tentatively adopted hypothesis. Very few observations made by scientists have any other origin. As Darwin said, "all observation must be *for or against some view,* if it is to be of any service."

Selection of significant features. This is closely related to the last point. Some occurrence impresses us as "significant": the rainbow has been so regarded, for instance, throughout recorded history. Upon what aspect of the rainbow shall we turn our attention? To the colors, the shape, the position in the sky, the accompanying clouds or other conditions of the sky—or even to our own state of health and the moral shortcomings of our society? In the absence of previous knowledge, all of these suggestions, and an indefinite number of others, are *equally plausible.* When the scientist decides to concentrate upon one aspect of the phenomenon rather than another, it is because his previously acquired knowledge gives some intimation of *what to look for.*

There is one further and most important consequence: The selection made partly determines what shall be seen. To a casual observer all canaries look alike; it is only to the investigator who has determined to record minute differences in appearance that each bird comes to have a look as distinctive and individual as that of any human. There is in short an *increase in discrimination determined by selectivity of attention.*

Observation of the sort required in fruitful scientific study is, accordingly, an art which has to be acquired by deliberate and prolonged training. Especially is this the case in the use of instruments: To be able to "read" an instrument means to have been trained to notice the relevant and discard the accidental or unimportant. The various special sciences demand different types of observation and call for appropriately differentiated types of training.

Neglect of "illusory" experiences. A particularly important case of the selection of significant features of experiences occurs when, as frequently happens, certain aspects of an experience (or even the entire experience) are rejected as "illusory."

The distinction between "illusion" and "reality," or between "correct" and "mistaken" experiences is a familiar one. Spots seen to rise and fall against a clear sky are attributed to defects in vision; a stick "seen" to be bent upon immersion in water is not believed to have changed its shape. The scientist similarly discards certain aspects of his experience as illusory. The colored fringes of an object seen through a microscope are neglected; and in all readings of measuring instruments the variations which result when successive attempts at determination are made are treated as "errors." Such picking and choosing among the data of experience is a universal rule in scientific observation; the well-trained scientist must know what observations *not* to notice.

What right, it may be said, has the scientist to legislate for nature? And what becomes of his vaunted objectivity and respect for fact if he exercises the right to neglect features genuinely present in his experiences? If the scientist were a mere recorder of phenomena there would be no answer to this accusation: For the bent stick *does* look bent, the mosquito leg is *seen* to have colored fringes, the *recorded* weight of an object does vary from reading to reading. But such observations, as we have said, are made "for or against some view," that is, in the light of hypotheses and generalizations of which they are instances. A scientist is not interested (as a painter might be) in how the bent stick *looks* merely; he wishes to discover laws *connecting* the various appearances of the stick. He is, therefore, entitled to neglect such features of the actual experience as he pleases *provided the neglected features do not contradict the laws he proclaims.* In establishing the measurable length of a stick, he may properly neglect its "bent look"; in counting the number of bristles on an insect's foot he is justified in paying no attention to the color.

The case of the deviations in the observed weight of an object is a little more complicated. Here the scientist is looking for some *constant,* a property which will be a permanent feature of observations made upon it by himself and other observers on other occasions. Now it is a matter of experience that by taking the average of the numbers furnished by a balance (or using some more complicated procedure to obtain a *calculated weight*) such a constant *can* be found. The calculated weight proves to be a feature of the individual experience which agrees with experiences of other qualified observers in a wide range of similar conditions.

It will be noted that the "illusory" features of the experience are not permanently *rejected*. The distinction between "illusion" and "reality" in a scientific observation is a *provisional* one between features usable in generalizations and features temporarily not so usable. It is the ultimate (and probably unattainable) aim of science to account for *all* observed features of phenomena. Thus the phenomena of the bent stick and the colored microscopic image are explained in optics; variations in the reading of a balance can be elucidated by study of the rigidity and elasticity of instruments; and so forth. At any given time, however, even the most advanced sciences have a multitude of unexplained phenomena labelled "for future attention."

Public verification and the elimination of bias. The criteria which determine the selection of acceptable features of scientific observation now begin to be clear. In order to be acceptable, a feature of an observation must be: (a) capable of being presented again *in similar conditions;* (b) if possible, connected with other *constants* by means of generalizations.

How dissimilar may conditions be, before they cease to count as "similar"? To a color-blind man, blood may *always* have the same color as coffee; yet such identity of color would not be acceptable as a scientific constant. It is required that any individual observation shall be capable of confirmation by *any* qualified observer, that is, anybody who is in a position, through training, to understand the conditions of the alleged experience, manipulate the tools and instruments required to produce it, and respond to tests certifying him as a 'normal' observer.

A central aim of scientific investigation is to submit the first crude experiences of the individual to the continuing control of confirmatory investigation by the whole body of scientists. Science rests upon the fidelity and integrity of the individual scientist, and the day when individual researchers began to report what some authority decreed would mark the beginning of the end of genuine science. (This is one reason why the so-called "experiments" conducted by elementary students of the sciences bear so little resemblance to the real thing; the student knows or can guess what is expected of him, and therefore more or less consciously "cooks" the answer.) Yet the report of the individual scientist gets no more credit than it can win through the critical repetition of the observations by other scientists. This availability of scientific observation to the inspection of any suitably qualified scientist is commonly referred to by use of the term *public verifiability.*

An individual observation is said to be publicly veri*fiable* when it *could* be confirmed by any suitably qualified scientist; it is said to be publicly veri*fied* when it *has* been so confirmed by a sufficient number of other observers. (It should be noted that observations are sometimes accepted which have not been publicly *verified*. The photographic record of a new star made by a reputable astronomer is not rejected on the ground that he alone made the observation; but it would be required that *other* astronomers should be *able* to make corroborating observations. Astronomy has no dealings with stars which can *in principle* be seen only by a single, favored, individual.)

The requirement of public verification has been sometimes abused by being enlisted to discredit startling innovations and deviations from current scientific orthodoxies. Yet it is the best instrument we have against personal bias and prejudice. The history of science has shown again and again the importance of this test (and the corresponding test for scientific generalizations); and all pessimistic commonplaces concerning the diversity of human opinions must take account of the historical demonstration that men *can* reach universal agreement—at least about scientific topics.

Search for abstract structures. Stress upon public verification has important consequences on the practice of scientific observation. It leads first to emphasis upon features of experience concerning which agreement can in practice be reached. Since sensations of touch, smell, and hearing are both vague and variable, modern science relies almost exclusively upon *vision;* and what needs to be seen tends to be increasingly narrowed down to the position of a pointer on a numbered scale (the so-called "pointer-readings" or "coincidence observations"). All scientists, of course, continue to use the vaguer, more variable, and richer experiences with which life abounds—if only to recognize each other and their instruments; and careful analysis of *all* that is involved in performing a typical scientific observation would show how much reliance is still placed upon such vague observation. At the crucial moments, however, when all finally depends upon "getting the observation right" (timing the eclipse, counting the particles, and so forth) the scientist will be found characteristically intent upon the position of some line (a pointer, the surface of a mercury column, or the like) relative to the numbered gradations of a scale.

This particularly important example of "pointer-readings" illustrates the tendency for the objects of scientific discourse to become increasingly abstract. What the scientist sees is *not* what "any man" would see: the situation to be observed is defined in the light of increasingly more complex theory, and what is recorded becomes increasingly something selected, abstracted, or calculated from the "direct" observation. The "felt warmth" of an object is replaced in turn by the readings of a mercury thermometer, a "calculated value" which is "corrected for errors," and later by a still more complex structure. It is for this reason that the reports of scientific investigation becomes increasingly hard for the layman to follow. It is not merely that the scientist has come gradually to discover unusual and hidden phenomena; the cause of the obscurity is still more to be found in the transformation imposed upon common-sense concepts by the criterion of public verifiability.

The Nature of Scientific Experiment

The distinction between observation and experiment. We have seen that the term "observation" may refer to a whole series of more or less sophisticated procedures. The simplest (and least useful) type of observation consists in the uncritical report by a casual observer of something seen (or otherwise learned through the senses). This is a long remove from the procedure used by a skilled scientist, highly trained in the choice of significant features of an experience, using delicate instruments, and applying calculation to obtain the results of observation in a form amenable to public verification.

Yet even the most sophisticated and elaborate observation is not an *experiment*—though every experiment requires the taking of observations. In order to understand the nature of the difference, we may consider, as a very simple illustration, the experiment, which Galileo is said to have performed, of dropping a heavy and a light body simultaneously from a high tower. An attempt of this kind, to show that the time of flight is independent of the mass of the body concerned, would unhesitatingly be described as an *experiment.* Yet if Galileo had *happened* to notice the time taken by different objects to fall the same height he would, just as unhesitatingly, be said to have performed a series of *observations.*

The difference between the two cases seems to consist in the following points: (a) The experiment was *deliberately undertaken;* (b) involved the setting up of an *artificial situation* contrived by the scientist; (c) was arranged to answer a *definite question;* (d) involved systematic *variation of factors* in the situation observed. (Only the last of these calls for further explanation: by the "variation of factors" we mean the attempt to reproduce the situation with change in only one factor at a time. . . . Thus Galileo dropped two bodies, identical as far as possible in *all* respects except for the difference in their mass.)

Of the four differences between experiment and observation listed in the last paragraph, the first and third are differences of degree alone; for we have already seen that scientific observation, in its most highly developed forms, tends to be undertaken deliberately as a test of a definite hypothesis, or in order to answer a definite question. We shall therefore concentrate upon the artificiality and induced variability which seem especially characteristic of scientific experiment. But before going further we shall do well to check our tentative conclusions by examining some *example* of scientific experimentation. We choose for this purpose Newton's famous work on the spectrum, as reported in his own original communication to the Royal Society (1671).

An Example of Experimentation

Sir,

To perform my late promise to you, I shall without further ceremony acquaint you, that in the beginning of the year 1666 (at which time I applied myself to the grinding of Optic glasses of other figures than *Spherical*) I procured me a triangular glass-prisme, to try therewith the celebrated *Phaenomena* of *Colours*. And in order thereto having darkened my chamber, and made a small hole in my windowshuts, to let in a convenient quantity of the Suns light, I placed my prisme at his entrance, that it might be thereby refracted to the opposite wall. It was at first a very pleasing divertisement, to view the vivid and intense colours produced thereby; but after a while applying myself to consider them more circumspectly, I became surprised to see them in an *oblong* form; which, according to the received laws of Refraction, I expected should have been *circular*. They were terminated at the sides with *streight* lines, but at the ends, the decay of light was so gradual, that it was difficult to determine justly, what was their figure; yet they seemed *semicircular*.

Comparing the length of this coloured *Spectrum* with its breadth, I found it about five times greater; a disproportion so extravagant, that it excited me to a more than ordinary curiosity of examining, from whence it might proceed. I could scarce think, that the various *Thickness* of the glass, or the termination with shadow or darkness, could have any Influence on light to produce such an effect; yet I thought it not amiss, first to examine those circumstances, and so *tryed* what would happen by transmitting light through parts of the glass of divers thicknesses or through holes in the window of divers bignesses or by setting the Prisme without so, that the light might pass through it, and be refracted before it was terminated by the hole: but I found none of those circumstances material. The fashion of the colours was in all these cases the same.

Then I suspected, whether by any *unevenness* in the glass, or other contingent irregularity, these colours might thus be dilated. And to try this, I took another Prisme like the former, and so placed it, that the light, passing through them both, might be refracted in contrary ways, and so by the latter returned into that course, from which the former had diverted it. For, by this means I thought, the *regular* effects of the first Prisme would be destroyed by the second Prisme, but the irregular ones more augmented, by the multiplicity of refraction. . . .

(*Philosophical Transactions*, Number 80, Feb. 19, 1671.)

A series of further experiments finally led Newton to conclude "that Light consists of rays differently refrangible," *i.e.* is composed of different kinds of light having varying refractive powers.

We notice the following points of interest in this account. The first observations in the series seem to have been made out of curiosity and with little intention of performing a deliberate experiment. The stimulus to serious investigation is provided by recognition of a significant conflict between observation and the theoretical prediction ("I became surprised to see them in an *oblong* form; which, according to the received laws of refraction, I expected should have been circular"). The subsequent experiments are directed toward *explaining* the observed phenomenon (the oblong shape of the spectrum); and consist in *systematic variation* of the factors in the experimental situation. Thus the hypothesis that the spread of the light is due to the thickness of a prism is tested by passing the light through various thicknesses of the prism, *while keeping all else unchanged*. Next the hypothesis that the shape of the aperture by which the light is admitted is responsible is eliminated in a similar fashion. And so forth.

This example, then, confirms our view of the importance of systematic variation of conditions in an experiment.

Artificiality of experiments. The experiences which come to people in the surroundings of everyday living occur within a relatively small range of climatic and other physical conditions. Early scientists took every opportunity to obtain observations made in *unusual* circumstances (as by climbing mountains, descending under water, or, after the invention of efficient pumps, observing phenomena in a vacuum). Today an important aspect of experimental technique consists in producing exceptionally high or low temperatures, artificially intensified electrical charges, or other exceptional circumstances not otherwise encountered. The method of "going to extremes" has proved especially valuable: "When the scientist studies extremes he is often as not rewarded by both knowledge of abnormal facts and also by a new viewpoint on the normal."

In calling the conditions of an experiment "artificial," we must not be misled by the word into supposing that the scientist somehow makes or creates the phenomena investigated. Liquid helium at a temperature close to absolute zero is still a "natural" substance; what is "artificial" in the experiments in which it is used is the creation of conditions in which its "natural properties" can be observed.

The kind of artificiality which is most fruitful in experimentation consists in the creation of conditions in which one factor at a time can be varied in independence of the others. Sometimes this can be done by *isolating* factors from other interfering factors (as in the electrical insulation of apparatus for experimental research in electricity, the preparation of "chemically pure" substances for chemical research, and so forth). The "shielding" or "isolation" of relevant factors in an experiment is often the hardest part of the undertaking, and may call for the highest kind of ingenuity and resourceful-ness.

Systematic variation of factors. This is the crux of scientific experimenta-tion. Any random observation will be an instance of indefinitely many factors that may contribute to the phenomenon attracting attention. If a group of children suddenly make exceptional progress in their studies, the result might plausibly be attributed to the personality of the teacher, the quality of the textbook used, the competitive atmosphere of the school, ex-ceptional endowment of the children, or to a host of other factors. On gen-eral grounds we might expect the result to be due to a *combination* of factors not detectable by superficial observation. Scientific investigation of such a question requires conditions to be created in which each suspected factor can be varied independently of the others.

A powerful means of effecting this is the use of so-called *control experi-ments.* Thus, if the question studied is the effect of adding iron to the diet of fish, *two* groups of fish will be used, chosen to be as alike as possible in species, average weight and length, and so on. One group will then be fed small quantities of iron, while the other *control group* will be treated simi-larly in all other respects. Increased growth in the iron-eating group may, in such conditions, be held to be reasonably significant. (It is much harder to design similar conditions for educational experiments. If it were possible to establish two schools whose students and teachers were all identical twins, we might begin to approximate to the best conditions.) . . .

Obstacles to Observation and Experiment

We can place the results of our discussion in a different perspective by considering the conditions which limit the possibility and effectiveness of scientific observation and experiment. . . .

The difficulty of correcting personal bias. In order for scientific investiga-tion to be possible, it is necessary, as we have seen, to develop some system-atic method of counteracting the interference produced by the observer's idiosyncrasies and prejudices. The intention on the part of the observer to be impartial, and to "observe the facts as they really are" is essential. *But good intentions are not enough.* For in advance of detailed knowledge of a partic-ular subject, it is impossible to determine what is "objective fact" and what "illusion" or "error." (We saw that the "objective" was distinguished from the "illusory" or "subjective" as that which leads to dependable knowledge, *i.e.* that which can be brought within the scope of sound *generalizations.*) From the heights of our superior knowledge, it is tempting to say that the early alchemists who expected to find "spirits" in chemical substances were victims of a characteristically human bias in favor of finding *human* traits in nature. Yet the expectation that iron has a "spirit" or "soul" is *antecedently* as reasonable as any other; if chemists waste no time today in looking for the "temperament" or "characters" of different kinds of matter (in the sense of those terms applicable to human beings) it is because the accumulation of scientific knowledge has shown such inquiries to be fruitless.

In comparatively undeveloped fields of inquiry, where the elimination of bias has most importance, objectivity is hardest to achieve. It is easy to say that the unbiased observation is that which will ultimately win the credence of all "qualified observers"; the practical difficulty is that of deciding who shall *count* as a "qualified observer." We meet here a circularity very characteristic of scientific procedure: the elimination of bias waits upon the acquisition of reliable information; the acquisition of reliable information waits upon the elimination of bias.

Subjects, such as history, which deal with fragmentary and ambiguous data from the vanished past, are in a particularly difficult position. For whatever data are used are bound to be a minute selection from the total; and personal bias in form of some preferred criteria of significance is unavoidable.

Inaccessibility of data. Events which are very remote in space or time, and those involving extremely large or extremely small magnitudes and velocities are obviously hard to observe even by the unbiased observer. Though the generation of living matter may be a purely chemical phenomenon, it is conceivable that we shall never have *enough time* to reproduce the proper conditions; it has been supposed that space is full of dark stars, which we have no way of observing, or even of many too remote for light-signals from them to have reached us. But the difficulties created by the restricted range of our sense-organs are being constantly overcome through the creation of appropriate instruments of observation.

The difficulty of perceiving significant data. This is closely related to the difficulty of recognizing bias. If a scientist from Mars (where there is no music) were to listen to a human violinist, he might perceive nothing more significant than the scraping of horse-hair over catgut; yet the composer's musical ideas are truly present in the musical performance *for those who are prepared to find them.* Scientific observation, we have seen, is an *active* process, in which the observer *interrogates* nature. The difficulty in psychology or economics or other young sciences is to know *what questions to ask.* "The problem of science is not to discover examples of laws when we know what kinds of law to look for; it is to know for what kind of law to look." (N. R. Campbell, *What Is Science?* p. 76.) Once again we take note of the circularity of scientific precedure: Without knowledge of generalizations, no significant observations; without significant observations, no generalizations.

The difficulty of creating experimental situations. In trying to answer some questions of urgent human interest, it may be impossible to arrange for the variation of conditions, and the use of control situations, as required in scientific experiment. Many people would like to know how far Hitler was responsible for the second World War. A god who could make the history of the world "repeat itself" with the *sole* exception that the infant Hitler *died at birth* might have a "scientific" answer to the question; mere mortals must rely upon weaker procedures of analogy, comparison with similar historical conditions, and so forth. Even where experiment is theoretically possible, it may be restrained by humanitarian considerations. We hesitate to infect *humans* with lethal diseases, or deliberately to create socially maladjusted communities.

When no other difficulties arise, it may be practically impossible to insure isolation of one factor from others. This is typically the case in the social sciences, where any factor of interest (say juvenile delinquency) tends to be highly complex and related to an unmanageable variety of other factors.

One special difficulty of this general type is due to *interference by instruments*. Introduction of *any* instrument produces some change, no matter how small, in the situation observed. In certain important cases, such disturbances are not trivial and cannot safely be neglected as irrelevant. The study of ultramicroscopic phenomena in physics is particularly embarrassed by this difficulty; trying to learn the properties of electrons (or other infinitesimal particles) by bombarding them with other electrons is like trying to discover the properties of rocks by shooting cannon-balls at them. Similar difficulties arise in other sciences; the conclusions of the biologist are likely to be mistaken to the extent that he is compelled to study the properties of tissue *removed from the living animal;* a society in which Gallup pollsters and other social investigations are active often shows characteristics not found in undisturbed societies.

The moral of these difficulties. A catalogue of the obstacles to scientific observation and experiment can be made to appear very impressive. To draw pessimistic conclusions concerning the value of scientific method in this account would be unreasonable, nevertheless. The triumphs of scientific method in the most complex fields of inquiry are sufficient demonstration that the obstacles to observation and experiment can be overcome. Only a very rash or a very foolish critic would chart the boundaries of possible scientific investigation; the cure for lack of scientific knowledge of a subject is more and better scientific study.

Fact and Hypothesis[*]

IRVING MARMER COPI [1917–   ] was educated at the University of Michigan, where he took his doctorate in 1948. After teaching for one year at Illinois, he returned to Michigan. He has written on logic, scientific method, and the philosophy of language.

The job of science, we all know, is to discover facts; but a haphazard collection of facts cannot be said to constitute a science. To be sure, some parts of science may focus on this or that particular fact. A geographer, for example, may be interested in describing the exact configuration of a particular coastline, or a geologist in the precise nature of rock strata in a particular locality. But in the more advanced sciences, bare descriptive knowledge of this or that particular fact is of little importance. The scientist is eager to search out more general truths, of which particular facts are instances and for which they constitute evidence. Isolated particular facts may be known —in a sense—by direct observation. That a particular released object falls, that this ball moves more slowly down an inclined plane than it did when dropped directly downwards, that the tides ebb and flow, all these are matters of fact open to direct inspection. But the scientist seeks more than a mere record of such phenomena; he strives to understand them. To this end he seeks to formulate general laws which state the patterns of all such occurrences and the systematic relationships between them. The scientist is engaged in a search for the natural laws according to which all particular events occur and the fundamental principles which underlie them.

This preliminary exposition of the theoretical aims of science can perhaps be made clearer by means of an example. By careful observation, and the application of geometrical reasoning to the data thus collected, the Italian physicist and astronomer Galileo (1564–1642) succeeded in formulating the laws of falling bodies, which gave a very general description of the behavior of bodies at the surface of the earth. At about the same time the great German astronomer Kepler (1571–1630), basing his reasonings very largely on the astronomical data collected by Tycho Brahe (1546–1601), formulated the laws of planetary motion, which gave an accurate description of the elliptical orbits traveled by the planets round the sun. Each of these two great scientists succeeded in unifying the various phenomena in his own field

[*] From Copi: *Introduction to Logic*, Chapter 13. Copyright, 1953, by The Macmillan Company. Reprinted by permission of The Macmillan Company.

of investigation by formulating the interrelations between them: Kepler in celestial mechanics, Galileo in terrestrial mechanics. Their discoveries were great achievements, but they were, after all, separate and apart. Just as isolated particular facts challenge the scientist to unify and explain them by discovering their lawful connections, so a plurality of general laws challenges the scientist to unify and explain them by discovering a still more general principle which subsumes the several laws as special cases. In the case of Kepler's and Galileo's laws, this challenge was met by one of the greatest scientific geniuses of all time, Sir Isaac Newton (1642–1727). By means of his Theory of Gravitation, together with his three Laws of Motion, Newton unified and explained celestial and terrestrial mechanics by showing them both to be deducible within the framework of a single more fundamental *theory*. The scientist seeks not merely to know what the facts are, but to explain them, and to this end he devises *theories*. To understand exactly what is involved here, we must consider the general nature of explanation itself.

EXPLANATIONS: SCIENTIFIC AND UNSCIENTIFIC. In everyday life it is the unusual or startling for which we demand explanations. An office boy may arrive at work on time every morning for ever so long, and no curiosity will be aroused. But let him come an hour late one day, and his employer will demand an *explanation*. What is it that is wanted when an explanation for something is requested? An example will help to answer this question. The office boy might reply that he had taken the seven-thirty bus to work as usual, but the bus had been involved in a traffic accident which had entailed considerable delay. In the absence of any other transportation, the boy had had to wait for the bus to be repaired, and that had taken a full hour. This account would probably be accepted as a satisfactory explanation. It can be so regarded because from the statements which constitute the explanation the fact to be explained follows logically and no longer appears puzzling. An explanation is a group of statements or a story from which the thing to be explained can logically be inferred and whose assumption removes or diminishes its problematic or puzzling character. . . . It thus appears that explanation and inference are very closely related. They are, in fact, the same process regarded from opposite points of view. Given certain premises, any conclusion which can logically be inferred from them is regarded as being explained by them. And given a fact to be explained, we say that we have found an explanation for it when we have found a set of premises from which it can logically be inferred.

Of course some proposed explanations are better than others. The chief criterion for evaluating explanations is *relevance*. If the tardy office boy had offered as explanation for his late arrival the fact that there is a war in China or a famine in India, that would properly be regarded as a very poor explanation, or rather as "no explanation at all." Such a story would have "nothing to do with the case"; it would be *irrelevant*, because from it the fact to be explained can *not* be inferred. The relevance of a proposed explanation, then, corresponds exactly to the cogency of the argument by which the fact to be explained is inferred from the proposed explanation. Any acceptable explanation must be relevant, but not all stories which are relevant in this sense are acceptable explanations. There are other criteria for deciding the worth or acceptability of proposed explanations.

The most obvious requirement to propose is that the explanation be *true*. In the example of the office boy's lateness, the crucial part of his explanation was a particular fact, the traffic accident, of which he was (presumably) an eyewitness. But the explanations of science are for the most part *general* rather than particular. The keystone of Newtonian Mechanics is the Law of Universal Gravitation, whose statement is:

Every particle of matter in the universe attracts every other particle with a force which is directly proportional to the product of the masses of the particles and inversely proportional to the square of the distance between them.

Newton's law is not directly verifiable in the same way that a bus accident is at the time it occurs. There is simply no way in which we can inspect *all* particles of matter in the universe and see that they do attract each other in precisely the way that Newton's law asserts. Few propositions of science are *directly* verifiable as true. In fact, none of the important ones are. For the most part they concern *unobservable* entities, such as molecules and atoms, electrons and protons, and the like. Hence the proposed requirement of truth is not *directly* applicable to most scientific explanations. Before considering more useful criteria for evaluating scientific theories, it will be helpful to compare scientific with unscientific explanations.

Science is supposed to be concerned with facts, and yet in its further reaches we find it apparently committed to highly speculative notions which are far removed from the possibility of direct experience. How then are scientific explanations to be distinguished from those which are frankly mythological or superstitious? An unscientific "explanation" of the regular motions of the planets was the doctrine that each heavenly body was the abode of an "Intelligence" or "Spirit" which controlled its movement. A certain humorous currency was achieved during World War II by the unscientific explanation of certain aircraft failures as being due to "gremlins," which were said to be invisible but mischievous little men who played pranks on aviators. The point to note here is that from the point of view of observability and direct verifiability, there is no great difference between modern scientific theories and the unscientific doctrines of mythology or theology. One can no more see or touch a Newtonian "particle," an atom, or electron, than an "Intelligence" or a "gremlin." What then are the differences between scientific and unscientific explanations?

There are two important and closely related differences between the kind of explanation sought by science and the kind provided by superstitions of various sorts. The first significant difference lies in the attitudes taken towards the explanations in question. The typical attitude of one who really accepts an unscientific explantion is dogmatic. What he accepts is regarded as being absolutely true and beyond all possibility of improvement or correction. During the Middle Ages and the early modern period the word of Aristotle was the ultimate authority to which scholars appealed for deciding questions of fact. . . . The scientist's attitude towards his explanations is altogether different. Every explanation in science is put forward tentatively and provisionally. A proposed explanation is regarded as a mere hypothesis, more or less probable on the basis of the available facts or relevant evidence. It must be admitted that the scientist's vocabulary is a little misleading on this point. When what was first suggested as a "hypothesis" becomes well confirmed, it is frequently elevated to the position of a "theory." And when, on the basis of a great mass of evidence, it achieves well nigh universal acceptance, it is promoted to the lofty status of a "law." This terminology is not always strictly adhered to: Newton's discovery is still called the "Law of Gravitation," while Einstein's contribution, which supersedes or at least improves on Newton's, is referred to as the "Theory of Relativity." The vocabulary of "hypothesis," "theory," and "law" is unfortunate, since it obscures the important fact that *all* of the general propositions of science are regarded as hypotheses, never as dogmas.

Closely allied with the difference in the way they are regarded is the second and more fundamental difference between scientific and unscientific explanations or theories. This second difference lies in the basis for accepting or rejecting the view in question. Many unscientific views are mere prejudices, which their adherents could scarcely give any reason for holding. Since they are regarded as "certain," however, any challenge or question is likely to be regarded as an affront and met with abuse. If one who accepts an unscientific explanation *can* be persuaded to discuss the basis for its acceptance, there are only a few grounds on which he will attempt to "defend" it. It is true because "we've always believed it," or because "everyone knows it." These all too familiar phrases express appeals to tradition or popularity rather than evidence. . . . In general, unscientific beliefs are held independently of anything we should regard as *evidence* in their favor. Because they are *absolute,* questions of evidence are regarded as having little or no importance.

The case is quite different in the realm of science. Since every scientific explanation is regarded as a hypothesis, it is regarded as worthy of acceptance only to the extent that there is *evidence* for it. As a hypothesis, the question of its truth or falsehood is *open,* and there is continual search for more and more evidence to decide that question. The term "evidence" as used here refers ultimately to experience; *sensible* evidence is the ultimate court of appeal in verifying scientific propositions. Science is *empirical* in holding that sense experience is the *test of truth* for all its pronouncements. Consequently, it is of the essence of a *scientific* proposition that it be capable of being tested by observation.

Some propositions can be tested *directly.* To decide the truth or falsehood of the proposition which asserts that it is now raining outside, we need only look out the window. To tell whether a traffic light shows green or red, all we have to do is to look at it. But the propositions which scientists usually offer as explanatory hypotheses are not of this type. Such general propositions as Newton's Laws or Einstein's Theory are not *directly testable* in this fashion. They can, however, be tested *indirectly.* The *indirect method* of testing the truth of a proposition is familiar to all of us, though we may not be familiar with this name for it. For example, if his employer had been suspicious of the office boy's explanation of his tardiness, he might have checked up on it by telephoning the bus company to find out whether an accident had really happened to the seven-thirty bus. If the bus company's report checked with the boy's story, this would serve to dispel the employer's suspicions; whereas if the bus company denied that an accident had occurred, it would probably convince the employer that his office boy's story was false. This inquiry would constitute an *indirect test* of the office boy's explanation.

The pattern of *indirect testing* or *indirect verification* consists of two parts. First one deduces from the proposition to be tested one or more other propositions which *are* capable of being tested *directly.* Then these consequences are tested and found to be either true or false. If the consequences are false, any proposition which implies them must be false also. On the other hand, if the consequences are true, they are evidence for the truth of the proposition being tested, which is thus confirmed *indirectly.*

It should be noted that indirect testing is never demonstrative or certain. To deduce directly testable conclusions from a proposition usually requires additional premises. The conclusion that the bus company will *reply* that the seven-thirty bus had an accident this morning does not follow validly from the proposition that the seven-thirty bus *did* have an accident. Additional premises are needed, for example, that all accidents are reported to the company's office, that the reports are not mislaid or forgotten, and the company does not make a policy of denying its accidents. So the bus company's denying that an accident occurred would not demonstrate the office boy's story to be false, for the discrepancy might be due to the falsehood of one of the other premises mentioned. Those others, however, ordinarily have such a high degree of probability that a negative reply on the part of the bus company would render the office boy's story very doubtful indeed.

Similarly, establishing the truth of a conclusion does not demonstrate the truth of the premises from which it was deduced. We know very well that a valid argument may have a true conclusion even though its premises are not all true. In the present example, the bus company might affirm that an accident occurred to the seven-thirty bus because of some mistake in their records, even though no accident had occurred. So the inferred consequent *might* be true even though the *premises* from which it was deduced were not. In the usual case, though, that is highly unlikely; so that a successful or affirmative direct testing of a conclusion serves to render probable the premises from which it was deduced.

It must be admitted that every proposition, scientific or unscientific, which is a relevant explanation for any observable fact, has *some* evidence in its favor, namely the fact to which it is relevant. Thus the regular motions of the planets must be conceded to constitute evidence for the (unscientific) theory that the planets are inhabited by "Intelligences" which cause them to move in just the orbits which are observed. The motions themselves are as much evidence for that myth as they are for Newton's or Einstein's theories. The difference lies in the fact that that is the *only* evidence for the unscientific hypothesis. Absolutely no other *directly* testable propositions can be deduced from the myth. On the other hand, a very large number of directly testable propositions can be deduced from the scientific explanations mentioned. Here, then, is *the* difference between scientific and unscientific explanations. A scientific explanation for a given fact will have directly testable propositions deducible from it other than the one asserting the fact to be explained. But an unscientific explanation will have no other directly testable propositions deducible from it. It is of the essence of a scientific proposition to be empirically verifiable. . . .

EVALUATING SCIENTIFIC EXPLANATIONS. The question naturally arises as to how scientific explanations are to be evaluated, that is, judged as good or bad, or at least as better or worse. This question is especially important because there is usually more than a single scientific explanation for one and the same fact. A man's abrupt behavior may be explained either by the hypothesis that he is shy or by the hypothesis that he is unfriendly. In a criminal investigation two different and incompatible hypotheses about the identity of the criminal may equally well account for the known facts. In the realm of science proper, that an object expands when heated is explained by both the caloric theory of heat and the kinetic theory. The caloric theory regarded heat as an invisible weightless fluid called "caloric," with the power of penetrating, expanding, and dissolving bodies, or dissipating them in vapor. The kinetic theory, on the other hand, regards the heat of a body as consisting of random motions of the molecules of which the body is composed. These are *alternative* scientific explanations which serve equally well to explain some of the phenomena of thermal expansion. They cannot both be true, however, and the problem is to evaluate or choose between them.

What is wanted here is a list of conditions which a good hypothesis can be expected to fulfill. It must not be thought that such a list of conditions can constitute a *recipe* by whose means anyone at all can construct good hypotheses. No one has ever pretended to lay down a set of rules for the invention or discovery of hypotheses. It is likely that none could ever be laid down, for that is the *creative* side of the scientific enterprise. Ability to create is a function of a person's imagination and talent and cannot be reduced to a mechanical process. A great scientific hypothesis, with wide explanatory powers like those of Newton's or Einstein's, is as much the product of genius as a great work of art. There is no formula for discovering new hypotheses, but there are certain rules to which acceptable hypotheses can be expected to conform. These can be regarded as the criteria for evaluating hypotheses.

There are five criteria which are used in judging the worth or acceptability of hypotheses. They may be listed as (1) relevance, (2) testability, (3) compatibility with previously well established hypotheses, (4) predictive or explanatory power, and (5) simplicity. The first two have already been discussed, but we shall review them briefly here.

1. *Relevance.* No hypothesis is ever proposed for its own sake but is always intended as an explanation of some fact or other. Therefore it must be *relevant* to the fact which it is intended to explain, that is, the fact in question must be deducible from the proposed hypothesis—either from the hypothesis alone or from it together with certain causal laws which may be presumed to have already been established as highly probable, or from these together with certain assumptions about particular initial conditions. A hypothesis which is not relevant to the fact it is intended to explain simply fails to explain it and can be regarded as having failed to fulfill its intended function. A good hypothesis must be *relevant*.

2. *Testability.* The chief distinguishing characteristic of scientific hypotheses (as contrasted with unscientific ones) is that they are testable. That is, there must be the possibility of making observations which tend to

confirm or disprove any scientific hypothesis. It need not be *directly* testable, of course. As has already been observed, most of the really important scientific hypotheses are formulated in terms of such unobservable entities as electrons or electromagnetic waves. As one contemporary research scientist has written: "A physicist of this century, interested in the basic structure of matter, deals with radiation he cannot see, forces he cannot feel, particles he cannot touch." But there must be some way of getting from statements about such unobservables to statements about directly observable entities such as tables and chairs, or pointer readings, or lines on a photographic plate. In other words, there must be some connection between any scientific hypothesis and empirical data or facts of experience.

3. *Compatibility with Previously Well Established Hypotheses.* The requirement that an acceptable hypothesis must be compatible or consistent with other hypotheses which have already been well confirmed is an eminently reasonable one. Science, in seeking to encompass more and more facts, aims at achieving a *system* of explanatory hypotheses. Of course such a system must be self-consistent, for no self-contradictory set of propositions could possibly be true—or even intelligible. Ideally, the way in which scientists hope to make progress is by gradually expanding their hypotheses to comprehend more and more facts. For such progress to be made each new hypothesis must be consistent with those already confirmed. Thus Leverrier's hypothesis that there was an additional but not yet charted planet beyond the orbit of Uranus was perfectly consistent with the main body of accepted astronomical theory. A new theory must *fit in* with older theories if there is to be orderly progress in scientific inquiry.

It is possible, of course, to overestimate the importance of the third criterion. Although the ideal of science may be the gradual growth of theoretical knowledge by the addition of one new hypothesis after another, the actual history of scientific progress has not always followed that pattern. Many of the most important of new hypotheses have been inconsistent with older theories and have in fact replaced them rather than fitted in with them. Einstein's Relativity Theory was of that sort, shattering many of the preconceptions of the older Newtonian theory. The phenomenon of radioactivity, first observed during the last decade of the Nineteenth Century, led to the overthrow—or at least the modification—of many cherished theories which had almost achieved the status of absolutes. One of these was the principle of the Conservation of Matter, which asserted that matter could neither be created nor destroyed. The hypothesis that radium atoms undergo spontaneous disintegration was inconsistent with that old established principle—but it was the principle which was relinquished in favor of the newer hypothesis.

The foregoing is not intended to give the impression that scientific progress is a helter-skelter process in which theories are abandoned right and left in favor of newer and shinier ones. Older theories are not so much abandoned as corrected. Einstein himself has always insisted that his own work is a modification rather than a rejection of Newton's. The principle of the Conservation of Matter was modified by being absorbed into the more comprehensive principle of the Conservation of Mass-Energy. Every established theory has been established through having proved adequate to explain a considerable mass of data, of observed facts. And it cannot be dethroned or discredited by any new hypothesis unless that new hypothesis can account for the same facts as well or even better. There is nothing capricious about the development of science. Every change represents an improvement, a more comprehensive and thus more adequate explanation of the way in which the world manifests itself in experience. Where inconsistencies occur between hypotheses, the greater age of one does not automatically prove it to be correct and the newer one wrong. The *presumption* is in favor of the older one if it has already been extensively confirmed. But if the new one in conflict with it *also* receives extensive confirmation, considerations of age or priority are definitely irrelevant. Where there is a conflict between two hypotheses, we must turn to the observable facts to decide between them. Ultimately, our last court of appeal in deciding between rival hypotheses is experience. What our third criterion, compatibility with previously well established hypotheses, comes to is this: the totality of hypotheses accepted at any time should be consistent with each other, and—other things being equal—of two new hypotheses, the one which fits in better with the accepted body of scientific theory is to be preferred. The question of what is involved in "other things being equal" takes us directly to our fourth criterion.

4. *Predictive or explanatory power.* By the predictive or explanatory power of a hypothesis is meant the range of observable facts that can be deduced from it. This criterion is related to, but different from, that of testability. A hypothesis is testable if *some* observable fact is deducible from it. If one of two testable hypotheses has a greater number of observable facts deducible from it than from the other, then it is said to have greater predictive or explanatory power. For example, Newton's hypothesis of universal gravitation together with his three laws of motion had greater predictive power than either Kepler's or Galileo's hypotheses, because all observable consequences of the latter two were also consequences of the former, and the former had many more besides. An observable fact which can be deduced from a given hypothesis is said to be explained by it and also can be said to be *predicted* by it. The greater the predictive power of a hypothesis,

the more it explains, and the better it contributes to our understanding of the phenomena with which it is concerned.

Our fourth criterion has a negative side which is of crucial importance. If a hypothesis is inconsistent with any well attested fact of observation, the hypothesis is false and must be rejected. Where two different hypotheses are both relevant to explaining some set of facts and both are testable, and both are compatible with the whole body of already established scientific theory, it may be possible to choose between them by deducing incompatible propositions from them which are directly testable. If H_1 and H_2, two different hypotheses, entail incompatible consequences, it may be possible to set up a *crucial experiment* to decide between them. Thus if H_1 entails that under circumstance C phenomenon P will occur, while H_2 entails that under circumstance C phenomenon P will not occur, then all we need to decide between H_1 and H_2 is to realize circumstance C and observe the presence or absence of phenomenon P. If P occurs, this is evidence *for* H_1 and *against* H_2, while if P does not occur, this is evidence *against* H_1 and *for* H_2.

This kind of crucial experiment to decide between rival hypotheses may not always be easy to carry out, for the required circumstance C may be difficult or impossible to realize. Thus the decision between Newtonian Theory and Einstein's General Theory of Relativity had to await a total eclipse of the sun—a situation or circumstance which it is clearly beyond the present powers of man to produce. In other cases the crucial experiment may have to await the development of new instruments, either for the production of the required *circumstances*, or for the observation or measurement of the predicted phenomenon. The proponents of rival astronomical hypotheses must frequently mark time while awaiting the construction of new and more powerful telescopes, for example. . . .

5. *Simplicity.* It sometimes happens that two rival hypotheses satisfy the first four criteria equally well. Historically the most important pair of such hypotheses were those of Ptolemy (fl. 127–151) and Copernicus (1473–1543). Both were intended to explain all of the then known data of astronomy. According to the Ptolemaic theory, the earth is the center of the universe, and the heavenly bodies move about it in orbits which require a very complicated geometry of epicycles to describe. Ptolemy's theory was relevant, testable, and compatible with previously well established hypotheses, satisfying the first three criteria perfectly. According to the Copernican theory, the sun rather than the earth is at the center, and the earth itself moves around the sun along with the other planets. Copernicus' theory too satisfied the first three criteria perfectly. And with respect to the fourth criterion, the two theories were almost exactly on a par. (True enough, the Copernican theory seemed to predict a stellar parallax which could not be observed, but

this failure was easily accounted for by the auxiliary hypothesis that the fixed stars were too far away for any parallax to be noticed.) To all intents and purposes, the Ptolemaic and Copernican theories were of equal predictive or explanatory power. There was only one significant difference between the two rival hypotheses. Although both required the clumsy method of epicycles to account for the observed positions of the various heavenly bodies, *fewer* such epicycles were required within the Copernican theory. The Copernican system was therefore *simpler,* and on this basis it was accepted by all later astronomers, despite the greater age and equal predictive power of the Ptolemaic system, and in the teeth of persecution by the Medieval Church!

The criterion of simplicity is a perfectly natural one to invoke. In ordinary life as well as in science, the simplest theory which fits all the available facts is the one we tend to accept. In court trials of criminal cases the prosecution attempts to develop a hypothesis which includes the guilt of the accused and fits in with all the available evidence. Opposing him, the defense attorney seeks to set up a hypothesis which includes the innocence of the accused and also fits all the available evidence. Often both sides succeed, and then the case is usually decided—or *ought* to be decided—in favor of that hypothesis which is simpler or more "natural." Simplicity, however, is a very difficult term to define. Not all controversies are as straightforward as the Ptolemaic-Copernican one, in which the latter's greater simplicity consisted merely in requiring a smaller number of epicycles. And of course "naturalness" is an almost hopelessly deceptive term—for it seems much more "natural" to believe that the earth is still while the apparently moving sun really does move. The fifth and last criterion, simplicity, is an important and frequently decisive one, but it is vague and not always easy to apply.

Physical Theory and Experiment[*]

PIERRE M. M. DUHEM [1861–1916] was one of the outstanding theoretical physicists of his time. His principal contributions were to thermodynamics, but he also wrote extensively on other branches of mathematical physics and on the history and philosophy of science. He taught at the Universities of Lille and Rennes, and from 1895 until his death he was Professor at Bordeaux University. His principal work was a comprehensive treatment of many branches of physics, which appeared in eight volumes under the title *Le Système du Monde*.

An Experiment in Physics Can Never Condemn an Isolated Hypothesis but Only a Whole Theoretical Group

The physicist who carries out an experiment, or gives a report of one, implicitly recognizes the accuracy of a whole group of theories. Let us accept this principle and see what consequences we may deduce from it when we seek to estimate the role and logical import of a physical experiment.

In order to avoid any confusion we shall distinguish two sorts of experiments: experiments of *application,* which we shall first just mention, and experiments of *testing,* which will be our chief concern.

You are confronted with a problem in physics to be solved practically; in order to produce a certain effect you wish to make use of knowledge acquired by physicists; you wish to light an incandescent bulb; accepted theories indicate to you the means for solving the problem; but to make use of these means you have to secure certain information; you ought, I suppose, to determine the electromotive force of the battery of generators at your disposal; you measure this electromotive force: that is what I call an experiment of application. This experiment does not aim at discovering whether accepted theories are accurate or not; it merely intends to draw on these theories. In order to carry it out, you make use of instruments that these same theories legitimize; there is nothing to shock logic in this procedure.

But experiments of application are not the only ones the physicist has to perform; only with their aid can science aid practice, but it is not through

[*] From Duhem: *The Aim and Structure of Physical Theory,* translated from the French by Philip P. Wiener. Reprinted by permission of the Princeton University Press. Copyright 1954 by Princeton University Press. Translated from the second edition, published in 1914 by Marcel Rivière & Cie, Paris, under the title *La Théorie Physique: Son Objet, Sa Structure.*

them that science creates and develops itself; besides experiments of application, we have experiments of testing.

A physicist disputes a certain law; he calls into doubt a certain theoretical point. How will he justify these doubts? How will he demonstrate the inaccuracy of the law? From the proposition under indictment he will derive the prediction of an experimental fact; he will bring into existence the conditions under which this fact should be produced; if the predicted fact is not produced, the proposition which served as the basis of the prediction will be irremediably condemned.

F. E. Neumann assumed that in a ray of polarized light the vibration is parallel to the plane of polarization, and many physicists have doubted this proposition. How did O. Wiener undertake to transform this doubt into a certainty in order to condemn Neumann's proposition? He deduced from this proposition the following consequence: If we cause a light beam reflected at 45° from a plate of glass to interfere with the incident beam polarized perpendicularly to the plane of incidence, there ought to appear alternately dark and light interference bands parallel to the reflecting surface; he brought about the conditions under which these bands should have been produced and showed that the predicted phenomenon did not appear, from which he concluded that Neumann's proposition is false, viz., that in a polarized ray of light the vibration is not parallel to the plane of polarization.

Such a mode of demonstration seems as convincing and as irrefutable as the proof by reduction to absurdity customary among mathematicians; moreover, this demonstration is copied from the reduction to absurdity, experimental contradiction playing the same role in one as logical contradiction plays in the other.

Indeed, the demonstrative value of experimental method is far from being so rigorous or absolute: the conditions under which it functions are much more complicated than is supposed in what we have just said; the evaluation of results is much more delicate and subject to caution.

A physicist decides to demonstrate the inaccuracy of a proposition; in order to deduce from this proposition the prediction of a phenomenon and institute the experiment which is to show whether this phenomenon is or is not produced, in order to interpret the results of this experiment and establish that the predicted phenomenon is not produced, he does not confine himself to making use of the proposition in question; he makes use also of a whole group of theories accepted by him as beyond dispute. The prediction of the phenomenon, whose nonproduction is to cut off debate, does not derive from the proposition challenged if taken by itself, but from the proposition at issue joined to that whole group of theories; if the predicted phenomenon is not produced, not only is the proposition questioned at fault, but so is the whole theoretical scaffolding used by the physicist. The only thing the experiment teaches us is that among the propositions used to predict the phenomenon and to establish whether it would be produced, there is at least one error; but where this error lies is just what it does not tell us. The physicist may declare that this error is contained in exactly the proposition he wishes to refute, but is he sure it is not in another proposition? If he is, he accepts implicitly the accuracy of all the other propositions he has used, and the validity of his conclusion is as great as the validity of his confidence.

Let us take as an example the experiment imagined by Zenker and carried out by O. Wiener. In order to predict the formation of bands in certain circumstances and to show that these did not appear, Wiener did not make use merely of the famous proposition of F. E. Neumann, the proposition which he wished to refute; he did not merely admit that in a polarized ray vibrations are parallel to the plane of polarization; but he used, besides this, propositions, laws, and hypotheses constituting the optics commonly accepted: he admitted that light consists in simple periodic vibrations, that these vibrations are normal to the light ray, that at each point the mean kinetic energy of the vibratory motion is a measure of the intensity of light, that the more or less complete attack of the gelatine coating on a photographic plate indicates the various degrees of this intensity. By joining these propositions, and many others that would take too long to enumerate, to Neumann's proposition, Wiener was able to formulate a forecast and establish that the experiment belied it. If he attributed this solely to Neumann's proposition, if it alone bears the responsibility for the error this negative result has put in evidence, then Wiener was taking all the other propositions he invoked as beyond doubt. But this assurance is not imposed as a matter of logical necessity; nothing stops us from taking Neumann's proposition as accurate and shifting the weight of the experimental contradiction to some other proposition of the commonly accepted optics; as H. Poincaré has shown, we can very easily rescue Neumann's hypothesis from the grip of Wiener's experiment on the condition that we abandon in exchange the hypothesis which takes the mean kinetic energy as the measure of the light intensity; we may, without being contradicted by the experiment, let the vibration be parallel to the plane of polarization, provided that we measure the light intensity by the mean potential energy of the medium deforming the vibratory motion.

These principles are so important that it will be useful to apply them to another example; again we choose an experiment regarded as one of the most decisive ones in optics.

We know that Newton conceived the emission theory for optical phenomena. The emission theory supposes light to be formed of extremely thin projectiles, thrown out with very great speed by the sun and other sources of light; these projectiles penetrate all transparent bodies; on account of the various parts of the media through which they move, they undergo attractions and repulsions; when the distance separating the acting particles is very small these actions are very powerful, and they vanish when the masses between which they act are appreciably far from each other. These essential hypotheses joined to several others, which we pass over without mention, lead to the formulation of a complete theory of reflection and refraction of light; in particular, they imply the following proposition: The index of refraction of light passing from one medium into another is equal to the velocity of the light projectile within the medium it penetrates, divided by the velocity of the same projectile in the medium it leaves behind.

This is the proposition that Arago chose in order to show that the theory of emission is in contradiction with the facts. From this proposition a second follows: Light travels faster in water than in air. Now Arago had indicated an appropriate procedure for comparing the velocity of light in air with the velocity of light in water; the procedure, it is true, was inapplicable, but Foucault modified the experiment in such a way that it could be carried out; he found that the light was propagated less rapidly in water than in air. We may conclude from this, with Foucault, that the system of emission is incompatible with the facts.

I say the *system* of emission and not the *hypothesis* of emission; in fact, what the experiment declares stained with error is the whole group of propositions accepted by Newton, and after him by Laplace and Biot, that is, the whole theory from which we deduce the relation between the index of refraction and the velocity of light in various media. But in condemning this system as a whole by declaring it stained with error, the experiment does not tell us where the error lies. Is it in the fundamental hypothesis that light consists in projectiles thrown out with great speed by luminous bodies? Is it in some other assumption concerning the actions experienced by light corpuscles due to the media through which they move? We know nothing about that. It would be rash to believe, as Arago seems to have thought, that Foucault's experiment condemns once and for all the very hypothesis of emission, i.e., the assimilation of a ray of light to a swarm of projectiles. If physicists had attached some value to this task, they would undoubtedly have succeeded in founding on this assumption a system of optics that would agree with Foucault's experiment.

In sum, the physicist can never subject an isolated hypothesis to experimental test, but only a whole group of hypotheses; when the experiment is in disagreement with his predictions, what he learns is that at least one of the hypotheses constituting this group is unacceptable and ought to be modified; but the experiment does not designate which one should be changed.

We have gone a long way from the conception of the experimental method arbitrarily held by persons unfamiliar with its actual functioning. People generally think that each one of the hypotheses employed in physics can be taken in isolation, checked by experiment, and then, when many varied tests have established its validity, given a definitive place in the system of physics. In reality, this is not the case. Physics is not a machine which lets itself be taken apart; we cannot try each piece in isolation and, in order to adjust it, wait until its solidity has been carefully checked. Physical science is a system that must be taken as a whole; it is an organism in which one part cannot be made to function except when the parts that are most remote from it are called into play, some more so than others, but all to some degree. If something goes wrong, if some discomfort is felt in the functioning of the organism, the physicist will have to ferret out through its effect on the entire system which organ needs to be remedied or modified without the possibility of isolating this organ and examining it apart. The watchmaker to whom you give a watch that has stopped separates all the wheelworks and examines them one by one until he finds the part that is defective or broken. The doctor to whom a patient appears cannot dissect him in order to establish his diagnosis; he has to guess the seat and cause of the ailment solely by inspecting disorders affecting the whole body. Now, the physicist concerned with remedying a limping theory resembles the doctor and not the watchmaker. . . .

Good Sense Is the Judge of Hypotheses Which Ought to Be Abandoned

When certain consequences of a theory are struck by experimental contradiction, we learn that this theory should be modified but we are not told by the experiment what must be changed. It leaves to the physicist the task of finding out the weak spot that impairs the whole system. No absolute principle directs this inquiry, which different physicists may conduct in very different ways, without having the right to accuse one another of illogicality. For instance, one may be obliged to safeguard certain fundamental hypotheses while he tries to reestablish harmony between the consequences of the theory and the facts by complicating the schematism in which these hypotheses are applied, by invoking various causes of error, and by multiplying corrections. The next physicist, disdainful of these complicated artificial procedures, may decide to change some one of the essential assumptions supporting the entire system. The first physicist does not have the right to condemn in advance the boldness of the second one, nor does the latter have the right to treat the timidity of the first physicist as absurd. The methods they follow are justifiable only by experiment, and if they both succeed in satisfying the requirements of experiment each is logically permitted to declare himself content with the work that he has accomplished.

That does not mean that we cannot very properly prefer the work of one of the two to that of the other. Pure logic is not the only rule for our judgments; certain opinions which do not fall under the hammer of the principle of contradiction are in any case perfectly unreasonable. These motives which do not proceed from logic and yet direct our choices, these "reasons which reason does not know" and which speak to the ample "mind of finesse" but not to the "geometric mind," constitute what is appropriately called good sense.

Now, it may be good sense that permits us to decide between two physicists. It may be that we do not approve of the haste with which the second one upsets the principles of a vast and harmoniously constructed theory whereas a modification of detail, a slight correction, would have sufficed to put these theories in accord with the facts. On the other hand, it may be that we may find it childish and unreasonable for the first physicist to maintain obstinately at any cost, at the price of continual repairs and many tangled-up stays, the worm-eaten columns of a building tottering in every part, when by razing these columns it would be possible to construct a simple, elegant, and solid system.

But these reasons of good sense do not impose themselves with the same implacable rigor that the prescriptions of logic do. There is something vague and uncertain about them; they do not reveal themselves at the same time with the same degree of clarity to all minds. Hence, the possibility of lengthy quarrels between the adherents of an old system and the partisans of a new doctrine, each camp claiming to have good sense on its side, each party finding the reasons of the adversary inadequate. The history of physics would furnish us with innumerable illustrations of these quarrels at all times and in all domains. Let us confine ourselves to the tenacity and ingenuity with which Biot by a continual bestowal of corrections and accessory hypotheses maintained the emissionist doctrine in optics, while Fresnel opposed this doctrine constantly with new experiments favoring the wave theory.

In any event this state of indecision does not last forever. The day arrives when good sense comes out so clearly in favor of one of the two sides that the other side gives up the struggle even though pure logic would not forbid its continuation. After Foucault's experiment had shown that light traveled faster in air than in water, Biot gave up supporting the emission hypothesis; strictly, pure logic would not have compelled him to give it up, for Foucault's experiment was *not* the crucial experiment that Arago thought he saw in it, but by resisting wave optics for a longer time Biot would have been lacking in good sense.

Since logic does not determine with strict precision the time when an inadequate hypothesis should give way to a more fruitful assumption, and since recognizing this moment belongs to good sense, physicists may hasten this judgment and increase the rapidity of scientific progress by trying consciously to make good sense within themselves more lucid and more vigilant. Now nothing contributes more to entangle good sense and to disturb its insight than passions and interests. Therefore, nothing will delay the decision which should determine a fortunate reform in a physical theory more than the vanity which makes a physicist too indulgent towards his own system and too severe towards the system of another. We are thus led to the conclusion so clearly expressed by Claude Bernard: The sound experimental criticism of a hypothesis is subordinated to certain moral conditions; in order to estimate correctly the agreement of a physical theory with the facts, it is not enough to be a good mathematician and skillful experimenter; one must also be an impartial and faithful judge.

SUGGESTED READINGS

John Stuart Mill's *System of Logic* is one of the first attempts to set forth the essentials of modern scientific method. Probably its most famous contribution is the discussion of the four methods for establishing causal connections, Book III, Chapters 7 and 8. For sharp criticism of these methods see F. H. Bradley's *Principles of Logic*, Book II, Part II, Chapter 3. Also useful are H. W. B. Joseph, *Introduction to Logic*, Chapter 10, and L. S. Stebbing, *Modern Introduction to Logic*, Chapter 17.

In *The Logic of Scientific Discovery*, Chapter 2, Karl Popper discusses the importance of being clear about methodology. This has also been a matter of considerable concern to many practicing scientists. Among the recently influential works on this topic are two by Norman Campbell: *What Is Science?* and the larger, more technical *Foundations of Science*. Another frequently discussed attempt by a noted scientist to explain science is E. Schrodinger's essay, "On the Peculiarity of the Scientific World-View," reprinted in his *What is Life?*

C. S. Peirce's essay, "The Fixation of Belief," is an important attempt to show that scientific method produces the most valuable kind of knowledge. In "How to Make Our Ideas Clear," Peirce proposes to use scientific method in explaining the meanings of terms as well as in testing the truth of assertions. These essays are available in Peirce's *Collected Papers*, Volume V, and in many anthologies. The connection of scientific method and meaning has assumed great importance in the last decades. Hans Reichenbach in *The Rise of Scientific Philosophy*, Part I, discusses this development. M. Schlick's "Meaning and Verification" gives a classical statement of the view that only assertions testable by scientific techniques are meaningful; this essay is reprinted in H. Feigl and M. Brodbeck, *Readings in the Philosophy of Science*. C. G. Hempel discusses various problems with this criterion of meaning in "The Empiricist Criterion of Meaning," reprinted in *Logical Positivism*, edited by A. J. Ayer.

Mathematics and Experience

There seems to be an important difference between the truths of pure mathematics (for example, $6 - 2 = 4$) and the truths of empirical science (for example, Newton's law of universal gravitation). The former are apparently certain and indubitable, perhaps even self-evident; whereas any empirical assertion is only *probably* true. The contrast between the certainty of mathematical truths and the uncertainty of empirical beliefs has led to much speculation, most of which has been couched in terms of the following important distinction.

It is common among philosophers to distinguish between two kinds of knowledge, that which is *a posteriori* (after, or dependent on, experience) and that which is *a priori* (prior to, or independent of, experience). The distinction is most easily explained by reference to a corresponding distinction between *a posteriori* and *a priori statements*, which may be illustrated as follows:

(1) All bachelors are unhappy.
(2) All bachelors are unmarried.

Statement (1) we call an *a posteriori* statement, because to find out whether it is true or false we must appeal to experience; that is, we must actually observe bachelors, or we must send bachelors a questionnaire asking them whether they are unhappy or in some such way collect evidence that will tend to prove or disprove that all bachelors are unhappy. Since the evidence acquired by such an appeal to experience is not logically conclusive, we could never, as a result of it, be in a position to say that an *a posteriori* statement is *certainly* true.

The case is quite different with statement (2), which is an *a priori* statement. In the first place, no observation of bachelors is relevant to its truth or falsity. In the second place, we can apparently be *certain* that it is true. No matter what investigations we carry out, we can be sure that we will never find a married bachelor.

A reason sometimes assigned to account for this difference is that *a priori* statements are *analytic*. By saying that a statement is analytic we mean that its truth depends solely on the meanings of the terms employed in it. If we know the meanings of "bachelor" and "unmarried," for example, we *know* that all bachelors are unmarried. The truth of *synthetic* (that is, nonanalytic) statements, on the other hand, depends on the nature of the world and not simply on the relations among our concepts. The concept "bachelor" does not imply that people called bachelors must be unhappy. To find out whether they are, we must consult experience.

MILL holds that the propositions of mathematics are empirical (in the sense that they derive from experience), that they are synthetic (in the sense that they depend on the nature of the world rather than on our concepts), and that they differ from the propositions of physics and other sciences in being more general and confirmed to a greater degree than those of the other empirical sciences. They rest on basic laws derived from repeated experience, so that mathematics, like the rest of science, rests on experiential, inductive foundations.

This view of mathematical truth is challenged by HEMPEL. Instead of assimilating the methods of mathematics to those of the other sciences, Hempel, along with most contemporary philosophers, sharply distinguishes between empirical propositions and those propositions that have absolute certainty because they depend simply upon the analysis of concepts. Clearly, if the only statements that are *certainly* true are analytic statements, then we can have no absolutely certain knowledge *concerning the world.* The certainty that we have in pure mathematics would rest simply on the nature of the concepts mathematicians use. On this view, the truths of mathematics are (in the words of Bertrand Russell) "of the same nature as the Great Truth that there are three feet in a yard,"—a "Truth" which tells what the word "yard" means, but doesn't tell us the length of anything. However, these truths are not without their uses: mathematics is regarded as a kind of language, and one which is singularly well suited to the expression and elaboration of the concepts and theories of certain scientific disciplines.

There are, in general, two main ways of taking issue with such a position. Some contemporary philosophers have attempted to show that the distinction between "analytic" and "synthetic" statements cannot be clearly and rigorously drawn. But critics have more often held that in addition to *a priori* statements such as (2) above, which are granted to be merely analytic, there are also synthetic *a priori* propositions. This is the view defended by EWING in his criticism of Hempel's position, which Ewing refers to as "the linguistic theory of *a priori* propositions."

Mathematics and Experience*

JOHN STUART MILL [1806–1873] was the leading British philosopher of his time. In his *System of Logic* he sought to lay the foundations for inductive logic and to reduce all mathematical and logical reasoning to a species of induction. In other works he also defended an empiricist approach, holding a position not far removed from that of Hume. His *Principles of Political Economy* was the standard exposition of economic theory for more than a generation. The works of Mill which are most widely read today are his ethical and political writings, in particular *Utilitarianism* and *On Liberty*.

. . . [W]herein lies the peculiar certainty always ascribed to the sciences which are entirely, or almost entirely, deductive? Why are they called the Exact Sciences? Why are mathematical certainty, and the evidence of demonstration, common phrases to express the very highest degree of assurance attainable by reason? Why are mathematics by almost all philosophers, and (by some) even those branches of natural philosophy which, through the medium of mathematics, have been converted into deductive sciences, considered to be independent of the evidence of experience and observation, and characterised as systems of Necessary Truth?

The answer I conceive to be, that this character of necessity ascribed to the truths of mathematics, and even (with some reservations to be hereafter made) the peculiar certainty attributed to them, is an illusion; in order to sustain which, it is necessary to suppose that those truths relate to, and express the properties of purely imaginary objects. It is acknowledged that the conclusions of geometry are deduced, partly at least, from the so-called Definitions, and that those definitions are assumed to be correct representations, as far as they go, of the objects with which geometry is conversant. Now we have pointed out that, from a definition as such, no proposition, unless it be one concerning the meaning of a word, can ever follow; and that what apparently follows from a definition, follows in reality from an implied assumption that there exists a real thing conformable thereto. This assumption in the case of the definitions of geometry, is not strictly true: there exist no real things exactly conformable to the definitions. There exist no points without magnitude; no lines without breadth, nor perfectly straight; no circles with all their radii exactly equal, nor squares with all their angles per-

* From Mill: *System of Logic* (1st edition, 1843), 8th edition, Longmans, Green, and Co., 1872.

fectly right. It will perhaps be said that the assumption does not extend to
the actual, but only to the possible existence of such things. I answer that,
according to any test we have of possibility, they are not even possible.
Their existence, so far as we can form any judgment, would seem to be
inconsistent with the physical constitution of our planet at least, if not of the
universe. To get rid of this difficulty, and at the same time to save the credit
of the supposed system of necessary truth, it is customary to say that the
points, lines, circles, and squares which are the subject of geometry, exist in
our conceptions merely, and are part of our minds; which minds, by working
on their own materials, construct an *a priori* science, the evidence of which is
purely mental, and has nothing whatever to do with outward experience. By
howsoever high authorities this doctrine may have been sanctioned, it appears to me psychologically incorrect. The points, lines, circles, and squares
which any one has in his mind, are (I apprehend) simply copies of the
points, lines, circles, and squares which he has known in his experience. Our
idea of a point I apprehend to be simply our idea of the *minimum visible,*
the smallest portion of surface which we can see. A line as defined by
geometers is wholly inconceivable. We can reason about a line as if it had no
breadth; because we have a power, which is the foundation of all the control
we can exercise over the operations of our minds; the power, when a perception is present to our senses or a conception to our intellects, of *attending* to
a part only of that perception or conception, instead of the whole. But we
cannot *conceive* a line without breadth; we can form no mental picture of
such a line; all the lines which we have in our minds are lines possessing
breadth. If any one doubts this, we may refer him to his own experience. I
much question if any one who fancies that he can conceive what is called a
mathematical line, thinks so from the evidence of his consciousness: I suspect it is rather because he supposes that unless such a conception were possible, mathematics could not exist as a science: a supposition which there
will be no difficulty in showing to be entirely groundless.

Since, then, neither in nature, nor in the human mind, do there exist any
objects exactly corresponding to the definitions of geometry, while yet that
science cannot be supposed to be conversant about non-entities; nothing
remains but to consider geometry as conversant with such lines, angles, and
figures as really exist; and the definitions, as they are called, must be regarded as some of our first and most obvious generalisations concerning
those natural objects. The correctness of those generalisations, *as* generalisations, is without a flaw: the equality of all the radii of a circle is true of all
circles, so far as it is true of any one: but it is not exactly true of any circle; it
is only nearly true; so nearly that no error of any importance in practice will
be incurred by feigning it to be exactly true. When we have occasion to ex-

tend these inductions or their consequences, to cases in which the error would be appreciable—to lines of perceptible breadth or thickness, parallels which deviate sensibly from equidistance, and the like—we correct our conclusions by combining with them a fresh set of propositions relating to the aberration; just as we also take in propositions relating to the physical or chemical properties of the material, if those properties happen to introduce any modification into the result; which they easily may, even with respect to figure and magnitude, as in the case, for instance, of expansion by heat. So long, however, as there exists no practical necessity for attending to any of the properties of the object except its geometrical properties, or to any of the natural irregularities in those, it is convenient to neglect the consideration of the other properties and of the irregularities, and to reason as if these did not exist: accordingly, we formally announce in the definitions, that we intend to proceed on this plan. But it is an error to suppose, because we resolve to confine our attention to a certain number of the properties of an object, that we therefore conceive, or have an idea of, the object denuded of its other properties. We are thinking, all the time, of precisely such objects as we have seen and touched, and with all the properties which naturally belong to them; but, for scientific convenience, we feign them to be divested of all properties, except those which are material to our purpose, and in regard to which we design to consider them.

The peculiar accuracy, supposed to be characteristic of the first principles of geometry thus appears to be fictitious. The assertions on which the reasonings of the science are founded do not, any more than in other sciences, exactly correspond with the fact, but we suppose that they do so for the sake of tracing the consequences which follow from the supposition. The opinion of Dugald Stewart respecting the foundations of geometry, is, I conceive, substantially correct; that it is built on hypotheses; that it owes to this alone the peculiar certainty supposed to distinguish it; and that in any science whatever, by reasoning from a set of hypotheses, we may obtain a body of conclusions as certain as those of geometry, that is, as strictly in accordance with the hypotheses, and as irresistibly compelling assent, *on condition* that those hypotheses are true.

When, therefore, it is affirmed that the conclusions of geometry are necessary truths, the necessity consists in reality only in this, that they correctly follow from the suppositions from which they are deduced. Those suppositions are so far from being necessary, that they are not even true; they purposely depart, more or less widely, from the truth. The only sense in which necessity can be ascribed to the conclusions of any scientific investigation, is that of legitimately following from some assumption, which, by the conditions of the inquiry, is not to be questioned. In this relation, of course, the derivative truths of every deductive science must stand to the inductions, or assumptions, on which the science is founded, and which, whether true or untrue, certain or doubtful in themselves, are always supposed certain for the purposes of the particular science. . . .

It remains to inquire, what is the ground of our belief in axioms—what is the evidence on which they rest? I answer, they are experimental truths; generalisations from observation. The proposition, Two straight lines cannot enclose a space—or, in other words, two straight lines which have once met do not meet again, but continue to diverge—is an induction from the evidence of our senses.

This opinion runs counter to a scientific prejudice of long standing and great strength, and there is probably no proposition enunciated in this work for which a more unfavourable reception is to be expected. It is, however, no new opinion; and even if it were so, would be entitled to be judged, not by its novelty, but by the strength of the arguments by which it can be supported.

. . . [T]he truth of the axiom, Two straight lines cannot enclose a space, even if evident independently of experience, is also evident from experience. Whether the axiom needs confirmation or not, it receives confirmation in almost every instant of our lives, since we cannot look at any two straight lines which intersect one another without seeing that from that point they continue to diverge more and more. Experimental proof crowds in upon us in such endless profusion, and without one instance in which there can be even a suspicion of an exception to the rule, that we should soon have stronger ground for believing the axiom, even as an experimental truth, than we have for almost any of the general truths which we confessedly learn from the evidence of our senses. Independently of *a priori* evidence we should certainly believe it with an intensity of conviction far greater than we accord to any ordinary physical truth: and this too at a time of life much earlier than that from which we date almost any part of our acquired knowledge, and much too early to admit of our retaining any recollection of the history of our intellectual operations at that period. Where then is the necessity for assuming that our recognition of these truths has a different origin from the rest of our knowledge, when its existence is perfectly accounted for by supposing its origin to be the same? when the causes which produce belief in all other instances exist in this instance, and in a degree of strength as much superior to what exists in other cases as the intensity of the belief itself is superior? The burden of proof lies on the advocates of the contrary opinion: it is for them to point out some fact inconsistent with the supposition that this part of our knowledge of nature is derived from the same sources as every other part. . . .

From these considerations it would appear that Deductive or Demonstrative Sciences are all, without exception, Inductive Sciences; that their evidence is that of experience; but that they are also, in virtue of the peculiar character of one indispensable portion of the general formulae according to which their inductions are made, Hypothetical Sciences. Their conclusions are only true on certain suppositions, which are, or ought to be, approximations to the truth, but are seldom, if ever, exactly true; and to this hypothetical character is to be ascribed the peculiar certainty which is supposed to be inherent in demonstration.

What we have now asserted, however, cannot be received as universally true of Deductive or Demonstrative Sciences, until verified by being applied to the most remarkable of all those sciences, that of Numbers; the theory of the Calculus; Arithmetic and Algebra.

. . . [T]here is in every step of an arithmetical or algebraical calculation a real induction, a real inference of facts from facts; and . . . what disguises the induction is simply its comprehensive nature and the consequent extreme generality of the language. All numbers must be numbers of something; there are no such things as numbers in the abstract. *Ten* must mean ten bodies, or ten sounds, or ten beatings of the pulse. But though numbers must be numbers of something, they may be numbers of anything. Propositions, therefore, concerning numbers have the remarkable peculiarity that they are propositions concerning all things whatever; all objects, all existences of every kind, known to our experience. All things possess quantity; consist of parts which can be numbered; and in that character possess all the properties which are called properties of numbers. That half of four is two, must be true whatever the word four represents, whether four hours, four miles, or four pounds weight. We need only conceive a thing divided into four equal parts (and all things may be conceived as so divided) to be able to predicate of it every property of the number four, that is, every arithmetical proposition in which the number four stands on one side of the equation. Algebra extends the generalisation still farther: every number represents that particular number of all things without distinction, but every algebraical symbol does more, it represents all numbers without distinction. As soon as we conceive a thing divided into equal parts, without knowing into what number of parts, we may call it a or x, and apply to it, without danger of error, every algebraical formula in the books. The proposition, $2(a + b) = 2a + 2b$, is a truth co-extensive with all nature. Since then algebraical truths are true of all things whatever, and not, like those of geometry, true of lines only or of angles only, it is no wonder that the symbols should not excite in our minds ideas of any things in particular. When we demonstrate the forty-seventh proposition of Euclid, it is not necessary that the words should raise in us an image of all right-angled triangles, but only of some one right-angled triangle; so in algebra we need not, under the symbol *a*, picture to ourselves all things whatever, but only some one thing; why not, then, the letter itself? The mere written characters, *a, b, x, y, z,* serve as well for representatives of things in general, as any more complex and apparently more concrete conception. That we are conscious of them, however, in their character of things, and not of mere signs, is evident from the fact that our whole process of reasoning is carried on by predicating of them the properties of things. In resolving an algebraic equation, by what rules do we proceed? By applying at each step to *a, b,* and *x,* the proposition that equals added to equals make equals; that equals taken from equals leave equals; and other propositions founded on these two. These are not properties of language, or of signs as such but of magnitudes, which is as much as to say, of all things. The inferences, therefore, which are successively drawn, are inferences concerning things, not symbols; though as any things whatever will serve the turn, there is no necessity for keeping the idea of the Thing at all distinct, and consequently the process of thought may, in this case, be allowed without danger to do what all processes of thought, when they have been performed often, will do if permitted, namely, to become entirely mechanical. Hence the general language of algebra comes to be used familiarly without exciting ideas, as all other general language is prone to do from mere habit, though in no other case than this can it be done with complete safety. But when we look back to see from whence the probative force of the process is derived, we find that at every single step, unless we suppose ourselves to be thinking and talking of the things and not the mere symbols, the evidence fails.

There is another circumstance, which, still more than that which we have now mentioned, gives plausibility to the notion that the propositions of arithmetic and algebra are merely verbal. That is, that when considered as propositions respecting Things, they all have the appearance of being identical propositions. The assertion, Two and one is equal to three, considered as an assertion respecting objects, as for instance "two pebbles and one pebble are equal to three pebbles," does not affirm equality between two collections of pebbles, but absolute identity. It affirms that if we put one pebble to two pebbles, those very pebbles are three. The objects, therefore, being the very same, and the mere assertion that "objects are themselves" being insignificant, it seems but natural to consider the proposition Two and one is equal to three, as asserting mere identity of signification between the two names.

This, however, though it looks so plausible, will not bear examination. The expression "two pebbles and one pebble," and the expression "three pebbles," stand indeed for the same aggregation of objects, but they by no means stand for the same physical fact. They are names of the same objects, but of those objects in two different states: though they *de*note the same things, their *con*notation is different. Three pebbles in two separate parcels, and three pebbles in one parcel, do not make the same impression on our senses; and the assertion that the very same pebbles may by an alteration of place and arrangement be made to produce either the one set of sensations or the other, though a very familiar proposition, is not an identical one. It is a truth known to us by early and constant experience—an inductive truth; and such truths are the foundation of the science of Numbers. The fundamental truths of that science all rest on the evidence of sense; they are proved by showing to our eyes and our fingers that any given number of objects, ten balls, for example, may by separation and rearrangement exhibit to our senses all the different sets of numbers the sum of which is equal to ten. All the improved methods of teaching arithmetic to children proceed on a knowledge of this fact. All who wish to carry the child's *mind* along with them in learning arithmetic; all who wish to teach numbers, and not mere ciphers—now teach it through the evidence of the senses, in the manner we have described.

Mathematics and the *A Priori**

CARL GUSTAV HEMPEL [1905–   ], born in Germany, took his Ph.D. at Berlin in 1934. He has taught at Queens College and Yale University and is now Professor of Philosophy at Princeton. He is one of the foremost exponents of logical empiricism and has written extensively on problems in logic and scientific methodology.

THE PROBLEM. It is a basic principle of scientific inquiry that no proposition and no theory is to be accepted without adequate grounds. In empirical science, which includes both the natural and the social sciences, the grounds for the acceptance of a theory consist in the agreement of predictions based on the theory with empirical evidence obtained either by experiment or by systematic observation. But what are the grounds which sanction the ac-

* From Hempel: "On the Nature of Mathematical Truth," in *American Mathematical Monthly*, LII (1945), pp. 543–556. Reprinted by permission of *American Mathematical Monthly* and the author. [*Note:* The following pages omit the more technical portions of this article. The article in its entirety is also available in Feigl and Sellars: *Readings in Philosophical Analysis*, Appleton-Century-Crofts, 1949.]

ceptance of mathematics? That is the question I propose to discuss in the present paper. For reasons which will become clear subsequently, I shall use the term "mathematics" here to refer to arithmetic, algebra, and analysis—to the exclusion, in particular, of geometry.

ARE THE PROPOSITIONS OF MATHEMATICS SELF-EVIDENT TRUTHS? One of the several answers which have been given to our problem asserts that the truths of mathematics, in contradistinction to the hypotheses of empirical science, require neither factual evidence nor any other justification because they are "self-evident." This view, however, which ultimately relegates decisions as to mathematical truth to a feeling of self-evidence, encounters various difficulties. First of all, many mathematical theorems are so hard to establish that even to the specialist in the particular field they appear as anything but self-evident. Secondly, it is well known that some of the most interesting results of mathematics—especially in such fields as abstract set theory and topology—run counter to deeply ingrained intuitions and the customary kind of feeling of self-evidence. Thirdly, the existence of mathematical conjectures (such as those of Goldbach and of Fermat), which are quite elementary in content and yet undecided up to this day, certainly shows that not all mathematical truths can be self-evident. And finally, even if self-evidence were attributed only to the basic postulates of mathematics, from which all other mathematical propositions can be deduced, it would be pertinent to remark that judgments as to what may be considered as self-evident are subjective; they may vary from person to person and certainly cannot constitute an adequate basis for decisions as to the objective validity of mathematical propositions.

IS MATHEMATICS THE MOST GENERAL EMPIRICAL SCIENCE? According to another view, advocated especially by John Stuart Mill, mathematics is itself an empirical science which differs from the other branches such as astronomy, physics, chemistry, etc., mainly in two respects: its subject matter is more general than that of any other field of scientific research, and its propositions have been tested and confirmed to a greater extent than those of even the most firmly established sections of astronomy or physics. Indeed, according to this view, the degree to which the laws of mathematics have been borne out by the past experiences of mankind is so overwhelming that— unjustifiably—we have come to think of mathematical theorems as qualitatively different from the well-confirmed hypotheses or theories of other branches of science: we consider them as certain, while other theories are thought of as at best "very probable" or very highly confirmed.

But this view, too, is open to serious objections. From a hypothesis which is empirical in character—such as, for example, Newton's law of gravitation —it is possible to derive predictions to the effect that under certain specified conditions certain specified observable phenomena will occur. The actual occurrence of these phenomena constitutes confirming evidence, their non-occurrence disconfirming evidence for the hypothesis. It follows in particular that an empirical hypothesis is theoretically disconfirmable; i.e., it is possible to indicate what kind of evidence, if actually encountered, would disconfirm the hypothesis. In the light of this remark, consider now a simple "hypothesis" from arithmetic: $3 + 2 = 5$. If this is actually an empirical generalization of past experiences, then it must be possible to state what kind of evidence would oblige us to concede the hypothesis was not generally true after all. If any disconfirming evidence for the given proposition can be thought of, the following illustration might well be typical of it: We place some microbes on a slide, putting down first three of them and then another two. Afterwards we count all the microbes to test whether in this instance 3 and 2 actually added up to 5. Suppose now that we counted 6 microbes altogether. Would we consider this as an empirical disconfirmation of the given proposition, or at least as a proof that it does not apply to microbes? Clearly not; rather, we would assume we had made a mistake in counting or that one of the microbes had split in two between the first and second count. But under no circumstances could the phenomenon just described invalidate the arithmetical proposition in question; for the latter asserts nothing whatever about the behavior of microbes; it merely states that any set consisting of $3 + 2$ objects may also be said to consist of 5 objects. And this is so because the symbols "$3 + 2$" and "5" denote the same number: they are synonymous by virtue of the fact that the symbols "2," "3," "5," and "$+$" are *defined* (or tacitly understood) in such a way that the above identity holds as a consequence of the meaning attached to the concepts involved in it.

THE ANALYTIC CHARACTER OF MATHEMATICAL PROPOSITIONS. The statement that $3 + 2 = 5$, then, is true for similar reasons as, say, the assertion that no sexagenarian is 45 years of age. Both are true simply by virtue of definitions or of similar stipulations which determine the meaning of the key terms involved. Statements of this kind share certain important characteristics: Their validation naturally requires no empirical evidence; they can be shown to be true by a mere analysis of the meaning attached to the terms which occur in them. In the language of logic, sentences of this kind are called analytic or true *a priori*, which is to indicate that their truth is logically independent of, or logically prior to, any experiential evidence. And while the statements of empirical science, which are synthetic and can be validated only *a posteriori*, are constantly subject to revision in the light of new evidence, the truth of an analytic statement can be established definitely, once and for all. However, this characteristic "theoretical certainty" of analytic propositions has to be paid for at a high price: An analytic statement conveys no factual information. Our statement about sexagenarians, for example, asserts nothing that could possibly conflict with any factual evidence: it has no factual implications, no empirical content; and it is precisely for this reason that the statement can be validated without recourse to empirical evidence.

Let us illustrate this view of the nature of mathematical propositions by reference to another, frequently cited, example of a mathematical—or rather logical—truth, namely the proposition that whenever $a = b$ and $b = c$ then $a = c$. On what grounds can this so-called "transitivity of identity" be asserted? Is it of an empirical nature and hence at least theoretically disconfirmable by empirical evidence? Suppose, for example, that a, b, c, are certain shades of green, and that as far as we can see, $a = b$ and $b = c$, but clearly $a \neq c$. This phenomenon actually occurs under certain conditions; do we consider it as disconfirming evidence for the proposition under consideration? Undoubtedly not; we would argue that if $a \neq c$, it is impossible that $a = b$ and also $b = c$; between the terms of at least one of these latter pairs, there must obtain a difference, though perhaps only a subliminal one. And we would dismiss the possibility of empirical disconfirmation, and indeed the idea that an empirical test should be relevant here, on the grounds that identity is a transitive relation by virtue of its definition or by virtue of the basic postulates governing it. Hence, the principle in question is true *a priori*.

I have argued so far that the validity of mathematics rests neither on its alleged self-evidential character nor on any empirical basis, but derives from the stipulations which determine the meaning of the mathematical concepts, and that the propositions of mathematics are therefore essentially "true by definition." . . . The propositions of mathematics have, therefore, the same unquestionable certainty which is typical of such propositions as "All bachelors are unmarried," but they also share the complete lack of empirical content which is associated with that certainty: The propositions of mathematics are devoid of all factual content; they convey no information whatever on any empirical subject matter.

On the Applicability of Mathematics to Empirical Subject Matter. This result seems to be irreconcilable with the fact that after all mathematics has proved to be eminently applicable to empirical subject matter, and that indeed the greater part of present-day scientific knowledge has been reached only through continual reliance on and application of the propositions of mathematics. Let us try to clarify this apparent paradox by reference to some examples.

Suppose that we are examining a certain amount of some gas, whose volume v, at a certain fixed temperature, is found to be 9 cubic feet when the pressure p is 4 atmospheres. And let us assume further that the volume of the gas for the same temperature and $p = 6$ at., is predicted by means of

Boyle's law. Using elementary arithmetic we reason thus: For corresponding values of v and p, $vp = c$, and $v = 9$ when $p = 4$; hence $c = 36$. Therefore, when $p = 6$, then $v = 6$. Suppose that this prediction is borne out by subsequent test. Does that show that the arithmetic used has a predictive power of its own, that its propositions have factual implications? Certainly not. All the predictive power here deployed, all the empirical content exhibited stems from the initial data and from Boyle's law, which asserts that $vp = c$ for *any* two corresponding values of v and p, hence also for $v = 9$, $p = 4$, and for $p = 6$ and the corresponding value of v. The function of the mathematics here applied is not predictive at all; rather, it is analytic or explicative: it renders explicit certain assumptions or assertions which are included in the content of the premises of the argument (in our case, these consist of Boyle's law plus the additional data); mathematical reasoning reveals that those premises contain—hidden in them, as it were,—an assertion about the case as yet unobserved. In accepting our premises—so arithmetic reveals— we have—knowingly or unknowingly—already accepted the implication that the v-value in question is 6. Mathematical as well as logical reasoning is a conceptual technique of making explicit what is implicitly contained in a set of premises. The conclusions to which this technique leads asserts nothing that is *theoretically new* in the sense of not being contained in the content of the premises. But the results obtained may well be *psychologically new:* we may not have been aware, before using the techniques of logic and mathematics, what we committed ourselves to in accepting a certain set of assumptions or assertions.

A similar analysis is possible in all other cases of applied mathematics, including those involving, say, the calculus. Consider, for example, the hypothesis that a certain object, moving in a specified electric field, will undergo a constant acceleration of 5 feet/sec². For the purpose of testing this hypothesis, we might derive from it, by means of two successive integrations, the prediction that if the object is at rest at the beginning of the motion then the distance covered by it at any time t is $5/2t^2$ feet. This conclusion may clearly be psychologically new to a person not acquainted with the subject, but it is not theoretically new; the content of the conclusion is already contained in that of the hypothesis about the constant acceleration. And indeed, here as well as in the case of the compression of a gas, a failure of the prediction to come true would be considered as indicative of the factual incorrectness of at least one of the premises involved (*f. ex.,* of Boyle's law in its application to the particular gas), but never as a sign that the logical and mathematical principles involved might be unsound.

Thus, in the establishment of empirical knowledge, mathematics (as well as logic) has, so to speak, the function of a theoretical juice extractor: the techniques of mathematical and logical theory can produce no more juice of factual information than is contained in the assumptions to which they are applied; but they may produce a great deal more juice of this kind than might have been anticipated upon a first intuitive inspection of those assumptions which form the raw material for the extractor. . . .

But while mathematics in no case contributes anything to the content of our knowledge of empirical matters, it is entirely indispensable as an instrument for the validation and even for the linguistic expression of such knowledge: The majority of the more far-reaching theories in empirical science—including those which lend themselves most eminently to prediction or to practical application—are stated with the help of mathematical concepts; the formulation of these theories makes use, in particular, of the number system, and of functional relationships among different metrical variables. Furthermore, the scientific test of these theories, the establishment of predictions by means of them, and finally their practical application, all require the deduction, from the general theory, of certain specific consequences; and such deduction would be entirely impossible without the techniques of mathematics which reveal what the given general theory implicitly asserts about a certain special case.

Thus, the analysis outlined on these pages exhibits the system of mathematics as a vast and ingenious conceptual structure without empirical content and yet an indispensable and powerful theoretical instrument for the scientific understanding and mastery of the world of our experience.

Synthetic *A Priori* Truth°

ALFRED CYRIL EWING [1899–   ] received his education at Oxford and has lectured on philosophy at Cambridge University since 1931. He was Visiting Professor of Philosophy at Princeton and Northwestern Universities in 1949 and has taught in India. He has written extensively on metaphysics, ethics, social philosophy, and the history of philosophy.

In the theory of knowledge, the first point that confronts us is the sharp distinction between two kinds of knowledge which have been called respectively *a priori* and empirical. Most of our knowledge we obtain by observation of the external world (sense-perception) and of ourselves (intro-

° Reprinted with permission of The Macmillan Company from *Fundamental Questions of Philosophy* by A. C. Ewing. First published in 1951 by Routledge and Kegan Paul, Ltd. Permission to reprint also granted by Routledge and Kegan Paul, Ltd.

spection). This is called empirical knowledge. But some knowledge we can obtain by simply thinking. That kind of knowledge is called *a priori*. Its chief exemplifications are to be found in logic and mathematics. In order to see that $5 + 7 = 12$ we do not need to take five things and seven things, put them together, and then count the total number. We can know what the total number will be simply by thinking.

Another important difference between *a priori* and empirical knowledge is that in the case of the former we do not see merely that something, S, is in fact P, but that it must be P and why it is P. I can discover that a flower is yellow (or at least produces sensations of yellow) by looking at it, but I cannot thereby see why it is yellow or that it must be yellow. For anything I can tell it might equally well have been a red flower. But with a truth such as that $5 + 7 = 12$ I do not see merely that it is a fact but that it must be a fact. It would be quite absurd to suppose that $5 + 7$ might have been equal to 11 and just happened to be equal to 12, and I can see that the nature of 5 and 7 constitutes a fully adequate and intelligible reason why their sum should be 12 and not some other number. It is indeed conceivable that some of the things which make the two groups of 5 and 7 might, when they were put together, fuse like drops of water, or even vanish, so that there were no longer 12 things; but what is inconceivable is that there could *at the same time* be $5 + 7$ things of a certain kind at once in a certain place and yet less than 12 things of that kind in that place. Before some of the things fused or vanished they would be $5 + 7$ in number and also 12 in number, and after the fusion or disappearance they would be neither $5 + 7$ nor 12. When I say in this connection that something is inconceivable, I do not mean merely or primarily that we cannot conceive it—this is not a case of a mere psychological inability like the inability to understand higher mathematics. It is a positive insight: we definitely see it to be impossible that certain things could happen. This we do not see in the case of empirical propositions which are false: they are not true but might for anything we know have been true. It is even conceivable, so far as we can see, that the fundamental laws of motion might have been quite different from what they are, but we can see that there could not have been a world which contradicted the laws of arithmetic. This is expressed by saying that empirical propositions are *contingent*, but true *a priori* propositions *necessary*. What we see to be necessary is not indeed that arithmetic should apply to the universe. It is conceivable that the universe might have been constituted entirely of a homogeneous fluid, and then, since there would have been no distinction between different things, it is difficult to see how arithmetic could have applied to it. What we do see is that arithmetic must be true of whatever can be numbered at all.

We must not be misled here by the fact that in order to come to understand arithmetic we originally required examples. Once we have learnt the beginnings of arithmetic in the kindergarten with the help of examples, we do not need examples any more to grasp it, and we can see the truth of many arithmetical propositions, e.g. that $3112 + 2467 = 5579$, of which we have never had examples. We have probably never taken 3112 things and 2467 things, put them together and counted the resulting set, but we still know that this is what the result of the counting would be. If it were empirical knowledge, we could not know it without counting. The examples are needed, not to prove anything, but only in order to enable us to come to understand in the first instance what is meant by number. . . .

Another important field for *a priori* knowledge is logic. The laws of logic must be known *a priori* or not at all. They certainly are not a matter for empirical observation, and the function of logical argument is just to give us conclusions which we have not discovered by observation. The argument would be superfluous if we had observed them already. We are able to make inferences because there is sometimes a logical connection between one or more propositions (the premise or premises) and another proposition, the conclusion, such that the latter must be true if the former is. Then, if we know the former, we can assert the latter on the strength of it, thus anticipating any experience. To take an example, there is a story that Mr. X., a man of high reputation and great social standing, had been asked to preside at a big social function. He was late in coming, and so a Roman Catholic priest was asked to make a speech to pass the time till his arrival. The priest told various anecdotes, including one which recorded his embarrassment when as confessor he had to deal with his first penitent and the latter confessed to a particularly atrocious murder. Shortly afterwards Mr. X. arrived, and in his own speech he said: "I see Father———is here. Now, though he may not recognize me, he is an old friend of mine, in fact I was his first penitent." It is plain that such an episode would enable one to infer that Mr. X. had committed a murder without having observed the crime. The form of inference involved: The first penitent was a murderer, Mr. X. was the first penitent, therefore Mr. X. was a murderer—is of the famous kind to which logicians have given the name of *syllogism*. The importance of syllogisms had often been exaggerated, but they are as important as any kind of inference, and we cannot deny that in many cases a syllogism has given people information of which they were not in any ordinary sense aware before they used the syllogism and which they did not acquire by observation. Inference is only possible because there are special connections between the propositions involved such that one necessarily follows from others. It is a chief function of logic to study these connections, of which that expressed in the syllogism is by no means the only one. . . .

A *priori* knowledge, while most prominent in mathematics and logic, is not limited to these subjects. For instance, we can see *a priori* that the same surface cannot have two different colours all over at the same time, or that a thought cannot have a shape. Philosophers have been divided into *rationalists* and *empiricists* according to whether they stressed the *a priori* or the empirical element more. The possibility of metaphysics depends on *a priori* knowledge, for our experience is quite inadequate to enable us to make on merely empirical grounds any sweeping generalizations of the kind the metaphysician desires. The term *a priori* covers both self-evident propositions, i.e. those which are seen to be true in their own right, and those which are derived by inference from propositions themselves self-evident.

At the present time even empiricist philosophers recognize the impossibility of explaining away *a priori* propositions as merely empirical generalizations, but they are inclined to the view that *a priori* propositions and *a priori* reasoning are merely concerned with language, and so cannot tell us anything new about the real world. Thus it is said that, when we make an inference, the conclusion is just part of the premises expressed in different language. If so, inference would be of use merely for clarifying our language and would involve no real advance in knowledge. Some inferences are of this type, e.g. A is a father, therefore A is male. But are they all? That would be hard indeed to square with the *prima facie* novelty of many conclusions. Take, for instance, the proposition that the square on the hypotenuse of a right-angled triangle is equal to the sum of the squares on the other two sides. Such a proposition can be inferred from the axioms and postulates of Euclid, but it certainly does not seem to be included in their meaning. Otherwise we should know it as soon as we understood the axioms and postulates. The example I gave of the murder discovered by a logical argument seems to be another case of a fact not known at all beforehand by the reasoner which is discovered by his reasoning. Extreme empiricist philosophers contend that this appearance of novelty is really illusory, and that in some sense we knew the conclusion all along; but they have never succeeded in making clear in what sense we did so. It is not enough to say that the conclusion is implicit in the premises. "Implicit" means "implied by," and of course a conclusion is implied by its premises, if the inference is correct at all. But this admission leaves quite open the question whether or not a proposition can follow from a different one which does not contain it as part of itself; and since we obviously can by deductive inference come to know things which we did not know before in any ordinary sense of "know," we must treat the empiricist's claim as unjustified till he has produced a clearly defined sense of "implicit in" or "contained in" which leaves room for that novelty in inference which we all cannot help really admitting. In any ordinary sense of "know" the conclusion is not in the cases I have mentioned known prior to the inference, and since the premises are and indeed must be known before we know the conclusion, it is therefore in no ordinary sense of "part" part of the premises.

It is indeed sometimes said that the premises include the conclusion in a confused form, but it is obvious that the beginner in geometry cannot be said to be aware of Pythagoras's theorem even in a confused form though he may know all the premises from which it can be deduced. Nor does awareness of the propositions that A was B's first penitent and that B's first penitent was a murderer include even confusedly the awareness that A was a murderer as long as the premises are not combined. When they are combined therefore something new appears that was not present to consciousness before in any way; there is a new discovery. We can also show by definite logical argument that the interpretation we are discussing does not enable one to avoid the admission of novelty in inference. For, what is it to know something in a confused form? It is surely to know some general attributes present in a whole but not others. To be aware of p even confusedly must involve discriminating some general attributes in p, and those are given in the premises, which are admittedly understood in some degree. If we do not discriminate any attributes, the confusion is too great for argument to be possible at all. Now it is admitted that, when we reach the conclusion, we do discriminate attributes which we did not discriminate before, even if they are alleged to have been contained in the confused whole which was present to our minds before we started inferring. It is further admitted that the conclusion follows necessarily from the premises. Therefore the general attributes which we discriminate at the time when we knew only the premises and not the conclusion must be linked with the attributes we discriminate afterwards in such a way that the latter follow necessarily from the former. So we still have to admit that sheer *a priori* inference can enable us to discover new attributes. In some cases it may take a good while to draw the inference, in other cases it may be practically instantaneous as soon as the premises are known and combined, but whether it takes a long or a short time to draw the inference cannot be relevant to the principle.

Nevertheless, the view that inference cannot yield new conclusions dies hard, and so it will not be superfluous to bring further arguments. (1) "This has shape" admittedly follows logically from "this has size" and vice versa. If the view I am criticizing were true, "this has size" would, therefore, have to include in its meaning "this has shape," and "this has shape" would also have to include in its meaning "this has size." But this would only be possible if the two sentences meant exactly the same thing, which they obviously do not. (2) Take an argument such as—Montreal is to the north of New York,

New York is to the north of Washington, therefore Montreal is to the north of Washington. If the view I am discussing is true, the conclusion is part of the premises. But it is not part of either premise by itself, otherwise both premises would not be needed. So the only way in which it could be part of both together would be if it were divisible into two propositions one of which was part of the first and the other part of the second. I defy anybody to divide it in this way. (3) The proposition "Socrates was a philosopher" certainly entails the proposition "if Socrates had measles some philosophers have had measles," but it cannot be that the second proposition is included in the first. For the first proposition certainly does not include the notion of measles.

What is really the same view is often expressed by saying that all *a priori* propositions are "analytic." A distinction has commonly been drawn between *analytic* propositions, in which the predicate is in the notion of the subject already formed before the proposition is asserted, so that the proposition gives no new information, and *synthetic* propositions in which the predicate is not so contained and which are thus capable of giving new information. Analytic propositions are essentially verbal, being all true by definition, e.g. all fathers are male. As an example of a synthetic proposition we could take any proposition established by experience such as "I am cold" or "It is snowing," but empiricists often assert that there are no synthetic *a priori* propositions. That this view cannot be justified may be shown at once. The proposition that there are no synthetic *a priori* propositions, since it cannot be established by empirical observations, would be, if justified, itself a synthetic *a priori* proposition, and we cannot affirm it as a synthetic *a priori* proposition that there are no synthetic *a priori* propositions. We may therefore dismiss off-hand any arguments for the theory. Such arguments, whatever they were, would have to involve synthetic *a priori* propositions. . . .

The analytic view seems plausible when we are concerned with the simplest propositions of logic and arithmetic, but we must not assume that a proposition is analytic because it is obvious. Though it may be very difficult to determine precisely where analytic propositions end and synthetic propositions begin, we cannot use this as a ground for denying the latter. It is very difficult to say precisely where blue ends and green begins, since the different shades run into each other imperceptibly, but we cannot therefore argue that all blue is really green. Taking arithmetic, even if there is a good deal of plausibility in saying that $2 + 2$ is included in the meaning of "4," there is none in saying $95 - 91$ or $\dfrac{216}{2} = \dfrac{287 + 25}{3}$ are so included. Yet, if the analytic view were true, all the infinite numerical combinations which could be seen *a priori* to be equal to 4 would have to be included in the meaning of "4."

Some empiricists, without committing themselves to the view that all *a priori* propositions are analytic, still say these are a matter of arbitrary choice or verbal convention. They are influenced here by a modern development in the view of geometry. It used to be held that the axioms of Euclid expressed a direct insight into the nature of physical space, but this is denied by modern scientists, and the view is taken that they are arbitrary postulates which geometricians make because they are interested in what would follow *if* they were true. Whether they are true or not is then a matter of empirical fact to be decided by science. But, even if this suggests that the premises of our *a priori* arguments may be arbitrary postulates, this does not make the subsequent steps arbitrary. From the postulates of Euclid it follows that the three angles of a triangle are equal to two right angles. If the original postulates are arbitrary, it is not certain that the conclusion is true of the real world; but it is still not an arbitrary matter that it follows from the postulates. The postulates may well be false, but there can be no doubt that *if* they were true the conclusions must be so, and it is in this hypothetical working out of the consequences of postulates which may not be true that pure geometry consists. The *a priori* necessity of pure geometry is not therefore in the least invalidated by modern developments. What is *a priori* is that the conclusions follow from the axioms and postulates, and this is not at all affected by the (empirical) discovery that not all the axioms and postulates exactly apply to the physical world. (Applied Euclidean geometry is possible in practice because it is an empirical fact that they approximately apply. The divergencies only show themselves when we consider unusually great velocities or distances.)

If not only the postulates but the successive stages in the inference were themselves arbitrary, we might just as well infer from the same premises that the angles of a triangle were equal to a million right angles or to none at all. All point in inference would be lost. Dictators may do a great deal, but they cannot alter the laws of logic and mathematics; these laws would not change even if by a system of intensive totalitarian education every human being were persuaded to fall in with a world dictator's whim in the matter and believe they were different from what they are. Nor can they change with alterations in language, though they may be expressed differently. That the truth of *a priori* propositions does not just depend on the nature of language can be easily seen when we consider that, even if we do not know any Fijian or Hottentot, we can know that also in these languages and not only in the languages we know the proposition $5 + 7 = 12$ must be true. It is of course true that by altering the meaning of the words we could make the proposition we expressed by "$5 + 7 = 12$" false, e.g. if I used "12" in a new sense to mean what other people mean by "11," but then it would be a different proposition. I could play the same trick with empirical propositions and say truly, e.g., that "fire does not burn" or "there is an elephant in this room" if I used "burn" to mean "drown" or "elephant" to mean "table." This does not in the least impair the obviousness of the contrary propositions established by experience. Finally, as we argued above that the proposition that there can be no synthetic *a priori* propositions would itself, if justified, have to be a synthetic *a priori* proposition, so we may argue that the proposition that all *a priori* propositions are a matter of arbitrary linguistic convention would, if true, have to be itself a matter of arbitrary linguistic convention. It therefore could not be vindicated by any argument and would be merely a matter of a new usage of words arbitrarily established by the persons who assert it, since it certainly does not express the usual meaning of "*a priori* propositions." So we must reject any attempt to explain away the *a priori* as a genuine source of new knowledge. If the attempt had succeeded, we should have had to admit that philosophy in anything like its old sense was impossible, for philosophy clearly cannot be based merely on observation.

The views we have been criticizing contain the following elements of truth. (1) A *priori* propositions can be seen to be true and the conclusions of an inference seem to follow from their premises without any further observation, provided we understand the meaning of the words used. But to say that q follows from p once we understand the meaning of the words is not to say that q is part of the meaning of the words used to express p. "Follow from" and "be part of" are not synonyms. (2) If q follows from p you cannot assert p and deny q without contradicting yourself, but this is only to say that in that case the denial of q implies the denial of p. It is not to say that q is part of what you assert when you assert p, unless we already assume that what is implied is always part of what implies it, i.e. beg the question at issue. (3) An *a priori* proposition cannot be fully understood without being seen to be true. It may be impossible to understand something fully without understanding something else not included in it at all, so it may still be synthetic.

People have been inclined to deny synthetic *a priori* propositions because they could not see how one characteristic could necessarily involve another, but that this could not happen would be itself a synthetic *a priori* metaphysical proposition. People have also thought that it was necessary to give some sort of explanation of *a priori* knowledge, and could not see how this could be done except in terms of language. To this I should reply that there is no reason to suppose that *a priori* knowledge requires some special explanation any more than does our ability to attain knowledge empirically by observation. Why not take it as an ultimate fact? Human beings certainly cannot explain everything, whether there is ultimately an explanation for it or not.

SUGGESTED READINGS

The problem of synthetic *a priori* truth is central to Kant's great *Critique of Pure Reason* (translated by N. Kemp Smith), and the Introduction to that work gives a very clear statement of the problem as Kant saw it. S. Körner's short book on Kant gives a good account of his view. There are various commentaries on the *Critique:* those by A. C. Ewing and H. J. Paton (more advanced) are especially useful. A. J. Ayer, in Chapter IV of *Language, Truth and Logic,* gives a simple positivistic analysis in clear terms. A. Pap, *Semantics and Necessary Truth,* especially Chapters 1–7, is a more advanced study. For short essays on various facets on the problem, see H. Hahn, "Logic, Mathematics, and the Knowledge of Nature," reprinted in *Logical Positivism,* edited by A. J. Ayer; K. Popper, "Why Are the Calculuses of Logic and Mathematics Applicable to Reality?" in *Proceedings of the Aristotelian Society, Supplementary Volume,* 1946; M. Schlick, "Is There a Factual Apriori?," and E. Nagel, "Logic Without Ontology," both reprinted in *Readings in Philosophical Analysis,* edited by H. Feigl and W. Sellars.

Some of the most important pioneering work in the philosophy of mathematics was done by A. N. Whitehead and B. Russell. Whitehead has written an excellent short book, *Introduction to Mathematics,* and Russell's *Introduction to Mathematical Philosophy* gives a good account of why Whitehead and Russell thought mathematics could be derived from logic. Russell owed much to G. Frege, whose *Foundations of Arithmetic* (translated by J. L. Austin) is a classic work, but quite difficult.

An important article by W. Quine, "Two Dogmas of Empiricism," reprinted in his *From a Logical Point of View,* challenges the validity of the distinction between analytic and synthetic, and suggests quite a different approach to the problems in which those concepts are involved. Quine has been much criticised: see, for example, H. P. Grice and P. Strawson, "In Defense of a Dogma" in *Philosophical Review,* 1956.

Causation and Law

If we are asked to explain what we mean by "cause," we would no doubt find that our most common usage involves two points: if *a* causes *b*, then (1) *a* and *b* must be spatially contiguous, and (2) *a* must be temporally prior to *b*. When we say, for example, that a falling rock *causes* a pane of glass to break, we mean (in part, at least) that the rock and the glass actually come in contact (spatial contiguity) and that the rock must strike the glass before the glass breaks (temporal priority). We should not be inclined to say that a falling rock broke the glass if the rock never struck the glass nor if it struck the glass after the glass had broken.

But this is not all that we mean by "cause." There may be many events spatially contiguous with and immediately prior to a given effect, but not all of them will be thought of as *causes* of that effect. I might, for example, be speaking as I drop a rock on the glass. But the resulting sound waves in the air, though spatially contiguous with the glass, and temporally prior to its breaking, would not be regarded as *causes* of the effect.

Why wouldn't we grant that the sound waves were causes of the damage? One way of replying would be to say that there is no *necessary connection* between the sound waves and the effect in question; what connection there is, is "irrelevant." According to this conception of cause, when we say that *a* causes *b*, we mean that, in addition to contiguity and immediate temporal priority, there is a *necessary* connection between the two events, that the cause *a* exerted a *power* or *force* which produced the effect *b*.

This common conception of "cause" raises serious problems. Is it, for example, legitimate to hold that a cause must be spatially contiguous with its effect? Does a cause always occur *before* the effect, or can cause and effect be simultaneous? Most important of all, there are problems concerning the family of notions, "necessary connection," "power," and "force." These notions were subjected to severe criticism by HUME.

Hume's criticism of the notion of cause has been enormously influential in the philosophy of science. Before Hume, it had been assumed by most philosophers that the primary aim of scientific investigations was to study "causes." Later philosophers, motivated in part by Hume, and in part by a careful analysis of what scientists were doing, tended to stress the role of *laws* in science. Such laws do not use "cause-effect" terminology, nor do they refer to necessary connections, powers, or forces. They describe uniformities and regularities in nature (Hume's "constant conjunctions") and wherever possible express them in mathematical formulas.

WHITEHEAD argues against one of Hume's main tenets and, by implication, against those philosophical views of science that are influenced by Hume's attack on necessary connection. Whitehead maintains that our daily experience continually provides instances of precisely that sort of necessity or causal efficacy which Hume questioned and that moreover, Hume to the contrary, our awareness of this causal efficacy is direct and immediate.

A more recent attack on Hume's analysis of the basis for our belief in the causal relation is provided by HART and HONORÉ in their discussion of how the notion of a "cause" is applied to legal contexts. According to their account there are many contexts, especially legal ones, in which "cause" is applied in a way that has little to do with "constant conjunction," or anything of the sort (though in special cases certain kinds of scientific findings may be relevant to deciding an issue). When we ask, for example, what caused Smith's death, we are unlikely to be interested in answers like "A piece of metal was lodged in his heart, and we know (by the Humean criterion of 'cause') that whenever this happens the victim dies." Rather we suppose that there is some reasonable on-going state of affairs that has somehow, perhaps unexpectedly, been tampered with—and that the "cause" of the event we are interested in is Brown's shooting the revolver. Hart and Honoré argue that the legal usage is closer to our ordinary view of causation than that "manufactured for us" by Hume and his followers.

The Idea of Necessary Connection*

D A V I D H U M E [1711–1776], philosopher, historian, and political economist, was born in Scotland, and educated at Edinburgh University. Although his *Treatise of Human Nature* (1739–1740) contains the most complete account of his philosophical views, *An Enquiry Concerning Human Understanding* (1748), from which the following selection is taken, is the best known of his works. Hume is ranked among the greatest critical philosophers of modern times.

Part I

There are no ideas, which occur in metaphysics, more obscure and uncertain, than those of *power, force, energy* or *necessary connexion,* of which it is every moment necessary for us to treat in all our disquisitions. We shall, therefore, endeavour, in this section, to fix, if possible, the precise meaning of these terms, and thereby remove some part of that obscurity, which is so much complained of in this species of philosophy.

It seems a proposition, which will not admit of much dispute, that all our ideas are nothing but copies of our impressions, or, in other words, that it is impossible for us to *think* of any thing, which we have not antecedently

* From Hume: *An Enquiry Concerning Human Understanding,* Sections 7 and 5.

felt, either by our external or internal senses. . . . To be fully acquainted, therefore, with the idea of power or necessary connexion, let us examine its impression; and in order to find the impression with greater certainty, let us search for it in all the sources, from which it may possibly be derived.

When we look about us towards external objects, and consider the operation of causes, we are never able, in a single instance, to discover any power or necessary connexion; any quality, which binds the effect to the cause, and renders the one an infallible consequence of the other. We only find, that the one does actually, in fact, follow the other. The impulse of one billiard-ball is attended with motion in the second. This is the whole that appears to the *outward* senses. The mind feels no sentiment or *inward* impression from this succession of objects: Consequently, there is not, in any single, particular instance of cause and effect, any thing which can suggest the idea of power or necessary connexion.

From the first appearance of an object, we never can conjecture what effect will result from it. But were the power or energy of any cause discoverable by the mind, we could foresee the effect, even without experience; and might, at first, pronounce with certainty concerning it, by mere dint of thought and reasoning.

In reality, there is no part of matter, that does ever, by its sensible qualities, discover any power or energy, or give us ground to imagine, that it could produce any thing, or be followed by any other object, which we could denominate its effect. Solidity, extension, motion; these qualities are all complete in themselves, and never point out any other event which may result from them. The scenes of the universe are continually shifting, and one object follows another in an uninterrupted succession; but the power or force, which actuates the whole machine, is entirely concealed from us, and never discovers itself in any of the sensible qualities of body. We know, that, in fact, heat is a constant attendant of flame; but what is the connexion between them, we have no room so much as to conjecture or imagine. It is impossible, therefore, that the idea of power can be derived from the contemplation of bodies, in single instances of their operation; because no bodies ever discover any power, which can be the original of this idea.

Since, therefore, external objects as they appear to the senses, give us no idea of power or necessary connexion, by their operation in particular instances, let us see, whether this idea be derived from reflection on the operations of our own minds, and be copied from any internal impression. It may be said, that we are every moment conscious of internal power; while we feel, that, by the simple command of our will, we can move the organs of our body, or direct the faculties of our mind. An act of volition produces motion in our limbs, or raises a new idea in our imagination. This influence of the will we know by consciousness. Hence we acquire the idea of power or energy; and are certain, that we ourselves and all other intelligent beings are possessed of power. . . .

We shall proceed to examine this pretension; and first with regard to the influence of volition over the organs of the body. This influence, we may observe, is a fact, which, like all other natural events, can be known only by experience, and can never be foreseen from any apparent energy or power in the cause, which connects it with the effect, and renders the one an infallible consequence of the other. The motion of our body follows upon the command of our will. Of this we are every moment conscious. But the means, by which this is effected; the energy, by which the will performs so extraordinary an operation; of this we are so far from being immediately conscious, that it must for ever escape our most diligent enquiry.

For *first;* is there any principle in all nature more mysterious than the union of soul with body; by which a supposed spiritual substance acquires such an influence over a material one, that the most refined thought is able to actuate the grossest matter? Were we empowered, by a secret wish, to remove mountains, or control the planets in their orbit; this extensive authority would not be more extraordinary, nor more beyond our comprehension. But if by consciousness we perceived any power or energy in the will, we must know this power; we must know its connexion with the effect; we must know the secret union of soul and body, and the nature of both these substances; by which the one is able to operate, in so many instances, upon the other.

Secondly, We are not able to move all the organs of the body with a like authority; though we cannot assign any reason besides experience, for so remarkable a difference between one and the other. Why has the will an influence over the tongue and fingers, not over the heart or liver? This question would never embarrass us, were we conscious of a power in the former case, not in the latter. . . .

Thirdly, We learn from anatomy, that the immediate object of power in voluntary motion, is not the member itself which is moved, but certain muscles, and nerves, and animal spirits, and, perhaps, something still more minute and more unknown, through which the motion is successively propagated, ere it reach the member itself whose motion is the immediate object of volition. Can there be a more certain proof, that the power, by which this whole operation is performed, so far from being directly and fully known by an inward sentiment or consciousness, is, to the last degree, mysterious and unintelligible? Here the mind wills a certain event: Immediately another event, unknown to ourselves, and totally different from the one intended, is produced: This event produces another, equally unknown: Till at last, through a long succession, the desired event is produced. But if the original power were felt, it must be known: Were it known, its effect also must be known; since all power is relative to its effect. And *vice versa*, if the effect be not known, the power cannot be known nor felt. How indeed can we be conscious of a power to move our limbs, when we have no such power; but only that to move certain animal spirits, which, though they produce at last the motion of our limbs, yet operate in such a manner as is wholly beyond our comprehension?

We may, therefore, conclude . . . that our idea of power is not copied from any sentiment or consciousness of power within ourselves, when we give rise to animal motion, or apply our limbs to their proper use and office. That their motion follows the command of the will is a matter of common experience, like other natural events: But the power or energy by which this is effected, like that in other natural events, is unknown and inconceivable. . . .

The generality of mankind never find any difficulty in accounting for the more common and familiar operations of nature—such as the descent of heavy bodies, the growth of plants, the generation of animals, or the nourishment of bodies by food: But suppose that, in all these cases, they perceive the very force or energy of the cause, by which it is connected with its effect, and is for ever infallible in its operation. They acquire, by long habit, such a turn of mind, that, upon the apppearance of the cause, they immediately expect with assurance its usual attendant, and hardly conceive it possible that any other event could result from it. It is only on the discovery of extraordinary phænomena, such as earthquakes, pestilence, and prodigies of any kind, that they find themselves at a loss to assign a proper cause, and to explain the manner in which the effect is produced by it. It is usual for men, in such difficulties to have recourse to some invisible intelligent principle as the immediate cause of that event which surprises them, and which, they think, cannot be accounted for from the common powers of nature. But philosophers, who carry their scrutiny a little farther, immediately perceive that, even in the most familiar events, the energy of the cause is as unintelligible as in the most unusual, and that we only learn by experience the frequent *Conjunction* of objects, without being ever able to comprehend anything like *Connexion* between them. . . .

Part II

But to hasten a conclusion of this argument, which is already drawn out to too great a length: We have sought in vain for an idea of power or necessary connexion in all the sources from which we could suppose it to be derived. It appears that, in single instances of the operation of bodies, we never can, by our utmost scrutiny, discover any thing but one event following another, without being able to comprehend any force or power by which the cause operates, or any connexion between it and its supposed effect. The same difficulty occurs in contemplating the operations of mind on body—where we observe the motion of the latter to follow upon the volition of the former, but are not able to observe or conceive the tie which binds together the motion and volition, or the energy by which the mind produces this effect. The authority of the will over its own faculties and ideas is not a whit more comprehensible: So that, upon the whole, there appears not, throughout all nature, any one instance of connexion which is conceivable by us. All events seem entirely loose and separate. One event follows another; but we never can observe any tie between them. They seem *conjoined,* but never *connected.* And as we can have no idea of any thing which never appeared to our outward sense or inward sentiment, the necessary conclusion *seems* to be that we have no idea of connexion or power at all, and that these words are absolutely without any meaning, when employed either in philosophical reasonings or common life.

But there still remains one method of avoiding this conclusion, and one source which we have not yet examined. When any natural object or event is presented, it is impossible for us, by any sagacity or penetration, to discover, or even conjecture, without experience, what event will result from it, or to carry our foresight beyond that object which is immediately present to the memory and senses. Even after one instance or experiment where we have observed a particular event to follow upon another, we are not entitled to form a general rule, or foretell what will happen in like cases; it being justly esteemed an unpardonable temerity to judge of the whole course of nature from one single experiment, however accurate or certain. But when one particular species of event has always, in all instances, been conjoined with another, we make no longer any scruple of foretelling one upon the appearance of the other, and of employing that reasoning, which can alone assure us of any matter of fact or existence. We then call the one object, *Cause;* the other, *Effect.* We suppose that there is some connexion between them; some power in the one, by which it infallibly produces the other, and operates with the greatest certainty and strongest necessity.

It appears, then, that this idea of a necessary connexion among events arises from a number of similar instances which occur of the constant conjunction of these events; nor can that idea ever be suggested by any one of these instances, surveyed in all possible lights and positions. But there is nothing in a number of instances, different from every single instance, which is supposed to be exactly similar; except only, that after a repetition of similar instances, the mind is carried by habit, upon the appearance of one event, to expect its usual attendant, and to believe that it will exist. This connexion, therefore, which we *feel* in the mind, this customary transition of the imagination from one object to its usual attendant, is the sentiment or impression from which we form the idea of power or necessary connexion. Nothing farther is in the case. Contemplate the subject on all sides; you will never find any other origin of that idea. This is the sole difference between one instance, from which we can never receive the idea of connexion, and a number of similar instances, by which it is suggested. The first time a man saw the communication of motion by impulse, as by the shock of two billiard balls, he could not pronounce that the one event was *connected*: but only that it was *conjoined* with the other. After he has observed several instances of this nature, he then pronounces them to be *connected*. What alteration has happened to give rise to this new idea of *connexion?* Nothing but that he now *feels* these events to be *connected* in his imagination, and can readily foretell the existence of one from the appearance of the other. When we say, therefore, that one object is connected with another, we mean only that they have acquired a connexion in our thought, and give rise to this inference, by which they become proofs of each other's existence: A conclusion which is somewhat extraordinary, but which seems founded on sufficient evidence. Nor will its evidence be weakened by any general diffidence of the understanding, or sceptical suspicion concerning every conclusion which is new and extraordinary. No conclusions can be more agreeable to scepticism than such as make discoveries concerning the weakness and narrow limits of human reason and capacity.

And what stronger instance can be produced of the surprising ignorance and weakness of the understanding than the present? For surely, if there be any relation among objects which it imports to us to know perfectly, it is that of cause and effect. On this are founded all our reasonings concerning matter of fact or existence. By means of it alone we attain any assurance concerning objects which are removed from the present testimony of our memory and senses. The only immediate utility of all sciences, is to teach us, how to control and regulate future events by their causes. Our thoughts and enquiries are, therefore, every moment, employed about this relation: Yet so imperfect are the ideas which we form concerning it, that it is impossible to give any just definition of cause, except what is drawn from something extraneous and foreign to it. Similar objects are always conjoined with similar. Of this we have experience. Suitably to this experience, therefore, we may define a cause to be *an object, followed by another, and where all the objects similar to the first are followed by objects similar to the second.* Or in other words, *where, if the first object had not been, the second never had existed.* The appearance of a cause always conveys the mind, by a customary transition, to the idea of the effect. Of this also we have experience. We may, therefore, suitably to this experience, form another definition of cause, and call it, *an object followed by another, and whose appearance always conveys the thought to that other.* But though both these definitions be drawn from circumstances foreign to the cause, we cannot remedy this inconvenience, or attain any more perfect definition, which may point out that circumstance in the cause, which gives it a connexion with its effect. We have no idea of this connexion, nor even any distinct notion what it is we desire to know, where we endeavour at a conception of it. We say, for instance, that the vibration of this string is the cause of this particular sound. But what do we mean by that affirmation? We either mean *that this vibration is followed by this sound, and that all similar vibrations have been followed by similar sounds: Or, that this vibration is followed by this sound, and that upon the appearance of one the mind anticipates the senses, and forms immediately an idea of the other.* We may consider the relation of cause and effect in either of these two lights; but beyond these, we have no idea of it.

To recapitulate, therefore, the reasonings of this section: Every idea is copied from some preceding impression or sentiment; and where we cannot find any impression, we may be certain that there is no idea. In all single instances of the operation of bodies or minds, there-is nothing that produces any impression, nor consequently can suggest any idea of power or necessary connexion. But when many uniform instances appear, and the same object is always followed by the same event; we then begin to entertain the notion of cause and connexion. We then *feel* a new sentiment or impression, to wit, a customary connexion in the thought or imagination between one object and its usual attendant; and this sentiment is the original of that idea which we seek for. For as this idea arises from a number of similar instances, and not from any single instance, it must arise from that circumstance, in which the number of instances differ from every individual instance. But this customary connexion or transition of the imagination is the only circumstance in which they differ. In every other particular they are alike. The first instance which we saw of motion communicated by the shock of two billiard balls (to return to this obvious illustration) is exactly similar to any instance that may, at present, occur to us; except only, that we could not, at first, *infer* one event from the other; which we are enabled to do at present, after so long a course of uniform experience.

Custom, then, is the great guide of human life. It is that principle alone which renders our experience useful to us, and makes us expect, for the future, a similar train of events with those which have appeared in the past.

Without the influence of custom, we should be entirely ignorant of every matter of fact beyond what is immediately present to the memory and senses. We should never know how to adjust means to ends, or to employ our natural powers in the production of any effect. There would be an end at once of all action, as well as of the chief part of speculation.

But here it may be proper to remark, that though our conclusions from experience carry us beyond our memory and senses, and assure us of matters of fact which happened in the most distant places and most remote ages, yet some fact must always be present to the senses or memory, from which we may first proceed in drawing these conclusions. A man, who should find in a desert country the remains of pompous buildings, would conclude that the country had, in ancient times, been cultivated by civilized inhabitants; but did nothing of this nature occur to him, he could never form such an inference. We learn the events of former ages from history; but then we must peruse the volumes in which this instruction is contained, and thence carry up our inferences from one testimony to another, till we arrive at the eyewitnesses and spectators of these distant events. In a word, if we proceed not upon some fact, present to the memory or senses, our reasonings would be merely hypothetical; and however the particular links might be connected with each other, the whole chain of inferences would have nothing to support it, nor could we ever, by its means, arrive at the knowledge of any real existence. If I ask why you believe any particular matter of fact, which you relate, you must tell me some reason; and this reason will be some other fact, connected with it. But as you cannot proceed after this manner, *in infinitum,* you must at last terminate in some fact, which is present to your memory or senses; or must allow that your belief is entirely without foundation.

What, then, is the conclusion of the whole matter? A simple one; though, it must be confessed, pretty remote from the common theories of philosophy. All belief of matter of fact or real existence is derived merely from some object, present to the memory or senses, and a customary conjunction between that and some other object. Or in other words; having found, in many instances, that any two kinds of objects—flame and heat, snow and cold—have always been conjoined together; if flame or snow be presented anew to the senses, the mind is carried by custom to expect heat or cold, and to *believe* that such a quality does exist, and will discover itself upon a nearer approach. This belief is the necessary result of placing the mind in such circumstances. It is an operation of the soul, when we are so situated, as unavoidable as to feel the passion of love, when we receive benefits; or hatred, when we meet with injuries. All these operations are a species of natural instincts, which no reasoning or process of the thought and understanding is able either to produce or to prevent.

Experiencing Causal Connection[*]

ALFRED NORTH WHITEHEAD [1861–1947] was one of the most eminent mathematicians and philosophers of our time. Born in England, he took his B.A. at Cambridge University and for the next forty years taught mathematics in Cambridge and London. In 1924 he was appointed Professor of Philosophy at Harvard, a post which he held until his retirement in 1937. With Bertrand Russell he wrote *Principia Mathematica* (1910–1913), a work which opened up vast new fields in mathematics. His extensive contributions to philosophy are no less notable.

The discussion of the problem, constituted by the connection between causation and perception, has been conducted by the various schools of thought derived from Hume and Kant under the misapprehension generated by an inversion of the true constitution of experience. The inversion was explicit in the writings of Hume and of Kant: for both of them presentational immediacy was the primary fact of perception, and any apprehension of causation was, somehow or other, to be elicited from this primary fact. . . .

Owing to its long dominance, it has been usual to assume as an obvious fact the primacy of presentational immediacy. We open our eyes and our other sense-organs; we then survey the contemporary world decorated with sights, and sounds, and tastes; and then, by the sole aid of this information about the contemporary world, thus decorated, we draw what conclusions we can as to the actual world. No philospher really holds that this is the sole source of information: Hume and his followers appeal vaguely to 'memory' and to 'practice,' in order to supplement their direct information; and Kant wrote other 'Critiques' in order to supplement his *Critique of Pure Reason*. But the general procedure of modern philosophical 'criticism' is to tie down opponents strictly to the front door of presentational immediacy as the sole source of information, while one's own philosophy makes its escape by a back door veiled under the ordinary usages of language.

If this 'Humian' doctrine be true, certain conclusions as to 'behavior' ought to follow—conclusions which, in the most striking way, are not verified. It is almost indecent to draw the attention of philosophers to the minor transactions of daily life, away from the classic sources of philosophic knowledge; but, after all, it is the empiricists who began this appeal to Caesar.

According to Hume, our behaviour presupposing causation is due to the

* From Whitehead: *Process and Reality*, pp. 263 ff. Copyright, 1929, by The Macmillan Company. Reprinted by permission of The Macmillan Company, New York.

repetition of associated presentational experiences. Thus the vivid presentment of the antecedent percepts should vividly generate the behaviour, in
action or thought, towards the associated consequent. The clear, distinct,
overwhelming perception of the one is the overwhelming reason for the subjective transition to the other. For behaviour, interpretable as implying
causation, is on this theory the subjective response to presentational immediacy. According to Hume this subjective response is the beginning and the
end of all that there is to be said about causation. In Hume's theory the response is response to presentational immediacy, and to nothing else. Also the
situation elicited in response is nothing but an immediate presentation, or
the memory of one. Let us apply this explanation to reflex action: in the
dark, the electric light is suddenly turned on and the man's eyes blink. There
is a simple physiological explanation of this trifling incident.

But this physiological explanation is couched wholly in terms of causal
efficacy: it is the conjectural record of the travel of a spasm of excitement
along nerves to some nodal centre, and of the return spasm of contraction
back to the eyelids. The correct technical phraseology would not alter the
fact that the explanation does not involve any appeal to presentational
immediacy. . . . At the most there is a tacit supposition as to what a
physiologist, who in fact was not there, might have seen if he had been
there, and if he could have vivisected the man without affecting these occurrences, and if he could have observed with a microscope which also in fact
was absent. Thus the physiological explanation remains from the point
of view of Hume's philosophy, a tissue of irrelevancies. It presupposes a side
of the universe about which, on Hume's theory, we must remain in blank
ignorance.

Let us now dismiss physiology and turn to the private experience of the
blinking man. The sequence of percepts, in the mode of presentational immediacy, are flash of light, feeling of eye-closure, instant of darkness. The
three are practically simultaneous; though the flash maintains its priority
over the other two, and these two latter percepts are indistinguishable as to
priority. According to the philosophy of organism [*i.e.*, Whitehead's philoso-
phy], the man also experiences another percept in the mode of causal
efficacy. He feels that the experiences of the *eye* in the matter of the flash are
causal of the blink. The man himself will have no doubt of it. In fact, it is
the feeling of causality which enables the man to distinguish the priority of
the flash; and the inversion of the argument, whereby the temporal sequence
'flash to blink' is made the premise for the 'causality' belief, has its origin in
pure theory. The man will explain his experience by saying, 'The flash made
me blink'; and if his statement be doubted, he will reply, 'I know it, because
I felt it.'

The philosophy of organism accepts the man's statement, that the flash *made* him blink. But Hume intervenes with another explanation. He first points out that in the mode of presentational immediacy there is no percept of the flash *making* the man blink. In this mode there are merely the two percepts—the flash and the blink—combining the two latter of the three percepts under the one term 'blink.' Hume refuses to admit the man's protestation, that the compulsion to blink is just what he did feel. The refusal is based on the dogma, that all percepts are in the mode of presentational immediacy—a dogma not to be upset by a mere appeal to direct experience. Besides Hume has another interpretation of the man's experience: what the man really felt was his *habit* of blinking after flashes. The word 'association' explains it all, according to Hume. But how can a 'habit' be felt, when a 'cause' cannot be felt? Is there any presentational immediacy in the feeling of a 'habit'? Hume by a sleight of hand confuses a 'habit of feeling blinks after flashes' with a *'feeling of the habit* of feeling blinks after flashes.'

We have here a perfect example of the practice of applying the test of presentational immediacy to procure the critical rejection of some doctrines, and of allowing other doctrines to slip out by a back door, so as to evade the test. The notion of causation arose because mankind lives amid experiences in the mode of causal efficacy.

We will keep to the appeal to ordinary experience, and consider another situation, which Hume's philosophy is ill equipped to explain. The 'causal feeling' according to that doctrine arises from the long association of well-marked presentations of sensa, one precedent to the other. It would seem therefore that inhibitions of sensa, given in presentational immediacy, should be accompanied by a corresponding absence of 'causal feeling'; for the explanation of how there is 'causal feeling' presupposes the well-marked familiar sensa, in presentational immediacy. Unfortunately the contrary is the case. An inhibition of familiar sensa is very apt to leave us a prey to vague terrors respecting a circumambient world of causal operations. In the dark there are vague presences, doubtfully feared; in the silence, the irresistible causal efficacy of nature presses itself upon us; in the vagueness of the low hum of insects in an August woodland, the inflow into ourselves of feelings from enveloping nature overwhelms us; in the dim consciousness of half-sleep, the presentations of sense fade away, and we are left with the vague feeling of influences from vague things around us. It is quite untrue that the feelings of various types of influences are dependent upon the familiarity of well-marked sensa in immediate presentment. Every way of omitting the sensa still leaves us a prey to vague feelings of influence. Such feelings, divorced from immediate sensa, are pleasant, or unpleasant, according to mood; but they are always vague as to spatial and temporal definition, though their explicit dominance in experience may be heightened in the absence of sensa.

Further, our experience of our various bodily parts are primarily perceptions of them as *reasons* for 'projected' sensa: the hand is the *reason* for the projected touch-sensum, the *eye* is the *reason* for the projected sight-sensum. Our bodily experience is primarily an experience of the dependence of presentational immediacy upon causal efficacy. Hume's doctrine inverts this relationship by making causal efficacy, as an experience, dependent upon presentational immediacy. This doctrine, whatever be its merits, is not based upon any appeal to experience.

The Everyday Idea of Cause*

HERBERT L. A. HART [1907–   ] practiced law for a number of years after taking his degree from New College, Oxford. He has taught at Harvard and since 1952 has been Professor of Jurisprudence at Oxford. In addition to numerous articles he has published *The Concept of Law* (1961).
ANTONY MAURICE HONORÉ [1921–   ] has made numerous contributions to the study of causation from a legal point of view. He is at present Rhodes Reader in Roman-Dutch Law at Oxford.

I

Both the historian and the lawyer frequently assert that one particular event was the 'effect' or 'the consequence' or 'the result' of another or of some human action; or that one event or human action 'caused' or was 'the cause of' another event: somewhat less frequently they assert that one person 'caused' another to do something or 'made' him do it. In such language, a variety of related concepts are deployed which have bred many problems, and practitioners of both disciplines have given divergent accounts of its meaning. Philosophers, whose discussions of causation, protracted over centuries, have certainly contributed something to the understanding of causation in the natural sciences, till very recently have contributed little to further understanding here: lawyers, indeed, have seen this and said very clearly that the issues which philosophers discuss fail to illumine the specific aspects of causation which trouble them. So they have rejected philosophical

* From H. L. A. Hart and A. M. Honoré: *Causation in the Law,* Oxford, copyright 1959. Reprinted by permission of The Clarendon Press, Oxford.

theories usually with the insistence that the lawyer's causal problems are not 'scientific inquests' but are to be determined 'on common-sense principles.' Similar dissatisfaction with what the philosopher has hitherto tendered as an analysis of the meaning of causation is often expressed by saying that this analysis, though doubtless adequate for the scientist's causal notions, distorts what the historian does, or attempts to do, in identifying the causes of particular events.

Why has philosophy been thought irrelevant here while relevant to science? What similarity between law and history, and which of the many differences between these two and science account for this? Among many factors an important one is this. The lawyer and the historian are both primarily concerned to make causal statements about *particulars,* to establish that on some particular occasion some particular occurrence was the effect or consequence of some other particular occurrence. The causal statements characteristic of these disciplines are of the form 'This man's death on this date was caused by this blow.' Their characteristic concern with causation is not to discover connexions between types of events, and so not to *formulate* laws or generalizations, but is often to *apply* generalizations, which are already known or accepted as true and even platitudinous, to particular concrete cases. In this and other respects the causal statements of the lawyer and the historian are like the causal statements most frequent in ordinary life: they are singular statements identifying in complex situations certain particular events as causes, effects, or consequences of other particular events. Such singular causal statements have their own special problems and it is these that most trouble the lawyer and historian. By contrast, in the experimental sciences, by which so much of the philosophical discussion of causation has been influenced, the focus of attention is the discovery of generalizations and the construction of theories. What is typically asserted here is a connexion between kinds of events, and particular causal statements, made in the tidy controlled setting of the laboratory, have *only* the derivative interest of instances and present no special difficulties.

Since Hume, European philosophy has been dominated by the doctrine that the generalizations or laws which it is the prime business of the experimental sciences to discover, constitute the very essence of the notion of causation. Hence even singular causal statements which appear to be confined to the connexion between two particular occurrences are in fact covertly general; their causal character is derivative and lies *wholly* in the fact that the particular events with which they are concerned exemplify some generalization asserting that kinds or classes of events are invariably connected. So the very distinction between mere *post hoc* (A's blow was followed by B's death) and *propter hoc* (A's blow caused B's death) lies just in the fact that the latter, but not the former, depends upon and implies the truth of one or more general propositions relating directly or indirectly events of these two kinds. This analysis of the very notion of cause in terms of generalizations or laws asserting invariable connexion between kinds of events seemed to dissolve many of the perplexities and obscurities which had so long attended it, and which had made men think that, in using causal language, they were committed to belief in the existence of unobservable 'forces,' or 'powers' which some events had to 'produce' others, or to mysterious relationships which constituted the causal connexion between particular events. All this was condemned by the philosophical analysis of cause as so much confusion, due to the neglect of the simple fact that every singular causal statement was an instance of one or more general propositions asserting invariable sequence, and that causal connexion consisted solely in this.

The Humean analysis certainly swept away much lumber. Above all it offered to the scientist a more or less adequate account of those aspects of causation with which he is concerned: it freed him from the need to worry about the old obscure notions of unobservable powers and forces, for it told him, in effect, that there was nothing in these notions, or in the idea of cause itself, over and above the generalizations and laws which it was his business to discover. There are, however, other difficulties connected with causation not touched by this analysis. They are felt by those who, like the historian and the lawyer, are not primarily concerned to discover laws or generalizations, but often apply known or accepted generalizations to particular cases; they are difficulties peculiar to singular causal statements. The most notorious of these difficulties is this: when generalizations are used to identify the cause of a particular event on a particular occasion, the question arises whether something should be said to be the cause of something else, or only its 'occasion,' 'a mere condition,' or 'part of the circumstances' in which the cause operated. This is an inseparable feature of the historian's and the lawyer's and the plain man's use of causal notions. Plainly, the distinction has little to do with the generalizations which may be required to establish any singular causal statement, but very much to do with the particular context and purpose for which a particular causal inquiry is made and answered.

In most cases where a fire has broken out the lawyer, the historian, and the plain man would refuse to say that the cause of the fire was the presence of oxygen, though no fire would have occurred without it: they would reserve the title of cause for something of the order of the short-circuit, the dropping of a lighted cigarette, or lightning. Yet there are contexts where it would be natural to say that the presence of the oxygen was the cause of the fire. We have only to consider a factory where delicate manufacturing processes are carried on, requiring the exclusion of oxygen, to make it perfectly sensible to identify as the cause of a fire the presence of oxygen introduced by someone's mistake. The general laws which we may need to demonstrate causal connexion in these two cases of fire will not tell us that in one case oxygen can be sensibly cited as the cause and in the other not. Yet in making this distinction it is plain that our choice, though responsive to the varying context of the particular occasions, is not arbitrary or haphazard. The question is, 'What sort of principles guide our thoughts?' Legal theorists have often written as if only the lawyer, in manipulating the concept of cause, was faced with such a task of selection, and with the need to draw a distinction between causes and mere conditions or circumstances. They have often said this under the influence of a somewhat inaccurate version of John Stuart Mill's doctrine which we later consider, and have insisted that, apart from legal rules, or the special requirements of legal 'policy,' or conceptions of justice, every factor necessary for the occurrence of an event is equally entitled to be called 'the cause.' Yet this is not the case: neither the plain man, nor the historian, uses the expression 'cause,' or any related expression, in this way. For the contrast of cause with mere conditions is an inseparable feature of all causal thinking, and constitutes as much of the meaning of causal expressions as the implicit reference to generalizations does.

A related difficulty, also peculiar to the application of causal notions to particular cases, is the following. If we are puzzled by someone's sudden death and ask for the cause there seem to be natural limits forbidding us to give in answer, on the one hand events which are too near in time to the death, and on the other events which are too remote in time. If a man has been shot it would usually be stupid or inappropriate, though not false, to give as the cause of his death the fact that his blood-cells were deprived of oxygen, and equally inappropriate to give the manufacturer's action in selling the gun to his father from whom he had inherited it. What considerations control the normal refusal to cite or accept the first answer or to carry things back as far as the second? Again it seems clear the choice is not arbitrary here, but has to do with the context of the inquiry, who asks the question and why.

Much the same is true if we consider causal statements as pressing connexions forwards, not backwards, in time. The historian, the lawyer, and the plain man are often concerned to work out consequences in this way and so to deploy, in identifying the consequences of some particular event, not one but several generalizations concerning the regular course of events. In doing this there are some cases where it seems natural to pursue connexions 'through' a sequence of independent events: A lights a fire in the open, a mild breeze gets up and the fire spreads and consumes the adjoining house. Here the breeze was independent of the man's action in lighting the fire, but in the terms of the law's favourite though perhaps most misleading metaphor, it does not 'break the chain of causation.' It would be correct and natural to say that A's action was the cause of the destruction of the house. But if a man shoots at his wife intending to kill her, and she takes refuge in her parents' house where she is injured by a falling tile, though we may believe, on the strength of various general propositions, that if the man had not shot at his wife she would not have been injured (just as we may believe also, on the strength of general propositions, that if A had not lit the fire the house would not have been destroyed), this would not justify the assertion that the man had caused his wife's injury either in a legal context or in any other. It is obvious that, when we pursue causal connexion in particular cases through a series of events, we have to take account, not only of generalizations which may inform us what sorts of events are necessary or sufficient conditions of the occurrence of others, but also of considerations of a quite different order, concerning the way in which generalizations may be combined and applied in particular cases. Again, this is not a peculiarity of the legal use of causal notions, but a feature of their use in all branches of thought where particular causal statements are made.

The character of the distinction between causes and conditions, and the principles imposing limits on the pressing of causal connexions backwards or forwards in time, are the source of most of the difficulties in understanding the causal concepts with which the lawyer works, and they have received very little attention in the traditional philosophical discussions of cause. Perhaps a shift in philosophical method is really necessary before these problems could be seen to be as central as they are to our understanding of causation. They come into view only when the philosopher is prepared to forego, at least temporarily, larger questions concerning the 'status' or 'validity' or the 'necessity' of the idea of causation, and to examine and chart in some detail the actual use made in given disciplines or in ordinary discourse of the key expressions like 'cause,' 'consequence,' and 'effects.' Such things emerge only when we observe the way in which a shifting context affects the force and meaning of these expressions.

II

Human beings have learnt, by making appropriate movements of their bodies, to bring about desired alterations in objects, animate or inanimate, in their environment, and to express these simple achievements by transitive verbs like push, pull, bend, twist, break, injure. The process involved here consists of an initial immediate bodily manipulation of the thing affected and often takes little time. Men have, however, learnt to extend the range of their actions and have discovered that by doing these relatively simple actions they can, in favourable circumstances, bring about secondary changes, not only in the objects actually manipulated, but in other objects. Here the process initiated by bodily movements and manipulation may be protracted in space or time, may be difficult to accomplish and involve a series of changes, sometimes of noticeably different kinds. Here we use the correlative terms 'cause' and 'effect' rather than simple transitive verbs: the effect is the desired secondary change and the cause is our action in bringing about the primary change in the things manipulated or those primary changes themselves. So we cause one thing to move by striking it with another, glass to break by throwing stones, injuries by blows, things to get hot by putting them on fires. Here the notions of cause and effect come together with the notion of means to ends and of producing one thing by doing another. Cases of this exceedingly simple type are not only those where the expressions cause and effect have their most obvious application; they are also paradigms for the understanding of the causal language used of very different types of case. This is so for two reasons: first some important point of resemblance, or at least analogy, with these simple cases is traceable in the wider range to which causal language is extended; and, secondly, expressions which have a literal use in the simple cases have come to be used in a metaphorical and sometimes baffling way in cases far outside their scope. It is therefore important to consider certain prominent features of these simple cases which affect the general use of causal language in this way.

Human action in the simple cases, where we produce some desired effect by the manipulation of an object in our environment, is an interference in the natural course of events which *makes a difference* in the way these develop. In an almost literal sense, such an interference by human action is an intervention or intrusion of one kind of thing upon another distinct kind of thing. Common experience teaches us that, left to themselves, the things we manipulate, since they have a 'nature' or characteristic way of behaving, would persist in states or exhibit changes different from those which we have learnt to bring about in them by our manipulation. The notion, that a cause is essentially something which interferes with or intervenes in the course of events which would normally take place, is central to the common-sense concept of cause, and at least as essential as the notions of invariable or constant sequence so much stressed by Mill and Hume. Analogies with the interference by human beings with the natural course of events in part control, even in cases where there is literally no human intervention, what is to be identified as the cause of some occurrence; the cause, though not a literal intervention, is a *difference* to the normal course which accounts for the difference in the outcome.

In these basic cases involving human manipulation the cause is not only an intervention but one which characteristically involves movement of things; for when we bring about changes in things by manipulating them or other things, the first stages of this process consist of movements of our own body or parts of it, and consequently movements of things or parts of the things which we manipulate. Very often these initiating movements are accompanied by experiences characteristically associated with the exertion of pressure or force. The prominent part played in the simple cases by movement is responsible for two related ways of speaking about causes. First, it has bred a whole host of metaphors: causes quite outside the range of the simple cases we are considering are spoken of as 'forces' 'being active,' 'operating,' 'coming to rest,' having 'power' or 'potency,' 'active force,' even when it is clearly realized that what is thus spoken of does not consist of movement or of anything like it. We find, for example, courts using such expressions freely: even the question whether the sale of a gun to a child was the cause of some injury has been discussed in the form of the inquiry as to whether or not the sale was an 'active force' that had 'come to rest' when the child's mother took the gun from him. Conversely, preoccupation with the basic simple cases, where causes literally are movements, is the undiagnosed source of the difficulties which some theorists have experienced in seeing how a 'static condition' or a 'negative condition' or an omission could be the cause of anything. Mill in his footnotes argued against just such an objection, but the analogies with a thing which is active or moves have darkened many a discussion of causation. The position here is a curious, though not unfamiliar one when the terminology used in a given type of case is extended to cases which are only partly analogous. On the one hand it is perfectly common and intelligible in ordinary life to speak of static conditions or negative events as causes: there is no convenient substitute for statements that the lack of rain was the cause of the failure of the corn crop, the icy condition of the road was the cause of the accident, the failure of the signalman to pull the lever was the cause of the train smash. On the other hand the theorist, when he attempts to analyse the notion of a cause, is haunted by the sense that since these ways of speaking diverge from the paradigm cases where causes are events or forces, they must be somehow improper. The corrective is to see that in spite of differences between these cases and the simply paradigms, the very real analogies are enough to justify the extension of causal language to them.

In these simple cases, where we speak of a deliberate human intervention or the primary changes initiated by it as the cause of an occurrence, we rely upon general knowledge and commit ourselves to a general proposition of some kind; but this is something very different from causal 'laws' or general propositions asserting invariable sequence which Mill regarded as essential to causal connexion. When we assert that A's blow made B's nose bleed or A's exposure of the wax to the flame caused it to melt, the general knowledge used here is knowledge of the familiar 'way' to produce, by manipulating things, certain types of change which do not normally occur without our intervention. If formulated they are broadly framed generalizations, more like recipes in which we assert that doing one thing will 'under normal conditions' produce another than statements of 'invariable sequence' between a complex set of specified conditions and an event of the given kind. Mill's description of common sense 'selecting' the cause from such a set of conditions is a *suggestio falsi* so far as these simple causal statements are concerned; for, though we may gradually come to know more and more of the conditions required for our interventions to be successful, we do not 'select' from them the one we treat as the cause. Our intervention is regarded as the cause from the start before we learn more than a few of the other necessary conditions. We simply continue to call it the cause when we know more.

It is, moreover, a marked feature of these simple causal statements that we do not regard them as asserted unjustifiably or without warrant in a particular case if the maker of them cannot specify any considerable number of the further required conditions. It is perfectly legitimate to say that A's blow caused B's nose to bleed and to feel confidence in the truth of his statement, though we could not formulate or would have very little confidence in a generalization purporting to specify conditions under which blows are invariably followed by bleeding from the nose. Yet even at this simple level where the cause is our own deliberate intervention *propter hoc* is recognized to be different from *post hoc*. It is *possible* that just at the moment A struck, B independently ruptured a blood-vessel; experience may alert us to such possibilities, and science teach us how to recognize them. Yet this would be a remarkable coincidence and there is a presumption, which is normally fulfilled (but rebuttable), that when we deliberately intervene in nature to bring about effects which in fact supervene, no other explanation of their occurrence is to be found. Hence to make this type of causal statement is justified if there is no ground for believing this normally fulfilled presumption not to hold good. It is, however, a feature of this, as of other types of empirical statement, that exceptionally they are not vindicated in the result and have to be withdrawn. But this does not mean that in asserting these causal statements we claim that they are instances of some general proposition asserting invariable sequence.

SUGGESTED READINGS

The literature on the concept of cause is vast. B. Russell suggests that much of the debate is unimportant because science does not use the concept: see his "On the Notion of Cause," in *Mysticism and Logic*. Most philosophers have felt that even if this is true the notion deserves attention. Kant attempted to reply to Hume in his *Critique of Pure Reason;* however, students who wish to find out about Kant's views might do well to begin with his *Prolegomena to Any Future Metaphysic* (translated by Lucas), in which Kant tried, not very successfully, to give a clear introduction to his philosophy. For elementary exposition of the problems connected with causation, see L. S. Stebbing, *Modern Introduction to Logic,* Chapter 15, and A. Pap, *Introduction to the Philosophy of Science,* Part IV. In *The Structure of Science* E. Nagel has an excellent section on causation, regularity, and law (Chapter 4), and another excellent, somewhat more difficult chapter, the tenth, on causality and indeterminism in modern science.

There are important discussions of causation in P. Duhem, *Aim and Structure of Physical Theory,* Chapter V, and in M. Schlick, "Causation in Everyday Life and in Recent Science," reprinted in H. Feigl and W. Sellars, *Readings in Philosophical Analysis.* The essays by E. Mach ("The Significance and Purpose of Natural Laws") and H. Margenau ("Meaning and Scientific Status of Causality") in the anthology edited by A. Danto and S. Morgenbesser, *Philosophy of Science,* are more advanced. C. S. Peirce's essays, "The Reality of Thirdness" and "The Doctrine of Necessity Examined" are also difficult but are well worth study. They are in his *Collected Papers,* Volumes V and VI, respectively, and in V. Tomas (editor) *Essays in the Philosophy of Science.*

Induction

Any hypothesis or theory based on the empirical method is, as we know, a general conclusion inferred from specific instances. For example, the statement "If a person lacks vitamin C for a protracted period of time, he will get beri-beri," and the statement "If the volume of a gas is kept constant, the pressure will vary with the temperature," are generalizations drawn from specific observations and experiments. Yet both statements refer not only to the data from which they were derived and by which they have been confirmed, but also to further, as yet unobserved cases. The first refers to *all* instances in which persons lack vitamin C and the second to *all* instances in which a gas (*any* gas) is subjected to changes in temperature while its volume remains constant.

In going beyond the evidence on the basis of which hypotheses are suggested and tentatively confirmed, we are assuming that what holds true in the cases we have examined will, if conditions are sufficiently similar, also hold true in other cases. The unobserved cases about which we make inferences may be of two types: (1) those that already exist or have existed, but have not been examined and (2) those that still lie in the future. In both types of case we are generalizing on the basis of known instances to further instances, and we feel that our generalizations are justified.

But what justification is there for our reliance on these inferences? It is this question that is termed "the problem of induction." This problem, raised in its modern form by Hume, is stated with great clarity in the following reading by RUSSELL, who argues that the inductive principle cannot be justified on the basis of experience. WILL, considering the type of case that concerns the future, holds that Hume and Russell misconceive the problem. In the only reasonable sense of the word "future," he argues, our inferences from past to future cases are justified.

On Induction*

BERTRAND RUSSELL [1872–   ] is among the most distinguished and influential of living philosophers. He has written voluminously on almost every aspect of philosophy: the philosophy of science, the theory of knowledge, the mind-body problem, ethics, political philosophy, and the history of philosophy. With Alfred North Whitehead he wrote *Principia Mathematica* (1910–1913), a monumental work that gave a new direction to studies in the foundations of mathematics. Has taught and lectured at most of the principal universities in Europe and America.

If we are to know of the existence of matter, of other people, of the past before our individual memory begins, or of the future, we must know general principles of some kind by means of which such inferences can be drawn. It must be known to us that the existence of some one sort of thing, A, is a sign of the existence of some other sort of thing, B, either at the same time as A or at some earlier or later time, as, for example, thunder is a sign of the earlier existence of lightning. If this were not known to us, we could never extend our knowledge beyond the sphere of our private experience; and this sphere . . . is exceedingly limited. The question we have now to consider is whether such an extension is possible, and if so, how it is effected.

Let us take as an illustration a matter about which none of us, in fact, feel the slightest doubt. We are all convinced that the sun will rise tomorrow. Why? Is this belief a mere blind outcome of past experience, or can it be justified as a reasonable belief? It is not easy to find a test by which to judge whether a belief of this kind is reasonable or not, but we can at least ascertain what sort of general beliefs would suffice, if true, to justify the judgment that the sun will rise to-morrow, and the many other similar judgements upon which our actions are based.

It is obvious that if we are asked why we believe that the sun will rise to-morrow, we shall naturally answer, 'Because it always has risen every day.' We have a firm belief that it will rise in the future, because it has risen in the past. If we are challenged as to why we believe that it will continue to rise as heretofore, we may appeal to the laws of motion: the earth, we shall say, is a freely rotating body, and such bodies do not cease to rotate unless something interferes from outside, and there is nothing outside to interfere with

* From Russell: *The Problems of Philosophy*, Chapter 6. Copyright 1912, The Home University Library. Reprinted by permission of Oxford University Press.

the earth between now and to-morrow. Of course it might be doubted whether we are quite certain that there is nothing outside to interfere, but this is not the interesting doubt. The interesting doubt is as to whether the laws of motion will remain in operation until to-morrow. If this doubt is raised, we find ourselves in the same position as when the doubt about the sunrise was first raised.

The *only* reason for believing that the laws of motion will remain in operation is that they have operated hitherto, so far as our knowledge of the past enables us to judge. It is true that we have a greater body of evidence from the past in favour of the laws of motion than we have in favour of the sunrise, because the sunrise is merely a particular case of fulfilment of the laws of motion, and there are countless other particular cases. But the real question is: Do *any* number of cases of a law being fulfilled in the past afford evidence that it will be fulfilled in the future? If not, it becomes plain that we have no ground whatever for expecting the sun to rise tomorrow, or for expecting the bread we shall eat at our next meal not to poison us, or for any of the other scarcely conscious expectations that control our daily lives. It is to be observed that all such expectations are only *probable*; thus we have not to seek for a proof that they *must* be fulfilled, but only for some reason in favour of the view that they are *likely* to be fulfilled.

Now in dealing with this question we must, to begin with, make an important distinction, without which we should soon become involved in hopeless confusions. Experience has shown us that, hitherto, the frequent repetition of some uniform succession or coexistence has been a *cause* of our expecting the same succession or coexistence on the next occasion. Food that has a certain appearance generally has a certain taste, and it is a severe shock to our expectations when the familiar appearance is found to be associated with an unusual taste. Things which we see become associated, by habit, with certain tactile sensations which we expect if we touch them; one of the horrors of a ghost (in many ghost-stories) is that it fails to give us any sensations of touch. Uneducated people who go abroad for the first time are so surprised as to be incredulous when they find their native language not understood.

And this kind of association is not confined to men; in animals also it is very strong. A horse which has been often driven along a certain road resists the attempt to drive him in a different direction. Domestic animals expect food when they see the person who usually feeds them. We know that all these rather crude expectations of uniformity are liable to be misleading. The man who has fed the chicken every day throughout its life at last wrings its neck instead, showing that more refined views as to the uniformity of nature would have been useful to the chicken.

But in spite of the misleadingness of such expectations, they nevertheless exist. The mere fact that something has happened a certain number of times causes animals and men to expect that it will happen again. Thus our instincts certainly cause us to believe that the sun will rise to-morrow, but we may be in no better a position than the chicken which unexpectedly has its neck wrung. We have therefore to distinguish the fact that past uniformities *cause* expectations as to the future, from the question whether there is any reasonable ground for giving weight to such expectations after the question of their validity has been raised.

The problem we have to discuss is whether there is any reason for believing in what is called 'the uniformity of nature.' The belief in the uniformity of nature is the belief that everything that has happened or will happen is an instance of some general law to which there are *no* exceptions. The crude expectations which we have been considering are all subject to exceptions, and therefore liable to disappoint those who entertain them. But science habitually assumes, at least as a working hypothesis, that general rules which have exceptions can be replaced by general rules which have no exceptions. 'Unsupported bodies in air fall' is a general rule to which balloons and aeroplanes are exceptions. But the laws of motion and the law of gravitation, which account for the fact that most bodies fall, also account for the fact that balloons and aeroplanes can rise; thus the laws of motion and the law of gravitation are not subject to these exceptions.

The belief that the sun will rise to-morrow might be falsified if the earth came suddenly into contact with a large body which destroyed its rotation; but the laws of motion and the law of gravitation would not be infringed by such an event. The business of science is to find uniformities, such as the laws of motion and the law of gravitation, to which, so far as our experience extends, there are no exceptions. In this search science has been remarkably successful, and it may be conceded that such uniformities have held hitherto. This brings us back to the question: Have we any reason, assuming that they have always held in the past, to suppose that they will hold in the future?

It has been argued that we have reason to know that the future will resemble the past, because what was the future has constantly become the past, and has always been found to resemble the past, so that we really have experience of the future, namely of times which were formerly future, which we may call past futures. But such an argument really begs the very question at issue. We have experience of past futures, but not of future futures, and the question is: Will future futures resemble past futures? This question is not to be answered by an argument which starts from past futures alone. We have therefore still to seek for some principle which shall enable us to know that the future will follow the same laws as the past.

The reference to the future in this question is not essential. The same question arises when we apply the laws that work in our experience to past things of which we have no experience—as, for example, in geology, or in theories as to the origin of the Solar System. The question we really have to ask is: 'When two things have been found to be often associated, and no instance is known of the one occurring without the other, does the occurrence of one of the two, in a fresh instance, give any good ground for expecting the other?' On our answer to this question must depend the validity of the whole of our expectations as to the future, the whole of the results obtained by induction, and in fact practically all the beliefs upon which our daily life is based.

It must be conceded, to begin with, that the fact that two things have been found often together and never apart does not, by itself, suffice to *prove* demonstratively that they will be found together in the next case we examine. The most we can hope is that the oftener things are found together, the more probable it becomes that they will be found together another time, and that, if they have been found together often enough, the probability will amount *almost* to certainty. It can never quite reach certainty, because we know that in spite of frequent repetitions there sometimes is a failure at the last, as in the case of the chicken whose neck is wrung. Thus probability is all we ought to seek.

It might be urged, as against the view we are advocating, that we know all natural phenomena to be subject to the reign of law, and that sometimes, on the basis of observation, we can see that only one law can possibly fit the facts of the case. Now to this view there are two answers. The first is that, even if *some* law which has no exceptions applies to our case, we can never, in practice, be sure that we have discovered that law and not one to which there are exceptions. The second is that the reign of law would seem to be itself only probable, and that our belief that it will hold in the future, or in unexamined cases in the past, is itself based upon the very principle we are examining.

The principle we are examining may be called the *principle of induction,* and its two parts may be stated as follows:

(*a*) When a thing of a certain sort A has been found to be associated with a thing of a certain other sort B, and has never been found dissociated from a thing of the sort B, the greater the number of cases in which A and B have been associated, the greater is the probability that they will be associated in a fresh case in which one of them is known to be present;

(*b*) Under the same circumstances, a sufficient number of cases of association will make the probability of a fresh association nearly a certainty, and will make it approach certainty without limit.

As just stated, the principle applies only to the verification of our expecta-

tion in a single fresh instance. But we want also to know that there is a probability in favour of the general law that things of the sort A are *always* associated with things of the sort B, provided a sufficient number of cases of
association are known, and no cases of failure of association are known. The
probability of the general law is obviously less than the probability of the
particular case, since if the general law is true, the particular case must also
be true, whereas the particular case may be true without the general law
being true. Nevertheless the probability of the general law is increased by
repetitions, just as the probability of the particular case is. We may therefore repeat the two parts of our principle as regards the general law, thus:

(*a*) The greater the number of cases in which a thing of the sort A has been
found associated with a thing of the sort B, the more probable it is (if
no cases of failure of association are known) that A is always associated
with B;

(*b*) Under the same circumstances, a sufficient number of cases of the association of A with B will make it nearly certain that A is always associated with B, and will make this general law approach certainty without limit.

It should be noted that probability is always relative to certain data. In
our case, the data are merely the known cases of coexistence of A and B.
There may be other data, which *might* be taken into account, which would
gravely alter the probability. For example, a man who had seen a great
many white swans might argue, by our principle, that on the data it was
probable that all swans were white, and this might be a perfectly sound
argument. The argument is not disproved by the fact that some swans are
black, because a thing may very well happen in spite of the fact that some
data render it improbable. In the case of the swans, a man might know that
colour is a very variable characteristic in many species of animals, and that,
therefore, an induction as to colour is peculiarly liable to error. But this
knowledge would be a fresh datum, by no means proving that the probability relatively to our previous data had been wrongly estimated. The fact,
therefore, that things often fail to fulfil our expectations is no evidence that
our expectations will not *probably* be fulfilled in a given case or a given class
of cases. Thus our inductive principle is at any rate not capable of being
disproved by an appeal to experience.

The inductive principle, however, is equally incapable of being *proved* by
an appeal to experience. Experience might conceivably confirm the inductive
principle as regards the cases that have been already examined; but as regards unexamined cases, it is the inductive principle alone that can justify
any inference from what has been examined to what has not been examined.
All arguments which, on the basis of experience, argue as to the future or the

unexperienced parts of the past or present, assume the inductive principle; hence we can never use experience to prove the inductive principle without begging the question. Thus we must either accept the inductive principle on the ground of its intrinsic evidence, or forgo all justification of our expectations about the future. If the principle is unsound, we have no reason to expect the sun to rise to-morrow, to expect bread to be more nourishing than a stone, or to expect that if we throw ourselves off the roof we shall fall. When we see what looks like our best friend approaching us, we shall have no reason to suppose that his body is not inhabited by the mind of our worst enemy or of some total stranger. All our conduct is based upon associations which have worked in the past, and which we therefore regard as likely to work in the future; and this likelihood is dependent for its validity upon the inductive principle.

The general principles of science, such as the belief in the reign of law, and the belief that every event must have a cause, are as completely dependent upon the inductive principle as are the beliefs of daily life. All such general principles are believed because mankind have found innumerable instances of their truth and no instances of their falsehood. But this affords no evidence for their truth in the future, unless the inductive principle is assumed.

Thus all knowledge which, on a basis of experience tells us something about what is not experienced, is based upon a belief which experience can neither confirm nor confute, yet which, at least in its more concrete applications, appears to be as firmly rooted in us as many of the facts of experience.

Will the Future Be Like the Past?[*]

FREDERICK LUDWIG WILL [1909–   ] has been teaching philosophy at Illinois since 1938. His writing has been especially concerned with problems related to scientific method.

A

The standard argument for complete inductive scepticism, for the belief that inductive procedures have no rational and no empirical justification whatever, is the one stated in a small variety of ways in the writings of

[*] From F. Will: "Will the Future Be Like the Past?", Mind, N.S., LVI (1947), pp. 332–347. Reprinted by permission of Mind and the author.

Hume. If one consults these writings in search of an answer to the question of inductive validity one finds the same clear answer argued first in technical detail in the *Treatise*, secondly compressed into a few non-technical paragraphs in the *Abstract of a Treatise of Human Nature*, and thirdly, presented again in a non-technical but somewhat fuller version in a chapter in the *Enquiry Concerning Human Understanding*. There is no basis whatever for any conclusion concerning future matters, according to this argument; there is no way whatever in which such conclusions can be established to be certainly true or even probable. For in the first place no such conclusion can be demonstrated by reasoning alone, since they are all conclusions about matters of fact, and since it is the case that the denial of any assertion of a matter of fact is not self-contradictory. But if one gives up the rationalistic aspiration to demonstrate propositions about matters of fact or existence *a priori,* and turns instead to experience, this road, though apparently more promising at first, likewise ends by leading one exactly nowhere. Clearly no statement about future matters of fact can be established by observation. Future things cannot be observed. Any event or state of affairs which can be observed is by definition not in the future. The only recourse which remains therefore is the inductive procedure of employing present or past observations and inferring therefrom the nature of the future. But this procedure to which we are all forced, or rather, to which we all should be forced, if we did not, in company with the animals, use it naturally from birth, is in the light of close analysis completely indefensible. For such reasoning assumes, and is quite invalid without the assumption, that the future will be like the past.

[A]ll inferences from experience suppose, as their foundation, that the future will resemble the past, and that similar powers will be conjoined with similar sensible qualities. If there be any suspicion that the course of nature may change, and that the past may be no rule for the future, all experience becomes useless, and can give rise to no inference or conclusion. . . .

Will the future "resemble the past"? Or be "conformable to the past"? These are the ways in which in the *Enquiry* Hume expresses the question concerning the uniformity of nature, restricting to its reference toward the future the question which already had been asked in broader terms in the *Treatise*. There, without the temporal restriction, it is argued that the principle of inductive conclusions, the principle upon which reason would proceed if reason determined us in these matters, is *"that instances, of which we have had no experience, must resemble those, of which we have had experience, and that the course of nature continues always uniformly the same."*

However the principle is stated, the argument about it remains the same.

It is indispensable, if inductive conclusions are to be justified; but just as it is absolutely indispensable, so, and this is the measure of our logical misfortune, it cannot be established as certain or as probable in any way. . . .

Any further doubts about the doubtfulness of this principle which is the main-spring of inductive inference are quickly disposed of. No one who understands the principle with its reference to unobserved instances will suggest that it can be simply observed to be true. It is still true that one cannot observe the future, or the unobserved generally. And, finally, no one who has a sound logical conscience and appreciates the indispensability of the principle to induction generally will tolerate the suggestion that the principle may be established by inductions from experience. Such a process would be circular.

It is impossible, therefore, that any arguments from experience can prove this resemblance of the past to the future; since all these arguments are founded on the supposition of that resemblance.

And again:

. . . all our experimental conclusions proceed upon the supposition that the future will be conformable to the past. To endeavour, therefore, the proof of this last supposition by probable arguments, or arguments regarding existence, must be evidently going in a circle, and taking that for granted, which is the very point in question.

On this point the *Treatise* . . . and the *Abstract* speak with one voice. One final quotation from the latter may serve to summarise the conclusion.

'Tis evident that *Adam* with all his science, would never have been able to *demonstrate,* that the course of nature must continue uniformly the same, and that the future must be comformable to the past. What is possible can never be demonstrated to be false; and 'tis possible the course of nature may change, since we can conceive such a change. Nay, I will go farther, and assert, that he could not so much as prove by any *probable* arguments, that the future must be conformable to the past. All probable arguments are built on the supposition, that there is this conformity betwixt the future and the past, and therefore can never prove it. This conformity is a *matter of fact,* and if it must be proved, will admit of no proof but from experience. But our experience in the past can be a proof of nothing for the future, but upon a supposition, that there is a resemblance betwixt them. This therefore is a point, which can admit of no proof at all, and which we take for granted without any proof. . . .

B

Granted that there is empirical evidence which has been used to establish various scientific laws, all that it is evidence for, he [the sceptic] insists, is the assertion that *in the past* these laws were true, that in the past differences in time have made no difference. This evidence is absolutely worthless for inferences which speak about the future unless it is possible to assume that the future will be like the past. But stop! That is part of what one is trying to show, that is, that mere differences in temporal position, whether past or future, make no difference in these laws of nature. That the future will be like the past means, among other things, that in the future these laws will hold, that in this specific respect differences in time will make no difference. This cannot be inductively confirmed, the sceptic is saying, because any inductive argument for it assumes it and is therefore, as evidence, completely valueless.

One major source of the plausibility of the sceptic's reasoning lies in the analogies which knowing the future easily suggests and in terms of which one is apt to think and be misled. Is this not, one may ask, like any case of sampling? And must one not take care, when reasoning inductively from samples, that one's samples are fair? If a scientist reasons concerning the behaviour of oxygen, nitrogen, or hydrogen on Mars, if such elements there be on Mars, on the basis of the known behaviour of these elements on the earth, he is assuming that in some respects the samples of the elements on the other planet are like those we have here. Similarly in reasoning about the future behaviour of these elements on the basis of present and past behaviour one must assume that future samples of these elements will be like present and past ones. Now if it is the case that past samples may be regarded as evidence about future ones only upon such an assumption, then no examination of past samples, however extensive, can be regarded as yielding evidence for the assumption itself. Any reasoning which did attempt to employ such samples as evidence for the assumption would be forced to use the assumption as a principle in the reasoning and would therefore beg the whole question at issue.

A physical representation of the kind of analogy presented here might be as follows: Suppose that there was somewhere in the world an enclosure beyond which it was impossible for anyone ever to go or to make any observations. Nothing could be seen, heard, or in any other way perceived beyond the border. The territory beyond the enclosure, forever barred from human perception, is the land of Future. The territory within the enclosure is the land of Present and Past, but since it is overwhelmingly the latter, it all goes under the name of Past. Now suppose that someone within the enclosure is interested in some proposition about the way things behave beyond the enclosure, say, a simple and homely proposition about chickens, to the effect that beyond the enclosure roosters fight more than hens. And he wonders what evidence, if any, there is for this proposition. Of course he cannot observe this to be true. He must base it upon his observation in the land of

Past; and if he does base it upon the observed fact that roosters in the land of Past fight more than hens, he must assume that in this respect chickens beyond the enclosure behave like chickens within it, so that, knowing that in the latter area roosters are the more pugnacious, he may employ this knowledge as evidence that things are this way also in the former area. This is an assumption which no empirical evidence, confined as it must be to evidence in Past, can be employed to support. Any attempt to support it with such evidence must itself assume that in respect to the phenomena involved differences between Past and Future are negligible; and since that is exactly what the reasoning is attempting to establish, the process is patently circular.

This is the kind of metaphor which makes friends, and influences people, in this case, to draw the wrong conclusions. There are several faults in the analogy. The chief one is that, as represented, the border between Past and Future is stationary, while in the temporal situation it is not. To duplicate the temporal situation in this respect the analogy should represent the border as constantly moving, revealing as it does constantly, in territory which has hitherto been Future, hens and roosters similar as regards difference in disposition to those already observed in Past. The matter of evidence for the proposition about hens and roosters is then also different. If this proposition is in a position analogous to the beliefs about uniformity which are represented in modern scientific laws, the situation is something like this. Previously inhabitants in Past had drawn more sweeping conclusions concerning the difference between the disposition to fight of male and female chickens. They have discovered recently that in respect to young chicks and pullets this generalisation did not hold. They have therefore revised the proposition to exclude all the known negative instances and speak only and more surely of the behaviour of hens and roosters, meaning by these latter terms just fully grown and developed female and male chickens.

So far as there is any record, chickens in Past have verified this rule; so far as there is any record, every chicken revealed by the ever receding border has likewise verified it; so far as there is any record there has not been one negative instance. Is it not the case that the inhabitants of Past do have evidence for the proposition that all chickens obey this rule, those already in Past, which they call "Past-chickens," and those also which are not yet in Past but which will be subsequently revealed by the moving border, and which they call not unnaturally "Future-chickens"? They have a vast number of positive instances of the rule, and no negative instances, except those in respect to which the rule has already been revised. In view of the present evidence that in all cases, year after year and century after century, the progressively revealed chickens have verified and do verify this rule, must one not conclude that the inhabitants of Past do have evidence for this proposition, and that anyone is wrong who says that they have actually no evidence one way or other?

The sceptic, however, is still prepared to argue his case, and his argument, in terms of the present analogy, has a now familiar ring. That the inhabitants of Past have no evidence whatsoever about the behaviour of Future-chickens, he will insist; and as grounds he will point out that although the border does progressively recede and reveal chickens like those previously observed in Past, these are really not Future-chickens. By the very fact that they have been revealed they are no longer Future-chickens, but are now Past-chickens. Observation of them is not observation of Future-chickens, and any attempt to reason from such observation to conclusions about Future-chickens must therefore assume that Future-chickens are like Past-chickens. For the inhabitants of Past, in these efforts to know the land beyond the border, this is both an inescapable and unknowable presumption.

What should one say of an argument of this kind? Only through some logical slip, one feels strongly, would it be possible to arrive at such a conclusion. One would have thought that the receding border was a matter upon which the inhabitants of Past may legitimately congratulate themselves in the light of their interest in learning what Future-chickens, when they become Past, are going to be like. If the border had not yet begun to recede they would indeed be in an unfortunate position for securing such knowledge. But happily this is not the case. The border is constantly receding. And granting that it will constantly recede, revealing always more of the land of Future, and even granting also that this means that there is an inexhaustible area to be revealed, the inhabitants of Past are in the fortunate position that with the progressive recession they may learn more and more about chickens, Past and Future. They may derive hypotheses from their experience of what has already been revealed and proceed further to test these by the progressive revelations of Future, in the light of which they may be confirmed, refuted, or revised. The sceptic's argument amounts to the assertion that all this apparent good fortune is really illusory and that the sorry Pastians are actually in no better position with respect to knowing about Future-chickens and Future-things generally than they would be if the border never moved at all. For the movement of the border does not reveal Future-chickens, since Future is by definition the land beyond the border. No matter how much or how little is revealed, by the very fact that it is revealed and on this side of the border it is not Future but Past, and therefore, since the land of Future always is beyond observation, no empirical method can produce any evidence that what is in that land is in any way similar to what is not. That this rendering of the sceptic's position, though in the language of the above metaphor, is undistorted and fair may be seen by consulting the words of an illustrious modern sceptic and follower of Hume, Bertrand Russell. In his chapter, "On Induction," in *The Problems of Philosophy*, Russell expressed the matter in this fashion:

> It has been argued that we have reason to know that the future will resemble the past, because what was the future has constantly become the past, and has always been found to resemble the past, so that we really have experience of the future, which we may call past futures. But such an argument really begs the very question at issue. We have experience of past futures, but not of future futures, and the question is: Will future futures resemble past futures? This question is not to be answered by an argument which starts from past futures alone. We have therefore still to seek for some principle which shall enable us to know that the future will follow the same laws as the past.

This is the central difficulty urged by Hume, Russell, and others in arguing that there can never be any empirical evidence that the future will be like the past. Empirically, in Russell's language, it is possible to have evidence only that this has been true of past and possibly present futures, not that it will be true of future futures. It is the situation in the land of Past all over again. There are generalisations which are constantly being confirmed by experience. But every time a confirming instance occurs it is nullified as evidence by the argument that it is not really a confirming instance at all. For by the fact that it has occurred it is an instance of a past future, and therefore it tells nothing whatever about future futures. In treating of the land of Past it was suggested that there is involved in arguing in this manner a logical slip or error. It remains to investigate how this is the case.

C

Suppose that in 1936, to take but a short span of time, a man says that in the above-defined sense the future will be like the past. In 1936, if he could somehow have shown that 1937 would be like 1936, this would have been evidence for his statement, as even a sceptic would admit. But in 1937, when he does establish that 1937 is like 1936, it has somehow ceased to be evidence. So long as he did not have it, it was evidence; as soon as he gets it it ceases to be. The constant neutralisation of the evidence which is effected in this argument is effected by the same kind of verbal trick which children play upon one another in fun. Child A asks child B what he is going to do tomorrow. B replies that he is going to play ball, go swimming, or what not. Thereupon A says, "You can't do that."

B: Why not?

A: Because to-morrow never comes. When to-morrow comes it won't be to-morrow; it will be to-day. You can never play to-morrow; you can only play to-day.

Again, if a prophet announces that next year will bring a utopia, and if each succeeding year, when the predicted utopia does not come, he defends himself by pointing out that he said "next year" and that obviously this is not next year, no reasonable person would pay much attention to him. Such a person would realise, on a moment's reflexion, that the prophet is being deceptive with the word "next." In 1936, "next year" means "1937"; in 1937 it means "1938." Since every year "next year" means a different year, a year yet to come, what the prophet says can never be verified or disproved. If in 1936 he meant by this phrase 1937, as he sensibly should, then this statement can be verified or refuted in 1937. But if, when 1937 comes, he insists that he did not mean 1937, but "next year," and if in 1938 he again insists that he did not mean that year, and so on, then what he seems to be meaning by "next year" is the $n + 1$th year where n is the ever-progressing number of the present year. No one should alter his present activities or his plans for the future on the basis of such a prediction, for, of course, it really is not a prediction. While in the form of a statement about the future it does not say anything about the future, anything which could possibly be true or false in the infinity of time, if infinity it is, which yet remains to transpire. For what the prophet is saying is that utopia will come next year, and by his own interpretation of the words "next year" he is affirming that next year will never come. In other words, at the time which never comes, and hence when nothing occurs, a utopia will occur. This is not even sensible speech; it is a contradiction.

In a similar though less simple way those who employ the sceptical argument about uniformity to show that there is no evidence whatever for any statement about the future are being themselves deceived and are deceiving others by their use of expressions like "next," "future," "future future," and "past future." The man who said in 1936 that the future would be like the past, that mere differences in temporal position make no difference in the behaviour of nature which is described in scientific laws, meant, as he sensibly should, that this was true of the years 1937, 1938, and so on. He said something of the form "all A's are B's" and it has been possible since 1936 to examine the A's of 1937 to 1946 and to see whether what he said is confirmed or disproved by the available evidence. If, however, now that it is 1946, and all this evidence is in, he should remark that since it is 1946 the years 1937–46 are no longer future and therefore have ceased to be evidence for the proposition, then he is guilty of using, or rather abusing, the word "future" in the way in which the prophet in the previous example was abusing the word "next." For the only basis for his contention that the observed A's are not confirming evidence, or what is the same thing, that they are confirming instances only if one assumes quite circularly that the future is like the past, is in his illusive use of the word "future." Time does pass, and, because it does, the present is a constantly changing one; and the point of reference for the use of words like "future" and "past" is accordingly different. The correct conclusion to be drawn from the fact that time passes is that the future is constantly being revealed and that, in consequence, we have had and shall have the opportunity to learn more and more accurately what the laws of nature's behaviour are and how therefore the future will be like the past. . . .

There are then, two senses of the word "future" to be carefully discriminated. They may be designated future-1 and future-2. In the sense of future-1, when one speaks about the future he is speaking of events which have not occurred, of things which do not exist, but of events and things which, with the constant movement of the line of the present, may sometime occur or exist. In the sense of future-2 when one speaks about the future he is speaking of the time which is always beyond the line of the moving present, of a time which never comes, which by definition can never come, no matter how far the line of the present moves.

Interpreted in the sense of future-1 there are beliefs about the way the future will be like the past, which have been and are being confirmed constantly by the uniform experience of countless positive instances in everyday life and in vast areas of science. Because they have been thus confirmed they constitute a vast set of assumptions with which scientists and laymen approach their problems in the various areas to which the confirmation applies. It is when these beliefs are interpreted in the sense of future-2 that the sceptics are able to produce a plausible argument to show that these beliefs are not empirically confirmable and are hence unknowable. But, when these are so interpreted, the argument has no bearing whatever, favourable or unfavourable, upon the soundness or success of any inductive inquiry. It asserts that specific types of events occur in specific ways, not in 1945, 1955, or any other year which will ever come, but in a year and a time which will never come. That one cannot produce empirical evidence for the statement that at a time which never comes and when no events occur, events will occur in these rather than other ways, may be readily admitted. But this is no good reason for scepticism. No scepticism is entailed by this admission so long as it is made with the understanding that there is evidence about the other kind of future, the kind which will come and in which events do occur. And it is this latter kind of future only, of these two kinds, with which our inductions are concerned. It is this kind of future alone about which our inductions predict, and this kind alone which will ever confirm or refute our assertions. It is, therefore, not sensible for anyone to worry, in his inductive reasoning, about the character of a future which by definition can never come, about his incapacity to prove that if this future did come, which is itself a contradictory condition, it would have this or that character. And no one would worry about such a thing for an instant unless misled by fallacious reasoning such as that which has just been exposed.

SUGGESTED READINGS

J. S. Mill tried to answer Hume's questions about induction in Book III, Chapters 3–5, of his *System of Logic*, but no one has been very happy with his solution. For a clear criticism, not only of Mill's kind of solution but of the problem as Hume raised it, see M. Black, "The Justification of Induction," in his *Language and Philosophy*. Older treatments of the problem include L. S. Stebbing, *Modern Introduction to Logic*, Chapters 14 and 21, and H. W. B. Joseph, *Introduction to Logic*, Chapters 18 and 19. In *Probability and Induction* W. Kneale has discussed with admirable lucidity a wide range of problems pertaining to these two topics; in Part II he gives an historical account of major theories of induction.

C. S. Peirce discusses induction in various essays, many of which are to be found in Volume II of his *Collected Papers;* beginning on page 483 there is an extensive discussion of Mill on induction. In Volume VI there is an interesting paper on "The Order of Nature" (pp. 283 ff). K. Popper argues that induction is no special problem because science proceeds, not by proving hypotheses true, but by rejecting false hypotheses and using only those that survive rigorous testing. For his views, see *The Logic of Scientific Discovery*, especially Chapters 1, 4, and 10.

For further advanced discussions see J. J. Katz, *The Problem of Induction and Its Solution;* S. Barker, *Induction and Hypothesis;* R. B. Braithwaite, *Scientific Explanation*, Chapter 9; J. M. Keynes, *Treatise on Probability;* and the interesting article by H. Feigl in *Philosophical Analysis*, edited by M. Black.

Is Science Limited?

Scientific method has been the subject of criticism from a variety of points of view. Criticism is directed sometimes against the method as it is used, in a rudimentary way, in everyday life, and sometimes against the highly developed form it assumes in the advanced sciences, as well as against both of these extremes. Those critics who offer alternatives to supplement or replace the methods of science are motivated (in part, at least) by the hope of avoiding what they take to be defects inherent in those methods.

Rationalism

Neither in daily life nor in science do empirical methods give *certainty*. In daily life we trust the senses, which are notoriously fallible. We rely on hearsay and authority, and we fall into inconsistencies. We usually do not have explicit reasons for believing what we believe. And even when we use the developed methods of science, we fail to achieve certainty; at best we get highly probable conclusions.

Furthermore, both in science and in daily life empirical methods are *piecemeal*. In facing everyday problems, we are usually content to attack the difficulties that lie close at hand, and we rarely examine our problems in a coherent and systematic order. In science the situation is somewhat the same. Whereas scientists do test their hypotheses for consistency with other hypotheses, they employ the motto "divide and rule": nature is split up into fields, each of which is studied by specialists. Even within a particular discipline, investigations concern specific, delimited problems, and questions *first* studied rarely (except by accident) concern the most general and ultimate aspects of the field. In fact, most contemporary scientists would be inclined to doubt the wisdom of proceeding directly to an examination of the most universal and basic issues in any field of specialization.

Rationalists, on the other hand, seek both certainty and systematic completeness. Modeling their inquiries on earlier conceptions of mathematics (particularly geometry), they attempt to rely not on experience but on reason alone. According to the rationalist position, "the natural light of reason" suffices to establish basic axioms of universal import, and permits us to deduce specific consequences from them. Such axioms, which rationalists regard as self-evident and indubitable, are held to be independent of experience, so that experience could not prove them false. They would provide a sure foundation for all further knowledge, and truths deduced from the axioms would constitute a single, unified, all-embracing system.

It is this ideal of knowledge that DESCARTES states and defends.

146

Intuitionism

Etymologically, the term "intuition" refers to any direct "looking at or into"; it refers, that is, to direct and unmediated methods of getting knowledge. We can speak of "rational intuition," referring to an immediate insight (without reasoning and without proof) into, say, mathematical or logical relationships. We can also speak of "sensuous intuition," referring to the immediate awareness or beholding of data given to the senses. Philosophers have in fact used both expressions. However, as the term has come to be most widely used, "intuition" refers to a method based on neither reason nor the senses. Intuitionists hold that men have a special faculty or capacity, a special way of knowing, which is independent both of their senses and of their capacity for reasoning.

The knowledge obtained by this faculty is believed to be more certain, and above all more important, than knowledge gained in any other way. Its importance lies in the fact that it is not knowledge of the external, superficial aspects of things, but of their inner core: their purposes, their inner forces, their hidden character. According to intuitionists, it is by intuition that we know ourselves, that we know the character, moods, and motives of others, and that we experience the real nature of time, motion, and other fundamental aspects of the universe. For intuitionists an intellectual, analytic approach leads us away from the real nature of things, into abstractions and relations; it is through intuition alone that we can grasp concrete actualities in their uniqueness.

The selection from BERGSON expresses the intuitionist position in one of its most widely held and influential forms.

Pragmatism

Strictly speaking, pragmatism is not an alternative to empirical methods. It is rather an alternative interpretation of them, springing from a reconsideration of problems concerning truth and belief.

In the particular version of pragmatism which JAMES defended, one of the central contentions is that knowledge serves human purposes and that the only test of whether our beliefs are true is whether they have fruitful consequences. In daily life, for example, we regard a belief as true if its results help us to fulfill our purposes. And in science too we verify hypotheses through our experience of specific consequences to which they lead. According to James, religious beliefs must be established in the same way. Religious beliefs, it is true, do not have consequences that lend themselves to testing through the methods applicable in the sciences. But this very independence from scientific verification permits us to accept them because of *other* consequences—their effects on our personal lives and actions. Our religious faith is tested by reference to its practical influence, and its truth is established by its capacity to transform our lives. Just as we accept a scientific belief because of its fruitful consequences in the investigation of nature, so we have a right to accept a religious commitment because of its fruitful consequences in making our personal lives richer and fuller.

In James' view, therefore, religious faith and scientific knowledge are by no means opposed; although each has its special field of application and special conditions of verification, the truths of religious faith and scientific knowledge are established by an identical criterion: fruitful consequences in practice.

Science and Common Sense

RYLE is concerned to remind us of certain facts that we are likely to forget when we consider the remarkable "world" that scientists, especially physical scientists, are sometimes thought to inhabit. Naively, we might think of them as picking up extremely small particles of matter (called "electrons") with extremely small tweezers and then subjecting them to examination under microscopes of extraordinarily high power. Ryle is concerned, in part, to point out that physicists live in the same world we all live in, and that if what they say is to make any sense at all, it must be made sense of in terms of our ordinary macroscopic notions (door-knobs that help us get into the laboratory, "big" levers and pulleys, after pulling which we look at "big" dials and gauges, and so on). One way in which we might think of science as being limited is that its results and methods *must* be somehow anchored in the everyday world we all inhabit.

Rationalism *

R E N É   D E S C A R T E S [1596–1650] was educated at the Jesuit college at La Flèche and soon became distinguished for his works on mathematics and the sciences. His greatest contribution to these fields was his invention of analytic geometry. From mathematics he drew the inspiration for his philosophy, attempting to answer philosophical and theological problems by the same rigorous method of reasoning which mathematics employs. Because of his originality and his influence on subsequent thought, he is generally regarded as the founder of modern philosophy.

Rule I

The end of study should be to direct the mind towards the enunciation of sound and correct judgments on all matters that come before it.

Whenever men notice some similarity between two things, they are wont to ascribe to each, even in those respects in which the two differ, what they have found to be true of the other. Thus they erroneously compare the sci-

---

* From Descartes: *Rules for the Direction of the Mind,* translated by Elizabeth S. Haldane and G. R. T. Ross, in *The Philosophical Works of Descartes,* Volume I. Copyright, 1911, by the Cambridge University Press. Reprinted by permission of the Cambridge University Press.

ences, which entirely consist in the cognitive exercise of the mind, with the
arts, which depend upon an exercise and disposition of the body. They see
that not all the arts can be acquired by the same man, but that he who restricts himself to one, most readily becomes the best executant, since it is not
so easy for the same hand to adapt itself both to agricultural operations and
to harp-playing, or to the performance of several such tasks as to one alone.
Hence they have held the same to be true of the sciences also, and distinguishing them from one another according to their subject matter, they have
imagined that they ought to be studied separately, each in isolation from all
the rest. But this is certainly wrong. For since the sciences taken all together
are identical with human wisdom, which always remains one and the same,
however applied to different subjects, and suffers no more differentiation
proceeding from them than the light of the sun experiences from the variety
of the things which it illumines, there is no need for minds to be confined at
all within limits; for neither does the knowing of one truth have an effect like
that of the acquisition of one art and prevent us from finding out another, it
rather aids us to do so. . . . Hence we must believe that all the sciences are
so inter-connected, that it is much easier to study them all together than to
isolate one from all the others. . . .

Rule II

*Only those objects should engage our attention, to the sure and indubitable
knowledge of which our mental powers seem to be adequate.*

Science in its entirety is true and evident cognition. He is no more learned
who has doubts on many matters than the man who has never thought of
them; nay he appears to be less learned if he has formed wrong opinions on
any particulars. Hence it were better not to study at all than to occupy one's
self with objects of such difficulty, that, owing to our inability to distinguish
true from false, we are forced to regard the doubtful as certain; for in those
matters any hope of augmenting our knowledge is exceeded by the risk of
diminishing it. Thus in accordance with the above maxim we reject all such
merely probable knowledge and make it a rule to trust only what is completely known and incapable of being doubted. . . .

But if we adhere closely to this rule we shall find left but few objects of
legitimate study. For there is scarce any question occurring in the sciences
about which talented men have not disagreed. But whenever two men come
to opposite decisions about the same matter one of them at least must certainly be in the wrong, and apparently there is not even one of them in the
right; for if the reasoning of the second was sound and clear he would be
able so to lay it before the other as finally to succeed in convincing *his* understanding also. Hence apparently we cannot attain to a perfect knowledge

in any such case of probable opinion, for it would be rashness to hope for more than others have attained to. Consequently if we reckon correctly, of the sciences already discovered, Arithmetic and Geometry alone are left, to which the observance of this rule reduces us. . . .

Now let us proceed to explain more carefully our reasons for saying that of all the sciences known as yet, Arithmetic and Geometry alone are free from any taint of falsity or uncertainty. We must note then that there are two ways by which we arrive at the knowledge of facts, viz., by experience and by deduction. We must further observe that while our inferences from experience are frequently fallacious, deduction, or the pure illation of one thing from another, though it may be passed over, if it is not seen through, cannot be erroneous when performed by an understanding that is in the least degree rational. . . . My reason for saying so is that none of the mistakes which men can make (men, I say, not beasts) are due to faulty inference; they are caused merely by the fact that we base inferences upon poorly comprehended experiences, or that propositions are posited which are hasty and groundless.

This furnishes us with an evident explanation of the great superiority in certitude of Arithmetic and Geometry to other sciences. The former alone deal with an object so pure and uncomplicated, that they need make no assumptions at all which experience renders uncertain, but wholly consist in the rational deduction of consequences. They are on that account much the easiest and clearest of all, and possess an object such as we require, for in them it is scarce humanly possible for anyone to err except by inadvertence. And yet we should not be surprised to find that plenty of people of their own accord prefer to apply their intelligence to other studies. The reason for this is that every person permits himself the liberty of making guesses in the matter of an obscure subject with more confidence than in one which is clear, and that it is much easier to have some vague notion about any subject, no matter what, than to arrive at the real truth about a single question however simple that may be.

But one conclusion now emerges out of these considerations, viz. not, indeed, that Arithmetic and Geometry are the sole sciences to be studied, but only that in our search for the direct road towards truth we should busy ourselves with no object about which we cannot attain a certitude equal to that of the demonstrations of Arithmetic and Geometry.

Rule III

In the subjects we propose to investigate, our inquiries should be directed, not to what others have thought, nor to what we ourselves conjecture, but to what we can clearly and perspicuously behold and with certainty deduce; for knowledge is not won in any other way.

To study the writings of the ancients is right, because it is a great boon for us to be able to make use of the labours of so many men; and we should do so, both in order to discover what they have correctly made out in previous ages, and also that we may inform ourselves as to what in the various sciences is still left for investigation. But yet there is a great danger lest in a too absorbed study of these works we should become infected with their errors, guard against them as we may. For it is the way of writers, whenever they have allowed themselves rashly and credulously to take up a position in any controverted matter, to try with the subtlest of arguments to compel us to go along with them. But when, on the contrary, they have happily come upon something certain and evident, in displaying it they never fail to surround it with ambiguities, fearing, it would seem, lest the simplicity of their explanation should make us respect their discovery less, or because they grudge us an open vision of the truth.

Further, supposing now that all were wholly open and candid, and never thrust upon us doubtful opinions as true, but expounded every matter in good faith, yet since scarce anything has been asserted by any one man the contrary of which has not been alleged by another, we should be eternally uncertain which of the two to believe. It would be no use to total up the testimonies in favour of each, meaning to follow that opinion which was supported by the greater number of authors; for if it is a question of difficulty that is in dispute, it is more likely that the truth would have been discovered by few than by many. But even though all these men agreed among themselves, what they teach us would not suffice for us. For we shall not, e.g., all turn out to be mathematicians though we know by heart all the proofs that others have elaborated, unless we have an intellectual talent that fits us to resolve difficulties of any kind. Neither, though we have mastered all the arguments of Plato and Aristotle, if yet we have not the capacity for passing a solid judgment on these matters, shall we become Philosophers; we should have acquired the knowledge not of a science, but of history.

I lay down the rule also, that we must wholly refrain from ever mixing up conjectures with our pronouncements on the truth of things. This warning is of no little importance. There is no stronger reason for our finding nothing in the current Philosophy which is so evident and certain as not to be capable of being controverted, than the fact that the learned, not content with the recognition of what is clear and certain, in the first instance hazard the assertion of obscure and ill-comprehended theories, at which they have arrived merely by probable conjecture. Then afterwards they gradually attach complete credence to them, and mingling them promiscuously with what is true and evident, they finish by being unable to deduce any conclusion which does not appear to depend upon some proposition of the doubtful sort, and hence is not uncertain.

But lest we in turn should slip into the same error, we shall here take note of all those mental operations by which we are able, wholly without fear of illusion, to arrive at the knowledge of things. Now I admit only two, viz., intuition and deduction.

By *intuition* I understand, not the fluctuating testimony of the senses, nor the misleading judgment that proceeds from the blundering constructions of imagination, but the conception which an unclouded and attentive mind gives us so readily and distinctly that we are wholly freed from doubt about that which we understand. Or, what comes to the same thing, *intuition* is the undoubting conception of an unclouded and attentive mind, and springs from the light of reason alone; it is more certain than deduction itself, in that it is simpler, though deduction, as we have noted above, cannot by us be erroneously conducted. Thus each individual can mentally have intuition of the fact that he exists, and that he thinks; that the triangle is bounded by three lines only, the sphere by a single superficies, and so on. Facts of such a kind are far more numerous than many people think, disdaining as they do . . . to direct their attention upon such simple matters. . . .

This evidence and certitude, however, which belongs to intuition, is required not only in the enunciation of propositions, but also in discursive reasoning of whatever sort. For example consider this consequence: 2 and 2 amount to the same as 3 and 1. Now we need to see intuitively not only that 2 and 2 make 4, and that likewise 3 and 1 make 4, but further that the third of the above statements is a necessary conclusion from these two.

Hence now we are in a position to raise the question as to why we have, besides intuition, given this supplementary method of knowing, viz., knowing by *deduction,* by which we understand all necessary inference from other facts that are known with certainty. This, however, we could not avoid, because many things are known with certainty, though not by themselves evident, but only deduced from true and known principles by the continuous and uninterrupted action of a mind that has a clear vision of each step in the process. It is in a similar way that we know that the last link in a long chain is connected with the first, even though we do not take in by means of one and the same act of vision all the intermediate links on which that connection depends, but only remember that we have taken them successively under review and that each single one is united to its neighbour, from the first even to the last. Hence we distinguish this mental intuition from deduction by the fact that into the conception of the latter there enters a certain movement or succession, into that of the former there does not. Further deduction does not require an immediately presented evidence such as intuition possesses; its certitude is rather conferred upon it in some way by memory. The upshot of the matter is that it is possible to say that those propositions indeed which are immediately deduced from first principles are known now by intuition, now by deduction, i.e., in a way that differs according to our point of view. But the first principles themselves are given by intuition alone, while, on the contrary, the remote conclusions are furnished only by deduction.

These two methods are the most certain routes to knowledge, and the mind should admit no others. All the rest should be rejected as suspect of error and dangerous. . . .

Rule IV

There is need of a method for finding out the truth.

So blind is the curiosity by which mortals are possessed, that they often conduct their minds along unexplored routes, having no reason to hope for success, but merely being willing to risk the experiment of finding whether the truth they seek lies there. As well might a man burning with an unintelligent desire to find treasure, continuously roam the streets, seeking to find something that a passerby might have chanced to drop. This is the way in which most Chemists, many Geometricians, and Philosophers not a few prosecute their studies. I do not deny that sometimes in these wanderings they are lucky enough to find something true. But I do not allow that this argues greater industry on their part, but only better luck. But, however that may be, it were far better never to think of investigating truth at all, than to do so without a method. For it is very certain that unregulated inquiries and confused reflections of this kind only confound the natural light and blind our mental powers. Those who so become accustomed to walk in darkness weaken their eye-sight so much that afterwards they cannot bear the light of day. This is confirmed by experience; for how often do we not see that those who have never taken to letters, give a sounder and clearer decision about obvious matters than those who have spent all their time in the schools? Moreover by a method I mean certain and simple rules, such that, if a man observe them accurately, he shall never assume what is false as true, and will never spend his mental efforts to no purpose, but will always gradually increase his knowledge and so arrive at a true understanding of all that does not surpass his powers. . . .

Rule V

Method consists entirely in the order and disposition of the objects towards which our mental vision must be directed if we would find out any truth. We shall comply with it exactly if we reduce involved and obscure propositions step by step to those that are simpler, and then starting with the intuitive apprehension of all those that are absolutely simple, attempt to ascend to the knowledge of all others by precisely similar steps.

In this alone lies the sum of all human endeavour, and he who would approach the investigation of truth must hold to this rule as closely as he who enters the labyrinth must follow the thread which guided Theseus. But many people either do not reflect on the precept at all, or ignore it altogether, or presume not to need it. Consequently they often investigate the most difficult questions with so little regard to order, that, to my mind, they act like a man who should attempt to leap with one bound from the base to the summit of a house, either making no account of the ladders provided for his ascent or not noticing them. It is thus that all Astrologers behave, who, though in ignorance of the nature of the heavens, and even without having made proper observations of the movements of the heavenly bodies, expect to be able to indicate their effects. This is also what many do who study Mechanics apart from Physics, and readily set about devising new instruments for producing motion. Along with them go also those Philosophers who, neglecting experience, imagine that truth will spring from their brain like Pallas from the head of Zeus.

Now it is obvious that all such people violate the present rule. But since the order here required is often so obscure and intricate that not everyone can make it out, they can scarcely avoid error unless they diligently observe what is laid down in the following proposition.

Rule VI

In order to separate out what is quite simple from what is complex, and to arrange these matters methodically, we ought, in the case of every series in which we have deduced certain facts the one from the other, to notice which fact is simple, and to mark the interval, greater, less or equal, which separates all the others from this.

Although this proposition seems to teach nothing very new, it contains, nevertheless, the chief secret of method, and none in the whole of this treatise is of greater utility. For it tells us that all facts can be arranged in certain series, not indeed in the sense of being referred to some ontological genus such as the categories employed by Philosophers in their classification, but in so far as certain truths can be known from others; and thus, whenever a difficulty occurs we are able at once to perceive whether it will be profitable to examine certain others first, and which, and in what order.

Further, in order to do that correctly, we must note first that for the purpose of our procedure, which does not regard things as isolated realities, but compares them with one another in order to discover the dependence in knowledge of one upon the other, all things can be said to be either absolute or relative.

I call that absolute which contains within itself the pure and simple essence of which we are in quest. Thus the term will be applicable to whatever is considered as being independent, or a cause, or simple, universal, one, equal, like, straight, and so forth; and the absolute I call the simplest and the easiest of all, so that we can make use of it in the solution of questions.

But the relative is that which, while participating in the same nature, or at least sharing in it to some degree which enables us to relate it to the absolute and to deduce it from that by a chain of operations, involves in addition something else in its concept which I call relativity. Examples of this are found in whatever is said to be dependent, or an effect, composite, particular, many, unequal, unlike, oblique, etc. These relatives are the further removed from the absolute, in proportion as they contain more elements of relativity subordinate the one to the other. We state in this rule that these should all be distinguished and their correlative connection and natural order so observed, that we may be able by traversing all the intermediate steps to proceed from the most remote to that which is in the highest degree absolute. . . .

Finally we must note that our inquiry ought not to start with the investigation of difficult matters. Rather, before setting out to attack any definite problem, it behooves us first, without making any selection, to assemble those truths that are obvious as they present themselves to us, and afterwards, proceeding step by step, to inquire whether any others can be deduced from these, and again any others from these conclusions and so on, in order. This done, we should attentively think over the truths we have discovered and mark with diligence the reasons why we have been able to detect some more easily than others, and which these are. Thus, when we come to attack some definite problem we shall be able to judge what previous questions it were best to settle first. For example, if it comes into my thought that the number 6 is twice 3, I may then ask what is twice 6, viz., 12; again, perhaps I seek for the double of this, viz., 24, and again of this, viz., 48. Thus I may deduce that there is the same proportion between 3 and 6, as between 6 and 12, and likewise 12 and 24, and so on, and hence that the numbers 3, 6, 12, 24, 48, etc., are in continued proportion. But though these facts are all so clear as to seem almost childish, I am now able by attentive reflection to understand what is the form involved by all questions that can be propounded about the proportions or relations of things, and the order in which they should be investigated; and this discovery embraces the sum of the entire science of Pure Mathematics.

Rule VII

If we wish our science to be complete, those matters which promote the end we have in view must one and all be scrutinized by a movement of thought which is continuous and nowhere interrupted; they must also be included in an enumeration which is both adequate and methodical.

It is necessary to obey the injunctions of this rule if we hope to gain admission among the certain truths for those which, we have declared above, are not immediate deductions from primary and self-evident principles. For this deduction frequently involves such a long series of transitions from ground to consequent that when we come to the conclusion we have difficulty in recalling the whole of the route by which we have arrived at it. This is why I say that there must be a continuous movement of thought to make good this weakness of the memory. Thus, e.g., if I have first found out by separate mental operations what the relation is between the magnitudes *A* and *B*, then what between *B* and *C*, between *C* and *D*, and finally between *D* and *E*, that does not entail my seeing what the relation is between *A* and *E*, nor can the truths previously learnt give me a precise knowledge of it unless I recall them all. To remedy this I would run them over from time to time, keeping the imagination moving continuously in such a way that while it is intuitively perceiving each fact it simultaneously passes on to the next; and this I would do until I had learned to pass from the first to the last so quickly, that no stage in the process was left to the care of the memory, but I seemed to have the whole in intuition before me at the same time. This method will both relieve the memory, diminish the sluggishness of our thinking, and definitely enlarge our mental capacity.

But we must add that this movement should nowhere be interrupted. Often people who attempt to deduce a conclusion too quickly and from remote principles do not trace the whole chain of intermediate conclusions with sufficient accuracy to prevent them from passing over many steps without due consideration. But it is certain that wherever the smallest link is left out the chain is broken and the whole of the certainty of the conclusion falls to the ground. . . .

Rule VIII

If in the matters to be examined we come to a step in the series of which our understanding is not sufficiently well able to have an intuitive cognition, we must stop short there. We must make no attempt to examine what follows; thus we shall spare ourselves superfluous labour.

. . . If a man proposes to himself the problem of examining all the truths for the knowledge of which human reason suffices—and I think that this is a task which should be undertaken once at least in his life by every person who seriously endeavors to attain equilibrium of thought—he will, by the rules given above, certainly discover that nothing can be known prior to the understanding, since the knowledge of all things else depends upon this and not conversely. Then, when he has clearly grasped all those things which follow proximately on the knowledge of the naked understanding, he will enumerate among other things whatever instruments of thought we have other than the understanding; and these are only two, viz., imagination and sense. He will therefore devote all his energies to the distinguishing and examining of these three modes of cognition, and seeing that in the strict sense truth and falsity can be a matter of the understanding alone, though often it derives its origin from the other two faculties, he will attend carefully to every source of deception in order that he may be on his guard. He will also enumerate exactly all the ways leading to truth which lie open to us, in order that he may follow the right way. They are not so many that they cannot all be easily discovered and embraced in an adequate enumeration. And though this will seem marvellous and incredible to the inexpert, as soon as in each matter he has distinguished those cognitions which only fill and embellish the memory, from those which cause one to be deemed really more instructed, which it will be easy for him to do, he will feel assured that any absence of further knowledge is not due to lack of intelligence or of skill, and that nothing at all can be known by anyone else which he is not capable of knowing, provided only that he gives to it his utmost mental application.

Intuitionism*

HENRI BERGSON [1859–1941] has been one of the most widely read and influential of recent philosophers. He had spectacular success as a lecturer at the Collège de France, and he wrote a series of important philosophic works. Among them are *Time and Free-Will, Matter and Memory, Introduction to Metaphysics, Creative Evolution,* and *The Two Sources of Morality and Religion.* His teaching and writing won many honors: he was a member of the Legion of Honor and of the French Academy, and a winner of the Nobel Prize for Literature. He also served as president of the League of Nations Committee for Intellectual Cooperation.

A comparison of the definitions of metaphysics and the various conceptions of the absolute leads to the discovery that philosophers, in spite of their apparent divergencies, agree in distinguishing two profoundly different ways

* From Bergson: *An Introduction to Metaphysics,* translated by T. E. Hulme. Copyright, 1912, by G. P. Putnam's Sons. Reprinted by permission of G. P. Putnam's Sons.

of knowing a thing. The first implies that we move round the object; the second that we enter into it. The first depends on the point of view at which we are placed and on the symbols by which we express ourselves. The second neither depends on a point of view nor relies on any symbol. The first kind of knowledge may be said to stop at the *relative;* the second, in those cases where it is possible, to attain the *absolute.*

Consider, for example, the movement of an object in space. My perception of the motion will vary with the point of view, moving or stationary, from which I observe it. My expression of it will vary with the systems of axes, or the points of reference, to which I relate it; that is, with the symbols by which I translate it. For this double reason I call such motion *relative:* in the one case, as in the other, I am placed outside the object itself. But when I speak of an *absolute* movement, I am attributing to the moving object an interior and, so to speak, states of mind; I also imply that I am in sympathy with those states, and that I insert myself in them by an effort of imagination. Then, according as the object is moving or stationary, according as it adopts one movement or another, what I experience will vary. And what I experience will depend neither on the point of view I may take up in regard to the object, since I am inside the object itself, nor on the symbols by which I may translate the motion, since I have rejected all translations in order to possess the original. In short, I shall no longer grasp the movement from without, remaining where I am, but from where it is, from within, as it is in itself. I shall possess an absolute.

Consider, again, a character whose adventures are related to me in a novel. The author may multiply the traits of his hero's character, may make him speak and act as much as he pleases, but all this can never be equivalent to the simple and indivisible feeling which I should experience if I were able for an instant to identify myself with the person of the hero himself. Out of that indivisible feeling, as from a spring, all the words, gestures, and actions of the man would appear to me to flow naturally. They would no longer be accidents which, added to the idea I had already formed of the character, continually enriched that idea, without ever completing it. The character would be given to me all at once, in its entirety, and the thousand incidents which manifest it, instead of adding themselves to the idea and so enriching it, would seem to me, on the contrary, to detach themselves from it, without, however, exhausting it or impoverishing its essence. All the things I am told about the man provide me with so many points of view from which I can observe him. All the traits which describe him, and which can make him known to me only by so many comparisons with persons or things I know already, are signs by which he is expressed more or less symbolically. Symbols and points of view, therefore, place me outside him; they give me only what he has in common with others, and not what belongs to him and to him alone. But that which is properly himself, that which constitutes his essence, can not be perceived from without, being internal by definition, nor be expressed by symbols, being incommensurable with everything else. Description, history, and analysis leave me here in the relative. Coincidence with the person himself would alone give me the absolute.

It is in this sense, and in this sense only, that *absolute* is synonymous with *perfection*. Were all the photographs of a town, taken from all possible points of view, to go on indefinitely completing one another, they would never be equivalent to the solid town in which we walk about. Were all the translations of a poem into all possible languages to add together their various shades of meaning and, correcting each other by a kind of mutual retouching, to give a more and more faithful image of the poem they translate, they would yet never succeed in rendering the inner meaning of the original. A representation taken from a certain point of view, a translation made with certain symbols, will always remain imperfect in comparison with the object of which a view has been taken, or which the symbols seek to express. But the absolute, which is the object and not its representation, the original and not its translation, is perfect, by being perfectly what it is.

It is doubtless for this reason that the *absolute* has often been identified with the *infinite*. Suppose that I wished to communicate to some one who did not know Greek the extraordinarily simple impression that a passage in Homer makes upon me; I should first give a translation of the lines, I should then comment on my translation, and then develop the commentary; in this way, by piling up explanation on explanation, I might approach nearer and nearer to what I wanted to express; but I should never quite reach it. When you raise your arm, you accomplish a movement of which you have, from within, a simple perception; but for me, watching it from the outside, your arm passes through one point, then through another, and between these two there will be still other points; so that, if I began to count, the operation would go on for ever. Viewed from the inside, then, an absolute is a simple thing; but looked at from the outside, that is to say, relatively to other things, it becomes, in relation to these signs which express it, the gold coin for which we never seem able to finish giving small change. Now, that which lends itself at the same time both to an indivisible apprehension and to an inexhaustible enumeration is, by the very definition of the word, an infinite.

It follows from this that an absolute could only be given in an *intuition*, whilst everything else falls within the province of *analysis*. By intuition is meant the kind of *intellectual sympathy* by which one places oneself within an object in order to coincide with what is unique in it and consequently inexpressible. Analysis, on the contrary, is the operation which reduces the object to elements already known, that is, to elements common both to it and other objects. To analyze, therefore, is to express a thing as a function of something other than itself. All analysis is thus a translation, a development into symbols, a representation taken from successive points of view from which we note as many resemblances as possible between the new object which we are studying and others which we believe we know already. In its eternally unsatisfied desire to embrace the object around which it is compelled to turn, analysis multiplies without end the number of its points of view in order to complete its always incomplete representation, and ceaselessly varies its symbols that it may perfect the always imperfect translation. It goes on, therefore, to infinity. But intuition, if intuition is possible, is a simple act.

Now it is easy to see that the ordinary function of positive science is analysis. Positive science works, then, above all, with symbols. Even the most concrete of the natural sciences, those concerned with life, confine themselves to the visible form of living beings, their organs and anatomical elements. They make comparisons between these forms, they reduce the more complex to the more simple; in short, they study the workings of life in what is, so to speak, only its visual symbol. If there exists any means of possessing a reality absolutely instead of knowing it relatively, of placing oneself within it instead of looking at it from outside points of view, if having the intuition instead of making the analysis: in short, of seizing it without any expression, translation, or symbolic representation—metaphysics is that means. *Metaphysics, then, is the science which claims to dispense with symbols.*

There is one reality, at least, which we all seize from within, by intuition and not by simple analysis. It is our own personality in its flowing through time—our self which endures. We may sympathize intellectually with nothing else, but we certainly sympathize with our own selves.

When I direct my attention inward to contemplate my own self (supposed for the moment to be inactive), I perceive at first, as a crust solidified on the surface, all the perceptions which come to it from the material world. These perceptions are clear, distinct, juxtaposed or juxtaposable one with another; they tend to group themselves into objects. Next, I notice the memories which more or less adhere to these perceptions and which serve to interpret them. These memories have been detached, as it were, from the depth of my personality, drawn to the surface by the perceptions which resemble them; they rest on the surface of my mind without being absolutely myself. Lastly, I feel the stir of tendencies and motor habits—a crowd of virtual actions, more or less firmly bound to these perceptions and memories. All these clearly defined elements appear more distinct from me, the more distinct they are from each other. Radiating, as they do, from within outwards, they form, collectively, the surface of a sphere which tends to grow larger and lose itself in the exterior world. But if I draw myself in from the periphery towards the centre, if I search in the depth of my being that which is most uniformly, most constantly, and most enduringly myself, I find an altogether different thing.

There is, beneath these sharply cut crystals and this frozen surface, a continuous flux which is not comparable to any flux I have ever seen. There is a succession of states, each of which announces that which follows and contains that which precedes it. They can, properly speaking, only be said to form multiple states when I have already passed them and turn back to observe their track. Whilst I was experiencing them they were so solidly organized, so profoundly animated with a common life, that I could not have said where any one of them finished or where another commenced. In reality no one of them begins or ends, but all extend into each other. . . .

The unrolling of our duration resembles in some of its aspects the unity of an advancing movement and in others the multiplicity of expanding states; and, clearly, no metaphor can express one of these two aspects without sacrificing the other. If I use the comparison of a spectrum with its thousand shades, I have before me a thing already made, whilst duration is continually in the making. If I think of an elastic which is being stretched, or of a spring which is extended or relaxed, I forget the richness of color, characteristic of duration that is lived, to see only the simple movement by which consciousness passes from one shade to another. The inner life is all this at once: variety of qualities, continuity of progress, and unity of direction. It cannot be represented by images.

But it is even less possible to represent it by *concepts,* that is by abstract, general, or simple ideas. It is true that no image can reproduce exactly the original feeling I have of the flow of my own conscious life. But it is not even necessary that I should attempt to render it. If a man is incapable of getting for himself the intuiton of the constitutive duration of his own being, nothing will ever give it to him, concepts no more than images. Here the single aim of the philosopher should be to promote a certain effort, which in most men is usually fettered by habits of mind more useful to life. Now the image has at least this advantage, that it keeps us in the concrete. No image can replace the intuition of duration, but many diverse images, borrowed from very different orders of things, may, by the convergence of their action, direct consciousness to the precise point where there is a certain intuition to be seized. . . . Concepts on the contrary—especially if they are simple have the disadvantage of being in reality symbols substituted for the object they symbolize, and demand no effort on our part. Examined closely, each of them, it would be seen, retains only that part of the object which is common to it and to others, and expresses, still more than the image does, a *comparison* between the object and others which resemble it. But as the comparison has made manifest a resemblance, as the resemblance is a property of the object, and as a property has every appearance of being a *part* of the object which possesses it, we easily persuade ourselves that by setting concept beside concept we are reconstructing the whole of the object with its parts, thus obtaining, so to speak, its intellectual equivalent. In this way we believe that we can form a faithful representation of duration by setting in line the concepts of unity, multiplicity, continuity, finite or infinite divisibilty, etc. There precisely is the illusion. There also is the danger. Just in so far as abstract ideas can render service to analysis, that is, to the scientific study of the object in its relations to other objects, so far are they incapable of replacing intuition, that is, the metaphysical investigation of what is essential and unique in the object. For on the one hand these concepts, laid side by side, never actually give us more than an artificial reconstruction of the object, of which they can only symbolize certain general, and, in a way, impersonal aspects; it is therefore useless to believe that with them we can seize a reality of which they present to us the shadow alone. And, on the other hand, besides the illusion there is also a very serious danger. For the concept generalizes at the same time as it abstracts. The concept can only symbolize a particular property by making it common to an infinity of things. . . . Thus the different concepts that we form of the properties of a thing inscribe round it so many circles, each much too large and none of them fitting it exactly. . . . Let it suffice us for the moment to have shown that our duration . . . can be suggested to us indirectly by images, but that it can never—if we confine the word concept to its proper meaning—be enclosed in a conceptual representation. . . .

We do penetrate into it, however, and that can only be by an effort of intuition. In this sense, an inner, absolute knowledge of the duration of the self by the self is possible. But if metaphysics here demands and can obtain an intuition, science has none the less need of an analysis. Now it is a confusion between the function of analysis and that of intuition which gives birth to the discussions between the schools and the conflicts between systems.

Psychology, in fact, proceeds like all the other sciences by analysis. It resolves the self, which has been given to it at first in a simple intuition, into sensations, feelings, ideas, etc., which it studies separately. It substitutes, then, for the self a series of elements which form the facts of psychology. But are these *elements* really *parts?* That is the whole question, and it is because it has been evaded that the problem of human personality has so often been stated in insoluble terms.

It is incontestable that every psychical state, simply because it belongs to a person, reflects the whole of a personality. Every feeling, however simple it may be, contains virtually within it the whole past and present of the being experiencing it, and, consequently, can only be separated and constituted into a "state" by an effort of abstraction or of analysis. But it is no less incontestable that without this effort of abstraction or analysis there would be no possible development of the science of psychology. What, then, exactly, is the operation by which a psychologist detaches a mental state in order to erect it into a more or less independent entity? He begins by neglecting that special coloring of the personality which cannot be expressed in known and common terms. Then he endeavors to isolate, in the person already thus simplified, some aspect which lends itself to an interesting inquiry. If he is considering inclination, for example, he will neglect the inexpressible shade which colors it, and which makes the inclination mine and not yours; he will fix his attention on the movement by which our personality *leans towards* a certain object: he will isolate this attitude, and it is this special aspect of the personality, this snapshot of the mobility of the inner life, this "diagram" of concrete inclination, that he will erect into an independent fact. There is in this something very like what an artist passing through Paris does when he makes, for example, a sketch of a tower of Notre Dame. The tower is inseparably united to the building, which is itself no less inseparably united to the ground, to its surroundings, to the whole of Paris, and so on. It is first necessary to detach it from all these; only one aspect of the whole is noted, that formed by the tower of Notre Dame. Moreover, the special form of this tower is due to the grouping of the stones of which it is composed, but the artist does not concern himself with these stones, he notes only the silhouette of the tower. For the real and internal organization of the thing he substitutes, then, an external and schematic representation. So that, on the whole, his sketch corresponds to an observation of the object from a certain point of view and to the choice of a certain means of representation. But exactly the same thing holds true of the operation by which the psychologist extracts a single mental state from the whole personality. This isolated psychical state is hardly anything but a sketch, the commencement of an artificial reconstruction; it is the whole considered under a certain elementary aspect in which we are specially interested and which we have carefully noted. It is not a part, but an element. It has not been obtained by a natural dismemberment, but by analysis.

Now beneath all the sketches he has made at Paris the visitor will probably, by way of memento, write the word "Paris." And as he has really seen Paris, he will be able, with the help of the original intuition he had of the whole, to place his sketches therein, and so join them up together. But there is no way of performing the inverse operation; it is impossible, even with an infinite number of accurate sketches, and even with the word "Paris" which indicates that they must be combined together, to get back to an intuition that one has never had, and to give oneself an impression of what Paris is like if one has never seen it. This is because we are not dealing here with real *parts,* but with mere *notes* of the total impression.

That personality has unity cannot be denied; but such an affirmation teaches one nothing about the extraordinary nature of the particular unity presented by personality. That our self is multiple I also agree, but then it must be understood that it is a multiplicity which has nothing in common with any other multiplicity. What is really important for philosophy is to know exactly what unity, what multiplicity, and what reality superior both to abstract unity and multiplicity the multiple unity of the self actually is. Now philosophy will know this only when it recovers possession of the simple intuition of the self by the self. Then, according to the direction it chooses for its descent from this summit, it will arrive at unity or multiplicity, or at any one of the concepts by which we try to define the moving life of the self. But no mingling of these concepts would give anything which at all resembles the self that endures.

If we are shown a solid cone, we see without any difficulty how it narrows towards the summit and tends to be lost in a mathematical point, and also how it enlarges in the direction of the base into an indefinitely increasing circle. But neither the point nor the circle, nor the juxtaposition of the two on a plane, would give us the least idea of a cone. The same thing holds true of the unity and multiplicity of mental life, and of the zero and the infinite towards which empiricism and rationalism conduct personality.

Concepts, as we shall show elsewhere, generally go together in couples and represent two contraries. There is hardly any concrete reality which cannot be observed from two opposing standpoints, which cannot consequently be subsumed under two antagonistic concepts. Hence a thesis and an antithesis which we endeavor in vain to reconcile logically, for the very simple reason that it is impossible, with concepts and observations taken from outside points of view, to make a thing. But from the object, seized by intuition, we pass easily in many cases to the two contrary concepts; and as in that way thesis and antithesis can be seen to spring from reality, we grasp at the same time how it is that the two are opposed and how they are reconciled.

It is true that to accomplish this, it is necessary to proceed by a reversal of the usual work of the intellect. *Thinking* usually consists in passing from concepts to things, and not from things to concepts. To know a reality, in the usual sense of the word "know," is to take ready-made concepts, to portion them out and to mix them together until a practical equivalent of the reality is obtained. But it must be remembered that the normal work of the intellect is far from being disinterested. We do not aim generally at knowledge for the sake of knowledge, but in order to take sides, to draw profit—in short, to satisfy an interest. We inquire up to what point the object we seek to know is *this* or *that,* to what known class it belongs, and what kind of action, bearing, or attitude it should suggest to us. These different possible actions and attitudes are so many *conceptual directions* of our thought, determined once for all; it remains only to follow them: in that precisely consists the application of concepts to things. To try to fit a concept on an object is simply to ask what we can do with the object, and what it can do for us. To label an object with a certain concept is to mark in precise terms the kind of action or attitude the object should suggest to us. All knowledge, properly so called, is then oriented in a certain direction, or taken from a certain point of view. It is true that our interest is often complex. This is why it happens that our knowledge of the same object may face several successive directions and may be taken from various points of view. It is this which constitutes, in the usual meaning of the terms, a "broad" and "comprehensive" knowledge of the object; the object is then brought not under one single concept, but under several in which it is supposed to "participate." How does it participate in all these concepts at the same time? This is a question which does not concern our practical action and about which we need not trouble. It is, therefore, natural and legitimate in daily life to proceed by the juxtaposition and portioning out of concepts; no philosophical difficulty will arise from this procedure, since by a tacit agreement we shall abstain from philosophizing. But to carry this *modus operandi* into philosophy, to pass here also from concepts to the thing, to use in order to obtain a disinterested knowledge of an object (that this time we desire to grasp as it is in itself) a manner of knowing inspired by a determinate interest, consisting by definition in an externally-taken view of the object, is to go against the end that we have chosen, to condemn philosophy to an eternal skirmishing between the schools and to install contradiction in the very heart of the object and of the method. Either there is no philosophy possible, and all knowledge of things is a practical knowledge aimed at the profit to be drawn from them, or else philosophy consists in placing oneself within the object itself by an effort of intuition.

The Will to Believe*

WILLIAM JAMES [1842–1910], the son of an eminent intellectual and brother of the novelist Henry James, was the most celebrated and influential exponent of pragmatism of his time. He received most of his early education abroad, attended Harvard Medical School, and then taught anatomy and physiology at Harvard College. However, as his interests in psychology and philosophy grew, he turned to the teaching of these subjects. In 1876 he founded the first American experimental laboratory for psychology, and in 1890 his great text, *The Principles of Psychology*, appeared. In his later years his attention was almost exclusively devoted to philosophy. His primary interest was the development of a pragmatic point of view that would do equal justice to the claims of the exact sciences and to the claims of moral and religious experience.

I have brought with me to-night something like a sermon on justification by faith to read to you,—I mean an essay in justification *of* faith, a defence of our right to adopt a believing attitude in religious matters, in spite of the fact that our merely logical intellect may not have been coerced. 'The Will to Believe,' accordingly, is the title of my paper.

I have long defended to my own students the lawfulness of voluntarily adopted faith; but as soon as they have got well imbued with the logical spirit, they have as a rule refused to admit my contention to be lawful philosophically, even though in point of fact they were personally all the time chock-full of some faith or other themselves. I am all the while, however, so profoundly convinced that my own position is correct, that your invitation has seemed to me a good occasion to make my statements more clear. Perhaps your minds will be more open than those with which I have hitherto had to deal. I will be as little technical as I can, though I must begin by setting up some technical distinctions that will help us in the end.

Let us give the name of *hypothesis* to anything that may be proposed to our belief; and just as the electricians speak of live and dead wires, let us speak of any hypothesis as either *live* or *dead*. A live hypothesis is one which appeals as a real possibility to him to whom it is proposed. If I ask you to believe in the Mahdi, the notion makes no electric connection with your

* From James: "The Will to Believe," an address to the Philosophical Clubs of Yale and Brown Universities, published in the *New World*, 1896. Also available in James: *Essays on Faith and Morals*, Longmans, Green and Company, 1949.

nature,—it refuses to scintillate with any credibility at all. As an hypothesis it is completely dead. To an Arab, however (even if he be not one of the Mahdi's followers), the hypothesis is among the mind's possibilities: it is alive. This shows that deadness and liveness in an hypothesis are not intrinsic properties, but relations to the individual thinker. They are measured by his willingness to act. The maximum of liveness in an hypothesis means willingness to act irrevocably. Practically, that means belief; but there is some believing tendency wherever there is willingness to act at all.

Next, let us call the decision between two hypotheses an *option*. Options may be several kinds. They may be—1, *living* or *dead;* 2, *forced* or *avoidable;* 3, *momentous* or *trivial;* and for our purposes we may call an option a *genuine* option when it is of the forced, living, and momentous kind.

1. A living option is one in which both hypotheses are live ones. If I say to you: "Be a theosophist or be a Mohammedan," it is probably a dead option, because for you neither hypothesis is likely to be alive. But if I say: "Be an agnostic or be a Christian," it is otherwise: trained as you are, each hypothesis makes some appeal, however small, to your belief.

2. Next, if I say to you: "Choose between going out with your umbrella or without it," I do not offer you a genuine option, for it is not forced. You can easily avoid it by not going out at all. Similarly, if I say, "Either love me or hate me," "Either call my theory true or call it false," your option is avoidable. You may remain indifferent to me, neither loving nor hating, and you may decline to offer any judgment as to my theory. But if I say, "Either accept this truth or go without it," I put on you a forced option, for there is no standing place outside of the alternative. Every dilemma based on a complete logical disjunction, with no possibility of not choosing, is an option of this forced kind.

3. Finally, if I were Dr. Nansen and proposed to you to join my North Pole expedition, your option would be momentous; for this would probably be your only similar opportunity, and your choice now would either exclude you from the North Pole sort of immortality altogether or put at least the chance of it into your hands. He who refuses to embrace a unique opportunity loses the prize as surely as if he tried and failed. *Per contra*, the option is trivial when the opportunity is not unique, when the stake is insignificant, or when the decision is reversible if it later prove unwise. Such trivial options abound in the scientific life. A chemist finds an hypothesis live enough to spend a year in its verification: he believes in it to that extent. But if his experiments prove inconclusive either way, he is quit for his loss of time, no vital harm being done.

It will facilitate our discussion if we keep all these distinctions well in mind. . . .

The thesis I defend is, briefly stated, this: *Our passional nature not only lawfully may, but must, decide an option between propositions, whenever it is a genuine option that cannot by its nature be decided on intellectual grounds; for to say, under such circumstances, "Do not decide, but leave the question open," is itself a passional decision,—just like deciding yes or no,—and is attended with the same risk of losing the truth.* The thesis thus abstractly expressed will, I trust, soon become quite clear. But I must first indulge in a bit more of preliminary work. . . .

There are two ways of looking at our duty in the matter of opinion,—ways entirely different, and yet ways about whose difference the theory of knowledge seems hitherto to have shown very little concern. *We must know the truth;* and *we must avoid error,*—these are our first and great commandments as would-be knowers; but they are not two ways of stating an identical commandment, they are two separable laws. Although it may indeed happen that when we believe the truth A, we escape as an incidental consequence from believing the falsehood B, it hardly ever happens that by merely disbelieving B we necessarily believe A. We may in escaping B fall into believing other falsehoods, C or D, just as bad as B; or we may escape B by not believing anything at all, not even A.

Believe truth! Shun error!—these, we see, are two materially different laws; and by choosing between them we may end by coloring differently our whole intellectual life. We may regard the chase for truth as paramount, and the avoidance of error as secondary; or we may, on the other hand, treat the avoidance of error as more imperative, and let truth take its chance. Clifford, in an instructive passage, exhorts us to the latter course. Believe nothing, he tells us, keep your mind in suspense forever, rather than by closing it on insufficient evidence incur the awful risk of believing lies. You, on the other hand, may think that the risk of being in error is a very small matter when compared with the blessings of real knowledge, and be ready to be duped many times in your investigation rather than postpone indefinitely the chance of guessing true. I myself find it impossible to go with Clifford. We must remember that these feelings of our duty about either truth or error are in any case only expressions of our passional life. Biologically considered, our minds are as ready to grind out falsehood as veracity, and he who says, "Better go without belief forever than believe a lie!" merely shows his own preponderant private horror of becoming a dupe. He may be critical of many of his desires and fears, but this fear he slavishly obeys. He cannot imagine any one questioning its binding force. For my own part, I have also a horror of being duped; but I can believe that worse things than being duped may happen to a man in this world: so Clifford's exhortation has to my ears a thoroughly fantastic sound. It is like a general informing his soldiers that it is better to keep out of battle forever than to risk a single wound. Not so are victories either over enemies or over nature gained. Our errors are surely not such awfully solemn things. In a world where we are so certain to incur them in spite of all our caution, a certain lightness of heart seems healthier than this excessive nervousness on their behalf. At any rate, it seems the fittest thing for the empiricist philosopher.

And now, after all this introduction, let us go straight at our question. I have said, and now repeat it, that not only as a matter of fact do we find our passional nature influencing us in our opinions, but that there are some options between opinions in which this influence must be regarded both as an inevitable and as a lawful determinant of our choice.

I fear here that some of you my hearers will begin to scent danger, and lend an inhospitable ear. Two first steps of passion you have indeed had to admit as necessary,—we must think so as to avoid dupery, and we must think so as to gain truth; but the surest path to those ideal consummations, you will probably consider, is from now onwards to take no further passional step.

Well, of course, I agree as far as the facts will allow. Wherever the option between losing truth and gaining it is not momentous, we can throw the chance of *gaining truth* away, and at any rate save ourselves from any chance of *believing falsehood,* by not making up our minds at all till objective evidence has come. In scientific questions, this is almost always the case; and even in human affairs in general, the need of acting is seldom so urgent that a false belief to act on is better than no belief at all. Law courts, indeed, have to decide on the best evidence attainable for the moment, because a judge's duty is to make law as well as to ascertain it, and (as a learned judge once said to me) few cases are worth spending much time over: the great thing is to have them decided on *any* acceptable principle, and got out of the way. But in our dealings with objective nature we obviously are recorders, not makers, of the truth; and decisions for the mere sake of deciding promptly and getting on to the next business would be wholly out of place. Throughout the breadth of physical nature facts are what they are quite independently of us, and seldom is there any such hurry about them that the risks of being duped by believing a premature theory need be faced. The questions here are always trivial options, the hypotheses are hardly living (at any rate not living for us spectators), the choice between believing truth or falsehood is seldom forced. The attitude of sceptical balance is therefore the absolutely wise one if we would escape mistakes. What difference, indeed, does it make to most of us whether we have or have not a theory of the Röntgen rays, whether we believe or not in mind-stuff, or have a conviction about the causality of conscious states? It makes no difference. Such options are not forced on us. On every account it is better not to make them, but still keep weighing reasons *pro et contra* with an indifferent hand.

I speak, of course, here of the purely judging mind. For purposes of discovery such indifference is to be less highly recommended, and science would be far less advanced than she is if the passionate desires of individuals to get their own faiths confirmed had been kept out of the game. See for example the sagacity which Spencer and Weismann now display. On the other hand, if you want an absolute duffer in an investigation, you must, after all, take the man who has no interest whatever in its results: he is the warranted incapable, the positive fool. The most useful investigator, because the most sensitive observer, is always he whose eager interest in one side of the question is balanced by an equally keen nervousness lest he become deceived. Science has organized this nervousness into a regular *technique,* her so-called method of verification; and she has fallen so deeply in love with the method that one may even say she has ceased to care for truth by itself at all. It is only truth as technically verified that interests her. The truth of truths might come in merely affirmative form, and she would decline to touch it. Such truth as that, she might repeat with Clifford, would be stolen in defiance of her duty to mankind. Human passions, however, are stronger than technical rules. As Pascal says, "The heart has its reasons, that reason knows not of"; and however indifferent to all but the bare rules of the game the umpire, the abstract intellect, may be, the concrete players who furnish him the materials to judge of are usually, each one of them, in love with some pet 'live hypothesis' of his own. Let us agree, however, that wherever there is no forced option, the dispassionately judicial intellect with no pet hypothesis, saving us, as it does, from dupery at any rate, ought to be our ideal.

The question next arises: Are there not somewhere forced options in our speculative questions, and can we (as men who may be interested at least as much in positively gaining truth as in merely escaping dupery) always wait with impunity till the coercive evidence shall have arrived? It seems *a priori* improbable that the truth should be so nicely adjusted to our needs and powers as that. In the great boarding-house of nature, the cakes and the butter and the syrup seldom come out so even and leave the plates so clean. Indeed, we should view them with scientific suspicion if they did.

Moral questions immediately present themselves as questions whose solution cannot wait for sensible proof. A moral question is a question not of what sensibly exists, but of what is good, or would be good if it did exist. Science can tell us what exists; but to compare the *worths,* both of what exists and of what does not exist, we must consult not science, but what Pascal calls our heart. Science herself consults her heart when she lays it down that

the infinite ascertainment of fact and correction of false belief are the supreme goods for man. Challenge the statement, and science can only repeat
it oracularly, or else prove it by showing that such ascertainment and correction bring man all sorts of other goods which man's heart in turn declares.
The question of having moral beliefs at all or not having them is decided by
our will. Are our moral preferences true or false, or are they only odd biological phenomena, making things good or bad for *us*, but in themselves indifferent? How can your pure intellect decide? If your heart does not *want* a
world of moral reality, your head will assuredly never make you believe in
one. Mephistophelian scepticism, indeed, will satisfy the head's play-instincts
much better than any rigorous idealism can. Some men (even at the student
age) are so naturally cool-hearted that the moralistic hypothesis never has
for them any pungent life, and in their supercilious presence the hot young
moralist always feels strangely ill at ease. The appearance of knowingness is
on their side, of *naïveté* and gullibility on his. Yet, in the inarticulate heart of
him, he clings to it that he is not a dupe, and that there is a realm in which
(as Emerson says) all their wit and intellectual superiority is no better than
the cunning of a fox. Moral scepticism can no more be refuted or proved by
logic than intellectual scepticism can. When we stick to it that there *is* truth
(be it of either kind), we do so with our whole nature, and resolve to stand
or fall by the results. The sceptic with his whole nature adopts the doubting
attitude; but which of us is the wiser, Omniscience only knows.

Turn now from these wide questions of good to a certain class of questions
of fact, questions concerning personal relations, states of mind between one
man and another. *Do you like me or not?*—for example. Whether you do or
not depends, in countless instances, on whether I meet you half-way, am
willing to assume that you must like me, and show you trust and expectation. The previous faith on my part in your liking's existence is in such cases
what makes your liking come. But if I stand aloof, and refuse to budge an
inch until I have objective evidence, until you shall have done something
apt, as the absolutists say, *ad extorquendum assensum* [for extorting my
assent], ten to one your liking never comes. How many women's hearts are
vanquished by the mere sanguine insistence of some man that they *must*
love him! He will not consent to the hypothesis that they cannot. The desire
for a certain kind of truth here brings about that special truth's existence;
and so it is in innumerable cases of other sorts. Who gains promotions,
boons, appointments, but the man in whose life they are seen to play the
part of live hypotheses, who discounts them, sacrifices other things for their
sake before they have come, and takes risks for them in advance? His faith
acts on the powers above him as a claim, and creates its own verification.

A social organism of any sort whatever, large or small, is what it is because each member proceeds to his own duty with a trust that the other members will simultaneously do theirs. Wherever a desired result is achieved by the co-operation of many independent persons, its existence as a fact is a pure consequence of the precursive faith in one another of those immediately concerned. A government, an army, a commercial system, a ship, a college, an athletic team, all exist on this condition, without which not only is nothing achieved, but nothing is even attempted. A whole train of passengers (individually brave enough) will be looted by a few highwaymen, simply because the latter can count on one another, while each passenger fears that if he makes a movement of resistance, he will be shot before any one else backs him up. If we believed that the whole car-full would rise at once with us, we should each severally rise, and train-robbing would never even be attempted. There are, then, cases where a fact cannot come at all unless a preliminary faith exists in its coming. *And where faith in a fact can help create the fact,* that would be an insane logic which should say that faith running ahead of scientific evidence is the 'lowest kind of immorality' into which a thinking being can fall. Yet such is the logic by which our scientific absolutists pretend to regulate our lives!

In truths dependent on our personal action, then, faith based on desire is certainly a lawful and possibly an indispensable thing.

But now, it will be said, these are all childish human cases, and have nothing to do with great cosmical matters, like the question of religious faith. Let us then pass on to that. Religions differ so much in their accidents that in discussing the religious question we must make it very generic and broad. What then do we now mean by the religious hypothesis? Science says things are; morality says some things are better than other things; and religion says essentially two things.

First, she says that the best things are the more eternal things, the overlapping things, the things in the universe that throw the last stone, so to speak, and say the final word. "Perfection is eternal,"—this phrase of Charles Secrétan seems a good way of putting this first affirmation of religion, an affirmation which obviously cannot yet be verified scientifically at all.

The second affirmation of religion is that we are better off even now if we believe her first affirmation to be true.

Now, let us consider what the logical elements of this situation are *in case the religious hypothesis in both its branches be really true.* (Of course, we must admit that possibility at the outset. If we are to discuss the question at all, it must involve a living option. If for any of you religion be a hypothesis that cannot, by any living possibility be true, then you need go no farther. I speak to the 'saving remnant' alone.) So proceeding, we see, first that religion offers itself as a *momentous* option. We are supposed to gain, even now, by our belief, and to lose by our nonbelief, a certain vital good. Secondly, religion is a *forced* option, so far as that good goes. We cannot escape the issue by remaining sceptical and waiting for more light, because, although we do avoid error in that way *if religion be untrue*, we lose the good, *if it be true*, just as certainly as if we positively chose to disbelieve. It is as if a man should hesitate indefinitely to ask a certain woman to marry him because he was not perfectly sure that she would prove an angel after he brought her home. Would he not cut himself off from that particular angel-possibility as decisively as if he went and married some one else? Scepticism, then, is not avoidance of option; it is option of a certain particular kind of risk. *Better risk loss of truth than chance of error,*—that is your faith-vetoer's exact position. He is actively playing his stake as much as the believer is; he is backing the field against the religious hypothesis, just as the believer is backing the religious hypothesis against the field. To preach scepticism to us as a duty until 'sufficient evidence' for religion be found, is tantamount therefore to telling us, when in presence of the religious hypothesis, that to yield to our fear of its being error is wiser and better than to yield to our hope that it may be true. It is not intellect against all passions, then; it is only intellect with one passion laying down its law. And by what, forsooth, is the supreme wisdom of this passion warranted? Dupery for dupery, what proof is there that dupery through hope is so much worse than dupery through fear? I, for one, can see no proof; and I simply refuse obedience to the scientist's command to imitate his kind of option, in a case where my own stake is important enough to give me the right to choose my own form of risk. If religion be true and the evidence for it be still insufficient, I do not wish, by putting your extinguisher upon my nature (which feels to me as if it had after all some business in this matter), to forfeit my sole chance in life of getting upon the winning side,—that chance depending, of course, on my willingness to run the risk of acting as if my passional need of taking the world religiously might be prophetic and right.

All this is on the supposition that it really may be prophetic and right, and that, even to us who are discussing the matter, religion is a live hypothesis which may be true. Now, to most of us religion comes in a still further way that makes a veto on our active faith even more illogical. The more perfect and more eternal aspect of the universe is represented in our religions as having personal form. The universe is no longer a mere *It* to us, but a *Thou*, if we are religious; and any relation that may be possible from person to person might be possible here. For instance, although in one sense we are passive portions of the universe, in another we show a curious autonomy, as if we were small active centres on our own account. We feel, too, as if the appeal of religion to us were made to our own active good-will, as if evidence might be forever withheld from us unless we met the hypothesis half-way. To take a trivial illustration: just as a man who in a company of gentle-men made no advances, asked a warrant for every concession, and believed no one's word without proof, would cut himself off by such churlishness from all the social rewards that a more trusting spirit would earn,—so here, one who should shut himself up in snarling logicality and try to make the gods extort his recognition willy-nilly, or not get it at all, might cut himself off forever from his only opportunity of making the gods' acquaintance. This feeling, forced on us we know not whence, that by obstinately believing that there are gods (although not to do so would be so easy both for our logic and our life) we are doing the universe the deepest service we can, seems part of the living essence of the religious hypothesis. If the hypothesis *were* true in all its parts, including this one, then pure intellectualism, with its veto on our making willing advances, would be an absurdity; and some participa-tion of our sympathetic nature would be logically required. I, therefore, for one, cannot see my way to accepting the agnostic rules for truth-seeking, or wilfully agree to keep my willing nature out of the game. I cannot do so for this plain reason, that *a rule of thinking which would absolutely prevent me from acknowledging certain kinds of truth if those kinds of truth were really there, would be an irrational rule.* That for me is the long and short of the formal logic of the situation, no matter what the kinds of truth might ma-terially be.

I confess I do not see how this logic can be escaped. But sad experience makes me fear that some of you may still shrink from radically saying with me, *in abstracto,* that we have the right to believe at our own risk any hy-pothesis that is live enough to tempt our will. I suspect, however, that if this is so, it is because you have got away from the abstract logical point of view altogether, and are thinking (perhaps without realizing it) of some particu-lar religious hypothesis which for you is dead. The freedom to 'believe what we will' you apply to the case of some patent superstition; and the faith you think of is the faith defined by the schoolboy when he said, "Faith is when you believe something that you know ain't true." I can only repeat that this is misapprehension. *In concreto,* the freedom to believe can only cover living options which the intellect of the individual cannot by itself resolve; and liv-ing options never seem absurdities to him who has them to consider. When I look at the religious question as it really puts itself to concrete men, and when I think of all the possibilities which both practically and theoretically it involves, then this command that we shall put a stopper on our heart, in-stincts, and courage, and *wait*—acting of course meanwhile more or less as if religion were *not* true—till doomsday, or till such time as our intellect and senses working together may have raked in evidence enough,—this command, I say, seems to me the queerest idol ever manufactured in the philosophic cave. Were we scholastic absolutists, there might be more excuse. If we had an infallible intellect with its objective certitudes, we might feel ourselves disloyal to such a perfect organ of knowledge in not trusting to it exclusively, in not waiting for its releasing word. But if we are empiricists, if we believe that no bell in us tolls to let us know for certain when truth is in our grasp, then it seems a piece of idle fantasticality to preach so solemnly our duty of waiting for the bell. Indeed we *may* wait if we will,—I hope you do not think that I am denying that,—but if we do so, we do so at our peril as much as if we believed. In either case we *act*, taking our life in our hands. No one of us ought to issue vetoes to the other, nor should we bandy words of abuse. We ought, on the contrary, delicately and profoundly to respect one another's mental freedom: then only shall we bring about the intellectual republic; then only shall we have that spirit of inner tolerance without which all our outer tolerance is soulless, and which is empiricism's glory; then only shall we live and let live, in speculative as well as in practical things. . . .

Let me end by a quotation from Fitz-James Stephen, "What do you think of yourself? What do you think of the world? . . . These are questions with which all must deal as it seems good to them. They are riddles of the Sphinx, and in some way or other we must deal with them. . . . In all important transactions of life we have to take a leap in the dark. . . . If we decide to leave the riddles unanswered, that is a choice; if we waver in our answer, that, too, is a choice: but whatever choice we make, we make it at our peril. If a man chooses to turn his back altogether on God and the future, no one can prevent him; no one can show beyond reasonable doubt that he is mistaken. If a man thinks otherwise and acts as he thinks, I do not see that any one can prove that *he* is mistaken. Each must act as he thinks best; and if he is wrong, so much the worse for him. We stand on a mountain pass in the midst of whirling snow and blinding mist, through which we get glimpses now and then of paths which may be deceptive. If we stand still we shall be frozen to death. If we take the wrong road we shall be dashed to pieces. We do not certainly know whether there is any right one. What must we do? 'Be strong and of a good courage.' Act for the best, hope for the best, and take what comes. . . . If death ends all, we cannot meet death better."

The World of Science and the Everyday World*

GILBERT RYLE [1900–   ] is Waynflete Professor of Metaphysical Philosophy at Oxford and is the editor of the British periodical *Mind*. He has been highly influential in recent developments in British and American philosophy. His main work, *The Concept of Mind* (1949), is a systematic attempt to use the methods of linguistic analysis to clarify problems about mental events and mental entities. In *Dilemmas* (1954) he applied similar methods to a wide range of problems. More recently he has written a study of Plato entitled *Plato's Progress* (1966).

We often worry ourselves about the relations between what we call 'the world of science' and 'the world of real life' or 'the world of common sense.' Sometimes we are even encouraged to worry about the relations between 'the desk of physics' and the desk on which we write.

When we are in a certain intellectual mood, we seem to find clashes between the things that scientists tell us about our furniture, clothes and limbs and the things that we tell about them. We are apt to express these felt rivalries by saying that the world whose parts and members are described by scientists is different from the world whose parts and members we describe ourselves, and yet, since there can be only one world, one of these seeming worlds must be a dummy-world. Moreover, as no one nowadays is hardy enough to say 'Bo' to science, it must be the world that we ourselves describe which is the dummy-world. Before directly confronting this issue, let me remind you of a partly parallel issue which, though it exercised our great-grandfathers and grandfathers, does not any longer seriously exercise us.

When Economics was entering its adolescence as a science, thinking people were apt to feel themselves torn between two rival accounts of Man. According to the new, tough-minded account presented by the economists, Man was a creature actuated only by considerations of gain and loss—or at least he was this in so far as he was enlightened. The conduct of his life, or at least of his rational life, was governed by the principles of Supply and Demand, Diminishing Returns, Gresham's law and a few others. But Man as thus depicted seemed to be disastrously different from Man as depicted by

* From Ryle: *Dilemmas*, 1954, Chapter 5. Reprinted by permission of the publishers, Cambridge University Press.

the preacher, the biographer, the wife or the man himself. Which, then, was the real man and which the dummy-man, the Economic Man or the Every-day Man?

The choice was a hard one. How could one vote against the Economic Man without taking sides with the unscientific against the scientific story? There seemed to be a deadly rivalry between what economists said about the motives and policies of human beings and what ordinary people said about the motives and policies of the people with whom they lived—and it was the latter story that seemed doomed to be condemned. The brother, whom I ordinarily describe as hospitable, devoted to his branch of learning, and unexcited about his bank-balance, must be a dummy-brother if I am to take science seriously. My real brother, my Economic Brother, is concerned only to maximize his gains and minimize his losses. Those of his efforts and outlays which do not pay are done in ignorance of the state of the market or else from stupidity in making his calculations about it.

We have, I think, outgrown this feeling that our grandparents had, that we have to choose between the Economic Brother and the brother whom we know. We no longer think or are even tempted to imagine that what the economist says about the marketings of men who want to minimize losses and maximize gains is a general diagnosis of people's motives and intentions. We realize that there is no incompatibility between (1) saying that my brother is not much interested in exchange-transactions, and (2) saying that if and when he is engaged in such a transaction with the intention of trying to come out of it as well as possible, then he does, other things being equal, choose the cheaper of two otherwise similar articles and invest his savings where risks of loss are relatively slight and prospects of dividends are rela-tively good. This means that we no longer suppose that the economist is offering a characterization or even a mis-characterization of my brother or of anyone else's brother. He is doing something quite different. He is offering an account of certain marketing-tendencies, which applies to or covers my brother in so far as he concerns himself in marketing matters. But it does not say that he must or does often or does ever concern himself in such matters. In fact it does not mention him at all. Certainly it talks about the Consumer, or it talks about the Tenant, or the Investor, or the Employee. But in an im-portant way this anonymous character is neither my brother nor *not* my brother but someone else's brother. He has not got a surname, though people who have got surnames often are, among thousands of other things that they are, consumers, investors, tenants and employees. In one way the economist is not talking about my brother or anyone else's brother at all. He does not know or need to know that I have a brother, or what kind of a man he is. Nothing that the economist says would require to be changed if my brother's character or mode of life changed. Yet in another way the economist certainly is talking about my brother, since he is talking about anyone, whoever he may be and whatever he may be like, who makes purchases, invests his savings or earns a wage or salary, and my brother does or might fill these bills.

Æsop told a story of a dog who dropped his bone in order to secure the tempting reflection of the bone. No child thinks that this was meant to be just an anecdote about a real dog. It was meant to convey a lesson about human beings. But which human beings? Hitler perhaps. Yet Æsop did not know that there was going to be a Hitler. Well, about Everyman. But there is no such person as Everyman. Æsop's story was, in one way, about Hitler or about anyone else you choose to name. In another way it was not about any person that you can name. When we are clear about these different ways in which a person is and is not what a moral or economic statement is about, we cease to think either that my brother is a well-camouflaged Economic Man or that the economist is asking us to believe in fables. The mortal conflict which our grandfathers felt to exist between economics and real life no longer bothers us very much—at least until we become edified enough to think not about our brothers, but about the Capitalist and the Worker. They, of course, are quite different from people's brothers.

But we have not, I think, outgrown the feeling that there is a feud between the world of physical science and the world of real life, and that one of these worlds, presumably, sad to say, the familiar one, is a dummy. I want to persuade you that this notion is the product of an influential variety of cross-purposes between theories, and to show you some of the sources of these cross-purposes.

As a preface to the serious part of the argument I want to deflate two over-inflated ideas, from which derives not the cogency but some of the persuasiveness of the argument for the irreconcilability of the world of science with the everyday world. One is the idea of *science*, the other that of *world*.

(*a*) There is no such animal as 'Science.' There are scores of sciences. Most of these sciences are such that acquaintanceship with them or, what is even more captivating, hearsay knowledge about them has not the slightest tendency to make us contrast their world with the everyday world. Philology is a science, but not even popularizations of its discoveries would make anyone feel that the world of philology cannot be accommodated by the world of familiar people, things and happenings. Let philologists discover everything discoverable about the structures and origins of the expressions that we use; yet their discoveries have no tendency to make us write off as mere dummies the expressions that we use and that philologists also use. The sole dividedness of mind that is induced in us by learning any of the lessons of philology is akin to that which we sometimes experience when told, say, that our old, familiar paper-weight was once an axe-head used by a prehistoric warrior. Something utterly ordinary becomes also, just for the moment, charged with history. A mere paper-weight becomes also, just for the moment, a death-dealing weapon. But that is all.

Nor do most of the other sciences give us the feeling that we live our daily lives in a bubble-world. Botanists, entomologists, meteorologists, and geologists do not seem to threaten the walls, floors and ceilings of our common dwelling-place. On the contrary, they seem to increase the quantity and improve the arrangement of its furniture. Nor even, as might be supposed, do all branches of physical science engender in us the idea that our everyday world is a dummy-world. The discoveries and theories of astronomers and astro-physicists may make us feel that the earth is very small, but only by making us feel that the heavens are very big. The gnawing suspicion that both the terrestrial and the super-terrestrial alike are merely painted stage-canvas is not begotten by even hearsay knowledge of the physics of the immense. It is not begotten, either, by hearsay knowledge of the physics of the middle-sized. The theory of the pendulum, the cannon-ball, the water-pump, the fulcrum, the balloon and the steam-engine does not by itself drive us to vote between the everyday world and the so-called world of science. Even the comparatively minute can be accommodated by us without theoretical heart-searchings in our everyday world. Pollen-grains, frost crystals and bacteria, though revealed only through the microscope, do not by themselves make us doubt whether middle-sized and immense things may not belong where rainbows and mirages or even dreams belong. We always knew that there were things too small to be seen with the naked eye; the magnifying-glass and the microscope have surprised us not by establishing their existence but by disclosing their variety and, in some cases, their importance.

No, there are, I think, two branches of science which, especially when in collusion with one another, produce what I may describe as the 'poison-pen effect,' the effect of half-persuading us that our best friends are really our worst enemies. One is the physical theory of the ultimate elements of matter; the other is that one wing of human physiology which investigates the mechanism and functioning of our organs of perception. I do not think it makes much difference to the issue whether these ultimate elements of matter are described as the Greek atomists described them or as the twentieth-century nuclear physicist describes them. Nor do I think that it makes much difference whether we consider old-fashioned guesses or recent conclusive discoveries about the mechanism of perception. The upsetting moral drawn by Epicurus, Galileo, Sydenham and Locke is precisely that drawn by Eddington, Sherrington and Russell. The fact that this upsetting moral was once drawn from a piece of speculation and is now drawn from well-established scientific theory makes no difference. The moral drawn is not a piece of good science now, and it was not a piece of bad science then.

So the so-called world of science which, we gather, has the title to replace our everyday world is, I suggest, the world not of science in general but of atomic and sub-atomic physics in particular, enhanced by some slightly incongruous appendages borrowed from one branch of neuro-physiology.

(*b*) The other idea which needs prefatory deflation is that of *world*. When we hear that there is a grave disparity between our everyday world and the world of science or, a little more specifically, the world of one wing of physical science, it is difficult for us to shake off the impression that there are some physicists who by dint of their experiments, calculations and theorizing have qualified themselves to tell us everything that is really important about the cosmos, whatever that may be. Where theologians used to be the people to tell us about the creation and management of the cosmos, now these physicists are the experts—for all that in the articles and books that they write for their colleagues and pupils the word 'world' seldom occurs, and the grand word 'cosmos,' I hope, never occurs. There is some risk of a purely verbal muddle here. We know that a lot of people are interested in poultry and would not be surprised to find in existence a periodical called 'The Poultry World.' Here the word 'world' is not used as theologians use it. It is a collective noun used to label together all matters pertaining to poultry-keeping. It could be paraphrased by 'field' or 'sphere of interest' or 'province.' In this use there could be no question of a vendetta between the poultry world and the Christian world, since, while 'world' could be paraphrased by 'cosmos' in the phrase 'Christian world,' it could not be so paraphrased in the other.

It is obviously quite innocuous to speak of the physicist's world, if we do so in the way in which we speak of the poultry-keeper's world or the entertainment world. We could correspondingly speak of the bacteriologist's world and the marine zoologist's world. In this use there is no connotation of cosmic authority, for the word 'world' in this use does not mean '*the* world' or 'the cosmos.' On the contrary, it means the *department* of interests which physicists' interests constitute. . . .

I am now going to try to bring out the underlying logical pattern of the view that the truths of physical theory leave no room for the truths of daily life, and this I do by means of a long drawn out analogy with which I hope you will bear for some little time. An undergraduate member of a college is one day permitted to inspect the college accounts and to discuss them with the auditor. He hears that these accounts show how the college has fared during the year. 'You will find,' he is told, 'that all the activities of the college are represented in these columns. Undergraduates are taught, and here are the tuition-fees that they pay. Their instructors teach, and here are the stipends that they receive. Games are played, and here are the figures; so much for rent of the ground, so much for the wages of the groundsman, and so on. Even your entertainments are recorded; here is what was paid out to the butchers, grocers and fruiterers, here are the kitchen-charges, and here is what you paid in your college battels.' At first the undergraduate is merely mildly interested. He allows that these columns give him a different sort of view of the life of the college from the patchwork-quilt of views that he had previously acquired from his own experiences of working in the library, playing football, dining with his friends, and the rest. But then under the influence of the auditor's grave and sober voice he suddenly begins to wonder. Here everything in the life of the college is systematically marshalled and couched in terms which, though colourless, are precise, impersonal and susceptible of conclusive checking. To every plus there corresponds an equal and opposite minus; the entries are classified; the origins and destinations of all payments are indicated. Moreover, a general conclusion is reached; the financial position of the college is exhibited and compared with its position in previous years. So is not this expert's way, perhaps, the right way in which to think of the life of the college, and the other muddled and emotionally charged ways to which he had been used the wrong ways?

At first in discomfort he wriggles and suggests 'May not these accounts give us just one part of the life of the college? The chimney-sweep and the inspector of electricity-meters see their little corners of the activities of the college; but no one supposes that what they have to tell is more than a petty fragment of the whole story. Perhaps you, the auditor, are like them and see only a small part of what is going on.' But the auditor rejects this suggestion. 'No,' he says, 'here are the payments to the chimney-sweep at so much per chimney swept, and here are the payments to the Electricity Board at so much a unit. Everybody's part in the college life, including my own, is down here in figures. There is nothing departmental in the college accounts. Everything is covered. What is more, the whole system of accountancy is uniform for all colleges and is, at least in general pattern, uniform for all businesses, government departments and town councils. No speculations or hypotheses are admitted; our results are lifted above the horizons of opinion and prejudice by the sublime Principle of Double Entry. These accounts tell the objective truth about the entire life of the whole college; the stories that you tell about it to your brothers and sisters are only picturesque travesties of the audited facts. They are only dreams. Here are the realities.' What is the undergraduate to reply? He cannot question the accuracy, comprehensiveness or exhaustiveness of the accounts. He cannot complain that they cover five or six sides of college life, but do not cover the other sixteen sides. All the sides that he can think of are indeed duly covered.

Perhaps he is acute enough to suspect that there has been some subtle trick played by this word 'covered.' The tuition he had received last term from the lecturer in Anglo-Saxon was indeed covered, yet the accounts were silent about what had been taught and the auditor betrayed no inquisitiveness about what progress the student had made. He, too, the undergraduate himself, had been covered in scores of sections of the accounts, as a recipient of an Exhibition, as a pupil of the lecturer in Anglo-Saxon and so on. He had been covered, but not characterized or mischaracterized. Nothing was said about him that would not have fitted a much taller Exhibitioner or a much less enthusiastic student of Anglo-Saxon. Nothing had been said about him personally at all. He has not been described, though he has been financially accounted for.

Take a special case. In one way the auditor is very much interested in the books that the librarian buys for the college library. They must be scrupulously accounted for, the price paid for each must be entered, the fact of the actual receipt of the book must be recorded. But in another way the auditor need not be at all interested in these books, since he need not have any idea what the books contain or whether anybody reads them. For him the book is merely what is indicated by the price mark on its jacket. For him the differences between one book and another are differences in shillings. The figures in the section devoted to library accounts do indeed cover every one of the actual books bought; yet nothing in these figures would have been different had these books been different in subject-matter, language, style and binding, so long as their prices were the same. The accounts tell neither lies nor the truth about the contents of any of the books. In the reviewer's sense of 'describe,' they do not describe any of the books, though they scrupulously cover all of the books.

Which, now, is the real and which the bubble-book, the book read by the undergraduate or the book whose price is entered in the library-accounts? Clearly there is no answer. There are not two books, nor yet one real book, side by side with another bubble-book—the latter, queerly, being the one that is useful for examinations. There is just a book available for students, and an entry in the accounts specifying what the college paid for it. There could have been no such entry had there not been the book. There could not be a library stocked with mere book-prices; though also there could not be a well-conducted college which had a library full of books but required no library accounts to be kept.

The library used by the student is the same library as that accounted for by the accountant. What the student finds in the library is what the accountant tells the pounds, shillings and pence of. I am suggesting, you see, that it is in partially the same way that the world of the philologist, the marine-biologist, the astronomer and the housewife is the same world as that of the physicist; and what the pedestrian and the bacteriologist find in the world is what the physicist tells him about in his double-entry notation. . . .

I hope that this protracted analogy has satisfied you at least that there is a genuine logical door open for us; that at least there is no general logical objection to saying that physical theory, while it covers the things that the more special sciences explore and the ordinary observer describes, still does not put up a rival description of them; and even that for it to be true in its way, there must be descriptions of these other kinds which are true in their quite different way or ways. It need not be a matter of rival worlds of which one has to be a bubble-world, nor yet a matter of different sectors or provinces of one world, such that what is true of one sector is false of the other.

In the way in which a landscape-painter paints a good or bad picture of a range of hills, the geologist does not paint a rival picture, good or bad, of those hills, though what he tells us the geology of are the same hills that the painter depicts or misdepicts. The painter is not doing bad geology and the geologist is not doing good or bad landscape painting. In the way in which the joiner tells us what a piece of furniture is like and gets his description right or wrong (no matter whether he is talking about its colour, the wood it is made of, its style, carpentry or period), the nuclear physicist does not proffer a competing description, right or wrong, though what he tells us the nuclear physics of covers what the joiner describes. They are not giving conflicting answers to the same questions or to the same sort of question, though the physicist's questions are, in a rather artificial sense of 'about,' about what the joiner gives his information about. The physicist does not mention the furniture; what he does mention are, so to speak, bills for such goods as, *inter alia*, bits of furniture.

Part of this point is sometimes expressed in this way. As the painter in oils on one side of the mountain and the painter in water-colours on the other side of the mountain produce very different pictures, which may still be excellent pictures of the same mountain, so the nuclear physicist, the theologian, the historian, the lyric poet and the man in the street produce very different, yet compatible and even complementary pictures of one and the same 'world.' But this analogy is perilous. It is risky enough to say that the accountant and the reviewer both give descriptions of the same book, since in the natural sense of 'describe' in which the reviewer does describe or misdescribe the book, the accountant does neither. But it is far riskier to characterize the physicist, the theologian, the historian, the poet and the man in the street as all alike producing 'pictures,' whether of the same object or of different objects. The highly concrete word 'picture' smothers the enormous differences between the businesses of the scientist, historian, poet and theologian even worse than the relatively abstract word 'description' smothers the big differences between the businesses of the accountant and the reviewer. It is just these smothered differences which need to be brought out into the open. If the seeming feuds between science and theology or between fundamental physics and common knowledge are to be dissolved at all, their dissolution can come not from making the polite compromise that both parties are really artists of a sort working from different points of view and with different sketching materials, but only from drawing uncompromising contrasts between their businesses. To satisfy the tobacconist and the tennis-coach that there need be no professional antagonisms between them, it is not necessary or expedient to pretend that they are really fellow-workers in some joint but unobvious missionary enterprise. It is better policy to remind them how different and independent their trades actually are. Indeed, this smothering effect of using notions like *depicting, describing, explaining,* and others to cover highly disparate things reinforces other tendencies to assimilate the dissimilar and unsuspiciously to impute just those parities of reasoning, the unreality of which engenders dilemmas.

SUGGESTED READINGS

The rise of modern science in the seventeenth century had a profound influence on philosophic thought, and throughout the modern period philosophers have been confronted by the question of whether or not the methods of science are limited. Do these methods need to be corrected by the use of other, perhaps nonrational, approaches to reality? Do they need to be supplemented by their methods? One of the most interesting books on the importance of science, and various reactions to it throughout history, is A. N. Whitehead's *Science and the Modern World.* For an attempt to discuss systematically the various forms of thought other than the scientific, see E. Cassirer, *Essay on Man,* a work that presents briefly the main points of his massive *Philosophy of Symbolic Forms.* S. Langer is influenced by Cassirer, but in *Philosophy in a New Key* she presents much original material on art and myth. A fascinating attempt to understand prescientific modes of thought is presented by Henri Frankfort and others in *Before Philosophy.*

Bergson and James are two of the focal points of contemporary discussions of the limits of science: almost all of the works of these thinkers are relevant to various aspects of the topic. In addition Kierkegaard and

Nietzsche have had a profound influence on contemporary thought in precisely this area of philosophic discussion. Among their works Kierkegaard's *Concluding Unscientific Postscript* (an extract from which is given in Section VI) and the first part of Nietzsche's *Beyond Good and Evil* contain particularly significant statements of their points of view.

Whereas the discussions in the present section are concerned with the limits of the physical sciences, doubts as to the scope and power of scientific method in dealing with social life have been expressed at least as widely. An interesting and readable survey of a number of writers concerned with these problems and with related problems of social action is given in H. Stuart Hughes, *Consciousness and Society*.

Two Current Issues:
A. The Concept
of Explanation

Until about twenty-five years ago, most discussions of scientific methodology centered around the concept of cause and problems concerning induction. More recently, however, another aspect of methodology has been receiving vigorous discussion, namely, the concept of *explanation*. In a classic paper, HEMPEL and OPPENHEIM, taking as their model the kind of explanations found in science, argued that to explain an event is to subsume it under certain general laws. We can explain the fact that a vase broke, for example, by (1) citing a "covering law" to the effect that whenever an object of such-and-such brittleness strikes a solid surface (such as a floor) with such-and-such force, the object breaks, and by (2) noting that the vase in question met the antecedent (initial) conditions, i.e., it *was* an object with the proper sort of brittleness and it did meet the floor with the required force.

Many philosophers have accepted this notion of explanation as being adequate in all cases, and have done much to clarify it from a formal or mathematical point of view. But there have been others, for example, PASSMORE, who have maintained that this view of explanation does not do justice to our ordinary ways of talking and thinking about explanations. If we are interested in giving an account, or an explanation, of the assassination of a president, we are not likely to be satisfied with the remark that when bits of metal strike a person's brain, he dies. We want to know something about the motives of the criminal, the techniques used, and so on. According to this view, the explanations considered by Hempel and Oppenheim occur only in restricted types of cases.

The Logic of Explanation[*]

CARL GUSTAVE HEMPEL [1905–   ]. See p. 95.
PAUL OPPENHEIM [1885–   ], born in Germany, earned his Ph.D. at
the University of Giessen. He has long been a resident of the United States. In his
publications he has dealt especially with the theory of knowledge and the philosophy of science.

§ 1. INTRODUCTION. To explain the phenomena in the world of our experience, to answer the question "why?" rather than only the question
"what?", is one of the foremost objectives of all rational inquiry; and especially, scientific research in its various branches strives to go beyond a mere
description of its subject matter by providing an explanation of the phenomena it investigates. While there is rather general agreement about this chief
objective of science, there exists considerable difference of opinion as to the
function and the essential characteristics of scientific explanation. In the
present essay, an attempt will be made to shed some light on these issues by
means of an elementary survey of the basic pattern of scientific explanation. . . .

§ 2. SOME ILLUSTRATIONS. A mercury thermometer is rapidly immersed in
hot water; there occurs a temporary drop of the mercury column, which is
then followed by a swift rise. How is this phenomenon to be explained? The
increase in temperature affects at first only the glass tube of the thermometer; it expands and thus provides a larger space for the mercury inside,
whose surface therefore drops. As soon as by heat conduction the rise in
temperature reaches the mercury, however, the latter expands, and as its
coefficient of expansion is considerably larger than that of glass, a rise of the
mercury level results.—This account consists of statements of two kinds.
Those of the first kind indicate certain conditions which are realized prior to,
or at the same time as, the phenomenon to be explained; we shall refer to
them briefly as antecedent conditions. In our illustration, the antecedent
conditions include, among others, the fact that the thermometer consists of a
glass tube which is partly filled with mercury, and that it is immersed into
hot water. The statements of the second kind express certain general laws; in

[*] From C. G. Hempel and P. Oppenheim: "Studies in the Logic of Explanation,"
Part I: "Elementary Survey of Scientific Explanation," PHILOSOPHY OF SCIENCE,
Vol. 15, No. 2, April 1948, pages 135–146. Copyright ©, 1948, The Williams and Wil-
kins Company, Baltimore, Md. U.S.A.

our case, these include the laws of the thermic expansion of mercury and of glass, and a statement about the small thermic conductivity of glass. The two sets of statements, if adequately and completely formulated, explain the phenomenon under consideration: They entail the consequence that the mercury will first drop, then rise. Thus, the event under discussion is explained by subsuming it under general laws, i.e., by showing that it occurred in accordance with those laws, by virtue of the realization of certain specified antecedent conditions.

Consider another illustration. To an observer in a row boat, that part of an oar which is under water appears to be bent upwards. The phenomenon is explained by means of general laws—mainly the law of refraction and the law that water is an optically denser medium than air—and by reference to certain antecedent conditions—especially the facts that part of the oar is in the water, part in the air, and that the oar is practically a straight piece of wood.—Thus, here again, the question "Why does the phenomenon happen?" is construed as meaning "according to what general laws, and by virtue of what antecedent conditions does the phenomenon occur?"

So far, we have considered exclusively the explanation of particular events occurring at a certain time and place. But the question "Why?" may be raised also in regard to general laws. Thus, in our last illustration, the question might be asked: Why does the propagation of light conform to the law of refraction? Classical physics answers in terms of the undulatory theory of light, i.e. by stating that the propagation of light is a wave phenomenon of a certain general type, and that all wave phenomena of that type satisfy the law of refraction. Thus, the explanation of a general regularity consists in subsuming it under another, more comprehensive regularity, under a more general law.—Similarly, the validity of Galileo's law for the free fall of bodies near the earth's surface can be explained by deducing it from a more comprehensive set of laws, namely Newton's laws of motion and his law of gravitation, together with some statements about particular facts, namely the mass and the radius of the earth.

§ 3. The Basic Pattern of Scientific Explanation. From the preceding sample cases let us now abstract some general characteristics of scientific explanation. We divide an explanation into two major constituents, the explanandum and the explanans. By the explanandum, we understand the sentence describing the phenomenon to be explained (not that phenomenon itself); by the explanans, the class of those sentences which are adduced to account for the phenomenon. As was noted before, the explanans falls into two subclasses; one of these contains certain sentences $C_1, C_2, \ldots, C_k$ which state specific antecedent conditions; the other is a set of sentences $L_1, L_2, \ldots L_r$ which represent general laws.

If a proposed explanation is to be sound, its constituents have to satisfy certain conditions of adequacy, which may be divided into logical and empirical conditions. For the following discussion, it will be sufficient to formulate these requirements in a slightly vague manner. . . .

I. *Logical conditions of adequacy*

(R1) The explanandum must be a logical consequence of the explanans; in other words, the explanandum must be logically deducible from the information contained in the explanans, for otherwise, the explanans would not constitute adequate grounds for the explanandum.

(R2) The explanans must contain general laws, and these must actually be required for the derivation of the explanandum.—We shall not make it a necessary condition for a sound explanation, however, that the explanans must contain at least one statement which is not a law; for, to mention just one reason, we would surely want to consider as an explanation the derivation of the general regularities governing the motion of double stars from the laws of celestial mechanics, even though all the statements in the explanans are general laws.

(R3) The explanans must have empirical content; i.e., it must be capable, at least in principle, of test by experiment or observation.—This condition is implicit in (R1); for since the explanandum is assumed to describe some empirical phenomenon, it follows from (R1) that the explanans entails at least one consequence of empirical character, and this fact confers upon it testability and empirical content. But the point deserves special mention because, as will be seen in §4, certain arguments which have been offered as explanations in the natural and in the social sciences violate this requirement.

II. *Empirical condition of adequacy*

(R4) The sentences constituting the explanans must be true. That in a sound explanation, the statements constituting the explanans have to satisfy some condition of factual correctness is obvious. But it might seem more appropriate to stipulate that the explanans has to be highly confirmed by all the relevant evidence available rather than that it should be true. This stipulation however, leads to awkward consequences. Suppose that a certain phenomenon was explained at an earlier stage of science, by means of an explanans which was well supported by the evidence then at hand, and which had been highly disconfirmed by more recent empirical findings. In such a case, we would have to say that originally the explanatory account was a correct explanation, but that it ceased to be one later, when unfavorable evidence was discovered. This does not appear to accord with sound common usage which directs us to say that on the basis of the limited initial evidence, the truth of the explanans, and thus the soundness of the explanation, had been quite probable, but that the ampler evidence now available made it highly probable that the explanans was not true, and hence that the account in question was not— and had never been—a correct explanation. . . .

Some of the characteristics of an explanation which have been indicated so far may be summarized in the following schema:

$$
\text{Logical deduction}
\left\{
\begin{array}{ll}
C_1, C_2, \ldots, C_k & \text{Statements of antecedent} \\
& \text{conditions} \\
\\
L_1, L_2, \ldots, L_r & \text{General Laws}
\end{array}
\right\} \text{Explanans}
$$

$$
\begin{array}{ll}
E & \left.\begin{array}{l}\text{Description of the} \\ \text{empirical phenomenon} \\ \text{to be explained}\end{array}\right\} \text{Explanandum}
\end{array}
$$

Let us note here that the same formal analysis, including the four necessary conditions, applies to scientific prediction as well as to explanation. The difference between the two is of a pragmatic character. If E is given, i.e. if we know that the phenomenon described by E has occurred, and a suitable set of statements $C_1, C_2, \ldots, C_k, L_1, L_2, \ldots, L_r$ is provided afterwards, we speak of an explanation of the phenomenon in question. If the latter statements are given and E is derived prior to the occurrence of the phenomenon it describes, we speak of a prediction. It may be said, therefore, that an explanation is not fully adequate unless its explanans, if taken account of in time, could have served as a basis for predicting the phenomenon under consideration.—Consequently, whatever will be said in this article concerning the logical characteristics of explanation or prediction will be applicable to either, even if only one of them should be mentioned.

It is this potential predictive force which gives scientific explanation its importance: only to the extent that we are able to explain empirical facts can we attain the major objective of scientific research, namely not merely to record the phenomena of our experience, but to learn from them, by basing upon them theoretical generalizations which enable us to anticipate new occurrences and to control, at least to some extent, the changes in our environment.

Many explanations which are customarily offered, especially in prescientific discourse, lack this predictive character, however. Thus, it may be explained that a car turned over on the road "because" one of its tires blew out while the car was travelling at high speed. Clearly, on the basis of just this information, the accident could not have been predicted, for the explanans provides no explicit general laws by means of which the prediction might be effected, nor does it state adequately the antecedent conditions which would be needed for the prediction.—The same point may be illustrated by reference to W. S. Jevons's view that every explanation consists in pointing out a resemblance between facts, and that in some cases this process may require no reference to laws at all and "may involve nothing more than a single identity, as when we explain the appearance of shooting stars by showing that they are identical with portions of a comet." But clearly, this identity does not provide an explanation of the phenomenon of shooting stars unless we presuppose the laws governing the development of heat and light as the effect of friction. The observation of similarities has explanatory value only if it involves at least tacit reference to general laws.

In some cases, incomplete explanatory arguments of the kind here illustrated suppress parts of the explanans simply as "obvious"; in other cases, they seem to involve the assumption that while the missing parts are not obvious, the incomplete explanans could at least, with appropriate effort, be so supplemented as to make a strict derivation of the explanandum possible. This assumption may be justifiable in some cases, as when we say that a lump of sugar disappeared "because" it was put into hot tea, but it is surely not satisfied in many other cases. Thus, when certain peculiarities in the work of an artist are explained as outgrowths of a specific type of neurosis, this observation may contain significant clues, but in general it does not afford a sufficient basis for a potential prediction of those peculiarities. In cases of this kind, an incomplete explanation may at best be considered as indicating some positive correlation between the antecedent conditions adduced and the type of phenomenon to be explained, and as pointing out a direction in which further research might be carried on in order to complete the explanatory account.

The type of explanation which has been considered here so far is often referred to as causal explanation. If E describes a particular event, then the antecedent circumstances described in the sentences $C_1, C_2, \ldots, C_k$ may be said jointly to "cause" that event, in the sense that there are certain empirical regularities, expressed by the laws $L_1, L_2, \ldots, L_r$, which imply that whenever conditions of the kind indicated by $C_1, C_2, \ldots, C_k$ occur, an event of the kind described in E will take place. Statements such as L_1, $L_2, \ldots, L_r$, which assert general and unexceptional connections between specified characteristics of events, are customarily called causal, or deterministic laws. They are to be distinguished from the so-called statistical laws which assert that in the long run, an explicitly stated percentage of all cases satisfying a given set of conditions are accompanied by an event of a certain specified kind. Certain cases of scientific explanation involve "subsumption" of the explanandum under a set of laws of which at least some are statistical in character. Analysis of the peculiar logical structure of that type of subsumption involves difficult special problems. The present essay will be restricted to an examination of the causal type of explanation, which has retained its significance in large segments of contemporary science, and even in some areas where a more adequate account calls for reference to statistical laws.

§ 4. Explanation in the Non-Physical Sciences. Motivation and Teleological Approaches. Our characterization of scientific explanation is so far based on a study of cases taken from the physical sciences. But the general principles thus obtained apply also outside this area. Thus, various types of behavior in laboratory animals and in human subjects are explained in psychology by subsumption under laws or even general theories of learning or conditioning; and while frequently, the regularities invoked cannot be stated with the same generality and precision as in physics or chemistry, it is clear, at least, that the general character of those explanations conforms to our earlier characterization.

Let us now consider an illustration involving sociological and economic factors. In the fall of 1946, there occurred at the cotton exchanges of the United States a price drop which was so severe that the exchanges in New York, New Orleans, and Chicago had to suspend their activities temporarily. In an attempt to explain this occurrence, newspapers traced it back to a large-scale speculator in New Orleans who had feared his holdings were too large and had therefore begun to liquidate his stocks; smaller speculators had then followed his example in a panic and had thus touched off the critical decline. Without attempting to assess the merits of the argument, let us note that the explanation here suggested again involves statements about antecedent conditions and the assumption of general regularities. The former include the facts that the first speculator had large stocks of cotton, that there were smaller speculators with considerable holdings, that there existed the institution of the cotton exchanges with their specific mode of operation, etc. The general regularities referred to are—as often in semi-popular explanations—not explicitly mentioned; but there is obviously implied some form of the law of supply and demand to account for the drop in cotton prices in terms of the greatly increased supply under conditions of practically unchanged demand; besides, reliance is necessary on certain regularities in the behavior of individuals who are trying to preserve or improve their economic position. Such laws cannot be formulated at present with satisfactory precision and generality, and therefore, the suggested explanation is surely incomplete, but its intention is unmistakably to account for the phenomenon by integrating it into a general pattern of economic and socio-psychological regularities.

We turn to an explanatory argument taken from the field of linguistics. In Northern France, there exist a large variety of words synonymous with the English "bee," whereas in Southern France, essentially only one such word is in existence. For this discrepancy, the explanation has been suggested that in the Latin epoch, the South of France used the word "apicula," the North the word "apis." The latter, because of a process of phonologic decay in Northern France, became the monosyllabic word "é"; and monosyllables tend to be eliminated, especially if they contain few consonantic elements, for they are apt to give rise to misunderstandings. Thus, to avoid confusion, other words were selected. But "apicula," which was reduced to "abelho," remained clear enough and was retained, and finally it even entered into the standard language, in the form "abbeille." While the explanation here described is incomplete in the sense characterized in the previous section, it clearly exhibits reference to specific antecedent conditions as well as to general laws.

While illustrations of this kind tend to support the view that explanation in biology, psychology, and the social sciences has the same structure as in the physical sciences, the opinion is rather widely held that in many instances, the causal type of explanation is essentially inadequate in fields other than physics and chemistry, and especially in the study of purposive behavior. Let us examine briefly some of the reasons which have been adduced in support of this view.

One of the most familiar among them is the idea that events involving the activities of humans singly or in groups have a peculiar uniqueness and irrepeatability which makes them inaccessible to causal explanation because the latter,—with its reliance upon uniformities, presupposes repeatability of the phenomena under consideration. This argument which, incidentally, has also been used in support of the contention that the experimental method is inapplicable in psychology and the social sciences, involves a misunderstanding of the logical character of causal explanation. Every individual event, in the physical sciences no less than in psychology or the social sciences, is unique in the sense that it, with all its peculiar characteristics, does not repeat itself. Nevertheless, individual events may conform to, and thus be explainable by means of, general laws of the causal type. For all that a causal law asserts is that any event of a specified kind, i.e. any event having certain specified characteristics, is accompanied by another event which in turn has certain specified characteristics; for example, that in any event involving friction, heat is developed. And all that is needed for the testability and applicability of such laws is the recurrence of events with the antecedent characteristics, i.e. the repetition of those characteristics, but not of their individual instances. Thus, the argument is inconclusive. It gives occasion, however, to emphasize an important point concerning our earlier analysis: When we spoke of the explanation of a single event, the term "event" referred to the occurrence of some more or less complex characteristic in a specific spatio-temporal location or in a certain individual object, and not to *all* the characteristics of that object, or to all that goes on in that space-time region.

A second argument that should be mentioned here contends that the establishment of scientific generalizations—and thus of explanatory principles—for human behavior is impossible because the reactions of an individual in a given situation depend not only upon that situation, but also upon the previous history of the individual.—But surely, there is no *a priori* reason why generalizations should not be attainable which take into account this dependence of behavior on the past history of the agent. That indeed the given argument "proves" too much, and is therefore a *non sequitur*, is made evident by the existence of certain physical phenomena, such as magnetic hysteresis and elastic fatigue, in which the magnitude of a specific physical effect depends upon the past history of the system involved, and for which nevertheless certain general regularities have been established.

A third argument insists that the explanation of any phenomenon involving purposive behavior calls for reference to motivations and thus for teleological rather than causal analysis. Thus, for example, a fuller statement of the suggested explanation for the break in the cotton prices would have to indicate the large-scale speculator's motivations as one of the factors determining the event in question. Thus, we have to refer to goals sought, and this, so the argument runs, introduces a type of explanation alien to the physical sciences. Unquestionably, many of the—frequently incomplete—explanations which are offered for human actions involve reference to goals and motives; but does this make them essentially different from the causal explanations of physics and chemistry? One difference which suggests itself lies in the circumstance that in motivated behavior, the future appears to affect the present in a manner which is not found in the causal explanations of the physical sciences. But clearly, when the action of a person is motivated, say, by the desire to reach a certain objective, then it is not the as yet unrealized future event of attaining that goal which can be said to determine his present behavior, for indeed the goal may never be actually reached; rather—to put it in crude terms—it is (a) his desire, present before the action, to attain that particular objective, and (b) his belief, likewise present before the action, that such and such a course of action is most likely to have the desired effect. The determining motives and beliefs, therefore, have to be classified among the antecedent conditions of a motivational explanation, and there is no formal difference on this account between motivational and causal explanation.

Neither does the fact that motives are not accessible to direct observation by an outside observer constitute an essential difference between the two kinds of explanation; for also the determining factors adduced in physical explanations are very frequently inaccessible to direct observation. This is the case, for instance, when opposite electric charges are adduced in explanation of the mutual attraction of two metal spheres. The presence of those charges, while eluding all direct observation, can be ascertained by various kinds of indirect test, and that is sufficient to guarantee the empirical character of the explanatory statement. Similarly, the presence of certain motivations may be ascertainable only by indirect methods, which may include reference to linguistic utterances of the subject in question, slips of the pen or of the tongue, etc.; but as long as these methods are "operationally determined" with reasonable clarity and precision, there is no essential difference in this respect between motivational explanation and causal explanation in physics.

A potential danger of explanation by motives lies in the fact that the method lends itself to the facile construction of ex-post-facto accounts without predictive force. It is a widespread tendency to "explain" an action by ascribing it to motives conjectured only after the action has taken place. While this procedure is not in itself objectionable, its soundness requires that (1) the motivational assumptions in question be capable of test, and (2) that suitable general laws be available to lend explanatory power to the assumed motives. Disregard of these requirements frequently deprives alleged motivational explanations of their cognitive significance.

The explanation of an action in terms of the motives of the agent is sometimes considered as a special kind of teleological explanation. As was pointed out above, motivational explanation, if adequately formulated, conforms to the conditions for causal explanation, so that the term "teleological" is a misnomer if it is meant to imply either a non-causal character of the explanation or a peculiar determination of the present by the future. If this is borne in mind, however, the term "teleological" may be viewed, in this context, as referring to causal explanations in which some of the antecedent conditions are motives of the agent whose actions are to be explained.

Teleological explanations of this kind have to be distinguished from a much more sweeping type, which has been claimed by certain schools of thought to be indispensable especially in biology. It consists in explaining characteristics of an organism by reference to certain ends or purposes which the characteristics are said to serve. In contradistinction to the cases examined before, the ends are not assumed here to be consciously or subconsciously pursued by the organism in question. Thus, for the phenomenon of mimicry, the explanation is sometimes offered that it serves the purpose of protecting the animals endowed with it from detention by its pursuers and thus tends to preserve the species.—Before teleological hypotheses of this kind can be appraised as to their potential explanatory power, their meaning has to be clarified. If they are intended somehow to express the idea that the purposes they refer to are inherent in the design of the universe, then clearly they are not capable of empirical test and thus violate the requirement (R3) stated in §3. In certain cases, however, assertions about the purposes of biological characteristics may be translatable into statements in non-teleological terminology which assert that those characteristics function in a specific manner which is essential to keeping the organism alive or to preserving the species. An attempt to state precisely what is meant by this latter assertion —or by the similar one that without those characteristics, and other things being equal, the organism or the species would not survive—encounters considerable difficulties. But these need not be discussed here. For even if we assume that biological statements in teleological form can be adequately translated into descriptive statements about the life-preserving function of certain biological characteristics, it is clear that (1) the use of the concept of purpose is not essential in these contexts, since the term "purpose" can be completely eliminated from the statements in question, and (2) teleological assumptions, while now endowed with empirical content, cannot serve as explanatory principles in the customary contexts. Thus, e.g., the fact that a given species of butterflies displays a particular kind of coloring cannot be inferred from—and therefore cannot be explained by means of—the statement that this type of coloring has the effect of protecting the butterflies from detection by pursuing birds, nor can the presence of red corpuscles in the human blood be inferred from the statement that those corpuscles have a specific function in assimilating oxygen and that this function is essential for the maintenance of life.

One of the reasons for the perseverance of teleological considerations in biology probably lies in the fruitfulness of the teleological approach as a heuristic device: Biological research which was psychologically motivated by a teleological orientation, by an interest in purposes in nature, has frequently led to important results which can be stated in non-teleological terminology and which increase our scientific knowledge of the causal connections between biological phenomena.

Another aspect that lends appeal to teleological considerations is their anthropomorphic character. A teleological explanation tends to make us feel that we really "understand" the phenomenon in question, because it is accounted for in terms of purposes, with which we are familiar from our own experience of purposive behavior. But it is important to distinguish here understanding in the psychological sense of a feeling of empathic familiarity from understanding in the theoretical, or cognitive, sense of exhibiting the phenomenon to be explained as a special case of some general regularity. The frequent insistence that explanation means the reduction of something unfamiliar to ideas or experiences already familiar to us is indeed misleading. For while some scientific explanations do have this psychological effect, it is by no means universal: The free fall of a physical body may well be said to be a more familiar phenomenon than the law of gravitation, by means of which it can be explained; and surely the basic ideas of the theory of relativity will appear to many to be far less familiar than the phenomena for which the theory accounts.

"Familiarity" of the explicans is not only not necessary for a sound explanation—as we have just tried to show—, but it is not sufficient either. This is shown by the many cases in which a proposed explicans sounds suggestively familiar, but upon closer inspection proves to be a mere metaphor, or an account lacking testability, or a set of statements which includes no general laws and therefore lacks explanatory power. A case in point is the neovitalistic attempt to explain biological phenomena by reference to an entelechy or vital force. The crucial point here is not—as it is sometimes made out to be—that entelechies cannot be seen or otherwise directly observed; for that is true also of gravitational fields, and yet, reference to such fields is essential in the explanation of various physical phenomena. The decisive difference between the two cases is that the physical explanation provides (1) methods of testing, albeit indirectly, assertions about gravitational fields, and (2) general laws concerning the strength of gravitational fields, and the behavior of objects moving in them. Explanations by entelechies satisfy the analogue of neither of these two conditions. Failure to satisfy the first condition represents a violation of (R3); it renders all statements about entelechies inaccessible to empirical test and thus devoid of empirical meaning. Failure to comply with the second condition involves a violation of (R2). It deprives the concept of entelechy of all explanatory import; for explanatory power never resides in a concept, but always in the general laws in which it functions. Therefore, notwithstanding the flavor of familiarity of the metaphor it invokes, the neovitalistic approach cannot provide theoretical understanding.

The preceding observations about familiarity and understanding can be applied, in a similar manner, to the view held by some scholars that the explanation, or the understanding, of human actions requires an empathic understanding of the personalities of the agents. This understanding of another person in terms of one's own psychological functioning may prove a useful heuristic device in the search for general psychological principles which might provide a theoretical explanation; but the existence of empathy on the part of the scientist is neither a necessary nor a sufficient condition for the explanation, or the scientific understanding, of any human action. It is not necessary, for the behavior of psychotics or of people belonging to a culture very different from that of the scientist may sometimes be explainable and predictable in terms of general principles even though the scientist who establishes or applies those principles may not be able to understand his subjects empathically. And empathy is not sufficient to guarantee a sound explanation, for a strong feeling of empathy may exist even in cases where we completely misjudge a given personality. Moreover, as the late Dr. Zilsel has pointed out, empathy leads with ease to incompatible results; thus, when the population of a town has long been subjected to heavy bombing attacks, we can understand, in the empathic sense, that its morale should have broken down completely, but we can understand with the same ease also that it should have developed a defiant spirit of resistance. Arguments of this kind often appear quite convincing; but they are of an *ex post facto* character and lack cognitive significance unless they are supplemented by testable explanatory principles in the form of laws or theories.

Familiarity of the explanans, therefore, no matter whether it is achieved through the use of teleological terminology, through neovitalistic metaphors, or through other means, is no indication of the cognitive import and the predictive force of a proposed explanation. Besides, the extent to which an idea will be considered as familiar varies from person to person and from time to time, and a psychological factor of this kind certainly cannot serve as a standard in assessing the worth of a proposed explanation. The decisive requirement for every sound explanation remains that it subsume the explanandum under general laws.

Varieties of Explanation *

John Arthur Passmore [1914–   ] studied at the University of Sydney and taught there from 1935 until 1949. After teaching in New Zealand, he became Professor of Philosophy at the Australian National University in Canberra in 1958. He has published *Hume's Intentions* (1952) and *One Hundred Years of Philosophy* (1957), as well as many articles.

In everyday life there is a wide variety of circumstances under which we may offer, or be offered, what we should describe as "an explanation" of an occurrence. Consider the following:

(1) "As I got into the street-car, I noticed a large brown cylinder which was emitting a continuous clicking noise. The driver explained that I was to put my fare into it."

In this instance, I am confronted by an object which I do not know how to use. The explanation tells me how to use it, "what it is for."

(2) "On the menu, there was something called 'scrod.' The waitress explained that this is young cod."

As in case (1), I am being taught how to use something—a word. But the explanation now takes the form of a definition.

(3) "I asked him why I had to submit a report on a student at mid-term. He explained that this is the common custom in American universities."

My puzzlement in this case revolved about what I took to be an unusual procedure; the explanation consists in telling me that it is not unusual, that there is nothing to be puzzled about.

(4) "One of my students did not hand in his mid-term paper. I asked him to explain."

Here what I seek as an explanation is an excuse, a justification.

(5) "I found one passage in his essay very obscure. I asked him about it, and he explained what he was getting at."

To explain is, in this case, to elucidate, to paraphrase, to make clear how something fits into a general context.

* From Passmore: "Explanation in Everyday Life, in Science, and in History." Reprinted from *History and Theory*, Volume II, Number 2, by permission of Wesleyan University Press. Copyright © 1962 by Wesleyan University.

(6) "I asked him how he had got home, and he explained that he first caught a subway, then a street-car, then a taxi."

The explanation fills in detail. I already know that he got home; the explanation tells me by what stages he did so.

(7) "I thought Mary was winking at me, but they explained that she had a tic."

In this case, to explain is to re-classify, or re-interpret.

(8) "I had always been told that all Americans were hearty hail-fellow well-met sort of people, but he explained that this is only true of the Mid-Western."

"Explained to me" because I am puzzled about the discrepancy between what I had been told and what I have experienced; the explanation tells me that I have wrongly taken to be a universal characteristic of Americans what is, in fact, characteristic only of a special class of American.

(9) "I asked him why he wrote badly, and he explained that his school course laid very little stress on English composition."

The explanation, in this case, refers to precedent conditions—this is a typical causal explanation.

These types of cases, no doubt, flow into one another; on the other hand, there may be, almost certainly are, other distinguishable instances. Enough has been said, however, to indicate under what a variety of circumstances a piece of information can be offered as an explanation. The only common factor, so far as I can see, is that in each instance I am puzzled; the explanation sets out to resolve my puzzlement. It is not just that there is something I do not know; there is something I do not know when I ask: "At what time does the train leave for New York?", but that is not a request for an explanation. Being puzzled is a special sort of not knowing, not knowing "what to make of" a situation. The puzzling situation presents characteristics which are, from our point of view, unexpected; it interrupts the smoothness of our dealings with the world. The explanation, if we accept it, gets us moving again.

An explanation need not even be a reply to a question; we may offer an explanation to somebody who is standing before a turnstile and obviously does not know what to do next, or to a child whose voice sounds puzzled as he reads aloud. In such an instance, although we are not puzzled ourselves, we recognize what there is about the situation which, in some sense, "calls for" an explanation. This is a matter of experience; we have to know that the turnstile is an unusual one, or that the child has never met the kind of behavior about which he is now reading. For, of course, no situation is intrinsically puzzling. It is puzzling only to somebody who has not yet developed particular habits, particular forms of expectation. The turnstile is not puzzling to a daily commuter, although it may be quite baffling to a visitor from abroad. The Boston-bred will, no doubt, have learned the meaning of "scrod," or acquired the habit of putting his fare into a cylinder, not by asking for explanations but simply by imitation; he will not be puzzled by the withdrawn behavior of New Englanders because he will not expect anything else of his neighbors.

Before we start asking for explanations we have already acquired a multitude of such routine, habitual expectations. We know the English language, we know how menus are constructed; when we ask the waitress what scrod is, we expect an answer which will define it, in English, as a kind of food. She knows this, too; she will not answer, except in a pert mood: "a monosyllable," or even: "a kind of food"; although, in a different social context, just such an answer would be the appropriate one. If, indeed, pointing to the word "with" on the menu, or even "dinner," we ask the waitress, in English: "What does that mean?", she will be wholly bewildered. In this sort of context, this relationship between ourselves and the waitress, the question makes no sense.

More generally, an assumption of unfamiliarity is written into every request for an explanation; only those who realize what is unfamiliar to us will have any idea what question we are asking. Suppose I came home on a cold winter's night. The heating system is on; the house is warm; the front door is wide open. Then if I were to ask my wife: "Why is the heating system on?", "Why is the house warm?", she would think I was disturbed in mind. "Why is the front door open?", on the other hand, is a perfectly natural question— here is the break in routine. (In mid-summer, on the contrary, the first two questions would be quite natural; the last, quite likely, would be incomprehensible.)

That is why cases where I can be said to offer an explanation fade into cases where I say that no explanation is necessary. Suppose, asked why I am travelling by jeep to some point in Central Australia, I reply: "There is no alternative." The question presupposed that there was an alternative, that I could have gone by aeroplane, for example. What I have done is to reject that presupposed alternative; in one sense, my reply consists in asserting that my action needs no explanation, that there is nothing puzzling in my choosing a jeep. Yet, reporting this, it would be quite natural to say: "He explained that he had no alternative."

Similarly, when I ask why I have to submit a mid-term report on a student and receive the answer that this is an American custom, I am being told not to be puzzled. It is presumed that I have supposed this to be a demand made upon me in particular, or uniquely by my university; now this supposition is destroyed. Again, it would be natural to report this reply as: "He explained that this was the American custom." But one might also say: "I thought the behavior of this university needed some special explanation, but I found that it was just conforming to custom."

Everything depends, then, on what I know and what I want to know. If I am asked by an adult human being why Jones died, it will be no explanation to reply: "All men are mortal," for so much, it can be presumed, he knows already; that is not the unfamiliar feature of the situation that is bothering him. To a child, on the other hand, who is quite unfamiliar with the fact of death, such an answer can be an explanation, and all the explanation he needs. Similarly, when a stranger to America asks: "Why does the drugstore sell cigars?", it will normally be safe to presume that he is, wrongly, supposing that the drugstore is unique; the answer: "In America, drugstores do" will perfectly suffice as an explanation. He can go on to ask: "Why do they?", but he need not do so, and usually will not do so. In any case, this is a different question, one that is always permissible but never obligatory.

It follows from all this that there can be no purely formal definition of an explanation. The schema:

$$\text{All X are Y, P is an X, } \therefore \text{ P is a Y}$$

can sometimes be used to explain why P is a Y, but it can also be used to test the hypothesis that all X are Y, to prove that P is Y, to calculate that it is Y, to predict that it will be Y. How the schema is used will depend on what we know and what we want to know; and these are not formal considerations. To revert to my previous example, we cannot say *a priori* that: "All American drugstores sell cigars, this is an American drugstore, therefore this drugstore sells cigars," is or is not an explanation. Addressed to a stranger, it can serve to explain why the drugstore sells cigars; addressed to a travelled American, who is really wondering why any American drugstore sells cigars but may express his puzzle by a reference to a particular case, it is no explanation at all. Sometimes it will be used to convince a doubter that he ought to enter the drugstore; it will be meant as a proof that this is where cigars are to be found. Sometimes it will be a formal prediction. Explaining, in short, is a particular way of using a form of argument; it has no logical form peculiar to it.

For each type of explanation, however, there is a way of deciding whether the explanation is a good one. A student who, when asked: "Why didn't you hand in your essay?", replies that he felt lazy, has not given a good explanation; for, in the context, a good explanation has to be an acceptable excuse. A "filling-out" explanation must leave no gaps; if I live ten miles from the university, it will not do to reply to the question: "How did you get home in the snow-storm?" with the answer: "Three miles by bus and then a mile walk." A good explanation of a passage by Shakespeare stands in a special sort of interpretative relation to the original text.

Few scientists would accept such a liberal interpretation of "explanation". In the *Phaedo*, Plato represents Socrates as protesting against the already-apparent tendency of Greek scientists to assimilate all explanations to explanation by precedent conditions. Aristotle's doctrine of the "four causes" —more accurately, the "four types of explanation"—temporarily stemmed the tide; but, by the end of the seventeenth century, the battle was substantially over. Hume does not for a moment doubt that an adequate explanation of any phenomenon must refer to precedent conditions. Definition, classification, interpretation, instructions for using, all came to be regarded as auxiliaries to explanation rather than as modes of explanation; justification and excuse-making were wholly excluded from enquiry; the mere removal of misconceptions was not dignified with the name of explanation. Physicists, indeed, came to suggest that their concern lies with functional relations rather than with causal relations; such an equation as $P_1 V_1 = P_2 V_2$, they pointed out, makes no reference to precedent conditions. But by itself it does not explain, either; and when it is used as an ingredient in an explanation— to explain why, for example, the volume of gas in a pump diminishes—the explanation is of a causal character. At the very least, one can say, the scientific assumption has been that explanation always consists in using a general law as a means of explaining the behavior of a particular case or kind of case.

Historians have not been so restricted or restrictive. They regard themselves as "explaining" *how* Rome was supplied with water, *what* a phrase in mediaeval law means, *that* Socrates' attitude to his wife was "common form" in Athens, as well as *why* Luther's revolt against the Roman Catholic Church was supported by the German Princes. Often enough, they count justifying as explaining; and if they detail the route taken by the British detachment from Boston to Lexington, consider themselves as "explaining" how it got there. . . .

Science, of course, developed out of our everyday activities. There were explanations, as there was proof, long before there was science. Nor has the connection with everyday procedures been entirely lost; the scientist, too, looks for an explanation when he is puzzled and tries, in his explanations, to remove that puzzlement. In important respects, however, he sets out to realize what, in everyday experience, only appears as an ideal limit.

Take first the case of intelligibility. The scientist has a great deal to do with changing our standards of intelligibility; he educates us into accepting explanations of weather-changes which refer to pressure systems, or explanations of disease which refer to viruses and bacteria. But he begins, as often as not, by taking as unintelligible, as being in need of an explanation, what seems to us already to be satisfactorily clear. In this sense, Karl Popper is right when, in opposition to the view (strongly supported by what we have so far said) that explanation derives the unfamiliar from the familiar, he argues that scientific explanation proceeds from the familiar to the unfamiliar.

Thus we are not ordinarily puzzled in the slightest degree by the fact that if a porcelain vase is dropped from a height on to a hard floor it will break. That is just a familiar brute fact, which we use in explaining why a particular ornament has broken, but do not feel under any obligation to explain. The scientist, on the other hand, may begin to wonder why the vase breaks; not in the sense of wondering how this particular vase comes to get broken, but, rather, why porcelain vases break when dropped and metal vases do not. Very soon, indeed, he completely loses interest in the fate of our favourite vase—although its mishap might happen to be the stimulus which led him to reflect about fragility. The vase is transformed into a particular structure of molecules; our dropping it and the solid floor are expressed as forces. So, when the physical scientist explains why the vase breaks when we drop it, he no longer refers to familiar forms of connection between everyday objects—propositions like "the floor is hard" do not appear in his explanations—but to unfamiliar relations between unfamiliar objects. Indeed, unless we have been specially trained, the scientist's explanation will mean nothing to us. We understand a man who tells us a picture appears on the television screen because he pushed a button, but all this talk about ionized particles. . . .

The scientist often works with quite special conceptions of intelligibility. Very often he presumes, in the fashion traditional to rationalistic philosophies, that some form of connection is intrinsically intelligible and that all explanations ought to exhibit one of these intrinsically-intelligible forms. For example, in everyday life explanations very often refer to ends or purposes; over considerable periods of human history this, indeed, has been the "normal form" of intelligible explanations. The Platonic-Aristotelian reaction against Milesian science tried to establish the teleological form of explanation as the truly intelligible pattern for science. The general tendency of science, however—although with powerful resistance from within biology— has been to argue that this sort of connection is not really intelligible; that a thing's "purpose" consists in certain of the effects which its activities produce (or, in the case of human action, which they set out to produce), and that it is unintelligible to suggest that these effects, or attempted effects, explain the activities themselves. Thus, whereas in everyday life it is quite natural to reply to the question: "Why did Jane go to town?" with the answer: "To buy a new hat," a "really intelligible" explanation, on this view, will refer to the stimulus of an advertisement, or of the sight of her neighbor's new hat, operating upon a Jane conceived of either as a mechanism of response or as a field of forces. Jane's going to town and her buying a hat will now be considered as stages in the response to a stimulus; they will not be related as explicandum to explanation.

There are very good reasons for taking this view: it is, indeed, unintelligible to suggest that something that might not exist at all (for the hat might not be bought) can be an explanation of something that does happen (the trip to town). Of course, in everyday life, when the psychologist is asked why his wife has gone to town, he will continue to reply: "To buy a hat," and will expect to be understood; just as the biologist might, when asked by his children why men have two eyes, explain that it enables them to tell more precisely where objects are; or the physicist, asked why the vase breaks, and the saucepan does not, might reply that the vase if fragile. In each case however, he would think that he had not given the "real" explanation, but only a rough-and-ready clue to the real explanation. . . .

Now, at last, for history. In an article mainly addressed to the historian, the delay in reaching my proper purpose may seem to be both interminable and unjustifiable. It is deliberate; for, as I began by suggesting, very many of the difficulties and controversies which have recently emerged in the discussions of explanation in history flow from underlying misconceptions about the nature of explanation in general. The historian who is genuinely interested in the philosophy of history will have to widen his interests to consider many of the traditional problems of philosophy.

Unlike the scientist, the historian cannot presume that his audience, even when he is writing only for fellow-historians, is acquainted with any general principles which are usable as explanations, except such as are familiar to every educated man. Studying history does not consist in learning novel general propositions, but rather in becoming acquainted in depth with a particular historical period. The historian may know, as other people do not know, just what was the state of the English monasteries at the time of the Reformation or just what changes occurred during the composition of the Declaration of Independence; he would be delighted to know "what song the sirens sang, and what name Achilles took when he hid amongst the women"; but he is seldom a great reader of theoretical works. It is true that there are certain sorts of generalization of which the historian is master; but they are generalizations with a very limited range, propositions like: "In the Edinburgh of the early eighteenth century, it was still unsafe publicly to express unorthodox views on theology," which may be used to explain the cautious behavior of some particular critic of Christianity. But as for general propositions not thus limited in time and space, he has none of his own to deploy. Thus his standards of intelligibility are precisely those of the ordinary man; he presumes only such general modes of connection as are already familiar in everyday life. The general reader, attempting to read a major contribution to history, may find himself bored by the detail, but the explanatory principles involved, the arguments employed, the transitions from point to point, will certainly not bewilder him, as he will almost certainly be bewildered by any major contribution to science.

The historian's explanations, again, are couched in wholly familiar terms. The physicist transforms the wind, the curtain, the vase, the wooden floor into masses, velocities, accelerations; for the traditional historian, as for the ordinary man, they are the wind, the curtain, the vase, the wooden floor. The Marxists, indeed, set out to transform history in this respect; social and personal actions were to be transformed into productive forces, social institutions into productive relations. Tolstoy, I suppose, anticipated a similar transformation when, in *War and Peace,* he suggested that the historian should explain historical occurrences by referring to "the common, infinitesimally small elements by which the masses are moved." But no "scientific history," in this sense of the phrase, has yet recommended itself to the general body of historians. They still talk in terms of people, of parties, of States; neither explanation nor explicandum is represented as a complex of unfamiliar concepts.

Nowadays, no doubt, the historian may use economic or psychological explanations. He may write, for example, that "as a result of the sharp rise in interest rates, there was considerable unemployment"; but this is only because he thinks he can now presume that this mode of connection is familiar to his readers. (As, on the other side, even the most devout of historians do not now explain historical events in terms of the intervention of supernatural forces.) It is not the historian's job to defend an economic theory, in the sense in which it certainly is his concern to show that on some particular occasion there was in fact a rise in interest rates, or that there was in fact unemployment. Whether he be a narrative historian like Wedgwood or Runciman, or a cross-sectional historian like Huizinga, he will not wish to pause in his historical exposition in order to justify the use of a particular mode of connection in his explanations.

On the side of adequacy much the same is true; the historian will not, in general, be fussier than his fellow-men. He will explain the Duke of Guise's death as being the result of an assassin's stab, although he knows that not all stab wounds kill. The man certainly was stabbed, he certainly died, and it is natural to presume, unless there is some special reason for believing to the contrary, that the wound was of the kind that kills. Perhaps his associates took advantage of his helpless state to kill him off in some other way; but such abstract possibilities do not generally disturb the sleep of historians.

The fact that the historian is not in general predicting, or retrodicting, but already knows the facts and is simply connecting them in familiar ways, makes it possible for him to be somewhat casual. However, if he knows that the Duke of Guise was stabbed, but can only deduce that he died; or knows he died, but not from what cause, much more caution and detail will be necessary, and he will feel the need for stricter general principles. For example, economics, in theory, can be of particular usefulness to the historian because, with its help, he can sometimes infer the existence of economic phenomena which were not, in times less conscious of economic questions, specifically recorded; and then use them in explanation of other, recorded, phenomena. But few historians, in practice, happily engage in reasoning of this sort, unless they are what, perhaps significantly, are ordinarily described as "pre-historians"; they generally do not care to infer that, say, popular discontent was increased by a rise in prices if that rise in prices cannot be actually documented.

Suppose a historian is faced by some such puzzle as why the belief in witchcraft declined so rapidly in the latter half of the seventeenth century. How does he set about explaining it? If he is writing a summarized text, he may content himself with such a near-tautology as the explanation that men lost their belief in witchcraft "because they became more enlightened." But in general he prefers to present a picture, in considerable detail, of the way in which this man or that (generally described as "typical") came to change his beliefs. By looking carefully at such an instance, or a few such instances, we are to "see" what happened. In part, the historian prefers this mode of presentation because—and this fact must be kept firmly in mind—the historian *likes* detail, otherwise he could never endure to be an historian. His readers like it, too, otherwise they would not be reading history. Listen to an historian's conversation, or his contributions to a faculty meeting; it will soon be apparent that the anecdotal development of a particular case rather than the enunciation of a general principle is his natural mode of communicating his thoughts, especially when he is thinking at his best. Like a novelist, he helps us to see how a change occurred, by showing it in process; in so doing he appeals to our sense of what connections are "natural", not to unfamiliar principles. He relies upon our agreeing, for example, that men will prefer courses of action which make them more powerful, or wealthier, or which bring preferment for their family, unless they have peculiarities of character which the historian will then have to bring out descriptively. That matters could not have happened otherwise, he could rarely show us, and does not need to. Generally speaking, he knows what happened and has only the task of emphasizing the moments in its development which, we shall agree, were particularly significant. Which moments were significant, only our experience can tell us; we believe that it "matters", in understanding Burke's political career, how his speeches were received in the House of Commons, but not what he ordinarily ate for breakfast. . . .

 For the most part, then, there is nothing much to say about historical explanation; nothing that cannot be said about explanation in everyday life. Scientific explanation is the peculiar thing—the odd-man-out—in the general use of explanation; peculiar in its overriding concern with what is only, from the historian's as from the everyday point of view, one type of explanation; in its search for strictly necessary and sufficient conditions which can be formulated as equations; in its transformation of its subject matter; in its setting up of certain patterns of explanation is peculiarly intelligible. Most of the time, of course, the historian is not even attempting to explain, as the scientist understands explanation. He is telling us what happened on some interesting occasion, as we might describe our adventures on a trip abroad— except that the occasion will be an important moment in the development of a society. Or he is picturing for us the state of society at a given time, trying to portray what Huizinga calls "the picture of an age." Occasionally something he says will be puzzling, or he thinks it might puzzle us, and so he suggests an explanation which will have that sort of adequacy and intelligibility we expect in everyday life.

Very often an explanation will have already been offered by contemporary witnesses; these may disagree or, perhaps, their explanation will be of the sort we do not now regard as intelligible or adequate. Then the historian may suggest an alternative explanation, based on a careful discussion of the detail in the original document. Only in this respect, in his skill in handling documents, does he differ notably from the ordinary narrator. Even that skill is more often directed towards finding out what actually happened than towards an explanation of it. It is all very casual and informal; no wonder historians are often puzzled to know what philosophers of history are fussing about! In fact, however, it often becomes too casual, too informal, too uninformed about, say, the discoveries of anthropologists, economists, or psychologists (all of whom the historian, in England especially, often regards with the darkest suspicion). The historian can at least be expected to consider how far new theoretical work bears on his habits of explanation; and he does not always live up to that level. What we cannot expect of him is that he should adopt the standards of the physicist or of the physiologist.

For his task has no relation to theirs; he is not attempting to develop a body of theory, but to show us something about the way in which a particular course of events developed.

SUGGESTED READINGS

. Hempel's views have been presented in numerous essays, most of which have now been collected into a single volume, *Aspects of Scientific Explanation*. He has also written an introductory *Philosophy of Science*, which deals with this as well as other problems. K. Popper's account of explanation may be found in Section 12 of *The Logic of Scientific Discovery*. In Chapters 2 and 3 of *The Structure of Science* E. Nagel presents a thorough discussion of most of the issues connected with the nature of explanation.

Numerous books deal with various aspects of explanation: I. Scheffler, *Anatomy of Inquiry*, Part I, is particularly good. He has also written an article criticising Hempel: "Explanation, Prediction, and Abstraction," which is reprinted in A. Danto and S. Morgenbesser, *Philosophy of Science*. On a similar topic, M. Scriven's "The Temporal Asymmetry of Explanation and Prediction" in *Delaware Studies in the Philosophy of Science*, Volume I, edited by B. Baumrin, is valuable though not easy. A. Grünbaum deals with some of these and other problems in "Temporally Asymmetric Principles, Parity between Explanation and Prediction, and Mechanism vs. Teleology," in *Philosophy of Science*, XXIX (1962). There is an interesting and suggestive approach to a different sort of view on explanation in S. Bromberger, "Why Questions," in *Mind and Cosmos*, edited by R. Colodny.

Various attempts have been made to discuss the problem of explanation from the point of view of social rather than natural science. R. Brown, *Explanation in Social Science*, and Q. Gibson, *The Logic of Social Inquiry*, are two examples, neither entirely successful. M. Natanson's *Philosophy of the Social Sciences* is a useful anthology, with articles from a phenomenological approach as well as more analytically oriented writings.

B. Historical Explanation

Historians explain, or seem to explain, why events happened in certain ways and not in others. This fact must itself be accounted for by a fully adequate theory of explanation, yet it poses a special problem for theories drawn from the types of explanations used in the physical sciences. Scientists are interested in establishing and accounting for laws and other regularities and recurrences and historians are interested in establishing and accounting for particular events. The apparent difference has given rise to one of the most important contemporary controversies concerning historical explanation.

COLLINGWOOD, himself a professional historian, insists that the methods of acquiring knowledge of history are unlike those used to obtain knowledge of the nonhuman world. We can only understand a human action by coming to know the thoughts of the agent. But this way of understanding what happens is not available for use in accounting for, say, earthquakes or atomic disintegration. Collingwood argues that when we have come to understand a man's action by knowing the particular thoughts that led him to do it, we do not need any further explanation: in particular, we do not need to subsume the action under any general laws that would explain a number of similar actions. Human action can be understandable even though it is unique.

JOYNT and RESCHER disagree with this view. Adopting what is essentially the Hempel-Oppenheim model of scientific explanation, they argue that simple, law-like generalities are available for and indispensable to an understanding of human action. They try to show how such laws are actually used by historians for the explanation of particular facts.

The Uniqueness of Historical Thought

R. G. COLLINGWOOD [1889–1943]. See p. 18.

What history is, what it is about, how it proceeds, and what it is for, are questions which to some extent different people would answer in different ways. But in spite of differences there is a large measure of agreement between the answers. . . .

(a) *The definition of history.* Every historian would agree, I think, that

* From R. G. Collingwood, *The Idea of History*, Oxford: at The Clarendon Press, 1946. Reprinted by permission of The Clarendon Press, Oxford.

history is a kind of research or inquiry. What kind of inquiry it is I do not yet ask. The point is that generically it belongs to what we call the sciences: that is, the forms of thought whereby we ask questions and try to answer them. Science in general, it is important to realize, does not consist in collecting what we already know and arranging it in this or that kind of pattern. It consists in fastening upon something we do not know, and trying to discover it. Playing patience with things we already know may be a useful means towards this end, but it is not the end itself. It is at best only the means. It is scientifically valuable only in so far as the new arrangement gives us the answer to a question we have already decided to ask. That is why all science begins from the knowledge of our own ignorance: not our ignorance of everything, but our ignorance of some definite thing—the origin of parliament, the cause of cancer, the chemical composition of the sun, the way to make a pump work without muscular exertion on the part of a man or a horse or some other docile animal. Science is finding things out: and in that sense history is a science.

(b) *The object of history.* One science differs from another in that it finds out things of a different kind. What kind of things does history find out? I answer, *res gestae:* actions of human beings that have been done in the past. Although this answer raises all kinds of further questions many of which are controversial, still, however they may be answered, the answers do not discredit the proposition that history is the science of *res gestae,* the attempt to answer questions about human actions done in the past.

(c) *How does history proceed?* History proceeds by the interpretation of evidence: where evidence is a collective name for things which singly are called documents, and a document is a thing existing here and now, of such a kind that the historian, by thinking about it, can get answers to the questions he asks about past events. Here again there are plenty of difficult questions to ask as to what the characteristics of evidence are and how it is interpreted. But there is no need for us to raise them at this stage. However they are answered, historians will agree that historical procedure, or method, consists essentially of interpreting evidence.

(d) Lastly, *what is history for?* This is perhaps a harder question than the others; a man who answers it will have to reflect rather more widely than a man who answers the three we have answered already. He must reflect not only on historical thinking but on other things as well, because to say that something is 'for' something implies a distinction between A and B, where A is good for something and B is that for which something is good. But I will suggest an answer, and express the opinion that no historian would reject it, although the further questions to which it gives rise are numerous and difficult.

My answer is that history is 'for' human self-knowledge. It is generally thought to be of importance to man that he should know himself: where knowing himself means knowing not his merely personal peculiarities, the things that distinguish him from other men, but his nature as man. Knowing yourself means knowing, first, what it is to be a man; secondly, knowing what it is to be the kind of man you are; and thirdly, knowing what it is to be the man *you* are and nobody else is. Knowing yourself means knowing what you can do; and since nobody knows what he can do until he tries, the only clue to what man can do is what man has done. The value of history, then, is that it teaches us what man has done and thus what man is. . . .

THE SCIENCE OF HUMAN NATURE. Man, who desires to know everything, desires to know himself. Nor is he only one (even if, to himself, perhaps the most interesting) among the things he desires to know. Without some knowledge of himself, his knowledge of other things is imperfect: for to know something without knowing that one knows it is only a half-knowing, and to know that one knows is to know oneself. Self-knowledge is desirable and important to man, not only for its own sake, but as a condition without which no other knowledge can be critically justified and securely based.

Self-knowledge, here, means not knowledge of man's bodily nature, his anatomy and physiology; nor even a knowledge of his mind, so far as that consists of feeling, sensation, and emotion; but a knowledge of his knowing faculties, his thought or understanding or reason. How is such knowledge to be attained? It seems an easy matter until we think seriously about it; and then it seems so difficult that we are tempted to think it impossible. Some have even reinforced this temptation by argument, urging that the mind, whose business it is to know other things, has for that very reason no power of knowing itself. But this is open sophistry: first you say what the mind's nature is, and then you say that because it has this nature no one can know that it has it. Actually, the argument is a counsel of despair, based on recognizing that a certain attempted method of studying the mind has broken down, and on failure to envisage the possibility of any other.

It seems a fair enough proposal that, in setting out to understand the nature of our own mind, we should proceed in the same way as when we try to understand the world about us. In studying the world of nature, we begin by getting acquainted with the particular things and particular events that exist and go on there; then we proceed to understand them, by seeing how they fall into general types and how these general types are interrelated. These interrelations we call laws of nature; and it is by ascertaining such laws that we understand the things and events to which they apply. The same method, it might seem, is applicable to the problem of understanding mind. Let us begin by observing, as carefully as possible, the ways in which our own minds and those of others behave under given circumstances; then, having become acquainted with these facts of the mental world, let us try to establish the laws which govern them.

Here is a proposal for a 'science of human nature' whose principles and methods are conceived on the analogy of those used in the natural sciences. . . .

It was no doubt inevitable that in the seventeenth and eighteenth centuries, dominated as they were by the new birth of physical science, the eternal problem of self-knowledge should take shape as the problem of constructing a science of human nature. To any one reviewing the field of human research, it was evident that physics stood out as a type of inquiry which had discovered the right method of investigating its proper object, and it was right that the experiment should be made of extending this method to every kind of problem. But since then a great change has come over the intellectual atmosphere of our civilization. The dominant factor in this change has not been the development of other natural sciences like chemistry and biology, or the transformation of physics itself since more began to be known about electricity, or the progressive application of all these new ideas to manufacture and industry, important though these have been; for in principle they have done nothing that might not have been foreseen as implicit in seventeenth-century physics itself. The really new element in the thought of today as compared with that of three centuries ago is the rise of history. . . .

THE FIELD OF HISTORICAL THOUGHT. I must begin by attempting to delimit the proper sphere of historical knowledge as against those who, maintaining the historicity of all things, would resolve all knowledge into historical knowledge. Their argument runs in some such way as this.

The methods of historical research have, no doubt, been developed in application to the history of human affairs: but is that the limit of their applicability? They have already before now undergone important extensions: for example, at one time historians had worked out their methods of critical interpretation only as applied to written sources containing narrative material, and it was a new thing when they learnt to apply them to the unwritten data provided by archaeology. Might not a similar but even more revolutionary extension sweep into the historian's net the entire world of nature? . . .

If we put this question to the ordinary historian, he will answer it in the negative. According to him, all history properly so called is the history of human affairs. His special technique, depending as it does on the interpretation of documents in which human beings of the past have expressed or betrayed their thoughts, cannot be applied just as it stands to the study of natural processes; and the more this technique is elaborated in its details, the farther it is from being so applicable. There is a certain analogy between the archaeologist's interpretation of a stratified site and the geologist's interpretation of rock-horizons with their associated fossils; but he difference is no less clear than the similarity. The archaeologist's use of his stratified relics depends on his conceiving them as artifacts serving human purposes and thus expressing a particular way in which men have thought about their own life; and from his point of view the palaeontologist, arranging his fossils in a time-series, is not working as an historian, but only as a scientist thinking in a way which can at most be described as quasi-historical.

Upholders of the doctrine under examination would say that here the historian is making an arbitrary distinction between things that are really the same, and that his conception of history is an unphilosophically narrow one, restricted by the imperfect development of his technique; very much as some historians, because their equipment was inadequate to studying the history of art or science or economic life, have mistakenly restricted the field of historical thought to the history of politics. The question must therefore be raised, why do historians habitually identify history with the history of human affairs? In order to answer this question, it is not enough to consider the characteristics of historical method as it actually exists, for the question at issue is whether, as it actually exists, it covers the whole field which properly belongs to it. We must ask what is the general nature of the problems which this method is designed to solve. When we have done so, it will appear that the special problem of the historian is one which does not arise in the case of natural science.

The historian, investigating any event in the past, makes a distinction between what may be called the outside and the inside of an event. By the outside of the event I mean everything belonging to it which can be described in terms of bodies and their movements: the passage of Caesar, accompanied by certain men, across a river called the Rubicon at one date, or the spilling of his blood on the floor of the senate-house at another. By the inside of the event I mean that in it which can only be described in terms of thought: Caesar's defiance of Republican law, or the clash of constitutional policy between himself and his assassins. The historian is never concerned with either of these to the exclusion of the other. He is _investigating not mere events_ (where by a mere event I mean one which has only an outside and no inside) but actions, and an action is the unity of the outside and inside of an event. He is interested in the crossing of the Rubicon only in its relation to Republican law, and in the spilling of Caesar's blood only in its relation to a constitutional conflict. His work may begin by discovering the outside of an event, but it can never end there; he must always remember that the event was an action, and that his main task is to think himself into this action, to discern the thought of its agent.

In the case of nature, this distinction between the outside and the inside of an event does not arise. The events of nature are mere events, not the acts of agents whose thought the scientist endeavours to trace. It is true that the scientist, like the historian, has to go beyond the mere discovery of events; but the direction in which he moves is very different. Instead of conceiving the event as an action and attempting to rediscover the thought of his agent, penetrating from the outside of the event to its inside, the scientist goes beyond the event, observes its relation to others, and thus brings it under a general formula or law of nature. To the scientist, nature is always and merely a 'phenomenon,' not in the sense of being defective in reality, but in the sense of being a spectacle presented to his intelligent observation; whereas the events of history are never mere phenomena, never mere spectacles for contemplation, but things which the historian looks, not at, but through, to discern the thought within them.

In thus penetrating to the inside of events and detecting the thought which they express, the historian is doing something which the scientist need not and cannot do. In this way the task of the historian is more complex than that of the scientist. In another way it is simpler: the historian need not and cannot (without ceasing to be an historian) emulate the scientist in searching for the causes or laws of events. For science, the event is discovered by perceiving it, and the further search for its cause is conducted by assigning it to its class and determining the relation between that class and others. For history, the object to be discovered is not the mere event, but the thought expressed in it. To discover that thought is already to understand it. After the historian has ascertained the facts, there is no further process of inquiring into their causes. When he knows what happened, he already knows why it happened.

This does not mean that words like 'cause' are necessarily out of place in reference to history; it only means that they are used there in a special sense. When a scientist asks 'Why did that piece of litmus paper turn pink?' he means 'On what kinds of occasions do pieces of litmus paper turn pink?' When an historian asks 'Why did Brutus stab Caesar?' he means 'What did Brutus think, which made him decide to stab Caesar?' The cause of the event, for him, means the thought in the mind of the person by whose agency the event came about: and this is not something other than the event, it is the inside of the event itself.

The processes of nature can therefore be properly described as sequences of mere events, but those of history cannot. They are not processes of mere events but processes of actions, which have an inner side, consisting of processes of thought; and what the historian is looking for is these processes of thought. All history is the history of thought.

But how does the historian discern the thoughts which he is trying to discover? There is only one way in which it can be done: by re-thinking them in his own mind. The historian of philosophy, reading Plato, is trying to know what Plato thought when he expressed himself in certain words. The only way in which he can do this is by thinking it for himself. This, in fact, is what we mean when we speak of 'understanding' the words. So the historian of politics or warfare, presented with an account of certain actions done by Julius Caesar, tries to understand these actions, that is, to discover what thoughts in Caesar's mind determined him to do them. This implies envisaging for himself the situation in which Caesar stood, and thinking for himself what Caesar thought about the situation and the possible ways of dealing with it. The history of thought, and therefore all history, is the re-enactment of past thought in the historian's own mind.

This re-enactment is only accomplished, in the case of Plato and Caesar respectively, so far as the historian brings to bear on the problem all the powers of his own mind and all his knowledge of philosophy and politics. It is not a passive surrender to the spell of another's mind; it is a labour of active and therefore critical thinking. The historian not only re-enacts past thought, he re-enacts it in the context of his own knowledge and therefore, in re-enacting it, criticizes it, forms his own judgement of its value, corrects whatever errors he can discern in it. This criticism of the thought whose history he traces is not something secondary to tracing the history of it. It is an indispensable condition of the historical knowledge itself. Nothing could be a completer error concerning the history of thought than to suppose that the historian as such merely ascertains, 'what so-and-so thought,' leaving it to some one else to decide 'whether it was true.' All thinking is critical thinking; the thought which re-enacts past thoughts, therefore, criticizes them in re-enacting them.

It is now clear why historians habitually restrict the field of historical knowledge to human affairs. A natural process is a process of events, an historical process is a process of thoughts. Man is regarded as the only subject of historical process, because man is regarded as the only animal that thinks, or thinks enough, and clearly enough, to render his actions the expressions of his thoughts. The belief that man is the only animal that thinks at all is no doubt a superstition; but the belief that man thinks more, and more continuously and effectively, than any other animal, and is the only animal whose conduct is to any great extent determined by thought instead of by mere impulse and appetite, is probably well enough founded to justify the historian's rule of thumb.

It does not follow that all human actions are subject-matter for history; and indeed historians are agreed that they are not. But when they are asked how the distinction is to be made between historical and non-historical human actions, they are somewhat at a loss how to reply. From our present point of view we can offer an answer: so far as man's conduct is determined by what may be called his animal nature, his impulses and appetites, it is non-historical; the process of those activities is a natural process. Thus, the historian is not interested in the fact that men eat and sleep and make love and thus satisfy their natural appetites; but he is interested in the social customs which they create by their thought as a framework within which these appetites find satisfaction in ways sanctioned by convention and morality. . . .

Man has been defined as an animal capable of profiting by the experience of others. Of his bodily life this would be wholly untrue: he is not nourished because another has eaten, or refreshed because another has slept. But as regards his mental life it is true; and the way in which this profit is realized is by historical knowledge. The body of human thought or mental activity is a corporate possession, and almost all the operations which our minds perform are operations which we learned to perform from others who have performed them already. Since mind is what it does, and human nature, if it is a name for anything real, is only a name for human activities, this acquisition of ability to perform determinate operations is the acquisition of a determinate human nature. Thus the historical process is a process in which man creates for himself this or that kind of human nature by re-creating in his own thought the past to which he is heir.

The Problem of Uniqueness in History[*]

Carey B. Joynt [1924–   ] is Chairman of the International Relations Department at Lehigh University. He is the author of numerous articles on international affairs and on historical methodology.

Nicholas Rescher [1928–   ] has taught at Princeton and at Lehigh; since 1961 he has been Professor of Philosophy at the University of Pittsburgh and Associate Director of its Center for the Philosophy of Science. He is editor of the *American Philosophical Quarterly* and his written extensively on logic, philosophy of science, and the history of philosophy.

INTRODUCTION. The claim is frequently made that the mode of explanation to be found in history differs radically and fundamentally from the types of explanation found in the natural or social sciences. This difference is said to

[*] From Joynt and Rescher: "The Problem of Uniqueness in History." Reprinted from *History and Theory*, Volume I, Number 2, by permission of Wesleyan University Press. Copyright © 1960 by Wesleyan University.

lie in the fact that history, unlike science, must always deal with "the description of a situation or state of affairs which is unique." It is argued that the exclusive objects of historical understanding are unique, particular, concrete events: the historian, it is contended, is primarily concerned with describing and analyzing the *unique* features of his data, unlike the scientist who looks to the *generic*.

It is the thesis of this paper that such a claim for history (which, when properly understood, contains a large measure of truth) cannot, without severe qualifications, survive objections which can be brought against it. Practicing historians, it is true, sometimes try to defend the claim of history to uniqueness, but as a rule these efforts are swept aside by the critics as special pleading that does not come to grips with the substantive arguments which can be marshalled against them.

In the interests of clarity and truth it should be frankly recognized, to begin with, that, in a significant sense, every particular event whatsoever is unique. . . . That is to say, it would seem to be an elemental fact about the universe that all events whatsoever are unique. Every concrete natural occurrence is unique, even the occurrence of a so-called "recurrent" phenomenon like a sunrise or of "repeatable" events like the melting of a lump of sugar in a teacup.

Events are rendered non-unique *in thought only,* by choosing to use them as examples of a type or class. We refer alike to "an appearance of a comet" or "a sea-fight with sailing ships," and our use of such terms, when examined, suggests that the occurrences of natural history (in the sense of non-human history) do not differ as regards uniqueness from the events of human history. Whether an event is selected for treatment as a unique, concrete particular, or is treated as the non-unique exemplar of a class of events, is essentially a matter of human interest and perspective. Galileo, rolling a ball down an inclined plane treated each roll as identical for it served his purposes so to do, just as an historian speaking of the Black Death could, if he wished, treat each unique death as identical in its contribution to a class of events called "a plague." Like the scientist, the historian resolves the dilemma of uniqueness by the use of a large variety of classes in his discussions: "nations," "wars," "revolutions," "assassinations," "budgets," and the like. The list is endless. It cannot be maintained that the use of such classes sets history apart in that they fail to exhaust the unique structure of a particular person or event, for exactly the same holds true of all scientific classification. Only *some* of the features of a given particular are described in such a classification, and no set of generic classifications could conceivably exhaust the structure of the particular objects or events so described.

Bearing these general but fundamental comments in mind, let us now examine in more detail the claim that history deals, in some sense, with unique events. Three particular areas can be utilized to throw considerable light upon this central problem: the relation of history to the "historical" sciences, the role of generalizations in history, and the requirements of interpretation in history.

THE RELATION OF HISTORY TO THE 'HISTORICAL' SCIENCES. History, it is clear, has no monopoly on the study of the past. The biologist who describes the evolution of life, the sociologist or anthropologist who delves into the development of human organizations and institutions, the philologist who analyzes the growth and change of languages, the geologist who studies the development of our planet, and the physical cosmologist who investigates the evolution of the cosmos, all deal with essentially "historical" questions, that is to say, with the events and occurrences of the past. Many diverse areas of scientific inquiry have the past as the "target" of their researches. It is therefore natural and appropriate to ask: How does history (history proper, i.e., *human* history) differ from these other "historical" sciences?

In attempting a reply to this question, we must recognize that it is simply not enough to insist that history deals with the doings of men in the context of civilized society, however true this remark may be. The bio-medical student of human ecology is also concerned with man and his social environment, and of course anthropologists and sociologists study the activities of men in the context of human institutions, past no less than present. Consequently, there can be no adequate grounds for maintaining that history is to be distinguished from the "historical" sciences on the basis of subject-matter considerations alone.

Nor can a warrant for the distinction be said to inhere in the methodology of research. For here also there is no hard-and-fast barrier of separation between history and the sciences. History conforms fully to the standard hypothetico-deductive paradigm of scientific inquiry, usually described in the following four steps:

1. Examination of the data.
2. Formulation of an explanatory hypothesis.
3. Analysis of the consequences of the hypothesis.
4. Test of these consequences against additional data.

Historical research follows just this pattern: the historian assembles his chronological data, frames an interpretative hypothesis to explain them, examines the consequences of this hypothesis and seeks out the additional data by which the adequacy of this hypothesis can be tested. The universal characteristics of scientific procedure characterize the work of the historian also. And even if the specific form which this generic process takes in history were to differ from that which it assumes in other areas of science in certain points of detail, this would be irrelevant to the matter at issue. Botany has less need for the algebraic theory of matrices than does quantum-mechanics or the economics of production-processes; however, this does not mean that such differences in mathematical requirements can be used as a basis for claiming that these fields can be delimited on methodological grounds.

It thus appears that the definitive characteristics of history are to be found neither in its subject-matter nor in its methods. Does it follow that there is no essential difference between history and the "historical" sciences? Not at all! But to see the precise character of the distinction we must examine closely the relative role of datum and theory, of fact and law in various sciences.

Throughout the various sciences, including all of those sciences which we have here characterized as "historical," we find that the object of the science is the study of a certain range of basic "fact" with a view to the discovery of generalizations, ideally universal laws, which govern the range of phenomena constituting this factual domain. In consequence, particular facts have a strictly *instrumental* status for the sciences. The "facts" serve as data, as means to an end: the law. In the sciences, the particular events that comprise the facts studied play an indispensable but nonetheless strictly subordinate role: the focus of interest is the general law, and the particular fact is simply a means to this end.

In history, on the other hand, this means-end relationship is, in effect, reversed. Unlike the scientist, the historian's interest lies, first and foremost, in the particular facts of his domain. But of course he is not solely interested in historical facts and in describing them. For this is mere chronology, which may constitute the inevitable starting-point for history, but is by no means to be confused with history itself. The historian is not simply interested in dating events and describing them, but in *understanding them*. And "understanding" calls for interpretation, classification, and assessment, which can only be attained by grasping the relationship of causal and conceptual interrelation among the chronological particulars. . . .

It is just at this point that scientific generalizations and laws enter upon the scene. They provide the necessary means for understanding particular facts; they furnish the fundamental patterns of interrelationships that constitute the links through which the functional connections among particular events may be brought to view.

Now if this analysis is correct, it is clear that the historian in effect reverses the means-end relationship between fact and theory that we find in science. For the historian *is* interested in generalizations, and *does* concern himself with them. But he does so not because generalizations constitute the aim and objective of his discipline, but because they help him to illuminate the particular facts with which he deals. History seeks to provide an *understanding of specific occurrences,* and has recourse to such laws and generalizations— largely borrowed from the sciences, but also drawn from ordinary human experience—which can be of service in this enterprise. But here the role of generalizations is strictly instrumental: they provide aids towards understanding particular events. The scientist's means-end relation of facts to laws is thus inverted by the historian.

Correspondingly, the very way in which history concerns itself with the past is quite different from that of the "historical" sciences. The historian is interested in the particular facts regarding the past *for themselves,* and not in an instrumental role as data for laws. Indeed, unlike the researcher in "historical" science, the historian is not a *producer* of general laws, but a *consumer* of them. His position *vis-à-vis* the sciences is essentially parasitic. The generalizations provided by anthropology, sociology, psychology, etc., are used by the historian in the interests of his mission of facilitating our understanding of the past. . . . The difference, then, between history and the "historical" sciences resides neither in subject-matter nor in method, but in the objectives of the research, and the consequent perspective that is taken in looking at the past. History does not collect facts to establish laws; rather, it seeks to exploit laws to explain facts. In this lies part of history's claim to uniqueness.

To obtain a clearer view of this essentially distinctive and characteristic relationship of fact and law in history, it will be necessary to examine more closely the role played by generalizations in history.

THE ROLE OF GENERALIZATIONS IN HISTORY. The question of the role of generalizations in history bears intimately upon the problem of the uniqueness of historical events. Since generalizations must, in the nature of things, deal with *types* or *classes* of events, it follows that they can have pertinence to specific, particular events only insofar as these are typical and classifiable, i.e., just insofar as they are *not* unique. Thus, determination of the extent to which generalizations can play a legitimate and useful role in history offers the best means of pin-pointing those ways in which historical events can properly be said to be "unique."

Perhaps the most famous thesis regarding the role of generalization in history is the doctrine which holds that there is one single grand law governing the fate of nations, empires, civilizations or cultures. On such a view, all of the really major and large-scale transactions of history fall inevitably into one and the same basic pattern. The principal and characteristic function of the historian is to discern and then articulate this supreme generalization which pervades the regularity inherent in the historical process, a procedure familiar to readers, in the present century, through the work of Spengler and Toynbee. On a view of this nature, uniqueness has at best a very restricted role in history, being limited to points of detail, in virtue of the predominant status of the basic pattern of regularity.

In reaction against this kind of thesis, various theorists have taken their position at the very opposite extreme, and have espoused the view that generalization has no place whatever in history. This view may be characterized as "historical nihilism." On this conception, the supreme fact of historical study is the total absence of generalizations from the historical domain. Pervasive uniqueness becomes the order of the day. The historian, it is argued, inevitably deals with non-repeatable particulars. Generalization is not only unwarranted, it drastically impedes all understanding of the data of history.

Our own view lies squarely between these two contrasting positions. The plain fact is that no grand generalization of the "pattern of history" has ever been formulated which is both (1) sufficiently specific to be susceptible to a critical test against the data and (2) sufficiently adequate to survive such a test. Thus it is not, in our judgment, to such a thesis that one can look for an acceptable account of the place of generalization in history. On the other hand, it is demonstrable that failure of the grand generalization approach to history in no way justifies ruling generalizations out of the historical pale. To see why this is so requires a closer look at the role of laws and generalizations in history.

To begin with, it is clear that the historian must make use of the general laws of the sciences. He cannot perform his job heedless of the information provided by science regarding the behavior of his human materials. The teachings of human biology, of medicine, or of psychology can be ignored by the historian only at his own peril. The facts offered by these sciences regarding the mortality and morbidity of men, their physical needs for nourishment, sleep, etc., their psychological make-up, and the like represent essentially unchanging constants in the functioning of the human materials with which history deals. Nor can the physical sciences which describe the behavior of man's environment, again by means of general laws, be ignored by the historian. History must ever be re-written if only because the progress of science leads inescapably to a deepening in our understanding of historical events. And because the general laws of the sciences deal with the fundamental constancies of nature, and not with idiosyncratic particulars, their role in historical understanding is a primary locus for *non-uniqueness* in history.

Going beyond this, it is important to recognize that the general laws of the natural sciences do not constitute the only basis of generalization in history. These sciences give us the characterization of the physical, biological and psychological boundary conditions within which man must inevitably operate. But there are also sets of boundary conditions which stem from man's *cultural* rather than his physical environment. These bring to the scene of historical explanation the general laws of the social sciences, which create further conditions of non-uniqueness.

Nor is this the whole story. We must now consider another mode of generalization that has pivotal importance in historical explanation, namely generalizations which represent not the strictly universal laws to which we are accustomed from the sciences, but *limited* generalizations. Such limited generalizations are rooted in *transitory regularities,* deriving from the existence of temporally restricted technological or institutional patterns. Some explanation regarding these is in order.

In any given state of technological development, various definite rules can be laid down regarding the performance of various functions within this particular state of technology. An example from the history of military technology may help to clarify this. Consider the statement: "In the seafights of sailing vessels in the period of 1653–1805, large formations were too cumbersome for effectual control as single units." On first view, this statement might seem to be a mere descriptive list of characteristics of certain particular engagements: a shorthand version of a long conjunction of statements about large-scale engagements during the century and a half from Texel (1653) to Trafalgar (1805). This view is incorrect, however, because the statement in question is more than an assertion regarding the characteristics of certain actual engagements. Unlike mere description, it is a true generalization in that it can serve to explain developments in cases to which it makes no reference. Furthermore, the statement has counterfactual force. It asserts that in literally any large-scale fleet action fought under the conditions in question (sailing vessels of certain types, with particular modes of armament, and with then extant communications methods) effectual control of a great battle line is hopeless. It is claimed, for example, that had Villeneuve issued from Cadiz some days earlier or later he would all the same have encountered difficulty in the management of the great allied battle fleet of over thirty sail of the line, and Nelson's stratagem of dividing his force into two virtually independent units under prearranged plans would have facilitated effective management equally well as at Trafalgar.

The statement in question is thus no mere descriptive summary of particular events; it functions on the more general plane of law-like statements in that it can serve as a basis for explanation, and exert counterfactual force. To be sure, the relevant individual descriptive statements which are known do provide a part of the appropriate evidence for the historical generalization. But the content of the statement itself lies beyond the sphere of mere description, and in taking this wider role historical generalizations become marked as genuine law-like statements.

Nevertheless, such historical generalizations are not unrestricted or universal in the manner in which the laws of the physical sciences are, i.e., they are not valid for all times and places. An historical generalization is limited, either tacitly or expressly, to applicability within specific geographic and temporal bounds. Usually, historical generalizations are formulated by explicit use of proper names: names of places, of groups of persons, of periods of time, of customs or institutions, of systems of technology, of culture, or the like. The restriction of application in such cases is overt in the formulation of the law. Sometimes, however, such limited generalizations are formulated as unconditionally universal statements. But in such cases the statement properly interpreted takes on a conditional form of such a kind that its applicability is *de facto* tightly restricted. If sailing ships and contemporary naval technology and ordnance *were* reinstated, the tactical principles developed from the time of Tromp and de Ruyter to that of Rodney and Nelson would prove valid guidance. But the applicability of these tactical principles is conditional upon the fulfillment of conditions which cannot reasonably be expected to recur. (This is not true of certain experimental situations in physics like the Michelson-Morley experiment—which merely are rarely repeated.) It is clear that analogous examples of limited generalizations can be drawn from every field of technology: production, agriculture, communication, resource exploitation, medical practice, etc. And such technology-based generalizations will inevitably be of limited scope, being valid for only a particular period and era.

A second major source of limited generalizations is constituted by the entire sphere of institutional practices. Social customs, legal and political institutions, economic organization, and other institutional areas, all constitute sources of such limited generalizations. Thus a limited generalization can be based, for example, upon the U.S. practices of holding a presidential election every four years, and a population census every ten. Here again we have regularities which are limited, in temporal (and of course geographic) scope to an era during which certain fundamental institutional practices are relatively constant. Such institutional patterns will of course be of immense value to the historian in providing an explanation for the relevant events. He will seek to discover such institutional regularities precisely because they afford him the means to an explanation of occurrences. Events within a limited period can be understood and explained in terms of the limited generalizations which capture the particular institutional structure of this era. And the existence of institutionalized patterns of regularity again makes for a limitation upon the extent to which "uniqueness" obtains with respect to the data with which the historian deals.

It should be noted, however, that the utilization in historical explanations of limited generalizations based upon reference to temporary technological and institutional eras does not provide the basis for a fundamental separation between history and the natural sciences. Such reliance upon transitory regularities does not make a place for uniqueness in history in any absolute sense. After all, the past stages of biological and cosmological evolution are also non-repetitive. And thus the "historical" departments of the natural sciences must also deal with non-recurring eras. And in these domains, limited generalizations can—and sometimes are—also formulated. But as a rule the scientist is concerned with such limited regularities only as a way-station en route to the universal laws which are the main focus of his interest, and therefore tends, by and large, to be relatively aloof to the peculiarly limited generalizations which also could be formulated for his domain. But the historian, whose interest must focus upon the understanding of particular events and not the formulation of universal generalizations, has a much larger stake in limited generalizations.

The upshot of the present analysis of the role of generalizations in history can thus be summarized as follows. History must and does use generalizations: first as a consumer of scientific laws, secondly as a producer of limited generalizations formulated in the interests of its explanatory mission and its focus upon specific particulars. The use of all of these types of generalizations in history is indispensable for the historian's discharge of his interpretative mission. Interpretation demands that he be able to spell out the linkages of causation and of influence between events, and this can only be done in the light of connecting generalizations. To see this more clearly, and to attain a fuller perspective of the place of interpretation in history, we turn now to an analysis of what is involved in historical interpretation.

THE REQUIREMENTS OF INTERPRETATION IN HISTORY. The considerations so far brought forward do not, however, fully meet the hard core of the claim so clearly and forcefully stated by Dray that "historical events and conditions are often unique simply in the sense of being different from others with *which it would be natural to group them under a classification term*" so that the historian is "almost invariably concerned with [an event] as *different* from other members of its class." Thus the thesis claiming a characteristic role for uniqueness in history is based in the final analysis upon the assertion that historical events are "unique" in the sense that *all* classifications used will fail at a critical juncture to illuminate adequately the event in question, since the event differs in its essential characteristics from its associates in these classes.

This claim of Dray's contains a vital element of truth, but it would be an error to press this thesis too far. The sad fact is that a history composed of strictly non-repeatable occurrences would be mere chronicle. Any efforts to establish connections among events, and to exhibit their mutual relevance and significance would be excluded by a strict application of Dray's dictum. But, of course, history deals not only with what has happened, but with the assessment of the significance of what has occurred. The historian is interested in Napoleon not only as a person with a unique assemblage of characteristics, but as the leader of a national group in a crucial period of its history. The moment one leaves the bare statement of brute fact and occurrence, and turns to interpretation, stark and atomic uniqueness is necessarily left behind. Interpretation and explanation force the historian to become involved in the problem of causation, and hence to abandon uniqueness. . . .

The wide divide separating a mere narrative chronicle from an historical account proper can best be illustrated by an example. Consider the following narrative: "On July 28, 1914 Austria-Hungary declared war on Serbia. On July 30 the Russians ordered general mobilization. On August 1 Germany declared war on Russia and on August 3 on France. The British declaration of war occurred on August 14, 1914."

As it stands this is mere narrative, in that it confines itself to a bare recital of events. In its stark nakedness it deals only with brute fact. It is a mere skeleton, lifeless, and by itself possessed of only small meaning and significance. Yet it presents within its few lines the beginnings of a tragedy which, before its end, shook the civilized world to its very foundations.

For such a passage to acquire meaning and significance—in order for it to become history—the events described must be interpreted and explained. A perusal of adequate historical accounts based on these events, whatever final form they assume, will be found to deal with a wide variety of patterns involving both generalizations and general notions in the explanation they seek to provide. Thus in our example, the events will be portrayed in terms of the balance of power, rival alliance systems, the impact of military men upon civilian leaders, the problems of cohesion in a nation-state, and the problems of decision-making under conditions of radical uncertainty, to name but a few. If one examines a detailed account of how the government of one state alone viewed the decision to act or to stand aside, a fascinating picture emerges of men weighing anxiously the news arriving in the diplomatic telegrams, deeply divided as to their best course of action on grounds both practical and moral, and finally when the invasion of Belgium had begun, presenting its decisions for ratification or rejection before the institution of Parliament to which it was responsible.

An examination of any satisfactory historical account of a series of events shows clearly the indispensable role played by categories, classifications and generalizations (whether universal or limited in range). Such concepts will contribute in two main ways to the reconstruction of events by the historian.

In the first place, the concepts enable the historian to *select* important and relevant facts from the infinite number of facts which are available to him. It often occurs that the body of pertinent fact is overwhelming in scope, and that the task of the historian requires judicious selection. . . .

Secondly, such generic concepts have particular importance for the *explanation* of the events in question. Their use essentially determines the meaning and significance of the account which finally emerges from the historian's efforts. They are, in short, absolutely crucial to the attempt of the historian to interpret his material, to raise it above the level of narrative and chronology to the status of true history. By utilizing, in the example cited above, the concepts of alliance systems, and of the organizational role of the military in their impact upon civilian statesmen, the historian can demonstrate that France believed the Triple Entente was necessary to her survival as a Great Power, and that Germany's policy decisions were heavily influenced by the general strategy of the Schlieffen plan. In this way, definite causal patterns are erected through the use of general concepts. Similarly, it can be demonstrated that the existing technology of the period played a vital part in the eventual decisions of the various powers to order general mobilization, or to issue an ultimatum to their opponents to cease such a procedure lest war follow. Here then we find limited generalizations serving to delineate the institutional boundary conditions under which men operated, enabling the historian to set up a general pattern into which particular events can be fitted and from which certain definite conclusions can justifiably be derived.

There can be little doubt that the use of categories, classes, and generalizations are absolutely essential to, and perform a vital function for, the adequate discharge of the historian's task. Indeed, taken together, they constitute the framework and structure of history, the setting in which the recital of particulars unfolds. They constitute the hard core of explanation and interpretation and, by their presence and the vital nature of the role they play, go a very long way indeed towards qualifying the claim that history deals solely or even primarily with the unique features of particular events.

SUGGESTED READINGS

A theory in some respects similar to Collingwood's is presented in the rather difficult but quite important work by Benedetto Croce, *History, Its Theory and Practice,* translated by D. Ainslee. C. G. Hempel's essay, "The Function of General Laws in History," applies his basic view of explanation to history. This article, originally in the *Journal of Philosophy* (1944), has been reprinted, along with selections from Croce and a great many other writers, in P. Gardiner's anthology, *Theories of History.* The paper by E. Nagel in Part II of that volume is quite useful; it is also to be found in a wide-ranging anthology edited by H. Meyerhoff, *The Philosophy of History in Our Time.* A more recent anthology containing essays written along analytic lines is W. H. Dray's *Philosophical Analysis and History.* All of the essays in it are valuable but difficult.

There have been recently a number of books on the general topic of philosophy of history, and all of these discuss historical explanation. W. H. Dray and W. H. Walsh have both written useful introductory books entitled *Philosophy of History.* P. Gardiner in *The Nature of Historical Explanation* and W. H. Dray in *Laws and Explanation in History* debate the specific issue at a more advanced level. In *Philosophy and the Historical Understanding,* especially Chapters 4 and 5, W. B. Gallie presents a rather different view of some interest. Two recent full-scale treatments of the area are A. C. Danto's *Analytic Philosophy of History* and M. G. White's *Foundations of Historical Knowledge.*

Some light is shed on the problems of history by considering the problems arising from the social sciences generally. Excerpts from writers on a wide range of topics in this area will be found in D. Braybrooke's short anthology *Philosophical Problems of the Social Sciences,* and in M. Natanson's more substantial collection *Philosophy and the Social Sciences.* Chapters 12 and 13 of E. Nagel's *The Structure of Science* contain a thorough and careful systematic discussion of the major issues.

III ❧ KNOWLEDGE AND BELIEF

One of the ways in which we distinguish between knowledge and belief crops up in our everyday ways of talking. When asked the whereabouts of a friend, we might say, "I *believe* he is upstairs in his room; but I *know* he is around here someplace—I just saw him a minute ago." Our ordinary ways of speaking suggest that the difference between knowledge and belief lies in the amount of conviction we have: belief implies that we have a sensible but tentative guess at what the true nature of the situation is, but when we say we *know,* we speak with greater certainty.

Even in this case we *might* be led to doubt the evidence of our senses. It is just barely possible that we did not see our friend a minute ago, but rather someone else who bore a striking resemblance to him. Our experiences with the errors that we and others make can lead us to ask more penetrating questions about how and when we feel that our beliefs are certain enough to call them "knowledge." And in particular we might be led to ask what the sources of our doubt are or what *kind* of thing can be doubted.

Some philosophers have felt that, although we might be mistaken in identifying or describing what we see, we cannot be mistaken in *seeing* what we see. According to this view, some aspects of our experience are simply given to us: perceptions impinge upon us, and mistakes arise when we interpret these perceptions. I may want, after the fact, to withdraw my claim to have seen a cat, but I may also want to insist that I had seen something that looked enough like a cat to justify my belief.

These questions about what may be doubted and what the role of perception is in making claims to knowledge lead naturally to another question, namely, how should we describe the truth we seek? It seems at first glance, at any rate, that if we are to make any sense of our doubts, there must be some criterion external to us according to which some of our beliefs are true and others false.

These four questions—What can be doubted? What is given to us in perception? What is the relation between perception and the world outside us? What is the nature of truth?—are discussed from several points of view in the following selections.

Doubt

The phrase "Cartesian doubt" refers to a principle stated by DESCARTES, according to which we should begin our philosophical considerations by doubting whatever might lead us into error. We have all been misled on more than one occasion by our senses and by the inferences we draw from what we think we have observed or remembered, and so it seems that none of these faculties can be trusted. Descartes proposes as a test case the possibility that there is some evil demon whose sole purpose it is to deceive us on all possible occasions: if we could successfully escape the clutches of such a demon by establishing one proposition about which we could not be mistaken, we would have a starting point from which to build a comprehensive positive philosophy. Descartes thinks that each of us is in a position to discover at least one such proposition. Each of us is aware of his own thoughts, feelings, desires, and doubts. Hence each of us can say: "Because I have these feelings, desires, thoughts, and doubts, I could not be mistaken in thinking that I exist—for in order even to doubt or to be mistaken, I must exist."

The idea of the deceitful demon led Descartes to suggest that he could be deceived in waking life even as he was in sleep. This thesis has some plausibility: we have all experienced dreams that were sufficiently life-like to frighten us and have all had moments at which life seemed like a dream. But BOUWSMA holds that Descartes' argument rests on a mistake. He attempts to show this by examining the notion of deceit. We cannot, he says, be *deceived* in our sleep (as we can be deceived by a liar when we are awake) simply because the notion of "deceit" does not permit this sort of application. This "conceptual fact," he holds, reveals a basic flaw in Descartes' argument.

Meditations I and II[*]

RENÉ DESCARTES [1596–1650]. See p. 148.

I. Concerning the Things of which we may doubt

It is now several years since I first became aware how many false opinions I had from my childhood been admitting as true, and how doubtful was everything I have subsequently based on them. Accordingly I have ever since been convinced that if I am to establish anything firm and lasting in the sciences, I must once for all, and by a deliberate effort, rid myself of all those opinions to which I have hitherto given credence, starting entirely anew, and building from the foundations up. But as this enterprise was evidently one of great magnitude, I waited until I had attained an age so mature that I could no longer expect that I should at any later date be better able to execute my design. This is what has made me delay so long; and I should now be failing in my duty, were I to continue consuming in deliberation such time for action as still remains to me.

Today, then, as I have suitably freed my mind from all cares, and have secured for myself an assured leisure in peaceful solitude, I shall at last apply myself earnestly and freely to the general overthrow of all my former opinions. In doing so, it will not be necessary for me to show that they are one and all false; that is perhaps more than can be done. But since reason has already persuaded me that I ought to withhold belief no less carefully from things not entirely certain and indubitable than from those which appear to me manifestly false, I shall be justified in setting all of them aside, if in each case I can find any ground whatsoever for regarding them as dubitable. Nor in so doing shall I be investigating each belief separately—that, like inquiry into their falsity, would be an endless labor. The withdrawal of foundations involves the downfall of whatever rests on these foundations, and what I shall therefore begin by examining are the principles on which my former beliefs rested.

Whatever, up to the present, I have accepted as possessed of the highest truth and certainty I have learned either from the senses or through the senses. Now these senses I have sometimes found to be deceptive; and it is

* From *Descartes' Philosophical Writings*, translated by Norman Kemp Smith. Reprinted by permission of the publishers, Macmillan & Co., Ltd., London, and The Macmillan Company of Canada, Ltd.

only prudent never to place complete confidence in that by which we have even once been deceived.

But, it may be said, although the senses sometimes deceive us regarding minute objects, or such as are at a great distance from us, there are yet many other things which, though known by way of sense, are too evident to be doubted; as, for instance, that I am in this place, seated by the fire, attired in a dressing-gown, having this paper in my hands, and other similar seeming certainties. Can I deny that these hands and this body are mine, save perhaps by comparing myself to those who are insane, and whose brains are so disturbed and clouded by dark bilious vapors that they persist in assuring us that they are kings, when in fact they are in extreme poverty; or that they are clothed in gold and purple when they are in fact destitute of any covering; or that their head is made of clay and their body of glass, or that they are pumpkins. They are mad; and I should be no less insane were I to follow examples so extravagant.

None the less I must bear in mind that I am a man, and am therefore in the habit of sleeping, and that what the insane represent to themselves in their waking moments I represent to myself, with other things even less probable, in my dreams. How often, indeed, have I dreamt of myself being in this place, dressed and seated by the fire, whilst all the time I was lying undressed in bed! At the present moment it certainly seems that in looking at this paper I do so with open eyes, that the head which I move is not asleep, that it is deliberately and of set purpose that I extend this hand, and that I am sensing the hand. The things which happen to the sleeper are not so clear nor so distinct as all of these are. I cannot, however, but remind myself that on many occasions I have in sleep been deceived by similar illusions; and on more careful study of them I see that there are no certain marks distinguishing waking from sleep; and I see this so manifestly that, lost in amazement, I am almost persuaded that I am now dreaming.

Let us, then, suppose ourselves to be asleep, and that all these particulars —namely, that we open our eyes, move the head, extend the hands—are false and illusory; and let us reflect that our hands perhaps, and the whole body, are not what we see them as being. Nevertheless we must at least agree that the things seen by us in sleep are as it were like painted images, and cannot have been formed save in the likeness of what is real and true. The types of things depicted, eyes, head, hands, etc.—these at least are not imaginary, but true and existent. For in truth when painters endeavor with all possible artifice to represent sirens and satyrs by forms the most fantastic and unusual, they cannot assign them natures which are entirely new, but only make a certain selection of limbs from different animals. Even should they excogitate something so novel that nothing similar has ever before been seen, and that their work represents to us a thing entirely fictitious and false, the colors used in depicting them cannot be similarly fictitious; they at least must truly exist. And by this same reasoning, even should those general things, viz., a body, eyes, a head, hands and such like, be imaginary, we are yet bound to admit that there are things simpler and more universal which are real existents and by the intermixture of which, as in the case of the colors, all the images of things of which we have any awareness be they true and real or false and fantastic, are formed. To this class of things belong corporeal nature in general and its extension, the shape of extended things, their quantity or magnitude, and their number, as also the location in which they are, the time through which they endure, and other similar things.

This, perhaps, is why we not unreasonably conclude that physics, astronomy, medicine, and all other disciplines treating of composite things are of doubtful character, and that arithmetic, geometry, etc., treating only of the simplest and most general things and but little concerned as to whether or not they are actual existents, have a content that is certain and indubitable. For whether I am awake or dreaming, 2 and 3 are 5, a square has no more than four sides; and it does not seem possible that truths so evident can ever be suspected of falsity.

Yet even these truths can be questioned. That God exists, that He is all-powerful and has created me such as I am, has long been my settled opinion. How, then, do I know that He has not arranged that there be no Earth, no heavens, no extended thing, no shape, no magnitude, no location, while at the same time securing that all these things appear to me to exist precisely as they now do? Others, as I sometimes think, deceive themselves in the things which they believe they know best. How do I know that I am not myself deceived every time I add 2 and 3, or count the sides of a square, or judge of things yet simpler, if anything simpler can be suggested? But perhaps God has not been willing that I should be thus deceived, for He is said to be supremely good. If, however, it be repugnant to the goodness of God to have created me such that I am constantly subject to deception, it would also appear to be contrary to His goodness to permit me to be sometimes deceived, and that He does permit this is not in doubt.

There may be those who might prefer to deny the existence of a God so powerful, rather than to believe that all other things are uncertain. Let us, for the present, not oppose them; let us allow, in the manner of their view, that all which has been said regarding God is a fable. Even so we shall not have met and answered the doubts suggested above regarding the reliability of our mental faculties; instead we shall have given added force to them. For in whatever way it be supposed that I have come to be what I am, whether by fate or by chance, or by a continual succession and connection of things, or by some other means, since to be deceived and to err is an imperfection, the likelihood of my being so imperfect as to be the constant victim of deception will be increased in proportion as the power to which they assign my origin is lessened. To such argument I have assuredly nothing to reply; and thus at last I am constrained to confess that there is no one of all my former opinions which is not open to doubt, and this not merely owing to want of thought on my part, or through levity, but from cogent and maturely considered reasons. Henceforth, therefore, should I desire to discover something certain, I ought to refrain from assenting to these opinions no less scrupulously than in respect of what is manifestly false.

But it is not sufficient to have taken note of these conclusions; we must also be careful to keep them in mind. For long-established customary opinions perpetually recur in thought, long and familiar usage having given them the right to occupy my mind, even almost against my will, and to be masters of my belief. Nor shall I ever lose this habit of assenting to and of confiding in them, not at least so long as I consider them as in truth they are, namely, as opinions which, though in some fashion doubtful (as I have just shown), are still, none the less, highly probable and such as it is much more reasonable to believe than to deny. [This is why I shall, as I think, be acting prudently if, taking a directly contrary line, I of set purpose employ every available device for the deceiving of myself, feigning that all these opinions are entirely false and imaginary. Then, in due course, having so balanced my old-time prejudices by this new prejudice that I cease to incline to one side more than to another, my judgment, no longer dominated by misleading usages, will not be hindered by them in the apprehension of things. In this course there can, I am convinced, be neither danger nor error.] What I have under consideration is a question solely of knowledge, not of action, so that I cannot for the present be at fault as being over-ready to adopt a questioning attitude.

Accordingly I shall now suppose, not that a true God, who as such must be supremely good and the fountain of truth, but that some malignant genius exceedingly powerful and cunning has devoted all his powers in the deceiving of me; I shall suppose that the sky, the earth, colors, shapes, sounds and all external things are illusions and impostures of which this evil genius has availed himself for the abuse of my credulity; I shall consider myself as having no hands, no eyes, no flesh, no blood, nor any senses, but as falsely opining myself to possess all these things. Further, I shall obstinately persist in this way of thinking; and even if, while so doing, it may not be within my power to arrive at the knowledge of any truth, there is one thing I have it in me to do, viz., to suspend judgment, refusing assent to what is false. Thereby, thanks to this resolved firmness of mind, I shall be effectively guarding myself against being imposed upon by this deceiver, no matter how powerful or how craftily deceptive he may be.

This undertaking is, however, irksome and laborious, and a certain indolence drags me back into the course of my customary life. Just as a captive who has been enjoying in sleep an imaginary liberty, should he begin to suspect that his liberty is a dream, dreads awakening, and conspires with the agreeable illusions for the prolonging of the deception, so in similar fashion I gladly lapse back into my accustomed opinions. I dread to be wakened, in fear lest the wakefulness may have to be laboriously spent, not in the tranquilizing light of truth, but in the extreme darkness of the above-suggested questionings.

II. *Concerning the Nature of the Human Mind, and how it is more easily known than the Body*

So disquieting are the doubts in which yesterday's meditation has involved me that it is no longer in my power to forget them. Nor do I yet see how they are to be resolved. It is as if I had all of a sudden fallen into very deep water, and am so disconcerted that I can neither plant my feet securely on the bottom nor maintain myself by swimming on the surface. I shall, however, brace myself for a great effort, entering anew on the path which I was yesterday exploring; that is, I shall proceed by setting aside all that admits even of the very slightest doubt, just as if I had convicted it of being absolutely false; and I shall persist in following this path, until I have come upon something certain, or, failing in that, until at least I know, and know with certainty, that in the world there is nothing certain.

Archimedes, that he might displace the whole earth, required only that there might be some one point, fixed and immovable, to serve in leverage; so likewise I shall be entitled to entertain high hopes if I am fortunate enough to find some one thing that is certain and indubitable.

I am supposing, then, that all the things I see are false; that of all the happenings my memory has ever suggested to me, none has ever so existed; that I have no senses; that body, shape, extension, movement and location are but mental fictions. What is there, then, which can be esteemed true? Perhaps this only, that nothing whatsoever is certain.

But how do I know that there is not something different from all the things I have thus far enumerated and in regard to which there is not the least occasion for doubt? Is there not some God, or other being by whatever name we call Him, who puts these thoughts into my mind? Yet why suppose such a being? May it not be that I am myself capable of being their author?

Am I not myself at least a something? But already I have denied that I have a body and senses. This indeed raises awkward questions. But what is it that thereupon follows? Am I so dependent on the body and senses that without them I cannot exist? Having persuaded myself that outside me there is nothing, that there is no heaven, no Earth, that there are no minds, no bodies, am I thereby committed to the view that I also do not exist? By no means. If I am persuading myself of something, in so doing I assuredly do exist. But what if, unknown to me, there be some deceiver, very powerful and very cunning, who is constantly employing his ingenuity in deceiving me? Again, as before, without doubt, if he is deceiving me, I exist. Let him deceive me as much as he will, he can never cause me to be nothing so long as I shall be thinking that I am something. And thus, having reflected well, and carefully examined all things, we have finally to conclude that this declaration, *Ego sum, ego existo,* is necessarily true every time I propound it or mentally apprehend it.

But I do not yet know in any adequate manner what I am, I who am certain that I am; and I must be careful not to substitute some other thing in place of myself, and so go astray in this knowledge which I am holding to be the most certain and evident of all that is knowable by me. This is why I shall now meditate anew on what, prior to my venturing on these questionings, I believed myself to be. I shall withdraw those beliefs which can, even in the least degree, be invalidated by the reasons cited, in order that at length, of all my previous beliefs, there may remain only what is certain and indubitable.

What then did I formerly believe myself to be? Undoubtedly I thought myself to be a man. But what is a man? Shall I say a rational animal? No, for then I should have to inquire what is "animal," what "rational"; and thus from the one question I should be drawn on into several others yet more difficult. I have not, at present, the leisure for any such subtle inquiries. Instead, I prefer to meditate on the thoughts which of themselves sprang up in my mind on my applying myself to the consideration of what I am, considerations suggested by my own proper nature. I thought that I possessed a face, hands, arms, and that whole structure to which I was giving the title "body," composed as it is of the limbs discernible in a corpse. In addition, I took notice that I was nourished, that I walked, that I sensed, that I thought, all of which actions I ascribed to the soul. But what the soul might be I did not stop to consider; or if I did, I imaged it as being something extremely rare and subtle, like a wind, a flame or an ether, and as diffused throughout my grosser parts. As to the nature of "body," no doubts whatsoever disturbed me. I had, as I thought, quite distinct knowledge of it; and had I been called upon to explain the manner in which I then conceived it, I should have explained myself somewhat thus: by body I understand whatever can be determined by a certain shape, and comprised in a certain location, whatever so fills a certain space as to exclude from it every other body, whatever can be apprehended by touch, sight, hearing, taste or smell, and whatever can be moved in various ways, not indeed of itself but something foreign to it by which it is touched and impressed. For I nowise conceived the power of self-movement, of sensing or knowing, as pertaining to the nature of body: on the contrary I was somewhat astonished on finding in certain bodies faculties such as these.

But what am I now to say that I am, now that I am supposing that there exists a very powerful, and if I may so speak, malignant being, who employs all his powers and skill in deceiving me? Can I affirm that I possess any one of those things which I have been speaking of as pertaining to the nature of body? On stopping to consider them with closer attention, and on reviewing all of them, I find none of which I can say that it belongs to me; to enumerate them again would be idle and tedious. What then, of those things which I have been attributing not to body, but to the soul? What of nutrition or of walking? If it be that I have no body, it cannot be that I take nourishment or that I walk. Sensing? There can be no sensing in the absence of body; and besides I have seemed during sleep to apprehend things which, as I afterwards noted, had not been sensed. Thinking? Here I find what does belong to me: it alone cannot be separated from me. *I am, I exist*. This is certain. How often? As often as I think. For it might indeed be that if I entirely ceased to think, I should thereupon altogether cease to exist. I am not at present admitting anything which is not necessarily true; and, accurately speaking, I am therefore [taking myself to be] only a thinking thing, that is to say, a mind, an understanding or reason—terms the significance of which has hitherto been unknown to me. I am, then, a real thing, and really existent. What thing? I have said it, a thinking thing.

And what more am I? I look for aid to the imagination. [But how mistakenly!] I am not that assemblage of limbs we call the human body; I am not a subtle penetrating air distributed throughout all these members; I am not a wind, a fire, a vapor, a breath or anything at all that I can image. I am supposing all these things to be nothing. Yet I find, while so doing, that I am still assured that I am a something.

But may it not be that those very things which, not being known to me, I have been supposing non-existent, are not really different from the self that I know? As to that I cannot say, and am not now discussing it. I can judge only of things that are known to me. Having come to know that I exist, I am inquiring as to what I am, this I that I thus know to exist. Now quite certainly this knowledge, taken in the precise manner as above, is not dependent on things the existence of which is not yet known to me; consequently and still more evidently it does not depend on any of the things which are feigned by the imagination. Indeed this word *feigning* warns me of my error; for I should in truth be feigning were I to *image* myself to be a something; since imaging is in no respect distinguishable from the contemplating of the shape or image of a *corporeal* thing. Already I know with certainty that I exist, and that all these imaged things, and in general whatever relates to the nature of body, may possibly be dreams merely or deceptions. Accordingly, I see clearly that it is no more reasonable to say, "I will resort to my imagination in order to learn more distinctly what I am," than if I were to say, "I am awake and apprehend something that is real, true; but as I do not yet apprehend it sufficiently well, I will of express purpose go to sleep, that my dreams may represent it to me with greater truth and evidence." I know therefore that nothing of all I can comprehend by way of the imagination pertains to this knowledge I [already] have of myself, and that if the mind is to determine the nature of the self with perfect distinctness, I must be careful to restrain it, diverting it from all such imaginative modes of apprehension.

[What then is it that I am? A thinking thing. What is a thinking thing? It is a thing that doubts, understands, affirms, denies, wills, abstains from willing, that also can be aware of images and sensations.]

Assuredly if all these things pertain to me, I am indeed a something. And how could it be they should not pertain to me? Am I not that very being who doubts of almost everything, who none the less also apprehends certain things, who affirms that one thing only is true, while denying all the rest, who yet desires to know more, who is averse to being deceived, who images many things, sometimes even despite his will, and who likewise apprehends many things which seem to come by way of the senses? Even though I should be always dreaming, and though he who has created me employs all his ingenuity in deceiving me, is there any one of the above assertions which is not as true as that I am and that I exist? Any one of them which can be distinguished from my thinking? Any one of them which can be said to be separate from the self? So manifest is it that it is I who doubt, I who apprehend, I who desire, that there is here no need to add anything by way of rendering it more evident. It is no less certain that I can apprehend images. For although it may happen (as I have been supposing) that none of the things imaged are true, the imaging, *quâ* active power, is none the less really in me, as forming part of my thinking. Again, I am the being who senses, that is to say, who apprehends corporeal things, as if by the organs of sense, since I do in truth see light, hear noise, feel heat. These things, it will be said, are false, and I am only dreaming. Even so, it is none the less certain that it seems to me that I see, that I hear, and that I am warmed. This is what in me is rightly called sensing, and as used in this precise manner is nowise other than thinking.

From all this I begin to know what I am somewhat better than heretofore. But it still seems to me—for I am unable to prevent myself continuing in this way of thinking—that corporeal things, which are reconnoitered by the senses, and whose images inform thought, are known with much greater distinctness than that part of myself (whatever it be) which is not imageable —strange though it may be to be thus saying that I know and comprehend more distinctly those things which I am supposing to be doubtful and unknown, and as not belonging to me, than others which are known to me, which appertain to my proper nature and of the truth of which I am convinced—in short are known more distinctly than I know myself. But I can see how this comes about: my mind delights to wander and will not yet suffer itself to be restrained within the limits of truth.

Let us, therefore, once again allow the mind the freest reign, so that when afterwards we bring it, more opportunely, under due constraint, it may be the more easily controlled. Let us begin by considering the things which are commonly thought to be the most distinctly known, viz., the bodies which we touch and see; not, indeed, bodies in general, for such general notions are usually somewhat confused, but one particular body. Take, for example, this piece of wax; it has been but recently taken from the hive; it has not yet lost the sweetness of the honey it contained; it still retains something of the odor of the flowers from which it has been gathered; its color, its shape, its size, are manifest to us; it is hard, cold, easily handled, and when struck upon with the finger emits a sound. In short, all that is required to make a body known with the greatest possible distinctness is present in the one now before us. But behold! While I am speaking let it be moved toward the fire. What remains of the taste exhales, the odor evaporates, the color changes, the shape is destroyed, its size increases, it becomes liquid, it becomes hot and can no longer be handled, and when struck upon emits no sound. Does the wax, notwithstanding these changes, still remain the same wax? We must admit that it does; no one doubts that it does, no one judges otherwise. What, then, was it I comprehended so distinctly in knowing the piece of wax? Certainly, it could be nothing of all that I was aware of by way of the senses, since all the things that came by way of taste, smell, sight, touch and hearing, are changed, and the wax none the less remains.

Perhaps it has all along been as I am now thinking, viz., that the wax was not that sweetness of honey, nor that pleasing scent of flowers, nor that whiteness, that shape, that sound, but a body which a little while ago appeared to me decked out with those modes, and now appears decked out with others. But what precisely is it that I am here imaging? Let us attentively consider the wax, withdrawing from it all that does not belong to it, that we may see what remains. As we find, what then alone remains is a something extended, flexible and movable. But what is this "flexible," this "movable"? What am I then imaging? That the piece of wax from being round in shape can become square, or from being square can become triangular? Assuredly not. For I am apprehending that it admits of an infinity of similar shapes, and am not able to compass this infinity by way of images. Consequently this comprehension of it cannot be the product of the faculty of imagination.

What, we may next ask, is its extension? Is it also not known [by way of the imagination]? It becomes greater when the wax is melted, greater when the wax is made to boil, and ever greater as the heat increases; and I should not be apprehending what the wax truly is, if I did not think that this piece of wax we are considering allows of a greater variety of extensions than I have ever imaged. I must, therefore, admit that I cannot by way of images comprehend what this wax is, and that it is by the mind alone that I [adequately] apprehend it. I say this particular wax, for as to wax in general that is yet more evident. Now what is this wax which cannot be [adequately] apprehended save by the mind? Certainly the same that I see, touch, image, and in short, the very body that from the start I have been supposing it to be. And what has especially to be noted is that our [adequate] apprehension of it is not a seeing, nor a touching, nor an imaging, and has never been such, although it may formerly have seemed so, but is solely an inspection of the mind which may be imperfect and confused, as it formerly was, or clear and distinct, as it now is, according as my attention is directed less or more to the constituents composing the body.

I am indeed amazed when I consider how weak my mind is and how prone to error. For although I can, dispensing with words, [directly] apprehend all this in myself, none the less words have a hampering hold upon me, and the accepted usages of ordinary speech tend to mislead me. Thus when the wax is before us we say that we see it to be the same wax as that previously seen, and not that we judge it to be the same from its retaining the same color and shape. From this I should straightway conclude that the wax is known by ocular vision, independently of a strictly mental inspection, were it not that perchance I recall how when looking from a window at beings passing by on the street below, I similarly say that it is men I am seeing, just as I say that I am seeing the wax. What do I see from the window beyond hats and cloaks, which might cover automatic machines? Yet I judge those to be men. In analogous fashion, what I have been supposing myself to see with the eyes I am comprehending solely with the faculty of judgment, a faculty proper not to my eyes but to my mind.

But aiming as I do at knowledge superior to the common, I should be ashamed to draw grounds for doubt from the forms and terms of ordinary speech. I prefer therefore to pass on, and to ask whether I apprehended the wax on my first seeing it, and while I was still believing that I knew it by way of the external senses, or at least by the *sensus communis,* as they call it, that is to say by the imaginative faculty, more perfectly and more evidently than I now apprehend it after having examined with greater care what it is and in what way it can be known. It would indeed be foolish to have doubts as to the answer to this question. Was there anything in that first apprehension which was distinct? What did I apprehend that any animal might not have seen? When, however, I distinguish the wax from its external forms; when stripped as it were of its vestments I consider it in complete nakedness, it is certain that though there may still be error in my judgment, I could not be thus apprehending it without a mind that is human.

What now shall I say of the mind itself, i.e., of myself? For as yet I do not admit in myself anything but mind. What am I to say in regard to this I which seems to apprehend this piece of wax so distinctly? Do I not know myself much more truly and much more certainly, and also much more distinctly and evidently, than I do the wax? For if I judge that the wax is or exists because I see it, evidently it follows, with yet greater evidence that I myself am or exist, inasmuch as I am thus seeing it. For though it may be that what I see is not in truth wax, and that I do not even possess eyes with which to see anything, yet assuredly when I see, or (for I no longer allow the distinction) when I think I see, it cannot be that I myself who think am not a something. So likewise, if I judge that the wax exists because I touch it, it will follow that I am; and if I judge that the imagination, or some other cause whatever it be, persuades me that the wax exists, the same conclusion follows [viz., that I am *thinking* by way of an image and *thinking* what I thus image to be independently existing]. And what I have here said regarding the piece of wax may be said in respect of all other things which are external to me.

And yet a further point: if the apprehension of the wax has seemed to me more determinate and distinct when sight and touch, and many causes besides, have rendered it manifest to me, how much more evidently and distinctly must I now know myself, since all the reasons which can aid in the apprehension of wax, or of any body whatsoever, afford yet better evidence of the nature of my mind. Besides, in the mind itself there are so many more things which can contribute to the more distinct knowledge of it, that those which come to it by way of the body scarcely merit being taken into account.

Thus, then, I have been brought step by step to the conclusion I set out to establish. For I now know that, properly speaking, bodies are cognized not by the senses or by the imagination, but by the understanding alone. They are not thus cognized because seen or touched, but only in so far as they are apprehended understandingly. Thus, as I now recognize, nothing is more easily or more evidently apprehended by me than my mind. Difficult, however, as it is to rid oneself of a way of thinking to which the mind has been so long accustomed, it is well that I should halt for some time at this point, that by prolonged meditation I may more deeply impress upon myself this new knowledge.

"On Many Occasions I Have in Sleep Been Deceived"—Descartes*

O E T S K. B O U W S M A [1898–   ] taught for many years at the University of Nebraska. He has given the John Locke Lectures at Oxford and has written numerous articles, many of which are collected in his *Philosophical Essays*.

I want in this paper to discuss a fragment of a sentence from Descartes. We are all acquainted with the context of the sentence, since the argument into which it enters is the ever-popular argument concerning dreams. The fragment is the hinge upon which the argument turns. The fragment is: ". . . on many occasions I have in sleep been deceived. . . ." This comes to: In dreams we are deceived.

We might now consider this sentence under the heading: Is it so? and what makes Descartes or anyone else think that it is so? This is direct and looks simple. It is not, and, as is usually the case in studying what any philosopher says, we shall need to ask: What does he mean? So let us turn to this first.

What, then, does Descartes mean when he says: "On many occasions I have in sleep been deceived. . . ."? And now I can imagine someone remarking: "What's all the mystery? You know what it is to be deceived and you know what it is to sleep and you know what it is to be in sleep, and so that's it. You are deceived in sleep." This makes it seem as simple as: On many occasions I have in Chicago been deceived or murdered, or something like that. There is nothing strange about that. And what might happen in Chicago might happen in sleep or anywhere else. You run all these syllables together, and everything comes out all right. This is, I think, a valuable suggestion, and is succinct and neat. All the same, this frightens me. Let me ask: But what is it like to be deceived in Chicago? You meet someone on State Street. You are new in the city. He tells you a hard luck story. His wife ran off with all his money and his children, and now he has no money to support them. Would you lend him a goodly sum just to tide the family over? He will pay you again as soon as he can arrange a loan with a loan company which he owns. You are bulging with money and you give him a goodly sum. The next day you meet the man attending sessions of the American Philosophical Association. You both laugh, and you think it's a big joke. He buys you a dinner with your money. He's a generous, good-natured philosopher. Visiting the pier in Chicago, you go to see the big boats. While you are watching, suddenly you see a woman, having leaped from somewhere into the cold water. Poor unfortunate! Forlorn love, perhaps. Deserted by some scoundrel. There is no one to help. You throw aside your coat, leap onto the railing of the pier where you are standing, and swim out to the struggling woman. You expect a fight. She will resist your rescue. You are a good swimmer. As you approach her, she seems suddenly quiet, relaxed, as though she were out for a float. You halloo to her and seize her by the collar of her dress. And, then? Why, the woman you would have saved is a mannikin out of a store window, done up in frills and fancies. You drop your burden, swim back to the pier, clamber up to where you were, and there you are greeted with "Bravos!" from six boys. You throw six boys into the water. On another occasion you ask someone how a certain machine works, and he gives you a completely bogus account. Other people ask, and now you tell them the bogus account you heard. A week later someone else tells you how the machine works.

As you can see in these cases being deceived isn't what anyone goes in for. Apart from the loss of money, and the wet clothes on the pier and your complete loss of confidence in your judgment concerning what someone says concerning how a machine works, the fact is that in all these cases you were deceived. No one wants to be deceived. It's humiliating. Are you going to tell your friends about the man who got your money, about the doll you saved from the whale, about your lectures on how the machine runs? They will laugh at you. You'd better keep your naive soul under wraps and be a chump in private. And after this, stay home. What now, then, goes with being deceived? Sheepishness, apologies, "Of course, I should have known better," and resolution not to let it happen again, "Next time I'll be on my guard."

Now, let us consider what it would be like to treat dreams as cases of deception. So someone tells you with a sad face, remorseful, or at least, regretful, in what it was he was deceived. He may blame himself or he may blame his fate. "How was I to know it was only a doll?" "How was I to know I wasn't King?" It's a grim business. He may react with bitterness. "Every night I go to bed there's the same prospect. I'll be bamboozled again. And every morning I wake again exasperated." He did his best, but his best was of no avail. It isn't fair! The injustice of it! For notice that dreams come just when a man is least able to defend himself, when he is as helpless as a log, fast asleep. One might as honorably steal blankets and bottles from a baby's crib. It's worse than doing a man dirt behind his back. At least, such a man may turn. And what is worse, there is no hope that in the future one may escape. One may stay away from Chicago. One may talk back to tellers of hard-luck stories. One may also get one's revenge, throwing six boys into the deep. But there's no staying away from dreams. They are unavoidable. A man must sleep or die. And there is no such thing as learning to cope with dreams. They always get the best of one. "The lot of man is not a happy one." If a man is to walk through this life by day with trepidation, wary, full of guile, think of his state when going to sleep. One thing is sure, he will be taken in. And he cannot even choose how. Afterwards there's only the memory of this humiliation. Also, one never does find out just how the deception is worked. There are no sleeves to search, no hats to ransack. One doesn't even know where to look. If there is a magician in the place, he is gone by the time one discovers there was one.

And in case now this should be the proper reaction of a man to his dreaming, what should our behavior be, we who listen to one who tells his dreams? Is it not to weep? For notice the man comes to confess. Original sin. I dreamed last night. I was deceived. Or he comes to lament. Original defect. Original predicament. In either case, how are we to react? His shame is our shame. His defect is our defect. Proud man, who aspires to truth and big talk by day, is every night brought low, to his high-mind's undoing. So how are we to speak, to act, when someone tells his dream? Are we to say: "Well, that's your funeral"? For shame! His funeral is our funeral. "The bell it tolls for thee." You, too, dream. So, then, hear his lamentation. Remember: No one likes to be deceived—at least, no self-respecting man or ostrich does.

There is no sand to bliss your ignorance. There was a popular song some years ago entitled: "Don't tell me what you dreamed last night; I've been reading Freud." And now we have something similar: "Don't tell me that you dreamed last night; I've been reading Descartes." Freud, of course, is interested in *what* you dreamed last night, and Descartes chiefly in *that* you dreamed last night. Is there not embarrassment in either case? I have, in any case, been startled to discover how much of a parallel one could, for a certain purpose, construct in this case.

And now notice that if, as was said above, we are to understand the fragment of Descartes' sentence on the model of "on many occasions I have in Chicago been deceived," then it appears that Descartes' sentence must come to most people as a surprise and news. And furthermore even on those who are inclined to say what Descartes says, it seems not to make any impression. They go on telling their dreams as nonchalantly as they always have, and they are not in the least ashamed. Have these people then no conscience that they publish what should be their shame, so lightly? People do not usually go about telling their exploits as dupes. Isn't it odd then that a man should take this relish in his own deception or in telling his dreams? And that others should relish it, too? Is deception any the less deception because deception is so common? There are, of course, some people who shy away from telling their dreams. ("Has this man no feeling of his business, that he sings at grave-making?") But these people shy away from telling their dreams, not because they don't like to admit to being deceived, but, on the contrary, because they cannot stand the truth, and cannot stand other people's enduring what they themselves cannot stand, the truth. The truth is something scandalous, and dreams are supposed to shout it loud to those who have that particular sort of trained ears. It seems, accordingly, that some people say: "Dreams lie." Other people say: "Dreams never lie."

It has been suggested that dreaming might be thought of as a form of practical joke, or kidding, and that if one took a dream in this way and the joke didn't go too far, no legs broken, just a plain case of falling off one's chair, or wiping a smudge off one's face, then, of course, one would take the dream like a good sport and join in the fun. And, then, of course, there would be no occasion for this humiliation and commiseration. In this case someone would tell his dream and everyone would understand that the teller of the dream was telling about a practical joke played on him while he slept. He would set the table on a roar. And, then, someone would ask: "And who do you think did it? Who was the kidder kidded you?" After all, a practical joke without the joker, or kidding without the kidder, is bare. There would be little relish in that. And, then, of course, he would tell who it was or whom he suspected. And, then, there would be more laughter. And who, then, was it? It might be anyone, but where one has no reason for suspecting anyone, and one has no practical-joking friend, well, there's always Queen Mab. Who did it, then? "Queen Mab, the galloping imp. If I catch her, I'll tickle her antenna." Is this, then, how we are to understand Descartes? Does Descartes think that when he dreamed, Queen Mab, or some other spinner, put on a show for him, pretending to him it was his very self sitting before the fire, etc.? There is no trace of this, either. Descartes is neither humiliated by the deception nor does he regard it as sport. Descartes is plainly puzzled.

"On many occasions I have in sleep been deceived." This sentence may also bring back scenes of childhood. In at least fifty-one homes in Chicago this morning some young mother has found her little boy hiding under the blankets. "Why, Peter, why are you hiding?" And little Peter says, whimpering, "I don't want the bear to get me." And, of course, the bear doesn't get Peter. Bears won't touch anything under blankets. Then his mother says: "There isn't any bear. You've been dreaming." And almost certainly that is the case. Perhaps something like this happens a number of times. Some morning he gets up in a hurry to look for Jimmy in the garden behind a bush. They've been playing hide-and-seek. But Jimmy isn't there. And Peter comes into the house quite disappointed. So his mother comforts him again. "You dreamed it, honey. Jimmy isn't in the garden." By the time he's three Peter has caught on. He doesn't hide under the covers anymore, and he doesn't rush out of sleep into the garden to look for Jimmy. Now, there may be some older people who are like Peter. Once or twice a year, early in the morning, they find this man, up in a tree, quite distressed, and in his pajamas, all rumpled. He too is hiding from the bear. Now one might say about Peter and about this man that they have in sleep been deceived. Peter's mother didn't put it this way. She said: "There isn't any bear, honey. You've been dreaming." We might also say that they have not learned the meaning of "I dreamed." Once they catch on to that, they no longer hide. And they wouldn't even dream of saying: "I was deceived."

Is it possible then that Descartes meant something like: "On many occasions I have in sleep been deceived" and on waking, hid from a bear? Not at all possible. And now I want to say that that man who said, "Well, you know what it is to be deceived and you know what 'in sleep' is, and so on, and so you should understand Descartes' sentence," doesn't help us to understand. For they say that they dream, and that they are deceived in dreams, and yet do not show the least shame or regret, or react as they might to kidding or to a practical joke. And what sort of deception is this that a man has no regard for, that doesn't affect him at all? These are, after all, sensitive souls, who would normally be offended at a lie. But they tell their dreams with zest. "Last night I was deceived, in my sleep." "Oh, I much more." "Very interesting. Very interesting!" "Very vivid flim-flam." A dirty trick, I say. In any case I should like now to approach this sentence from a slightly different angle.

Let us ask: Just how did Descartes come to say this? Can we figure out how he found this out? I think we all know that the Positivists, under the embarrassments of some misunderstanding, have reminded us that we can sometimes get a perspective of the meaning of an expression, a sentence, or at least some part of the meaning, if we pursue questions of this sort. So, perhaps, we may in this way also get some clue as to what this sentence means. How then did Descartes discover that in dreams we are deceived? I want in the first place to set aside a suggestion which comes from some of our distinguished members who say that some other nameless people say that Descartes got what he says from ordinary language, that is, from what a lot of other nameless, ordinary people say. In this case, then, someone would ask Descartes: Why do you say that? and he would reply, "If you take note of what people say when they tell their dreams, at breakfast, for instance, you will discover—it was a surprise to me, too!—that some people in telling their dreams begin: Last night I dreamed—. . ., and others begin: Last night I was deceived in my sleep. These expressions are used interchangeably and the same people use both expressions, now one, now the other. So my sentence comes to: 'I dreamed . . .,' means the same as: 'In sleep I was deceived.'" He might add, of course, that this is of no significance whatsoever. If this interchangeability strikes you as odd, this may be because you are used to speaking German, and in German there is no such equivalence. Let me insist that were there such equivalence, this would not be of the slightest significance, of no more significance than: Some people say "I dreamed . . .," all the bassos say this in a low voice, and some other people say "I dreamed," all the sopranos say this in a high voice, and "I dreamed" means "I dreamed," high voice or low voice. But did Descartes get his sentence, then, in this way? Of course not. There isn't a trace of this in ordinary language. And if these nameless ones, ordinaries, said anything like this, may they live to see better days. Of course, it is possible that they said something which looks or sounds a little like this, and there may have been some misunderstanding concerning just what they said. In any case this won't help to understand Descartes.

And, now, since we have considered the suggestion that Descartes came to say what he said by way of noticing what Tom, Dick, and Harry and their triplet sisters say, someone else may suggest that Descartes came to say what he said by way of noticing what extraordinary people say, speaking extraordinary language. But since Descartes is himself chief among such extraordinary people, and since, in any case, that extraordinary people do or do not say those extraordinary things would be of no significance in trying to understand them, then we'll not pursue this suggestion, either.

Before I go on to consider some other possibility, I'd like to take another look at Descartes' sentence. Let's take the sentence: In dreams we are deceived. I want particularly to notice the word "dream." Suppose someone tells his dream. He says: "Last night I dreamed I was Icarus and drove the sun-chariot through the sky." (He had been reading about rocket-ships.) His brother says: "Well, that was an interesting dream." Someone comes in and asks: "What was an interesting dream?" and his brother says: "He dreamed last night that he was Icarus and drove the sun-chariot through the sky." My question is: When a man tells his dream, is what he tells his dream, or is it conceivable, for instance, that a man should tell his dream and that he should get it wrong? Is there something else which is his dream, and which he merely reports and concerning which he now may make mistakes? Consider. They say that there are some people who never dream. How they understand what it is they do not do, I don't know. Perhaps all there is to it is that they never tell dreams, though it must sometimes also strike them as strange that other people do. In any case, one could understand how they might compete at breakfast and make up stories which they would introduce as dreams, "Last night I dreamed . . ." Someone might ask: "Did you really dream that?"

"Of course, can't you hear me?"

"But dreaming isn't telling dreams."

"What, then?"

And, then, the bonafide dreamer is stumped. He says, "We dream, of course." After a pause, he goes on. "There are goings-on in the night."

"Where?"

"In our sleep."

"In your sleep? Where's that?"

And now the dreamer has nothing to show for all his trouble. He has no more to show than does the person who makes up a story. Now my question can be put in this way: Is Descartes saying something about the goings-on in the night or is he saying something about what the teller of dreams tells? Is a dream what a man says it is, and in this respect like the Constitution, which is what the supreme court says it is? Is Descartes saying that there is something deceptive about the goings-on in the night in the way in which there is something deceptive about the goings-on on the stage when a magician puts on a show? The woman isn't actually sawed in two. It only appears to be so. So, too, you didn't actually drive the sun-chariot. You only seemed to drive the sun-chariot. And is it now as by a kind of review of the dream, the goings-on, that he discovers that there was a deception, just as after the magic show he may figure out just how it was the magician waved his scarf to flutter your attention? My impression is that this is certainly how Descartes thinks of dreams. He runs into trouble, then, precisely because in looking back upon the dream he can discover nothing which gives the goings-on away (they are not what they seem) in the way in which he can discover what gives the goings-on away in the case of the magician.

What I have now written, I have written to give some explanation of why it won't do to explain Descartes' saying what he said merely by noticing, in the way described, what people say. Did he then try, as I have suggested, to review his dreams, the goings-on, and so discover that in dreams we are deceived? Let's suppose he tried. But might he not in that case have discovered that in the case of some dreams at least men are not deceived, and would it not then have been accidental that he, Descartes, was always deceived? Consider. King Pharaoh believed in dreams. He dreamed and believed in his dream, but he could not make out what the dream said. It was a dream about seven lean kine and seven fat kine. There was also Joseph, an accomplished dreamer, and a believer in dreams and an interpreter of dreams. Dreams are in this respect very much like foreign languages. There is also in the scriptures a prophet who interpreted dreams and on one occasion told the King, the King being much disturbed by a dream which he could not remember, what the King had dreamed. All this need not strike us as very remarkable in 1957. There are many of the Joseph brotherhood today who also interpret dreams. Their maxim is: Dreams never lie. Of course, interpreters may misinterpret, but this is because the language in which dreams are written is very difficult. It seems in any case that Pharaoh, in the dream cited, and by way of the interpreter got a long range weather forecast, seven years of plenty and then seven years of drought. And now if later someone had asked King Pharaoh whether he was deceived in dreams, he would certainly have replied: "Perhaps. But there was one dream which told me true. In it I was not deceived. Everything came out just as the dream said." Of course, there might be other dreams of which he might have said: "We never made out that one." And of another he might have said: "That dream lied. The interpretation was correct, unmistakable. But the grasshoppers never did come." In those days dreams commonly forecast the future. In our day they forecast nothing but the past. My point now in introducing this consideration is that in this instance we have a context, a way of taking dreams, in which Descartes' language has an intelligible employment. Are we deceived in dreams? Sometimes. Some people say: Never. That Descartes has nothing of this sort in mind is clear from this that he says that we are always deceived in dreams. And if we are always deceived in dreams, then interpretation is meaningless. It is only by way of dreams whose meaning is unmistakable, and which come true, that one is provided with a key. Clearly Descartes did not take dreams in this way. But how, then, did he take them?

There is another interesting expression in the scriptures—namely, "And there appeared to him in a dream. . . ."—and then there follows some message, an order or a warning of some sort. No doubt there are people in all times who understand certain dreams in this way. "My mother came to me in a dream last night. . . ." Now here again there would be occasion for the use of the expression: "On many occasions I have in sleep been deceived" or "not been deceived," and then one could go on to say "by my mother," "by a blonde angel," "by a parrot," etc. In any case, this too will not do. Descartes is not thinking of any special dreams. It is true, of course, that Descartes once dreamed a dream which he, himself, interpreted as warning him about his past life and as directing him to pursue the vocation which he later followed. In this connection Descartes employs the words "revelation" and "spirit of truth." Descartes also writes that "the genius that had heightened in him the enthusiasm which had been burning in him for the past several days had forecast these dreams to him before he had retired to his bed." It seems in any case that Descartes might have written of this dream in this way: On at least one occasion I have in sleep been led into the truth. I am not saying that this is in any way inconsistent with: In dreams we are deceived, since we have not as yet managed to tie any meaning to this. It still looks strange.

Up to this point I have been busy trying to show that there is something peculiar about Descartes' sentence. I pointed out that if, for instance, a man says that he was deceived last night, meaning that he dreamed last night, he shows no embarrassment about this and no resentment. How can he be so cheerful about this? Does he think that somehow, like Descartes in the sixth meditation, he will laugh last, when, that is, God gives him the signal? I may add that neither is it a recommendation. To Descartes it must have seemed more like the discovery of something quite familiar. Then I went on to say that Descartes' sentence certainly is not a grammatical one, intended to describe how we use certain expressions, interchangeably, that is. And last I set up for comparison such a use of Descartes' sentence as Pharaoh and other readers of dreams make and whatever it is that Descartes has done.

Now I should like to return to the first question I introduced at the beginning of this essay. The question is: Is it so?—that is, is it so that we are deceived in dreams? And my answer is: It is neither so nor not so. Either answer is based on a misunderstanding. Are berries right or wrong? How would you answer that—yes or no? It is true, of course, that the question I asked does not look at all, nor strike one at all, as like this one about berries.

No one could take the latter seriously. Nevertheless, I want to suggest that however serious one may be in dealing with my question, which is also Descartes' question, one will not get out of the woods until one also comes to see that it is also *like* the question about berries. The latter is, of course, a deliberate misdemeanor, if, that is, it can be said to be demeanor at all. There is nothing deliberate about Descartes' question, and, of course, it is much more important than a misdemeanor. Now, then, I want to explain this.

It may be noted that Descartes does not explain his sentence. He gives no reasons. It must, then, have seemed to him to require no reasons. It may even now seem strange that his sentence should be brought to this sort of question. Doesn't everybody know that in dreams we are deceived? Whatever explanation is given of Descartes' sentence must also explain this that it is difficult even to bring it into question. I should like then to suggest that Descartes never did discover this, that he never did deliberately make it up as though he were saying some new thing, and, also, he never figured it out. Even when it led him into such difficulties, he never questioned it. What then? Well, it's rather as though he were stricken with this sentence—struck by it as with something with which he is as familiar and at home as he is with his hands and feet. It is native to him in his language, and so too the matter of resistance never comes up. One doesn't resist one's hands and feet. The sentence has by insinuation, on the sly, made its way. But how then? By way of an allurement, a seduction, a charm, a compulsion, a sorcery. And what now exercises these strange powers? The evil genius? I do not think so. In any case I mean to say that Descartes, like all the rest of us, is lured, seduced, charmed, compelled by an analogy, an analogy of a special sort, an analogy which keeps one's mind in a certain fixed position, and of which he is himself unaware. And this is how it comes about that Descartes says that in dreams we are deceived.

It has been said that seeing through an analogy is like seeing through spectacles. Imagine, then, that you are seeing through spectacles on the lenses of which designs are drawn. Imagine now, further, that when you look at designs on a paper, you see the lines which are part of the design on the lenses of your spectacles as part of the design on the paper. This will, obviously, result in some confusion, and until you become aware of the design on the lenses of your spectacles, you will not see clearly the design on the paper. You must remove those spectacles. The analogy to which I have referred plays a part like that of the design on the lenses of your spectacles. The analogy, it must be remembered, is not out in the open. It is nothing Descartes speaks of. ("Even your best friends [I, for instance] won't tell you.") It is submerged, underground. It is, accordingly, like a design on the lenses of one's spectacles of which one is completely unaware. No wonder, then, that one sees in a confused way the design on the paper.

Before I go on now I should like to raise this caution. The explanation I will give touches the fringes only of an account of all language and of philosophy, of such magnificence and depth, that I am unceasingly amazed that any mere human being should ever have come upon it. And now my caution. If we compare the account to which I have referred, to some gorgeous tapestry, an intellectual design of Bayeux proportions and needle-fine, then my sketch of an explanation of the fragment from Descartes must be compared to some tiny segment, cut out of the splendid frame, and now pale and tattered and a sorry thing. I have the heart to present it only as it now gives me occasion to tell you where I got it. I wish that my essay might for this purpose have more push. And now this further. I will present the sketch of an explanation of Descartes' sentence. It is not, however, presented as *the* explanation. The routes by which one may in the mazes of language lose one's way and so find oneself in the confines of some bewildering nowhere are many. Let us say, in the words of Socrates, that one "may venture to think, not improperly or unworthily, that something of the kind is true."

And now I should like to explain the analogy. The analogy is described as "grammatical." In the case of: Are berries right or wrong? there is no grammatical analogy which could explain this. I called it a misdemeanor, but one might call it a crime. Except for the purpose of illustrating crime, or some mischief, it has no excuse. It makes no sense, either philosophical or otherwise. Nevertheless, it bears a certain similarity to "In dreams we are deceived." Remember now that neither of these sentences is here said to be an analogy, though, of course, there may be an analogy between them. The latter sentence, however, bears the traces of an analogy—the grammatical one, that is—and it is this analogy which explains the form of the sentence and our fascination.

What now do I mean by a grammatical analogy? Consider the following sentences:

Peter tells his dream.
Peter tells a story.
Peter tells what happened.

Here we have on the surface of these sentences obvious similarities. "Peter tells." But there is more than that. If Peter tells, Peter talks; and this will be so, no matter what Peter tells. Furthermore, if Peter tells his dream, Peter remembers his dream. If Peter tells a story, he remembers the story (unless he is making it up). If Peter tells what happened, Peter remembers what happened. Also, if Peter tells, someone listens, even if it is Peter who listens.

And what is told is interesting or uninteresting or dull or stupid and so on, in any case. Peter may practice telling. He may be an accomplished teller or again a bungler in telling, and all those may apply in any case. He may in the midst of telling forget what he was to tell. His facial expression, (How did he look when he came to this part? Very grave.), his gestures, (He raised his hand at this point.) and his zest in telling (His eyes shone.), all three are relevant. In connection with his telling you may ask all these sorts of questions, again, no matter what he is telling. This now is what I mean by the grammatical analogy. The sentence forms which go, in this instance, with the first telling, a context, go with the others, too. So one may say: The language pattern involved in telling a dream is like that involved in telling what happened. This is right. There are those similarities.

But suppose now that someone went on to say, "And so telling a dream is like telling what happened." Though this may be true, this may also be misleading. For he may now also suppose that all these sentences have the same meaning in these different contexts. Accordingly, he may say remembering is remembering, and whether, then, you remember a dream, or remember a story, or remember what happened, it's all the same. This, of course, is wrong. For notice, in the case of remembering a dream it makes no sense to say. "You got it wrong. That's not how it was." His dream is what he remembers, what he tells. But in case of telling a story or in case of telling what happened, one may certainly remember it wrong. We'll get the book and see. We can check. This is what the book says, and this is what you said. The book says: "Words, words, words, words," and you said, "Buzz, buzz, buzz." And as for what happened, your memory is unreliable. We'll visit the scene, and see, Mr. Falstaff, whether all those dead bodies are still lying on the field. It won't particularly matter in this case whether he is remembering or whether he is lying. What is misleading in such cases is the use of similar expressions or even the same sentences which then tempt us to assume an analogy or sameness in meaning. The point is that the expression may be the same and the meaning different. This is especially tempting when there is generally a wide area both of analogous grammar and analogous meaning. (Who would ever have supposed that the difference between remembering a dream and remembering what happened could be of philosophical significance?) It may be useful also to note that in case Peter tells a story he is making up ("Tell us a story, Uncle Peter"), he remembers nothing at all, and that doesn't mean he is actively forgetting. But it has been suggested that making up stories is a form of discovery, like taking notes on the scene of the happening.

We have noticed the similarity in the grammatical or the sentence pattern of these various bits of discourse, and we have also noticed that beyond this there is also a divergence of pattern. And now I should like to stress a point already made. If someone tells what happened, then, of course, it makes sense to ask such questions as: Are you sure? Did you observe carefully? Were there other witnesses? What do they say?, and to retort with: "You're wrong. That's not how it was." But when it now comes to someone's telling his dream, none of these questions is allowed. And this is not because for some arbitrary reason one doesn't want these questions asked, as though he wanted to hide something, keeping the witnesses of one's dream from testifying. This is a part of the essence of the dream. But certain questions in relation to the telling of a dream are intelligible and certain others which are intelligible in relation to telling what happened are not intelligible in relation to the telling of a dream. In this way one can see both the coincidence and the divergence of these two distinct language patterns.

And now among these several forms of discourse, certainly, that of telling what happened is basic, fundamental. We no doubt learn it first and throughout our lives it is of primary importance. It dominates. The others may be regarded as variations on a theme. One might, then, unwittingly expect that the pattern of it should be repeated in the others. There are now special reasons why there should be this disposition in the case of dreams. In the first place you may tell as your dream, on Monday, what you may tell as what happened, on next Tuesday. This weighed very heavily in Descartes' discussion. Furthermore, you remember your dream and you remember what happened. I have already noticed the misleading character of this parallel. Besides this, in connection with remembering one's dream, one may be visited with vivid imagery, just as one may in remembering what happened. Now, then, I am suggesting that it is the momentum of this grammatical analogy which carries one along the whole way. This is the source of that allurement, that push, that sorcery, which I mentioned earlier.

And so this is how one comes to say that in dreams we are deceived. We can, I think, trace a likely course of this seduction. Thinking in general about what you tell when you tell your dream and what you tell when you tell what happened, you may say, comparing the two, that when you tell your dream, you tell what is not so, what never happened, and when you tell what happened, well, that's what is so. Now this looks like: What you told as your dream is false, and what you told as what happened is true. What is not noticed in this case is that the distinction between what happened and what did not happen, between true and false, falls within the pattern of telling what happened, and is excluded from the pattern of telling one's dream. This shows how easy in language it is to go through an open switch.

Above I used the phrase "thinking in general." It is in this circumstance that one goes through the open switch. The switches are always open. But when one listens to someone telling his dream, one does not go through such open switches. Try this on someone who is telling his dream.

"Ah! So you were deceived?"

"Deceived?"

"Why, yes. Did you not at the time of your dream have the attitude of acceptance? Did you not at the time of your dream believe in your dream, believe in the bear?"

And now what is the teller of dreams to say? Is he to say: "Why, yes, I did have the attitude of acceptance, I did believe in the bear." Where does such language come from? Well, clearly, it comes from the analogy with telling what happened, but not at all in a simple way since the phrases introduced here come, not directly from the context of what happened and of seeing what happened, but from this language as seen through still another analogy. There are cases in which in seeing one is not sure as to what one is seeing. This, of course, is shown in the language. "I am not sure, but I believe that it's a bear." There are other cases in which one may say, "He believes that it's a bear," or "He's sure it's a bear," when one may oneself be uncertain or may know that there is no bear. One might judge in such a circumstance by the way in which someone else approaches what he takes to be a bear. The phrase "attitude of acceptance" suggests that the question: Shall I accept? has come up and that one has then assumed the attitude of acceptance. (What the heck! One has to take a chance.) This way of looking at perception goes along with the sense-datum theory, such that every time you look at the broad side of a barn something comes between you and the broad-side of a barn (if there is a broad-side of a barn), and you finally make the plunge. After all, they are your cows, and you'd better do some accepting, gambling on the friendliness of sense-data, or of whoever has charge (animal faith) or fret the whole of your milking time away. This is one how, some how, of looking at perception and of telling what happened with which it gets mixed up. Now, then, the point is that if you look at perception in this way (the most ordinary perception involves "acceptance" and "belief"), and if, then, you go on to look at dreams as a form of perception, why then, naturally, you look at dreams, also, as involving "acceptance" and "belief." It turns out, then, to be a case of a lost gamble, misplaced confidence, which you have the further illusion of having uncovered. Descartes' metaphysical embarrassment arises from the fact that he cannot figure out that he ever did uncover this.

Suppose someone said: "No. No, indeed. I wasn't deceived. I saw at once it wasn't a bear. Why, some of the stuffing was showing at the seams. It was a puppet show, that's what it was. And I could see the strings." That he cannot find the stuffed bear or the puppets after he wakes, proves nothing.

There are and have been so many stuffed bears and so many puppet shows. What is dreaming but a baffling sort of television? Where did that program come from? It's a big omniverse.

Having said that what is told as one's dream is false, one has also to explain the remembering. How is it possible that I should, at the time of the telling the dream, and so telling what is false, what never happened, how is it possible that I should remember so vividly what never happened? And now what is there to do but draw further on the analogy in which one is already entangled? And so we get the picture of dreaming already referred to above. As you have been a witness to goings-on, of what happened, in case you tell what happens, so too you must have been a witness to goings-on, of what happened in your sleep, in case you tell your dream. That you remember and tell what you now know did not happen, shows plainly that you were deceived. It may help to remind ourselves that people who tell what happened are sometimes mistaken. Suppose now that someone who was a witness to some happening got it all wrong—unaccountably wrong.

Imagine someone who looks out the window which looks out upon a garden with a green lawn and trees and bushes, etc. He looks, and then he rubs his eyes and says: "You know what I saw?" And he tells you about Andromache on the walls of Troy. This would be very odd. He looks out of the window, and he tells what he saw. Perhaps, in such a case, it would do no good at all to take him back to the window. He might see Andromache on the walls of Troy again. One might now think of one's dream in this way. "I looked, and I saw, and lo, and behold!, this is what I saw." He tells his dream. He doesn't remember, however, where it was that he was looking. If one always dreamed, looking out of the window, then, of course, one could always return to the window and make sure that one did not see Andromache on the wall. Since you don't know where you were when in your sleep you were seeing,—who is to say that in such a case you are where your eyes are?—how is one to say that from wherever you were you could not see Andromache on the walls of Troy? Here all the ordinary barriers of perception are done away. So there's no such thing as going back to the window, either to say that Andromache was standing on the wall or that she wasn't. Only if she wasn't, can you say that you were deceived. Descartes has said that he was deceived. But can he show now that he did not see Andromache on the wall, or that he was nowhere in the vicinity, when he in his sleep saw what he saw? He doesn't know what he saw. So, how does he now know that he did not see Andromache on the wall? This is precisely, it—that he doesn't know he didn't, and so he doesn't know he was deceived.

This may help further to show how the analogy with telling what happened befogs one's view of telling one's dream.

I have now also answered my second question: What makes Descartes or anyone else think so? He is under the domination, the influence, of the analogy which I have described. And need I add, and so are all the rest of us? It is not easy to withstand even if one is aware of it. This sentence, then, as we have seen, arises like a bloom out of a confusion, and it serves to gather round its head that cloud, the skepticism of the senses. So, with ridding ourselves of the confusion, we rid ourselves of the sentence, and so also of the problem of skepticism. Eternal vigilance is still the price of keeping in the clear. "And is not that grand!"

And now if there are analogies which mislead, and so confuse, are there not also analogies which may lead us back and help us to see? Try this. If you hit a man on the head, he may be stunned and dazed. When he recovers, he says: "OooOh, I saw stars!" Now, then, was he deceived? Would you be interested in showing him that he did not? Are you to say: "No, you didn't. It's mid-afternoon?" Or are you to say that you doubt that he saw stars, and you don't know whether he did or did not? Suppose he offers to hit you on the head so that you can see for yourself. Are you to insist that they are not the same stars we ordinarily see? Suppose he says: "Oooooh, I saw the big dipper." How do you know he didn't? Why isn't a concussion like night? Of course, you may not be at all inclined to say that he was deceived. How much must he say in order for you to say that he was deceived? Suppose you hit him on the head, again, a little harder, and, now, when he recovers, he cries: "Oooh, I saw . . . ," and then he tells you a story. It sounds to you like a dream. I am not now asking at what point you would say he was pretending, but at what point you would say that he was deceived. There is, of course, no question about whether or not he saw stars, anymore than there is a question about whether or not a man dreamed. The question is as to why in the case of a man's dream one is inclined to say that he was deceived, whereas, in the case of a man's seeing stars one is not so inclined. Suppose a man said: "Last night I dreamed I saw stars," and he doesn't mean that he dreamed someone hit him on the head. Was he deceived? Of course, in the latter case in which the man dreamed, he was not hit on the head. Would this, then, show that he was deceived? How? I am not saying that the analogy between "I saw stars" and "I dreamed . . ." is complete. I am only suggesting that this analogy may help to lay the spell of the other one.

This reminds me. It is significant that in connection with dreams we ask: What caused him to dream? and sometimes we are satisfied with a sort of explanation. "He ate too much." "He was so excited yesterday at the zoo." "I always dream when I'm low on thyroid." "It was our conversation just before we went to bed." No one explains a dream by saying: "Oh, he wasn't paying attention" or "He was half asleep." The fact is, he was asleep. Nor does one say "He was asleep."

In case of deception, no one says: "He mistook the dry pavement in the sunlight at noon for a wet pavement, or a mirage for an oasis, because, as you know, he ate baked eel at dinner and that always gives him indigestion." Or "Yesterday he was so excited about the monkey at the zoo. Remember how he looked into the monkey's eyes! And today he can't tell a hawk from a hand-saw." One may say: "He was pre-occupied with something—thinking hard about how he would tell his mother and of how he would introduce her to his mother. So he was not attending." Or "But the pavement in sunlight at noon does look like a wet pavement."

Dreams have an explanation in the sense just illustrated. So do deceptions. The difference in the explanation is a difference in the concepts. We explicate the concepts by bringing out these differences. In the case of "I saw stars," the explanation is: "I was hit on the head." And this explanation does not compete with: "They're shooting off fire-works on the beach." In case the former is the explanation, the second is ruled out, whether they are shooting off fire-works on the beach or not.

Of course, there is a maze in the case of dreams. Everybody knows that. The question is: What sort of maze is this?

Consider: Someone says: "It's a horse." Someone else says: "It's a zebra. Horses and zebras are common in this circus." Still another says: "Zebras are horses." So what are you to do? Well, get some horses and get some zebras, and examine them closely. Now, then, are zebras horses? Here now is a similar case. Someone says: "It's a dream." Someone else says: "It's a deception." Still another says: "Dreams are deceptions." So what are you to do? Well, get some dreams and get some deceptions, and examine them closely. Compare. But this is not so easy to do. "Go, and catch a falling star." Go, and catch a dream. Dreams, let me tell you, are not so easy to come by. And deceptions also are hard to get. If, now, you could get hold of a dream and make it stand still ("I saw a dream walking") and could get hold of a deception (Deception stalks) and make it stand still, and if then you could walk around them, doing your subtlest, why, then, you should be able to settle this matter. The problem now reduces itself to a matter of technique. Is there a net for catching dreams and a net for catching deceptions? A dream in one hand, held, hardly a wisp, between your thumb and forefinger, and a deception in the other, held, scarcely a whisper, between your thumb and forefinger—that would be ideal. Butter-fingers!

This analogy, which is also powerful, makes it seem as if the problem concerning dreams were one which is to be settled only by means of further information which remains inaccessible to us. Dreams are more volatile than helium. Dreams explode silently at the mere approach of an enquiring one. In the case of the horses and zebras, presumably, someone finds out more about horses and zebras and in this process there is a refinement of concepts. If horses and zebras invisibled faster than light and disappeared (Pfut!) at the mere shadow of a curiosity about them, why, these scientists would have to give up. Of course, even in such a case, it seems as though horses and zebras are tame enough, so long as no one asks questions. "And thereby," as Shakespeare says, "hangs a tale." For dreams and deceptions, too, are tame enough, so long as no one asks certain questions. I have tried in this paper also to show in what sense one can make a dream and a deception stand still to be examined. One examines concepts—namely, the concepts "dream" and "deception." To do this is to remind oneself of the meanings of these expressions in the patterns of language and circumstance into which they enter. I have not led a dream zebra out, to stand alongside a deception zebra alongside a real zebra, and inspected. I have counted no hairs. With what eye should I inspect? Not with these blue eyes. All the same, I have the urge.

Try to think of the differences in meanings of sentences in terms of the figure of the differences in the branchings of the limbs of trees. There may be similarities in the patterns of such branchings. Two limbs of a tree up to a point show the same branchings off and then may come divergences which are present in one and not in the other. Squirrels commonly have no trouble because of such resemblances and such divergences among branches. They leap and run and frisk. And normally this is also the case with human beings in following routes of language—that is, when they are busy, when, for instance, there are nuts to get. But there are cases in which one takes one's lead in getting perspective of the branchings of one limb of meaning, from the design of the branchings of another, by reason of a dominant similarity. And so one has the illusion that there are divergent branchings when there are none, or none when there are some. The slightest pressure here may give one a strange feeling, a feeling as of suspense between heaven and earth. And this reminds me that philosophy has sometimes been described in this way, as thought in suspense between heaven and earth, one of the children of plenty and of want, a lovechild. In any case, if you rest your foot on the absence of the branchings of a limb, on the mere shadow of the branchings of a limb, cast by a similar limb, you may have the illusion of resting securely, up a tree, or you may feel yourself in unstable equilibrium, quite up in the air. But I am not concerned here to speak of squirrels up a tree, or of a man up in the air. I am trying to present a certain way of looking at confusion, the sort of confusion I see in: We are deceived in dreams. Off the limb: Peter-told-his-dream, there is no branch: Peter-was-deceived.

This essay is a clear instance of mitigated plagiarism. My hope is that the plagiarism shows through.

SUGGESTED READINGS

For a general book on Descartes, see N. K. Smith, *New Studies in the Philosophy of Descartes.* Richard H. Popkin has written a useful *History of Skepticism from Erasmus to Descartes.*

Some standard skeptical arguments are restated briefly in B. Russell, *Problems of Philosophy,* Chapter 1. Chapter 2 of A. J. Ayer's *Problem of Knowledge* is another useful review of skeptical arguments. For an extremely detailed and careful statement of the view that empirical beliefs are at best probable, see C. I. Lewis, *Analysis of Knowledge and Valuation,* Part II, which is discussed at length by N. Malcolm in his essay in *Philosophical Analysis* (edited by M. Black). One of the central modern statements of opposition to skepticism is G. E. Moore's "Proof of an External World," now available in his *Philosophical Papers.* Using arguments somewhat similar to Moore's, Thomas Reid defends common sense against some of Hume's skeptical arguments in Essay VII, Chapter 4, of the *Essays on the Intellectual Powers.* Another type of criticism of skeptical arguments is directed against Descartes by H. A. Prichard in *Knowledge and Perception* (see especially pages 71–80). There is a fairly large literature on the argument to skepticism from dreams: for example, see Norman Malcolm, *Dreaming,* and the review of this book by D. Pears in *Mind,* 1961.

One of the main types of skepticism is skepticism about the existence of minds other than one's own. This has been exhaustively discussed from a Wittgensteinian point of view by J. Wisdom in a series of difficult and fascinating articles reprinted as *Other Minds.* There is an excellent essay by J. L. Austin on "Other Minds" in his *Philosophical Papers.* Chapter 3 of P. F. Strawson's *Individuals* contains a very powerful criticism of Descartes (see especially Section 4).

The Given

    We all know what it is like to "recognize" a friend from the back, go up and clap him on the shoulder, and when he turns around, find him to be some one we never saw before. Although we may have been mistaken in recognizing our friend from the back, there is still a truth about the situation that we will never retract: "That *looked like* Henry!" and in spite of the fact that it wasn't Henry, we still claim that he had a Henry-like look. Other examples are not hard to come by. We "see" railroad tracks converging at a distance, but we "know" that they really do not converge. And similar situations arise in science: we "see" a vapor trail in a cloud chamber, and on this basis we speak of the path of an electron. In both these cases something is immediately presented, but in neither case do we say that the object is as it appears. It would seem, at any rate, that certain facts are given to us in experience and that from these we infer whatever else we know.

    PRICE defends this position. We may be mistaken in interpreting what confronts our eyes (i.e., thinking, or inferring, that it is Henry), but what confronts our eyes (Henry-like appearances) is inescapably *there*. AUSTIN on the other hand argues that there is no "privileged" class of assertions of the kind Price envisages: anything we may say about how things "look" or "appear" is, depending on the context, subject to correction.

The Given in Perception [*]

HENRY HABBERLY PRICE [1899–   ] recently retired from the Wykeham Professorship of Logic at Oxford, where he taught for many years. His attempt to present a tenable version of classical empiricism is embodied in two important volumes, *Hume's Theory of the External World* (1940) and *Thinking and Experience* (1953), in addition to the book from which the present selection is taken.

    Every man entertains a great number of beliefs concerning material things, e.g. that there is a square-topped table in this room, that the earth is a spheroid, that water is composed of hydrogen and oxygen. It is plain that

[*] From Price: *Perception*, London, 1932. Reprinted by permission of Methuen and Co., Ltd.

all these beliefs are based on sight and on touch (from which organic sensation cannot be separated): based upon them in the sense that <u>if we had not had certain particular experiences of seeing and touching, it would be neither *possible* nor *reasonable* to entertain these beliefs</u>. Beliefs about imperceptibles such as molecules or electrons or X-rays are no exception to this. Only they are based not directly on sight and touch, but indirectly. Their direct basis consists of certain other beliefs concerning scientific instruments, photographic plates, and the like. Thus over and above any intrinsic uncertainty that they themselves may have, whatever uncertainty attaches to these more basic beliefs is communicated to them. It follows that in any attempt either to analyse or to justify our beliefs concerning material things, the primary task is to consider beliefs concerning perceptible or 'macroscopic' objects such as chairs and tables, cats and rocks. It follows, too, that no theory concerning 'microscopic' objects can possibly be used to throw doubt upon our beliefs concerning chairs or cats or rocks, so long as these are based directly on sight and touch. <u>Empirical Science can never be more trustworthy than perception</u>, upon which it is based; and it can hardly fail to be *less* so, since among its non-perceptual premises there can hardly fail to be some which are neither self-evident nor demonstrable. Thus the not uncommon view that the world which we perceive is an illusion and only the 'scientific' world of protons and electrons is real, is based upon a gross fallacy, and would destroy the very premises upon which Science itself depends.

My aim in this book is to examine those experiences in the way of seeing and touching upon which our beliefs concerning material things are based, and to inquire in what way and to what extent they justify these beliefs. Other modes of sense-experience, e.g. hearing and smelling, will be dealt with only incidentally. For it is plain that they are only auxiliary. If we possessed them, but did not possess either sight or touch, we should have no beliefs about the material world at all, and should lack even the very conception of it. Possessing sight or touch or both, we can use experiences of these other senses as signs of obtainable but not at the moment actual experiences of seeing or touching, and thereby gain indirectly information which these inferior senses in themselves provide no hint of.

It may appear to some people that Science, particularly Physiology, can answer these questions for us. But it should already be clear that this is a mistake. Thus if it be said that when a man sees something, e.g. a tomato, light rays emanating from the object impinge upon his retina and this stimulates the optic nerve, which in turn causes a change in the optic centers in his brain, which causes a change in his mind: there are two comments to be made. 1. No doubt this is in fact a perfectly true account, but what are our *grounds* for believing it? Obviously they are derived from observation, and mainly if not entirely from visual observation. Thus the Physiologist has not explained in the least how visual observation justifies a man in holding a certain belief about a tomato, e.g. that it is spherical. All he has done is to put forward certain *other* beliefs concerning a retina and a brain. Those other beliefs have themselves to be justified in exactly the same way as the first belief, and we are as far as ever from knowing what way that is. Instead of answering our question, we have found another instance of it. Nor is this result surprising. Since the premises of Physiology are among the propositions into whose validity we are inquiring, it is hardly likely that its conclusions will assist us. 2. In any case, Science only professes to tell us what are the *causes* of seeing and touching. But we want to know what seeing and touching themselves *are*. This question lies outside the sphere of Science altogether.

Thus there is no short cut to our goal. We must simply examine seeing and touching for ourselves and do the best we can. What, then, is it to see or to touch something? Let us confine ourselves to sight for the moment and return to the instance of the tomato.

When I see a tomato there is much that I can doubt. I can doubt whether it is a tomato, that I am seeing, and not a cleverly painted piece of wax. I can doubt whether there is any material thing there at all. Perhaps what I took for a tomato was really a reflection; perhaps I am even the victim of some hallucination. One thing however I cannot doubt: that there exists a red patch of a round and somewhat bulgy shape, standing out from a background of other colour-patches, and having a certain visual depth, and that this whole field of colour is directly present to my consciousness. What the red patch is, whether a substance, or a state of a substance, or an event, whether it is physical or psychical or neither, are questions that we may doubt about. But that something is red and round then and there I cannot doubt. Whether the something persists even for a moment before and after it is present to my consciousness, whether other minds can be conscious of it as well as I, may be doubted. But that it now *exists*, and that *I* am conscious of it—by me at least who am conscious of it this cannot possibly be doubted. And when I say that it is 'directly' present to my consciousness, I mean that my consciousness of it is not reached by inference, nor by any other intellectual process (such as abstraction or intuitive induction), nor by any passage from sign to significate. There obviously must be some sort or sorts of presence to consciousness which can be called 'direct' in this sense, else we should have an infinite regress. Analogously, when I am in the situations called 'touching something,' 'hearing it,' 'smelling it,' etc., in each case there is something which at that moment indubitably exists—a pressure (or present patch), a noise, a smell; and that something is directly present to my consciousness.

This peculiar and ultimate manner of being present to consciousness is called *being given,* and that which is thus present is called a *datum.* The corresponding mental attitude is called *acquaintance, intuitive apprehension,* or sometimes *having.* Data of this special sort are called *sense-data.* And the acquaintance with them is conveniently called *sensing;* though sometimes, I think, this word is used in another sense. It is supposed by some writers that sense-data are mental events, and these writers appear to think that the word 'sensing,' if used at all, ought to mean the coming-into-being of sense-data, not the intuitive apprehension of them. (For their coming-into-being will then be a mental process.) This seems to be a very inconvenient usage. We need some word for the intuitive apprehension of sense-data. We cannot say 'perceiving' (for that, as we shall see, has at least two other meanings already). And 'sensing' is the obvious word to use. At any rate in this book we shall always use it in this sense. When we have occasion to speak of the process which is the coming-into-being of a sense-datum we shall call it *sense-datum-genesis.*

It is true that the term 'given' or 'datum' is sometimes used in a wider and looser sense to mean 'that, the inspection of which provides a premise for inference.' Thus the data of the historian are the statements which he finds in documents and inscriptions; the data of the general are the facts reported by his aircraft and his intelligence service; the data of the detective are the known circumstances and known results of the crime; and so on. But it is obvious that these are only data relatively and for the purpose of answering a certain question. They are really themselves the results of inference, often of a very complicated kind. We may call them data *secundum quid.* But eventually we must get back to something which is a datum *simpliciter,* which is not the result of any previous intellectual process. It is with data *simpliciter,* or rather with one species of them, that we are concerned.

How do sense-data differ from other data, e.g. from those of memory or introspection? We might be tempted to say, in the manner in which they come to be given, viz. as a result of the stimulation of a sense-organ. This will not do. For first, the sense-organs are themselves material things, and it seems quite likely that the term 'material thing' cannot be defined except by reference to sense-data; and if so we should have a vicious circle. And secondly, even though we doubted the existence of all material things, including our own body and its organs, it would still be perfectly obvious that sense-data differ from other sorts of data. The only describable differentia that they seem to have is this, that they lead us to conceive of and believe in the existence of certain material things, whether there are in fact any such things or not. (Visual and tactual sense-data do this directly, the others indirectly, as explained above.) But it seems plain that there is also another characteristic common and peculiar to them, which may be called 'sensuousness.' This is obvious on inspection, but it cannot be described.

Does sensing differ from other forms of intuitive apprehension? Or is there only one sort of intuitive apprehension, and does the difference between (say) sensing, remembering and the contemplation of mental images lie only in the nature of the apprehension? The question is difficult, nor does it seem very important. Perhaps we may say that there are two sorts of intuitive apprehension, one directed upon *facts*, e.g. the fact that I am puzzled or was puzzled, or again the fact that $2 + 2 = 4$, or that courage is good; another directed upon *particular existents*, e.g. this colour-patch or this noise or that visual image, or again upon this feeling of disgust and that act of wondering. The first is apprehension *that*, the second is apprehension *of*. The term *acquaintance* is properly reserved for the second, and we shall so use it in future.

Are there several different sorts of acquaintance, e.g. sensing, self-consciousness, and contemplation of mental images? I cannot see that there are. The difference seems to be wholly on the side of the data. If so, *a fortiori* there are not different kinds of sensing. Visual sensing will simply be the acquaintance with colour-patches, auditory sensing the acquaintance with sounds, and so on; the acquaintance being the same in each case. No doubt there will be different kinds of *sense-datum-genesis*, just as there are different kinds of sense-data. And if any one likes to use the term 'visual sensing' to mean the genesis of colour-patches and 'auditory sensing' to mean the genesis of noises, he may; and of course he is then entitled to say that there *are* different kinds of sensing. But this has not the slightest tendency to show that there are different kinds of sensing in *our* sense of the word (which is also the usual one).

If the term sense-datum is taken in the strictly limited meaning that we have given it, I do not see how any one can doubt that there are sense-data. . . .

It is now clear that all our beliefs about the material world are based directly or indirectly upon the sensing of visual and tactual sense-data, meaning by 'based' that if we were not from time to time acquainted with visual and tactual sense-data, these beliefs could neither exist nor be justified. But is this their whole basis? Plainly it is not. To see that it is not, we have only to consider any such belief, and ask what exactly it is that the belief is about. For instance, I believe that this tomato is red, smooth, soft, and sweet-tasting. It is obvious that this is not a belief about a sense-datum. For no single sense-datum has all these qualities. Further, I believe that the tomato is ripe and vitaminous: and these characteristics do not seem to characterize any sense-datum at all. It follows that though sensing is *necessary* for the holding of such beliefs, it is certainly not *sufficient*. There must be some further process or act, by which the subjects of such beliefs are brought before the mind.

It is true that according to Berkeley and many other philosophers material things are wholly composed of sense-data. But even so, sensing would not be sufficient. For even on this view, a material thing is not *a* sense-datum, but a complicated *group* of sense-data. And it is plain that even if all the members of the group are sensed, yet the group itself is not given in sense. In order to bring the group before the mind, we should have to 'collect' the sense-data (to use a term of Mr. Russell's)—or perhaps this would *be* the bringing of it before the mind. And the collecting would have to include at least two processes distinct from sensing. The sense-data are sensed successively, so that memory will be required. And even when (with the help of memory) a number of sense-data past and present are assembled before the mind, we have still to recognize that they stand in such and such relations to each other, say of similarity or spatial collocation or what not; otherwise, though aware of the members, we are not aware of the group. Nor would that be all. For it would probably be admitted, first, that such a group would have no finite number of members; and secondly, that sense-data are private, i.e. that no one mind can sense sense-data sensed by any other mind, while the group is not restricted to any one mind's sense-data. It would follow that no one mind *could* sense all the sense-data which (on this view) compose an object. And even if these admissions were not made, still it is certain that hardly any one who entertains beliefs about a particular material object has in fact sensed more than a very few of the data which are alleged to compose it; it is quite possible that he has only sensed one of them, i.e. has 'just glanced at' the thing as we say, or 'just felt it.' Thus the so-called collecting will have to include the *supplementation* of the given members of the group by not-given ones; i.e. the knowing or believing that in addition to the colour-patches, pressures, smells, etc., actually given to me as I observe the object, there is a vastly—perhaps infinitely—greater multitude of colour-patches, pressures, smells, etc., related to them in the appropriate object-composing manner, but not actually given to me at all. The most we could say would be that, in the case of beliefs based directly on observation, at least one member of the group must have been actually sensed by the holder of the belief, and each of the members *could* be sensed by some observer, human or animal.

Thus even if a material object is wholly composed of sense-data, sensing is not a sufficient (though it is a necessary) condition of holding beliefs about it. Some further mental process or attitude is needed. And *a fortiori* this will be true on other theories concerning the nature of material objects. . . .

And it is natural to consider first the view called *Naive Realism*. The name is not a very suitable one (for the view is hardly a faithful analysis of the unreflective assumptions of the plain or naive man), but it is well known and serves as a convenient label.

Naive Realism . . . holds that my consciousness of an object is the *knowing that* there exists an object to which the sense-datum now sensed by me belongs. Perceptual consciousness would not be acquaintance or intuitive apprehension of a particular, as sensing is. It would be knowledge about, or apprehension of a fact. But it would be like sensing in that it would be knowledge, and not mere belief or mere taking for granted.

Secondly, Naive Realism holds that in the case of a visual or tactual sense-datum, *belonging to* means the same as *being a part of the surface of*: in that literal sense in which the surface of one side of this page is part of the whole surface of this page. Thus if we ask a Naive Realist what sort of thing it is whose existence he knows of in an act of perceptual consciousness, he answers: It is that which visual and tactual sense-data are parts of the surface of. And having a surface, it must be a three-dimensional entity located in space. No doubt he would add that it persists through time and has various causal properties, and that it makes no difference to these spatial and temporal characteristics and these causal properties whether we sense the sense-data belonging to it or not; for this is universally admitted to be part of the meaning of the term 'material thing.'

It is commonly held that the *Argument from Illusion* (as it is called) is sufficient to refute Naive Realism. And this seems substantially true. But what exactly the argument proves is not very clear. The fact seems to be that there are really two distinct arguments: for want of better names we will call them respectively the Phenomenological Argument and the Causal Argument. Contrary to common opinion, the first is by far the more important. It seeks to show directly that there are visual and tactual sense-data which cannot be identical with parts of the surfaces of material objects. The second seeks to show that visual and tactual sense-data only exist while certain processes, other than sensing but contemporary with it, are going on in the nervous system and perhaps in the mind of the being who senses them. And it is inferred from this that they cannot be identical with parts of the surfaces of objects; for such an object (and therefore the surfaces of it) *ex hypothesi* continues to exist at times when we are not sensing, and it is now contended that at those times the sense-data do not exist.

It is not at all easy to state either of these arguments clearly, and in a form which will survive obvious criticisms. The first thing to do is to say what the term 'illusion' means. We must be careful not to define it in causal terms, for this, as we shall see, would lead to a vicious circle. I suggest the following provisional definition: An illusory sense-datum of sight or touch is a sense-datum which is such that we tend to take it to be part of the surface of a material object, but if we take it so we are wrong. It is not necessary that we should *actually* so take it. Thus if I were to see a mirage knowing it to be a mirage, I should not be deceived. But the sense-datum would be none the less illusory: since I do *tend* to take it for part of the surface of a pool of water, and if I actually did I should be wrong. Nor have we begged the question against Naive Realism in saying this. For we have only been saying what the term 'illusory' *means:* whether there are really any instances of it, remains to be seen.

Does the notion of illusoriness apply to data of the other senses? Could there be an illusory sound or smell? It seems clear that there could. But here for 'being part of the surface of' we must substitute something like 'emanating from.' By *s* emanates from O we should mean roughly (1) *s* is caused by O, (2) *s* is more intense in the neighborhood of O than elsewhere.

Now there is no doubt that there are illusory visual and tactual sense-data in the sense defined. Let us begin with visual ones. First, *Perspective* provides plenty of instances. We all know that stereoscopic vision is possible only within a relatively narrow range. Outside this range there is what is called Collapse of Planes, and objects undergo various sorts of 'distortion.' Thus a distant hillside which is full of protuberances, and slopes upwards at quite a gentle angle, will appear flat and vertical, like a scene painted on cardboard. This means that the sense-datum, the colour-expanse which we sense, actually *is* flat and vertical. And if so, it cannot be part of the surface of something protuberant and gently sloping.

Again in *Reflection* the sense-datum is dislocated from the object and reversed as to right and left. Often too it is 'distorted,' i.e. its shape differs from the shape of the object, as with the reflection of a tree in water ruffled by a breeze, or that of a lamp in the polished surface of a shoe. In *Refraction* there is distortion and commonly dislocation too, as with things seen through uneven glass. The like occurs with *physiological* disorders: as for instance in seeing double, where there are two sense-data which cannot both be parts of the surface of the object, for at least one is in the wrong place, and moreover both are flattened. (It is worth remembering that in binocular vision things not in focus are always seen double; and that in the visual experience of an insect every piece of matter is probably multiplied fifty or a hundred fold.) The phenomena of giddiness provide an analogous instance, particularly that giddiness which precedes a fainting fit, where the walls of the room not only 'turn round' but 'move in and out.' *After-images,* which are sense-data completely cut off as it were from the thing, changing and moving independently of its changes and motions, and even capable of existing after its destruction, are the transitional cases between these distorted and dislocated sense-data, and the completely 'wild' ones which are characteristic of *Hallucination*. In hallucination the sense-datum fails to belong to any object in any way at all, though of course the sentient still *takes* it to belong to one. Total hallucination in which the entire field of view consists of 'wild' data is probably confined to lunatics and delirious patients. But partial hallucination, where part of the field of view is wild and part is not, is far from uncommon; for emotion and habitual expectations often cause one to see what one expects to see, for instance (to take some cases from the writer's own experience) they cause one to see 3 instead of 8 when one is waiting for No. 3 bus, or to see a log of wood with protruding branches as a recumbent black and white cow, or a cyclist carrying a milk-can in one hand as a pedestrian leading a goat. In such cases the sense-datum is 'cooked' and supplemented by the mind. And such 'cookery' may be negative as well as positive: some part of what is physically before our eyes has at a certain moment no visual sense-datum belonging to it though other parts have (Negative Hallucination). The failure to see misprints, and sometimes entire words, will illustrate this. When we see the right word instead of the misprint—the most common case—there is a combination of negative and positive hallucination.

Nor must we forget that there are illusions of touch as well as of sight, though they are much less frequent. It will not do to say, with some philosophers, that at least all tactual sense-data are parts of the surfaces of material objects, even if many visual ones are not. Thus a man whose leg has been amputated feels pressure upon his now non-existent foot: i.e. he has a tactual sense-datum similar to those which he used to have before; but there is now no foot with part of whose surface it could be identical. Again, a case has been described in which the patient's brain was operated upon while he remained conscious: when the appropriate region of it was stimulated with a mild electric current, he reported that he felt as if some one was stroking his finger, though nobody was. Thus he sensed a certain tactual sense-datum in the absence of the material thing to which such a datum would ordinarily belong. It is less often realized that there is something corresponding to perspective in touch. Thus a sixpence feels bigger if laid on the tongue than if laid on the back of the hand; and a pair of fixed compass-points drawn across the face appear to diverge as they pass the lips. And it has been pointed out that there are occasional after-images of touch. Thus when my hat is taken off my head, I still continue to feel it there for a time: and the same is true if some small object such as a matchbox is placed on one's head for a minute or two and then removed.

The Phenomenological form of the Argument from illusion simply points to such facts as these and contends that they directly refute Naive Realism. And it certainly does seem clear that there are a great many visual and tactual sense-data which cannot possibly be parts of the surface of material objects in any natural sense of the words 'surface' and 'part.' It follows that perceptual consciousness cannot always be a form of knowing, as the Naive Realists say it is, for it is certainly sometimes erroneous. The Causal Argument uses the same facts in another way. According to it, they show that sense-data vary with variations in the medium between the observer and the object, with variations in the observer's sense-organs, and with variations in his nervous system. And we never find a sense-datum in the absence of a sense-organ and a nervous system, and in sight, hearing and smell we always find a medium as well. Such constant conjunction and concomitant variation, it is urged, are obviously signs of causal dependence. Moreover, this causal dependence is in all cases a dependence on the *brain*. For the states of the intervening medium and of the sense-organs and afferent nerves only make a difference to the sense-datum in so far as they make a difference to processes in that: otherwise they are irrelevant. And the state of the external object itself is only relevant in so far as it indirectly affects the brain, while in hallucination the external object is dispensed with altogether. Further, this dependence of sense-data upon the brain is a *complete* dependence. There is no quality possessed by sense-data which is not subject to this concomitant variation. Thus sense-data are not merely affected by brain-processes, but entirely produced by them. It even begins to seem conceivable that they are themselves cerebral events qualified in a certain way.

If all this is so, no sense-datum can continue to exist in the absence of the cerebral processes which generate it, and therefore no sense-datum can be part of the surface of an external (i.e. extra-cerebral) object, e.g. of a table. If the sense-datum *is* a cerebral event, this is obvious. If it is produced by cerebral events without being one, the conclusion still follows. For when we cease from sensing, the table *ex hypothesi* remains unchanged. But it now appears that when we cease from sensing, the sense-datum itself ceases to exist: it is not merely that the colour-patch or pressure ceases to be a datum, i.e. ceases to be sensed by a mind; it is altogether abolished. (Not that it depends for its existence upon being sensed—that is absurd, since sensing is a form of knowing—but upon another process which only occurs when sensing does.) But if no change occurs in the object when I cease from sensing, then the abolition of the sense-datum cannot be a change in the object, and therefore the sense-datum cannot have been a part of its surface; and we may add, cannot have been a constituent of the object in any other way either.

It might be thought that both arguments could be met by drawing a distinction between *normal* and *abnormal* sense-data. We should then say that normal sense-data of sight and touch *are* parts of the surfaces of material things and are *not* dependent on processes in the observer's brain: while abnormal ones are dependent on processes in the brain and are not part of the surfaces of material things, but are related to the things in some more complicated way. The material thing would still be the remote though not the immediate cause of them, and they might still resemble parts of its surface though they would not *be* such parts. This is a considerable modification in the original theory, but quite a plausible one. We should also have to modify the original account of perceptual consciousness. When I sense an abnormal sense-datum, we must say, I merely *believe* that there exists a material thing part of whose surface it is: only when I sense a normal one do I *know* that there exists such a material thing.

But this will not do. The difficulty is that there is no qualitative difference between normal sense-data as such and abnormal sense-data as such. Indeed the whole trouble about abnormal sense-data is precisely that they simulate normal ones. Otherwise it would not even be possible for us to be deceived by them; they would be strange, but they would not be illusory. We shall give two examples. The abnormal crooked sense-datum of a straight stick standing in water is qualitatively indistinguishable from a normal sense-datum of a crooked stick. Again a mirror-image of a right-hand glove 'looks exactly like' a real left-hand glove; i.e. the two sense-data are indistinguishable, though one is abnormal, the other normal. Is it not incredible that two entities so similar in all these qualities should really be so utterly different: that the one should be a real constituent of a material object, wholly independent of the observer's mind and organism, while the other is merely the fleeting product of his cerebral processes?

We may also appeal to considerations of continuity. When a cricket ball, for instance, is seen from twenty yards off, the sense-datum is flat and therefore abnormal. From a short distance, say two yards, which is within the range of stereoscopic vision, the sense-datum is no longer flat but bulgy and accordingly normal. (We will suppose that there are no complications arising from bad light or drugs or ocular disorders.) But what about intermediate distances? I start from two yards off, and walk slowly backwards, keeping my eye on the ball. At a certain point in my walk, the sense-datum just begins to be flattened; and this must mean that the normal sense-datum is replaced by an abnormal one. There is all the difference in the world between these two sense-data, if the theory is correct. The first is a physical entity, which continues to exist whether my body is present or not, the second is a mere cerebral product. We should expect at least a jerk or a flicker as the one is replaced by the other. But in point of fact we find nothing of the sort. There is a sensibly continuous transition from the bright bulgy patch sensed from two yards off to the faint, small flat one sensed from twenty yards off, without any break at all. Moreover, if the last normal member of the series be taken (and according to the theory there must be a last one), then it will be possible to find an abnormal member which differs from it as little as you please, in size, colour, and bulginess. Now it seems most extraordinary that there should be a total difference of nature where there is only an infinitesimal difference of quality. It also seems most extraordinary that so radical a replacement should be brought about by an infinitesimal backward movement of the observer's body.

Nor is the other part of the theory more plausible. There is no discernible difference in our consciousness when we pass from sensing a normal sense-datum to sensing an abnormal one, or vice versa. In both cases there is acquaintance with something, and in both cases there is also 'perceptual consciousness.' What the nature of this 'perceptual consciousness' may be we are to consider later, but certainly it is the same in both cases. It is impossible to hold that it is knowledge in the one and mere belief in the other.

It might indeed be thought that we could avoid this particular difficulty by making the knowledge less determinate. Might there not be different sorts of 'belonging to'? Normal sense-data might then belong to the thing in one way and abnormal in some other way. And this would enable us to admit that the consciousness is of the same nature in both cases. In each case, it might then be maintained, it is knowledge; and what we know is that there exists some material thing or other to which this sense-datum belongs in some way or other: in which way, and therefore also what particular sort of material thing, would remain to be determined later. But apart from the difficulty of understanding how this determining is to be done, the existence of hallucinations is a fatal objection to the theory. In hallucination, for instance in the visions of delirium, the sense-datum is completely wild; it does not belong to any material thing in any way at all. The pink sense-datum, to take the usual case, not only does not belong to a pink rat, as a sentient himself assumes: it does not *belong to* anything, and indeed owns no allegiance of any sort except to the disordered nervous system which generates it.

Thus if these two arguments are correct, Naive Realism is certainly false. If they are correct, it cannot be held that all visual and tactual sense-data are parts of the surfaces of material objects, and considerations of continuity suggest strongly that none are. Nor can it be held that all instances of perceptual consciousness are instances of knowing: and it is strongly suggested that none are. The positive conclusion is that all sense-data are produced by processes in the brains of the beings who sense them.

Perception and Incorrigibility*

JOHN LANGSHAW AUSTIN [1911–1960] was White's Professor of Moral Philosophy at the University of Oxford. Although he published little during his lifetime, he was one of the most influential teachers and philosophers of the contemporary analytic movement. Some volumes of his writings have been published posthumously: *Philosophical Papers* (1961), *How to Do Things with Words* (1962), and *Sense and Sensibilia* (1962).

The pursuit of the incorrigible is one of the most venerable bugbears in the history of philosophy. It is rampant all over ancient philosophy, most conspicuously in Plato, was powerfully re-animated by Descartes, and bequeathed by him to a long line of successors. . . . In some cases the motive seems to be a comparatively simple hankering for something to be *absolutely certain*—a hankering which can be difficult enough to satisfy if one rigs it so that certainty is absolutely unattainable; in other cases, such as Plato's perhaps, what is apparently sought for is something that will be *always true*. But in the case now before us, which descends directly from Descartes, there is an added complication in the form of a general doctrine about knowledge. And it is of course knowledge, not perception at all, in which these philosophers are really interested. In Ayer's case this shows itself in the title of his book, as well as, *passim*, in his text; Price is more seriously interested than is Ayer in the actual facts about perception, and pays more attention to them —but still, it is worth noticing that, after raising the initial question, 'What is it to *see* something?,' his very next sentence runs, 'When I see a tomato there is much that I *can doubt*.' This suggests that he too is really interested, not so much in what seeing is, as in what one *can't* doubt.

In a nutshell, the doctrine about knowledge, 'empirical' knowledge, is that it has *foundations*. It is a structure the upper tiers of which are reached by inferences, and the foundations are the *data* on which these inferences are based. (So of course—as it appears—there just have to be sense-data.) Now the trouble with inferences is that they may be mistaken; whenever we take a step, we may put a foot wrong. Thus—so the doctrine runs—the way to identify the upper tiers of the structure of knowledge is to ask whether one

* From J. L. Austin: *Sense and Sensibilia*, reconstructed by G. J. Warnock from the manuscript notes, Oxford, 1962. Reprinted by permission of The Clarendon Press, Oxford.

might be mistaken, whether there is something that one *can doubt;* if the answer is Yes, then one is not at the basement. And conversely, it will be characteristic of the *data* that in their case no doubt is possible, no mistake can be made. So to find the data, the foundations, look for *the incorrigible.* . . .

We must now consider the rights and wrongs of all this. . . . It seems to be fairly generally realized nowadays that, if you just take a bunch of sentences (or propositions, to use the term Ayer prefers) impeccably formulated in some language or other, there can be no question of sorting them out into those that are true and those that are false; for (leaving out of account so-called 'analytic' sentences) the question of truth and falsehood does not turn only on what a sentence *is,* nor yet on what it *means,* but on, speaking very broadly, the circumstances in which it is uttered. Sentences are not *as such* either true or false. But it is really equally clear, when one comes to think of it, that for much the same reasons there could be no question of picking out from one's bunch of sentences those that are evidence for others, those that are 'testable,' or those that are 'incorrigible.' What kind of sentence is uttered as providing evidence for what depends, again, on the circumstances of particular cases; there is no kind of sentence which *as such* is evidence-providing, just as there is no kind of sentence which *as such* is surprising, or doubtful, or certain, or incorrigible, or true. Thus, while Carnap is quite right in saying that there is no special kind of sentence which *has* to be picked out as supplying the evidence for the rest, he is quite wrong in supposing that *any* kind of sentence *could* be picked out in this way. It is not that it doesn't much matter how we do it; there is really no question of doing such a thing at all. And thus Ayer is also wrong in holding, as he evidently does hold, that the evidence-providing kind of sentences are always sense-datum sentences, so that *these* are the ones that ought to be picked out.

This idea that there is a certain kind, or form, of sentence which as such is incorrigible and evidence-providing seems to be prevalent enough to deserve more detailed refutation. Let's consider incorrigibility first of all. The argument begins, it appears, from the observation that there are sentences which can be identified as intrinsically more adventurous than others, in uttering which we stick our necks out further. If for instance I say 'That's Sirius,' I am wrong if, though it is a star, that star is not Sirius; whereas, if I had said only 'That's a star,' its not being Sirius would leave me unshaken. Again, if I had said only, 'That looks like a star,' I could have faced with comparative equanimity the revelation that it isn't a star. And so on. Reflections of this kind apparently give rise to the idea that there is or could be a kind of sentence in the utterance of which I take no chances *at all,* my commitment is absolutely minimal; so that in principle *nothing* could show that I had made a mistake, and my remark would be 'incorrigible.'

But in fact this ideal goal is completely unattainable. There isn't, there couldn't be, any kind of sentence which as such is incapable, once uttered, of being subsequently amended or retracted. Ayer himself, though he is prepared to say that sense-datum sentences are incorrigible, takes notice of one way in which they couldn't be; it is, as he admits, always possible in principle that, however non-committal a speaker intends to be, he may produce the *wrong word,* and subsequently be brought to admit this. But Ayer tries, as it were, to laugh this off as a quite trivial qualification; he evidently thinks that he is conceding here only the possibility of slips of the tongue, purely 'verbal' slips (or of course of lying). But this is not so. There are more ways than these of bringing out the wrong word. I may say 'Magenta' wrongly either by a mere slip, having meant to say 'Vermilion'; or because I don't know quite what 'magenta' means, what shade of colour is called *magenta;* or again, because I was unable to, or perhaps just didn't, really notice or attend to or properly size up the colour before me. Thus, there is always the possibility, not only that I may be brought to admit that 'magenta' wasn't the right word to pick on for the colour before me, but *also* that I may be brought to see, or perhaps remember, that the colour before me just wasn't *magenta.* And this holds for the case in which I say, 'It seems, to me personally, here and now, as if I were seeing something magenta,' just as much as for the case in which I say, 'That is magenta.' The first formula may be more cautious, but it isn't *incorrigible.*

Yes, but, it may be said, even if such cautious formulas are not *intrinsically* incorrigible, surely there will be plenty of cases in which what we say by their utterance will *in fact* be incorrigible—cases in which, that is to say, nothing whatever could actually be produced as a cogent ground for retracting them. Well, yes, no doubt this is true. But then exactly the same thing is true of utterances in which quite different forms of words are employed. For if, when I make some statement, it is true that nothing whatever could in fact be produced as a cogent ground for retracting it, this can only be because I am in, have got myself into, the very best possible position for making that statement—I have, and am entitled to have, *complete* confidence in it when I make it. But whether this is so or not is not a matter of what *kind of sentence* I use in making my statement, but of what *the circumstances are* in which I make it. If I carefully scrutinize some patch of colour in my visual field, take careful note of it, know English well, and pay scrupulous attention to just what I'm saying, I may say, 'It seems to me now as if I were seeing something pink'; and nothing whatever could be produced as showing that I had made a mistake. But equally, if I watch for some time an animal a few feet in front of me, in a good light, if I prod it perhaps, sniff, and take note of the noises it makes, I may say, 'That's a pig'; and this too will be 'incorrigible,' nothing could be produced that would show that I had made a mistake. Once one drops the idea that there is a special *kind of sentence* which is *as such* incorrigible, one might as well admit (what is plainly true anyway) that *many* kinds of sentences may be uttered in making statements which are *in fact* incorrigible—in the sense that, when they are made, the circumstances are such that they are quite certainly, definitely, and un-retractably *true.*

Consider next the point about evidence—the idea that there is, again, some special kind of sentences whose function it is to formulate the evidence on which other kinds are based. There are at least two things wrong with this.

First, it is not the case, as this doctrine implies, that whenever a 'material-object' statement is made, the speaker must have or could produce evidence for it. This may sound plausible enough; but it involves a gross misuse of the notion of 'evidence.' The situation in which I would properly be said to have *evidence* for the statement that some animal is a pig is that, for example, in which the beast itself is not actually on view, but I can see plenty of pig-like marks on the ground outside its retreat. If I find a few buckets of pig-food, that's a bit more evidence, and the noises and the smell may provide better evidence still. But if the animal then emerges and stands there plainly in view, there is no longer any question of collecting evidence; its coming into view doesn't provide me with more *evidence* that it's a pig, I can now just *see* that it is, the question is settled. And of course I might, in different cir-cumstances, have just seen this in the first place, and not had to bother with collecting evidence at all. Again, if I actually see one man shoot an-other, I may *give* evidence, as an eye-witness, to those less favourably placed; but I don't *have* evidence for my own statement that the shooting took place, I actually *saw* it. Once again, then, we find that you have to take into account, not just the words used, but the situation in which they are used; one who says 'It's a pig' will sometimes have evidence for saying so, sometimes not; one can't say that the *sentence* 'It's a pig,' as such, is of a kind for which evidence is essentially required.

But secondly, as the case we've considered has already shown, it is not the case that the formulation of evidence is the function of any special sort of sentence. The evidence, if there is any, for a 'material-object' statement will usually be formulated in statements of just the same kind; but in general, *any* kind of statement could state evidence for *any* other kind, if the circum-stances were appropriate. It is not true in general, for instance, that general statements are 'based on' singular statements and not vice versa; my belief that *this* animal will eat turnips may be based on the belief that most pigs eat turnips; though certainly, in different circumstances, I might have supported the claim that most pigs eat turnips by saying that this pig eats them at any rate. Similarly, and more relevantly perhaps to the topic of perception, it is not true in general that statements of how things are are 'based on' statements of how things appear, look, or seem and not vice versa. I may say, for instance, 'That pillar is bulgy' on the ground that it looks bulgy; but equally I might say, in different circumstances, 'That pillar looks bulgy'—on the ground that I've just built it, and I *built* it bulgy.

We are now in a position to deal quite briefly with the idea that 'material-object' statements are *as such* not conclusively verifiable. This is just as wrong as the idea that sense-datum statements are as such incorrigible (it is not just 'misleading,' as Ayer is prepared to allow that it might be). Ayer's doctrine is that 'the notion of certainty does not apply to propositions *of this kind.*' And his ground for saying this is that, in order to verify a proposition of this kind conclusively, we should have to perform the self-contradictory feat of completing 'an infinite series of verifications'; however many tests we may carry out with favourable results, we can never complete all the possible tests, for these are infinite in number; but nothing *less* than all the possible tests would be *enough*.

Now why does Ayer (and not he alone) put forward this very extraordinary doctrine? It is, of course, not true in general that statements about 'material things', as such, *need* to be 'verified.' If, for instance, someone remarks in casual conversation, 'As a matter of fact I live in Oxford,' the other party to the conversation may, if he finds it worth doing, verify this assertion, but the *speaker* of course, has no need to do this—he knows it to be true (or, if he is lying, false). Strictly speaking, indeed, it is not just that he has no *need* to verify his statement; the case is rather that, since he already knows it to be true, nothing whatever that he might do could *count* as his 'verifying' it. Nor need it be true that he is in this position by virtue of having verified his assertion at some previous stage; for of how many people really, who know quite well where they live, could it be said that they have at any time *verified* that they live there? When could they be supposed to have done this? In what way? And why? What we have here, in fact, is an erroneous doctrine which is a kind of mirror-image of the erroneous doctrine about evidence we discussed just now; the idea that statements about 'material things' *as such* need to be verified is just as wrong as, and wrong in just the same way as, the idea that statements about 'material things' *as such* must be based on evidence. And both ideas go astray, at bottom, through the pervasive error of neglecting *the circumstances in which* things are said—of supposing that *the words alone* can be discussed, in a quite general way.

But even if we agree to confine ourselves to situations in which statements can be, and do need to be, verified, the case still looks desperate. Why on earth should one think that such verification can't ever be conclusive? If, for instance, you tell me there's a telephone in the next room, and (feeling mistrustful) I decide to verify this, how could it be thought *impossible* for me to do this conclusively? I go into the next room, and certainly there's something there that looks exactly like a telephone. But is it a case perhaps of *trompe l'oeil* painting? I can soon settle that. Is it just a dummy perhaps, not really connected up and with no proper works? Well, I can take it to pieces a bit and find out, or actually use it for ringing somebody up—and perhaps get them to ring me up too, just to make sure. And of course, if I do all these things, I *do* make sure; what more could possibly be required? This object has already stood up to amply enough tests to establish that it really is a telephone; and it isn't just that, for everyday or practical or ordinary purposes, enough is *as good as* a telephone; what meets all these tests just *is* a telephone, no doubt about it.

However, as is only to be expected, Ayer has a reason for taking this extraordinary view. He holds, as a point of general doctrine, that, though in his view statements about 'material things' are never strictly equivalent to statements about sense-data, yet 'to say anything about a material thing is to say something, but not the same thing about classes of sense-data'; or, as he sometimes puts it, a statement about a 'material thing' *entails* 'some set of statements or other about sense-data.' But—and this is his difficulty—there is no *definite* and *finite* set of statements about sense-data entailed by any statement about a 'material thing.' Thus, however assiduously I check up on the sense-datum statements entailed by a statement about a 'material thing,' I can never exclude the possibility that there are *other* sense-datum statements, which it also entails, but which, if checked, would turn out to be untrue. But of course, if a statement may be found to entail a false statement, then it itself may thereby be found to be false; and this is a possibility which, according to the doctrine, cannot in principle be finally eliminated. And since, again according to the doctrine, verification just consists in thus checking sense-datum statements, it follows that verification can *never* be conclusive.

Of the many objectionable elements in this doctrine in some ways the strangest is the use made of the notion of entailment. What does the sentence, 'That is a pig,' *entail?* Well, perhaps there is somewhere, recorded by some zoological authority, a statement of the necessary and sufficient conditions for belonging to the species *pig*. And so perhaps, if we use the word 'pig' strictly in that sense, to say of an animal that it's a pig will entail that it satisfies those conditions, whatever they may be. But clearly it isn't this

sort of entailment that Ayer has in mind; nor, for that matter, is it particularly relevant to the use that non-experts make of the word 'pig.' But what
other kind of entailment is there? We have a pretty rough idea what pigs
look like, what they smell and sound like, and how they normally behave;
and no doubt, if something didn't look at all right for a pig, behave as pigs
do, or make pig-like noises and smells, we'd say that it wasn't a pig. But
are there—do there *have* to be—*statements* of the term, 'It looks . . . ,' 'It
sounds . . . ,' 'It smells . . . ,' of which we could say straight off that
'That is a pig' entails them? Plainly not. We learn the word 'pig,' as we
learn the vast majority of words for ordinary things, ostensively—by being
told, in the presence of the animal, '*That* is a pig'; and thus, though certainly
we learn what sort of thing it is to which the word 'pig' can and can't be
properly applied, we don't go through any kind of intermediate stage of relating the word 'pig' to a lot of *statements* about the way things look, or
sound, or smell. The word is just not introduced into our vocabulary in this
way. Thus, though of course we come to have certain expectations as to
what will and won't be the case when a pig is in the offing, it is wholly
artificial to represent these expectations in the guise of *statements entailed by*
'That is a pig.' And for just this reason it is, at best, wholly artificial to speak
as if *verifying* that some animal is a pig consists in checking up on the statements entailed by 'That is a pig.' If we do think of verification in this way,
certainly difficulties abound; we don't know quite where to begin, how to
go on, or where to stop. But what this shows is, not that 'That is a pig' is
very difficult to verify or incapable of being conclusively verified, but that
this is an impossible travesty of verification. If the procedure of verification
were rightly described in this way, then indeed we couldn't say just what
would constitute conclusive verification that some animal was a pig. But
this doesn't show that there is actually any difficulty at all, usually, in
verifying that an animal is a pig, if we have occasion to do so; it shows
only that what verification *is* has been completely misrepresented.

We may add to this the rather different but related point that, though certainly we have more or less definite views as to what objects of particular
kinds will and won't do, and of how they will and won't re-act in one situation or another, it would again be grossly artificial to represent these in the
guise of definite entailments. There are vast numbers of things which I take
it for granted that a telephone won't do, and doubtless an infinite number of
things which it never enters my head to consider the possibility that it might
do; but surely it would be perfectly absurd to say that 'This is a telephone'
entails the whole galaxy of statements to the effect that it doesn't and won't
do these things, and to conclude that I haven't *really* established that anything is a telephone until, *per impossibile*, I have confirmed the whole infi-

nite class of these supposed entailments. Does 'This is a telephone' *entail* 'You couldn't eat it'? Must I try to eat it, and fail, in the course of making sure that it's a telephone?

The conclusions we have reached so far, then, can be summed up as follows:

1. There is no *kind* or *class* of sentences ('propositions') of which it can be said that *as such*
   (a) they are incorrigible;
   (b) they provide the evidence for other sentences; and
   (c) they must be checked in order that other sentences may be verified.
2. It is not true of sentences about 'material things' that *as such*
   (a) they must be supported by or based on evidence;
   (b) they stand in need of verification; and
   (c) they cannot be conclusively verified.

Sentences in fact—as distinct from *statements made in particular circumstances*—cannot be divided up *at all* on these principles, into two groups or any other number of groups. And this means that the general doctrine about knowledge which I sketched at the beginning of this section, which is the real bugbear underlying doctrines of the kind we have been discussing, is *radically* and *in principle* misconceived. For even if we were to make the very risky and gratuitous assumption that what some particular person knows at some particular place and time could systematically be sorted out into an arrangement of foundations and super-structure, it would be a mistake in principle to suppose that the same thing could be done for knowledge *in general*. And this is because there *could* be no *general* answer to the questions what is evidence for what, what is certain, what is doubtful, what needs or does not need evidence, can or can't be verified. If the Theory of Knowledge consists in finding grounds for such an answer, there is no such thing.

SUGGESTED READINGS

B. Russell's important paper, "Knowledge by Acquaintance and Knowledge by Description," is reprinted in *Mysticism and Logic*. G. E. Moore's early views on sense-data are now available in Chapter II of *Some Main Problems of Philosophy*. Most modern discussion of the given is influenced in one way or another by the work of these two philosophers. A. J. Ayer gives a clear statement of an empiricist position in *Foundations of Empirical*

Knowledge, Chapters 1 and 2, and in the volume he edited, *Logical Positiv-ism,* he includes statements by several positivists; see especially the papers by Neurath and Schlick.

Peirce and John Dewey anticipate some aspects of Austin's attack on the concept of a "given." For Peirce, see the two very difficult essays, "Questions Concerning Certain Faculties Claimed for Man" and "Some Consequences of Four Incapacities," both in Volume V of his *Collected Papers* (and in P. P. Wiener's collection *Values in a Universe of Chance*). W. Gallie's *Peirce* is a good introduction to these essays. For Dewey, see *Essays in Experimental Logic* (Chapter 4) and the essay "Context and Thought," reprinted in *On Experience, Nature, and Freedom,* edited by R. Bernstein. The difficult but valuable essay by W. Sellars, "Empiricism and the Philosophy of Mind," in *Science, Perception and Reality,* similarly attacks the idea that there must be some one type of entity which in any situation is given and from which all construction of knowledge must begin.

For a useful collection of statements by "Realists" of a variety of persua-sions, see R. M. Chisholm (editor), *Realism and the Background of Percep-tion,* especially selections 8 and 9.

Perception and the External World

The usual commonsense view of our knowledge of the external world assumes:
(1) that there is a world of physical objects existing independently of our perceptions or conceptions of it; and (2) that when we perceive things we are aware of them as they really are. Common sense takes it for granted that a desk, for example, not only exists independently of anyone's experiencing it, but that it really *is*, in itself, as it appears to us: it is the size, shape, and color that we perceive it to be.

The commonsense view does not seem to deal adequately with two types of difficulty. In the first place, a desk appears to have different sizes, shapes, and colors when seen from different positions or under different illuminations; yet common sense holds it to be one and the same desk that we perceive under all these conditions and assumes that its *real* qualities remain unaffected by our position or by the lighting. In the second place, when we contrast the description of the world given by physicists with a description of the world as it appears in direct perception, the two descriptions are very different. Contemporary physical theories describe material objects such as desks as being configurations of electrical charges in rapid motion. According to such descriptions, material objects are not "solid," nor are they colored; in most respects, if not all, they are utterly different from what we regard as material objects on the basis of direct perception.

These difficulties have been attacked in a number of ways. BERKELEY defends the view that the only real substances are minds. The first part of the selection gives his classic attack on the existence of an independent *material* world and answers some of the objections that might be raised against it. In the second part he puts forward his own positive form of Idealism. LOVEJOY represents the view of Critical Realism. He argues for the hypothesis that a physical world exists independently of experience and holds that we can learn something of its nature by inferences based upon experience. LEWIS also defends realism, but does so from a pragmatic point of view: our knowledge of the external world depends on the fact that our concepts do the work they are intended to do. MOORE on the other hand claims that our initial feelings were right all along; the commonsense view of the world is one we all share, and indeed all we need. The selection from MERLEAU-PONTY defends the view that perception is primary as a source of our knowledge of the world we live in and that we should not think of such knowledge as "mediated" by the concepts of common sense or those of science.

Idealism*

GEORGE BERKELEY [1685–1753] was an Anglican minister, an important figure in literary circles, and one of the most acute of British philosophers. Before he was twenty, the main principles of his pluralistic idealism were fully formed. His major works, *A Treatise on the Principles of Human Knowledge* and *Three Dialogues between Hylas and Philonous*, were published in 1710 and 1713. The analysis of knowledge which they contain has had great influence on all subsequent philosophy.

THE UNREALITY OF A MATERIAL WORLD. It is evident to any one who takes a survey of the *objects of human knowledge*, that they are either *ideas* actually imprinted on the senses; or else such as are perceived by attending to the passions and operations of the mind; or lastly, *ideas* formed by help of memory and imagination—either compounding, dividing, or barely representing those originally perceived in the aforesaid ways. By sight I have the ideas of light and colours, with their several degrees and variations. By touch I perceive hard and soft, heat and cold, motion and resistance; and of all these more and less either as to quantity or degree. Smelling furnishes me with odours; the palate with tastes; and hearing conveys sounds to the mind in all their variety of tone and composition.

And as several of these are observed to accompany each other, they come to be marked by one name, and so to be reputed as one *thing*. Thus, for example, a certain colour, taste, smell, figure and consistence having been observed to go together, are accounted one distinct thing, signified by the name apple; other collections of ideas constitute a stone, a tree, a book, and the like sensible things; which as they are pleasing or disagreeable excite the passions of love, hatred, joy, grief, and so forth. . . .

That neither our thoughts, nor passions, nor ideas formed by the imagination, exist without the mind is what everybody will allow. And to me it seems no less evident that the various sensations or ideas imprinted on the Sense, however blended or combined together (that is, whatever objects they compose), cannot exist otherwise than in a mind perceiving them. I think an intuitive knowledge may be obtained of this, by any one that shall

---

* From Berkeley: *A Treatise Concerning the Principles of Human Knowledge* (1710). [*Note*: The following selections are all from Part I and are given in the following order. The Unreality of a Material World: paragraphs 1, 3, 8–11, 14–15, 18–20, 23, 34, 37–38, 40–45; The True Nature of the World: paragraphs 2, 25–27, 136–139, 28–31, 145–149.]

attend to what is meant by the term *exist* when applied to sensible things. . . . There was an odour, that is, it was smelt; there was a sound, that is, it was heard; a colour or figure, and it was perceived by sight or touch. This is all that I can understand by these and the like expressions. For as to what is said of the *absolute* existence of unthinking things, without any relation to their being perceived, that is to me perfectly unintelligible. Their *esse* is *percipi;* nor is it possible they should have any existence out of the minds or thinking things which perceive them. . . .

But, say you, though the ideas themselves do not exist without the mind, yet there may be things like them, whereof they are copies or resemblances; which things exist without the mind, in an unthinking substance. I answer, an idea can be like nothing but an idea; a colour or figure can be like nothing but another colour or figure. If we look but never so little into our thoughts, we shall find it impossible for us to conceive a likeness except only between our ideas. Again, I ask whether those supposed *originals,* or external things, of which our ideas are the pictures or representations, be themselves perceivable or no? If they are, then *they* are ideas, and we have gained our point: but if you say they are not, I appeal to any one whether it be sense to assert a colour is like something which is invisible; hard or soft, like something which is intangible; and so of the rest.

Some there are who make a distinction betwixt *primary* and *secondary* qualities. By the former they mean extension, figure, motion, rest, solidity or impenetrability, and number; by the latter they denote all other sensible qualities, as colours, sounds, tastes, and so forth. The ideas we have of these last they acknowledge not to be the resemblances of anything existing without the mind, or unperceived; but they will have our ideas of the *primary qualities* to be patterns or images of things which exist without the mind, in an unthinking substance which they call Matter. By Matter, therefore, we are to understand an inert, senseless substance, in which extension, figure, and motion do actually subsist. But it is evident, from what we have already shewn, that extension, figure and motion are only ideas existing in the mind, and an idea can be like nothing but another idea; and that consequently neither they nor their archetypes can exist in an unperceiving substance. Hence, it is plain that the very notion of what is called *Matter* or *corporeal substance,* involves a contradiction in it. Insomuch that I should not think it necessary to spend more time in exposing its absurdity. But, because the tenet of the existence of Matter seems to have taken so deep a root in the minds of philosophers, and draws after it so many ill consequences, I choose rather to be thought prolix and tedious than omit anything that might conduce to the full discovery and extirpation of that prejudice.

They who assert that figure, motion, and the rest of the primary or original qualities do exist without the mind, in unthinking substances, do at the same time acknowledge that colours, sounds, heat, cold, and such-like secondary qualities, do not; which they tell us are sensations, existing in the mind alone, that depend on and are occasioned by the different size, texture, and motion of the minute particles of matter. This they take for an undoubted truth, which they can demonstrate beyond all exception. Now, if it be certain that those *original* qualities are inseparably united with the other sensible qualities, and not, even in thought, capable of being abstracted from them, it plainly follows that *they* exist only in the mind. But I desire any one to reflect, and try whether he can, by any abstraction of thought, conceive the extension and motion of a body without all other sensible qualities. For my own part, I see evidently that it is not in my power to frame an idea of a body extended and moving, but I must withal give it some colour or other sensible quality, which is acknowledged to exist only in the mind. In short, extension, figure, and motion, abstracted from all other qualities, are inconceivable. Where therefore the other sensible qualities are, there must these be also, to wit, in the mind and nowhere else.

Again, *great* and *small, swift* and *slow,* are allowed to exist nowhere without the mind; being entirely relative, and changing as the frame or position of the organs of sense varies. The extension therefore which exists without the mind is neither great nor small, the motion neither swift nor slow; that is, they are nothing at all. But, say you, they are extension in general, and motion in general. Thus we see how much the tenet of extended moveable substances existing without the mind depends on that strange doctrine of *abstract ideas.* And here I cannot but remark how nearly the vague and indeterminate description of Matter, or corporeal substance, which the modern philosophers are run into by their own principles, resembles that antiquated and so much ridiculed notion of *materia prima,* to be met with in Aristotle and his followers. Without extension solidity cannot be conceived: since therefore it has been shewn that extension exists not in an unthinking substance, the same must also be true of solidity. . . .

I shall farther add, that, after the same manner as modern philosophers prove certain sensible qualities to have no existence in Matter, or without the mind, the same thing may be likewise proved of all other sensible qualities whatsoever. Thus, for instance, it is said that heat and cold are affections only of the mind, and not at all patterns of real beings, existing in the corporeal substances which excite them; for that the same body which appears cold to one hand seems warm to another. Now, why may we not as well argue that figure and extension are not patterns or resemblances of qualities existing in Matter; because to the same eye at different stations, or eyes of a different texture at the same station, they appear various, and cannot therefore be the images of anything settled and determinate without the mind? Again, it is proved that sweetness is not really in the sapid thing; because the thing remaining unaltered the sweetness is changed into bitter, as in case of a fever or otherwise vitiated palate. Is it not as reasonable to say that motion is not without the mind; since if the succession of ideas in the mind become swifter, the motion, it is acknowledged, shall appear slower, without any alteration in any external object?

In short, let any one consider those arguments which are thought manifestly to prove that colours and tastes exist only in the mind, and he shall find they may with equal force be brought to prove the same thing of extension, figure, and motion. Though it must be confessed this method of arguing does not so much prove that there is no extension or colour in an outward object, as that we do not know by sense which is the true extension or colour of the object. But the arguments foregoing plainly shew it to be impossible that any colour or extension at all, or other sensible quality whatsoever, should exist in an unthinking subject without the mind, or in truth that there should be any such thing as an outward object. . . .

[Supposing] it were possible that solid, figured, moveable substances may exist without the mind, corresponding to the ideas we have of bodies, yet how is it possible for us to know this? Either we must know it by Sense or by Reason. As for our senses, by them we have the knowledge only of our sensations, ideas, or those things that are immediately perceived by sense, call them what you will: but they do not inform us that things exist without the mind, or unperceived, like to those which are perceived. This the materialists themselves acknowledge.—It remains therefore that if we have any knowledge at all of external things, it must be by reason inferring their existence from what is immediately perceived by sense. But I do not see what reason can induce us to believe the existence of bodies without the mind, from what we perceive, since the very patrons of Matter themselves do not pretend there is any necessary connexion betwixt them and our ideas? I say it is granted on all hands (and what happens in dreams, frensies, and the like, puts it beyond dispute) that it is possible we might be affected with all the ideas we have now, though no bodies existed without resembling them. Hence it is evident the supposition of external bodies is not necessary for the producing our ideas; since it is granted they are produced sometimes, and might possibly be produced always, in the same order we see them in at present, without their concurrence.

But, though we might possibly have all our sensations without them, yet perhaps it may be thought easier to conceive and explain the manner of their production, by supposing external bodies in their likeness rather than otherwise; and so it might be at least probable there are such things as bodies that excite their ideas in our minds. But neither can this be said. For, though we give the materialists their external bodies, they by their own confession are never the nearer knowing how our ideas are produced; since they own themselves unable to comprehend in what manner body can act upon spirit, or how it is possible it should imprint any idea in the mind. Hence it is evident the production of ideas or sensations in our minds, can be no reason why we should suppose Matter or corporeal substances; since that is acknowledged to remain equally inexplicable with or without this supposition. If therefore it were possible for bodies to exist without the mind, yet to hold they do so must needs be a very precarious opinion; since it is to suppose, without any reason at all, that God has created innumerable beings that are entirely useless, and serve to no manner of purpose.

In short, if there were external bodies, it is impossible we should ever come to know it; and if there were not, we might have the very same reasons to think there were that we have now. . . .

But, say you, surely there is nothing easier than for me to imagine trees, for instance, in a park, or books existing in a closet, and nobody by to perceive them. I answer, you may so, there is no difficulty in it. But what is all this, I beseech you, more than framing in your mind certain ideas which you call *books* and *trees*, and at the same time omitting to frame the idea of any one that may perceive them? But do not you yourself perceive or think of them all the while? This therefore is nothing to the purpose: it only shews you have the power of imagining, or forming ideas in your mind; but it does not shew that you can conceive it possible the objects of your thought may exist without the mind. To make out this, it is necessary that you conceive them existing unconceived or unthought of; which is a manifest repugnancy. When we do our utmost to conceive the existence of external bodies, we are all the while only contemplating our own ideas. But the mind, taking no notice of itself, is deluded to think it can and does conceive bodies existing unthought of, or without the mind, though at the same time they are apprehended by, or exist in, itself. A little attention will discover to any one the truth and evidence of what is here said, and make it unnecessary to insist on any other proofs against the existence of *material substance.* . . .

Before we proceed any farther it is necessary we spend some time in answering Objections which may probably be made against the Principles we have hitherto laid down. In doing of which, if I seem too prolix to those of quick apprehensions, I desire I may be excused, since all men do not equally apprehend things of this nature; and I am willing to be understood by every one.

First, then, it will be objected that by the foregoing principles all that is real and substantial in nature is banished out of the world, and instead thereof a chimerical scheme of *ideas* takes place. All things that exist exist only in the mind; that is, they are purely notional. What therefore becomes of the sun, moon, and stars? What must we think of houses, rivers, mountains, trees, stones; nay, even of our own bodies? Are all these but so many chimeras and illusions on the fancy?—To all which, and whatever else of the same sort may be objected, I answer, that by the Principles premised we are not deprived of any one thing in nature. Whatever we see, feel, hear, or any wise conceive or understand, remains as secure as ever, and is as real as ever. . . .

It will be urged that thus much at least is true, to wit, that we take away all *corporeal substances*. To this my answer is, that if the word *substance* be taken in the vulgar sense, for a *combination* of sensible qualities, such as extension, solidity, weight, and the like—this we cannot be accused of taking away: but if it be taken in a philosophic sense, for the support of accidents or qualities without the mind—then indeed I acknowledge that we take it away, if one may be said to take away that which never had any existence, not even in the imagination.

But after all, say you, it sounds very harsh to say we eat and drink ideas, and we are clothed with ideas. I acknowledge it does so—the word *idea* not being used in common discourse to signify the several combinations of sensible qualities which are called *things;* and it is certain that any expression which varies from the familiar use of language will seem harsh and ridiculous. But this doth not concern the truth of the proposition, which in other words is no more than to say, we are fed and clothed with those things which we perceive immediately by our senses. The hardness or softness, the colour, taste, warmth, figure, and suchlike qualities, which combined together constitute the several sorts of victuals and apparel, have been shewn to exist only in the mind that perceives them: and this is all that is meant by calling them *ideas*. . . .

But, say what we can, some one perhaps may be apt to reply, he will still believe his senses, and never suffer any arguments, how plausible soever, to prevail over the certainty of them. Be it so; assert the evidence of sense as high as you please, we are willing to do the same. That what I see, hear, and feel doth exist, that is to say, is perceived by me, I no more doubt than I do of my own being. But I do not see how the testimony of sense can be alleged as a proof for the existence of anything which is *not* perceived by sense. . . .

Secondly, it will be objected that there is a great difference betwixt real fire for instance, and the idea of fire, betwixt dreaming or imagining oneself burnt, and actually being so. (If you suspect it to be only the idea of fire which you see, do but put your hand into it and you will be convinced with a witness.) This and the like may be urged in opposition to our tenets.—To all which the answer is evident from what hath been already said; and I shall only add in this place, that if real fire be very different from the idea of fire, so also is the real pain that it occasions very different from the idea of the same pain, and yet nobody will pretend that real pain either is, or can possibly be, in an unperceiving thing, or without the mind, any more than its idea.

Thirdly, it will be objected that we see things actually without or at a distance from us, and which consequently do not exist in the mind; it being absurd that those things which are seen at the distance of several miles should be as near to us as our own thoughts.—In answer to this, I desire it may be considered that in a dream we do oft perceive things as existing at a great distance off, and yet for all that, those things are acknowledged to have their existence only in the mind.

But, for the fuller clearing of this point, it may be worth while to consider how it is that we perceive distance, and things placed at a distance, by sight. For, that we should in truth *see* external space, and bodies actually existing in it, some nearer, others farther off, seems to carry with it some opposition to what hath been said of their existing nowhere without the mind. The consideration of this difficulty it was that gave birth to my *Essay towards a New Theory of Vision,* which was published not long since. Wherein it is shewn that distance or outness is neither immediately of itself perceived by sight, nor yet apprehended or judged of by lines and angles, or anything that hath a necessary connexion with it; but that it is only suggested to our thoughts by certain visible ideas, and sensations attending vision, which in their own nature have no manner of similitude or relation either with distance or things placed at a distance; but, by a connexion taught us by experience, they come to signify and suggest them to us, after the same manner that words of any language suggest the ideas they are made to stand for. . . . So that in strict truth the ideas of sight, when we apprehend by them distance, and things placed at a distance, do not suggest or mark out to us things actually existing at a distance, but only admonish us what ideas of touch will be imprinted in our minds at such and such distances of time, and in consequence of such or such actions. . . .

Fourthly, it will be objected that from the foregoing principles it follows things are every moment annihilated and created anew. The objects of sense exist only when they are perceived: the trees therefore are in the garden, or the chairs in the parlour, no longer than while there is somebody by to perceive them. Upon shutting my eyes all the furniture in the room is reduced to nothing, and barely upon opening them it is again created.—In answer to all which, I refer the reader to what has been said, and desire he will consider whether he means anything by the actual existence of an idea distinct from its being perceived. For my part, after the nicest inquiry I could make, I am not able to discover that anything else is meant by those words; and I once more entreat the reader to sound his own thoughts, and not suffer himself to be imposed on by words. If he can conceive it possible either for his ideas or their archetypes to exist without being perceived, then I give up the cause. But if he cannot, he will acknowledge it is unreasonable for him to stand up in defence of he knows not what, and pretend to charge on me as an absurdity, the not assenting to those propositions which at bottom have no meaning in them. . . .

THE TRUE NATURE OF THE WORLD. But, besides all that endless variety of ideas or objects of knowledge, there is likewise Something which knows or perceives them, and exercises divers operations, as willing, imagining, remembering, about them. This perceiving, *active* being is what I call *mind, spirit, soul,* or *myself.* By which words I do not denote any one of my ideas, but a thing entirely distinct from them, wherein they exist, or, which is the same thing, whereby they are perceived; for the existence of an idea consists in being perceived. . . .

[Now,] all our ideas, sensations, notions, or the things which we perceive, by whatsoever names they may be distinguished, are visibly *inactive:* there is nothing of power or agency included in them. So that one idea or object of thought cannot produce or make any alteration in another. To be satisfied of the truth of this, there is nothing else requisite but a bare observation of our ideas. For, since they and every part of them exist only in the mind, it follows that there is nothing in them but what is perceived; but whoever shall attend to his ideas, whether of sense or reflexion, will not perceive in them any power or activity; there is, therefore, no such thing contained in them. A little attention will discover to us that the very being of an idea implies passiveness and inertness in it; insomuch that it is impossible for an idea to do anything, or, strictly speaking, to be the cause of anything: neither can it be the resemblance or pattern of any active being. Whence it plainly follows that extension, figure, and motion cannot be the cause of our sensations. To say, therefore, that these are the effects of powers resulting from the configuration, number, motion, and size of corpuscles, must certainly be false.

[But] we perceive a continual succession of ideas; some are anew excited, others are changed or totally disappear. There is therefore, *some* cause of these ideas, whereon they depend, and which produces and changes them. That this cause cannot be any quality or idea or combination of *ideas,* is clear from the preceding paragraph. . . . It must therefore be a *substance;* but it has been shewn that there is no corporeal or material substance: it remains therefore that the cause of ideas is an incorporeal active substance or Spirit.

A Spirit is one simple, undivided, active being—as it perceives ideas it is called the *understanding*, and as it produces or otherwise operates about them it is called the *will*. Hence there can be no *idea* formed of a soul or spirit; for all ideas whatever, being passive and inert, they cannot represent unto us, by way of image or likeness, that which acts. A little attention will make it plain to any one, that to have an idea which shall be *like* that active Principle of motion and change of ideas is absolutely impossible. Such is the nature of Spirit, or that which acts, that it cannot be of itself perceived, but only by the effects which it produceth. . . .

It will perhaps be said that we want a *sense* (as some have imagined) proper to know substances withal; which, if we had, we might know our own soul as we do a triangle. To this I answer, that in case we had a new sense bestowed upon us, we could only receive thereby some new *sensations* or *ideas of sense*. But I believe nobody will say that what he means by the terms *soul* and *substance* is only some particular sort of idea or sensation. We may therefore infer that, all things duly considered, it is not more reasonable to think our faculties defective, in that they do not furnish us with an *idea* of Spirit, or active thinking substance, than it would be if we should blame them for not being able to comprehend a *round square*.

From the opinion that Spirits are to be known after the manner of an idea or sensation have arisen many absurd and heterodox tenets, and much scepticism about the nature of the soul. It is even probable that this opinion may have produced a doubt in some whether they had any soul at all distinct from their body; since upon inquiry they could not find they had an idea of it. That an *idea,* which is inactive, and the existence whereof consists in being perceived, should be the image or likeness of an agent subsisting by itself, seems to need no other refutation than barely attending to what is meant by those words. But perhaps you will say that though an idea cannot resemble a Spirit in its thinking, acting, or subsisting by itself, yet it may in some other respects; and it is not necessary that an idea or image be in all respects like the original.

I answer, If it does not in those mentioned, it is impossible it should represent it in any other thing. Do but leave out the power of willing, thinking, and perceiving ideas, and there remains nothing else wherein the idea can be like a spirit. For, by the word *spirit* we mean only that which thinks, wills, and perceives; this, and this alone, constitutes the signification of that term. If therefore it is impossible that any degree of those powers should be represented in an idea, it is evident there can be no idea of a Spirit.

But it will be objected that, if there is no *idea* signified by the terms, *soul, spirit,* and *substance,* they are wholly insignificant, or have no meaning in them. I answer, those words do mean or signify a real thing; which is neither an idea nor like an idea, but that which perceives ideas, and wills, and reasons about them. . . .

I find I can excite ideas in my mind at pleasure, and vary and shift the scene as oft as I think fit. It is no more than *willing*, and straightway this or that idea arises in my fancy; and by the same power it is obliterated and makes way for another. This making and unmaking of ideas doth very properly denominate the mind active. Thus much is certain and grounded on experience: but when we talk of unthinking agents, or of exciting ideas exclusive of volition, we only amuse ourselves with words.

But, whatever power I may have over my own thoughts, I find the ideas actually perceived by Sense have not a like dependence of *my* will. When in broad daylight I open my eyes, it is not in my power to choose whether I shall see or no, or to determine what particular objects shall present themselves to my view: and so likewise as to the hearing and other senses; the ideas imprinted on them are not creatures of *my* will. There is therefore some other Will or Spirit that produces them.

ϪThe ideas of Sense are more strong, lively, and distinct than those of the Imagination; they have likewise a steadiness, order, and coherence, and are not excited at random, as those which are the effects of human wills often are, but in a regular train or series—the admirable connexion whereof sufficiently testifies the wisdom and benevolence of its Author. Now the set rules, or established methods, wherein the Mind we depend on excites in us the ideas of Sense, are called *the laws of nature;* and these we learn by experience, which teaches us that such and such ideas are attended with such and such other ideas, in the ordinary course of things. Ϫ

This gives us a sort of foresight, which enables us to regulate our actions for the benefit of life. And without this we should be eternally at a loss: we could not know how to act for anything that might procure us the least pleasure, or remove the least pain of sense. That food nourishes, sleep refreshes, and fire warms us; that to sow in the seed-time is the way to reap in the harvest; and in general that to obtain such or such ends, such or such means are conducive—all this we know, not by discovering any *necessary connexion* between our ideas, but only by the observation of the *settled laws* of nature; without which we should be all in uncertainty and confusion, and a grown man no more know how to manage himself in the affairs of life than an infant just born. . . .

[Now,] from what hath been said, it is plain that we cannot know the existence of *other spirits* otherwise than by their operations, or the ideas by them, excited in us. I perceive several motions, changes, and combinations of ideas, that inform me there are certain particular agents like myself, which accompany them, and concur in their production. Hence, the knowledge I have of other spirits is not immediate, as is the knowledge of my ideas; but depending on the intervention of ideas, by me referred to agents or spirits distinct from myself, as effects or concomitant signs.

But, though there be some things which convince us human agents are concerned in producing them, yet it is evident to every one that those things which are called the Works of Nature, that is, the far greater part of the ideas or sensations perceived by us, are *not* produced by, or dependent on, the wills of *men*. There is therefore some other Spirit that causes them; since it is repugnant that they should subsist by themselves. But, if we attentively consider the constant regularity, order, and concatenation of natural things, the surprising magnificence, beauty and perfection of the larger, and the exquisite contrivance of the smaller parts of the creation, together with the exact harmony and correspondence of the whole, but above all the never-enough-admired laws of pain and pleasure, and the instincts or natural inclinations, appetites, and passions of animals;—I say if we consider all these things, and at the same time attend to the meaning and import of the attributes One, Eternal, Infinitely Wise, Good, and Perfect, we shall clearly perceive that they belong to the aforesaid Spirit, 'who works in all' and 'by whom all things consist.'

Hence, it is evident that God is known as certainly and immediately as any other mind or spirit whatsoever, distinct from ourselves. We may even assert that the existence of God is far more evidently perceived than the existence of men; because the effects of Nature are infinitely more numerous and considerable than those ascribed to human agents. There is not any one mark that denotes a man, or effect produced by him, which does not more strongly evince the being of that Spirit who is the Author of Nature. For it is evident that, in affecting other persons, the will of man hath no other object than barely the motion of the limbs of his body; but that such a motion should be attended by, or excite any idea in the mind of another, depends wholly on the will of the Creator. He alone it is who, 'upholding all things by the word of His power,' maintains that intercourse between spirits whereby they are able to perceive the existence of each other. And yet this pure and clear Light which enlightens everyone is itself invisible to the greatest part of mankind.

It seems to be a general pretence of the unthinking herd that they cannot *see* God. Could we but see Him, say they, as we see a man, we should believe that He is, and believing obey His commands. But alas, we need only open our eyes to see the Sovereign Lord of all things, with a *more* full and clear view than we do any one of our fellow-creatures. Not that I imagine we see God (as some will have it) by a direct and immediate view; or see corporeal things, not by themselves, but by seeing that which represents them in the essence of God, which doctrine is, I must confess, to me incomprehensible. But I shall explain my meaning. A human spirit or person is not perceived by sense, as not being an idea. When therefore we see the colour, size, figure, and motions of a man, we perceive only certain sensations or ideas excited in our own minds; and these being exhibited to our view in sundry distinct collections, serve to mark out unto us the existence of finite and created spirits like ourselves. Hence it is plain we do not see a man, if by *man* is meant, that which lives, moves, perceives, and thinks as we do: but only such a certain collection of ideas, as directs us to think there is a distinct principle of thought and motion, like to ourselves, accompanying and repre- sented by it. And after the same manner we see God: all the difference is that, whereas some one finite and narrow assemblage of ideas denotes a par- ticular human mind, whithersoever we direct our view we do at all times and in all places perceive manifest tokens of the Divinity; everything we see, hear, feel, or anywise perceive by sense, being a sign or affect of the power of God; as is our perception of those very motions which are produced by men.

It is therefore plain that nothing can be more evident to any one that is capable of the least reflexion than the existence of God, or a Spirit who is intimately present to our minds, producing in them all that variety of ideas or sensations which continually affect us, on whom we have an absolute and entire dependence, in short 'in whom we live, and move, and have our being.'

The Commonsense View of the World*

GEORGE EDWARD MOORE [1873–1958] was educated at Cambridge University and taught there from 1911 until his retirement in 1939. Moore was one of the leaders in the development of analytic philosophy. His works on the theory of knowledge and on ethics have had a pervasive influence on contempo- rary British and American philosophy.

In what follows I have merely tried to state, one by one, some of the most important points in which my philosophical position differs from positions which have been taken up by *some* other philosophers. . . .

* From Moore: "A Defence of Common Sense," in *Philosophical Papers*, 1959. Re- printed by permission of the publisher, George Allen and Unwin, Ltd., London.

The first point is a point which embraces a great many other points. And it is one which I cannot state as clearly as I wish to state it, except at some length. The method I am going to use for stating it is this. I am going to begin by enunciating, under the heading (1), a whole long list of propositions, which may seem, at first sight, such obvious truisms as not to be worth stating: they are, in fact, a set of propositions, every one of which (in my own opinion) I *know*, with certainty, to be true. I shall, next, under the heading (2), state a single proposition which makes an assertion about a whole set of *classes* of propositions—each class being defined, as the class consisting of all propositions which resemble *one* of the propositions in (1) in a certain respect. (2), therefore, is a proposition which could not be stated, until the list of propositions in (1), or some similar list, had already been given. (2) is itself a proposition which may seem such an obvious truism as not to be worth stating: and it is also a proposition which (in my own opinion) I *know*, with certainty, to be true. But, nevertheless, it is, to the best of my belief, a proposition with regard to which many philosophers have, for different reasons, differed from me; even if they have not directly denied (2) itself, they have held views incompatible with it. My first point, then, may be said to be that (2), together with all its implications, some of which I shall expressly mention, is true.

(1) I begin, then, with my list of truisms, every one of which (in my own opinion) I *know*, with certainty, to be true. The propositions to be included in this list are the following:

There exists at present a living human body, which is *my* body. This body was born at a certain time in the past, and has existed continuously ever since, though not without undergoing changes; it was, for instance, much smaller when it was born, and for some time afterwards, than it is now. Ever since it was born, it has been either in contact with or not far from the surface of the earth; and, at every moment since it was born, there have also existed many other things, having shape and size in three dimensions (in the same familiar sense in which it has), from which it has been *at various distances* (in the familiar sense in which it is now at a distance both from that mantelpiece and from that bookcase, and at a greater distance from the bookcase than it is from the mantelpiece); also there have (very often, at all events) existed some other things of this kind with which it was *in contact* (in the familiar sense in which it is now in contact with the pen I am holding in my right hand and with some of the clothes I am wearing). Among the things which have, in this sense, formed part of its environment (i.e. have been either in contact with it, or at *some* distance from it, however *great*) there have, at every moment since its birth, been large numbers of other living human bodies, each of which has, like it, (*a*) at some time been born, (*b*) continued to exist from some time after birth, (*c*) been, at every moment of its life after birth, either in contact with or not far from the surface of the earth; and many of these bodies have already died and ceased to exist. But the earth had existed also for many years before my body was born; and for many of these years, also, large numbers of human bodies had, at every moment, been alive upon it; and many of these bodies had died and ceased to exist before it was born. Finally (to come to a different class of propositions), I am a human being, and I have, at different times since my body was born, had many different experiences, of each of many different kinds: e.g. I have often perceived both my own body and other things which formed part of its environment, including other human bodies; I have not only perceived things of this kind, but have also observed facts about them, such as, for instance, the fact which I am now observing, that that mantelpiece is at present nearer to my body than that bookcase; I have been aware of other facts, which I was not at the time observing, such as, for instance, the fact, of which I am now aware, that my body existed yesterday and was then also for some time nearer to that mantelpiece than to that bookcase; I have had expectations with regard to the future, and many beliefs of other kinds, both true and false; I have thought of imaginary things and persons and incidents, in the reality of which I did not believe; I have had dreams; and I have had feelings of many different kinds. And, just as my body has been the body of a human being, namely myself, who has, during his lifetime, had many experiences of each of these (and other) different kinds; so, in the case of very many of the other human bodies which have lived upon the earth, each has been the body of a different human being, who has, during the lifetime of that body, had many different experiences of each of these (and other) different kinds.

(2) I now come to the single truism which, as will be seen, could not be stated except by reference to the whole list of truisms, just given in (1). This truism also (in my own opinion) I *know*, with certainty, to be true; and it is as follows:

In the case of *very many* (I do not say *all*) of the human beings belonging to the class (which includes myself) defined in the following way, i.e. as human beings who have had human bodies, that were born and lived for some time upon the earth, and who have, during the lifetime of those bodies, had many different experiences of each of the kinds mentioned in (1), it is true that each has frequently, during the life of his body, known, with regard to *himself* or *his* body, and with regard to some time earlier than any of the times at which I wrote down the propositions in (1), a proposition *corresponding* to each of the propositions in (1), in the sense that it asserts with regard to *himself* or *his* body and the earlier time in question (namely, in each case, the time at which he knew it), just what the corresponding proposition in (1) asserts with regard to *me* or *my* body and the time at which I wrote that proposition down.

In other words what (2) asserts is only (what seems an obvious enough truism) that each of *us* (meaning by 'us,' very many human beings of the class defined) has frequently *known,* with regard to *him*self or *his* body and the time at which he knew it, everything which, in writing down my list of propositions in (1), I was claiming to know about *myself* or *my* body and the time at which I wrote that proposition down, i.e. just as *I* knew (when I wrote it down) 'There exists at present a human living body which is my body,' so each of us has frequently known with regard to himself and some other time the different but corresponding proposition, which *he* could *then* have properly expressed by, 'There exists *at present* a human body which is *my* body'; just as *I* know 'Many human bodies other than mine have before now lived on the earth,' so each of us had frequently known the different but corresponding proposition 'Many human bodies other than *mine* have before *now* lived on the earth'; just as *I* know 'Many human beings other than my-self have before now perceived, and dreamed, and felt,' so each of *us* has frequently known the different but corresponding proposition, 'Many human beings other than *myself* have before *now* perceived, and dreamed, and felt'; and so on, in the case of *each* of the propositions enumerated in (1). . . .

In what I have just said, I have assumed that there is some meaning which is *the* ordinary or popular meaning of such expressions as 'The earth has ex-isted for many years past.' And this, I am afraid, is an assumption which some philosophers are capable of disputing. They seem to think that the question 'Do you believe that the earth has existed for many years past?' is not a plain question, such as should be met either by a plain 'Yes' or 'No,' or by a plain 'I can't make up my mind,' but is the sort of question which can be properly met by: 'It all depends on what you mean by "the earth" and "exists" and "years": if you mean so and so, and so and so, and so and so, then I do; but if you mean so and so, and so and so, and so and so, or so and so, and so and so, and so and so, or so and so, and so and so, and so and so, then I don't, or at least I think it is extremely doubtful.' It seems to me that such a view is as profoundly mistaken as any view can be. Such an expres-sion as 'The earth has existed for many years past' is the very type of an unambiguous expression, the meaning of which we all understand. Anyone who takes a contrary view must, I suppose, be confusing the question whether we understand its meaning (which we all certainly do) with the entirely different question whether we *know what it means,* in the sense that we are able to *give a correct analysis* of its meaning. The question what is the correct analysis of *the* proposition meant *on any occasion* (for, of course,

as I insisted in defining (2), a different proposition is meant at every different time at which the expression is used) by 'The earth has existed for many
years past' is, it seems to me, a profoundly difficult question, and one to
which, as I shall presently urge, no one knows the answer. But to hold that
we do not know what, in certain respects, is the analysis of what we understand by such an expression, is an entirely different thing from holding that
we do not understand the expression. It is obvious that we cannot even raise
the question how what we do understand by it is to be analysed, unless we
do understand it. So soon, therefore, as we know that a person who uses
such an expression is using it in its ordinary sense, we understand his meaning. So that in explaining that I was using the expressions used in (1) in
their ordinary sense (those of them which have an ordinary sense, which is
not the case with quite all of them), I have done all that is required to make
my meaning clear.

But now, assuming that the expressions which I have used to express (2)
are understood, I think, as I have said, that many philosophers have really
held views incompatible with (2). . . .

[Many] philosophers . . . have held, I think, that though each of us
knows propositions corresponding to *some* of the propositions in (1),
namely to those which merely assert that *I* myself have had in the past experiences of certain kinds at many different times, yet none of us knows *for
certain* any propositions either of the type (*a*) which assert the existence of
material things or of the type (*b*) which assert the existence of *other* selves,
beside myself, and that *they* also have had experiences. They admit that we
do in fact *believe* propositions of both these types, and that they *may* be
true: some would even say that we know them to be highly probable; but
they deny that we ever know them, *for certain,* to be true. Some of them
have spoken of such beliefs as 'beliefs of Common Sense,' expressing thereby
their conviction that beliefs of this kind are very commonly entertained by
mankind: but they are convinced that these things are, in all cases, only *believed,* not known for certain; and some have expressed this by saying that
they are matters of Faith, not of Knowledge.

Now the remarkable thing which those who take this view have not, I
think, in general duly appreciated, is that, in each case, the philosopher who
takes it is making an assertion about 'us'—that is to say, not merely about
himself, but about *many other human beings as well*. When he says 'No
human being has ever *known* of the existence of other human beings,' he is
saying: 'There have been many other human beings beside myself, and none
of them (including myself) has ever known of the existence of other human
beings.' If he says: 'These beliefs are beliefs of Common Sense, but they are
not matters of *knowledge*', he is saying: 'There have been many other

human beings, beside myself, who have shared these beliefs, but neither I nor any of the rest has ever known them to be true.' In other words, he asserts with confidence that these beliefs *are* beliefs of Common Sense, and seems often to fail to notice that, *if* they are, they must be true; since the proposition that they are beliefs of Common Sense is one which logically entails propositions both of type (*a*) and of type (*b*); it logically entails the proposition that many human beings, beside the philosopher himself, have had human bodies, which lived upon the earth, and have had various experiences, including beliefs of this kind. This is why this position . . . seems to me to be self-contradictory . . . it is making a proposition about *human knowledge* in general, and therefore is actually asserting the existence of many human beings . . . It is true that a philosopher who says 'There have existed many human beings beside myself, and none of us has ever known of the existence of any human beings beside himself,' is only contradicting himself if what he holds is 'There have *certainly* existed many human beings beside myself' or, in other words, '*I know* that there have existed other human beings beside myself.' But this, it seems to me, is what such philosophers have in fact been generally doing. They seem to me constantly to betray the fact that they regard the proposition that those beliefs *are* beliefs of Common Sense, or the proposition that they themselves are not the only members of the human race, as not merely true, but *certainly* true; and *certainly* true it cannot be, unless one member, at least, of the human race, namely themselves, has *known* the very things which that member is declaring that no human being has ever known.

Nevertheless, my position that I *know*, with certainty, to be true all of the propositions in (1), is certainly not a position, the denial of which entails both of two incompatible propositions. If I do *know* all these propositions to be true, then, I think, it is quite certain that other human beings also have known corresponding propositions: that is to say (2) also *is* true, and *I* know it to be true. But do I really *know* all the propositions in (1) to be true? Isn't it possible that I merely believe them? Or know them to be highly probable? In answer to this question, I think I have nothing better to say than that it seems to me that I *do* know them, with certainty. It is, indeed, obvious that, in the case of most of them, I do not know them *directly*: that is to say, I only know them because, in the past, I have known to be true *other* propositions which were evidence for them. If, for instance, I do know that the earth had existed for many years before I was born, I certainly only know this because I have known other things in the past which were evidence for it. And I certainly do not know exactly what the evidence was. Yet all this seems to me to be no good reason for doubting that I do know it. We are all, I think, in this strange position that we do *know* many things, with regard to which we *know* further that we must have had evidence for them, and yet we do not know *how* we know them, i.e. we do not know what the evidence was. If there is any 'we,' and if we know that there is, this must be so: for that there is a 'we' is one of the things in question. And that I do know that there is a 'we,' that is to say, that many other human beings, with human bodies, have lived upon the earth, it seems to me that I do know, for certain.

If this first point in my philosophical position, namely my belief in (2), is to be given any name, which has actually been used by philosophers in classifying the positions of other philosophers, it would have, I think, to be expressed by saying that I am one of those philosophers who have held that the 'Common Sense view of the world' is, in certain fundamental features, *wholly* true. But it must be remembered that, according to me, *all* philosophers, without exception, have agreed with me in holding this: and that the real difference, which is commonly expressed in this way, is only a difference between those philosophers, who have *also* held views inconsistent with these features in 'the Common Sense view of the world,' and those who have not.

Critical Realism*

ARTHUR ONCKEN LOVEJOY [1873–1962] was professor of philosophy at Johns Hopkins until his retirement in 1938. He was the most vigorous exponent of critical realism in recent philosophy. In addition, he has had considerable influence on American literary studies through his work on the history of ideas.

The content of our actual experience does not consist . . . of entities which, upon *any* plausible theory of the constitution of the physical world, can be supposed to be members of that world. It consists of particulars which (1) arise through the functioning of percipient organisms, (2) are present only within the fields of private awareness of such organisms, (3) are destitute of certain of the essential properties and relations . . . of the "physical" . . . , and (4) possess properties which physical things lack. They *are*, in short, essentially of the nature of "ideas," as Descartes and Locke (for the most part) used that term. And it is through these entities that any knowledge which we may attain of the concrete characters of the

* From Lovejoy: *The Revolt Against Dualism*, Chapter 8. Copyright, 1930, by Open Court Publishing Company. Reprinted by permission of Open Court Publishing Company.

physical world, and of any other realities extraneous to our several private
fields of awareness, must be mediated; so that we are brought back to
Locke's conclusion, despite the heroic efforts of so many philosophers of our
age to escape from it: "it is evident that the mind knows not things immediately, but by the intervention of the ideas it has of them." If the word "nature" is used—though I think it is unhappily so used—to mean exclusively
the world as it is, or may conceivably be, apart from all experience, *i.e.*,
apart from the processes of conscious perception and thought and phantasy
and feeling, then between "nature" and experience there is a radical discontinuity; for the occurrence of those processes adds to the sum of reality not
only particular existents, but kinds of existents, which "nature"—if so
defined—though it engenders them, cannot plausibly be supposed to contain.

It may, however, seem . . . that these arguments explode the foundations
of all realism. Especially may the developments in recent physics appear to
some to have this effect. . . . The theory of relativity is generally conceived
to have rendered dubious and equivocal, if not to have disproved, the
spatiality of physical objects in their macroscopic aspect; and the latest hypotheses concerning the minute components of "matter" and their relation to
energy-quanta to have, so to say, disembodied matter itself. And what is left
is a set of mathematical formulas useful for predicting the sequences of perceptions, but which many physicists find it impossible to construe as descriptions of physical reality. Thus Jeans, speaking of intra-atomic processes and
of radiation, writes: "It is difficult to form even the remotest conception of
the realities underlying all these phenomena. . . . Indeed, it may be
doubted whether we shall ever properly understand the realities involved;
they may well be so fundamental as to be beyond the grasp of the human
mind." Similarly Eddington concludes his recent summary of the philosophical implications—and non-implications—of contemporary science by assuring us that all that physics has to report about external nature is that "something unknown is doing we don't know what"; that when, for example, we
see an elephant sliding down a hill, the impression of the "bulkiness" of the
elephant which we experience "presumably has some direct counterpart in
the external world," but that this "counterpart must be of a nature beyond
our apprehension," and that "science can make nothing of it." . . .

This new agnosticism among the physicists, then, manifestly verges upon
phenomenalism. . . . So little seems to be left of the physical world of the
older realism that the residuum may appear hardly worth salvaging. Thus
the result, not merely of the present discussion, but of recent reflection in
general, will doubtless be regarded by idealists as tending to vindicate *their*
type of monism. . . . If it is admitted that, as Locke declared, "the mind, in

all its thoughts and reasonings, hath no immediate object but its own ideas," then the consequences which Locke's successors drew from this proposition must, we shall be told, again be drawn. And if the new physics—also setting out from realistic preconceptions—reduces the so-called physical universe to a bare *x*, of which we can say, at most, only that there must be in it *some* difference corresponding to every difference in our perceptual content, then the term "physical," as applied to it, ceases to have any distinctive meaning.

In this situation it seems worth while to consider afresh what reasons—other than "instincts," to which some realists seem to me to appeal too simply—can be given for believing that there is a world of existing particulars which are nobody's "ideas"—which, in other words, are independent of awareness—and to ask how much, or what sort, of knowledge of that world it is permissible to suppose that we can attain. . . .

The case for physical realism should not, I think, be made to rest primarily or wholly . . . upon the assumed necessity of postulating external causal objects to account for our percepts—objects about which we can infer no more than that there are differences of some kind in them, corresponding numerically, but not necessarily or probably in their qualities, to the differences between percepts. It is true that if there *are* external objects, and if they cannot be identical with our data, we must be able to infer so much, at least, about them, if we are to base any judgments whatever concerning them upon perception. And it is also true that our disposition to assume that our experiences have causes is somewhat too disparagingly described when it is called mere "animal faith." It is a faith, indeed; but . . . it is a highly critical and extremely attenuated faith. And it is a part of the general faith that reality has a greater degree of orderliness, of interconnection of parts, and therefore of intelligibility, than is manifested in the confused phantasmagoria of unsupplemented sensation. But it is not the primary form of that faith; it is derivative from something more fundamental. For there is no obvious gain in the coherency and intelligibility of the world if you merely take an isolated momentary bit of perceptual content and assert concerning it: This must have had a cause external in some sense to itself.

The more fundamental postulate to which I refer—and the better reason for accepting realism—will begin to appear if we consider what the "independence" which might be ascribed to physical reals, and would constitute the first essential of their physicality, would be. It would have to do primarily with the *time* of their existence. Consciousness in general, and the consciousness of this or that sensible object in particular, is fluctuating and intermittent. For you an object now exists and now does not exist; when you are in deep sleep or a swoon the whole world is non-existent. The primary function of "real objects," the way in which the belief in them helps us to regard the universe as more coherent than sense-experience, consists (as was implied in our definition of the notion of a "physical world") in their filling the temporal gaps between actual perceptions. The "independence" of a thing means, concretely, its continued existence, or the continuance of a connected series of events of which it is a member, at times when it is not being attended to by me, nor necessarily by any one like me. The starting-point of the argument for physical realism, I suggest, is the plain man's normal and reasonable belief that the processes of nature do not stop when he stops noticing them. It is not the "outerness" of the object perceived, *when* it is perceived, but the *persistence of something which is in some manner connected with what is perceived, during the interperceptual intervals,* that is the primary natural postulate out of which the belief in an external world, in objects which exist though they are not given in experience, arises. How irrepressible this belief is may be judged from the emphatic affirmation of it even by phenomenalists who ostensibly refuse to admit any metempirical realities. Thus Petzoldt, after declaring that "there is no scientific meaning in the assumption that there exists behind experience something-or-other as its bearer or generator," forthwith proceeds to castigate those who will not believe in "a perdurance of objects which is independent of us"—who fail to regard the fact that "things always turn up again quite independently of whether I have had my eyes open or not, at the place they previously had, or at some place wholly independent of my thought." Petzoldt, in short, apparently finds it superfluous to suppose that there are any common and independent realities behind our experiences, but impossible to conceive that there are none between our experiences. . . .

The belief in the continuance of things or processes between perceptions is not a blank act of faith, as would be the postulation of an external causal object for a single momentary percept; it may be said to be—not, indeed, rigorously verified—but strengthened by one of the most familiar of empirical facts—namely, that the same uniform causal sequences of natural events which may be observed within experience appear to go on in the same manner when not experienced. You build a fire in your grate of a certain quantity of coal, of a certain chemical composition. Whenever you remain in the room there occurs a typical succession of sensible phenomena according to an approximately regular schedule of clocktime; in, say, a half-hour the coal is half consumed; at the end of the hour the grate contains only ashes. If you build a fire of the same quantity of the same material under the same conditions, leave the room, and return after any given time has elapsed, you get approximately the same sense-experiences as you would have had at the corresponding moment if you had remained in the room. You infer, therefore, that the fire has been burning as usual during your absence, and that

CONTINUANCE of INDEPENDENCE

being perceived is not a condition necessary for the occurrence of the process. But a consistent idealist or phenomenalist cannot say this. He is committed to the proposition either that the fire has not been or, at all events, cannot legitimately be assumed to have been, burning when no one was perceiving it; his doctrine amounts to a gratuitous assumption of the universal jumpiness or temporal discontinuity of causal sequences. The most that he can admit—and he cannot admit less—is that fires and other natural processes behave *as if* they went on when unobserved; if he desires to make this seem more intelligible, he may invoke some pre-established harmony, or resort to a species of occasionalism—assuming that when you return to the room after an hour God (as Descartes would have said) deceives you by putting into your mind a percept of a grate full of ashes, though *these* ashes are not the effects of any fire. But such "explanations" of the facts are plainly arbitrary and far-fetched; they multiply types of causal agency beyond necessity. And to be content with a mere *Philosophie des Als-Ob* [philosophy of 'As-If'] in such a case—to say that, although nothing at all that was like a fire or would have caused you to perceive a fire, if you had remained in the room, was really happening while you were absent, nevertheless all goes on as though the fire had been burning during that interval—this, surely, is a singularly strained and artificial notion, wholly foreign to the normal propensities of our intelligence.

Naïve realism, however, infers more from this type of act than is warranted; it supposes that while you were not in the room *exactly the same* phenomena were going on as you would have experienced had you been there—the play of color in the flames, the qualities experienced by you in thermal sensation, and so on. To suppose this is to assume that certain of the factors in the case—namely, your presence in the room and your psychophysical constitution—make no difference in the content of your experience. This positive assumption of the complete irrelevance of certain actual antecedents or concomitants of a given effect is not only gratuitous and improbable, but is in conflict with familiar empirical evidences of the concomitant variation of sense-data with differences in the perceptible natures or states of percipients. What is reasonably inferrible is that some process capable of causing an organism, constituted as you are, to have the perceptual experience of a burning fire, has been continuously going on while you were not in such relations to it as actually to perceive any fire. The causal theory of perception is thus derivative from, not logically prior to, the postulate of the continuance of the orderly sequences of nature during interperceptual intervals. The world of external causal entities or events is the world that you are obliged to assume when you accept the evidence for such continuance, while recognizing the probability that your own makeup, as a body or a mind or both, plays some part in determining the qualitative character of your percepts. The specific qualities characteristic of the potentially unperceived, that is, interperceptual, process, remain, so far as these considerations go, undetermined; you cannot, thus far, tell how much of what you experience is due to external events, how much to the nature of "that which is acted upon" by these events. But this does not weaken the reasons for believing that there *are* such temporally persistent and therefore independent events. . . .

It is perhaps worth remarking—though not too much weight should be given to the fact—that men of science . . . are radically agnostic about the physical world only intermittently, or when the wind is in a certain quarter. Thus physicists and astronomers are accustomed to debate, from the standpoint of the relativity theory, whether the universe is finite or infinite in extent, and, if it can be shown to be finite, of just what shape it is, and how many million years would be required for a ray of light to complete "the journey round the whole of space" and return to its starting-point. And, as Jeans tells us, "it has been quite seriously suggested that two faint nebulae," previously supposed to be extremely remote from us, "may actually be our two nearest neighbors in the sky, M 33 and M 31, seen the long way round space"—*i.e.*, that "we see the fronts of two objects when we look at M 33 and M 31 and the backs of the same two objects when we point our telescopes in exactly the opposite directions." This, Jeans remarks, is perhaps "only a conjecture"; but "many more startling conjectures in astronomy have . . . proved to be true." The raising of such questions and conjectures seems superfluous, not to say meaningless, unless it is assumed that there is a physical world which has extension and in which it is possible for light to travel, *i.e.*, to reach successively different positions. The habitual fashion of speech of our astronomers and physicists plainly betrays the fact that they conceive themselves to be concerned with the problem of ascertaining the probable nature of relatively persistent physical realities behind, and causally related to, the diversities of our transitory perceptual data.

But it will, no doubt, be said that this is merely a careless or syncopated way of expressing themselves which men of science have fallen into—or, if seriously meant by them, that it is at all events of no philosophical moment. None of these hypotheses and discussions really relate to a "background"—to the characters of realities either actually or potentially outside sense-experience. There are no such existent particulars in the universe as M 33 and M 31, no "long way" and "short way round space," no "shape," either spherical or cylindrical, ascribable to the physical whole of things; there is just "something, we don't know what." All such terms express merely a conceptual frame-work devised for theoretical purposes, a series of scientific fictions. Our perceptual experience takes place as if such entities existed and such events occurred; it is therefore useful to employ the notions of them; but the only factual elements in the scheme consist of private sense-data of individual physicists, *plus,* perhaps, certain unknown quantities of which merely the number may be supposed to be correspondent with the number of differences in the percepts.

From this conception of the character of the business in which the physicist is engaged one consequence not always noted seems to follow. If all specific hypotheses relating to things other than perceptual data are to be regarded as fictions, certain classes of hypotheses frequently advanced and discussed must be illegitimate. For though it may be useful to interpolate in thought fictitious processes *between* actual perceptions, it can hardly be useful to extrapolate them beyond the region of any possible perception. Yet astronomers are accustomed to advance hypotheses concerning, for example, the sources of solar energy, from which they draw inferences as to the past and future duration of organic life upon the earth, and the state of this planet and of the solar system long before man's appearance and long after his disappearance. They describe for us the birth of the earth through the tidal action of some other celestial body which (fortunately for us) approached near to the sun probably some 2000 million years ago. They usually affirm the almost certain truth of the second law of thermodynamics, and therefore predict the eventual, though unimaginably remote, "heat-death" of the physical world. Now the events described by these propositions in astronomy and physics are presumably neither actual nor possible experiences of any mortal; nor can the propositions be considered fictions which somehow enable us to infer past or predict future actual experiences. If, then, the sole legitimate subject-matter of science consists of percepts and their inter-connections, together with the number of correlated differences in an otherwise entirely undefined background, no propositions concerning the origin and early history of our system, or the ultimate distribution of energy, would be admissible in science. The temporal range of the discourse of the astronomer would be limited to the history of our species, or at most of percipient organisms. All else would be gratuitous, if not meaningless, fairy-tales—neither true nor useful. If, on the other hand, cosmogonies, histories of the solar system, accounts of what took place in early geological time, and the like, are to be regarded as legitimate and significant parts of the province of science, it can only be upon the condition that these hypotheses are propounded as descriptions of events that actually happened without observation. The descriptions must in any case, of course, be admitted to be highly incomplete and abstract; but they do not, if of any scientific consequence, reduce to the vague proposition that "something, we don't know what," happened before, and will happen after, the presence of human or other percipients upon the cosmic scene.

But even these considerations are less than conclusive with respect to the question with which we are now concerned: whether any intelligible and consistent theory, in terms of particular existences or events, which would accord with, coördinate, and account for the uniformities and differences of our sense-experiences, can be formulated. . . . *If* a theory, and only one theory, of this kind appears attainable, the fact constitutes a positive reason for regarding that theory as a probable (though doubtless exceedingly inadequate) account of the constitution of the independent causal background of experience. If everything in perception—when we "study it carefully and in detail"—takes place as if certain extra-perceptual events were occurring, in accordance with certain laws, as the common determinants of the otherwise inexplicable similarities and diversities of the data of different percipients, and if through such a theory we are led to the discovery of perceptible facts previously unknown, it is simpler and more in harmony with the normal assumptions of our reason to suppose that those events do occur, rather than that they do not. Though the universe *may* be a systematic and elaborate deception, in which everything in our experience intricately conspires with everything else to suggest to us beliefs which are not true, it does not seem necessary or rational to start with the supposition that this is the case. . . .

We shall take three conclusions as already established: (a) there is an order of existences or events which persists when unperceived; (b) this is causally related to our sensa; (c) the particulars belonging to it cannot be identical with our sensa. Our problem, then, is whether, given these premises and the common facts of every-day experience, we can reach any further probable propositions concerning the extra-perceptual, neutral, causal order. One such proposition, manifestly, is that we have power to act upon this order. Processes which apparently go on unperceived can be initiated by percipient beings. And the unobserved causal processes will vary (as their subsequently observed effects will show) with variations in the specific characters of our sense-data while we are initiating those processes; *e.g.,* if I build my fire of wood instead of coal, the time required for it to burn out will be shorter and the ashes which I find on returning to the room will be of a different quality. It is equally a fact of every-day experience that . . . if I merely imagine or dream of a fire in the grate, I do not—after ceasing so to dream or imagine—experience the visual and tactual content called ashes. Purely visual content is not found by us to be sufficient to start fires (or to give sensible evidence of the physical equivalent of a fire having started in the extra-perceptual world), or to be correlated with the initiation by us of any physical process. The same fact is illustrated by the comparative sterility of pink rats. If I am able to initiate a physical process, my action (if experienced at all by myself) is experienced in the form of tactual and kinaesthetic as well as (in some cases) visual sense-data; it is, in short, one of the primary discoveries of experience that tactual and kinaesthetic sensations have a different and more constant relation to the physical causal order than do visual percepts or images. The former are the phases of our experience in which we as percipients appear to have causal contact with that order. And it is reasonable to suppose that this fact throws some light upon the nature of the external causal world.

Furthermore, if, like everyone else, we assume that there are many percipients, and that they can through language convey some information to one another about the characteristics of their respective sense-data, we find that each of them is able to act upon the other percipients, that is, to determine in some degree what experiences they shall have; and that this action upon them is usually, and probably always, conditioned upon initiating (in the sense and in the manner already indicated) physical processes. If I light a fire, other men as well as myself will feel the heat; they may, in consequence of my action, observe a sensible fire continuously while I do not; while if I imagine or dream of a fire, their experience remains unaffected. One of the two principal reasons why we do not regard dream-fires as indications of the occurrence of events (at least the kind of events ordinarily connected with sensible fires) in the persistent and therefore independent world is that they do not cause others to have sensations of warmth or to find perceptible ashes in their perceptible grates. Purely private percepts are called illusory, not merely because they happen to be private, but because they do not causally interact directly, or in the manner in which other qualitatively similar percepts do, with the world which is the medium of communication and interaction between us.

Now what observably happens when I thus act upon the external world and through it affect other men's experiences and my own subsequent experiences, is usually that with my perceptible body I push and pull other perceptible objects about in my perceptual space. And with the movements which I thus determine as data of my own perception there may be—under conditions empirically definable—correlated perceptions of movement in the experience of others. They report to me that they see what they call my body moving, and other objects moving in ways uniformly connected with my bodily movements. That their percepts of what they call my body are not my body itself is true—if the arguments on this matter previously set forth are correct; and it is also true that the perceptual objects which they see moving in consequence of my bodily movements are not existentially nor qualitatively identical with those which I see, nor yet with any entity in the neutral causal order. The question may nevertheless be asked: Are the causal processes in the external world which are initiated by motions (*i.e.*, by those which I perceive) and which terminate in motions (*i.e.*, those which other men perceive) also of the nature of motions? The idealist answers definitely in the negative; the phenomenalist and the all-but agnostic physicist answer that we have, at any rate, no reason whatever for thinking so. But there are, I think, certain considerations which, though not demonstrative, make an affirmative answer to the question the more plausible.

(a) In the first place, it is at least not *impossible* that the processes which cause and link together the percepts of different times and different persons are of the same general sort as the causal sequences which empirically occur within our perceptual experience. No fact of experience, obviously, can prove the contrary.

(b) It is a simpler assumption about the unperceived causal processes that they are of the same sort as those perceived, rather than of some wholly different sort. In making such an assumption we still follow the rule of continuity in our conjectures about that which we cannot directly experience. We do not postulate differences in the nature of things beyond necessity. If I suppose that, when I have the experience of moving my body and pushing and pulling something about, thereby producing effects in the neutral causal order, I *am* pushing or pulling something about, and that this *is* a way in which effects in that order are produced, I am enabled to conceive of the external world with which I am in relation in action as fundamentally homogeneous with the perceptual world; and though it may not be so, it appears to me more sensible to proceed upon the hypothesis that it is, so long as there is no good evidence to the contrary.

(c) The spaces in which our perceptible effective bodily movements take place, whether or not they are literally parts of a single Space, are at all events congruent; they fit together in a remarkable way. For example, a hundred men from as many different places are summoned to attend an international conference in Geneva. They thereupon consult maps, timetables, Baedekers, to find the routes to take in order to reach that city. These useful works were prepared by yet other men. They do not, however, purport to be descriptions of the arrangement of things in private perceptual spaces of their authors; they profess to represent a set of spatial relations which will hold good in the perceptual experience of any inhabitant of the earth. The routes which they describe are not routes to a hundred private Genevas, but to a single Geneva conceived to have a determinate position in some common or public spatial order. And by a series of movements of their own legs, assisted by motions of trains and steamships, which follow spatial directions symbolized in the maps and guidebooks, the delegates to the conference presently find themselves having similar (though not identical) visual and tactual percepts, for example, percepts of the Quai Mont Blanc, and in a position in which they can sit down in the same room and talk to one another. The result may be that the construction of battleships in certain other places will be discontinued. The idealistic or phenomenalistic account of this affair is that there is no common space such as is represented by the maps, and that no motion of what could strictly be called the body of any delegate took place. What happened was merely that their minds—which were throughout in no place at all—after first having private percepts of maps and then having visual and other sensations of motion, resulting, perhaps, in sensations of sea-sickness, subsequently experienced certain resemblant sense-percepts which they mistakenly called by the single name "Geneva," and others which they called the bodies and voices of their fellow delegates. In reality, therefore, the delegates never met. Their private sequences of sense-data, for no known or conjecturable reason, happened eventually to coincide in part; at approximately the time when one of them had the kinaesthetic sensations of opening his mouth and using his vocal organs, the others had correspondent visual sensations and also certain sound-sensations of (more or less) intelligible words; but they were no nearer one another when this occurred than at the beginning. Now this is, no doubt, conceivable, in the sense that it is not formally self-contradictory; but it seems to me incredibly far-fetched, and I cannot avoid the suspicion that the human species (including physicists and even idealistic philosophers) is constitutionally incapable of really believing it—of thinking in this fashion of this type of experience. Men have always believed, and will, doubtless, continue to believe, that the way to arrive at a place is to go there; and they will always be recalcitrant to a view which requires them to hold, or to regard it as probable, that (for example) the ill-fated passengers of the *Titanic* were not really in the same ship or even in the same space. So long as the experienced bodily movements of a number of separate percipients thus fit into a single spatial pattern; so long as, in consequence of motions in convergent directions in that pattern (and not otherwise), the percipients find themselves face to face; so long as (to vary the illustration) through such bodily movements (and not otherwise) they are enabled not only to destroy the bodies of other men but also to bring all *their* perceiving to an end, by firing bullets in the direction in which the other men's bodies are perceived—so long men will naturally conceive of the processes in the common world through which their respective sense-data are caused as occurring in a single common spatial or spatio-temporal order and as consisting of motions therein. That this conceived common space is literally identical with their perceived spaces they may find reason to doubt; that the bodies which effectively move in it have all the properties of the bodies sensibly perceived, or are particulars existentially identical with them, they will find good reasons for denying. But the fact that their apprehension of bodies must be recognized by them to be mediate or representational and to contain "psychic additions" and distortions need not, and pretty certainly will not, prevent them from thinking that they have bodies—unique bodies, that is, each of which belongs to one percipient, and is not merely the multitudinous aggregate of the percepts of it—bodies which are therefore assignable to the public spatial system, which have positions relative to other bodies, which can change these positions, and in doing so cause changes in other bodies and modify thereby the sense-content, or even bring to an end the existence, of other percipient beings.

In all this, it may be said, I am forgetting the theory of relativity, which shows that there is no general frame of nature, no common space or time for different percipients. But I have never observed relativistic physicists hesitating to assume that the imaginary voyagers whom they describe as roving about the heavens at enormous speeds can send light-signals to one another, whatever their relative velocities or the length of their journeys; and I find such physicists always assuming that these signals will take time in passing from one "system" to another, and that their course will be deflected if they happen to pass through the gravitational fields to be found in the neighborhood of material bodies. That relativity physics dispenses, and shows the plain man how to dispense, with the notions of a general spatial order (whatever its novel geometrical properties) or of moving entities therein, consequently still seems to me difficult to make out; and I surmise, therefore, that the plain man's prejudice in favor of the belief that he has a body which moves in a public space, and that, in general, the causal processes in the persistent neutral world consist (at least in part) of the motions of bodies, will not by this doctrine be corrected, but rather confirmed.

Pragmatic Realism[*]

CLARENCE IRVING LEWIS [1883–1964] is best known for his influential contributions to logic and for his distinguished books on the theory of knowledge and on valuation. He began his career in philosophy at the University of California, and from 1920 until 1953 he taught at Harvard. After his retirement he held teaching positions at Princeton and Stanford.

The history of philosophy since Descartes has been largely shaped by acceptance of the alternatives; either (1) knowledge is not relative to the mind, or (2) the content of knowledge is not the real, or (3) the real is dependent on mind.

Kant, and phenomenalism in general, recognizes the relativity of knowledge, the dependence of the phenomenal object on the mind, and hence the impossibility of knowing the real as it is in itself. Idealism, taking the relativity of knowledge as its main premise, argues to the unqualified dependence of reality upon mind by holding the alternative—that there is no valid knowledge of the real—to be logically impossible. Realists in general seek to reconcile the possibility of knowing reality with its independence of the mind by one or another attempt to escape the relativity of knowledge.

However, the alternatives accepted are false alternatives. This whole historical development, so far as it turns upon them, is a mistake. There is no contradiction between the relativity of knowledge and the independence of its object. If the real object can be known at all, it can be known only in its relation to a mind; and if the mind were different the nature of the object as known might well be different. Nevertheless the description of the object as known is true description of an independent reality.

This sounds at first like unintelligible paradox. But, as I shall hope to convince the reader, relativity of this sort, which is entirely compatible with independence, is commonplace, capable of illustration for all sorts of relations which have nothing directly to do with knowledge.

If this position can be successfully maintained, then the fundamental premises of phenomenalism and idealism fall to the ground, some of the main difficulties posed by skepticism are met, and the general attitude of common-sense realism can be reinstated without attempting to do the impossible and avoid the relativity of knowledge. . . .

Reality, so far as it can be given in experience or known, is relative to the

[*] From *Mind and the World Order*, Chapter 6, by Clarence Irving Lewis; copyright 1929 by Charles Scribner's Sons. Reprinted by permission of the publishers.

knower. It can be apprehended only as it does or would appear to some perceiver in some actual or possible experience. But that the only character which can be attributed to anything real is a character described in relative terms—relative to some experience—does not deny to it an independent nature, and does not deny that this nature can be known. On the contrary, true knowledge is absolute because it conveys an absolute truth, though it can convey such truth only in relative terms.

There is much here that is in no wise peculiar to knowledge but has to do with the logic of relativity in general. It is equally true of weight, for example, that it can only be described in relative terms, but that the property of the object, so described, is independent of the particular standard in terms of which the description is given. The situation in which truth can be told only in relative terms, is obviously a common one, if not universal. But this relational truth may nevertheless be absolute. To put the matter in general terms: If relative to R, A is X, and relative to S, A is Y, neither X nor Y is an absolute predicate of A. But "A is X relative to R" and "A is Y relative to S," are absolute truths. Moreover they may be truths about the independent nature of A. Generally speaking, if A had no independent character, it would not be X relative to R or Y relative to S. These relative (or relational) characters, X and Y, are partial but absolutely valid revelations of the nature of A. If we should add, "There is no truth about A which can be told without reference to its relation to R or S, or some other such," we should then have a very good paradigm to the relativity of knowledge.

To make this clear, let us turn to a few simple examples of relativity, some of which have nothing specially to do with knowledge.

The size of Cæsar's toga is relative to the yardstick. But if we say, "The number of square yards in the toga is determined by the yardstick," the statement is over-simple. Given the toga, its size in yards is determined by the yardstick; given the yardstick, the number of yards in the toga is determined by the toga itself. If the toga had not a determinate sizableness independent of the yardstick, or if the yardstick had no size independent of the toga, then there would be no such fact as the number of yards in the toga; the relation would be utterly indeterminate. This independent character of the toga, or of the yardstick, is what we should be likely to call its "absolute" size. This can only be described in terms of *some* measure, though the description will vary according to what this measure is. The size of the toga in yards is relative to the yardstick, but it is nevertheless an independent property of the toga, a true report of which is given by correct measurement in yards. Thus what is relative is also independent; if it had no "absolute" character, it would have no character in relative terms.

This example leads naturally to another—another sense in which size is relative. One might be moved to observe that this conceptual relativity of size is something which goes round in a circle. The toga is of so many yards; a yard, so many feet. But how big is a yard or a foot? Eventually this goes back to something like the king's foot, which is a fact of the same order as the toga. A size is relative to *other* sizes; but *some* size must be an absolute so-bigness, immediately apprehended, or there is no size at all. This would be to maintain the eventual reference of the concept to something immediate. But it is well to note in passing that, except in precisely such relative terms, the absolute so-bigness of the king's foot is also an absolute inexpressible.

Size as an absolute and immediately given so-bigness is quite similarly relative when this size is attributed to the object. As Berkeley put it: How big is a mite's foot? As big as it looks to the mite or as big as it looks to us? We here confront a relativity of sense-experience which concerns its supposed truth to the real object. Size, as perceived, varies with distance from the perceiver. And there is no possibility of perceiving size at all except at *some* distance. Perceived size is a function of two terms, distance and X. The distance being fixed, differences of perceived size are attributable to differences in X. The perceived size is, so to speak, the value of the function. This is a function of two variables; its value, perceived size, is not determined by distance alone; it depends also on X. Distance being specified, and the value of the function, perceived size, being given, X is thereby determined. Distance being known, the perceived size is a true revelation of X, which we may call the independent size of the object.

If it be asked, "But what precisely is this independent size in any intelligible terms," we can carry our mathematical analogy one step further. (It is, in fact, a little more than an analogy, for the logic of functions is not confined to mathematics.) The independent size, X, of the perceived object is the integration of the function, its perceived size or perceived sizes, over the whole range of the other variable, distance. That is, all the perceived sizes, at different distances, belong to or are parts of the objectively real size of the thing perceived. The analogy holds good, further, in that from the value of the function, perceived size, for any given distance, its value for other distances are predictable. If, now, we remember that the conceptual interpretation of the immediately presented as the size of an objectively real thing, is precisely such implicit prediction, from its perceived size at this distance, of perceived sizes at other distances (among other things), we shall observe that the "independent size of the object" is precisely the content of a correct concept by which its size as presented is understood. For such a correct conceptual interpretation, *any one* of its perceived sizes is a true revelation of this independent property.

If any one ask for an absolute size which perception or knowledge could copy or be true to in any fundamentally different sense, I can only say that the meaning of his inquiry escapes me, and I believe it escapes him also.

It is obvious that what is here pointed out for size, holds for properties in general. Just as size may be in terms of the king's foot or the platinum bar in the Bureau of Standards, so color, for example, may be determined by reference to the sun's spectrum or the color-pyramid. This is conceptual relativity. Thus, in turn, we may seem to be thrown back on color as perceived, the visual quality just as we perceive it. But this, as a property of the real thing, is something which can hardly be supposed to represent simple coincidence of mind and object, because color, as perceived, varies with illumination. Except in light of *some* candle-power color cannot be seen at all, but the perceptual content itself varies with variation of the candle-power. Does this mean that we never see color as it is? Or that we see it as it is only at some standard illumination, arbitrarily determined? Or that we always see it as it is, when we see it at all, if what we see enables us to predict our altered visual experience of the object under other conditions?

Similarly for shape. Conceptually a shape is relative to other shapes. It can be described only in relation to standard shapes, such as square and round or by analysis into elements of shape, such as angles (measured by reference to a standard) and linear measure (obviously again relative). And shape as immediately presented configuration, if referred to the object, is relative to perspective.

The logic is the same throughout. Relativity is not incompatible with, but *requires,* an independent character in what is thus relative. And second, though what is thus relative cannot be known apart from such relation, still the other term or terms of the relation being given, all such relative knowledge is true knowledge of that independent character which, together with the other term or terms of this relationship, determines this content of our relative knowledge. The concept, or conceptual interpretation, *transcends* this relativity precisely because what the concept comprises is this relational pattern in which the independent nature of what is apprehended is exhibited in experience.

CRITIQUE OF PHENOMENALISM. This being so, the nature of the fallacy committed by phenomenalism becomes apparent. From the relativity of knowledge to the mind, it argues to the impossibility of knowing the independent real. This is as if the question about the size of Cæsar's toga were to be answered: "Its size in our yards is so and so; in terms of some other measure which other creatures might apply, it would be different. Apart from yards or some other measure, size has no meaning. So you see that the real toga in itself is something outside the category of size. Whether it can have size at all or, if so, what that size would be, we can never know." The premise is correct. The conclusion *non sequitur*.

It may seem that our illustrations are not precisely to the point since neither distance nor degree of illumination or angle of perspective, etc., is a property of the perceiving mind or of the sense-organs. But such illustrations have the advantage of making it clear that the logic of relativity is unaltered whether the object in question is an independent real, supposedly beyond or behind its appearances altogether, or is recognized to be the merely phenomenal object. The penny whose apparent size and configuration are relative to distance and perspective is recognized to be phenomenal and wholly knowable whether it is admitted to be independently real or not. If the relativity of its various appearances to perspective, distance and so on, does not defeat the possibility of our knowing the *phenomenal* object, how can relativity to mind, the logic of which is point for point identical, defeat the possibility of knowing the *independently real object?*

The one ground on which it might be urged with some show of reason that the relativity of the content of knowledge to the mind prevents true knowledge of the real, is that the nature of one term in this relation—the mind itself—is not known. That is, it might be said that we cannot stand outside ourselves and critically bound our own limitations. The elliptical appearance of the penny—it may be urged—conveys true knowledge because I know my angle of vision, and know how this appearance would vary as my perspective was altered. If all objects were seen from one angle only—as all objects are perpetually viewed from within the limitations of the human mind—then the relativity of perceived shape to perspective would lead to a confusion of configuration as (always) perceived with an absolute shape, which it is not.

There is much here that is worthy of careful attention, though the point is not sufficient to establish the phenomenalist's conclusion. . . .

We must distinguish between the notion that unrecognized limitations of the human mind would mean any *deceitfulness* or *erroneousness* of knowledge—a failure to accord with the true nature of the real—and the quite different notion that such limitations would mean a corresponding degree of *ignorance* of reality. When this distinction is drawn, the whole point of phenomenalism, as regards the relation of mind to independent reality, will be found to be lost; because when we grant to his arguments the utmost which can be granted, the conclusion to which they point is that our knowledge of the independent object is veridical but partial, not that it is untrue to absolute reality.

Our analogy may be of further assistance here. It is true that if we were restricted to one angle of perspective, one distance, etc., this would lead to *limitation* of knowledge. If we were restricted to perception at five feet, whether we knew it or not, that would mean a real limitation of our knowledge, because we could not understand or predict the systematic variation of perceived size with distance, which is an *additional* insight into the nature of that independent *X*, the size of the object, which is one term of the relation which determines size as perceived. Because we are able to see things at a wide range of distances, we learn to predict from our image at any one distance the appearance of the thing at other distances. Though the momentary perception is limited to a single distance, the breadth of previous experience, and knowledge of this momentary condition, enable us to transcend the momentary limitation. A *permanent* limitation could *not* be thus transcended.

However, we must not confuse limitation of knowledge with misrepresentation or mistake. Any sort of limitation of sense-organs or mind which should be reflected in perception, so far from meaning that we do not perceive things as they are, means that in certain respects we are freed from all possibility of error and are fatally certain to perceive things as they are, though to perceive and understand only part of what we otherwise might. The penny which looks elliptical may deceive us into thinking that it *is* elliptical, precisely because we are capable of viewing things from other angles than the present one. If we were limited to just one angle of vision, we should be restricted in our knowledge but we should thereby be freed from all possible mistakes of perspective. Similarly, if the image I have of a mite's foot should register on the retina of an intelligent mite, it would lead to error. But the limitation which prevents him from seeing his foot as it looks to me, at the same time prevents him from suffering certain illusions about his feet which would otherwise be possible.

That we humans do not have senses which register directly the whole known range of harmonic motions, means that there is much of reality which, until we learned to call upon various indirect modes of observation, was beyond our knowledge. And our inability to imagine how certain ranges of vibration might register upon sense-organs which should be sensitive to them, is as much a limitation as the blind man's inability to imagine color. But just as blindness does not condemn a man to false perception or even false interpretation (although it does make it practically necessary to run more risks and hazard judgment in the absence of desirable clues), so in general subjective limitations cannot render knowledge untrue to its object. At most they only mean greater ignorance and consequently greater likelihood of false judgment. The exigencies of life to be met remain just as numerous; the basis of judgment is more meager; hence error will probably be more frequent. Yet it remains true that no experience, however limited, is or can be intrinsically misrepresentative.

How much of reality we can grasp, doubtless depends upon our human limitations. The relativity of knowledge to the mind means such limitations, but it does not mean that the real object is a *ding an sich* [thing-in-itself]. Unless we grossly suppose that what humans can know is all there is to know, such limitation can lead to no untruth of our knowledge to reality. In this matter, as in many others, theory seems to suffer from a tendency to extremes—to hold either that the reality we know is all there is, or else that we cannot truly know any. The golden mean seems both modest and sensible. Knowledge has two opposites, ignorance and error. The relativity of perception may mean ignorance or it may not. If I can observe things from every angle, the restriction to one perspective at a time will not mean necessary ignorance, especially since other perspectives can be predicted from the present one. But if perception were restricted to a single angle, that relativity would mean ignorance. This will be true for limitations of the mind in general.

Ignorance of whatever sort increases the likelihood of error, because it means that in practice we must go forward on grounds of judgment less sufficient. But the given itself is never misrepresentative; always it is true revelation of the real, however partial. The notion that it can be untrue to the real reflects both a misapprehension of the significance of the truth of judgment and the old and meaningless fallacy that the function of sensory awareness in knowledge is to provide a qualitative replica of the independent object. Ignorance, however great, cannot make of reality a *ding an sich;* it does not vitiate such knowledge as we have, and that knowledge is of the independent reality. . . .

CRITIQUE OF IDEALISM. The idealist argues from this relativity of knowledge to the mind to the conclusion that the object is completely mind-dependent. In this, he misinterprets the nature of relativity and forgets the possibility that the object as known may be coincidently determined by two conditions and thus relative to both. . . .

The fallacy of idealism lies in arguing: "The nature of the thing as known always depends on the nature of the mind. Therefore the object cannot exist or have character independent of the mind." This is as if one should argue "The mass and velocity of an alpha-particle always depends on its motion relative to the observer. Therefore it can have no mass and velocity, and cannot exist, independent of this relative motion." In one sense of the word "independent" it *is* true that the mass and velocity of an alpha-particle has no meaning independent of its relative motion. And in a strictly parallel sense, it is true that the nature of the object, independent of the knowing mind, is undetermined; and independent of any and every mind, is meaningless. But there is no need for us to trip over the ambiguities of the word. The mass and velocity of an alpha-particle at least has two independent conditions; its motion relative to the observer is only one of them. We cannot argue from "dependent on its relative motion" to "completely determined by its relative motion." Similarly we cannot argue from the fact that it is meaningless to try to describe a thing out of relation to mind to the quite different thesis that the real object known is completely determined by the mind which knows it. If it should be said that while the object is not determined by its particular relation to a particular mind, it is determined by relation to mind in general, we may revert to the analogy once more. Mass and velocity apart from relation to some frame of motion is always undetermined; but it is *not* determined by such relation in general (if that means anything).

To revert to a previous illustration, the idealistic argument may be parodied: "The size of Cæsar's toga is relative to the yardstick or to some other standard of measure. No size without a yardstick. The size of things is through and through yardstickian. To be sure, the fallible yardstick in my hand may not determine size in general, but the yardstick in the Bureau of Standards determines both my yardstick and all sizes that there are. It creates size."

If the mind were the *only* condition of the thing as known, then the nature of the mind being specified, objects in general would be completely determined. One could say, "Given human mind possessed of such and such organs and interpreting data in such and such categories, what will be the reality it knows?" And there would be an answer in general and in particular.

Idealism has often boggled over the fact that it could not deduce the particular content of experience and knowledge. The questions, "Why do I have just this experience? Why do I find just this reality and no other?" must have an answer. Either that or it must be recognized that the particularity of experience is itself an ultimate—if inexplicable—datum; that the given is a condition of reality independent of the mind. Berkeley, of course, has his reply to this question: There is a reality, God, independent of my mind, which is responsible. The post-Kantian idealists, not sharing Berkeley's empiricism, have either neglected this problem or, like Fichte, have said that it is no part of the business of philosophy to deduce the particular. But he fails to face the question: Granted the idealistic thesis, *can* the particular be deduced? Philosophy, he might rightly claim, is not interested in the fact that I now see a blue blotter or that there are elephants in Africa. But his claim is that *all* the conditions of experience and reality are contained in mind. Outside of minds is nothing which could determine, or help determine, what minds know. If that be true, then mind being specified, not only the form or general character of knowledge but also the content in all its particularity, must be determined. It would still not be the business of philosophy to make the deduction for each particular item, because the particular items would not be of general interest. But it *is* a matter of general interest that all such items are thus deducible—if that be a fact. We might expect some inductive proof of this deducibility—the deduction of the elephants in Africa—as an illustration. If the mathematician should tell us, "All the facts of physics can be deduced from the system of quaternions," but should reply to our request for a deduction of the law of gravitation by saying, "Particular physical facts are of no interest to the mathematician and no part of his business," we should draw our own conclusions.

That idealism may argue that reality is exclusively mental or spiritual by maintaining that the condition of this particularity is *another* spiritual being, we are not here concerned. Such argument (or dogmatic assertion) is metaphysical and is, or should be, quite distinct from the argument from the relativity of knowledge.

It is a much more important consideration, I believe, that unless the content of knowledge is recognized to have a condition independent of the mind, the peculiar significance of knowledge is likely to be lost. For the purpose of knowledge is to be true to something which is beyond it. Its intent is to be governed and dictated to in certain respects. It is a real act with a real purpose because it seeks something which it knows it may miss. If knowledge had no condition independent of the knowing act, would this be so?

THE INDEPENDENCE OF THE OBJECT. It is most important to discover precisely what, in terms of knowledge, can be meant by "the independence of the object." Whether the subject-object relation is universal in reality or not, clearly the answer must be compatible with its universality in *knowledge*. It must, further, be independent of any supposed qualitative identity of the content or perception with the object, since such identity is probably meaningless and in any case is unverifiable.

It may be asked, "What would it mean for a mind to know an object, when the supposition of the qualitative identity of given content of perception with the object is ruled out?" The answer, in terms of the theory here presented, will be clear: It means that we are able to interpret validly certain given items of experience as sign of other possible experience, the total content of such further possible experience, related to the given in certain categorial ways, being attributed to the object, as constituting what we know of it and *what we mean by attributing reality to it*. If this conception seems to leave us in the air about the "nature of the object," let us first inquire what further question it is to which we seek the answer. We might find that there is no such further question which is meaningful.

In terms of experience and knowledge, the independence of reality—its independence of the knowing mind—means, first, the *givenness* of what is given; our realization that we do not create this content of experience and cannot, by the activity of thinking, alter it. Second, it means the truth of those "If—then" propositions in which the process of possible experience, starting from the given, could be expressed. The "if" here depends upon our own active nature for its meaning, as has been pointed out, but the content of the "then" clause, and the truth of the proposition as a whole, are things with respect to which the knowing mind is not dictator but dictated to. I may confront the given with different attitudes and purposes; I may be differently active toward it and, starting from it, I may proceed into the future in different ways. But *what I should then find;* what eventuations of experience are genuinely possible; that is something independent of any purpose or attitude of mine. These, I seek correctly to anticipate in my present interpretation of the given. If they do not obtain in reality, my present "knowledge" is false. Whether they obtain or not, is determined independently of my mind. If not, then it is not determined at all, and knowledge and error are, both of them, purely subjective and meaningless.

Third, the independence of reality means the transcendence by reality of our present knowledge of it; it means that I can ask significant questions about my object which *have* an answer when that answer is something which I cannot give. In terms of experience this means that, starting from the given in certain ways, I can safely predict the accrual of *something* the particular nature of which I cannot now determine. For example, if I examine the contents of this drawer, either I shall find a piece of chalk or I shall find none. So much I know; but I do not know now—and cannot discover merely by taking thought—*which* of these alternatives I should find true. There is that in the object which I do not now know; I know something to be determined in reality which is neither implicitly nor explicitly determined in my knowledge of it. This, and all similar questions I could ask and could not now answer, witness the independence of my object.

The Primacy of Perception[*]

MAURICE MERLEAU-PONTY [1908–1961] was made Professor of Philosophy at the Collège de France in 1953, the youngest man ever to occupy this position. He was influential not only as a philosopher but as a commentator on current affairs as well. Among his books now available in English are *Phenomenology of Perception, The Structure of Behavior, Signs, Sense and Nonsense,* and *In Praise of Philosophy.*

Preliminary Summary of the Argument

1. Perception as an original modality of consciousness

The unprejudiced study of perception by psychologists has finally revealed that the perceived world is not a sum of objects (in the sense in which the sciences use this word), that our relation to the world is not that of a thinker to an object of thought, and finally that the unity of the perceived thing, as perceived by several consciousnesses, is not comparable to the unity of a proposition [*théorème*], as understood by several thinkers, any more than perceived existence is comparable to ideal existence.

As a result we cannot apply the classical distinction of form and matter to perception, nor can we conceive the perceiving subject as a consciousness which "interprets," "deciphers," or "orders" a sensible matter according to an ideal law which it possesses. Matter is "pregnant" with its form, which is to say that in the final analysis every perception takes place within a certain horizon and ultimately in the "world." We experience a perception and its horizon "in action" [*pratiquement*] rather than by "posing" them or explicitly "knowing" them. Finally the quasi-organic relation of the perceiving subject and the world involves, in principle, the contradiction of immanence and transcendence.

2. The generalization of these results

Do these results have any value beyond that of psychological description? They would not if we could superimpose on the perceived world a world of ideas. But in reality the ideas to which we recur are valid only for a period of our lives or for a period in the history of our culture. Evidence is never

* From Merleau-Ponty: *The Primacy of Perception and Other Essays,* edited by James M. Edie, Northwestern University Press, 1964. Translation copyright © 1964. Reprinted by permission of Northwestern University Press.

apodictic, nor is thought timeless, though there is some progress in objectifi-
cation and thought is always valid for more than an instant. The certainty of
ideas is not the foundation of the certainty of perception but is, rather, based
on it—in that it is perceptual experience which gives us the passage from
one moment to the next and thus realizes the unity of time. In this sense all
consciousness is perceptual, even the consciousness of ourselves.

3. Conclusions

The perceived world is the always presupposed foundation of all rationality, all value and all existence. This thesis does not destroy either rationality
or the absolute. It only tries to bring them down to earth. . . .

[The Full Presentation]

. . . The point of departure for these remarks is that the perceived world
comprises relations and, in a general way, a type of organization which has
not been recognized by classical psychology and philosophy.

If we consider an object which we perceive but one of whose sides we do
not see, or if we consider objects which are not within our visual field at this
moment—*i.e.*, what is happening behind our back or what is happening in
America or at the South Pole—how should we describe the existence of these
absent objects or the nonvisible parts of present objects?

Should we say, as psychologists have often done, that I *represent* to myself
the sides of this lamp which are not seen? If I say these sides are representations, I imply that they are not grasped as actually existing; because what is
represented is not here before us, I do not actually perceive it. It is only a
possible. But since the unseen sides of this lamp are not imaginary, but only
hidden from view (to see them it suffices to move the lamp a little bit), I
cannot say that they are representations.

Should I say that the unseen sides are somehow anticipated by me, as perceptions which would be produced necessarily if I moved, given the structure of the object? If, for example, I look at a cube, knowing the structure of
the cube as it is defined in geometry, I can anticipate the perceptions which
this cube will give me while I move around it. Under this hypothesis I would
know the unseen side as the necessary consequence of a certain law of the
development of my perception. But if I turn to perception itself, I cannot
interpret it in this way because this analysis can be formulated as follows: It
is *true* that the lamp has a back, that the cube has another side. But this
formula, "It is true," does not correspond to what is given to me in perception. Perception does not give me truths like geometry but presences.

 I grasp the unseen side as present, and I do not affrm that the back of the
lamp exists in the same sense that I say the solution of a problem exists. The
hidden side is present in its own way. It is in my vicinity.

Thus I should not say that the unseen sides of objects are simply possible perceptions, nor that they are the necessary conclusions of a kind of analysis or geometrical reasoning. It is not through an intellectual synthesis which would freely posit the total object that I am led from what is given to what is not actually given; that I am given, together with the visible sides of the object, the nonvisible sides as well. It is, rather, a kind of practical synthesis: I can touch the lamp, and not only the side turned toward me but also the other side; I have only to extend my hand to hold it.

The classical analysis of perception reduces all our experience to the single level of what, for good reasons, is judged to be true. But when, on the contrary, I consider the whole setting [*l'entourage*] of my perception, it reveals another modality which is neither the ideal and necessary being of geometry nor the simple sensory event, the "*percipi*," and this is precisely what remains to be studied now.

But these remarks on the setting [*entourage*] of what is perceived enable us better to see the perceived itself. I perceive before me a road or a house, and I perceive them as having a certain dimension: the road may be a country road or a national highway; the house may be a shanty or a manor. These identifications presuppose that I recognize the true size of the object, quite different from that which appears to me from the point at which I am standing. It is frequently said that I restore the true size on the basis of the apparent size by analysis and conjecture. This is inexact for the very convincing reason that the apparent size of which we are speaking is not perceived by me. It is a remarkable fact that the uninstructed have no awareness of perspective and that it took a long time and much reflection for men to become aware of a perspectival deformation of objects. Thus there is no deciphering, no mediate inference from the sign to what is signified, because the alleged signs are not given to me separately from what they signify.

In the same way it is not true that I deduce the true color of an object on the basis of the color of the setting or of the lighting, which most of the time is not perceived. At this hour, since daylight is still coming through the windows, we perceive the yellowness of the artificial light, and it alters the color of objects. But when daylight disappears this yellowish color will no longer be perceived, and we will see the objects more or less in their true colors. The true color thus is not deduced, taking account of the lighting, because it appears precisely when daylight disappears.

If these remarks are true, what is the result? And how should we understand this "I perceive" which we are attempting to grasp?

We observe at once that it is impossible, as has often been said, to decompose a perception, to make it into a collection of sensations, because in it the whole is prior to the parts—and this whole is not an ideal whole. The meaning which I ultimately discover is not of the conceptual order. If it were a concept, the question would be how I can recognize it in the sense data, and it would be necessary for me to interpose between the concept and the sense-data certain intermediaries, and then other intermediaries between these intermediaries, and so on. It is necessary that meaning and signs, the form and matter of perception, be related from the beginning and that, as we say, the matter of perception be "pregnant with its form."

In other words, the synthesis which constitutes the unity of the perceived objects and which gives meaning to the perceptual data is not an intellectual synthesis. Let us say with Husserl that it is a "synthesis of transition" [*synthèse de transition*]—I anticipate the unseen side of the lamp because I can touch it—or a "horizonal synthesis" [*synthèse d'horizon*]—the unseen side is given to me as "visible from another standpoint," at once given but only immanently. What prohibits me from treating my perception as an intellectual act is that an intellectual act would grasp the object either as possible or as necessary. But in perception it is "real"; it is given as the infinite sum of an indefinite series of perspectival views in each of which the object is given but in none of which is it given exhaustively. It is not accidental for the object to be given to me in a "deformed" way, from the point of view [*place*] which I occupy. That is the price of its being "real." The perceptual synthesis thus must be accomplished by the subject, which can both delimit certain perspectival aspects in the object, the only ones actually given, and at the same time go beyond them. This subject, which takes a point of view, is my body as the field of perception and action [*pratique*]—in so far as my gestures have a certain reach and circumscribe as my domain the whole group of objects familiar to me. Perception is here understood as a reference to a whole which can be grasped, in principle, only through certain of its parts or aspects. The perceived thing is not an ideal unity in the possession of the intellect, like a geometrical notion, for example; it is rather a totality open to a horizon of an indefinite number of perspectival views which blend with one another according to a given style, which defines the object in question.

Perception is thus paradoxical. The perceived thing itself is paradoxical; it exists only in so far as someone can perceive it. I cannot even for an instant imagine an object in itself. As Berkeley said, if I attempt to imagine some place in the world which has never been seen, the very fact that I imagine it makes me present at that place. I thus cannot conceive a perceptible place in which I am not myself present. But even the places in which I find myself are never completely given to me; the things which I see are things for me only under the condition that they always recede beyond their immediately given aspects. Thus there is a paradox of immanence and transcendence in perception. Immanence, because the perceived object cannot be foreign to him who perceives; transcendence, because it always contains something more than what is actually given. And these two elements of perception are not, properly speaking, contradictory. For if we reflect on this notion of perspective, if we reproduce the perceptual experience in our thought, we see that the kind of evidence proper to the perceived, the appearance of "something," requires both this presence and this absence.

Finally, the world itself, which (to give a first, rough definition) is the totality of perceptible things and the thing of all things, must be understood not as an object in the sense the mathematician or the physicist give to this word—that is, a kind of unified law which would cover all the partial phenomena or as a fundamental relation verifiable in all—but as the universal style of all possible perceptions. We must make this notion of the world, which guides the whole transcendental deduction of Kant, though Kant does not tell us its provenance, more explicit. "If a world is to be possible," he says sometimes, as if he were thinking before the origin of the world, as if he were assisting at its genesis and could pose its *a priori* conditions. In fact, as Kant himself said profoundly, we can only think the world because we have already experienced it; it is through this experience that we have the idea of being, and it is through this experience that the words "rational" and "real" receive a meaning simultaneously.

If I now consider not the problem of knowing how it is that there are things for me or how it is that I have a unified, unique, and developing perceptual experience of them, but rather the problem of knowing how my experience is related to the experience which others have of the same objects, perception will again appear as the paradoxical phenomenon which renders being accessible to us.

If I consider my perceptions as simple sensations, they are private; they are mine alone. If I treat them as acts of the intellect, if perception is an inspection of the mind, and the perceived object an idea, then you and I are talking about the same world, and we have *the right* to communicate among ourselves because the world has become an ideal existence and is the same for all of us—just like the Pythagorean theorem. But neither of these two formulas accounts for our experience. If a friend and I are standing before a landscape, and if I attempt to show my friend something which I see and which he does not yet see, we cannot account for the situation by saying that I see something in my own world and that I attempt, by sending verbal messages, to give rise to an analogous perception in the world of my friend. There are not two numerically distinct worlds plus a mediating language which alone would bring us together. There is—and I know it very well if I become impatient with him—a kind of demand that what I see be seen by him also. And at the same time this communication is required by the very thing which I am looking at, by the reflections of sunlight upon it, by its color, by its sensible evidence. The thing imposes itself not as true for every intellect, but as real for every subject who is standing where I am.

I will never know how you see red, and you will never know how I see it; but this separation of consciousnesses is recognized only after a failure of communication, and our first movement is to believe in an undivided being between us. There is no reason to treat this primordial communication as an illusion, as the sensationalists do, because even then it would become inexplicable. And there is no reason to base it on our common participation in the same intellectual consciousness because this would suppress the undeniable plurality of consciousnesses. It is thus necessary that, in the perception of another, I find myself in relation with another "myself," who is, in principle, open to the same truths as I am, in relation to the same being that I am. And this perception is realized. From the depths of my subjectivity I see another subjectivity invested with equal rights appear, because the behavior of the other takes place within my perceptual field. I understand this behavior, the words of another; I espouse his thought because this other, born in the midst of my phenomena, appropriates them and treats them in accord with typical behaviors which I myself have experienced. Just as my body, as the system of all my holds on the world, founds the unity of the objects which I perceive, in the same way the body of the other—as the bearer of symbolic behaviors and of the behavior of true reality—tears itself away from being one of my phenomena, offers me the task of a true communication, and confers on my objects the new dimension of intersubjective being or, in other words, of objectivity. Such are, in a quick résumé, the elements of a description of the perceived world. . . .

We willingly admit that we cannot rest satisfied with the description of the perceived world as we have sketched it up to now and that it appears as a psychological curiosity if we leave aside the idea of the true world, the world as thought by the understanding. This leads us, therefore, to the second point which I propose to examine: what is the relation between intellectual consciousness and perceptual consciousness?

Before taking this up, let us say a word about the other objection which was addressed to us: you go back to the unreflected [irréfléchi]; therefore you renounce reflection. It is true that we discover the unreflected. But the unreflected we go back to is not that which is prior to philosophy or prior to reflection. It is the unreflected which is understood and conquered by reflection. Left to itself, perception forgets itself and is ignorant of its own accomplishments. Far from thinking that philosophy is a useless repetition of life I think, on the contrary, that without reflection life would probably dissipate itself in ignorance of itself or in chaos. But this does not mean that reflection should be carried away with itself or pretend to be ignorant of its origins. By fleeing difficulties it would only fail in its task.

Should we now generalize and say that what is true of perception is also true in the order of the intellect and that in a general way all our experience, all our knowledge, has the same fundamental structures, the same synthesis of transition, the same kind of horizons which we have found in perceptual experience?

No doubt the absolute truth or evidence of scientific knowledge would be opposed to this idea. But it seems to me that the acquisitions of the philosophy of the sciences confirm the primacy of perception. Does not the work of the French school at the beginning of this century, and the work of Brunschvicg, show that scientific knowledge cannot be closed in on itself, that it is always an approximate knowledge, and that it consists in clarifying a pre-scientific world the analysis of which will never be finished? Physico-mathematical relations take on a physical sense only to the extent that we at the same time represent to ourselves the sensible things to which these relations ultimately apply. Brunschvicg reproached positivism for its dogmatic illusion that the law is truer than the fact. The law, he adds, is conceived exclusively to make the fact intelligible. The perceived happening can never be reabsorbed in the complex of transparent relations which the intellect constructs because of the happening. But if this is the case, philosophy is not only consciousness of these relations; it is also consciousness of the obscure element and of the "non-relational foundation" on which these relations are based. Otherwise it would shirk its task of universal clarification. When I think the Pythagorean theorem and recognize it as true, it is clear that this truth is not for this moment only. Nevertheless later progress in knowledge will show that it is not yet a final, unconditioned evidence and that, if the Pythagorean theorem and the Euclidean system once appeared as final, unconditioned evidences, that is itself the mark of a certain cultural epoch. Later developments would not annul the Pythagorean theorem but would put it back in its place as a partial, and also an abstract, truth. Thus here also we do not have a timeless truth but rather the recovery of one time by another time, just as, on the level of perception, our certainty about perceiving a given thing does not guarantee that our experience will not be contradicted, or dispense us from a fuller experience of that thing. Naturally it is necessary to establish here a difference between ideal truth and perceived truth. I do not propose to undertake this immense task just now. I am only trying to show the organic tie, so to speak, between perception and intellection. Now it is incontestable that I dominate the stream of my conscious states and even that I am unaware of their temporal succession. At the moment when I am thinking or considering an idea, I am not divided into the instants of my life. But it is also incontestable that this domination of time, which is the work of thought, is always somewhat deceiving. Can I seriously say that I will always hold the ideas I do at present—and mean it? Do I not know that in six months, in a year, even if I use more or less the same formulas to express my thoughts, they will have changed their meaning slightly? Do I not know that there is a life of ideas, as there is a meaning of everything I experience, and that every one of my most convincing thoughts will need additions and then will be, not destroyed, but at least integrated into a new unity? This is the only conception of knowledge that is scientific and not mythological.

Thus perception and thought have this much in common—that both of them have a future horizon and a past horizon and that they appear to themselves as temporal, even though they do not move at the same speed nor in the same time. We must say that at each moment our ideas express not only the truth but also our capacity to attain it at that given moment. Skepticism begins if we conclude from this that our ideas are always false. But this can only happen with reference to some idol of absolute knowledge. We must say, on the contrary, that our ideas, however limited they may be at a given moment—since they always express our contact with being and with culture—are capable of being true provided we keep them open to the field of nature and culture which they must express. And this possibility is always open to us, just because we are temporal. The idea of going straight to the essence of things is an inconsistent idea if one thinks about it. What is given is a route, an experience which gradually clarifies itself, which gradually rectifies itself and proceeds by dialogue with itself and with others. Thus what we tear away from the dispersion of instants is not an already-made reason; it is, as has always been said, a natural light, our openness to *something*. What saves us is the possibility of a new development, and our power of making even what is false, true—by thinking through our errors and replacing them within the domain of truth. . . .

The . . . psychologists who have described the perceived world as I did above, the Gestalt psychologists, have never drawn the philosophical conclusions of their description. In that respect they remain within the classical framework. Ultimately they consider the structures of the perceived world as the simple result of certain physical and physiological processes which take place in the nervous system and completely determine the *gestalten* and the experience of the *gestalten*. The organism and consciousness itself are only functions of external physical variables. Ultimately the real world is the physical world as science conceives it, and it engenders our consciousness itself.

But the question is whether Gestalt theory, after the work it has done in calling attention to the phenomena of the perceived world, can fall back on the classical notion of reality and objectivity and incorporate the world of the *gestalten* within this classical conception of reality. Without doubt one of the most important acquisitions of this theory has been its overcoming of the classical alternatives between objective psychology and introspective psychology. Gestalt psychology went beyond this alternative by showing that the object of psychology is the structure of behavior, accessible both from within and from without. In his book on the chimpanzees, Köhler applied this idea and showed that in order to describe the behavior of a chimpanzee it is necessary, in characterizing this behavior, to bring in notions such as the "melodic line" of behavior. These are anthropomorphic notions, but they can be utilized objectively because it is possible to agree on interpreting "melodic" and "non-melodic" behaviors in terms of "good solutions" and "bad solutions." The science of psychology thus is not something constructed outside the human world; it is, in fact, a property of the human world to make the distinction between the true and the false, the objective and the fictional. When, later on, Gestalt psychology tried to explain itself—in spite of its own discoveries—in terms of a scientistic or positivistic ontology, it was at the price of an internal contradiction which we have to reject.

Coming back to the perceived world as we have described it above, and basing our conception of reality on the phenomena, we do not in any way sacrifice objectivity to the interior life, as Bergson has been accused of doing. As Gestalt psychology has shown, structure, *Gestalt*, meaning are no less visible in objectively observable behavior than in the experience of ourselves —provided, of course, that objectivity is not confused with what is measurable. Is one truly objective with respect to man when he thinks he can take him as an object which can be explained as an intersection of processes and causalities? Is it not more objective to attempt to constitute a true science of human life based on the description of typical behaviors? Is it objective to apply tests to man which deal only with abstract aptitudes, or to attempt to grasp the situation of man as he is present to the world and to others by means of still more tests?

Psychology as a science has nothing to fear from a return to the perceived world, nor from a philosophy which draws out the consequences of this return. Far from hurting psychology, this attitude, on the contrary, clarifies the philosophical meaning of its discoveries. For there are not two truths; there is not an inductive psychology and an intuitive philosophy. Psychological induction is never more than the methodological means of bringing to light a certain typical behavior, and if induction includes intuition, conversely intuition does not occur in empty space. It exercises itself on the facts, on the material, on the phenomena brought to light by scientific research. There are not two kinds of knowledge, but two different degrees of clarification of the same knowledge. Psychology and philosophy are nourished by the same phenomena; it is only that the problems become more formalized at the philosophical level.

But the philosophers might say here that we are giving psychology too big a place, that we are compromising rationality by founding it on the texture of experience, as it is manifested in perceptual experience. But either the demand for an absolute rationality is only a wish, a personal preference which should not be confused with philosophy, or this point of view, to the extent that it is well-founded, satisfies it as well as, or even better than, any other. When philosophers wish to place reason above the vicissitudes of history they cannot purely and simply forget what psychology, sociology, ethnography, history, and psychiatry have taught us about the conditioning of human behavior. It would be a very romantic way of showing one's love for reason to base its reign on the disavowal of acquired knowledge. What can be validly demanded is that man never be submitted to the fate of an external nature or history and stripped of his consciousness. Now my philosophy satisfies this demand. In speaking of the primacy of perception, I have never, of course, meant to say (this would be a return to the theses of empiricism) that science, reflection, and philosophy are only transformed sensations or that values are deferred and calculated pleasures. By these words, the "primacy of perception," we mean that the experience of perception is our presence at the moment when things, truths, values are constituted for us; that perception is a nascent *logos;* that it teaches us, outside all dogmatism, the true conditions of objectivity itself; that it summons us to the tasks of knowledge and action. It is not a question of reducing human knowledge to sensation, but of assisting at the birth of this knowledge, to make it as sensible as the sensible, to recover the consciousness of rationality. This experience of rationality is lost when we take it for granted as self-evident, but is, on the contrary, rediscovered when it is made to appear against the background of non-human nature.

SUGGESTED READINGS

A brilliant statement of a classical empiricist position on perception and physical objects is to be found in John Stuart Mill's *Examination of Sir William Hamilton's Philosophy,* Chapter 11. At greater length and with much more attention to detail, H. H. Price, in *Hume's Theory of the Ex-*

ternal World, has presented a view that is basically the same as Mill's, in the form of a commentary on Hume's views in his *Treatise of Human Nature* (especially Book I, Part IV, Chapter 2). Berkeley's theory of perception is discussed in G. J. Warnock's *Berkeley,* which is a good general introduction to his system.

Major attempts to use the sense-datum theory are C. D. Broad's *Scientific Thought,* Part II (especially Chapters 7 and 8); and C. I. Lewis' *Analysis of Knowledge and Valuation,* Part II. G. Paul's "Is there a Problem about Sense-Data," is an early criticism of the theory; it is reprinted in A. Flew, *Logic and Language,* I. I. Berlin, "Empirical Propositions and Hypothetical Statements," *Mind,* 1950, discusses the problems involved in trying to reduce statements about physical objects to statements about perceptions. H. H. Price discusses a causal theory of perception in Chapter 4 of *Perception,* and more recently H. P. Grice revived interest in that view in "The Causal Theory of Perception," a difficult paper published in the *Proceedings of the Aristotelian Society,* 1961. R. M. Chisholm, in *Perceiving,* proposes an original and ingenious theory which has received considerable attention recently. R. J. Hirst's *Perception and the External World* is a useful anthology with a bibliography.

Truth

Philosophers are popularly supposed to be in search of truth, and many philosophers would agree that this is one of their important tasks. But searching for truth has some properties in common with searching for a lion: in both cases one has to know ahead of time how to recognize what is sought.

Two classical theories about what is to be looked for are represented in the readings from RUSSELL and BRADLEY. Russell (following Aristotle) holds that what we say (or think) is *true* just in case it corresponds to reality. Independent of any of us, there is a realm of *facts* ("The Empire State building is in New York," "It was raining last Tuesday," and so on), and our beliefs are *true* if they accord with these facts. Bradley, on the other hand, holds that there is no knowledge that is independent of feeling and sensation, and that consequently there is no reason to believe in the existence of the "independent facts" required to make sense of the correspondence theory of truth advocated by Russell. The principal test of the "truth" of our ideas consists in coherence: if our ideas fit together properly, then they should be said to be *true*, since there is no other way to test them.

Pragmatists agree that there is no realm of "facts" existing independently of our experience, waiting to be discovered. Something *becomes* a fact through our discovery of it; it ceases to be a fact when experience rejects it. What is important is not truth in the traditional, absolute sense—truth in this sense could never be known. What *is* important is to reach a solution of specific problems that arise in experience. These problems, whether scientific, personal, or social, can be resolved only by action; if our action solves the problem, then the belief that led to the action was a true belief. And this is the case for all actions: performing experiments, carrying out decisions, adopting social policies, or whatever. In short, what works in practice will decide which of our alternative beliefs is true. And not only is the fruitful functioning of a belief in experience the real test of its truth, it is the *only* verifiable meaning we have for the concept of truth itself. In the selection from JAMES, pragmatism is put forward as the correct interpretation of scientific method and the truths it yields.

Truth and Falsehood*

BERTRAND RUSSELL [1872–   ]. See p. 131.

Our knowledge of truths, unlike our knowledge of things, has an opposite, namely *error*. So far as things are concerned, we may know them or not know them, but there is no positive state of mind which can be described as erroneous knowledge of things, so long, at any rate, as we confine ourselves to knowledge by acquaintance. Whatever we are acquainted with must be something; we may draw wrong inferences from our acquaintance, but the acquaintance itself cannot be deceptive. Thus there is no dualism as regards acquaintance. But as regards knowledge of truths, there is a dualism. We may believe what is false as well as what is true. We know that on very many subjects different people hold different and incompatible opinions: hence some beliefs must be erroneous. Since erroneous beliefs are often held just as strongly as true beliefs, it becomes a difficult question how they are to be distinguished from true beliefs. How are we to know, in a given case, that our belief is not erroneous? This is a question of the very greatest difficulty, to which no completely satisfactory answer is possible. There is, however, a preliminary question which is rather less difficult, and that is: What do we *mean* by truth and falsehood? It is this preliminary question which is to be considered in this chapter.

In this chapter we are not asking how we can know whether a belief is true or false: we are asking what is meant by the question whether a belief is true or false. It is to be hoped that a clear answer to this question may help us to obtain an answer to the question what beliefs are true, but for the present we ask only 'What is truth?' and 'What is falsehood?' not 'What beliefs are true?' and 'What beliefs are false?' It is very important to keep these different questions entirely separate, since any confusion between them is sure to produce an answer which is not really applicable to either.

There are three points to observe in the attempt to discover the nature of truth, three requisites which any theory must fulfil.

(1) Our theory of truth must be such as to admit of its opposite, falsehood. A good many philosophers have failed adequately to satisfy this condition: they have constructed theories according to which all our thinking

---

* From Russell: *The Problems of Philosophy*, Home University Library, Oxford University Press, 1912. Reprinted by permission of The Oxford University Press.

ought to have been true, and have then had the greatest difficulty in finding a place for falsehood. In this respect our theory of belief must differ from our theory of acquaintance, since in the case of acquaintance it was not necessary to take account of any opposite.

(2) It seems fairly evident that if there were no beliefs there could be no falsehood, and no truth either, in the sense in which truth is correlative to falsehood. If we imagine a world of mere matter, there would be no room for falsehood in such a world, and although it would contain what may be called 'facts,' it would not contain any truths, in the sense in which truths are things of the same kind as falsehoods. In fact, truth and falsehood are properties of beliefs and statements: hence a world of mere matter, since it would contain no beliefs or statements, would also contain no truth or falsehood.

(3) But, as against what we have just said, it is to be observed that the truth or falsehood of a belief always depends upon something which lies outside the belief itself. If I believe that Charles I died on the scaffold, I believe truly, not because of any intrinsic quality of my belief, which could be discovered by merely examining the belief, but because of an historical event which happened two and a half centuries ago. If I believe that Charles I died in his bed, I believe falsely: no degree of vividness in my belief, or of care in arriving at it, prevents it from being false, again because of what happened long ago, and not because of any intrinsic property of my belief. Hence, although truth and falsehood are properties of beliefs, they are properties dependent upon the relations of the beliefs to other things, not upon any internal quality of the beliefs.

The third of the above requisites leads us to adopt the view—which has on the whole been commonest among philosophers—that truth consists in some form of correspondence between belief and fact. It is, however, by no means an easy matter to discover a form of correspondence to which there are no irrefutable objections. By this partly—and partly by the feeling that, if truth consists in a correspondence of thought with something outside thought, thought can never know when truth has been attained—many philosophers have been led to try to find some definition of truth which shall not consist in relation to something wholly outside belief. The most important attempt at a definition of this sort is the theory that truth consists in *coherence*. It is said that the mark of falsehood is failure to cohere in the body of our beliefs, and that it is the essence of a truth to form part of the completely rounded system which is The Truth.

There is, however, a great difficulty in this view, or rather two great difficulties. The first is that there is no reason to suppose that only *one* coherent body of beliefs is possible. It may be that, with sufficient imagination, a novelist might invent a past for the world that would perfectly fit on to what we know, and yet be quite different from the real past. In more scientific matters, it is certain that there are often two or more hypotheses which account for all the known facts on some subject, and although, in such cases, men of science endeavour to find facts which will rule out all the hypotheses except one, there is no reason why they should always succeed.

In philosophy, again, it seems not uncommon for two rival hypotheses to be both able to account for all the facts. Thus, for example, it is possible that life is one long dream, and that the outer world has only that degree of reality that the objects of dreams have; but although such a view does not seem inconsistent with known facts, there is no reason to prefer it to the common-sense view, according to which other people and things do really exist. Thus coherence as the definition of truth fails because there is no proof that there can be only one coherent system.

The other objection to this definition of truth is that it assumes the meaning of 'coherence' known, whereas, in fact, 'coherence' presupposes the truth of the laws of logic. Two propositions are coherent when both may be true, and are incoherent when one at least must be false. Now in order to know whether two propositions can both be true, we must know such truths as the law of contradiction. For example, the two propositions, 'this tree is a beech' and 'this tree is not a beech,' are not coherent, because of the law of contradiction. But if the law of contradiction itself were subjected to the test of coherence, we should find that, if we choose to suppose it false, nothing will any longer be incoherent with anything else. Thus the laws of logic supply the skeleton or framework within which the test of coherence applies, and they themselves cannot be established by this test.

For the above two reasons, coherence cannot be accepted as giving the *meaning* of truth, though it is often a most important *test* of truth after a certain amount of truth has become known.

Hence we are driven back to *correspondence with fact* as constituting the nature of truth. It remains to define precisely what we mean by 'fact,' and what is the nature of the correspondence which must subsist between belief and fact, in order that belief may be true.

In accordance with our three requisites, we have to seek a theory of truth which (1) allows truth to have an opposite, namely falsehood, (2) makes truth a property of beliefs, but (3) makes it a property wholly dependent upon the relation of the beliefs to outside things.

The necessity of allowing for falsehood makes it impossible to regard belief as a relation of the mind to a single object, which could be said to be what is believed. If belief were so regarded, we should find that, like acquaintance, it would not admit of the opposition of truth and falsehood, but would have to be always true. This may be made clear by examples. Othello believes falsely that Desdemona loves Cassio. We cannot say that this belief consists in a relation to a single object, 'Desdemona's love for Cassio,' for if there were such an object, the belief would be true. There is in fact no such object, and therefore Othello cannot have any relation to such an object. Hence his belief cannot possibly consist in a relation to this object.

It might be said that his belief is a relation to a different object, namely 'that Desdemona loves Cassio'; but it is almost as difficult to suppose that there is such an object as this, when Desdemona does not love Cassio, as it was to suppose that there is 'Desdemona's love for Cassio.' Hence it will be better to seek for a theory of belief which does not make it consist in a relation of the mind to a single object.

It is common to think of relations as though they always held between *two* terms, but in fact this is not always the case. Some relations demand three terms, some four, and so on. Take, for instance, the relation 'between.' So long as only two terms come in, the relation 'between' is impossible: three terms are the smallest number that render it possible. York is between London and Edinburgh; but if London and Edinburgh were the only places in the world, there could be nothing which was between one place and another. Similarly *jealousy* requires three people: there can be no such relation that does not involve three at least. Such a proposition as 'A wishes B to promote C's marriage with D' involves a relation of four terms; that is to say, A and B and C and D all come in, and the relation involved cannot be expressed otherwise than in a form involving all four. Instances might be multiplied indefinitely, but enough has been said to show that there are relations which require more than two terms before they can occur.

The relation involved in *judging* or *believing* must, if falsehood is to be duly allowed for, be taken to be a relation between several terms, not between two. When Othello believes that Desdemona loves Cassio, he must not have before his mind a single object, 'Desdemona's love for Cassio,' or 'that Desdemona loves Cassio,' for that would require that there should be objective falsehoods, which subsist independently of any minds; and this, though not logically refutable, is a theory to be avoided if possible. Thus it is easier to account for falsehood if we take judgement to be a relation in which the mind and the various objects concerned all occur severally; that is to say, Desdemona and loving and Cassio must all be terms in the relation which subsists when Othello believes that Desdemona loves Cassio. This relation, therefore, is a relation of four terms, since Othello also is one of the terms of the relation. When we say that it is a relation of four terms, we do not mean that Othello has a certain relation to Desdemona, and has the same relation to loving and also to Cassio. This may be true of some other relation than believing; but believing, plainly, is not a relation which Othello has to *each* of the three terms concerned, but to *all* of them together: there is only one example of the relation of believing involved, but this one example knits together four terms. Thus the actual occurrence, at the moment when Othello is entertaining his belief, is that the relation called 'believing' is knitting together into one complex whole the four terms Othello, Desdemona, loving, and Cassio. What is called belief or judgement is nothing but this relation of believing or judging, which relates a mind to several things other than itself. An *act* of belief or of judgement is the occurrence between certain terms at some particular time, of the relation of believing or judging.

We are now in a position to understand what it is that distinguishes a true judgement from a false one. For this purpose we will adopt certain definitions. In every act of judgement there is a mind which judges, and there are terms concerning which it judges. We will call the mind the *subject* in the judgement, and the remaining terms the *objects*. Thus, when Othello judges that Desdemona loves Cassio, Othello is the subject, while the objects are Desdemona and loving and Cassio. The subject and the objects together are called the *constituents* of the judgement. It will be observed that the relation of judging has what is called a 'sense' or 'direction.' We may say, metaphorically, that it puts its objects in a certain *order*, which we may indicate by means of the order of the words in the sentence. (In an inflected language, the same thing will be indicated by inflections, e.g. by the difference between nominative and accusative.) Othello's judgement that Cassio loves Desdemona differs from his judgement that Desdemona loves Cassio, in spite of the fact that it consists of the same constituents, because the relation of judging places the constituents in a different order in the two cases. Similarly, if Cassio judges that Desdemona loves Othello, the constituents of the judgement are still the same, but their order is different. This property of having a 'sense' or 'direction' is one which the relation of judging shares with all other relations. The 'sense' of relations is the ultimate source of order and series and a host of mathematical concepts; but we need not concern ourselves further with this aspect.

We spoke of the relation called 'judging' or 'believing' as knitting together into one complex whole the subject and the objects. In this respect, judging is exactly like every other relation. Whenever a relation holds between two or more terms, it unites the terms into a complex whole. If Othello loves Desdemona, there is such a complex whole as 'Othello's love for Desdemona.' The terms united by the relation may be themselves complex, or may be simple, but the whole which results from their being united must be complex. Wherever there is a relation which relates certain terms, there is a complex object formed of the union of those terms; and conversely, wherever there is a complex object, there is a relation which relates its constituents. When an act of believing occurs, there is a complex, in which 'believing' is the uniting relation, and subject and objects are arranged in a certain order by the 'sense' of the relation of believing. Among the objects, as we saw in considering 'Othello believes that Desdemona loves Cassio,' one must be a relation—in this instance, the relation 'loving.' But this relation, as it occurs in the act of believing, is not the relation which creates the unity of the complex whole consisting of the subject and the objects. The relation 'loving,' as it occurs in the act of believing, is one of the objects—it is a brick in the structure, not the cement. The cement is the relation 'believing.' When the belief is *true*, there is another complex unity, in which the relation which was one of the objects of the belief relates the other objects. Thus, e.g., if Othello believes *truly* that Desdemona loves Cassio, then there is a complex unity, 'Desdemona's love for Cassio,' which is composed exclusively of the *objects* of the belief, in the same order as they had in the belief, with the relation which was one of the objects occurring now as the cement that binds together the other objects of the belief. On the other hand, when a belief is *false*, there is no such complex unity composed only of the objects of the belief. If Othello believes *falsely* that Desdemona loves Cassio, then there is no such complex unity as 'Desdemona's love for Cassio.'

Thus a belief is *true* when it *corresponds* to a certain associated complex, and *false* when it does not. Assuming, for the sake of definiteness, that the objects of the belief are two terms and a relation, the terms being put in a certain order by the 'sense' of the believing, then if the two terms in that order are united by the relation into a complex, the belief is true; if not, it is false. This constitutes the definition of truth and falsehood that we were in search of. Judging or believing is a certain complex unity of which a mind is a constituent; if the remaining constituents, taken in the order which they have in the belief, form a complex unity, then the belief is true; if not, it is false.

Thus although truth and falsehood are properties of beliefs, yet they are in a sense extrinsic properties, for the condition of the truth of a belief is something not involving beliefs, or (in general) any mind at all, but only the *objects* of the belief. A mind, which believes, believes truly when there is a *corresponding* complex not involving the mind, but only its objects. This correspondence ensures truth, and its absence entails falsehood. Hence we account simultaneously for the two facts that beliefs (*a*) depend on minds for their *existence*, (*b*) do not depend on minds for their *truth*.

We may restate our theory as follows: If we take such a belief as 'Othello believes that Desdemona loves Cassio,' we will call Desdemona and Cassio the *object-terms,* and loving the *object-relation.* If there is a complex unity 'Desdemona's love for Cassio,' consisting of the object-terms related by the object-relation in the same order as they have in the belief, then this complex unity is called the *fact corresponding to the belief.* Thus a belief is true when there is a corresponding fact, and is false when there is no corresponding fact.

It will be seen that minds do not *create* truth or falsehood. They create beliefs, but when once the beliefs are created, the mind cannot make them true or false, except in the special case where they concern future things which are within the power of the person believing, such as catching trains. What makes a belief true is a *fact,* and this fact does not (except in exceptional cases) in any way involve the mind of the person who has the belief.

Truth and Coherence*

F R A N C I S H E R B E R T B R A D L E Y [1846–1924] was one of the major influences in the development of Hegelian idealism in Great Britain and the United States. He lived a secluded life as a Fellow of Merton College, Oxford, devoting his energies to philosophy and producing several important works: *Ethical Studies* (1876), *Principles of Logic* (1883), and *Appearance and Reality* (1893).

. . . What I maintain is that in the case of facts of perception and memory the test [of truth] which we do apply, and which we must apply, is that of system. I contend that this test works satisfactorily, and that no other test will work. And I argue in consequence that there are no judgements of sense which are in principle infallible. . . .

The reason for maintaining independent facts and infallible judgements, as I understand it, is twofold. (1) Such data, it may be said, can be actually shown. And (2) in any case they must exist, since without them the intelligence cannot work. . . .

(1) I doubt my ability to do justice to the position of the man who claims to show ultimate given facts exempt from all possible error. In the case of any datum of sensation or feeling, to prove that we have this wholly unmod-

* From Bradley: *Essays on Truth and Reality,* Oxford, 1914, Chapter 7. Reprinted by permission of The Clarendon Press, Oxford.

ified by what is called 'apperception' seems a hopeless undertaking. And how far it is supposed that such a negative can be proved I do not know. What, however, is meant must be this, that we somehow and somewhere have verifiable facts of perception and memory, and also judgements, free from all chance of error.

I will begin hereby recalling a truth familiar but often forgotten. . . . In your search for independent facts and for infallible truths you may go so low that, when you have descended beyond the level of error, you find yourself below the level of any fact or of any truth which you can use. What you seek is particular facts of perception or memory, but what you get may be something not answering to that character. I will go on to give instances of what I mean, and I think that in every case we shall do well to ask this question, 'What on the strength of our ultimate fact are we able to contradict?'

(*a*) If we take the instance of simple unrelated sensations or feelings, *a*, *b*, *c*—supposing that there are such things—what judgement would such a fact enable us to deny? We could on the strength of this fact deny the denial that *a*, *b* and *c* exist in any way, manner or sense. But surely this is not the kind of independent fact of which we are in search.

(*b*) From this let us pass to the case of a complex feeling containing, at once and together, both *a* and *b*. On the ground of this we can deny the statement that *a* and *b* cannot or do not ever anyhow co-exist in feeling. This is an advance, but it surely leaves us far short of our goal.

(*c*) What we want, I presume, is something that at once is infallible and that also can be called a particular fact of perception or memory. And we want, in the case of perception, something that would be called a fact for observation. We do not seem to reach this fact until we arrive somewhere about the level of 'I am here and now having a sensation or complex of sensations of such or such a kind.' The goal is reached; but at this point, unfortunately, the judgement has become fallible, so far at least as it really states particular truth.

(*a*) In such a judgement it is in the first place hard to say what is meant by the 'I.' If, however, we go beyond feeling far enough to mean a self with such or such a real existence in time, then memory is involved, and the judgement at once, I should urge, becomes fallible. . . . Thus the statement made in the judgement is liable to error, or else the statement does not convey particular truth.

(*β*) And this fatal dilemma holds good when applied to the 'now' and 'here.' If these words mean a certain special place in a certain special series or order, they are liable to mistake. But, if they fall short of this meaning, then they fail to state individual fact. My feeling is, I agree, not subject to error in the proper sense of that term, but on the other side my feeling does not of itself deliver truth. And the process which gets from it a deliverance as to individual fact is fallible.

Everywhere such fact depends on construction. And we have here to face not only the possibility of what would commonly be called mistaken interpretation. We have in addition the chance of actual sense-hallucination. And, worse that this, we have the far-reaching influence of abnormal suggestion and morbid fixed idea. This influence may stop short of hallucination, and yet may vitiate the memory and the judgement to such an extent that there remains no practical difference between idea and perceived fact. And, in the face of these possibilities, it seems idle to speak of perceptions and memories secure from all chance of error. Or on the other side banish the chance of error, and with what are you left? You then have something which (as we have seen) goes no further than to warrant the assertion that such and such elements can and do co-exist—somehow and somewhere, or again that such or such a judgement happens—without any regard to its truth and without any specification of its psychical context. And no one surely will contend that with this we have particular fact.

The doctrine that perception gives us infallible truth rests on a foundation which in part is sound and in part fatally defective. That what is felt is felt, and cannot, so far as felt, be mistaken—so much as this must be accepted. But the view that, when I say 'this,' 'now,' 'here,' or 'my,' what I feel, when so speaking, is carried over intact into my judgement, and that my judgement in consequence is exempt from error, seems wholly indefensible. It survives, I venture to think, only because it never has understood its complete refutation. That which I designate, is not and cannot be carried over into my judgement. The judgement may in a sense answer to that which I feel, but none the less it fails to contain and to convey my feeling. And on the other hand, so far as it succeeds in expressing my meaning, the judgement does this in a way which makes it liable to error. Or, to put it otherwise, the perceived truth, to be of any use, must be particularized. So far as it is stated in a general form, it contains not only that which you meant to say but also, and just as much, the opposite of that which you meant. And to contend for the infallibility of such a truth seems futile. On the other side so far as your truth really is individualized, so far as it is placed in a special construction and vitally related to its context, to the same extent the element of interpretation or implication is added. And, with this element obviously comes the possibility of mistake. And we have seen above that, viewed psychologically, particular judgements of perception immune from all chance of error seem hardly tenable.

(2) I pass now to the second reason for accepting infallible data of perception. Even if we cannot show these (it is urged) we are bound to assume

them. For in their absence our knowledge has nothing on which to stand, and this want of support results in total scepticism.

It is possible of course here to embrace both premises and conclusion, and to argue that scepticism is to be preferred to an untrue assumption. And such a position I would press on the notice of those who uphold infallible judgements of sense and memory. But personally I am hardly concerned in this issue, for I reject both the conclusion and the premises together. Such infallible and incorrigible judgements are really not required for our knowledge, and, since they cannot be shown, we must not say that they exist. . . .

I agree that we depend vitally on the sense-world, that our material comes from it, and that apart from it knowledge could not begin. To this world, I agree, we have for ever to return, not only to gain new matter but to confirm and maintain the old. I agree that to impose order from without on sheer disorder would be wholly impracticable, and that, if my sense-world were disorderly beyond a certain point, my intelligence would not exist. And further I agree that we cannot suppose it possible that *all* the judgements of perception and memory which for me come first, could in fact for me be corrected. I cannot, that is, imagine the world of my experience to be so modified that in the end none of these accepted facts should be left standing. But so far, I hasten to add, we have not yet come to the real issue. There is still a chasm between such admissions and the conclusion that there are judgements of sense which possess truth absolute and infallible.

We meet here a false doctrine largely due to a misleading metaphor. My known world is taken to be a construction built upon such and such foundations. It is argued, therefore, to be in principle a superstructure which rests upon these supports. You can go on adding to it no doubt, but only so long as the supports remain; and, unless they remain, the whole building comes down. But the doctrine, I have to contend, is untenable, and the metaphor ruinously inapplicable. The foundation in truth is provisional merely. In order to begin my construction I take the foundation as absolute—so much certainly is true. But that my construction continues to rest on the beginnings of my knowledge is a conclusion which does not follow. It does not follow that, if these are allowed to be fallible, the whole building collapses. For it is in another sense that my world rests upon the data of perception.

My experience is solid, not so far as it is a superstructure but so far as in short it is a system. My object is to have a world as comprehensive and coherent as possible, and, in order to attain this object, I have not only to reflect but perpetually to have recourse to the materials of sense. I must go to this source both to verify the matter which is old and also to increase it by what is new. And in this way I must depend upon the judgements of perception. Now it is agreed that, if I am to have an orderly world, I cannot possibly accept all 'facts.' Some of these must be relegated, as they are, to the world of error, whether we succeed or fail in modifying and correcting them. And the view which I advocate takes them all as in principle fallible. On the other hand, that view denies that there is any necessity for absolute facts of sense. Facts for it are true, we may say, just so far as they work, just so far as they contribute to the order of experience. If by taking certain judgements of perception as true, I can get more system into my world, then these 'facts' are so far true, and if by taking certain 'facts' as errors I can order my experience better, then so far these 'facts' are errors. And there is no 'fact' which possesses an absolute right. Certainly there are truths with which I begin and which I personally never have to discard, and which therefore remain in fact as members of my known world. And of some of these certainly it may be said that without them I should not know how to order my knowledge. But it is quite another thing to maintain that every single one of these judgements is in principle infallible. The absolute indispensable fact is in my view the mere creature of false theory. Facts are valid so far as, when taken otherwise than as 'real,' they bring disorder into my world. And there are to-day for me facts such that, if I take them as mistakes, my known world is damaged and, it is possible, ruined. But how does it follow that I cannot to-morrow on the strength of new facts gain a wider order in which these old facts can take a place as errors? The supposition may be improbable, but what you have got to show is that it is in principle impossible. A foundation used at the beginning does not in short mean something fundamental at the end, and there is no single 'fact' which in the end can be called fundamental absolutely. It is all a question of relative contribution to my known world-order.

'Then no judgement of perception will be more than probable?' Certainly that is my contention. 'Facts' are justified because and as far as, while taking them as real, I am better able to deal with the incoming new 'facts' and in general to make my world wider and more harmonious. The higher and wider my structure, and the more that any particular fact or set of facts is implied in that structure, the more certain are the structure and the facts. And, if we could reach an all-embracing ordered whole, then our certainty would be absolute. But, since we cannot do this, we have to remain content with relative probability. Why is this or that fact of observation taken as practically certain? It is so taken just so far as it is *not* taken in its own right. (i) Its validity is due to such and such a person perceiving it under such and such conditions. This means that a certain intellectual order in the person is necessary as a basis, and again that nothing in the way of sensible or mental distortion intervenes between this order and what is given. And (ii) the observed fact must agree with our world as already arranged, or at least must not upset this. If the fact is too much contrary to our arranged world we provisionally reject it. We eventually accept the fact only when after confirmation the hypothesis of its error becomes still more ruinous. We are forced then more or less to rearrange our world, and more or less perhaps to reject some previous 'facts.' The question throughout is as to what is better or worse for our order as a whole.

Why again to me is a remembered fact certain, supposing that it is so? Assuredly not because it is infallibly delivered by the faculty of Memory, but because I do not see how to reconcile the fact of its error with my accepted world. Unless I go on the principle of trusting my memory, apart from any special reason to the contrary, I cannot order my world so well, if indeed I can order it at all. The principle here again is system. . . .

The same account holds with regard to the facts of history. For instance, the guillotining of Louis XVI is practically certain, because, to take this as error, would entail too much disturbance of my world. Error is possible here of course. Fresh facts conceivably might come before me such as would compel me to modify in part my knowledge as so far arranged. And in this modified arrangement the execution of Louis would find its place as an error. But the reason for such a modification would have to be considerable, while, as things are, no reason exists. . . . To take memory as in general trustworthy, where I have no special reason for doubt, and to take the testimony of those persons, whom I suppose to view the world as I view it, as being true, apart from special reason on the other side—these are principles by which I construct my ordered world, such as it is. And because by any other method the result is worse, therefore for me these principles are true. On the other hand to suppose that any 'fact' of perception or memory is so certain that no possible experience could justify me in taking it as error, seems to me injurious if not ruinous. On such a principle my world of knowledge would be ordered worse, if indeed it could be ordered at all. For to accept all the 'facts,' as they offer themselves, seems obviously impossible; and, if it is we who have to decide as to which facts are infallible, then I ask how we are to decide. The ground of validity, I maintain, consists in successful contribution. That is a principle of order, while any other principle, so far as I see, leads to chaos.

'But,' it may still be objected, 'my fancy is unlimited. I can therefore invent an imaginary world even more orderly than my known world. And further this fanciful arrangement might possibly be made so wide that the world of perception would become for me in comparison small and inconsiderable. Hence, my perceived world, so far as not supporting my fancied arrangement, might be included within it as error. Such a consequence would or might lead to confusion in theory and to disaster in practice. And yet the result follows from your view inevitably, unless after all you fall back upon the certainty of perception.'

To this possible objection, I should reply first, that it has probably failed to understand rightly the criterion which I defend. The aspect of comprehensiveness has not received here its due emphasis. The idea of system demands the inclusion of all possible material. Not only must you include everything to be gained from immediate experience and perception, but you must also be ready to act on the same principle with regard to fancy. But this means that you cannot confine yourself within the limits of this or that fancied world, as suits your pleasure or private convenience. You are bound also, so far as is possible, to recognize and to include the opposite fancy.

This consideration to my mind ruins the above hypothesis on which the objection was based. The fancied arrangement not only has opposed to it the world of perception. It also has against it any opposite arrangement and any contrary fact which I can fancy. And, so far as I can judge, these contrary fancies will balance the first. Nothing, therefore, will be left to outweigh the world as perceived, and the imaginary hypothesis will be condemned by our criterion.

. . . I may state the view which has commended itself to my mind. Truth is an ideal expression of the Universe, at once coherent and comprehensive. It must not conflict with itself, and there must be no suggestion which fails to fall inside it. Perfect truth in short must realize the idea of a systematic whole. And such a whole . . . possesses essentially the two characters of coherence and comprehensiveness.

Pragmatism*

WILLIAM JAMES [1842–1910]. See page 166.

THE METHOD OF PRAGMATISM. Some years ago, being with a camping party in the mountains, I returned from a solitary ramble to find everyone engaged in a ferocious metaphysical dispute. The *corpus* of the dispute was a squirrel—a live squirrel supposed to be clinging to one side of a tree-trunk; while over against the tree's opposite side a human being was imagined to

---

* From James: *Pragmatism, A New Name for Some Old Ways of Thinking*, Lectures II and VI. Copyright, 1907, by William James; Longmans, Green and Company, New York. Permission to reprint granted by Paul R. Reynolds & Son, 599 Fifth Avenue, New York 17, N. Y.

stand. This human witness tries to get sight of the squirrel by moving rapidly round the tree, but no matter how fast he goes, the squirrel moves as fast in the opposite direction, and always keeps the tree between himself and the man, so that never a glimpse of him is caught. The resultant metaphysical problem now is this: *Does the man go round the squirrel or not?* He goes round the tree, sure enough, and the squirrel is on the tree; but does he go round the squirrel? In the unlimited leisure of the wilderness, discussion had been worn threadbare. Everyone had taken sides, and was obstinate; and the numbers on both sides were even. Each side, when I appeared therefore appealed to me to make it a majority. Mindful of the scholastic adage that whenever you meet a contradiction you must make a distinction, I immediately sought and found one, as follows: "Which party is right," I said, "depends on what you *practically mean* by 'going round' the squirrel. If you mean passing from the north of him to the east, then to the south, then to the west, and then to the north of him again, obviously the man does go round him, for he occupies these successive positions. But if on the contrary you mean being first in front of him, then on the right of him, then behind him, then on his left, and finally in front again, it is quite as obvious that the man fails to go round him, for by the compensating movements the squirrel makes, he keeps his belly turned towards the man all the time, and his back turned away. Make the distinction, and there is no occasion for any farther dispute. You are both right and both wrong according as you conceive the verb 'to go round' in one practical fashion or the other."

Although one or two of the hotter disputants called my speech a shuffling evasion, saying they wanted no quibbling or scholastic hair-splitting, but meant just plain honest English 'round,' the majority seemed to think that the distinction had assuaged the dispute.

I tell this trivial anecdote because it is a peculiarly simple example of what I wish now to speak of as *the pragmatic method*. The pragmatic method is primarily a method of settling metaphysical disputes that otherwise might be interminable. Is the world one or many?—fated or free?—material or spiritual?—here are notions either of which may or may not hold good of the world; and disputes over such notions are unending. The pragmatic method in such cases is to try to interpret each notion by tracing its respective practical consequences. What difference would it practically make to any one if this notion rather than that notion were true? If no practical difference whatever can be traced, then the alternatives mean practically the same thing, and all dispute is idle. Whenever a dispute is serious, we ought to be able to show some practical difference that must follow from one side or the other's being right.

A glance at the history of the idea will show you still better what pragmatism means. The term is derived from the same Greek word πρᾶγμα meaning action, from which our words 'practice' and 'practical' come. It was first introduced into philosophy by Mr. Charles Peirce in 1878. In an article entitled 'How to Make Our Ideas Clear,' in the 'Popular Science Monthly' for January of that year Mr. Peirce, after pointing out that our beliefs are really rules for action, said that, to develop a thought's meaning, we need only determine what conduct it is fitted to produce: that conduct is for us its sole significance. And the tangible fact at the root of all our thought-distinctions, however subtle, is that there is no one of them so fine as to consist in anything but a possible difference of practice. To attain perfect clearness in our thoughts of an object, then, we need only consider what conceivable effects of a practical kind the object may involve—what sensations we are to expect from it, and what reactions we must prepare. Our conception of these effects, whether immediate or remote, is then for us the whole of our conception of the object, so far as that conception has positive significance at all.

This is the principle of Peirce, the principle of pragmatism. . . . To take in the importance of Peirce's principle, one must get accustomed to applying it to concrete cases. I found a few years ago that Ostwald, the illustrious Leipzig chemist, had been making perfectly distinct use of the principle of pragmatism in his lectures on the philosophy of science, though he had not called it by that name.

"All realities influence our practice," he wrote me, "and that influence is their meaning for us. I am accustomed to put questions to my classes in this way: In what respects would the world be different if this alternative or that were true? If I can find nothing that would become different, then the alternative has no sense."

That is, the rival views mean practically the same thing, and meaning, other than practical, there is for us none. Ostwald in a published lecture gives this example of what he means. Chemists have long wrangled over the inner constitution of certain bodies called 'tautomerous.' Their properties seemed equally consistent with the notion that an instable hydrogen atom oscillates inside of them, or that they are instable mixtures of two bodies. Controversy raged, but never was decided. "It would never have begun," says Ostwald, "if the combatants had asked themselves what particular experimental fact could have been made different by one or the other view being correct. For it would then have appeared that no difference of fact could possibly ensue; and the quarrel was as unreal as if, theorizing in primitive times about the raising of dough by yeast, one party should have invoked a 'brownie,' while another insisted on an 'elf' as the true cause of the phenomenon."

It is astonishing to see how many philosophical disputes collapse into insignificance the moment you subject them to this simple test of tracing a concrete consequence. There can *be* no difference anywhere that doesn't *make* a difference elsewhere—no difference in abstract truth that doesn't express itself in a difference in concrete fact and in conduct consequent upon that fact, imposed on somebody, somehow, somewhere, and somewhen. The whole function of philosophy ought to be to find out what definite difference it will make to you and me, at definite instants of our life, if this world-formula or that world-formula be the true one. . . .

Pragmatism represents a perfectly familiar attitude in philosophy, the empiricist attitude, but it represents it, as it seems to me, both in a more radical and in a less objectionable form than it has ever yet assumed. A pragmatist turns his back resolutely and once for all upon a lot of inveterate habits dear to professional philosophers. He turns away from abstraction and insufficiency, from verbal solutions, from bad *a priori* reasons, from fixed principles, closed systems, and pretended absolutes and origins. He turns towards concreteness and adequacy, towards facts, towards action and towards power. That means the empiricist temper regnant and the rationalist temper sincerely given up. It means the open air and possibilities of nature, as against dogma, artificiality, and the pretence of finality in truth.

At the same time it does not stand for any special results. It is a method only. But the general triumph of that method would mean an enormous change in what I called in my last lecture the 'temperament' of philosophy. Teachers of the ultra-rationalistic type would be frozen out, much as the courtier type is frozen out in republics, as the ultramontane type of priest is frozen out in protestant lands. Science and metaphysics would come much nearer together, would in fact work absolutely hand in hand.

Metaphysics has usually followed a very primitive kind of quest. You know how men have always hankered after unlawful magic, and you know what a great part in magic *words* have always played. If you have his name, or the formula of incantation that binds him, you can control the spirit, genie, afrit, or whatever the power may be. Solomon knew the names of all the spirits, and having their names, he held them subject to his will. So the universe has always appeared to the natural mind as a kind of enigma, of which the key must be sought in the shape of some illuminating or power-bringing word or name. That word names the universe's *principle*, and to possess it is after a fashion to possess the universe itself. 'God,' 'Matter,' 'Reason,' 'the Absolute,' 'Energy,' are so many solving names. You can rest when you have them. You are at the end of your metaphysical quest.

But if you follow the pragmatic method, you cannot look on any such word as closing your quest. You must bring out of each word its practical cash-value, set it at work within the stream of your experience. It appears less as a solution, then, than as a program for more work, and more particularly as an indication of the ways in which existing realities may be *changed*.

Theories thus become instruments, not answers to enigmas, in which we can rest. We don't lie back upon them, we move forward, and, on occasion, make nature over again by their aid. Pragmatism unstiffens all our theories, limbers them up and sets each one at work. Being nothing essentially new, it harmonizes with many ancient philosophic tendencies. It agrees with nominalism for instance, in always appealing to particulars; with utilitarianism in emphasizing practical aspects; with positivism in its disdain for verbal solutions, useless questions and metaphysical abstractions.

All these, you see, are *anti-intellectualist* tendencies. Against rationalism as a pretension and a method pragmatism is fully armed and militant. But, at the outset, at least, it stands for no particular results. It has no dogmas, and no doctrines save its method. As the young Italian pragmatist Papini has well said, it lies in the midst of our theories, like a corridor in a hotel. Innumerable chambers open out of it. In one you may find a man writing an atheistic volume; in the next some one on his knees praying for faith and strength; in a third a chemist investigating a body's properties. In a fourth a system of idealistic metaphysics is being excogitated; in a fifth the impossibility of metaphysics is being shown. But they all own the corridor, and all must pass through it if they want a practicable way of getting into or out of their respective rooms.

No particular results then, so far, but only an attitude of orientation, is what the pragmatic method means. *The attitude of looking away from first things, principles, 'categories,' supposed necessities; and of looking towards last things, fruits, consequences, facts.*

So much for the pragmatic method! . . . Meanwhile the word pragmatism has come to be used in a still wider sense, as meaning also a certain *theory of truth.* . . .

THE PRAGMATIC THEORY OF TRUTH. I am well aware how odd it must seem to some of you to hear me say that an idea is 'true' so long as to believe it is profitable to our lives. That it is *good*, for as much as it profits you will gladly admit. If what we do by its aid is good, you will allow the idea itself to be good in so far forth, for we are the better for possessing it. But is it not a strange misuse of the word 'truth,' you will say, to call ideas also 'true' for this reason?

To answer this difficulty fully is impossible at this stage of my account. . . . Let me now say only this, that truth is *one species of good*, and not, as is usually supposed, a category distinct from good, and co-ordinate with it.

The true is the name of whatever proves itself to be good in the way of belief, and good, too, for definite, assignable reasons. Surely you must admit this, that if there were *no* good for life in true ideas, or if the knowledge of them were positively disadvantageous and false ideas the only useful ones, then the current notion that truth is divine and precious, and its pursuit a duty, could never have grown up or become a dogma. In a world like that, our duty would be to *shun* truth, rather. But in this world, just as certain foods are not only agreeable to our taste, but good for our teeth, our stomach, and our tissues; so certain ideas are not only agreeable to think about, or agreeable as supporting other ideas that we are fond of, but they are also helpful in life's practical struggles. If there be any life that it is really better we should lead, and if there be any idea which, if believed in, would help us to lead that life, then it would be really *better for us* to believe in that idea, *unless, indeed, belief in it incidentally clashed with other greater vital benefits.*

'What would be better for us to believe'! This sounds very like a definition of truth. It comes very near to saying 'what we *ought* to believe': and in *that* definition none of you would find any oddity. Ought we ever not to believe what it is *better for us* to believe? And can we then keep the notion of what is better for us, and what is true for us, permanently apart? . . .

Truth, as any dictionary will tell you, is a property of certain of our ideas. It means their 'agreement,' as falsity means their disagreement, with 'reality.' Pragmatists and intellectualists both accept this definition as a matter of course. They begin to quarrel only after the question is raised as to what may precisely be meant by the term 'agreement,' and what by the term 'reality,' when reality is taken as something for our ideas to agree with.

In answering these questions the pragmatists are more analytic and painstaking, the intellectualists more offhand and irreflective. The popular notion is that a true idea must copy its reality. Like other popular views, this one follows the analogy of the most usual experience. Our true ideas of sensible things do indeed copy them. Shut your eyes and think of yonder clock on the wall, and you get just such a true picture or copy of its dial. But your idea of its 'works' (unless you are a clockmaker) is much less of a copy, yet it passes muster, for it in no way clashes with the reality. Even though it should shrink to the mere word 'works,' that word still serves you truly; and when you speak of the 'time-keeping function' of the clock, or of its spring's 'elasticity,' it is hard to see exactly what your ideas can copy.

You perceive that there is a problem here. Where our ideas cannot copy definitely their object, what does agreement with that object mean? . . . The great assumption of the intellectualists is that truth means essentially an inert static relation. When you've got your true idea of anything, there's an end of the matter. You're in possession; you *know*; you have fulfilled your thinking destiny. You are where you ought to be mentally; you have obeyed your categorical imperative; and nothing more need follow on that climax of your rational destiny. Epistemologically you are in stable equilibrium.

Pragmatism, on the other hand, asks its usual question. "Grant an idea or belief to be true," it says, "what concrete difference will its being true make in any one's actual life? How will the truth be realized? What experiences will be different from those which would obtain if the belief were false? What, in short, is the truth's cash-value in experiential terms?"

The moment pragmatism asks this question, it sees the answer: *True ideas are those that we can assimilate, validate, corroborate and verify. False ideas are those that we can not.* That is the practical difference it makes to us to have true ideas; that, therefore, is the meaning of truth, for it is all that truth is known-as.

This thesis is what I have to defend. The truth of an idea is not a stagnant property inherent in it. Truth *happens* to an idea. It *becomes* true, is *made* true by events. Its verity *is* in fact an event, a process: the process namely of its verifying itself, its veri-*fication*. Its validity is the process of its valid-*ation*.

But what do the words verification and validation themselves pragmatically mean? They again signify certain practical consequences of the verified and validated idea. It is hard to find any one phrase that characterizes these consequences better than the ordinary agreement-formula—just such consequences being what we have in mind whenever we say that our ideas 'agree' with reality. They lead us, namely, through the acts and other ideas which they instigate, into or up to, or towards, other parts of experience with which we feel all the while—such feeling being among our potentialities—that the original ideas remain in agreement. The connexions and transitions come to us from point to point as being progressive, harmonious, satisfactory. This function of agreeable leading is what we mean by an idea's verification. Such an account is vague and it sounds at first quite trivial, but it has results which it will take the rest of my hour to explain.

Let me begin by reminding you of the fact that the possession of true thoughts means everywhere the possession of invaluable instruments of action: and that our duty to gain truth, so far from being a blank command from out of the blue, or a 'stunt' self-imposed by our intellect, can account for itself by excellent practical reasons.

The importance to human life of having true beliefs about matters of fact is a thing too notorious. We live in a world of realities that can be infinitely useful or infinitely harmful. Ideas that tell us which of them to expect count as the true ideas in all this primary sphere of verification, and the pursuit of such ideas is a primary human duty. The possession of truth, so far from being here an end in itself, is only a preliminary means towards other vital satisfactions. If I am lost in the woods and starved, and find what looks like a cow-path, it is of the utmost importance that I should think of a human habitation at the end of it, for if I do so and follow it, I save myself. The true thought is useful here because the house which is its object is useful. The practical value of true ideas is thus primarily derived from the practical importance of their objects to us. Their objects are, indeed, not important at all times. I may on another occasion have no use for the house; and then my idea of it, however verifiable, will be practically irrelevant, and had better remain latent. Yet since almost any object may some day become temporarily important, the advantage of having a general stock of *extra* truths, of ideas that shall be true of merely possible situations, is obvious. We store such extra truths away in our memories, and with the overflow we fill our books of reference. Whenever such an extra truth becomes practically relevant to one of our emergencies, it passes from cold-storage to do work in the world and our belief in it grows active. You can say of it then either that 'it is useful because it is true' or that 'it is true because it is useful.' Both these phrases mean exactly the same thing, namely that here is an idea that gets fulfilled and can be verified. True is the name for whatever idea starts the verification-process, useful is the name for its completed function in experience. True ideas would never have been singled out as such, would never have acquired a class-name, least of all a name suggesting value, unless they had been useful from the outset in this way.

From this simple cue pragmatism gets her general notion of truth as something essentially bound up with the way in which one moment in our experience may lead us towards other moments which it will be worth while to have been led to. Primarily, and on the common-sense level, the truth of a state of mind means this function of *a leading that is worth while*. When a moment in our experience, of any kind whatever, inspires us with a thought that is true, that means that sooner or later we dip by that thought's guidance into the particulars of experience again and make advantageous connexion with them. This is a vague enough statement, but I beg you to retain it, for it is essential.

Our experience meanwhile is all shot through with regularities. One bit of it can warn us to get ready for another bit, can 'intend' or be 'significant of' that remoter object. The object's advent is the significance's verification. Truth, in these cases, meaning nothing but eventual verification, is manifestly incompatible with waywardness on our part. Woe to him whose beliefs play fast and loose with the order which realities follow in his experience; they will lead him nowhere or else make false connexions.

By 'realities' or 'objects' here, we mean either things of common sense, sensibly present, or else common-sense relations, such as dates, places, distances, kinds, activities. Following our mental image of a house along the cow-path, we actually come to see the house; we get the image's full verification. *Such simply and fully verified leadings are certainly the originals and prototypes of the truth-process.* Experience offers indeed other forms of truth-process, but they are all conceivable as being primary verifications arrested, multiplied or substituted one for another.

Take, for instance, yonder object on the wall. You and I consider it to be a 'clock,' altho no one of us has seen the hidden works that make it one. We let our notion pass for true without attempting to verify. If truths mean verification-process essentially, ought we then to call such unverified truths as this abortive? No, for they form the overwhelmingly large number of the truths we live by. Indirect as well as direct verifications pass muster. Where circumstantial evidence is sufficient, we can go without eye-witnessing. Just as we here assume Japan to exist without ever having been there, because it *works* to do so, everything we know conspiring with the belief, and nothing interfering, so we assume that thing to be a clock. We *use* it as a clock, regulating the length of our lecture by it. The verification of the assumption here means its leading to no frustration or contradiction. Verifi*ability* of wheels and weights and pendulum is as good as verification. For one truth-process completed there are a million in our lives that function in this state of nascency. They turn us *towards* direct verification; lead us into the *surroundings* of the objects they envisage; and then, if everything runs on harmoniously, we are so sure that verification is possible that we omit it, and are usually justified by all that happens. . . .

Primarily, no doubt, to agree means to copy, but we saw that the mere word 'clock' would do instead of a mental picture of its works, and that of many realities our ideas can only be symbols and not copies. 'Past time,' 'power,' 'spontaneity,'—how can our mind copy such realities?

To 'agree' in the widest sense with a reality *can only mean to be guided either straight up to it or into its surroundings, or to be put into such working touch with it as to handle either it or something connected with it better than if we disagreed.* Better either intellectually or practically! And often agreement will only mean the negative fact that nothing contradictory from the quarter of that reality comes to interfere with the way in which our ideas guide us elsewhere. To copy a reality is, indeed, one very important way of agreeing with it, but it is far from being essential. The essential thing is the process of being guided. Any idea that helps us to *deal,* whether practically or intellectually, with either the reality or its belongings, that doesn't entangle our progress in frustrations, that *fits*, in fact, and adapts our life to the reality's whole setting, will agree sufficiently to meet the requirement. It will hold true of that reality.

Thus, *names* are just as 'true' or 'false' as definite mental pictures are. They set up similar verification-processes, and lead to fully equivalent practical results.

All human thinking gets discursified; we exchange ideas; we lend and borrow verifications, get them from one another by means of social intercourse. All truth thus gets verbally built out, stored up, and made available for every one. Hence, we must *talk* consistently just as we must *think* consistently: for both in talk and thought we deal with kinds. Names are arbitrary, but once understood they must be kept to. We mustn't now call Abel 'Cain' or Cain 'Abel.' If we do, we ungear ourselves from the whole book of Genesis, and from all its connexions with the universe of speech and fact down to the present time. We throw ourselves out of whatever truth that entire system of speech and fact may embody.

The overwhelming majority of our true ideas admit of no direct or face-to-face verification—those of past history, for example, as of Cain and Abel. The stream of time can be remounted only verbally, or verified indirectly by the present prolongations of effects of what the past harbored. Yet if they agree with these verbalities and effects, we can know that our ideas of the past are true. *As true as past time itself was,* so true was Julius Cæsar, so true were antediluvian monsters, all in their proper dates and settings. That past time itself was, is guaranteed by its coherence with everything that's present. True as the present *is*, the past *was* also.

Agreement thus turns out to be essentially an affair of leading—leading that is useful because it is into quarters that contain objects that are important. True ideas lead us into useful verbal and conceptual quarters as well as directly up to useful sensible termini. They lead to consistency, stability and flowing human intercourse. They lead away from excentricity and isolation, from foiled and barren thinking. The untrammelled flowing of the leading-process, its general freedom from clash and contradiction, passes for its indirect verification; but all roads lead to Rome, and in the end and eventually, all true processes must lead to the face of directly verifying sensible experiences *somewhere,* which somebody's ideas have copied.

Such is the large loose way in which the pragmatist interprets the word agreement. He treats it altogether practically. He lets it cover any process of conduction from a present idea to a future terminus, provided only it run prosperously. It is only thus that 'scientific' ideas, flying as they do beyond common sense, can be said to agree with their realities. It is, as I have already said, *as if* reality were made of ether, atoms or electrons, but we mustn't think so literally. The term 'energy' doesn't even pretend to stand for anything 'objective.' It is only a way of measuring the surface of phenomena so as to string their changes on a simple formula.

Yet in the choice of these man-made formulas we can not be capricious with impunity any more than we can be capricious on the common-sense practical level. We must find a theory that will *work*; and that means something extremely difficult; for our theory must mediate between all previous truths and certain new experiences. It must derange common sense and previous belief as little as possible, and it must lead to some sensible terminus or other that can be verified exactly. To 'work' means both these things; and the squeeze is so tight that there is little loose play for any hypothesis. Our theories are wedged and controlled as nothing else is. Yet sometimes alternative theoretic formulas are equally compatible with all the truths we know, and then we choose between them for subjective reasons. We choose the kind of theory to which we are already partial; we follow 'elegance' or 'economy.' Clerk-Maxwell somewhere says it would be 'poor scientific taste' to choose the more complicated of two equally well-evidenced conceptions; and you will all agree with him. Truth in science is what gives us the maximum possible sum of satisfactions, taste included, but consistency both with previous truth and with novel fact is always the most imperious claimant. . . .

Our account of truth is an account of truths in the plural, of processes of leading, realized *in rebus,* and having only this quality in common, that they *pay.* They pay by guiding us into or towards some part of a system that dips at numerous points into sense-percepts, which we may copy mentally or not, but with which at any rate we are now in the kind of commerce vaguely designated as verification. Truth for us is simply a collective name for verification-process, just as health, wealth, strength, etc., are names for other processes connected with life, and also pursued because it pays to pursue them. Truth is *made,* just as health, wealth and strength are made, in the course of experience. . . .

'The true,' to put it very briefly, is only the expedient in the way of our thinking, just as 'the right' is only the expedient in the way of our behaving. Expedient in almost any fashion; and expedient in the long run and on the whole of course; for what meets expediently all the experience in sight won't necessarily meet all farther experiences equally satisfactorily. Experience, as we know, has ways of *boiling over,* and making us correct our present formulas.

The 'absolutely' true, meaning what no farther experience will ever alter, is that ideal vanishing-point towards which we imagine that all our temporary truths will some day converge. It runs on all fours with the perfectly wise man, and with the absolutely complete experience; and, if these ideals are ever realized, they will all be realized together. Meanwhile we have to live to-day by what truth we can get to-day, and be ready tomorrow to call it falsehood. Ptolemaic astronomy, euclidean space, aristotelian logic, scholastic metaphysics, were expedient for centuries, but human experience has boiled over those limits, and we now call these things only relatively true, or true within those borders of experience. 'Absolutely' they are false; for we know that those limits were casual, and might have been transcended by past theorists just as they are by present thinkers.

When new experiences lead to retrospective judgments, using the past tense, what these judgments utter *was* true, even tho no past thinker had been led there. We live forwards, a Danish thinker has said, but we understand backwards. The present sheds a backward light on the world's previous processes. They may have been truth-processes for the actors in them. They are not so for one who knows the later revelations of the story.

This regulative notion of a potential better truth to be established later, possibly to be established some day absolutely, and having powers of retroactive legislation, turns its face, like all pragmatist notions, towards concreteness of fact, and towards the future. Like the half-truths, the absolute truth will have to be *made*, made as a relation incidental to the growth of a mass of verification-experience, to which the half-true ideas are all along contributing their quota.

I have already insisted on the fact that truth is made largely out of previous truths. Men's beliefs at any time are so much experience *funded*. But the beliefs are themselves parts of the sum total of the world's experience, and become matter, therefore, for the next day's funding operations. So far as reality means experienceable reality, both it and the truths men gain about it are everlastingly in process of mutation—mutation towards a definite goal, it may be—but still mutation.

SUGGESTED READINGS

On Idealistic views of truth, see A. C. Ewing, *Idealism*, Chapter 5, which gives a useful general account. For a standard defence of the coherence theory H. H. Joachim's rather difficult book *The Nature of Truth* should be consulted.

The correspondence theory of truth, in a revised and quite sophisticated version, was defended by J. L. Austin and attacked by P. F. Strawson in papers originally published in the *Proceedings of the Aristotelian Society,*

Supplementary Volume, 1950, and reprinted in G. Pitcher, *Truth*. These are difficult but rewarding. Austin attempts to reply to Strawson in "Unfair to Facts," *Philosophical Papers*. G. J. Warnock carries on the debate in a paper in the Pitcher volume and another in *Knowledge and Experience*, edited by C. D. Rollins.

C. S. Peirce's version of a pragmatic theory of truth must in part be gleaned from a variety of papers, but he discusses truth quite explicitly in *Collected Papers*, Volume V (pages 388 ff). There are criticisms of the pragmatic theory of truth in several chapters of F. H. Bradley's *Essays on Truth and Reality*, but they are directed against James rather than Peirce. G. E. Moore criticized James quite destructively in the third essay reprinted in *Philosophical Studies*.

One of the most important views of truth put forward in recent years is that propounded by A. Tarski. He gives a good short exposition of it in "The Semantic Conception of Truth," *Philosophy and Phenomenological Research*, 1944, reprinted in H. Feigl and W. Sellars, *Readings in Philosophical Analysis*. Tarski's view is criticized by M. Black in *Language and Philosophy*.

W. Sellars discusses "Truth and Correspondence" in *Science, Perception, and Reality*.

IV ❧ MIND, BODY, AND FREEDOM

One of the principal philosophic problems raised by the development of science concerns the relation between the physical and mental worlds. Since the time of Kepler, Galileo, and Newton, it has been fashionable to try to explain all physical phenomena in terms of physical laws, particularly the laws of mechanics. But there is no *a priori* reason to believe that these laws which work so well for, say, astronomical bodies will also do as well for *our* bodies. Everyone acknowledges, of course, that our bodies are subject to laws of gravity, just as every material object is. But it also seems that *we* can direct the motions of our bodies and that we do so by some methods not taken into account by the laws of mechanics.

How to describe correctly the relations between our "selves" and our bodies has been a problem of much controversy. We might ask first what a "self" is? Evidently it is not the same sort of thing as a rock, or a door, or a human being's body; the first group of the following readings consider this question. But even if we have answers here, there are still questions to raise about how selves make their impact on the world of physical objects, including the human bodies they "inhabit." If the mind is not itself a physical object, how can it influence the behavior of physical objects?

Another obvious question arises immediately from the last one. Are we free to choose and to act as we wish? Introspective evidence leads us to believe that, within limits, we are "free agents"; but the close connections between our minds and our brains may suggest that this feeling of freedom is illusory and that our behavior is governed by laws that are just as ineluctable as those that govern the movement of stars. Some philosophers have held not only that as individuals we have no control over our own behavior, but that even the course of history is independent of our wishes. But these views have also received strong criticism, as is indicated in the following readings.

361

The Self

A question to which "Cartesian doubt" gives rise (see Section III) is that of the existence and character of the self. We have ample evidence from psychologists that children *learn* how to differentiate their bodies from the surrounding environment and that this distinction between self and environment, or self and other, is not something we are born with.

According to HUME, our basis for believing in the identity of persons lies in the fact that each of us has a series of impressions, which we gather into a bundle and call a "self." When we wake up in the morning, we think of ourselves as the "same person" who went to bed the night before, but this is only because we can in this way tie our experiences together. On Hume's view, no one has ever confronted his "self" in experience. McTAGGART denies this view on two grounds. First, if the Humean view were correct, we would have no way of distinguishing the "bundles" that belong to (or constitute) you from those belonging to (or constituting) me. If this were all that was involved, why shouldn't you have my toothache or I have your memories? And secondly, McTaggart also claims that we have an immediate and direct awareness of the self. I know by direct acquaintance that when I remember my youth, it is I, *myself*, who am remembering my youth, and not someone else.

The locus of selfhood is placed elsewhere by MEAD. It is not simply a collection of impressions, as Hume would have us believe, nor is it something with which we are immediately acquainted. The self is rather a notion we come to be familiar with through living in a society; "selves" arise from our continuing daily intercourse with others.

Of Personal Identity*

DAVID HUME [1711–1776]. See page 110.

There are some philosophers, who imagine we are every moment intimately conscious of what we call our SELF; that we feel its existence and its continuance in existence; and are certain, beyond the evidence of a demonstration, both of its perfect identity and simplicity. The strongest sensation,

* From Hume: *Treatise of Human Nature*, Book I, 1739.

the most violent passion, say they, instead of distracting us from this view, only fix it the more intensely, and make us consider their influence on *self* either by their pain or pleasure. To attempt a farther proof of this were to weaken its evidence; since no proof can be deriv'd from any fact, of which we are so intimately conscious; nor is there any thing, of which we can be certain, if we doubt of this.

Unluckily all these positive assertions are contrary to that very experience, which is pleaded for them, nor have we any idea of *self*, after the manner it is here explain'd. For from what impression cou'd this idea be deriv'd? This question 'tis impossible to answer without a manifest contradiction and absurdity; and yet 'tis a question, which must necessarily be answer'd, if we wou'd have the idea of self pass for clear and intelligible. It must be some one impression, that gives rise to every real idea. But self or person is not any one impression, but that to which our several impressions and ideas are suppos'd to have a reference. If any impression gives rise to the idea of self, that impression must continue invariably the same, thro' the whole course of our lives; since self is suppos'd to exist after that manner. But there is no impression constant and invariable. Pain and pleasure, grief and joy, passions and sensations succeed each other, and never all exist at the same time. It cannot, therefore, be from any of these impressions, or from any other, that the idea of self is deriv'd; and consequently there is no such idea.

But farther, what must become of all our particular perceptions upon this hypothesis? All these are different, and distinguishable, and separable from each other, and may be separately consider'd, and may exist separately, and have no need of any thing to support their existence. After what manner, therefore, do they belong to self; and how are they connected with it? For my part, when I enter most intimately into what I call *myself,* I always stumble on some particular perception or other, of heat or cold, light or shade, love or hatred, pain or pleasure. I never can catch *myself* at any time without a perception, and never can observe any thing but the perception. When my perceptions are remov'd for any time, as by sound sleep; so long am I insensible of *myself,* and may truly be said not to exist. And were all my perceptions remov'd by death, and cou'd I neither think, nor feel, nor see, nor love, nor hate after the dissolution of my body, I shou'd be entirely annihilated, nor do I conceive what is farther requisite to make me a perfect non-entity. If any one upon serious and unprejudic'd reflexion, thinks he has a different notion of *himself,* I must confess I can reason no longer with him. All I can allow him is, that he may be in the right as well as I, and that we are essentially different in this particular. He may, perhaps, perceive something simple and continu'd, which he calls *himself;* tho' I am certain there is no such principle in me.

But setting aside some metaphysicians of this kind, I may venture to affirm of the rest of mankind, that they are nothing but a bundle or collection of different perceptions, which succeed each other with an inconceivable rapidity, and are in a perpetual flux and movement. Our eyes cannot turn in their sockets without varying our perceptions. Our thought is still more variable than our sight; and all our other senses and faculties contribute to this change; nor is there any single power of the soul, which remains unalterably the same, perhaps for one moment. The mind is a kind of theatre, where several perceptions successively make their appearance; pass, re-pass, glide away, and mingle in an infinite variety of postures and situations. There is properly no *simplicity* in it at one time, nor *identity* in different; whatever natural propension we may have to imagine that simplicity and identity. The comparison of the theatre must not mislead us. They are the successive perceptions only, that constitute the mind; nor have we the most distant notion of the place, where these scenes are represented, or of the materials, of which it is compos'd.

What then gives us so great a propension to ascribe an identity to these successive perceptions, and to suppose ourselves possest of an invariable and uninterrupted existence thro' the whole course of our lives? In order to answer this question, we must distinguish betwixt personal identity, as it regards our thought or imagination, and as it regards our passions or the concern we take in ourselves. The first is our present subject; and to explain it perfectly we must take the matter pretty deep, and account for that identity, which we attribute to plants and animals: there being a great analogy betwixt it, and the identity of a self or person.

We have a distinct idea of an object, that remains invariable and uninterrupted thro' a suppos'd variation of time; and this idea we call that of *identity* or *sameness*. We have also a distinct idea of several different objects existing in succession, and connected together by a close relation; and this to an accurate view affords as perfect a notion of *diversity*, as if there was no manner of relation among the objects. But tho' these two ideas of identity, and a succession of related objects be in themselves perfectly distinct, and even contrary, yet 'tis certain, that in our common way of thinking they are generally confounded with each other. That action of the imagination, by which we consider the uninterrupted and invariable object, and that by which we reflect on the succession of related objects, are almost the same to the feeling, nor is there much more effort of thought requir'd in the latter case than in the former. The relation facilitates the transition of the mind from one object to another, and renders its passage as smooth as if it contemplated one continu'd object. This resemblance is the cause of the confusion and mistake, and makes us substitute the notion of identity, instead of that of related objects. However at one instant we may consider the related succession as variable or interrupted, we are sure the next to ascribe to it a perfect identity, and regard it as invariable and uninterrupted. Our propensity to this mistake is so great from the resemblance above-mention'd, that we fall into it before we are aware; and tho' we incessantly correct ourselves by reflexion, and return to a more accurate method of thinking, yet we cannot long sustain our philosophy, or take off this biass from the imagination. Our last resource is to yield to it, and boldly assert that these different related objects are in effect the same, however interrupted and variable. In order to justify to ourselves this absurdity, we often feign some new and unintelligible principle, that connects the objects together, and prevents their interruption or variation. Thus we feign the continu'd existence of the perceptions of our senses, to remove the interruption; and run into the notion of a *soul,* and *self,* and *substance,* to disguise the variation. But we may farther observe, that where we do not give rise to such a fiction, our propension to confound identity with relation is so great, that we are apt to imagine something unknown and mysterious, connecting the parts, beside their relation; and this I take to be the case with regard to the identity we ascribe to plants and vegetables. And even when this does not take place, we still feel a propensity to confound these ideas, tho' we are not able fully to satisfy ourselves in that particular, nor find any thing invariable and uninterrupted to justify our notion of identity.

Thus the controversy concerning identity is not merely a dispute of words. For when we attribute identity, in an improper sense, to variable or interrupted objects, our mistake is not confin'd to the expression, but is commonly attended with a fiction, either of something invariable and uninterrupted, or of something mysterious and inexplicable, or at least with a propensity to such fictions. . . .

The identity, which we ascribe to the mind of man, is only a fictitious one, and of a like kind with that which we ascribe to vegetables and animal bodies. It cannot, therefore, have a different origin, but must proceed from a like operation of the imagination upon like objects.

But lest this argument shou'd not convince the reader; tho' in my opinion perfectly decisive; let him weigh the following reasoning, which is still closer and more immediate. 'Tis evident, that the identity, which we attribute to the human mind, however perfect we may imagine it to be, is not able to run the several different perceptions into one, and make them lose their characters of distinction and difference, which are essential to them. 'Tis still true, that every distinct perception, which enters into the composition of the mind, is a distinct existence, and is different, and distinguishable, and separable from every other perception, either contemporary or successive.

But, as, notwithstanding this distinction and separability, we suppose the whole train of perceptions to be united by identity, a question naturally arises concerning this relation of identity; whether it be something that really binds our several perceptions together, or only associates their ideas in the imagination. That is, in other words, whether in pronouncing concerning the identity of a person, we observe some real bond among his perceptions, or only feel one among the ideas we form of them. This question we might easily decide, if we wou'd recollect what has been already prov'd at large, that the understanding never observes any real connexion among objects, and that even the union of cause and effect, when strictly examin'd, resolves itself into a customary association of ideas. For from thence it evidently follows, that identity is nothing really belonging to these different perceptions, and uniting them together; but is merely a quality, which we attribute to them, because of the union of their ideas in the imagination, when we reflect upon them. Now the only qualities, which can give ideas an union in the imagination, are these three relations above-mention'd. These are the uniting principles in the ideal world, and without them every distinct object is separable by the mind, and may be separately consider'd, and appears not to have any more connexion with any other object, than if disjoin'd by the greatest difference and remoteness. 'Tis, therefore, on some of these three relations of resemblance, contiguity and causation, that identity depends; and as the very essence of these relations consists in their producing an easy transition of ideas; it follows, that our notions of personal identity, proceed entirely from the smooth and uninterrupted progress of the thought along a train of connected ideas, according to the principles above-explain'd.

The only question, therefore, which remains, is, by what relations this uninterrupted progress of our thought is produc'd, when we consider the successive existence of a mind or thinking person. And here 'tis evident we must confine ourselves to resemblance and causation, and must drop contiguity, which has little or no influence in the present case.

To begin with *resemblance;* suppose we cou'd see clearly into the breast of another, and observe that succession of perceptions, which constitutes his mind or thinking principle, and suppose that he always preserves the memory of a considerable part of past perceptions; 'tis evident that nothing cou'd more contribute to the bestowing a relation on this succession amidst all its variations. For what is the memory but a faculty, by which we raise up the images of past perceptions? And as an image necessarily resembles its object, must not the frequent placing of these resembling perceptions in the chain of thought, convey the imagination more easily from one link to another, and make the whole seem like the continuance of one object? In this particular, then, the memory not only discovers the identity, but also contributes to its production, by producing the relation of resemblance among the perceptions. The case is the same whether we consider ourselves or others.

As to *causation;* we may observe, that the true idea of the human mind, is to consider it as a system of different perceptions or different existences, which are link'd together by the relation of cause and effect, and mutually produce, destroy, influence, and modify each other. Our impressions give rise to their correspondent ideas; and these ideas in their turn produce other impressions. One thought chaces another, and draws after it a third, by which it is expell'd in its turn. In this respect, I cannot compare the soul more properly to any thing than to a republic or commonwealth, in which the several members are united by the reciprocal ties of government and subordination, and give rise to other persons, who propagate the same republic in the incessant changes of its parts. And as the same individual republic may not only change its members, but also its laws and constitutions; in like manner the same person may vary his character and disposition, as well as his impressions and ideas, without losing his identity. Whatever changes he endures, his several parts are still connected by the relation of causation. And in this view our identity with regard to the passions serves to corroborate that with regard to the imagination, by the making our distant perceptions influence each other, and by giving us a present concern for our past or future pains or pleasures.

As memory alone acquaints us with the continuance and extent of this succession of perceptions, 'tis to be consider'd, upon that account chiefly, as the source of personal identity. Had we no memory, we never shou'd have any notion of causation, nor consequently of that chain of causes and effects, which constitute our self or person. But having once acquir'd this notion of causation from the memory, we can extend the same chain of causes, and consequently the identity of our persons beyond our memory, and can comprehend times, and circumstances, and actions, which we have entirely forgot, but suppose in general to have existed. For how few of our past actions are there, of which we have any memory? Who can tell me, for instance, what were his thoughts and actions on the first of *January* 1715, the 11th of *March* 1719, and the 3d of *August* 1733? Or will he affirm, because he has entirely forgot the incidents of these days, that the present self is not the same person with the self of that time; and by that means overturn all the most establish'd notions of personal identity? In this view, therefore, memory does not so much *produce* as *discover* personal identity, by shewing us the relation of cause and effect among our different perceptions. 'Twill be incumbent on those, who affirm that memory produces entirely our personal identity, to give a reason why we can thus extend our identity beyond our memory.

The whole of this doctrine leads us to a conclusion, which is of great importance in the present affair, *viz.* that all the nice and subtile questions concerning personal identity can never possibly be decided, and are to be regarded rather as grammatical than as philosophical difficulties. Identity depends on the relations of ideas; and these relations produce identity, by means of that easy transition they occasion. But as the relations, and the easiness of the transition may diminish by insensible degrees, we have no just standard, by which we can decide any dispute concerning the time, when they acquire or lose a title to the name of identity. All the disputes concerning the identity of connected objects are merely verbal, except so far as the relation of parts gives rise to some fiction or imaginary principle of union, as we have already observ'd.

The Self as Substance*

JOHN MCTAGGART ELLIS MCTAGGART [1866–1925], after completing his undergraduate studies at the University of Cambridge, taught there until his death. His principal work was an elaborate metaphysical system, a version of Hegelian idealism, which was published under the title *The Nature of Existence* (Volume I, 1921; Volume II, 1927). He also wrote three commentaries on Hegel and a short book, *Some Dogmas of Religion* (1906), on the philosophy of religion.

. . . What then do we mean by a self? I should say that the quality of being a self is a simple quality which is known to me because I perceive—in the strict sense of the word—one substance as possessing this quality. This substance is myself. And I believe that every self-conscious being—that is, every self who knows that he is a self—directly perceives himself in this manner. . . .

The reasons which have led me to accept the view that the self is known to itself by direct perception were suggested to me by a passage of Mr Russell's article "Knowledge by Acquaintance and Knowledge by Description." Mr Russell did not work out his position in detail—which was not essential for the main design of his paper. And he has now ceased to hold the position at all. I remain, however, convinced of the truth of the view, the first suggestion of which I owe to him.

* From *McTaggart: The Nature of Existence*, Volume II, 1927, Chapter 36. Reprinted by permission of the publisher, Cambridge University Press.

The argument is as follows. I can judge that I am aware of certain things —for example, of the relation of equality. I assert, then, the proposition "I am aware of equality." This proposition, whether true or false, has certainly a meaning. And, since I know what the proposition means, I must know each constituent of it. I must therefore know "I." Whatever is known must be known by acquaintance or by description. If, therefore, "I" cannot be known by description, it must be known by acquaintance, and I must be aware of it.

Now how could "I" be described in this case? The description must be an exclusive description . . . since I do not know "I" by description unless I know enough about it to distinguish it from everything else. Can I describe "I" as that which is aware of equality? But it is obvious that this is not an exclusive description of "I." It could not be an exclusive description of "I" unless I was the only person who was ever aware of equality. And it is obvious that this is not certain, and that it is possible that some one besides me was, is, or will be aware of equality. (In point of fact, I have, of course, overwhelming empirical evidence for the conclusion that some other persons *are* aware of equality.) Thus we cannot get an exclusive description of "I" in this way. . . .

An attempt has been made to describe "I" in another manner. It is no longer described as that which is aware of something, or which has a mental state. It is described as a whole of which certain mental states are parts. The classical statement of this view is Hume's. "I may venture to affirm of . . . mankind, that they are nothing but a bundle or collection of different perceptions which succeed each other with an inconceivable rapidity and are in a perpetual flux or movement."

This gives, of course, a very different view of the self from that which is generally held. In the first place, the knowledge of the self is logically subsequent to the knowledge of the mental states. We can know the states without knowing the self, but we can only know the self by means of our knowledge of the states. In the second place, it would seem that the theory holds that this relation of knowledge corresponds to a relation in the things themselves. The ultimate realities are the mental states, and the selves are only secondary, since they are nothing but aggregates of the states. In the third place we must no longer say that the self perceives, thinks, or loves, or that it has a perception of thought or an emotion. We can only say that the bundle includes a perception, a thought, or an emotion, as one of its parts.

On this theory, then, when I use the word "I," I know what "I" means by description, and it is described as meaning that bundle of mental states of which my use of the word is one member. Is this satisfactory?

In the first place we must note that it is by no means every group of mental states which is a bundle in Hume's sense of the word, that is to say, an aggregate of mental states which form a self. For any two mental states form a group by themselves. And there are an infinite number of groups, of each of which both G and H are members. All these groups are not bundles. The emotions of James II on the acquittal of the seven Bishops, and the volitions of William III at the Boyne, are to be found together in an infinite number of groups. But no one supposes—neither Hume nor anyone else—that they belong to the same self. They are therefore not in the same bundle.

But, since every group is not a bundle, we say nothing definite when we say that two mental states are in the same bundle, unless we are able to distinguish bundles from other groups. How is this to be done? Can we distinguish them by saying that the members of bundles have relations to one another which the members of groups which are not bundles do not have? But what would such relations be?

They could not be spatial relations, nor relations of apparent spatiality. For in many cases—as with emotions and abstract thoughts—the states have no special relation to anything which is or appears as spatial. And in cases in which they do have those relations, I can judge, for example, that I have seen Benares and Piccadilly and that Jones has seen Regent Street. Or again I can judge that I have seen Piccadilly and Regent Street, and that Smith has seen Benares. Thus perceptions of sensa which appear as related to objects close together may be in the same bundle or in different bundles, and the same is true of sensa which appear as related to objects distant from one another.

Neither can they be temporal relations, or relations of apparent temporality. For some cases we say that experiences separated by years belong to the same bundle, and in some cases to different bundles. And in some cases we say that simultaneous experiences belong to the same bundle, and in some cases to different bundles.

They cannot be relations of similarity or dissimilarity. For in every bundle there are states which are similar and dissimilar to other states in that bundle, and which are similar and dissimilar to states in other bundles. Nor can it be causation. For my happiness to-day may have no causal connection with my misery yesterday, whereas, if I am malignant, it may be caused by the misery of Jones to-day.

Again the relation cannot be the relation of knowledge. For I can know both my own misery and that of Jones. Nor can it be the relation of apparent perception. For, of my state of misery yesterday and my state of happiness to-day, neither apparently perceives the other. Nor can they be apparently perceived by the same state, for one has ceased some time before the other began.

The relation we are looking for, then, cannot be any of these. Nor do I see any other *direct* relation between the states which could determine the bundle to which they belong. There seems only one alternative left. The relation must be an indirect relation, and it must be through the self. We must say that those states, and those only, which are states of the same self, form the bundle of parts of that self.

There is no difficulty about this, if, as I have maintained, a self is aware of himself by perception. But it is fatal to the attempt to know "I" by description. It would obviously be a vicious circle if I described "I" as being that bundle of states of which my use of the word is a member, and then distinguished that bundle from other groups by describing it as that group of mental states which are states of "I."

One more attempt to know "I" by description must be considered. It might be admitted that, if we adhered to a purely presentationist position like Hume's, the bundles could not be described except by their relations to selves. But, it might be said, if we admit the existence of matter (or of some substance which appears as matter), they could be described in another way. For then, it might be considered, we could say that states belong to the same self when, and only when, the same living body (or what appears as such) stands in a certain relation of causality to both of them. In that sense the meaning of "I am angry" would be that the same living body stood in that relation of causality both to the state of anger and to the judgment about it.

I have said "a certain relation of causality" because it is clear that not all relations of causality would do. The movements of an actor's body may cause aesthetic emotions in each of a thousand spectators, but these emotions admittedly belong to different selves. It might perhaps suffice if we say that the relation between the living body and the mental state must not be mediated by the intervention of any other living body.

The view that *every* mental state has a cerebral state which stands in such a relation to it, is by no means established, and is rejected by many eminent psychologists. But, even if it were accepted, the theory which we are here considering would break down.

It is to be noticed that all that makes states part of the same self is the indirect relation through the body. It is not any direct relation between the states, which is *caused* by the indirect relation, but which would perhaps be perceived even if the indirect relation was not known. It could not be this, for we have seen that no direct relation can be found such that each state in a self has it to all other states in the self and to no other states.

But if there is no relation but the indirect relation, then no man has any reason to say that any two states belong to the same self unless he has a reason to believe them to be caused by the same body. And this means that the vast majority of such statements as "I was envious yesterday" are absolutely untrustworthy. In the first place, by far the greater number of them have been made by people who have never heard of the doctrine that emotions and judgments are caused by bodily states. They could not, therefore, have any reason to believe that the envy and the judgment were caused by the same body. And therefore they could have no reason to believe that they belong to the same self. But, as we have seen, in asserting "I was envious yesterday" I am asserting that the envy and the judgment belong to the same self.

In the second place, even those people who have heard of the doctrine that all mental states are caused by bodily states and who accept it, do not, in far the greater number of cases, base their judgments that two states belong to the same self on a previous conviction that they are caused by the same body. And, indeed, in the case of an emotion and a judgment it is impossible that they should do so. For it would be impossible for any man to observe his brain, and to observe it in two states which he could identify as the causes of the emotion and the judgment respectively. And his only ground for believing that they were caused by the same living body would depend on his recognizing them as belonging to the same self. It is impossible therefore that he can legitimately base his belief that they belong to the same self on the ground that they were caused by the same body.

Thus this theory would involve that every judgment of the type "I am x," or "I was x," or "I did x," where x is anything that a substance can be or do, is totally untrustworthy. Such scepticism, even if not absolutely self-contradictory, which I think it is, is so extreme that it may be regarded as a *reductio ad absurdum*.

But we may go further. "I was envious yesterday" has no meaning for anyone who does not know the meaning of "I." Now if "I" can only be known by description, and the only description which is true of it is "that group of mental states, caused by the same living body, of which the envy and my judgment are members," it follows that anyone who does not describe "I" in that way, will not know what "I" means, and so will mean nothing when he says "I was envious yesterday." But the assertion that the meaning of "I was envious yesterday" depends on the acceptance, by the man who makes it, of the doctrine of the cerebral causation of all mental states, is clearly preposterous.

We may now, I think, conclude that the meaning of "I" cannot be known by description, and that, since the meaning of "I" is certainly known—or all propositions containing it would be meaningless—it must be known by acquaintance. Each self, then, who knows the meaning of "I" (it is quite possible that many selves have not reached this knowledge), must do it by perceiving himself.

The Self as Social *

GEORGE HERBERT MEAD [1863–1931] studied at Oberlin and Harvard; in 1893 he went to the University of Chicago, where he taught for the rest of his life. He was very much influenced by the American pragmatic movement, especially by his colleague John Dewey. He was primarily interested in social philosophy, and the development of the field of sociology in the United States owes much to him. His principal works are *Mind, Self and Society* (1934) and *Philosophy of the Act* (1938).

THE SELF AND THE ORGANISM. In our statement of the development of intelligence we have already suggested that the language process is essential for the development of the self. The self has a character which is different from that of the physiological organism proper. The self is something which has a development; it is not initially there, at birth, but arises in the process of social experience and activity, that is, develops in the given individual as a result of his relations to that process as a whole and to other individuals within that process. The intelligence of the lower forms of animal life, like a great deal of human intelligence, does not involve a self. In our habitual actions, for example, in our moving about in a world that is simply there and to which we are so adjusted that no thinking is involved, there is a certain amount of sensuous experience such as persons have when they are just waking up, a bare thereness of the world. Such characters about us may exist in experience without taking their place in relationship to the self. One must, of course, under those conditions, distinguish between the experience that immediately takes place and our own organization of it into the experience of the self. One says upon analysis that a certain item had its place in his experience, in the experience of his self. We do inevitably tend at a certain level of sophistication to organize all experience into that of a self. We do so intimately identify our experiences, especially our affective experiences, with

* Reprinted from *Mind, Self and Society* by George H. Mead, by permission of The University of Chicago Press. Copyright 1934 by the University of Chicago. All rights reserved. Published 1934.

the self that it takes a moment's abstraction to realize that pain and pleasure can be there without being the experience of the self. Similarly, we normally organize our memories upon the string of our self. If we date things we always date them from the point of view of our past experiences. We frequently have memories that we cannot date, that we cannot place. A picture comes before us suddenly and we are at a loss to explain when that experience originally took place. We remember perfectly distinctly the picture, but we do not have it definitely placed, and until we can place it in terms of our past experience we are not satisfied. Nevertheless, I think it is obvious when one comes to consider it that the self is not necessarily involved in the life of the organism, nor involved in what we term our sensuous experience, that is, experience in a world about us for which we have habitual reactions.

We can distinguish very definitely between the self and the body. The body can be there and can operate in a very intelligent fashion without there being a self involved in the experience. The self has the characteristic that it is an object to itself, and that characteristic distinguishes it from other objects and from the body. It is perfectly true that the eye can see the foot, but it does not see the body as a whole. We cannot see our backs; we can feel certain portions of them, if we are agile, but we cannot get an experience of our whole body. There are, of course, experiences which are somewhat vague and difficult of location, but the bodily experiences are for us organized about a self. The foot and hand belong to the self. We can see our feet, especially if we look at them from the wrong end of an opera glass, as strange things which we have difficulty in recognizing as our own. The parts of the body are quite distinguishable from the self. We can lose parts of the body without any serious invasion of the self. The mere ability to experience different parts of the body is not different from the experience of a table. The table presents a different feel from what the hand does when one hand feels another, but it is an experience of something with which we come definitely into contact. The body does not experience itself as a whole, in the sense in which the self in some way enters into the experience of the self.

It is the characteristic of the self as an object to itself that I want to bring out. This characteristic is represented in the word "self," which is a reflexive, and indicates that which can be both subject and object. This type of object is essentially different from other objects, and in the past it has been distinguished as conscious, a term which indicates an experience with, an experience of, one's self. It was assumed that consciousness in some way carried this capacity of being an object to itself. In giving a behavioristic statement of consciousness we have to look for some sort of experience in which the physical organism can become an object to itself.

When one is running to get away from someone who is chasing him, he is entirely occupied in this action, and his experience may be swallowed up in the objects about him, so that he has, at the time being, no consciousness of self at all. We must be, of course, very completely occupied to have that take place, but we can, I think, recognize that sort of a possible experience in which the self does not enter. We can, perhaps, get some light on that situation through those experiences in which in very intense action there appear in the experience of the individual, back of this intense action, memories and anticipations. Tolstoi as an officer in the war gives an account of having pictures of his past experience in the midst of his most intense action. There are also the pictures that flash into a person's mind when he is drowning. In such instances there is a contrast between an experience that is absolutely wound up in outside activity in which the self as an object does not enter, and an activity of memory and imagination in which the self is the principal object. The self is then entirely distinguishable from an organism that is surrounded by things and acts with reference to things, including parts of its own body. These latter may be objects like other objects, but they are just objects out there in the field, and they do not involve a self that is an object to the organism. This is, I think, frequently overlooked. It is that fact which makes our anthropomorphic reconstructions of animal life so fallacious. How can an individual get outside himself (experientially) in such a way as to become an object to himself? This is the essential psychological problem of selfhood or of self-consciousness; and its solution is to be found by referring to the process of social conduct or activity in which the given person or individual is implicated. The apparatus of reason would not be complete unless it swept itself into its own analysis of the field of experience; or unless the individual brought himself into the same experiential field as that of the other individual selves in relation to whom he acts in any given social situation. Reason cannot become impersonal unless it takes an objective, non-affective attitude toward itself; otherwise we have just consciousness, not self-consciousness. And it is necessary to rational conduct that the individual should thus take an objective, impersonal attitude toward himself, that he should become an object to himself. For the individual organism is obviously an essential and important fact or constituent element of the empirical situation in which it acts; and without taking objective account of itself as such, it cannot act intelligently, or rationally. . . .

A CONTRAST OF INDIVIDUALISTIC AND SOCIAL THEORIES OF THE SELF. The differences between the type of social psychology which derives the selves of individuals from the social process in which they are implicated and in which they empirically interact with one another, and the type of social psychology which instead derives that process from the selves of the individuals involved in it, are clear. The first type assumes a social process or social order as the logical and biological precondition of the appearance of the selves of the individual organisms involved in that process or belonging to that order. The other type, on the contrary, assumes individual selves as the presuppositions, logically and biologically, of the social process or order within which they interact.

The difference between the social and the individual theories of the development of mind, self, and the social process of experience or behavior is analogous to the difference between the evolutionary and the contract theories of the state as held in the past by both rationalists and empiricists. The latter theory takes individuals and their individual experiencing—individual minds and selves—as logically prior to the social process in which they are involved, and explains the existence of that social process in terms of them; whereas the former takes the social process of experience or behavior as logically prior to the individuals and their individual experiencing which are involved in it, and explains their existence in terms of that social process. But the latter type of theory cannot explain that which is taken as logically prior at all, cannot explain the existence of minds and selves; whereas the former type of theory can explain that which it takes as logically prior, namely, the existence of the social process of behavior, in terms of such fundamental biological or physiological relations and interactions as reproduction, or the co-operation of individuals for mutual protection or for the securing of food.

Our contention is that mind can never find expression, and could never have come into existence at all, except in terms of a social environment; that an organized set or pattern of social relations and interactions (especially those of communication by means of gestures functioning as significant symbols and thus creating a universe of discourse) is necessarily presupposed by it and involved in its nature. And this entirely social theory or interpretation of mind—this contention that mind develops and has its being only in and by virtue of the social process of experience and activity, which it hence presupposes, and that in no other way can it develop and have its being—must be clearly distinguished from the partially (but only partially) social view of mind. On this view, though mind can get expression only within or in terms of the environment of an organized social group, yet it is nevertheless in some sense a native endowment—a congenital or hereditary biological attribute—of the individual organism, and could not otherwise exist or manifest itself in the social process at all; so that it is not itself essentially a social phenomenon, but rather is biological both in its nature and in its origin, and is social only in its characteristic manifestations or expressions. According to this latter view, moreover, the social process presupposes, and in a sense is a product of, mind; in direct contrast is our opposite view that mind presupposes, and is a product of, the social process. The advantage of our view is that it enables us to give a detailed account and actually to explain the genesis and development of mind; whereas the view that mind is a congenital biological endowment of the individual organism does not really enable us to explain its nature and origin at all: neither what sort of biological endowment it is, nor how organisms at a certain level of evolutionary progress come to possess it. Furthermore, the supposition that the social process presupposes, and is in some sense a product of, mind seems to be contradicted by the existence of the social communities of certain of the lower animals, especially the highly complex social organizations of bees and ants, which apparently operate on a purely instinctive or reflex basis, and do not in the least involve the existence of mind or consciousness in the individual organisms which form or constitute them. And even if this contradiction is avoided by the admission that only at its higher levels—only at the levels represented by the social relations and interactions of human beings—does the social process of experience and behavior presuppose the existence of mind or become necessarily a product of mind, still it is hardly plausible to suppose that this already ongoing and developing process should suddenly, at a particular stage in its evolution, become dependent for its further continuance upon an entirely extraneous factor, introduced into it, so to speak, from without.

The individual enters as such into his own experience only as an object, not as a subject; and he can enter as an object only on the basis of social relations and interactions, only by means of his experiential transactions with other individuals in an organized social environment. It is true that certain contents of experience (particularly kinaesthetic) are accessible only to the given individual organism and not to any others; and that these private or "subjective," as opposed to public or "objective," contents of experience are usually regarded as being peculiarly and intimately connected with the individual's self, or as being in a special sense self-experiences. But this accessibility solely to the given individual organism of certain contents of its experience does not affect, nor in any way conflict with, the theory as to the social nature and origin of the self that we are presenting; the existence of private or "subjective" contents of experience does not alter the fact that self-consciousness involves the individual's becoming an object to himself by taking the attitudes of other individuals toward himself within an organized setting of social relationships, and that unless the individual had thus become an object to himself he would not be self-conscious or have a self at all. Apart from his social interactions with other individuals, he would not relate the private or "subjective" contents of his experience to himself, and he could not become aware of himself as such, that is, as an individual, a person, merely by means or in terms of these contents of his experience; for in order to become aware of himself as such he must, to repeat, become an object to himself, or enter his own experience as an object, and only by social means—only by taking the attitudes of others toward himself—is he able to become an object to himself.

It is true, of course, that once mind has arisen in the social process it makes possible the development of that process into much more complex forms of social interaction among the component individuals than was possible before it had arisen. But there is nothing odd about a product of a given process contributing to, or becoming an essential factor in, the further development of that process. The social process, then, does not depend for its origin or initial existence upon the existence and interactions of selves; though it does depend upon the latter for the higher stages of complexity and organization which it reaches after selves have arisen within it.

SUGGESTED READINGS

Plato's dialogue *Phaedo* contains several arguments for immortality which depend on the sort of position about the nature of the soul which Hume attacks. It may be of interest to see how one of Hume's most important empiricist predecessors works out a theory of the self which is not as radical as Hume's: see John Locke, *Essay Concerning Human Understanding*, Book II, Chapter 27. J. S. Mill tried to work out a nonskeptical Humean position concerning the self, as he tried to work out such a view concerning external objects. He presents his view in Chapter 12 of his *Examination of Sir William Hamilton's Philosophy* but confesses that he thinks it is inadequate. Hume also felt his own view inadequate: see the Appendix to the *Treatise of Human Nature*.

McTaggart's positive views are complicated and difficult; some idea of them may be obtained from the essay "Personality" in his *Philosophical Studies*. He also discusses F. H. Bradley's very different position, which the latter presents in *Appearance and Reality*, Chapter 9, and in "What is the Real Julius Caesar?", *Essays on Truth and Reality*, Chapter 14.

William James' *Principles of Psychology*, Volume I, Chapter 10, is a very readable and interesting study of "The Consciousness of the Self." Recent writers on the self have been influenced by Chapter 6 of G. Ryle, *The Concept of Mind*, and by P. Strawson's essay "Persons," which originally appeared in Volume II of *Minnesota Studies in the Philosophy of Science*, edited by H. Feigl *et al.*, and has been reprinted in D. Gustafson, *Essays in Philosophical Psychology*.

There is a careful, thorough, and useful discussion of problems concerning the unity of mind in C. D. Broad's *Mind and Its Place in Nature*, Chapter 13.

The Mind-Body Problem

Although such characteristics as birth, growth, reproduction, and death are shared by all living things, there are traits that are specifically human. These specifically human traits have always been felt to be the most important characteristics of men.

There have been many attempts to describe those essential features that distinguish men from the rest of nature. "Man" has been defined, for instance, in terms of rationality, in terms of the ability to use symbols, and in terms of culture. All these conceptions of human nature point to specifically human traits: abstract thinking, the power of communication, the ability to pass on to succeeding generations the accumulated results of individual and social experience. All these definitions are of ancient origin. Aristotle, for example, described man not merely as a biological organism, but as a rational and political (i.e., social) animal.

Many philosophers have been led to believe that these unique features of human beings can be explained only on the assumption that man has a dual nature—a *material* body endowed with an *immaterial* mind or soul. This is the view of *dualism*. According to dualism, there is an irreducible difference between body and mind; it is not possible to explain what happens in the mind solely in terms of what occurs in the body.

This view is examined and defended by PRATT, who, after considering some difficulties in the dualist position and various alternatives to it, concludes that dualism is the only tenable hypothesis.

Whether or not we accept dualism, we are still left with the question: What kind of system is the self? According to BLANSHARD, the self differs radically from any mechanical system. It is a teleological (i.e., purposive) system that cannot be explained adequately by laws describing the relations among its parts.

RYLE, on the other hand, claims that the whole problem is mistakenly conceived; it is, as he calls it, a "category-mistake" to say that human beings come in two parts, one of which is physical (the body), the other mental (the mind). By our ways of talking about behavior, we have simply been misled into thinking that there is inside us a nonphysical entity that directs the motion of our bodies, much as a truck-driver drives a truck. But Ryle argues that this view of the matter is simply a philosopher's fairy-tale.

Ryle and Blanshard both reject dualism, but for different reasons. Another nondualist view is put forward by SMART, who holds that the mind-body problem can be solved simply by identifying mental events with physical ones, i.e., with brain processes. His primary purpose is to show that supposedly valid arguments against this position are not as convincing as they may seem.

Matter and Spirit[*]

JAMES BISSETT PRATT [1875–1944] taught philosophy at Williams College from 1905 until his death. He wrote extensively on the mind-body problem, on the philosophy of religion, and on Oriental religions.

The crucial significance of the mind-body relation is no new discovery. Not only the ancient Greek philosophers, but thousands of years before them primitive men the world over made it the starting point of their thought and based upon their particular solution of this question nearly the whole of their philosophy of life and nature. But while they understood very well the decisive position of this problem they had little inkling of its real difficulty, nor did they even imagine the varied ways in which the mind-body relation is capable of being expressed. As a fact, since the days of the Greek philosophers some eight or nine different solutions have been offered, and as much of the best philosophic thought has busied itself with this problem for many centuries it seems unlikely that anything very radically new will be suggested in the future. In fact it can be shown in something like mathematical fashion that we have in our hands already all the possible solutions. For either body and mind are causally related or they are not. If for the present we leave on one side the denial of such relationship, the number of possible ways in which they may be related is obviously limited. I hasten to add that I mean the word *"causally"* as used above to be taken in sufficiently large fashion to include every kind of implication or influence; and that for our present purposes the word *body*, or *matter*, may be interpreted in either realistic or idealistic fashion. Whatever interpretation we put upon matter, idealists and realists alike will acknowledge that the words matter and mind have distinguishable meanings. With so much agreed upon, we can easily work out the chief ways in which the two may conceivably be related. If for the moment we omit detailed variations within the principal groups, there are four and only four of such possible relations. Firstly, mind and body may mutually influence each other [Interaction]. Secondly, body may alone be causally effective and mind merely a result [Materialism]. Thirdly, mind and body may flow on parallel with each other, each causally efficient within its own banks, so to speak, but neither ever affecting the other [Parallelism]. Fourthly, mind alone may be efficient, and body merely a resultant or ap-

* From Pratt: *Matter and Spirit*, Chapter 1, 2, and 4. Published, 1922, by The Macmillan Company. Reprinted by permission of Mrs. James Bissett Pratt.

pearance of mind [Idealistic Parallelism]. Variations of detail may be suggested and have been suggested within most of these principal types of relationship; but plainly no other relationship of a general nature is thinkable. . . .

If, then, mind and body are causally related their relation must be one of the four kinds here suggested. And if, either by positive arguments in favor of one of these views, or negatively through the elimination of three of them, we can determine which of the four is true, we shall find not only that this particular problem is solved, but that we have a new and piercing light into many a hitherto obscure corner of our universe—a light which may dissipate not only some of our theoretical doubts but even some of our practical uncertainties.

APPARENT DIFFICULTIES OF INTERACTION. The first of the four general views that I mentioned above, commonly referred to as the theory of Interaction, is naturally the first to present itself to the naïve mind. It appears indeed to rest upon actually observed facts—in sensation we seem to find a physical process operating upon our consciousness, and in volition we feel ourselves, as psychical beings, operating upon the physical world. It is not strange, therefore, that Interaction should be the first theory of mind and body to be explicitly developed, both by the individual and by the race. Primitive man founded his animistic philosophy upon it; and both Socrates and Plato were convinced interactionists. They made a sharp distinction between body and soul, a distinction which they regarded as of the utmost importance; and it could easily be shown that most of their moral and religious teachings and much of their cosmic speculation would go to pieces if based on any other foundation than the interaction theory. It was an essential part of the larger Platonic dualism, and it formed the basis of Plato's firm conviction of the soul's immortality. The rise of Christianity brought additional strength to the doctrine, for the Christian Fathers regarded body and soul as distinct entities and in their mutual influence upon each other they found much of the cosmic struggle centering. It was not strange that with Christianity and Platonism uniting their forces in its support the doctrine of Interaction should have held the field almost without a rival for well over 1,500 years.

With the rise of modern natural science, however, new considerations and new motives appeared upon the scene which were destined to put Interaction upon the defensive and give its rivals an enormous advantage. A new conception of physical nature came over men's minds. Mathematical and mechanical laws were found to dominate regions of the universe where their presence had hardly been suspected. Everywhere quality came to be reduced to quantity, the indefinite to the measurable. Once the mechanistic explanation was thoroughly applied to the inorganic world the attempt to extend it to the realms of life and mind became inevitable. And this for two reasons. The world of living matter being made of the same elements as the inorganic world, and forming as it does so minute a portion of the whole of Nature, it seemed most improbable that the laws which hold everywhere else should be subject to exception in this little corner. And secondly it was seen that the extension of mechanical law to this last region would make the entire physical universe an open book to science, all of it at length being susceptible to the same sort of description, explanation, and prediction. The door to this last conquest of mechanistic science was, oddly enough, opened by the greatest interactionist of his century, René Descartes. For, though he maintained that body and mind were absolutely distinct in man, he taught that animals were merely automata, and that all their actions must be accounted for on mechanical principles only. It was but a step from this to the suggestion that in man also consciousness, though of course present, never interfered with the activities of the body and that all these might be explained by physical laws alone. Two further advances of Science, made in the 19th Century, added enormously to the strength of this naturalistic attack upon Interaction. These were the formulation of the law of the conservation of energy and the Darwinian doctrine of evolution. For if no energy can ever be created or destroyed, plainly mind cannot interfere with bodily processes; and since man is descended from the lower animals there is no reason why his actions should not be explicable by the same general law as theirs.

Thus it has come about that when the natural scientist approaches the mind-body problem he almost invariably rules out Interaction first of all, as being quite out of the question. This procedure he justifies by two general reasons. The first is the incompatibility, already referred to, of Interaction with the mechanical view of physical nature, and in particular with the law of the conservation of energy. The second reason is of a more philosophical sort—the difficulty, namely, that has been pointed out ever since the days of Descartes in seeing how two such diverse things as matter and mind could possibly affect each other. How indeed can one imagine an *idea* producing a *motion* in the matter of the brain? As easily, says Clifford, might we picture the two halves of a heavy train kept together by the feelings of amity between the stoker and the guard.

MATERIALISM. The naturalistic movement, having discredited Interaction, was bound to offer some theory of mind and body in its place. As a fact it offered two, each of which in turn possessed two or more variations. I refer to Materialism and Parallelism. . . . [Materialism] has two subtypes although its adherents have not always recognized the fact nor distinguished them clearly enough in their own minds for us to be invariably certain which of the two types, in any given case, they are upholding. The first of these materialistic views maintains that consciousness *is a form of brain activity;* —that it is either some fine and subtle kind of matter, or (more commonly) some form of energy, either kinetic or potential. This type of Materialism had a considerable vogue in Büchner's day, but fortunately for your patience we need not dwell upon it, for it has been pretty generally discredited. To say that consciousness *is* a form of matter or of motion is to use words without meaning. The identification of consciousness and motion indeed can never be refuted; but only because he who does not see the absurdity of such a statement can never be made to see anything. Argument against any given position must regularly take the general form of the *reductio ad absurdum.* He therefore, who chooses at the beginning a position which is as absurd as any that can be imagined is in the happy situation of being armor proof against all argument. He can never be "reduced to the absurd" because he is already there. If he cannot see that, though consciousness and motion may be *related* as intimately as you please, we *mean* different things by the two words, that though consciousness may be *caused* by motion, it *is* not itself what we mean by motion any more than it is green cheese—if he cannot see this there is no arguing with him. But while we certainly cannot convince him we may properly ignore him in all discussions of the subject; for he has put himself in a position where all discussion is impossible.

We turn, therefore, to the much more defensible form of Materialism which declares that while consciousness is not to be identified with anything physical it is caused by physical processes that occur in the brain, and that it, on its side, never influences either the brain processes nor any subsequent portions of its own stream. In the words of Professor Warren: "Intelligence is a function not of conscious 'intuition' but of the connection between afferent and efferent nerve tracts. It denotes an adjustment between the environmental situation and the responsive activity, and this adjustment is brought about either by inherited neural paths or by individually acquired connections. The motor impulse in every case presumably follows the path of least resistance. There is no need to assume a non-physical 'guiding' agent in order to explain why the nervous current comes to follow certain paths rather than others." "The mechanics of intelligent activity follows the same pattern as other movements and transformations of energy. . . . The laws of physics and chemistry hold for intelligent organisms as well as for atoms and electrons." Consciousness, in other words, is always a result, never a cause; every portion of every psychic state is fully determined by the accompanying or preceding brain state. It is the universal mechanical laws of the physical world that produce and regulate and fix our thoughts; our preceding thoughts and the laws of logic having no real efficacy in the matter whatever. Consciousness, in short, is but "a lyric cry in the midst of business." In support of this proposition the materialist points first of all to the scientific presuppositions that we have already discussed—the universality of mechanical law, the conservation of energy, the evolution of man and of man's consciousness. More specifically he dwells upon the following considerations. Comparative anatomy shows a fairly close correlation between brain capacity and mental ability. Recent studies in brain anatomy have enabled us to locate in various definite portions of the cortex the centers of sensation and the centers that control muscular action. The destruction of any of these centers results in the destruction or derangement of the corresponding functions of consciousness. It would seem, therefore, to follow, he argues, that consciousness is dependent upon brain.

The facts and principles to which the materialist appeals, however, are not conclusive. Both the parallelist and even the discouraged interactionist have their answers. United for once against a common foe, they point out that the facts of brain anatomy and physiology upon which the materialist relies are perfectly compatible with both Parallelism and Interaction. The interactionist has never denied—on the contrary, he has affirmed—that certain processes in the brain produce changes in consciousness; and the parallelist always insists that for every mental process there is a correlated brain process. In fact the parallelist goes farther than this and asserts that not only are the facts in question consistent with all three theories, but that the general principles of Naturalism, to which the materialist first of all appealed, are really inconsistent with Materialism. For if some of the physical energy in the brain is used in producing something (viz. consciousness) which is not physical, the doctrine of the conservation of energy is abrogated; you will have physical energy being destroyed—destroyed, that is, from the point of view of the physical world which alone in this question needs to be considered.

There are, moreover, certain further considerations which seem to make the materialistic position quite untenable. The materialist has appealed to the evolution of human consciousness. Consciousness was not created, he tells us; it has developed, and is to be accounted for by Natural Selection. This view is obviously essential to his position, and in fact it was this view of the origin and development of consciousness that has led many a scientist to a materialistic interpretation of the relation of mind and body. Possibly something might be said on the other side. Possibly Natural Selection does not tell the whole story. Let us, however, take the materialist at his word and see for ourselves the exact consequences and implications of his evolutionary view. Consciousness, then, developed through the action of Natural Selection. That is to say, those individuals and those species whose reactions were influenced by conscious factors, such as sensation, pleasure, pain, memory, judgment, etc., had an advantage over their unconscious or less conscious rivals and were enabled thereby the better to escape danger, procure food, and rear their young. This naturalistic explanation will hold both for consciousness in general and for each conscious function in particular. Thus the emotion of fear with its strong impulse to flee or hide was selected and developed because of its biological utility, because the animal who felt afraid in certain circumstances was more likely to escape danger than one who had no conscious reaction to a really dangerous situation. In other words, both consciousness as a whole and each of its parts, aspects, or functions has been selected and developed because of its beneficial *effect* upon the behavior of the organism. Had it had no such effect, animal organisms would have developed as purely unconscious automata. So says the evolutionist and so says the materialist.

But, alas for the absent-minded materialist, he has forgotten one thing—in fact just the most fundamental principle of his whole mind-body doctrine. This fundamental principle, as you will all recall, is the assertion that consciousness has and can have no effect upon behavior whatsoever. Consciousness, says Materialism, is always an effect, never a cause. It was, indeed, just fear of allowing consciousness any influence over bodily activities that prompted the whole materialistic movement. Since consciousness, therefore, can have no influence, good or bad, upon the reactions of the organism, the evolutionary explanation of it, as due to Natural Selection, must be false. What then will the materialist suggest? Special creation is not to his taste; he will not be likely to turn to the Creator and ask for His assistance. Yet he may well feel that nothing short of divine intervention will save him in his sudden and bitter discovery that he had unintentionally, inadvertently, but none the less inevitably and irretrievably, declared war upon Darwin and all the evolutionists.

Let us continue a little farther the line of thought suggested by the materialist's denial of efficiency to consciousness. Since consciousness never interferes with physical processes, never affects them in any way, the whole of man's civilization, the sum total of his achievements, both material and spiritual, must be ascribed to purely physical laws. The whole tremendous mass of it through all the ages would have come about just the same if no scientist or inventor had ever had a thought, no poet or artist a sentiment, no moral or religious teacher an aspiration or ideal, no patriot a feeling of loyalty, no mother an emotion of love. But leaving these things on one side, let us consider in more detail one aspect of the denial of the efficiency of consciousness which should be of particular interest to our materialistic friend.

Consciousness, he will remind us, is always an effect and never a cause. And this means, if Materialism is to be self-consistent, that every psychic state, every feeling and every thought, is determined in its totality by the correlated brain process and never in any degree by any preceding psychic state. To say that a thought is even in a minute degree a co-cause of the following thought would be to wreck Materialism. In the process known as reasoning, therefore, it is a mistake to suppose that consciousness of logical relations has anything whatever to do with the result. It is not logical necessity but mechanical necessity that squeezes out our so-called reasoned conclusions. Take the familiar syllogism:

> All men are mortal
> Socrates is a man
> ∴ Socrates is mortal

The materialist assures us that we should be falling back into the primitive superstitions of a pre-naturalistic age should we suppose that either of the premises had anything to do with our arriving at the conclusion. We finally assert that Socrates is mortal not because we have in mind the mortality of all men and the humanity of Socrates, nor for any other logical or psychological reason; but because certain mechanical processes in our brains force that thought into consciousness. Thus no conclusion is ever arrived at because of logical necessity. There is no logical necessity among mental processes but only physical necessity. The truth is, according to Materialism, we think the way we have to think, the way our mechanical brains constrain us to think. We may happen to think logically; but if we do, this is not because logic had anything to do with our conclusion, but because the brain molecules shake down, so to speak, in a lucky fashion. It is plain, therefore, that no conclusion that we men can reach can ever claim to be based on logic. It is forever impossible to demonstrate that any thesis is logically necessary. If we happen to entertain it we do, that is all; for demonstration is out of the question.

This seems plainly to be the inevitable outcome of the materialist doctrine. And it gives an interesting and somewhat surprising turn to the discussion. For suppose at this point we ask the materialist why he maintains that Materialism is true. If he hopes to convince us he can only reply he considers Materialism true because it is the logical conclusion from certain admitted facts, or that the falseness of all other theories can be logically demonstrated. . . . The hopeless self-contradiction of such a position is obvious. With one breath the materialist asserts that his doctrine is logically demonstrable and that there is no such thing as logical demonstration. As Bradley has put it, no theory can be true which is inconsistent with the possibility of our knowing it to be true. . . .

PARALLELISM. In turning from Materialism to Parallelism we are in fact following the example of most Nineteenth Century materialists. For it was in Parallelism that nearly all of them took refuge when the difficulties of their former doctrine were fully revealed; and their choice of refuge was well made. For Parallelism seems to possess all the naturalistic advantages of Materialism with none of its difficulties. Unlike both Materialism and Interaction, it is no naïve and primitive doctrine, but a careful, artistic, and self-conscious effort to avoid the difficulties which proved so serious to its rivals. With these difficulties in mind it has aimed chiefly at three things. (1) The first of these is the application of the mechanical laws of Naturalism to all physical processes, those of the human brain included. Every physical event, the behavior of men as well as the falling of stones, must be entirely explicable on purely physical principles; and the law of the conservation of energy must be nowhere infringed. This is the primary motive of Parallelism and by strict adherence to it the difficulties of Interaction are clearly avoided. (2) But of almost equal importance to the parallelist (if we may believe his protestations) is his second aim, namely to retain the independence of consciousness within its own realm and thereby to avoid the difficulties of Materialism. To apply mechanical laws to all human behavior and yet to retain belief in the independence of consciousness, of course, seems at first sight a difficult feat; but the parallelist is persuaded he can achieve it by avoiding, finally, a pitfall into which both the interactionist and the materialist fell,— namely the belief in causal action between two such diverse entities as mind and body. (3) Causal action, says the parallelist, may be found in the physical stream, or in the psychical stream, or in both, but never crossing from one to the other. Bodily events and mental events flow parallel to each other in coordinate series, but without mutual influence. But though there is no interchange of causal activity between the two streams there is a strict concomitance. For every mental state there is a corresponding bodily state and vice versa; and this one-to-one correspondence holds not only of the mental and bodily states as wholes but also of their parts—as indeed it obviously must if the doctrine is to be self-consistent.

Such is the theory of Parallelism in general. So much all its adherents, as I understand them, maintain. But the theory is a very elaborate and subtle one, and, as might be expected, it has several sub-types or variations. Conceivably there are at least five possible ways in which mind and body might be represented as a running parallel to each other without causal relation. The first of these is frankly dualistic, while the four others have more or less of a monistic slant. Dualistic Parallelism simply states the parallelist view (as I have attempted to do above) without explanation. But this bald form of the doctrine need not detain us, inasmuch as no one, so far as I know, has ever defended it. It has no real adherents for obvious reasons. If mind and body be regarded as two separate kinds of being, neither of them in any way dominating or influencing the other, their unfailing concomitance would be one of the most astonishing facts in the universe—an unbroken succession of unaccountable coincidences which could at best be attributed only to some sort of miraculous agency or Pre-established Harmony. For a somewhat similar reason we may dismiss, as almost all parallelists have done, a second possible form of the doctrine, which would make the physical series fundamental, and the psychical merely an epiphenomenon; . . . it is plainly open either to the difficulties of Dualistic Parallelism just considered or to the equally serious difficulties of Materialism. There remain for our consideration the two great forms of Parallelism to one or the other of which practically all the adherents of the school belong. These are the so-called Double Aspect View, in its two subordinate types, and Idealistic Parallelism.

The Double Aspect View depicts the mental and the bodily series as equally real, yet does not, like mere Dualistic Parallelism, leave us with a series of unexplained coincidences on our hands, but shows us why the two series are always parallel. This reason is to be found in the hypothesis that mind and body are not independent and substantive things but are merely two aspects of the same Reality. The commonest illustration is that of the curved line, which on one side is convex, on the other concave. Suppose such a line with many curvings and twistings; the succession of concavities and convexities on one side would correspond exactly to the convexities and concavities on the other, and yet without any interchange of causal activity between them. Many other illustrations have been suggested, one of the most recent being that of Professor Warren—the relation, namely, between the mass and the surface of a physical object. These two vary concomitantly, yet neither is the cause of the other.

Unfortunately for my exposition and your understanding, there are two forms of this doctrine; and it is not always easy in reading the expositions of its adherents to know which is the one intended. That both mind and body are merely aspects of something else is strenuously maintained, but just what they are aspects of is not always clear. A careful reading, however, discloses two distinct suggestions. Sometimes it is maintained that mind and body are aspects of each other; sometimes that they are aspects of some known or unknown *Tertium Quid*. I think the first of these doctrines should not detain us a great while. If mind and matter are not aspects of some third reality they presumably constitute between them at any rate the major part of the actual universe. If now one of these two forms of reality is nothing but an aspect of the other, and if the other likewise is nothing but an aspect of the one, our universe shrinks into two mere appearances which are not the appearances of anything and do not appear to any one. We are presented merely with two shadows, each the shadow of the other. It is hard to take such a suggestion seriously; and in reading grave expositions of this view one feels transported into the Wonderland where Alice had her remarkable adventures, and one seems to see the smile of the Cheshire Cat still hanging on in the sky, long after the cat itself has completely dissolved into thin air.

If we are to accept the Double Aspect View, then plainly we must assert that mind and body are aspects of some third thing, the true reality back of the two diverse appearances. This proposition seems in many ways exceedingly attractive. Questions, however, throng upon one the moment one seeks to be clear about the real meaning intended. How shall one construe this *Tertium Quid* which by hypothesis is neither mental nor physical? If it be really neither of these can we know anything about it? And if it be an Unknowable, how can we get from it any real explanation? We have constructed it only for the sake of explaining by its aid certain facts of our life; but how can we hope to explain the known by recourse to the Unknowable —"that refuge of ignorance"? Nor can it be said that the illustrations proposed really throw any light whatever on our problem. We can see very well how the convex and concave sides of a line parallel and must parallel each other. But we see this because convexities and concavities are both curves— both the same sort of thing—and because, knowing what a line is we see how its two sides follow from its nature. But can it be seriously maintained that this in the least helps us to see how two things admittedly so diverse as mind and body can be two sides of a Something-I-know-not-what? The best that can be said for the proposition is that inasmuch as we know nothing of the Unknowable we know not what aspects it may have. But surely such an assertion is far from illuminating; and instead of being a positive theory concerning empirically known facts it is merely a confession of ignorance about an arbitrarily assumed entity so constructed that no one ever could know it. . . .

IDEALISTIC PARALLELISM. Of the list of possible answers to the mind-body problem with which we started there remains but one unexamined. For Idealistic Parallelism is identical with the fourth *general* type of theory to which reference was made in the first lecture—that, namely, according to which mind alone is efficient while body is merely the resultant or appearance of it. We start our consideration of it, therefore, very favorably inclined in advance. When we come to closer terms with it, moreover, we find it in possession of one very obvious and weighty advantage over all its rivals. It is able, namely, to render unto Caesar the things that are Caesar's and unto God the things that are God's. While giving a perfectly definite account of what it means and while making it abundantly clear why mental and physical processes run always parallel, it is able to grant mechanical science full swing throughout the entire sphere of the physical with no least exception, and yet maintain not only that mind is independent of body but that mind is the true reality, and body merely its appearance.

In stating this great merit of Idealistic Parallelism I have, in fact, stated the theory itself. The only genuine reality, it maintains, is psychical in its nature. Body, on the other hand, is merely the phenomenon of mind,—the way in which one center of consciousness appears to another. And not only is this true of our brains and our bodies but of the whole physical world. For if this kind of Parallelism is to be consistent with itself it must be extended to a universal Parallelism. It must give a panpsychic interpretation of everything. Though this fact has not been fully realized by all adherents of the doctrine it can easily be shown to be necessary. For the changes that occur within one's experience and which, like sensations, cannot be accounted for by preceding events within it, must be explained by reference to the outer world; and since all causal influence of the physical upon the psychical is precluded by Parallelism, this outer world must be interpreted as being, upon its inner side and in its true nature, of the same psychic sort as our own experience—though presumably of a much lower and simpler order. This panpsychic interpretation is, in fact, gladly and eagerly accepted and proclaimed by the more philosophical advocates of Idealistic Parallelism. For the physical world as a whole being thus interpreted in idealistic fashion, the values of the spirit appear at length safe. Materialism is forever overcome. Yet, as Paulsen points out, it is overcome "not in the sense of being altogether false and groundless, for it surely is not that. Its demand that everything that exists be explained physically is perfectly well founded and this demand Parallelism fully satisfies. The physicist must still assume the universe to be a physical nexus embracing the whole of reality. Materialism, however, is vanquished in so far as it now appears to be a one-sided view of existence that can and must be supplemented. . . . The corporeal world is at bottom but an accidental concept, an inadequate representation of existence in our sensibility."

Thus the age-long conflict between the demands of natural science and the needs of the spirit seems at length ended by a peace that is fully satisfying and honorable to both sides. The philosophical defender of the concept of causality is shown to be justified in his contention that between two such diverse entities as mind and matter are commonly depicted as being, there can be no interchange of causal influence. The natural scientist is allowed to stride through the whole of the physical universe explaining every minutest event within it on purely mechanistic principles. The law of the conservation of energy is nowhere questioned. No private domain is hedged off, even within man's brain, in which the laws of physical science are refused absolute dominion. No interference is allowed with them even by the human will. And yet the whole of this complete, mechanistic physical world is shown to be merely the outer side, the phenomenal appearance, of the true reality within—a reality which in itself is not physical at all. The truth of the matter is seen to be spirit. . . .

The physical and chemical laws are thus nowhere interfered with, not even in human purposeful activity. The absolute universality of mechanical law is preserved. That is the First and Great Commandment of Parallelism. And the Second is like unto it. Physical processes never interfere with psychical processes. The two series simply accompany each other. So much for the parallelist side of Idealistic Parallelism. Now for the idealist side. The physical and psychical series always and invariably and exactly accompany each other *because* the physical is merely the appearance of the psychical. . . . Matter everywhere is merely the appearance of mind; it is merely the effect—actual or possible—produced by various psychic centers upon the sensibilities of various perceivers. . . .

It will be seen that the physical is as completely stripped of causal efficiency by this view as the psychical was stripped of it by Materialism. No physical state, on the hypothesis of Idealistic Parallelism, ever causes another physical state, but each is directly caused by a psychical state.

Such a theory seems odd enough in all conscience. Yet the oddest part of it remains to be mentioned. . . . Though the psychical series is the only one that *acts,* the only one with any causal efficacy, it always acts in such a way that its appearance—the physical series—will invariably unroll *in accordance with mechanical laws.* . . . The real events (the psychical series) must take care, whatever else they do, to preserve appearances—to maintain scrupulously the scientific regularity of their physical phenomena. . . .

Thus it is really the mechanical laws of the appearance or of the merely possible appearance that determine the activity of the real being back of the appearance. The appearance of the mind—namely the brain—has no causal efficacy whatever, not even within its own series; throughout the life of almost every one of us it never is even a real appearance but only a possible one. Yet the mechanical laws of its behavior, and not the teleological, rational, aesthetic, hedonic relations between ideas and impulses, dominate every process not only within the physical but also within the psychical series. The action of the reality is altogether determined by the laws of its merely possible appearance. It is a remarkable case of the tail wagging the dog.

The seriousness of this situation must be realized quite irrespective of its incongruity. It involves the necessity of really giving up all teleology even in the mental life. It means that it is not the consciousness of logic and of purpose, nor the laws which introspective psychology studies, that control the flow of our thoughts, the course of our reasonings, and the sequence of our actions upon our purposes; not psychical laws determine these things but the same mechanical laws, never guessed at in introspection, which govern the dance of atoms in the chemist's retort and the fall of snowflakes in the polar regions. . . . For plainly no one who holds to the universality of mechanical law can consistently maintain the efficiency of consciousness. If non-purposeful, non-logical, non-aesthetic laws absolutely and alone control human behavior, then purposeful, logical, aesthetic laws do not control it and are incapable of influencing it. One cannot eat one's cake and keep it too.

The necessity of giving up the efficacy of consciousness need not be fatal to Parallelism. But if one means to maintain it, he should do so with his eyes open. He should realize all that is involved. The consequences of such a position are varied. Let me remind you of two of them, bearing, namely, upon biological evolution and human activity. As to the first, the parallelist must face the same dilemma as that which proved so difficult for the materialist. . . . For if the mechanical laws of matter and energy determine every case of human or animal activity, then plainly the conscious processes of instinct, pleasure, pain, desire, and thought do not influence activity. Hence they have contributed nothing toward the preservation of individual or species; and therefore their preservation and development cannot be in the least explained by the Darwinian principle of Natural Selection.

The parallelist must account for the evolution of the race as best he can without any help from consciousness. He must do the same for the advance of human civilization and for the productions and activities of individuals. In the words of Paulsen himself, the parallelist must "explain the author of the *Critique of Pure Reason* just as he would explain clock work." Well, perhaps he can do it. But I submit that the proposition is so preposterous that unless we are shown more compelling reasons than the parallelist has as yet furnished, most of us will look further in the hope of finding a position which will demand of us a little less primitive credulity. . . .

INTERACTION. Our last lecture came to a rather disappointing close. We had passed in review all the leading, and probably all the possible, hypotheses as to the relation of mind and body, and none of them had proved entirely satisfactory or acceptable. . . .

Parallelism in its leading forms we studied in considerable detail and, I think, in no unsympathetic spirit; and I see no conceivable reason for altering the unfavorable judgment to which we were forced. Materialism also we analyzed with some care; and the great difficulties which it involved were so patent that I feel sure nothing would be gained by a reconsideration of its assertions. Of all the proposed solutions of our problem Interaction alone was put aside with a rather summary and inadequate consideration. We hardly more than glanced at it, as you will remember, and not yet realizing how difficult was our problem, we hurried on to more promising suggestions. Having seen now, through a slow and I fear painful course of reasoning, how fallacious were all these promises, we owe it in fairness to ourselves to give to Interaction the same sort of serious consideration that we have given to each of the other hypotheses.

What then, we must ask ourselves, were the difficulties which we found with Interaction which made us pass it by as unsatisfactory? . . .

These difficulties were two-fold. Interaction, namely, involved an impossible view of causation, and secondly it was inconsistent with the universality of mechanical law. This second difficulty divided itself into a more specific and a more general consideration. On the one hand Interaction seemed plainly incompatible with the principle of the conservation of energy; and on the other it as plainly made impossible unobstructed domination over all the world of matter and motion by the laws of physics, chemistry, and biology.

The first of these difficulties, the causal one, is plainly a question that can be settled only by philosophy. This seems too obvious to deserve mention, yet oddly enough it is quite forgotten by many objectors. In their opinion the matter is to be settled not by philosophy or thought but by imagination. Thus a distinguished scientist bids us "try to imagine the idea of a beefsteak binding two molecules together." We are assured we cannot do this, and the conclusion is immediately drawn that therefore mind and body can never influence each other. A remarkably simple and valuable scientific method this. Consistently adopted and skillfully applied it will solve all problems of science and philosophy. Is the earth indeed spherical? The contemporaries of Columbus settled it conclusively in the negative by an appeal to this method. Try to imagine people standing with their feet up and their heads down! "It is impossible." If, however, we are dissatisfied with this easy method of settling the problem of the possible causal relation of body and mind, we shall appeal, as I have said, not to the imagination but to philosophy.

Is Interaction, then, incompatible with causation? Is it conceivable or not that two things so diverse as matter and mind may be causally related? If philosophy is to settle this question it must first of all ask another and antecedent question, namely, what do we mean by causation? Now philosophers are far from being agreed on the details of this matter, but fortunately for us they are nearly all agreed on so much of the answer as is relevant to our

problem. There are two negative characteristics of causation which were settled once for all by David Hume nearly three hundred years ago and which
have seldom been seriously questioned by reputable philosophers since. The
first of these negative characteristics of causation is the absence from it of
any rational necessity. Neither causal relation nor the lack of it can be
predicated by reason of any two objects or events, prior to experience. Without observing the actions of two objects you can never tell in advance
whether one of them can effect the other or cannot do so. Causation, according to Hume, is merely regular and invariable sequence, and whether or not
it holds between two kinds of things is to be determined only by experience.
The second negative characteristic of causation which Hume pointed out is
the absence of any observable "power" passing over from cause to effect or
of any "real tie" binding them together. Watch one object or event cause another; you can never see any power in the first nor any tie between them.
You see simply one event following another. As I have already said, Hume's
position on these two matters has been almost universally accepted by both
philosophy and science. We can neither see causation in any other sense
than that of regular sequence nor argue to it deductively in any given instance. Prior to experience it is absurd for us to attempt to say what can and
what cannot cause something else. Whether a given thing is the cause of another is in every case to be settled purely by appeal to experience. So much,
we are safe in saying, practically all contemporary thinkers will admit; and
not a few would go further and declare, with Bertrand Russell, that science
no longer looks for causes "because there are no such things," and that "the
law of causality is a relic of a bygone age." In place of the older notion of
causes and effects, these thinkers would substitute a certain uniformity of
nature capable of being expressed in various differential equations.

Having now seen what causation means, let us return to the mind-body
problem. We are asked, How can two things so dissimilar affect each other
at all? To which the obvious reply is the further question, Why can they not?
Is it so certain that dissimilar things must fail to influence each other?
Whether they can do so or not must be settled not by an appeal to the
imagination but by an appeal to experience. Our inability to answer the
question, How can the sun attract the earth, is not generally held to make it
impossible for the sun actually to do so. Likewise in dealing with body and
mind, our question is not how one acts upon the other, but the simpler question, Do the two seem to be related in such fashion that certain bodily
events are regularly followed by certain mind events, and certain mind
events by certain bodily events? Prior to the appeal to experience, the *a
priori* denial of the possibility of such causal relation is pure dogma.

What, then, has experience—experience rather than theory—to say on this

matter? If I am not tremendously mistaken, experience speaks here in no uncertain terms. And I refer to the simplest and commonest experiences of
every day. If the electricity were suddenly turned off from this room, our
visual sensations would all cease; if it were turned on again they would
immediately return. And this experiment could be repeated endlessly with
invariably the same result. Here, surely, we seem to have a case of invariable
sequence if it is to be found anywhere, the physical change, being regularly
followed by the psychical change. Nor is regularity any more difficult to find
in the reverse direction. I will to raise my hand and my hand rises; and this
experiment and innumerable others like it can be repeated as long as the
skeptical investigator wishes to stay and watch it. Surely if we are to be persuaded that physical stimuli have nothing to do with the production of sensations, or that will actions have nothing to do with the movements of our
muscles, the persuader must rely upon something else than an appeal to experience. There seems, in fact, something almost perverse in the assertion, so
popular in certain naturalistic circles, that the principle of simplicity demands that we explain human conduct without any reference to the conscious thoughts and purposes which so indubitably and so obviously precede
or accompany it. There they are, ready at hand as a means of explanation,
and without them the activities of human beings are notoriously inexplicable. As Becher has put it in his work *Gehirn und Seele,* if an astronomer
finds an irregularity in the motion of a known star which he cannot explain,
he assumes an unknown factor; but if another star whose influence has not
yet been reckoned in is present, the astronomer is not prevented from bringing it into his calculation by any "principle of simplicity." . . .

There is therefore nothing in the nature of causation inconsistent with the
view that mind and body act on each other; and experience would seem to
indicate that such causal interaction is one of the commonest things observable. The first accusation against Interaction falls, therefore, to the
ground. The second accusation raised against it, however, is much more
difficult to deny, namely that the interaction of mind and body is incompatible with the principle of the conservation of energy. . . .

The difficulty of harmonizing Interaction with this theory is evident. If no
energy can ever be created or destroyed how can the physical energy of the
brain affect the mind, and how can the mind ever affect the brain? Should
we not have in the one case the destruction, in the other the creation of energy? . . . For if the sum total of the energy of the universe, in minds and
in matter, be constant, then the amount at the disposal of each mind will be
absolutely definite and absolutely limited and it will be quite impossible for
the mind to create any new energy. . . . Thus mind, instead of being a genuine source of creative energy or a real power in the control of it, will be

merely a kind of passive reservoir for its temporary storage or a channel for its flow. . . .

So far as I can see, the only way in which the efficiency of consciousness can be preserved is by insisting upon the creative power of the mind. If *it*—it and not merely something of which it is the channel—is to have genuine influence upon conduct, it must be an originator of action absolutely undetermined by the laws of energy, it must be able to make something that is *new*. It is hard to see how it can do this unless it be a genuine creator of energy.

My personal conclusion is, therefore, that Interaction, in the sense in which it is really of importance, is not compatible with the theory of the constancy of energy. The two are antithetical. What must we conclude from this? That Interaction is therefore impossible? Perhaps so. Yet before doing this we must, if our method is to be logical or scientific, first ask how we know that the theory of the constancy of energy in the universe is true. . . .

How shall we prove that in the relations between mind and matter no energy is ever created or destroyed? Within the inorganic world the amount of energy may well be constant. This indeed has never been proved and probably never will be. It is a postulate; but it is one that we are probably all willing to make. But the question of the universal application of the theory to the inorganic world is not the question we are talking about. What evidence is there that it applies also to conscious and reasoning beings? . . .

The only argument in favor of such a view is the argument from analogy that since the theory holds in the inorganic world therefore it must hold in the organic and conscious world. In other words, it is part of the general view that not only the conservation of energy but all the laws of physics and chemistry must have absolute and unmodified application to the whole material world and that they can never be interfered with by anything else. It was the necessary denial of this universal applicability, it will be remembered, that formed the chief difficulty of Interaction. Here, then, we have the decisive issue in its most crucial form. . . . In the light of all our actual experience is it or is it not probable that those laws which hold absolutely for the non-organic world hold also and with equal absoluteness for the organic and conscious world? . . . The upholders of the view that the physical laws of the brain completely determine the action of the mind will refer us to such things as reflex action and habit in normal beings, to the localization of function and the phenomena of aphasia. But plainly the first two of these are perfectly consistent with a view which, like Interaction, agrees that the body is a machine but insists that it is a machine which to some extent is run by the mind. And as to aphasia, though there is no time for even a cursory treatment of the subject, let me remind you that while the earliest investigations of the disease by Broca, Wernicke, and their contemporaries made it appear that memories were stored up in definite brain centers and that memory and presumably thought were altogether dependent upon particular cerebral structures, the most recent work upon the subject has quite upset this entire theory. The whole question is in many ways still vague and unsettled, but the three following points seem pretty well established. Firstly, memory images are not stored up in particular parts of the brain. Upon this the leading authorities are agreed; definite memories *seem* to be created by the mind and to be conditioned upon some general type of brain *set* such as that which Bergson suggests in his interactionist hypothesis. Secondly, even when no images can be formed it is still possible for the patient to think, to mean, to will. He may be unable to get the meaning of others, because he has forgotten their language; but he is still very conscious of his own meaning and his own wishes and able to cling persistently to a definite purpose even though unable to put the purpose into words. He seems, in short, to be intensely conscious, yet without definite images or symbols. Thirdly, by persistent activity of the will much of the language loss in aphasia may be regained through a laborious process of reëducation. Presumably this means the training of new centers to do the work of those destroyed by the original lesion. In any case it seems to indicate clearly the activity of the mind. . . .

So far, then, as I am aware, there is absolutely no experimental or empirical evidence of any kind which gives any support whatever to the denial of the mind's power to modify the workings of the laws of physics and chemistry. On the other hand, we have the unhesitating and universal testimony of every unspoiled individual consciousness, and the equally unquestionable evidence of everyday experience that mind can and does determine conduct. The very structure of the nervous system as an organizaton of forces in unstable equilibrium, and the nature of consciousness as ever tending toward action and always interested in it indicate, as our greatest psychologist pointed out, the same conclusion. In the words of Professor James, "it is quite inconceivable that consciousness should have nothing to do with a business which it so faithfully attends." Moreover, as I have so often repeated, to insist that mechanical laws completely determine all the actions of the human brain and the human body just as they determine the processes of the inorganic world, is to accept the responsibility of explaining the whole of every individual's conduct and the whole of human history with no reference to thought, purpose, or feeling.

To prove the truth or the probability of such a view would require most serious considerations and most cogent reasons. But, as I think we have sufficiently seen, the upholders of this position have not a single relevant empirical fact to rely upon, and not an argument to appeal to, unless it be that of a thoroughly question-begging analogy.

Instead of arguments we are presented with motives. These motives are two in number. The less important is self-defensive in form. We are told that the belief in the universality of physical law is a postulate necessary for science, and that if it be denied the whole of natural science will come tumbling down, its very foundations having been destroyed. But what nonsense is this! If we refuse to admit that the laws which control inorganic matter also absolutely dominate that small portion of the material world in which matter comes into relation with personality, how many of the claims of physical science will thereby be undermined? In the whole realm of physics and of chemistry, of astronomy and geology, not one. Mechanical science will be forced to give up its claims to absolute sway only in that tiny realm where personality, or perhaps where life, begins to have influence. In this connection it is interesting to note that the demand for the absolute universality of physical laws comes, as a rule, not from the physicists, not from the chemists, but from a small number of biologists, a larger number of psychologists, and most of all from the naturalistic school of the philosophers. The mechanistic philosophers are much more royalist than their king, and the demand for the universal sway of the mechanical seems to vary directly with the square of the distance from headquarters.

The other motive which prompts Naturalism in its attempt to deny the efficiency of mind is of a more positive and ambitious sort. It is, namely, the desire to make all forms of matter, of motion, and of energy susceptible to the same sort of description, explanation, and prediction; the wish to get a single world formula under which everything that happens may be subsumed. "We have achieved the impersonal point of view," hymns one of the most ecstatic of the behaviorists, "in the interpretation of stars and stones and trees and bacteria and guinea pigs. Our next step is to achieve it for the phenomena of human behavior." Thus shall we at length achieve that consummation devoutly to be wished, that thoroughly scientific point of view, from which we shall be unable to find in man anything essentially different from what we observe in stones, bacteria, and guinea pigs. There is, to be sure, absolutely no evidence to show that such an achievement is possible, no argument to indicate that the actual world is such as to submit to such a formula; but the great longing heart of Naturalism demands that it shall be so, and the naturalistic philosopher solemnly declares that it is so—it is so because it must be so. It would be impossible to find in the most sentimental and unreasoning forms of religious experience a more extreme case of the pious wish or the Will to Believe. . . .

And when one stops to face squarely this proposition that mind has no effect on conduct,—when, I say, one stops to face it squarely, and leaving aside pet theories, gives it serious consideration in the light of all that one knows of oneself and of other men and of human history and civilization— the proposition reveals itself to the steady gaze as unspeakably preposterous. In the words of Professor Lovejoy, "Never, surely, did a sillier or more self-stultifying idea enter the human mind than the idea that thinking as such— that is to say, remembering, planning, reasoning, forecasting,—is a vast irrelevancy having no part in the causation of man's behavior or in the shaping of his fortunes—a mysterious redundancy in the cosmos which would follow precisely the same course without it."

We are told we must deny the efficiency of consciousness because of the difficulty in believing in any exceptions to the action of mechanical law and the difficulty of imagining how mind can act on matter. I submit that to be so nice with little difficulties, and so omnivorous with monstrosities that approach the mentally impossible is a case of straining at one poor gnat and swallowing a whole caravan of camels. Like others I find it *difficult* to *imagine* an idea affecting a brain molecule; but I think I am also like nearly everybody else when I find it *impossible* to believe that thought and purpose have had nothing to do with building up human civilization and creating human literature and philosophy. How the opponents of Interaction manage to believe these things I confess I find it very difficult indeed to imagine.

Teleology and the Self *

BRAND BLANSHARD [1892–   ] taught philosophy at Michigan and Swarthmore before going to Yale in 1945. His two-volume work, *The Nature of Thought*, is an original development of idealism as applied to contemporary philosophic issues.

Theories about the nature of mind are too numerous even to be listed here. Nevertheless in their bearing on our present interest they break into two large camps, and as to these we must know where we stand. . . . There are those, on the one hand, who think that mind is to be explained by resolv-

* From Blanshard: *The Nature of Thought*, Volume I, pp. 475 ff. Copyright, 1940. Reprinted by permission of George Allen and Unwin, Ltd.

ing it into simpler elements, ascertaining the laws of these elements, and then compounding these laws to explain the behaviour of the whole. There are others who think it can be explained only through the end it is seeking to realize, and that the stages of its growth, either racial or individual, are to be understood as steps in a self-guided ascent. The one group holds, to speak in metaphor, that mind develops by being pushed from behind, the other, by being drawn from ahead. Both appeal in support of their views to the facts of evolution, but one group interprets evolution in mechanistic terms, the other in teleological. . . .

The issue between these schools is clear cut. They agree that mind as we know it has in some sense evolved; they differ as to whether this evolution is to be explained by levelling up or levelling down. At the "top" of the scale, in the human mind, we have events that would seem very clearly to require purpose for their explanation; at the "bottom," in non-living matter, we have a causality that to all appearances is of an extremely different kind, excluding purpose altogether. Can one of these types of causality be reduced to the other? According to the mechanist we can level down. Mind, he says, has obviously evolved from matter; if we are to understand it, we must follow its generation in accordance with the laws of matter; and while in this process of generation there is much that remains obscure, such obscurity cannot hide the fact that matter *has* produced mind, nor even in general its way of doing this. For there is one kind of explanation which has succeeded over such an enormous range of facts that we can only suppose it again applicable here. It is a kind to which others are always reduced as soon as possible, and which nothing, so far, has conclusively resisted; indeed, to show in detail that anything is amenable to it has come to serve as the ideal of scientific explanation. Thus when we say that the mind is a proper subject for science at all, we are saying in effect that mechanistic explanation applies to it. . . .

The teleological view of mind is at the opposite pole from mechanism. It holds that whatever may be true of inorganic matter or even of the matter of living bodies, mechanism breaks down utterly when it comes to the characteristic behaviour of mind. Take, for example, any instance of intelligent action. Suppose I wish to attend a concert, and go to the telephone to reserve a seat. I cross the room and pick up the receiver. Why? The mechanist would say that it was because my body, particularly my brain, was constituted thus and so, and had certain stimuli acting upon it; and that with a full knowledge of body and stimuli my behaviour could be predicted and explained. It will not do for the teleologist to reply merely that we do not actually have such knowledge. This any sensible mechanist admits. He adds, however, that one can no more show in this way that such behaviour escapes mechanical law than one can demonstrate a particular planet to escape the law of gravitation by showing that its orbit is not yet wholly accounted for. To refute the mechanistic theory, the teleologist must show not only that it fails in knowledge but that it is bound always to fail, that there is something in the nature of mind which stands permanently, because in principle, beyond the reach of such theory, no matter how far extended by future knowledge.

This the teleologist does seek to show. He holds that any extension of mechanism short of abandonment of it in principle would still miss the essential reason why I went to the telephone. That reason is that I *wanted* to attend the concert. And he insists that we shall never bring that want into the scope of a mechanical scheme by merely increasing the power of our microscopes, for it is not, like matter in motion, the sort of thing that an observer could observe, even if he were infinitely sharp-eyed. Our action has an inner aspect as real as the outer, and from the inner point of view, the action is essentially the pursuit of an end, a means to this end. Though my interest in the end and my decision to pursue it seem to have no possible place among moving particles, the teleologist is just as certain that they contribute to my behaviour as any mechanist could be that the motion of a colliding billiard ball has something to do with the motion of a second. And he would go on to say that whenever you find intelligence at work, you must explain it in the same way.

Is it possible to find a middle ground between these violently opposing theories? Many believe it is, and have adopted as their middle position what is called 'emergent evolution.' This, too, has various forms, but in the most popular of these it differs from the older mechanism by giving up even the presumption that nature is predictable. It points out that one might have an exhaustive knowledge of the components of a compound taken separately and yet be helpless to predict how they would behave when put together. To use the stock example, one might learn all that it was theoretically possible to learn about hydrogen and oxygen, and their behaviour towards all substances except each other, and yet be unable to predict that when put together they would behave like water. A particle which obeys one set of laws when acting alone may obey a different set when it becomes a member of an aggregate. And according to many emergent evolutionists, this principle is enough in itself to bridge the interval between behaviour at the bottom of the scale and behaviour at the top. For just as a particle may behave otherwise when a member of an aggregate than when alone, so an aggregate may behave otherwise when a member of a larger aggregate than when a member of a smaller one. A particle may escape the laws of pure physics by entering into a chemical compound; this compound may escape purely chemical law when it enters into an organism; the organism may escape biological law when the cells combine to produce sentience, and so on up to the most complex forms of human or superhuman behaviour. And thus the chasm is spanned. The difference between the mechanical and the purposive is not a sheer antithesis but a difference in the structure and complexity of the wholes concerned.

But it is hard to see in this view any real compromise or conciliation. Mechanism is fully represented in it while true purposiveness is left out. One need not question the facts; it may quite well be true that at certain points in the scale there are eruptions of something quite unpredictable in terms of the older and simpler laws. What is questionable is the claim that we really have here a bridge between mechanism and teleology. What we rather have is a less simple kind of mechanism which is as remote as its predecessor from truly purposive behaviour. Old-fashioned mechanism said that you could deduce the behaviour of aggregates from the nature and laws of their components. Emergent evolutionism says that you cannot so deduce it because such behaviour is not the function of the individual elements either separately or in sum, but of a new pattern or structure that supervenes when these come together. For the teleogist, what is there to choose between these doctrines? He is persuaded that a certain behaviour is adopted because it is a means to an end. He is told that it occurs because the pattern of the organism has now become so complex as to make such reactions necessary. Is this purposiveness? He cannot see that it is. The mechanistic family resemblance is too strong. Hydrogen acts in a certain way because it possesses a certain nature; water acts in another way because it possesses a more complex nature; but in both the type of causality is the same. And while purposive causality does seem confined to patterns of some complexity, it is idle to say that this complexity explains it or makes it intelligible. Emergent evolutionism therefore does not reconcile the extremes. The chasm remains in principle unbridged.

Conciliation failing, the question recurs whether either type can extrude the other. Can we level down or level up? Can the domain of mechanism be extended to include the domain of mind and expel teleology from the province it claims; or can teleology be extended to cover events in nature generally and leave mechanism without a kingdom? The latter question need not be pressed, but the first demands an answer. I shall hold that the answer is No; that however successful in the outlying provinces mechanistic explanation may be, mind itself is irreducibly purposive and will elude the grasp of mechanism always. By way of evidence I shall mention three processes of mind whose nature, if closely observed, will place them, I think, beyond the reach of such explanation. These are the processes of (1) growth, (2) choice, and (3) inference.

(1) There is nothing in the movements of particles, or aggregates of particles, that corresponds to what we mean by development in a mind. Analogy begins only when, in the lower forms of life, such as the seed that becomes a plant, the adequacy of mechanism has already ceased to be obvious. For the mechanist, the growth or evolution of anything can only mean an addition to its particles, or a rearrangement of them, or both. The process is typified in the enlargement of a snowball as it rolls downhill or the formation of new patterns when the pieces in a kaleidoscope are redisposed. But such change is not growth or development. For *what* grows in such cases? The particles? They remain precisely the same as before; they are, at most, reordered. The aggregate of particles? But no physical aggregate can even increase in size, let alone truly grow or develop; the aggregate that forms the snowball at one moment has not enlarged at the next; it has merely had other particles disposed in a blanket around it. . . .

When we take growth or development when we know it best, and try to describe accurately what happens when, for example, we pass from a worse to a better understanding of something, or from feeble to full responsiveness to a musical passage, it seems merely meaningless to say that what is going on is a rearrangement of atoms or the enlargement of an aggregate of these, even if the atoms, by some miracle, have now become sensations or some other sort of mental entity. What it does appear to be is a process in which the germinal becomes the mature, the potential the actual; in which I become what I had it in me to become; in which, as I review it, I can see that what I am at present was there in embryo, working itself out to completion, and laying the movement at every step under constraint through the character of what was to emerge. It is true that each stage conditions the next. But why are these stages serial? Why does each as it arises move on in a single direction? Because, as we can see at the end, the same immanent purpose was working at each stage. *Where* the movement was taking us at any step we could not say exactly, but with the completion of the process it becomes clear that the fulfilment we have reached, if new, is not wholly new, and differs from what went before only as a maturer form of the same; that this identical and continuous element has been working in darkness, freeing itself from irrelevancy, organizing its matter, enlarging its scope, until it is fully formed and ripe. We shall misconceive the process radically if we regard it as an adding or rearranging of units, for it is essentially a coming to be on the part of that which is not yet actual, in which the form of what emerges controls the course of its own emergence. This, to the mechanist, may be mysticism. If that is his verdict after examining the process we mean, we shall respect it. But if what he examines is, as is too likely, some utterly different process of nervous, muscular, or cerebral change, substituted by confusion for the process here meant, the verdict will be merely irrelevant.

(2) The teleological nature of mind is shown similarly in *choice*. Choice would most naturally be conceived by the mechanist as a conflict of physical forces, issuing in the predominance of one. It has often been maintained, both by mechanists and others, that something like this happens when a mind is torn between conflicting impulses. And there are no doubt cases of such conflict where the analogy is worth drawing. When one offers a squirrel a nut, the hesitant approaches and retreats suggest a quasi-physical tug-of-war between the impulses of fear and hunger. But this is not a case of choice. Choice proper begins when we are able to contemplate and compare two prospective experiences. Now comparison is rendered possible only by the possession of something in common by the things compared. In the case of ethical choice the common element is good or value, and choice involves the recognition that the good or value we seek will be realized more fully in one course than in another. This seeking after good or value is not one desire among others, which competes with them and in succeeding annuls them. It is something that is present in its degree in all desires, and must reach its end if at all by working through them. Similarly with the end itself. It is not a particular good competing with other particular goods, but that whose presence in varying measure in all of them makes reasonable preference possible. Indeed choice is at bottom another kind of the same process we found in development, in which that which existed *in posse* actualizes itself in maturer form. Now the process of discerning an end to be realized more fully in one good than in another is certainly far removed from the process of being driven by the stronger impulse; and it is so plainly and radically different from any movement or collision of atoms or conflict of forces which can occur in the physical world that analogies between them are more likely to confuse than to clarify.

(3) *Inference* falls, even more clearly perhaps than development and choice, beyond the range of mechanism. . . . The point may be put in either of two ways: either mechanism knows nothing of necessity while inference cannot do without it; or as the self-development of an idea, inference is another species of the process we have just been considering. Mechanism is content to take its laws as descriptions of fact rather than as statements of necessity. The law that A causes B, for example, is not a statement that A's nature necessitates B's; it does not pretend to say more than that A regularly *is* followed by B. This kind of mechanism has often been applied to mental process under the name of 'association'; and just as conflicting forces have a rough analogy with conflicting impulses, so the behaviour of units or particles that regularly go together is not wholly unlike what happens in consciousness, when, with guidance and tension relaxed, ideas gambol idly. But

as an account of inference it is grossly false. For in all inference that is really such, if the thought of B follows the thought of A, it is precisely because A and B are linked by the bond of necessity; A is felt as incomplete and not wholly intelligible unless its relation to B is perceived. Inference is no vaudeville stage where Act 1, the prestidigitator, may be followed with equal propriety by the performing seals or a song. If it were, there would, at bottom, be no distinction between Euclid and a day-dream. Inference is a process in which the nature of A, together with an immanent ideal of intelligible system, controls what shall emerge as B. A is recognized as a fragment, torn from a larger whole, and the mind in seeking this whole is compelled to develop A along some lines rather than others. . . . In ultimate principle, inference is one with growth and choice.

These instances show, I think, that when confronted by the distinctive activities of mind, mechanism is inadequate.

The Ghost in the Machine[*]

GILBERT RYLE [1900–   ]. See p. 176.

THE OFFICIAL DOCTRINE. There is a doctrine about the nature and place of minds which is so prevalent among theorists and even among laymen that it deserves to be described as the official theory. Most philosophers, psychologists and religious teachers subscribe, with minor reservations, to its main articles and, although they admit certain theoretical difficulties in it, they tend to assume that these can be overcome without serious modifications being made to the architecture of the theory. It will be argued here that the central principles of the doctrine are unsound and conflict with the whole body of what we know about minds when we are not speculating about them.

The official doctrine, which hails chiefly from Descartes, is something like this. With the doubtful exceptions of idiots and infants in arms every human being has both a body and a mind. Some would prefer to say that every human being is both a body and a mind. His body and his mind are ordinarily harnessed together, but after the death of the body his mind may continue to exist and function.

[*] From Ryle: *The Concept of Mind,* 1949, Chapter 1. Published by Hutchinson's University Library, London, and Barnes and Noble, Inc., New York. Reprinted by permission of Hutchinson Publishing Group, Ltd., and Barnes and Noble, Inc.

Human bodies are in space and are subject to the mechanical laws which govern all other bodies in space. Bodily processes and states can be inspected by external observers. So a man's bodily life is as much a public affair as are the lives of animals and reptiles and even as the careers of trees, crystals and plants.

But minds are not in space, nor are their operations subject to mechanical laws. The workings of one mind are not witnessable by other observers; its career is private. Only I can take direct cognisance of the states and processes of my own mind. A person therefore lives through two collateral histories, one consisting of what happens in and to his body, the other consisting of what happens in and to his mind. The first is public, the second private. The events in the first history are events in the physical world, those in the second are events in the mental world.

It has been disputed whether a person does or can directly monitor all or only some of the episodes of his own private history; but, according to the official doctrine, of at least some of these episodes he has direct and unchallengeable cognisance. In consciousness, self-consciousness and introspection he is directly and authentically apprised of the present states and operations of his mind. He may have great or small uncertainties about concurrent and adjacent episodes in the physical world, but he can have none about at least part of what is momentarily occupying his mind.

It is customary to express this bifurcation of his two lives and of his two worlds by saying that the things and events which belong to the physical world, including his own body, are external, while the workings of his own mind are internal. This antithesis of outer and inner is of course meant to be construed as a metaphor, since minds, not being in space, could not be described as being spatially inside anything else, or as having things going on spatially inside themselves. But relapses from this good intention are common and theorists are found speculating how stimuli, the physical sources of which are yards or miles outside a person's skin, can generate mental responses inside his skull, or how decisions framed inside his cranium can set going movements of his extremities. . . .

As a necessary corollary of this general scheme there is implicitly prescribed a special way of construing our ordinary concepts of mental powers and operations. The verbs, nouns and adjectives, with which in ordinary life we describe the wits, characters and higher-grade performances of the people with whom we have to do, are required to be construed as signifying special episodes in their secret histories, or else as signifying tendencies for such episodes to occur. When someone is described as knowing, believing or guessing something, as hoping, dreading, intending or shirking something, as designing this or being amused at that, these verbs are supposed to denote the occurrence of specific modifications in his (to us) occult stream of consciousness. Only his own privileged access to this stream in direct awareness and introspection could provide authentic testimony that these mental-conduct verbs were correctly or incorrectly applied. The onlooker, be he teacher, critic, biographer or friend, can never assure himself that his comments have any vestige of truth. Yet it was just because we do in fact all know how to make such comments, make them with general correctness and correct them when they turn out to be confused or mistaken, that philosophers found it necessary to construct their theories of the nature and place of minds. Finding mental-conduct concepts being regularly and effectively used, they properly sought to fix their logical geography. But the logical geography officially recommended would entail that there could be no regular or effective use of these mental-conduct concepts in our descriptions of, and prescriptions for, other people's minds.

THE ABSURDITY OF THE OFFICIAL DOCTRINE. Such in outline is the official theory. I shall often speak of it, with deliberate abusiveness, as 'the dogma of the Ghost in the Machine.' I hope to prove that it is entirely false, and false not in detail but in principle. It is not merely an assemblage of particular mistakes. It is one big mistake and a mistake of a special kind. It is, namely, a category-mistake. It represents the facts of mental life as if they belonged to one logical type or category (or range of types or categories), when they actually belong to another. The dogma is therefore a philosopher's myth. In attempting to explode the myth I shall probably be taken to be denying well-known facts about the mental life of human beings, and my plea that I aim at doing nothing more than rectify the logic of mental-conduct concepts will probably be disallowed as mere subterfuge.

I must first indicate what is meant by the phrase 'Category-mistake.' This I do in a series of illustrations.

A foreigner visiting Oxford or Cambridge for the first time is shown a number of colleges, libraries, playing fields, museums, scientific departments and administrative offices. He then asks 'But where is the University? I have seen where the members of the Colleges live, where the Registrar works, where the scientists experiment and the rest. But I have not yet seen the University in which reside and work the members of your University.' It has then to be explained to him that the University is not another collateral institution, some ulterior counterpart to the colleges, laboratories and offices which he has seen. The University is just the way in which all that he has already seen is organized. When they are seen and when their co-ordination is understood, the University has been seen. His mistake lay in his innocent assumption that it was correct to speak of Christ Church, the Bodleian Library, the Ashmolean Museum *and* the University, to speak, that is, as if 'the University' stood for an extra member of the class of which these other units are members. He was mistakenly allocating the University to the same category as that to which the other institutions belong.

The same mistake would be made by a child witnessing the march-past of a division, who, having had pointed out to him such and such battalions, batteries, squadrons, etc., asked when the division was going to appear. He would be supposing that a division was a counterpart to the units already seen, partly similar to them and partly unlike them. He would be shown his mistake by being told that in watching the batttalions, batteries and squadrons marching past he had been watching the division marching past. The march past was not a parade of battalions, batteries, squadrons *and* a division; it was a parade of the battalions, batteries and squadrons *of* a division.

One more illustration. A foreigner watching his first game of cricket learns what are the functions of the bowlers, the batsmen, the fielders, the umpires and the scorers. He then says 'But there is no one left on the field to contribute the famous element of team-spirit. I see who does the bowling, the batting and the wicket-keeping; but I do not see whose role it is to exercise *esprit de corps.*' Once more, it would have to be explained that he was looking for the wrong type of thing. Team-spirit is not another cricketing-operation supplementary to all of the other special tasks. It is, roughly, the keenness with which each of the special tasks is performed, and performing a task keenly is not performing two tasks. Certainly exhibiting team-spirit is not the same thing as bowling or catching, but nor is it a third thing such that we can say that the bowler first bowls *and* then exhibits team-spirit or that a fielder is at a given moment *either* catching *or* displaying *esprit de corps.*

These illustrations of category-mistakes have a common feature which must be noticed. The mistakes were made by people who did not know how to wield the concepts *University, division* and *team-spirit.* Their puzzles arose from inability to use certain items in the English vocabulary.

The theoretically interesting category-mistakes are those made by people who are perfectly competent to apply concepts, at least in the situations with which they are familiar, but are still liable in their abstract thinking to allocate those concepts to logical types to which they do not belong. An instance of a mistake of this sort would be the following story. A student of politics has learned the main differences between the British, the French and the American Constitutions, and has learned also the differences and connections between the Cabinet, Parliament, the various Ministries, the Judicature and the Church of England. But he still becomes embarrassed when asked questions about the connections between the Church of England, the Home Office and the British Constitution. For while the Church and the Home

Office are institutions, the British Constitution is not another institution in the same sense of that noun. So inter-institutional relations which can be asserted or denied to hold between the Church and the Home Office cannot be asserted or denied to hold between either of them and the British Constitution. 'The British Constitution' is not a term of the same logical type as 'the Home Office' and 'the Church of England.' In a partially similar way, John Doe may be a relative, a friend, an enemy or a stranger to Richard Roe; but he cannot be any of these things to the Average Taxpayer. He knows how to talk sense in certain sorts of discussions about the Average Taxpayer, but he is baffled to say why he could not come across him in the street as he can come across Richard Roe. . . .

THE ORIGIN OF THE CATEGORY-MISTAKE. One of the chief intellectual origins of what I have yet to prove to be the Cartesian category-mistake seems to be this. When Galileo showed that his methods of scientific discovery were competent to provide a mechanical theory which should cover every occupant of space, Descartes found in himself two conflicting motives. As a man of scientific genius he could not but endorse the claims of mechanics, yet as a religious and moral man he could not accept, as Hobbes accepted, the discouraging rider to those claims, namely that human nature differs only in degree of complexity from clockwork. The mental could not be just a variety of the mechanical.

He and subsequent philosophers naturally but erroneously availed themselves of the following escape-route. Since mental-conduct words are not to be construed as signifying the occurrence of mechanical processes, they must be construed as signifying the occurrence of non-mechanical processes; since mechanical laws explain movements in space as the effects of other movements in space, other laws must explain some of the non-spatial workings of minds as the effects of other non-spatial workings of minds. The difference between the human behaviours which we describe as intelligent and those which we describe as unintelligent must be a difference in their causation; so, while some movements of human tongues and limbs are the effects of mechanical causes, others must be the effects of non-mechanical causes, i.e. some issue from movements of particles of matter, others from workings of the mind.

The differences between the physical and the mental were thus represented as differences inside the common framework of the categories of 'thing,' 'stuff,' 'attribute,' 'state,' 'process,' 'change,' 'cause,' and 'effect.' Minds are things, but different sorts of things from bodies; mental processes are causes and effects, but different sorts of causes and effects from bodily movements. And so on. Somewhat as the foreigner expected the University to be an extra edifice, rather like a college but also considerably different, so the repudiators of mechanism represented minds as extra centres of causal processes, rather like machines but also considerably different from them. Their theory was a para-mechanical hypothesis.

That this assumption was at the heart of the doctrine is shown by the fact that there was from the beginning felt to be a major theoretical difficulty in explaining how minds can influence and be influenced by bodies. How can a mental process, such as willing, cause spatial movements like the movements of the tongue? How can a physical change in the optic nerve have among its effects a mind's perception of a flash of light? This notorious crux by itself shows the logical mould into which Descartes pressed his theory of the mind. It was the self-same mould into which he and Galileo set their mechanics. Still unwittingly adhering to the grammar of mechanics, he tried to avert disaster by describing minds in what was merely an obverse vocabulary. The workings of minds had to be described by the mere negatives of the specific descriptions given to bodies; they are not in space, they are not motions, they are not modifications of matter, they are not accessible to public observation. Minds are not bits of clockwork, they are just bits of not-clockwork.

As thus represented, minds are not merely ghosts harnessed to machines, they are themselves just spectral machines. Though the human body is an engine, it is not quite an ordinary engine, since some of its workings are governed by another engine inside it—this interior governor-engine being one of a very special sort. It is invisible, inaudible and it has no size or weight. It cannot be taken to bits and the laws it obeys are not those known to ordinary engineers. Nothing is known of how it governs the bodily engine.

A second major crux points the same moral. Since, according to the doctrine, minds belong to the same category as bodies and since bodies are rigidly governed by mechanical laws, it seemed to many theorists to follow that minds must be similarly governed by rigid non-mechanical laws. The physical world is a deterministic system, so the mental world must be a deterministic system. Bodies cannot help the modifications that they undergo, so minds cannot help pursuing the careers fixed for them. *Responsibility, choice, merit* and *demerit* are therefore inapplicable concepts—unless the compromise solution is adopted of saying that the laws governing mental processes, unlike those governing physical processes, have the congenial attribute of being only rather rigid. The problem of the Freedom of the Will was the problem how to reconcile the hypothesis that minds are to be described in terms drawn from the categories of mechanics with the knowledge that higher-grade human conduct is not of a piece with the behaviour of machines.

It is an historical curiosity that it was not noticed that the entire argument was broken-backed. Theorists correctly assumed that any sane man could already recognise the differences between, say, rational and non-rational utterances or between purposive and automatic behaviour. Else there would have been nothing requiring to be salved from mechanism. Yet the explanation given presupposed that one person could in principle never recognise the difference between the rational and the irrational utterances issuing from other human bodies, since he could never get access to the postulated immaterial causes of some of their utterances. Save for the doubtful exception of himself, he could never tell the difference between a man and a Robot. It would have to be conceded, for example, that, for all that we can tell, the inner lives of persons who are classed as idiots or lunatics are as rational as those of anyone else. Perhaps only their overt behaviour is disappointing; that is to say, perhaps 'idiots' are not really idiotic, or 'lunatics' lunatic. Perhaps, too, some of those who are classed as sane are really idiots. According to the theory, external observers could never know how the overt behaviour of others is correlated with their mental powers and processes and so they could never know or even plausibly conjecture whether their applications of mental-conduct concepts to these other people were correct or incorrect. It would then be hazardous or impossible for a man to claim sanity or logical consistency even for himself, since he would be debarred from comparing his own performances with those of others. In short, our characterisations of persons and their performances as intelligent, prudent and virtuous or as stupid, hypocritical and cowardly could never have been made, so the problem of providing a special causal hypothesis to serve as the basis of such diagnoses would never have arisen. The question, 'How do persons differ from machines?' arose just because everyone already knew how to apply mental-conduct concepts before the new causal hypothesis was introduced. This causal hypothesis could not therefore be the source of the criteria used in those applications. Nor, of course, had the causal hypothesis in any degree improved our handling of those criteria. We still distinguish good from bad arithmetic, politic from impolitic conduct and fertile from infertile imaginations in the ways in which Descartes himself distinguished them before and after he speculated how the applicability of these criteria was compatible with the principle of mechanical causation.

He had mistaken the logic of his problem. Instead of asking by what criteria intelligent behaviour is actually distinguished from non-intelligent behaviour, he asked 'Given that the principle of mechanical causation does not tell us the difference, what other causal principle will tell it us?' He realised that the problem was not one of mechanics and assumed that it must therefore be one of some counterpart to mechanics. Not unnaturally psychology is often cast for just this role.

When two terms belong to the same category, it is proper to construct conjunctive propositions embodying them. Thus a purchaser may say that he bought a left-hand glove and a right-hand glove, but not that he bought a left-hand glove, a right-hand glove and a pair of gloves. 'She came home in a flood of tears and a sedan-chair' is a well-known joke based on the absurdity of conjoining terms of different types. It would have been equally ridiculous to construct the disjunction 'She came home either in a flood of tears or else in a sedan-chair.' Now the dogma of the Ghost in the Machine does just this. It maintains that there exist both bodies and minds; that there occur physical processes and mental processes; that there are mechanical causes of corporeal movements and mental causes of corporeal movements. I shall argue that these and other analogous conjunctions are absurd; but, it must be noticed, the argument will not show that either of the illegitimately conjoined propositions is absurd in itself. I am not, for example, denying that there occur mental processes. Doing long division is a mental process and so is making a joke. But I am saying that the phrase 'there occur mental processes' does not mean the same sort of thing as 'there occur physical processes,' and, therefore, that it makes no sense to conjoin or disjoin the two.

If my argument is successful, there will follow some interesting consequences. First, the hallowed contrast between Mind and Matter will be dissipated, but dissipated not by either of the equally hallowed absorptions of Mind by Matter or of Matter by Mind, but in quite a different way. For the seeming contrast of the two will be shown to be as illegitmate as would be the contrast of 'she came home in a flood of tears' and 'she came home in a sedan-chair.' The belief that there is a polar opposition between Mind and Matter is the belief that they are terms of the same logical type.

It will also follow that both Idealism and Materialism are answers to an improper question. The 'reduction' of the material world to mental states and processes, as well as the 'reduction' of mental states and processes to physical states and processes, presuppose the legitimacy of the disjunction 'Either there exist minds or there exist bodies (but not both).' It would be like saying, 'Either she bought a left-hand and a right-hand glove or she bought a pair of gloves (but not both).'

It is perfectly proper to say, in one logical tone of voice, that there exist minds and to say, in another logical tone of voice, that there exist bodies. But these expressions do not indicate two different species of existence, for 'existence' is not a generic word like 'coloured' or 'sexed.' They indicate two different senses of 'exist,' somewhat as 'rising' has different senses in 'the tide is rising,' 'hopes are rising,' and 'the average age of death is rising.' A man would be thought to be making a poor joke who said that three things are now rising, namely the tide, hopes and the average age of death. It would be just as good or bad a joke to say that there exist prime numbers and Wednesdays and public opinions and navies; or that there exist both minds and bodies.

Minds and Brains*

JOHN JAMIESON CARSWELL SMART [1920–   ] studied at Glasgow and Oxford and is now Hughes Professor of Philosophy at the University of Adelaide, in Australia. He has contributed many articles to philosophical journals.

. . . I wish to argue for the view that conscious experiences are simply *brain processes.* This is a view which almost every elementary student of philosophy is taught to refute. I shall try to show that the standard refutations of the view are fallacious.

Many of our ordinary psychological concepts seem to refer to inner processes. Of course this is not so with all of them. Some of them seem to be able to be elucidated in a behaviouristic way: to say that someone is vain is to say that he tends to show off, or look at himself often in the mirror, or something of that sort. To say that he is interested in mathematics is to say that he has a tendency to read mathematical books, to work out problems, to talk in terms of mathematical analogies, and so on. Similarly with the emotions: 'anger,' 'fear,' 'joy,' and the like can plausibly be said to refer to characteristic behaviour patterns. Again various adverbial phrases can be elucidated in a behaviouristic way. As Ryle has pointed out, the phrase 'thinking what he is doing' in 'he is driving the car thinking what he is doing' refers to certain tendencies to behave in various ways: for example, to apply the brakes when one sees a child about to run on to the road. To drive a car thinking what you are doing is not like walking and whistling. You can walk without whistling and you can whistle without walking, but you cannot do the 'thinking what you are doing' part of 'driving the car thinking what you are doing' without the driving of the car. (Similarly, you can walk gracefully, but you cannot do the being graceful part of the performance without doing the walking part of it.) This helps to elucidate the well-known difficulty of thinking without words. Certain kinds of thinking are pieces of intel-

* From Smart: *Philosophy and Scientific Realism,* London and New York, 1963. Reprinted by permission of Routledge and Kegan Paul, Ltd., London, and of Humanities Press, Inc., New York.

ligent talking to oneself. Consider the way in which I 'thinkingly' wrote the last sentence. I can no more do the 'thinking' part without the talking (or writing) part than a man can do the being graceful part apart from the walking (or some equivalent activity).

If all our psychological concepts were capable of a behaviouristic or quasi-behaviouristic analysis this would be congenial for physicalism. . . . Unfortunately, however, there are a good many psychological concepts for which a behaviouristic account seems impossible.

Suppose that I report that I am having an orange-yellow roundish after-image. Or suppose again that I report that I have a pain. It seems clear that the content of my report cannot be exclusively a set of purely behavioural facts. There seems to be some element of 'pure inner experience' which is being reported, and to which only I have direct access. You can observe my behaviour, but only I can be aware of my own after-image or my own pain. I suspect that the notion of a 'pain' is partly akin to that of an emotion: that is, the notion of pain seems essentially to involve the notion of distress, and distress is perhaps capable of an elucidation in terms of a characteristic behaviour pattern. But this is not all that a pain is: there is an immediately felt sensation which we do not have in other cases of distress. (Consider by contrast the distress of a mother because her son goes out gambling. The son gives his mother much pain, but he does not necessarily give her *a* pain.) In the case of the after-image there is not this 'emotional 'component of distress, and it seems easier to consider such 'neat' inner experiences. I shall therefore concentrate on the case where I report the experience of having an after-image. . . .

The first argument against the identification of experiences and brain processes can be put as follows: Aristotle, or for that matter an illiterate peasant, can report his images and aches and pains, and yet nevertheless may not know that the brain has anything to do with thinking. (Aristotle thought that the brain was an organ for cooling the blood.) Therefore what Aristotle or the peasant reports cannot *be* a brain process, though it can, of course, be something which is (unknown to Aristotle or the peasant) causally connected with a brain process.

The reply to this argument is simply this: when I say that experiences are brain processes I am asserting this *as a matter of fact*. I am not asserting that 'brain process' is part of what we *mean* by 'experience.' A couple of analogies will show what is wrong with the argument. Suppose that a man is acquainted with Sir Walter Scott and knows him as 'the author of *Waverley*.' He may never have heard of Ivanhoe. Yet the author of *Waverley* can be (and was) the very same person as the author of *Ivanhoe*. Again, consider lightning. According to modern science, lightning is a movement of electric charges from one ionised layer of cloud to another such layer or to the earth. This is what lightning really is. This fact was not known to Aristotle. And yet Aristotle presumably knew the meaning of the Greek word for 'lightning' perfectly well.

I wish to make it clear that I have used these examples mainly to make a *negative* point: I do not wish to claim that the relation between the expression 'I am having an after image' and 'there is such-and-such a brain process going on in me' is in *all* respects like that between 'there is the author of *Waverley*' and 'there is the author of *Ivanhoe*,' or like that between 'that is lightning' and 'that is a motion of electric charges.' The point I wish to make at present is simply that these analogies show the weakness of the . . . argument against identifying experiences and brain processes. I am, however, suggesting also that it may be the true nature of our inner experiences, as revealed by science, to be brain processes, just as to be a motion of electric charges is the true nature of lightning, what lightning really is. Neither the case of lightning nor the case of inner experiences is like that of explaining a footprint by reference to a burglar. It is not the true nature of a footprint to be a burglar.

In short, there can be contingent statements of the form 'A is identical with B,' and a person may know that something is an A without knowing it is a B. An illiterate peasant might well be able to talk about his sensations without knowing about his brain processes, just as he can talk about lightning, though he knows nothing about lightning. . . .

A related objection which is sometimes put up against the brain process thesis runs as follows. It will be pointed out that the hypothesis that sensations are connected with brain processes shares the tentative character of all scientific hypotheses. It is possible, though in the highest degree unlikely, that our present physiological theories will one day be given up, and it will seem as absurd to connect sensations with the brain as it now does to connect them with the heart. It follows that when we report a sensation we are not reporting a brain process.

This argument falls to the ground once it is realised that assertions of identity can be factual and contingent. The argument certainly does prove that when I say 'I have a yellowish-orange after-image' I cannot *mean* that I have such-and-such a brain process. (Any more than that if a man says 'there goes the author of *Waverley*' he *means* 'there goes the author of *Ivanhoe*.' The two sentences are not inter-translatable.) But the argument does not prove that what we report (*e.g.* the having of an after-image) is not *in fact* a brain process. It could equally be said that it is conceivable (though in the highest degree unlikely) that the electrical theory of lightning should be given up. This shows indeed that 'that is lightning' does not *mean* the same as 'that is a motion of electric charges.' But for all that, lightning is *in fact* a motion of electric charges. . . . Now it may be said that if we identify an experience and a brain process and if this identification is, as I hold it is, a *contingent* or *factual* one, then the experience must be identified as having some property not logically deducible from the properties whereby we identify the brain process. To return to our analogy of the contingent identification of the author of *Waverley* with the author of *Ivanhoe*. If the property of being the author of *Waverley* is the analogue of the neurophysiological properties of a brain process, what is the analogue of the property of being author of *Ivanhoe?* There is an inclination to say: 'an irreducible, emergent, introspectible property.'

How do I get round this objection? I do so as follows. The man who reports a yellowish-orange after-image does so in effect as follows: '*What is going on in me is like what is going on in me when* my eyes are open, the lighting is normal, etc., etc., and there really is a yellowish-orange patch on the wall.' In this sentence the word 'like' is meant to be used in such a way that something can be like itself: an identical twin is not only like his brother but is like himself too. With this sense of 'like' the above formula will do for a report that one is having a veridical sense datum too. Notice that the italicised words '*what is going on in me is like what is going on in me when* . . .' are topic-neutral. A dualist will think that what is going on in him when he reports an experience is in fact a non-physical process (though his report does not say that it is), an ancient Greek may think that it is a process in his heart, and I think that it is a process in my brain. The report itself is neutral to all these possibilities. This extreme 'openness' and 'topic neutrality' of reports of experiences perhaps explains why the 'raw feels' or immediate qualia of internal experiences have seemed so elusive. 'What is going on in me is like what is going on in me when . . .' is a colourless phrase, just as the word 'somebody' is colourless. If I say 'somebody is coming through the garden' I may do so because I see my wife coming through the garden. Because of the colourless feel of the word 'somebody' a very naïve hearer (like the king in *Alice in Wonderland*, who got thoroughly confused over the logical grammar of 'nobody') might suspect that 'somebody is coming through the garden' is about some very elusive and ghostly entity, instead of, in fact, that very colourful and flesh and blood person, my wife.

For this account to be successful, it is necessary that we should be able to report two processes as like one another without being able to say in what respect they are alike. An experience of having an after-image may be classified as like the experience I have when I see an orange, and this likeness, on my view, must consist in a similarity of neuro-physiological pattern. But of course we are not immediately aware of the pattern; at most we are able to report the similarity. Now it is tempting, when we think in a metaphysical and *a priori* way, to suppose that reports of similarities can be made only on a basis of the conscious apprehension of the features in respect of which these similarities subsist. But when we think objectively about the human being as a functioning mechanism this metaphysical supposition may come to seem unwarranted. It is surely more easy to construct a mechanism which will record (on a punched tape, for example) bare similarities in a class of stimuli than it is to construct a machine which will provide a report of the features in which these similarities consist. It therefore seems to me quite possible that we should be able to make reports to the effect that 'what is going on in me is like what goes on in me when . . .' without having any idea whatever of what in particular is going on in me (*e.g.* whether a brain process, a heart process, or a spiritual process).

I must make it clear that I am not producing the phrase 'What is going on in me is like what goes on in me when . . .' as a *translation* of a sensation report. It is rather meant to give in an informal way what a sensation report purports to be about. For example, it has been objected that it is no good translating 'I have a pain' as 'what is going on in me is like what goes on when a pin is stuck into me,' since, to put it crudely, pains have nothing in particular to do with pins, and certainly someone might learn the word 'pain' without ever having learned the word 'pin.' When, however, I say that 'I have a pain' is to the effect of 'what is going on in me is like what goes on in me when a pin is stuck into me,' my intention is simply to indicate the way in which learning to make sensation reports is learning to report likenesses and unlikenesses of various internal processes. There is indeed no need to learn the word 'pain' by having a pin stuck into one. A child may, for example, be introduced to the word 'pain' when he accidentally grazes his knee. But sensation talk must be learned with reference to some environmental stimulus situation or another. Certainly it need not be any *particular* one, such as the sticking in of pins.

The above considerations also show how we can reply to another objection which is commonly brought against the brain-process theory. The experience, it will be said, is not in physical space, whereas the brain process is. Hence the experience is not a brain process. This objection seems to beg the question. If my view is correct the experience *is* in physical space: in my brain. The truth behind the objection is that the experience is not reported as something spatial. It is reported only (in effect) in terms of 'what is going on in me is like what goes on in me when. . . .' This report is so 'open' and general that it is indeed neutral between my view that what goes on in me goes on in physical space and the psychophysical dualist's view that what goes on in me goes on in a non-spatial entity. This is without prejudice to the statement that what goes on in me is something which in fact *is* in physical space. On my view sensations do in fact have all sorts of neurophysiological properties. For they are neurophysiological processes. . . .

We must now pass on to consider another objection. This is that our experiences are private, immediately known only to ourselves, whereas brain processes are public, observable (in principle) by any number of external observers. If someone sincerely says that he is having a certain experience, then no one can contradict him. But if the physiologist reports something in the brain, then it is always *in principle* possible to say: 'Perhaps you are mistaken; you may be having an illusion or hallucination or something of the sort.' It will be remembered that I suggested that in reporting sensations we are in fact reporting likenesses and unlikenesses of brain processes. Now it may be objected (as has been done by K. E. M. Baier): 'Suppose that you had some electro-encephalograph fixed to your brain, and you observed that, according to the electro-encephalograph, you did *not* have the sort of brain process that normally goes on when you have a yellow sense datum. Nevertheless, if you had a yellow sense datum you would not give up the proposition that you had such a sense datum, no matter *what* the encephalograph said.' This part of the objection can be easily answered. I simply reply that the brain-process theory was put forward as a factual identification, not as a logically necessary one. I can therefore agree that it is logically possible that the electro-encephalograph experiment should turn out as envisaged in the objection, but I can still believe *that this will never in fact happen.* If it did happen I should doubtless give up the brain-process theory. . . .

However, it is incumbent on anyone who wishes to dispute the brain-process theory to produce experiences which are known to possess irreducibly 'psychic' properties, not merely 'topic neutral' ones. So far I do not think that anyone has done so.

SUGGESTED READINGS

Chapters 3 and 4 of C. H. Whiteley's short *Introduction to Metaphysics* contain a good elementary survey of some of the problems of mind and body, as does R. Taylor's more recent *Metaphysics*, Chapters 1–3. The best survey of various doctrines on the relation of mind and body is C. D. Broad's massive *The Mind and Its Place in Nature;* see especially the Introduction and Section A. In Section D, he treats problems concerning immortality. This topic is more exhaustively discussed by C. J. Ducasse in *Nature, Mind, and Death.* For those interested in following out debates on immortality, A.

Flew has prepared an anthology, *Body, Mind and Death,* which contains short excerpts from numerous classical and modern authors, as well as a good bibliography. Two other useful anthologies are G. N. A. Vesey, *Body and Mind,* and J. R. Smythies, *Brain and Mind:* the titles reflect their somewhat different orientations.

Ryle's *Concept of Mind* was reviewed by J. Wisdom, and this review, together with an important paper by U. T. Place, "Is Consciousness a Brain Process?", and several other essays, may be found in *Philosophy of Mind,* edited by V. C. Chappell. S. Hampshire has edited an anthology with the same title which contains more recent papers, mostly quite advanced and difficult. The paper by R. Rorty in this volume examines some of the objections drawn from ordinary language to the claim that consciousness is a brain process.

One of the most interesting attempts to give a criterion of the mental that will distinguish it sharply from the physical is that made by the great Austrian philosopher Franz Brentano. The crucial chapter of his *Psychology* is printed in translation in the first chapter in R. Chisholm, *Realism and the Background of Phenomenology.* For a brief survey of Brentano's work, see H. Spiegelberg, *The Phenomenological Movement,* Volume I, Part I, Chapter 1.

Freedom and Determinism

No one will deny that, within limits, men can do what they want or that they can achieve many of the ends they seek. In our culture a man may well fulfill his desire to become a doctor, or a lawyer, or to go into some particular business. On the other hand, no one will deny that a man's ability to achieve his goals is, at least in some degree, limited by his personal capacities and his social environment. A person of limited intelligence cannot become a great theoretical physicist, nor can a member of a primitive Australian culture achieve engineering feats that demand a vast background of theoretical and practical knowledge of physics.

Furthermore, everyone admits that men feel free to choose as they want, to decide upon one course of action rather than another. One feels free to decide to eat at one time rather than another, to study or go to a movie, to become a lawyer or not. On the other hand, our freedom of choice is sometimes clearly limited. Our deliberations may be influenced by long-standing habits, for example, or by fatigue, or rage, or illness.

The problem of human freedom, therefore, has two distinguishable but closely related aspects: *freedom of choice* and *freedom of action*. Concerning choice, we may ask what factors are responsible for a man's decision to commit himself to one alternative rather than another. Regarding action, we may ask what factors are responsible for a man's ability to achieve his ends, once he has committed himself to one alternative rather than another. Granting the role of personal and social factors in *influencing* one's choice and in *limiting* one's ability to do what is chosen, are these factors sufficient (1) to *determine* what our choice will be, and (2) to *determine* whether our goal will be achieved in action? In particular, does "effort" count? Can the effort one makes be a decisive factor either in the choice one makes or in the attainment of the goal one chooses?

Indeterminists (*libertarians*) hold that the effort one makes is a decisive factor and that this exertion of effort is not (in normal cases) determined by personal conditions or environmental factors, but by the *independent* will of the agent. *Determinists*, on the other hand, deny that those aspects of a man's character that we refer to as his "will" are themselves undetermined. According to this view, all human actions and all subjective phenomena (such as desire, deliberation, or feelings of freedom or constraint) are strictly the result of empirical conditions and are subject to explanation by natural laws.

In the selection which follows, WOOD formulates the position traditionally adopted by determinists and defends it against objections. RYLE analyzes the concept of "volition," and suggests that the common view of the "will," as a special kind of cause, is without foundation. JAMES, on the other hand, would accept the libertarian position regarding freedom of choice and would argue that only through an espousal of this position can freedom of action be won. For James, any appeal to the authority of science on behalf of determinism is a fallacious argument. For GRÜNBAUM, on the contrary, current critiques of determinism rest on misconceptions of scientific method and lead to a less satisfactory justification of our ordinary moral beliefs than does the position of determinism itself.

The Free-Will Controversy*

L E D G E R W O O D [1901–   ] has taught philosophy at Princeton since 1927. In addition to journal articles he has published books on the theory of knowledge and the history of philosophy.

Few philosophical controversies have been waged with greater acrimony than the controversy between the libertarians and the determinists; the vigour with which both sides of the question have been espoused is due not only to the metaphysical importance of the issue—which is indeed considerable—but most especially to its moral and religious implications. No other philosophical issues, with the exception of those pertaining to God and the immortality of the soul, are of greater ethical and theological moment. So thoroughly has the question been debated that further consideration of it may seem futile. Has not the evidence been so completely canvassed on both sides of the controversy that further discussion will be a fruitless reiteration of long familiar arguments? The free-will problem is considered by many contemporary thinkers an admittedly unsolved but completely outmoded problem to which they respond with impatience or complete indifference. This attitude toward the problem is quite indefensible since the question of the freedom of the will is one of those perennially significant philosophical issues which takes on new meaning in every age and is particularly significant in the context of contemporary science and philosophy. Recent psychology, in large measure through the influence of Freud, has achieved a more penetrating analysis of human motivation by bringing to the fore certain hitherto obscure factors which are operative in volition. The psychology of the subconscious by filling in apparent gaps in the psychological causation of volition has furthered the case for determinism. Furthermore, behaviouristic psychology by subjecting all human behaviour, including so-called volitional acts, to a mechanistic formula bears directly on the free-will issue and

* From Wood: "The Free-Will Controversy," in *Philosophy*, XVI (1941), pp. 386–397. Reprinted by permission of The Royal Institute of Philosophy and the author.

like the Freudian psychology seems to strengthen the deterministic position. Recent developments in the physical sciences are not without their significance for the free-will issue; the principle of indeterminacy in quantum mechanics has been eagerly seized upon by the libertarians in the belief that it affords a physical foundation for their position. Finally, in philosophy proper the progress of philosophical analysis and of the philosophical theory of meaning renders possible a more exact statement of the free-will issue and permits a more just appraisal of the traditional arguments on both sides of the free-will controversy than has hitherto been possible. . . .

The question of the freedom of the will, reduced to its barest essentials, is simply this: *Are all human acts of will causally produced by antecedent conditions or are at least some volitional actions exempt from causal determination?* The determinist insists that all actions, even the most carefully planned and deliberate, can be causally explained and that if we knew enough about a man's hereditary traits and the environmental influences which have moulded his character, we could predict just how he would behave under any specified set of circumstances. The free-willist or libertarian, on the other hand, asserts that there are at least some human actions of the volitional type in which the individual by the exercise of his will-power, acts independently of conditioning factors; that some, and perhaps all, volitional acts are causally indeterminate, that is to say, are not conjoined in any uniform way with antecedent conditions. The uniform antecedents of free acts are, on this view, undiscoverable for the simple reason that they do not exist. . . . The free-willist introduces an element of indeterminacy into human behaviour; he admits an effect, namely, the volitional action, without a sufficient and adequate natural cause. . . .

I propose to give a brief résumé of the free-will controversy, examining first the arguments for the freedom of the will and then stating the case for determinism. Although the position taken throughout the present paper is avowedly deterministic, the attempt will be made to state with fairness the case for and against both of the rival positions and on the basis of these arguments, to give a just appraisal of the two positions. The strength of the deterministic position will be found to lie not only in the positive evidence which may be adduced to support it, but also in its easy ability to meet the arguments advanced by the free-willists.

ARGUMENTS FOR THE FREEDOM OF THE WILL. The arguments of the free-willist are for the most part humanistic and non-scientific in character and may be conveniently considered under the following heads:

(1) the introspective or psychological argument,
(2) the moral and religious arguments,
(3) the argument from physical indeterminacy.

(1) *The introspective or psychological argument.* Most advocates of the free-will doctrine believe that the mind is directly aware of its freedom in the very act of making a decision, and thus that freedom is an immediate datum of our introspective awareness. "I feel myself free, *therefore*, I am free," runs the simplest and perhaps the most compelling of the arguments for freedom. In the elaboration of his argument, the free-willist offers a detailed description of what, in his opinion, is introspectively observable whenever the self makes a free choice. Suppose I find myself forced to choose between conflicting and incompatible lines of action. At such a time, I stand, so to speak, at the moral cross-roads, I deliberate, and finally by some mysterious and inexplicable power of mind, I decide to go one way rather than the other. Deliberative decision, if this description is correct, is analysable into these three constituents: (a) the envisaging of two or more incompatible courses of action, (b) the review of considerations favourable and unfavourable to each of the conflicting possibilities of action, and (c) the choice among the alternative possibilities.

Deliberative, or so-called "moral" decisions, are fairly numerous in the lives of all of us and are made on the most trivial occasions, as well as on matters of grave import. The university undergraduate's resolution of the conflict between his desire to see the latest cinema at the local playhouse and his felt obligation to devote the evening to his studies, trivial and inconsequential as it may seem, is the *type* of all moral decisions and differs in no essential respect from such a momentous decision as his choice of a life career. Each of these decisions to the extent that it is truly deliberative involves (a) the imaginative contemplation of alternative actions, (b) the weighing of considerations *for* and *against* the several alternatives involving, perhaps, an appeal to ideals and values approved by the moral agent, and finally (c) the choice between the several possibilities of action. At the moment of making the actual decision, the mind experiences a *feeling* of self-assertion and of independence of determining influences both external and internal. The libertarian rests his case for free-will on the authenticity of this subjective feeling of freedom.

The phenomenon of decision after deliberation is an indubitable *fact* which determinist and free-willist alike must acknowledge, but the real issue is whether this fact warrants the *construction* which the free-willist puts upon it. The determinist, replying to the introspective argument, urges that the *feeling* of freedom is nothing but a sense of relief following upon earlier tension and indecision. After conflict and uncertainty, the pent-up energies of the mind—or rather of the underlying neural processes—are released and this process is accompanied by an inner sense of power. Thus the feeling of freedom or of voluntary control over one's actions is a mere subjective illusion which cannot be considered evidence for psychological indeterminacy.

Besides the direct appeal to the sense of freedom, there is a psychological argument which *infers* freedom from the mind's ability to resolve an equilibrium of opposing motives. The allegedly "prerogative" or "critical" instance of free-will, is that in which the will makes a choice between two or more actions which are equally attractive, or equally objectionable. If, after a careful weighing of all the considerations *for* and *against* each of the alternative actions, the mind finds the rival claimants exactly equal, a decision is possible, argues the libertarian, only by a free act of will. We weigh the motives against one another, find the scale balanced, and then, in the words of William James, . . . "we feel, in deciding, as if we ourselves by our wilful act inclined the beam." This argument from the equilibrium of motives is indeed plausible, but the determinist has a ready reply. *If* the motives really had been exactly equal and opposite, then the mind would have remained indefinitely in a state of suspended judgment and consequent inaction or would, in Hamlet fashion, have oscillated between the two incompatibles, never able to yield to one or to the other. The analogy of the balanced scale would lead one to expect the will under these circumstances to do just this. Indeed, there are undoubtedy some pathological minds which are in a perpetual tug-of-war between conflicting tendencies of action and whose wills, as a consequence, are completely paralysed. But in normal minds the "motives" on the one side or the other become momentarily stronger because of some new external factor injected into the situation or because of the inner reorganization of forces and then action immediately ensues. Often the decision is determined by accidental and contingent circumstances—a literal flip of the coin—or perhaps one allows one's action to be decided by a chance idea or impulse, that is to say, by a "mental flip of the coin." In any case the fact that a decision is actually made testifies to the eventual inequality of the opposing forces. Under no circumstances is it necessary to resort to a mysterious, inner force of will to "incline the beam" one way rather than the other.

Still another introspective fact cited by the libertarian in support of his doctrine is that the moral agent is in retrospect convinced that he might, *if he had chosen,* have followed a course of action different from that which he actually pursued. The belief that there are genuine alternatives of action and that the choice between them is indeterminate is usually stronger in prospect and in retrospect than at the time of actual decision. The alternatives exist in prospect as imaginatively envisaged possibilities of action and in retrospect as the memory of the state of affairs before the agent had, so to speak, "made up his mind." Especially in retrospect does the agent recall his earlier decision with remorse and repentance, dwelling sorrowfully upon rejected possibilities of action which now loom up as opportunities missed. How frequently one hears the lament: "I regret that decision; I should, and I could, have acted otherwise." Now the contemplation of supposed alternatives of action along with the sentiment of regret produces the illusion of indeterminate choice between alternatives, but a careful analysis of the import of the retrospective judgment, "I could have acted otherwise than I did," will, I believe, disclose it to be an empirically meaningless statement. If I decided in favour of this alternative, rather than that, it can only mean that the circumstances being what they were, and I in the frame of mind I was at the time, no other eventuation was really possible. My statement that I could have acted differently expresses only my memory of an earlier state of suspense, indecision, and uncertainty, intensified by my present remorse and the firm determination that if, in the future, I am faced with a similar choice, I shall profit by my earlier mistake. There is, however, in the deliberative situation no evidence of genuine alternatives of action, or the indeterminacy of my choice between them.

(2) *The moral arguments.* The moral argument assumes a variety of forms, but they all agree in their attempt to infer volitional freedom of the moral agent from some feature of the moral situation. The most characteristic feature of moral action is that it seems to be directed toward the realization of an ideal or the fulfilment of an obligation. But, argues the free-willest, it is of the very nature of an ideal or an obligation that it shall be *freely* embraced; the acceptance or rejection of a moral ideal and the acknowledgement of an obligation as binding can only be accounted for on the assumption of the agent's free choice. The very existence of moral ideals, norms, or standards which, though *coercive* are not *compulsive*, testifies to the freedom of the agent who acknowledges them. Thus did Kant in his famous formula: "I ought, therefore I can" directly infer the agent's freedom from his recognition of moral obligation.

The moral argument is so loose in its logic that, unable to put one's finger on its fallacy, one is tempted to resort to the logicians' "catch-all," and call it a *non sequitur.* A moral agent's adoption of a moral ideal or recognition of a moral obligation simply does *not* imply that he possesses a free-will in the sense of psychological indeterminacy. An adequate critique of the moral argument would require a detailed psychological account of the genesis of moral ideals and duties without recourse to freedom of the libertarian sort and I am convinced that such an account is forthcoming. The emergence of ideals in the mind of an individual moral agent along with the feeling that such ideals are coercive is largely non-volitional and even when it rises to the volitional level and represents a choice between competing ideas, there is even then no reason for abandoning psychological determinism. The moral

argument for freedom is found, on close examination, to be the psychological argument in disguise and like it, is introspectively false; there is no indication or volitional freedom either in the original adoption of moral standards nor in subsequent moral decisions in accordance with those standards
once they have been embraced.

The moral argument for freedom has sometimes been stated from the
point of view not of the moral agent but of the moral critic who passes judgment on the action of another or even upon his own actions. A judgment of
praise or blame, of approval or condemnation, so the argument runs,
imputes freedom to the agent whose action is judged. When I praise your
unselfish and benevolent acts, I imply that you could, if you had chosen,
have been cruel and selfish instead. Condemnation of another's conduct
seems even more surely to suggest that he acted willingly, or rather "wilfully." Otherwise, would it not be in order to pity rather than condemn the
wrong-doer? Should we not say with condescension, "Poor misguided fool,
he can't help what he does, he is simply that kind of man"? Instead, we reprove his action and by so doing implicitly acknowledge that he is a free
moral agent. A novel variant of this argument is contained in William
James's essay "The Dilemma of Determinism." The determinist, so James
argues, finds himself in a curious logical predicament whenever he utters a
judgment of regret. If I, a determinist, pass an adverse judgment on my own
or another's actions, I thereby acknowledge that they ought not to have
been, that others ought to have been performed in their place. But how can
I meaningfully make such a statement if these particular actions, and no
others, were possible? "What sense can there be in condemning ourselves for
taking the wrong way, unless the right way was open to us as well?" James
advanced the moral argument, not as an absolute *proof* of freedom (he admits that it is not intellectually coercive), but rather as a belief to be *freely*
embraced. As a pragmatically effective, moral fiction, freedom has much to
be said in its favour: the belief in freedom no doubt fosters moral earnest-
ness, whereas the belief in determinism may, at least in certain persons,
induce moral lassitude. Most defenders of the free-will doctrine do not,
however, share James's cautious restraint; they advance the moral argument
as a conclusive proof of an indeterminate free-will. . . .

The determinist finds no difficulty in assimilating to his deterministic
scheme the facts of moral approval and disapproval. Moral valuation is not
the detached and disinterested judgment of a moral critic, but is an instru-
mentality for the social propagation of norms of conduct. Morality is essentially a social pehenomenon; society has gradually evolved its patterns of social behaviour which it imposes upon its individual members by means of
various sanctions including the favourable or adverse judgments which

members of society pass upon one another. Judgments of moral valuation rest upon the socially constituted norms of action and are the media through which these norms are communicated from individual to individual. I reprove your unsocial or antisocial behaviour in the belief that my adverse judgment may influence you to desist therefrom. When I pass a moral judgment on another, far from implying his free-will, I tacitly assume that my judgment of him, in so far as he takes cognizance of it, operates as a determining influence on his conduct. Thus moral criticism when interpreted naturalistically harmonizes with the theory of moral determinism.

Another moral argument, closely paralleling the argument from obligation, stresses the concept of moral responsibility. The free-willist considers freedom a *sine qua non* of responsibility; his argument runs: "Without freedom, there can be no responsibility, but there *must* be responsibility, hence man is free." . . . The concept of moral responsibility no doubt admits of precise empirical definition and exemplification; there is a real distinction between responsible and irresponsible actions. But when responsibility is analysed in this empirical and positivistic fashion, it will be found in no wise to imply volitional freedom. A careful analysis of responsible actions will show them to be if anything no more indeterminate than nonresponsible and irresponsible actions. And this brings us to the second criticism of the argument from responsibility: *viz.,* the failure to establish the alleged implication of the concept of freedom by the concept of responsibility. The concepts of freedom and responsibility are by no means indissolubly connected; on the contrary, the freedom of indeterminacy, far from guaranteeing responsibility, would, if it existed, actually be prejudicial to it. If freedom is the complete divorce of the will from antecedent conditions, including my moral character, I cannot then be held accountable for my actions. A will which descends upon me like "a bolt from the blue" is not *my* will and it is manifestly unfair to take me to task for its caprices. . . .

(3) *The argument from physical indeterminacy.* Free-willists have recently derived not a little encouragement from the advent of the principle of physical indeterminacy which even if it does not suffice to demonstrate freedom of the will, at least seems to remove a serious obstacle to its acceptance. If there is a real indeterminacy at the subatomic level of quantum mechanics, this affords at least the *possibility* of the physiological and ultimately of the psychological indeterminacy which constitutes the freedom of the will. Recent quantum theory seems on the surface to afford a physical basis for a volitional indeterminacy much as the swerve of the atoms involved by the ancient Epicureans seemed to justify their free-will doctrine. But the contemporary argument is defective and in very much the same respects as its historic prototype.

Against the modern version of the indeterminacy argument, it may be urged in the first place that the physical theory of indeterminacy merely expresses an observational difficulty encountered in the attempt to determine both the position and the velocity of an electron and that consequently it posits a methodological and not the physical or ontological indeterminacy which is requisite for the purposes of the free-will doctrine. But secondly, even supposing that the indeterminacy principle is physical and not merely methodological, it has not been shown that this subatomic indeterminacy manifests itself in the behaviour of ordinary mass-objects and in particular that it is exemplified in just those neural processes which are supposedly the basis of the act of free-will. The psychophysical correlation of a neural indeterminacy with its psychological counterpart, could be effected only by the introspective observation of the volitional indeterminacy along with the underlying physical indeterminacy, and thus the evidence of introspection is an essential link in the argument from physical indeterminacy. The physical theory of indeterminacy is at the present time far from demonstrating the existence of or giving a complete picture of the *modus operandi* of a free-will and thus the freedom of indeterminacy remains, even on the background of physical indeterminacy, a mere speculative possibility.

THE CASE FOR DETERMINISM. Whereas the evidence for the free-will doctrine is largely humanistic and moralistic, the case for determinism is an appeal to scientific evidence; the determinist finds that the sciences of *physiology, psychology,* and *sociology* afford evidence that human behaviour is no exception to the casual uniformity of nature.

(1) *Physiological evidence.* The more we know about the physiological and neural processes which go on inside the human organism, even when it reacts to the most complicated of stimuli, the more evident it becomes that there is no break in the continuous chain of causation. Physiology gives us a reasonably clear picture of the mechanism of human behaviour. The behaviourists, the most recent recruits to the cause of determinism, have with infinite patience applied the objective method of the physiologists to human conduct; they have described in the minutest detail the mechanism of reflexes and the manner of their conditioning. There seems to remain no missing link in the causal chain from stimulus to ultimate response—even when that response is long "delayed." Delayed responses are mediated by very complex neural processes which on their subjective side are called conflict, indecision, and deliberation, but they are no exception to the behaviouristic formula.

(2) *Psychological evidence.* While the deterministic thesis receives its most obvious support from physiology and behaviouristic psychology, introspective psychology makes its contribution also. An unbiased introspective examination of volition supports the theory of psychological determinism. The more carefully I scrutinize my decisions, the more clearly do I discern the motives which determine them. If one's powers of introspection were sufficiently developed, one could presumably after any decision discover the exact psychological influences which rendered that particular decision inevitable. Doubtless for a complete explanation of certain decisions it is necessary in addition to the conscious antecedents of the volitional act to recover the more recondite sub-conscious and unconscious influences; the extensive researches of the Freudians into the submerged factors in human motivation provide the explanation of otherwise inexplicable mental acts and therefore tend to supply the missing links in the chain of psychic causation. Indeed, the existence of consciously inexplicable conscious events was one of the most compelling reasons for the original positing of an unconscious or subconscious mind. It remains true, however, that a fairly complete account of the psychological causation of volitional decisions is possible even without recourse to an unconscious mind.

Perhaps the best classical statement of the case for psychological determinism was given by David Hume. Hume, whose introspective subtlety has rarely been surpassed, commits himself unequivocally to psychological determinism in his assertion that "There is a great uniformity among the actions of men. . . . *The same motives always produce the same actions.*" Every historian, as Hume points out, appeals to this principle in judging the accuracy of historical documents; he asks himself whether the reported actions conform to what is known of human nature. And we might add, the same criterion is appealed to even in the evaluation of works of fiction. The novelist or the playwright gives a portrayal of his characters, he places them in definite situations, and then describes how they act. If his account of their behaviour under these precisely defined circumstances violates any of the recognized laws of human motivation, his literary and dramatic artistry is to that extent defective. Thus the principle of psychological determinism serves as a recognized canon on historical, literary, and dramatic criticism, and while this does not "prove" the correctness of psychological determinism, it does afford confirmation of it from an unsuspected quarter.

(3) *Sociological evidence.* The social sciences yield abundant evidence for a deterministic view of human behaviour. The fact that the conduct of large aggregates of individuals is expressible in terms of statistical law, although it is by no means a conclusive proof of individual determinism, certainly points in that direction. I may not be able to predict how you as an individual will behave in any specified circumstances, but I can formulate a

statistical law applicable to a large group of individuals of which you are a member. It is difficult to reconcile the possibility of the laws of groups or mass action with individual free-will.

The conclusion reached as a result of the survey of the arguments on both sides of the free-will controversy is that the strength of the deterministic position lies not only in the overwhelming array of psychological, physiological, and sociological evidence for the uniformity of human behaviour, but also in its ability to meet the psychological, moral, and religious "proofs" of free-will. Accordingly, we seem fully justified in concluding that a capricious free-will, that is to say, a will capable of acting independently of antecedent conditions, psychological or physiological, is a philosophical absurdity.

The Dilemma of Determinism[*]

WILLIAM JAMES [1842–1910]. See page 166.

A common opinion prevails that the juice has ages ago been pressed out of the free-will controversy, and that no new champion can do more than warm up stale arguments which every one has heard. This is a radical mistake. I know of no subject less worn out, or in which inventive genius has a better chance of breaking open new ground,—not, perhaps, of forcing a conclusion or of coercing assent, but of deepening our sense of what the issue between the two parties really is, of what the ideas of fate and of free-will imply. . . .

The arguments I am about to urge all proceed on two suppositions: first, when we make theories about the world and discuss them with one another, we do so in order to attain a conception of things which shall give us subjective satisfaction; and, second, if there be two conceptions, and the one seems to us, on the whole, more rational than the other, we are entitled to suppose that the more rational one is the truer of the two. I hope that you are all willing to make these suppositions with me; for I am afraid that if there be any of you here who are not, they will find little edification in the rest of what I have to say. I cannot stop to argue the point; but I myself believe that all the magnificent achievements of mathematical and physical science—our

[*] From James: "The Dilemma of Determinism," An address to the Harvard Divinity Students published in the Unitarian Review, 1884. Also available in James: Essays on Faith and Morals, Longmans, Green and Co., 1949.

doctrines of evolution, of uniformity of law, and the rest—proceed from our indomitable desire to cast the world into a more rational shape in our minds than the shape into which it is thrown there by the crude order of our experience. The world has shown itself, to a great extent, plastic to this demand of ours for rationality. How much farther it will show itself plastic no one can say. Our only means of finding out is to try; and I, for one, feel as free to try conceptions of moral as of mechanical or of logical rationality. If a certain formula for expressing the nature of the world violates my moral demand, I shall feel as free to throw it overboard, or at least to doubt it, as if it disappointed my demand for uniformity of sequence, for example; the one demand being, so far as I can see, quite as subjective and emotional as the other is. The principle of causality, for example,—what is it but a postulate, an empty name covering simply a demand that the sequence of events shall some day manifest a deeper kind of belonging of one thing with another than the mere arbitrary juxtaposition which now phenomenally appears? It is as much an altar to an unknown god as the one that Saint Paul found at Athens. All our scientific and philosophic ideals are altars to unknown gods. Uniformity is as much so as is free-will. If this be admitted, we can debate on even terms. But if any one pretends that while freedom and variety are, in the first instance, subjective demands, necessity and uniformity are something altogether different, I do not see how we can debate at all.

To begin, then, I must suppose you acquainted with the usual arguments on the subject. I cannot stop to take up the old proofs from causation, from statistics, from the certainty with which we can foretell one another's conduct, from the fixity of character, and all the rest. But there are two *words* which usually encumber these classical arguments, and which we must immediately dispose of if we are to make any progress. One is the eulogistic word *freedom*, and the other is the opprobrious word *chance*. The word 'chance' I wish to keep, but I wish to get rid of the word 'freedom.' Its eulogistic associations have so far overshadowed all the rest of its meaning that both parties claim the sole right to use it, and determinists to-day insist that they alone are freedom's champions. Old-fashioned determinism was what we may call *hard* determinism. It did not shrink from such words as fatality, bondage of the will, necessitation, and the like. Nowadays, we have a *soft* determinism which abhors harsh words, and, repudiating fatality, necessity, and even predetermination, says that its real name is freedom; for freedom is only necessity understood, and bondage to the highest is identical with true freedom. . . .

Now, all this is a quagmire of evasion under which the real issue of fact has been entirely smothered. . . . But there *is* a problem, an issue of fact and not of words, an issue of the most momentous importance, which is often decided without discussion in one sentence,—nay, in one clause of a sentence,—by those very writers who spin out whole chapters in their efforts to show what 'true' freedom is; and that is the question of determinism, about which we are to talk to-night.

Fortunately, no ambiguities hang about this word or about its opposite, indeterminism. Both designate an outward way in which things may happen, and their cold and mathematical sound has no sentimental associations that can bribe our partiality either way in advance. Now, evidence of an external kind to decide between determinism and indeterminism is strictly impossible to find. Let us look at the difference between them and see for ourselves. What does determinism profess?

It professes that those parts of the universe already laid down absolutely appoint and decree what the other parts shall be. The future has no ambiguous possibilities hidden in its womb: the part we call the present is compatible with only one totality. Any other future complement than the one fixed from eternity is impossible. The whole is in each and every part, and welds it with the rest into an absolute unity, an iron block, in which there can be no equivocation or shadow of turning.

> With earth's first clay they did the last man knead,
> And there of the last harvest sowed the seed.
> And the first morning of creation wrote
> What the last dawn of reckoning shall read.

Indeterminism, on the contrary, says that the parts have a certain amount of loose play on one another, so that the laying down of one of them does not necessarily determine what the others shall be. It admits that possibilities may be in excess of actualities, and that things not yet revealed to our knowledge may really in themselves be ambiguous. Of two alternative futures which we conceive, both may now be really possible; and the one become impossible only at the very moment when the other excludes it by becoming real itself. Indeterminism thus denies the world to be one unbending unit of fact. It says there is a certain ultimate pluralism in it; and, so saying, it corroborates our ordinary unsophisticated view of things. To that view, actualities seem to float in a wider sea of possibilities from out of which they are chosen; and, *somewhere*, indeterminism says, such possibilities exist, and form a part of truth.

Determinism, on the contrary, says they exist *nowhere*, and that necessity on the one hand and impossibility on the other are the sole categories of the real. Possibilities that fail to get realized are, for determinism, pure illusions: they never were possibilities at all. There is nothing inchoate, it says, about this universe of ours, all that was or is or shall be actual in it having been from eternity virtually there. The cloud of alternatives our minds escort this mass of actuality withal is a cloud of sheer deceptions, to which 'impossibilities' is the only name that rightfully belongs.

The issue, it will be seen, is a perfectly sharp one, which no eulogistic terminology can smear over or wipe out. The truth *must* lie with one side or the other, and its lying with one side makes the other false.

The question relates solely to the existence of possibilities, in the strict sense of the term, as things that may, but need not, be. Both sides admit that a volition, for instance, has occurred. The indeterminists say another volition might have occurred in its place: the determinists swear that nothing could possibly have occurred in its place. Now, can science be called in to tell us which of these two point-blank contradicters of each other is right? Science professes to draw no conclusions but such as are based on matters of fact, things that have actually happened; but how can any amount of assurance that something actually happened give us the least grain of information as to whether another thing might or might not have happened in its place? Only facts can be proved by other facts. With things that are possibilities and not facts, facts have no concern. If we have no other evidence than the evidence of existing facts, the possibility-question must remain a mystery never to be cleared up.

And the truth is that facts practically have hardly anything to do with making us either determinists or indeterminists. Sure enough, we make a flourish of quoting facts this way or that; and if we are determinists, we talk about the infallibility with which we can predict one another's conduct; while if we are indeterminists, we lay great stress on the fact that it is just because we cannot foretell one another's conduct, either in war or statecraft or in any of the great and small intrigues and businesses of men, that life is so intensely anxious and hazardous a game. But who does not see the wretched insufficiency of this so-called objective testimony on both sides? What fills up the gaps in our minds is something not objective, not external. What divides us into possibility men and anti-possibility men is different faiths or postulates,—postulates of rationality. To this man the world seems more rational with possibilities in it,—to that man more rational with possibilities excluded; and talk as we will about having to yield to evidence, what makes us monists or pluralists, determinists or indeterminists, is at bottom always some sentiment like this.

The stronghold of the deterministic sentiment is the antipathy to the idea of chance. As soon as we begin to talk indeterminism to our friends, we find a number of them shaking their heads. This notion of alternative possibility, they say, this admission that any one of several things may come to pass, is, after all, only a roundabout name for chance; and chance is something the notion of which no sane mind can for an instant tolerate in the world. What is it, they ask, but barefaced crazy unreason, the negation of intelligibility and law? And if the slightest particle of it exist anywhere, what is to prevent the whole fabric from falling together, the stars from going out, and chaos from recommencing her topsy-turvy reign?

Remarks of this sort about chance will put an end to discussion as quickly as anything one can find. I have already told you that 'chance' was a word I wished to keep and use. Let us then examine exactly what it means, and see whether it ought to be such a terrible bugbear to us. I fancy that squeezing the thistle boldly will rob it of its sting.

The sting of the word 'chance' seems to lie in the assumption that it means something positive, and that if anything happens by chance, it must needs be something of an intrinsically irrational and preposterous sort. Now, chance means nothing of the kind. It is a purely negative and relative term, giving us no information about that of which it is predicated, except that it happens to be disconnected with something else,—not controlled, secured, or necessitated by other things in advance of its own actual presence. As this point is the most subtle one of the whole lecture, and at the same time the point on which all the rest hinges, I beg you to pay particular attention to it. What I say is that it tells us nothing about what a thing may be in itself to call it 'chance.' It may be a bad thing, it may be a good thing. It may be lucidity, transparency, fitness incarnate, matching the whole system of other things, when it has once befallen, in an unimaginably perfect way. All you mean by calling it 'chance' is that this is not guaranteed, that it may also fall out otherwise. . . .

Nevertheless, many persons talk as if the minutest dose of disconnectedness of one part with another, the smallest modicum of independence, the faintest tremor of ambiguity about the future, for example, would ruin everything, and turn this goodly universe into a sort of insane sand-heap or nulliverse, no universe at all. Since future human volitions are as a matter of fact the only ambiguous things we are tempted to believe in, let us stop for a moment to make ourselves sure whether their independent and accidental character need be fraught with such direful consequences to the universe as these.

What is meant by saying that my choice of which way to walk home after the lecture is ambiguous and matter of chance as far as the present moment is concerned? It means that both Divinity Avenue and Oxford Street are called; but that only one, and that one *either* one, shall be chosen. Now, I ask you seriously to suppose that this ambiguity of my choice is real; and then to make the impossible hypothesis that the choice is made twice over, and each time falls on a different street. In other words, imagine that I first walk through Divinity Avenue, and then imagine that the powers governing the universe annihilate ten minutes of time with all that it contained, and set me back at the door of this hall just as I was before the choice was made. Imagine then that, everything else being the same, I now make a different choice and traverse Oxford Street. You, as passive spectators, look on and see the two alternative universes,—one of them with me walking through Divinity Avenue in it, the other with the same me walking through Oxford Street. Now, if you are determinists you believe one of these universes to have been from eternity impossible: you believe it to have been impossible because of the intrinsic irrationality or accidentality somewhere involved in it. But looking outwardly at these universes, can you say which is the impossible and accidental one, and which the rational and necessary one? I doubt if the most ironclad determinist among you could have the slightest glimmer of light on this point. In other words, either universe *after the fact* and once there would, to our means of observation and understanding, appear just as rational as the other. There would be absolutely no criterion by which we might judge one necessary and the other matter of chance. Suppose now we relieve the gods of their hypothetical task and assume my choice, once made, to be made forever. I go through Divinity Avenue for good and all. If, as good determinists, you now begin to affirm, what all good determinists punctually do affirm, that in the nature of things I *couldn't* have gone through Oxford Street,—had I done so it would have been chance, irrationality, insanity, a horrid gap in nature,—I simply call your attention to this, that your affirmation is what the Germans call a *Machtspruch*, a mere conception fulminated as a dogma and based on no insight into details. Before my choice, either street seemed as natural to you as to me. Had I happened to take Oxford Street, Divinity Avenue would have figured in your philosophy as the gap in nature; and you would have so proclaimed it with the best deterministic conscience in the world.

But what a hollow outcry, then, is this against a chance which, if it were present to us, we could by no character whatever distinguish from a rational necessity! . . . The more one thinks of the matter, the more one wonders that so empty and gratuitous a hubbub as this outcry against chance should have found so great an echo in the hearts of men. It is a word which tells us absolutely nothing about what chances, or about the *modus operandi* of the chancing; and the use of it as a war-cry shows only a temper of intellectual absolutism, a demand that the world shall be a solid block, subject to one control,—which temper, which demand, the world may not be bound to gratify at all. In every outwardly verifiable and practical respect, a world in which the alternatives that now actually distract *your* choice were decided by pure chance would be by *me* absolutely undistinguished from the world in which I now live. I am, therefore, entirely willing to call it, so far as your choices go, a world of chance for me. To *yourselves,* it is true, those very acts of choice, which to me are so blind, opaque, and external, are the opposites of this, for you are within them and effect them. To you they appear as decisions; and decisions, for him who makes them, are altogether peculiar psychic facts. Self-luminous and self-justifying at the living moment at which they occur, they appeal to no outside moment to put its stamp upon them or make them continuous with the rest of nature. Themselves it is rather who seem to make nature continuous; and in their strange and intense function of granting consent to one possibility and withholding it from another, to transform an equivocal and double feature into an inalterable and simple past.

But with the psychology of the matter we have no concern this evening. The quarrel which determinism has with chance fortunately has nothing to do with this or that psychological detail. It is a quarrel altogether metaphysical. Determinism denies the ambiguity of future volitions, because it affirms that nothing future can be ambiguous. But we have said enough to meet the issue. Indeterminate future volitions *do* mean chance. . . .

We have seen what determinism means: we have seen that indeterminism is rightly described as meaning chance; and we have seen that chance, the very name of which we are urged to shrink from as from a metaphysical pestilence, means only the negative fact that no part of the world, however big, can claim to control absolutely the destinies of the whole. But although, in discussing the word 'chance,' I may at moments have seemed to be arguing for its real existence, I have not meant to do so yet. We have not yet ascertained whether this be a world of chance or no; at most, we have agreed that it seems so. And I now repeat what I said at the outset, that, from any strict theoretical point of view, the question is insoluble. To deepen our theoretic sense of the *difference* between a world with chances in it and a deterministic world is the most I can hope to do; and this I may now at last begin upon, after all our tedious clearing of the way.

I wish first of all to show you just what the notion that this is a deterministic world implies. The implications I call your attention to are all bound up with the fact that it is a world in which we constantly have to make what I shall, with your permission, call judgments of regret. Hardly an hour passes in which we do not wish that something might be otherwise; and happy indeed are those of us whose hearts have never echoed the wish of Omar Khayam—

> That we might clasp, ere closed, the book of fate,
> And make the writer on a fairer leaf
> Inscribe our names, or quite obliterate.

Ah! Love, could you and I with fate conspire
To mend this sorry scheme of things entire,
  Would we not shatter it to bits, and then
Remould it nearer to the heart's desire?

Now, it is undeniable that most of these regrets are foolish, and quite on a par in point of philosophic value with the criticisms on the universe of that friend of our infancy, the hero of the fable The Atheist and the Acorn,—

Fool! had that bough a pumpkin bore,
Thy whimsies would have worked no more, etc.

Even from the point of view of our own ends, we should probably make a botch of remodelling the universe. How much more then from the point of view of ends we cannot see! Wise men therefore regret as little as they can. But still some regrets are pretty obstinate and hard to stifle,—regrets for acts of wanton cruelty or treachery, for example, whether performed by others or by ourselves. Hardly any one can remain *entirely* optimistic after reading the confession of the murderer at Brockton the other day: how, to get rid of the wife whose continued existence bored him, he inveigled her into a desert spot, shot her four times, and then, as she lay on the ground and said to him, "You didn't do it on purpose, did you, dear?" replied, "No, I didn't do it on purpose," as he raised a rock and smashed her skull. Such an occurrence, with the mild sentence and self-satisfaction of the prisoner, is a field for a crop of regrets, which one need not take up in detail. We feel that, although a perfect mechanical fit to the rest of the universe, it is a bad moral fit, and that something else would really have been better in its place.

But for the deterministic philosophy the murder, the sentence, and the prisoner's optimism were all necessary from eternity; and nothing else for a moment had a ghost of a chance of being put into their place. To admit such a chance, the determinists tell us, would be to make a suicide of reason; so we must steel our hearts against the thought. And here our plot thickens, for we see the first of those difficult implications of determinism and monism which it is my purpose to make you feel. If this Brockton murder was called for by the rest of the universe, if it had to come at its preappointed hour, and if nothing else would have been consistent with the sense of the whole, what are we to think of the universe? Are we stubbornly to stick to our judgment of regret, and say, though it *couldn't* be, yet it *would* have been a better universe with something different from this Brockton murder in it? That, of course, seems the natural and spontaneous thing for us to do; and yet it is nothing short of deliberately espousing a kind of pessimism. The judgment of regret calls the murder bad. Calling a thing bad means, if it mean anything at all, that the thing ought not to be, that something else ought to be in its stead. Determinism, in denying that anything else can be in its stead, virtually defines the universe as a place in which what ought to be is impossible,—in other words, as an organism whose constitution is afflicted with an incurable taint, an irremediable flaw. The pessimism of a Schopenhauer says no more than this,—that the murder is a symptom; and that it is a vicious symptom because it belongs to a vicious whole, which can express its nature no otherwise than by bringing forth just such a symptom as that at this particular spot. Regret for the murder must transform itself, if we are determinists and wise, into a larger regret. It is absurd to regret the murder alone. Other things being what they are, *it* could not be different. What we should regret is that whole frame of things of which the murder is one member. I see no escape whatever from this pessimistic conclusion, if, being determinists, our judgment of regret is to be allowed to stand at all.

The only deterministic escape from pessimism is everywhere to abandon the judgment of regret. That this can be done, history shows to be not impossible. The devil, *quoad existentiam*, may be good. That is, although he be a *principle* of evil, yet the universe, with such a principle in it, may practically be a better universe than it could have been without. On every hand, in a small way, we find that a certain amount of evil is a condition by which a higher form of good is brought. There is nothing to prevent anybody from generalizing this view, and trusting that if we could but see things in the largest of all ways, even such matters as this Brockton murder would appear to be paid for by the uses that follow in their train. An optimism *quand même*, a systematic and infatuated optimism like that ridiculed by Voltaire in his Candide, is one of the possible ideal ways in which a man may train himself to look on life. Bereft of dogmatic hardness and lit up with the expression of a tender and pathetic hope, such an optimism has been the grace of some of the most religious characters that ever lived.

> Throb thine with Nature's throbbing breast,
> And all is clear from east to west.

Even cruelty and treachery may be among the absolutely blessed fruits of time, and to quarrel with any of their details may be blasphemy. The only real blasphemy, in short, may be that pessimistic temper of the soul which lets it give way to such things as regrets, remorse, and grief.

Thus, our deterministic pessimism may become a deterministic optimism at the price of extinguishing our judgments of regret.

But does not this immediately bring us into a curious logical predicament? Our determinism leads us to call our judgments of regret wrong, because they are pessimistic in implying that what is impossible yet ought to be. But how then about the judgments of regret themselves? If they are wrong, other judgments, judgments of approval presumably, ought to be in their place. But as they are necessitated, nothing else *can* be in their place; and the universe is just what it was before,—namely, a place in which what ought to be appears impossible. We have got one foot out of the pessimistic bog, but the other one sinks all the deeper. We have rescued our actions from the bonds of evil, but our judgments are now held fast. When murders and treacheries cease to be sins, regrets are theoretic absurdities and errors. The theoretic and the active life thus play a kind of see-saw with each other on the ground of evil. The rise of either sends the other down. Murder and treachery cannot be good without regret being bad: regret cannot be good without treachery and murder being bad. Both, however, are supposed to have been foredoomed; so something must be fatally unreasonable, absurd, and wrong in the world. It must be a place of which either sin or error forms a necessary part. From this dilemma there seems at first sight no escape. . . .

The only consistent way of representing a pluralism and a world whose parts may affect one another through their conduct being either good or bad is the indeterministic way. What interest, zest, or excitement can there be in achieving the right way, unless we are enabled to feel that the wrong way is also a possible and a natural way,—nay, more, a menacing and an imminent way? And what sense can there be in condemning ourselves for taking the wrong way, unless we need have done nothing of the sort, unless the right way was open to us as well? I cannot understand the willingness to act, no matter how we feel, without the belief that acts are really good and bad. I cannot understand the belief that an act is bad, without regret at its happening. I cannot understand regret without the admission of real, genuine possibilities in the world. Only *then* is it other than a mockery to feel, after we have failed to do our best, that an irreparable opportunity is gone from the universe, the loss of which it must forever after mourn.

If you insist that this is all superstition, that possibility is in the eye of science and reason impossibility, and that if I act badly 'tis that the universe was foredoomed to suffer this defect, you fall right back into the dilemma, the labyrinth, of pessimism, from out of whose toils we have just wound our way.

Now, we are of course free to fall back, if we please. For my own part, though, whatever difficulties may beset the philosophy of objective right and wrong, and the indeterminism it seems to imply, determinism, with its alternative of pessimism or romanticism, contains difficulties that are greater still. But you will remember that I expressly repudiated awhile ago the pretension to offer any arguments which could be coercive in a so-called scientific fashion in this matter. And I consequently find myself, at the end of this long talk, obliged to state my conclusions in an altogether personal way. This personal method of appeal seems to be among the very conditions of the problem; and the most any one can do is to confess as candidly as he can the grounds for the faith that is in him, and leave his example to work on others as it may.

Let me, then, without circumlocution say just this. The world is enigmatical enough in all conscience, whatever theory we may take up toward it. The indeterminism I defend, the free-will theory of popular sense based on the judgment of regret, represents that world as vulnerable, and liable to be injured by certain of its parts if they act wrong. And it represents their acting wrong as a matter of possibility or accident, neither inevitable nor yet to be infallibly warded off. In all this, it is a theory devoid either of transparency or of stability. It gives us a pluralistic, restless universe, in which no single point of view can ever take in the whole scene; and to a mind possessed of the love of unity at any cost, it will, no doubt, remain forever inacceptable. A friend with such a mind once told me that the thought of my universe made him sick, like the sight of the horrible motion of a mass of maggots in their carrion bed.

But while I freely admit that the pluralism and the restlessness are repugnant and irrational in a certain way, I find that every alternative to them is irrational in a deeper way. The indeterminism with its maggots, if you please to speak so about it, offends only the native absolutism of my intellect,—an absolutism which, after all, perhaps, deserves to be snubbed and kept in check. But the determinism with its necessary carrion, to continue the figure of speech, and with no possible maggots to eat the latter up, violates my sense of moral reality through and through. When, for example, I imagine such carrion as the Brockton murder, I cannot conceive it as an act by which the universe, as a whole, logically and necessarily expresses its nature without shrinking from complicity with such a whole. And I deliberately refuse to keep on terms of loyalty with the universe by saying blankly that the murder, since it does flow from the nature of the whole, is not carrion. There are *some* instinctive reactions which I, for one, will not tamper with. . . .

Make as great an uproar about chance as you please, I know that chance means pluralism and nothing more. If some of the members of the pluralism are bad, the philosophy of pluralism, whatever broad views it may deny me, permits me, at least, to turn to the other members with a clean breast of affection and an unsophisticated moral sense. And if I still wish to think of the world as a totality, it lets me feel that a world with a *chance* in it of being altogether good, even if the chance never come to pass, is better than a world with no such chance at all. That 'chance' whose very notion I am exhorted and conjured to banish from my view of the future as the suicide of reason concerning it, that 'chance' is—what? Just this,—the chance that in moral respects the future may be other and better than the past has been. This is the only chance we have any motive for supposing to exist. Shame, rather, on its repudiation and its denial! For its presence is the vital air which lets the world live, the salt which keeps it sweet.

The Myth of Volitions*

GILBERT RYLE [1900–   ]. See p. 176.

It has for a long time been taken for an indisputable axiom that the Mind is in some important sense tripartite, that is, that there are just three ultimate classes of mental processes. The Mind or Soul, we are often told, has three parts, namely, Thought, Feeling and Will; or more solemnly, the Mind or Soul functions in three irreducibly different modes, the Cognitive mode, the Emotional mode and the Conative mode. This traditional dogma is not only not self-evident, it is such a welter of confusions and false inferences that it is best to give up any attempt to re-fashion it. It should be treated as one of the curios of theory.

The main object of this chapter is not, however, to discuss the whole trinitarian theory of mind but to discuss, and discuss destructively, one of its ingredients. I hope to refute the doctrine that there exists a Faculty, immaterial Organ, or Ministry, corresponding to the theory's description of the 'Will' and, accordingly, that there occur processes, or operations, corresponding to what it describes as 'volitions.' . . .

Volitions have been postulated as special acts, or operations, 'in the mind,' by means of which a mind gets its ideas translated into facts. I think of some state of affairs which I wish to come into existence in the physical world, but, as my thinking and wishing are unexecutive, they require the mediation of a further executive mental process. So I perform a volition which somehow puts my muscles into action. Only when a bodily movement has issued from such a volition can I merit praise or blame for what my hand or tongue has done.

It will be clear why I reject this story. It is just an inevitable extension of

* From Ryle: *The Concept of Mind,* 1949, Chapter 3. Published by Hutchinson's University Library, London, and Barnes and Noble, Inc., New York. Reprinted by Permission of Hutchinson Publishing Group, Ltd., and Barnes and Noble, Inc.

the myth of the ghost in the machine [i.e. Dualistic Interactionism]. It assumes that there are mental states and processes enjoying one sort of existence, and bodily states and processes enjoying another. An occurrence on the one stage is never numerically identical with an occurrence on the other. So, to say that a person pulled the trigger intentionally is to express at least a conjunctive proposition, asserting the occurrence of one act on the physical stage and another on the mental stage; and, according to most versions of the myth, it is to express a causal proposition, asserting that the bodily act of pulling the trigger was the effect of a mental act of willing to pull the trigger.

According to the theory, the workings of the body are motions of matter in space. The causes of these motions must then be *either* other motions of matter in space *or,* in the privileged case of human beings, thrusts of another kind. In some way which must forever remain a mystery, mental thrusts, which are not movements of matter in space, can cause muscles to contract. To describe a man as intentionally pulling the trigger is to state that such a mental thrust did cause the contraction of the muscles of his finger. . . .

The first objection to the doctrine that overt actions, to which we ascribe intelligence-predicates, are results of counterpart hidden operations of willing is this. Despite the fact that theorists have, since the Stoics and Saint Augustine, recommended us to describe our conduct in this way, no one, save to endorse the theory, ever describes his own conduct, or that of his acquaintances, in the recommended idioms. No one ever says such things as that at 10 a.m. he was occupied in willing this or that, or that he performed five quick and easy volitions and two slow and difficult volitions between midday and lunch-time. An accused person may admit or deny that he did something, or that he did it on purpose, but he never admits or denies having willed. Nor do the judge and jury require to be satisfied by evidence, which in the nature of the case could never be adduced, that a volition preceded the pulling of the trigger. Novelists describe the actions, remarks, gestures and grimaces, the daydreams, deliberations, qualms and embarrassments of their characters; but they never mention their volitions. They would not know what to say about them.

By what sorts of predicates should they be described? Can they be sudden or gradual, strong or weak, difficult or easy, enjoyable or disagreeable? Can they be accelerated, decelerated, interrupted, or suspended? Can people be efficient or inefficient at them? Can we take lessons in executing them? Are they fatiguing or distracting? Can I do two or seven of them synchronously? Can I remember executing them? Can I execute them, while thinking of other things, or while dreaming? Can they become habitual? Can I forget how to do them? Can I mistakenly believe that I have executed one, when I have not, or that I have not executed one, when I have? At which moment was the boy going through a volition to take the high dive? When he set foot on the ladder? When he took his first deep breath? When he counted off 'One, two, three—Go,' but did not go? Very, very shortly before he sprang? What would his own answer be to those questions?

Champions of the doctrine maintain, of course, that the enactment of volitions is asserted by implication, whenever an overt act is described as intentional, voluntary, culpable or meritorious; they assert too that any person is not merely able but bound to know that he is willing when he is doing so, since volitions are defined as a species of conscious process. So if ordinary men and women fail to mention their volitions in their descriptions of their own behaviour, this must be due to their being untrained in the dictions appropriate to the description of their inner, as distinct from their overt, behaviour. However, when a champion of the doctrine is himself asked how long ago he executed his last volition, or how many acts of will he executes in, say, reciting 'Little Miss Muffet' backwards, he is apt to confess to finding difficulties in giving the answer, though these difficulties should not, according to his own theory, exist.

If ordinary men never report the occurrence of these acts, for all that, according to the theory, they should be encountered vastly more frequently than headaches, or feelings of boredom; if ordinary vocabulary has no non-academic names for them; if we do not know how to settle simple questions about their frequency, duration or strength, then it is fair to conclude that their existence is not asserted on empirical grounds. The fact that Plato and Aristotle never mentioned them in their frequent and elaborate discussions of the nature of the soul and the springs of conduct is due not to any perverse neglect by them of notorious ingredients of daily life but to the historical circumstance that they were not acquainted with a special hypothesis the acceptance of which rests not on the discovery, but on the postulation, of these ghostly thrusts.

The second objection is this. It is admitted that one person can never witness the volitions of another; he can only infer from an observed overt action to the volition from which it resulted, and then only if he has any good reason to believe that the overt action was a voluntary action, and not a reflex or habitual action, or one resulting from some external cause. It follows that no judge, schoolmaster, or parent ever knows that the actions which he judges merit praise or blame; for he cannot do better than guess that the action was willed. Even a confession by the agent, if such confessions were ever made, that he had executed a volition before his hand did the deed would not settle the question. The pronouncement of the confession is only another overt muscular action. The curious conclusion results that though volitions were called in to explain our appraisals of actions, this explanation is just what they fail to provide. If we had no other antecedent grounds for applying appraisal-concepts to the actions of others, we should have no reasons at all for inferring from those actions to the volitions alleged to give rise to them.

Nor could it be maintained that the agent himself can know that any overt action of his own is the effect of a given volition. Supposing, what is not the case, that he could know for certain, either from the alleged direct deliverances of consciousness, or from the alleged direct findings of introspection, that he had executed an act of will to pull the trigger just before he pulled it, this would not prove that the pulling was the effect of that willing. The connection between volitions and movements is allowed to be mysterious, so, for all he knows, his volition may have had some other movement as its effect and the pulling of the trigger may have had some other event for its cause.

Thirdly, it would be improper to burke the point that the connection between volition and movement is admitted to be a mystery. It is a mystery not of the unsolved but soluble type, like the problem of the cause of cancer, but of quite another type. The episodes supposed to constitute the careers of minds are assumed to have one sort of existence, while those constituting the careers of bodies have another sort; and no bridge-status is allowed. Transactions between minds and bodies involve links where no links can be. That there should be any causal transactions between minds and matter conflicts with one part, that there should be none conflicts with another part of the theory. Minds, as the whole legend describes them, are what must exist if there is to be a causal explanation of the intelligent behaviour of human bodies; and minds, as the legend describes them, live on a floor of existence defined as being outside the causal system to which bodies belong.

Fourthly, although the prime function of volitions, the task for the performance of which they were postulated, is to originate bodily movements, the argument, such as it is, for their existence entails that some mental happenings also must result from acts of will. Volitions were postulated to be that which makes actions voluntary, resolute, meritorious and wicked. But predicates of these sorts are ascribed not only to bodily movements but also to operations which, according to the theory, are mental and not physical operations. A thinker may ratiocinate resolutely, or imagine wickedly; he may try to compose a limerick and he may meritoriously concentrate on his algebra. Some mental processes then can, according to the theory, issue from volitions. So what of volitions themselves? Are they voluntary or involuntary acts of mind? Clearly either answer leads to absurdities. If I cannot help willing to pull the trigger, it would be absurd to describe my pulling it as 'voluntary.' But if my volition to pull the trigger is voluntary, in the sense assumed by the theory, then it must issue from a prior volition and that from another *ad infinitum*. It has been suggested, to avoid this difficulty, that volitions can not be described as either voluntary or involuntary. 'Volition' is a term of the wrong type to accept either predicate. If so, it would seem to follow that it is also of the wrong type to accept such predicates as 'virtuous' and 'wicked,' 'good' and 'bad,' a conclusion which might embarrass those moralists who use volitions as the sheet-anchor of their systems.

In short, then, the doctrine of volitions is a causal hypothesis, adopted because it was wrongly supposed that the question, 'What makes a bodily movement voluntary?' was a causal question. This supposition is, in fact, only a special twist of the general supposition that the question, 'How are mental-conduct concepts applicable to human behaviour?' is a question about the causation of that behaviour.

Champions of the doctrine should have noticed the simple fact that they and all other sensible persons knew how to decide questions about the voluntariness and involuntariness of actions and about the resoluteness and irresoluteness of agents before they had ever heard of the hypothesis of the occult inner thrusts of actions. They might then have realised that they were not elucidating the criteria already in efficient use, but, tacitly assuming their validity, were trying to correlate them with hypothetical occurrences of a para-mechanical pattern. Yet this correlation could, on the one hand, never be scientifically established, since the thrusts postulated were screened from scientific observation; and, on the other hand, it would be of no practical or theoretical use, since it would not assist our appraisals of actions, depending as it would on the presupposed validity of those appraisals. Nor would it elucidate the logic of those appraisal-concepts, the intelligent employment of which antedated the invention of this causal hypothesis.

Before we bid farewell to the doctrine of volitions, it is expedient to consider certain quite familiar and authentic processes with which volitions are sometimes wrongly identified.

People are frequently in doubt what to do; having considered alternative courses of action, they then, sometimes, select or choose one of these courses. This process of opting for one of a set of alternative courses of action is sometimes said to be what is signified by 'volition'. But this identification will not do, for most voluntary actions do not issue out of conditions of indecision and are not therefore results of settlements of indecisions. Moreover it is notorious that a person may choose to do something but fail, from weakness of will, to do it; or he may fail to do it because some circumstance arises after the choice is made, preventing the execution of the act chosen. But the theory could not allow that volitions ever fail to result in action, else further executive operations would have to be postulated to account for the fact that sometimes voluntary actions are performed. And finally the process of deliberating between alternatives and opting for one of them is itself subject to appraisal-predicates. But if, for example, an act of choosing is describable as voluntary, then, on this suggested showing, it would have in its turn to be the result of a prior choice to choose, and that from a choice to choose to choose. . . .

The same objections forbid the identification with volitions of such other familiar processes as that of resolving or making up our minds to do something and that of nerving or bracing ourselves to do something. I may resolve to get out of bed or go to the dentist, and I may, clenching my fists and gritting my teeth, brace myself to do so, but I may still backslide. If the action is not done, then, according to the doctrine, the volition to do it is also unexecuted. Again, the operations of resolving and nerving ourselves are themselves members of the class of creditable or discreditable actions, so they cannot constitute the peculiar ingredient which, according to the doctrine, is the common condition of any performance being creditable or discreditable.

Science and Man[*]

A D O L F G R ü N B A U M [1923–   ] has been Andrew Mellon Professor of Philosophy at the University of Pittsburgh since 1960. He is best known for his writings on the philosophy of physics; his books include *Philosophical Problems of Space and Time* and *Modern Science and Feno's Paradoxes*.

The deterministic conception of *human behavior* is inspired by the view that man is an integral part and product of nature and that his behavior can reasonably be held to exhibit scientifically ascertainable regularities just as any other *macroscopic* sector of nature. Determinism must be distinguished from predictability, since there are at least two kinds of situations in which there may be no predictability even though determinism is true: (i) Though determinism may hold in virtue of the existence of one-to-one functional dependencies between specifiable attributes of events, some such attributes *may* be *"emergent"* in the sense of being unpredictable relatively to any and

[*] From Grünbaum: "Science and Man," reprinted from *Perspectives in Biology and Medicine*, Volume V, Number 4, 1962, by permission of the University of Chicago Press. Copyright 1962 by the University of Chicago. The original version of the essay has been extensively revised for this volume by the author.

all laws that could possibly have been discovered by us humans in advance of the first occurrence of the attribute(s) in question, and (ii) there are perverse persons who choose among alternative courses of action *not* in the light of the benefits that may accrue from the action but with a view to assuring that someone else's prediction of their choice behavior turns out to be false. And there are conditions under which such perverse persons are bound to succeed in behaving *contra*-predictively.

The opponent of determinism, or "indeterminist," maintains that determinism is *logically incompatible* with the known fact that people respond meaningfully to moral imperatives. Specifically, the indeterminist says: If each one of us makes decisions which are determined by the sum total of all the relevant influences upon us (heredity, environmental background, the stimuli affecting us at the moment, etc.), then no man can help doing what he does. And then the consequences are allegedly as follows: (a) It is impossible to account for our feeling that we are able to act freely except by dismissing it as devoid of any factual foundation. (b) It is useless to try to choose between good and bad courses of action. (c) It is meaningless to hold people responsible for their acts. (d) It is unjust to punish people for wrong-doing, or reward and praise them for good deeds. (e) It is mere self-delusion to feel remorse or guilt for past misdeeds.

Furthermore, the indeterminist often makes the ominous declaration that if determinism became known to the masses of people and were accepted by them, moral chaos would result, because—so he claims—everyone would forthwith drop his inhibitions. The excuse would be that he cannot help acting uninhibitedly, and people would fatalistically sink into a state of futility, laziness, and indifference. Moreover, we are told that if determinism were believed, the great fighters against injustice in human history would give up raising their voices in protest, since the truth of determinism would allegedly make such efforts useless.

Thus, the indeterminist goes on to contend that there is a basic *inconsistency* in *any* deterministic *and* activistic socio-political theory, the alleged inconsistency being the following: to *advocate* a social activism with the aim of thereby bringing about a future state whose eventuation the given theory regards as assured by historical causation. This argument is applied to any kind of deterministic theory independently of whether the explanatory variables of the historical process are held by that theory to be economic, climatic, sexual, demographic, geopolitical, or the inscrutable will of God. Accordingly, the indeterminist objects to such diverse doctrines as (a) Justice Oliver Wendell Holmes' dictum that the inevitable comes to pass through effort, and (b) St. Augustine's (and Calvin's) belief in divine foreordination, when coupled with the advocacy of Christian virtue. And correlatively, the indeterminist claims that if determinism is true, it is futile for men to discuss how to optimize the achievement of their ends by a change in personal or group behavior.

. . . [Another] argument that we shall consider is based on one of the consequences of the postulates of quantum physics. Results formulated by the Heisenberg Uncertainty Principle, which I shall state, have been claimed to show that there is at last a physical basis for the ethical claims of the philosophical indeterminist.

I shall argue that the quantum mechanical indeterminacies characterizing individual micro-processes of physics are *irrelevant* to the free-will problem.

The Argument from Morality

To introduce the objections to the indeterminist's argument from morality, we must remind the addict to the narcotic of Norman Vincent Peale's "positive thinking" of the following stubborn fact. If determinism did actually make moral imperatives meaningless by entailing that moral appraisals and exhortations rest on an illusion—which I shall argue it does not—then that would be simply tragic. But it could hardly be claimed that determinism is false on the mere grounds that its alleged consequences would be terrible. We would show concern for the sanity of anyone who would say that his house could not have burnt down because this fact would make him unhappy.

But is it actually the case that there are data from the field of human responses to moral rules which refute the deterministic hypothesis? I shall argue that the answer is decidedly negative. For I shall maintain that in important respects, the data are *not* what they are alleged to be. And in so far as they are, I shall argue that they are not evidence against determinism. Nay, I shall claim that in part, these data are first rendered intelligible by determinism. Furthermore, I shall show what precise meaning must be given to certain moral concepts like responsibility, remorse, and punishment within the context of a deterministic theory. Of course, determinism does exclude, as we shall see, *some* of the moral conceptions entertained by philosophical indeterminists. . . . But I shall maintain that this involves no actual loss for ethics. And we have already seen that even if it did, this would not constitute evidence against determinism. I wish to emphasize, however, that . . . the categorical truth of determinism can be established *not* by logical analysis alone but requires the working psychologist's empirical discovery of specific causal laws.

To establish the invalidity of the moral argument offered by the indeterminist, I shall now try to show that there is no incompatibility between the deterministic assumptions of scientific psychology, on the one hand, and the feelings of freedom which we actually do have, the meaningful assignment of responsibility, the infliction of punishment, and the existence of feelings of remorse or guilt on the other.

(a) CONFUSION OF DETERMINISM WITH FATALISM. The first point to be made clear is that determinism should never be identified with the prescientific and appallingly primitive doctrine of fatalism. The fatalist says that, in every situation, regardless of what we do, the outcome will be unaffected by our efforts. . . . Thus, if a diabetic is in glucose shock on a certain day, it is immaterial whether he is administered insulin or sugar: if his time is up on that day, he will die then in either case, and if he is destined to live beyond that day, he will survive it in either case. That a person dies at the time of his death is an utter triviality. And this triviality must *not* be permitted to confer plausibility on the fatalist's claim that a man dies when his time is up, since the fatalist intends this claim to assert that human effort to postpone death is *always* futile.

The latter false thesis of fatalism does not follow at all from determinism. The determinist believes that specifiable causes determine our actions and that these, in turn, determine the effects that will ensue from them. But this doctrine allows that human effort be efficacious in *some* contexts while being futile in others. Thus, determinism allows the existence of situations which are correctly characterized by Justice Oliver Wendell Holmes' epigram that the inevitable comes to pass through effort. The mere fact that both fatalism and determinism affirm the fixity or determinedness of future outcomes led indeterminists to infer fallaciously that determinism is committed to the futility of *all* human effort. The determinist maintains that existing causes determine or fix whether certain efforts will in fact be made at certain times while allowing that future outcomes are indeed effort-dependent in particular contexts. By contrast, the fatalist holds falsely that all outcomes are independent of the efforts made by us humans. But since the determinist's affirmation of the fixity of the outcome does *not* entail that the outcome is effort-independent, the futility of human effort in all cases cannot be deduced from determinism. As well deduce the following absurdity: determinism guarantees that explosions are always independent of the presence of detonating substances, because determinism affirms that in specified contexts the effects of the presence of explosives are determined!

The indeterminist illicitly identifies and confuses fatalism with determinism in several of his theses, as will now become apparent.

The predictions that might be made by contemporary historical determinists concerning the social organization of industrial society, for example, pertain to a society of which these forecasters are themselves members. Hence such predictions are self-referential. But these predictions are made by social prophets who, *qua* deterministic forecasters, consider their own society from *without* rather than as active contributors to its destiny. And the predictions made from that theoretically external perspective are *predicated* on the prior fulfilment of certain initial conditions which include the presence in that society of people—among whom they themselves may happen to be included—who are dissatisfied with the existing state of affairs and are therefore actively seeking the future realization of the externally predicted social state. To ignore that the determinist rests his social prediction in part on the existence of the latter initial conditions, just as much as a physicist makes a prediction of a thermal expansion conditional upon the presence of heat, is to commit the *fallacy of equating determinism with fatalism*. Thus, a person's role as *predictor* of social change from an "external" perspective, as it were, is quite compatible logically with his belief in the necessity of his being an *advocate* of social change internal to society. We see that the indeterminist has no valid grounds for maintaining that it is logically inconsistent for an historical determinist, *qua* participating citizen, to advocate that action be taken by his fellow-citizens to create the social system whose advent he is predicting on the basis of his theory. For it is plain now that the indeterminist's charge derives its semblance of plausibility from his confusion of determinism with fatalism in the context of self-referential predictions. This confusion is present in Arthur Koestler's claim in his *Darkness at Noon* that the espousal of historical determinism by Marxists is *logically inconsistent* with their reproaching the labor movement in capitalist countries for insufficient effort on behalf of socialism.

Equally fallacious is the indeterminist's claim that it is practically *futile* for a determinist to weigh alternative modes of social organization with a view to optimizing the organization of his own society. For the determinist does *not* maintain, in fatalist fashion, that the future state of society is independent of the decisions which men make in response to (a) facts (both physical and social), (b) their own *interpretation* of these facts (which, of course, is often false), and (c) their value-objectives. It is precisely because, on the deterministic theory, human decisions *are* causally dependent upon these factors that deliberation concerning optimal courses of action and social arrangements can be reasonably expected to issue in successful action rather than lose its significance by adventitiousness. In short, the causal determinedness of the outcome of a process of human deliberation does not at all render futile those deliberations which issue in true beliefs about the efficacy of specified actions.

(*b*) Confusion of Causal Determination and Compulsion. The second, more fundamental point to bear in mind is that psychological laws do *not* force us to do or desire anything against our will. These laws merely state what, as a matter of fact, we do or desire under certain conditions. Thus, if there were a psychological law enabling us to predict that under certain conditions a man will desire to commit a certain act, this law would *not* be making him act in a manner contrary to his own desires, for the desire would be his. It follows that neither the causes of our desires nor psychological laws, which state under what conditions our desires arise and issue in specified kinds of behavior, *compel* us in any way to act in a manner contrary to our own will. There is in the indeterminist's thinking a confusion of physical and psychological law, on the one hand, with statutory law, on the other. Psychological laws do not coerce us against our will and do not *as such* make for the frustration or contravention of our desires. By contrast, statutory laws do frustrate the desires of some and are passed only because of the need to do so. Such laws are violated when they contravene powerful desires. But natural laws (as distinct from erroneous guesses as to what they are) cannot be broken. Anyone who steps off the top of the Empire State Building shouting defiance and insubordination to the law of gravitation will not break that law, but rather will give a pathetic illustration of its applicability.

We act under *compulsion,* in the sense relevant here, *when we are literally being physically restrained from without in implementing the desires which we have upon reacting to the total stimulus situation in our environment.* For example, if I am locked up and *therefore* cannot make an appointment, then I would be compelled to miss my appointment. Or, if a stronger man literally forces my hand to press a button which I do not wish to press, then I would be compelled to blow up a bridge. The meaning of "compulsion" intended here should *not,* of course, be identified with the meaning of that term familiar to students of neuroses. In the case of neurotic compulsion, *the compulsive person does unreflectively what he wishes,* although his behavior is inspired by unwarranted anxiety, and hence is insensitive to normally deterring factors, as in the case of an obsession with germs issuing in handwashing every time a door knob is touched.

To emphasize the meaning of "compulsion" relevant to the issue before us, I wish to point out that when a bank-teller hands over cash during a stick-up upon feeling the revolver pressing against his ribs, he is *not* acting under *compulsion* in my sense, any more than you and I act under compulsion when deciding *not* to go out playing tennis during a heavy rain. When handing over the money in preference to being shot, the bank-teller is doing what he genuinely wishes to do *under the given conditions.* Of course, in the absence of the revolver, the teller would not have desired to surrender the cash in response to a mere request. By the same token, it was the heavy rain that induced the hopeful tennis player to wish to stay indoors. But both the bank-teller and the frustrated tennis player are doing what they wish to do in the face of the existing conditions. The relevant similarity of the bank-teller case to a case of genuine compulsion in my sense lies only in the fact that our legal system does *not* decree punishment either in a case of genuine compulsion, like having one's hand literally forced to blow up a bridge by pressing a button, or in a case of *voluntary* action, like that of the bank-teller. For, although the bank-teller is actually *physically free* to hold on to the money and sound the alarm, he is *not* punished for surrendering the money because the alternative to such surrender would be to sound the alarm *at the cost of his own life*. The armed bank robber can therefore be said to have "compelled" the teller to surrender the money *not* in our technical sense, but only in the sense that the robber's threat was the decisive determinant of the *particular kind of voluntary action* that was taken by the teller. Similarly, when deference to their duties under the law "compels" a judge to sentence a dear friend to imprisonment or "compels" a policeman to arrest his own kin, the behavior of the judge and of the policeman are each voluntary. Their behavior is compelled only in the *non*-technical sense of springing from motives which had to overcome their affection for the culprits. Thus, what is common to genuine compulsion and voluntarily deciding to hand over money in preference to dying is that both of them are treated *as excusing conditions*. But *causal determination is not identical with what we have called compulsion*. For *voluntary* behavior does *not* cease to be voluntary and become "compelled" in our technical sense just because there are causes for that behavior. Hence unless he can show that responsibility is rendered meaningless in the case of causation no less than in the case of technical compulsion, the indeterminist is *not* entitled to assert that if determinism were true, the assignment of responsibility to people for their acts would be meaningless.

It should not be thought that the indeterminist is now prepared to surrender, for he has yet to use his strongest weapon. Says he: "We are all familiar with the fact that when we look back upon past conduct, we frequently feel very strongly that we could have done otherwise. For example, some one might have chosen to come here today via a route different from the one he actually did use. If the determinist is right in saying that our behavior was unavoidably determined by earlier causes, this retrospective feeling of freedom either should not exist or else it is fraudulent. In either case, the burden of proof rests upon the determinist." The determinist gladly accepts this challenge, and his reply is as follows: Let us carefully examine the content of the feeling that on a certain occasion we could have acted other than the way we did, in fact, act. What do we find? Does the feeling we have inform us that we could have acted otherwise *under exactly the same kinds of relevant external and internal motivational conditions?* No, says the determinist, this feeling simply discloses that we were able to act in accord with our strongest desire at that time *instead of acting under compulsion* and that we could indeed have acted otherwise *if a different motive had prevailed at the time.* And this state of affairs is entirely in accord with determinism. For the absence of freedom prevails in cases of technical compulsion and *not* on the strength of psychological causation. Thus the determinist answer is that the content of this "consciousness of freedom" consists in our awareness that we were able to act in response to our strongest motive at the time, and that we were not "under compulsion" in that sense. We were able to do what we wanted. But the determinist reminds us that our feeling of "freedom" does *not* disclose that, given the motives which acted on us at the time and given their relative strength and temporal distribution, we could have acted differently from the way in which we did, in fact, act. *Neither do we feel that we could have responded to the weaker of two contending motives, or acted without a cause or motive, or chosen the motives which acted upon us.* I never wake up totally devoid of any content of consciousness and then ask my *blank* self: "With what motives shall I populate my consciousness this A.M.? Shall I have the aspirations of Al Capone or those of Albert Schweitzer?" Nor do I even know what the indeterminist means by the supposition that we could have chosen our own character from scratch: every decision to shape or choose one's character must be one's own, i.e., must be made by an already existing personality, constituted by a set of dispositions. The notion of choosing one's character involves an infinite regress, because an initial "I" is presupposed in the making of the choice. Choices which mould the subsequent development of one's character are fully compatible with determinism. Since the retrospective feeling of freedom that we have does *not* report any ability of making the kinds of choices envisioned by the indeterminist, its deliverances contain no facts incompatible with the claim of the determinist. . . .

. . . The analysis we have offered is applicable at once to the case of remorse, regret, or guilt. We sometimes experience remorse over past conduct when we reconsider that conduct in the light of *different* motives. Once we bring a different set of motives to bear on a given situation, we may feel that a different decision is called for. If our motives do not change, we do not regret a past deed no matter how reprehensible it would otherwise appear. Many a killer has honestly declared that if he had to choose again, he would do again precisely what he had done. In that case, the relevant motives had not changed. *Regret is an expression of our emotion toward the disvalue and injustice which issued from our past conduct, as seen in the light of the new motives.* The regret we experience can then act as a *deterrent* against the repetition of past behavior which issued in disvalue. If the determinist expresses regret concerning past misconduct, he is applying motives of self-improvement to himself but not indulging in retroactive self-blame. Retroactive blame is futile, since the past will never return again. Thus, by responsibility for misdeeds the determinist does *not* mean retroactive blameworthiness, but rather *liability to reformative or educative punishment*. Punishment is educative in the sense that, when properly administered, it institutes countercauses to the repetition of injurious conduct. For the determinist wishing to spare culprits no less than others *gratuitous* suffering, punishment is never an end in itself. It is *not* intended as a revenge-catharsis. The determinist rejects as barbarous the primitive vengeful idea of retaliatory, retributive, or vindictive punishment. He condemns hurting a man simply because he has hurt others, for the same reason that he would condemn stealing from a thief or cheating a swindler. He fails to see how the damage done by the wrongdoer is remedied by the mere infliction of pain or sorrow of the culprit, *unless* such infliction of pain promises to act as a causal deterrent against the repetition of evil conduct. For the determinist, the decision whether pain is to be inflicted on the culprit and, if so, to what extent, is governed solely by the conduciveness of such punishment to reform and re-education of the culprit and repairing his damage, where possible. The requirement that punishment can be expected to be reformatory does not itself specify what choice is to be made among two equally effective punishments of differing severity. But the use of the moral requirement that *gratuitous* suffering be avoided as a principle of justice does indeed make this choice unique. The mathematics professor at the University of Pennsylvania whose three-year-old daughter was murdered by an adolescent in Philadelphia nobly disavowed all cave-man revenge. But he did ask for greater preventive efforts in diagnosing potentially homicidal but seemingly exemplary adolescents.

The implementation of this conception requires psychological and sociological research into *causal* connections and the institution of a *rational prison system*. If kindness rather than punishment were to deter the potential criminal, then it is clearly rational to be kind. The design and organization of the prison system must be set up accordingly, and the social cost would probably be less. Revenge seekers do not care whether prison hardens criminals further, nor whether the social cost of protecting society increases further. Their motto is that of the English schoolmaster: "Be pure in heart boys, or I'll flog you until you are."

On the determinist view of punishment as educative, "punishment" of the [criminally] insane automatically takes the form of treatment, since their in-

sanity lies in the fact that, among other things, (a) they act in a socially injurious way, and (b) they do not, because of a mental malfunction, provide
a unified point, as it were, for applying a counter-motive by the usual kinds
of punishment.

Insanity and punishment should *not* be judged by the McNaughton criterion: "Did the wrong-doer *'really know'* the difference between right and
wrong at the time of the act?" For this criterion does *not* suffice to determine
whether a man is sane in the sense of being deterred from repeating his
crime by the same punishment that would deter the rest of us. Often a man
who is judged sane by the *traditional* criterion does *not* respond to the
standard punishment but is, in fact, attracted by the prospect of such
punishment.

Our legal and penal system is to a certain extent an inconsistent and
unresolved compromise between the revenge philosophy of medieval spir-
itism which prescribed tortures for the insane and a grudging recognition of
some of the findings of modern science concerning the conditions breeding
criminal behavior. For the humane determinist, there is no "tempering of
justice with mercy": the punishment is never made more severe than is believed necessary to reform the criminal or prevent him from continuing his
destructive behavior. "Tempering justice with mercy" is the philosophy of
either a revenge-seeker who has qualms or a man who is torn between the
revenge conception and the reformatory one. . . .

(*c*) OTHER ARGUMENTS OF THE INDETERMINIST. It is sometimes said that,
when applied to man, the deterministic doctrine becomes untenable by virtue of becoming self-contradictory. This contention is often stated as follows: "The determinist, by his own doctrine, must admit that his very acceptance of determinism was causally conditioned or determined. Since he
could not help accepting it, he cannot argue that he has chosen a true
doctrine." To justify this claim, it is first pointed out rightly that determinism
implies a causal determination of its own acceptance by its defenders. Then
it is further maintained, however, that since the determinist could not, by his
own theory, help accepting determinism, he can have no confidence in its
truth. Thus it is asserted that the determinist's acceptance of his own doctrine was forced upon him. I submit that this inference involves a radical
fallacy. The proponent of this argument is gratuitously invoking the view
that if our beliefs have causes, these causes *force* the beliefs in question upon
us, against our better judgment, as it were. Nothing could be further from
the truth: this argument is another case of confusing *causation* with *compulsion*. My belief that I am now addressing you derives from the fact that your
presence is causally inducing certain images on the retinas of my eyes, and

that these images, in turn, cause me to infer that corresponding people are actually present before me. The reason why I do not suppose that I am now witnessing a performance of *Aïda* is that the images which Aïda, Radames, and Amneris would produce are not now in my visual field. The causal generation of a belief in no way detracts from its reliability. In fact, if a given belief were not produced in us by definite causes, we should have no reason to accept that belief as a correct description of the world, rather than some other belief arbitrarily selected. Far from making knowledge either adventitious or impossible, the deterministic theory about the origin of our beliefs alone provides the basis for thinking that our judgments of the world are or may be true. Knowing and judging are indeed causal processes in which the facts we judge are determining elements along with the cerebral mechanism employed in their interpretation. It follows that although the determinist's assent to his own doctrine is caused or determined, the truth of determinism is not jeopardized by this fact; if anything, it is made credible.

More generally, both true beliefs and false beliefs have psychological causes. The difference between a true or warranted belief and a false or unwarranted one must therefore be sought *not* in *whether* the belief in question is caused; instead, the difference must be sought in the particular *character* of the psychological causal factors which issued in the entertaining of the belief: *a warrantedly held belief, which has the presumption of being true, is one to which a person gave assent in response to awareness of supporting evidence.* Assent in the face of awareness of a *lack* of supporting evidence is irrational, although there are indeed psychological causes in such cases for giving assent. . . .

I hope that these considerations have shown, therefore, that it is entirely possible to give a *causal* account of both rational *and* irrational beliefs and behavior. And since a causal account is based on principles and regularities which are based on evidence, it follows that we can indeed give a rational explanation of why it is that people do behave irrationally under certain conditions, no less than we can provide a causal account of their rational behavior.

Lastly, a remark on the belief that determinism would lead to moral cynicism: why should my belief that my motives for wishing to help someone are caused lessen my readiness to implement my desire to help that person? Lincoln's view that his own beliefs (ethical and other) were causally determined did not weaken in the least his desire to abolish Negro slavery, as demanded by his ethical theory; and similarly for Augustine, Calvin, Spinoza, and a host of lesser men. . . .

Does Quantum Physics Have Any Bearing on the Freedom of the Will?

Although we saw that there is no incompatibility between determinism and the *feeling* of freedom, it might be supposed that the discovery of micro-indeterminism in quantum theory has shown that the causal conception of human decision processes has to be abandoned and that grave doubt has been cast on the amenability of human behavior to scientific mastery. I wish to devote the remainder of my remarks to showing why I do *not* think that this is so.

There is an important class of experimental results in physics which seems to compel the conclusion that micro-entities like electrons cannot be held to be particles in the classical sense. That is, they cannot be assumed to be entities characterized by the simultaneous possession of such sharply defined pairs of attributes as exact positions and velocities, attributes which specified the state of a particle in classical mechanics and which we shall call "conjugates." In particular, the evidence is incompatible with the following philosophical conception: electrons describe *unknown* particle trajectories by possessing simultaneously sharp positions and velocities which merely elude *concurrent measurement*. Thus it is an error to interpret these results as indicating merely limited measurability of otherwise autonomously existing properties. Instead, the experimental findings would seem to support the conclusion that (a) of any pair of the classical conjugate properties of state, like exact position and velocity, *at most one* characterizes the electron in any given experimental context, and that (b) sharp position and velocity of micro-particles cannot be measured simultaneously because they do not jointly exist to be measured. Thus, the evidence in question shows that the repudiation of the particle conception of the electron does *not* rest on the *mere* fact that sharply defined values of position and velocity are not simultaneously measurable or are *operationally incompatible*.

In classical physics, pairs of conjugates were held to characterize a particle simultaneously. We can therefore call this classical *joint*-ascribability the "theoretical *conjunctiveness*" of these properties, and contrast it with the opposing claim of the new quantum theory that these properties are theoretically *disjunctive* in the sense that *at most one* of them can characterize the micro-entity at any given time. Bohr has formulated the philosophical upshot of the discoveries of quantum theory by saying that conjugate properties are "complementary." By this he means two things. First, the complementarity of conjugates asserts that they are theoretically disjunctive, because the experimental arrangements under which a sharp value of one of two conjugates can be said to characterize the micro-entity in question are physically *incompatible* with the conditions under which a sharp value of the corresponding other conjugate parameter belongs to the micro-entity; contrary to the classical conception, these conjugate properties do *not* belong to microphysical objects *independently* of the experimental arrangement into which they enter but are *context-dependent:* that is to say, they are relevant only to particular interactions in which the micro-object is coupled indivisibly to a particular kind of observational macro-setup. Second, Bohr speaks of complementarity to convey the fact that in any account of the totality of all interactions of micro-entities with observational macro-apparatus, there is a need for *each* of the conjugate properties taken separately. The so-called Heisenberg Uncertainty Principle gives mathematical expression to this complementarity of conjugates in the form of certain inequalities.

These preparatory remarks on elementary quantum theory enable us to see at once why the new theory is driven to supplant the classical *deterministic* linkage between the attributes of individual events in space and time by a merely probabilistic or statistico-deterministic linkage. In the classical physics of closed systems, there was a one-to-one or unique functional relation between the values of the *complete* set of state variables at one or more times and the corresponding values at other times. In particle mechanics, the theoretical conjunctiveness of exact position and velocity is a *necessary condition* for a deterministic prediction or retrodiction: no classical physicist would claim a deterministic linkage between the mere position of a particle at a given time and its state at other times, but requires both position *and* velocity at a given time to predict or postdict the state of the particle at other times. But the quantum mechanical thesis is that the necessary condition for a classical deterministic prediction *cannot* be fulfilled: for the classical state attributes are *not* theoretically *con*junctive but merely *disjunctive,* so that the necessary condition for a deterministic relation between the attributes of individual events in space and time is *not* fulfilled. No wonder then that the new theory regards a *statistical* description of atomic phenomena not as merely an expression of our ignorance but as a reflection of an irreducible feature of the physical facts themselves.

I now wish to examine the import of this quantum mechanical indeterminism for the possibility of the scientific study of man by stating what conclusions, if any, seem to me to be warranted by the logic of the situation.

Earlier, I have argued that our retrospective feeling of freedom that we could have acted otherwise does *not* tell us that our decisions are uncaused in the sense that they could have been different under the same kind of relevant circumstances; so far as I can see, our feeling of freedom merely discloses that often we can do what we wish, but *not* that we can will what desires we shall have. As we saw, the very concept of "I" or of self already involves a set of dispositions which come into play when this self finds itself with desires that it has not chosen.

I therefore regard as wholly ill-conceived the quest for indeterministic neurological correlates of the non-existent kind of feeling of freedom postulated by the philosophical free willist. For the non-existence of the latter kind of feeling seems to me to make it idle to try to find quantum processes in the nervous system which are its supposed physical correlates. But what of the neurological correlate of the feeling of freedom which I do experience; that is, the feeling that I can often do what I wish under given circumstances and that under *other* circumstances I might well have different desires and act differently. Here I cannot see that the evidence warrants any more than the following cautious statement made by Niels Bohr in stating the conclusions of his essay "Light and Life":

I should like to emphasize that considerations of the kind here mentioned are entirely opposed to any attempt of seeking new possibilities for a spiritual influence on the behavior of matter in the statistical description of atomic phenomena. For instance, it is impossible from our standpoint, to attach an unambiguous meaning to the view sometimes expressed that the probability of the occurrence of certain atomic processes in the body might be under the direct influence of the will. In fact, according to the generalized interpretation of the psycho-physical parallelism, the freedom of the will is to be considered as a feature of conscious life which corresponds to functions of the organism that not only evade a causal mechanical description but resist even a physical analysis carried to the extent required for an unambiguous application of the statistical laws of atomic mechanics.

What then is the bearing of quantum physics on the freedom of the will? It seems to me to be the following: even if the retrospective feeling of freedom *did* disclose anything incompatible with the causal generation of our decisions—which it does not—the discoveries of quantum physics could *not* be adduced to show that this feeling has a foundation in fact.

So much for arguments which rest on the supposition that *the feeling of freedom* poses a problem to whose solution either quantum theory or its alleged philosophical lessons are relevant. But what of the import of quantum theory for the existence of regularities in human conduct and its predictability *apart from any invocation of the feeling of freedom?* Does that theory provide grounds for impugning the possibility of a science of man?

Perhaps there are cases in which the human eye responds to as little energy as a single photon or in which a neuron is triggered by a physical process sufficiently microscopic to be subject to quantum indeterminacies. If these processes of vision or neural excitation then issue in decisions and actions on the part of humans in whose bodies they transpire, then one can say that quantum indeterminacies enter into human macro-conduct and one can speak of a corresponding reduction in predictability *in principle*. But unless it is shown that a significant number of human decisions fall into this category, it would seem that the vast bulk if not all human decisions and acts involve physical agencies of such magnitude that quantum indeterminacies become irrelevant to them and classical deterministic characterization holds to all intents and purposes.

It is hoped that this discussion of the alleged intangibility of man's inner life and of the bearing of quantum indeterminacy on human freedom has served to support the view that there are very important respects in which science can *and* ought to deal with man as with the rest of nature.

SUGGESTED READINGS

The problem of free will is of crucial importance for Christianity and has therefore been discussed by most major Christian philosophers and theologians. St. Augustine's treatise *On Free Will* (available in his *Earlier Writings*, edited by J. H. S. Burleigh) is a classic statement of the problem. St. Thomas Aquinas deals with the issues in several places, among them *Summa Contra Gentiles*, Book II, Chapters 64–73 and 85–93. The mechanistic views of Thomas Hobbes, one of the greatest of English philosophers, are briefly indicated in Chapters 6 and 21 of his *Leviathan*. Kant's views, though extremely difficult to understand, are of major importance. They are stated in Part III of the *Fundamental Principles of the Metaphysics of Morals* and in the *Critique of Pure Reason* (translated by N. K. Smith), Second Division (Transcendental Dialectic), Book II, Section 9, III. Much easier to grasp and no less important is Hume's discussion of the problem in his *Treatise of Human Nature*, Book II, Part III, Chapters 1 and 2. John Stuart Mill presents an admirably clear statement of a similar position in his *System of Logic*, Book VI, Chapter 2.

There has been a great deal of recent discussion of the topic. Many good papers are contained in *Free Will and Determinism*, edited by B. Berofsky. Especially valuable are the selections by Schlick, Foot, and Campbell. Jean-Paul Sartre's views are also represented. A. I. Melden, in *Free Action*, presents a detailed, though not always very careful, discussion from an analytic point of view. A short book edited by D. F. Pears, *Freedom and the Will*, contains a number of excellent introductory discussions. In the symposium edited by S. Hook, *Determinism and Freedom*, the papers by Black, Hart, Edwards, and Hospers are especially worthy of attention.

Two Current Issues:
A. Minds and Machines

The development of electronic computers in recent years has given a new twist to questions about the relations between "mental" and "mechanical" events and has stimulated an extraordinary amount of discussion. Since 1950 more than one thousand papers have been published on the question as to whether machines can "think."

How would we recognize an *entity* (to use a term that does not prejudge the issue as to whether the thing is an organism or a machine) as having a *mind?* We all feel that *people* have minds and can think; monkeys can also think, in the sense that they can solve some rather simple problems—so can rats, for that matter. Flies and mosquitoes also seem to get along reasonably well, but most of us feel that they don't have minds. And whatever we may mean by "having a mind," most of us would probably agree that a cash register has none, nor does even the most sophisticated of existing electronic computers. But just where does the cut-off line come?

TURING argues that if we put the vague, and hence unanswerable, question "Can machines think" into precise form (by specifying exactly how we would expect a "thinking machine" to act), then the answer is affirmative. The difficulties in designing a machine that we could properly call "intelligent" are difficulties in practice only, not in principle. GUNDERSON on the other hand claims that Turing oversimplifies the problem and that even a machine that met Turing's test might still be regarded properly as "not thinking."

Computing Machinery and Intelligence*

ALAN M. TURING [1912–1954] studied at Cambridge and taught mathematics there from 1946 to his death. He made substantial contributions to several branches of pure and applied mathematics, and he is best known for his work on the theory of computing machines. His important insights into "Turing machines" (as they have come to be called) were gained while he was still in his early twenties. In recognition of this and other work he was awarded the O.B.E. in 1946 and was made a Fellow of the Royal Society in 1951.

THE IMITATION GAME. I propose to consider the question "Can machines think?" This should begin with definitions of the meaning of the terms "machine" and "think." The definitions might be framed so as to reflect so far as possible the normal use of the words, but this attitude is dangerous. If the meaning of the words "machine" and "think" are to be found by examining how they are commonly used it is difficult to escape the conclusion that the meaning and the answer to the question, "Can machines think?" is to be sought in a statistical survey such as a Gallup poll. But this is absurd. Instead of attempting such a definition I shall replace the question by another, which is closely related to it and is expressed in relatively unambiguous words.

The new form of the problem can be described in terms of a game which we call the "imitation game." It is played with three people, a man (A), a woman (B), and an interrogator (C) who may be of either sex. The interrogator stays in a room apart from the other two. The object of the game for the interrogator is to determine which of the other two is the man and which is the woman. He knows them by labels X and Y, and at the end of the game he says either "X is A and Y is B" or "X is B and Y is A." The interrogator is allowed to put questions to A and B thus:

C: Will X please tell me the length of his or her hair? Now suppose X is actually A, then A must answer. It is A's object in the game to try to cause C to make the wrong identification. His answer might therefore be

"My hair is shingled, and the longest strands are about nine inches long."

In order that tones of voice may not help the interrogator the answers

* From Turing: "Computing Machinery and Intelligence," *Mind*, LIX (1950). Reprinted by permission of the Editor of *Mind*.

should be written, or better still, typewritten. The ideal arrangement is to have a teleprinter communicating between the two rooms. Alternatively the question and answers can be repeated by an intermediary. The object of the game for the third player (B) is to help the interrogator. The best strategy for her is probably to give truthful answers. She can add such things as "I am the woman, don't listen to him!" to her answers, but it will avail nothing as the man can make similar remarks.

We now ask the question, "What will happen when a machine takes the part of A in this game?" Will the interrogator decide wrongly as often when the game is played like this as he does when the game is played between a man and a woman? These questions replace our original, "Can machines think?"

CRITIQUE OF THE NEW PROBLEM. As well as asking, "What is the answer to this new form of the question," one may ask, "Is this new question a worthy one to investigate?" This latter question we investigate without further ado, thereby cutting short an infinite regress.

The new problem has the advantage of drawing a fairly sharp line between the physical and the intellectual capacities of a man. No engineer or chemist claims to be able to produce a material which is indistinguishable from the human skin. It is possible that at some time this might be done, but even supposing this invention available we should feel there was little point in trying to make a "thinking machine" more human by dressing it up in such artificial flesh. The form in which we have set the problem reflects this fact in the condition which prevents the interrogator from seeing or touching the other competitors, or hearing their voices. Some other advantages of the proposed criterion may be shown up by specimen questions and answers. Thus:

Q: Please write me a sonnet on the subject of the Forth Bridge.

A: Count me out on this one. I never could write poetry.

Q: Add 34957 to 70764.

A: (Pause about 30 seconds and then give as answer) 105621.

Q: Do you play chess?

A: Yes.

Q: I have K at my K1, and no other pieces. You have only K at K6 and R at R1. It is your move. What do you play?

A: (After a pause of 15 seconds) R-R8 mate.

The question and answer method seems to be suitable for introducing almost any one of the fields of human endeavor that we wish to include. We do not wish to penalize the machine for its inability to shine in beauty competitions, nor to penalize a man for losing in a race against an airplane. The conditions of our game make these disabilities irrelevant. The "witnesses" can brag, if they consider it advisable, as much as they please about their charms, strength or heroism, but the interrogator cannot demand practical demonstrations. . . .

THE MACHINES CONCERNED IN THE GAME. It is natural that we should wish to permit every kind of engineering technique to be used in our machines. We also wish to allow the possibility that an engineer or team of engineers may construct a machine which works, but whose manner of operation cannot be satisfactorily described by its constructors because they have applied a method which is largely experimental. Finally, we wish to exclude from the machines men born in the usual manner. It is difficult to frame the definitions so as to satisfy these three conditions. One might for instance insist that the team of engineers should be all of one sex, but this would not really be satisfactory, for it is probably possible to rear a complete individual from a single cell of the skin (say) of a man. To do so would be a feat of biological technique deserving of the very highest praise, but we would not be inclined to regard it as a case of "constructing a thinking machine." This prompts us to abandon the requirement that every kind of technique should be permitted. We are the more ready to do so in view of the fact that the present interest in "thinking machines" has been aroused by a particular kind of machine, usually called an "electronic computer" or "digital computer." Following this suggestion we only permit digital computers to take part in our game.

This restriction appears at first sight to be a very drastic one. I shall attempt to show that it is not so in reality. To do this necessitates a short account of the nature and properties of these computers. . . .

DIGITAL COMPUTERS. The idea behind digital computers may be explained by saying that these machines are intended to carry out any operations which could be done by a human computer. The human computer is supposed to be following fixed rules; he has no authority to deviate from them in any detail. We may suppose that these rules are supplied in a book, which is altered whenever he is put on to a new job. He has also an unlimited supply of paper on which he does his calculations. He may also do his multiplications and additions on a "desk machine," but this is not important.

If we use the above explanation as a definition we shall be in danger of circularity of argument. We avoid this by giving an outline of the means by which the desired effect is achieved. A digital computer can usually be regarded as consisting of three parts:

(1) Store.
(2) Executive unit.
(3) Control.

The store is a store of information, and corresponds to the human computer's paper, whether this is the paper on which he does his calculations or that on which his book of rules is printed. Insofar as the human computer does calculations in his head a part of the store will correspond to his memory.

The executive unit is the part which carries out the various individual operations involved in a calculation. What these individual operations are will vary from machine to machine. Usually fairly lengthy operations can be done such as "Multiply 3540675445 by 7076345687" but in some machines only very simple ones such as "Write down 0" are possible.

We have mentioned that the "book of rules" supplied to the computer is replaced in the machine by a part of the store. It is then called the "table of instructions." It is the duty of the control to see that these instructions are obeyed correctly and in the right order. The control is so constructed that this necessarily happens.

The information in the store is usually broken up into packets of moderately small size. In one machine, for instance, a packet might consist of ten decimal digits. Numbers are assigned to the parts of the store in which the various packets of information are stored, in some systematic manner. A typical instruction might say—

Add the number stored in position 6809 to that in 4302 and put the result back into the latter storage position.

Needless to say it would not occur in the machine expressed in English. It would more likely be coded in a form such as 6809430217. Here 17 says which of various possible operations is to be performed on the two numbers. In this case the operation is that described above, viz. "Add the number. . . ." It will be noticed that the instruction takes up 10 digits and so forms one packet of information, very conveniently. The control will normally take the instructions to be obeyed in the order of the positions in which they are stored, but occasionally an instruction such as

Now obey the instruction stored in position 5606, and continue from there

may be encountered, or again

If position 4505 contains 0 obey next the instruction stored in 6707, otherwise continue straight on.

Instructions of these latter types are very important because they make it possible for a sequence of operations to be repeated over and over again until some condition is fulfilled, but in doing so to obey, not fresh instructions on each repetition, but the same ones over and over again. To take a domestic analogy. Suppose Mother wants Tommy to call at the cobbler's every morning on his way to school to see if her shoes are done; she can ask him afresh every morning. Alternatively she can stick up a notice once and for all in the hall which he will see when he leaves for school and which tells him to call for the shoes, and also to destroy the notice when he comes back if he has the shoes with him.

The reader must accept it as a fact that digital computers can be constructed, and indeed have been constructed, according to the principles we have described, and that they can in fact mimic the actions of a human computer very closely. . . .

CONTRARY VIEWS ON THE MAIN QUESTION. We may now consider the ground to have been cleared and we are ready to proceed to the debate on our question, "Can machines think?" and the variant of it quoted at the end of the last section. We cannot altogether abandon the original form of the problem, for opinions will differ as to the appropriateness of the substitution and we must at least listen to what has to be said in this connection.

It will simplify matters for the reader if I explain first my own beliefs in the matter. Consider first the more accurate form of the question. I believe that in about fifty years' time it will be possible to program computers, with a storage capacity of about 10^9, to make them play the imitation game so well that an average interrogator will not have more than 70 per cent chance of making the right identification after five minutes of questioning. The original question, "Can machines think?" I believe to be too meaningless to deserve discussion. Nevertheless I believe that at the end of the century the use of words and general educated opinion will have altered so much that one will be able to speak of machines thinking without expecting to be contradicted. I believe further that no useful purpose is served by concealing these beliefs. The popular view that scientists proceed inexorably from well-established fact to well-established fact, never being influenced by any unproved conjecture, is quite mistaken. Provided it is made clear which are proved facts and which are conjectures, no harm can result. Conjectures are of great importance since they suggest useful lines of research.

I now proceed to consider opinions opposed to my own.

THE THEOLOGICAL OBJECTION. Thinking is a function of man's immortal soul. God has given an immortal soul to every man and woman, but not to any other animal or to machines. Hence no animal or machine can think.

I am unable to accept any part of this, but will attempt to reply in theological terms. I should find the argument more convincing if animals were classed with men, for there is a greater difference, to my mind, between the typical animate and the inanimate than there is between man and the other animals. The arbitrary character of the orthodox view becomes clearer if we consider how it might appear to a member of some other religious community. How do Christians regard the Moslem view that women have no souls? But let us leave this point aside and return to the main argument. It appears to me that the argument quoted above implies a serious restriction of the omnipotence of the Almighty. It is admitted that there are certain things that He cannot do such as making one equal to two, but should we not believe that He has freedom to confer a soul on an elephant if He sees fit? We might expect that He would only exercise this power in conjunction with a mutation which provided the elephant with an appropriately improved brain to minister to the needs of this soul. An argument of exactly similar form may be made for the case of machines. It may seem different because it is more difficult to "swallow." But this really only means that we think it would be less likely that He would consider the circumstances suitable for conferring a soul. The circumstances in question are discussed in the rest of this paper. In attempting to construct such machines we should not be irreverently usurping His power of creating souls, any more than we are in the procreation of children: rather we are, in either case, instruments of His will providing mansions for the souls that He creates.

However, this is mere speculation. I am not very impressed with theological arguments whatever they may be used to support. Such arguments have often been found unsatisfactory in the past. In the time of Galileo it was argued that the texts, "And the sun stood still . . . and hasted not to go down about a whole day" (Joshua x. 13) and "He laid the foundations of the earth, that it should not move at any time" (Psalm cv. 5) were an adequate refutation of the Copernican theory. With our present knowledge such an argument appears futile. When that knowledge was not available it made a quite different impression.

The "Heads in the Sand" Objection. "The consequences of machines thinking would be too dreadful. Let us hope and believe that they cannot do so."

This argument is seldom expressed quite so openly as in the form above. But it affects most of us who think about it at all. We like to believe that Man is in some subtle way superior to the rest of creation. It is best if he can be shown to be *necessarily* superior, for then there is no danger of him losing his commanding position. The popularity of the theological argument is clearly connected with this feeling. It is likely to be quite strong in intellectual people, since they value the power of thinking more highly than others, and are more inclined to base their belief in the superiority of Man on this power.

I do not think that this argument is sufficiently substantial to require refutation. Consolation would be more appropriate: perhaps this should be sought in the transmigration of souls.

THE MATHEMATICAL OBJECTION. There are a number of results of mathematical logic which can be used to show that there are limitations to the powers of discrete state machines. The best known of these results is known as Gödel's theorem, and shows that in any sufficiently powerful logical system statements can be formulated which can neither be proved nor disproved within the system, unless possibly the system itself is inconsistent. There are other, in some respects similar, results due to Church, Kleene, Rosser, and Turing. The latter result is the most convenient to consider, since it refers directly to machines. . . . The result in question refers to a type of machine which is essentially a digital computer with an infinite capacity. It states that there are certain things that such a machine cannot do. If it is rigged up to give answers to questions as in the imitation game, there will be some questions to which it will either give a wrong answer, or fail to give an answer at all however much time is allowed for a reply. There may, of course, be many such questions, and questions which cannot be answered by one machine may be satisfactorily answered by another. We are of course supposing for the present that the questions are of the kind to which an answer "Yes" or "No" is appropriate, rather than questions such as "What do you think of Picasso?" The questions that we know the machines must fail on are of this type, "Consider the machine specified as follows. . . . Will this machine ever answer 'Yes' to any question?" The dots are to be replaced by a description of some machine in a standard form. . . . When the machine described bears a certain comparatively simple relation to the machine which is under interrogation, it can be shown that the answer is either wrong or not forthcoming. This is the mathematical result: it is argued that it proves a disability of machines to which the human intellect is not subject.

The short answer to this argument is that although it is established that there are limitations to the powers of any particular machine, it has only been stated, without any sort of proof, that no such limitations apply to the human intellect. But I do not think this view can be dismissed quite so lightly. Whenever one of these machines is asked the appropriate critical question, and gives a definite answer, we know that this answer must be wrong, and this gives us a certain feeling of superiority. Is this feeling illusory? It is no doubt quite genuine, but I do not think too much importance should be attached to it. We too often give wrong answers to questions ourselves to be justified in being very pleased at such evidence of fallibility on the part of the machines. Further, our superiority can only be felt on such an occasion in relation to the one machine over which we have scored our petty triumph. There would be no question of triumphing simultaneously over *all* machines. In short, then, there might be men cleverer than any given machine, but then again there might be other machines cleverer again, and so on.

Those who hold to the mathematical argument would, I think, mostly be willing to accept the imitation game as a basis for discussion. Those who believe in the two previous objections would probably not be interested in any criteria.

THE ARGUMENT FROM CONSCIOUSNESS. This argument is very well expressed in Professor Jefferson's Lister Oration for 1949, from which I quote. "Not until a machine can write a sonnet or compose a concerto because of thoughts and emotions felt, and not by the chance fall of symbols, could we agree that machine equals brain—that is, not only write it but know that it had written it. No mechanism could feel (and not merely artificially signal, an easy contrivance) pleasure at its successes, grief when its valves fuse, be warmed by flattery, be made miserable by its mistakes, be charmed by sex, be angry or depressed when it cannot get what it wants."

This argument appears to be a denial of the validity of our test. According to the most extreme form of this view the only way by which one could be sure that a machine thinks is to *be* the machine and to feel oneself thinking. One could then describe these feelings to the world, but of course no one would be justified in taking any notice. Likewise according to this view the only way to know that a *man* thinks is to be that particular man. It is in fact the solipsist point of view. It may be the most logical view to hold but it makes communication of ideas difficult. A is liable to believe "A thinks but B does not" while B believes "B thinks but A does not." Instead of arguing continually over this point it is usual to have the polite convention that everyone thinks.

I am sure that Professor Jefferson does not wish to adopt the extreme and solipsist point of view. Probably he would be quite willing to accept the imitation game as a test. The game (with the player B omitted) is frequently used in practice under the name of *viva voce* to discover whether someone really understands something or has "learned it parrot fashion." Let us listen in to a part of such a *viva voce:*

Interrogator: In the first line of your sonnet which reads "Shall I compare thee to a summer's day," would not "a spring day" do as well or better?

Witness: It wouldn't scan.

Interrogator: How about "a winter's day." That would scan all right.

Witness: Yes, but nobody wants to be compared to a winter's day.

Interrogator: Would you say Mr. Pickwick reminded you of Christmas?

Witness: In a way.

Interrogator: Yet Christmas is a winter's day, and I do not think Mr.
    Pickwick would mind the comparison.

Witness: I don't think you're serious. By a winter's day one means a
    typical winter's day, rather than a special one like Christmas.

And so on. What would Professor Jefferson say if the sonnet-writing machine was able to answer like this in the *viva voce?* I do not know whether
he would regard the machine as "merely artificially signaling" these answers,
but if the answers were as satisfactory and sustained as in the above passage
I do not think he would describe it as "an easy contrivance." This phrase is, I
think, intended to cover such devices as the inclusion in the machine of a
record of someone reading a sonnet, with appropriate switching to turn it on
from time to time.

In short then, I think that most of those who support the argument from
consciousness could be persuaded to abandon it rather than be forced into
the solipsist position. They will then probably be willing to accept our test.

I do not wish to give the impression that I think there is no mystery about
consciousness. There is, for instance, something of a paradox connected with
any attempt to localize it. But I do not think these mysteries necessarily need
to be solved before we can answer the question with which we are concerned in this paper.

ARGUMENTS FROM VARIOUS DISABILITIES. These arguments take the
form, "I grant you that you can make machines do all the things you
have mentioned but you will never be able to make one to do X." Numerous features X are suggested in this connection. I offer a selection:

Be kind, resourceful, beautiful, friendly (p. 19), have initiative, have a sense of
humor, tell right from wrong, make mistakes (p. 19), fall in love, enjoy strawberries and cream (p. 19), make someone fall in love with it, learn from experience
(pp. 25f.), use words properly, be the subject of its own thought (p. 20), have as
much diversity of behavior as a man, do something really new (p. 20). (Some of
these disabilities are given special consideration as indicated by the page numbers.)

No support is usually offered for these statements. I believe they are mostly
founded on the principle of scientific induction. A man has seen thousands of
machines in his lifetime. From what he sees of them he draws a number of
general conclusions. They are ugly, each is designed for a very limited purpose, when required for a minutely different purpose they are useless, the
variety of behavior of any one of them is very small, etc., etc. Naturally he
concludes that these are necessary properties of machines in general. Many
of these limitations are associated with the very small storage capacity of

most machines. (I am assuming that the idea of storage capacity is extended in some way to cover machines other than discrete state machines. The exact definition does not matter as no mathematical accuracy is claimed in the present discussion.) A few years ago, when very little had been heard of digital computers, it was possible to elicit much incredulity concerning them, if one mentioned their properties without describing their construction. That was presumably due to a similar application of the principle of scientific induction. These applications of the principle are of course largely unconscious. When a burned child fears the fire and shows that he fears it by avoiding it, I should say that he was applying scientific induction. (I could of course also describe his behavior in many other ways.) The works and customs of mankind do not seem to be very suitable material to which to apply scientific induction. A very large part of space-time must be investigated if reliable results are to be obtained. Otherwise we may (as most English children do) decide that everybody speaks English, and that it is silly to learn French.

There are, however, special remarks to be made about many of the disabilities that have been mentioned. The inability to enjoy strawberries and cream may have struck the reader as frivolous. Possibly a machine might be made to enjoy this delicious dish, but any attempt to make one do so would be idiotic. . . .

The claim that "machines cannot make mistakes" seems a curious one. One is tempted to retort, "Are they any the worse for that?" But let us adopt a more sympathetic attitude, and try to see what is really meant. I think this criticism can be explained in terms of the imitation game. It is claimed that the interrogator could distinguish the machine from the man simply by setting them a number of problems in arithmetic. The machine would be unmasked because of its deadly accuracy. The reply to this is simple. The machine (programed for playing the game) would not attempt to give the *right* answers to the arithmetic problems. It would deliberately introduce mistakes in a manner calculated to confuse the interrogator. A mechanical fault would probably show itself through an unsuitable decision as to what sort of a mistake to make in the arithmetic. Even this interpretation of the criticism is not sufficiently sympathetic. But we cannot afford the space to go into it much further. It seems to me that this criticism depends on a confusion between two kinds of mistakes. We may call them "errors of functioning" and "errors of conclusion." Errors of functioning are due to some mechanical or electrical fault which causes the machine to behave otherwise than it was designed to do. In philosophical discussions one likes to ignore the possibility of such errors; one is therefore discussing "abstract machines." These abstract machines are mathematical fictions rather than physical objects. By definition they are incapable of errors of functioning. In this sense we can truly say that "machines can never make mistakes." Errors of conclusion can only arise when some meaning is attached to the output signals from the machine. The machine might, for instance, type out mathematical equations, or sentences in English. When a false proposition is typed we say that the machine has committed an error of conclusion. There is clearly no reason at all for saying that a machine cannot make this kind of mistake. It might do nothing but type out repeatedly "$0 = 1$." To take a less perverse example, it might have some method for drawing conclusions by scientific induction. We must expect such a method to lead occasionally to erroneous results.

The claim that a machine cannot be the subject of its own thought can of course only be answered if it can be shown that the machine has *some* thought with *some* subject matter. Nevertheless, "the subject matter of a machine's operations" does seem to mean something, at least to the people who deal with it. If, for instance, the machine was trying to find a solution of the equation $x^2 - 40x - 11 = 0$ one would be tempted to describe this equation as part of the machine's subject matter at that moment. In this sort of sense a machine undoubtedly can be its own subject matter. It may be used to help in making up its own programs, or to predict the effect of alterations in its own structure. By observing the results of its own behavior it can modify its own programs so as to achieve some purpose more effectively. These are possibilities of the near future, rather than Utopian dreams.

The criticism that a machine cannot have much diversity of behavior is just a way of saying that it cannot have much storage capacity. Until fairly recently a storage capacity of even a thousand digits was very rare.

The criticisms that we are considering here are often disguised forms of the argument from consciousness. Usually if one maintains that a machine *can* do one of these things, and describes the kind of method that the machine could use, one will not make much of an impression. It is thought that the method (whatever it may be, for it must be mechanical) is really rather base. Compare the parenthesis in Jefferson's statement quoted above.

LADY LOVELACE'S OBJECTION. . . . A variant of Lady Lovelace's objection states that a machine can "never do anything really new." This may be parried for a moment with the saw, "There is nothing new under the sun." Who can be certain that "original work" that he has done was not simply the growth of the seed planted in him by teaching, or the effect of following well-known general principles. A better variant of the objection says that a machine can never "take us by surprise." This statement is a more direct challenge and can be met directly. Machines take me by surprise with great frequency. This is largely because I do not do sufficient calculation to decide what to expect them to do, or rather because, although I do a calculation, I do it in a hurried, slipshod fashion, taking risks. Perhaps I say to myself, "I suppose the voltage here ought to be the same as there: anyway let's assume it is." Naturally I am often wrong, and the result is a surprise for me, for by the time the experiment is done these assumptions have been forgotten. These admissions lay me open to lectures on the subject of my vicious ways, but do not throw any doubt on my credibility when I testify to the surprises I experience.

I do not expect this reply to silence my critic. He will probably say that such surprises are due to some creative mental act on my part, and reflect no credit on the machine. This leads us back to the argument from consciousness, and far from the idea of surprise. It is a line of argument we must consider closed, but it is perhaps worth remarking that the appreciation of something as surprising requires as much of a "creative mental act" whether the surprising event originates from a man, a book, a machine or anything else.

The view that machines cannot give rise to surprises is due, I believe, to a fallacy to which philosophers and mathematicians are particularly subject. This is the assumption that as soon as a fact is presented to a mind all consequences of that fact spring into the mind simultaneously with it. It is a very useful assumption under many circumstances, but one too easily forgets that it is false. A natural consequence of doing so is that one then assumes that there is no virtue in the mere working out of consequences from data and general principles.

ARGUMENT FROM CONTINUITY IN THE NERVOUS SYSTEM. The nervous system is certainly not a discrete state machine. A small error in the information about the size of a nervous impulse impinging on a neuron, may make a large difference to the size of the outgoing impulse. It may be argued that, this being so, one cannot expect to be able to mimic the behavior of the nervous system with a discrete state system.

It is true that a discrete state machine must be different from a continuous machine. But if we adhere to the conditions of the imitation game, the interrogator will not be able to take any advantage of this difference. The situation can be made clearer if we consider some other simpler continuous machine. A differential analyzer will do very well. (A differential analyzer is a certain kind of machine not of the discrete state type used for some kinds of calculation.) Some of these provide their answers in a typed form, and so are suitable for taking part in the game. It would not be possible for a digital computer to predict exactly what answers the differential analyzer would give to a problem, but it would be quite capable of giving the right sort of answer. For instance, if asked to give the value of π (actually about 3.1416) it would be reasonable to choose at random between the values 3.12, 3.13,

3.14, 3.15, 3.16 with the probabilities of 0.05, 0.15, 0.55, 0.19, 0.06 (say). Under these circumstances it would be very difficult for the interrogator to distinguish the differential analyzer from the digital computer.

THE ARGUMENT FROM INFORMALITY OF BEHAVIOR. It is not possible to produce a set of rules purporting to describe what a man should do in every conceivable set of circumstances. One might for instance have a rule that one is to stop when one sees a red traffic light, and to go if one sees a green one, but what if by some fault both appear together? One may perhaps decide that it is safest to stop. But some further difficulty may well arise from this decision later. To attempt to provide rules of conduct to cover every eventuality, even those arising from traffic lights, appears to be impossible. With all this I agree.

From this it is argued that we cannot be machines. I shall try to reproduce the argument, but I fear I shall hardly do it justice. It seems to run something like this. "If each man had a definite set of rules of conduct by which he regulated his life he would be no better than a machine. But there are no such rules, so men cannot be machines." The undistributed middle is glaring. I do not think the argument is ever put quite like this, but I believe this is the argument used nevertheless. There may however be a certain confusion between "rules of conduct" and "laws of behavior" to cloud the issue. By "rules of conduct" I mean precepts such as "Stop if you see red lights," on which one can act, and of which one can be conscious. By "laws of behavior" I mean laws of nature as applied to a man's body such as "if you pinch him he will squeak." If we substitute "laws of behavior which regulate his life" for "laws of conduct by which he regulates his life" in the argument quoted the undistributed middle is no longer insuperable. For we believe that it is not only true that being regulated by laws of behavior implies being some sort of machine (though not necessarily a discrete state machine), but that conversely being such a machine implies being regulated by such laws. However, we cannot so easily convince ourselves of the absence of complete laws of behavior as of complete rules of conduct. The only way we know of for finding such laws is scientific observation, and we certainly know of no circumstances under which we could say, "We have searched enough. There are no such laws."

We can demonstrate more forcibly that any such statement would be unjustified. For suppose we could be sure of finding such laws if they existed. Then given a discrete state machine it should certainly be possible to discover by observation sufficient about it to predict its future behavior, and this within a reasonable time, say a thousand years. But this does not seem to be the case. I have set up on the Manchester computer a small program using only 100 units of storage, whereby the machine supplied with one sixteen figure number replies with another within two seconds. I would defy anyone to learn from these replies sufficient about the program to be able to predict any replies to untried values. . . .

The reader will have anticipated that I have no very convincing arguments of a positive nature to support my views. If I had I should not have taken such pains to point out the fallacies in contrary views. Such evidence as I have I shall now give.

Let us return for a moment to Lady Lovelace's objection, which stated that the machine can only do what we tell it to do. One could say that a man can "inject" an idea into the machine, and that it will respond to a certain extent and then drop into quiescence, like a piano string struck by a hammer. Another simile would be an atomic pile of less than critical size: an injected idea is to correspond to a neutron entering the pile from without. Each such neutron will cause a certain disturbance which eventually dies away. If, however, the size of the pile is sufficiently increased, the disturbance caused by such an incoming neutron will very likely go on and on increasing until the whole pile is destroyed. Is there a corresponding phenomenon for minds, and is there one for machines? There does seem to be one for the human mind. The majority of them seem to be "subcritical," i.e., to correspond in this analogy to piles of subcritical size. An idea presented to such a mind will on an average give rise to less than one idea in reply. A smallish proportion are supercritical. An idea presented to such a mind may give rise to a whole "theory" consisting of secondary, tertiary and more remote ideas. Animals' minds seem to be very definitely subcritical. Adhering to this analogy we ask, "Can a machine be made to be supercritical?"

The "skin of an onion" analogy is also helpful. In considering the functions of the mind or the brain we find certain operations which we can explain in purely mechanical terms. This we say does not correspond to the real mind: it is a sort of skin which we must strip off if we are to find the real mind. But then in what remains we find a further skin to be stripped off, and so on. Proceeding in this way do we ever come to the "real" mind, or do we eventually come to the skin which has nothing in it? In the latter case the whole mind is mechanical. (It would not be a discrete state machine however. We have discussed this.)

This last two paragraphs do not claim to be convincing arguments. They should rather be described as "recitations tending to produce belief." . . .

As I have explained, the problem is mainly one of programing. Advances in engineering will have to be made too, but it seems unlikely that these will not be adequate for the requirements. Estimates of the storage capacity of the brain vary from 10^{10} to 10^{15} binary digits. I incline to the lower values and believe that only a very small fraction is used for the higher types of thinking. Most of it is probably used for the retention of visual impressions. I should be surprised if more than 10^9 was required for satisfactory playing of the imitation game, at any rate against a blind man. (Note: The capacity of the *Encyclopaedia Britannica,* eleventh edition, is 2×10^9.) A storage capacity of 10^7 would be a very practicable possibility even by present techniques. It is probably not necessary to increase the speed of operations of the machines at all. Parts of modern machines which can be regarded as analogues of nerve cells work about a thousand times faster than the latter. This should provide a "margin of safety" which could cover losses of speed arising in many ways. Our problem then is to find out how to program these machines to play the game. At my present rate of working I produce about a thousand digits of program a day, so that about sixty workers, working steadily through the fifty years might accomplish the job, if nothing went into the wastepaper basket. Some more expeditious method seems desirable. . . .

We may hope that machines will eventually compete with men in all purely intellectual fields. But which are the best ones to start with? Even this is a difficult decision. Many people think that a very abstract activity, like the playing of chess, would be best. It can also be maintained that it is best to provide the machine with the best sense organs that money can buy, and then teach it to understand and speak English. This process could follow the normal teaching of a child. Things would be pointed out and named, etc. Again I do not know what the right answer is, but I think both approaches should be tried.

We can only see a short distance ahead, but we can see plenty there that needs to be done.

The Imitation Game[*]

KEITH GUNDERSON [1935–   ] studied at Macalester College and Oxford before taking his Ph.D. at Princeton in 1963. He is now teaching at the University of California in Los Angeles. He is the author of several articles on the mind-body problem and has published a number of poems.

I

Disturbed by what he took to be the ambiguous, if not meaningless, character of the question "Can machines think?", the late A. M. Turing in his article "Computing Machinery and Intelligence" [immediately preceding

[*] From Gunderson: "The Imitation Game," *Mind,* LXXIII (1964). Reprinted by permission of the Editor of *Mind.*

this selection] sought to replace that question in the following way. He said:

The new form of the problem can be described in terms of a game which we call the "imitation game." It is played with three people, a man (A), a woman (B), and an interrogator (C) who may be either sex. The interrogator stays in a room apart from the other two. The object of the game for the interrogator is to determine which of the other two is the man and which is the woman. He knows them by labels X and Y, and at the end of the game he says either "X is A and Y is B" or "X is B and Y is A." The interrogator is allowed to put questions to A and B thus:

C: "Will X please tell me the length of his or her hair?"

Now suppose X is actually A, then A must answer. It is A's object in the game to try to cause C to make the wrong identification. His answer might therefore be

"My hair is shingled, and the longest strands are about nine inches long."

In order that tones of voice may not help the interrogator the answers should be written, or better still, typewritten. The ideal arrangement is to have a teleprinter communicating between the two rooms. Alternatively the question and answers can be repeated by an intermediary. The object of the game for the third player (B) is to help the interrogator. The best strategy for her is probably to give truthful answers. She can add such things as "I am the woman, don't listen to him!" to her answers, but it will avail nothing as the man can make similar remarks.

We now ask the question, "What will happen when a machine takes the part of A in this game?" Will the interrogator decide wrongly as often as when the game is played between a man and a woman? These questions replace our original. "Can machines think?"

And Turing's answers to these latter questions are more or less summed up in the following passage: "I believe that in fifty years' time it will be possible to program computers, with a storage capacity of about 10^9, to make them play the imitation game so well that an average interrogator will not have more than 70 per cent chance of making the right identification after five minutes of questioning." And though he goes on to reiterate that he suspects that the original question "Can machines think?" is meaningless, and that it should be disposed of and replaced by a more precise formulation of the problems involved (a formulation such as a set of questions about the imitation game and machine capacities), what finally emerges is that Turing does answer the "meaningless" question after all, and that his answer is in the affirmative and follows from his conclusions concerning the capabilities of machines which might be successfully substituted for people in the imitation-game context.

It should be pointed out that Turing's beliefs about the possible capabilities and capacities of machines are not limited to such activities as playing the imitation game as successfully as human beings. He does not, for example, deny that it might be possible to develop a machine which would relish the taste of strawberries and cream, though he thinks it would be "idiotic" to attempt to make one, and confines himself on the whole in his positive account to considerations of machine capacities which could be illustrated in terms of playing the imitation game.

So we shall be primarily concerned with asking whether or not a machine, which could play the imitation game as well as Turing thought it might, would thus be a machine which we would have good reasons for saying was capable of thought and what would be involved in saying this.

Some philosophers have not been satisfied with Turing's treatment of the question "Can machines think?" But the imitation game itself, which indeed seems to constitute the hub of his positive treatment, has been little more than alluded to or remarked on in passing. I shall try to develop in a somewhat more detailed way certain objections to it, objections which, I believe, Turing altogether fails to anticipate. My remarks shall thus in the main be critically oriented, which is not meant to suggest that I believe there are no plausible lines of defense open to a supporter of Turing. I shall, to the contrary, close with a brief attempt to indicate what some of these might be and some general challenges which I think Turing has raised for the philosopher of mind. But these latter I shall not elaborate upon.

II

Let us consider the following question: "Can rocks imitate?" One might say that it is a question "too meaningless to deserve discussion." Yet it seems possible to reformulate the problem in relatively unambiguous words as follows:

The new form of the problem can be described in terms of a game which we call the "toe-stepping game." It is played with three people, a man (A), a woman (B), and an interrogator (C) who may be of either sex. The interrogator stays in a room apart from the other two. The door is closed, but there is a small opening in the wall next to the floor through which he can place most of his foot. When he does so, one of the other two may step on his toe. The object of the game for the interrogator is to determine, by the way in which his toe is stepped on, which of the other two is the man and which is the woman. He knows them by labels X and Y, and at the end of the game he says either "X is A and Y is B" or "X is B and Y is A." Now the interrogator—rather the person whose toe gets stepped on—may indicate before he puts his foot through the opening, whether X or Y is to step on it. Better yet, there might be a narrow division in the opening, one side for X and one for Y (one for A and one for B).

Now suppose C puts his foot through A's side of the opening (which may be labeled X or Y on C's side of the wall). It is A's object in the game to try to cause C to make the wrong identification. His step on the toe might therefore be quick and jabbing like some high-heeled woman.

The object of the game for the third player (B) is to help the person whose toe gets stepped on. The best strategy for her is probably to try to step on it in the most womanly way possible. She can add such things as a slight twist of a high heel to her stepping, but it will avail nothing as the man can step in similar ways, since he will also have at his disposal various shoes with which to vary his toe-stepping.

We now ask the question: "What will happen when a rock-box (a box filled with rocks of varying weights, sizes, and shapes) is constructed with an electric eye which operates across the opening in the wall so that it releases a rock which descends upon C's toe whenever C puts his foot through A's side of the opening, and thus comes to take the part of A in this game?" (The situation can be made more convincing by constructing the rock-box so that there is a mechanism pulling up the released rock shortly after its descent, thus avoiding telltale noises such as a rock rolling on the floor, etc.) Will then the interrogator—the person whose toe gets stepped on—decide wrongly as often as when the game is played between a man and a woman? These questions replace our original, "Can rocks imitate?"

I believe that in less than fifty years' time it will be possible to set up elaborately constructed rock-boxes, with large rock-storage capacities, so that they will play the toe-stepping game so well that the average person who would get his toe stepped on would not have more than 70 per cent chance of making the right identification after about five minutes of toe-stepping.

The above seems to show the following: what follows from the toe-stepping game situation surely is not that rocks are able to imitate (I assume no one would want to take that path of argument) but only that they are able to be rigged in such a way that they could be substituted for a human being in a toe-stepping game without changing any essential characteristics of that game. And this is claimed in spite of the fact that if a human being were to play the toe-stepping game as envisaged above, we would no doubt be correct in saying that that person was imitating, etc. To be sure, a digital computer is a more august mechanism than a rock-box, but Turing has not provided us with any arguments for believing that its role in the imitation game, as distinct from the net results it yields, is any closer a match for a human being executing such a role, than is the rock-box's execution of its role in the toe-stepping game a match for a human being's execution of a similar role. The parody comparison can be pushed too far. But I think it lays bare the reason why there is no contradiction involved in saying, "Yes, a machine can play the imitation game, but it can't think." It is for the same reason that there is no contradiction in saying, "Of course a rock-box of such-and-such a sort can be set up, but rocks surely can't imitate." For thinking (or imitating) cannot be fully described simply by pointing to net results such as those illustrated above. For if this were not the case it would be correct to say that a piece of chalk could think or compose because it was freakishly blown about by a tornado in such a way that it scratched a rondo on a blackboard, and that a phonograph could sing, and that an electric-eye could see people coming.

People may be let out of a building by either an electric-eye or a doorman. The end result is the same. But though a doorman may be rude or polite, the electric-eye neither practices nor neglects etiquette. Turing brandishes net results. But I think the foregoing at least indicates certain difficulties with any account of thinking or decision as to whether a certain thing is capable of thought which is based primarily on net results. And, of course, one could always ask whether the net results were really the same. But I do not wish to follow that line of argument here. It is my main concern simply to indicate where Turing's account, which is cast largely in terms of net results, fails because of this. It is not an effective counter to reply: "But part of the net results in question includes intelligent people being deceived!" For what would this add to the general argument? No doubt people could be deceived by rock-boxes! It is said that hi-fidelity phonographs have been perfected to the point where blindfolded music critics are unable to distinguish their "playing" from that of, let us say, the Budapest String Quartet. But the phonograph would never be said to have performed with unusual brilliance on Saturday, nor would it ever deserve an encore. . . .

III

But let us return to the imitation game itself. It is to be granted that if human beings were to participate in such a game, we would almost surely regard them as deliberating, deciding, wondering—in short, "thinking things over"—as they passed their messages back and forth. And if someone were to ask us for an example of Johnson's intellectual prowess or mental capabilities, we might well point to this game which he often played, and how he enjoyed trying to outwit Peterson and Hanson who also participated in it. But we would only regard it as one of the many examples we might give of Peterson's mental capacities. We would ordinarily not feel hard pressed to produce countless other examples of Peterson deliberating, figuring, wondering, reflecting, or what in short we can call thinking. We might, for example, relate how he works over his sonnets or how he argues with Hanson. Now, I do not want to deny that it is beyond the scope of a machine to do these latter things. I am not, in fact, here concerned with giving an answer to the question, "Can machines think?" What I instead want to emphasize is that what we would say about Peterson in countless other situations is bound to influence what we say about him in the imitation game. A rock rolls down a hill and there is, strictly speaking, no behavior or action on the part of the rock. But if a man rolls down a hill we might well ask if he was pushed or did it intentionally, whether he's enjoying himself, playing a game, pretending to be a tumbleweed, or what. We cannot think of a man as simply or purely rolling down a hill—unless he is dead. A fortiori, we cannot understand him being a participant in the imitation game apart from his dispositions, habits, etc., which are exhibited in contexts other than the imitation game. Thus we cannot hope to find any decisive answer to the question as to how we should characterize a machine which can play (well) the imitation game, by asking what we would say about a man who could play (well) the imitation game. Thinking, whatever positive characterization or account is correct, is not something which any one example will explain or decide. But the part of Turing's case which I've been concerned with rests largely on one example.

IV

The following might help to clarify the above. Imagine the dialogue below:

Vacuum Cleaner Salesman: Now here's an example of what the all-purpose Swish 600 can do. (He then applies the nozzle to the carpet and it sucks up a bit of dust.)

Housewife: What else can it do?

Vacuum Cleaner Salesman: What do you mean "What else can it do?" It just sucked up that bit of dust, didn't you see?

Housewife: Yes, I saw it suck up a bit of dust, but I thought it was all-purpose. Doesn't it suck up larger and heavier bits of straw or paper or mud? And can't it get in the tight corners? Doesn't it have other nozzles? What about the cat hair on the couch?

Vacuum Cleaner Salesman: It sucks up bits of dust. That's what vacuum cleaners are for.

Housewife: Oh, that's what it does. I thought it was simply an example of what it does.

Vacuum Cleaner Salesman: It is an example of what it does. What it does is to suck up bits of dust.

We ask: Who's right about examples? We answer: It's not perfectly clear that anyone is lying or unjustifiably using the word "example." And there's no obvious linguistic rule or regularity to point to which tells us that if S can only do x, then S's doing x cannot be an example of what S can do since being an example presupposes or entails or whatnot that other kinds of examples are forthcoming (sucking up mud, cat hair, etc.). Yet, in spite of this, the housewife has a point. One simply has a right to expect more from an all-purpose, Swish 600 than what has been demonstrated. Here clearly the main trouble is with "all-purpose" rather than with "example," though there may still be something misleading about saying, "Here's an example . . . ," and it would surely mislead to say, "Here's *just* an example . . . ," followed by ". . . of what the all-purpose Swish 600 can do." The philosophical relevance of all this to our own discussion can be put in the following rather domestic way: "thinking" is a term which shares certain features with "all-purpose" as it occurs in the phrase "all-purpose Swish 600." It is not used to designate or refer to one capability, capacity, disposition, talent, habit, or feature of a given subject any more than "all-purpose" in the above example is used to mark out one particular operation of a vacuum cleaner. Thinking, whatever positive account one might give of it, is not, for example, like swimming or tennis playing. The question as to whether Peterson can swim or play tennis can be settled by a few token examples of Peterson swimming or playing tennis. (And it might be noted it is hardly imaginable that the question as to whether Peterson could think or not would be raised. For in general it is not at all interesting to ask that question of contemporary human beings, though it might be interesting for contemporary human beings to raise it in connection with different anthropoids viewed at various stages of their evolution.) But if we suppose the question were raised in connection with Peterson the only appropriate sort of answer to it would be one like, "Good heavens, what makes you think he can't?" (as if anticipating news of some horrible brain injury inflicted on Peterson). And our shock would not be at his perhaps having lost a particular talent. It would not be like the case of a Wimbledon champion losing his tennis talent because of an amputated arm.

It is no more unusual for a human being to be capable of thought than it is for a human being to be composed of cells. Similarly, "He can think" is no more an answer to questions concerning Peterson's mental capacities or intelligence, than "He's composed of cells" is an answer to the usual type of question about Peterson's appearance. And to say that Peterson can think is not to say there are a few token examples of thinking which are at our fingertips, any more than to say that the Swish 600 is all-purpose is to have in mind a particular maneuver or two of which the device is capable. It is because thinking cannot be identified with what can be shown by any one example or type of example; thus Turing's approach to the question "Can a machine think?" via the imitation game is less than convincing. In effect he provides us below with a dialogue very much like the one above:

Turing: You know, machines can think.

Philosopher: Good heavens! Really? How do you know?

Turing: Well, they can play what's called the imitation game. (This is followed by a description of same.)

Philosopher: Interesting. What else can they do? They must be capable of a great deal if they can really think.

Turing: What do you mean, "What else can they do?" They play the imitation game. That's thinking, isn't it?

Etc.

But Turing, like the vacuum cleaner salesman, has trouble making his sale.

SUGGESTED READINGS

The idea that men are machines of some sort is quite old. Descartes thought that the bodies of men and animals were machines and that animals, not having souls, had no feelings. In the mid-eighteenth century J. O. de la Mettrie, a Frenchman, wrote a book entitled (in translation) *Man a Machine*. But it was not until the development of modern computing machinery that the identification of minds and machines became plausible enough to challenge much philosophical attention. A collection of recent papers has been made by A. R. Anderson: it is called *Minds and Machines*. S. Hook has edited a symposium, *Dimensions of Mind*, on various facets of the topic. The papers by M. Scriven, "The Compleat Robot: A Prolegomena to Androidology," and by A. Danto, "On Consciousness in Machines," should be consulted. H. Putnam's contribution to this symposium has been reprinted in Anderson's collection. Putnam has a later paper, "Robots: Machines or Artificially Created Life?", in the *Journal of Philosophy*, 1964.

A fair acquaintance with mathematics is required for thorough investigation of the technical sides of this problem. This is illustrated by two important books, J. von Neumann's *The Computer and the Brain* and W. R. Ashby's *Design for a Brain*. For some relief the student may wish to consult I. Asimov, *I, Robot*.

B. Historical Inevitability

The belief that mankind has a destiny which it is powerless to alter has taken innumerable forms, many of them religious. The most influential modern version of this ancient belief is the Marxist theory of historical materialism, represented here by the work of ENGELS, who contributed greatly to the formation of Marx's theories. According to Marx and Engels no single individual can change the course of history or alter the institutions of his society. Existing social institutions are the result of historical processes determined primarily by economic structure and economic laws. These in turn do not result from the ideas, beliefs, or desires of individuals: "It is not the consciousness of men that determines their existence," Marx wrote in a famous epigram, "on the contrary their social existence determines their consciousness." We are made what we are by the way our society produces and distributes economic goods. To attempt to change society is futile unless we obey the historical laws according to which one mode of production and distribution leads to another. Marx thought that the system of production dominant during his lifetime—*laissez-faire* capitalism—was fated to destroy itself and to be replaced by an entirely different system, where there would be no social classes because there would be no private ownership of the means of production. The change was inevitable, and anyone who tried to prevent it was wasting his energy as much as if he had tried singlehanded to prevent the tide from rising.

This form of determinism obviously has far-reaching consequences. If our thoughts and feelings are determined by the economic structure of our society, does this not imply some sort of ethical relativism? Marx and Engels think that it does and that the moral, religious, and historical beliefs of any social class are not so much objective reflections of reality as weapons used to preserve or increase the power of that social class. If the destiny of mankind is fixed, does this not mean that we are deluded when we plan to do certain things to change society? Does it not even imply that we are not free to choose?

Because of these implications—to say nothing here of the overwhelming importance of the social and political implications of the theory—philosophers have been much concerned with Marxist doctrine, and indeed with any doctrine of historical determinism which resembles it in these respects. Engels, in this classic presentation of historical materialism, states some of the most important theses of the Marxist view. BERLIN offers a number of criticisms of these doctrines—not of their details, but of the principles on which they rest. He discusses crucially important notions like that of objectivity and points out various ways in which determinist theories of history are confused about the nature of scientific laws. Finally, he offers a defence of the freedom of individuals to be able to act as they choose, a defence that leaves room for the hope that men may be able to control not only their own actions but the future of their society as well.

Communism and History[*]

F R I E D R I C H   E N G E L S [1820–1895] was a close collaborator of Karl Marx from 1845 until the latter's death in 1883. Together they wrote *The Communist Manifesto*, and they collaborated in developing the theory of dialectical and historical materialism. After Marx's death, Engels spent the remainder of his life in further writing and in editing, completing, and translating Marx's works.

INTRODUCTION. The French philosophers of the eighteenth century, who paved the way for the revolution, appealed to reason as the sole judge of all that existed. A rational state, a rational society were to be established; everything that ran counter to eternal reason was to be relentlessly set aside. In reality this eternal reason was no more than the idealized intellect of the middle class, just at that period developing into the bourgeoisie. When, therefore, the French Revolution had realized this rational society and this rational state, it became apparent that the new institutions, however rational in comparison with earlier conditions, were by no means absolutely rational. The rational state had suffered shipwreck. Rousseau's Social Contract had found its realization in the Reign of Terror, from which the bourgeoisie, who had lost faith in their own political capacity, had sought refuge first in the corruption of the Directorate, and ultimately in the protection of the Napoleonic despotism. The promised eternal peace had changed to an endless war of conquest. The rational society had fared no better. The antagonism between rich and poor, instead of being resolved in general well-being, had been sharpened by the abolition of the guild and other privileges, which had bridged it over, and of the benevolent institutions of the Church, which had mitigated its effects; the impetuous growth of industry on a capitalist basis raised the poverty and suffering of the working masses into a vital condition of society's existence. The number of crimes increased from year to year. And if the feudal depravities, formerly shamelessly flaunting in the light of day, though not abolished, were yet temporarily forced into the background, on the other hand the bourgeois vices, until then cherished only in privacy, now bloomed all the more luxuriantly. Trade developed more and more into swindling. The "fraternity" of the revolutionary motto was realized in the chicanery and envy of the competitive struggle. Corruption took the place of

[*] From Engels: *Herr Eugen Dühring's Revolution in Science* (*Anti-Dühring*), Part III, Chapter 1 and 2, and Part I, Chapter 11, 9, and 10; translated by Emile Burns, edited by C. P. Dutt. Reprinted by permission of International Publishers, New York.

violent oppression, and money replaced the sword as the chief lever of social power. The right of "the first night" passed from the feudal lords to the bourgeois manufacturers. Prostitution assumed proportions hitherto unknown. Marriage itself remained, as before, the legally recognized form, the official cloak of prostitution, and was also supplemented by widespread adultery. In a word, compared with the glowing promises of the prophets of the Enlightenment, the social and political institutions established by the "victory of reason" proved to be bitterly disillusioning caricatures. The only thing still lacking was people to voice this disillusionment, and these came with the turn of the century. In 1802 Saint-Simon's *Geneva Letters* appeared; Fourier's first work was published in 1808, although the groundwork of his theory dated from 1799; on the first of January, 1800, Robert Owen took over the management of New Lanark.

At this period, however, the capitalist mode of production, and with it the antagonism between bourgeoisie and proletariat, was as yet very undeveloped. Large-scale industry, which had only just arisen in England, was still unknown in France. But it is large-scale industry that on the one hand first develops the conflicts which make a revolution in the mode of production an urgent necessity—conflicts not only between the classes born of it, but also between the very productive forces and forms of exchange which it creates; and on the other hand it develops, precisely in these gigantic productive forces, also the means through which these conflicts can be resolved. If, therefore, about 1800, the conflicts arising from the new social order were only just beginning to develop, this is even more true of the means through which they were to be resolved. Though during the Reign of Terror the propertyless masses of Paris had been able to win the mastery for a moment, by doing so they had only proved how impossible their rule was in the then existing conditions. The proletariat, only then just separating itself from these propertyless masses as the nucleus of a new class, as yet quite incapable of independent political action, appeared as an oppressed, suffering estate of society, to which, in its incapacity to help itself, help could at most be brought from outside, from above.

This historical situation also dominated the founders of socialism. To the immature stage of capitalist production and the immature class position, immature theories corresponded. The solution of social problems, a solution which still lay hidden in the undeveloped economic conditions, was to be produced out of their heads. Society presented nothing but abuses; it was the task of the thinking intellect to remove them. What was required was to discover a new and more perfect social order and to impose this on society from without, by propaganda and where possible by the example of model experiments. These new social systems were from the outset doomed to be utopias; the more their details were elaborated, the more they necessarily receded into pure phantasy. . . . The utopians, were utopians because they could be nothing else at a time when capitalist production was as yet so little developed. They necessarily had to construct the outlines of a new society out of their own heads, because within the old society the elements of the new were not as yet generally apparent; for the basic plan of the new edifice they could only appeal to reason, just because they could not as yet appeal to contemporary history. . . .

THE MATERIALIST CONCEPTION OF HISTORY. The materialist conception of history starts from the principle that production, and with production the exchange of its products, is the basis of every social order; that in every society which has appeared in history the distribution of the products, and with it the division of society into classes or estates, is determined by what is produced and how it is produced, and how the product is exchanged. According to this conception, the ultimate causes of all social changes and political revolutions are to be sought, not in the minds of men, in their increasing insight into eternal truth and justice, but in changes in the mode of production and exchange; they are to be sought not in the *philosophy* but in the *economics* of the epoch concerned. The growing realization that existing social institutions are irrational and unjust, that reason has become nonsense and good deeds a scourge, is only a sign that changes have been taking place quietly in the methods of production and forms of exchange with which the social order, adapted to previous economic conditions, is no longer in accord. This also involves that the means through which the abuses that have been revealed can be got rid of must likewise be present, in more or less developed form, in the altered conditions of production. These means are not to be *invented* by the mind, but *discovered* by means of the mind in the existing material facts of production.

Where then, on this basis, does modern socialism stand?

The existing social order, as is now fairly generally admitted, is the creation of the present ruling class, the bourgeoisie. The mode of production peculiar to the bourgeoisie—called, since Marx, the capitalist mode of production—was incompatible with the local privileges and the privileges of birth as well as with the reciprocal personal ties of the feudal system; the bourgeoisie shattered the feudal system, and on its ruins established the bourgeois social order, the realm of free competition, freedom of movement, equal rights for commodity owners, and all the other bourgeois glories. The capitalist mode of production could now develop freely. From the time when steam and the new tool-making machinery had begun to transform the former manufacture into large-scale industry, the productive forces evolved under bourgeois direction developed at a pace that was previously unknown and to an unprecedented degree. But just as manufacture, and the handicraft industry which had been further developed under its influence, had previously come into conflict with the feudal fetters of the guilds, so large-scale industry, as it develops more fully, comes into conflict with the barriers within which the capitalist mode of production holds it confined. The new forces of production have already outgrown the bourgeois form of using them; and this conflict between productive forces and mode of production is not a conflict which has arisen in men's heads, as for example the conflict between original sin and divine justice; but it exists in the facts, objectively, outside of us, independently of the will or purpose even of the men who brought it about. Modern socialism is nothing but the reflex in thought of this actual conflict, its ideal reflection in the minds first of the class which is directly suffering under it—the working class.

In what, then, does this conflict consist?

Previous to capitalist production, that is to say, in the Middle Ages, small-scale production was general, on the basis of the private ownership by the workers of their means of production: the agricultural industry of the small peasant, freeman or serf, and the handicraft industry of the towns. The instruments of labor—land, agricultural implements, the workshop and tools —were the instruments of labor of individuals, intended only for individual use, and therefore necessarily puny, dwarfish, restricted. But just because of this they belonged, as a rule, to the producer himself. To concentrate and enlarge these scattered, limited means of production, to transform them into the mighty levers of production of the present day, was precisely the historic role of the capitalist mode of production and of its representative, the bourgeoisie. In Part IV of *Capital* Marx gives a detailed account of how, since the fifteenth century, this process has developed historically through the three stages of simple co-operation, manufacture and large-scale industry. But as Marx also points out, the bourgeoisie was unable to transform those limited means of production into mighty productive forces except by transforming them from individual means of production into *social* means of production, which could be used only *by a body of men as a whole*. The spinning wheel, the hand loom and the blacksmith's hammer were replaced by the spinning machine, the mechanical loom and the steam hammer; and the factory, making the co-operation of hundreds and thousands of workers necessary, took the place of the individual workroom. And, like the means of production, production itself changed from a series of individual operations into a series of social acts, and the products from the products of individuals into social products. The yarn, the cloth and the metal goods which now came from the factory were the common product of many workers through whose hands it had to pass successively before it was ready. No individual can say of such products: I made it, that is *my* product. . . .

In commodity production as it had developed in the Middle Ages, the question could never arise of who should be the owner of the product of labor. The individual producer had produced it, as a rule, from raw material which belonged to him and was often produced by himself, with his own instruments of labor, and by his own manual labor or that of his family. There was no need whatever for the product to be appropriated by him; it belonged to him as an absolute matter of course. His ownership of the product was therefore based *upon his own labor*. Even where outside help was used, it was as a rule subsidiary, and in many cases received other compensation in addition to wages; the guild apprentice and journeyman worked less for the sake of their board and wages than to train themselves to become master craftsmen. Then came the concentration of the means of production in large workshops and manufactories, their transformation into means of production that were in fact social. But the social means of production and the social products were treated as if they were still, as they had been before, the means of production and the products of individuals. Hitherto, the owner of the instruments of labor had appropriated the product because it was as a rule his own product, the auxiliary labor of other persons being the exception; now, the owner of the instruments of production continued to appropriate the product, although it was no longer *his* product, but exclusively the product of *other's labor*. Thus, therefore, the products, now socially produced, were not appropriated by those who had really set the means of production in motion and really produced the products, but by the *capitalists*. Means of production and production itself had in essence become social. But they were subjected to a form of appropriation which has as its presupposition private production by individuals, with each individual owning his own product and bringing it on to the market. The mode of production is subjected to this form of appropriation, although it removes the presuppositions on which the latter was based. In this contradiction, which gives the new mode of production its capitalist character, *the whole conflict of today is already present in germ*. The more the new mode of production gained the ascendancy on all decisive fields of production and in all countries of decisive economic importance, pressing back individual production into insignificant areas, the *more glaring necessarily became the incompatibility of social production with capitalist appropriation*.

The first capitalist found, as we have said, the form of wage labor already in existence; but wage labor as the exception, as an auxiliary occupation, as a supplementary, as a transitory phase. The agricultural laborer who occasionally went to work as a day laborer had a few acres of his own land, from which if necessary he could get his livelihood. The regulations of the guilds ensured that the journeyman of today became the master craftsman of tomorrow. But as soon as the means of production had become social and were concentrated in the hands of capitalists, this situation changed. Both the means of production and the products of the small, individual producer lost more and more of their value; there was nothing left for him to do but to go to the capitalist and work for wages. Wage labor, hitherto an exception and subsidiary, became the rule and the basic form of all production, hitherto an auxiliary occupation, it now became the laborer's exclusive activity. The occasional wage worker became the wage worker for life. The number of life-long wage workers was also increased to a colossal extent by the simultaneous disintegration of the feudal system, the dispersal of the retainers of the feudal lords, the eviction of peasants from their homesteads, etc. The separation between the means of production concentrated in the hands of the capitalists, on the one side, and the producers now possessing nothing but their labor power, on the other, was made complete. *The contradiction between social production and capitalist appropriation became manifest as the antagonism between proletariat and bourgeoisie. . . .*

With the extension of commodity production, however, and especially with the emergence of the capitalist mode of production, the laws of commodity production, previously latent, also began to operate more openly and more potently. The old bonds were loosened, the old dividing barriers broken through, the producers more and more transformed into independent, isolated commodity producers. The anarchy of social production became obvious, and was carried to further and further extremes. But the chief means through which the capitalist mode of production accentuated this anarchy in social production was the direct opposite of anarchy: the increasing organization of production on a social basis in each individual productive establishment. This was the lever with which it put an end to the former peaceful stability. In whatever branch of industry it was introduced, it could suffer no older method of production to exist alongside it; where it laid hold of a handicraft, that handicraft was wiped out. The field of labor became a field of battle. The great geographical discoveries and the colonization which followed on them multiplied markets and hastened on the transformation of handicraft into manufacture. The struggle broke out not only between the individual local producers; the local struggles developed into national struggles, the trade wars of the seventeenth and eighteenth centuries. In the end large-scale industry and the creation of the world market made the struggle universal, and at the same time gave it an unparalleled intensity. Between individual capitalists, as between whole industries and whole countries, advantages in natural or artificial conditions of production decide life or death. The vanquished are relentlessly cast aside. It is the Darwinian struggle for individual existence, transferred from Nature to society with intensified fury. The standpoint of the animal in Nature appears as the last word in human development. The contradiction between social production and capitalist appropriation reproduces itself as *the antagonism between the organization of production in the individual factory and the anarchy of production in society as a whole.*

The capitalist mode of production moves in these two forms of the contradiction immanent in it from its very nature, without hope of escaping from that "vicious circle" which Fourier long ago discovered. But what Fourier in his day was as yet unable to see is that this circle is gradually narrowing; that the motion is rather in the form of a spiral and must meet its end, like the motion of the planets, by collision with the centre. It is the driving force of the social anarchy of production which transforms the immense majority of men more and more into proletarians, and it is in turn the proletarian masses who will ultimately put an end to the anarchy of production. It is the infinite perfectibility of the machine in large-scale industry into a compulsory commandment for each individual industrial capitalist to make his machinery more and more perfect, under penalty of ruin. But the perfecting of machinery means rendering human labor superfluous. If the introduction and increase of machinery meant the displacement of millions of hand workers by a few machine workers, the improvement of machinery means the displacement of larger and larger numbers of the machine workers themselves, and ultimately the creation of a mass of available wage workers exceeding the average requirements of capital for labor. . . .

Thus it comes about that the excessive labor of some becomes the necessary condition for the lack of employment of others, and that large-scale industry, which hunts all over the world for new consumers, restricts the consumption of the masses at home to a famine minimum and thereby undermines its own internal market. "The law that always equilibrates the relative surplus population, or industrial reserve army, to the extent and energy of accumulation, this law rivets the laborer to capital more firmly than the wedges of Vulcan did Prometheus to the rock. It establishes an accumulation of misery, corresponding with accumulation of capital. Accumulation of wealth at one pole is, therefore, at the same time accumulation of misery, agony of toil, slavery, ignorance, brutality, mental degradation, at the opposite pole, *i.e.,* on the side of the class that *produces its own product in the form of capital.*"

And to expect any other distribution of the products from the capitalist mode of production is like expecting the electrodes of a battery, while they are in contact with the battery, not to decompose water, not to develop oxygen at the positive pole and hydrogen at the negative. . . .

And in fact, since 1825, when the first general crisis broke out, the whole industrial and commercial world, the production and exchange of all civilized peoples and of their more or less barbarian dependent people have been dislocated practically once in every ten years. Trade comes to a standstill, the markets are glutted, the products lie in great masses, unsaleable, ready money disappears, credit vanishes, the factories are idle, the working masses go short of food because they have produced too much food, bankruptcy follows upon bankruptcy, forced sale upon forced sale. The stagnation lasts for years, both productive force and products are squandered and destroyed on a large scale, until the accumulated masses of commodities are at last disposed of at a more or less considerable depreciation, until production and exchange gradually begin to move again. By degrees the pace quickens; it becomes a trot; the industrial trot passes into a gallop, and the gallop in turn passes into the mad onrush of a complete industrial, commercial, credit, and speculative steeplechase, only to land again in the end, after the most breakneck jumps—in the ditch of a crash. And so on again and again. . . .

In these crises, the contradiction between social production and capitalist appropriation comes to a violent explosion. The circulation of commodities is for the moment reduced to nothing; the means of circulation, money, becomes an obstacle to circulation; all the laws of commodity production and commodity circulation are turned upside down. The economic collision has reached its culminating point: *the mode of production rebels against the mode of exchange; the productive forces rebel against the mode of production, which they have outgrown.*

The fact that the social organization of production within the factory has developed to the point at which it has become incompatible with the anarchy of production in society which exists alongside it and above it—this fact is made palpable to the capitalists themselves by the violent concentration of capital which takes place during crises through the ruin of many big and even more small capitalists. The whole mechanism of the capitalist mode of production breaks down under the pressure of the productive forces which it itself created. It is no longer able to transform the whole of this mass of means of production into capital; they lie idle, and for this very reason the industrial reserve army must also lie idle. Means of production, means of subsistence, available laborers, all the elements of production and of general wealth are there in abundance. But "abundance becomes the source of distress and want" (Fourier), because it is precisely abundance that prevents the conversion of the means of production and subsistence into capital. For in capitalist society the means of production cannot begin to function unless they have first been converted into capital, into means for the exploitation of human labor power. The necessity for the means of production and subsistence to take on the form of capital stands like a ghost between them and the workers. It alone prevents the coming together of the material and personal levers of production; it alone forbids the means of production to function, the workers to work and to live. Thus on the one hand the capitalist mode of production stands convicted of its own incapacity any longer to control these productive forces. And on the other hand these productive forces themselves press forward with increasing force to put an end to the contradiction, to rid themselves of their character as capital, *to the actual recognition of their character as social productive forces.* . . .

If the crises revealed the incapacity of the bourgeoisie any longer to control the modern productive forces, the conversion of the great organizations for production and communication into joint-stock companies and state property shows that for this purpose the bourgeoisie can be dispensed with. All the social functions of the capitalists are now carried out by salaried employees. The capitalist has no longer any social activity save the pocketing of revenues, the clipping of coupons and gambling on the Stock Exchange, where the different capitalists fleece each other of their capital. Just as at first the capitalist mode of production displaced the workers, so now it displaces the capitalists, relegating them, just as it did the workers, to the superfluous population, even if in the first instance not to the industrial reserve army.

But the conversion into either joint-stock companies or state property does not deprive the productive forces of their character as capital. In the case of joint-stock companies this is obvious. And the modern state, too, is only the organization with which bourgeois society provides itself in order to maintain the general external conditions of the capitalist mode of production against encroachments either by the workers or by individual capitalists. The modern state, whatever its form, is an essentially capitalist machine; it is the state of the capitalists, the ideal collective body of all capitalists. The more productive forces it takes over, the more it becomes the real collective body of all the capitalists, the more citizens it exploits. The workers remain wage-earners, proletarians. The capitalist relationship is not abolished; it is rather pushed to an extreme. But at this extreme it changes into its opposite. State ownership of the productive forces is not the solution of the conflict, but it contains within itself the formal means, the handle to the solution.

This solution can only consist in the recognition in practice of the social nature of the modern productive forces; that is, therefore, the mode of production, appropriation and exchange must be brought into accord with the social character of the means of production. And this can only be brought about by society, openly and without deviation, taking possession of the productive forces which have outgrown all control other than that of society itself. Thereby the social character of the means of production and of the products—which today operates against the producers themselves, periodically breaking through the mode of production and exchange and enforcing itself only as a blind law of Nature, violently and destructively—is quite consciously asserted by the producers, and is transformed from a cause of disorder and periodic collapse into the most powerful lever of production itself.

The forces operating in society work exactly like the forces operating in Nature: blindly, violently, destructively, so long as we do not understand them and fail to take them into account. But when once we have recognized them and understood how they work, their direction and their effects, the gradual subjection of them to our will and the use of them for the attainment of our aims depends entirely upon ourselves. And this is quite especially true of the mighty productive forces of the present day. So long as we obstinately refuse to understand their nature and their character—and the capitalist mode of production and its defenders set themselves against any such attempt—so long do these forces operate in spite of us, against us, and so long do they control us, as we have shown in detail. But once their nature is grasped, in the hands of the producers working in association they can be transformed from demoniac masters into willing servants. This is the difference between the destructive force of electricity in a thunderstorm and the tamed electricity of the telegraph and the arc light; the difference between a conflagration and fire in the service of man. A similar manipulation of the productive forces of the present day, on the basis of their real nature at last recognized by society, opens the way to the replacement of the anarchy of social production by a socially planned regulation of production in accordance with the needs both of society as a whole and of each individual. The capitalist mode of appropriation, in which the product enslaves first the producer, and then also the appropriator, will thereby be replaced by the mode of appropriation of the product based on the nature of the modern means of production themselves: on the one hand direct social appropriation as a means to the maintenance and extension of production, and on the other hand direct individual appropriation as a means to life and pleasure.

By more and more transforming the great majority of the population into proletarians, the capitalist mode of production brings into being the force which, under penalty of its own destruction, is compelled to carry out this revolution. By more and more driving towards the conversion of the vast socialized means of production into state property, it itself points the way for the carrying through of this revolution. *The proletariat seizes the State power, and transforms the means of production in the first instance into State property.* But in doing this, it puts an end to itself as the proletariat, it puts an end to all class differences and class antagonisms, it puts an end also to the state as the state. Former society, moving in class antagonisms, had need of the state, that is, an organization of the exploiting class at each period for the maintenance of its external conditions of production, that is, therefore, for the forcible holding down of the exploited class in the conditions of oppression (slavery, villeinage or serfdom, wage labor) determined by the existing mode of production. The state was the official representative of society as a whole, its embodiment in a visible corporation; but it was this only in so far as it was the State of that class which itself, in its epoch, represented society as a whole; in ancient times, the state of the slave-owning citizens; in the Middle Ages, of the feudal nobility; in our epoch, of the bourgeoisie. When ultimately it becomes really representative of society as a whole, it makes itself superfluous. As soon as there is no longer any class of society to be held in subjection; as soon as, along with class domination and the struggle for individual existence based on the former anarchy of production, the collisions and excesses arising from these have also been abolished, there is nothing more to be repressed which would make a special repressive force, a state, necessary. The first act in which the state really comes forward as the representative of society as a whole—the taking possession of the means of production in the name of society—is at the same time its last independent act as a state. The interference of the state power in social relations becomes superfluous in one sphere after another, and then ceases of itself. The government of persons is replaced by the administration of things and the direction of the process of production. The state is not "abolished," *it withers away.* It is from this standpoint that we must appraise the phrase "free people's state"—both its justification at times for agitational purposes, and its ultimate scientific inadequacy—and also the demand of the so-called anarchists that the state should be abolished overnight. . . .

The seizure of the means of production by society puts an end to commodity production, and therewith to the domination of the product over the producer. Anarchy in social production is replaced by conscious organization on a planned basis. The struggle for individual existence comes to an end. And at this point, in a certain sense, man finally cuts himself off from the animal world, leaves the conditions of animal existence behind him and enters conditions which are really human. The conditions of existence forming man's environment, which up to now have dominated man, at this point pass under the dominion and control of man, who now for the first time becomes the real conscious master of Nature, because and in so far as he has become master of his own social organization. The laws of his own social activity, which have hitherto confronted him as external, dominating laws of Nature, will then be applied by man with complete understanding, and hence will be dominated by man. Men's own social organization which has hitherto stood in opposition to them as if arbitrarily decreed by Nature and history, will then become the voluntary act of men themselves. The objective, external forces which have hitherto dominated history, will then pass under the control of men themselves. It is only from this point that men, with full consciousness, will fashion their own history; it is only from this point that the social causes set in motion by men will have, predominantly and in constantly increasing measure, the effects willed by men. It is humanity's leap from the realm of necessity into the realm of freedom. . . .

NECESSITY AND FREEDOM. Hegel was the first to state correctly the relation between freedom and necessity. To him, freedom is the appreciation of necessity. "Necessity is *blind* only *in so far as it is not understood.*" Freedom does not consist in the dream of independence of natural laws, but in the knowledge of these laws, and in the possibility this gives of systematically making them work towards definite ends. This holds good in relation both to the laws of external nature and to those which govern the bodily and mental life of men themselves—two classes of laws which we can separate from each other at most only in thought but not in reality. Freedom of the will therefore means nothing but the capacity to make decisions with real knowledge of the subject. Therefore the *freer* a man's judgment is in relation to a definite question, with so much the greater *necessity* is the content of this judgment determined; while the uncertainty, founded on ignorance, which seems to make an arbitrary choice among many different and conflicting possible decisions, shows by this precisely that it is not free, that it is controlled by the very object it should itself control. Freedom therefore consists in the control over ourselves and over external nature which is founded on knowledge of natural necessity; it is therefore necessarily a product of historical development. The first men who separated themselves from the animal kingdom were in all essentials as unfree as the animals themselves, but each step forward in civilization was a step towards freedom. On the threshold of human history stands the discovery that mechanical motion can be transformed into heat: the production of fire by friction; at the close of the development so far gone through stands the discovery that heat can be transformed into mechanical motion: the steam engine.—And, in spite of the gigantic and liberating revolution in the social world which the steam engine is carrying through—and which is not yet half completed—it is beyond 'estion that the generation of fire by friction was of even greater effectiveness for the liberation of mankind. For the generation of fire by friction gave man for the first time control over one of the forces of Nature, and thereby separated him for ever from the animal kingdom. The steam engine will never bring about such a mighty leap forward in human development, however important it may seem in our eyes as representing all those immense productive forces dependent on it—forces which alone make possible a state of society in which there are no longer class distinctions or anxiety over the means of subsistence for the individual, and in which for the first time there can be talk of real human freedom and of an existence in harmony with the established laws of Nature. . . .

MORALITY. What morality is preached to us today? There is first Christian-feudal morality, inherited from past centuries of faith; and this again has two main subdivisions, Catholic and Protestant moralities, each of which in turn has no lack of further subdivisions from the Jesuit-Catholic and Orthodox-Protestant to loose "advanced" moralities. Alongside of these we find the modern bourgeois morality and with it too the proletarian morality of the future, so that in the most advanced European countries alone the past, present and future provide three great groups of moral theories which are in force simultaneously and alongside of each other. Which is then the true one? Not one of them, in the sense of having absolute validity; but certainly that morality which contains the maximum of durable elements is the one which, in the present, represents the overthrow of the present, represents the future: that is, the proletarian.

But when we see that the three classes of modern society, the feudal aristocracy, the bourgeoisie and the proletariat, each have their special morality, we can only draw the one conclusion, that men, consciously or unconsciously, derive their moral ideas in the last resort from the practical relations on which their class position is based—from the economic relations in which they carry on production and exchange.

But nevertheless there is much that is common to the three moral theories mentioned above—is this not at least a portion of a morality which is externally fixed? These moral theories represent three different stages of the same historical development, and have therefore a common historical background, and for that reason alone they necessarily have much in common. Even more. In similar or approximately similar stages of economic development moral theories must of necessity be more or less in agreement. From the moment when private property in movable objects developed, in all societies in which this private property existed there must be this moral law in common: Thou shalt not steal. Does this law thereby become an eternal moral law? By no means. In a society in which the motive for stealing has been done away with, in which therefore at the very most only lunatics would ever steal, how the teacher of morals would be laughed at who tried solemnly to proclaim the eternal truth: Thou shalt not steal!

We therefore reject every attempt to impose on us any moral dogma whatsoever as an eternal, ultimate and forever immutable moral law on the pretext that the moral world too has its permanent principles which transcend history and the differences between nations. We maintain on the contrary that all former moral theories are the product, in the last analysis, of the economic stage which society had reached at that particular epoch. And as society has hitherto moved in class antagonisms, morality was always a class morality; it has either justified the domination and the interests of the ruling class, or, as soon as the oppressed class has become powerful enough, it has represented the revolt against this domination and the future interests of the oppressed. That in this process there has on the whole been progress in morality, as in all other branches of human knowledge, cannot be doubted. But we have not yet passed beyond class morality. A really human morality which transcends class antagonisms and their legacies in thought becomes possible only at a stage of society which has not only overcome class contradictions but has even forgotten them in practical life. . . .

EQUALITY. The feudal middle ages developed in its womb the class which was destined in the future course of its evolution to be the standard-bearer of the modern demand for equality: the bourgeoisie. . . . But the revolution in the economic conditions of society [at the end of the feudal period] was not followed by any immediate corresponding change in its political structure. The state order remained feudal, while society became more and more bourgeois. . . . Where economic relations required freedom and equality of rights, the political system opposed them at every step with guild restrictions and special privileges. Local privileges, differential duties, exceptional laws of all kinds in trade affected not only foreigners or people living in the colonies, but often enough also whole categories of the nationals of each country; the privileges of the guilds everywhere and ever anew formed barriers to the path of development of manufacture. Nowhere was the path open and the chances equal for all the bourgeois competitors—and yet this was the first and ever more pressing need.

The demand for liberation from feudal fetters and the establishment of equality of rights by the abolition of feudal inequalities was bound soon to assume wider dimensions from the moment when the economic advance of society first placed it on the order of the day. If it was raised in the interests of industry and trade, it was also necessary to demand the same equality of rights for the great mass of the peasantry who, in every degree of bondage from total serfdom upwards, were compelled to give the greater part of their labor time to their feudal lord without payment and in addition to pay innumerable other dues to him and to the state. On the other hand, it was impossible to avoid the demand for the abolition also of feudal privileges, the freedom from taxation of the nobility, the political privileges of the various feudal estates. And as people were no longer living in a world empire such as the Roman Empire had been, but in a system of independent states dealing with each other on an equal footing and at approximately the same stage of bourgeois development, it was a matter of course that the demand for equality should assume a general character reaching out beyond the individual state, that freedom and equality should be proclaimed as *human rights*. And it is significant of the specifically bourgeois character of these human rights that the American Constitution, the first to recognize the rights of man, in the same breath confirmed the slavery of the colored races then existing in America: class privileges were prescribed, race privileges sanctioned.

As is well known, however, from the moment when, like a butterfly from the chrysalis, the bourgeoisie arose out of the burghers of the feudal period, when this "estate" of the Middle Ages developed into a class of modern society, it was always and inevitably accompanied by its shadow, the proletariat. And in the same way the bourgeois demand for equality was accompanied by the proletarian demand for equality. From the moment when the bourgeois demand for the abolition of class privileges was put forward, alongside of it appeared the proletarian demand for the abolition of the *classes themselves*—at first in religious form, basing itself on primitive Christianity, and later drawing support from the bourgeois equalitarian theories themselves. The proletarians took the bourgeoisie at their word: equality must not be merely apparent, must not apply merely to the sphere of the state, but must also be real, must be extended to the social and economic sphere. And especially since the French bourgeoisie, from the great revolution on, brought bourgeois equality to the forefront, the French proletariat answered blow for blow with the demand for social and economic equality, and equality became the battle-cry particularly of the French proletariat.

The demand for equality in the mouth of the proletariat has therefore a double meaning. It is either—as was the case at the very start, for example in the peasants' war—the spontaneous reaction against the crying social inequalities, against the contrast of rich and poor, the feudal lords and their serfs, surfeit and starvation; as such it is the simple expression of the revolutionary instinct, and finds its justification in that, and indeed only in that. Or, on the other hand, the proletarian demand for equality has arisen as the reaction against the bourgeois demand for equality, drawing more or less correct and more far-reaching demands from this bourgeois demand, and serving as an agitational means in order to rouse the workers against the capitalists on the basis of the capitalists' own assertions: and in this case it stands and falls with bourgeois equality itself. In both cases the real content of the proletarian demand for equality is the demand for the *abolition of classes.* Any demand for equality which goes beyond that, of necessity passes into absurdity. . . .

The idea of equality, therefore, both in its bourgeois and in its proletarian form, is itself a historical product, the creation of which required definite historical conditions which in turn themselves presuppose a long previous historical development. It is therefore anything but an eternal truth.

Historical Inevitability*

I S A I A H B E R L I N [1901–   ] was appointed to the Chichele Professorship of Social and Political Theory at Oxford in 1957. He has taught at Oxford for many years and has also visited at several universities in the United States. In addition to articles on nineteenth-century intellectual history, he has published *Karl Marx* (1939) and *The Hedgehog and the Fox* (1953).

The notion that one can discover large patterns or regularities in the procession of historical events is naturally attractive to those who are impressed by the success of the natural sciences in classifying, correlating, and, above all, predicting. They consequently seek to extend historical knowledge to fill gaps in the past (and, at times, to build into the limitless gap of the future) by applying 'scientific' method: by setting forth, armed with a metaphysical or empirical system, from such islands of certain, or virtually certain, knowledge of the facts as they claim to possess. And no doubt a great deal has been done, and will be done, in historical as in other fields by arguing from the known to the unknown, or from the little known to the even less known. But whatever value the perception of patterns or uniformities may have in stimulating or verifying specific hypotheses about the past or the future, it has played, and is increasingly playing, another and more dubious role in determining the outlook of our time. It has affected not merely ways of observing and describing the activities and characters of human beings, but moral and political and religious attitudes towards them. For among the questions that are bound to arise in any consideration of how and why human beings act and live as they do, are questions of human motive and responsibility. In

* From Berlin: *Historical Inevitability,* Oxford University Press, 1954. Reprinted by permission of the Oxford University Press.

describing human behaviour it has always been artificial and over-austere to omit questions of the character, purposes, and motives of individuals. And in considering these one automatically evaluates not merely the degree and kind of influence of this or that motive or character upon what happens, but also its moral or political quality in terms of whatever scale of values one consciously or semiconsciously accepts in one's thought or action. How did this or that situation arise? Who or what was or is (or will be, or could be) responsible for a war, a revolution, an economic collapse, a renaissance of arts and letters, a discovery or an invention or a spiritual transformation altering the lives of men? It is by now a familiar story that there exist personal and impersonal theories of history. On the one hand, theories according to which the lives of entire peoples and societies have been decisively influenced by exceptional individuals—or, alternatively, doctrines according to which what happens occurs as a result not of the wishes and purposes of identifiable individuals, but of those of large numbers of unspecified persons, with the qualification that these collective wishes and goals are not solely or even largely determined by impersonal factors, and are therefore not wholly or even largely deducible from knowledge of natural forces alone, such as environment, or climate, or physical, physiological, and psychological processes. On either view, it becomes the business of historians to investigate who wanted what, and when, and where, in what way; how many men avoided or pursued this or that goal, and with what intensity; and further to ask under what circumstances such wants or fears have proved effective, and to what extent, and with what consequences.

Against this kind of interpretation, in terms of the purposes and characters of individuals, there is a cluster of views (to which the progress of the natural sciences has given a great and growing prestige) according to which all explanations in terms of human intentions rest on a mixture of vanity and stubborn ignorance. These views rest on the assumption that belief in the importance of the motives is delusive; that the behaviour of men is in fact made what it is by factors largely beyond the control of individuals; for instance, by the influence of physical factors, or of environment, or of custom; or by the 'natural' growth of some larger unit—a race, a nation, a class, a biological species; or (according to some writers) by some entity conceived in even less empirical terms—a 'spiritual organism,' a religion, a civilization, a Hegelian (or Buddhist) World Spirit; entities whose career or manifestations on earth are the object either of empirical or of metaphysical inquiries —depending on the cosmological outlook of particular thinkers. Those who incline to this kind of impersonal interpretation of historical change, whether because they believe that it possesses greater scientific value (i.e. enables them to predict the future, or 'retrodict' the past, more successfully or precisely), or because they believe that it embodies some crucial insight into the nature of the universe, are committed by it to placing the ultimate responsibility for what happens upon impersonal or 'trans-personal' or 'super-personal' entities or 'forces,' the evolution of which is regarded as being identical with human history. It is true that the more cautious and clear-headed among such theorists try to meet the objections of empirically minded critics by adding in a footnote, or as an afterthought, that, whatever their terminology, they are on no account to be taken to believe that there literally exist such creatures as civilizations or races or spirits of nations living side by side with the individuals who compose them; that they fully realize that all institutions 'in the last analysis' consist of individual men and women, and are not themselves personalities but only convenient devices —idealized models, or labels, or metaphors—different ways of classifying, grouping, explaining, or predicting the properties or behaviour of individual human beings in terms of their more important (i.e. historically effective) empirical characteristics. Nevertheless these protestations too often turn out to be mere lip-service to principles which those who profess them do not really believe. Such writers seldom write or think as if they took these deflationary *caveats* over-seriously; and the more candid or naïve among them do not even pretend to subscribe to them. Thus nations or cultures or civilizations for Fichte or Hegel (and Spengler; and one is inclined, though somewhat hesitantly, to add Professor Arnold Toynbee) are certainly not merely convenient collective terms for individuals possessing certain characteristics in common; but are more 'real' and more 'concrete' than the individuals who compose them. Individuals remain 'abstract' precisely because they are mere 'elements' or 'aspects,' 'moments' artificially abstracted for *ad hoc* purposes, and literally without existence (or, at any rate, 'historical' or 'philosophical' or 'real' being) apart from the wholes of which they form a part, much as the colour of a thing, or its shape, or its value are 'elements' or 'attributes' or 'modes' or 'aspects' of concrete objects—isolated for convenience, but thought of as existing independently—on their own—only because of some weakness or confusion in the analysing intellect. Marx and the Marxists are more ambiguous. We cannot be quite sure what to make of such a category as a social 'class' whose emergence and struggles, victories and defeats, condition the lives of individuals, sometimes against, and most often independently of, such individuals' conscious or expressed purposes. Classes are never proclaimed to be literally independent entities: they are constituted by individuals in their interaction (mainly economic). Yet to seek to explain, or put a moral or political value on the actions of individuals by examining such individuals one by one, even to the limited extent to which such examination is possible, is considered by Marxists to be not merely impracticable and time-wasting, but absurd in a more fundamental sense—because the 'true' (or 'deeper') causes of human behaviour lie not in the specific circumstances of an individual life or in the individual's thoughts or volitions (as a psychologist or biographer or a novelist might describe them) but in a pervasive interrelationship between a vast variety of such lives with their natural and man-made environment. Men do as they do, and think as they think, largely as a 'function of' the inevitable evolution of the 'class' as a whole—from which it follows that the history and development of classes can be studied independently of the biographies of their component individuals. It is the 'structure' and the 'evolution' of the class alone that (causally) matters in the end. This is, *mutatis mutandis,* similar to the attitude taken by those who identify race with culture, whether they be benevolent internationalists like Herder who thought that different races can and should admire, love, and assist one another as individuals can and do, because races are in some sense individuals (or super-individuals); or by the ferocious champions of national or racial self-assertion and war, like Gobineau or Houston Stewart Chamberlain or Hitler. And the same note, sometimes mild and civilized, sometimes harshly aggressive, is heard in the voices of all those upholders of collectivist *mystiques* who appeal from individual to tradition, or to the collective consciousness (or 'Unconscious') of a race or a nation or a culture, or, like Carlyle, feel that abstract nouns deserve capital letters, and tell us that Tradition or History (or 'The Past,' or 'The Masses') are wiser than we, or that the great society of the quick and the dead, of our ancestors and of generations yet unborn, has larger purposes than any single creature, purposes of which our lives are but a puny fragment, and that we belong to this larger unity with the 'deepest' and perhaps least conscious parts of ourselves. There are many versions of this belief, with varying proportions of empiricism and mysticism, 'tender'- and 'tough'-mindedness, optimism and pessimism, collectivism and individualism; but what all such views have in common is the fundamental distinction on which they rest between, on the one hand, 'real' and 'objective,' and, on the other, 'subjective' or 'arbitrary,' judgments, based respectively on acceptance or rejection of this ultimately mystical act of self-identification with a 'reality' which 'transcends' empirical experience.

For Hegel, for Marx, for Spengler (and for almost all thinkers for whom history is 'more' than past events, namely a theodicy) this reality takes on the form of an objective 'march of history.' The process may be thought of as being in time and space or beyond them; as being cyclical or spiral or rectilinear, or as occurring in the form of a peculiar zigzag movement, sometimes called dialectical; as continuous and uniform, or irregular, broken by sudden leaps to 'new levels'; as due to the changing forms of one single 'force,' or of conflicting elements locked (as in some ancient myth) in an eternal Pyrrhic struggle; as the history of one deity or 'force' or 'principle,' or of several; as being destined to end well or badly; as holding out to human beings the prospect of eternal beatitude, or eternal damnation, or of both in turn, or of neither. But whatever version of the story is accepted—and it is never a scientific, that is, empirically testable theory, stated in quantitative terms, still less a description of what our eyes see and our ears hear—the moral of it is always one and the same: that we must learn to distinguish the 'real' course of things from the dreams and fancies and 'rationalizations' which we construct for our solace or amusement; for these may comfort us for a while, but will betray us cruelly in the end. There is, we are told, a nature of things and it has a pattern in time: 'things are what they are and their consequences will be what they will be; why then should we seek to be deceived?' What, then, must we do to avoid deception? At the very least—if we cannot swallow the notion of super-personal 'spirits' or 'forces'—we must admit that all events occur in discoverable, uniform, unaltering patterns; for if some did not, how could we find the laws of all such occurrences? And without universal order—a system of true laws—how could history be 'intelligible'? how could it 'make sense,' 'have meaning,' be more than a picaresque account of a succession of random episodes, a mere collection (as Descartes, for this very reason, seems to have thought) of old wives' tales? Our values—what we think good and bad, important and trivial, right and wrong, noble and contemptible—all these are conditioned by the place we occupy in the pattern, on the moving stair. We praise and blame, worship and condemn whatever fits or does not fit the interests and needs and ideals that we seek to satisfy—the ends that (being made as we are) we cannot help pursuing —according to our lights, that is, our own perception of our condition, our place in 'Nature.' Such attitudes are held to be 'rational' and 'objective' to the degree to which we perceive this condition accurately, that is, understand where we are in terms of the great world plan, the movement whose regularities we discern as well as our historical sense and knowledge permits. To each condition and generation its own perspectives of the past and future, depending upon where it has arrived, what it has left behind, and whither it is moving; its values depend on this same awareness. To condemn the Greeks or the Romans or the Assyrians or the Aztecs for this or that folly or vice, may be no more than to say that what they did or wished or thought conflicts with our own view of life, which is the true or 'objective' view for the stage which we have reached, and which is perceived less or more clearly according to the depth and accuracy of our understanding of what this stage is, and of the manner in which it is developing. If the Romans and the Aztecs judged differently from us, they may have judged no less well and truly and 'objectively' to the degree to which they understood their own condition and their own very different stage of development. For us to condemn their scale of values is valid enough for our condition, which is the sole frame of reference we can use. And if they had known us, they might have condemned us as harshly and, because their circumstances and values were what they inevitably were, with equal validity. According to this view there is no point of rest outside the general movement where we or they can take up a stand, no static, absolute standards in terms of which things and persons can be finally evaluated. Hence the only attitudes correctly described, and rightly condemned, as relative, subjective and irrational, are forms of failure to relate our judgment to our own truest interests, that is, to what will fulfil our natures most fully—to all that the next step in the inevitable development necessarily holds in store. Some thinkers of this school view subjective aberrations with compassion and condone them as temporary attitudes from which the enlightenment of the future will for ever preserve mankind. Others gloat exultantly or ironically over the inevitable doom of those who misinterpret, and therefore fall foul of, the inexorable march of events. But whether the tone is charitable or sardonic, whether one condemns the errors of foolish individuals or the blind mob, or applauds their inevitable annihilation, this attitude rests on the belief that everything is caused to appear as it does by the machinery of history itself—by the impersonal forces of class, race, culture, History, The Life-Force, Progress, The Spirit of the Age. Given this organization of our lives which we did not create and cannot alter, it, and it alone, is ultimately responsible for everything. To blame or praise individuals or groups of individuals for acting rightly or wrongly, so far as this entails a suggestion that they are in some sense genuinely free to choose between alternatives, and may therefore be justly and reasonably blamed or praised for choosing as they did and do, is a vast blunder, a return to some primitive or naïve conception of human beings as being able somehow to evade total control of their lives by forces natural or supernatural, a relapse into a childish animism which the study of any scientific or metaphysical system should swiftly dispel. For if such choices were real, the determined world structure which alone, on this view, makes possible complete explanation, whether scientific or metaphysical, could not exist. And this is ruled out as unthinkable; 'reason rejects it'; it is confused, delusive, superficial, a piece of puerile megalomania, pre-scientific, unworthy of civilized men. . . .

The proposition that everything that we do and suffer is part of a fixed pattern; that Laplace's observer (supplied with adequate knowledge of facts and laws) could at any moment of historical time describe correctly every past and future event including those of 'inner' life, that is, human thoughts, feelings, acts, and so on, has often been entertained, and different implications have been drawn from it; belief in its truth has dismayed some and inspired others. But whether such determinism is a valid theory or not, it seems clear that acceptance of it does not in fact colour the ordinary thoughts of the majority of human beings, nor those of historians, nor even those of natural scientists outside the laboratory. For if it did, the language of the believers would reflect this fact and be very different from that of the rest of us. There is a class of expressions which we constantly use (and can scarcely do without) like 'you should not (or need not) have done this'; 'why did you make this terrible mistake?'; 'I could do it, but I would rather not'; 'why did the King of Ruritania abdicate?', because, unlike the King of Abyssinia, he lacked the strength of will to resist'; '*must* the Commander-in-Chief be quite so stupid?' Expressions of this type plainly involve the notion of more than the merely logical possibility of the realization of alternatives other than those which were in fact realized, namely of differences between situations in which individuals can be reasonably regarded as being responsible for their acts, and those in which they can not. For no one will wish to deny that we do often argue about the best among the possible courses of action open to human beings in the present and past and future, in fiction and in dreams; that historians (and judges and juries) do attempt to establish, as well as they are able, what these possibilities are; that the ways in which these lines are drawn mark the frontiers between reliable and unreliable history; that what is called realism (as opposed to fancy or ignorance of life or utopian dreams) consists precisely in the placing of what occurred (or might occur) in the context of what could have happened (or could happen), and in the demarcation of this from what could not; that this is all (as I think Sir Lewis Namier once suggested) that the sense of history, in the end, comes to; that upon this capacity all historical (as well as legal) justice depends; that it alone makes it possible to speak of criticism, or praise and blame, as just or deserved or absurd or unfair; and that this is the sole and obvious reason why accidents, *force majeure*—being by definition unavoidable—are necessarily outside the category of responsibility and consequently beyond the bounds of criticism, of the attribution of praise and blame. The difference between the expected and the exceptional, the difficult and the easy, the normal and the perverse, rests upon the drawing of these same lines. All this seems too self-evident to argue. It seems superfluous to add that all the discussions of historians about whether a given policy could or could not have been prevented, and what view should therefore be taken of the acts and characters of the actors, are intelligible only on the assumption of the reality of human choices. If determinism were a valid theory of human behaviour, these distinctions would be as inappropriate as the attribution of moral responsibility to the planetary system or the tissues of a living cell.

These categories permeate all that we think and feel so pervasively and universally, that to think them away, and conceive what and how we should be thinking, feeling, and talking without them, or in the framework of their opposites, is psychologically well-nigh impossible—as impracticable as, let us say, to pretend that we live in a world in which space, time, or number in the normal sense no longer exist. We may indeed always argue about specific situations, about whether a given occurrence is best explained as the inevitable effect of antecedent events beyond human control, or on the contrary as due to free human choice; free not merely in the sense that the case would have been altered if we had chosen—tried to act—differently; but that nothing prevented us from so choosing. It may well be that the growth of science and historical knowledge does in fact tend to show—make probable—that much of what was hitherto attributed to the acts of the unfettered wills of individuals can be satisfactorily explained only by the working of other, non-human, impersonal factors; that we have, in our ignorance or vanity, extended the realm of human freedom much too far. Yet the very meaning of such terms as 'cause' and 'inevitable' depends on the possibility of contrasting them with at least their imaginary opposites. These alternatives may be improbable, but they must at least be conceivable, if only for the purpose of contrasting them with causal necessities and law-observing uniformities. Unless we attach some meaning to the notion of free acts, i.e. acts not wholly determined by antecedent events or by the nature and 'dispositional characteristics' of either persons or things, it is difficult to see how we come to distinguish acts to which responsibility is attached from mere segments in a physical, or psychical, or psycho-physical causal chain of events—a distinction signified (even if all particular applications of it are mistaken) by the cluster of expressions which deal with open alternatives and free choices. Yet it is this distinction that underlines our normal attribution of values, in particular the notion that praise and blame can be just and not merely useful or effective. If the determinist hypothesis were true and adequately accounted for the actual world, there is a clear sense in which (despite all the extraordinary casuistry which has been employed to avoid this conclusion) the notion of human responsibility, as ordinarily understood would no longer apply to any actual, but only to imaginary or conceivable, states of affairs. I do not here wish to say that determinism is necessarily false, only that we neither speak nor think as if it could be true, and that it is difficult, and perhaps impossible, to conceive what our picture of the world would be if we seriously believed it; so that to speak, as some theorists of history (and scientists with a philosophical bent) tend to do, as if one might accept the determinist hypothesis, and yet to continue to think and speak much as we do at present, is to breed intellectual confusion. If the belief in freedom—which rests on the assumption that human beings do occasionally choose, and that their choices are not wholly accounted for by the kind of causal explanations which are accepted in, say, physics or biology—if this is a necessary illusion, it is so deep and so pervasive that it is not felt as such. No doubt we can try to convince ourselves that we are systematically deluded. But unless we attempt to think out the implications of this possibility, and alter our modes of thoughts and speech to allow for it accordingly, this hypothesis remains hollow; that is, we find it impossible even to entertain it seriously, if our behaviour is to be taken as evidence of what we can and what we cannot bring ourselves to believe or suppose not merely in theory, but in practice. . . .

When everything has been said in favour of attributing responsibility for character and action to natural and institutional causes; when everything possible has been done to correct blind or over-simple interpretations of conduct which fix too much blame on individuals and their free acts; when, in fact, there is strong evidence to show that it was difficult or impossible for men to do otherwise than they did, given their material environment or education or the influence upon them of various 'social pressures'; when every relevant psychological and sociological consideration has been taken into account, every impersonal factor given due weight; after 'hegemonist,' nationalist, and other historical heresies have been exposed and refuted; after every effort has been made to induce history to aspire, so far as it can without open absurdity, after the pure condition of a science; after all these severities, we continue to praise and to blame. We blame others as we blame ourselves; and the more we know, the more, it may be, we are disposed to blame. Certainly it will surprise us to be told that the better we understand our own actions—our own motives and the circumstances surrounding them —the freer from self-blame we shall inevitably feel. The contrary is surely often true. The more deeply we investigate the course of our own conduct, the more blameworthy our behaviour may seem to us to be, the more remorse we may be disposed to feel; and if this holds for ourselves, it is not reasonable to expect us necessarily, and in all cases, to withhold it from others. Our situations may differ from theirs, but not always so widely as to make all comparisons unfair. We ourselves may be accused unjustly, and so become acutely sensitive to the dangers of unjustly blaming others. But because blame can be unjust and the temptation to utter it very strong, it does not follow that it is never just; and because judgments can be based on ignorance, can spring from violent, or perverse, or silly, or shallow, or unfair notions, it does not follow that the opposites of these qualities do not exist at all; that we are mysteriously doomed to a degree of relativism and subjectivism in history, from which we are no less mysteriously free, or at any rate more free, in our normal daily thought and transactions with one another.

Indeed, the major fallacy of this position must by now be too obvious to need pointing out. We are told that we are creatures of nature or environment, or of history, and that this colours our temperament, our judgments, our principles. Every judgment is relative, every evaluation subjective, made what and as it is by the interplay of the factors of its own time and place, individual or collective. But relative to what? Subjective in contrast with what? Involved in some ephemeral pattern as opposed to what conceivable, presumably timeless, independence of such distorting factors? Relative terms (especially pejoratives) need correlatives, or else they turn out to be without meaning themselves, mere gibes, propagandist phrases designed to throw discredit, and not to describe or analyse. We know what we mean by disparaging a judgment or a method as subjective or biased—we mean that proper methods of weighing evidence have been too far ignored; or that what are normally called facts have been overlooked or suppressed or perverted; or that evidence normally accepted as sufficient to account for the acts of one individual or society is, for no good reason, ignored in some other case similar in all relevant respects; or that canons of interpretation are arbitrarily altered from case to case, that is, without consistency or principle; or that we have reasons for thinking that the historian in question wished to establish certain conclusions for reasons other than those justified by the evidence according to canons of valid inference accepted as normal in his day or in ours, and that this has blinded him to the criteria and methods normal in his field for verifying facts and proving conclusions; or all, or any, of these together; or other considerations like them. These are the kinds of ways in which superficiality is, in practice, distinguished from depth, bias from objectivity, perversion of facts from honesty, stupidity from perspicacity, passion and confusion from detachment and lucidity. And if we grasp these rules correctly, we are fully justified in denouncing breaches of them on the part of anyone; why should we not? But, it may be objected, what of words such as we have used so liberally above—'valid,' 'normal,' 'proper,' 'relevant,' 'perverted,' 'suppression of facts,' 'interpretation'—what do they signify? Is the meaning and use of these crucial terms so very fixed and unambiguous? May not that which is thought relevant or convincing in one generation be regarded as irrelevant in the next? What are unquestioned facts to one historian may, often enough, seem merely a suspicious piece of theorizing to another. This is indeed so. Rules for the weighing of evidence do change. The accepted data of one age seem to its remote successors shot through with metaphysical presuppositions so queer as to be scarcely intelligible. All objectivity, we shall again be told, is subjective, is what it is relatively to its own time and place; all veracity, reliability, all the insights and gifts of an intellectually fertile period are such only relatively to their own 'climate of opinion'; nothing is eternal, everything flows. Yet frequently as this kind of thing has been said, and plausible as it may seem, it remains in this context mere rhetoric. We do distinguish facts, not indeed from the valuations which enter into their very texture, but from interpretations of them; the borderline may not be distinct, but if I say that Stalin is dead and General Franco still alive, my statement may be accurate or mistaken, but nobody in his senses could, as words are used, take me to be advancing a theory or an interpretation. But if I say that Stalin exterminated a great many peasant proprietors because in his infancy he had been swaddled by his nurse, and that this made him aggressive, while General Franco has not done so because he did not go through this kind of experience, no one but a very naïve student of the social sciences would take me to be claiming to assert a fact, and that, no matter how many times I begin my sentences with the words: 'It is a fact that.' And I shall not readily believe you if you tell me that for Thucydides (or even for some Sumerian scribe) no fundamental distinction existed between relatively 'hard' facts and relatively 'disputable' interpretations. The borderline has, no doubt, always been wide and vague; it may be a shifting frontier, more distinct in some terrains than in others, but unless we know where, within certain limits, it lies, we fail to understand descriptive language altogether. The modes of thought of the ancients or of any cultures remote from our own are comprehensible to us only in the degree to which we share some, at any rate, of their basic categories; and the distinction between fact and theory is basic among these. I may dispute whether a given historian is profound or shallow, objective in his methods and impartial in his judgments, or borne on the wings of some obsessive hypothesis or overpowering emotion: but what I mean by these contrasted terms will not be utterly different for those who disagree with me, else there would be no argument; and will not, if I can claim to decipher texts at all correctly, be so widely different in different cultures and times and places as to make all communication systematically misleading and delusive. 'Objective,' 'true,' 'fair,' are words of large content, their uses are many, their edges often blurred. Ambiguities and confusions are always possible and often dangerous. Nevertheless such terms do possess meanings, which may, indeed, be fluid, but stay within limits recognized by normal usage, and refer to standards commonly accepted by those who work in relevant fields; and that not merely within one generation or society, but across large stretches of time and space. The mere claim that these crucial terms, these concepts or categories or standards, change in meaning or application, is to assume that such changes can to some degree be traced by methods which themselves are *pro tanto* not held liable to such change; for if these change in their turn, then, *ex hypothesi,* they do so in no way discoverable by us. And if not discoverable, then not discountable, and therefore of no use as a stick with which to beat us for our alleged subjectiveness or relativity, our delusions of grandeur and permanence, of the absoluteness of our standards in a world of ceaseless change. Such charges resemble suggestions sometimes casually advanced, that life is a dream. We protest that 'everything' cannot be a dream, for then, with nothing to contrast with dreams, the notion of a 'dream' loses all specific reference. We may be told that we shall have an awakening: that is, have an experience in relation to which the recollection of our present lives will be somewhat as remembered dreams now are, when compared to our normal waking experience at present. That may be true; but as things are, we can have little or no empirical experience for or against this hypothesis. We are offered an analogy one term of which is hidden from our view; and if we are invited, on the strength of it, to discount the reality of our normal waking life, in terms of another form of experience which is literally not describable and not utterable in terms of our daily experience and normal language—an experience of whose criteria for discriminating between realities and dreams we cannot in principle have any inkling—we may reasonably reply that we do not understand what we are asked to do; that the proposal is quite literally meaningless Indeed, we may advance the old, but nevertheless sound, platitude that one cannot cast doubt on everything at once, for then nothing is more dubious than anything else, and there are no standards of comparison and nothing is altered. So too, and for the same reason, we may reject as empty those general warnings which beg us to remember that all norms and criteria, factual, logical, ethical, political, aesthetic, are hopelessly infected by historical or social or some other kind of conditioning; that all are but temporary makeshifts, none are stable or reliable; for time and chance will bear them all away. But if all judgments are thus infected, there is nothing whereby we can discriminate between various degrees of infection, and if everything is relative, subjective, accidental, biased, nothing can be judged to be more so than anything else. If words like 'subjective' and 'relative,' 'prejudiced' and 'biased,' are terms not of comparison and contrast—do not imply the possibility of their own opposites, of 'objective' (or at least 'less subjective') of 'unbiased' (or at least 'less biased'), what meaning have they for us? To use them in order to refer to everything whatever, to use them as absolute terms, and not as correlatives, is nothing but a rhetorical perversion of their normal sense, a kind of general *memento mori,* an invocation to all of us to remember how weak and ignorant and trivial we are, a stern and virtuous maxim, and merited perhaps, but not a serious doctrine concerned with the question of the attribution of responsibility in history, relevant to any particular group of moralists or statesmen or human beings. . . .

One of the deepest of human desires is to find a unitary pattern in which the whole of experience, past, present and future, actual, possible and unfulfilled, is symmetrically ordered. . . . From the days of Herder and Saint-Simon, Hegel and Marx, to those of Spengler and Toynbee and their imitators, claims have been made widely varying in degree of generality and confidence, to be able to trace a structure of history (always *a priori* for all protests to the contrary), to discover the one and only true pattern into which alone all facts will be found to fit. But this is not, and can never be, accepted by any serious historian who wishes to establish the truth as it is understood by the best critics of his time, working by standards accepted as realistic by his most scrupulous and enlightened fellow workers. For he does not perceive one unique schema as the truth—the only real framework in which alone the facts truly lie; he does not distinguish the one real, cosmic pattern from false ones, as he certainly seeks to distinguish real facts from fiction. The same facts can be arranged in many patterns, seen from many perspectives, displayed in many lights, all of them equally valid, although some will be more suggestive or fertile in one field than in another, or unify many fields in some illuminating fashion, or, alternatively, bring out disparities and open chasms; some of these patterns will lie closer than others to the metaphysical or religious outlook of this or that historian or historical thinker. Yet through it all the facts themselves will remain relatively 'hard'. Relatively, but, of course, not absolutely; and whenever obsession by a given pattern causes a given writer to interpret the facts too artificially, to fill the gaps in his knowledge too smoothly, without sufficient regard to the empirical evidence, other historians will instinctively perceive that some kind of violence is being done to the facts, that the relation between evidence and interpretation is in some way abnormal; and that this is so not because there is doubt about the facts, but because there is an obsessive pattern at work. Freedom from such *idées fixes*—the degree of such freedom—distinguishes true history from the mythology of a given period; for there is no historical thought, properly speaking, save where facts are distinct not merely from fiction, but from theory and interpretation in a lesser or greater degree. We shall be reminded that there is no sharp break between history and mythology; or history and metaphysics; and that in the same sense there is no sharp line between 'facts' and theories: that no absolute touchstone can in principle be produced; and this is true enough, but from it nothing startling follows. That these differences exist only metaphysicians have disputed. Yet history as an independent discipline did, nevertheless, emerge; and that is tantamount to saying that the frontier between facts and cosmic patterns, empirical or metaphysical or theological, indistinct as it may be, is a central and 'objective' concept for all those who take the problems of history seriously. So long as we remain historians the two levels must be kept distinct, and the evidence of historical facts can never tend to prove or disprove metaphysical or theological patterns. The attempt, therefore, to shuffle off responsibility, which at an empirical level seems to rest upon this or that historical individual or society or set of opinions held or propagated by them, on to some metaphysical machinery which, because it is impersonal, excludes the very idea of moral responsibility, must always be invalid; and the desire to do so may, as often as not, be written down to the wish to escape from an untidy, cruel, and above all seemingly purposeless world, into a realm where all is harmonious, clear, intelligible, mounting towards some perfect culmination which satisfies the demands of 'reason,' or an aesthetic feeling, or a metaphysical impulse or religious craving; where nothing, above all, can be the object of criticism or complaint or condemnation or despair.

The matter is more serious when empirical arguments are advanced for an historical determinism which excludes the notion of personal responsibility. We are here no longer dealing with the metaphysics of history—the theodicies, say, of Schelling or Carlyle—as obvious substitutes for religion. We have before us the great sociological theories of history—the materialistic or scientific interpretations which began with Montesquieu and the *philosophes,* and led to the great schools of the nineteenth century, from the Saint-Simonians and the 'left wing' Hegelians to the followers of Comte, Marx, Darwin, and the liberal economists; from Freud, Pareto, Sorel to the ideologists of Fascism. Of these Marxism is much the boldest, the most intelligent and the least successful in its gallant and desperate attempt to treat history as a science. Arising out of them we have the vast proliferation of anthropological and sociological studies of civilized societies, with their tendency to trace all character and behaviour to the same kind of relatively irrational and unconscious causes as those which are held to have so successfully explained the behaviour of primitive societies. We have witnessed the rebirth of the notion of the 'sociology of knowledge,' which suggests that not only our methods but our conclusions and our reasons for believing them, in the entire realm of knowledge, can be shown to be wholly or largely determined by the stage reached in the development of our class or group, or nation or culture, or whatever other unit may be chosen; followed, in due course, by the fusion of these often unconvincing, but, usually, at least quasiscientific, doctrines with such non-empirical figments—at times all but personified powers both good and bad—as the 'Collectivist Spirit,' or 'The Myth of the Twentieth Century,' or 'The Contemporary Collapse of Values' (sometimes called 'The Crisis of Faith'), or 'Modern Man,' or 'The Last Stage of Capitalism.' All these modes of speech have peopled the air with supernatural entities of great power, Neo-Platonic and Gnostic spirits, angels and demons who play with us as they will, or, at any rate, make demands on us which, we are told, we ignore at our peril. There has grown up in our modern time a quasi-sociological mythology which, in the guise of scientific concepts, has developed into a new animism—certainly a more primitive and naïve religion than the traditional European faiths which it seeks to replace. This new cult leads troubled persons to ask such questions as 'Is war inevitable?', or 'Must collectivism triumph?', or 'Is civilization doomed?' These questions, and the tone in which they are posed, and the way in which they are discussed, imply a belief in the occult presence of vast impersonal entities— wars, collectivism, doom—agencies and forces at large in the world, which we have but little power to control or deflect. Sometimes these are said to 'embody themselves' in great men, titanic figures, who because they are at one with their age, achieve superhuman results—Napoleon, Bismarck, Lenin; sometimes in the actions of classes—the great capitalist combines, which work for ends that their members scarcely understand themselves, ends towards which their economic and social position 'inevitably' drive them; sometimes of huge inchoate entities called 'The Masses,' which do the work of history, little knowing of what mighty forces they are the 'creative vehicles.' Wars, revolutions, dictatorships, military and economic transformations are apt to be conceived like the genii of some oriental demonology, djinns, which once set free from the jars in which they have been confined for centuries, become uncontrollable, and capriciously play with the lives of men and nations. It is perhaps not to be wondered at that with so luxurious a growth of similes and metaphors, many innocent persons nowadays tend to believe that their lives are dominated not merely by relatively stable, easily identifiable, material factors—physical nature and the laws dealt with by the natural sciences; but by even more powerful and sinister, and far less intelligible, factors—the struggles of classes which members of these classes may not intend—the collision of social forces, the incidences of slumps and booms, which, like tides and harvests, can scarcely be controlled by those whose lives depend upon them—above all, by inexorable 'societal' and 'behavioural' patterns, to quote but a few sacred words from the barbarous vocabulary of the new mythologies. Cowed and humbled by the panoply of the new divinities, men are eager, and seek anxiously, for knowledge and comfort in the sacred books and in the new orders of priesthood which affect to tell them about the attributes and habits of their new masters. And the books and their expositors do speak words of comfort: demand creates supply. Their message is simple and very ancient. In a world where such monsters clash, individual human beings can have but little responsibility for what they do, the discovery of the new, terrifying, impersonal forces may render life infinitely more dangerous, yet if they serve no other purpose, they do, at any rate, divest their victims of all responsibility—from all those moral burdens which men in less enlightened days used to carry with such labour and anguish. So that what we have lost on the swings we make up on the roundabouts: if we lose freedom of action, at any rate we can no longer blame or be blamed for a world largely out of our control. The terminology of praise and condemnation turns out to be uncivilized and obscurantist. To record what occurs and why, in impersonal chronicles, as was done by detached and studious monks in other times of violence and strife, is represented as more honourable and more dignified, and more in keeping with the noble humility and integrity of a scholar, who in a time of doubt and crisis will at least preserve his soul if he abstains from the easy path of self-indulgence in moral sentiments. Agonizing doubts about the conduct of individuals caught in historical crises and the feeling of hope and despair, guilt, pride, and remorse, which accompany such reflections, are taken from us; like soldiers in an army driven by forces too great to resist, we lose those neuroses which depend on the fear of having to choose among alternatives. Where there is no choice there is no anxiety; and a happy release from responsibility. Some human beings have always preferred the peace of imprisonment, a contented security, a sense of having at last found one's proper place in the cosmos, to the painful conflicts and perplexities of the disordered freedom of the world beyond the walls.

Yet this is odd. For the assumptions upon which this kind of determinism has been erected are, when examined, exceedingly unplausible. What are these forces and these inexorable historical laws? What historiographer, what sociologist, what anthropologist can claim to have produced empirical generalizations remotely comparable to the great uniformities of the natural sciences? It is a commonplace to say that sociology still awaits its Newton, but even this seems much too audacious a claim; it has yet to find its Euclid and its Archimedes, before it can begin to dream of a Copernicus. On one side a patient and useful accumulation of facts, taxonomy, comparative studies, cautious and limited hypotheses, still hamstrung by too many exceptions to have any appreciable predictive power; on the other, imposing, sometimes ingenious, theoretical constructions, obscured by picturesque metaphors and a bold mythology, often stimulating to workers in other fields; and between these, a vast gap, such as has not existed in historical times between the theories and the factual evidence of the natural sciences. It is idle for sociology to plead that she is still young and has a glorious future. The eponymous hero to honour whose memory these words are being uttered, Auguste Comte, founded it a full hundred years ago, and its great conquests are still to come. It has affected other disciplines most fruitfully, notably history to which it has added a dimension. But it has as yet succeeded in discovering so few laws, hypotheses, wide generalizations, supported by adequate evidence, that its plea to be treated as a science can scarcely be entertained, nor are these few poor laws sufficiently revolutionary to make it seem an urgent matter to test their truth. In the great field of sociology (unlike her more speculative but far more effective younger sister, psychology), the loose generalizations of common sense, unsystematic rules of thumb, still, at times, seem more useful than their 'scientific' equivalents.

Social determinism is, at least historically, closely bound up with the ideals of sociology. And it may, indeed, be a true doctrine. But if it is true, and if we begin to take it seriously, then, indeed, the changes in our language, our moral notions, our attitudes toward one another, our views of history, of society and of everything else will be too profound to be even adumbrated. The concepts of praise and blame, innocence and guilt, and individual responsibility, from which we started, are but a small element in the structure, which would collapse or disappear. If social and psychological determinism were established as an accepted truth, our world would be transformed far more radically than was the teleological world of the classical and middle ages by the triumphs of mechanistic principles or those of natural selection. Our words—our modes of speech and thought—would be transformed in literally unimaginable ways; the notions of choice, of voluntary action, of responsibility, freedom, are so deeply embedded in our outlook, that our new life, as creatures in a world genuinely lacking these concepts, can, I should maintain, literally not be conceived by us. But there is, as yet, no need to alarm ourselves unduly. We are speaking only of pseudo-scientific ideals; the reality is not in sight. The evidence for a thoroughgoing determinism is not to hand; and if there is a persistent tendency to believe in it in some theoretical fashion, that is surely due far more to a 'scientistic' or metaphysical ideal, or to a longing to lay down moral burdens, or minimize individual responsibility and transfer it to impersonal forces which can be safely accused of causing all our discontents, than to any increase in our powers of critical reflection or any improvement in our scientific techniques. Belief in historical determinism of this type is, of course, very widespread, particularly in its Marxist, its psychological, and its sociological forms; and in what I should like to call its 'historiosophical' form too, by which I mean metaphysico-theological theories of history, which attract many who have lost their faith in older religious orthodoxies. Yet perhaps this attitude, so prevalent recently, is ebbing; and a contrary trend is discernible today. Our best historians use empirical tests in sifting facts, make microscopic examinations of the evidence, deduce no patterns, and show no false fear in attributing responsibility to individuals. Their specific attributions and analyses may be mistaken, but both they and their readers would be surprised to be told that their very activity had been superseded and stultified by the advances of sociology, or by some deeper metaphysical insight, like that of oriental stargazers by the discoveries of Kepler and his disciples. In their own queer way, some modern existentialists, too, proclaim the crucial importance of individual acts of choice. The condemnation by some among them of all philosophical systems as equally hollow, and of all moral, as of other doctrines, as equally worthless simply because they are systems and doctrines, may be absurd; but the more serious of them are no less insistent than Kant upon the reality of human autonomy, that is, upon the possibility of free self-commitment to an act or a form of life for what it is in itself. Whether recognition of freedom in this last sense does or does not entitle one logically to preach to others, or judge the past, is another matter. At any rate, it shows a commendable strength of intellect to have seen through the pretensions of those all-explanatory, all-justifying theodicies which promised to assimilate the human sciences to the natural in the quest for a unified schema of all there is, and have conspicuously failed to keep their word.

It needs more than infatuation with a programme to overthrow some of the most deeply rooted moral and intellectual habits of human beings, whether they be plumbers or historians. We are told that it is foolish to judge Charlemagne or Napoleon, or Genghis Khan or Hitler or Stalin for their massacres. For that is at most a comment upon ourselves and not upon 'the facts.' Likewise we are told that it is absurd to praise those benefactors of humanity whom the followers of Comte so faithfully celebrated, or at least that to do so is not our business as historians: because as historians our categories are 'neutral' and differ from our categories as ordinary human beings as those of chemists undeniably do. We are also told that as historians it is our task to describe, let us say, the great revolutions of our own time without so much as hinting that certain individuals involved in them not merely caused, but were responsible for, great misery and destruction—using such words according to the standards not merely of the twentieth century, which is soon over, or of our declining capitalist society, but of the human race at all the times and in all the places in which we have known it; and we are further told that we should practise such objectivity out of respect for some imaginary scientific canon which distinguishes between facts and values very sharply, so sharply that it enables us to regard the former as being objective, 'inexorable' and therefore self-justifying, and the latter merely as a subjective gloss upon events—due to the moment, the milieu, the individual temperament—and consequently unworthy of serious scholarship, of the great, hard edifice of dispassionate historical construction. To this we can only answer that to accept this doctrine is to do violence to the basic notions of our morality, to misrepresent our sense of our past, and to ignore

the most general concepts and categories of normal thought. The time will
come when men will wonder how this view, which combines a misunderstanding of empirical methods with cynicism exaggerated to the point of ec-
centricity, can ever have achieved such remarkable fame and influence and
respectability. For it is not scientific; nor can its reputation be due entirely to
a commendable fear of undue arrogance or philistinism, or of too bland and
uncritical an imposition of our own dogmas and standards upon others. In
part it is due to a genuine misunderstanding of the philosophical implications of the natural sciences, the great prestige of which has been misappro-
priated by many a fool and impostor since their earliest triumphs. But prin-
cipally it seems to me to spring from a desire to resign our responsibility, to
cease from judging provided we be not judged ourselves and, above all, are
not compelled to judge ourselves—from a desire to flee for refuge to some
vast amoral, impersonal, monolithic whole—nature or history, or class, or
race, or the 'harsh realities of our time,' or the irresistible evolution of the
social structure, that will absorb and integrate us into its limitless, neutral
texture, which it is senseless to evaluate or criticize, and which we resist to
our certain doom. This is a mirage which has often appeared in the history
of mankind, always at moments of confusion and inner weakness. It is one of
the great *alibis,* pleaded by those who cannot and do not wish to face the
facts of human responsibility, the existence of a limited but nevertheless real
area of human freedom, either because they have been too deeply wounded
or frightened to wish to return to the traffic of normal life, or because they
are filled with moral indignation against the false values and the, to them,
abhorrent moral codes of their own society, or class, or profession, and take
up arms against all ethical codes as such, as a dignified means of casting off
a morality which is to them, perhaps justifiably, repulsive. Nevertheless, such
views, although they may spring from a natural reaction against too much
moral rhetoric, are a desperate remedy. Those who hold them use history as
a method of escape from a world which has, for some reason, grown odious
to them into a fantasy where impersonal entities avenge their grievances and
set everything right, to the greater or lesser discomfiture of their persecutors,
real and imaginary. And in the course of this they describe the normal lives
lived by men in terms which fail to mark the most important psychological
and moral distinctions known to us. This they do in the service of an imaginary science, and, like the astrologers and magicians whom they have succeeded, cast up their eyes to the clouds, and speak in immense, unsubstan-
tiated images and similes, in deeply misleading metaphors and allegories,
and make use of hypnotic formulae with little regard for experience, or rational argument, or tests of proven reliability. Thereby they throw dust in
their own eyes as well as ours, obstruct our vision of the real world, and fur-

ther confuse an already sufficiently bewildered public about the relations of value to fact, and, even more, the nature and methods of the natural sciences and historical studies.

SUGGESTED READINGS

Parts II and III of Collingwood's *Idea of History* contain a good historical survey of speculative views of history up to and beyond Marx and Engels. Karl Löwith, in *Meaning and History*, surveys a similar history in an unusual and stimulating fashion. There are numerous volumes on Marx and Marxism. Perhaps the best brief introduction is I. Berlin, *Karl Marx*. M. M. Bober's *Karl Marx's Interpretation of History* is a detailed scholarly study. For a useful anthology of readings in the sources of Marxism, many of which deal explicitly with the problem of historical inevitability, L. Feuer's *Marx and Engels: Basic Writings* may be recommended.

For those interested in non-Marxist attempts to discover basic patterns of historical development, Part I of P. Gardiner's *Theories of History* contains a good set of selections. Among recent writers of a speculative cast of mind outside the Marxist ambit the most ambitious is A. J. Toynbee, whose twelve-volume *Study of History* has been condensed into two volumes by D. C. Somerville. For criticism of Toynbee, the reader should consult H. Trevor-Roper, "Arnold Toynbee's Millennium" in *Men and Events*; P. Geyl, *Debates with Historians*; and M. Samuel, *The Professor and the Fossil*...

The most famous attack on the possibility of the sort of philosophy of history that Engels presents is that by K. Popper: see *The Poverty of Historicism* and *The Open Society and Its Enemies*, especially Chapters 13–17 and 22. A. C. Danto, *Analytical Philosophy of History*, argues against the possibility of a speculative philosophy of history, but to see the full force of his argument one must study the whole volume. A brief account of his view is reprinted in the Dray anthology listed under the readings on Historical Explanation. The short introductory books there mentioned also deal generally with the topic of speculative philosophy of history.

V ❧ THE NATURE
AND STRUCTURE OF
MORALITY

Introduction

Moral judgments are part of our everyday experience; we all make such judgments, about ourselves and about others. We are all familiar with the feeling that although we acted in one way, we should have acted in another. We also distinguish between how men do treat each other and how they ought to treat each other, between what a country's laws are and what they ought to be. All such judgments presuppose a distinction between what *is in fact* the case and what *ought to be* the case.

An inquiry into what men ought to do is quite different from an inquiry into what men actually do. In the latter case, we *describe* behavior and try to explain how it occurred; but in the former we *evaluate* actions and motives for action, and speak of conduct as right or wrong, good or bad. It is for this reason that ethics is termed "normative": it deals with norms or standards for human conduct, not merely with the actual behavior of men.

Now what standard should we use in evaluating conduct? Should a man, for example, always be guided by his conscience? Should he act simply for his own pleasure? Should he always act for the greatest happiness of the greatest number? In everyday life we are often unclear about our standard—not only about what standard we ought to adopt, but even what standard we do in fact apply. And we are likely to be inconsistent, using one standard when we judge our own actions and another when we judge the actions of other people. Furthermore, it seems that there are a variety of standards in actual use: in other societies, and even within our own, people sometimes call actions good or right which we would call bad or wrong. Faced by these ambiguities, inconsistencies, and conflicts, we may wonder if there is *any* standard for judging how men ought to act.

Whether there *is* a universally valid moral standard, and if so, *what* that standard is, are the central questions in ethics. To reach a reasoned conclusion regarding these related problems, we must consider alternative views, tracing out their presuppositions concerning human nature and human knowledge and examining their implications for the conduct of men.

Theory and Data in Ethics

Even the least reflective of men pass moral judgments that do not rest on or spring from theories. In what relation, then, do pretheoretical moral beliefs stand to a philosophical theory of morality? All philosophers have agreed that a system of ethics must give some account of the pretheoretical moral beliefs of mankind. GASS argues for the view that these opinions are the fundamental data against which any theory of morality must be checked and that any theory which fails to agree in its conclusions with these basic opinions is to be rejected for just that reason. Some of the philosophers represented in later selections agree with Gass on this point; others, such as Nietzsche, do not. A conclusion on this point is extremely important, for without it one will not be able to give a clear account of the considerations that are decisive in evaluating alternative possible ethical theories.

The Case of the Obliging Stranger*

W I L L I A M G A S S [1924–   ] received his Ph.D. at Cornell. He is Professor of Philosophy at Purdue University. In addition to his work in philosophy, he has published several short stories and a novel, *Omensetter's Luck* (1966).

I

Imagine I approach a stranger on the street and say to him, "If you please, sir, I desire to perform an experiment with your aid." The stranger is obliging, and I lead him away. In a dark place conveniently by, I strike his head with the broad of an axe and cart him home. I place him, buttered and trussed, in an ample electric oven. The thermostat reads 450° F. Thereupon I go off to play poker with friends and forget all about the obliging stranger in the stove. When I return, I realize I have overbaked my specimen, and the experiment, alas, is ruined.

Something has been done wrong. Or something wrong has been done.

Any ethic that does not roundly condemn my action is vicious. It is interesting that none is vicious for this reason. It is also interesting that no more

* From Gass, "The Case of the Obliging Stranger," *Philosophical Review*, LXVI (1957). Reprinted by permission of the editor and the author.

convincing refutation of any ethic could be given than by showing that it approved of my baking the obliging stranger.

This is really all I have to say, but I shall not stop on that account. Indeed, I shall begin again.

II

The geometer cannot demonstrate that a line is beautiful. The beauty of lines is not his concern. We do not chide him when he fails to observe uprightness in his verticals, when he discovers no passions between sinuosities. We would not judge it otherwise than foolish to berate him for neglecting to employ the methods successful in biology or botany merely because those methods dealt fairly with lichens and fishes. Nor do we despair of him because he cannot give us reasons for doing geometry which will equally well justify our drilling holes in teeth. There is a limit, as Aristotle said, to the questions which we may sensibly put to each man of science; and however much we may desire to find unity in the purposes, methods, and results of every fruitful sort of inquiry, we must not allow that desire to make mush of their necessary differences.

Historically, with respect to the fundamental problems of ethics, this limit has not been observed. Moreover, the analogy between mathematics and morals, or between the methods of empirical science and the good life, has always been unfairly one-sided. Geometers never counsel their lines to be moral, but moralists advise men to be like lines and go straight. There are triangles of lovers, but no triangles in love. And who says the organism is a state?

For it is true that the customary methods for solving moral problems are the methods which have won honors by leaping mathematical hurdles on the one hand or scientific and physical ones on the other: the intuitive and deductive method and the empirical and inductive one. Nobody seems to have minded very much that the moral hurdle has dunked them both in the pool beyond the wall, for they can privately laugh at each other for fools, and together they can exclaim how frightfully hard is the course.

The difficulty for the mathematical method is the discovery of indubitable moral first premises which do not themselves rest on any inductive foundation and which are still applicable to the complicated tissue of factors that make up moral behavior. The result is that the premises are usually drawn from metaphysical speculations having no intimate relation to moral issues or from rational or mystical revelations which only the intuiter and his followers are willing to credit. For the purposes of deduction, the premises have to be so broad and, to satisfy intuition, so categorically certain, that they become too thin for touch and too heavy for bearing. All negative in-

stances are pruned as unreal or parasitic. Consequently, the truth of the ultimate premises is constantly called into question by those who have intuited
differently or have men and actions in mind that they want to call good and
right but cannot.

Empirical solutions, so runs the common complaint, lop off the normative
branch altogether and make ethics a matter of expediency, taste, or conformity to the moral etiquette of the time. One is told what people do, not what
they ought to do; and those philosophers who still wish to know what people
ought to do are told, by some of the more uncompromising, that they can
have no help from empiricism and are asking a silly question. Philosophers,
otherwise empiricists, who admit that moral ends lie beyond the reach of factual debate turn to moral sentiment or some other *bonum ex machina*, thus
generously embracing the perplexities of both methods.

III

Questions to which investigators return again and again without success
are very likely improperly framed. It is important to observe that the ethical
question put so directly as "What is good?" or "What is right?" aims in its
answer not, as one might immediately suppose, at a catalogue of the world's
good, right things. The moralist is not asking for a list of sheep and goats.
The case of the obliging stranger is a case of immoral action, but this admission is not an answer, even partially, to the question, "What is wrong?"

Furthermore, the ethical question is distressingly short. "Big" questions, it
would seem, ought to be themselves big, but they almost never are; and they
tend to grow big simply by becoming short—too short, in fact, ever to receive an answer. I might address, to any ear that should hear me, the rather
less profound-sounding, but none the less similar question, "Who won?" or
perhaps the snappier, "What's a winner?" I should have to ask this question
often because, if I were critical, I should never find an answer that would
suit me; while at the same time there would be a remarkable lot of answers
that suited a remarkable lot of people. The more answers I had—the more
occasions on which I asked the question—the more difficult, the more important, the more "big" the question would become.

If the moralist does not want to hear such words as "Samson," "money," or
"brains" when he asks his question, "What is good?", what does he want to
hear? He wants to hear a word like "power." He wants to know what is good
in the things that are good that makes them good. It should be perfectly
clear it is not the things themselves that he thinks good or bad but the qualities they possess, the relations they enter into, or the consequences they
produce. Even an intuitionist, who claims to perceive goodness directly, perceives a property of things when he perceives goodness, and not any *thing,*

except incidentally. The wrong done the obliging stranger was not the act of cooking him but was something belonging to the act in some one of many possible ways. It is not I who am evil (if I am not mad) but something which I *have* that is; and while, of course, I may be adjudged wicked for having whatever it is I have that is bad, it is only because I have it that I am wicked—as if I owned a vicious and unruly dog.

I think that so long as I look on my act in this way, I wrong the obliging stranger a second time.

The moralist, then, is looking for the ingredient that perfects or spoils the stew. He wants to hear the word "power." He wants to know what is good in what is good that makes it good; and the whole wretched difficulty is that one is forced to reply either that what is good in what is good makes the good in what is good good, or that it is, in fact, made good by things which are not in the least good at all. So the next question, which is always, "And why is power good?" is answered by saying that it is good because it is power and power is good; or it is put off by the promise that power leads to things worth much; or it is shrugged aside with the exclamation, "Well, that's life!" This last is usually accompanied by an exhortation not to oppose the inevitable course of nature.

You cannot ask questions forever. Sooner or later the questioning process is brought up short by statements of an apparently dogmatic sort. Pleasure is sought for pleasure's sake. The principle of utility is susceptible of no demonstration. Every act and every inquiry aims at well-being. The nonnatural property of goodness fastens itself to its object and will remain there whatever world the present world may madly become. Frustrated desires give rise to problems, and problems are bad. We confer the title of The Good upon our natural necessities.

I fail to see why, if one is going to call a halt in this way, the halt cannot be called early, and the evident, the obvious, the axiomatic, the indemonstrable, the intrinsic, or whatever one wants to name it, be deemed those clear cases of moral goodness, badness, obligation, or wrong which no theory can cloud, and for which men are prepared to fight to the last ditch. For if someone asks me, now I am repentant, why I regard my act of baking the obliging stranger as wrong, what can I do but point again to the circumstances comprising the act? "Well, I put this fellow in an oven, you see. The oven was on, don't you know." And if my questioner persists, saying: "Of course, I know all about *that;* but what I want to know is, why is *that* wrong?", I should recognize there is no use in replying that it is wrong because of the kind of act it is, a wrong one, for my questioner is clearly suffering from a sort of *folie de doute morale* which forbids him to accept any final answer this early in the game, although he will have to accept precisely the same kind of answer at some time or other.

Presumably there is some advantage in postponing the stop, and this advantage lies in the explanatory power of the higher-level answer. It cannot be that my baking the stranger is wrong for no reason at all. It would then be inexplicable. I do not think this is so, however. It is not inexplicable; it is transparent. Furthermore, the feeling of elucidation, of greater insight or knowledge, is a feeling only. It results, I suspect, from the satisfaction one takes in having an open mind. The explanatory factor is always more inscrutable than the event it explains. The same questions can be asked of it as were asked of the original occasion. It is either found in the situation and brought forward to account for all, as one might advance pain, in this case, out of the roaster; or it resides there mysteriously, like an essence, the witch in the oven; or it hovers, like a coil of smoke, as hovers the greatest unhappiness of the greatest number.

But how ludicrous are the moralist's "reasons" for condemning my baking the obliging stranger. They sound queerly unfamiliar and out of place. This is partly because they intrude where one expects to find denunciation only and because it is true they are seldom if ever *used*. But their strangeness is largely due to the humor in them.

Consider:

My act produced more pain than pleasure.
Baking this fellow did not serve the greatest good to the greatest number.
I acted wrongly because I could not consistently will that the maxim of my action become a universal law.
God forbade me, but I paid no heed.
Anyone can apprehend the property of wrongness sticking plainly to the whole affair.
Decent men remark it and are moved to tears.

But I should say that my act was wrong even if my stranger were tickled into laughter while he cooked; or even if his baking did the utmost good it could; or if, in spite of all, I could consistently will that whatever maxim I might have had might become a universal law; or even if God had spoken from a bush to me, "Thou shalt!" How redundant the property of wrongness, as if one needed *that*, in such a case! And would the act be right if the whole world howled its glee? Moralists can say, with conviction, that the act is wrong; but none can *show* it.

Such cases, like that of the obliging stranger, are cases I call clear. They have the characteristic of moral transparency, and they comprise the core of our moral experience. When we try to explain why they are instances of good or bad, of right or wrong, we sound comic, as anyone does who gives elaborate reasons for the obvious, especially when these reasons are so shame-faced before reality, so miserably beside the point. What we must explain is not why these cases have the moral nature they have, for that needs no explaining, but *why they are so clear*. It is an interesting situation: any moralist will throw over his theory if it reverses the decision on cases like the obliging stranger's. The most persuasive criticism of any ethical system has always been the demonstration, on the critic's part, that the system countenances moral absurdities, despite the fact that, in the light of the whole theoretical enterprise, such criticisms beg the question. Although the philosopher who is caught by a criticism of this sort may protest its circularity or even manfully swallow the dreadful conclusion, his system has been scotched, if it has not been killed. . . .

I think we decide cases where there is some doubt by stating what it is about them that puzzles us. We hunt for more facts, hoping that the case will clear:

"She left her husband with a broken hand and took the children."

"She did!"

"He broke his hand on her head."

"Dear me; but even so!"

"He beat her every Thursday after tea and she finally couldn't stand it any longer."

"Ah, of course, but the poor children?"

"He beat them, too."

"My, my, and was there no other way?"

"The court would grant her no injunction."

"Why not?"

"Judge Bridlegoose is a fool."

"Ah, of course, she did right, no doubt about it."

If more facts do not clear the case, we redescribe it, emphasizing first this fact and then that until it is clear, or until we have several clear versions of the original muddle. Many ethical disputes are due to the possession, by the contending parties, of different accounts of the same occasion, all satisfactorily clear, and this circumstance gives the disputants a deep feeling for the undoubted rightness of each of their versions. Such disputes are particularly acrimonious, and they cannot be settled until an agreement is reached about the true description of the case.

There are, of course, conflicts of duty which are perfectly clear. I have promised to meet you at four to bowl, but when four arrives I am busy rescuing a baby from the jaws of a Bengal tiger and cannot come. Unclear conflicts we try to clarify. And it sometimes happens that the tug of obligations is so equal as to provide no reasonable solution. If some cases are clear, others are undecidable.

It is perfectly true that principles are employed in moral decisions— popular principles, I mean, like the golden rule and the laws of God. Principles really obscure matters as often as they clear them. They are generally flags and slogans to which the individual is greatly attached. Attack the principle and you attack the owner: his good name, his reputation, his sense of righteousness. Love me, love my maxims. People have been wrongly persuaded that principles decide cases and that a principle which fails in one case fails in all. So principles are usually vehicles for especially powerful feelings and frequently get in the way of good sense. We have all observed the angry arguer who grasps the nettle of absurdity to justify his bragging about the toughness of his skin.

I should regard useful principles as summaries of what may be present generally in clear cases, as for instance: cases where pain is present are more often adjudged bad than not. We might, if the reverse were true for pleasure, express our principle briefly in hedonistic terms: pleasure is the good. But there may be lots of principles of this sort, as there may be lots of rather common factors in clear cases. Principles state more or less prevalent identifying marks, as cardinals usually nest in low trees, although there is nothing to prevent them from nesting elsewhere, and the location of the nest is not the essence of the bird. When I appeal to a principle, then, the meaning of my appeal consists of the fact that before me is a case about which I can reach no direct decision; of the fact that the principle I invoke is relevant, since not every principle is (the laws of God do not cover everything, for instance). In this way I affirm my loyalty to those clear cases the principle so roughly summarizes and express my desire to remain consistent with them. . . .

Ethics, I wish to say, is about something, and in the rush to establish principles, to elicit distinctions from a recalcitrant language, and to discover "laws," those lovely things and honored people, those vile seducers and ruddy villains our principles and laws are supposed to be based upon and our ethical theories to be about are overlooked and forgotten.

SUGGESTED READINGS

The question "What are the moral beliefs of common sense?" is surprisingly difficult to answer fully. H. Sidgwick, in *The Methods of Ethics,* Book III, Chapters 2–11, presents the most careful investigation a modern philosopher has ever made of the subject. In Book III, Chapter 8, and in Book IV, Chapter 3, he presents his own view of the relations between common sense morality and the ethical theory he thinks is most likely to be correct. For a very different view of the relation between data and theory, the reader should consult F. H. Bradley's essay, "My Station and Its Duties," in Ethical Studies (especially pp. 193–194). Thomas Reid, a Scottish philosopher of the late eighteenth century, presents with great clarity yet another view on the issue in his *Essays on the Active Powers of the Human Mind*, Essay V, "Of Morals," Chapters 1 and 2.

For some recent discussions touching on these problems the reader may consult G. C. Field, *Moral Theory*, Chapter 1; E. F. Carritt, *Ethical and Political Thinking*, Chapter 1; P. H. Nowell-Smith, *Ethics*, Chapters 1 and 2; and B. Mayo, *Ethics and the Moral Life*, Chapter 1.

For more general introductions to the problems of contemporary ethical theory, a beginning student can profit from the whole of W. K. Frankena's *Ethics* or J. D. Mabbott's *Introduction to Ethics*. As historical surveys of the period, M. Warnock's *Ethics Since* 1900 and G. C. Kerner's *The Revolution in Ethical Theory* are helpful.

Good as the Standard

One major tradition in ethics holds that the morality of an action depends on its consequences: an action is right if it leads to good consequences, wrong if it leads to bad. According to this tradition, therefore, no act is intrinsically right or wrong; in every case one must take into account what results from the act. One can only say that *in general* certain types of action, like telling the truth or keeping a promise, are right because they usually tend to bring about good consequences. But any *particular* case of truth-telling or promise-keeping might be wrong: in special circumstances more good might result from lying or breaking one's promise. Ethical theories which determine the rightness of an action in terms of the good it promotes are called *teleological* theories (from the Greek *telos*, meaning goal or end).

Any teleological theory is faced with the question of *whose* good ought to be taken into account. According to *egoism* a person is obliged to promote only his own good. But most teleologists do not grant priority to one's own good. A *universalistic* theory maintains that each person's good counts equally and that one is obliged to promote the greatest good on the whole. Such a theory does not demand that we sacrifice ourselves for the lesser good of someone else, but it does require that we give no preference to our own good or to that of our family or friends.

There is still another question that teleological theories must consider: What is "the good" that ought to be promoted? In other words, what is the nature of the end in terms of which we judge whether an act is right or wrong? Many answers have been proposed to this question; but the two most frequently given have identified the good either with *pleasure* or with *self-realization*. Both answers have had a variety of forms, depending on the interpretation given "pleasure" or "self-realization." *Hedonists*, although agreeing that pleasure is the only thing valuable in itself, have differed as to whether pleasure is the same as happiness, whether it is a state of bodily excitation, or whether it is freedom from pain. Even more marked differences are found among those who uphold the theory of *self-realization*. They would all agree that the only good worthy of pursuit for its own sake is the development or fulfilment of the self, but their views of the nature of the self are sometimes quite different. These varying views lead to different conceptions of the kind of life in which fulfilment of the self is achieved.

In the past decades another form of teleological theory, *ideal utilitarianism*, has gained in prominence. This theory, unlike hedonism and self-realization, denies that "the good" can be equated with any one thing. According to ideal utilitarianism, many different things in our individual and social experience are valuable in themselves. Friendship and justice, for example, and traits of character such as courage and generosity, would be classified by most ideal utilitarians as good in themselves. All these intrinsically good things should be sought for their own sakes, not merely as means to pleasure or self-realization.

The passages from BENTHAM constitute what is perhaps the most famous and influential statement of modern hedonism. They give the foundations of his moral system, on which he based his theories of legislation and social reform.

According to NIETZSCHE the standard of goodness is power: to evaluate actions or motives for action, we must decide whether they enhance or diminish an individual's power. His theory constitutes a bitter attack on Christian ideals, which he claimed were simply disguised expressions of man's general lust for power, originated by the weak to chain the strong. His aim was to "transvaluate values," to expose the hypocrisy of an ethics of meekness and to reassert the nobility of strength and joy and pride. The following selection from Nietzsche presents his conception of the nobility of power.

MOORE defends ideal utilitarianism. Unlike the hedonists, Moore asserts that value cannot be defined in terms of interest nor equated with pleasure. He argues that "good" is indefinable, but that we can directly apprehend what things are good in themselves. A right action is one that brings into existence the maximum amount of intrinsic value, taking all consequences into account.

The Good as Pleasure*

JEREMY BENTHAM [1748–1832] was the leading figure in the early phase of the British utilitarian movement in philosophy and politics. He was primarily interested in legal reform, and he constantly sought a philosophic basis for the reforms he advocated. In this connection he wrote his highly influential works on the theory of law and on ethics.

THE PRINCIPLE OF UTILITY. Nature has placed mankind under the governance of two sovereign masters, *pain* and *pleasure*. It is for them alone to point out what we ought to do, as well as to determine what we shall do. On the one hand the standard of right and wrong, on the other the chain of causes and effects, are fastened to their throne. They govern us in all we do, in all we say, in all we think; every effort we can make to throw off our subjection, will serve but to demonstrate and confirm it. In words a man may pretend to abjure their empire: but in reality he will remain subject to it all the while. The *principle of utility* recognizes the subjection, and assumes it for the foundation of that system, the object of which is to rear the fabric of

* From Bentham: *An Introduction to the Principles of Morals and Legislation*, Chapters 1, 2, 4, and 10.

felicity by the hands of reason and of law. Systems which attempt to question it, deal in sounds instead of sense, in caprice instead of reason, in darkness instead of light.

But enough of metaphor and declamation: it is not by such means that moral science is to be improved.

The principle of utility is the foundation of the present work; it will be proper therefore at the outset to give an explicit and determinate account of what is meant by it. By the principle of utility is meant that principle which approves or disapproves of every action whatsoever, according to the tendency which it appears to have to augment or diminish the happiness of the party whose interest is in question; or what is the same thing in other words, to promote or to oppose that happiness. I say of every action whatsoever; and therefore not only of every action of a private individual, but of every measure of government.

By utility is meant that property in any object, whereby it tends to produce benefit, advantage, pleasure, good, or happiness (all this in the present case comes to the same thing) or (what comes again to the same thing) to prevent the happening of mischief, pain, evil, or unhappiness to the party whose interest is considered: if that party be the community in general, then the happiness of the community: if a particular individual, then the happiness of that individual.

The interest of the community is one of the most general expressions that can occur in the phraseology of morals: no wonder that the meaning is often lost. When it has a meaning, it is this. The community is a fictitous *body*, composed of the individual persons who are considered as constituting as it were its *members*. The interest of the community then is, what?—the sum of the interests of the several members who compose it.

It is in vain to talk of the interest of the community, without understanding what is the interest of the individual. A thing is said to promote the interest, or to be *for* the interest, of an individual, when it tends to add to the sum total of his pleasures: or, what comes to the same thing, to diminish the sum total of his pains.

An action then may be said to be comformable to the principle of utility, or, for shortness' sake, to utility (meaning with respect to the community at large) when the tendency it has to augment the happiness of the community is greater than any it has to diminish it.

A measure of government (which is but a particular kind of action, performed by a particular person or persons) may be said to be conformable to or dictated by the principle of utility, when in like manner the tendency which it has to augment the happiness of the community is greater than any which it has to diminish it. . . .

Of an action that is comformable to the principle of utility, one may always say either that it is one that ought to be done, or at least that it is not one that ought not to be done. One may also say, that it is right it should be done; at least that it is not wrong it should be done: that it is a right action; at least that it is not a wrong action. When thus interpreted, the words *ought*, and *right* and *wrong*, and others of that stamp, have a meaning: when otherwise, they have none.

PRINCIPLES ADVERSE TO THAT OF UTILITY. If the principle of utility be a right principle to be governed by, and that in all cases, it follows from what has been just observed, that whatever principle differs from it in any case must necessarily be a wrong one. To prove any other principle, therefore, to be a wrong one, there needs no more than just to show it to be what it is, a principle of which the dictates are in some point or other different from those of the principle of utility: to state it is to confute it.

A principle may be different from that of utility in two ways: 1. By being constantly opposed to it: this is the case with a principle which may be termed the principle of *asceticism*. 2. By being sometimes opposed to it, and sometimes not, as it may happen: this is the case with another, which may be termed the principle of *sympathy* and *antipathy*.

By the principle of asceticism I mean that principle, which, like the principle of utility, approves or disapproves of any action, according to the tendency which it appears to have to augment or diminish the happiness of the party whose interest is in question; but in an inverse manner: approving of actions in as far as they tend to diminish his happiness; disapproving of them in as far as they tend to augment it. . . .

The principle of asceticism seems originally to have been the reverie of certain hasty speculators, who having perceived, or fancied, that certain pleasures, when reaped in certain circumstances, have, at the long run, been attended with pains more than equivalent to them, took occasion to quarrel with everything that offered itself under the name of pleasure. Having then got thus far, and having forgot the point which they set out from, they pushed on, and went so much further as to think it meritorious to fall in love with pain. Even this, we see, is at bottom but the principle of utility misapplied.

The principle of utility is capable of being consistently pursued; and it is but tautology to say, that the more consistently it is pursued, the better it must ever be for humankind. The principle of asceticism never was, nor never can be, consistently pursued by any living creature. Let but one tenth part of the inhabitants of this earth pursue it consistently, and in a day's time they will have turned it into a hell.

Among principles adverse to that of utility, that which at this day seems to have most influence in matters of government, is what may be called the principle of sympathy and antipathy. By the principle of sympathy and antipathy, I mean that principle which approves or disapproves of certain actions, not on account of their tending to augment the happiness, nor yet on account of their tending to diminish the happiness of the party whose interest is in question, but merely because a man finds himself disposed to approve or disapprove of them: holding up that approbation or disapprobation as a sufficient reason for itself, and disclaiming the necessity of looking out for any extrinsic ground. Thus far in the general department of morals; and in the particular department of politics, measuring out the quantum (as well as determining the ground) of punishment, by the degree of the disapprobation.

It is manifest, that this is rather a principle in name than in reality; it is not a positive principle of itself, so much as a term employed to signify the negation of all principle. What one expects to find in a principle is something that points out some external consideration, as a means of warranting and guiding the internal sentiments of approbation and disapprobation; this expectation is but ill fulfilled by a proposition, which does neither more nor less than hold up each of those sentiments as a ground and standard for itself.

In looking over the catalogue of human actions (says a partizan of this principle) in order to determine which of them are to be marked with the seal of disapprobation, you need but to take counsel of your own feelings: whatever you find in yourself a propensity to condemn, is wrong for that very reason. For the same reason it is also meet for punishment: in what proportion it is adverse to utility, or whether it be adverse to utility at all, is a matter that makes no difference. In that same *proportion* also it is meet for punishment; if you hate much, punish much; if you hate little, punish little; punish as you hate. If you hate not at all, punish not at all; the fine feelings of the soul are not to be overborne and tyrannized by the harsh and rugged dictates of political utility.

The various systems that have been formed concerning the standard of right and wrong, may all be reduced to the principle of sympathy and antipathy. One account may serve for all of them. They consist all of them in so many contrivances for avoiding the obligation of appealing to any external standard, and for prevailing upon the reader to accept of the author's sentiment or opinion as a reason for itself.

THE HEDONISTIC CALCULUS. Pleasures, then, and the avoidance of pains, are the *ends* which the legislator has in view: it behooves him therefore to understand their *value*. Pleasures and pains are the *instruments* he has to work with: it behooves him therefore to understand their force, which is again, in other words, their value.

To a person considered *by himself*, the value of a pleasure or pain considered *by itself*, will be greater or less, according to the four following circumstances:

1. Its *intensity*.
2. Its *duration*.
3. Its *certainty* or *uncertainty*.
4. Its *propinquity* or *remoteness*.

These are the circumstances which are to be considered in estimating a pleasure or a pain considered each of them by itself. But when the value of any pleasure or pain is considered for the purpose of estimating the tendency of any *act* by which it is produced, there are two other circumstances to be taken into the account; these are,

5. Its *fecundity*, or the chance it has of being followed by sensations of the *same* kind: that is, pleasures, if it be a pleasure: pains, if it be a pain.
6. Its *purity*, or the chance it has of *not* being followed by sensations of the *opposite* kind: that is, pains, if it be a pleasure: pleasures, if it be a pain.

These two last, however, are in strictness scarcely to be deemed properties of the pleasures or the pain itself; they are not, therefore, in strictness to be taken into the account of the value of that pleasure or that pain. They are in strictness to be deemed properties only of the act, or other event, by which such pleasure or pain has been produced; and accordingly are only to be taken into the account of the tendency of such act or such event.

To a *number* of persons, with reference to each of whom the value of a pleasure or a pain is considered, it will be greater or less, according to seven circumstances: to wit, the six preceding ones: viz.

1. Its *intensity*.
2. Its *duration*.
3. Its *certainty* or *uncertainty*.
4. Its *propinquity* or *remoteness*.
5. Its *fecundity*.
6. Its *purity*.

And one other; to wit:

7. Its *extent;* that is, the number of persons to whom it *extends;* or (in other words) who are affected by it.

To take an exact account then of the general tendency of any act, by which the interests of a community are affected, proceed as follows. Begin with any one person of those whose interests seem most immediately to be affected by it: and take an account,

1. Of the value of each distinguishable *pleasure* which appears to be produced by it in the *first* instance.
2. Of the value of each *pain* which appears to be produced by it in the *first* instance.
3. Of the value of each pleasure which appears to be produced by it *after* the first. This constitutes the *fecundity* of the first *pleasure* and the *impurity* of the first *pain*.
4. Of the value of each *pain* which appears to be produced by it after the first. This constitutes the *fecundity* of the first *pain*, and the *impurity* of the first *pleasure*.
5. Sum up all the values of all the *pleasures* on the one side, and those of all the *pains* on the other. The balance, if it be on the side of pleasure, will give the *good* tendency of the act upon the whole, with respect to the interests of that *individual* person; if on the side of pain, the *bad* tendency of it upon the whole.
6. Take an account of the *number* of persons whose interests appear to be concerned; and repeat the above process with respect to each. *Sum up* the numbers expressive of the degrees of *good* tendency, which the act has, with respect to each individual, in regard to whom the tendency of it is *good* upon the whole: do this again with respect to each individual, in regard to whom the tendency of it is *bad* upon the whole. Take the *balance;* which, if on the side of *pleasure,* will give the general *good tendency* of the act, with respect to the total number or community of individuals concerned; if on the side of *pain,* the general *evil tendency,* with respect to the same community.

It is not to be expected that this process should be strictly pursued previously to every moral judgment, or to every legislative or judicial operation. It may, however, be always kept in view: and as near as the process actually pursued on these occasions approaches to it, so near will such process approach to the character of an exact one.

Motives. With respect to goodness and badness, as it is with everything else that is not itself either pain or pleasure, so is it with motives. If they are good or bad, it is only on account of their effects: good, on account of their tendency to produce pleasure, or avert pain: bad, on account of their tendency to produce pain, or avert pleasure. Now the case is, that from one and the same motive, and from every kind of motive, may proceed actions that are good, others that are bad, and others that are indifferent. . . .

It appears then that there is no such thing as any sort of motive which is a bad one in itself: nor, consequently, any such thing as a sort of motive which in itself is exclusively a good one. And as to their effects, it appears too that these are sometimes bad, at other times either indifferent or good, and this appears to be the case with every sort of motive. *If any sort of motive then is either good or bad on the score of its effects, this is the case only on individual occasions, and with individual motives;* and this is the case with one sort of motive as well as with another. *If any sort of motive then can, in consideration of its effects, be termed with any propriety a bad one,* it can only be with reference to the balance of all the effects it may have had of both kinds within a given period, that is, of its most usual tendency.

What then? (it will be said) are not lust, cruelty, avarice, bad motives? Is there so much as any one individual occasion, in which motives like these can be otherwise than bad? No, certainly: and yet the proposition, that there is no one *sort* of motive but what will on many occasions be a good one, is nevertheless true. The fact is, that these are names which, if properly applied, are never applied but in the cases where the motives they signify happen to be bad. The names of these motives, considered apart from their effects, are sexual desire, displeasure, and pecuniary interest. To sexual desire, when the effects of it are looked upon as bad, is given the name of lust. Now lust is always a bad motive. Why? Because if the case be such, that the effects of the motive are not bad, it does not go, or at least ought not to go, by the name of lust. The case is, then, that when I say, "Lust is a bad motive," it is a proposition that merely concerns the import of the word lust; and which would be false if transferred to the other word used for the same motive, sexual desire. Hence we see the emptiness of all those rhapsodies of common-place morality, which consist in the taking of such names as lust, cruelty, and avarice, and branding them with marks of reprobation: applied to the *thing*, they are false; applied to the *name*, they are true indeed, but nugatory. Would you do a real service to mankind, show them the cases in which sexual desire *merits* the name of lust; displeasure, that of cruelty, and pecuniary interest, that of avarice.

The Good as Power[*]

FRIEDRICH NIETZSCHE [1844–1900] was Professor of Philology at Basel but gave up his academic career to spend the remainder of his life in writing. He was a severe critic of contemporary culture, a moralist who sought to analyze and overturn Christian values, and a philosophic exponent of irrationalism.

Every elevation of the type "man," has hitherto been the work of an aristocratic society—and so will it always be—a society believing in a long scale of gradations of rank and differences of worth among human beings, and requiring slavery in some form or other. Without the *pathos of distance,* such as grows out of the incarnated difference of classes, out of the constant outlooking and downlooking of the ruling caste on subordinates and instruments, and out of their equally constant practice of obeying and commanding, or keeping down and keeping at a distance—that other more mysterious pathos could never have arisen, the longing for an ever new widening of distance within the soul itself, the formation of ever higher, rarer, further, more extended, more comprehensive states, in short, just the elevation of the type "man," the continued "self-surmounting of man," to use a moral formula in a supermoral sense. To be sure, one must not resign oneself to any humanitarian illusions about the history of the origin of an aristocratic society (that is to say, of the preliminary condition for the elevation of the type "man"): the truth is hard. Let us acknowledge unprejudicedly how every higher civilisation hitherto has *originated!* Men with a still natural nature, barbarians in every terrible sense of the word, men of prey, still in possession of unbroken strength of will and desire for power, threw themselves upon weaker, more moral, more peaceful races (perhaps trading or cattle-rearing communities), or upon old mellow civilisations in which the final vital force was flickering out in brilliant fireworks of wit and depravity. At the commencement, the noble caste was always the barbarian caste: their superiority did not consist first of all in their physical, but in their psychical power—they were more *complete* men (which at every point also implies the same as "more complete beasts").

Corruption—as the indication that anarchy threatens to break out among the instincts, and that the foundation of the emotions, called "life," is con-

---

[*] From Nietzsche: *Beyond Good and Evil,* Chapter 9, authorized translation by Helen Zimmern. Copyright, 1907, by The Macmillan Company. Reprinted by permission of The Macmillan Company and Mrs. Maud Rosenthal.

vulsed—is something radically different according to the organisation in which it manifests itself. When, for instance, an aristocracy like that of France at the beginning of the Revolution, flung away its privileges with sublime disgust and sacrificed itself to an excess of its moral sentiments, it was corruption:—it was really only the closing act of the corruption which had existed for centuries, by virtue of which that aristocracy had abdicated step by step its lordly prerogatives and lowered itself to a *function* of royalty (in the end even to its decoration and parade-dress). The essential thing, however, in a good and healthy aristocracy is that it should *not* regard itself as a function either of the kingship or the commonwealth, but as the *significance* and highest justification thereof—that it should therefore accept with a good conscience the sacrifice of a legion of individuals, who, *for its sake*, must be suppressed and reduced to imperfect men, to slaves and instruments. Its fundamental belief must be precisely that society is *not* allowed to exist for its own sake, but only as a foundation and scaffolding, by means of which a select class of beings may be able to elevate themselves to their higher duties, and in general to a higher *existence:* like those sun-seeking climbing plants in Java—they are called *Sipo Matador,*—which encircle an oak so long and so often with their arms, until at last, high above it, but supported by it, they can unfold their tops in the open light, and exhibit their happiness.

To refrain mutually from injury, from violence, from exploitation, and put one's will on a par with that of others: this may result in a certain rough sense in good conduct among individuals when the necessary conditions are given (namely, the actual similarity of the individuals in amount of force and degree of worth, and their co-relation within one organisation). As soon, however, as one wished to take this principle more generally, and if possible even as *the fundamental principle of society*, it would immediately disclose what it really is—namely, a Will to the *denial* of life, a principle of dissolution and decay. Here one must think profoundly to the very basis and resist all sentimental weakness: life itself is *essentially* appropriation, injury, conquest of the strange and weak, suppression, severity, obtrusion of its own forms, incorporation, and at the least, putting it mildest, exploitation;—but why should one for ever use precisely these words on which for ages a disparaging purpose has been stamped? Even the organisation within which, as was previously supposed, the individuals treat each other as equal—it takes place in every healthy aristocracy—must itself, if it be a living and not a dying organisation, do all that towards other bodies, which the individuals within it refrain from doing to each other: it will have to be the incarnated Will to Power, it will endeavour to grow, to gain ground, attract to itself and acquire ascendency—not owing to any morality or immorality, but because it *lives*, and because life *is* precisely Will to Power. On no point, however, is the ordinary consciousness of Europeans more unwilling to be corrected than on this matter; people now rave everywhere, even under the guise of science, about coming conditions of society in which "the exploiting character" is to be absent:—that sounds to my ears as if they promised to invent a mode of life which should refrain from all organic functions. "Exploitation" does not belong to a depraved, or imperfect and primitive society: it belongs to the *nature* of the living being as a primary organic function, it is a consequence of the intrinsic Will to Power, which is precisely the Will to Life.— Granting that as a theory this is a novelty—as a reality it is the *fundamental fact* of all history: let us be so far honest towards ourselves!

In a tour through the many finer and coarser moralities which have hitherto prevailed or still prevail on the earth, I found certain traits recurring regularly together, and connected with one another, until finally two primary types revealed themselves to me, and a radical distinction was brought to light. There is *master-morality* and *slave-morality*;—I would at once add, however, that in all higher and mixed civilisations, there are also attempts at the reconciliation of the two moralities; but one finds still oftener the confusion and mutual misunderstanding of them, indeed, sometimes their close juxtaposition—even in the same man, within one soul. The distinctions of moral values have either originated in a ruling caste, pleasantly conscious of being different from the ruled—or among the ruled class, the slaves and dependents of all sorts. In the first case, when it is the rulers who determine the conception "good," it is the exalted, proud disposition which is regarded as the distinguishing feature, and that which determines the order of rank. The noble type of man separates from himself the beings in whom the opposite of this exalted, proud disposition displays itself: he despises them. Let it at once be noted that in this first kind of morality the antithesis "good" and "bad" means practically the same as "noble" and "despicable";—the antithesis "good" and "*evil*" is of a different origin. The cowardly, the timid, the insignificant, and those thinking merely of narrow utility are despised; moreover, also, the distrustful, with their constrained glances, the self-abasing, the dog-like kind of men who let themselves be abused, the mendicant flatterers, and above all the liars:—it is a fundamental belief of all aristocrats that the common people are untruthful. "We truthful ones"—the nobility in ancient Greece called themselves. It is obvious that everywhere the designations of moral value were at first applied to *men,* and were only derivatively and at a later period applied to *actions*; it is a gross mistake, therefore, when historians of morals start with questions like, "Why have sympathetic actions been praised?" The noble type of man regards *himself* as a determiner of values; he does not require to be approved of; he passes the judgment:

"What is injurious to me is injurious in itself"; he knows that it is he himself only who confers honour on things; he is a *creator of values*. He honours whatever he recognises in himself: such morality is self-glorification. In the foreground there is the feeling of plenitude, of power, which seeks to over-flow, the happiness of high tension, the consciousness of a wealth which would fain give and bestow:—the noble man also helps the unfortunate, but not—or scarcely—out of pity, but rather from an impulse generated by the superabundance of power. The noble man honours in himself the powerful one, him also who has power over himself, who knows how to speak and how to keep silence, who takes pleasure in subjecting himself to severity and hardness, and has reverence for all that is severe and hard. "Wotan placed a hard heart in my breast," says an old Scandinavian Saga: it is thus rightly expressed from the soul of a proud Viking. Such a type of man is even proud of *not* being made for sympathy; the hero of the Saga therefore adds warn-ingly: "He who has not a hard heart when young, will never have one." The noble and brave who think thus are the furthest removed from the morality which sees precisely in sympathy, or in acting for the good of others, or in *désintéressement,* the characteristic of the moral; faith in oneself, pride in oneself, a radical enmity and irony towards "selflessness," belong as defi-nitely to noble morality, as do a careless scorn and precaution in presence of sympathy and the "warm heart."—It is the powerful who *know* how to hon-our, it is their art, their domain for invention. The profound reverence for age and for tradition—all law rests on this double reverence,—the belief and prejudice in favour of ancestors and unfavourable to newcomers, is typical in the morality of the powerful; and if, reversely, men of "modern ideas" be-lieve almost instinctively in "progress" and the "future," and are more and more lacking in respect for old age, the ignoble origin of these "ideas" has complacently betrayed itself thereby. A morality of the ruling class, how-ever, is more especially foreign and irritating to present-day taste in the sternness of its principle that one has duties only to one's equals; that one may act towards beings of a lower rank, towards all that is foreign, just as seems good to one, or "as the heart desires," and in any case "beyond good and evil"; it is here that sympathy and similar sentiments can have a place. The ability and obligation to exercise prolonged gratitude and prolonged revenge—both only within the circle of equals,—artfulness in retaliation, *raffinement* of the idea in friendship, a certain necessity to have enemies (as outlets for the emotions of envy, quarrelsomeness, arrogance—in fact, in order to be a good *friend*): all these are typical characteristics of the noble morality, which, as has been pointed out, is not the morality of "modern ideas," and is therefore at present difficult to realise, and also to unearth and disclose.—It is otherwise with the second type of morality, *slave-morality.*

Supposing that the abused, the oppressed, the suffering, the unemancipated, the weary, and those uncertain of themselves, should moralise, what will be the common element in their moral estimates? Probably a pessimistic suspicion with regard to the entire situation of man will find expression, perhaps a condemnation of man, together with his situation. The slave has an unfavourable eye for the virtues of the powerful; he has a scepticism and distrust, a *refinement* of distrust of everything "good" that is there honoured —he would fain persuade himself that the very happiness there is not genuine. On the other hand, *those* qualities which serve to alleviate the existence of sufferers are brought into prominence and flooded with light; it is here that sympathy, the kind, helping hand, the warm heart, patience, diligence, humility, and friendliness attain to honour; for here these are the most useful qualities, and almost the only means of supporting the burden of existence. Slave-morality is essentially the morality of utility. Here is the seat of the origin of the famous antithesis "good" and "*evil*":—power and dangerousness are assumed to reside in the evil, a certain dreadfulness, subtlety, and strength, which do not admit of being despised. According to slave-morality, therefore, the "evil" man arouses fear; according to master-morality, it is precisely the "good" man who arouses fear and seeks to arouse it, while the bad man is regarded as the despicable being. The contrast attains its maximum when, in accordance with the logical consequences of slave-morality, a shade of depreciation—it may be slight and well-intentioned—at last attaches itself even to the "good" man of this morality; because, according to the servile mode of thought, the good man must in any case be the *safe* man: he is good-natured, easily deceived, perhaps a little stupid, *un bonhomme*. Everywhere that slave-morality gains the ascendency, language shows a tendency to approximate the significations of the words "good" and "stupid." . . .

At the risk of displeasing innocent ears, I submit that egoism belongs to the essence of a noble soul, I mean the unalterable belief that to a being such as "we," other beings must naturally be in subjection, and have to sacrifice themselves. The noble soul accepts the fact of his egoism without question, and also without consciousness of harshness, constraint, or arbitrariness therein, but rather as something that may have its basis in the primary law of things:—if he sought a designation for it he would say: "It is justice itself." He acknowledges under certain circumstances, which made him hesitate at first, that there are other equally privileged ones; as soon as he has settled this question of rank, he moves among those equals and equally privileged ones with the same assurance, as regards modesty and delicate respect, which he enjoys in intercourse with himself—in accordance with an innate heavenly mechanism which all the stars understand. It is an *additional* instance of his egoism, this artfulness and self-limitation in intercourse with his equals—every star is a similar egoist; he honours *himself* in them, and in the rights which he concedes to them, he has no doubt that the exchange of honours and rights, as the *essence* of all intercourse, belongs also to the natural condition of things. The noble soul gives as he takes, prompted by the passionate and sensitive instinct of requital, which is at the root of his nature. The notion of "favour" has, *inter pares,* neither significance nor good repute; there may be a sublime way of letting gifts as it were light upon one from above, and of drinking them thirstily like dew-drops; but for those arts and displays the noble soul has no aptitude. His egoism hinders him here: in general, he looks "aloft" unwillingly—he looks either *forward,* horizontally and deliberately, or downwards—*he knows that he is on a height.*

Ideal Utilitarianism [*]

GEORGE EDWARD MOORE [1837–1958]. See p. 295.

INTRINSIC VALUE. Ethics is undoubtedly concerned with the question what good conduct is; but, being concerned with this, it obviously does not start at the beginning, unless it is prepared to tell us what is good as well as what is conduct. For 'good conduct' is a complex notion: all conduct is not good; for some is certainly bad and some may be indifferent. And on the other hand, other things, beside conduct, may be good; and if they are so, then, 'good' denotes some property, that is common to them and conduct; and if we examine good conduct alone of all good things, then we shall be in danger of mistaking for this property, some property which is not shared by those other things: and thus we shall have made a mistake about Ethics even in this limited sense; for we shall not know what good conduct really is. This is a mistake which many writers have actually made, from limiting their enquiry to conduct. And hence I shall try to avoid it by considering first what is good in general; hoping, that if we can arrive at any certainty about this, it will be much easier to settle the question of good conduct: for we all know pretty well what 'conduct' is. This, then, is our first question: What is good? and What is bad? and to the discussion of this question (or these questions) I give the name of Ethics, since that science must, at all events, include it. . . .

What, then, is good? How is good to be defined? Now, it may be thought that this is a verbal question. A definition does indeed often mean the expressing of one word's meaning in other words. But this is not the sort of definition I am asking for. Such a definition can never be of ultimate importance in any study except lexicography. If I wanted that kind of definition I should have to consider in the first place how people generally used the word 'good'; but my business is not with its proper usage, as established by custom. I should, indeed, be foolish, if I tried to use it for something which it did not usually denote: if, for instance, I were to announce that, whenever I used the word 'good,' I must be understood to be thinking of that object which is usually denoted by the word 'table.' I shall, therefore, use the word in the sense in which I think it is ordinarily used; but at the same time I am not anxious to discuss whether I am right in thinking that it is so used. My business is solely with that object or idea, which I hold, rightly or wrongly, that the word is generally used to stand for. What I want to discover is the nature of that object or idea, and about this I am extremely anxious to arrive at an agreement.

But, if we understand the question in this sense, my answer to it may seem a very disappointing one. If I am asked 'What is good?' my answer is that good is good, and that is the end of the matter. Or if I am asked 'How is good to be defined?' my answer is that it cannot be defined, and that is all I have to say about it. But disappointing as these answers may appear, they are of the very last importance. To readers who are familiar with philosophic terminology, I can express their importance by saying that they amount to this: That propositions about the good are all of them synthetic and never analytic; and that is plainly no trivial matter. And the same thing may be expressed more popularly, by saying that, if I am right, then nobody can foist upon us such an axiom as that 'Pleasure is the only good' or that 'The good is the desired' on the pretence that this is 'the very meaning of the word.'

Let us, then, consider this position. My point is that 'good' is a simple notion, just as 'yellow' is a simple notion; that, just as you cannot, by any manner of means, explain to any one who does not already know it, what yellow is, so you cannot explain what good is. Definitions of the kind that I was asking for, definitions which describe the real nature of the object or notion denoted by a word, and which do not merely tell us what the word is used to mean, are only possible when the object or notion in question is something complex. You can give a definition of a horse, because a horse has many different properties and qualities, all of which you can enumerate. But when you have enumerated them all, when you have reduced a horse to his simplest terms, then you can no longer define those terms. They are simply something which you think of or perceive, and to any one who cannot think of or perceive them, you can never, by any definition, make their nature known. It may perhaps be objected to this that we are able to describe to others, objects which they have never seen or thought of. We can, for instance, make a man understand what a chimera is, although he has never heard of one or seen one. You can tell him that it is an animal with a lioness's head and body, with a goat's head growing from the middle of its back, and with a snake in place of a tail. But here the object which you are describing is a complex object; it is entirely composed of parts, with which we are all perfectly familiar—a snake, a goat, a lioness; and we know, too, the manner in which those parts are to be put together, because we know what is meant by the middle of a lioness's back, and where her tail is wont to grow. And so it is with all objects, not previously known, which we are able to define: they are all complex; all composed of parts, which may themselves, in the first instance, be capable of similar definition, but which must in the end be reducible to simplest parts, which can no longer be defined. But yellow and good, we say, are not complex: they are notions of that simple kind, out of which definitions are composed and with which the power of further defining ceases. . . .

'Good,' then, if we mean by it that quality which we assert to belong to a thing, when we say that the thing is good, is incapable of any definition, in the most important sense of that word. The most important sense of 'definition' is that in which a definition states what are the parts which invariably compose a certain whole; and in this sense 'good' has no definition because it is simple and has no parts. It is one of those innumerable objects of thought which are themselves incapable of definition, because they are the ultimate terms by reference to which whatever *is* capable of definition must be defined. That there must be an indefinite number of such terms is obvious, on reflection; since we cannot define anything except by an analysis, which, when carried as far as it will go, refers us to something, which is simply different from anything else, and which by that ultimate difference explains the peculiarity of the whole which we are defining: for every whole contains some parts which are common to other wholes also. There is, therefore, no intrinsic difficulty in the contention that 'good' denotes a simple and indefinable quality. There are many other instances of such qualities.

Consider yellow, for example. We may try to define it, by describing its physical equivalent; we may state what kind of light-vibrations must stimulate the normal eye, in order that we may perceive it. But a moment's reflection is sufficient to shew that those light-vibrations are not themselves what we mean by yellow. *They* are not what we perceive. Indeed we should never have been able to discover their existence, unless we had first been struck by the patent difference of quality between the different colours. The most we can be entitled to say of those vibrations is that they are what corresponds in space to the yellow which we actually perceive.

Yet a mistake of this simple kind has commonly been made about 'good.' It may be true that all things which are good are *also* something else, just as it is true that all things which are yellow produce a certain kind of vibration in the light. And it is a fact, that Ethics aims at discovering what are those other properties belonging to all things which are good. But far too many philosophers have thought that when they named those other properties they were actually defining good; that these properties, in fact, were simply not 'other,' but absolutely and entirely the same with goodness. This view I propose to call the 'naturalistic fallacy.' . . .

THE NATURALISTIC FALLACY AND HEDONISM. Suppose a man says 'I am pleased'; and suppose that is not a lie or a mistake but the truth. Well, if it is true, what does that mean? It means that his mind, a certain definite mind, distinguished by certain definite marks from all others, has at this moment a certain definite feeling called pleasure. 'Pleased' *means* nothing but having pleasure, and though we may be more pleased or less pleased, and even, we may admit for the present, have one or another kind of pleasure; yet in so far as it is pleasure we have, whether there be more or less of it, and whether it be of one kind or another, what we have is one definite thing, absolutely indefinable, some one thing that is the same in all the various degrees and in all the various kinds of it that there may be. We may be able to say how it is related to other things: that, for example, it is in the mind, that it causes desire, that we are conscious of it, etc., etc. We can, I say, describe its relation to other things, but define it we can *not*. And if anybody tried to define pleasure for us as being any other natural object; if anybody were to say, for instance, that pleasure *means* the sensation of red, and were to proceed to deduce from that that pleasure is a colour, we should be entitled to laugh at him and to distrust his future statements about pleasure. Well, that would be the same fallacy which I have called the naturalistic fallacy. That 'pleased' does not mean 'having the sensation of red,' or anything else whatever, does not prevent us from understanding what it does mean. It is enough for us to know that 'pleased' does mean 'having the sensation of pleasure,' and though pleasure is absolutely indefinable, though pleasure is pleasure and nothing else whatever, yet we feel no difficulty in saying that we are pleased. The reason is, of course, that when I say 'I am pleased,' I do *not* mean that 'I' am the same thing as 'having pleasure.' And similarly no difficulty need be found in my saying that 'pleasure is good' and yet not meaning that 'pleasure' is the same thing as 'good,' that pleasure *means* good, and that good *means* pleasure. If I were to imagine that when I said 'I am pleased,' I meant that I was exactly the same thing as 'pleased,' I should not indeed call that a naturalistic fallacy, although it would be the same fallacy as I have called naturalistic with reference to Ethics. The reason of this is obvious enough. When a man confuses two natural objects with one another, defining the one by the other, if for instance, he confuses himself, who is one natural object, with 'pleased' or with 'pleasure' which are others, then there is no reason to call the fallacy naturalistic. But if he confuses 'good,' which is not in the same sense a natural object, with any natural object whatever, then there is a reason for calling that a naturalistic fallacy; its being made with regard to 'good' marks it as something quite specific, and this specific mistake deserves a name because it is so common. As for the reasons why good is not to be considered a natural object, they may be reserved for discussion in another place. But, for the present, it is sufficient to notice this: Even if it were a natural object, that would not alter the nature of the fallacy nor diminish its importance one whit. All that I have said about it would remain quite equally true: only the name which I have called it would not be so appropriate as I think it is. And I do not care about the name: what I do care about is the fallacy. It does not matter what we call it, provided we recognise it when we meet with it. It is to be met with in almost every book on Ethics; and yet it is not recognised: and that is why it is necessary to multiply illustrations of it, and convenient to give it a name. It is a very simple fallacy indeed. When we say that an orange is yellow, we do not think our statement binds us to hold that 'orange' means nothing else than 'yellow,' or that nothing can be yellow but an orange. Supposing the orange is also sweet! Does that bind us to say that 'sweet' is exactly the same thing as 'yellow,' that 'sweet' must be defined as 'yellow'? And supposing it be recognised that 'yellow' just means 'yellow' and nothing else whatever, does that make it any more difficult to hold that oranges are yellow? Most certainly it does not: on the contrary, it would be absolutely meaningless to say that oranges were yellow, unless yellow did in the end mean just 'yellow' and nothing else whatever—unless it was absolutely indefinable. We should not get any very clear notion about things, which are yellow—we should not get very far with our science, if we were bound to hold that everything which was yellow, *meant* exactly the same thing as yellow. We should find we had to hold that an orange was exactly the same thing as a stool, a piece of paper, a lemon, anything you like. We could prove any number of absurdities; but should we be the nearer to the truth? Why, then, should it be different with 'good'? Why, if good is good and indefinable, should I be held to deny that pleasure is good? Is there any difficulty in holding both to be true at once? On the contrary, there is no meaning in saying that pleasure is good, unless good is something different from pleasure. . . .

INTRINSIC VALUE AND RIGHT ACTION. Our first conclusion as to the subject-matter of Ethics is, then, that there is a simple, indefinable, unanalysable object of thought by reference to which it must be defined. By what name we call this unique object is a matter of indifference, so long as we clearly recognise what it is and that it does differ from other objects. The words which are commonly taken as the signs of ethical judgments all do refer to it; and they are expressions of ethical judgments solely because they do so refer. . . . But, although all such judgments do refer to that unique notion which I have called 'good,' they do not all refer to it in the same way. They may either assert that this unique property does always attach to the thing in question, or else they may assert only that the thing in question is *a cause or necessary condition* for the existence of other things to which this unique property does attach. The nature of these two species of universal ethical judgments is extremely different; and a great part of the difficulties, which are met with in ordinary ethical speculation, are due to the failure to distinguish them clearly. Their difference has, indeed, received expression in ordinary language by the contrast between the terms 'good as means' and 'good in itself,' 'value as a means' and 'intrinsic value.' But these terms are apt to be applied correctly only in the more obvious instances; and this seems to be due to the fact that the distinction between the conceptions which they denote has not been made a separate object of investigation. This distinction may be briefly pointed out as follows.

Whenever we judge that a thing is 'good as a means,' we are making a judgment with regard to its causal relations: we judge *both* that it will have a particular kind of effect, *and* that that effect will be good in itself. But to find causal judgments that are universally true is notoriously a matter of extreme difficulty. The late date at which most of the physical sciences became exact, and the comparative fewness of the laws which they have succeeded in establishing even now, are sufficient proofs of this difficulty. With regard, then, to what are the most frequent objects of ethical judgments, namely actions, it is obvious that we cannot be satisfied that any of our universal causal judgments are true, even in the sense in which scientific laws are so. We cannot even discover hypothetical laws of the form 'exactly this action will always, under these conditions, produce exactly that effect.' But for a correct ethical judgment with regard to the effects of certain actions we require more than this in two respects. (1) We require to know that a given action will produce a certain effect, *under whatever circumstances it occurs.* But this is certainly impossible. It is certain that in different circumstances the same action may produce effects which are utterly different in all respects upon which the value of the effects depends. Hence we can never be entitled to more than a *generalisation*—to a proposition of the form 'This result *generally* follows this kind of action'; and even this generalisation will only be true, if the circumstances under which the action occurs are generally the same. This is in fact the case, to a great extent, within any one particular age and state of society. But, when we take other ages into account, in many most important cases the normal circumstances of a given kind of action will be so different, that the generalisation which is true for one will not be true for another. With regard then to ethical judgments which assert that a certain kind of action is good as a means to a certain kind of effect, none will be *universally* true; and many, though *generally* true at one period, will be generally false at others. But (2) we require to know not only that *one* good effect will be produced, but that, among all subsequent events affected by the action in question, the balance of good will be greater than if any other possible action had been performed. In other words, to judge that an action is generally a means to good is to judge not only that it generally does *some* good, but that it generally does the greatest good of which the circumstances admit. In this respect ethical judgments about the effects of action involve a difficulty and a complication far greater than that involved in the establishment of scientific laws. For the latter we need only consider a single effect; for the former it is essential to consider not only this, but the effects of that effect, and so on as far as our view into the future can reach. It is, indeed, obvious that our view can never reach far enough for us to be certain that any action will produce the best possible effects. We must be content, if the greatest possible balance of good seems to be produced within a limited period. But it is important to notice that the whole series of effects within a period of considerable length is actually taken account of in our common judgments that an action is good as a means; and that hence this additional complication, which makes ethical generalisations so far more difficult to establish than scientific laws, is one which is involved in actual ethical discussions, and is of practical importance. The commonest rules of conduct involve such considerations as the balancing of future bad health against immediate gains; and even if we can never settle with any certainty how we shall secure the greatest possible total of good, we try at least to assure ourselves that probable future evils will not be greater than the immediate good.

There are, then, judgments which state that certain kinds of things have good effects; and such judgments, for the reasons just given, have the important characteristics (1) that they are unlikely to be true, if they state that the kind of thing in question *always* had good effects, and (2) that, even if they only state that it *generally* has good effects, many of them will only be true of certain periods in the world's history. On the other hand there are judgments which state that certain kinds of things are themselves good; and these differ from the last in that, if true at all, they are all of them universally true. It is, therefore, extremely important to distinguish these two kinds of possible judgments. Both may be expressed in the same language: in both cases we commonly say 'Such and such a thing is good.' But in the one case 'good' will mean 'good as means,' *i.e.* merely that the thing is a means to good—will have good effects: in the other case it will mean 'good as end' —we shall be judging that the thing itself has the property which, in the first case, we asserted only to belong to its effects. It is plain that these are very different assertions to make about a thing; it is plain that either or both of them may be made, both truly and falsely, about all manner of things; and it is certain that unless we are clear as to which of the two we mean to assert, we shall have a very poor chance of deciding rightly whether our assertion is true or false. It is precisely this clearness as to the meaning of the question asked which has hitherto been almost entirely lacking in ethical speculation. Ethics has always been predominantly concerned with the investigation of a limited class of actions. With regard to these we may ask *both* how far they are good in themselves *and* how far they have a general tendency to produce good results. And the arguments brought forward in ethical discussion have always been of both classes—both such as would prove the conduct in question to be good in itself and such as would prove it to be good as a means. But that these are the only questions which any ethical discussion can have to settle, and that to settle the one is *not* the same thing as to settle the other—these two fundamental facts have in general escaped the notice of ethical philosophers. Ethical questions are commonly asked in an ambiguous form. It is asked 'What is a man's duty under these circumstances?' or 'Is it right to act in this way?' or 'What ought we to aim at securing?' But all these questions are capable of further analysis; a correct answer to any of them involves both judgments of what is good in itself and causal judgments. This is implied even by those who maintain that we have a direct and immediate judgment of absolute rights and duties. Such a judgment can only mean that the course of action in question is *the* best thing to do; that, by acting so, every good that *can* be secured will have been secured. Now we are not concerned with the question whether such a judgment will ever be true. The question is: What does it imply, if it is true? And the only possible answer is that, whether true or false, it implies both a proposition as to the degree of goodness of the action in question, as compared with other things, and a number of causal propositions. For it cannot be denied that the action will have consequences: and to deny that the consequences matter is to make a judgment of their intrinsic value, as compared with the action itself. In asserting that the action is *the* best thing to do, we assert that it together with its consequences presents a greater sum of intrinsic value than any possible alternative. And this condition may be realised by any of the three cases: —(a) If the action itself has greater intrinsic value than any alternatives, whereas both its consequences and those of the alternatives are absolutely devoid either of intrinsic merit or intrinsic demerit; or (b) if, though its consequences are intrinsically bad, the balance of intrinsic value is greater than would be produced by any alternative; or (c) if, its consequences being intrinsically good, the degree of value belonging to them and it conjointly is greater than that of any alternative series. In short, to assert that a certain line of conduct is, at a given time, absolutely right or obligatory, is obviously to assert that more good or less evil will exist in the world, if it be adopted than if anything else be done instead. But this implies a judgment as to the value both of its own consequences and of those of any possible alternative. And that an action will have such and such consequences involves a number of causal judgments. . . .

ORGANIC WHOLES. There remains one point which must not be omitted in a complete description of the kind of questions which Ethics has to answer. The main division of those questions is, as I have said, into two; the question what things are good in themselves, and the question to what other things these are related as effects. The first of these, which is the primary ethical question and is presupposed by the other, includes a correct comparison of the various things which have intrinsic value (if there are many such) in respect of the degree of value which they have; and such comparison involves a difficulty of principle which has greatly aided the confusion of intrinsic value with mere 'goodness as a means.' It has been pointed out that one difference between a judgment which asserts that a thing is good in itself, and a judgment which asserts that it is a means to good, consists in the fact that the first, if true of one instance of the thing in question, is necessarily true of all; whereas a thing which has good effects under some circumstances may have bad ones under others. Now it is certainly true that all judgments of intrinsic value are in this sense universal; but the principle which I have now to enunciate may easily make it appear as if they were not so but resembled the judgment of means in being merely general. There is, as will presently be maintained, a vast number of different things, each of which has intrinsic value; there are also very many which are positively bad; and there is a still larger class of things, which appear to be indifferent. But a thing belonging to any of these three classes may occur as part of a whole, which includes among its other parts other things belonging both to the same and to the other two classes; and these wholes, as such, may also have intrinsic value. The paradox, to which it is necessary to call attention, is that *the value of such a whole bears no regular proportion to the sum of the values of its parts.* It is certain that a good thing may exist in such a relation to another good thing that the value of the whole thus formed is immensely greater than the sum of the values of the two good things. It is certain that a whole formed of a good thing and an indifferent thing may have immensely greater value than that good thing itself possesses. It is certain that two bad things or a bad thing and an indifferent thing may form a whole much worse than the sum of badness of its parts. And it seems as if indifferent things may also be the sole constituents of a whole which has great value, either positive or negative. Whether the addition of a bad thing to a good whole may increase the positive value of the whole, or the addition of a bad thing to a bad may produce a whole having positive value, may seem more doubtful; but it is, at least, possible, and this possibility must be taken into account in our ethical investigations. However we may decide particular questions, the principle is clear. *The value of a whole must not be assumed to be the same as the sum of the values of its parts.*

A single instance will suffice to illustrate the kind of relation in question. It seems to be true that to be conscious of a beautiful object is a thing of great intrinsic value; whereas the same object, if no one be conscious of it, has certainly comparatively little value, and is commonly held to have none at all. But the consciousness of a beautiful object is certainly a whole of some sort in which we can distinguish as parts the object on the one hand and the being conscious on the other. Now this latter factor occurs as part of a different whole, whenever we are conscious of anything; and it would seem that some of these wholes have at all events very little value, and may even be indifferent or positively bad. Yet we cannot always attribute the slightness of their value to any positive demerit in the object which differentiates them from the consciousness of beauty; the object itself may approach as near as possible to absolute neutrality. Since, therefore, mere consciousness does not always confer great value upon the whole of which it forms a part, even though its object may have no great demerit, we cannot attribute the great superiority of the consciousness of a beautiful thing over the beautiful thing itself to the mere addition of the value of consciousness to that of the beautiful thing. Whatever the intrinsic value of consciousness may be, it does not give to the whole of which it forms a part a value proportioned to the sum of its value and that of its object. If this be so, we have here an instance of a whole possessing a different intrinsic value from the sum of that of its parts; and whether it be so or not, what is meant by such a difference is illustrated by this case.

There are, then, wholes which possess the property that their value is different from the sum of the values of their parts; and the relations which subsist between such parts and the whole of which they form a part have not hitherto been distinctly recognised or received a separate name. Two points are especially worthy of notice. (1) It is plain that the existence of any such part is a necessary condition for the existence of that good which is constituted by the whole. And exactly the same language will also express the relation between a means and the good thing which is its effect. But yet there is a most important difference between the two cases, constituted by the fact that the part is, whereas the means is not, a part of the good thing for the existence of which its existence is a necessary condition. The necessity by which, if the good in question is to exist, the means to it must exist is merely a natural or causal necessity. If the laws of nature were different, exactly the same good might exist, although what is now a necessary condition of its existence did not exist. The existence of the means has no intrinsic value; and its utter annihilation would leave the value of that which it is now necessary to secure entirely unchanged. But in the case of a part of such a whole as we are now considering, it is otherwise. In this case the good in question cannot conceivably exist, unless the part exist also. The necessity which connects the two is quite independent of natural law. What is asserted to have intrinsic value is the existence of the whole; and the existence of the whole includes the existence of its part. Suppose the part removed, and what remains is *not* what was asserted to have intrinsic value; but if we suppose a means removed, what remains is just what *was* asserted to have intrinsic value. And yet (2) the existence of the part may *itself* have no more intrinsic value than that of the means. It is this fact which constitutes the paradox of the relation which we are discussing. It has just been said that what has intrinsic value is the existence of the whole, and that this includes the existence of the part; and from this it would seem a natural inference that the existence of the part has intrinsic value. But the inference would be as false as if we were to conclude that, because the number of two stones was two, each of the stones was also two. The part of a valuable whole retains exactly the same value when it is, as when it is not, a part of that whole. If it had value under other circumstances, its value is not any greater, when it is part of a far more valuable whole; and if it had no value by itself, it has none still, however great be that of the whole of which it now forms a part. We are not then justified in asserting that one and the same thing is under some circumstances intrinsically good, and under others not so; as we are justified in asserting of a means that it sometimes does and sometimes does not produce good results. And yet we are justified in asserting that it is far more desirable that a certain thing should exist under some circumstances than under others; namely when other things will exist in such relations to it as to form a more valuable whole. *It* will not have more intrinsic value under these circumstances than under others; *it* will not necessarily even be a means to the existence of things having more intrinsic value: but it will, like a means, be a necessary condition for the existence of that which *has* greater intrinsic value, although, unlike a means, it will itself form a part of this more valuable existent. . . .

OUR KNOWLEDGE OF INTRINSIC VALUE. My discussion hitherto has fallen under two main heads. Under the first, I tried to show what 'good'—the adjective 'good'—*means*. This appeared to be the first point to be settled in any treatment of Ethics, that should aim at being systematic. It is necessary we should know this, should know what good means, before we can go on to consider what is good—what things or qualities are good. It is necessary we should know it for two reasons. The first reason is that 'good' is the notion upon which all Ethics depends. We cannot hope to understand what we mean, when we say that this is good or that is good, until we understand quite clearly, not only what 'this' is or 'that' is (which the natural sciences and philosophy can tell us) but also what is meant by calling them good, a matter which is reserved for Ethics only. Unless we are quite clear on this point, our ethical reasoning will be always apt to be fallacious. We shall think that we are proving that a thing is 'good,' when we are really only proving that it is something else; since unless we know what 'good' means, unless we know what is meant by that notion in itself, as distinct from what is meant by any other notion, we shall not be able to tell when we are dealing with it and when we are dealing with something else, which is perhaps like it, but yet not the same. And the second reason why we should settle first of all this question 'What good means?' is a reason of method. It is this, that we can never know on what *evidence* an ethical proposition rests, until we know the nature of the notion which makes the proposition ethical. We cannot tell what is possible, by way of proof, in favour of one judgment that 'This or that is good,' or against another judgment 'That this or that is bad,' until we have recognised what the nature of such propositions must always be. In fact, it follows from the meaning of good and bad, that such propositions are all of them, in Kant's phrase, 'synthetic': they all must rest in the end upon some proposition which must be simply accepted or rejected, which cannot be logically deduced from any other proposition. This result, which follows from our first investigation, may be otherwise expressed by saying that the fundamental principles of Ethics must be self-evident. But I am anxious that this expression should not be misunderstood. The expression 'self-evident' means properly that the proposition so called is evident or true, by *itself* alone; that it is not an inference from some proposition other than *itself*. The expression does *not* mean that the proposition is true, because it is evident to you or me or all mankind, because in other words it appears to us to be true. . . .

So much, then, for the first step in our ethical method, the step which established that good is good and nothing else whatever. . . . A second step was taken when we began to consider proposed self-evident principles of Ethics. In this second division, resting on our result that good means good, we begin the discussion of propositions asserting that such and such a thing or quality or concept was good. Of such a kind was the principle of Intuitionistic or Ethical Hedonism—the principle that 'Pleasure alone is good.' Following the method established by our first discussion, I claimed that the untruth of this proposition was self-evident. I could do nothing to *prove* that it was untrue; I could only point out as clearly as possible what it means, and how it contradicts other propositions which appear to be equally true. My only object in all this was, necessarily, to convince. But even if I did convince, that does not prove that we are right. It justifies us in *holding* that we are so; but nevertheless we may be wrong. On one thing, however, we may justly pride ourselves. It is that we have had a better chance of answering our question rightly, than Bentham or Mill or Sidgwick or others who have contradicted us. For we have *proved* that these have never even asked themselves the question which they professed to answer. They have confused it with another question: small wonder, therefore, if their answer is different from ours. We must be quite sure that the same question has been put, before we trouble ourselves at the different answers that are given to it. For all we know, the whole world would agree with us, if they could once clearly understand the question upon which we want their votes. Certain it is, that in all those cases where we found a difference of opinion, we found also that the question had *not* been clearly understood. Though, therefore, we cannot prove that we are right, yet we have reason to believe that everybody, unless he is mistaken as to what he thinks, will think the same as we. It is as with a sum in mathematics. If we find a gross and palpable error in the calculations, we are not surprised or troubled that the person who made this mistake has reached a different result from ours. We think he will admit that his result is wrong, if his mistake is pointed out to him. For instance if a man has to add up $5 + 7 + 9$, we should not wonder that he made the result to be 34, if he started by making $5 + 7 = 25$. And so in Ethics, if we find, as we did, that 'desirable' is confused with 'desired,' or that 'end' is confused with 'means,' we need not be disconcerted that those who have committed these mistakes do not agree with us. The only difference is that in Ethics, owing to the intricacy of its subject-matter, it is far more difficult to persuade anyone either that he has made a mistake or that that mistake affects his result.

. . . [T]o the fundamental question of Ethics—the question: 'What things are goods or ends in themselves?'— . . . we have hitherto obtained only a negative answer: the answer that pleasure is certainly not the *sole*

good. . . . [I]t appears that the question we have to answer is far less difficult than the controversies of Ethics might have led us to expect. Indeed,
once the meaning of the question is clearly understood, the answer to it, in
its main outlines, appears to be so obvious, that it runs the risk of seeming to
be a platitude. By far the most valuable things, which we know or can imagine, are certain states of consciousness, which may be roughly described as
the pleasures of human intercourse and the enjoyment of beautiful objects.
No one, probably, who has asked himself the question, has ever doubted
that personal affection and the appreciation of what is beautiful in Art or
Nature, are good in themselves; nor, if we consider strictly what things are
worth having *purely for their own sakes,* does it appear probable that any
one will think that anything else has *nearly* so great a value as the things
which are included under these two heads. I have myself urged . . . that
the mere existence of what is beautiful does appear to have *some* intrinsic
value; but I regard it as indubitable . . . that such mere existence of what is
beautiful has value, so small as to be negligible, in comparison with that
which attaches to the *consciousness* of beauty. This simple truth may, indeed, be said to be universally recognised. What has *not* been recognised is
that it is the ultimate and fundamental truth of Moral Philosophy. That it is
only for the sake of these things—in order that as much of them as possible
may at some time exist—that any one can be justified in performing any
public or private duty; that they are the *raison d'être* of virtue; that it is
they—these complex wholes *themselves,* and not any constituent or characteristic of them—that from the rational ultimate end of human action and
the sole criterion of social progress: these appear to be truths which have
been generally overlooked. . . .

With regard . . . to great positive evils, I think it is evident that, if we
take all due precautions to discover *precisely what* those things are, of
which, *if they existed absolutely by themselves,* we should judge the existence to be a great evil, we shall find most of them to be organic unities of
exactly the same nature as those which are the greatest positive goods. That
is to say, they are cognitions of some object, accompanied by some emotion.
Just as neither a cognition nor an emotion, *by itself,* appeared capable of
being greatly good, so (with one exception), neither a cognition nor an emotion, *by itself,* appears capable of being greatly evil. And just as a whole
formed of both, even without the addition of any other element, appeared
undoubtedly capable of being a great good, so such a whole, *by itself,* appears capable of being a great evil. With regard to the *third* element, which
was discussed as capable of adding greatly to the value of a good, namely,
true belief, it will appear that it has different relations towards different
kinds of evils. In some cases the addition of true belief to a positive evil

seems to constitute a far worse evil; but in other cases it is not apparent that it makes any difference.

The greatest positive evils may be divided into the following three classes.

(1) The first class consists of those evils, which seem always to include an enjoyment or admiring contemplation of things which are themselves either evil or ugly. That is to say these evils are characterised by the fact that they include precisely the same emotion, which is also essential to the greatest unmixed goods, from which they are differentiated by the fact that this emotion is directed towards an inappropriate object. In so far as this emotion is either a slight good in itself or a slightly beautiful object, these evils would therefore be cases of what I have called 'mixed' evils; but, as I have already said, it seems very doubtful whether an emotion, completely isolated from its object, has either value or beauty: it certainly has not much of either. It is, however, important to observe that the very same emotions, which are often loosely talked of as the greatest or the only goods, may be essential constituents of the very worst wholes: that, according to the nature of the cognition which accompanies them, they may be conditions either of the greatest good, or of the greatest evil.

In order to illustrate the nature of evils of this class, I may take two instances—cruelty and lasciviousness. That these are great intrinsic evils, we may, I think, easily assure ourselves, by imagining the state of a man, whose mind is solely occupied by either of these passions, in their worst form. If we then consider what judgment we should pass upon a universe which consisted *solely* of minds thus occupied, without the smallest hope that there would ever exist in it the smallest consciousness of any object other than those proper to these passions, or any feeling directed to any such object, I think we cannot avoid the conclusion that the existence of such a universe would be a far worse evil than the existence of none at all. But, if this be so, it follows that these two vicious states are not only, as is commonly admitted, bad as means, but also bad in themselves. . . .

(2) The second class of great evils are undoubtedly mixed evils; but I treat them next, because, in a certain respect, they appear to be the *converse* of the class last considered. Just as it is essential to this last class that they should include an emotion, appropriate to the cognition of what is good or beautiful, but directed to an inappropriate object; so to this second class it is essential that they should include a cognition of what is good or beautiful, but accompanied by an inappropriate emotion. In short, just as the last class may be described as cases of the love of what is evil or ugly, so this class may be described as cases of the hatred of what is good or beautiful. . . .

(3) The third class of great positive evils appears to be the class of *pains*.

With regard to these it should first be remarked that, as in the case of pleasure, it is not pain itself, but only the consciousness of pain, towards which our judgments of value are directed. Just as . . . it was said that pleasure, however intense, which no one felt, would be no good at all; so it appears that pain, however intense, of which there was no consciousness, would be no evil at all.

It is, therefore, only the consciousness of intense pain, which can be maintained to be a great evil. But that this, *by itself,* may be a great evil, I cannot avoid thinking. The case of pain thus seems to differ from that of pleasure: for the mere consciousness of pleasure, however intense, does not, *by itself,* appear to be a *great* good, even if it has some slight intrinsic value. . . .

I have now completed such remarks as seemed most necessary to be made concerning intrinsic values. It is obvious that for the proper answering of this, the fundamental question of Ethics, there remains a field of investigation as wide and as difficult, as was assigned to Practical Ethics in my last chapter. There is as much to be said concerning what results are intrinsically good, and in what degrees, as concerning what results it is possible for us to bring about: both questions demand, and will repay, an equally patient enquiry. Many of the judgments, which I have made in this chapter, will, no doubt, seem unduly arbitrary: it must be confessed that some of the attributions of intrinsic value, which have seemed to me to be true, do not display that symmetry and system which is wont to be required of philosophers. But if this be urged as an objection, I may respectfully point out that it is none. We have no title whatever to assume that the truth on any subject-matter will display such symmetry as we desire to see—or (to use the common vague phrase) that it will possess any particular form of 'unity.' To search for 'unity' and 'system,' at the expense of truth, is not, I take it, the proper business of philosophy, however universally it may have been the practice of philosophers. And that all truths about the Universe possess to one another all the various relations, which may be meant by 'unity,' can only be legitimately asserted, when we have carefully distinguished those various relations and discovered what those truths are. In particular, we can have no title to assert that ethical truths are 'unified' in any particular manner, except in virtue of an enquiry conducted by the method which I have endeavoured to follow and to illustrate. The study of Ethics would, no doubt, be far more simple, and its results far more 'systematic,' if, for instance, pain were an evil of exactly the same magnitude as pleasure is a good; but we have no reason whatever to assume that the Universe is such that ethical truths must display this kind of symmetry: no argument against my conclusion, that pleasure and pain do *not* thus correspond, can have any weight whatever, failing a careful examination of the instances which have led me to form it. Nevertheless I am content that the results of this chapter should be taken rather as illustrating the method which must be pursued in answering the fundamental question of Ethics, and the principles which must be observed, than as giving the correct answer to that question. That things intrinsically good or bad are many and various; that most of them are 'organic unities,' in the peculiar and definite sense to which I have confined the term; and that our only means of deciding upon their intrinsic value and its degree, is by carefully distinguishing exactly what the thing is, about which we ask the question, and then looking to see whether it has or has not the unique predicate 'good' in any of its various degrees: these are the conclusions, upon the truth of which I desire to insist.

SUGGESTED READINGS

The first volume of Sir L. Stephen's *English Utilitarians* concerns Bentham, and there are useful books on Nietzsche by W. Kaufmann and A. C. Danto. Moore is discussed widely in contemporary literature on ethics: see the references following the selections on "Reason and Morality" at the end of Section V.

Basic writings concerning the good include Plato's *Republic,* especially Book VI; Aristotle's *Nichomachean Ethics,* Books I, VII (Chapters 11–14), and X; St. Augustine, *City of God,* especially Book XIX; St. Thomas Aquinas, *Summa Contra Gentiles,* Book II, Chapter 1–37, 62–63; and Thomas Hobbes, *Leviathan,* Chapters 6, 10, 11, 13, and 14. Hobbes is the first great modern moral and political philosopher; his work anticipates Bentham in numerous ways. In *Utilitarianism* John Stuart Mill tries to remove some of the difficulties found with Bentham's view. For an extremely detailed statement of utilitarianism, see H. Sidgwick, *Methods of Ethics,* Book IV. G. E. Moore, in the first two chapters of *Ethics,* makes an extraordinarily painstaking attempt to state the basic utilitarian thesis, free of hedonistic commitments, as carefully as possible. Mill's position is criticized vehemently by F. H. Bradley in *Ethical Studies,* Essay III. For more temperate criticism, see H. Rashdall, *Theory of Good and Evil,* I, Chapters 2 and 3. R. M. Blake, in "Why Not Hedonism?—A Protest," *Int. Journal of Ethics,* XXXVII (1926–27), attempts to reply to some of the standard criticisms of hedonism.

Good samples of the discussion of the issues raised by Moore will be found in Sections II and IV of W. Sellars and J. Hospers, *Readings in Ethical Theory.* G. H. von Wright, in *Varieties of Goodness,* distinguishes numerous different senses of "good." J. O. Urmson's paper, "Grading," *Mind,* LIX (1950), is reasonably clear and comprehensible and has been quite influential.

Duty as the Standard

A number of important ethical theories hold that certain actions are immediately right or wrong, regardless of their consequences. We often feel that promises are directly binding, and we do not consider whether keeping the promise will promote more good than breaking it. Similarly, our sense of justice, or fair play, may lead us to object to certain social inequalities, simply because we believe these inequalities ought not to exist, and not because we know their abolition will, on the whole, have good consequences. Theories which, on the basis of considerations like these, take rightness and wrongness to be intrinsic properties of some actions or types of action are called *deontological* theories. They stress our obligation to do our duty, whether we like it or not, and insist that we can determine the morality of an action without weighing its long-run consequences.

There are three types of deontological theory. The first type maintains that in *specific situations* we immediately discern where our duty lies. When we are called upon to act, we immediately know what action would be right in that particular situation and what action would be wrong. The second form of deontological theory holds that we immediately know that certain *types* of action are *always* right and others wrong. Thus what constitutes our duty can be formulated in a set of moral rules. The third type of theory seeks to establish a *supreme law* of duty which would justify specific moral rules and serve as a standard for assessing our individual moral judgments.

The selection from BUTLER represents the first form of deontological theory, according to which we immediately sense what action is right or wrong in a specific situation. An "action," in Butler's sense of the word, is not merely some instance of behavior; a human action results from a motive, is done with an end in view, and is carried out under particular circumstances. In this full sense of the word Butler regards actions as "fitting" or "unfitting," their fittingness or unfittingness being discerned by a moral faculty in us. And if we examine what it is that we approve as right and condemn as wrong, we find that the basic principles of morality are veracity, justice, and regard for the common good.

KANT'S position is, in a sense, the opposite of Butler's. For Butler our duty is made clear to us by our insight into the moral requirements of specific situations; for Kant, who represents the third type of deontological position, our duty stems from a single supreme law of morality. According to this law we are acting in a morally right way only if we are able to will that everybody else should act in the same way. This gives us a genuinely objective standard, one that is independent of our desires and of accidental circumstances. On the basis of this ultimate principle Kant sought to show that those actions that are wrong are really "self-contradictory": we cannot will that all man should do them, but are in every case making exceptions in favor of ourselves.

ROSS defends the second type of deontological theory, which stands midway between the positions of Butler and Kant. He holds that specific *moral rules* cannot be deduced from a single supreme principle. But neither are such rules generalizations from our insight into the moral requirements of particular cases. For example, Ross holds that the rule "we ought not injure others" is directly apprehended as being, in itself, morally binding. He admits, however, that circumstances may arise in which two or more moral rules conflict. When they do, no supreme rule will help us decide what we should do; we must depend upon our moral insight to tell us which rule is the more binding in that particular case. But such conflicts do not rob moral rules of their inherent validity; we still recognize that each prescribes a type of conduct that is intrinsically right.

The Nature of Virtue[*]

JOSEPH BUTLER [1692–1752], Bishop of Durham, was a leading Anglican theologian of the eighteenth century. The publication of some of his early sermons on ethics was a notable contribution to the development of ethical theory. His most famous work, *The Analogy of Religion*, is a rational defense of revealed religion.

That which renders beings capable of moral government is their having a moral nature and moral faculties of perception and of action. Brute creatures are impressed and actuated by various instincts and propensions; so also are we. But additional to this, we have a capacity of reflecting upon actions and characters, and making them an object to our thought; and in doing this, we naturally and unavoidably approve some actions, under the peculiar view of their being virtuous and of good desert, and disapprove others as vicious and of ill desert. That we have this moral approving and disapproving faculty is certain from our experiencing it in ourselves, and recognizing it in each other. It appears from our exercising it unavoidably, in the approbation and disapprobation even of feigned characters; from the words "right" and "wrong," "odious" and "amiable," "base" and "worthy," with many others of like signification in all languages applied to actions and characters; from the many written systems of morals which suppose it, since it cannot be imagined that all these authors, throughout all these treatises, had absolutely no meaning at all to their words, or a meaning merely chimerical; from our nat-

---

[*] From Butler: "Dissertation on the Nature of Virtue" (Appendix II) in *Analogy of Religion*.

ural sense of gratitude, which implies a distinction between merely being the instrument of good and intending it; from the like distinction every one makes between injury and mere harm, which Hobbes says is peculiar to mankind, and between injury and just punishment, a distinction plainly natural, prior to the consideration of human laws. It is manifest great part of common language, and of common behavior over the world, is formed upon supposition of such a moral faculty, whether called conscience, moral reason, moral sense, or divine reason; whether considered as a sentiment of the understanding or as a perception of the heart, or, which seems the truth, as including both. Nor is it at all doubtful in the general what course of action this faculty, or practical discerning power within us, approves and what it disapproves. For, as much as it has been disputed wherein virtue consists, or whatever ground for doubt there may be about particulars, yet, in general, there is in reality an universally acknowledged standard of it. It is that which all ages and all countries have made profession of in public; it is that which every man you meet puts on the show of; it is that which the primary and fundamental laws of all civil constitutions over the face of the earth make it their business and endeavor to enforce the practice of upon mankind, namely, justice, veracity and regard to common good. It being manifest then, in general, that we have such a faculty or discernment as this, it may be of use to remark some things more distinctly concerning it.

First, it ought to be observed that the object of this faculty is actions, comprehending under that name active or practical principles—those principles from which men would act if occasions and circumstances gave them power; and which, when fixed and habitual in any person, we call his character. It does not appear that brutes have the least reflex sense of actions, as distinguished from events, or that will and design, which constitute the very nature of actions as such, are at all an object to their perception. But to ours they are; and they are the object, and the only one, of the approving and disapproving faculty. Acting, conduct, behavior, abstracted from all regard to what is in fact and event the consequence of it, is itself the natural object of the moral discernment, as speculative truth and falsehood is of speculative reason. Intention of such and such consequences, indeed, is always included, for it is part of the action itself; but though the intended good or bad consequences do not follow, we have exactly the same sense of the action as if they did. In like manner we think well or ill of characters, abstracted from all consideration of the good or the evil, which persons of such characters have it actually in their power to do. We never, in the moral way, applaud or blame either ourselves or others for what we enjoy or what we suffer, or for having impressions made upon us, which we consider as altogether out of our power, but only for what we do or would have done had it been in our power; or for what we leave undone, which we might have done or would have left undone, though we could have done it.

Secondly, our sense or discernment of actions as morally good or evil implies in it a sense or discernment of them as of good or ill desert. It may be difficult to explain this perception so as to answer all the questions which may be asked concerning it; but everyone speaks of such and such actions as deserving punishment; and it is not, I suppose, pretended that they have absolutely no meaning at all to the expression. Now the meaning plainly is not that we conceive it for the good of society that the doer of such actions should be made to suffer. For if, unhappily, it were resolved that a man who, by some innocent action, was infected with the plague should be left to perish lest, by other people's coming near him, the infection should spread, no one would say he deserved this treatment. Innocence and ill desert are inconsistent ideas. Ill desert always supposes guilt; and if one be no part of the other, yet they are evidently and naturally connected in our mind. The sight of a man in misery raises our compassion toward him, and, if this misery be inflicted on him by another, our indignation against the author of it. But when we are informed that the sufferer is a villain and is punished only for his treachery or cruelty, our compassion exceedingly lessens, and in many instances our indignation wholly subsides. Now what produces this effect is the conception of that in the sufferer which we call ill desert. Upon considering then, or viewing together, our notion of vice and that of misery, there results a third—that of ill desert. And thus there is in human creatures an association of the two ideas, natural and moral evil, wickedness and punishment. If this association were merely artificial or accidental, it were nothing; but being most unquestionably natural, it greatly concerns us to attend to it, instead of endeavoring to explain it away.

It may be observed further, concerning our perception of good and of ill desert, that the former is very weak with respect to common instances of virtue. One reason of which may be that it does not appear to a spectator, how far such instances of virtue proceed from a virtuous principle, or in what degree this principle is prevalent; since a very weak regard to virtue may be sufficient to make men act well in many common instances. And on the other hand, our perception of ill desert in vicious actions lessens, in proportion to the temptations men are thought to have had to such vices. For vice in human creatures consisting chiefly in the absence or want of the virtuous principle, though a man be overcome, suppose, by tortures, it does not from thence appear to what degree the virtuous principle was wanting. All that appears is that he had it not in such a degree as to prevail over the temptation; but possibly he had it in a degree which would have rendered him proof against common temptations.

Thirdly, our perception of vice and ill desert arises from, and is the result of, a comparison of actions with the nature and capacities of the agent. For the mere neglect of doing what we ought to do would, in many cases, be determined by all men to be in the highest degree vicious. And his determination must arise from such comparison, and be the result of it; because such neglect would not be vicious in creatures of other natures and capacities, as brutes. And it is the same also with respect to positive vices, or such as consist in doing what we ought not. For every one has a different sense of harm done by an idiot, madman, or child, and by one of mature and common understanding, though the action of both, including the intention, which is part of the action, be the same; as it may be, since idiots and madmen, as well as children, are capable not only of doing mischief, but also of intending it. Now this difference must arise from somewhat discerned in the nature or capacities of one, which renders the action vicious; and the want of which, in the other, renders the same action innocent or less vicious; and this plainly supposes a comparison, whether reflected upon or not, between the action and capacities of the agent, previous to our determining an action to be vicious. And hence arises a proper application of the epithets "incongruous," "unsuitable," "disproportionate," "unfit" to actions which our moral faculty determines to be vicious.

Fourthly, it deserves to be considered whether men are more at liberty, in point of morals, to make themselves miserable without reason than to make other people so, or dissolutely to neglect their own greater good, for the sake of a present lesser gratification, than they are to neglect the good of others whom nature has committed to their care. It should seem that a due concern about our own interest or happiness, and a reasonable endeavor to secure and promote it, which is, I think, very much the meaning of the word "prudence" in our language—it should seem that this is virtue, and the contrary behavior faulty and blamable, since, in the calmest way of reflection, we approve of the first, and condemn the other conduct, both in ourselves and others. This approbation and disapprobation are altogether different from mere desire of our own or of their happiness, and from sorrow upon missing it. For the object or occasion of this last kind of perception is satisfaction or uneasiness, whereas the object of the first is active behavior. In one case, what our thoughts fix upon is our condition, in the other, our conduct. It is true, indeed, that nature has not given us so sensible a disapprobation of imprudence and folly, either in *ourselves* or *others,* as of falsehood, injustice and cruelty; I suppose, because that constant habitual sense of private interest and good, which we always carry about with us, renders such sensible disapprobation less necessary, less wanting, to keep us from imprudently neglecting our own happiness and foolishly injuring ourselves, than it is necessary and wanting to keep us from injuring others to whose good we cannot have so strong and constant a regard; and also because imprudence and folly appearing to bring its own punishment more immediately and constantly than injurious behavior, it less needs the additional punishment which would be inflicted upon it by others had they the same sensible indignation against it as against injustice and fraud and cruelty. Besides, unhappiness being in itself the natural object of compassion, the unhappiness which people bring upon themselves, though it be willfully, excites in us some pity for them; and this, of course, lessens our displeasure against them. But still it is matter of experience that we are formed so as to reflect very severely upon the greater instances of imprudent neglect and foolish rashness, both in ourselves and others. In instances of this kind, men often say of themselves with remorse, and of others with some indignation, that they deserved to suffer such calamities because they brought them upon themselves and would not take warning. Particularly when persons come to poverty and distress by a long course of extravagance and after frequent admonitions, though without falsehood or injustice; we plainly do not regard such people as alike objects of compassion with those who are brought into the same condition by unavoidable accidents. From these things it appears that prudence is a species of virtue, and folly of vice, meaning by "folly" somewhat quite different from mere incapacity—a thoughtless want of that regard and attention to our own happiness which we had capacity for. And this the word properly includes, and, as it seems, in its usual acceptation, for we scarcely apply it to brute creatures.

However, if any person be disposed to dispute the matter, I shall very willingly give him up the words "virtue" and "vice," as not applicable to prudence and folly, but must beg leave to insist that the faculty within us, which is the judge of actions, approves of prudent actions, and disapproves imprudent ones; I say prudent and imprudent *actions* as such, and considered distinctly from the happiness or misery which they occasion. And, by the way, this observation may help to determine what justness there is in that objection against religion, that it teaches us to be interested and selfish.

Fifthly, without inquiring how far, and in what sense, virtue is resolvable into benevolence, and vice into the want of it, it may be proper to observe that benevolence and the want of it, singly considered, are in no sort the whole of virtue and vice. For if this were the case, in the review of one's own character, or that of others, our moral understanding and moral sense would be indifferent to everything but the degrees in which benevolence prevailed, and the degrees in which it was wanting. That is, we should neither approve of benevolence to some persons rather than to others, nor disapprove injustice and falsehood upon any other account than merely as an overbalance of happiness was foreseen likely to be produced by the first, and of misery by the second. But now, on the contrary, suppose two men competitors for anything whatever, which would be of equal advantage to each of them; though nothing indeed would be more impertinent than for a stranger to busy himself to get one of them preferred to the other, yet such endeavor would be virtue, in behalf of a friend or benefactor, abstracted from all consideration of distant consequences, as that examples of gratitude, and the cultivation of friendship, would be of general good to the world. Again, suppose one man should, by fraud or violence, take from another the fruit of his labor, with intent to give it to a third who he thought would have as much pleasure from it as would balance the pleasure which the first possessor would have had in the enjoyment, and his vexation in the loss of it; suppose also that no bad consequences would follow, yet such an action would surely be vicious. Nay further, were treachery, violence and injustice not otherwise vicious than as foreseen likely to produce an overbalance of misery to society, then, if in any case a man could procure to himself as great advantage by an act of injustice as the whole foreseen inconvenience, likely to be brought upon others by it, would amount to, such a piece of injustice would not be faulty or vicious at all; because it would be no more than, in any other case, for a man to prefer his own satisfaction to another's in equal degrees. The fact then appears to be that we are constituted so as to condemn falsehood, unprovoked violence, injustice, and to approve of benevolence to some, preferably to others, abstracted from all consideration which conduct is likeliest to produce an overbalance of happiness or misery. And therefore, were the Author of Nature to propose nothing to himself as an end but the production of happiness, were his moral character merely that of benevolence, yet ours is not so. Upon that supposition, indeed, the only reason of his giving us the above-mentioned approbation of benevolence to some persons rather than others, and disapprobation of falsehood, unprovoked violence, and injustice, must be that he foresaw this constitution of our nature would produce more happiness than forming us with a temper of mere general benevolence. But still, since this is our constitution, falsehood, violence, injustice must be vice in us, and benevolence to some, preferably to others, virtue, abstracted from all consideration of the overbalance of evil or good, which they may appear likely to produce.

Now if human creatures are endued with such a moral nature as we have been explaining, or with a moral faculty the natural object of which is actions, moral government must consist in rendering them happy and unhappy, in rewarding and punishing them as they follow, neglect or depart from, the moral rule of action interwoven in their nature, or suggested and enforced by this moral faculty—in rewarding and punishing them upon account of their so doing.

I am not sensible that I have, in this fifth observation, contradicted what any author designed to assert. But some of great and distinguished merit have, I think, expressed themselves in a manner which may occasion some danger to careless readers, of imagining the whole of virtue to consist in singly aiming, according to the best of their judgment, at promoting the happiness of mankind in the present state; and the whole of vice in doing what they foresee, or might foresee, is likely to produce an overbalance of unhappiness in it; than which mistakes, none can be conceived more terrible. For it is certain that some of the most shocking instances of injustice, adultery, murder, perjury, and even of persecution, may, in many supposable cases, not have the appearance of being likely to produce an overbalance of misery in the present state; perhaps sometimes may have the contrary appearance. For this reflection might easily be carried on, but I forbear. The happiness of the world is the concern of him who is the Lord and the Proprietor of it; nor do we know what we are about when we endeavor to promote the good of mankind in any ways but those which he had directed—that is indeed in all ways not contrary to veracity and justice. I speak thus upon supposition of persons really endeavoring, in some sort, to do good without regard to these. But the truth seems to be that such supposed endeavors proceed, almost always, from ambition, the spirit of the party, or some indirect principle, concealed perhaps in great measure from persons themselves. And though it is our business and our duty to endeavor, within the bounds of veracity and justice, to contribute to the ease, convenience, and even cheerfulness and diversion of our fellow creatures, yet, from our short views, it is greatly uncertain whether this endeavor will in particular instances produce an overbalance of happiness upon the whole, since so many and distant things must come into the account. And that which makes it our duty is that there is some appearance that it will, and no positive appearance sufficient to balance this, on the contrary side; and also, that such benevolent endeavor is a cultivation of that most excellent of all virtuous principles, the active principle of benevolence.

However, though veracity as well as justice is to be our rule of life, it must be added, otherwise a snare will be laid in the way of some plain men, that the use of common forms of speech, generally understood, cannot be falsehood; and in general, that there can be no designed falsehood without designing to deceive. It must likewise be observed that, in numberless cases, a man may be under the strictest obligations to what he foresees will deceive, without his intending it. For it is impossible not to foresee that the words and

actions of men, in different ranks and employments, and of different educa-
tions, will perpetually be mistaken by each other; and it cannot but be so
whilst they will judge with the utmost carelessness, as they daily do, of what
they are not, perhaps, enough informed to be competent judges of, even
though they considered it with great attention.

The Categorical Imperative*

IMMANUEL KANT [1724–1804] is ranked among the most profound and
original thinkers in the history of philosophy. He was a professor at Koenigsberg,
East Prussia, where he taught philosophy and a wide variety of other subjects. He
made one significant contribution to astronomy—the formulation of the nebular
hypothesis. His greatest philosophic work, The Critique of Pure Reason (1781),
formulated a fundamentally new view of the relation between knowledge and the
external world. In addition, his writings on ethics and aesthetics were contributions of the very highest order to both of these fields.

THE GOOD WILL. Nothing can possibly be conceived in the world, or even
out of it, which can be called good without qualification, except a Good Will.
Intelligence, wit, judgment, and the other *talents* of the mind, however they
may be named, or courage, resolution, perseverance, as qualities of temperament, are undoubtedly good and desirable in many respects; but these gifts
of nature may also become extremely bad and mischievous if the will which
is to make use of them, and which, therefore, constitutes what is called *character*, is not good. It is the same with the *gifts of fortune.* Power, riches,
honour, even health, and the general well-being and contentment with one's
condition which is called *happiness*, inspire pride, and often presumption, if
there is not a good will to correct the influence of these on the mind, and
with this also to rectify the whole principle of acting, and adapt it to its end.
The sight of a being who is not adorned with a single feature of a pure and
good will, enjoying unbroken prosperity, can never give pleasure to an impartial rational spectator. Thus a good will appears to constitute the indispensable condition even of being worthy of happiness.

There are even some qualities which are of service to this good will itself,
and may facilitate its action, yet which have no intrinsic unconditional value,
but always presuppose a good will, and this qualifies the esteem that we

* From Kant: *Fundamental Principles of the Metaphysics of Morals*, Sections 1 and 2.
Translated by T. K. Abbott.

justly have for them, and does not permit us to regard them as absolutely good. Moderation in the affections and passions, self-control, and calm deliberation are not only good in many respects, but even seem to constitute part of the intrinsic worth of the person; but they are far from deserving to be called good without qualification, although they have been so unconditionally praised by the ancients. For without the principles of a good will, they may become extremely bad; and the coolness of a villain not only makes him far more dangerous, but also directly makes him more abominable in our eyes than he would have been without it.

A good will is good not because of what it performs or effects, not by its aptness for the attainment of some proposed end, but simply by virtue of the volition, that is, it is good in itself, and considered by itself is to be esteemed much higher than all that can be brought about by it in favour of any inclination, nay, even of the sum total of all inclinations. Even if it should happen that, owing to special disfavour of fortune, or the niggardly provision of a step-motherly nature, this will should wholly lack power to accomplish its purpose, if with its greatest efforts it should yet achieve nothing, and there should remain only the good will (not, to be sure, a mere wish, but the summoning of all means in our power), then, like a jewel, it would still shine by its own light, as a thing which has its whole value in itself. . . .

DUTY VS. INCLINATION. We have then to develop the notion of a will which deserves to be highly esteemed for itself, and is good without a view to anything further, a notion which exists already in the sound natural understanding, requiring rather to be cleared up than to be taught, and which in estimating the value of our actions always takes the first place, and constitutes the condition of all the rest. In order to do this, we will take the notion of duty, which includes that of a good will, although implying certain subjective restrictions and hindrances. These, however, far from concealing it, or rendering it unrecognizable, rather bring it out by contrast, and make it shine forth so much the brighter.

I omit here all actions which are already recognized as inconsistent with duty, although they may be useful for this or that purpose, for with these the question whether they are done *from duty* cannot arise at all, since they even conflict with it. I also set aside those actions which really conform to duty, but to which men have *no* direct *inclination*, performing them because they are impelled thereto by some other inclination. For in this case we can readily distinguish whether the action which agrees with duty is done *from duty*, or from a selfish view. It is much harder to make this distinction when the action accords with duty, and the subject has besides a *direct* inclination to it. For example, it is always a matter of duty that a dealer should not overcharge an inexperienced purchaser; and wherever there is much commerce the prudent tradesman does not overcharge, but keeps a fixed price for everyone, so that a child buys of him as well as any other. Men are thus *honestly* served; but this is not enough to make us believe that the tradesman has so acted from duty and from principles of honesty: his own advantage required it; it is out of the question in this case to suppose that he might besides have a direct inclination in favour of the buyers, so that, as it were, from love he should give no advantage to one over another. Accordingly the action was done neither from duty nor from direct inclination, but merely with a selfish view.

On the other hand, it is a duty to maintain one's life; and in addition, everyone has also a direct inclination to do so. But on this account the often anxious care which most men take for it has no intrinsic worth, and their maxim has no moral import. They preserve their life *as duty requires,* no doubt, but not *because duty requires.* On the other hand, if adversity and hopeless sorrow have completely taken away the relish for life; if the unfortunate one, strong in mind, indignant at his fate rather than desponding or dejected, wishes for death, and yet preserves his life without loving it—not from inclination or fear, but from duty—then his maxim has a moral worth.

To be beneficent when we can is a duty; and besides this, there are many minds so sympathetically constituted that, without any other motive of vanity or self-interest, they find a pleasure in spreading joy around them, and can take delight in the satisfaction of others so far as it is their own work. But I maintain that in such a case an action of this kind, however proper, however amiable it may be, has nevertheless no true moral worth, but is on a level with other inclinations, e.g. the inclination to honour, which, if it is happily directed to that which is in fact of public utility and accordant with duty, and consequently honourable, deserves praise and encouragement, but not esteem. For the maxim lacks the moral import, namely, that such actions be done *from duty,* not from inclination. Put the case that the mind of that philanthropist was clouded by sorrow of his own, extinguishing all sympathy with the lot of others, and that while he still has the power to benefit others in distress, he is not touched by their trouble because he is absorbed with his own; and now suppose that he tears himself out of this dead insensibility, and performs the action without any inclination to it, but simply from duty, then first has his action its genuine moral worth. Further still; if nature has put little sympathy in the heart of this or that man; if he, even though an upright man, is by temperament cold and indifferent to the sufferings of others, perhaps because in respect of his own he is provided with the special gift of patience and fortitude, and he supposes, or even requires, that others should have the same—and such a man would certainly not be the meanest product of nature—but if nature had not specially framed him for a philanthropist, would he not still find in himself a source from whence to give himself a far higher worth than that of a good-natured temperament could be? Unquestionably. It is just in this that the moral worth of the character is brought out which is incomparably the highest of all, namely, that he is beneficent, not from inclination, but from duty. . . .

[Thus the first proposition of morality is that an action must be done from duty if it is to have moral worth.] The second proposition is: That an action done from duty derives its moral worth, *not from the purpose* which is to be attained by it, but from the maxim by which it is determined, and therefore does not depend on the realization of the object of the action, but merely on the *principle of volition* by which the action has taken place, without regard to any object of desire. It is clear from what precedes that the purposes which we may have in view in our actions, or their effects regarded as ends and springs of the will, cannot give to actions any unconditional or moral worth. In what, then, can their worth lie, if it is not to consist in the will and in reference to its expected effect? It cannot lie anywhere but in the *principle of the will* without regard to the ends which can be attained by the actions. For the will stands between its *a priori* principle, which is formal, and its *a posteriori* spring, which is material, as between two roads, and as it must be determined by something, it follows that it must be determined by the formal principle of volition when an action is done from duty, in which case every material principle has been withdrawn from it.

The third proposition, which is a consequence of the two preceding, I would express thus: *Duty is the necessity of acting from respect for the law.* I may have *inclination* for an object as the effect of my proposed action, but I cannot have *respect* for it, just for this reason, that it is an effect and not an energy of will. Similarly, I cannot have respect for inclination, whether my own or another's; I can at most, if my own, approve it; if another's, sometimes even love it; i.e. look on it as favourable to my own interest. It is only what is connected with my will as a principle, by no means as an effect— what does not subserve my inclination, but overpowers it, or at least in case of choice excludes it from its calculation—in other words, simply the law of itself, which can be an object of respect, and hence a command. Now an action done from duty must wholly exclude the influence of inclination, and with it every object of the will, so that nothing remains which can determine the will except objectively the *law*, and subjectively *pure respect* for this practical law, and consequently the maxim that I should follow this law even to the thwarting of all my inclinations.

Thus the moral worth of an action does not lie in the effect expected from it, nor in any principle of action which requires to borrow its motive from this expected effect. For all these effects—agreeableness of one's condition, and even the promotion of the happiness of others—could have been also brought about by other causes, so that for this there would have been no need of the will of a rational being; whereas it is in this alone that the supreme and unconditional good can be found. The pre-eminent good which we call moral can therefore consist in nothing else than *the conception of law in itself, which certainly is only possible in a rational being,* in so far as this conception, and not the expected effect, determines the will. . . .

HYPOTHETICAL AND CATEGORICAL IMPERATIVES. The conception of an objective principle, in so far as it is obligatory for a will, is called a command (of reason), and the formula of the command is called an *Imperative.* All imperatives are expressed by the word ought. . . . They say that something would be good to do or to forbear, but they say it to a will which does not always do a thing because it is conceived to be good to do it. . . .

Now all imperatives command either *hypothetically* or *categorically.* . . . If the action is good only as a means *to something else,* then the imperative is hypothetical; if it is conceived as good *in itself* and consequently as being necessarily the principle of a will which of itself conforms to reason, then it is *categorical.* . . .

Accordingly, the hypothetical imperative only says that the action is good for some purpose, *possible* or *actual.* In the first case it is a Problematical, in the second an Assertorial practical principle [see 1*a* and 1*b*, below]. The categorical imperative which declares an action to be objectively necessary in itself without reference to any purpose, i.e. without any other end, is valid as an Apodictic practical principle [see 2, below]. . . .

[1*a*] All sciences have a practical part, consisting of problems expressing that some end is possible for us, and of imperatives directing how it may be attained. These may, therefore, be called in general imperatives of Skill. Here there is no question whether the end is rational and good, but only what one must do in order to attain it. The precepts for the physician to make his patient thoroughly healthy, and for a poisoner to ensure certain death, are of equal value in this respect, that each serves to effect its purpose perfectly. Since in early youth it cannot be known what ends are likely to occur to us in the course of life, parents seek to have their children taught a *great many things,* and provide for their *skill* in the use of means for all sorts of arbitrary ends, of none of which can they determine whether it may not perhaps hereafter be an object to their pupil, but which it is at all events *possible* that he might aim at; and this anxiety is so great that they commonly neglect to form and correct their judgment on the value of the things which may be chosen as ends.

[1*b*] There is *one* end, however, which may be assumed to be actually such to all rational beings (so far as imperatives apply to them, viz. as de-

pendent beings), and, therefore, one purpose which they not merely *may* have, but which we may with certainty assume that they all actually *have* by a natural necessity, and this is *happiness*. The hypothetical imperative which expresses the practical necessity of an action as means to the advancement of happiness is Assertorial. We are not to present it as necessary for an uncertain and merely possible purpose, but for a purpose which we may presuppose with certainty and *a priori* in every man, because it belongs to his being. Now skill in the choice of means to his own greatest well-being may be called *prudence*, in the narrowest sense. And thus the imperative which refers to the choice of means to one's own happiness, i.e. the precept of prudence, is still always *hypothetical;* the action is not commanded absolutely, but only as means to another purpose.

[2] Finally, there is an imperative which commands a certain conduct immediately, without having as its condition any other purpose to be attained by it. This imperative is Categorical. It concerns not the matter of the action, or its intended result, but its form and the principle of which it is itself a result; and what is essentially good in it consists in the mental disposition, let the consequence be what it may. This imperative may be called that of Morality. . . .

When I conceive a hypothetical imperative, in general I do not know beforehand what it will contain until I am given the condition. But when I conceive a categorical imperative, I know at once what it contains. For as the imperative contains besides the law only the necessity that the maxims shall conform to this law, while the law contains no conditions restricting it, there remains nothing but the general statement that the maxim of the action should conform to a universal law, and it is this conformity alone that the imperative properly represents as necessary.

The Categorical Imperative (first formulation). There is therefore but one categorical imperative, namely, this: *Act only on that maxim whereby thou canst at the same time will that it should become a universal law.*

Now if all imperatives of duty can be deduced from this one imperative as from their principle, then, although it should remain undecided whether what is called duty is not merely a vain notion, yet at least we shall be able to show what we understand by it and what this notion means.

Since the universality of the law according to which effects are produced constitutes what is properly called *nature* in the most general sense (as to form), that is the existence of things so far as it is determined by general laws, the imperative of duty may be expressed thus: *Act as if the maxim of thy action were to become by thy will a universal law of nature.*

We will now enumerate a few duties, adopting the usual division of them into duties to ourselves and to others, and into perfect and imperfect duties.

1. A man reduced to despair by a series of misfortunes feels wearied of life, but is still so far in possession of his reason that he can ask himself whether it would not be contrary to his duty to himself to take his own life. Now he inquires whether the maxim of his action could become a universal law of nature. His maxim is: From self-love I adopt it as a principle to shorten my life when its longer duration is likely to bring more evil than satisfaction. It is asked then simply whether this principle founded on self-love can become a universal law of nature. Now we see at once that a system of nature of which it should be a law to destroy life by means of the very feeling whose special nature it is to impel to the improvement of life would contradict itself, and therefore could not exist as a system of nature; hence that maxim cannot possibly exist as a universal law of nature, and consequently would be wholly inconsistent with the supreme principle of all duty.

2. Another finds himself forced by necessity to borrow money. He knows that he will not be able to repay it, but sees also that nothing will be lent to him, unless he promises stoutly to repay it in a definite time. He desires to make this promise, but he has still so much conscience as to ask himself: Is it not unlawful and inconsistent with duty to get out of a difficulty in this way? Suppose, however, that he resolves to do so, then the maxim of his action would be expressed thus: When I think myself in want of money, I will borrow money and promise to repay it, although I know that I never can do so. Now this principle of self-love or of one's own advantage may perhaps be consistent with my whole future welfare; but the question now is, Is it right? I change then the suggestion of self-love into a universal law, and state the question thus: How would it be if my maxim were a universal law? Then I see at once that it could never hold as a universal law of nature, but would necessarily contradict itself. For supposing it to be a universal law that everyone when he thinks himself in a difficulty should be able to promise whatever he pleases, with the purpose of not keeping his promise, the promise itself would become impossible, as well as the end that one might have in view in it, since no one would consider that anything was promised to him, but would ridicule all such statements as vain pretenses.

3. A third finds in himself a talent which with the help of some culture might make him a useful man in many respects. But he finds himself in comfortable circumstances, and prefers to indulge in pleasure rather than to take pains in enlarging and improving his happy natural capacities. He asks, however, whether his maxim of neglect of his natural gifts, besides agreeing with his inclination to indulgence, agrees also with what is called duty. He sees then that a system of nature could indeed subsist with such a universal law although men (like the South Sea islanders) should let their talents rest, and resolve to devote their lives merely to idleness, amusement, and propa-

gation of their species—in a word, to enjoyment; but he cannot possibly *will* that this should be a universal law of nature, or be implanted in us as such by a natural instinct. For, as a rational being, he necessarily wills that his faculties be developed, since they serve him, and have been given him, for all sorts of possible purposes.

4. A fourth, who is in prosperity, while he sees that others have to contend with great wretchedness and that he could help them, thinks: What concern is it of mine? Let everyone be as happy as Heaven pleases, or as he can make himself; I will take nothing from him nor even envy him, only I do not wish to contribute anything to his welfare or to his assistance in distress! Now no doubt if such a mode of thinking were a universal law, the human race might very well subsist, and doubtless even better than in a state in which everyone talks of sympathy and good-will, or even takes care occasionally to put it into practice, but, on the other side, also cheats when he can, betrays the rights of men, or otherwise violates them. But although it is possible that a universal law of nature might exist in accordance with that maxim, it is impossible to *will* that such a principle should have the universal validity of a law of nature. For a will which resolved this would contradict itself, inasmuch as many cases might occur in which one would have need of the love and sympathy of others, and in which, by such a law of nature, sprung from his own will, he would deprive himself of all hope of the aid he desires.

These are a few of the many actual duties, or at least what we regard as such, which obviously fall into two classes on the one principle that we have laid down. We must be *able to will* that a maxim of our action should be a universal law. This is the canon of the moral appreciation of the action generally. Some actions are of such a character that their maxim cannot without contradiction be even *conceived* as a universal law of nature, far from it being possible that we should *will* that it *should* be so. In others this intrinsic impossibility is not found, but still it is impossible to *will* that their maxim should be raised to the universality of a law of nature, since such a will would contradict itself. It is easily seen that the former violate strict or rigorous (inflexible) duty; the latter only laxer (meritorious) duty. Thus it has been completely shown by these examples how all duties depend as regards the nature of the obligation (not the object of the action) on the same principle. . . .

The Categorical Imperative (second formulation). The will is conceived as a faculty of determining oneself to action *in accordance with the conception of certain laws.* And such a faculty can be found only in rational beings. Now that which serves the will as the objective ground of its self-determination is the *end,* and if this is assigned by reason alone, it must hold for all rational beings. On the other hand, that which merely contains the ground of possibility of the action of which the effect is the end, this is called the *means*. . . .

The ends which a rational being proposes to himself at pleasure as *effects* of his actions (material ends) are all only relative, for it is only their relation to the particular desires of the subject that gives them their worth, which therefore cannot furnish principles universal and necessary for all rational beings and for every volition, that is to say practical laws. Hence all these relative ends can give rise only to hypothetical imperatives.

Supposing, however, that there were something *whose existence* has *in itself* an absolute worth, something which, being *an end in itself,* could be a source of definite laws, then in this and this alone would lie the source of a possible categorical imperative, i.e. a practical law.

Now I say: man and generally any rational being *exists* as an end in himself, *not merely as a means* to be arbitrarily used by this or that will, but in all his actions, whether they concern himself or other rational beings, must be always regarded at the same time as an end. All objects of the inclinations have only a conditional worth; for if the inclinations and the wants founded on them did not exist, then their object would be without value. . . . Thus the worth of any object which is *to be acquired* by our action is always conditional. Beings whose existence depends not on our will but on nature's, have, if they are not rational beings, only a relative value as means, and are therefore called *things;* rational beings, on the contrary, are called *persons,* because their very nature points them out as ends in themselves, that is as something which must not be used merely as means, and so far therefore restricts freedom of action (and is an object of respect). These, therefore, are not merely subjective ends whose existence has a worth *for us* as an effect of our action, but *objective ends,* that is things whose existence is an end in itself: an end moreover for which no other can be substituted, which they should subserve *merely* as means, for otherwise nothing whatever would possess *absolute worth;* but if all worth were conditioned and therefore contingent, then there would be no supreme practical principle of reason whatever.

If then there is a supreme practical principle or, in respect of the human will, a categorical imperative, it must be one which, being drawn from the conception of that which is necessarily an end for everyone because it is *an end in itself,* constitutes an *objective* principle of will, and can therefore serve as a universal practical law. The foundation of this principle is: *rational nature exists as an end in itself.* Man necessarily conceives his own existence as being so: so far then this is a *subjective* principle of human actions. But every other rational being regards its existence similarly, just on the same rational principle that holds for me: so that it is at the same time an objective principle, from which as a supreme practical law all laws of the will must be capable of being deduced. Accordingly the practical imperative will be as follows: *So act as to treat humanity, whether in thine own person or in that of any other, in every case as an end withal, never as means only.* We will now inquire whether this can be practically carried out.

To abide by the previous examples:

Firstly, under the head of necessary duty to oneself: He who contemplates suicide should ask himself whether his action can be consistent with the idea of humanity as *an end in itself.* If he destroys himself in order to escape from painful circumstances, he uses a person merely as *a means* to maintain a tolerant condition up to the end of life. But a man is not a thing, that is to say, something which can be used merely as means, but must in all his actions be always considered as an end in himself. I cannot, therefore, dispose in any way of a man in my own person so as to mutilate him, to damage or kill him. (It belongs to ethics proper to define this principle more precisely, so as to avoid all misunderstanding, e.g. as to the amputation of the limbs in order to preserve myself; as to exposing my life to danger with a view to preserve it, &c. This question is therefore omitted here.)

Secondly, as regards necessary duties, or those of strict obligation, towards others; he who is thinking of making a lying promise to others will see at once that he would be using another man *merely as a means,* without the latter containing at the same time the end in himself. For he whom I propose by such a promise to use for my own purposes cannot possibly assent to my mode of acting towards him, and therefore cannot himself contain the end of this action. This violation of the principle of humanity in other men is more obvious if we take in examples of attacks on the freedom and property of others. For then it is clear that he who transgresses the rights of men intends to use the person of others merely as means, without considering that as rational beings they ought always to be esteemed also as ends, that is, as beings who must be capable of containing in themselves the end of the very same action.

Thirdly, as regards contingent (meritorious) duties to oneself; it is not enough that the action does not violate humanity in our own person as an end in itself, it must also *harmonize with* it. Now there are in humanity capacities of greater perfection which belong to the end that nature has in view in regard to humanity in ourselves as the subject: to neglect these might perhaps be consistent with the *maintenance* of humanity as an end in itself, but not with the *advancement* of this end.

Fourthly, as regards meritorious duties towards others: the natural end which all men have is their own happiness. Now humanity might indeed subsist, although no one should contribute anything to the happiness of others, provided he did not intentionally withdraw anything from it; but after all, this would only harmonize negatively, not positively, with *humanity*, as *an end in itself*, if everyone does not also endeavour, as far as in him lies, to forward the ends of others. For the ends of any subject which is in an end in himself, ought as far as possible to be *my* ends also, if that conception is to have its *full* effect with me.

This principle, that humanity and generally every rational nature is *an end in itself* (which is the supreme limiting condition of every man's freedom of action), is not borrowed from experience, *firstly*, because it is universal, applying as it does to all rational beings whatever, and experience is not capable of determining anything about them; *secondly*, because it does not present humanity as an end to men (subjectively), that is as an object which men do of themselves actually adopt as an end; but as an objective end, which must as a law constitute the supreme limiting condition of all our subjective ends.

The Right and the Good[*]

W I L L I A M D A V I D R O S S [1877–   ], formerly of Oriel College, Oxford, edited the Oxford edition of Aristotle, translating several of the works himself. He was also influential in reviving the deontological tradition in ethics. His ethical works present the most systematic statement of this position in recent philosophy.

The real point at issue between hedonism and utilitarianism on the one hand and their opponents on the other is not whether 'right' *means* 'productive of so and so'; for it cannot with any plausibility be maintained that it does. The point at issue is that to which we now pass, viz. whether there is any general character which makes right acts right, and if so, what it is. Among the main historical attempts to state a single characteristic of all right actions which is the foundation of their rightness are those made by egoism and hedonistic utilitarianism. But I do not propose to discuss these, not because the subject is unimportant, but because it has been dealt with so often and so well already, and because there has come to be so much agreement among moral philosophers that neither of these theories is satisfactory. A much more attractive theory has been put forward by Professor Moore:

that what makes actions right is that they are productive of more *good* than could have been produced by any other action open to the agent.

   This theory is in fact the culmination of all the attempts to base rightness on productivity of some sort of result. The first form this attempt takes is the attempt to base rightness on conduciveness to the advantage or pleasure of the agent. This theory comes to grief over the fact, which stares us in the face, that a great part of duty consists in an observance of the rights and a furtherance of the interests of others, whatever the cost to ourselves may be. Plato and others may be right in holding that a regard for the rights of others never in the long run involves a loss of happiness for the agent, that 'the just life profits a man.' But this, even if true, is irrelevant to the rightness of the act. As soon as a man does an action *because* he thinks he will promote his own interests thereby, he is acting not from a sense of its rightness but from self-interest.

   To the egoistic theory hedonistic utilitarianism supplies a much-needed amendment. It points out correctly that the fact that a certain pleasure will be enjoyed by the agent is no reason why he *ought* to bring it into being rather than an equal or greater pleasure to be enjoyed by another, though, human nature being what it is, it makes it not unlikely that he *will* try to bring it into being. But hedonistic utilitarianism in its turn needs a correction. On reflection it seems clear that pleasure is not the only thing in life that we think good in itself, that for instance we think the possession of a good character, or an intelligent understanding of the world, as good or better. A great advance is made by the substitution of 'productive of the greatest good' for 'productive of the greatest pleasure.'

   Not only is this theory more attractive than hedonistic utilitarianism, but its logical relation to that theory is such that the latter could not be true unless *it* were true, while it might be true though hedonistic utilitarianism were not. It is in fact one of the logical bases of hedonistic utilitarianism. For the view that what produces the maximum pleasure is right has for its bases the views (1) that what produces the maximum good is right, and (2) that pleasure is the only thing good in itself. . . . If, therefore, it can be shown that productivity of the maximum good is not what makes all right actions right, we shall *a fortiori* have refuted hedonistic utilitarianism.

   When a plain man fulfils a promise because he thinks he ought to do so, it seems clear that he does so with no thought of its total consequences, still less with any opinion that these are likely to be the best possible. He thinks in fact much more of the past than of the future. What makes him think it right to act in a certain way is the fact that he has promised to do so—that and, usually, nothing more. That his act will produce the best possible consequences is not his reason for calling it right. What lends colour to the theory we are examining, then, is not the actions (which form probably a great majority of our actions) in which some such reflection as 'I have promised' is the only reason we give ourselves for thinking a certain action right, but the exceptional cases in which the consequences of fulfilling a promise (for instance) would be so disastrous to others that we judge it right not to do so. It must of course be admitted that such cases exist. If I have promised to meet a friend at a particular time for some trivial purpose, I should certainly think myself justified in breaking my engagement if by doing so I could prevent a serious accident or bring relief to the victims of one. And the supporters of the view we are examining hold that my thinking so is due to my thinking that I shall bring more good into existence by the one action than by the other. A different account may, however, be given of the matter, an account which will, I believe, show itself to be the true one. It may be said that besides the duty of fulfilling promises I have and recognize a duty of relieving distress, and that when I think it right to do the latter at the cost of not doing the former, it is not because I think I shall produce more good thereby but because I think it the duty which is in the circumstances more of a duty. This account surely corresponds much more closely with what we really think in such a situation. If, so far as I can see, I could bring *equal amounts* of good into being by fulfilling my promise and by helping some one to whom I had made no promise, I should not hesitate to regard the former as my duty. Yet on the view that what is right is right because it is productive of the most good I should not so regard it.

There are two theories, each in its way simple, that offer a solution of such cases of conscience. One is the view of Kant, that there are certain duties of perfect obligation, such as those of fulfilling promises, of paying debts, of telling the truth, which admit of no exception whatever in favour of duties of imperfect obligation, such as that of relieving distress. The other is the view of, for instance, Professor Moore and Dr. Rashdall, that there is only the duty of producing goods, and that all 'conflicts of duties' should be resolved by asking 'by which action will most good be produced?' But it is more important that our theory fit the facts than that it be simple, and the account we have given above corresponds (it seems to me) better than either of the simpler theories with what we really think, *viz.* that normally promise-keeping, for example, should come before benevolence, but that when and only when the good to be produced by the benevolent act is very great and the promise comparatively trivial, the act of benevolence becomes our duty.

In fact the theory of 'ideal utilitarianism,' if I may for brevity refer so to the theory of Professor Moore, seems to simplify unduly our relations to our fellows. It says, in effect, that the only morally significant relation in which my neighbours stand to me is that of being possible beneficiaries by my action. They do stand in this relation to me, and this relation is morally significant. But they may also stand to me in the relation of promisee to promiser, of creditor to debtor, of wife to husband, of child to parent, of friend to friend, of fellow countryman to fellow countryman, and the like; and each of these relations is the foundation of a *prima facie* duty, which is more or less incumbent on me according to the circumstances of the case. When I am in a situation, as perhaps I always am, in which more than one of these *prima facie* duties is incumbent on me, what I have to do is to study the situation as fully as I can until I form the considered opinion (it is never more) that in the circumstances one of them is more incumbent than any other; then I am bound to think that to do this *prima facie* duty is my duty in the situation. . . .

There is nothing arbitrary about these *prima facie* duties. Each rests on a definite circumstance which cannot seriously be held to be without moral significance. Of *prima facie* duties I suggest, without claiming completeness or finality for it, the following division.

(1) Some duties rest on previous acts of my own. These duties seem to include two kinds, (*a*) those resting on a promise or what may fairly be called an implicit promise, such as the implicit undertaking not to tell lies which seems to be implied in the act of entering into conversation (at any rate by civilized men), or of writing books that purport to be history and not fiction. These may be called the duties of fidelity. (*b*) Those resting on a previous wrongful act. These may be called the duties of reparation. (2) Some rest on previous acts of other men, i.e. services done by them to me. These may be loosely described as the duties of gratitude. (3) Some rest on the fact or possibility of a distribution of pleasure or happiness (or of the means thereto) which is not in accordance with the merit of the persons concerned; in such cases there arises a duty to upset or prevent such a distribution. These are the duties of justice. (4) Some rest on the mere fact that there are other beings in the world whose condition we can make better in respect of virtue, or of intelligence, or of pleasure. These are the duties of beneficence. (5) Some rest on the fact that we can improve our own condition in respect of virtue or of intelligence. These are the duties of self-improvement. (6) I think that we should distinguish from (4) the duties that may be summed up under the title of 'not injuring others.' No doubt to injure others is incidentally to fail to do them good; but it seems to me clear that non-maleficence is apprehended as a duty distinct from that of beneficence, and as a duty of a more stringent character. It will be noticed that this alone among the types of duty has been stated in a negative way. An attempt might no doubt be made to state this duty, like the others, in a

positive way. It might be said that it is really the duty to prevent ourselves from acting either from an inclination to harm others or from an inclination to seek our own pleasure, in doing which we should incidentally harm them. But on reflection it seems clear that the primary duty here is the duty not to harm others, this being a duty whether or not we have an inclination that if followed would lead to our harming them; and that when we have such an inclination the primary duty not to harm others gives rise to a consequential duty to resist the inclination. The recognition of this duty of non-maleficence is the first step on the way to the recognition of the duty of beneficence; and that accounts for the prominence of the commands 'thou shalt not kill,' 'thou shalt not commit adultery,' 'thou shalt not steal,' 'thou shalt not bear false witness,' in so early a code as the Decalogue. But even when we have come to recognize the duty of beneficence, it appears to me that the duty of non-maleficence is recognized as a distinct one, and as *prima facie* more binding. We should not in general consider it justifiable to kill one person in order to keep another alive, or to steal from one in order to give alms to another.

The essential defect of the 'ideal utilitarian' theory is that it ignores, or at least does not do full justice to, the highly personal character of duty. If the only duty is to produce the maximum of good, the question who is to have the good—whether it is myself, or my benefactor, or a person to whom I have made a promise to confer that good on him, or a mere fellow man to whom I stand in no such special relation—should make no difference to my having a duty to produce that good. But we are all in fact sure that it makes a vast difference. . . .

If the objection be made, that this catalogue of the main types of duty is an unsystematic one resting on no logical principle, it may be replied, first, that it makes no claim to being ultimate. It is a *prima facie* classification of the duties which reflection on our moral convictions seems actually to reveal. And if these convictions are, as I would claim that they are, of the nature of knowledge, and if I have not misstated them, the list will be a list of authentic conditional duties, correct as far as it goes though not necessarily complete. The list of *goods* put forward by the rival theory is reached by exactly the same method—the only sound one in the circumstances—*viz.* that of direct reflection on what we really think. Loyalty to the facts is worth more than a symmetrical architectonic or a hastily reached simplicity. If further reflection discovers a perfect logical basis for this or for a better classification, so much the better.

It may, again, be objected that our theory that there are these various and often conflicting types of *prima facie* duty leaves us with no principle upon which to discern what is our actual duty in particular circumstances. But this objection is not one which the rival theory is in a position to bring forward.

For when we have to choose between the production of two heterogeneous goods, say knowledge and pleasure, the 'ideal utilitarian' theory can only fall back on an opinion, for which no logical basis can be offered, that one of the goods is the greater; and this is no better than a similar opinion that one of two duties is the more urgent. And again, when we consider the infinite variety of the effects of our actions in the way of pleasure, it must surely be admitted that the claim which *hedonism* sometimes makes, that it offers a readily applicable criterion of right conduct, is quite illusory.

I am unwilling, however, to content myself with an *argumentum ad hominem,* and I would contend that in principle there is no reason to anticipate that every act that is our duty is so for one and the same reason. Why should two sets of circumstances, or one set of circumstances, *not* possess different characteristics, any one of which makes a certain act our *prima facie* duty? When I ask what it is that makes me in certain cases sure that I have a *prima facie* duty to do so and so, I find that it lies in the fact that I have made a promise; when I ask the same question in another case, I find the answer lies in the fact that I have done a wrong. And if on reflection I find (as I think I do) that neither of these reasons is reducible to the other, I must not on any *a priori* ground assume that such a reduction is possible. . . .

It is necessary to say something by way of clearing up the relation between *prima facie* duties and the actual or absolute duty to do one particular act in particular circumstances. If, as almost all moralists except Kant are agreed, and as most plain men think, it is sometimes right to tell a lie or to break a promise, it must be maintained that there is a difference between *prima facie* duty and actual or absolute duty. When we think ourselves justified in breaking, and indeed morally obliged to break, a promise in order to relieve some one's distress, we do not for a moment cease to recognize a *prima facie* duty to keep our promise, and this leads us to feel, not indeed shame or repentance, but certainly compunction, for behaving as we do; we recognize, further, that it is our duty to make up somehow to the promisee for the breaking of the promise. We have to distinguish from the characteristic of being our duty that of tending to be our duty. Any act that we do contains various elements in virtue of which it falls under various categories. In virtue of being the breaking of a promise, for instance, it tends to be wrong; in virtue of being an instance of relieving distress it tends to be right. Tendency to be one's duty may be called a parti-resultant attribute, i.e. one which belongs to an act in virtue of some one component in its nature. *Being* one's duty is a toti-resultant attribute, one which belongs to an act in virtue of its whole nature and of nothing less than this. . . .

Another instance of the same distinction may be found in the operation of natural laws. *Qua* subject to the force of gravitation towards some other body, each body tends to move in a particular direction with a particular velocity; but its actual movement depends on *all* the forces to which it is subject. It is only by recognizing this distinction that we can preserve the absoluteness of laws of nature, and only by recognizing a corresponding distinction that we can preserve the absoluteness of the general principles of morality. But an important difference between the two cases must be pointed out. When we say that in virtue of gravitation a body tends to move in a certain way, we are referring to a causal influence actually exercised on it by another body or other bodies. When we say that in virtue of being deliberately untrue a certain remark tends to be wrong, we are referring to no causal relation, to no relation that involves succession in time, but to such a relation as connects the various attributes of a mathematical figure. And if the word 'tendency' is thought to suggest too much a causal relation, it is better to talk of certain types of act as being *prima facie* right or wrong (or of different persons as having different and possibly conflicting claims upon us), than of their tending to be right or wrong.

Something should be said of the relation between our apprehension of the *prima facie* rightness of certain types of act and our mental attitude towards particular acts. It is proper to use the word 'apprehension' in the former case and not in the latter. That an act, *qua* fulfilling a promise, or *qua* effecting a just distribution of good, or *qua* returning services rendered, or *qua* promoting the good of others, or *qua* promoting the virtue or insight of the agent, is *prima facie* right, is self-evident; not in the sense that it is evident from the beginning of our lives, or as soon as we attend to the proposition for the first time, but in the sense that when we have reached sufficient mental maturity and have given sufficient attention to the proposition it is evident without any need of proof, or of evidence beyond itself. It is self-evident just as a mathematical axiom, or the validity of a form of inference, is evident. The moral order expressed in these propositions is just as much part of the fundamental nature of the universe (and, we may add, of any possible universe in which there were moral agents at all) as is the spatial or numerical structure expressed in the axioms of geometry or arithmetic. In our confidence that these propositions are true there is involved the same trust in our reason that is involved in our confidence in mathematics; and we should have no justification for trusting it in the latter sphere and distrusting it in the former. In both cases we are dealing with propositions that cannot be proved, but that just as certainly need no proof. . . .

In what has preceded, a good deal of use has been made of 'what we really think' about moral questions; a certain theory has been rejected because it does not agree with what we really think. It might be said that this is in principle wrong; that we should not be content to expound what our present moral consciousness tells us but should aim at a criticism of our existing moral consciousness in the light of theory. Now I do not doubt that the moral consciousness of men has in detail undergone a good deal of modification as regards the things we think right, at the hands of moral theory. But if we are told, for instance, that we should give up our view that there is a special obligatoriness attaching to the keeping of promises because it is self-evident that the only duty is to produce as much good as possible, we have to ask ourselves whether we really, when we reflect, *are* convinced that this is self-evident, and whether we really *can* get rid of our view that promise-keeping has a bindingness independent of productiveness of maximum good. In my own experience I find that I cannot, in spite of a very genuine attempt to do so; and I venture to think that most people will find the same, and that just because they cannot lose the sense of special obligation, they cannot accept as self-evident, or even as true, the theory which would require them to do so. In fact it seems, on reflection, self-evident that a promise, simply as such, is something that *prima facie* ought to be kept, and it does *not*, on reflection, seem self-evident that production of maximum good is the only thing that makes an act obligatory. And to ask us to give up at the bidding of a theory our actual apprehension of what is right and what is wrong seems like asking people to repudiate their actual experience of beauty, at the bidding of a theory which says 'only that which satisfies such and such conditions can be beautiful'. If what I have called our actual apprehension is (as I would maintain that it is) truly an apprehension, i.e. an instance of knowledge, the request is nothing less than absurd. . . .

It would be a mistake to found a natural science on 'what we really think', i.e. on what reasonably thoughtful and well-educated people think about the subjects of the science before they have studied them scientifically. For such opinions are interpretations, and often misinterpretations, of sense-experience; and the man of science must appeal from these to sense-experience itself, which funishes his real data. In ethics no such appeal is possible. We have no more direct way of access to the facts about rightness and goodness and about what things are right or good, than by thinking about them; the moral convictions of thoughtful and well-educated people are the data of ethics just as sense-perceptions are the data of a natural science. Just as some of the latter have to be rejected as illusory, so have some of the former; but as the latter are rejected only when they are in conflict with other more accurate sense-perceptions, the former are rejected only when they are in conflict with other convictions which stand better the test of reflection. The existing body of moral convictions of the best people is the cumulative product of the moral reflection of many generations, which has developed an extremely delicate power of appreciation of moral distinctions; and this the theorist cannot afford to treat with anything other than the greatest respect.

SUGGESTED READINGS

A. Duncan-Jones has written a short book on Butler. For an interesting recent discussion of conscience, see B. Mayo, *Ethics and the Moral Life*, Chapters 8 and 9; for a criticism of the concept, see J. F. M. Hunter, "Conscience," *Mind*, 1963.

In grappling with Kant, the student will obtain some help from H. J. Paton's *The Categorical Imperative*, which is a detailed commentary on the *Foundations of the Metaphysics of Morals*. Paton's translation of that work, entitled *The Moral Law*, is accompanied by notes and a brief commentary. C. D. Broad, *Five Types of Ethical Theory*, has good chapters on Butler and on Kant.

Ross derived much of his thinking from H. A. Prichard, whose short but very difficult paper, "Does Moral Philosophy Rest on a Mistake?" (*Mind*, 1912), is reprinted in Prichard's *Moral Obligation* and in W. Sellars and J. Hospers, *Readings in Ethical Theory*. A clear elementary statement of a similar view is given in E. F. Carritt, *Ethical and Political Thinking*, Chapters 1–9. One important kind of criticism of this view is given in P. F. Strawson, "Ethical Intuitionism," reprinted in Sellars and Hospers.

Essays in Moral Philosophy, edited by A. I. Melden, contains a good essay by H. L. A. Hart discussing the differences between "Legal and Moral Obligation," as well as a discussion by M. Singer of "Moral Rules and Principles." Singer here applies the theory stated briefly in "Generalization in Ethics" (*Mind*, 1955), which is an attempt at a restatement of a Kantian type of position.

Utilitarians, though they take "good" as basic, must provide a theory of obligation. J. S. Mill sets forth his view mainly in Chapter 5 of *Utilitarianism* and in Book VI, Chapter 12 of the *System of Logic*. W. K. Frankena discusses this and other utilitarian views very clearly in *Ethics*, Chapter 3.

Two Current Issues:
A. Relativism

Anthropological evidence indicates that in all societies men possess a moral conscience, a sense of right and wrong. In every culture some actions and motives for action are approved as "right" or "good," and others are disapproved as "wrong" or "bad." On the other hand, what particular actions and motives are praised and what are blamed seems to vary greatly from culture to culture. Whether this variability reflects ultimate differences in moral standards, or whether there is in fact some invariance in these standards, is an important question on which not all investigators agree.

Cultural relativists hold that there is an indefinite variability in moral standards. Their position is based in part on a survey of different cultures. Such studies show, they maintain, that what is deemed worthy of approval or disapproval in one society is different, both in detail and on the whole, from that of another. However, their view is also put forward on general theoretical grounds. *First,* they claim that all moral standards are merely reflections of *mores,* of ways of doing things that happened to arise and be approved within a particular culture. In other words, a moral standard is simply an historical product, sanctioned by custom. *Second,* they claim that the only source of an individual's moral judgments lies in the mores of the group in which he is reared. All men are malleable: if brought up in one culture, they will adopt one set of moral norms; if brought up in another, they will adopt a different set. Taken together, these two assertions lead the cultural relativist to deny that any moral standard is universally valid and to regard any criticism of the standards of others as a mere expression of the particular norms that the critic has been trained to accept.

BENEDICT defends the position of cultural relativism by attempting to show that even our most general concepts of what is normal or abnormal are culturally determined. KROEBER and KLUCKHOHN, on the other hand, interpret the evidence of anthropology as in no way implying an ultimate variability in the standards of different cultures. The selection from ASCH, a social psychologist, criticizes the psychological assumptions on the basis of which cultural relativists seek to prove that our moral judgments have their source wholly in the *mores* of the group.

The Concept of the Normal[*]

Ruth Fulton Benedict [1887–1948] taught anthropology at Columbia University. She did field work on American Indian cultures, but is best known for her theoretical writings. During the Second World War she served with the Bureau of Overseas Intelligence and in 1946 published a work on the patterns of Japanese culture.

Modern social anthropology has become more and more a study of the varieties and common elements of cultural environment and the consequences of these in human behavior. For such a study of diverse social orders primitive peoples fortunately provide a laboratory not yet entirely vitiated by the spread of a standardized world-wide civilization. Dyaks and Hopis, Fijians and Yakuts are significant for psychological and sociological study because only among these simpler peoples has there been sufficient isolation to give opportunity for the development of localized social forms. In the higher cultures the standardization of custom and belief over a couple of continents has given a false sense of the inevitability of the particular forms that have gained currency, and we need to turn to a wider survey in order to check the conclusions we hastily base upon this near-universality of familiar customs. Most of the simpler cultures did not gain the wide currency of the one which, out of our experience, we identify with human nature, but this was for various historical reasons, and certainly not for any that gives us as its carriers a monopoly of social good or of social sanity. Modern civilization, from this point of view, becames not a necessary pinnacle of human achievement but one entry in a long series of possible adjustments.

These adjustments, whether they are in mannerisms like the ways of showing anger, or joy, or grief in any society, or in major human drives like those of sex, prove to be far more variable than experience in any one culture would suggest. In certain fields, such as that of religion or of formal marriage arrangements, these wide limits of variability are well known and can be fairly described. In others it is not yet possible to give a generalized account, but that does not absolve us of the task of indicating the significance of the work that has been done and of the problems that have arisen.

One of these problems relates to the customary modern normal-abnormal categories and our conclusions regarding them. In how far are such cate-

[*] From Benedict: "Anthropology and the Abnormal" in *The Journal of General Psychology*, X (1934), pp. 59–82. Reprinted by permission of The Journal Press.

gories culturally determined, or in how far can we with assurance regard them as absolute? In how far can we regard inability to function socially as diagnostic of abnormality, or in how far is it necessary to regard this as a function of the culture?

As a matter of fact, one of the most striking facts that emerge from a study of widely varying cultures is the ease with which our abnormals function in other cultures. It does not matter what kind of "abnormality" we choose for illustration, those which indicate extreme instability, or those which are more in the nature of character traits like sadism or delusions of grandeur or of persecution, there are well-described cultures in which these abnormals function at ease and with honor, and apparently without danger or difficulty to the society.

The most notorious of these is trance and catalepsy. Even a very mild mystic is aberrant in our culture. But most peoples have regarded even extreme psychic manifestations not only as normal and desirable, but even as characteristic of highly valued and gifted individuals. . . . It is hard for us, born and brought up in a culture that makes no use of the experience, to realize how important a rôle it may play and how many individuals are capable of it, once it has been given an honorable place in any society. . . .

The most spectacular illustrations of the extent to which normality may be culturally defined are those cultures where an abnormality of our culture is the cornerstone of their social structure. It is not possible to do justice to these possibilities in a short discussion. A recent study of an island of northwest Melanesia by Fortune [*Sorcerers of Dobu*] describes a society built upon traits which we regard as beyond the border of paranoia. In this tribe the exogamic groups look upon each other as prime manipulators of black magic, so that one marries always into an enemy group which remains for life one's deadly and unappeasable foes. They look upon a good garden crop as a confession of theft, for everyone is engaged in making magic to induce into his garden the productiveness of his neighbors'; therefore no secrecy in the island is so rigidly insisted upon as the secrecy of a man's harvesting of his yams. Their polite phrase at the acceptance of a gift is, "And if you now poison me, how shall I repay you this gift?" Their preoccupation with poisoning is constant; no woman ever leaves her cooking pot for a moment unattended. Even the great affinal economic exchanges that are characteristic of this Melanesian culture area are quite altered in Dobu since they are incompatible with this fear and distrust that pervades the culture. They go farther and people the whole world outside their own quarters with such malignant spirits that all-night feasts and ceremonials simply do not occur here. They have even rigorous religiously enforced customs that forbid the sharing of seed even in one family group. Anyone else's food is deadly poison to you, so that communality of stores is out of the question. For some months before harvest the whole society is on the verge of starvation, but if one falls to the temptation and eats up one's seed yams, one is an outcast and a beachcomber for life. There is no coming back. It involves, as a matter of course, divorce and the breaking of all social ties.

Now in this society where no one may work with another and no one may share with another, Fortune describes the individual who was regarded by all his fellows as crazy. He was not one of those who periodically ran amok and, beside himself and frothing at the mouth, fell with a knife upon anyone he could reach. Such behavior they did not regard as putting anyone outside the pale. They did not even put the individuals who were known to be liable to these attacks under any kind of control. They merely fled when they saw the attack coming on and kept out of the way. "He would be all right tomorrow." But there was one man of sunny, kindly disposition who liked work and liked to be helpful. The compulsion was too strong for him to repress it in favor of the opposite tendencies of his culture. Men and women never spoke of him without laughing; he was silly and simple and definitely crazy. Nevertheless, to the ethnologist used to a culture that has, in Christianity, made his type the model of all virtue, he seemed a pleasant fellow.

An even more extreme example, because it is of a culture that has built itself upon a more complex abnormality, is that of the North Pacific Coast of North America. The civilization of the Kwakiutl, at the time when it was first recorded in the last decades of the nineteenth century, was one of the most vigorous in North America. It was built up on an ample economic supply of goods, the fish which furnished their food staple being practically inexhaustible and obtainable with comparatively small labor, and the wood which furnished the material for their houses, their furnishings, and their arts being, with however much labor, always procurable. They lived in coastal villages that compared favorably in size with those of any other American Indians and they kept up constant communication by means of sea-going dug-out canoes.

It was one of the most vigorous and zestful of the aboriginal cultures of North America, with complex crafts and ceremonials, and elaborate and striking arts. It certainly had none of the earmarks of a sick civilization. The tribes of the Northwest Coast had wealth, and exactly in our terms. That is, they had not only a surplus of economic goods, but they made a game of the manipulation of wealth. It was by no means a mere direct transcription of economic needs and the filling of those needs. It involved the idea of capital, of interest, and of conspicuous waste. It was a game with all the binding rules of a game, and a person entered it as a child. His father distributed wealth for him, according to his ability, at a small feast or potlatch, and each gift the receiver was obliged to accept and to return after a short interval with interest that ran to about 100 per cent a year. By the time the child was grown, therefore, he was well launched, a larger potlatch had been given for him on various occasions of exploit or initiation, and he had wealth either out at usury or in his own possession. Nothing in the civilization could be enjoyed without validating it by the distribution of this wealth. Everything that was valued, names and songs as well as material objects, were passed down in family lines, but they were always publicly assumed with accompanying sufficient distributions of property. It was the game of validating and exercising all the privileges one could accumulate from one's various forbears, or by gift, or by marriage, that made the chief interest of the culture. Everyone in his degree took part in it, but many, of course, mainly as spectators. In its highest form it was played out between rival chiefs representing not only themselves and their family lines but their communities, and the object of the contest was to glorify oneself and to humiliate one's opponent. On this level of greatness the property involved was no longer represented by blankets, so many thousand of them to a potlatch, but by higher units of value. These higher units were like our bank notes. They were incised copper tablets, each of them named, and having a value that depended upon their illustrious history. This was as high as ten thousand blankets, and to possess one of them, still more to enhance its value at a great potlatch, was one of the greatest glories within the compass of the chiefs of the Northwest Coast.

The details of this manipulation of wealth are in many ways a parody on our own economic arrangements, but it is with the motivations that were recognized in this contest that we are concerned in this discussion. The drives were those which in our own culture we should call megalomaniac. There was an uncensored self-glorification and ridicule of the opponent that it is hard to equal in other cultures outside of the monologues of the abnormal. . . . All of existence was seen in terms of insult. Not only derogatory acts performed by a neighbor or an enemy, but all untoward events, like a cut when one's axe slipped, or a ducking when one's canoe overturned, were insults. All alike threatened first and foremost one's ego security, and the first thought one was allowed was how to get even, how to wipe out the insult. . . .

In their behavior at great bereavements this set of the culture comes out most strongly. Among the Kwakiutl it did not matter whether a relative had died in bed of disease, or by the hand of an enemy, in either case death was an affront to be wiped out by the death of another person. The fact that one had been caused to mourn was proof that one had been put upon. A chief's sister and her daughter had gone up to Victoria, and either because they drank bad whiskey or because their boat capsized they never came back. The chief called together his warriors. "Now I ask you, tribes, who shall wail? Shall I do it or shall another?" The spokesman answered, of course, "Not you, Chief. Let some other of the tribes." Immediately they set up the war pole to announce their intention of wiping out the injury, and gathered a war party. They set out, and found seven men and two children asleep and killed them. "Then they felt good when they arrived at Sebaa in the evening."

The point which is of interest to us is that in our society those who on that occasion would feel good when they arrived at Sebaa that evening would be the definitely abnormal. There would be some, even in our society, but it is not a recognized and approved mood under the circumstances. On the Northwest Coast those are favored and fortunate to whom that mood under those circumstances is congenial, and those to whom it is repugnant are unlucky. This latter minority can register in their own culture only by doing violence to their congenial responses and acquiring others that are difficult for them. The person, for instance, who, like a Plains Indian whose wife has been taken from him, is too proud to fight, can deal with the Northwest Coast civilization only by ignoring its strongest bents. If he cannot achieve it, he is the deviant in that culture, their instance of abnormality. . . .

Behavior honored upon the Northwest Coast is one which is recognized as abnormal in our civilization, and yet it is sufficiently close to the attitudes of our own culture to be intelligible to us and to have a definite vocabulary with which we may discuss it. The megalomaniac paranoid trend is a definite danger in our society. It is encouraged by some of our major preoccupations, and it confronts us with a choice of two possible attitudes. One is to brand it as abnormal and reprehensible, and is the attitude we have chosen in our civilization. The other is to make it an essential attribute of ideal man, and this is the solution in the culture of the Northwest Coast.

These illustrations, which it has been possible to indicate only in the briefest manner, force upon us the fact that normality is culturally defined. An adult shaped to the drives and standards of either of these cultures, if he were transported into our civilization would fall into our categories of abnormality. He would be faced with the psychic dilemmas of the socially unavailable. In his own culture, however, he is the pillar of society, the end result of socially inculcated mores, and the problem of personal instability in his case simply does not arise.

No one civilization can possibly utilize in its mores the whole potential range of human behavior. Just as there are great numbers of possible phonetic articulations, and the possibility of language depends on a selection and standardization of a few of these in order that speech communication may be possible at all, so the possibility of organized behavior of every sort, from the fashions of local dress and houses to the dicta of a people's ethics and religion, depends upon a similar selection among the possible behavior traits. In the field of recognized economic obligations or sex tabus this selection is as non-rational and subconscious a process as it is in the field of phonetics. It is a process which goes on in the group for long periods of time and is historically conditioned by innumerable accidents of isolation or of contact of peoples. In any comprehensive study of psychology, the selection that different cultures have made in the course of history within the great circumference of potential behavior is of great significance.

Every society, beginning with some slight inclination in one direction or another, carries its preference farther and farther, integrating itself more and more completely upon its chosen basis, and discarding those types of behavior that are uncongenial. Most of those organizations of personality that seem to us most incontrovertibly abnormal have been used by different civilizations in the very foundations of their institutional life. Conversely the most valued traits of our normal individuals have been looked on in differently organized cultures as aberrant. Normality, in short, within a very wide range, is culturally defined. It is primarily a term for the socially elaborated segment of human behavior in any culture; and abnormality, a term for the segment that that particular civilization does not use. The very eyes with which we see the problem are conditioned by the long traditional habits of our own society.

It is a point that has been made more often in relation to ethics than in relation to psychiatry. We do not any longer make the mistake of deriving the morality of our own locality and decade directly from the inevitable constitution of human nature. We do not elevate it to the dignity of a first principle. We recognize that morality differs in every society, and is a convenient term for socially approved habits. Mankind has always preferred to say, "It is morally good," rather than "It is habitual," and the fact of this preference is matter enough for a critical science of ethics. But historically the two phrases are synonymous.

The concept of the normal is properly a variant of the concept of the good. It is that which society has approved. A normal action is one which falls well within the limits of expected behavior for a particular society. Its variability among different peoples is essentially a function of the variability of the behavior patterns that different societies have created for themselves, and can never be wholly divorced from a consideration of culturally institutionalized types of behavior.

Each culture is a more or less elaborate working-out of the potentialities of the segment it has chosen. In so far as a civilization is well integrated and consistent within itself, it will tend to carry farther and farther, according to its nature, its initial impulse toward a particular type of action, and from the point of view of any other culture those elaborations will include more and more extreme and aberrant traits.

Each of these traits, in proportion as it reinforces the chosen behavior patterns of that culture, is for that culture normal. Those individuals to whom it is congenial either congenitally, or as the result of childhood sets, are accorded prestige in that culture, and are not visited with the social contempt or disapproval which their traits would call down upon them in a society that was differently organized. On the other hand, those individuals whose characteristics are not congenial to the selected type of human behavior in that community are the deviants, no matter how valued their personality traits may be in a contrasted civilization.

The Dobuan who is not easily susceptible to fear of treachery, who enjoys work and likes to be helpful, is their neurotic and regarded as silly. On the Northwest Coast the person who finds it difficult to read life in terms of an insult contest will be the person upon whom fall all the difficulties of the culturally unprovided for. The person who does not find it easy to humiliate a neighbor, nor to see humiliation in his own experience, who is genial and loving, may, of course, find some unstandardized way of achieving satisfactions in his society, but not in the major patterned responses that his culture requires of him. If he is born to play an important rôle in a family with many hereditary privileges, he can succeed only by doing violence to his whole personality. If he does not succeed, he has betrayed his culture; that is, he is abnormal.

I have spoken of individuals as having sets toward certain types of behavior, and of these sets as running sometimes counter to the types of behavior which are institutionalized in the culture to which they belong. From all that we know of contrasting cultures it seems clear that differences of temperament occur in every society. The matter has never been made the subject of investigation, but from the available material it would appear that these temperament types are very likely of universal recurrence. That is, there is an ascertainable range of human behavior that is found wherever a sufficiently large series of individuals is observed. But the proportion in which behavior types stand to one another in different societies is not universal. The vast majority of the individuals in any group are shaped to the fashion of that culture. In other words, most individuals are plastic to the moulding force of the society into which they are born. In a society that values trance, as in India, they will have supernormal experience. In a society that institutionalizes homosexuality, they will be homosexual. In a society that sets the gathering of possessions as the chief human objective, they will amass property. The deviants, whatever the type of behavior the culture has institutionalized, will remain few in number, and there seems no more difficulty in moulding the vast malleable majority to the "normality" of what we consider an aberrant trait than to the normality of such accepted behavior patterns as acquisitiveness. The small proportion of the number of the deviants in any culture is not a function of the sure instinct with which that society has built itself upon the fundamental sanities, but of the universal fact that, happily, the majority of mankind quite readily take any shape that is presented to them.

Values and Relativity[*]

A L F R E D L O U I S K R O E B E R [1876–1960] taught anthropology at the University of California. In addition to his notable contributions as an investigator of American cultures, Kroeber was one of America's leading theoretical anthropologists.

C L Y D E K L U C K H O H N [1905–1960] was Professor of Anthropology at Harvard. He was a leader in recent attempts to relate anthropological findings to the theory of value and in the movement to apply the methods of anthropology to contemporary political and social problems.

We know by experience that sincere comparison of cultures leads quickly to recognition of their "relativity." What this means is that cultures are differently weighted in their values, hence are differently structured, and differ both in part-functioning and in total-functioning; and that true understanding of cultures therefore involves recognition of their particular value systems. Comparisons of cultures must not be simplistic in terms of an arbitrary or preconceived universal value system, but must be multiple, with each culture first understood in terms of its own particular value system and therefore its own idiosyncratic structure. After that, comparison can with gradually increasing reliability reveal to what degrees values, significances, and qualities are common to the compared cultures, and to what degree distinctive. In proportion as common structures and qualities are discovered, the uniquenesses will mean more. And as the range of variability of differentiations becomes better known, it will add to the significance of more

[*] From Kroeber and Kluckhohn: Culture, A Critical Review of Concepts and Definitions; Papers of The Peabody Museum, Harvard University, XLVII (1952), no. 1, pp. 174–179. Reprinted by permission of The Peabody Museum and the authors.

universal or common features—somewhat as knowledge of variability deepens significance of a statistical mean. . . .

The inescapable fact of cultural relativism does not justify the conclusion that cultures are in all respects utterly disparate monads and hence strictly noncomparable entities. If this were literally true, a comparative science of culture would be *ex hypothesi* impossible. It is unfortunately the case that up to this point anthropology has not solved very satisfactorily the problem of describing cultures in such a way that objective comparison is possible. . . .

In principle, however, there is a generalized framework that underlies the more apparent and striking facts of cultural relativity. All cultures constitute so many somewhat distinct answers to essentially the same questions posed by human biology and by the generalities of the human situation. These are the considerations explored by Wissler under the heading of "the universal culture pattern" and by Murdock under the rubric of "the least common denominators of cultures." Every society's patterns for living must provide approved and sanctioned ways for dealing with such universal circumstances as the existence of two sexes; the helplessness of infants; the need for satisfaction of the elementary biological requirements such as food, warmth, and sex; the presence of individuals of different ages and of differing physical and other capacities. The basic similarities in human biology the world over are vastly more massive than the variations. Equally, there are certain necessities in social life for this kind of animal regardless of where that life is carried on or in what culture. Cooperation to obtain subsistence and for other ends requires a certain minimum of reciprocal behavior, of a standard system of communication, and indeed of mutually accepted values. The facts of human biology and of human group living supply, therefore, certain invariant points of reference from which cross-cultural comparison can start without begging questions that are themselves at issue. As Wissler pointed out, the broad outlines of the ground plan of all cultures is and has to be about the same because men always and everywhere are faced with certain unavoidable problems which arise out of the situation "given" by nature. Since most of the patterns of all cultures crystallize around the same foci, there are significant respects in which each culture is not wholly isolated, self-contained, disparate but rather related to and comparable with all other cultures.

Nor is the similarity between cultures, which in some ways transcends the fact of relativity, limited to the sheer forms of the universal culture pattern. There are at least some broad resemblances in content and specifically in value content. Considering the exuberant variation of cultures in most respects, the circumstance that in some particulars almost identical values prevail throughout mankind is most arresting. No culture tolerates indiscriminate lying, stealing, or violence within the in-group. The essential universality of the incest taboo is well-known. No culture places a value upon suffering as an end in itself; as a means to the ends of the society (punishment, discipline, etc.), yes; as a means to the ends of the individual (purification, mystical exaltation, etc.), yes; but of and for itself, never. We know of no culture in either space or time, including the Soviet Russian, where the official ideology denies an after-life, where the fact of death is not ceremonialized. Yet the more superficial conception of cultural relativity would suggest that at least one culture would have adopted the simple expedient of disposing of corpses in the same way most cultures do dispose of dead animals—*i.e.*, just throwing the body out far enough from habitations so that the odor is not troubling. When one first looks rather carefully at the astonishing variety of cultural detail over the world one is tempted to conclude: human individuals have tried almost everything that is physically possible and nearly every individual habit has somewhere at some time been institutionalized in at least one culture. To a considerable degree this is a valid generalization—but not completely. In spite of loose talk (based upon an uncritical acceptance of an immature theory of cultural relativity) to the effect that the symptoms of mental disorder are completely relative to culture, the fact of the matter is that all cultures define as abnormal individuals who are permanently inaccessible to communication or who fail to maintain some degree of control over their impulse life. Social life is impossible without communication, without some measure of order: the behavior of any "normal" individual must be predictable—within a certain range—by his fellows and interpretable by them.

To look freshly at values of the order just discussed is very difficult because they are commonplaces. And yet it is precisely because they are *common*places that they are interesting and important. Their vast theoretical significance rests in the fact that despite all the influences that predispose toward cultural variation (biological variation, difference in physical environments, and the processes of history) all of the very many different cultures known to us have converged upon these universals. It is perfectly true (and for certain types of enquiry important) that the value "thou shalt not kill thy fellow tribesman" is not concretely identical either in its cognitive or in its affective aspects for a Navaho, an Ashanti, and a Chukchee. Nevertheless the central conception is the same, and there is understanding between representatives of different cultures as to the general intent of the prohibition. . . .

There is nothing supernatural or even mysterious about the existences of these universalities in culture content. Human life is—and has to be—a moral life (up to a point) because it is a social life. It may safely be presumed that human groups which failed to incorporate certain values into their nascent cultures or which abrogated these values from their older tradition dissolved as societies or perished without record. Similarly, the biological sameness of the human animal (needs and potentialities) has also contributed to convergences.

The fact that a value is a universal does not, of course, make it an absolute. It is possible that changed circumstances in the human situation may lead to the gradual disappearance of some of the present universals. However, the mere existence of universals after so many millennia of culture history and in such diverse environments suggests that they correspond to something extremely deep in man's nature and/or are necessary conditions to social to life.

When one moves from the universals or virtual universals to values which merely are quite widespread, one would be on most shaky ground to infer "rightness" or "wrongness," "better" or "worse" from relative incidence. A value may have a very wide distribution in the world at a particular time just because of historical accidents such as the political and economic power of one nation at that time. Nations diffuse their culture into the areas their power reaches. Nevertheless this does not mean one must take all cultural values except universals as of necessarily equal validity. Slavery or cannibalism may have a place in certain cultures that is not evident to the ethnocentric Christian. Yet even if these culture patterns play an important part in the smooth functioning of these societies, they are still subject to a judgment which is alike moral and scientific. This judgment is not just a projection of values, local in time and space, that are associated with Western culture. Rather, it rests upon a *consensus gentium* and the best scientific evidence as to the nature of raw human nature—*i.e.*, that human nature which all cultures mold and channel but never entirely remake. To say that certain aspects of Naziism were morally wrong, is not parochial arrogance. It is—or can be—an assertion based both upon cross-cultural evidence as to the universalities in human needs, potentialities, and fulfillments and upon natural science knowledge with which the basic assumptions of any philosophy must be congruent.

Any science must be adequate to explain both the similarities and the differences in the phenomena with which it deals. Recent anthropology has focussed its attention preponderantly upon the differences. They are there; they are very real and very important. Cultural relativism has been completely established and there must be no attempt to explain it away or to depreciate its importance because it is inconvenient, hard to take, hard to live with. Some values are almost purely cultural and draw their significance only from the matrix of that culture. Even the universal values have their special phrasings and emphases in accord with each distinct culture. . . .

At the same time one must never forget that cultural differences, real and important though they are, are still so many variations on themes supplied by raw human nature and by the limits and conditions of social life. In some ways culturally altered human nature is a comparatively superficial veneer. The common understandings between men of different cultures are very broad, very general, very easily obscured by language and many other observable symbols. True universals or near universals are apparently few in number. But they seem to be as deep-going as they are rare. Relativity exists only within a universal framework. Anthropology's facts attest that the phrase "a common humanity" is in no sense meaningless. This is also important. . . .

In sum, cultures are distinct yet similar and comparable. As Steward has pointed out, the features that lend uniqueness are the secondary or variable ones. Two or more cultures can have a great deal of content—and even of patterning—in common and still there is distinctness; there are universals, but relativistic autonomy remains a valid principle. Both perspectives are true and important, and no false either-or antinomy must be posed between them. Once again there is a proper analogy between cultures and personalities. Each human being is unique in his concrete totality, and yet he resembles all other human beings in certain respects and some particular human beings a great deal. It is no more correct to limit each culture to its distinctive features and organization, abstracting out as "pre-cultural" or as "conditions of culture" the likenesses that are universal, than to deny to each personality those aspects that derive from its cultural heritage and from participation in common humanity.

A Psychological Critique of Relativism[*]

SOLOMON ELLIOTT ASCH [1907–] is Professor of Psychology at Swarthmore. He is well known for his empirical investigations in social psychology, as well as for his systematic work, *Social Psychology*.

THE THESIS OF CULTURAL RELATIVISM. That ideas of what is right and wrong differ poses a sharp problem for a theory of human nature. We can discern in the history of thought two opposed solutions. Traditional thinking

[*] From Asch: *Social Psychology*, Chapter 13. Copyright, 1952, by Prentice-Hall, Inc., Englewood Cliffs, N. J. Reprinted by permission of Prentice-Hall, Inc.

adopts an absolutist position. It asserts that we are capable of grasping certain actions as unconditionally right and other acts as intrinsically wrong. This is a view difficult to maintain in the light of historical evidence; it has no means of coping with the facts of cultural diversity. Knowledge of divergent social practices has cast increasing doubt on the absolutist interpretation and provoked a reaction against it. The reaction has taken the form of a denial that there are any fixed principles of value in human relations and of the assertion that these are historically conditioned or relative to the society. This is the position of ethical relativism. It is this conclusion, which is of considerable consequence to the social sciences, that we shall consider here.

The case for the relativistic interpretation of values has appeared to many overwhelmingly strong. There is undeniably a profound cultural determination at work. Quite regularly most individuals adopt the prevailing beliefs and values. Social conditions not only enforce particular practices; they also inculcate the conviction of their rightness. Although historical and comparative investigation demonstrate the lack of fixity of human institutions, their practitioners adhere to them in an absolute way; every parochial system appears to its upholders as universally valid. The varied and often contradictory beliefs about marriage or property ownership cannot all have equal validity, yet each is treated by its supporters as unquestionable. It also appears that people misconceive the ways in which they arrive at their beliefs and values. Each acts as if he has gone through a process of judging and evaluating his views independently. But an unbiased examination will show that he could not have developed them himself and that had fate cast him under other skies, he would have been a faithful member of Russian or Eskimo society. Our assumption about the rationality and self-evidence of our values is itself, it would seem, a socially bred illusion—dogmatism parading under a veneer of reason. These considerations are the ground for the conclusion that custom decides what is right and wrong and that these distinctions are subjective, egocentric expressions of preference. It seems to follow that terms such as duty and justice refer simply to what individuals have been taught to like and fear.

To say that social forces can induce people to judge the same action as right or wrong is to make an assertion about people and to imply something of importance about the processes of forming and changing evaluations and standards. The tenets of relativism have not been stated rigorously; we shall need to state them and particularly to reveal the psychological assumptions upon which they rest. We find that there has developed independently within psychology a theory that offers a foundation for the thesis of relativism: stimulus-response theories of learning and motivation have this surprising property. It is now our task to examine the relation of this aspect of stimulus-response psychology to the facts. . . .

THE PSYCHOLOGICAL BASIS OF CULTURAL RELATIVISM. Cultural relativism finds a strict psychological foundation in the propositions of stimulus-response psychology about needs and learning. In particular they offer an apparently cogent explanation of the formation of different reactions to identical conditions. Stimulus-response theory asserts that one can at will attach to a given situation S_1 any of a number of acts, feelings, and evaluations, depending on the consequences that follow. To situation S_1 any of responses R_X, R_Y, R_Z are possible. Which of the responses will become connected to the situation S_1 depends on which response will be followed by reward. It follows that we can, by the manipulation of rewards and punishments, attach to the *same* situation either of two *opposed* responses. There are situations that approximate outwardly to this interpretation. A signal in a conditioning experiment can be connected with food or with shock; a word can designate one object or another wholly unlike it. The stimulus-response account presupposes a thoroughgoing relation of arbitrariness between situation and action and between action and consequence. Let us now see how this interpretation is applied to practices and convictions.

The extension is accomplished simply by the assertion that beliefs, customs, and values are also "responses," learned in precisely the same way as one learns the connection between a person and his name or between a person and his telephone number. We learn to believe that which rewards and to disbelieve that which incurs pain. Therefore the manipulation of rewards and punishments can determine us to judge the same action as good or bad, true or false. For an organism governed by rewards and punishments these are the only possible and necessary "proofs." The laws of learning grind out truth and falsehood indifferently; rewards and punishments are the sole content and criterion of right and wrong. It follows that our ideas of right and wrong, beautiful or ugly are decided by social sanctions and that identical actions can be made desirable or despicable. It is on this basis that we are said to learn that gangsters are bad and that democracy is desirable. These are standards that we have "accepted"; nothing in the nature of democracy and crime points to their value. Life in society is therefore likened to the running of a maze in which the paths are arbitrarily fixed and which one learns to run in the search for satisfaction and avoidance of pain. "Culture, as conceived by social scientists, is a statement of the design of the human maze, of the type of reward involved, and of what responses are to be rewarded. It is in this sense a recipe for learning." . . . When today we encounter the statement that culture is "learned" it often refers not only to the necessity of past experience but also to the arbitrary effect of experience described here.

Deeply embedded in this view is the assumption that aside from a few biological needs there are no factor forces or tendencies in men. All else is "plasticity," the capacity to be shaped in almost indefinitely different ways by rewards and punishments. The temper of this position was clearly expressed in the following well-known statement by J. B. Watson:

> Give me a dozen healthy infants, well-formed, and my own specific world to bring them up in and I'll guarantee to take any one at random and train him to become any type of specialist I might select—doctor, lawyer, artist, merchant-chief, and yes, even beggar-man and thief, regardless of his talents, penchants, tendencies, abilities, vocations, and race of his ancestors. [*Behaviorism*. New York: W. W. Norton, 1930, p. 82.]

The core of the same thought has been expressed more recently in the following statement:

> Man's biological nature is neither good nor bad, aggressive nor submissive, war-like nor peaceful, but neutral in these respects. He is capable of developing in either direction depending on what he is compelled to learn by his environment and by his culture. It is a mistake to assume that he can learn war more easily than peace. His learning machinery is not prejudiced, as is sometimes thought, toward the acquirement of bad habits. The bias is in his social environment. [M. A. May: *A Social Psychology of War and Peace*. New Haven: Yale University Press, 1944, p. 20.]

This position presupposes a dynamically empty organism, lacking autonomous tendencies beyond primary needs and lacking directed forces toward nature or society, which can therefore be turned with equal ease in opposed directions. To be sure, men can learn. But the fact of learning has the peculiar property of not altering them in any way that is significant for a conception of their character, since the habits they form contain nothing of comprehension or insight. Stimulus-response theory excludes the direct perception of social necessities or the guidance of sociological events by conscious direction. The following may serve as an illustration. We find that people react in one way when they find that someone has been untruthful and in a quite different way when he has been truthful. How is this to be understood? The stimulus-response answer is that such actions have in the past been connected with different consequences. What is of interest about the answer is not that it emphasizes the results of action, but its disregard of the idea that truthfulness and untruthfulness are comprehended in terms of their structure—in terms of what they signify for the relation between one person and another—and that they are evaluated on that basis. Instead of concluding that the requirement of truthfulness grows out of a grasp of the causal relation between act and consequence, it treats of truthfulness as a habit that has survived in the course of a trial and error process. This view is responsible for the conclusion that human nature is like water, which takes on whatever shape is imparted to it.

It is not difficult to see how this starting point decides the general interpretation of social action. If convictions and decisions are exclusively the outcome of arbitrary forces upon people who believe what they are made to believe, then one must not deceive oneself into holding that they are other than an expression of bias. In the sense of cultural relativism your values are not yours; they are those of the *Times,* or the *Tribune,* or whatever source of special pleading has succeeded in gaining access to you. You are a mouthpiece with society pulling the strings. At the center of these formulations is a definite assumption about the kind of dependence that prevails between individuals and groups. A plastic individual meets an established social order; the relation is that of hammer and anvil. Such views recommend themselves to many because of their objectivistic character; they appear to assume so much less than other psychologies. It remains to be seen whether they do not contain large assumptions.

Earlier we noted some difficulties in this mode of thinking; here we may simply repeat them. (1) It fails to describe the concrete cognitive and emotional operations one encounters in the social setting. In the present context it simply ignores the fact that people make ethical discriminations and that they sense requirements, and assumes that they are initially blank as far as these distinctions are concerned. . . . It is in these terms that we have to understand the insistence that norms and values are first "external" to the individual and are then "internalized." In the context of the theory, "external" means action alien to the individual's character, tendencies, and capacities; "internal" refers to the blind adoption of these ways. The process of "socialization" is, according to this view, the uncritical adoption of beliefs and values. (2) The stimulus-response account of human needs and rewards is more restricted than observation leads us to conclude. Even if one could assume that the constructs "drive," "reward," "response," were adequate to the actions of infra-human organisms (from the observation of which they are largely derived), it would remain highly questionable whether they apply without modification to social action. In their first intention these terms refer to very particular phenomena, such as deprivation of food, turning a corner, avoiding a shock. It would seem necessary to show that they are relevant to social phenomena. But this is assumed, not proven. Therefore the assertions that society may be likened to a maze and that culture is learned are little more than reiterations of a belief that the rat's learning of a maze (or a particular interpretation of it) is all we need for the understanding of customs and institutions.

RELATIONAL DETERMINATION VERSUS RELATIVISM. The insufficiencies of an absolutist psychological theory of ethical judgments are obvious. It has no means for dealing with cultural diversity (or, for that matter, with intra-individual diversity). On the other hand, although the observations to which relativism refers have greatly widened the horizon of the social sciences, the psychological interpretation they have received poses equally serious difficulties. It is often assumed that these positions are the sole alternatives. Is there not, however, a way to understand the diversities of human practices and convictions without at the same time denying the authentic role of ethical discrimination? We will attempt to show that there is an alternative that fits the facts more closely.

It is now necessary to consider a point about value-judgments that was only adumbrated in the preceding chapter. When we evaluate an act as right or wrong we do so with reference to its place and setting. We evaluate acts always as parts of given conditions. We consider it wrong to take food away from a hungry child, but not if he is overeating. We consider it right to fulfill a promise, but not if it is a promise to commit a crime. Each of these examples is evidence that requiredness is not a property that belongs to an action irrespective of its setting and relations. Every judgment of the value of an act takes into account the particular circumstances under which it occurs. There follows the important consequence that the *same* act may be evaluated as right because it is fitting under one set of conditions, and as wrong because it violates the requirements of another set of conditions. (Whether there are some acts that we evaluate as right or wrong under all circumstances is a difficult question that we may leave open in an elementary discussion.)

It has been customary to hold that diverse evaluations of the same act are automatic evidence for the presence of different principles of evaluation. The preceding examples point to an error in this interpretation and to the need for a distinction between relational determination and relativism. Indeed, an examination of the relational factors that determine the demands we sense may point to the operation of constant principles in situations that differ in concrete details. We shall explore now the bearing of the fact of relational determination upon the culturally determined diversities of evaluation.

The essential proposition of ethical relativism states that one can connect to the identical situation different and even opposed evaluations. Comparative observations of cultures seem to support this view abundantly. Infanticide, as we have seen, receives different evaluations, as do numerous other practices. It seems to follow that the content of our most basic convictions is variable and that there is hardly a principle that, cherished under one social climate, is not violated in another. These observations apparently contradict the conclusion that we sense the demands of conditions. Relativism asserts this contradiction, claiming that evaluations are subjective habits and preferences.

Some years ago Duncker and Wertheimer examined this problem and called attention to a fundamental oversight in the relativistic position. Duncker showed that the conclusion of relativism rests exclusively on the diverse connections observed between outer conditions and practices. But psychological analysis requires that we take cognizance of certain intermediate steps. We act toward a given situation in terms of its meaning—what we understand of it and what experience has taught us about it. On this basis we make evaluations and sense requirements that guide action. The terms of which we must take cognizance in the analysis of actions that have value-character are: (a) the externally given conditions; (b) the meaning they have for the actor; (c) the evaluations and requirements that available knowledge and understanding produce; and (d) the resulting actions. Now the thesis of relativism points to a lack of constancy in the relation between (a) and (d). It fails however to deal with the intervening terms. In particular, it does not consider the relation of evaluation (c) to the given cognitive conditions (b). But relativism, if it is to be psychologically valid, must assert that one can attach different evaluations to situations that have the same cognitive and emotional content. If, for example, we are to speak of relativism with reference to infanticide we must assume that the *same* action which is tolerated under one set of conditions is outlawed under other conditions. This assumption is as a rule dubious. The character of the object "infant" may not be the same under all conditions. In the first few days of life, an infant may be regarded as not yet human, in the way that many regard the embryo. (It should be noted that infanticide, when practiced, occurs only during the first few days following birth.) Therefore, the act of killing will not have the same meaning under all conditions. Precisely the same issue arises in connection with the killing of parents. In the society that follows this practice there prevails the belief that people continue to lead in the next world the same existence as in the present and that they maintain forever the condition of health and vigor they had at the time of death. It is therefore a filial duty of the son to dispatch his parents, an act that has the full endorsement of the parent and of the community.

Duncker suggests that different and apparently opposed practices and values are frequently not the consequence of diversity in ethical principles but of differences in the comprehension of a situation—differences in "situational meaning." The same external situation may possess quite varied meanings, depending upon the existing level of knowledge and upon other conditions. The resulting differences of action may therefore not be due to a diversity of principle. The meaning of a situation is usually a dependent part of a wider context. In a society in which supernatural beings are part of the cognitive scene, it will be plausible and convincing to impute illness to a purposeful, human-like agency. Consequently, the exorcising of illness by prayer and incantation will, under the given conditions, have a marked relevance. It will not signify that the persons in question are employing novel principles of causation or that they possess different modes of perceiving causation. Similarly, the concept of "stranger" may vary greatly; it may decide whether we shall slay him or treat him essentially like ourselves. The relativistic argument, by failing to take into account the psychological content of the situation, equates things that are psychologically different and only externally the same. It seeks for a mechanical regularity between external situation and action instead of a structural identity between the psychological content of a situation and the act. If we consider the psychological content, we have to conclude that the same action may represent psychologically different contents and that different actions may be functionally identical. To establish whether human beings actually possess contradictory values, it would be necessary to show that the relations between situational meanings and evaluation, or between the terms (b) and (c) above, can vary. This relativism has decidedly failed to do.

Implicit in the preceding discussion is the conclusion that the fact of cultural differences cannot be automatically converted into an argument for a relativism of values. Cultural differences are compatible with identity in values. Indeed, the assumption of variance dictates the conclusion that practices will differ with circumstances. If action and experience are a function of given conditions, we must expect that the former will vary with the latter. To expect uniform practices among societies is as reasonable as to expect all those with poor eyesight to wear identical lenses or for a person to face all situations with the same emotion. This point is well understood when the facts of material culture are under discussion. We consider it reasonable that the Bantu do not build igloos and that Eskimos do not live in thatched huts. Instead of stating conclusions about the relativism of building practices we quite properly take into account the climate, the materials available, and the level of knowledge. The same mode of thinking is indicated when we speak of values, if we do not assume in advance that they are arbitrary. When an Eskimo family permits an old person to expose himself to death this must be viewed in relation to their situation, their problems, and the alternatives open to them. The act does not have the same meaning for them that it would have for us today; Eskimos do not have homes for the aged or retirement pensions. If we take the given circumstances into account the possibility is present for understanding diverse actions in terms of the same operations of valuing.

What can we say about the relation between "situational meaning" and evaluation? In general, anthropological evidence does not furnish proof of relativism in the relation between the meaning of situations and their evaluation. We do not know of societies in which bravery is despised and cowardice held up to honor, in which generosity is considered a vice and ingratitude a virtue. It seems rather, as Duncker proposed, that the relations between valuation and meaning are invariant. It is not usual to find groups placing a different valuation upon, or experiencing different obligations toward, a situation that they understand in an identical way. It seems rather that certain ethical discriminations are universally known. We still have to hear of a society to which modesty, courage, and hospitality are not known.

Throughout the preceding discussion we have assumed one far-reaching form of "relativism" to be present: that pertaining to knowledge and understanding. Historical conditions determine the extent and level of knowledge and therefore the content and evaluation of given conditions. We may illustrate the general fact with a simple instance. A need, such as hunger, does not innately refer to its adequate object. It is only when the hungry infant is fed that he can form a craving for milk or sweets and search for them subsequently. Obviously the object must be experienced (or heard about) if it is to become relevant to one's needs. One cannot crave an object one has not experienced. It will necessarily happen that in different societies there will be quite different food preferences. Here we have a concrete, if simple, instance of what many call relativism, although it is more properly an example of relational determination. What can it teach us? First, the variation is not unlimited; however different in quality and in adequacy, an article of food will generally become an object of craving because it has food-value. When two groups come in contact, each will continue to prefer its diet; here we have a difference that is to a degree arbitrary. But again we find that the differences are not as unlimited as a sketchy analysis suggests. To the extent that different diets are equally nutritious, a preference for the one that is familiar is a fact upon which one cannot place undue importance. It is more significant to ask about the changes in diet that follow increased knowledge. The answer is fairly obvious.

In the sense described there is a considerable relativism as a result of differences in level of knowledge. One cannot be intelligent about things one does not know; one cannot long for the sea or for mountains if one is not aware of their existence. One can have no desire for fame if one has no historical perspective; one cannot be fired with zeal to contribute to knowledge if science is unknown. Do not these facts commit us to a new relativism with the same practical consequences as the old? It seems to me that they do not. They demonstrate what no one questions—that knowledge and action change in accordance with material and social conditions.

A serious appraisal of the role of cognitive factors permits us to clarify an important problem about values. It may have seemed that to emphasize the probability of invariance between evaluation and action and the presence of certain universal ethical discriminations leaves no place for the growth or change of values. But it should be evident that changes of knowledge and understanding make necessary the evolution of values. When knowledge spreads that men have basic qualities in common, it becomes more difficult to oppress them. When we find that differences between races are chiefly socially determined, it becomes less easy to practice segregation and colonialism. When we learn that criminals have emotions and strong social tendencies we can no longer sustain a purely punitive attitude toward them. With an increased appreciation of the role of reflection and knowledge some come to feel the obligation to be intelligent. Increasing knowledge of human characteristics teaches us the value of the human person. As we learn more of the conditions that affect the development of persons we feel the obligation to improve the material conditions of mankind. In this way alone can we understand the more humane treatment of mental patients, the feeble-minded, and other disadvantaged groups. In this sense there can be a development in the notions of justice and the emergence of novel moral insight. There is reason to say that ideas have an immense effect on evaluation and action.

Many of the most significant changes in human relations have had, it must be added, a relatively expedient basis. Slaves have not usually been freed by an outburst of pity in their owners, nor has the improvement in the conditions of workers been due primarily to a more humane attitude among owners of wealth. There was no ethical impulse back of the industrial revolution, which made possible for the first time in history the freeing of mankind from want and oppression. These changes took place because they coincided with narrower interests. Yet it would not be right to hold this explanation as wholly adequate. Improvements in working conditions, the growth of public education and universal suffrage did, to be sure, wait upon definite technical developments. But these changes would not have come about if not for the tremendous role of the feeling of injustice by those who were oppressed and even by some who profited from existing exploitation. The demand for a shorter working day and for higher wages derives its strength not only from the force workers command when they unite; their force has its source to a profound degree in considerations of value. Under new conditions people perceive opportunities to improve their lot and to achieve values that earlier they could not realize or perhaps clearly conceive. These aspirations must be present and must function to take advantage of existing conditions. If we look closely we find that technical conditions and new relations of power do not alone account for social changes. Technical changes can work to give those concerned with justice an advantage, can win over those who are not zealous, and can weaken the position of those who are determined to maintain their advantage at all costs.

What are the consequences of these ideas for understanding cultural differences in evaluation? Perhaps the main effect is to make the practices of peoples more comprehensible by divesting them, not of interest, but of bizarreness and grotesqueness. Once we abandon certain assumptions about the externality of man's relation to the surroundings, a wholly different view of cultural differences unfolds before us. These need no longer appear as responses to manipulation by social conditions or as the final signs of limitation and subjectivity. We can now see them also as the necessary consequence of permanent human tendencies coming to expression under particular conditions. It also becomes clear that the first step in understanding action or conviction is to establish the way in which it appears to the actor and the reason it appears to him to be right. This is the way to proceed if we take seriously human capacities for comprehension and for formulating explanations within the limitations of knowledge and experience. We need to establish the core of relevance that action or belief has for its practitioners; to do so we need to see action in its context.

Considered from the standpoint of method, relativism deals with social data in a piecemeal way. The impressiveness of its conclusions rests almost entirely on the divorce of data from their context. It lists the diversity of practices in response to the same external conditions, tearing them out of their context. In consequence it obscures their concrete content and dynamics. It should also be mentioned here that an adequate examination must include a reference to the repercussions that standards and values have upon those who are under their sway. The reactions to regulations, the problems they solve, and the conflicts they generate are as pertinent as is their existence and observance. Those views that stress the almost unlimited malleability of human character tend to overlook the inevitable concomitants of conditions, which it would be hard to understand relativistically. Unless we look at interrelations we remove the possibility of understanding either cultural differences or similarities.

In general, it is not enough to catalogue existing similarities and differences; these are only the starting point of inquiry. It is more important to show that cultural variations are facts having direction. To consider cultural differences in terms of change and direction is immediately to transcend the static position of relativism. It is not enough to say that some societies observe rules of cleanliness and others do not. It would be more consequential to ask whether one can as readily teach one group to adopt the habits of cleanliness as another to surrender them; whether one can as readily convert an American community to curing illness by sorcery as persuade a primitive group to adopt modern medical practices. It is not enough to say for example that the musical tastes of Japanese and Europeans differ. It is more significant to ask what the reactions of Japanese and Europeans would be to both forms of music when they have mastered each. If we proceed in this way we are likely to find that changes have a direction and that often the direction is irreversible because of the sensible character of some psychological processes. Instead of comparing men and societies as they are, it is more fruitful to study the tendencies they show in the course of change.

This discussion has not attempted to settle the extent to which values are invariant, but rather to suggest a way of thinking about their identities and differences. In particular, it has described an alternative to the positions of absolutism and relativism. In contrast to the former, we have taken into account the facts of cultural diversity. At the same time we have tried to go beyond the sheer factual demonstration of diversity. The first two positions, although entirely opposed in their conclusions, are at one on an essential point of theory. They reach opposed conclusions on the basis of the same technical assumption of elementarism; therefore they agree that the sole alternatives are between them. Indeed, it would be right to say that each rests its case on the failure of the other. Relativism argues that if there are valid standards they must everywhere be the same and that the variability of standards is evidence that they are arbitrary. Absolutism, on the other hand, seeks to preserve the validity of standards at the cost of ignoring observed differences. If, however, we take into account the structural properties of experience and action we can understand that standards are relative without abandoning the concept of a human nature. It is necessary to acknowledge that science, art, and moral convictions at no time express completely the facts of the world or human needs; in this general sense there is relativism. But we need also to see these achievements as part of the history of human development, as the strivings of an authentic human nature. If we follow this path we will not treat all social facts as equally arbitrary or identify what is with what is right. Instead we will consider what societies do to realize human possibilities or to stunt them.

SUGGESTED READINGS

Some philosophers have written empirical studies of the ethical codes of primitive peoples: two such works are R. B. Brandt's *Hopi Ethics* and John Ladd's *The Structure of a Moral Code,* which deals with the Navaho. Usually, however, such work is done by anthropologists. Robert Redfield's *The Primitive World and Its Transformations* is an excellent example of recent discussion. The philosopher A. Macbeath summarizes much empirical work in his *Experiments in Living.* Among older works, those of E. Westermarck should be especially noted; in *Ethical Relativity* he produced one of the classic statements of the doctrine. For philosophical criticism of it, see B. Blanshard, *Reason and Goodness,* Chapter 5.

The first two chapters of W. T. Stace's *The Concept of Morals* contain a simple and clear presentation of relativism. R. B. Brandt has a more advanced analysis in Chapter 5 of his *Ethical Theory.* A. Edel presents a lengthy discussion in *Ethical Judgement,* Part I. In *The Logic of Moral Discourse,* Chapter 2, Paul Edwards gives a clear introductory discussion of the relations between relativism and subjectivisim, and criticises the two views. Since these two types of view are related, in some of their versions, the reader may wish to see G. E. Moore's important criticisms of subjectivism, in *Ethics,* Chapters 3 and 4. Moore's views are an expansion of points made by H. Sidgwick in *The Methods of Ethics,* Book I, Chapter 3. B. Mayo defends relativism against some of the usual criticisms in Chapter 3 of *Ethics and the Moral Life.* A. Murphy, *The Theory of Practical Reason,* Chapter 13, though difficult, is valuable in presenting a view which attempts to give an adequate place to the variety of moral codes without accepting moral relativism.

B. Reason and Morality

Although the problem of relativism continues to be an important issue in ethical theory, recent discussions have tended to focus attention on the issue of whether ethical assertions are capable of rational justification. One of the first accounts of moral judgments to bring this topic into the forefront of recent discussion was the contention of A. J. AYER that moral utterances are neither true nor false. Such utterances are on his view not even meaningful in the same sense as are, say, statements in physics or chemistry. They are more like such exclamations as "Ouch!" or "Wow!" We do not regard these utterances as true or false: they are "noncognitive" and nonrational, expressing feelings and emotions.

Ayer's view was regarded as a serious challenge to the rationality of morality by many philosophers, and many of them tried to offer alternative views on the role of reason in morality. HARE's view is in many ways close to Ayer's. He thinks of ethical utterances as being like commands, which are neither true nor false. But he holds that one can give reasons for commands and therefore one can give reasons for at least some of one's moral beliefs. The most fundamental moral beliefs, however, cannot, according to Hare, be proved. Hence the foundation of one's system of morality must simply be accepted by making a "decision" for which no reason can be given. BAIER rejects this view, arguing instead that one can give good reasons for adopting "the moral point of view." Once one has adopted this stance, he can distinguish true from false moral beliefs and can give reasons to support his judgment in any particular case. The reasons that can be given are essentially reasons appealing to self-interest. Baier thinks that it would be unreasonable to reject these considerations, so that if his claims are generally sound he has given a rational foundation to morality. MURPHY presents quite a different attempt to show how morality is rational. He rejects both Hare's groundless "decision" and Baier's egoistic foundation and argues that only a man who is already to some extent moral can raise or even understand moral questions. To be moral is to have at least some moral beliefs and to have some understanding of what it is to support these with reasons. To try to argue with a man who is not moral in this way is hopeless, but this does not show, Murphy thinks, that there is no "real" foundation for morality. What it shows is that such a person needs the kind of training children need before they are in a position to discuss morality.

The Emotive Theory[*]

Alfred Jules Ayer [1910–   ] was educated at Oxford and taught there and at London before assuming his present professorship at Oxford. His articles and books, of which *Language, Truth and Logic* is the most widely known, have been stimulating and influential contributions to analytic philosophy.

The ordinary system of ethics, as elaborated in the works of ethical philosophers, is very far from being a homogeneous whole. Not only is it apt to contain pieces of metaphysics, and analyses of non-ethical concepts: its actual ethical contents are themselves of very different kinds. We may divide them, indeed, into four main classes. There are, first of all, propositions which express definitions of ethical terms, or judgments about the legitimacy or possibility of certain definitions. Secondly, there are propositions describing the phenomena of moral experience, and their causes. Thirdly, there are exhortations to moral virtue. And, lastly, there are actual ethical judgments. It is unfortunately the case that the distinction between these four classes, plain as it is, is commonly ignored by ethical philosophers; with the result that it is often very difficult to tell from their works what it is that they are seeking to discover or prove.

In fact, it is easy to see that only the first of our four classes, namely that which comprises the propositions relating to the definitions of ethical terms, can be said to constitute ethical philosophy. The propositions which describe the phenomena of moral experience, and their causes, must be assigned to the science of psychology, or sociology. The exhortations to moral virtue are not propositions at all, but ejaculations or commands which are designed to provoke the reader to action of a certain sort. Accordingly, they do not belong to any branch of philosophy or science. As for the expressions of ethical judgments, we have not yet determined how they should be classified. But inasmuch as they are certainly neither definitions nor comments upon definitions, nor quotations, we may say decisively that they do not belong to ethical philosophy. A strictly philosophical treatise on ethics should therefore make no ethical pronouncements. But it should, by giving an analysis of ethical terms, show what is the category to which all such pronouncements belong. And this is what we are now about to do.

[*] From Ayer: *Language, Truth and Logic,* Chapter 6. Victor Gollancz Ltd., London; Dover Publications, New York. Copyright, 1936, by Victor Gollancz Ltd. Reprinted by permission of Victor Gollancz Ltd. and Dover Publications.

A question which is often discussed by ethical philosophers is whether it is possible to find definitions which would reduce all ethical terms to one or two fundamental terms. But this question, though it undeniably belongs to ethical philosophy, is not relevant to our present enquiry. We are not now concerned to discover which term, within the sphere of ethical terms, is to be taken as fundamental; whether, for example, "good" can be defined in terms of "right" or "right" in terms of "good," or both in terms of "value." What we are interested in is the possibility of reducing the whole sphere of ethical terms to non-ethical terms. We are enquiring whether statements of ethical value can be translated into statements of empirical fact.

That they can be so translated is the contention of those ethical philosophers who are commonly called subjectivists, and of those who are known as utilitarians. For the utilitarian defines the rightness of actions, and the goodness of ends, in terms of the pleasure, or happiness, or satisfaction, to which they give rise; the subjectivist, in terms of the feelings of approval which a certain person, or group of people, has towards them. Each of these types of definition makes moral judgements into a sub-class of psychological or sociological judgments; and for this reason they are very attractive to us. For, if either was correct, it would follow that ethical assertions were not generically different from the factual assertions which are ordinarily contrasted with them; and the account which we have already given of empirical hypotheses would apply to them also.

Nevertheless we shall not adopt either a subjectivist or a utilitarian analysis of ethical terms. We reject the subjectivist view that to call an action right, or a thing good, is to say that it is generally approved of, because it is not self-contradictory to assert that some actions which are generally approved of are not right, or that some things which are generally approved of are not good. And we reject the alternative subjectivist view that a man who asserts that a certain action is right, or that a certain thing is good, is saying that he himself approves of it, on the ground that a man who confessed that he sometimes approved of what was bad or wrong would not be contradicting himself. And a similar argument is fatal to utilitarianism. We cannot agree that to call an action right is to say that of all the actions possible in the circumstances it would cause, or be likely to cause, the greatest happiness, or the greatest balance of pleasure over pain, or the greatest balance of satisfied over unsatisfied desire, because we find that it is not self-contradictory to say that it is sometimes wrong to perform the action which would actually or probably cause the greatest happiness, or the greatest balance of pleasure over pain, or of satisfied over unsatisfied desire. And since it is not self-contradictory to say that some pleasant things are not good, or that some bad things are desired, it cannot be the case that the sentence "x is good" is equivalent to "*x* is pleasant," or to "*x* is desired." And to every other variant of utilitarianism with which I am acquainted the same objection can be made. And therefore we should, I think, conclude that the validity of ethical judgements is not determined by the felicific tendencies of actions, any more than by the nature of people's feelings; but that it must be regarded as "absolute" or "intrinsic," and not empirically calculable.

If we say this, we are not, of course, denying that it is possible to invent a language in which all ethical symbols are definable in non-ethical terms, or even that it is desirable to invent such a language and adopt it in place of our own; what we are denying is that the suggested reduction of ethical to non-ethical statements is consistent with the conventions of our actual language. That is, we reject utilitarianism and subjectivism, not as proposals to replace our existing ethical notions by new ones, but as analyses of our existing ethical notions. Our contention is simply that, in our language, sentences which contain normative ethical symbols are not equivalent to sentences which express psychological propositions, or indeed empirical propositions of any kind.

It is advisable here to make it plain that it is only normative ethical symbols, and not descriptive ethical symbols, that are held by us to be indefinable in factual terms. There is a danger of confusing these two types of symbols, because they are commonly constituted by signs of the same sensible form. Thus a complex sign of the form "*x* is wrong" may constitute a sentence which expresses a moral judgement concerning a certain type of conduct, or it may constitute a sentence which states that a certain type of conduct is repugnant to the moral sense of a particular society. In the latter case, the symbol "wrong" is a descriptive ethical symbol, and the sentence in which it occurs expresses an ordinary sociological proposition; in the former case, the symbol "wrong" is a normative ethical symbol, and the sentence in which it occurs does not, we maintain, express an empirical proposition at all. It is only with normative ethics that we are at present concerned; so that whenever ethical symbols are used in the course of this argument without qualification, they are always to be interpreted as symbols of the normative type.

In admitting that normative ethical concepts are irreducible to empirical concepts, we seem to be leaving the way clear for the "absolutist" view of ethics—that is, the view that statements of value are not controlled by observation, as ordinary empirical propositions are, but only by a mysterious "intellectual intuition." A feature of this theory, which is seldom recognized by its advocates, is that it makes statements of value unverifiable. For it is notorious that what seems intuitively certain to one person may seem doubtful, or even false, to another. So that unless it is possible to provide some criterion by which one may decide between conflicting intuitions, a mere appeal to intuition is worthless as a test of a proposition's validity. But in the case of moral judgements, no such criterion can be given. Some moralists claim to settle the matter by saying that they "know" that their own moral judgements are correct. But such an assertion is of purely psychological interest, and has not the slightest tendency to prove the validity of any moral judgement. For dissentient moralists may equally well "know" that their ethical views are correct. And, as far as subjective certainty goes, there will be nothing to choose between them. When such differences of opinion arise in connection with an ordinary empirical proposition, one may attempt to resolve them by referring to, or actually carrying out, some relevant empirical test. But with regard to ethical statements, there is, on the "absolutist" or "intuitionist" theory, no relevant empirical test. We are therefore justified in saying that on this theory ethical statements are held to be unverifiable. They are, of course, also held to be genuine synthetic propositions.

Considering the use which we [wish to make] of the principle that a synthetic proposition is significant only if it is empirically verifiable, it is clear that the acceptance of an "absolutist" theory of ethics would undermine the whole of our main argument. And as we have already rejected the "naturalistic" theories which are commonly supposed to provide the only alternative to "absolutism" in ethics, we seem to have reached a difficult position. We shall meet the difficulty by showing that the correct treatment of ethical statements is afforded by a third theory, which is wholly compatible with our radical empiricism.

We begin by admitting that the fundamental ethical concepts are unanalysable, inasmuch as there is no criterion by which one can test the validity of the judgements in which they occur. So far we are in agreement with the absolutists. But, unlike the absolutists, we are able to give an explanation of this fact about ethical concepts. We say that the reason why they are unanalysable is that they are mere pseudo-concepts. The presence of an ethical symbol in a proposition adds nothing to its factual content. Thus if I say to someone, "You acted wrongly in stealing that money," I am not stating anything more than if I had simply said, "You stole that money." In adding that this action is wrong I am not making any further statement about it. I am simply evincing my moral disapproval of it. It is as if I had said, "You stole that money," in a peculiar tone of horror, or written it with the addition of some special exclamation marks. The tone, or the exclamation marks, adds nothing to the literal meaning of the sentence. It merely serves to show that the expression of it is attended by certain feelings in the speaker.

If now I generalise my previous statement and say, "Stealing money is wrong," I produce a sentence which has no factual meaning—that is, expresses no proposition which can be either true or false. It is as if I had written "Stealing money!!"—where the shape and thickness of the exclamation marks show, by a suitable convention, that a special sort of moral disapproval is the feeling which is being expressed. It is clear that there is nothing said here which can be true or false. Another man may disagree with me about the wrongness of stealing, in the sense that he may not have the same feelings about stealing as I have, and he may quarrel with me on account of my moral sentiments. But he cannot, strictly speaking, contradict me. For in saying that a certain type of action is right or wrong, I am not making any factual statement, not even a statement about my own state of mind. I am merely expressing certain moral sentiments. And the man who is ostensibly contradicting me is merely expressing his moral sentiments. So that there is plainly no sense in asking which of us is in the right. For neither of us is asserting a genuine proposition.

What we have just been saying about the symbol "wrong" applies to all normative ethical symbols. Sometimes they occur in sentences which record ordinary empirical facts besides expressing ethical feeling about those facts: sometimes they occur in sentences which simply express ethical feeling about a certain type of action, or situation, without making any statement of fact. But in every case in which one would commonly be said to be making an ethical judgement, the function of the relevant ethical word is purely "emotive." It is used to express feeling about certain objects, but not to make any assertion about them.

It is worth mentioning that ethical terms do not serve only to express feeling. They are calculated also to arouse feeling, and so to stimulate action. Indeed some of them are used in such a way as to give the sentences in which they occur the effect of commands. Thus the sentence "It is your duty to tell the truth" may be regarded both as the expression of a certain sort of ethical feeling about truthfulness and as the expression of the command "Tell the truth." The sentence "You ought to tell the truth" also involves the command "Tell the truth," but here the tone of the command is less emphatic. In the sentence "It is good to tell the truth" the command has become little more than a suggestion. And thus the "meaning" of the word "good," in its ethical usage, is differentiated from that of the word "duty" or the word "ought." In fact we may define the meaning of the various ethical words in terms both of the different feelings they are ordinarily taken to express, and also the different responses which they are calculated to provoke.

We can now see why it is impossible to find a criterion for determining the validity of ethical judgements. It is not because they have an "absolute" validity which is mysteriously independent of ordinary sense-experience, but because they have no objective validity whatsoever. If a sentence makes no statement at all, there is obviously no sense in asking whether what it says is true or false. And we have seen that sentences which simply express moral judgements do not say anything. They are pure expressions of feeling and as such do not come under the category of truth and falsehood. They are unverifiable for the same reason as a cry of pain or a word of command is unverifiable—because they do not express genuine propositions.

Thus, although our theory of ethics might fairly be said to be radically subjectivist, it differs in a very important respect from the orthodox subjectivist theory. For the orthodox subjectivist does not deny, as we do, that the sentences of a moralizer express genuine propositions. All he denies is that they express propositions of a unique non-empirical character. His own view is that they express propositions about the speaker's feelings. If this were so, ethical judgements clearly would be capable of being true or false. They would be true if the speaker had the relevant feelings, and false if he had not. And this is a matter which is, in principle, empirically verifiable. Furthermore they could be significantly contradicted. For if I say, "Tolerance is a virtue," and someone answers, "You don't approve of it," he would, on the ordinary subjectivist theory, be contradicting me. On our theory, he would not be contradicting me, because, in saying that tolerance was a virtue, I should not be making any statement about my own feelings or about anything else. I should simply be evincing my feelings, which is not at all the same thing as saying that I have them.

The distinction between the expression of feeling and the assertion of feeling is complicated by the fact that the assertion that one has a certain feeling often accompanies the expression of that feeling, and is then, indeed, a factor in the expression of that feeling. Thus I may simultaneously express boredom and say that I am bored, and in that case my utterance of the words, "I am bored," is one of the circumstances which make it true to say that I am expressing or evincing boredom. But I can express boredom without actually saying that I am bored. I can express it by my tone and gestures, while making a statement about something wholly unconnected with it, or by an ejaculation, or without uttering any words at all. So that even if the assertion that one has a certain feeling always involves the expression of that feeling, the expression of a feeling assuredly does not always involve the assertion that one has it. And this is the important point to grasp in considering the distinction between our theory and the ordinary subjectivist theory. For whereas the subjectivist holds that ethical statements actually assert the existence of certain feelings, we hold that ethical statements are expressions and excitants of feeling which do not necessarily involve any assertions.

We have already remarked that the main objection to the ordinary subjectivist theory is that the validity of ethical judgements is not determined by the nature of their author's feelings. And this is an objection which our theory escapes. For it does not imply that the existence of any feelings is a necessary and sufficient condition of the validity of an ethical judgement. It implies, on the contrary, that ethical judgements have no validity.

There is, however, a celebrated argument against subjectivist theories which our theory does not escape. It has been pointed out by Moore that if ethical statements were simply statements about the speaker's feelings, it would be impossible to argue about questions of value. To take a typical example: if a man said that thrift was a virtue, and another replied that it was a vice, they would not, on this theory, be disputing with one another. One would be saying that he approved of thrift, and the other that *he* didn't; and there is no reason why both these statements should not be true. Now Moore held it to be obvious that we do dispute about questions of value, and accordingly concluded that the particular form of subjectivism which he was discussing was false.

It is plain that the conclusion that it is impossible to dispute about questions of value follows from our theory also. For as we hold that such sentences as "Thrift is a virtue" and "Thrift is a vice" do not express propositions at all, we clearly cannot hold that they express incompatible propositions. We must therefore admit that if Moore's argument really refutes the ordinary subjectivist theory, it also refutes ours. But, in fact, we deny that it does refute even the ordinary subjectivist theory. For we hold that one really never does dispute about questions of value.

This may seem, at first sight, to be a very paradoxical assertion. For we certainly do engage in disputes which are ordinarily regarded as disputes about questions of value. But, in all such cases, we find, if we consider the matter closely, that the dispute is not really about a question of value, but about a question of fact. When someone disagrees with us about the moral value of a certain action or type of action, we do admittedly resort to argument in order to win him over to our way of thinking. But we do not attempt to show by our arguments that he has the "wrong" ethical feeling towards a situation whose nature he has correctly apprehended. What we attempt to show is that he is mistaken about the facts of the case. We argue that he has misconceived the agent's motive: or that he has misjudged the effects of the action, or its probable effects in view of the agent's knowledge; or that he has failed to take into account the special circumstances in which the agent was placed. Or else we employ more general arguments about the effects which actions of a certain type tend to produce, or the qualities which are usually manifested in their performance. We do this in the hope that we have only to get our opponent to agree with us about the nature of the empirical facts for him to adopt the same moral attitude towards them as we do. And as the people with whom we argue have generally received the same moral education as ourselves, and live in the same social order, our expectation is usually justified. But if our opponent happens to have undergone a different process of moral "conditioning" from ourselves, so that, even when he acknowledges all the facts, he still disagrees with us about the moral value of the actions under discussion, then we abandon the attempt to convince him by argument. We say that it is impossible to argue with him because he has a distorted or undeveloped moral sense; which signifies merely that he employs a different set of values from our own. We feel that our own system of values is superior, and therefore speak in such derogatory terms of his. But we cannot bring forward any arguments to show that our system is superior. For our judgement that it is so is itself a judgement of value, and accordingly outside the scope of argument. It is because argument fails us when we come to deal with pure questions of value, as distinct from question of facts, that we finally resort to mere abuse.

In short, we find that argument is possible on moral questions only if some system of values is presupposed. If our opponent concurs with us in expressing moral disapproval of all actions of a given type t, then we may get him to condemn a particular action A, by bringing forward arguments to show that A is of type t. For the question whether A does or does not belong to that type is a plain question of fact. Given that a man has certain moral principles, we argue that he must, in order to be consistent, react morally to certain things in a certain way. What we do not and cannot argue about is the validity of these moral principles. We merely praise or condemn them in the light of our own feelings.

If anyone doubts the accuracy of this account of moral disputes, let him try to construct even an imaginary argument on a question of value which does not reduce itself to an argument about a question of logic or about an empirical matter of fact. I am confident that he will not succeed in producing a single example. And if that is the case, he must allow that its involving the impossibility of purely ethical arguments is not, as Moore thought, a ground of objection to our theory, but rather a point in favour of it.

Having upheld our theory against the only criticism which appeared to threaten it, we may now use it to define the nature of all ethical enquiries. We find that ethical philosophy consists simply in saying that ethical concepts are pseudo-concepts and therefore unanalysable. The further task of describing the different feelings that the different ethical terms are used to express, and the different reactions that they customarily provoke, is a task for the psychologist. There cannot be such a thing as ethical science, if by ethical science one means the elaboration of a "true" system of morals. For we have seen that, as ethical judgements are mere expressions of feeling, there can be no way of determining the validity of any ethical system, and, indeed, no sense in asking whether any such system is true. All that one may legitimately enquire in this connection is, What are the moral habits of a given person or group of people, and what causes them to have precisely those habits and feelings? And this enquiry falls wholly within the scope of the existing social sciences.

Imperatives, Morality, and Reasons[*]

RICHARD M. HARE [1919–   ], formerly a Fellow of Balliol College, is now Professor of Philosophy at Oxford. His two books, *The Language of Morals* (1952) and *Freedom and Reason* (1963), have been at the center of much recent discussion of philosophical ethics.

PRESCRIPTIVE LANGUAGE. If we were to ask of a person 'What are his moral principles?' the way in which we could be most sure of a true answer would be by studying what he *did*. He might, to be sure, profess in his conversation all sorts of principles, which in his actions he completely disregarded; but it would be when, knowing all the relevant facts of a situation, he was faced with choices or decisions between alternative courses of action, between alternative answers to the question 'What shall I do?', that he would reveal in what principles of conduct he really believed. The reason why actions are in a peculiar way revelatory of moral principles is that the function of moral principles is to guide conduct. The language of morals is one sort of prescriptive language. And this is what makes ethics worth studying: for the question 'What shall I do?' is one that we cannot for long evade; the problems of conduct, though sometimes less diverting than crossword puzzles, *have to be solved* in a way that crossword puzzles do not. We cannot wait to see the solution in the next issue, because on the solution of the problems depends what happens in the next issue. Thus, in a world in which the problems of conduct become every day more complex and tormenting, there is a great need for an understanding of the language in which these problems are posed and answered. . . .

[*] From Hare: *The Language of Morals*, Oxford, 1952, Chapters 1–4. Reprinted by permission of The Clarendon Press, Oxford, and the author.

I shall proceed from the simple to the more complex. I shall deal first with the simplest form of prescriptive language, the ordinary imperative sentence. The logical behaviour of this type of sentence is of great interest to the student of moral language because, in spite of its comparative simplicity, it raises in an easily discernible form many of the problems which have beset ethical theory. . . .

The temptation to reduce imperatives to indicatives is very strong, and has the same source as the temptation to analyse value-words in the way called 'naturalistic.' This is the feeling that the 'proper' indicative sentence, of which there is thought to be only one kind, is somehow above suspicion in a way that other sorts of sentence are not; and that therefore, in order to put these other sorts of sentence above suspicion, it is necessary to show that they are *really* indicatives. This feeling was intensified when the so-called 'verificationist' theory of meaning became popular. This theory, which is in many ways a very fruitful one in its proper sphere, holds, to put it roughly, that a sentence does not have meaning unless there is something that would be the case if it were true. Now this is a very promising account of one of the ways in which a certain class of sentences (the typical indicatives) have meaning. Obviously, if a sentence is claimed to express a statement of fact, and yet we have no idea what would be the case if it were true, then that sentence is (to us) meaningless. But if this criterion of meaningfulness, which is useful in the case of statements of fact, is applied indiscriminately to types of utterance which are not intended to express statements of fact, trouble will result. Imperative sentences do not satisfy this criterion, and it may be that sentences expressing moral judgements do not either; but this only shows that they do not express statements in the sense defined by the criterion; and this sense may be a narrower one than that of normal usage. It does not mean that they are meaningless, or even that their meaning is of such a character that no logical rules can be given for their employment.

The feeling, that only 'proper indicatives' are above suspicion, can survive (surprisingly) the discovery that there are perfectly good significant sentences of our ordinary speech which are not reducible to indicatives. It survives in the assumption that any meaning which is discovered for these sentences must necessarily be of some logically inferior status to that of indicatives. This assumption has led philosophers such as Professor A. J. Ayer, in the course of expounding their most valuable researches into the logical nature of moral judgements, to make incidental remarks which have raised needless storms of protest. The substance of Ayer's theory is that moral judgements do not ordinarily function in the same way as the class of indicative sentences marked out by his verification-criterion. But by his way of stating his view, and his assimilation of moral judgements to other (quite distinct) types of sentence which are also marked off from typical indicatives by this criterion, he stirred up dust which has not yet subsided. All this might be closely paralleled by a similar treatment of imperatives—and it seems that writers of the same general line of thought as Ayer would have said the same sort of thing about imperatives as they did about moral judgements. Suppose that we recognize the obvious fact that imperatives are not like typical indicatives. Suppose, further, that we regard only typical indicatives as above suspicion. It will be natural then to say 'Imperatives do not state anything, they only express wishes.' Now to say that imperatives express wishes is, like the first theory which we considered, unexceptionable on the colloquial plane; we would indeed say, if someone said 'Keep my name out of this,' that he had expressed a wish to have his name kept out of it. But nevertheless the extreme ambiguity of the word 'express' may generate philosophical confusion. We speak of expressing statements, opinions, beliefs, mathematical relations, and so on; and if it is in one of these senses that the word is used, the theory, though it tells us little, is harmless. But unfortunately it is also used in ways which are unlike these; and Ayer's use (in speaking of moral judgements) of the word 'evince' as its rough synonym was dangerous. Artists and composers and poets are said to express their own and our feelings; oaths are said to express anger; and dancing upon the table may express joy. Thus to say that imperatives express wishes may lead the unwary to suppose that what happens when we use one, is this: we have welling up inside us a kind of longing, to which, when the pressure gets too great for us to bear, we give vent by saying an imperative sentence. Such an interpretation, when applied to such sentences as 'Supply and fit to door mortise dead latch and plastic knob furniture,' is unplausible. And it would seem that value judgements also may fail to satisfy the verification-criterion, and indeed be in some sense, like imperatives, prescriptive, without having this sort of thing said about them. It is perfectly unexceptionable, on the colloquial plane, to say that the sentence 'A is good' is used to express approval of A (*The Shorter Oxford English Dictionary* says: 'Approve: . . . to pronounce to be good'); but it is philosophically misleading if we think that the approval which is expressed is a peculiar warm feeling inside us. If the Minister of Local Government expresses approval of my town plan by getting his underlings to write to me saying 'The Minister approves of your plan' or 'The Minister thinks your plan is the best one,' I shall in no circumstances confirm the letter by getting a private detective to observe the Minister for signs of emotion. In this case, to have such a letter sent *is* to approve. . . .

. . . We shall need, in this inquiry, to consider only the inference from universal imperative sentences, together with indicative minor premisses, to singular imperative conclusions. . . . If it were impossible to make inferences of this kind, the word 'all' would have no meaning in commands. But this type of inference does raise a further difficulty, because one of the premisses is in the indicative, and one in the imperative. The inference is:

> Take all the boxes to the station.
> This is one of the boxes.
> ∴ Take this to the station.

It might be asked how we are to know, given two premisses in different moods, in what mood the conclusion is to be. The problem of the effect upon inferences of the moods of premisses and conclusion has been ignored by logicians who have not looked beyond the indicative mood; though there is no reason why they should have ignored it. . . .

Let me first state two of the rules that seem to govern this matter; we may leave till later the question of their justification. The rules are:

(1) *No indicative conclusion can be validly drawn from a set of premisses which cannot be validly drawn from the indicatives among them alone.*

(2) *No imperative conclusion can be validly drawn from a set of premisses which does not contain at least one imperative.*

It is only the second rule which will concern us in this inquiry. There is a very important apparent exception to this rule, the so-called 'hypothetical imperative,' with which I shall deal in the next chapter. For the moment, however, let us take the rule as it stands. It is of the most profound importance for ethics. . . . If we admit, as I shall later maintain, that it must be part of the function of a moral judgement to prescribe or guide choices, that is to say, to entail an answer to some question of the form 'What shall I do?' —then it is clear, from the second of the rules just stated, that no moral judgement can be a pure statement of fact. . . .

INFERENCE. The rule that an imperative cannot appear in the conclusion of a valid inference, unless there is at least one imperative in the premisses, may be confirmed by an appeal to general logical considerations. For it is now generally regarded as true by definition that (to speak roughly at first) nothing can appear in the conclusion of a valid deductive inference which is not, from their very meaning, implicit in the conjunction of the premisses. It follows that, if there is an imperative in the conclusion, not only must *some* imperative appear in the premisses, but that very imperative must be itself implicit in them.

Since these considerations have a wide bearing on moral philosophy, it will be as well to explain them in greater detail. Few people now think, as Descartes seems to have done, that we can arrive at scientific conclusions about matters of empirical fact, like the circulation of the blood, by deductive reasoning from self-evident first principles. The work of Wittgenstein and others has to a great extent made clear the reasons for the impossibility of doing this. It has been argued, convincingly in my opinion, that all deductive inference is analytic in character; that is to say, that the function of a deductive inference is not to get from the premisses 'something further' not implicit in them (even if that is what Aristotle meant), but to make explicit what was implicit in the conjunction of the premisses. . . .

[These] considerations about inference . . . mean that a Cartesian procedure, either in science or in morals, is doomed from the very start. If any science is intended to give us conclusions of substance about matters of fact, then, if its method is deductive, these conclusions must be implicit in the premisses. This means that, before we fully understand the meanings of our Cartesian first principles, we have to know that they (with the addition only of definitions of terms) entail such various propositions as, that all mules are barren, or that a man's heart is on the left-hand side of his body, or that the sun is so many miles from the earth. But if all these facts are implicit in the first principles, the latter can hardly be called self-evident. We find out about facts like these at least in part by observation; no amount of reasoning from axioms will take its place. The position of pure mathematics has been much discussed and is still obscure; it seems best to regard the axioms of pure mathematics and logic as definitive of the terms used in them. But this much, at any rate, may be said, that if a science purports to tell us facts like the above, it cannot, like pure mathematics, be based on deductive reasoning and nothing else. It was the mistake of Descartes to assimilate to pure mathematics studies which are of a wholly different character.

It does not follow, from the fact that deduction, whether in the form of pure mathematics or of logic, cannot take the place of observation, that deduction is therefore altogether useless as an adjunct to observation. Science makes use of expressions which would be altogether meaningless unless we could deduce. The sentence 'There are three gramme weights on the balance and no more' would be meaningless to anyone who could not deduce from it 'There is one gramme weight on the balance, and one other, and one other, and no more,' and vice versa.

The same considerations hold good in ethics. Many of the ethical theories which have been proposed in the past may without injustice be called

'Cartesian' in character; that is to say, they try to deduce particular duties from some self-evident first principle. Often factual observations are admitted among the premises; but this, though it makes the theories which admit them incompletely 'Cartesian,' does not affect my argument. A Cartesian procedure in morals is as illusory as it is in science. If we may take it that, as I shall show later, a piece of genuinely evaluative moral reasoning must have as its end-product an imperative of the form 'Do so-and-so,' it follows that its principles must be of such a kind that we can deduce such particular imperatives from them, in conjunction with factual minor premisses. If, for example, a moral system is to enjoin me not to say this particular thing which is false, its principles must contain implicitly or explicitly an imperative to the effect that what is false is not to be said in circumstances like those in which I now am. And, similarly, they must contain other imperatives such as will regulate my conduct in all manner of circumstances, both foreseen and unforeseen. But it is obvious that such a set of principles could not possibly be self-evident. It is not easier, but more difficult, to assent to a very general command like 'Never say what is false' than it is to assent to the particular command 'Do not say this particular thing which is false,' just as it is more difficult and dangerous to adopt the hypothesis that all mules are barren than to acknowledge the undoubted fact that this mule which has just died has had no progeny. A decision never to say what is false involves a decision in advance about a very great number of individual cases, with only the information about them that they are all cases of saying what is false. It is not, surely, casuistry of an objectionable kind to want to avoid committing ourselves in this fashion. It is quite true that, when we have had experience of making such decisions, we may eventually find ourselves able to accept the general principle. But suppose that we were faced, for the first time, with the question 'Shall I now say what is false?' and had no past decisions, either of our own or of other people, to guide us. How should we then decide the question? Not, surely, by inference from a self-evident general principle, 'Never say what is false'; for if we could not decide even whether to say what was false in these particular circumstances, how could we possibly decide whether to say what was false in innumerable circumstances whose details were totally unknown to us, save in this respect, that they were all cases of saying what was false?

The same point may be put in another way. It is an established principle of logic that if one proposition entails another, then the negation of the second entails the negation of the first. An analogous principle, somewhat stronger, is also valid, that if I know that one proposition entails another, to be in doubt about assenting to the second is *eo ipso* to be in doubt about assenting to the first. For instance, if I know that the proposition 'All mules are barren and this is a mule' entails the proposition 'This (mule) is barren,' it follows that if I am in doubt about assenting to the proposition 'This (mule) is barren,' I must be in doubt about assenting to the proposition 'All mules are barren and this is a mule'; and this means that I must be in doubt about either 'All mules are barren' or 'This is a mule.' Now if we apply an exactly parallel reasoning to our case about saying what is false, we get the following result. Since I am in doubt, *ex hypothesi*, whether or not to make this false statement, I must be in doubt about assenting to the command 'Do not make this statement.' But if I am in doubt about this command, I must *eo ipso* be in doubt, either about the factual premiss 'This statement is false' (and this alternative is ruled out *ex hypothesi*), or else, as must be the case, about the imperative premiss 'Never say what is false.' It follows that no general principle can be self-evident which is to be of assistance in deciding particular questions about which we are in doubt.

The impossibility of a 'Cartesian' moral system may be shown in another way, closely akin to the one just explained. It is not in the least clear what could be meant by calling any proposition, least of all a general principle of conduct, 'self-evident.' If such a principle is to be in some sense impossible to reject, this, it seems to me, can only be for one of two reasons. First, it might be said that a principle of conduct was impossible to reject, if it were *self-contradictory* to reject it. But if it is self-contradictory to reject a principle, this can only be because the principle is analytic. But if it is analytic, it cannot have any content; it cannot tell me to do one thing rather than another. The term 'analytic,' which we shall have occasion to use a good deal, may be defined with sufficient precision as follows: A sentence is analytic if, and only if, either (1) the fact that a person dissents from it is a sufficient criterion for saying that he has misunderstood the speaker's meaning or (2) it is entailed by some sentence which is analytic in sense (1). A sentence which is not analytic or self-contradictory is called synthetic. These definitions are of course not exact; a full discussion of the meanings of 'analytic' and 'synthetic' is outside the scope of this book.

Secondly, it might be suggested that a principle of conduct might be impossible to reject, in the sense that its rejection was a psychological impossibility. But what is or is not a psychological impossibility is a contingent matter; it may be a psychological impossibility for *me* to reject a principle which the more hardened or sophisticated have no difficulty in discarding. We could never have any justification for asserting that no one could ever reject a principle, unless that principle were analytic. Moreover, the psychological impossibility of rejecting a principle would be a fact about the constitution of people's psyches; and from a fact, or the indicative sentence recording it, no imperative can be derived.

A third kind of interpretation is sometimes canvassed, which rests upon the introduction of a value-word. It might be suggested that, though a principle was both logically and psychologically possible to reject, it might be not *rational* to reject it (it might be impossible for a rational person to reject it). Sometimes instead of 'rational' we have other expressions, such as 'a morally developed or morally educated person' or 'a competent and impartial judge.' These are all value-expressions. We therefore have to ask 'What could be the criterion for deciding whether a person falls into one or other of these classes?' Clearly we cannot say that the rejection of the principle is itself evidence that the person who rejects it is not qualified in these ways; for in this case our criterion of self-evidence would be circular. There must therefore be some other means of finding out whether a person is rational. But the question whether a person is rational must be either a factual question or a question of value (or a combination of the two). If it is a purely factual question, then we cannot get imperative conclusions out of factual premisses such as 'So-and-so is rational' and 'So-and-so finds it impossible to reject the principle that . . . .' But if it is wholly or partly a question of value, then either the answer to it is self-evident in some sense (in which case again our criterion of self-evidence would be circular), or else we have at least one constituent in our reasoning which is neither factual nor self-evident. This third possibility, therefore, must be ruled out.

It follows from these considerations that if it is the function of general moral principles to regulate our conduct, *i.e.* to entail, in conjunction with indicative minor premisses, answers to questions of the form 'Shall I or shall I not do this particular thing?' then these general moral principles cannot be self-evident. If this view of the function of moral principles were accepted (and I shall later give reasons for doing so), it would provide a conclusive refutation of a large number of ethical theories. Suppose, for example, that we find a philosopher telling us that it is self-evident that we ought always to do what our conscience tells us; we must answer that, since we are often in doubt whether or not to do some act which our conscience tells us to do, this general principle cannot be self-evident. And even if it were the case that we never were in doubt on this point, this would be merely a fact about our psyches, and no imperative conclusions would follow from it. . . .

DECISIONS OF PRINCIPLE. There are two factors which may be involved in the making of any decision to do something. Of these, the first may at any rate theoretically be absent, the second is always present to some degree. They correspond to the major and minor premisses of the Aristotelian practical syllogism. The major premiss is a principle of conduct; the minor premiss is a statement, more or less full, of what we should in fact be doing if we did one or other of the alternatives open to us. Thus if I decide not to say something, because it is false, I am acting on a principle, 'Never (or never under certain conditions) say what is false,' and I must know that this, which I am wondering whether to say, is false.

Let us take the minor premiss first, since it presents less difficulty. We plainly cannot decide what to do unless we know at least something about what we should be doing if we did this or that. For example, suppose that I am an employer, and am wondering whether or not to sack a clerk who habitually turns up at the office after the hour at which he has undertaken to turn up. If I sack him I shall be depriving his family of the money on which they live, perhaps giving my firm a reputation which will lead clerks to avoid it when other jobs are available, and so on; if I keep him, I shall be causing the other clerks to do work which otherwise would be done by this clerk; and the affairs of the office will not be transacted so quickly as they would if all the clerks were punctual. These would be the sorts of consideration that I should take into account in making my decision. They would be the effects on the total situation of the alternative actions, sacking him or not sacking him. It is the effects which determine what I should be doing; it is between the two sets of effects that I am deciding. The whole point about a decision is that it makes a difference to what happens; and this difference is the difference between the effects of deciding one way, and the effects of deciding the other.

It sometimes seems to be implied by writers on ethics that it is immoral, on certain sorts of occasion, to consider the effects of doing something. We ought, it is said, to do our duty no matter what the effects of doing it. As I am using the word 'effects,' this cannot be maintained. I am not making a claim for 'expediency' (in the bad sense) as against 'duty.' Even to do our duty—in so far as it is *doing* something—is effecting certain changes in the total situation. It is quite true that, of the changes that it is possible to effect in the total situation, most people would agree that we ought to consider certain kinds more relevant than others (which than which, it is the purpose of moral principles to tell us). I do not think that the immediacy or remoteness of the effects makes any difference, though their certainty or uncertainty does. The reason why it is considered immoral to fail to right an injustice whose effects will maximize pleasure, is not that in such a choice the effects are considered when they should not have been; it is that certain of the effects—namely, the maximization of pleasure—are given a relevance which they should not have, in view of the prior claim of those other effects which would have consisted in the righting of the injustice. . . .

[I]t is most important, in a verbal exposition of an argument about what to do, not to allow value-words in the minor premiss. In setting out the facts of the case, we should be as factual as we can. Those versed in the logic of these words, and therefore forewarned against its pitfalls, may in the interests of brevity neglect this precaution; but for the inexperienced it is very much better to keep value-expressions where they belong, in the major premiss. This will prevent the inadvertent admission of an ambiguous middle term . . . I do not mean that in discussing the facts of the case we should not admit any words which could possibly have an evaluative meaning; for this, in view of the way in which evaluative meaning pervades our language, would be well-nigh impossible. I only mean that we must be sure that, as we are using the words in the minor premiss, there are definite tests (not themselves involving evaluation) for ascertaining its truth or falsity. In the last paragraph I was using the word 'pleasure' in such a sense, though it is not always so used.

The relation between the two premisses may perhaps be made clearer by considering an artificial example. Let us suppose that a man has a peculiar kind of clairvoyance such that he can know everything about the effects of all the alternative actions open to him. But let us suppose that he has so far formed for himself, or been taught, no principles of conduct. In deciding between alternative courses of action, such a man would know, fully and exactly, between what he was deciding. We have to ask to what extent, if any, such a man would be handicapped, in coming to a decision, by not having any formed principles. It would seem beyond doubt that he could choose between two courses; it would be strange, even, to call such a choice necessarily arbitrary or ungrounded; for if a man knows to the last detail exactly what he is doing, and what he might otherwise have done, his choice is not arbitrary in the sense in which a choice would be arbitrary if made by the toss of a coin without any consideration of the effects. But suppose that we were to ask such a man 'Why did you choose this set of effects rather than that? Which of the many effects were they that led you to decide the way you did?' His answer to this question might be of two kinds. He might say 'I can't give any reasons; I just felt like deciding that way; another time, faced with the same choice, I might decide differently.' On the other hand, he might say 'It was this and this that made me decide; I was deliberately avoiding such and such effects, and seeking such and such.' If he gave the first of these two answers, we might in a certain sense of that word call his decision arbitrary (though even in that case he had *some* reason for his choice, namely, that he felt that way); but if he gave the second, we should not.

Let us see what is involved in this second type of answer. Although we have assumed that the man has no formed principles, he shows, if he gives the second answer, that he has started to form principles for himself; for to choose effects *because* they are such and such is to begin to act on a principle that such and such effects are to be chosen. We see in this example that in order to act on principle it is not necessary in some sense to have a principle already, before you act; it may be that the decision to act in a certain way, because of something about the effects of acting in that way, *is* to subscribe to a principle of action—though it is not necessarily to adopt it in any permanent sense. . . .

We must not think that, if we can decide between one course and another without further thought (it seems self-evident to us, which we should do), this necessarily implies that we have some mysterious intuitive faculty which tells us what to do. A driver does not know when to change gear by intuition; he knows it because he has learnt and not forgotten; what he knows is a principle, though he cannot formulate the principle in words. The same is true of moral decisions which are sometimes called 'intuitive.' We have moral 'intuitions' because we have learnt how to behave, and have different ones according to how we have learnt to behave.

It would be a mistake to say that all that had to be done to a man to make him into a good driver was to tell him, or otherwise inculcate into him, a lot of general principles. This would be to leave out the factor of decision. Very soon after he begins to learn, he will be faced with situations to deal with which the provisional principles so far taught him require modification; and he will then have to decide what to do. He will very soon discover which decisions were right and which wrong, partly because his instructor tells him, and partly because having seen the effects of the decisions he determines in future not to bring about such effects. On no account must we commit the mistake of supposing that decisions and principles occupy two separate spheres and do not meet at any point. All decisions except those, if any, that are completely arbitrary are to some extent decisions of principle. We are always setting precedents for ourselves. It is not a case of the principle settling everything down to a certain point, and decision dealing with everything below that point. Rather, decision and principles interact throughout the whole field. Suppose that we have a principle to act in a certain way in certain circumstances. Suppose then that we find ourselves in circumstances which fall under the principle, but which have certain other peculiar features, not met before, which make us ask 'Is the principle really intended to cover cases like this, or is it incompletely specified—is there here a case belonging to a class which should be treated as exceptional?' Our answer to this question will be a decision, but a decision of principle, as is shown by the use of the value-word 'should.' If we decide that this should be an exception, we thereby modify the principle by laying down an exception to it.

Suppose, for example, that in learning to drive I have been taught always to signal before I slow down or stop, but have not yet been taught what to do when stopping in an emergency; if a child leaps in front of my car, I do not signal, but keep both hands on the steering-wheel; and thereafter I accept the former principle with this exception, that in cases of emergency it is better to steer than to signal. I have, even on the spur of the moment, made a decision of principle. To understand what happens in cases like this is to understand a great deal about the making of value-judgments. . . .

It would be folly, however, to say that there is only one way of learning a skill or any other body of principles, or of justifying a particular decision made in the practice of it. There are many ways, and I have tried to make the above account sufficiently general to cover all of them. It is sometimes said by writers on morals that we have to justify an act by reference to its effects, and that we tell which effects are to be sought, which avoided, by reference to some principle. Such a theory is that of the utilitarians, who bid us look at the effects, and examine these in the light of the principle of utility, to see which effects would maximize pleasure. Sometimes, on the other hand, it is said . . . that an act is justified directly by reference to the principles which it observes, and these principles in their turn by reference to the effects of always observing them. Sometimes it is said that we should observe principles and ignore the effects—though for the reasons given above 'effects' cannot be here intended in the sense in which I have been using it. What is wrong with these theories is not what they say, but their assumption that they are telling us the only way to justify actions, or decide what actions to do. We do, indeed, justify and decide on actions in all these ways; for example, sometimes, if asked why we did A, we say, 'Because it was a case falling under principle P,' and if asked to justify P in turn, we go into the effects of observing it and of not observing it. But sometimes, when asked the same question 'Why did you do A?' we say 'Because if I hadn't, E would have happened,' and if asked what was wrong about E happening, we appeal to some principle.

The truth is that, if asked to justify as completely as possible any decision, we have to bring in both effects—to give content to the decision—and principles, and the effects in general of observing those principles, and so on, until we have satisfied our inquirer. Thus a complete justification of a decision would consist of a complete account of its effects, together with a complete account of the principles which it observed, and the effects of observing those principles—for, of course, it is the effects (what obeying them in fact consists in) which give content to the principles too. Thus, if pressed to justify a decision completely, we have to give a complete specification of the way of life of which it is a part. This complete specification it is impossible in practice to give; the nearest attempts are those given by the great religions, especially those which can point to historical persons who carried out the way of life in practice. Suppose, however, that we can give it. If the inquirer still goes on asking 'But why *should* I live like that?' then there is no further answer to give him, because we have already, *ex hypothesi*, said everything that could be included in this further answer. We can only ask him to make up his own mind which way he ought to live; for in the end everything rests upon such a decision of principle. He has to decide whether to accept that way of life or not; if he accepts it, then we can proceed to justify the decisions that are based upon it; if he does not accept it, then let him accept some other, and try to live by it. The sting is in the last clause. To describe such ultimate decisions as arbitrary, because *ex hypothesi* everything which could be used to justify them has already been included in the decision, would be like saying that a complete description of the universe was utterly unfounded, because no further fact could be called upon in corroboration of it. This is not how we use the words 'arbitrary' and 'unfounded.' Far from being arbitrary, such a decision would be the most well-founded of decisions, because it would be based upon a consideration of everything upon which it could possibly be founded.

It will be noticed how, in talking of decisions of principle, I have inevitably started talking value-language. Thus we decide that the principle *should* be modified, or that it is *better* to steer than to signal. This illustrates the very close relevance of what I have been saying in the first part of this book to the problems of the second part; for to make a value-judgement is to make a decision of principle.

Moral Argument, Self-Interest, and Morality[*]

K u r t E. M. B a i e r [1917–   ], born in Vienna, studied at the Universities of Melbourne and Oxford. After teaching at Melbourne and Cornell, he came in 1962 to the University of Pittsburgh, where he is now Professor of Philosophy. He has written on ethics and philosophical psychology.

MORAL CONVICTIONS CAN BE TRUE OR FALSE. It is often argued that our moral convictions are merely expressions of our feelings, emotions, or attitudes, or that they are commands or pseudo commands, and that, therefore, they cannot be true or false. It might be added that they must have some kind of imperatival force, for it must be possible to act in accordance with or contrary to them. But one cannot act in accordance with or contrary to truths or facts. Truths or facts are compatible with any sort of behavior. Truths are, therefore, useless in morality. There we need something in the nature of precepts.

This argument is unsound. Moral convictions can be true or false and also imperatival. To say 'Killing is wrong' is to say that killing constitutes the contravention of a certain sort of rule or commandment, 'Don't kill,' 'Thou shalt not kill.' Hence, 'Killing is wrong' may be true or false, for it may or may not be the contravention of such a rule. On the other hand, it also makes this remark imperatival, for killing is thereby declared to be the contravention of a rule or commandment. If, in a train, I say to my neighbor, 'No smoking in here,' I say something which can be true or false (for it may or may not be a nonsmokers') and also imperatival (for if it is a nonsmokers', then there is a rule forbidding smoking in the compartment). Thus, what makes 'No smoking in here' and 'Killing is wrong' capable of being true or false is the fact that the rules alluded to by these remarks are capable of passing a certain test. 'No smoking in here' can be true (or false), because the rule 'No smoking in this compartment' is (or is not) properly laid down by the Railway Company which is (or is not) entitled to do so. Our main task will, of course, be to show what are the appropriate tests which a moral rule must pass in order that remarks alluding to it should be said to be true. We have to answer questions such as what are the tests which the rule 'Thou shalt not kill' must pass if it is to be true that killing is wrong.

The proof that moral convictions could be true or false and also imperatival seems to me to constitute quite a strong argument in favor of saying that they actually are true or false, for this is what we all naturally think. The only reason why we have doubts is that philosophers have various reasons for saying that propositions cannot be both imperatival and true or false. However, in view of the great popularity of the emotive and imperativalist theories, it is perhaps not out of place to devote some additional space to establishing this conclusion.

My main contention is that we could not properly speak of *a morality*, as opposed to a system of conventions, customs, or laws, until the question of the correctness or incorrectness, truth or falsity, of the rules prevalent in a community is asked, until, in other words, the prevalent rules are subjected to certain tests. It is only when the current rules are no longer regarded as sacrosanct, as incapable of alteration or improvement, only when the current rules are contrasted with other possible, improved, ideal rules, that a group can be said to have a morality as opposed to a mere set of taboos. . . .

TRUE MORALITIES AND ABSOLUTE MORALITY. Our discussion has brought to light an essential characteristic of a morality: that it should make sense to ask, 'But are these moral convictions true?' or 'Is this moral code correct?' or words to that effect. The question implies that the moral rules and convictions of any group can and should be subjected to certain tests. It implies a distinction between this and that morality on the one hand and true morality on the other.

Let us be quite clear, however, what this distinction amounts to. It is not, in the first place, that between 'a morality' and 'morality as such,' which is analogous to the distinction between a legal system and law as such or between a disease and disease as such. Talking about a morality, say Greek or Tikopia or *fin de siècle* morality, is like talking about Roman, canonic, or Napoleonic law, or about Bright's disease, cancer, or leprosy. But talking about morality as such or the nature of morality is like talking about law as such or the nature of law, disease as such or the nature of disease. When talking in this way, we are drawing attention to the essentials of the concept. We are thinking of the conditions which something must satisfy in order to be properly called 'a morality,' 'a legal system,' 'a disease.' . . .

I shall, then, distinguish between true moralities and absolute morality. True moralities are actually embodied moralities, those forming part of a given way of life of a society or an individual, which would pass a certain test, if they were subjected to it. Absolute morality, on the other hand, is that set of moral convictions, whether held by anyone or not, which is true quite irrespective of any particular social conditions in which they might be embodied. Every true morality must contain as its core the convictions belonging to absolute morality, but it may also contain a lot more that could not be contained in every other true morality. . . .

POINTS OF VIEW. What, then, is the test (if any) which a moral conviction must pass in order to be called true? Many philosophers have held that there is not and cannot be such a test. They would perhaps admit that we may reduce our moral convictions to a few basic moral principles, or perhaps even only one, from which all others can be derived, but they would hold that at least one such principle must simply be selected as we please. Such basic principles are matters for deciding, not for finding out.

I shall argue, on the contrary, that our moral convictions are true if they can be seen to be required or acceptable *from the moral point of view.* . . .

Suppose the problem under discussion is whether or not a certain traffic roundabout should be erected at a certain intersection. I can look at this from various points of view, that of a pedestrian or a motorist, a local politician or a manufacturer of roundabouts, and so on. In cases such as these, we have in mind the point of view of self-interest as applied to certain special positions or jobs or functions in a society. To look at our problem from the point of view of a motorist is to ask whether the erection of a roundabout at this intersection is in the interest of a motorist. For different points of view there may, of course, be different, even opposing, answers to the same practical questions. The roundabout may be in the interest of a motorist but not of a pedestrian, in the interest of a manufacturer of roundabouts but not of a local politician who depends for his votes on the poorer section (the pedestrians) of the population.

However, a point of view is not necessarily defined by the principle of self-interest or its more specific application to a particular position in society. We can, for instance, look at this problem from the point of view of town planners or traffic experts, who may favor the roundabout because their special task is to solve traffic problems. Their point of view is defined by the principle 'Favor anything that keeps the traffic flowing; oppose anything that is likely to cause traffic holdups.' But the erection of the roundabout can hardly be said to be *in their interest.* They do not derive any personal advantage or benefit from the scheme. There are many such disinterested points of view, for example, the point of view of a social worker, a social reformer, an advocate of public health schemes, a missionary.

A person is of good will if he adopts the moral point of view as supreme, that is, as overriding all other points of view. When asking the question 'What shall I do?' or 'What is to be done?' such a person will always engage in moral deliberation, survey and weigh the moral considerations, and give them greater weight than any others. A person has adopted the moral point of view when he reviews the facts in the light of *his* moral convictions. We do not require him to test his moral convictions every time, but only because we presume that he already has true moral convictions. This presumption may be false. He may simply have accepted without much questioning the moral convictions of his group, or he may have departed from them without getting any nearer the truth. In such a case, he merely *means* to adopt the moral point of view, but has not succeeded. He has adopted something which he wrongly believes to be the moral point of view. He must still be called a person of good will because of his intentions, but he cannot arrive at true answers to his question.

Clearly, our central problem is to define the moral point of view. . . .

[THE MORAL POINT OF VIEW.] Throughout the history of philosophy, by far the most popular candidate for the position of the moral point of view has been self-interest. There are obvious parallels between these two standpoints. Both aim at the good. Both are rational. Both involve deliberation, the surveying and weighing of reasons. The adoption of either yields state-

ments containing the word 'ought.' Both involve the notion of self-mastery
and control over the desires. It is, moreover, plausible to hold that a person
could not have a reason for doing anything whatsoever unless his behavior
was designed to promote his own good. Hence, if morality is to have the support of reason, moral reasons must be self-interested, hence the point of view
of morality and self-interest must be the same. On the other hand, it seems
equally obvious that morality and self-interest are very frequently opposed.
Morality often requires us to refrain from doing what self-interest recom-
mends or to do what self-interest forbids. Hence morality and self-interest
cannot be the same points of view.

Self-interest and morality. Can we save the doctrine that the moral point
of view is that of self-interest? One way of circumventing the difficulty just
mentioned is to draw a distinction between two senses of 'self-interest,'
shortsighted and enlightened. The shortsighted egoist always follows his
short-range interest without taking into consideration how this will affect
others and how their reactions will affect him. The enlightened egoist, on
the other hand, knows that he cannot get the most out of life unless he pays
attention to the needs of others on whose good will he depends. On this
view, the standpoint of (immoral) egoism differs from that of morality in
that it fails to consider the interests of others even when this costs little or
nothing or when the long-range benefits to oneself are likely to be greater
than the short-range sacrifices.

This view can be made more plausible still if we distinguish between
those egoists who consider each course of action on its own merits and those
who, for convenience, adopt certain rules of thumb which they have found
will promote their long-range interest. Slogans such as 'Honesty is the best
policy,' 'Give to charity rather than to the Department of Internal Revenue,'
'Always give a penny to a beggar when you are likely to be watched by your
acquaintances,' 'Treat your servants kindly and they will work for you like
slaves,' 'Never be arrogant to anyone—you may need his services one day,'
are maxims of this sort. They embody the "wisdom" of a given society. The
enlightened long-range egoist may adopt these as rules of thumb, that is, as
prima-facie maxims, as rules which he will observe unless he has good evidence that departing from them will pay him better than abiding by them.
It is obvious that the rules of behavior adopted by the enlightened egoist
will be very similar to those of a man who rigidly follows our own moral
code.

Sidgwick appears to believe that egoism is one of the legitimate "methods
of ethics," although he himself rejects it on the basis of an "intuition" that it
is false. He supports the legitimacy of egoism by the argument that everyone
could consistently adopt the egoistic point of view. "I quite admit that when

the painful necessity comes for another man to choose between his own happiness and the general happiness, he must as a reasonable being prefer his own, i.e. it is right for him to do this on my principle." The consistent enlightened egoist satisfies the categorical imperative, or at least one version of it, 'Act only on that maxim whereby thou canst at the same time will that it should become a universal law.'

However, no "intuition" is required to see that this is not the point of view of morality, even though it can be universally adopted without self-contradiction. In the first place, a consistent egoist adopts for all occasions the principle 'everyone for himself' which we allow (at most) only in conditions of chaos, when the normal moral order breaks down. Its adoption marks the return to the law of the jungle, the state of nature, in which the "softer," "more chivalrous" ways of morality have no place.

This point can be made more strictly. It can be shown that those who adopt consistent egoism cannot make moral judgments. Moral talk is impossible for consistent egoists. But this amounts to a *reductio ad absardum* of consistent egoism.

Let B and K be candidates for the presidency of a certain country and let it be granted that it is in the interest of either to be elected, but that only one can succeed. It would then be in the interest of B but against the interest of K if B were elected, and vice versa, and therefore in the interest of B but against the interest of K if K were liquidated, and vice versa. But from this it would follow that B ought to liquidate K, that it is wrong for B not to do so, that B has not "done his duty" until he has liquidated K; and vice versa. Similarly K, knowing that his own liquidation is in the interest of B and therefore anticipating B's attempts to secure it, ought to take steps to foil B's endeavors. It would be wrong for him not to do so. He would "not have done his duty" until he had made sure of stopping B. It follows that if K prevents B from liquidating him, his act must be said to be both wrong and not wrong—wrong because it is the prevention of what B ought to do, his duty, and wrong for B not to do it; not wrong because it is what K ought to do, his duty, and wrong for K not to do it. But one and the same act (logically) cannot be both morally wrong and not morally wrong. Hence in cases like these morality does not apply.

This is obviously absurd. For morality is designed to apply in just such cases, namely, those where interests conflict. But if the point of view of morality were that of self-interest, then there could *never* be moral solutions of conflicts of interest. However, when there are conflicts of interest, we always look for a "higher" point of view, one from which such conflicts can be settled. Consistent egoism makes everyone's private interest the "highest court of appeal." But by 'the moral point of view' we *mean* a point of view which is a court of appeal for conflicts of interest. Hence it cannot (logically) be identical with the point of view of self-interest. Sidgwick is, therefore, wrong in thinking that consistent egoism is one of the "legitimate methods of ethics." He is wrong in thinking that an "intuition" is required to see that it is not the correct moral point of view. That it is not can be seen in the same way in which we can "see" that the Court of Petty Sessions is not the Supreme Court.

Morality involves doing things on principle. Another feature of consistent egoism is that the rules by which a consistent egoist abides are merely rules of thumb. A consistent egoist has only one supreme principle, to do whatever is necessary for the realization of his one aim, the promotion of his interest. He does not have *principles,* he has only an aim. If one has adopted the moral point of view, then one acts on principle and not merely on rules of thumb designed to promote one's aim. This involves conforming to the rules whether or not doing so favors one's own or anyone else's aim.

Kant grasped this point even if only obscurely. He saw that adopting the moral point of view involves acting on principle. It involves conforming to rules even when doing so is unpleasant, painful, costly, or ruinous to oneself. Kant, furthermore, argued rightly that, since moral action is action on principle (and not merely in accordance with rules of thumb), a moral agent ought not to make exceptions in his own favor, and he interpreted this to mean that moral rules are absolutely inflexible and without exceptions. Accordingly he concluded that if 'Thou shalt not kill' states a moral rule, then any and every act correctly describable as an act of killing someone must be said to be morally wrong.

Kant also saw that this view required him to reject some of our deepest moral convictions; we certainly think that the killing of a man in self-defense or by the hangman is not morally wrong. Kant was prepared to say that our moral convictions are wrong on this point. Can we salvage these moral convictions? The only alternative, to say that acting on principle does not require us not to make exceptions in our own favor, seems to be equally untenable.

It is therefore not surprising that many philosophers have abandoned Kant's (and the commonsense) view that the moral rightness of an act is its property of being in accordance with a moral rule or principle. Thus, the deontologists claim that rightness is a simple property which we can "see" or "intuit" in an act, and the utilitarians, that rightness is a complex property, namely, the tendency of an act to promote the greatest happiness of the greatest number. But, as is well known, these accounts are not plausible and lead to considerable difficulties.

However, this whole problem arises only because of a confusion, the confusion of the expression 'making an exception to a rule' with the expression 'a rule has an exception.' As soon as this muddle is cleared away, it can be seen that Kant is right in saying that acting on principle implies making no exception in anyone's favor, but wrong in thinking that therefore all moral rules must be absolutely without exception.

'No parking in the city' has a number of recognized exceptions which are part of the rule itself, for example, 'except in the official parking areas,' 'except in front of a parking meter,' 'except on Saturday mornings and after 8 P.M. every day.' A person who does not know the recognized exceptions does not completely know the rule, for these exceptions more precisely define its range of application. A policeman who is not booking a motorist parking in front of a parking meter is not granting exemption to (making an exception in favor of) this motorist. On the contrary, he is administering the rule correctly. If he did apply the no-parking rule to the motorist, *he* would be applying it where *it* does not apply, because this is one of the recognized exceptions which are *part of* the rule. On the other hand, a policeman who does not book a motorist parking his vehicle in a prohibited area at peak hour on a busy day is making an exception in the motorist's favor. If he does so because the man is his friend, he illegitimately grants an exemption. If he does so because the motorist is a doctor who has been called to attend to a man lying unconscious on the pavement, this is a "deserving case" and he grants the exemption legitimately.

Apply this distinction to the rules of a given morality. Notice first that moral rules differ from laws and regulations in that they are not administered by special administrative organs such as policemen and magistrates. Everyone "administers" them himself. Nevertheless, it makes sense to speak of making exceptions in one's own favor. For one may refuse to apply the rule to oneself when one knows that it does apply, that is to say, one may refuse to observe it even when one knows one should. And what is true of making exceptions in one's own favor is true also of making them in favor of someone else. It is almost as immoral to make exceptions in favor of one's wife, son, or nephew as in favor of oneself.

When we say, therefore, that a person who has killed a burglar in self-defense has not done anything wrong, we are not making an exception in the houseowner's favor. It is much nearer the truth to say that, in our morality, the rule 'Thou shalt not kill' *has several recognized exceptions,* among them 'in self-defense.' We can say that a man does not know fully our moral rule 'Thou shalt not kill' if he does not know that it has, among others, this exception.

Like other rules of reason, our moral convictions are so only *presumptively*. Killing is wrong *unless* it is killing in self-defense, killing by the hangman, killing of an enemy in wartime, accidental killing, and possibly mercy killing. If it is one of these types of killing, then it is *not* wrong.

Even if it is one of the wrongful acts of killing, it is so only *prima facie*, other things being equal. For there may have been an overriding moral reason in favor of killing the man, for example, that he is about to blow up a train and that this is the only way of stopping him.

One further point should be made to avoid misunderstanding. Unlike laws and regulations, moral rules have not been laid down by anyone. Knowing moral rules cannot, therefore, involve knowing exactly what a certain person has enjoined and forbidden and what exceptions he has allowed, because there is no such person. In the case of regulation and laws, it was precisely this knowledge which enabled us to draw the distinction between saying that someone was granting an exception and saying that he was merely applying the rule which, for cases of this sort, provided for an exception. Our distinction seems to collapse for moral rules.

However, the answer to this is simple. When a magistrate is empowered to make exceptions or grant exemptions in "deserving cases," the question of what is a "deserving case" is not of course answered in the regulation itself. If it were, the magistrate would not be exercising his power to grant exemption, but would simply apply the regulation as provided in it. How, then, does the magistrate or policeman know what is a deserving case? The doctor who parks his car in a prohibited spot in order to attend to an injured man is such a case, namely, a *morally deserving* case. The principles in accordance with which policemen or magistrates grant exemptions to existing regulations are moral principles. In the case of moral rules, there cannot be any distinction between exceptions which are part of the rule and deserving cases. *Only* deserving cases can be part of the moral rule, and *every* deserving case is properly part of it. Hence while in the case of laws and regulations there is a reason for going beyond the exceptions allowed in the regulation itself (when there is a morally deserving instance), in the case of moral rules there is no such reason. For all deserving cases are, from the nature of the case, part of the moral rule itself. Hence it is never right to make an exception to a moral rule in anyone's favor. Kant is therefore quite right in saying that it is always wrong to make exceptions to moral rules in one's own favor (and for that matter in anyone else's), but he is wrong in thinking that this makes moral rules inflexible.

All this follows from the very nature of moral principles. They are binding on everyone alike quite irrespective of what are the goals or purposes of the person in question. Hence self-interest cannot be the moral point of view, for it sets every individual one supreme goal, his own interest, which overrules all his other maxims.

Moral rules are meant for everybody. The point of view of morality is inadequately characterized by saying that *I* have adopted it if *I* act on principles, that is, on rules to which I do not make exceptions whenever acting on them would frustrate one or the other of my purposes or desires. It is characterized by greater universality than that. It must be thought of as a standpoint from which principles are considered as being acted on *by everyone.* Moral principles are not merely principles on which a person must always act without making exceptions, but they are principles *meant for everybody.* . . .

Moral rules must be for the good of everyone alike. The conditions so far mentioned are merely formal. They exclude certain sorts of rule as not coming up to the formal requirements. But moral rules should also have a certain sort of content. Observation of these rules should be *for the good of everyone alike.* Thrasymachus' view that justice is the advantage of the stronger, if true of the societies of his day, is an indictment of their legal systems from the moral point of view. It shows that what goes by the name of morality in these societies is no more than a set of rules and laws which enrich the ruling class at the expense of the masses. But this is wrong because unjust, however much the rules satisfy the formal criteria. For given certain initial social conditions, formal equality before the law may favor certain groups and exploit others.

There is one obvious way in which a rule may be for the good of everyone alike, namely, if it furthers the common good. When I am promoted and my salary is raised, this is to my advantage. It will also be to the advantage of my wife and my family and possibly of a few other people—it will not be to the advantage of my colleague who had hoped for promotion but is now excluded. It may even be to his detriment if his reputation suffers as a result. If the coal miners obtain an increase in their wages, then this is to the advantage of coal miners. It is for their common good. But it may not be to the advantage of anyone else. On the other hand, if production is raised and with it everyone's living standard, that is literally to everyone's advantage. The rule 'Work harder,' if it has these consequences, is for the common good of all.

Very few rules, if any, will be for the common good of everyone. But a rule may be in the interest of everyone alike, even though the results of the observation of the rule are not for the common good in the sense explained. Rules such as 'Thou shalt not kill,' 'Thou shalt not be cruel,' 'Thou shalt not lie' are obviously, in some other sense, for the good of everyone alike. What is this sense? It becomes clear if we look at these rules from the moral point of view, that is, that of an independent, unbiased, impartial, objective, dispassionate, disinterested observer. Taking such a God's-eye point of view, we can see that it is in the interest of everyone alike that everyone should abide by the rule 'Thou shalt not kill.' From the moral point of view, it is clear that it is in the interest of everyone alike if everyone alike should be allowed to pursue his own interest provided this does not adversely affect someone else's interests. Killing someone in the pursuit of my interests would interfere with his.

There can be no doubt that such a God's-eye point of view is involved in the moral standpoint. The most elementary teaching is based on it. The negative version of the so-called Golden Rule sums it up: 'Don't do unto others as you would not have them do unto you.' When we teach children the moral point of view, we try to explain it to them by getting them to put themselves in another person's place: 'How would you like to have that done to you!' 'Don't do evil,' the most readily accepted moral rule of all, is simply the most general form of stating this prohibition. For doing evil is the opposite of doing good. Doing good is doing for another person what, if he were following (self-interested) reason, he would do for himself. Doing evil is doing to another person what it would be contrary to reason for him to do to himself. Harming another, hurting another, doing to another what he dislikes having done to him are the specific forms this takes. Killing, cruelty, inflicting pain, maiming, torturing, deceiving, cheating, rape, adultery are instances of this sort of behavior. They all violate the condition of "reversibility," that is, that the behavior in question must be acceptable to a person whether he is at the "giving" or "receiving" end of it.

It is important to see just what is established by this condition of being for the good of everyone alike. In the first place, anyone is doing wrong who engages in nonreversible behavior. It is irrelevant whether he knows that it is wrong or not, whether the morality of his group recognizes it or not. Such behavior is "wrong in itself," irrespective of individual or social recognition, irrespective of the consequences it has. Moreover, every single act of such behavior is wrong. We need not consider the whole group or the whole of humanity engaging in this sort of behavior, but only a single case. Hence we can say that all nonreversible behavior is morally wrong; hence that anyone engaging in it is doing what, *prima facie,* he ought not to do. We need not consider whether this sort of behavior has harmful consequences, whether it is forbidden by the morality of the man's group, or whether he himself thinks it wrong.

The principle of reversibility does not merely impose certain prohibitions on a moral agent, but also certain positive injunctions. It is, for instance, wrong—an omission—not to help another person when he is in need and when we are in a position to help him. The story of the Good Samaritan makes this point. The positive version of the Golden Rule makes the same

point more generally: 'Do unto others as you would have them do unto you.'
Note that it is wrong—not merely not meritorious—to omit to help others
when they are in need and when you are in a position to help them. It does
not follow from this, however, that it is wrong not to promote the greatest
good of the greatest number, or not to promote the greatest amount of good
in the world. Deontologists and utilitarians alike make the mistake of thinking that it is one, or the only one, of our moral duties to "do the optimific
act." Nothing could be further from the truth. We do not have a duty to do
good to others or to ourselves, or to others and/or to ourselves in a judicious
mixture such that it produces the greatest possible amount of good in the
world. We are morally required to do good only to those who are actually in
need of our assistance. The view that we always ought to do the optimific
act, or whenever we have no more stringent duty to perform, would have
the absurd result that we are doing wrong whenever we are relaxing, since
on those occasions there will always be opportunities to produce greater
good than we can by relaxing. For the relief of suffering is always a greater
good than mere enjoyment. Yet it is quite plain that the worker who, after a
tiring day, puts on his slippers and listens to the wireless is not doing anything he ought not to, is not neglecting any of his duties, even though it may
be perfectly true that there are things he might do which produce more
good in the world, even for himself, than merely relaxing by the fireside. . . .

The supremacy of moral reasons. Are moral reasons really superior to reasons of self-interest as we all believe? Do we really have reason on our side
when we follow moral reasons against self-interest? What reasons could
there be for being moral? Can we really give an answer to 'Why should we
be moral?' It is obvious that all these questions come to the same thing.
When we ask, 'Should we be moral?' or 'Why should we be moral?' or 'Are
moral reasons superior to all others?' we ask to be shown the reason for
being moral. What is this reason?

Let us begin with a state of affairs in which reasons of self-interest are
supreme. In such a state everyone keeps his impulses and inclinations in
check when and only when they would lead him into behavior detrimental
to his own interest. Everyone who follows reason will discipline himself to
rise early, to do his exercises, to refrain from excessive drinking and smoking,
to keep good company, to marry the right sort of girl, to work and study
hard in order to get on, and so on. However, it will often happen that people's interests conflict. In such a case, they will have to resort to ruses or
force to get their own way. As this becomes known, men will become suspicious, for they will regard one another as scheming competitors for the
good things in life. The universal supremacy of the rules of self-interest must
lead to what Hobbes called the state of nature. At the same time, it will be

clear to everyone that universal obedience to certain rules overriding self-interest would produce a state of affairs which serves everyone's interest much better than his unaided pursuit of it in a state where everyone does the same. Moral rules are universal rules designed to override those of self-interest when following the latter is harmful to others. 'Thou shalt not kill,' 'Thou shalt not lie,' 'Thou shalt not steal' are rules which forbid the inflicting of harm on someone else even when this might be in one's interest.

The very *raison d'être* of a morality is to yield reasons which overrule the reasons of self-interest in those cases when everyone's following self-interest would be harmful to everyone. Hence moral reasons are superior to all others.

"But what does this mean?" it might be objected. "If it merely means that we do so regard them, then you are of course right, but your contention is useless, a mere point of usage. And how could it mean any more? If it means that we not only do so regard them, but *ought* so to regard them, then there must be *reasons* for saying this. But there could not be any reasons for it. If you offer reasons of self-interest, you are arguing in a circle. Moreover, it cannot be true that it is always in my interest to treat moral reasons as superior to reasons of self-interest. If it were, self-interest and morality could never conflict, but they notoriously do. It is equally circular to argue that there are moral reasons for saying that one ought to treat moral reasons as superior to reasons of self-interest. And what other reasons are there?"

The answer is that we are now looking at the world from the point of view of *anyone*. We are not examining particular alternative courses of action before this or that person; we are examining two alternative worlds, one in which moral reasons are always treated by everyone as superior to reasons of self-interest and one in which the reverse is the practice. And we can see that the first world is the better world, because we can see that the second world would be the sort which Hobbes describes as the state of nature.

This shows that I ought to be moral, for when I ask the question 'What ought I to do?' I am asking, 'Which is the course of action supported by the best reasons?' But since it has just been shown that moral reasons are superior to reasons of self-interest, I have been given a reason for being moral, for following moral reasons rather than any other, namely, they are better reasons than any other.

But is this always so? Do we have a reason for being moral whatever the conditions we find ourselves in? Could there not be situations in which it is not true that we have reasons for being moral, that, on the contrary, we have reasons for ignoring the demands of morality? Is not Hobbes right in saying that in a state of nature the laws of nature, that is, the rules of morality, bind only *in foro interno*?

Hobbes argues as follows.

(i) To live in a state of nature is to live outside society. It is to live in conditions in which there are no common ways of life and, therefore, no reliable expectations about other people's behavior other than that they will follow their inclination or their interest.

(ii) In such a state reason will be the enemy of co-operation and mutual trust. For it is too risky to hope that other people will refrain from protecting their own interests by the preventive elimination of probable or even possible dangers to them. Hence reason will counsel everyone to avoid these risks by preventive action. But this leads to war.

(iii) It is obvious that everyone's following self-interest leads to a state of affairs which is desirable from no one's point of view. It is, on the contrary, desirable that everybody should follow rules overriding self-interest whenever that is to the detriment of others. In other words, it is desirable to bring about a state of affairs in which all obey the rules of morality.

(iv) However, Hobbes claims that in the state of nature it helps nobody if a single person or a small group of persons begins to follow the rules of morality, for this could only lead to the extinction of such individuals or groups. In such a state, it is therefore contrary to reason to be moral.

(v) The situation can change, reason can support morality, only when the presumption about other people's behavior is reversed. Hobbes thought that this could be achieved only by the creation of an absolute ruler with absolute power to enforce his laws. We have already seen that this is not true and that it is quite different if people live in a society, that is, if they have common ways of life, which are taught to all members and somehow enforced by the group. Its members have reason to expect their fellows generally to obey its rules, that is, its religion, morality, customs, and law, even when doing so is not, on certain occasions, in their interest. Hence they too have reason to follow these rules.

Is this argument sound? One might, of course, object to step (i) on the grounds that this is an empirical proposition for which there is little or no evidence. For how can we know whether it is true that people in a state of nature would follow only their inclinations or, at best, reasons of self-interest, when nobody now lives in that state or has ever lived in it?

However, there is some empirical evidence to support this claim. For in the family of nations, individual states are placed very much like individual persons in a state of nature. The doctrine of the sovereignty of nations and the absence of an effective international law and police force are a guarantee that nations live in a state of nature, without commonly accepted rules that are somehow enforced. Hence it must be granted that living in a state of nature leads to living in a state in which individuals act either on impulse or

as they think their interest dictates. For states pay only lip service to morality. They attack their hated neighbors when the opportunity arises. They
start preventive wars in order to destroy the enemy before he can deliver his
knockout blow. Where interests conflict, the stronger party usually has his
way, whether his claims are justified or not. And where the relative strength
of the parties is not obvious, they usually resort to arms in order to determine "whose side God is on." Treaties are frequently concluded but, morally
speaking, they are not worth the paper they are written on. Nor do the partners regard them as contracts binding in the ordinary way, but rather as
public expressions of the belief of the governments concerned that for the
time being their alliance is in the interest of the allies. It is well understood
that such treaties may be canceled before they reach their predetermined
end or simply broken when it suits one partner. In international affairs, there
are very few examples of *Nibelungentreue*, although statesmen whose countries have profited from keeping their treaties usually make such high moral
claims.

It is, moreover, difficult to justify morality in international affairs. For suppose a highly moral statesman were to demand that his country adhere to a
treaty obligation even though this meant its ruin or possibly its extinction.
Suppose he were to say that treaty obligations are sacred and must be kept
whatever the consequences. How could he defend such a policy? Perhaps
one might argue that someone has to make a start in order to create mutual
confidence in international affairs. Or one might say that setting a good example is the best way of inducing others to follow suit. But such a defense
would hardly be sound. The less skeptical one is about the genuineness of
the cases in which nations have adhered to their treaties from a sense of
moral obligation, the more skeptical one must be about the effectiveness of
such examples of virtue in effecting a change of international practice.
Power politics still govern in international affairs.

We must, therefore, grant Hobbes the first step in his argument and admit
that in a state of nature people, as a matter of psychological fact, would not
follow the dictates of morality. But we might object to the next step that
knowing this psychological fact about other people's behavior constitutes a
reason for behaving in the same way. Would it not still be immoral for anyone to ignore the demands of morality even though he knows that others are
likely or certain to do so, too? Can we offer as a justification for morality the
fact that no one is entitled to do wrong just because someone else is doing
wrong? This argument begs the question whether it *is* wrong for anyone in
this state to disregard the demands of morality. It cannot be wrong to break
a treaty or make preventive war if we have no reason to obey the moral
rules. For to say that it is wrong to do so is to say that we ought not to do so.

But if we have no reason for obeying the moral rule, then we have no reason for overruling self-interest, hence no reason for keeping the treaty when keeping it is not in our interest, hence it is not true that we have a reason for keeping it, hence not true that we ought to keep it, hence not true that it is wrong not to keep it.

I conclude that Hobbes's argument is sound. Moralities are systems of principles whose acceptance by everyone as overruling the dictates of self-interest is in the interest of everyone alike, though following the rules of a morality is not of course identical with following self-interest. If it were, there could be no conflict between a morality and self-interest and no point in having moral rules overriding self-interest. Hobbes is also right in saying that the application of this system of rules is in accordance with reason only in social conditions, that is, when there are well-established ways of behavior.

The answer to our question 'Why should we be moral?' is therefore as follows. We should be moral because being moral is following rules designed to overrule self-interest whenever it is in the interest of everyone alike that everyone should set aside his interest. It is not self-contradictory to say this, because it may be in one's interest *not* to follow one's interest at times. We have already seen that enlightened self-interest acknowledges this point. But while enlightened self-interest does not require any genuine sacrifice from anyone, morality does. In the interest of the possibility of the good life for everyone, voluntary sacrifices are sometimes required from everybody. Thus, a person might do better for himself by following enlightened self-interest rather than morality. It is not possible, however, that *everyone* should do better for himself by following enlightened self-interest rather than morality. The best possible life *for everyone* is possible only by everyone's following the rules of morality, that is, rules which quite frequently may require individuals to make genuine sacrifices.

It must be added to this, however, that such a system of rules has the support of reason only where people live in societies, that is, in conditions in which there are established common ways of behavior. Outside society, people have no reason for following such rules, that is, for being moral. In other words, outside society, the very distinction between right and wrong vanishes.

Reason and the Moral Self [*]

ARTHUR EDWARD MURPHY [1901–1962] began his career at the University of California and subsequently taught at various universities in the United States: Chicago, Brown, Cornell, Illinois, Washington, and Texas. His primary interest was in moral philosophy and his books include *The Uses of Reason* (1943) and *The Theory of Practical Reason* (1965), from which the present selection was taken.

In the statement, "your brother needs your help," there is obviously a reference to matters of fact that must be factually certified if the statement is to present a rationally cogent ground for moral action. If the man in question is not my brother but an impostor, or if he does not need help, being in fact better off financially than I am, then no good reason for my helping him has been given. This reference to fact is basic and inescapable. "Because you promised" is not a good reason why I should attend X's lecture if I never promised to attend it. We need not elaborate the obvious.

But suppose the facts, in this sense, are admitted. He is my brother and he does need help that I, though perhaps at some sacrifice, could give him. As information this is unquestioned. Now what of it? "You ought, on this ground to give him the money." Is that another fact of the same sort, to be added to my store of information on the subject? No, it is supposed to follow from the facts already stated. Follow *how?* Can we deduce it syllogistically from the "premises" already supplied? No, we should need an additional normative premise for the purpose. All cases of helping needy brothers are cases of ought to be done actions. This is a case of helping a needy brother. Therefore this is an ought to be done action. Where did this normative major premise come from and how is its truth certified? Perhaps it is the conclusion of a prior syllogism. All actions that maximize happiness are cases of ought-to-be-done actions. All cases of helping brothers are cases of maximizing happiness. Therefore all cases of helping brothers are cases of ought to be done actions. The logic is impeccable, but we have again a major premise to be empirically or non-empirically (*a priori*) certified. This sort of thing can go on indefinitely and sometimes does. There seems no way out of

[*] From Murphy, *The Theory of Practical Reason,* copyright 1965 by The Open Court Publishing Company, LaSalle, Illinois. Reprinted by permission of The Open Court Publishing Company, LaSalle, Illinois.

it except to say at some point, "don't you *see* that this latest major premise (our "ethical first principle") is cognitively true?" or else to cut out the argument and issue orders, or to observe that, for persuasive purposes, the question of validity is "of no interest." Given this initial statement of the problem, the "isms" are hardly to be blamed for their attempts to cut, in this way, the Gordian knot that they themselves have tied.

There seems indeed to be no rational way out of this unhappy situation. But how did we get into it in the first place? Was this trip really necessary, or even well-advised? We have been looking for some additional premise that would establish the relevance as a ground for action of the information initially given. But it was not *as information* merely that "your brother needs your help" was thus presented and, if it is misunderstood as such, no accumulation of further premises, empirical or *a priori*, will "in the end" supply the cogency that has initially been missed. How shall the man who cannot understand that he has in these circumstances an obligation to the brother whom he has seen and lived with, "see" (in a quite different sense) that brotherhood in general entails the ought-to-be-doneness of helpful acts, or, perhaps, that all happiness maximizing actions have this remarkable property and that brother-helping acts are, in general, happiness-maximizing? A man who knows his duty only in this way does not in practice know what duty means, though he may nonetheless write books about its "meaning."

How *do* we come to understand that we have obligations to our brothers —that a brother's need is genuinely a ground of obligation for morally right action? We learn it, of course, as we share practically in the goods and the requirements of family life, *as* sons and brothers bound together by the ties of mutual concern that make the family a moral unit. This is not always as simple and easy a relationship as the word "brotherhood" suggests. Sibling rivalry has a part in it, and it may be suspected that if all men looked on each other as brothers they would still find much to quarrel about, as brothers do. But, where the family is indeed a moral unity, these quarrels are contained within the limits of an area of shared understanding and responsibility whose requirements of mutual regard and helpfulness are a *must* for right family living and are so understood by those for whom it is in fact a way of life. We *are* to some degree our brothers' keepers, and it was this *moral* truth that made Cain's crime so grave an offense. Hence the term "brother," in the statement of a ground of obligation is not a practically noncommittal term. To be a brother is not just to be a male sibling—it is a privilege, a burden and, whether we like it or not, a commitment. The man who understood in this way that his brother needed help would know in that acknowledgement, a reason why he ought to help him. And the man who could not in this way understand *some* obligation statements—whether those of brotherhood or some others—would never know why, on moral grounds, he *should* do anything rather than anything else, though he might see that he was prudentially well-advised to conform to rules that others understood as "obligations."

The reasons thus understood are, as are all practical reasons, reasons of the heart. It is not merely as ethical inquirers but as loving, hating, greedy, sympathetic, sociable and self-assertive beings, bound together in the ties of family life, that we understand such obligations and sometimes act accordingly. That is what it is to *be* a brother and it is as brothers that we are bound in this way to mutual helpfulness. What "brotherhood" would morally imply for a man who had no such emotions and "understood" moral requiredness only as he understood—say—a physical compulsion or the necessity that all triangles must have three sides we need not here inquire. For his sense of obligation would not be ours and ours, though he might accurately describe it sociologically, would have no moral significance for him. It is in this way that there is something peculiar, or distinctive, about moral obligation. If we choose, for analytic purposes, to ignore it, we may talk about something logically neater, epistemologically simpler or metaphysically deeper. But what we shall then be talking about will not be moral obligation, and we should not be surprised to find that it cannot in the end supply the moral relevance it ruled out of its calculations at the start.

"But, when we look at obligation statements in this light, what do we see?" "Don't you know? For there is nothing hidden." The "seeing" that is here required is not an intuition of self-evident (yet, in ethical theory, highly controversial) general principles of ought-to-be-doneness which are advanced, with complicated arguments, as the final grounds of moral right. It is that minimum of practical understanding required for membership in any community in which "right" can have a moral cogency for action, in which the requirements of a man's moral situation are recognized and used as grounds for warrantable claims that he is bound, as a brother, for example, or a citizen, to honor in his conduct. A man who could not in this way understand that "because you promised" was a reason why he ought to do a promised act would not know what it was to make a promise and to "bind" his conduct in this way, though he might be well aware that it was a rule of his society that sanctions of a predictable sort would be brought to bear on those who, having said "I promise," did not perform the action to which this locution was attached, and think it prudent to conform his behavior to this rule. A society in which men were bound together by no other ties than this would not be the fellowship of kindred minds that gives its moral meaning to the term "community." To be *morally* bound is in this way to be tied to others in a way of life whose mutual requirements can be understood and accepted as grounds for action. Anyone who has at some time shared responsibility in such a way of life knows what it is to have an obligation and why, on the ground it specifies, there are actions that he ought to do. The "why" of moral obligation is just *this* "why" and it is in this way that it is practically to be understood. For it is thus that practical reason can be, and sometimes is, a guide of life. . . .

Yet a man may "see" his duty and still not do it—or do it only when additional, non-moral incentives have been offered. Indeed he may. For the moral self is not the whole man, and no actual man is merely or completely such a self. *In so far as* he has this capacity and concern he has a motive for so acting, but he has other concerns and interests also and these will often make it hard for him to do what he regards as right. And frequently he will not do it. These other concerns, however, do not operate externally upon him as appetitive competitors for motivational control. They must somehow borrow the color of righteousness, or the odor of sanctity, if they are to bear the light of public scrutiny and be recognized as *his* reasons for so acting. Hence, the peculiarly twisted and contorted nature of moral evil. The moral conflict is not between appetites seeking information (including information about should-be-doneness) but between false "goods" and true, where the false must present themselves *as* true if they are to maintain their hold upon the will of men who know what it means to ask for justifying reasons for an action. There is endless room here for deception and for self-deception. But unless this concern for justification were present throughout, there would be no point in the deception and no practical sense in the misuse of justifying reasons. The irrationality of a moral agent—and we are often thus irrational—is not the non-rationality of appetites that need and could in principle have no other "justification" than that of their occurrence or non-occurrence. It is that of a will that perverts and misuses reasons to "justify" conduct that needs the sanction of a justification if it is to be willingly performed. With this aspect of the self and its agency we shall deal more fully in the next chapter. What is here essential is to see that so far from implying a psychological gap between justifying and motivating reasons, it shows the complex nature of their mutual involvement in moral action. As addressed to men concerned to justify their actions, justifying reasons are *so far* motivating reasons, and it is only in this way that they can, as reasons, have a practical bearing on our conduct. We do not always act on the terms they set, but if we had no tendency so to act, this kind of justification, as a guide to conduct, would have for us no sense. What sense it could then retain as a source of information about the normatively charged properties of actions the reader may be left, by this time, to judge for himself.

Does this mean that the man who is wholly indifferent to obligations *has* no obligations and is not to be held morally responsible for what he does? Yes. This may seem initially a drastic saying but all practical good sense supports it. Such a man would be not a moral agent but a moral idiot—he would have neither the concern nor the competence to act on moral grounds and considerations of moral right and wrong addressed to him or offered in appraisal of his conduct would be as irrelevant as attempts to carry on a conversation with a tree. We do not blame a tree for its taciturnity, though we may wish, on some occasions, that it could be more communicative. The difference of course is that we do not really expect such behavior of trees, while we do expect it of men, not as a prediction, merely, but in the sense in which England expects every man to do his duty. Some measure of such concern and competence is a must for adequate participation in all those human activities in which we trust others and ask for their trust in return, and we are reluctant to believe that in any human being it is wholly absent. Such trust is often misplaced, and there are obvious limits to its reliable application. But if it were always misplaced the activities in which it can sometimes be misplaced would cease to function, for no one would trust anyone else. If there are men, like us in other respects, who wholly lack this capacity they must for practical purposes be dealt with in other ways. We do not trust an alcoholic to keep his promise of abstinence and it would be morally idle to blame him for his failure to do so. He is not, in his condition, a man who can make a promise, though he may use with fervor the words that are normally appropriate in so doing. He must be "treated" in another way. And if we were all in this respect in the condition of the alcoholic, moral judgments would have no relevance to our conduct. Happily this is not the case. And hence it is to us the moral reasons, as ground of obligation, are significantly addressed. We often do not use them as we ought, but it is in the confidence that our fellows can rightly understand and use them that we can work with them as partners in a way of life that is in fact a moral *modus vivendi*. In this humble sense it is literally true that the just shall live by faith, for without this kind of faith there could be no practice in which "justice" as we understand it, had a moral use.

The practical point of such shared activities, as we have seen, is the attainment of goods that only in such activities are possible to man. Moral requirements make practical sense as requirements *for* the preservation of that level of mutual understanding, helpfulness, and respect which is the normative condition for the attainment of such goods. To understand the cogency of moral reasons, as grounds of obligation, in this light is not to substitute a nonmoral "why" for the "why" of moral justification. On the contrary, it is just by being in their own right the justification that, on moral grounds, was sought that moral reasons can perform this practically essential function.

Rightly used, they do their own justifying work, and only a man who can understand and accept them in this light can use them rightly. But it does help us to see the importance of being justified, the unique and irreplaceable part it has in any and all activities that make practical sense and can have a normatively significant fulfilment. We could not be ourselves without it. . . .

There is a persistent misunderstanding to which a theory of the sort so far outlined is open and which, if not explicitly corrected, will lead to a distorted picture of the nature and the work of practical reason. Right actions, we have said, are warrantable by reasons. It is only as thus warrantable that the characterization of an action as right has a normative force or cogency that makes practically justifying sense. And in answer to the questions: where do we get such reasons? and how can we understand and use them in this way? we have replied that we learn their use and cogency as we become responsibly participating members in the communities in which, in practice, the distinction between right and wrong ways of acting functions as a guide to justifiable conduct. Here training must precede questioning and argument. The man who in such training has learned the difference between right and wrong understands, in some instances at least, what it is to act justifiably or for good reasons, and the man who does not know this cannot significantly ask for the reason for an action for which a practically justifying "because" would provide a relevant answer. He would not have the understanding—the mastery of the conceptual structure of the practice— required to make practical sense of such a reason if he saw one.

So much, I have maintained, is true and of fundamental importance for our subject. But it is at just this point that the misunderstanding referred to above may arise, and too often does. For when we look for the content of the reasons that in this way and initially we learn, we find it in the accepted rules and approvals of the social groups in which such training actually is given. And if to act justifiably is simply to conform our actions to such rules, then the work of practical reason seems to be "in the end" just that of following learned instructions. In its beginning is its end, so far as being reasonable is concerned. . . .

Of course, the content of such training, as formulated in familiar maxims, will be the accepted moral precepts of the group in which the training is given. It is only on the basis of an agreed or understood consensus that there can be common grounds for action, and a ground that is not in its intention "common" is not a practical reason. If everything in a moral situation were arguable or questionable at once there could be no significant questioning or argument. And until the learner has acquired this working basis of understanding, until he knows in some cases what good reasons are, he will have nothing to reason with or about when he is called on in his own person to distinguish between actions that are right and wrong. *Of course* his having promised is a reason why he ought to do a promised act; a man who could not understand this, or other reasons of a similarly rudimentary nature, would be one with whom we could never hope to reach a moral understanding on the issues of our common life. But while this is the beginning of moral wisdom it cannot in principle, or in hard cases, be the end. For such reasons are not reasons for themselves, self-evident bits of final moral truth, to be cognitively cherished on their own account. They are grounds *for* actions to be done and whether in specific cases they are sufficient grounds, is a question that cannot be answered by an appeal to their initial unquestioning acceptance as reasons. And this question is inherent in their right use *as reasons* from the start, though, fortunately, in many instances, it need not be raised. In moral training, as in any other, we must begin with the rudiments. There cannot be exceptions to rules unless there are rules and the rule, as a moral maxim, is the norm for normal cases. But the rudiments must have the root of the matter in them, else the seed thus planted could not grow up to bear the fruit which is moral agency and moral judgment. And this root is precisely the understanding and use of the reasons taught *as reasons*—as grounds for action to be done not because that is the way we learned it, or because it is the done thing but because, for good and sufficient reasons, it is right. The learner thus equipped is launched on a voyage of discovery that can carry him a long way from his starting point. For the process of the use of reasons is a self-correcting process. The customary acceptances with which it begins are the grounds for action each of us has learned to respect in the local communities in which he was brought up to play his part well as a son, a team mate or a citizen. In many situations they are good enough. If they were not the group that taught him what it is to be a responsible agent would not be itself a moral community. But in changing conditions and in the larger situations with which he and his group, since it is never morally isolated, have to deal, they are sometimes not good enough. There are issues that cannot on their local and parochial terms be adequately met and other people's reasons to be weighed that are not those he learned in childhood to respect. And if he has not merely been "brought up" but has grown up he must come to understand and use the better reasons here required—better in the same way in which these are good, as requirements for a moral *modus vivendi*—but adequate, as those that he initially learned are not, to serve here as foundations for a good society. Moral learning is not for children merely; we must go on learning all our lives if the requirements of our moral situation are rightly to be met. The point of moral training is to supply a starting point and to develop the concern and capacity with which we can thus go on. It is a teaching that prepares us to go beyond our instructions and to solve a problem for ourselves. And it is in just this way that it is a training in the practical use of reason. . . .

To make our own standpoint clear, however, we must first state what, as we can understand them, moral problems—those in which a right use of practical reasons could be relevant and effective in reaching a solution—are, and what specifically the achievement of this solution demands of us as rational inquirers. In such a situation there must be ground for doubt, else there would be no occasion for inquiry or reflection. But equally, in such a situation, not everything is doubtful. Unless there were discoverable in it some factors that, as they stand, and without question, we could recognize as grounds of obligation, as reasons for or against the doing of an action, there would be nothing, morally, to be in doubt about, and no question as to the right or wrong of doing could significantly arise. And unless such factors were discoverably relevant to the specific point at issue, there could be no such doubt concerning it. A deed that we have no reason for either doing or not doing would be morally indifferent; we should be "free" to deal with it as we pleased—if we had any pleasure in the matter. The "why?" of justification would be impertinent.

Our actual problems of right action, as we know, are not at all like this. In them, from the start, the true issue is a moral one precisely because we do have reasons for or against its voluntary doing. To say that an action would be the giving of a sum of money is so far to leave the issue open as to whether or not it should be done. To specify it as a bribe is already to give a reason against its performance—to say why, unless there are better reasons to the contrary, it should not be done. We are not called upon to invent such reasons for themselves or to read into them by inference from "higher" truths a moral implication that they do not carry on their face. We learned their use and cogency in the process in which we became moral agents, and it is only as such agents that we have problems of this sort to solve. And the reasons that we have thus learned are normally sufficient to specify the moral merit of specific actions without pondering or doubt. They provide the working basis of the understanding on whose terms the distinction between right and wrong makes practical sense. Without such an agreement there would be no "game" in which its principles could be invoked as "rules" that in specific cases should be followed, and in the *why* which is the right use of such rules no normative significance or cogency could be discovered. This game would not be played; and it is inside this game and subject to its categorial requirements that we have moral problems.

When such reasons clearly apply, and where no counter reasons relevantly appear, a good man will see and do his duty without argument or question. The doubter who, in this situation, still demands a reason why he ought to do what will push him into action, is no longer asking what he ought to do, but demanding some extrinsic and additional inducement to perform it. And it is in this way that we should normally understand him. His is not a moral problem, and it is not on moral grounds that we can deal with him. But there are situations where our obvious and familiar reasons do not unequivocally apply—not because they have no moral cogency in such cases, but because they are not here sufficient as they stand to specify the moral merits of specific cases. The act that is the giving of a bribe is never *merely* that. It may also be a way of getting needed help from those whom only bribes can "persuade" to supply it. And if the cause for which the help is needed is a good one, which it is our responsibility to further where we can, there is so far a reason why the payment should be made. And these reasons as they stand conflict, not in the abstract or in principle—we ought in general both to support good causes *and* to refuse to pay bribes—but in the judgment on specific action that each, taken by itself, would warrant.

This is indeed a moral problem. And it arises not where we have no reasons, but are faced with a merely blank or groundless doubt, but where *prima facie* we have too many and no "principle" as yet, for their right combination. Either and neither of the alternatives presented can be justified "by reason" as the right one. We are damned if we do, and damned if we don't. And this is a situation in which we cannot rationally acquiesce. But how are we to deal with it? . . . The problem, let us say, concerns a rise in wages for the members of the Teamster's Union which we, as citizens, are invited to approve. Some grounds will normally be offered to support the claim to such a rise, and these will not be merely arbitrary or idle. The salary hike would enable the union to increase its security funds, and this in turn would contribute to the health and welfare of its members in their declining years. Taken by itself, this is a reason, and a good one, for the action proposed. And those who make it on this ground are entitled, as our fellow citizens trying in this characteristically American way to raise their living standard, to a fair and friendly hearing. And if we concentrate our attention, as do its advocates, exclusively upon the strength of this consideration taken simply by itself, the cogency of claims based upon it can be made to seem almost self-evident. It is thus that the issue is normally presented in the Union Halls where it originates.

But, as we all know, there is more *to* the problem than this. If the proposed advance in wages is likely to initiate an inflationary spiral and thus bring increased financial burdens to others in the community already in a comparatively unfavorable position and less able than the Teamsters to bear the cost of the expected price increase—widows, orphans, and college professors, for example—then there is a reason why it should not be approved and it too, as it stands, is a good one. And it can plausibly be so presented as to appear to be the only reason that ought to count in the present case. We can be sure, in fact, that there are those who will so present it. Between the relative merits of such competing reasons, how are we to judge? What ground, indeed, is there on which an impartial judgment can objectively be made? So far there seems to be none. Each party to the controversy has his own "right," and if he is prepared to stand intransigently upon it, will never lack for arguments with which to justify his cause. All he has to do is maintain in his supporters that state of mind in which it is morally self-evident that the counter-claims of others do not count. They represent instead the ruthless push for power of unscrupulous men whose conduct, as Congressional Investigations of Communists have shown, is by no means above reproach. *Or* they echo the special pleading of those vested interests that have always blocked the path of Industrial Democracy, the kind that advancing labor has had to fight in the past in battles in which its present leaders played a courageous part, and is prepared to fight again if need be, to advance its legitimate interests in our society. The reader will have no difficulty in recognizing this sort of argument; we have heard it all before and shall do so again, with dark references to the subversive and/or reactionary forces of the extreme left or right that are alleged to lurk behind it. And in all of this debate each side will exhort the other, and above all, the public, to be reasonable. But what, in such a case, would it be *like* to be reasonable?

If the competing claims existed quite alone, and in this naked conflict, there could in principle be no answer to this question. We should simply have to "see" that the one claim, with its supporting reason, was "stronger" than the other, and to judge its worth accordingly. Fortunately, in more normal instances, this is not the case. These claims do not exist, and cannot be supported, quite alone. They are made within a social situation in which *other* claims and interests than theirs are no less entitled to consideration, and in which the claims of all contenders must be contained within the structure of a moral order in which all alike can justly share. Only in this context and as grounds for a justification that can have equal cogency for all do their own proffered reasons make such moral sense as in fact they have. And this is true not merely in theory, where we like to talk about the common good, but in practice also. If the Teamsters' claim can be enforced on reluctant employers only by the use of unfair practices then it ought to be opposed at any cost. There are limits to the methods by which "advancing labor" can legitimately advance its cause, and "in the end," these are moral limits. When we have reached them there can be no compromise with evil, and any demands that can be shown to exceed them are thereby condemned. The trouble is that these limits, in particular cases, are sometimes hard to draw. But it is just *in* particular cases that we often have good grounds for drawing it. There are, in the first place, relevant factual questions to be asked. How much, specifically, would the proposal cost, not just in money, but in sacrifice from those adversely affected by it? On whom would this cost chiefly bear, and is it one that, in their present situation, they can be rightly asked to bear? Could the harm that would result from it be compensated for elsewhere, and the burden shifted to those in a better position to bear it? Is the proposal here made for the Teamsters' Union one we could accept not in their case only but in that of other unions also which, we may be sure, would be prompt to advance a comparable claim? Would concessions now made be just an incentive to more drastic demands to follow? What bearing on the efficiency of our national economy and, above all, on our relative power position in the world could it be expected to have? These, in their turn, are not easy questions, but they are often not beyond our power to answer reasonably, *if* we will inquire honestly about them, and a right answer there would clearly have some bearing on the merits of the specific case at issue. For they are all morally relevant considerations, and in their light we should be able to judge better what we ought to do. This better judgment, and the reasons that can adequately support it, are the goal of rational inquiry on moral issues.

What such inquiry can give us, if it is fairly carried through, is not just new information but, if we are prepared to see and weigh its moral relevance, a new light in which to understand the merits of the issue whose appraisal is here called for. For in our reasonable use of it we are acting not merely as partisans of one side or the other, whose case is to be defended at all costs, but as spokesmen for a good which, by a right combination of competing interests, can be practically the good of all. And this, if we are serious in our language, is what we mean by the common good which is normatively entitled, in such situations, to take precedence over that of any competing or divisive interest. The standpoint from which judgments of common good are made is in this sense that of the community—not an ideal or abstract community but that of the actual moral order in which diverse interests may pursue their several goods in common. This is not merely nor primarily a "larger" good in which everybody gets as big a cut as possible of what he wants. It may, in hard cases, be one in which the many are asked to sacrifice their special interests for the preservation and protection of a numerically smaller group whose minimal requirements for decent living must at all costs be met. Nor, in consequence, is it one on which all appetites will be equally appeased. There will inevitably be those who do not like it, and will go on pressing their more special claims. And so long as these pressures respect the limits of due process in a public argument, they will be entitled to a hearing. But it will constitute, if it is reasonable in fact and not merely in its pretensions, a working basis or *modus vivendi* in which all concerned can fairly be asked to go on together, and it must find its warrant in the answering judgment of those who are willing *in this way* to go on and on these terms to live and work together. It is in this way that just government, and the claims of all authority that claims normative cogency, rest on and are confirmed in the consent of the governed. Nothing more than this is needed for a right solution of all moral problems; nothing less will suffice. The preservation and development of that community of *understanding* in which it is reliably achieved is the point of responsible moral inquiry.

There will, of course, be cases where not all relevant questions can be conclusively answered, and where a judgment must be based on inconclusive grounds. Here we proceed at considerable moral risk and must be prepared to take the consequences. We may find out that a judgment confidently made was wrong and that in fact our verdict will not stand up under the demands of actual living. This is a wise and humbling reflection and may well lead us, where no judgment on our part is practically called for, to follow the biblical admonition: "Judge not." But there are situations in which we *are* called on to judge in our own persons between right and wrong and to act accordingly. As responsible moral agents we cannot avoid the responsibilities of such judgments. What are these responsibilities? Infallibility is not reasonably expected of us. But it is required of us that we do our best to reach a just decision. And until all discoverably relevant considerations in the situation have been weighed, in an appraised judgment on the merits of this specific case, we have not done our best. Nor have we done it if, once a verdict has been given, we close our eyes to further light on the subject. The "game" in which "decisions" are responsibly made does not end with the making of decisions. We must go on, in action shared with others, to live in the moral world whose structure they have gone some way to determine. The process of being reasonable is a continuing and a self-correcting process, and the capacity to change our minds in the light of what it has to teach us, is essential to its proper use. But to profit by our past mistakes we must be able to recognize these *as mistakes*, and it is only in the light of a better understanding, in this way achieved, that it can responsibly be done. This is what it is, in practice, to be morally reasonable in our conduct, and it is in the right exercise of this capacity that we can rightly live and learn together.

This is what it would be like to follow reason in its practical use. But why should we follow reason? By what *right* have its dictates taken precedence over the demands of other and "deeper" sides of our nature? Why should we do what our reason wants, when our hearts are set on something else? The answer is by this time obvious, but perhaps, in the murky atmosphere of contemporary thought, will bear repeating. "Reason" as such has no "right" to dictate anything, and it is never by dictation that it does its proper moral work. The right for which it speaks is a right it *finds* by honest searching, and if it is not thus findable by all who will *in this way* seek it, then it has no justifiable claim upon our hearts and wills. Nor has practical reason any axe of its own to grind in this discovery. It is not its *want* that that should prevail, for it is not one want among others but the concern that *all* wants shall be satisfied so far as this is possible within the structure of a moral order which all men of good will can accept as one in which *their* wants can be reasonably fulfilled. The question is not what *Reason* wants but what a man can rightly *will* as a responsible moral agent, as a self. It is only in this capacity that for him the question of right arises at all, and it is in these terms alone that a "should" has normative or justifying cogency. If you did not expect this kind of an answer, why did you ask the question? What else but this would *be* a relevant answer to it and only for a man in fact concerned to act rightly, i.e., reasonably, could such an answer have practical relevance or point. Is such action to his advantage? That depends, of course, on how he reckons his advantage. There is no guarantee that it will always give him what he wanted, and he would be a fool to expect it. Nor is it certified to satisfy all sides and levels of his "nature," for there is much in his nature that resists the requirements of moral order—as Freud has frequently insisted. It is what will satisfy him *as a self* or responsible agent and the only happiness it guarantees is that which *on these terms* is possible to him. And it sets the conditions on which he can live honorably with others in the shared enjoyment of a common and communicable good. To live in this way as a self is, as we have seen, not a gift of nature; it is a hard-won achievement, to be sustained with vigilance, and sometimes against great odds in a world not wholly friendly to the best in man. The time may come when we shall no longer care enough to pay this cost, when this "game" no longer will be played. And then the word "justification," if still uttered, will have a different meaning, for it will have some other use. Those who spoke the language would never know the answer to a question as to why they *should* be reasonable. They would have no means of understanding the question. In our present moral situation we are not such men. We do understand the question, and are concerned to offer a right answer to it. It is to such men thus concerned that this inquiry is relevantly addressed.

What, then, is a moral decision, and on what grounds, if any, is it rightly made? R. M. Hare's statement of the problem in *The Language of Morals* has set the pattern for its academic discussion in the past decade and will serve us here as a working model for our own. . . . Hare starts, as most ethical theorists do, with the traditional pattern of practical reasoning. In the making of any decision to do something, he tells us, two factors may be involved: a major premise which is a principle of conduct, e.g., never say what is false, and a minor premise which is a factual, and so far as possible, valuationally neutral statement of what we should be doing if we acted in one way or another in the particular situation, e.g., that the utterance of this assertion would in fact be saying something false. In deciding not to make this statement *because* it would be false I am acting on a principle of which the action in question is an instance. And this is what it is to have grounds for a decision. My principle is my ground and, as a major premise, it specifies univocally the moral right of cases that are factually certifiable as falling under it. We have heard this sort of thing before and know by this time what to think of it. For Hare, however, it is only a beginning. For the unique character of "decision" does not adequately appear in this decision to act, or not to act, on moral grounds.

Suppose, now, I am not satisfied to let the matter rest at this point. This statement would indeed be false, and to eschew false statements is my principle. But, nonetheless, I *decide* in this instance to make the statement. Here a further "decision" is required. For I decide now *not* to apply my principle or "reason" or so to qualify it that it allows exceptions of specific kinds. This does not make my principle more loose. On the contrary, with the allowable exceptions specified the general rule is tighter than before. And Hare, who clearly is a Kantian at heart, is all for tightness. But the decision to alter the principle in this way is one I make on my own responsibility. There is, presumably, no "principle" for it, or none that I have not, by a prior decision, legislated for myself. Thus we are confronted, not merely with decisions to do one thing rather than another, for a reason, but "decisions of principle" about the grounds or reasons I will follow in deciding, in the more familiar sense, to act in one way rather than another. It is important, I think, to note the difference between these two sorts of decision, though Hare does not do so. The former is clearly present in all voluntary action, which just is the doing, so far as it is unimpeded, of what in such action I decide to do. The latter is a horse of another color. It is not the doing of something for a reason, but a pure choosing or "deciding" of the reasons for which anything should be done. For the one I have reasons—those that, presumably I have in this instance chosen to accept as principles. For the other, what reasons or justification could I have? Any justification would be itself a reason which by prior decision I had chosen to accept. And by what reason would this choice be justified? Here finally, as Hare affirms, we must simply *decide*, presumably without a justification, and accept the responsibility for so doing. It is, he holds, the part of moral maturity to recognize this hard fact. A decision *of* principle cannot be made *on* principle, but requires a groundless fiat of the will. This fiat is the morally unique and ultimate decision which traditional ethical theories have neglected—"a factor which is the very essence of morals." We must "learn to use 'ought'-sentences in the realization that they can only be verified by reference to a standard or set of principles which we have by our own decision accepted and made our own." *This* is the "decision" whose "justification" is presented to us as at once a tragedy, a problem and a task. We must try to see what sense we can make of it. . . .

[F]irst of all we must see, as he does not, that the nightmare of "ultimate" and groundless choosing is a nightmare, the misbegotten product of a logical confusion of decision with subjective willfulness, and that the only "truth" involved in it is only the distortion that bad delusions too frequently produce. The "decision" to create *ex nihilo* a world of "values" on our responsibility is, fortunately, one that, as moral agents, we are never called upon to make. We are required to justify our decisions to *do* one thing rather than another, and we do this understandably when we give our reasons for so doing. Here it is the action, not the reason, that is the appropriate object of willed or decisive action, and it is *this* "decision," made often in the face of great obstacles and strong temptations, that is the appropriate object of rational justification. We do not, in such situations, choose our reasons. We are morally in no position to do so. The reasons we have learned to use in the whole course of our moral training are the very structure of our own moral being as agents or deciders; they constitute the normative order of the *Lebensform*, or form of life, in which the practice of moral justification has a normative authority as a guide for conduct. Where there is a question of the adequacy of a particular reason or "principle" to the issues of concrete action, we can refer, as Hare rightly notes, from such a "principle" to its qualification within the network of related principles which constitute the pattern of our "form of life." But to talk of deciding for a way of life in general and *in vacuo* is a sheer absurdity. We do not in this sense choose our way of life: we are stuck with it. Its "principles," not as social habits merely, into which we happen to have been born, but as normatively cogent grounds for right action, are the very fibre of our being *as* responsible selves or moral agents, and we could no more get outside them to decide, in value-free and unconditioned independence, what "values" are, than we could speak English without using the syntax of the language to express our thoughts. We may, of course, rebel against the standards we have learned and look elsewhere than to the family, the church or the nation into which we were born to find a worthy object for our ultimate allegiance. But if our rebellion is not merely aimless and blind, we have grounds for it and those grounds are produced by those very factors *in* our form of life which have taught us to be discontented with its presently inadequate acceptances and procedures. We could have no other ground than this on which to stand. The free thinker who turns against the church, and has good grounds for doing so, has learned the meaning of the freedom that he cherishes in a community that is, in its pretensions at least, a Christian society. And it is in the name of a truth which he there learned to value, a truth whose knowledge can genuinely make men free, that he justifies the shift in his allegiance. . . .

What neither he nor we can do is to drown our own moral roots and still make value judgments. We carry our moral past and its traditions with us, if not as a spiritual resource, then as a scar. There is no way that we can judge or justify anything save *on* the ground that it initially provides. We are not uncommitted shoppers in a world of *morally* possible alternative value-systems who may quite groundlessly "choose" one or another to our taste and *then* proceed to live with it. We do not choose our reasons when we choose to act for a reason. This prior "choice" calls for no justification, for it is never made. It would be in truth a moral absurdity, for it would *call* for a justification that could not be itself a justifying ground for action until, by a "responsible" but unjustifiable choice we ourselves had made it so. To see that a morally disembodied will thus legislating for itself and for all mankind is an absurdity is so far a gain in analytic understanding. But to accept the result as a fair account of our actual human situation is to show, I think, a rather cynically twisted sense of humor. Or, to put the whole matter in a form with which the reader should by this time be familiar, morally normative communications are significantly addressed to the concerned and competent, for only they would understand or know what to do with them. This understanding, hardly won through centuries of funded moral experience, *is* the ground for rational decision, the solid substance of our moral world, and for better or for worse, we and our moral responsibilities are *inside* it. Santayana once judiciously observed that "we cannot cease to think, and still continue to know." It is no less the case that we cannot stand outside the categorial structure of the practice in which "responsibility" makes sense, and still make moral judgments. Only a morally uprooted and disoriented thinker could seriously suppose that in this way he was morally free to choose his "values" without prior moral standards. And he, however much he might have to say about "ultimate decisions," could not make a moral judgment of the justification, i.e., the rightness, of decisions that require such justification in the shared work of our common life. He would have nothing to judge with.

SUGGESTED READINGS

The view that morality rests on feeling, not on reason, was given a classical exposition by Hume in *Treatise of Human Nature*, Book III, Part I (and more briefly in his *Inquiry Concerning the Principles of Morals*, Section I and Appendix I). The most important version of a modern restatement of the theory is that of C. L. Stevenson, *Ethics and Language*. (See his papers in W. Sellars and J. Hospers, *Readings in Ethical Theory*, which contains many other articles dealing with this and allied topics.) Emotivism has been criticised frequently: "Can Ethics Do Without Propositions?" by J. Harrison, *Mind*, 1950, is a typical technical attack. R. B. Brandt, *Ethical Theory*, Chapter 9, reviews most of the issues.

There have been numerous attempts to defend the rationality of morality. Section VIII of Sellars and Hospers contains some interesting papers discussing the problem of justifying a first principle of morality. S. E. Toulmin, in *Examination of the Place of Reason in Ethics*, surveys different views of the nature of morality and develops a suggestive new alternative. P. H. Nowell-Smith, in *Ethics*, gives a more complex analysis of moral discourse than Toulmin and rather a different view of the place of reason in moral argument. A clear exposition of the various positions and problems is to be found in Chapter 8 of W. K. Frankena's *Ethics*. In addition the reader may wish to consult articles by two especially interesting recent writers not represented in the foregoing selections: J. Rawls, "Outline of a Decision Procedure for Ethics," *Philosophical Review*, 1951, and P. Foot, "Moral Arguments," *Mind*, 1958.

VI ✺ RELIGION, THEISM, AND NATURALISM

Philosophers frequently raise questions important for religion, and the teachings of religion frequently propose answers to philosophic problems. For example, many religions hold that man has an immortal soul, and one of the problems of philosophy is to understand what can be meant by the term "soul," how the soul is related to the body, and therefore in what sense (if any) man is immortal. Many such problems are of importance both to philosophy and to religion. One of these problems, however, is of central importance in determining our views on all other issues common to both fields. This is the problem of religious knowledge. What, we may ask, are the grounds for our religious beliefs, and how are these beliefs related to our other knowledge?

This problem has various aspects. In the first place, we may ask whether the methods of knowledge we use in other fields are also capable of establishing religious truths. For example, can we prove the existence of God by means of reasoning based upon premises drawn from experience? We may also ask whether there are special ways of attaining religious knowledge, such as mystical experience or revelation. If we accept any such special avenue to religious truth, we must then inquire how this way of knowing is related to our usual ways of acquiring knowledge. Is it true, for example, that revelation and natural knowledge can never be in conflict? If we do not hold that there is this necessary harmony between them, which is to take precedence over the other?

There is another set of questions that arise when religion is made the object of philosophic reflection. The upshot of one's inquiries into these problems may be the conclusion that a belief in God is warranted rationally or is acceptable in some nonrational way. If so, what else ought one, to be consistent, accept? How does a belief in God fit into or give structure to a rational and coherent philosophical view of the world? Similarly, if one comes to the conclusion that belief in God is not warranted in any way, one will need to work out the implications of this for other aspects of thought. Moreover until one has a fairly good idea of how both theistic and nontheistic views can be developed, one is not in a position to assess the adequacy of those views. Equally for the religious and the nonreligious thinker, therefore, it is essential to have a clear grasp of the major alternatives.

The Nature of Religion

If one is to examine adequately the many philosophic problems that arise within the sphere of religion, it is well to look first at what religion is. Religion, however, is not easily defined. One difficulty lies in the diversity of forms that religion has assumed in different cultures. Even today there are conflicting and competing religions, and in the past there have been many more. The question arises, therefore, whether a given definition can be applied equally well to, say, Greek and Roman polytheism, Christianity, Buddhism, and Confucianism. A definition of religion which applies only to some of these historic religions and not others would be as inadequate as a definition of "organism" which applies to vertebrate animals only and not to invertebrates or to plants.

A second difficulty in defining religion is closely related to the first. It stems from the fact that we speak with equal propriety of religious *institutions* and of religious *experience*. For example, we speak of Christianity as a particular form of religion, and we compare its institutions and ceremonies with those of Greek polytheism; but we also speak of Christian attitudes and emotions and compare them with Greek religious attitudes and emotions. An adequate definition of religion, therefore, must take into account not only the great diversity in institutional forms of religion, but also a wide range of individual religious experience.

In spite of the diversity of religious institutions and experience, some factors are common to all religions. For example, religious experience always involves personal commitment, and every religious institution demands such a dedication of the self on the part of its believers. The extent of this commitment or dedication varies with different religions, but it is to be found, in some degree, in every religion, and in every religious person.

Religious commitment has a number of aspects. It always involves a way of life, an ethical ideal, to which the religious person dedicates himself because of its supreme importance. It also includes the acceptance of beliefs about nature, man, and the Divine—some view, that is, of the ultimate nature of the universe and man's place in it. And finally, in most cases it includes participation in religious ceremonies which express the common dedication of a community of believers. Each of these factors has been used as a basis for definitions of religion. However, an adequate definition cannot confine itself to any one of them: though there have been variations in emphasis, all have been present in religion at all times and in all cultures.

The selection from ROYCE formulates the view that every religion has three interconnected components: the practical, the emotional, and the theoretical. OMAN reviews some inadequate definitions of religion and, by utilizing concepts that have been in the forefront of theological and anthropological discussions of religion, puts forward a more inclusive definition.

Religion as Moral Code
and Theory[*]

J o s i a h R o y c e [1855–1916] took his doctorate in philosophy at Johns Hopkins in 1878. After teaching English at the University of California for four years, he accepted a position in Philosophy at Harvard. He became the most celebrated American exponent of absolute idealism and the teacher of many leading American philosophers of the next generation.

We speak commonly of religious feelings and of religious beliefs; but we find difficulty in agreeing about what makes either beliefs or feelings religious. A feeling is not religious merely because it is strong, nor yet because it is also morally valuable, nor yet because it is elevated. If the strength and the moral value of a feeling made it religious, patriotism would be religion. If elevation of feeling were enough, all higher artistic emotion would be religious. But such views would seem to most persons very inadequate. As for belief, it is not religious merely because it is a belief in the supernatural. Not merely is superstition as such very different from religion, but even a belief in God as the highest of beings need not be a religious belief. If La Place had needed what he called "that hypothesis," the Deity, when introduced into his celestial mechanics, would have been but a mathematical symbol, or a formula like Taylor's theorem,—no true object of religious veneration. On the other hand, Spinoza's impersonal Substance, or the Nirvana of the Buddhists, or any one of many like notions, may have, either as doctrines about the world or as ideals of human conduct, immense religious value. Very much that we associate with religion is therefore nonessential to religion. Yet religion is something unique in human belief and emotion, and must not be dissolved into any lower or more commonplace elements. What then is religion?

So much at all events seems sure about religion: it has to do with action. It is impossible without some appearance of moral purpose. A totally immoral religion may exist; but it is like a totally unseaworthy ship at sea, or like a rotten bank, or like a wild-cat mine. It deceives its followers. It pretends to guide them into morality of some sort. If it is blind or wicked, not its error makes it religious, but the faith of its followers in its worth. A religion may

[*] From Royce: *The Religious Aspect of Philosophy*, Chapter 1. Houghton, Mifflin Company, 1885.

teach the men of one tribe to torture and kill men of another tribe. But even such a religion would pretend to teach right conduct. Religion, however, gives us more than a moral code. A moral code alone, with its "Thou shalt," would be no more religious than is the civil code. A religion adds something to the moral code. And what it adds is, first, enthusiasm. Somehow it makes the faithful regard the moral law with devotion, reverence, love. By history, by parable, by myth, by ceremony, by song, by whatever means you will, the religion gives to the mere code life and warmth. A religion not only commands the faithful, but gives them something that they are glad to live for, and if need be to die for.

But not yet have we mentioned the element of religion that makes it especially interesting to a student of theoretical philosophy. So far as we have gone, ethical philosophy would criticise the codes of various religions, while theoretical philosophy would have no part in the work. But, in fact, religion always adds another element. Not only does religion teach devotion to a moral code, but the means that it uses to this end include a more or less complete theory of things. Religion says not merely *do and feel,* but also *believe.* A religion tells us about the things that it declares to exist, and most especially it tells us about their relations to the moral code and to the religious feeling. There may be a religion without a supernatural, but there cannot be a religion without a theoretical element, without a statement of some supposed matter of fact, as part of the religious doctrine.

These three elements, then, go to constitute any religion. A religion must teach some moral code, must in some way inspire a strong feeling of devotion to that code, and in so doing must show something in the nature of things that answers to the code or that serves to reinforce the feeling. A religion is therefore practical, emotional, and theoretical; it teaches us to do, to feel, and to believe, and it teaches the belief as a means to its teaching of the action and of the feeling.

. . . We have tried to give a definition that shall express, not merely what a Buddhist or a Catholic or a Comtist or an Hegelian means by his religion, but what all men everywhere mean by religion. They all want religion to define for them their duty, to give them the heart to do it, and to point out to them such things in the real world as shall help them to be steadfast in their devotion to duty. When people pray that they may be made happy, they still desire to learn what they are to do in order to become happy. When saints of any creed look up to their God as their only good, they are seeking for guidance in the right way. The savages of whom we hear so much nowadays have indeed low forms of religion, but these religions of theirs still require them to do something, and tell them why it is worth while to do this, and make them more or less enthusiastic in doing it. Among ourselves, the poor and the lonely, the desolate and the afflicted, when they demand religious comfort, want something that shall tell them what to do with life, and how to take up once more the burdens of their broken existence. And the religious philosopher must submit to the same test that humanity everywhere proposes to its religions. If one tries to regulate our diet by his theories, he must have the one object, whatever his theory, since he wants to tell us what is healthful for us. If he tells us to eat nothing but snow, that is his fault. The true object of the theory of diet remains the same. And so if men have expressed all sorts of one-sided, disheartening, inadequate views of religion, that does not make the object of religious theory less catholic, less comprehensive, less definitely human. A man who propounds a religious system must have a moral code, an emotional life, and some theory of things to offer us. With less we cannot be content. He need not, indeed, know or pretend to know very much about our wonderful world, but he must know something, and that something must be of definite value.

The Sphere of Religion*

JOHN WOOD OMAN [1860–1939] was a Presbyterian minister, teacher, and scholar, and the author of a number of works on systematic theology and the philosophy of religion. As Principal of Westminster College, Cambridge, he greatly influenced his contemporaries in the Presbyterian ministry.

RELIGION AS BELIEF IN GODS OR OBSERVANCE OF CULTS. Theories of religion may be divided according as they seek the essential distinguishing marks in its outward beliefs or practices, or in its inward faiths or emotions. Thus one is more historical and the other more psychological; one considers what men worship, the other how they worship; one what they believe, the other how they believe. It will be convenient, even though it cannot be done with absolute definiteness, to divide theories accordingly, and to consider these types in succession, beginning with the former, which emphasizes gods or cults.

* From Oman: "The Sphere of Religion" in Science, Religion, and Reality, edited by Joseph Needham. Copyright, 1925, by The Macmillan Company. (New edition, 1955: George Braziller, Inc., New York.) Reprinted by permission of The Society for Promoting Christian Knowledge, Northumberland Ave., London W.C.2, and George Braziller, Inc.

Probably the view which has found widest acceptance is that the distinctive mark of religion is the belief in gods. This is taken to belong to all religions and to belong to them only: and, in that case, it would be what we need for marking off the sphere of religion.

It cannot be questioned that this belief is a very prominent element in most religions. But, if we keep strictly to the idea of gods as personal beings, there is at all events one religion without it. Primitive Buddhism replaced at least all effective idea of gods by a rigid law of requital; and we may not exclude a religion which has claimed so many adherents for so long a time. Nor can we include all the objects of worship in other religions under the conception of personal gods or even of their dwelling places.

But, on the other hand, should we define gods more vaguely as unseen powers, while our definition would then cover all religion, it would include much else. Magic is also belief in unseen powers, and magic has been sharply distinguished from religion by the most profoundly religious persons, such as the Hebrew prophets. Further, there is a wide range of belief in vague unseen influences, such as has recently been called the "numinous," which may be merely the "spooky" and have no necessary connection with religion.

More recently the observance of some kind of worship or cult has been regarded as the distinctive characteristic of religion. For example, it has been argued that there is no common element in all forms of Christianity except that Jesus has been the centre of all forms of its cults, and that, so long as this continue, it will remain, in spite of all its variety, one religion. And this importance of the ritual could be maintained with still more certainty for other religions, such as Confucianism or Brahmanism.

But, even if the cult could be regarded as the mark of a particular religion, it could not, by any narrowing of the meaning of the word, be made to exclude all that is not religious. There are elements in many cults which are mere social tradition, and not in any strict sense religious. Still less can it, by any stretching of the meaning of the word, be made to include all that is religious. There have been beliefs which have been the more religious for remaining a secret of the heart, except in so far as they may work a visible change in the believer; and there are practices which have been the more religious for turning attention from public ceremonies to common human relations. The most conspicuous example in history is the religion of the Hebrew prophets, who constantly declared that a religion marked only by the cult was mere profane trampling of God's courts, and who made no attempt to replace the existing cult by a better, but declared that true religion was to do justly and love mercy and to walk humbly with one's God. Nor, though Jesus visited the synagogue and the temple, can it be said that his religion had much to do with either. In face of these examples to the contrary, it cannot be, as has been maintained, that what makes doctrines religious and not merely philosophical, and practices religious and not merely ethical, is their relation to the cult.

RELIGION AS A SPECIAL TYPE OF THOUGHT OR FEELING OR ACTING. More recently the tendency has been to define religion, not by the object, but by the manner of its belief; not by its cults, but by its piety. The reasons given are, first, that such inward marks of it are simpler and more certain than any attempt to combine the multitudinous outward forms; and, second, that the special quality of religion concerns a person's faith or piety and not the objects of his belief, which may be merely accepted from tradition.

The first reason, however, does not seem to be justified by experience, because there never has been any agreement even on so broad a question as the department of mind to which religion is to be assigned. If the marks are simple, this question ought to be elementary. Yet the answers given to it by the profoundest thinkers have radically disagreed. Kant held religion to be essentially belief in the reality and sovereignty of the moral order, and, therefore, to be dependent, in the last resort, upon a right attitude of the will. Schleiermacher denied that such an appendage to morality was of the nature of real religion at all, and found the sphere of religion in piety, which he described as a feeling of dependence that is absolute because it places us in immediate relation to the absolute, universal, final reality. Hegel rejected both views and regarded religion as intellectual exaltation into the region of eternal truth. Thus Kant placed religion in the sphere of will, Schleiermacher of feeling, and Hegel of reason. Such wide divergence between thinkers so serious and profound does not encourage the hope that the essential mark of religion will be easier to discover in the peculiar quality of religion in the soul than in its manifold outward manifestations; and, in point of fact, the question of what belongs to religion in history has never received quite such divergent answers as the question of what belongs to religion in psychology.

The second argument, that the essential quality of religion belongs to the soul that cherishes it, rests on the fact that no kind of religious belief would be of any religious value unless it were entertained by a conviction of a peculiar quality, and that no rite is truly religious except as it is done with piety. And, without doubt, when personal belief and reverence are wanting, religion is an unreality. . . . But that would not be in any sense a distinctive mark of religion.

DEFINITION OF RELIGION. Nothing is really truth for us except as it is our conviction, or beauty for us except as we truly perceive and feel it, or goodness except as it is good to our own insight. Truth, without our conviction of its truth, would be mere facts in an encyclopaedia; and morality, without our own conscience of right, mere rules of good form. Nevertheless, the special quality of truth is to be objectively valid and of goodness to be concerned with the actual moral order. And, in the same way, the special quality of religion is to be concerned with what is regarded not merely as real, but as the ultimate reality; and this is in no way altered by the importance of our personal relation to it.

This, as a matter of fact, is the only point on which Kant, Schleiermacher, and Hegel are agreed. The difference in their opinions about the seat of religion in the soul is as complete as the possibilities admit, seeing that there is only intellect, feeling, or will to which it could be ascribed. But they are at one in seeking religion where they think they discern the creative element in experience. Their real divergence does not concern religion, but has to do with the point where ultimate reality touches the human spirit, because for all alike the intercourse with the universe which creates all our experience is, so to speak, a religious intercourse. . . .

All these theories, therefore, though ascribing radically contradictory origins to religion in the mind, agree in seeking them where reality manifests itself to us. Their views of what religion is also differ with the seat to which they ascribe it, yet all agree that it is, or ought to be, victory and peace through providing for us a right relation to the ultimate reality. For Kant this reality is the moral order, for Schleiermacher the artistic harmony of the universe, for Hegel the cosmic process of reason; but for all, it is that which is absolute in its claim, and, for all, religion is the recognition of this claim and, through it, is emancipation from the fluctuating values of sense and victory over all that is changing and accidental. . . .

The essential quality of religion is the claim to deal with a special kind of environment . . . an unseen environment of absolute worth which demands worship. . . .

THE FACTORS OF EXPERIENCE. Our discussion so far has tended to show that, whether this environment be real or not, religion is an affirmation of what we may call broadly the supernatural, and that its quality is determined by this outward reference and not by any particular kind of subjective feeling or attitude, while its validity wholly depends on whether such an invisible world exist or not. Now this would seem to bring us so near to the Rationalist view of religion, as a matter of evidences for the existence of God, providence, and immortality, that the difference might not seem worth discussing. Even where difference does exist, the advantage may appear to be on the side of a theory which states what its supernatural is and establishes the existence of it by inference from the natural. And undoubtedly we have in its insistence that the essential question about religion concerns its truth, the reason why the Rationalist view of religion has been so widely held and why it endures to this day, for unless its object is real, nay, the ultimate reality, religion is a vain and most unnecessarily distressing illusion. Moreover, Rationalism was right in insisting that this question may not be evaded, and also that we may not escape the demand to answer it for ourselves. . . .

It is plainly not possible to go with any fullness here into a matter which would involve us in a whole theory of knowledge, and it must suffice to make some statements which may seem to be no more than assertions. We know all environment, not as impact or physical influx, but as meaning: and this meaning depends on (1) the unique character of the feeling it creates; (2) the unique value it has for us; (3) the immediate conviction of a special kind of objective reality, which is inseparable from this valuation; and (4) the necessity of thinking it in relation to the rest of experience and the rest of experience in relation to it.

In all experience these four aspects are indivisibly joined in one, and each loses its significance in isolation. The feeling depends on the value, and the value on the feeling; the conviction of reality is not an additional inference, but the valuation depends on the conviction of reality and the conviction of reality on the correctness of the valuation; the thinking of it in its place in our whole experience is not after we have received it, but is necessary for receiving it, and essential to the conviction of its reality. These elements are the same for the experience of things physical as for the experience of things spiritual. What does distinguish religion from all else is the unique quality of the feeling, of the valuation of the nature of the object, and of the way of thinking things together.

There is, however, a constant necessity to distinguish what we may not divide, nor is it specially difficult with the world of religion, because, as with every other environment, there is (1) a reflection of it in a feeling of its own special quality; (2) an immediate judgement of worth of a kind different from all others; (3) a conviction of a peculiar kind of reality; and (4) a special way of thinking it all together as one experience. For the first two I propose to distinguish two words which are only vaguely distinct in our language, and, as is often necessary in the use of terms for more technical purposes, to differentiate them somewhat more precisely than is done by common usage. These words are the "holy" and the "sacred." The "holy" I propose to use for the direct sense or feeling of the supernatural, and the "sacred" for its valuation as of absolute worth. The special object I shall call "the supernatural," and the thinking together "theology," both words, however, having a somewhat more definite meaning than they have in popular usage. By the sacred, in particular, all religion is distinguished, and all religious thinking is right thinking as it is about what is truly sacred. The supernatural is not a further inference from it as from effects to a cause, but is felt and valued in it; and, when separated from this manifestation, it is without content and deprived of all reality, because it no longer deals with an environment, but is mere abstract argument about the universe.

THE SENSE OF THE HOLY. Holy and sacred are only vaguely distinguishable in ordinary usage, and that rather by some difference in the feeling associated with the words than by any clear difference of application. But here, as has been explained, it is proposed to use them more definitely, making the sense of holiness apply to the special feeling of awe or reverence which certain ideas or objects evoke, while excluding from its meaning the valuation of them as of absolute worth, for which the term sacred is reserved.

In our language the "holy," used by itself, would mean something which stirs moral reverence. But, in such expressions as the "holy edifice" or the "holy sacrament," it is still used to express a vague feeling of an awe which is not of an ethical quality: and the history of religion shows that this is its original meaning. Even a "Holy God" did not originally mean a "God of purer eyes than to behold iniquity," but an awe-inspiring being, with the sense of holiness not unlike the feeling evoked by countless material objects. These different types of feeling may be distinguished as the "awesome holy" and the "ethical holy."

The more primitive form of the sense of the holy is here called the "awesome holy," because it is an awe so near akin to fear as to give colour to the theory that fear was the source of all religion, that, according to a very ancient theory, *timor fecit deos* [fear creates gods]. What is at least most immediately obvious in it is dread of some mysterious dangerous force, though a closer study shows that this is only the negative side of the sense of it as exalting, stimulating, re-enforcing. But even this seems to be conceived almost as a material fluid, and to have no spiritual and at least no ethical significance. In view of this there are writers who maintain that this primitive awesome holy has no connection with the ethical holy: and there are some who regard them as distinct to the end. This awe, which is held to be quite apart from moral reverence, is then taken to be the distinctive religious feeling. In this way, we are told, we keep religion and ethics to their own departments.

That they ought to be kept to their own departments might seem to be shown by the unfortunate history of their amalgamation, for religion has been made to depend upon ethics and ethics on religion in ways which have wronged both. Religion has been made a mere sanction of morals, whereupon it ceases to be religion; and morals a mere announcement of commands of the Diety, dependent on the blessing and ban of religion for its sanctions and motives, whereupon it ceases to be morals. Religion, if it be worth anything, must stand in its own right; while good is good to be done for its own sake and not because an omnipotent person has laid down rules and will maintain them by rewards and punishments.

But, though this is true, it is far from being the end of the matter. A religion which is not ethical is in danger of being superstition and not religion; and an ethic which has no appeal except to the visible and the useful is business, not morals. Historically, too, the religious sense of the holy becomes an ethical feeling. On the one hand, the natural evolution of the awesome holy is into moral reverence; and by that very thing we measure it as progress. On the other, morality has always been a religious development, directly related to the sense of the holy, and a real moral feeling can never be wholly divorced from something at least akin to its awe. . . .

The sense of the holy is stirred only by what is valued as sacred. From this sacred or absolute valuation it has its special quality as feeling, a certain absolute quality of awe or reverence, which at once distinguishes even its lowest forms from the merely uncanny or magical. The feelings both of the uncanny and of the magical are attached to our fears and wishes, and are to be subjected, as best we can, to our uses; whereas the holy is a feeling neither to be run away from nor to be put in subjection. Thus, if the feeling is attached to a sacred value, then it is the sense of the holy; but if to one of merely comparative value as it satisfies our desires or suits our convenience or our profit, the feeling with which we respond to it cannot be so described. . . .

THE JUDGEMENT OF THE SACRED. The sense of the holy, we have seen, has its own peculiar quality as feeling, being a direct response to a special kind of environment. But we have further seen that it goes inseparably with the valuation of this environment as sacred, and that the feeling can only be described through the values to which it is attached, the unique character of the feeling being made plain only by the absoluteness of the sacred with which it is bound up. The sacred, as used here, means this valuation as of absolute worth, and not anything less, being that which may not be brought down and compared with values of pleasure or ease or any visible good.

The interaction between this sense of the holy and this valuation as sacred is not all in one direction. On the one hand, the valuation may immediately follow the feeling, or, on the other, the feeling may immediately follow the valuation, though it is not, in either case, mere sequence. We value things because they appeal to our feelings, but we also feel about them largely as we value them. Yet, more frequently perhaps than any other feeling, the sense of the holy follows and depends on its value; and, on the whole, this becomes increasingly the case as the mind develops. We might even regard it as at least one mark of progress, that while the more primitive the life, the more the feelings determine the value; the more advanced the development, the more the values determine the feelings. . . .

Everything that is sacred is in the sphere of religion, and everything in the sphere of religion is sacred. Unless dogmas express beliefs valued as sacred, they are mere intellectual formulas; unless rites are the worship of a power valued as sacred, they are mere social ceremonies; unless God Himself embody all we value as sacred, he is a mere metaphysical hypothesis. Only when the valuation as sacred accompanies the sense of awe and reverence have we the religious holy, and only a reality having this absolute value is the religious supernatural. Therefore, if there is any one mark of the sphere of religion, it is this valuation of everything within it as sacred.

THE EXISTENCE OF THE SUPERNATURAL. If, as has been maintained, everything sacred is within the sphere of religion, and everything within the sphere of religion sacred, and this valuation interacts with a peculiar type of feeling to be described as the sense of the holy, we should seem to have discovered a mark by which the sphere of religion could be defined so as to include what belongs to it and exclude all else.

On that view, if, as has been further maintained, moral reverence is continuous with material awe and what we may call the ideal with the material sacred, when we speak of the sacredness of truth and beauty and goodness, we are, whether consciously or not, putting them into the sphere of religion. And there must be a sense in which this is right, because we cannot by any building up of natural values arrive at anything of absolute worth, and it is the sacredness of truth, in itself and for our own loyalty, which distinguishes it from mere facts in an encyclopaedia, while by the same mark beauty is distinguished from prettiness, and goodness from merely useful behaviour.

But, while the sacred to which they appeal and the reverence they stir are from the world of religion, it is vital to any right interest in them that each should be in a world of its own. We have the study of their norms or standards in logic, aesthetics, and ethics. Thus, on the one hand, even if their sacredness be in the same sphere as religion, they carry on their business in independence of it; and, on the other, religion is not a mere combination of them, nor yet something merely alongside of them. In seeking truth, we may not be influenced by religious considerations, but must regard only the reality we would know. And beauty, too, must just be beauty, and goodness goodness. If religion try to control such judgements, it corrupts them and is itself corrupted. Wherefore, while we cannot separate true thinking, feeling, and acting from religion without losing the absolute worth by which alone they can be valued, it becomes necessary to distinguish the business of religion from the business of logic, aesthetics, and ethics as sharply as we can.

The distinction, however, depends neither upon the feeling of holiness nor the judgement of sacredness, but upon the reality to which these belong—the existence of the supernatural. The supernatural is the special concern of religion, and nothing else is concerned with it in the same way as religion.

As here used the supernatural means the world which manifests more than natural values, the world which has values which stir the sense of the holy and demand to be esteemed as sacred. . . . The two are not in opposition, and are constantly interwoven, and there may be nothing wholly natural or wholly supernatural, but our interests in them are perfectly distinct, and very definitely distinguish aspects of our experience. Part of it is natural, in the sense that its values are comparative and to be judged as they serve our needs; and part of it supernatural, in the sense that its values are absolute, to which our needs must submit. We know the supernatural as it reflects itself in the sense of the holy and has for us absolute value, directly and without further argument, and henceforth we are concerned with its existence and its relation to us and our relation to it. We can make no more out of arguing abstractly about it than we should out of arguing abstractly, as men long did, about the natural. The supreme task, the task which has, more than any other, marked human progress, has been to discover the true sacred, and that means again to exercise the true sense of the holy. And, only on the basis of the right judgement inspired by the right feeling, can religion with profit ask: What is the sacred reality and how is it related to us and we to it?

SUGGESTED READINGS

The best way of putting oneself into a position to answer the question, "What is religion?", is to study a variety of the world's religions. The following books are helpful for this purpose: E. Conze, *Buddhism;* W. Briggs, *Anthology of Zen;* D. T. Suzuki, *Essays in Zen Buddhism;* L. Baeck, *The Essence of Judaism;* R. M. Brown, *The Spirit of Protestantism;* K. Adam, *The Spirit of Catholicism;* A. C. Bouquet, *Hinduism.* Comparative studies have been carried out in a number of different ways. E. Durkheim's *Elementary Forms of Religious Life* is by a great sociologist; R. Lowie, *Primitive Religion,* and J. G. Frazer, *The Golden Bough* (available in a one-volume abridgement) are by anthropologists; J. Wach, *Comparative Study of Religions,* is by a professor of theology. Chapter 4 of W. Kaufmann's *Critique of Religion and Philosophy* discusses various definitions of "religion" critically and sensibly. E. A. Burtt, *Types of Religious Philosophy,* Chapters 2–4, contains a good survey of traditional Western religion.

Recent discussions of the nature of religion have tended to center on the nature of religious language, the roles it plays in human life, the kinds of activity in which it plays these roles, and the ways in which it communicates religious thought and experience. R. B. Braithwaite, *An Empiricist's View of the Nature of Religious Belief,* gives a challenging account according to which religion is mainly morality plus fables. J. Wisdom's paper, "Gods," reprinted in his *Philosophy and Psychoanalysis,* gives quite a different view. P. Tillich's influential views may be found in *Dynamics of Faith,* Chapter 3, and in his essays in the symposium edited by S. Hook, *Religious Experience and Truth.* A clear account of the Thomist doctrine of analogical meaning is given in E. Mascall, *Existence and Analogy.* An elementary survey of views on the meaning of religious discourse is W. T. Blackstone, *Problem of Religious Language.*

Proofs of the Existence of God

The word "religion," like many other useful and important words in ordinary language, is quite vague. The beliefs and practices that may be referred to by it do not show any clear and sharp distinction from beliefs or practices that are not usually called "religious," and there is no very marked agreement as to just where the line should be drawn. People have called Marxism a religion, and some men are said to make money their god; there are religions with many deities and religions with none; there are religions that center on moral teaching and others for which such teaching is incidental. The form of religion best known in the civilizations of Western Europe and the Americas, however, is a religion involving both a belief in a deity and the advocacy of a set of moral standards. Insofar as a religion teaches the belief that God is a definite personal being separate from the rest of the universe, that religion is *theistic*. It is polytheistic or monotheistic, according as it teaches that there are many gods or only one. But it is to be distinguished from the *pantheistic* view, according to which God and the universe are in some manner one and the same, as well as from *atheistic* views, according to which there are no gods. To many theists, indeed, pantheists have seemed no more religious than atheists.

Some of the major philosophical problems that arise from and in the theistic view are discussed in the following readings. The present section is concerned with what is probably the central problem that arises in theistic religions: can we give a rational proof of the existence of God? An adequate discussion of this problem presupposes answers to two preliminary questions: what is the God of theism, and what do we mean by "proof?"

According to theists, God is actively present in the universe; He is *immanent*, or "indwelling" in it. But God is not to be identified with the universe. He also has being apart from it; God is *transcendent* as well as immanent. He is the omnipotent creator of the universe, its omnipresent conserver, and the ultimate source of all good. This conception of God as both immanent and transcendent is characteristic of theism. But it is important to realize that not all religions are theistic. According to the teachings of pantheistic religions, for example, the universe itself is Divine, and God is *not* a transcendent being, a being apart from the universe itself. Some religions also reject the theistic concept of God.

Secondly, what do we mean by a "proof" of the existence of God? It ought to be noted that any proof presupposes some premises. In Euclidean geometry, for instance, we can prove a great many theorems; but we must accept certain postulates or axioms from which these theorems are deduced. (It may be that in another context we could prove these initial premises, but in that case we would start from still other unproved premises.) This also holds for the proofs we are considering. Each proof accepts some fact of experience or some idea as basic and from this ground argues for the existence of God. One of the proofs of Aquinas, for example, starts from the fact of causation in the universe and argues from this premise to the being of God as First Cause. In a similar fashion, each proof moves from an initial premise to the conclusion that God exists.

One form of criticism of the rational proofs asserts that the proofs do not necessarily demonstrate the existence of the God of theism. It considers a pantheistic interpretation of God, for example, to be equally consistent with these arguments. Another type of criticism attacks the validity of the proofs themselves. It maintains that a careful analysis of the reasoning involved reveals fallacies in all of them and shows that the argument fails to sustain the conclusion that God exists.

We should remember, however, that the problem of whether we can *prove* God's existence must be distinguished from the more general question of the truth of theism. Of course, we will have reason for believing in theism if we accept one or more of the proofs. But if we reject these proofs, it does not follow that we must reject theism. Many people have considered the proofs inadequate, yet have accepted theism on other grounds. Rational proofs for the existence of God, in short, offer only one line of approach to the truth of theism.

In the selections which follow, the proof given by SAINT ANSELM is an *a priori* argument. From an initial definition of God, Saint Anselm reasons that we cannot, without contradiction, assert that God does not exist. SAINT THOMAS AQUINAS rejected this form of proof; all his arguments are *a posteriori*. They start from some fact given in experience, such as "motion" or "design," and proceed from this fact to the conclusion that God exists.

Both HUME and STACE reject rational proofs of the existence of God. The selection from Hume criticizes the argument from design; but his method of criticism is equally applicable to the arguments from motion and from causation. The approach of Stace is more general, defending the view that the Divine is forever beyond all proof or disproof.

The Ontological Argument*

S T . A N S E L M [1033–1109], the greatest theologian of the eleventh century, is most famous for his ontological proof of the existence of God. In 1093 he was appointed Archbishop of Canterbury; his pontificate was stormy and interrupted, due to the attempts of King William Rufus to abrogate rights formerly granted to the Church. Anselm was canonized in 1494.

After I had published, at the solicitous entreaties of certain brethren, a brief work (the Monologium) as an example of meditation on the grounds of faith, in the person of one who investigates, in a course of silent reasoning with himself, matters of which he is ignorant; considering that this book was knit together by the linking of many arguments, I began to ask myself whether there might be found a single argument which would require no other for its proof than itself alone; and alone would suffice to demonstrate that God truly exists, . . .

Truly there is a God, although the fool hath said in his heart, There is no God.

And so, Lord, do thou, who dost give understanding to faith, give me, so far as thou knowest it to be profitable, to understand that thou art that which we believe. And, indeed, we believe that thou art a being than which nothing greater can be conceived. Or is there no such nature, since the fool hath said in his heart, there is no God? (Psalms xiv. I). But, at any rate, this very fool, when he hears of this being of which I speak—a being than which nothing greater can be conceived—understands what he hears, and what he understands is in his understanding; although he does not understand it to exist.

For, it is one thing for an object to be in the understanding, and another to understand that the object exists. When a painter first conceives of what he will afterwards perform, he has it in his understanding, but he does not yet understand it to be, because he has not yet performed it. But after he has made the painting, he both has it in his understanding, and he understands that it exists, because he has made it.

Hence, even the fool is convinced that something exists in the understand-

* From Anselm: *Proslogium,* translated by Sidney Norton Deane, Preface, Chapter 2 and 3. Copyright, 1910, by The Open Court Publishing Company. Reprinted by permission of The Open Court Publishing Company.

ing, at least, than which nothing greater can be conceived. For, when he hears of this, he understands it. And whatever is understood, exists in the understanding. And assuredly that, than which nothing greater can be conceived, cannot exist in the understanding alone. For, suppose it exists in the understanding alone: then it can be conceived to exist in reality; which is greater.

Therefore, if that, than which nothing greater can be conceived, exists in the understanding alone, the very being, than which nothing greater can be conceived, is one, than which a greater can be conceived. But obviously this is impossible. Hence, there is no doubt that there exists a being, than which nothing greater can be conceived, and it exists both in the understanding and in reality.

God cannot be conceived not to exist—God is that, than which nothing greater can be conceived—That which can be conceived not to exist is not God.

And it assuredly exists so truly, that it cannot be conceived not to exist. For, it is possible to conceive of a being which cannot be conceived not to exist; and this is greater than one which can be conceived not to exist. Hence, if that, than which nothing greater can be conceived, can be conceived not to exist, it is not that, than which nothing greater can be conceived. But this is an irreconcilable contradiction. There is, then, so truly a being than which nothing greater can be conceived to exist, that it cannot even be conceived not to exist; and this being thou art, O Lord, our God.

So truly, therefore, dost thou exist, O Lord, my God, that thou canst not be conceived not to exist; and rightly. For, if a mind could conceive of a being better than thee, the creature would rise above the Creator; and this is most absurd. And, indeed, whatever else there is, except thee alone, can be conceived not to exist. To thee alone, therefore, it belongs to exist more truly than all other beings, and hence in a higher degree than all others. For, whatever else exists does not exist so truly, and hence in a less degree it belongs to it to exist. Why, then, has the fool said in his heart, there is no God (Psalms xiv. I), since it is so evident, to a rational mind, that thou dost exist in the highest degree of all? Why, except that he is dull and a fool?

Five Proofs of the Existence of God[*]

S A I N T T H O M A S A Q U I N A S [1225?–1274], a member of the Dominican Order, studied and taught at the great seats of learning of his time. His life was devoted to the clarification of Christian doctrine and its integration with Aristotle's metaphysics. In his monumental *Summa Theologica* he effected one of the greatest syntheses in the history of thought: a body of teachings in which natural human reason and Divine Revelation are held to be in harmony on all philosophic problems and in all matters of faith.

Whether God Exists?

Objection 1. It seems that God does not exist; because if one of two contraries be infinite, the other would be altogether destroyed. But the name *God* means that He is infinite goodness. If, therefore, God existed, there would be no evil discoverable; but there is evil in the world. Therefore God does not exist.

Obj. 2. Further, it is superfluous to suppose that what can be accounted for by a few principles has been produced by many. But it seems that everything we see in the world can be accounted for by other principles, supposing God did not exist. For all natural things can be reduced to one principle, which is nature; and all voluntary things can be reduced to one principle, which is human reason, or will. Therefore there is no need to suppose God's existence.

On the contrary, It is said in the person of God: *I am Who am* (Exod. iii. 14).

I answer that, The existence of God can be proved in five ways.

The first and more manifest way is the argument from motion. It is certain, and evident to our senses, that in the world some things are in motion. Now whatever is moved is moved by another, for nothing can be moved except it is in potentiality to that towards which it is moved; whereas a thing moves inasmuch as it is in act. For motion is nothing else than the reduction of something from potentiality to actuality. But nothing can be reduced from potentiality to actuality, except by something in a state of actuality.

[*] From Aquinas, *Summa Theologica*, translated, edited, and annotated by Anton C. Pegis. Reprinted by permission of Random House, Inc., New York, and Burns and Oates, Ltd., London.

Thus that which is actually hot, as fire, makes wood, which is potentially hot, to be actually hot, and thereby moves and changes it. Now it is not possible that the same thing should be at once in actuality and potentiality in the same respect, but only in different respects. For what is actually hot cannot simultaneously be potentially hot; but it is simultaneously potentially cold. It is therefore impossible that in the same respect and in the same way a thing should be both mover and moved, *i.e.*, that it should move itself. Therefore, whatever is moved must be moved by another. If that by which it is moved be itself moved, then this also must needs be moved by another, and that by another again. But this cannot go on to infinity, because then there would be no first mover, and, consequently, no other mover, seeing that subsequent movers move only inasmuch as they are moved by the first mover; as the staff moves only because it is moved by the hand. Therefore it is necessary to arrive at a first mover, moved by no other; and this everyone understands to be God.

The second way is from the nature of efficient cause. In the world of sensible things we find there is an order of efficient causes. There is no case known (neither is it, indeed, possible) in which a thing is found to be the efficient cause of itself; for so it would be prior to itself, which is impossible. Now in efficient causes it is not possible to go on to infinity, because in all efficient causes following in order, the first is the cause of the intermediate cause, and the intermediate is the cause of the ultimate cause, whether the intermediate cause be several, or one only. Now to take away the cause is to take away the effect. Therefore, if there be no first cause among efficient causes, there will be no ultimate, nor any intermediate, cause. But if in efficient causes it is possible to go on to infinity, there will be no first efficient cause, neither will there be an ultimate effect, nor any intermediate efficient causes; all of which is plainly false. Therefore it is necessary to admit a first efficient cause, to which everyone gives the name of God.

The third way is taken from possibility and necessity, and runs thus. We find in nature things that are possible to be and not to be, since they are found to be generated, and to be corrupted, and consequently, it is possible for them to be and not to be. But it is impossible for these always to exist, for that which can not-be at some time is not. Therefore, if everything can not-be, then at one time there was nothing in existence. Now if this were true, even now there would be nothing in existence, because that which does not exist begins to exist only through something already existing. Therefore, if at one time nothing was in existence, it would have been impossible for anything to have begun to exist; and thus even now nothing would be in existence—which is absurd. Therefore, not all beings are merely possible, but there must exist something the existence of which is necessary. But every necessary thing either has its necessity caused by another, or not. Now it is impossible to go on to infinity in necessary things which have their necessity caused by another, as has been already proved in regard to efficient causes. Therefore we cannot but admit the existence of some being having of itself its own necessity, and not receiving it from another, but rather causing in others their necessity. This all men speak of as God.

The fourth way is taken from the gradation to be found in things. Among beings there are some more and some less good, true, noble, and the like. But *more* and *less* are predicated of different things according as they resemble in their different ways something which is the maximum, as a thing is said to be hotter according as it more nearly resembles that which is hottest; so that there is something which is truest, something best, something noblest, and, consequently, something which is most being, for those things that are greatest in truth are greatest in being, as it is written in [Aristotle's] *Metaphysics* ii. Now the maximum in any genus is the cause of all in that genus, as fire, which is the maximum of heat, is the cause of all hot things, as is said in the same book. Therefore there must also be something which is to all beings the cause of their being, goodness, and every other perfection; and this we call God.

The fifth way is taken from the governance of the world. We see that things which lack knowledge, such as natural bodies, act for an end, and this is evident from their acting always, or nearly always, in the same way, so as to obtain the best result. Hence it is plain that they achieve their end, not fortuitously, but designedly. Now whatever lacks knowledge cannot move towards an end, unless it be directed by some being endowed with knowlege and intelligence; as the arrow is directed by the archer. Therefore some intelligent being exists by whom all natural things are directed to their end: and this being we call God.

Reply Obj. 1. As Augustine says: *Since God is the highest good, He would not allow any evil to exist in His works; unless His omnipotence and goodness were such as to bring good even out of evil.* This is part of the infinite goodness of God, that He should allow evil to exist, and out of it produce good.

Reply Obj. 2. Since nature works for a determinate end under the direction of a higher agent, whatever is done by nature must be traced back to God as to its first cause. So likewise whatever is done voluntarily must be traced back to some higher cause other than human reason and will, since these can change and fail; for all things that are changeable and capable of defect must be traced back to an immovable and self-necessary first principle, as has been shown.

On the Argument from Design[*]

DAVID HUME [1711–1776]. See page 110.

I must own, *Cleanthes*, said *Demea*, that nothing can more surprise me, than the light, in which you have, all along, put this argument. By the whole tenor of your discourse, one would imagine that you were maintaining the being of a God, against the cavils of atheists and infidels; and were necessitated to become a champion for that fundamental principle of all religion. But this, I hope, is not by any means a question among us. No man; no man, at least, of common sense, I am persuaded, ever entertained a serious doubt with regard to a truth so certain and self-evident. The question is not concerning the *being* but the *nature* of God. This, I affirm, from the infirmities of human understanding, to be altogether incomprehensible and unknown to us. The essence of that supreme mind, his attributes, the manner of his existence, the very nature of his duration; these and every particular, which regards so divine a Being, are mysterious to men. Finite, weak, and blind creatures, we ought to humble ourselves in his august presence, and, conscious of our frailties, adore in silence his infinite perfections, which eye hath not seen, ear hath not heard, neither hath it entered into the heart of man to conceive them. They are covered in a deep cloud from human curiosity: It is profaneness to attempt penetrating through these sacred obscurities: And next to the impiety of denying his existence, is the temerity of prying into his nature and essence, decrees and attributes.

But lest you should think, that my piety has here got the better of my philosophy, I shall support my opinion, if it needs any support, by a very great authority. I might cite all the divines almost, from the foundation of Christianity, who have ever treated of this or any other theological subject: But I shall confine myself, at present, to one equally celebrated for piety and philosophy. It is Father Malebranche, who, I remember, thus expresses himself. "One ought not so much (says he) to call God a spirit, in order to express positively what he is, as in order to signify that he is not matter. He is a Being infinitely perfect: Of this we cannot doubt. But in the same manner as we ought not to imagine, even supposing him corporeal, that he is clothed with a human body, as the Anthropomorphites asserted, under colour that

[*] From Hume: *Dialogues Concerning Natural Religion*, Part II.

that figure was the most perfect of any; so neither ought we to imagine, that the Spirit of God has human ideas, or bears *any* resemblance to our spirit; under colour that we know nothing more perfect than a human mind. We ought rather to believe, that as he comprehends the perfections of matter without being material . . . he comprehends also the perfections of created spirits, without being spirit, in the manner we conceive spirit: That his true name is, *He that is,* or in other words, Being without restriction, All Being, the Being infinite and universal."

After so great an authority, *Demea,* replied *Philo,* as that which you have produced, and a thousand more, which you might produce, it would appear ridiculous in me to add my sentiment, or express my approbation of your doctrine. But surely, where reasonable men treat these subjects, the question can never be concerning the *Being,* but only the Nature of the Deity. The former truth, as you well observe, is unquestionable and self-evident. Nothing exists without a cause; and the original cause of this universe (whatever it be) we call GOD; and piously ascribe to him every species of perfection. Whoever scruples this fundamental truth deserves every punishment, which can be inflicted among philosophers, to wit, the greatest ridicule, contempt and disapprobation. But as all perfection is entirely relative, we ought never to imagine, that we comprehend the attributes of this divine Being, or to suppose, that his perfections have any analogy or likeness to the perfections of a human creature. Wisdom, thought, design, knowledge; these we justly ascribe to him; because these words are honourable among men, and we have no other language or other conceptions, by which we can express our adoration of him. But let us beware, lest we think, that our ideas any wise correspond to his perfections, or that his attributes have any resemblance to these qualities among men. He is infinitely superior to our limited view and comprehension; and is more the object of worship in the temple, than of disputation in the schools.

In reality, *Cleanthes,* continued he, there is no need of having recourse to that affected scepticism, so displeasing to you, in order to come at this determination. Our ideas reach no farther than our experience: We have no experience of divine attributes and operations: I need not conclude my syllogism: You can draw the inference yourself. And it is a pleasure to me (and I hope to you too) that just reasoning and sound piety here concur in the same conclusion, and both of them establish the adorably mysterious and incomprehensible nature of the supreme Being.

Not to lose any time in circumlocutions, said *Cleanthes,* addressing himself to *Demea,* much less in replying to the pious declamations of *Philo;* I shall briefly explain how I conceive this matter. Look round the world: Contemplate the whole and every part of it: You will find it to be nothing but one great machine, subdivided into an infinite number of lesser machines, which again admit of subdivisions, to a degree beyond what human senses and faculties can trace and explain. All these various machines, and even their most minute parts, are adjusted to each other with an accuracy, which ravishes into admiration all men, who have ever contemplated them. The curious adapting of means to ends, throughout all nature, resembles exactly, though it much exceeds, the productions of human contrivance; of human design, thought, wisdom, and intelligence. Since therefore the effects resemble each other, we are led to infer, by all the rules of analogy, that the causes also resemble; and that the Author of nature is somewhat similar to the mind of man; though possessed of much larger faculties, proportioned to the grandeur of the work, which he has executed. By this argument *a posteriori*, and by this argument alone, do we prove at once the existence of a Deity, and his similarity to human mind and intelligence.

I shall be so free, *Cleanthes*, said *Demea*, as to tell you, that from the beginning, I could not approve of your conclusion concerning the similarity of the Deity to men; still less can I approve of the mediums, by which you endeavour to establish it. What! No demonstration of the being of a God! No abstract arguments! No proofs *a priori*! Are these, which have hitherto been so much insisted on by philosophers, all fallacy, all sophism? Can we reach no farther in this subject than experience and probability? I will not say, that this is betraying the cause of a Deity: But surely, by this affected candour, you give advantage to atheists, which they never could obtain, by the mere dint of argument and reasoning.

What I chiefly scruple in this subject, said *Philo*, is not so much, that all religious arguments are by *Cleanthes* reduced to experience, as that they appear not to be even the most certain and irrefragable of that inferior kind. That a stone will fall, that fire will burn, that the earth has solidity, we have observed a thousand and a thousand times; and when any new instance of this nature is presented, we draw without hesitation the accustomed inference. The exact similarity of the cases gives us a perfect assurance of a similar event; and a stronger evidence is never desired nor sought after. But wherever you depart, in the least, from the similarity of the cases, you diminish proportionably the evidence; and may at last bring it to a very weak *analogy*, which is confessedly liable to error and uncertainty. After having experienced the circulation of the blood in human creatures, we make no doubt that it takes place in men and other animals. The analogical reasoning is much weaker, when we infer the circulation of the sap in vegetables from our experience that the blood circulates in animals; and those, who hastily followed that imperfect analogy, are found, by more accurate experiments, to have been mistaken.

If we see a house, *Cleanthes,* we conclude, with the greatest certainty, that it had an architect or builder; because this is precisely that species of effect, which we have experienced to proceed from that species of cause. But surely you will not affirm, that the universe bears such a resemblance to a house, that we can with the same certainty infer a similar cause, or that the analogy is here entire and perfect. The dissimilitude is so striking, that the utmost you can here pretend to is a guess, a conjecture, a presumption concerning a similar cause; and how that pretension will be received in the world, I leave you to consider.

It would surely be very ill received, replied *Cleanthes;* and I should be deservedly blamed and detested, did I allow, that the proofs of a Deity amounted to no more than a guess or conjecture. But is the whole adjustment of means to ends in a house and in the universe so slight a resemblance? The economy of final causes? The order, proportion, and arrangement of every part? Steps of a stair are plainly contrived, that human legs may use them in mounting; and this inference is certain and infallible. Human legs are also contrived for walking and mounting; and this inference, I allow, is not altogether so certain, because of the dissimilarity which you remark; but does it, therefore, deserve the name only of presumption or conjecture?

Good God! cried *Demea,* interrupting him, where are we? Zealous defenders of religion allow, that the proofs of a Deity fall short of perfect evidence! And you, *Philo,* on whose assistance I depended, in proving the adorable mysteriousness of the divine nature, do you assent to all these extravagant opinions of *Cleanthes?* For what other name can I give them? Or why spare my censure, when such principles are advanced, supported by such an authority, before so young a man as *Pamphilus?*

You seem not to apprehend, replied *Philo,* that I argue with *Cleanthes* in his own way; and by showing him the dangerous consequences of his tenets, hope at last to reduce him to our opinion. But what sticks most with you, I observe, is the representation which *Cleanthes* has made of the argument *a posteriori;* and finding that that argument is likely to escape your hold and vanish into air, you think it so disguised, that you can scarcely believe it to be set in its true light. Now, however much I may dissent, in other respects, from the dangerous principles of *Cleanthes,* I must allow, that he has fairly represented that argument; and I shall endeavour so to state the matter to you, that you will entertain no farther scruples with regard to it.

Were a man to abstract from every thing which he knows or has seen, he would be altogether incapable, merely from his own ideas, to determine what kind of scene the universe must be, or to give the preference to one state or situation of things above another. For as nothing, which he clearly conceives, could be esteemed impossible or implying a contradiction, every chimera of his fancy would be upon an equal footing; nor could he assign any just reason, why he adheres to one idea or system, and rejects the others, which are equally possible.

Again; after he opens his eyes, and contemplates the world, as it really is, it would be impossible for him, at first, to assign the cause of any one event; much less, of the whole of things or of the universe. He might set his Fancy a rambling; and she might bring him in an infinite variety of reports and representations. These would all be possible; but being all equally possible, he would never, of himself, give a satisfactory account for his preferring one of them to the rest. Experience alone can point out to him the true cause of any phenomenon.

Now according to this method of reasoning, *Demea,* it follows (and is, indeed, tacitly allowed by *Cleanthes* himself) that order, arrangements, or the adjustment of final causes is not, of itself, any proof of design; but only so far as it has been experienced to proceed from that principle. For aught we can know *a priori* matter may contain the source or spring of order originally, within itself, as well as mind does; and there is no more difficulty in conceiving, that the several elements, from an internal unknown cause, may fall into the most exquisite arrangement, than to conceive that their ideas, in the great, universal mind, from a like internal, unknown cause, fall into that arrangement. The equal possibility of both these suppositions is allowed. But by experience we find (according to *Cleanthes*), that there is a difference between them. Throw several pieces of steel together, without shape or form; they will never arrange themselves so as to compose a watch: Stone, and mortar, and wood, without an architect, never erect a house. But the ideas in a human mind, we see, by an unknown, inexplicable economy, arrange themselves so as to form the plan of a watch or house. Experience, therefore, proves, that there is an original principle of order in mind, not in matter. From similar effects we infer similar causes. The adjustment of means to ends is alike in the universe, as in a machine of human contrivance. The causes, therefore, must be resembling.

I was from the beginning scandalised, I must own, with this resemblance, which is asserted, between the Deity and human creatures; and must conceive it to imply such a degradation of the supreme Being as no sound theist could endure. With your assistance, therefore, *Demea,* I shall endeavour to defend what you justly call the adorable mysteriousness of the divine nature, and shall refute this reasoning of *Cleanthes;* provided he allows, that I have made a fair representation of it.

When *Cleanthes* had assented, *Philo,* after a short pause, proceeded in the following manner.

That all inferences, *Cleanthes*, concerning fact, are founded on experience, and that all experimental reasonings are founded on the supposition, that similar causes prove similar effects, and similar effects similar causes; I shall not, at present, much dispute with you. But observe, I entreat you, with what extreme caution all just reasoners proceed in the transferring of experiments to similar cases. Unless the cases be exactly similar, they repose no perfect confidence in applying their past observation to any particular phenomenon. Every alteration of circumstances occasions a doubt concerning the event; and it requires new experiments to prove certainly, that the new circumstances are of no moment or importance. A change in bulk, situation, arrangement, age, disposition of the air, or surrounding bodies; any of these particulars may be attended with the most unexpected consequences: And unless the objects be quite familiar to us, it is the highest temerity to expect with assurance, after any of these changes, an event similar to that which before fell under our observation. The slow and deliberate steps of philosophers, here, if any where, are distinguished from the precipitate march of the vulgar, who, hurried on by the smallest similitude, are incapable of all discernment or consideration.

But can you think, *Cleanthes*, that your usual phlegm and philosophy have been preserved in so wide a step as you have taken, when you compared to the universe houses, ships, furniture, machines; and from their similarity in some circumstances inferred a similarity in their causes? Thought, design, intelligence, such as we discover in men and other animals, is no more than one of the springs and principles of the universe, as well as heat or cold, attraction or repulsion, and a hundred others, which fall under daily observation. It is an active cause, by which some particular parts of nature, we find, produce alterations on other parts. But can a conclusion, with any propriety, be transferred from parts to the whole? Does not the great disproportion bar all comparison and inference? From observing the growth of a hair, can we learn any thing concerning the generation of a man? Would the manner of a leaf's blowing, even though perfectly known, afford us any instruction concerning the vegetation of a tree?

But allowing that we were to take the *operations* of one part of nature upon another for the foundation of our judgment concerning the *origin* of the whole (which never can be admitted); yet why select so minute, so weak, so bounded a principle as the reason and design of animals is found to be upon this planet? What peculiar privilege has this little agitation of the brain which we call *thought*, that we must thus make it the model of the whole universe? Our partiality in our own favour does indeed present it on all occasions: But sound philosophy ought carefully to guard against so natural an illusion.

So far from admitting, continued *Philo*, that the operations of a part can afford us any just conclusion concerning the origin of the whole, I will not allow any one part to form a rule for another part, if the latter be very remote from the former. Is there any reasonable ground to conclude, that the inhabitants of other planets possess thought, intelligence, reason, or any thing similar to these faculties in men? When nature has so extremely diversified her manner of operation in this small globe; can we imagine, that she incessantly copies herself throughout so immense a universe? And if thought, as we may well suppose, be confined merely to this narrow corner, and has even there so limited a sphere of action; with what propriety can we assign it for the original cause of all things? The narrow views of a peasant, who makes his domestic economy the rule for the government of kingdoms, is in comparison a pardonable sophism.

But were we ever so much assured, that a thought and reason, resembling the human, were to be found throughout the whole universe, and were its activity elsewhere vastly greater and more commanding than it appears in this globe: Yet I cannot see, why the operations of a world, constituted, arranged, adjusted, can with any propriety be extended to a world, which is in its embryo-state, and is advancing towards that constitution and arrangement. By observation, we know somewhat of the economy, action, and nourishment of a finished animal; but we must transfer with great caution that observation to the growth of a foetus in the womb, and still more, to the formation of an animalcule in the loins of its parent. Nature, we find, even from our limited experience, possesses an infinite number of springs and principles, which incessantly discover themselves on every change of her position and situation. And what new and unknown principles would actuate her in so new and unknown a situation as that of the formation of a universe, we cannot, without the utmost temerity, pretend to determine.

A very small part of this great system, during a very short time, is very imperfectly discovered to us: And do we thence pronounce decisively concerning the origin of the whole?

Admirable conclusion! Stone, wood, brick, iron, brass, have not, at this time, in this minute globe of earth, an order or arrangement without human art and contrivance: Therefore the universe could not originally attain its order and arrangement, without something similar to human art. But is a part of nature a rule for another part very wide of the former? Is it a rule for the whole? Is a very small part a rule for the universe? Is nature in one situation, a certain rule for nature in another situation, vastly different from the former?

And can you blame me, *Cleanthes*, if I here imitate the prudent reserve of Simonides, who, according to the noted story, being asked by Hiero, *What*

God was? desired a day to think of it, and then two days more; and after that manner continually prolonged the term, without ever bringing in his definition or description? Could you even blame me, if I had answered at first, *that I did not know,* and was sensible that this subject lay vastly beyond the reach of my faculties? You might cry out sceptic and rallier as much as you pleased: But having found, in so many other subjects, much more familiar, the imperfections and even contradictions of human reason, I never should expect any success from its feeble conjectures, in a subject, so sublime, and so remote from the sphere of our observation. When two species of objects have always been observed to be conjoined together, I can *infer,* by custom, the existence of one wherever I see the existence of the other: And this I call an argument from experience. But how this argument can have place, where the objects, as in the present case, are single, individual, without parallel, or specific resemblance, may be difficult to explain. And will any man tell me with a serious countenance, that an orderly universe must arise from some thought and art, like the human, because we have experience of it? To ascertain this reasoning, it were requisite, that we had experience of the origin of worlds; and it is not sufficient surely, that we have seen ships and cities arise from human art and contrivance. . . .

Philo was proceeding in this vehement manner, somewhat between jest and earnest, as it appeared to me; when he observed some signs of impatience in *Cleanthes,* and then immediately stopped short. What I had to suggest, said *Cleanthes,* is only that you would not abuse terms, or make use of popular expressions to subvert philosophical reasonings. You know, that the vulgar often distinguish reason from experience, even where the question relates only to matter of fact and existence; though it is found, where that *reason* is properly analysed, that it is nothing but a species of experience. To prove by experience the origin of the universe from mind is not more contrary to common speech than to prove the motion of the earth from the same principle. And a caviller might raise all the same objections to the Copernican system, which you have urged against my reasonings. Have you other earths, might he say, which you have seen to move? Have. . . .

Yes! cried *Philo,* interrupting him, we have other earths. Is not the moon another earth, which we see to turn round its centre? Is not Venus another earth, where we observe the same phenomenon? Are not the revolutions of the sun also a confirmation, from analogy, of the same theory? All the planets, are they not earths, which revolve about the sun? Are not the satellites moons, which move round Jupiter and Saturn, and along with these primary planets, round the sun? These analogies and resemblances, with others, which I have not mentioned, are the sole proofs of the Copernican system: And to you it belongs to consider, whether you have any analogies of the same kind to support your theory.

In reality, *Cleanthes,* continued he, the modern system of astronomy is now so much received by all enquirers, and has become so essential a part even of our earliest education, that we are not commonly very scrupulous in examining the reasons upon which it is founded. It is now become a matter of mere curiosity to study the first writers on that subject, who had the full force of prejudice to encounter, and were obliged to turn their arguments on every side, in order to render them popular and convincing. But if we peruse Galileo's famous *Dialogues* concerning the system of the world, we shall find that that great genius, one of the sublimest that ever existed, first bent all his endeavours to prove, that there was no foundation for the distinction commonly made between elementary and celestial substances. The schools, proceeding from the illustrations of sense, had carried this distinction very far; and had established the latter substances to be ingenerable, incorruptible, unalterable, impassible; and had assigned all the opposite qualities to the former. But Galileo, beginning with the moon, proved its similarity in every particular to the earth; its convex figure, its natural darkness when not illuminated, its density, its distinction into solid and liquid, the variations of its phases, the mutual illuminations of the earth and moon, their mutual eclipses, the inequalities of the lunar surface, &c. After many instances of this kind, with regard to all the planets, men plainly saw, that these bodies became proper objects of experience; and that the similarity of their nature enabled us to extend the same arguments and phenomena from one to the other.

In this cautious proceeding of the astronomers, you may read your own condemnation, *Cleanthes;* or rather may see, that the subject in which you are engaged exceeds all human reason and enquiry. Can you pretend to show any such similarity between the fabric of a house, and the generation of a universe? Have you ever seen nature in any such situation as resembles the first arrangement of the elements? Have worlds ever been formed under your eye? and have you had leisure to observe the whole progress of the phenomenon, from the first appearance of order to its final consummation? If you have, then cite your experience, and deliver your theory.

The Divine as Beyond Proof *

WALTER TERENCE STACE [1886–   ] was born and educated in Britain, served in the British Civil Service in Ceylon for twenty-two years, and came to the United States in 1932 to teach philosophy at Princeton. Stace's works include books on Greek philosophy, Hegel, aesthetics, the theory of knowledge, morals and politics, and religion.

The pure religious consciousness lies in a region which is forever beyond all proof or disproof.

This is a necessary consequence of the "utterly other" character of God from the world, and of the "utterly other" character of the world from God. The eternal order is not the natural order, and the natural order is not the eternal order. The two orders intersect, but in the intersection each remains what it is. Each is wholly self-contained. Therefore it is impossible to pass, by any logical inference, from one to the other. This at once precludes as impossible any talk either of the proof or disproof of religion.

When philosophers and theologians speak of "proofs of the existence of God," or "evidences of Christianity," what they have in mind is always a logical passage from the natural order, or some fact in the natural order, to the divine order. They may, for instance, argue in the following way. Here is the world. That is a natural fact. It must have had a cause. Other natural facts are then pointed out which are supposed to show adaptations of means to end in nature. Bees pollinate flowers. Surely not by chance, nor following any purpose of their own. Or the heart has the function—which is interpreted as meaning the purpose—of pumping the blood. This teleological mechanism was not made by us, and the purpose evident in it is not our purpose. Therefore the cause of the world must have been an intelligent and designing mind. Doubtless I have much over-simplified the argument, and this version of it might not be accepted by the theologian as a statement of it which is to his liking. Certainly it is not a full statement. That, however, is not the point. The point is that, however the argument is stated, it necessarily starts from the natural order, or from selected facts in the natural order, and ends with a conclusion about the divine reality.

In other cases the natural fact from which the argument starts may be

---

some very astonishing occurrence, which we do not yet know how to explain, and which we therefore call a miracle. This is evidence, it is believed, of a divine intervention.

In all cases we use some fact or facts of the natural order as premises for our argument, and then leap, by an apparently logical inference, clear out of the natural order into the divine order, which thus appears as the conclusion of the argument. The point is that the premise is in the natural world, the conclusion in the divine world.

But an examination of the nature of inference shows that this is an impossible procedure. For inference proceeds always along the thread of some relation. We start with one fact, which is observed. This bears some relation to another fact, which is not observed. We pass along this relation to the second fact. The first fact is our premise, the second fact our conclusion. The relation, in the case of the deductive inference, is that of logical entailment. In non-deductive inferences other relations are used, of which the most common is that of causality. Thus, although the sun is now shining, and the sky is cloudless, I see that the ground is wet, and the trees are dripping with water. I infer that an April shower has passed over, and that it rained a few minutes ago. My inference has passed along the thread of a causal relation from an effect as premise to a cause as conclusion. To pass in this way from facts which are before my eyes, along a relational link, to other facts which are not before my eyes—which are inferred, not seen—is the universal character of inference.

But the natural order is the totality of all things which stand to each other in the one systematic network of relationships which is the universe. Therefore no inference can ever carry me from anything in the natural order to anything outside it. If I start from a natural fact, my inferential process, however long, can end only in another natural fact. A "first cause," simply by virtue of being a cause, would be a fact in the natural order. It is not denied that it might conceivably be possible to argue back from the present state of the world to an intelligent cause of some of its present characteristics— although I do not believe that any such argument is in fact valid. The point is that an intelligent cause of the material world, reached by any such inference, would be only another natural being, a part of the natural order. The point is that such a first cause *would not be God*. It would be at the most a demi-urge. I shall return to this point later.

If God does not lie at the end of any telescope, neither does He lie at the end of any syllogism. I can never, starting from the natural order, prove the divine order. The proof of the divine order must lie, somehow, within itself. It must be its own witness. For it, like the natural order, is complete in itself, self-contained.

But if, for these reasons, God can never be proved by arguments which take natural facts for their premises, for the very same reason He can never be disproved by such arguments. For instance, He cannot be disproved by pointing to the evil and pain in the world.

But if, by arguments of the kind we are considering, the divine order can never be proved, nevertheless God is not without witness. Nor is His being any the less a certainty. But the argument for anything within the divine order must start from within the divine order. The divine order, however, is not far off. It is not beyond the stars. It is within us—as also within all other things. God exists in the eternal moment which is in every man, either self-consciously present and fully revealed, or buried, more or less deeply, in the unconscious. We express this in poetic language if we say that God is "in the heart." It is in the heart, then, that the witness of Him, the proof of Him, must lie, and not in any external circumstance of the natural order. So far as theology is concerned, we had better leave the bees and their pollination of flowers alone.

That the divine cannot be made the subject of proof is merely another aspect of the truth that the mystical illumination is incapable of conceptualization. For this means that God is inaccessible to the logical intellect. The attempt to prove His existence is an attempt to reach Him through concepts, and is therefore foredoomed to failure. The doctrine of the negative divine implies the same conclusion. For its meaning is that the door to an understanding of God is barred against the concept, and therefore against logical argument. And all this comes to the same as saying that God is known only by intuition, not by the logical intellect.

The great error of the traditional proofs of the existence of God is that they take a symbolic truth for a literal truth, a truth of fact, and then try to prove that it is a fact. The religious doctrine speaks of God as a mind or person, purposively controlling the world for good ends, and filled with love for men and all creatures. This symbolic language is taken as stating literal facts, and then "evidences" of these facts are sought. The results are invariably disastrous for religion. The evidences are torn to shreds by the sceptic without difficulty, and it then seems to all the world as if religion has been destroyed, although, if religion were truly understood, it would be seen that it emerges entirely unscathed from these sceptical attacks.

For instance, it is desired to prove that God is good and loves His creatures. The only possible "evidences" for this, to be found in the natural order, will consist in the various "blessings" which men undoubtedly enjoy —in other words, the various good things which the world contains and the happiness which men often experience. But if these are pointed out, all the sceptic has to do is to point to the evil and misery in the world, most of which cannot by any conceivable stretch of imagination be attributed to man's own fault, although some can. (Presumably none of the agony suffered by animals can be thought of as due to their fault.) This is evidence on the other side, and entirely destroys the religious argument. For the conclusion which that argument seeks to reach is not that God is partly good, and partly evil, which is what would follow from an impartial balancing of the good and evil things in the world, but that God is wholly good. The only refuge of the religious man will consist in saying that, while the good in the world is evidence for God's goodness, the evil in the world is not evidence of His badness, but only of the fact that the existence of evil is for man a mystery and an insoluble problem. But obviously, from the point of view of logical argument, to which the religious man has foolishly committed himself, he cannot be allowed thus to quote the evidence which is in his favor, while refusing to take any account of the evidence against him, under the pretext that it is a mystery.

These defects come upon religious men because they take their doctrines to be literal statements of fact, and therefore amenable to proof by argument. It must now be added that these attempts at proof not only fail of their purpose, and so do no good to religion, but that they positively degrade it. For their effect is to drag down the divine and the eternal from their own sphere into the sphere of the natural and temporal. As has already been pointed out many times, if we argue back along the chain of causes to a first cause, and call this first cause God, we thereby make Him merely one among other things in the world, that is, in the natural order. All the other alleged proofs have the same effect. They thus make God finite. For the natural order is the order of finite things. If God is related to other things as their cause, then He is finite, since the otherness of these other things limits His being. This is the result of taking God's causality in a literal sense—in the sense, that is, in which we say that heat is the cause of the boiling of water. This also places God in time, because the causal relation is a time relation. But if the causality of God is taken symbolically, then it plainly cannot be proved by going backwards along the causal chain, since this procedure implies the literal understanding of the causal concept.

It is a logical impossibility to pass by inference from the natural order to the divine order. But it is not, of course, a logical impossibility to pass from one thing in the natural order to another. Therefore it is not a logical impossibility that there should be evidences of a vast mind running the affairs of nature. All sorts of purely naturalistic suggestions of this kind are possible. We cannot be sure that the human mind is the largest in the universe. Nor are disembodied minds a logical impossibility. The earth might therefore be presided over by a great invisible mind, who might take orders from a still greater mind in charge of the solar system. This spirit might in turn be subordinate to another spirit which supervises the galaxy. The solar system might be a single atom—the earth a single electron spinning round the nucleus—in the blood stream of some vast animal, whose body is the entire material universe. Such fantasies could conceivably be true. But they are superstitions nonetheless, because they are groundless, gratuitous, and lacking in any foundation of evidence. The point, however, is that no such vast mind running the universe, or a part of the universe, however enormous, magnificent, powerful, intelligent, good, it might be, could be God. For it would be merely another natural being, a part of the natural order, or perhaps the whole of it. God so thought of is a superstition, a gigantic and perhaps benevolent ghost, an immense, disembodied, and super-earthly clergyman. And some such superstition is what is implied by all the supposed proofs of His existence.

We return to our position that there is no logical reasoning which will carry us from the natural order to the divine order. There is no such thing as natural theology. God is either known by revelation—that is to say, by intuition—or not at all. And revelation is not something which took place in the past. It takes place in every moment of time, and in every heart—although it reaches a climactic moment in the illumination of the great mystic.

SUGGESTED READINGS

St. Anselm's ontological argument, which was also used by Descartes and others, has recently been defended by N. Malcolm, in an article (*Philosophical Review*, 1960) that led to considerable discussion. Malcolm's essay, together with a number of other essays on the argument, are reprinted in A. Plantinga, *The Ontological Argument*. R. Taylor, in *Metaphysics*, gives a good brief statement of the cosmological argument; for a more extended recent treatment, see A. Farrer, *Finite and Infinite*. The argument from design has been stated many times: William Paley's *Natural Theology* is an excellent eighteenth-century presentation, and Bishop Butler's *Analogy of Religion* is an earlier and more subtle version of a similar argument. For discussion of St. Thomas' five proofs, the books on him by F. Coplestone and by E. Gilson should be consulted. N. Kemp Smith's book on Hume is excellent; his edition of Hume's *Dialogues* has an extremely useful introduction.

Kant's famous objections to proofs of God's existence are to be found in his *Critique of Pure Reason*, Second Division, Book II, Chapter 3. Despite his rejection of all theoretical proofs for God, Kant thinks that the requirements imposed on us by morality give us a practical right to believe in God. His thought here is set forth in the *Critique of Practical Reason,* Book II, Chapter 2, especially Sections IV and V. In his *Commentary* on this work, L. W. Beck discusses these points in Chapter 14.

There is an elementary discussion of proofs of God's existence in W. Kaufmann, *Critique of Philosophy and Religion,* Chapter 5. A set of recent discussions is available in *New Essays in Philosophical Theology,* edited by A. Flew and A. MacIntyre: J. J. C. Smart examines a number of standard arguments for God's existence, and J. N. Findlay discusses whether God's existence can be disproved. John Hick's anthology, *The Existence of God,* contains numerous selections on this topic.

Mysticism

One way of seeking to establish the existence of God is through rational argument. We may, for example, argue that a careful analysis of our conception of God proves that God necessarily exists; or we may argue that His existence is logically implied by some particular fact of experience, such as the universality of causation, or the existence of minds, or the nature of morality. All such proofs of God's existence rely on inference: they do not assume that the existence of God is immediately known, but seek to establish it by reasoning.

According to *mysticism*, however, knowledge of God comes from direct experience, not from inference. For the mystic, God stands in no need of proof. The mystic need not argue for God's existence from other facts, since in the mystic state he has immediately experienced the presence of God. He finds in his experience of union with the Divine a certainty of God's reality which surpasses all other forms of knowing. In this union of the self with God all doubt disappears, and the reality of God is experienced more fully and richly than it can be known in any other way.

It might be charged, of course, that the certainty of God's reality which is attained in the mystic state is illusory. However, mystics answer this charge by citing the agreement among those who have experienced these states: throughout the ages there have been mystics, and their testimony bears common witness to the experience of union with the Divine.

The selection from JAMES portrays the essential characteristics of mystic states and shows their continuity with other, more familiar states of consciousness. James also shows how similar the experiences of mystics have been, and how pervasive mysticism has been in all religions. However, he is not merely concerned to depict the mystic state, he also evaluates the claim that such states offer proof of God's existence and yield knowledge of His nature.

JONES, who himself belongs in the mystic tradition, uses another approach. He is not concerned to defend the mystic experience as proof of the existence of God, but to demonstrate its importance in the whole economy of our lives—in thought as well as in action.

The Mystic's Way[*]

WILLIAM JAMES [1842–1910]. See page 166.

One may say truly, I think, that personal religious experience has its root and centre in mystical states of consciousness; so for us, who in these lectures are treating personal experience as the exclusive subject of our study, such states of consciousness ought to form the vital chapter from which the other chapters get their light. Whether my treatment of mystical states will shed more light or darkness, I do not know, for my own constitution shuts me out from their enjoyment almost entirely, and I can speak of them only at second hand. But though forced to look upon the subject so externally, I will be as objective and receptive as I can; and I think I shall at least succeed in convincing you of the reality of the states in question, and of the paramount importance of their function.

First of all, then, I ask, What does the expression "mystical states of consciousness" mean? How do we part off mystical states from other states?

The words "mysticism" and "mystical" are often used as terms of mere reproach, to throw at any opinion which we regard as vague and vast and sentimental, and without a base in either facts or logic. For some writers a "mystic" is any person who believes in thought-transference, or spirit-return. Employed in this way the word has little value: there are too many less ambiguous synonyms. So, to keep it useful by restricting it, I will simply propose to you four marks which, when an experience has them, may justify us in calling it mystical for the purpose of the present lectures. In this way we shall save verbal disputation, and the recriminations that generally go therewith.

1. INEFFABILITY. The handiest of the marks by which I classify a state of mind as mystical is negative. The subject of it immediately says that it defies expression, that no adequate report of its contents can be given in words. It follows from this that its quality must be directly experienced; it cannot be

imparted or transferred to others. In this peculiarity mystical states are more like states of feeling than like states of intellect. No one can make clear to another who has never had a certain feeling, in what the quality or worth of it consists. One must have musical ears to know the value of a symphony; one must have been in love one's self to understand a lover's state of mind. Lacking the heart or ear, we cannot interpret the musician or the lover justly, and are even likely to consider him weak-minded or absurd. The mystic finds that most of us accord to his experiences an equally incompetent treatment.

2. NOETIC QUALITY. Although so similar to states of feeling, mystical states seem to those who experience them to be also states of knowledge. They are states of insight into depths of truth unplumbed by the discursive intellect. They are illuminations, revelations, full of significance and importance, all inarticulate though they remain; and as a rule they carry with them a curious sense of authority for aftertime.

These two characters will entitle any state to be called mystical, in the sense in which I use the word. Two other qualities are less sharply marked, but are usually found. These are:—

3. TRANSIENCY. Mystical states cannot be sustained for long. Except in rare instances, half an hour, or at most an hour or two, seems to be the limit beyond which they fade into the light of common day. Often, when faded, their quality can but imperfectly be reproduced in memory; but when they recur it is recognized; and from one recurrence to another it is susceptible of continuous development in what is felt as inner richness and importance.

4. PASSIVITY. Although the oncoming of mystical states may be facilitated by preliminary voluntary operations, as by fixing the attention, or going through certain bodily performances, or in other ways which manuals of mysticism prescribe; yet when the characteristic sort of consciousness once has set in, the mystic feels as if his own will were in abeyance, and indeed sometimes as if he were grasped and held by a superior power. This latter peculiarity connects mystical states with certain definite phenomena of secondary or alternative personality, such as prophetic speech, automatic writing, or the mediumistic trance. When these latter conditions are well pronounced, however, there may be no recollection whatever of the phenomenon, and it may have no significance for the subject's usual inner life, to which, as it were, it makes a mere interruption. Mystical states, strictly so-called, are never merely interruptive. Some memory of their content always remains, and a profound sense of their importance. They modify the inner life of the subject between the times of their recurrence. Sharp divisions in this region are, however, difficult to make, and we find all sorts of gradations and mixtures.

These four characteristics are sufficient to mark out a group of states of consciousness peculiar enough to deserve a special name and to call for careful study. Let it then be called the mystical group.

Our next step should be to gain acquaintance with some typical examples. Professional mystics at the height of their development have often elaborately organized experiences and a philosophy based thereupon. But you remember what I said in my first lecture: phenomena are best understood when placed within their series, studied in their germ and in their over-ripe decay, and compared with their exaggerated and degenerated kindred. The range of mystical experience is very wide, much too wide for us to cover in the time at our disposal. Yet the method of serial study is so essential for interpretation that if we really wish to reach conclusions we must use it. I will begin, therefore, with phenomena which claim no special religious significance, and end with those of which the religious pretensions are extreme.

The simplest rudiment of mystical experience would seem to be that deepened sense of the significance of a maxim or formula which occasionally sweeps over one. "I've heard that said all my life," we exclaim, "but I never realized its full meaning until now." "When a fellow-monk," said Luther, "one day repeated the words of the Creed: 'I believe in the forgiveness of sins,' I saw the Scripture in an entirely new light; and straightway I felt as if I were born anew. It was as if I had found the door of paradise thrown wide open." This sense of deeper significance is not confined to rational propositions. Single words, and conjunctions of words, effects of light on land and sea, odors and musical sounds, all bring it when the mind is tuned aright. Most of us can remember the strangely moving power of passages in certain poems read when we were young, irrational doorways as they were through which the mystery of fact, the wildness and the pang of life, stole into our hearts and thrilled them. The words have now perhaps become mere polished surfaces for us; but lyric poetry and music are alive and significant only in proportion as they fetch these vague vistas of a life continuous with our own, beckoning and inviting, yet ever eluding our pursuit. We are alive or dead to the eternal inner message of the arts according as we have kept or lost this mystical susceptibility. . . .

Somewhat deeper plunges into mystical consciousness are met with in yet other dreamy states. Such feelings as these which Charles Kingsley describes are surely far from being uncommon, especially in youth:—

> When I walk the fields, I am oppressed now and then with an innate feeling that everything I see has a meaning, if I could but understand it. And this feeling of being surrounded with truths which I cannot grasp amounts to indescribable awe sometimes. . . . Have you not felt that your real soul was imperceptible to your mental vision, except in a few hallowed moments? . . .

The next step into mystical states carries us into a realm that public opinion and ethical philosophy have long since branded as pathological, though private practice and certain lyric strains of poetry seem still to bear witness to its ideality. I refer to the consciousness produced by intoxicants and anaesthetics, especially by alcohol. The sway of alcohol over mankind is unquestionably due to its power to stimulate the mystical faculties of human nature, usually crushed to earth by the cold facts and dry criticisms of the sober hour. Sobriety diminishes, discriminates, and says no; drunkenness expands, unites, and says yes. It is in fact the great exciter of the *Yes* function in man. It brings its votary from the chill periphery of things to the radiant core. It makes him for the moment one with truth. Not through mere perversity do men run after it. To the poor and the unlettered it stands in the place of symphony concerts and of literature; and it is part of the deeper mystery and tragedy of life that whiffs and gleams of something that we immediately recognize as excellent should be vouchsafed to so many of us only in the fleeting earlier phases of what in its totality is so degrading a poisoning. The drunken consciousness is one bit of the mystic consciousness and our total opinion of it must find its place in our opinion of that larger whole.

Nitrous oxide and ether, especially nitrous oxide, when sufficiently diluted with air, stimulate the mystical consciousness in an extraordinary degree. Depth beyond depth of truth seems revealed to the inhaler. This truth fades out, however, or escapes, at the moment of coming to; and if any words remain over in which it seemed to clothe itself, they prove to be the veriest nonsense. Nevertheless, the sense of a profound meaning having been there persists; and I know more than one person is persuaded that in the nitrous oxide trance we have a genuine metaphysical revelation.

Some years ago I myself made some observations on this aspect of nitrous oxide intoxication, and reported them in print. One conclusion was forced upon my mind at that time, and my impression of its truth has ever since remained unshaken. It is that our normal waking consciousness, rational consciousness as we call it, is but one special type of consciousness, whilst all about it, parted from it by the filmiest of screens, there lie potential forms of consciousness entirely different. We may go through life without suspecting their existence; but apply the requisite stimulus, and at a touch they are there in all their completeness, definite types of mentality which probably somewhere have their field of application and adaptation. No account of the universe in its totality can be final which leaves these other forms of consciousness quite disregarded. How to regard them is the question—for they are so discontinuous with ordinary consciousness. Yet they may determine attitudes though they cannot furnish formulas, and open a region though they fail to give a map. At any rate, they forbid a premature closing of our accounts with reality. Looking back on my own experiences, they all converge towards a kind of insight to which I cannot help ascribing some metaphysical significance. The keynote of it is invariably a reconciliation. It is as if the opposites of the world, whose contradictoriness and conflict make all our difficulties and troubles, were melted into unity. Not only do they, as contrasted species, belong to one and the same genus, but *one of the species,* the nobler and better one, *is itself the genus, and so soaks up and absorbs its opposite into itself.* This is a dark saying, I know, when thus expressed in terms of common logic, but I cannot wholly escape from its authority. I feel as if it must mean something, something like what the Hegelian philosophy means, if one could only lay hold of it more clearly. Those who have ears to hear, let them hear; to me the living sense of its reality only comes in the artificial mystic state of mind. . . .

J. A. Symonds records a mystical experience with chloroform, as follows:—

After the choking and stifling had passed away, I seemed at first in a state of utter blankness; then came flashes of intense light, alternating with blackness, and with a keen vision of what was going on in the room around me, but no sensation of touch. I thought that I was near death; when, suddenly, my soul became aware of God, who was manifestly dealing with me, handling me, so to speak, in an intense personal present reality. I felt him streaming in like light upon me. . . . I cannot describe the ecstasy I felt. Then, as I gradually awoke from the influence of the anaesthetics, the old sense of my relation to the world began to return, the new sense of my relation to God began to fade. . . .

Yet, this question remains, Is it possible that the inner sense of reality which succeeded, when my flesh was dead to impressions from without, to the ordinary sense of physical relations, was not a delusion but an actual experience? Is it possible that I, in that moment, felt what some of the saints have said they always felt, the undemonstrable but irrefragable certainty of God?

With this we make connection with religious mysticism pure and simple. Symonds's question takes us back to those examples which you will remember my quoting in the lecture on the Reality of the Unseen, of sudden realization of the immediate presence of God. The phenomenon in one shape or another is not uncommon.

'I know,' writes Mr. Trine, 'an officer on our police force who has told me that many times when off duty, and on his way home in the evening, there comes to him such a vivid and vital realization of his oneness with this Infinite Power, and this Spirit of Infinite Peace so takes hold of and so fills him, that it seems as if his feet could hardly keep to the pavement, so buoyant and so exhilarated does he become by reason of this inflowing tide.'

Certain aspects of nature seem to have a peculiar power of awakening such mystical moods. Most of the striking cases which I have collected have occurred out of doors. Literature has commemorated this fact in many passages of great beauty—this extract, for example, from Amiel's Journal Intime:—

Shall I ever again have any of those prodigious reveries which sometimes came to me in former days? One day, in youth, at sunrise, sitting in the ruins of the castle of Faucigny; and again in the mountains, under the noonday sun, above Lavey, lying at the foot of a tree and visited by three butterflies; once more at night upon the shingly shore of the Northern Ocean, my back upon the sand and my vision ranging through the milky way;—such grand and spacious, immortal, cosmogonic reveries, when one reaches to the stars, when one owns the infinite! Moments divine, ecstatic hours; in which our thought flies from world to world, pierces the great enigma, breathes with a respiration broad, tranquil, and deep as the respiration of the ocean, serene and limitless as the blue firmament; . . . instants of irresistible intuition in which one feels one's self great as the universe, and calm as a god. . . . What hours, what memories! The vestiges they leave behind are enough to fill us with belief and enthusiasm, as if they were visits of the Holy Ghost. . . .

We have now seen enough of this cosmic or mystic consciousness, as it comes sporadically. We must next pass to its methodical cultivation as an element of the religious life. Hindus, Buddhists, Mohammedans, and Christians all have cultivated it methodically.

In India, training in mystical insight has been known from time immemorial under the name of yoga. Yoga means the experimental union of the individual with the divine. It is based on persevering exercise; and the diet, posture, breathing, intellectual concentration, and moral discipline vary slightly in the different systems which teach it. The yogi, or disciple, who has by these means overcome the obscurations of his lower nature sufficiently, enters into the condition termed *samâdhi*, "and comes face to face with facts which no instinct or reason can ever know." He learns—

'That the mind itself has a higher state of existence, beyond reason, a superconscious state, and that when the mind gets to that higher state, then this knowledge beyond reasoning comes. . . . All the different steps in yoga are intended to bring us scientifically to the superconscious state or Samâdhi. . . . Just as unconscious work is beneath consciousness, so there is another work which is above consciousness, and which, also, is not accompanied with the feeling of egoism. . . . There is no feeling of *I*, and yet the mind works, desireless, free from restlessness, objectless, bodiless. Then the Truth shines in its full effulgence, and we know ourselves—for Samâdhi lies potential in us all—for what we truly are, free, immortal, omnipotent, loosed from the finite, and its contrasts of good and evil altogether, and identical with the Atman or Universal Soul.' . . .

In the Christian church there have always been mystics. Although many of them have been viewed with suspicion, some have gained favor in the eyes of the authorities. The experiences of these have been treated as precedents, and a codified system of mystical theology has been based upon them, in which everything legitimate finds its place. The basis of the system is "orison" or meditation, the methodical elevation of the soul towards God. Through the practice of orison the higher levels of mystical experience may be attained. . . .

The first thing to be aimed at in orison is the mind's detachment from outer sensations, for these interfere with its concentration upon ideal things. Such manuals as Saint Ignatius's Spiritual Exercises recommend the disciple to expel sensation by a gradual series of efforts to imagine holy scenes. The acme of this kind of discipline would be a semi-hallucinatory mono-ideism —an imaginary figure of Christ, for example, coming fully to occupy the mind. Sensorial images of this sort, whether literal or symbolic, play an enormous part in mysticism. But in certain cases imagery may fall away entirely, and in the very highest raptures it tends to do so. The state of consciousness becomes then insusceptible of any verbal description. Mystical teachers are unanimous as to this. . . . I cannot pretend to detail to you the sundry stages of the Christian mystical life. . . .

The cognitive aspects of them, their value in the way of revelation, is what we are directly concerned with, and it is easy to show by citation how strong an impression they leave of being revelations of new depths of truth. Saint Teresa is the expert of experts in describing such conditions, so I will turn immediately to what she says of one of the highest of them, the "orison of union."

'In the orison of union,' says Saint Teresa, 'the soul is fully awake as regards God, but wholly asleep as regards things of this world and in respect of herself. During the short time the union lasts, she is as it were deprived of every feeling, and even if she would, she could not think of any single thing. Thus she needs to employ no artifice in order to arrest the use of her understanding: it remains so stricken with inactivity that she neither knows what she loves, nor in what manner she loves, nor what she wills. In short, she is utterly dead to the things of the world and lives solely in God. . . . I do not even know whether in this state she has enough life left to breathe. It seems to me she has not; or at least that if she does breathe, she is unaware of it. Her intellect would fain understand something of what is going on within her, but it has so little force now that it can act in no way whatsoever. So a person who falls into a deep faint appears as if dead. . . .

'Thus does God, when he raises a soul to union with himself, suspend the natural action of all her faculties. She neither sees, hears, nor understands, so long as she is united with God. But this time is always short, and it seems even shorter than it is. God establishes himself in the interior of this soul in such a way, that when she returns to herself, it is wholly impossible for her to doubt that she has been in God, and God in her. This truth remains so strongly impressed on her that, even though many years should pass without the condition returning, she can neither forget the favor she received, nor doubt of its reality. If you, nevertheless, ask how it is possible that the soul can see and understand that she has been in God, since during the union she has neither sight nor understanding, I reply that she does not see it then, but that she sees it clearly later, after she has returned to herself, not by any vision, but by a certitude which abides with her and which God alone can give her. I knew a person who was ignorant of the truth that God's mode of being in everything must be either by presence, by power, or by essence, but who, after having received the grace of which I am speaking, believed this truth in the most unshakable manner. So much so that, having consulted a half-learned man who was as ignorant on this point as she had been before she was enlightened, when he replied that God is in us only by "grace," she disbelieved his reply, so sure she was of the true answer; and when she came to ask wiser doctors, they confirmed her in her belief, which much consoled her. . . .

'But how, you will repeat, *can* one have such certainty in respect to what one does not see? This question, I am powerless to answer. These are secrets of God's omnipotence which it does not appertain to me to penetrate. All that I know is that I tell the truth; and I shall never believe that any soul who does not possess this certainty has ever been really united to God.'

The kinds of truth communicable in mystical ways, whether these be sensible or supersensible, are various. Some of them relate to this world— visions of the future, the reading of hearts, the sudden understanding of texts, the knowledge of distant events, for example; but the most important revelations are theological or metaphysical. . . .

In spite of their repudiation of articulate self-description, mystical states in general assert a pretty distinct theoretic drift. It is possible to give the outcome of the majority of them in terms that point in definite philosophical directions. One of these directions is optimism, and the other is monism. We pass into mystical states from out of ordinary consciousness as from a less into a more, as from a smallness into a vastness, and at the same time as from an unrest to a rest. We feel them as reconciling, unifying states. They appeal to the yes-function more than to the no-function in us. In them the unlimited absorbs the limits and peacefully closes the account. Their very denial of every adjective you may propose as applicable to the ultimate truth—He, the Self, the Atman, is to be described by "No! no!" only, say the Upanishads—though it seems on the surface to be a no-function, is a denial made on behalf of a deeper yes. Whoso calls the Absolute anything in particular, or says that it is *this*, seems implicitly to shut it off from being *that*

—it is as if he lessened it. So we deny the "this," negating the negation which it seems to us to imply, in the interests of the higher affirmative attitude by which we are possessed. The fountain-head of Christian mysticism is Dionysius the Areopagite. He describes the absolute truth by negatives exclusively.

The cause of all things is neither soul nor intellect; nor has it imagination, opinion, or reason, or intelligence; nor is it reason or intelligence; nor is it spoken or thought. It is neither number, nor order, nor magnitude, nor littleness, nor equality, nor inequality, nor similarity, nor dissimilarity. It neither stands, nor moves, nor rests. . . . It is neither essence, nor eternity, nor time. Even intellectual contact does not belong to it. It is neither science nor truth. It is not even royalty or wisdom; not one; not unity; not divinity or goodness; nor even spirit as we know it.

But these qualifications are denied by Dionysius, not because the truth falls short of them, but because it so infinitely excels them. It is above them. It is *super*-lucent, *super*-splendent, *super*-essential, *super*-sublime, *super everything* that can be named. . . .

To this dialectical use, by the intellect, of negation as a mode of passage towards a higher kind of affirmation, there is correlated the subtlest of moral counterparts in the sphere of the personal will. Since denial of the finite self and its wants, since asceticism of some sort, is found in religious experience to be the only doorway to the larger and more blessed life, this moral mystery intertwines and combines with the intellectual mystery in all mystical writings. . . .

In Paul's language, I live, yet not I, but Christ liveth in me. Only when I become as nothing can God enter in and no difference between his life and mine remain outstanding.

This overcoming of all the usual barriers between the individual and the Absolute is the great mystic achievement. In mystic states we both become one with the Absolute and we become aware of our oneness. This is the everlasting and triumphant mystical tradition, hardly altered by differences of clime or creed. In Hinduism, in Neoplatonism, in Sufism, in Christian mysticism, in Whitmanism, we find the same recurring note, so that there is about mystical utterances an eternal unanimity which ought to make a critic stop and think, and which brings it about that the mystical classics have, as has been said, neither birthday nor native land. Perpetually telling of the unity of man with God, their speech antedates languages, and they do not grow old.

"That art Thou!" say the Upanishads, and the Vedantists add: "Not a part, not a mode of That, but identically That, that absolute Spirit of the World."

"As pure water poured into pure water remains the same, thus, O Gautama, is the Self of a thinker who knows. Water in water, fire in fire, ether in ether, no one can distinguish them: likewise a man whose mind has entered into the Self." . . .

In mystical literature such self-contradictory phrases as "dazzling obscurity," "whispering silence," "teeming desert," are continually met with. They prove that not conceptual speech, but music rather, is the element through which we are best spoken to by mystical truth. Many mystical scriptures are indeed little more than musical compositions.

"He who would hear the voice of Nada, 'the Soundless Sound,' and comprehend it, he has to learn the nature of Dhâranâ. . . . When to himself his form appears unreal, as do on waking all the forms he sees in dreams; when he has ceased to hear the many, he may discern the ONE—the inner sound which kills the outer. . . . For then the soul will hear, and will remember. And then to the inner ear will speak THE VOICE OF THE SILENCE. . . . And now thy *Self* is lost in SELF, *thyself* unto THYSELF, merged in that SELF from which thou first didst radiate. . . . Behold! thou hast become the Light, thou hast become the Sound, thou art thy Master and thy God. Thou art THYSELF the object of thy search: the VOICE unbroken, that resounds throughout eternities, exempt from change, from sin exempt, the seven sounds in one, the VOICE OF THE SILENCE."

These words, if they do not awaken laughter as you receive them, probably stir chords within you which music and language touch in common. Music gives us ontological messages which non-musical criticism is unable to contradict, though it may laugh at our foolishness in minding them. There is a verge of the mind which these things haunt; and whispers therefrom mingle with the operations of our understanding, even as the waters of the infinite ocean send their waves to break among the pebbles that lie upon our shores. . . .

That doctrine, for example, that eternity is timeless, that our "immortality," if we live in the eternal, is not so much future as already now and here, which we find so often expressed to-day in certain philosophic circles, finds its support in a "hear, hear!" or an "amen," which floats up from that mysteriously deeper level. We recognize the passwords to the mystical region as we hear them, but we cannot use them ourselves; it alone has the keeping of "the password primeval."

I have now sketched with extreme brevity and insufficiency, but as fairly as I am able in the time allowed, the general traits of the mystic range of consciousness. *It is on the whole pantheistic and optimistic, or at least the opposite of pessimistic. It is anti-naturalistic, and harmonizes best with twice-bornness and so-called other-worldly states of mind.*

My next task is to inquire whether we can invoke it as authoritative. Does it furnish any *warrant for the truth* of the twice-bornness and supernatural-ity and pantheism which it favors? I must give my answer to this question as concisely as I can.

In brief my answer is this—and I will divide it into three parts:—

(1) Mystical states, when well developed, usually are, and have the right to be, absolutely authoritative over the individuals to whom they come.
(2) No authority emanates from them which should make it a duty for those who stand outside of them to accept their revelations uncritically.
(3) They break down the authority of the non-mystical or rationalistic consciousness, based upon the understanding and the senses alone. They show it to be only one kind of consciousness. They open out the possibility of other orders of truth, in which, so far as anything in us vitally responds to them, we may freely continue to have faith.

I will take up these points one by one.

I.

As a matter of psychological fact, mystical states of a well-pronounced and emphatic sort *are* usually authoritative over those who have them. They have been "there," and know. It is vain for rationalism to grumble about this. If the mystical truth that comes to a man proves to be a force that he can live by, what mandate have we of the majority to order him to live in another way? We can throw him into a prison or a madhouse, but we cannot change his mind—we commonly attach it only the more stubbornly to its beliefs. It mocks our utmost efforts, as a matter of fact, and in point of logic it absolutely escapes our jurisdiction. Our own more "rational" beliefs are based on evidence exactly similar in nature to that which mystics quote for theirs. Our senses, namely, have assured us of certain states of fact; but mystical experiences are as direct perceptions of fact for those who have them as any sensations ever were for us. The records show that even though the five senses be in abeyance in them, they are absolutely sensational in their epistemological quality, if I may be pardoned the barbarous expression —that is, they are face to face presentations of what seems immediately to exist.

The mystic is, in short, *invulnerable,* and must be left, whether we relish it or not, in undisturbed enjoyment of his creed. Faith, says Tolstoy, is that by which men live. And faith-state and mystic state are practically convertible terms.

II.

But I now proceed to add that mystics have no right to claim that we ought to accept the deliverance of their peculiar experiences, if we are ourselves outsiders and feel no private call thereto. The utmost they can ever ask of us in this life is to admit that they establish a presumption. They form a consensus and have an unequivocal outcome; and it would be odd, mystics might say, if such a unanimous type of experience should prove to be altogether wrong. At bottom, however, this would only be an appeal to numbers, like the appeal of rationalism the other way; and the appeal to numbers has no logical force. If we acknowledge it, it is for "suggestive," not for logical reasons: we follow the majority because to do so suits our life.

But even this presumption from the unanimity of mystics is far from being strong. In characterizing mystic states as pantheistic, optimistic, etc., I am afraid I over-simplified the truth. I did so for expository reasons, and to keep the closer to the classic mystical tradition. The classic religious mysticism, it now must be confessed, is only a "privileged case." It is an *extract*, kept true to type by the selection of the fittest specimens and their preservation in "schools." It is carved out from a much larger mass; and if we take the larger mass as seriously as religious mysticism has historically taken itself, we find that the supposed unanimity largely disappears. To begin with, even religious mysticism itself, the kind that accumulates traditions and makes schools, is much less unanimous than I have allowed. It has been both ascetic and antinomianly self-indulgent within the Christian church. It is dualistic in Sankhya, and monistic in Vedanta philosophy. I called it pantheistic; but the great Spanish mystics are anything but pantheists. They are with few exceptions non-metaphysical minds, for whom "the category of personality" is absolute. The "union" of man with God is for them much more like an occasional miracle than like an original identity. How different again, apart from the happiness common to all, is the mysticism of Walt Whitman, Edward Carpenter, Richard Jeffries, and other naturalistic pantheists, from the more distinctively Christian sort. The fact is that the mystical feeling of enlargement, union, and emancipation has no specific intellectual content whatever of its own. It is capable of forming matrimonial alliances with material furnished by the most diverse philosophies and theologies, provided only they can find a place in their framework for its peculiar emotional mood. We have no right, therefore, to invoke its prestige as distinctively in favor of any special belief, such as that in absolute idealism or in the absolute monistic identity, or in the absolute goodness, of the world. It is only relatively in favor of all these things—it passes out of common human consciousness in the direction in which they lie.

So much for religious mysticism proper. But more remains to be told, for religious mysticism is only one half of mysticism. The other half has no accumulated traditions except those which the text-books on insanity supply. Open any one of these, and you will find abundant cases in which "mystical ideas" are cited as characteristic symptoms or enfeebled or deluded states of mind. In delusional insanity, paranoia, as they sometimes call it, we may have a *diabolical* mysticism, a sort of religious mysticism turned upside down. The same sense of ineffable importance in the smallest events, the same texts and words coming with new meanings, the same voices and visions and leadings and missions, the same controlling by extraneous powers; only this time the emotion is pessimistic: instead of consolations we have desolations; the meanings are dreadful; and the powers are enemies of life. It is evident that from the point of view of their psychological mechanism, the classic mysticism and these lower mysticisms spring from the same mental level, from that great subliminal or transmarginal region of which science is beginning to admit the existence, but of which so little is really known. That region contains every kind of matter: "seraph and snake" abide there side by side. To come from thence is no infallible credential. What comes must be sifted and tested, and run the gauntlet of confrontation with the total context of experience, just like what comes from the outer world of sense. Its value must be ascertained by empirical methods, so long as we are not mystics ourselves.

Once more, then, I repeat that non-mystics are under no obligation to acknowledge in mystical states a superior authority conferred on them by their intrinsic nature.

III.

Yet, I repeat once more, the existence of mystical states absolutely overthrows the pretension of non-mystical states to be the sole and ultimate dictators of what we may believe. As a rule, mystical states merely add a supersensuous meaning to the ordinary outward data of consciousness. They are excitements like the emotions of love or ambition, gifts to our spirit by means of which facts already objectively before us fall into a new expressiveness and make a new connection with our active life. They do not contradict these facts as such, or deny anything that our senses have immediately seized. It is the rationalistic critic rather who plays the part of denier in the controversy, and his denials have no strength, for there never can be a state of facts to which new meaning may not truthfully be added, provided the mind ascend to a more enveloping point of view. It must always remain an open question whether mystical states may not possibly be such superior points of view, windows through which the mind looks out upon a more extensive and inclusive world. The difference of the views seen from the different mystical windows need not prevent us from entertaining this supposition. The wider world would in that case prove to have a mixed constitution like that of this world, that is all. It would have its celestial and its infernal regions, its tempting and its saving moments, its valid experiences and its counterfeit ones, just as our world has them; but it would be a wider world all the same. We should have to use its experiences by selecting and subordinating and substituting just as is our custom in this ordinary naturalistic world; we should be liable to error just as we are now; yet the counting in of that wider world of meanings, and the serious dealing with it, might, in spite of all the perplexity, be indispensable stages in our approach to the final fullness of the truth.

The God of Mystical Experience*

RUFUS MATTHEW JONES [1863–1948] taught philosophy at Haverford College from 1889 almost until his death. He was a leading figure in the Society of Friends, and the active chairman of the American Friends Service Committee for twenty years. He wrote voluminously on the history of Quakerism and on the history and significance of the mystic tradition.

The interpreter of Mysticism labors under heavy handicaps. He is compelled, for one thing, to use a word that is loaded with uncertainty and confusion. For that reason he usually fails to convince persons who insist on having definiteness. Hosts of people, after all that has been written, still suppose that "mystical" is synonymous with the *mysterious*. The word is believed to stand for something dark, vague, deeply veiled and hidden. One hears "great argument about it and about," but evermore the darkness veils its meaning and the mystery abides. Still others use the word "mystical" to mean something occult or possibly uncanny. The Lady of the Lake, "clothed in white samite, mystic, wonderful," with a subtle secret magic, gave King Arthur his sword, Excalibur, and that use of the word "mystic" runs through human story and history. The Gnostic movements, the mystery religions, the lore of the Cabala, the teachings of theosophy, and the weird symbolizing of William Blake, are alike referred to as being "mystic."

The word has, again, been used in recent times, by psychologists and psychic researchers, for the phenomena of the mediumistic trance and séance. It has come to stand for table rappings and levitations and spirit-communications and ectoplasm and it often means any class of phenomena

---

* From Jones: *Pathways to the Reality of God*, Chapter 2. Copyright, 1931, by The Macmillan Company. Reprinted by permission of The Macmillan Company.

that do not come under scientific observation, or submit to careful laboratory methods. There is, too, a persistent tendency to apply the word "mystic" to mysterious voices which certain types of persons claim to hear—for example, the interior "voices" which Bunyan heard cry: "Sell him, sell him." Sometimes "communications" and "oracular messages" seem to be inwardly given to persons of this type. Then, again, the word is often used so loosely that it may mean any type of religion that is intense, emotional and vital, such, for example, as attends a conversion-experience or a personal dedication to a life of self-denying service.

One of the most frequent ways of using the word, especially in the history of Roman Catholic Mysticism, is to apply it exclusively to an extreme and rare type of contemplation, which culminates in ecstasy and which seems to the person himself to be a marriage union of the soul with God. The time-process seems to be obliterated in an eternal now and the finite being is absorbed into the Infinite One. That undoubtedly is the classical use of the word "mystical." From the nature of the case this experience of ecstasy and of absorption is something unutterable and incommunicable. It transcends everything temporal and finite, and it possesses none of the marks and characteristics of our usual concrete human events. It is not *like* anything else, consequently there are no terms of description for it. The great mystics of history who have claimed to have had this ecstatic experience, have thought of it as a supernatural gift of divine grace and have felt a peculiar exaltation of spirit as a result of it, but it is quite obvious that mystical experiences of that type could furnish no content of thought. Those who have had the experience are convinced by it that God is real, are certain that they have found Him and that they have been caught up into union with Him, but they cannot hint to human ears any descriptive circumstance about the actual character of God.

In spite of all these dark-fringed confusions which surround the word "mystical," I must nevertheless continue to use it, for there is no better term available and I must add to the general confusion by proposing still another way of using the overloaded word. If we were to give up using words because they have had a variety of meanings during their past racial history and because they carry a trail of crude and superstitious meanings in their wide range of denotation, we should be reduced to a small vocabulary. We are all the time "disinfecting" and rehabilitating words that have become corrupt or bedraggled in the age-long strife and commerce of ideas.

There is good historical ground for clarifying the word mysticism and setting it apart to mean a direct way of vital intercourse and correspondence between man and God. There are moments when one stops arguing and proving and finds himself enveloped by a Life that floods into him and "restores" him with health and joy. "I saw that there was an infinite ocean of light and love that flowed over the ocean of darkness," is the way George Fox expresses such an experience. "I am as certain as that I live that nothing is so near to me as God," is Meister Eckhart's testimony. Mysticism may, and, I think, should stand for that type of experience in which a person feels an overmastering conviction that actual contact is attained with a divine, life-giving, joy-bringing Presence. Léonce de Grandmaison, in his important little book on *Personal Religion,* defines mysticism quite similarly, when he says: "There exist moments brief and unforeseeable when man has the feeling of entering, not by effort . . . into immediate contact . . . with an infinite Goodness." One of the most convincing evidences of this vital "contact," one that seems to the mystic himself a demonstration of energies from beyond himself, is the transmutation of the inner life of the person to whom the experience comes. The mystic becomes "another man," and the "transmutation" that is wrought seems as divine as does the consciousness of Presence. The experience may rise to the state of ecstasy or of ineffable union, and it sometimes does, but ecstasy is by no means essential to mystic exaltation, nor is there any sound reason for regarding ecstasy as the loftiest form of mysticism. The construction of personality is more important than the memory of an "uplift."

The most characteristic aspect of the experience is the consciousness of what I have called divine Presence, or, at least, the consciousness of finding a new order of environment, in which the inner spirit feels at home. There are all degrees of this consciousness of being "at home" in the Life of the Spirit, from a mere awareness of fresh upwelling Life, that seems to come from beyond the self, to a rapturous sense of being enfolded by a larger life and of being in complete attainment of the goal of life. There are as many varieties of mystical experiences as there are varieties of the experience of love. Sometimes the consciousness of objective presence is clear and vivid and sometimes the usual limits and divisions of thought are transcended. In the fullest and richest moments of the experience the usual duality of a subject reflectively beholding an external object, which stands in sundered relation to it, is overpassed. It is a moment of fusion like that which comes in the enjoyment of great music or of surpassing beauty or sublimity, or of perfect love, a moment when the soul, abandoning its conscious, successive, bit-by-bit manner of knowing, responds to its object by a single undifferentiated act, all of one piece. Analysis and differentiation may come later, but for the moment the experience is fused and undifferentiated. . . . It is more than merged fusion of subject and object. With that fusion comes also an unwonted unification of the inner powers of the self. We leap beyond the ordinary step-by-step sequences of thought. The usual divergent and conflicting forces in us are overcome. Background inhibitions and marginal doubts for once disappear. "It should be" is no longer mocked by "here it cannot be." The radiations and centrifugal tendencies of the inner life vanish in an extraordinary state of integration, in which intellect and emotion and will-purpose are present in undifferentiated union. . . . But this condition of fusion and integration does not state the whole case. Mystical experience at its normal best is not only fused and integrated but is flooded and invaded with energies which seem to come from beyond the usual margins of the self. There is a vast increase of vitality. "Over-brimming" expresses the experience, perhaps, as well as any single word does. It feels like:

> Another morn risen on mid-noon.

The beyond, "the Yonder," has suddenly become "the here." What never could be is. *"Das Unbeschreibliche hier ist es gethan."* The finite is no longer set over against the Infinite, they seem to interpenetrate. The temporal appears to be lifted up into the Eternal, as a musical note is taken up into its place in an unbroken melody. The swimmer has found the sea and is swimming in it. The homesick exile has discovered the Homeland. What a recent writer has called "a concentration of the affections and a resulting experience of celestial joy" almost always are in evidence in the high tide of mystical experience. The late Poet Laureate, Robert Bridges, has well expressed the feeling in his lines:

> A glow of child-like wonder enthral'd me, as if sense
> Had come to a new birth purified, my mind enrapt
> Re-awakening to a fresh initiation of life.

We are, however, now especially concerned to discover whether the experience is anything more than a heightening of vitality and an increase of emotional intensity; whether in short it brings an increment of knowledge and extends the range of insight and truth. Do we know anything more about God after a mystical experience than we did before it came? Are the experiences knowledge-bringing and truth-expanding, or do they terminate in exuberance and emotional thrill?

It can be said without question that they are distinctly more than emotional upheavals. It is certain that they bring a vastly increased stock of energy to live by. There is an immense driving power in such experiences. They supply an extraordinary dynamic and a new capacity of initiative. William James is undoubtedly right when he says, though I do not quote him exactly, that the overcoming of all usual barriers is the great mystic achievement. Of St. Ignatius Loyola he says: "His mysticism made him assuredly one of the most powerfully practical human engines that ever lived," and he declares that St. Theresa's mystical experiences formed in her a "new centre of spiritual energy." Such increase of will-power, such clarification of insight upon the line of direction for one's life implies that there is at hand a stock of fresh truth, though it does not prove beyond contention that the experience has brought new knowledge.

But if we are to talk of "knowledge" in this connection it ought to be made frankly clear that we are not using the word to mean scientifically organized "knowledge." That is, the knowledge of facts accurately described and causally explained so that it can be treated as universal truth, the same for all minds. What happens in the moments of mystical experience is, rather, an enrichment of the individual mind, an increase of its range and depth, an enlarged outlook on life, an intensification of insight, a heightening of personality. It is much like what happens with the refinement and culture of artistic taste, or with the appreciation of beauty in any field. The thing that matters in these rapturous moments is not a new stock of facts or a discovery of what causes beauty. It is the incoming of power to discriminate with clearer insight and the formation of a new capacity to interpret what is essential to the type of reality with which one is dealing. In all these achievements of depth and power the particular, individual experience tends to reveal aspects of universality, though it cannot be ranked with the universality of scientific knowledge. The nearer one approaches to what is *essential* to any one of the values of life, the wider is the appeal it makes to others and the more universal is the response to it. But there can be no *compulsion* in these matters. We cannot use "must" here. The authority of truth and beauty and goodness is, and must always remain, its power to produce inward conviction in other minds. And we must be content with that.

It must be admitted at once that we have no specific *sense* for dealing with the world of ultimate reality in any way comparable to the physical sense with which we deal with objects in space. If we use the word "sense" in this new connection we must use it metaphorically and not literally. We possess no differentiated organ of sight, hearing or touch by which we can know, recognize or describe realities which we call "spiritual." Mystics do speak frequently, no doubt, of "contact," or of "seeing," or of "hearing," of being "invaded," or "flooded," or "enveloped," or of having "a sense of presence." But it is usually their vivid way of saying that they have a degree of assurance and conviction of God no less certain than that which they get through sense-contact with objects . . . Mary Austin, who has already been quoted, declared that her experience had "the feel of Presence," but she added that she "was conscious only of force, a source of energy." "No sense was in operation." There was something happening *inside*. "A portion of my innermost deep-self," she says, "was functioning; as much a part of my constitution as the clapper is to the bell." It is what the Psalmist called having "truth in the inward parts." She adopts the East Indian phrase, "the Sacred Middle" within herself to name "the innermost deep-self," "the conscious equipment" by which a person attains his first-hand "evidence of things not seen" and his acquaintance with "the substance of things hoped for." . . . All the great mystics speak in similar fashion. St. John of the Cross, one of the greatest mystics of all time, says that "the soul makes its greatest progress when it travels in the dark." In what he considers the highest moments of contemplation, "God communicates Himself no longer through the channels of sense, nor does He come to a mind that is busy with fancies, or imaginations, or reflections, or processes of thought"; the soul must first attain "the dark night of both senses and mind." In other words, what we usually call "knowledge" is for St. John of the Cross transcended and the soul apprehends without specific sense data.

A hardly less famous mystic, who wrote *The Cloud of Unknowing* in the early second half of the fourteenth century and who has recently, with some exaggeration, been called "the most subtle and original spiritual writer in the English language," finds the goal of life to be attained in an experience in which "nothing remains of thy working mind but a naked intent stretching unto God, not clothed in any special thought of God, how He is in Himself or in any of His works, but only that He is as He is." That reminds one very closely of the bare experience of a *that* without any *what*—"a mere boulder of impression."

But fortunately that is not all there is to say about the insight and the truth that are gained through mystical experience. It is assuredly worth something to attain "a naked intent stretching unto God." Our "intents" are never completely definable in terms of "content" either to ourselves or to others, but "intents" even when they do not quite come to focus in thought reveal some relation to reality and are effective as vital energies. It is out of these intensified moments of concentration that richer contents of thought and life emerge. The hush and silence, the peace and serenity, the withdrawal from the surface and the concentration at the center, do in some real way fructify the mind and give it what mystics boldly call "spiritual fecundity" and what Baron von Hügel calls "overflowing interior plenitude." This fructification of the deeper levels of the being may in the end be more important than the mere multiplication of facts. "Interior plenitude" is on the whole a greater gain than is the bare accumulation of information. An organizing, energizing, procreating force at the center of one's life counts for vastly more than would a few added items of knowledge. . . . J. A. Symonds declares that his experience of concentration and unification enabled him to "hire sunshine for leaden hours," and "to engender a mood of mind sufficient for the purpose of living." That does not necessarily mean increase of knowledge. It means, rather, increase of serenity through faith and conviction, and a new fortification of spirit through the intensification of the fused mental powers. But in the long run that inward condition does frequently enable the mind to reach farther than it reached before and to gain a content of life and truth that lay beyond it until then.

It has too often been assumed that mystical knowledge consists of ready-made oracular communications, i.e., secret messages, mysteriously given, or that new items of knowledge drop out of the void into the passive mind of the mystic. I do not make that claim. I am not interested in the question of ready-made communications. I do not pray for such bestowals and I make no defense of their validity. I am much more concerned to show that the human mind itself can become a sensitive spiritual organ of response than that new ranges of information are on rare occasions vouchsafed to a select and chosen few. My real claim, then, is this, that when the powers of the mind are fused and unified, overbrimmed and revitalized by intense mystical concentration and unification *the whole interior self becomes an immensely heightened organ of spiritual apprehension in correspondence with the real world to which it belongs. . . .*

The mystic in all periods bears witness to the truth of the transcendence of God. God is not glorified man. He is not the sum total of things—an all inclusive Pan. We do not attain Him by stretching our own stature. He is, in very truth, Other than we or the things we see. But, if the mystic is a safe guide, God is not an *"absolute* Other." There is something in us related to Him. There is a way through the soul of man to genuine fellowship and friendship with Him, and there is the possibility of a steadily growing acquaintance with His character. We are no more bankrupt in our capacity for finding God than in our capacity for finding harmony, or beauty, or moral goodness, or truth. We shall not find all there is of any of these values, but all we do find is real, and is good to live by. So also with our findings of God, they do not exhaust His being. They do not carry us to the full height of all that He is. But what we have proves to be solid building-material for life-purposes, and every spiritual gain that is achieved makes the next one more possible and more sure.

SUGGESTED READINGS

One of the standard works on mysticism is E. Underhill, *Mysticism*, but before reading it the student should read at least some writings by mystics themselves. The works of St. John of the Cross and of St. Teresa of Avila have been translated by E. Allison Peers; both of them were powerful writers, and St. John was a very fine poet. There are various translations, many of them quite old, of the crabbed and difficult writings of the influential German mystic Jakob Boehme (sometimes spelled "Behmen"). A useful introductory collection of excerpts from the mystics has been assembled by E. O'Brien, under the title *Varieties of Mystical Experience*. Of secondary works Baron F. von Hügel's massive two volume *Mystical Element in Religion*, Dean W. R. Inge's *Christian Mysticism*, and G. Scholem, *Major Trends in Jewish Mysticism* are standard scholarly works; but for a brief survey the reader would do well to turn to W. T. Stace, *Mysticism and Philosophy*.

Mysticism, as James makes clear in his writing, is only one of the "varieties of religious experience," and its other forms are equally important for an understanding of religion. A. N. Whitehead discusses the subject briefly in Chapter 2 of *Religion in the Making*. R. Otto's famous book *The Holy* is an important study of certain emotions that he takes to be distinctively religious. Two older classics should be mentioned: F. Schleiermacher's *On Religion*, especially the second "Speech," and S. T. Coleridge's *Confessions of an Inquiring Spirit* are both seminal works for modern theology. H. D. Lewis, *Our Experience of God*, is a good recent survey. For discussion of the extent to which religious experience can be used as evidence for the truth of religious assertions, see C. B. Martin, *Religious Belief*, Chapter 5, and R. Hepburn, *Christianity and Paradox*, Chapters 3 and 4. Ninian Smart's *Reasons and Faiths* is an excellent general treatment of a number of issues in the philosophy of religion.

Faith and Reason

Although every religion includes beliefs about the nature of the Divine and the universe and about human nature and destiny, these beliefs were, in most cases, originally expressed in nonphilosophic terms. In many religions philosophers and theologians have eventually reformulated them as systematic intellectual expressions of religious faith. In whatever form such beliefs are expressed, however, we must face the problem of how the content of religious faith is related to our other beliefs and convictions. Although there have been a variety of approaches to this problem, the following selections represent views of special importance in contemporary thought.

One widely held position, represented by SAINT THOMAS AQUINAS, maintains that natural knowledge and revelation complement each other. Natural knowledge is limited and must be supplemented by faith in divine revelation, but since both reason and revelation are God-given, neither can conflict with the other. Natural knowledge, for example, is sufficient to establish the existence of one eternal God. Revelation, on the other hand, is needed to fulfill our natural knowledge of God by imparting truths about His nature that would otherwise lie forever beyond our understanding. Reason and revelation, therefore, are in harmony; natural knowledge proves the reasonableness of God's revelation of Himself, and revelation fulfills the promise of our natural knowledge of God. And what is true of our knowledge of God is true of all knowledge of the universe and of man. Right reason is to be trusted, and reason's grasp of the nature of things is not discredited merely because it must be supplemented by faith in divine revelation.

A second solution to the problem of faith and knowledge, sharply contrasting with that of Saint Thomas Aquinas, is represented in the selection from BRUNNER. According to Brunner, reason is limited to dealing with impersonal things. Ultimate questions about God and His relations to man and the universe are susceptible of endless rational discussion, but of no definitive solution. Reason's pretensions to know God are, in fact, liable to serious error; for God, Who is wholly different, cannot be grasped by human faculties. He can be known *only* through His word—His act of self-communication. Religious faith is a responsive acceptance of the word of God, independent of any natural evidence or of any rational considerations. Such faith cannot be proved, for any "proof" would involve experience and reason and make God other than the "wholly different." But faith needs no proof: it bears its own certainty within itself in the immediate apprehension of God's word as truth.

In recent years a large number of thinkers have attempted to defend religious belief by arguing that it is so wholly unlike other forms of belief that none of the usual standards for acceptability can rightly be applied to it.

Some have argued that religious discourse has a function totally different from other types of discourse and that rational criticism of what is said in religious language betrays misunderstanding on the part of the critic. Others, arguing from the unique nature of that about which religious belief is concerned, have concluded that religious comprehension transcends normal types of understanding. The powerful and brilliantly written views of KIERKEGAARD are the ancestor of many contemporary positions of this sort. In the selection here Kierkegaard argues that the notion of truth as it applies to the propositions of religion is entirely different from the notion as it applies elsewhere. MURPHY criticises Kierkegaard by pointing out the consequences of adopting the position that religious truth is purely subjective, and he argues that no one who takes his religion seriously could accept those consequences.

The Harmony of Reason and Revelation*

S т. T н о м а s A q u i n a s [1225?–1274]. See page 688.

In what way it is possible to make known the divine truth. . . . Now in those things which we hold about God there is truth in two ways. For certain things that are true about God wholly surpass the capability of human reason, for instance that God is three and one: while there are certain things to which even natural reason can attain, for instance that God is, that God is one, and others like these, which even the philosophers proved demonstratively of God, being guided by the light of natural reason.

That certain divine truths wholly surpass the capability of human reason, is most clearly evident. For since the principle of all the knowledge which the reason acquires about a thing, is the understanding of that thing's essence, because according to the Philosopher's [*i.e.,* Aristotle's] teaching the principle of a demonstration is *what a thing is*, it follows that our knowledge about a thing will be in proportion to our understanding of its essence. Wherefore, if the human intellect comprehends the essence of a particular

* From Aquinas: *Summa Contra Gentiles*, Book 1, Chapter 3–8, translated by the English Dominican Fathers. Copyright, 1924, by Burns, Oates, and Washbourne, Ltd. Reprinted by permission of Burns, Oates, and Washbourne, Ltd., London, and Benziger Bros., New York.

thing, for instance a stone or a triangle, no truth about that thing will surpass the capability of human reason. But this does not happen to us in relation to God, because the human intellect is incapable by its natural power of attaining to the comprehension of His essence: since our intellect's knowledge, according to the mode of the present life, originates from the senses: so that things which are not objects of senses cannot be comprehended by the human intellect, except in so far as knowledge of them is gathered from sensibles. Now sensibles cannot lead our intellect to see in them what God is, because they are effects unequal to the power of their cause. And yet our intellect is led by sensibles to the divine knowledge so as to know about God that He is, and other such truths, which need to be ascribed to the first principle. Accordingly some divine truths are attainable by human reason, while others altogether surpass the power of human reason.

Again. The same is easy to see from the degrees of intellects. For if one of two men perceives a thing with his intellect with greater subtlety, the one whose intellect is of a higher degree understands many things which the other is altogether unable to grasp; as instanced in a yokel who is utterly incapable of grasping the subtleties of philosophy. Now the angelic intellect surpasses the human intellect more than the intellect of the cleverest philosopher surpasses that of the most uncultured. For an angel knows God through a more excellent effect than does man, for as much as the angel's essence, through which he is led to know God by natural knowledge, is more excellent than sensible things, even than the soul itself, by which the human intellect mounts to the knowledge of God. And the divine intellect surpasses the angelic intellect much more than the angelic surpasses the human. For the divine intellect by its capacity equals the divine essence, wherefore God perfectly understands of Himself what He is, and He knows all things that can be understood about Him: whereas the angel knows not what God is by his natural knowledge, because the angel's essence, by which he is led to the knowledge of God, is an effect unequal to the power of its cause. Consequently an angel is unable by his natural knowledge to grasp all that God understands about Himself: nor again is human reason capable of grasping all that an angel understands by his natural power. Accordingly just as a man would show himself to be a most insane fool if he declared the assertions of a philosopher to be false because he was unable to understand them, so, and much more, a man would be exceedingly foolish, were he to suspect of falsehood the things revealed by God through the ministry of His angels, because they cannot be the object of reason's investigations.

Furthermore. The same is made abundantly clear by the deficiency which every day we experience in our knowledge of things. For we are ignorant of many of the properties of sensible things, and in many cases we are unable to discover the nature of those properties which we perceive by our senses. Much less therefore is human reason capable of investigating all the truths about that most sublime essence. . . .

That the truth about divine things which is attainable by reason is fittingly proposed to man as an object of belief. While then the truth of the intelligible things of God is twofold, one to which the inquiry of reason can attain, the other which surpasses the whole range of human reason, both are fittingly proposed by God to man as an object of belief. We must first show this with regard to that truth which is attainable by the inquiry of reason, lest it appear to some, that since it can be attained by reason, it was useless to make it an object of faith by supernatural inspiration. Now three disadvantages would result if this truth were left solely to the inquiry of reason. One is that few men would have knowledge of God: because very many are hindered from gathering the fruit of diligent inquiry, which is the discovery of truth, for three reasons. Some indeed on account of an indisposition of temperament, by reason of which many are naturally indisposed to knowledge: so that no efforts of theirs would enable them to reach to the attainment of the highest degree of human knowledge, which consists in knowing God. Some are hindered by the needs of household affairs. For there must needs be among men some that devote themselves to the conduct of temporal affairs, who would be unable to devote so much time to the leisure of contemplative research as to reach the summit of human inquiry, namely the knowledge of God. And some are hindered by laziness. For in order to acquire the knowledge of God in those things which reason is able to investigate, it is necessary to have a previous knowledge of many things: since almost the entire consideration of philosophy is directed to the knowledge of God: for which reason metaphysics, which is about divine things, is the last of the parts of philosophy to be studied. Wherefore it is not possible to arrive at the inquiry about the aforesaid truth except after a most laborious study: and few are willing to take upon themselves this labour for the love of a knowledge, the natural desire for which has nevertheless been instilled into the mind of man by God.

The second disadvantage is that those who would arrive at the discovery of the aforesaid truth would scarcely succeed in doing so after a long time. First, because this truth is so profound, that it is only after long practice that the human intellect is enabled to grasp it by means of reason. Secondly, because many things are required beforehand, as stated above. Thirdly, because at the time of youth, the mind, when tossed about by the various movements of the passions, is not fit for the knowledge of so sublime a truth, whereas *calm gives prudence and knowledge.* Hence mankind would remain in the deepest darkness of ignorance, if the path of reason were the only available way to the knowledge of God: because the knowledge of God which especially makes men perfect and good, would be acquired only by the few, and by these only after a long time.

The third disadvantage is that much falsehood is mingled with the investigations of human reason, on account of the weakness of our intellect in forming its judgments, and by reason of the admixture of phantasms. Consequently many would remain in doubt about those things even which are most truly demonstrated, through ignoring the force of the demonstration: especially when they perceive that different things are taught by the various men who are called wise. Moreover among the many demonstrated truths, there is sometimes a mixture of falsehood that is not demonstrated, but assumed for some probable or sophistical reason which at times is mistaken for a demonstration. Therefore it was necessary that definite certainty and pure truth about divine things should be offered to man by the way of faith.

Accordingly the divine clemency has made this salutary commandment, that even some things which reason is able to investigate must be held by faith: so that all may share in the knowledge of God easily, and without doubt or error. . . .

That those things which cannot be investigated by reason are fittingly proposed to man as an object of faith. It may appear to some that those things which cannot be investigated by reason ought not to be proposed to man as an object of faith: because divine wisdom provides for each thing according to the mode of its nature. We must therefore prove that it is necessary also for those things which surpass reason to be proposed by God to man as an object of faith.

For no man tends to do a thing by his desire and endeavour unless it be previously known to him. Wherefore since man is directed by divine providence to a higher good than human frailty can attain in the present life, as we shall show in the sequel, it was necessary for his mind to be bidden to something higher than those things to which our reason can reach in the present life, so that he might learn to aspire, and by his endeavours to tend to something surpassing the whole state of the present life. And this is especially competent to the Christian religion, which alone promises goods spiritual and eternal: for which reason it proposes many things surpassing the thought of man: whereas the old law which contained promises of temporal things, proposed few things that are above human inquiry. It was with this motive that the philosophers, in order to wean men from sensible pleasures to virtue, took care to show that there are other goods of greater account than those which appeal to the senses, the taste of which things affords much greater delight to those who devote themselves to active or contemplative virtues.

Again it is necessary for this truth to be proposed to man as an object of faith in order that he may have truer knowledge of God. For then alone do we know God truly, when we believe that He is far above all that man can possibly think of God, because the divine essence surpasses man's natural knowledge, as stated above. Hence by the fact that certain things about God are proposed to man, which surpass his reason, he is strengthened in his opinion that God is far above what he is able to think.

There results also another advantage from this, namely, the checking of presumption which is the mother of error. For some there are who presume so far on their wits that they think themselves capable of measuring the whole nature of things by their intellect, in that they esteem all things true which they see, and false which they see not. Accordingly, in order that man's mind might be freed from this presumption, and seek the truth humbly, it was necessary that certain things far surpassing his intellect should be proposed to man by God.

That it is not a mark of levity to assent to the things that are of faith, although they are above reason. Now those who believe this truth, of *which reason affords a proof*, believe not lightly, as though *following foolish fables.* For divine Wisdom Himself, Who knows all things most fully, deigned to reveal to man *the secrets of God's wisdom:* and by suitable arguments proves His presence, and the truth of His doctrine and inspiration, by performing works surpassing the capability of the whole of nature, namely, the wondrous healing of the sick, the raising of the dead to life, a marvellous control over the heavenly bodies, and what excites yet more wonder, the inspiration of human minds, so that unlettered and simple persons are filled with the Holy Ghost, and in one instant are endowed with the most sublime wisdom and eloquence. And after considering these arguments, convinced by the strength of the proof, and not by the force of arms, nor by the promise of delights, but—and this is the greatest marvel of all—amidst the tyranny of persecutions, a countless crowd of not only simple but also of the wisest men, embraced the Christian faith, which inculcates things surpassing all human understanding, curbs the pleasures of the flesh, and teaches contempt of all worldly things. That the minds of mortal beings should assent to such things, is both the greatest of miracles, and the evident work of divine inspiration, seeing that they despise visible things and desire only those that are invisible. And that this happened not suddenly nor by chance, but by the disposition of God, is shown by the fact that God foretold that He would do so by the manifold oracles of the prophets, whose books we hold in veneration as bearing witness to our faith. This particular kind of proof is alluded to in the words of *Hebrews* 2:3-4: *Which,* namely the salvation of mankind, *having begun to be declared by the Lord, was confirmed with us by them that heard Him, God also bearing witness by signs and wonders, and divers . . . distributions of the Holy Ghost.*

Now such a wondrous conversion of the world to the Christian faith is a most indubitable proof that such signs did take place, so that there is no need to repeat them, seeing that there is evidence of them in their result. For it would be the most wondrous sign of all if without any wondrous signs the world were persuaded by simple and lowly men to believe things so arduous, to accomplish things so difficult, and to hope for things so sublime. Although God ceases not even in our time to work miracles through His saints in confirmation of the faith. . . .

That the truth of reason is not in opposition to the truth of the Christian faith. Now though the aforesaid truth of the Christian faith surpasses the ability of human reason, nevertheless those things which are naturally instilled in human reason cannot be opposed to this truth. For it is clear that those things which are implanted in reason by nature, are most true, so much so that it is impossible to think them to be false. Nor is it lawful to deem false that which is held by faith, since it is so evidently confirmed by God. Seeing then that the false alone is opposed to the true, as evidently appears if we examine their definitions, it is impossible for the aforesaid truth of faith to be contrary to those principles which reason knows naturally.

Again. The same thing which the disciple's mind receives from its teacher is contained in the knowledge of the teacher, unless he teach insincerely, which it were wicked to say of God. Now the knowledge of naturally known principles is instilled into us by God, since God Himself is the author of our nature. Therefore the divine Wisdom also contains these principles. Consequently whatever is contrary to these principles, is contrary to the divine Wisdom; wherefore it cannot be from God. Therefore those things which are received by faith from divine revelation cannot be contrary to our natural knowledge.

Moreover. Our intellect is stayed by contrary arguments, so that it cannot advance to the knowledge of truth. Wherefore if conflicting knowledges were instilled into us by God, our intellect would thereby be hindered from knowing the truth. And this cannot be ascribed to God.

Furthermore. Things that are natural are unchangeable so long as nature remains. Now contrary opinions cannot be together in the same subject. Therefore God does not instil into man any opinion or belief contrary to natural knowledge.

Hence the Apostle says (*Romans* 10:8): *The word is nigh thee even in thy heart and in thy mouth. This is the word of faith which we preach.* Yet because it surpasses reason some look upon it as though it were contrary thereto; which is impossible.

This is confirmed also by the authority of Augustine who says. . . *That which truth shall make known can nowise be in opposition to the holy books whether of the Old or of the New Testament.*

From this we may evidently conclude that whatever arguments are alleged against the teachings of faith, they do not rightly proceed from the first self-evident principles instilled by nature. Wherefore they lack the force of demonstration, and are either probable or sophistical arguments, and consequently it is possible to solve them.

In what relation human reason stands to the truth of faith. It would also seem well to observe that sensible things from which human reason derives the source of its knowledge, retain a certain trace of likeness to God, but so imperfect that it proves altogether inadequate to manifest the substance itself of God. For effects resemble their causes according to their own mode, since like action proceeds from like agent; and yet the effect does not always reach to a perfect likeness to the agent. Accordingly human reason is adapted to the knowledge of the truth of faith, which can be known in the highest degree only by those who see the divine substance, in so far as it is able to put together certain probable arguments in support thereof, which nevertheless are insufficient to enable us to understand the aforesaid truth as though it were demonstrated to us or understood by us in itself. And yet however weak these arguments may be, it is useful for the human mind to be practised therein, so long as it does not pride itself on having comprehended or demonstrated: since although our view of the sublimest things is limited and weak, it is most pleasant to be able to catch but a glimpse of them.

The Word and the World*

HEINRICH EMIL BRUNNER [1889–   ], Professor of Theology at Zurich, is an eminent figure in the Protestant Neo-Orthodox movement. The dominant theme of his works is the significance of Revelation for modern man.

When the modern man speaks of truth, he means that which every man is capable of knowing. Whether it be Euclid or Descartes, Newton or Einstein, who enounces it makes no difference. You may forget the discoverer of such truths, you may even forget that they had to be discovered and were not always known—all this has no influence upon the truths themselves. They are timeless, or, to use a common phrase, eternal truths. They are such that every one who is a human being can or could know them. We call them truths of reason. The word "reason" is used here in its older and wider sense as meaning all truth which man, just because and in so far as he is man, *ipso facto* knows or could know. Truth of reason in this sense includes not only what we now call rational, logical, mathematical, or scientific knowledge, but intuitive, irrational, emotional and even (if there be such) occult insight as well. For all of these belong to the nature of man as such, even though some individuals possess them in a higher degree than others. . . .

To this range of knowledge belongs even that which we call metaphysical or religious. I am not here concerned with the question whether these types of knowledge are true or otherwise. What is important here is simply that they lie within the sphere of human reason. Every man, however indistinctly, feels something of the holy or the numinous, that feeling which Otto's psychology of religion describes so vividly. And every man of reasonably developed intelligence is capable of following the argument of the metaphysicians. To-day we are experiencing a revival of metaphysics. Whether this will last or not, I do not know; whether it is a good thing or not is a matter of private opinion, and of no importance here. If you were to ask me for my opinion about metaphysics, I should answer that personally I have a very strong interest in metaphysics and dearly love to follow the debates of the metaphysicians. . . . Sometimes I feel very much inclined to put in my oar in their discussions, but after all it is as if I were looking at it all from a distance. Who will prove to be right in the end, the realist or the idealist, the pantheist or deist or theist, I do not know. Nobody does know, and I have good grounds for believing that their quarrels will remain unsettled till doomsday. For of course they cannot be settled. It seems to me to be characteristic of the human situation, that with an equal stringency of logic you can defend the one standpoint as well as the other. In any period when metaphysics is alive, it is alive in every one of its different types. But after all I remain conscious that where metaphysics is concerned, I am only an amateur.

Of one thing however I am certain, being a theologian and not a metaphysician—that all these philosophical wars and rumours of war have only a very remote significance for Christian faith, that the believer follows them more or less like a spectator with a certain air of detachment, and that even the findings of the psychologists of religion (Otto, for example) have only an indirect importance for his faith. Metaphysics as well as religion, the sense of the numinous no less than the idea of the Absolute, belong to general human reason, to the nature of man. And whatever you say about God from this point of view is human or rational knowledge.

Christian faith, however, is concerned with something very different. And it can exist as Christian faith only so long as it remains alive to the fact that it is dealing with this "something different," viz., a knowledge of God which in no way is founded in man, which by no means is obtainable by man through his religious or metaphysical faculties or through his religious experience. It is knowledge of God from beyond all human possibilities—truth which is given in the event which constitutes revelation, in the unique decisive occurrence of history, in the Word of God. Let us mark somewhat more sharply this contradiction which, in recent theology, has so often been blurred.

When I said that Christian faith, or, to speak more concretely, the Christian theologian is only indirectly interested in questions of metaphysics and philosophy of religion, I did not mean that they are of no importance. They are as important and interesting as anything that concerns the nature of man. Indeed, as touching the centre of man, they have a specific importance. But from the point of view of Christian faith, they have significance only for the knowledge of man, not for the knowledge of God. According to faith's own assertion, Christian knowledge of God has a different source and a different content. And both, this different source and this different content, come ultimately to the same thing.

Whether this assertion of Christian faith is true or not is evidently the vital question. But before we seek answer to it, it is necessary to make its meaning clear and to safeguard it from confusion, for instance from its confusion with religious, moral or metaphysical knowledge.

Everything which the apostles, who speak to us in the New Testament, the great Church Fathers, or the creeds of the Churches from the Apostles' Creed down to the Thirty-Nine Articles and the Westminster Confession, wanted to express is this one thing: that into the world of men with their ethics, their metaphysics and their religions, there has entered something different, something which is distinguished not gradually or quantitatively, but qualitatively and fundamentally, from everything which man can know from himself outward. And that something is the Word of God. . . . Christian belief stands or falls with the assertion that the Word of God is something other than ethics, metaphysics, or religion, something different in its source as well as in its content. . . .

Truth of reason, be it scientific, moral, metaphysical or religious, has this characteristic, that I can know it myself. . . . For the philosopher the things of the world, men, and history are objects of his thought and as such the basis for his conclusions, but he *himself* draws the conclusions. He can teach himself the truth, even the truth about God. In other words, this way to God is a monologue. God is present in this thinking only as an object, not as subject. Even where the religious thinker affirms that God is a person, it is he who thinks this personal object. His monologue is not interrupted. God is contained in the world of this thinker, perhaps as its cause, as its ground, as its depth or meaning; but in any case as the ground, the depth or the meaning of *his* world. God does not stand over against this world or this man, as a subject. He belongs to the monologue of this thinker, and to his world.

But Christian faith maintains (and in this belief it consists) that God Himself asserts Himself as a subject, that He interrupts the monologue of our thought of God, of our mystical feeling of God, and that He addresses me as "Thou." By this fact a threefold change takes place: in me, in the world, and in the conception of God.

In me. Before this interruption of the monologue takes place, I am—so to say—master of the world. God is somehow localized in it as its ground, or aim, or cause. But the movement in this relationship proceeds from me. I find God, I find Him in this my world as an object. . . . I am, if I may say so, secured in God *beforehand,* and any change in this relationship lies in my hands. If you speak of sin or guilt in this connection, these words mean nothing very serious or unsafe. If you speak of revelation, you mean simply the discovery of a new depth in my world. Salvation means self-salvation; it means this even where, as in mysticism, they speak of divine grace. The movement is the soul's, not God's.

But if it is God who speaks to me, this means that I cannot know God myself. I can know Him only by His self-communication. Before He speaks, He is absolute *mystery.* This is the secret of personality, of a subject in contradistinction to an object. An object is what I can think myself; a subject is what I cannot think. In my thinking it, it becomes an object. A subject is what exists as such for me only as he himself speaks to me; outside this communication he remains a mystery. But here we are not speaking of two human subjects; therefore the fact of the divine speaking implies something more. The God who speaks to me, speaks to me as Lord of my being. By the very fact of His asserting Himself in my world, I cease to be master in it. He asserts Himself by addressing me, He demands a response. He places me in a situation of *responsibility.* My relation to Him is now no more secure, but most insecure; for it is a relation which consists in decision. . . . The decision, however, can consist only in this, that I hear the claim which is directed to me, that I cast away all self-securities and live from that which I receive in this self-communication of God. This is what is meant by believing or faith. Faith, in contradistinction to every other relationship of religion, is the transcendent relationship; which means the relation towards the God who speaks to me from outside myself and whose secret is unfolded to me only in this communication through His Word. That is why, as we said previously, the content of the word "God" has undergone a change. He is no more the ground, the depth, the cause of my world; He is now the "Lord"! A thought-of God is never Lord. He does not stand above the world; He is tied to the thought-world, as the thought-world is tied to Him. But now, as the God who speaks Himself, He is personal. The thought-of person—say, the idea of God in theistic metaphysics—is not truly personal, because it does not assert itself over against me but is immanent in my thoughts. God is truly personal only in His personal self-manifestation, that is, in His Word. It is not by chance but by necessity that no metaphysics really knows the personal God, any more than mysticism or morals knows Him. The ultimate metaphysical concepts must remain abstract: the world-law, the world-value, the world-depths, the world-cause. And only where metaphysics draws upon Christian faith can the illusion arise that metaphysics knows a personal God. The personal God is known only where He makes Himself known in His Word.

And finally, there only is He known as the Creator. The Creator means something totally different from the world-ground or the world-cause. The Creator is the Lord of the world and of myself, the sovereign Self who needs no world in order to exist. He is the One in whose will the world has its ground; the One who for this reason *cannot* be known from the world, but only out of His Word. These three belong inseparably together: the Word of God, the personal Lord, the Creator.

This then is the Christian assertion about God and His relation to man and to the world. It is the Christian alone who makes this assertion, for it is he alone who knows this God who reveals Himself in His personal Word as the Lord and who by the faith in His Word relieves man from his false independence and his monologue existence. It can be proved that this alone is Christian faith. It can also be proved that the Christian faith alone and no other known religion is of this nature. But can it be proved that it is true? Let us ask what this question could mean. If it were to mean: Can it be scientifically proved that the Christian faith is true, it would be a sign that you have not understood what was said above. You can only prove general, timeless, and impersonal truth. In fact, to prove means nothing else than to link up an assertion with a system of general and timeless truth. To prove faith would mean placing faith within the sphere of general truths; and that is evidently nonsense, for it contradicts the definition of faith. There is a strict connection between general, timeless, and impersonal truths. But just as strict is the impossibility of proving faith. Otherwise it would not be faith. You cannot *prove* personal truth, you can only believe it. . . .

When the Christian speaks of faith, he means an act which is possible only in response to the Word of God; personal decision which in responsibility answers God's challenge. This character of personal decision is not a general feature of religion, but of Christian faith only; this faith carries its own certainty within itself, and does not admit of support by proof. That it is really *God's* Word, that it is *truth* which speaks to me and not a phantasmagoria of my soul, only the believer knows in apprehending God's Word as *God's*.

The question: Is it true? can, however, be understood in a second sense. Is that which the Christian Church or the Bible says about God's Word really trustworthy? It is the duty of theology to answer this question. More than that, theology essentially consists in an answer to this question. Hence the answer can only be given here in a very summary way. The question has to be formulated in two or more precise ones. First: Is *God* taken seriously in the Christian message, or, what amounts to the same thing, do the Christian statements about God express the Godhead of God? Second: Is *faith* taken seriously, *i.e.*, does the Christian statement about faith express the most incisive meaning of the word?

As to the first question, we should answer on the basis of what has been said: Only where God manifests Himself as subject, so that I can know only through Him who He is, is the divinity of God taken seriously. A God whom I myself could know, to whom I myself could give His name, whom I myself could think, is not really God. God's proper name can be pronounced and imparted only by Himself. Either God is the Other One, the wholly Other One, not as a neuter but as a person, or He is not really God; and if He *is* the Other One, it is He alone who can disclose His secret. "Thou shalt not make any image or likeness," because God is incomparable. "I am that I am"—this is His name. He is the One whose name, whose existence, cannot be known from anything else. The God whom we should know from the world, the God whom we should find in the depths of our soul or mind, would not be Himself; the freedom, the sovereignty, the lordship of God over the world cannot be known from the world; and the lordship and freedom of God over against us cannot be known from the depths of our mind. The real God, who has His own proper name, is the One who is known only by His telling us His own name. All other ideas of God are tinged with pantheism because the thought of God is reached from the world or from the human Ego.

We say the same thing when we say that this God alone is truly personal. That God is personal who asserts Himself over against us through His Word, the indissoluble subject who does not allow Himself to be turned into an object. The personality of God, which is the opposite of a God-idea, is His being over against us. An immanent God is not personal. But the transcendent God, that is to say, the unknown mysterious God, is knowable only by the act of His self-impartation in His Word, in which He Himself tells us His will, in the double sense—His demand and His gift, His commandment and His Word of grace.

A glance at non-Christian religions confirms empirically our conceptual statements. Neither India, nor China, nor Greece, nor Rome knows the personal God, in spite of certain approximations. In all these religions God and world form a continuum; or, where the world is denied as in Brahmanism, the distinction between God and *myself* is dissolved. God and self become identical. There is no I and Thou in dialogue, but only the monologue; or better still, the silence of the only one.

As to the second question: Man too becomes truly personal only when he is addressed by the Word of God, that is in faith. A moment ago we said that the Indian knows no divine Thou; to this we should have to add that that is why his own existence is not really personal. A human Ego which is more than appearance, which is an indissoluble person, exists only where there is a divine *Thou*. The mystic, the pantheist, the idealist, the romantic —not to speak of the materialists—do not know the personality of man. The human self somehow evaporates in an abstract medium, whether it be in an idea or an all-mind, in nature or in matter. Personality in the strict sense of the word, we said, in the sense of indissoluble personality, exists only where man's being is grounded in God's addressing him. There it is qualified as responsibility. For the monologue man, the Ego dwindles away with the *Thou*. He either confuses himself fantastically with the divine mind, or he confuses himself despairingly with a natural object. I can know myself as a person only where I see my existence grounded in responsibility, and that means where I know myself to be created by and in the Word of God. This knowledge, however, is identical with that act of decision which the Christian calls faith. There alone does man acquire a truly personal existence. . . .

And this is the sharpest meaning of the word *Faith* or *Belief*. To believe means to be dependent, but also to be dragged out of all self-securities, and to have my only security in God. Where man does not believe, he has his security in himself, in his reason, in his science, in his world, in his religion. To believe means to renounce all securities, not rashly but of necessity, by seeing that they are no securities before God. The man who does believe hangs in the hand of God, above the abyss of perdition. Such faith is possible only as a response to God's gracious Word. The difference between all immanent ideas of God found in mysticism or metaphysics and Christian faith is precisely this, that the former offer man a security in himself, whilst here man is thrown totally upon God. This is an expression of faith which we find solely in the Bible, because here alone God is known as the Lord of our being, who does not allow us to be our own masters. Therefore I hold that the answer of Christian faith alone is in the strict sense *trustworthy*.

To conclude, let me say a few words about the positive relation of faith to the knowledge of reason. So far we have been speaking about the distinction of the two. But this is not to be interpreted as if Christian faith had only a negative relation to reason. Even the Christian acknowledges reason as the greatest gift of the Creator, but that is as a gift and not as God. Above reason, there is the Creator of reason. Reason is not given us to know God, but to know the world. Where reason pretends to know God, it creates a reason-God, and that always is an idol. It is on this pretentious trespassing reason that faith declares war. I do not mean that we are not allowed to think metaphysically; but we are not allowed to put the God whom reason knows in the place of the living God, who can be known only in the personal decision of faith.

Truth Is Subjectivity *

SÖREN KIERKEGAARD [1813–1855] abandoned his studies for the Lutheran ministry in order to devote himself to writing a series of volumes designed to lay bare the true nature of Christianity—a vocation to which he felt himself specially called. Long almost unknown outside his native Denmark, he has in this century been recognized as an important forerunner of contemporary existentialism. Many of his books are now available in English: among them are *Either/Or, Fear and Trembling, Philosophical Fragments,* and *Concluding Unscientific Postscript.*

Being an individual man is a thing that has been abolished, and every speculative philosopher confuses himself with humanity at large, whereby he becomes something infinitely great—and at the same time nothing at all. He confounds himself with humanity in sheer distraction of mind, just as the opposition press uses the royal "we," and sailors say: "devil take me!" But when a man has indulged in oaths for a long time, he returns at last to the simple utterance, because all swearing is self-nugatory; and when one discovers that every street urchin can say "we," one perceives that it means a little more, after all, to be a particular individual. And when one finds that every basement-dweller can play the game of being humanity, one learns at last that being purely and simply a human being is a more significant thing than playing the society game in this fashion. And one thing more. When a basement-dweller plays this game everyone thinks it ridiculous; and yet it

* From Kierkegaard, *Concluding Unscientific Postscript,* translated by Swenson and Lowrie. Reprinted by permission of the Princeton University Press. Copyright 1941 by Princeton University Press.

is equally ridiculous for the greatest man in the world to do it. And one may very well permit oneself to laugh at him for this, while still entertaining a just and proper respect for his talents and his learning and so forth. . . .

Objectively we consider only the matter at issue, subjectively we have regard to the subject and his subjectivity; and behold, precisely this subjectivity is the matter at issue. This must constantly be borne in mind, namely, that the subjective pattern is not something about an objective issue, but is the subjectivity itself. For since the problem in question poses a decision, and since all decisiveness, as shown above, inheres in subjectivity, it is essential that every trace of an objective issue should be eliminated. If any such trace remains, it is at once a sign that the subject seeks to shirk something of the pain and crisis of the decision; that is, he seeks to make the problem to some degree objective. If the Introduction still awaits the appearance of another work before bringing the matter up for judgment, if the System still lacks a paragraph, if the speaker has still another argument up his sleeve, it follows that the decision is postponed. Hence we do not here raise the question of the truth of Christianity in the sense that when this has been determined, the subject is assumed ready and willing to accept it. No, the question is as to the mode of the subject's acceptance; and it must be regarded as an illusion rooted in the demoralization which remains ignorant of the subjective nature of the decision, or as an evasion springing from the disingenuousness which seeks to shirk the decision by an objective mode of approach, wherein there can in all eternity be no decision, to assume that the transition from something objective to the subjective acceptance is a direct transition, following upon the objective deliberation as a matter of course. On the contrary, the subjective acceptance is precisely the decisive factor; and an objective acceptance of Christianity is paganism or thoughtlessness.

Christianity proposes to endow the individual with an eternal happiness, a good which is not distributed wholesale, but only to one individual at a time. Though Christianity assumes that there inheres in the subjectivity of the individual, as being the potentiality of the appropriation of this good, the possibility for its acceptance, it does not assume that the subjectivity is immediately ready for such acceptance or even that it has, without further ado, a real conception of the significance of such a good. The development or transformation of the individual's subjectivity, its infinite concentration in itself over against the conception of an eternal happiness, that highest good of the infinite—this constitutes the developed potentiality of the primary potentiality which subjectivity as such presents. In this way Christianity protests every form of objectivity; it desires that the subject should be infinitely concerned about himself. It is subjectivity that Christianity is concerned with, and it is only in subjectivity that its truth exists, if it exists at all; objectively, Christianity has absolutely no existence. If its truth happens to be in only a single subject, it exists in him alone; and there is greater Christian joy in heaven over this one individual than over universal history and the System, which as objective entities are incommensurable with that which is Christian.

It is commonly assumed that no art or skill is required in order to be subjective. To be sure, every human being is a bit of a subject, in a sense. But now to strive to become what one already is: who would take the pains to waste his time on such a task, involving the greatest imaginable degree of resignation? Quite so. But for this very reason alone it is a very difficult task, the most difficult of all tasks in fact, precisely because every human being has a strong natural bent and passion to become something more and different. And so it is with all such apparently insignificant tasks: precisely their seeming insignificance makes them infinitely difficult. In such cases the task itself is not directly alluring, so as to support the aspiring individual; instead it works against him, and it needs an infinite effort on his part merely to discover that his task lies here, that this is his task—an effort from which he is otherwise relieved. To think about the simple things of life, about what the plain man also knows after a fashion, is extremely forbidding; for the differential distinction attainable even through the utmost possible exertion is by no means obvious to the sensual man. No indeed, thinking about the highfalutin is very much more attractive and glorious.

When one overlooks this little distinction, humoristic from the Socratic standpoint and infinitely anxious from the Christian, between being something like a subject so-called, and being a subject, or becoming one, or being what one is through having become what one is: then it becomes wisdom, the admired wisdom of our own age, that it is the task of the subject increasingly to divest himself of his subjectivity in order to become more and more objective. It is easy to see what this wisdom understands by being a subject of a sort. It understands by it quite rightly the accidental, the angular, the selfish, the eccentric, and so forth, all of which every human being can have enough of. Nor does Christianity deny that such things should be gotten rid of; it has never been a friend of loutishness. But the difference is, that philosophy teaches that the way is to become objective, while Christianity teaches that the way is to become subjective, *i.e.* to become a subject in truth. Lest this should seem a mere dispute about words, let me say that Christianity wishes to intensify passion to its highest pitch; but passion is subjectivity, and does not exist objectively. . . .

When the question of truth is raised in an objective manner, reflection is directed objectively to the truth, as an object to which the knower is related.

Reflection is not focused upon the relationship, however, but upon the question of whether it is the truth to which the knower is related. If only the object to which he is related is the truth, the subject is accounted to be in the truth. When the question of the truth is raised subjectively, reflection is directed subjectively to the nature of the individual's relationship: if only the mode of this relationship is in the truth, the individual is in the truth, even if he should happen to be thus related to what is not true. Let us take as an example the knowledge of God. Objectively, reflection is directed to the problem of whether this object is the true God; subjectively, reflection is directed to the question whether the individual is related to a something *in such a manner* that his relationship is in truth a God-relationship. . . .

The existing individual who chooses to pursue the objective way enters upon the entire approximation-process by which it is proposed to bring God to light objectively. But this is in all eternity impossible, because God is a subject, and therefore exists only for subjectivity in inwardness. The existing individual who chooses the subjective way apprehends instantly the entire dialectical difficulty involved in having to use some time, perhaps a long time, in finding God objectively; and he feels this dialectical difficulty in all its painfulness, because he must use God at that very moment, since every moment is wasted in which he does not have God. That very instant he has God, not by virtue of any objective deliberation but by virtue of the infinite passion of inwardness. The objective inquirer, on the other hand, is not embarrassed by such dialectical difficulties as are involved in devoting an entire period of investigation to finding God—since it is possible that the inquirer may die tomorrow; and if he lives he can scarcely regard God as something to be taken along if convenient, since God is precisely that which one takes *a tout prix,* which in the understanding of passion constitutes the true inward relationship to God.

It is at this point, so difficult dialectically, that the way swings off for everyone who knows what it means to think, and to think existentially; which is something very different from sitting at a desk like a fantastical being and writing about what one has never done, something very different from writing *de omnibus dubitandum,* and at the same time being as existentially credulous as the most sensuous of men. Here is where the way swings off, and the change is marked by the fact that, while objective knowledge rambles comfortably on by way of the long road of approximation without being impelled by the urge of passion, subjective knowledge counts every delay a deadly peril, and the decision so infinitely important and so instantly pressing that it is as if the opportunity had already passed unutilized.

Now when the problem is to reckon up on which side there is most truth, whether on the side of one who seeks the true God objectively, and pursues the approximate truth of the God-idea; or on the side of one who, driven by the infinite passion of his need of God, feels an infinite concern for his own relationship to God in truth (and to be at one and the same time on both sides equally is, as we have noted, not possible for an existing individual, but is merely the happy delusion of an imaginary I-am-I): the answer cannot be in doubt for anyone who has not been demoralized with the aid of science. If one who lives in the midst of Christianity goes up to the house of God, the house of the true God, with the true conception of God in his knowledge, and prays, but prays in a false spirit; and one who lives in an idolatrous community prays with the entire passion of the infinite, although his eyes rest upon the image of an idol: where is there most truth? The one prays in truth to God though he worships an idol; the other prays falsely to the true God, and hence worships in fact an idol.

When one man investigates objectively the problem of immortality, and another embraces an uncertainty with the passion of the infinite: where is there most truth, and who has the greater certainty? The one has entered upon a never-ending approximation, for the certainty of immortality lies precisely in the subjectivity of the individual; the other is immortal, and fights for his immortality by struggling with the uncertainty. Let us consider Socrates. Nowadays everyone dabbles in a few proofs; some have several such proofs, others fewer. But Socrates! He puts the question objectively in a problematic manner: *if* there is an immortality. Must he therefore be accounted a doubter in comparison with one of our modern thinkers with the three proofs? By no means. On this "if" he risks his entire life, he has the courage to meet death, and he has with the passion of the infinite so determined the pattern of his life that it must be found acceptable—*if* there is an immortality. Can any better proof be given for the immortality of the soul? But those who have the three proofs do not at all determine their lives in conformity therewith; if there is an immortality, it must feel disgust over their manner of life: can any better refutation be given of the three proofs? The "bit" of uncertainty that Socrates had helped him, because he himself contributed the passion of the infinite; the three proofs that the others have do not profit them at all, because they are and remain dead to spirit and enthusiasm, and their three proofs, in lieu of proving anything else, prove just this. A young girl may enjoy all the sweetness of love on the basis of what is merely a weak hope; but she is beloved, because she rests everything on this weak hope; but many a wedded matron more than once subjected to the strongest expressions of love has in so far indeed had proofs, but strangely enough has not enjoyed *quod erat demonstrandum*. The Socratic ignorance, which Socrates held fast with the entire passion of his inwardness, was thus an expression for the principle that the eternal truth is related to an existing individual, and that this truth must therefore be a paradox for him as long as he exists; and yet it is possible that there was more truth in the Socratic ignorance as it was in him, than in the entire objective truth of the System, which flirts with what the times demand and accommodates itself to *Privatdocents*.

The objective accent falls on WHAT is said, the subjective accent on HOW it is said. This distinction holds even in the aesthetic realm, and receives definite expression in the principle that what is in itself true may in the mouth of such and such a person become untrue. In these times this distinction is particularly worthy of notice for, if we wish to express in a single sentence the difference between ancient times and our own, we should doubtless have to say: "In ancient times only an individual here and there knew the truth; now all know it, but the inwardness of its appropriation stands in an inverse relationship to the extent of its dissemination. Aesthetically the contradiction that truth becomes untruth in this or that person's mouth is best construed comically. In the ethico-religious sphere, the accent is again on the "how." But this is not to be understood as referring to demeanor, expression, delivery, or the like; rather it refers to the relationship sustained by the existing individual, in his own existence, to the content of his utterance. Objectively the interest is focused merely on the thought-content, subjectively on the inwardness. At its maximum this inward "how" is the passion of the infinite, and the passion of the infinite is the truth. But the passion of the infinite is precisely subjectivity, and thus subjectivity becomes the truth. Objectively there is no infinite decision, and hence it is objectively in order to annul the difference between good and evil, together with the principle of contradiction, and therewith also the infinite difference between the true and the false. Only in subjectivity is there decision, to seek objectivity is to be in error. It is the passion of the infinite that is the decisive factor and not its content, for its content is precisely itself. In this manner subjectivity and the subjective "how" constitute the truth.

But the "how" which is thus subjectively accentuated, precisely because the subject is an existing individual, is also subject to a dialectic with respect to time. In the passionate moment of decision, where the road swings away from objective knowledge, it seems as if the infinite decision were thereby realized. But in the same moment the existing individual finds himself in the temporal order, and the subjective "how" is transformed into a striving, a striving which receives indeed its impulse and a repeated renewal from the decisive passion of the infinite, but is nevertheless a striving.

When subjectivity is the truth, the conceptual determination of the truth must include an expression for the antithesis to objectivity, a memento of the fork in the road where the way swings off; this expression will also indicate the tension of the subjective inwardness. Here is such a definition of truth: *An objective uncertainty held fast in an appropriation-process of the most passionate inwardness is the truth,* the highest truth attainable for an *existing individual.* At the point where the way swings off (and where this is cannot be specified objectively, since it is a matter of subjectivity), there objective knowledge is placed in abeyance. Thus the subject merely has, objectively, the uncertainty; but it is this which precisely increases the tension of that infinite passion which constitutes his inwardness. The truth is precisely the venture which chooses an objective uncertainty with the passion of the infinite. I contemplate nature in the hope of finding God, and I see omnipotence and wisdom; but I also see much else that disturbs my mind and excites anxiety. The sum of all this is an objective uncertainty. But it is for this very reason that the inwardness becomes as intense as it is, for it embraces this objective uncertainty with the entire passion of the infinite. In the case of a mathematical proposition the objectivity is given, but for this reason the truth of such a proposition is also an indifferent truth.

But the above definition of truth is an equivalent expression for faith. Without risk there is no faith. Faith is precisely the contradiction between the infinite passion of the individual's inwardness and the objective uncertainty. If I am capable of grasping God objectively, I do not believe, but precisely because I cannot do this I must believe. If I wish to preserve myself in faith I must constantly be intent upon holding fast the objective uncertainty, so that in the objective uncertainty I am out "upon the seventy thousand fathoms of water," and yet believe.

On Kierkegaard's Claim That Truth Is Subjectivity*

A R T H U R E D W A R D M U R P H Y [1901–1962]. See p. 652.

I propose in this paper to examine the claim of Kierkegaard that "truth is subjectivity," as this thesis is expounded and defended in his *Concluding Unscientific Postscript,* in an attempt to discover (a) what it means and (b)

---

* From *Reason and the Common Good: Selected Essays of Arthur E. Murphy,* edited by Hay, Singer, and Murphy, 1963. Reprinted by permission of Prentice-Hall, Inc., Englewood Cliffs, New Jersey.

what grounds, if any, there are for believing that what it says is true. Kierkegaard's discussion of this subject is characteristically devious and I cannot hope, within the limits of this paper, to cover all that he has to say about it. His thesis, however, is of some philosophical interest, since it purports to be not only a devastating refutation of Hegel but a way of showing the incapacity of philosophy to enlighten the ultimate issues of human existence. The considerations offered to support it have impressed many contemporary thinkers, including some philosophers, as both pertinent and profound. It seems proper, therefore, for those of us who are engaged in the common work of philosophical inquiry to make the best attempt we can to understand it. Those who regard it not as a proper subject for common understanding but as a work of esoteric edification will not find this a rewarding undertaking. They will be well advised at this point to turn their attention to matters more congenial to their taste and temperament.

The point of Kierkegaard's discussion of "truth," I take it, is to offer a justification of faith, in his special sense of "faith," by showing that the believer is "in the truth" subjectively in his groundless affirmation of what is rationally absurd, because this affirmation both brings him into the right relation to "the truth" on which his eternal happiness depends and "potentiates" his inwardness in existing to the highest degree. So to exist is to be "in the truth," whether what is affirmed is "objectively" true or not, and faith is thus justified by the truth subjectively "in" the believer, not by grounds (in this case, it is argued, there can be no grounds) for believing that what is affirmed—the being of God—is actually the case. "When the question of truth is raised in an objective manner, reflection is directed objectively to the truth as an object to which the knower is related. Reflection is not focussed upon the relationship, however, but upon the question of whether it is the truth to which the knower is related. If only the object to which he is related is the truth, the subject is accounted to be in the truth. When the question of truth is raised subjectively, reflection is directed subjectively to the nature of the individual's relationship; if only the mode of this relationship is in the truth, the individual is in the truth even if he should happen to be thus related to what is not true." [p. 178 (Swenson trans.)] A footnote adds, "The reader will observe that the question here is about eternal truth, or about the truth that is essentially related to existence, and it is precisely for the sake of clarifying it as inwardness or as subjectivity that this contrast is drawn."

"When the question of truth is raised in an objective manner . . ." *What* question? The question whether it is the truth to which the believer is related—whether there is any such "eternal truth" as faith affirms? That would be the "objective" way of putting it, the way that Kierkegaard reprehends. To *this* question he has no answer at all, except to say that it should

never have been asked. "When the question of truth is raised subjectively"
the answer Kierkegaard has to give shows at once that it is not the same
question that is being raised. For what he then tells us is that the believer is
"in the truth" in believing even when what he believes is not the truth. To
the question, "Is what my belief affirms true?" the answer is, "You are truly
existing in believing it to be so even if it is not." If the believer is concerned
about the object of his belief, the reality of God, this is no answer at all. It
becomes an answer only if he can be persuaded that "the truth" that matters
here is the tension, inwardness and existential profundity of his own manner
of being (as contrasted with the aesthetic, ethical and that of "religiousness
A"). The point of the whole discussion of truth as "subjectivity" is to recommend this change of reference.

This may be contested by those who like to regard Kierkegaard's thesis as
a justification of faith in the more familiar sense of ground for believing that
what the faith affirms is true, but there can really be no doubt about it.
Kierkegaard, on this point at least, has been at pains to make his meaning
clear. "Objectively we consider only the matter at issue, subjectively we have
regard to the subject and his subjectivity; and behold, precisely this subjectivity is the matter at issue. This must constantly be born in mind, namely,
that the subjective problem is not something about the objective issue, but is
the subjective itself" (p. 115). "Objectively the interest is focused on the
thought-content, subjectively on the inwardness. At its maximum this inward
'how' is the passion of the infinite, and the passion of the infinite is the truth.
But the passion of the infinite, is precisely subjectivity, and thus subjectivity
becomes the truth . . . Only in subjectivity is there decisiveness; to seek objectivity is to be in error. It is the passion of the infinite that is the decisive
factor, and not its content, for its content is precisely itself. In this manner
subjectivity and the subjective 'how' constitute the truth" (p. 181).

Thus to say that "truth is subjectivity" is not to bring any new support to
the claim of religious faith to objective truth. It is rather to shift attention
from this issue to another—that of the existential status of the individual in
believing, and to call this manner of existing "the truth." The conceptual determination of truth (when subjectivity is the truth) is this: "An objective
uncertainty held fast in an appropriation-process of the most passionate
inwardness is the truth, the highest truth attainable for an existing individual . . . But the above definition of truth is an equivalent expression for
faith" (p. 182). The man of faith is "in the truth" because his inwardness in
believing is the truth (as subjectivity) and "behold, precisely this subjectivity is the matter at issue." The point of Kierkegaard's discussion lies in making it "the issue," for the existing individual the only issue in which he is
existentially involved, the issue of his own existence. Given his definitions of

"subjectivity," "truth," and "faith," it seems to follow, as he claims, that such a "faith" *is* the truth, though why this self-centered passion should be identified as religious faith rather than sheer egocentricity is so far hardly clear. And why it should be dignified as the highest truth attainable for an existing individual is a further question. To this question we now turn.

Why is faith, or being subjectively *in* the truth, the *highest* truth attainable for an existing individual? Because (a) it potentiates "inwardness" to the highest degree and such inwardness is the highest manner of existing for an existing individual. And (b) it is the highest manner of existing because it brings man into the right relationship to "the truth" on which his eternal happiness depends, a truth which infinitely transcends his present temporal condition as an existing individual. Let us consider these points in order.

The "leap of faith" intensifies inwardness because it is a tremendous risk, an objectively groundless affirmation of the rationally incredible. Such affirmation generates passion and, by its objective absurdity, throws upon the individual the whole responsibility for the decision for or against eternal truth. This decision is the supreme expression of his decisiveness as an individual. To be in this way an individual is truly to exist; it is the mode of being proper to man as a synthesis of the eternal and the temporal situated in existence. In this sense, only the man of faith *truly* exists, though of course there are others who "exist" also—in their fashion. Here "truth" is a kind of being and the ontological superiority of this mode of being for the existing individual is the justification of faith.

Surely there is something wrong with this picture. If "the truth" is subjectivity, then the believer runs no risk when he leaps; he has it, or rather *is* it, in the very act of leaping. For the truth here in question is "eternal truth," the truth essentially related to man's existence, and Kierkegaard claims to have shown that *it* is inwardness or subjectivity. But if this is the case then eternal truth is not a transcendent goal but a present possession; the passionate individual is now in the highest state of existence he could possibly attain. Verily he *has* his reward, and his condition is one not for soul-searching but for self-congratulation. This note of self-congratulation is not absent from Kierkegaard's account of faith.

But this is surely very dialectical indeed. For if the believer has the truth he seeks where is the tension? If no tension, where is the inwardness? And if no inwardness, no authentic faith. So it looks as though, if truth is inwardness, the man of faith is not in the truth precisely in virtue of being in the truth. But then he is of all men most miserable and so after all is in the truth because he is not in the truth. Perhaps it would be better to say that he is in the truth only because he does not understand that to exist in passionate inwardness is to be in the truth and therefore, through a misunderstanding of

Kierkegaard's theory, goes on leaping for a truth he still supposes he does not possess. This would prove once more, and on a higher level, the importance of a lack of understanding to faith as inwardness. I offer it to the dialectical theologians for such use as they may care to make of it.

On a more mundane level it is pertinent, I think, to point out that, here as elsewhere, the alleged dialectic arises through a failure to make some elementary distinctions. In his discussion, Kierkegaard uses "the truth" to mean *both* the eternal truth at which the believer aims, which is emphatically *not* subjectivity since it infinitely transcends the believer's present state of being ("God does not exist, He is eternal") (p. 296) *and* the subjective condition of the believer in his agonizing separation from this truth (his "situation in existence") when he groundlessly affirms it. To be "in the truth" is not to possess this truth, but endlessly, and in this life vainly, to be trying to attain it. It is precisely because the believer is infinitely concerned with a truth that is not subjectivity and with its infinite transcendence that he is in the truth in his passionate and tortured affirmation of it. Kierkegaard recognizes this at times and even makes a point of it. "To ask with infinite interest about a reality that is not one's own, is faith, and this constitutes a paradoxical relation to the paradoxical . . . The believer differs from the ethicist in being infinitely interested in the reality of another (in the fact, for example, that God existed in time)" (p. 288).

Now the fact that God existed in time is not a fact of the believer's state of being; and his being "in the truth" (passionately decisive) in affirming it sheds no light on what he is here passionately concerned about, that this *is* a fact and one on which he can properly stake his chance of an eternal happiness. Thus being "in the truth" is no confirmation whatever of "the truth" that he is infinitely concerned about—the reality of another. In a way, this must be good news for Kierkegaardians. For this, once recognized, should drive the individual still further back into himself and potentiate inwardness to an even higher degree. But this is new evidence that he is in the truth in believing, and if subjectivity is the truth, then once more he has it and now in overflowing measure. In seeing that Kierkegaard's answer is no answer one becomes still more subjective and this, perhaps, is the Kierkegaardian answer. As he puts it in a revealing passage: "It is impossible to express with more intensive inwardness the principle that subjectivity is truth, than when subjectivity is in the first instance untruth, and yet subjectivity is the truth" (p. 191). We must add, however, that it is not merely "in the first instance" but eternally that subjectivity is not "the truth" that for example Christianity proclaimed. For it is not a truth about God but a state or existential condition of the believer and only a believer more concerned about his own inwardness than about God could find in it an adequate goal in his quest for religious truth.

There is good reason to conclude, I think, from the whole tenor of his life and writing that Kierkegaard was that kind of a believer. The point of his discussion is not that he has offered grounds for belief in the truth of *what* the Christian faith affirms but that, by shifting the reference of religious truth from God to man, he has shown that the groundlessness of faith fits his own unhappy inwardness and is, *in this way,* the truth. "Subjectivity culminates in passion, Christianity is the paradox, paradox and passion are a mutual fit, and the paradox is altogether suited to one whose situation is, to be in the extremity of existence" (p. 206). Nietzsche unkindly described Kant's practical reason as "a special kind of reason for cases in which one need not bother about reason." I think we might with more justice say that Kierkegaard has given us a kind of truth for cases in which we are told not to bother about truth. The paradox of this position is that it is only because we are profoundly bothered about the objective truth of faith that we are in the condition (passionate inwardness) which is here offered as the highest existential substitute for the eternal truth we seek. Whether such a paradoxical condition is existentially profound or merely self-defeating is a further question.

That what Kierkegaard has to tell us about faith fits the facts of his own subjectivity is clear enough. Rarely has a man been more persuasive in projecting his private ailments as "existential" profundities. His relations to his father and to Regina Olsen take on ontological significance, as the commentators love to tell us, and his fears and frustrations are dignified as an embodiment of the highest truth attainable to man—the truth of subjectivity. But *is* this condition of recessive inwardness the highest truth that is humanly attainable? If human existence is the incongruous juxtaposition of temporal and eternal that Kierkegaard says it is, if the Being on whom man's eternal happiness depends is an offense to his reason and (compare *Fear and Trembling*) to his morality as well, and if to embrace this offense without being offended is his only hope for salvation, *then* the unhappy passion of this desperate affirmation is indeed the response appropriate to his condition. But are any of these the case? The subjectivity of faith does not warrant their affirmation, for it is only if they are accepted as objective truth that faith is even subjectively justified as suited to man's existential situation. If what they assert is not the case then Kierkegaard's suffering is like the agony of a man self-submerged in two feet of water who refuses to stand up and breathe good air because his prostrate posture is the one appropriate to the situation in existence of a drowning man. "But this," as Kierkegaard likes to say, "is comic." Suppose that this were objectively true. And why are we not to suppose it? Because in so doing we should be existing only objectively, which is not truly to exist at all. What then is the criterion of "true" existence? Subjective inwardness. Why so? Because such inwardness is proper to man in the extremity of existence. Is he in such an extremity? In the state of passionate inwardness he feels himself to be and in faith affirms it. Is this affirmation true? It is true in the sense that in making it he is *in* the truth, that is, in the subjective condition proper to a man in the extremity of existence. This could go on almost endlessly, and in the *Postscript* it does.

The point I wish to make is that while it ostensibly turns away from the issue of objective truth, Kierkegaard's procedure presupposes such truth at every step in its retreat into recessive inwardness. His subjectivity is parasitic for its "existential" significance on the assumed objective truth of a doctrine about man and God whose right to claim such truth it strives at every point to discredit. Not only does it bite the hand that feeds it but it calls this questionable procedure faith. For whatever feeds recessive inwardness feeds faith. "Religiousness is indeed inwardness in existing and everything which serves to deepen this determinant heightens the religiousness, and the paradox-religiousness is the ultimate" (p. 506). This is the best that Kierkegaard has to offer. There is no better reason for believing that this is the highest existential condition attainable by man than for believing in the objective reality of God (as Kierkegaard describes Him), and for this, he has been at pains to tell us, there is no reason whatever. What have we left? Just subjectivity itself, as devoid of ontological as of divine support. "Subjectivity is truth; subjectivity is reality" (p. 306). Whose subjectivity? Kierkegaard's. And there the matter ends. Whether it is a dead end or an ultimate disclosure of reality, is for the reader to decide. But he will do well to remember that it can be at best a disclosure of the reality, not of God, but of Kierkegaard.

Of course faith is not knowledge and a man cannot fairly be asked to demonstrate the truth of that which, in the circumstances of his creaturely existence, he must accept on faith or not at all. But faith is at least an affirmation of the objective truth of what is believed, and objectivity, as a human attitude, is the concern that what is thus affirmed shall in fact be true and credible as such by such standards as are humanly available. It is unreasonable to limit such standards to the procedures of mathematics and the empirical sciences, since these would be inappropriate to the relation between God and man if such a relation did in fact exist. But to reject not merely a too narrow objectivity but a concern for the objective truth itself, and to make an existential virtue of the inflexible determination to retain a preconceived opinion at all costs is a danger not so much to reason as to faith itself. For when faith loses its concern for objective truth, it loses its transcendent reference and that means that it also loses its transcendent object. Only subjectivity is left. It is the peculiar merit of Kierkegaard's account that it has made this truth so explicit that hereafter it can hardly be missed. The remaining question is whether the substitute object now offered—subjectivity—is one that a man of faith, in the more usual sense of that term, can accept as the proper goal of his religious quest.

Kierkegaard frequently speaks of faith, as he understands it, as a God-relationship. The propriety of this description is questionable at least. It seems rather to be a self-relationship in which the believer, through the repulsion of the paradox, is driven back into himself. The ostensible object (God) serves as a kind of opaque surface which turns back the light and presents to the believer only a reflection of himself as inwardly existing. Here faith indeed has *found* an object, "whose content is precisely itself." But this is not the faith that is the substance of things hoped for, and the evidence of things not seen.

And finally, *of course* reason is not faith, nor a proper substitute for faith in the lives of men who, if they are to live at their human best, must reach for truth not seen as yet. But reason may nonetheless be an essential aid to any faith that aims at any truth beyond its own "existential" occurrence. It can, for example, resolve some of the dialectical paradoxes that are Kierkegaard's stock in trade in his attempted proof that religious truth must, for man as a rational creature, be absurd. It can remind us, in the judicious words of Whitehead, that the discovery of a contradiction in an argument proves nothing except that a mistake has been made somewhere, and that the borrowed dialectic on which Kierkegaard depends to discredit human reason is itself a misuse, not a proper use, of reason. As a way of *finding out* about the world in which our subjectivity is involved, reason can bring light into dark places, a light that only those who love their own opinions more than truth need be afraid to face. And at its objective best it guarantees an openness to truth in all aspects and dimensions of experience that can give us a larger world to live in, not with a fragment of our minds and hearts but with the whole of them. This wholeness, above all else, is what we miss in Kierkegaard. The *Philosophical Fragments* is well named, and the *Postscript* is a postscript to the *Fragments*. Kierkegaard has not shown that a rational faith is unattainable. But he has shown conclusively, I believe, that it requires a different method and a different object than those that such fragments of philosophy can articulate or understand.

SUGGESTED READINGS

The *Short Life of Kierkegaard* by W. Lowrie is helpful in understanding Kierkegaard's thought. The *Philosophical Fragments,* translated by D. Swenson, with introductions by N. Thulstrup and H. Hong, is one of Kierkegaard's most stimulating works, though it is rather difficult. *Fear and Trembling* is very readable and gives a good idea of some of his main views.

In W. Kaufmann's *Critique of Religion and Philosophy,* Chapters 6 and 8 introduce many of the topics that are central in recent discussions of faith, reason, and knowledge. Karl Barth's work is forbiddingly difficult, but extremely influential; his short book on the ontological argument, *Anselm: Fides Quaerens Intellectum,* gives some idea of his views. R. Bultmann's controversial ideas on "demythologizing" Christianity are available in English in *Kerygma and Myth* and (more briefly) in *Jesus Christ and Mythology.* R. Niebuhr discusses "The Truth in Myths" in *The Nature of Religious Experience,* edited by J. Bixler.

The controversial *Honest to God* by Bishop J. A. T. Robinson attempts to use many of these recent ideas on the nonliteral interpretation of religion and presents the results in a popular form. The storm aroused by the book is reflected in *The Honest to God Debate* edited by D. L. Edwards; it contains essays by J. Macquarrie, "How Is Theology Possible?" and A. MacIntyre, "God and the Theologians," which are especially worth reading. On this kind of theology, in general, the reader should consult the two-page "Sermonette," which concludes H. A. Wolfson's *Religious Philosophy.*

Theism as a World View

According to theism, the world of finite things is neither self-sustaining nor self-explanatory. The natural order points beyond itself to an infinite, transcendent Being on whom all finite things depend and in whom they find their fulfillment. The world as a whole and in all its parts is God's creation. It is a cosmos whose structure and order express a divine intelligence and whose meaning and value lie in a divine will.

This does not mean, however, that finite things are unreal or illusory. They have their own natures, and we can learn more and more about them, and how they are related to each other. But such knowledge of finite things is at best partial and limited, and we are inevitably led to seek a more ultimate explanation. We then find that a fully adequate explanation of anything requires that we understand the natural order in terms of an Infinite Being and His relation to the world.

Just as theists do not deny the reality of finite things, so they do not deny the reality of human values, nor substitute an unattainable morality for the highest forms of human activity. What is good or evil, virtuous or sinful, can be known by man, and man is fully responsible for his actions. In other words, theism does not set up a morality which runs counter to our own highest aspirations. Theists insist, however, that human values and moral norms have their *ultimate* source in a realm of being beyond the merely human. In their view, the highest forms of human experience presuppose God, as the final center of meaning and value.

Although God is the ultimate principle of explanation and the ultimate source of value, man can never fully understand His infinite nature by natural means. For man is finite, and his natural knowledge of an infinite being is limited by the conditions of his finitude. Nevertheless, all theists agree that only an acceptance of the reality of God renders all facets of human experience meaningful. To deny God's existence, and to regard man as merely a part of a wholly natural, purposeless order, would falsify the most distinctive traits of human nature and of man's experience of the world.

In the selection from GILSON, the traditional doctrine of Creation, as presented by Saint Thomas Aquinas, forms the starting point for a discussion of the relation of God to the world. In considering the doctrines of divine providence and divine conservation, Gilson is concerned to show that God is not only transcendent but also immanent, not merely the creator but also the sustainer of the world of finite things. Finally, in discussing divine concourse, he explains the harmony of natural and divine causation, and the reconciliation of causal explanation with divine purpose.

The selection from NIEBUHR contains a critique of recent philosophic tendencies which regard man as wholly a part of nature, and nature as self-sufficient and self-explanatory. Against the background of this criticism of naturalism, Niebuhr defends a Biblical-Christian interpretation of human life and human destiny.

God and the World*

ETIENNE HENRI GILSON [1884–   ], member of the French Academy, is one of the foremost contemporary Catholic philosophers. He is a distinguished historian of philosophy, and has had great influence as a teacher at Paris, Harvard, the Collège de France, and the Institute of Mediaeval Studies at Toronto.

DIVINE CREATION. The mode in which every created thing issues from its universal cause—which is God—goes by the name of "creation." Hence the importance of defining the nature of creation. We speak of creation whenever something which was not, begins to be. In other words, there is creation wherever a transition occurs from non-being to being, in other words, from nothingness to being. Applying this notion to all existing things, we may say that creation, which is the emanation of all being, consists in the act whereby all things pass from non-being or nothingness to being. This is the meaning of the expression that God has created the world from nothing. But it is important to note that in this assertion the preposition "from" signifies in no way the material causes; it means simply a sequence. God has not created the world from nothing in the sense that He caused it to issue from nothing as from a sort of pre-existing matter, but in the sense that, after the nothing, being appeared. "Creating from nothing," in short, means "not creating from something." This expression, far from putting any matter at the beginning of things, systematically excludes all conceivable matter, in the same way as when we say that someone is sad about nothing, we mean that his sadness has no cause.

Such a conception of the creative act encounters at once certain objections of philosophers whose whole habits of thought run counter to it. For the student of physics, for instance, an act is, by definition, a change, i.e., a sort of movement. But everything that passes from one place to another, or from

* From Gilson: The Philosophy of St. Thomas Aquinas, translated by Edward Bullough, edited by Rev. G. A. Elrington, Chapters 7 and 9. Copyright, 1925, by W. Heffer & Sons, Ltd. Reprinted by permission of W. Heffer & Sons, Ltd., and B. Herder Book Company.

one state to another, presupposes an initial place or state which is the point of departure of the movement or change, so that, where such a point of departure is lacking, the very notion of change would be inapplicable. For example: I move a body; it was consequently in a certain place, whence I have caused it to pass to another. Or I alter the colour of an object; the object must therefore have been of a certain colour in order that I should have been able to give it another. But in the case of creation, as just defined, it is just this point of departure which is lacking. Without the creation, there is nothing; after the creation, there is something. Is not then this passage from nothingness to being a contradictory notion, since it supposes that something which does not exist, nevertheless changes its condition, and that something which is nothing, becomes something? *Ex nihilo nihil fit* (from nothing, nothing comes): such is the initial objection of the philosopher against the very possibility of creation.

Yet this is an objection which holds only in proportion as you concede its starting-point. The student of physics argues from the notion of movement; he observes that the requisite conditions for the existence of movement are not met by the case of creation; hence he concludes that creation is impossible. In point of fact, the only legitimate conclusion of his argument is that creation is not a movement. In that case the argument would be quite legitimate. For it is perfectly true that every movement is the change of condition of a being, and if we talk of an act which yet is not a movement, we do not know how to picture it to ourselves. Whatever effort we may make, in consequence, we shall always *imagine* creation *as if it were* a change, a pictorial representation which makes it into something self-contradictory and impossible. In reality, creation is something quite else, something for which we have even no name, because it lies so entirely outside the range of human experience. To say that creation is the gift of being, is still a deceptive expression, for how can anything be given to something which is nothing? To say it is acceptance of being, is no better, for how can something which is nothing accept anything? However—let us say that in some manner it is the acceptance of being, without attempting to picture it to ourselves.

If such is indeed the mode of production signified by the term "creation," it is evident that God can create and is alone capable of creating. For it has been established that God is the universal Cause of all being. . . .

THE GOODNESS OF THE CREATED WORLD. We came to the conclusion in examining the very notion of "creation," that God alone is creator, since creation is the action proper to Him and nothing exists which has not been created by Him. Perhaps it may not be amiss to recall this general conclusion at the moment of beginning the examination of the corporeal world, because it is an old and widespread error to think that its nature is bad in itself, that it is consequently the work of another principle, itself bad and other than God. This is a doubly pernicious error, for, in the first place all existing things possess at least one common constitutive element, namely, their very being; consequently there must exist a single principle whence they derive this element and which causes them to be, of whatever kind they may otherwise be, whether invisible and spiritual, or visible and corporeal. As God is the cause of Being, His causality extends no less necessarily to bodies than to spirits. But a second argument, drawn from the end of things, may help to carry conviction: God Himself has no other end than Himself; things, on the contrary, have an end other than themselves, namely, God. This is an absolute truth which applies to every order of reality, to bodies no less than to spirits; but this fact must be linked with another, namely, that a being which exists for the sake of God, nevertheless, exists also for itself and for its own good. Thus in this sort of immense organism which is the Universe, every part exists, in the first place, for its own proper act and its own end, like the eye for the sake of seeing; but in addition, each of the inferior parts exists for the sake of the superior parts, as the creatures inferior to man for the sake of man; moreover, all these creatures, taken singly, exist only for the sake of the collective perfection of the Universe, and, finally, this collective perfection of creatures, taken in its totality, is there only as an imitation and representation of the glory of God Himself. This radical metaphysical optimism leaves nothing out which in any manner whatever deserves to have the name of being, the corporeal world no more than the rest: matter exists for the sake of form, inferior forms for the sake of higher forms, the higher forms with the view to God. Therefore, everything that is, is good and, consequently, also everything has God for its cause. . . .

DIVINE PROVIDENCE AND CONSERVATION. Concerning the beings thus constituted, it is important to realise that God governs them by His providence, that He is intimately present in their substance and operations, and that yet the closeness of His concurrence leaves their own efficacy wholly intact. That, in the first place, the world is governed, is evident to the least sophisticated minds as soon as they direct their attention to the universal order of things. But the very idea of God to which we have been led by the proofs of His existence, forces this fact upon us, because God is postulated by reason as the first principle of the universe, and since whatever is the principle of a thing is also its end, God cannot but be the end of all things, hence, relates them to Himself, directs them to Himself, which is precisely what "governing" means. The ultimate end, therefore, in view of which the creator administers the Universe, appears for that very reason as transcending things and external to them: here again, what is true of the principle is equally true of the end.

The aspect, richest in metaphysical consequences, which this governance of things by God presents to our mind, is that of the conservation of things. By a series of arguments which lead to the very heart of his metaphysics of bodies, St. Thomas develops, first of all, regardless of consequences the postulates implied in this divine conservation. Then having, so to speak, left things with nothing belonging to them in their own right, he shows that this divine concurrence which seems to deprive them of their own efficacy and being, is really what, on the contrary, confers these upon things.

Every effect depends upon its cause and depends upon it in strict proportion to the extent in which the cause has really produced the effect. Let us, for instance, take the case of a workman fashioning an object, or of an architect building a house: the object or the house owe to their authors the external form and the configuration of the parts which characterise them; but that is all; for the material of which the thing is made exists already in nature, so that the maker did not have to make it but confined himself to utilising it. Now, the precise kind of causal relation is very well formulated by the relation of dependence which links together the two terms: the object, once made, subsists independently of the workman, because since it does not owe to him its being, it can naturally do without him in order to preserve it. Exactly the same observation applies to the order of natural beings; for each produces other beings by virtue of a form which it has itself only received but of which it is not the cause, with the result that each can indeed produce the form but not the being by which its effects subsist. Consequently we find that a child continues to live after the death of its father, in exactly the same manner as a house continues to stand after the architect has gone: in both cases we are dealing with causes which bring it about that a thing *becomes* what it is, but not that it exists. Now, the situation is entirely different as regards the relation of things to God: in the first place, because God is not only the cause of the form taken on by things, but of the very being in virtue of which they exist, so that ceasing for a single instant to depend on their cause, they would cease to be altogether. The second reason is that there would be in a sense a contradiction in God making creatures which could do without Him. For a "creature" is essentially something which has its being from someone else, in distinction to God who has His being only from Himself and subsists independently. For a creature to be able to subsist for a single instant without divine concurrence, it would have to exist in and by itself for that instant, *i.e.*, it would have to be God. Thus, the first effect of providence exercised by God upon things is the immediate and permanent influence by which He assures their conservation. This influence is, in some way, simply the continuation of the creative action, and any interruption of this continued creation by which God maintains all things in being, would instantly reduce them to nothingness.

Proceeding further and following the divine influence into the very heart of things, we shall find that it extends beyond their existence, also to their causality. As, in fact, nothing is except by virtue of the divine Being, so nothing can do anything except again by virtue of divine efficacy. If, therefore, any being causes the existence of another being, it does so only because God confers upon it the power to do so—a truth, by the way, directly evident, if we bear in mind that being is the effect proper to God, since creation is His peculiar action and to produce being is, in the strict sense, to create.

But we must go further still and assert that what is true of the productive efficacy of beings is equally true of their operations: God is for all beings that operate, the cause and reason of their operating. Why this further consequence? The answer is that to act means always, more or less, to produce, because whatever produces nothing, does nothing. Now, it was just stated that every genuine production of being, however minute, belongs properly to God alone: every operation therefore presupposes God as cause. In addition, a being acts only by virtue of the faculties it possesses and by applying the natural forces it can make use of, to their effects. But neither these faculties nor these forces originate in the first place from the thing but from God, who is their author as universal cause; so that, when all is said and done, God is the principal cause of all actions performed by His creatures which are nothing but instruments in His hands.

So it is then finally at the very heart of things that God is everywhere present and acting by His efficacy; He supports them, animates them from within, guides them in their operations, applies them to their acts, so that they neither are nor do anything except by Him, just as they would neither exist nor act without Him. . . .

DIVINE CONCOURSE. Thomistic philosophy, in which the creature is nothing and does nothing without God, yet sets itself in opposition to every doctrine which does not leave to secondary causes the full measure of being and efficacy which belongs to them by right. . . . In the sensible world causes and effects follow with perfect regularity: a hot body always warms another in its vicinity, it never chills it; a human being never engenders anything but a human being; it is therefore evident that the nature of the effect produced is inseparably bound up with the nature of the producing cause. Now it is this constancy in the regulation of natural effects to secondary causes which makes it impossible to assume that the power of God simply takes their place; for if the action of God were not diversified in accordance with the different beings in which it operates, neither would the effects be diversified in the same manner as the things themselves, and the result would be that anything whatever would produce anything whatever. The existence of laws of nature consequently renders it impossible to suppose that God has created beings deprived of causality.

What is perhaps even more remarkable is that those who deny to secondary causes all efficacy in order to reserve to God the privilege of causality, do no less wrong to God than to the things themselves. The work manifests by its excellence the glory of the maker, and what a poor universe would that world be which were completely deprived of efficacy! In the first place, it would be an absurd world. If you give someone the principal, you do not deny him the accessory. What would be the sense of creating heavy bodies but incapable of moving downwards? If God has conferred upon things resemblance to Himself by giving them being, He must also have given them the activity which flows from this being and must, consequently, have granted to them the actions proper to them. Moreover, a universe of inert things would imply a first cause less perfect than a universe of active things, capable of communicating to each other their perfections by acting upon each other just as God has communicated to them something of His own perfection by creating them, linked and ordered by the mutual actions which they exercise on each other. The sentiment which impels certain philosophers to withdraw all from nature in order to glorify God, is inspired by an intention, good enough in itself but nevertheless blind. In actual fact, "detrahere actiones proprias rebus est divinae bonitati derogare," to deprive things of their proper actions is to detract from divine goodness.

The problem ultimately reduces itself to this, how to maintain without concession the two apparently contradictory truths: viz. that God does all that the creatures do, and yet the creatures do of themselves whatever they do. The point is consequently, how the same single effect can derive simultaneously from two different causes, God and the natural agent that produces it. This is at first sight an incomprehensible position from which the majority of philosophers seem to have recoiled, for it is difficult to see how one and the same action can proceed from two causes: if it is produced by a natural body, the cause cannot be God. Furthermore, if it proceeds from God, it is still less intelligible that it should at the same time be produced by a natural body, for the divine causality affects the very centre of the being and leaves nothing to be produced beyond its effects. The dilemma seems consequently inevitable, unless indeed we are content to place it into the very heart of things and leave it at that.

In reality this contradiction which metaphysical thought encounters here, is not so entirely irreducible as it appears, and is perhaps at bottom merely superficial. It would indeed be contradictory to admit that God and natural things were both the causes of natural effects at the same time and under the same aspect. They are, in fact, causes at the same time, but not under the same aspect, as a comparison may help us to realise.

When a workman produces a thing, he must necessarily make use of

utensils and instruments of all sorts. The choice of the instruments is guided
by their shape, and he himself does no more than to move them in order to
apply them and to cause them to produce their effects. When an axe splits a
piece of wood, it is the axe that is the cause of the effect produced, and yet
we can say with as much reason that the cause is also the carpenter who
wields the axe. At the same time it is impossible to divide the effect produced into two parts, one of which is due to the axe and the other to the
carpenter. It is the axe that produces the entire effect, and at the same time
the entire effect is also produced by the carpenter. The real difference lies in
this, that they do not produce the effect in the same manner, for the axe
splits the wood only by virtue of the efficacy which is conferred upon it by
the carpenter, so that, indeed, the carpenter is the primary and principal
cause, whereas the axe is the secondary and instrumental cause of the effect
produced. We must conceive an analogous relation between God as the first
cause, and the natural bodies which we observe operating around us. But
the relation is only analogous, because the divine influence penetrates the
secondary cause far more completely than the workman can ever penetrate
his utensil. God confers upon all things their being, their form, their movement and their efficacy; and yet this efficacy belongs all the same to them,
once they have received it, and it is they that perform their operations. Even
the lowliest being acts and produces its effect, although it does so by virtue
of all the superior causes to whose action it is subjected and whose efficacy is
transmitted to it in descending gradations. At the beginning of this whole
series stands God, entire and immediate cause of all the effects produced by
things and of the whole activity developed by them; at the lower end of the
series is the natural body, immediate cause of the operation proper to it and
performed by it, although it performs it simply by virtue of the efficacy conferred upon it by God.

Considering from this point of view the operations and movements that
take place continually in the universe, we observe that neither element in
this double causality can be considered as superfluous. In the first place, it is
evident that the divine operation is necessary for the production of natural
effects, since the secondary causes owe all their own efficacy to the first cause
which is God. But it is not superfluous that God, who indeed can produce by
Himself all the natural effects, should yet produce them by the intermediary
of certain other causes. These intermediaries which He has willed, are not
necessary to Him, because He could not do without them; but it is for their
own sake that He has willed them, and the existence of secondary causes is
not evidence of a lack of power, but of the immensity of His goodness. The
universe then, as conceived by St. Thomas, is not a mass of inert bodies
passively set in motion by a force transmitted through them, but an organ-

ism of active beings each one of which enjoys the efficacy which God has delegated to it at the same time as its being. At the first beginning of such a world, we must therefore postulate not so much a power that exercises its force, as an infinite goodness that communicates itself to the world: Love is the deepest spring of all causality.

A Christian View of Life and History[*]

R E I N H O L D   N I E B U H R [1892–   ] was educated at Elmhurst College, Eden Theological Seminary, and Yale Divinity School. He was a pastor in Detroit from 1915 to 1928. Since that time he has taught at Union Theological Seminary. He has written voluminously, edited two Christian journals of opinion, and taken an active part in liberal political movements. He is probably the most influential American spokesman for Neo-orthodoxy in contemporary Protestantism.

THE SPIRITUAL CRISIS OF OUR AGE. It would have been difficult for the generations of the twentieth century to survive the hazards and to face the perplexities of our age in any event, since every problem of human existence had been given a wider scope than known in previous ages. But our perplexities became the more insoluble and the perils to which we were exposed became the more dangerous because the men of this generation had to face the rigors of life in the twentieth century with nothing but the soft illusions of the previous two centuries to cover their spiritual nakedness. There was nothing in the creeds and dogmas of these centuries which would have enabled modern men either to anticipate or to understand the true nature of the terrors and tumults to which they would be exposed.

The history of mankind exhibits no more ironic experience than the contrast between the sanguine hopes of recent centuries and the bitter experiences of contemporary man. Every technical advance, which previous generations regarded as a harbinger or guarantor of the redemption of mankind from its various difficulties, has proved to be the cause, or at least the occasion, for a new dimension of ancient perplexities.

A single article of faith has given diverse forms of modern culture the unity of a shared belief. Modern men of all shades of opinion agreed in the belief that historical development is a redemptive process. . . .

[*] From *Faith and History* (Chapter 1, 5, 6, and 8) by Reinhold Niebuhr; copyright 1949 by Charles Scribner's Sons. Reprinted by permission of Charles Scribner's Sons, James Nisbet and Company, Ltd., and the author.

The goal toward which history was presumably moving was variously defined. The most unreflective forms of historical optimism in the nineteenth century assumed that increasing physical comfort and well-being were the guarantee of every other form of advance. Sometimes the enlarging human community was believed to be developing inevitably toward a universal community, for "clans and tribes, long narrowly self-regarding, are finally enlarged and compacted into nations; and nations move inevitably, however slowly, into relations with one another, whose ultimate goal is the unification of mankind." It may be recorded in passing that scarcely a single student in the modern era noted the marked difference between the task of unifying tribes, nations and empires and the final task of the unification of mankind. In the former case there is always some particular force of geography, language, common experience or the fear of a common foe which furnishes the core of cohesion. In the latter case unity must be achieved in defiance of the unique and particularistic forces of historical concretion.

Sometimes, as in H. G. Wells' *Outline of History*, the historical process is assumed to be moving toward the democratization, as well as the universalization, of the human community. The democratic culmination, toward which history was presumably moving was frequently defined in contradictory terms. Libertarians thought they saw a movement toward increasing liberty while equalitarians and collectivists thought they could discern a movement toward more intense social cohesion.

Nor was there agreement about the cause of historical advance. Social Darwinism as well as other forms of naturalism looked upon historical development as a mere extension of natural evolution. The Darwinists saw the guarantee of progress in the survival of the fittest. Others discerned a movement in both nature and history from consistent egoism to a greater and greater consideration of the interests of others.

More frequently historical development was regarded not so much as an extension of forces operative in nature as a negation of natural impulses through the growth of mind. The method of reason's trimph over the irrationalities of nature was, however, variously interpreted. The French Enlightenment assigned reason the primary function of discerning the "laws of nature" and of destroying man's abortive efforts to circumvent these laws. Comte, on the other hand, believed that a scientific political program would bring the irrational factors in man's common life under rational control. Condorcet believed that justice would triumph when universal education destroyed the advantage which the shrewd had over the simple. Or it was assumed that increasing rationality would gradually destroy the irrational (primarily religious) justifications of special privilege. Or that increasing reason would gradually prompt all men to grant their fellow men justice, the power of logic requiring that the interests of each individual be brought into a consistent scheme of value. More recently the psychological sciences have hoped for the increasing control or elimination of self-regarding impulses and the extension of human sympathy through the rational control of man's sub-rational life. . . .

Though there are minor dissonances the whole chorus of modern culture learned to sing the new song of hope in remarkable harmony. The redemption of mankind, by whatever means, was assured for the future. It was, in fact, assured by the future.

There were experiences in previous centuries which might well have challenged this unqualified optimism. But the expansion of man's power over nature proceeded at such a pace that all doubts were quieted, allowing the nineteenth century to become the "century of hope" and to express the modern mood in its most extravagant terms. History, refusing to move by the calendar, actually permitted the nineteenth century to indulge its illusions into the twentieth. Then came the deluge. Since 1914 one tragic experience has followed another, as if history had been designed to refute the vain delusions of modern man.

The "laws" and tendencies of historical development proved in the light of contemporary experience to be much more complex than any one has supposed. Every new freedom represented a new peril as well as a new promise. Modern industrial society dissolved ancient forms of political authoritarianism; but the tyrannies which grew on its soil proved more brutal and vexatious than the old ones. The inequalities rooted in landed property were levelled. But the more dynamic inequalities of a technical society became more perilous to the community than the more static forms of uneven power. The achievement of individual liberty was one of the genuine advances of bourgeois society. But this society also created atomic individuals who, freed from the disciplines of the older organic communities, were lost in the mass; and became the prey of demagogues and charlatans who transmuted their individual anxieties and resentments into collective political power of demonic fury.

The development of instruments of communication and transportation did create a potential world community by destroying all the old barriers of time and space. But the new interdependence of the nations created a more perplexing problem than anyone had anticipated. It certainly did not prompt the nations forthwith to organize a "parliament of man and federation of the world." Rather it extended the scope of old international frictions so that a single generation was subjected to two wars of global dimensions. Furthermore the second conflict left the world as far from the goal of global peace as the first. At its conclusion the world's peace was at the mercy of two competing alliances of world savers, the one informed by the bourgeois and the other by the proletarian creed of world redemption. Thus the civil war in the heart of modern industrial nations, which had already brought so much social confusion into the modern world, was re-enacted in the strife between nations. The development of atomic instruments of conflict aggravated the fears not only of those who lacked such instruments, but of those who had them. The fears of the latter added a final ironic touch to the whole destiny of modern man. The possession of power has never annulled the fears of those who wield it, since it prompts them to anxiety over its possible loss. The possession of a phenomenal form of destructive power in the modern day has proved to be so fruitful of new fears that the perennial ambiguity of man's situation of power and weakness became more vividly exemplified, rather than overcome. Thus a century which was meant to achieve a democratic society of world-scope finds itself at its half-way mark uncertain about the possibility of avoiding a new conflict of such proportions as to leave the survival of mankind, or at least the survival of civilization, in doubt.

The tragic irony of this refutation by contemporary history of modern man's conception of history embodies the spiritual crisis of our age. . . .

EXTRAVAGANT VIEWS OF FREEDOM AND VIRTUE. Though all human capacities are subject to development, and the cultural achievements and social institutions of mankind are capable of an indeterminate development, the extension of human power and freedom in either individual life or in the total human enterprise does not change the human situation essentially. Man remains a creature of nature on every stage of his development. There are certain bounds of human finiteness which no historical development can overcome. The preoccupation of modern culture with the remarkable increase in human power and freedom has inclined modern men to deny and to defy these fixed limits.

The tendency to overestimate the degree of increase of human freedom expresses itself most characteristically in the belief that the development of human capacities radically alters the human situation. The final form of the modern error about history is the belief that man's ambiguous position as both a creature and a creator of history is gradually changed until he may, in the foreseeable future, become the unequivocal master of historical destiny. This final and most absurd form of *Hybris* [overweening pride] persuades modern culture to reject all Biblical concepts of divine providence as expressions of human impotence and ignorance, no longer relevant to the modern man's situation of intelligence and power. . . .

If it should be true that history radically changes the human situation and that man's mastery over, rather than subordination to, the natural and historical process is the primary proof and fruit of that change, it would follow that religious conceptions of a providential purpose and pattern would become irrelevant through historical development. The warning of Christ, "Which of you by taking thought can add one cubit unto his stature?" (*Matthew* 6:27) seems from the viewpoint of modern pride a typical religious expression of impotence, which ceases to have meaning in a day in which technics have extended the power of the human foot in transportation, of the human hand in manufacture, and of the ear and eye in fabulous forms of communication. . . .

The curious belief of modern culture that religion is merely an expression of impotence, which man's growing power will overcome . . . is succinctly expressed in the observation of Bertrand Russell that fishermen with sailboats incline to the religious while those who boast the possession of motorboats divest themselves of religion. "Modern technics," declares Mr. Russell, "is giving man a sense of power which is changing his whole mentality. Until recently the physical environment was something that had to be accepted. But to the modern man physical environment is merely the raw material for manipulation and opportunity. It may be that God made the world, but there is no reason why we should not make it over." The modern man's sense of power does not stop with a sense of mastery over the immediate natural conditions of his life. "A cosmic process has come to consciousness," boasts Eustace Hayden, "and to the capacity for purposive self-control on the social level. . . . The task is to impose human purposes upon the cosmic process, to shape the course of the flowing stream of life."

The illusion of budding omnipotence, which inspires the charge that a religious sense of Providence is the expression of a primitive impotence, could not be stated more clearly. . . .

The extravagant estimate of the degree of freedom and power which may accrue to man through historical development is hardly as grievous an error as the estimate of the virtue of that freedom, implied in most modern interpretations of the human situation.

Since modern rationalism inherited the belief from classical rationalism that the evil in human nature is the consequence of natural finiteness and physical impulses, it naturally inclined to the conclusion that the development of rational capacities was, in itself, a process of gradual emancipation from evil. . . . Individual and collective egotism is believed to be the consequence of a primitive ignorance which must ultimately either yield to more enlightened and therefore more inclusive forms of self-interest, or which will be brought under the dominion of the moral force implicit in man's rational faculties.

In more recent scientific forms of this identification of virtue and reason, the hope is to bring the irrational stuff of human nature under control by more adequate psychiatric technics or by establishing rational political checks upon the irrational impulses of men.

In any event evil is always a force of the past, which must be overcome by present and future possibilities. The triumph of virtue is more or less guaranteed because historical development assures both the increasing purity of reason and the efficacy of its scientific technics. This error of identifying increasing freedom with increasing virtue is primarily responsible for the false estimates of history by contemporary culture. The increasing evils which arose with increasing power could be neither anticipated nor comprehended within terms of these presuppositions.

In its most naive form modern rationalism identifies technical competence with rational profundity and sees in the conquest of nature a proof of man's capacity to bring the irrational stuff of human nature under control. All that is necessary is to apply the "methods of science" as rigorously to the world of human affairs as to the realm of nature. In forms less crude there is some recognition of the wide gulf which separates the world of history from the world of nature; but confidence in the final dominion of reason over this more complex world is no less sanguine.

One reason why it never occurs to the typical modern that evil in human nature may be due to a corruption of human freedom, rather than to some inertia of nature or history, is because the human self in its integrity and unity has been lost.

THE HUMAN SITUATION. Despite all modern protests against dualism and idealism, the real self in its unity is dissolved into an intelligible and a sensible self. But the intelligible self is not really a self. It is pure mind. And the sensible self is not really a self. It is a congeries of physical impulses. . . .

This dismissal of the real self in the unity of its finiteness and freedom is responsible for the note of unreality in the more theoretic disciplines of our culture, as compared either with the common sense which informs the practical life of men or the profounder insights of poets and artists, seeking to portray life in its wholeness and complexity. The common sense of ordinary men is seldom under the illusion that the jealousies and envies which infect even the most intimate human relations are merely the defects of an undisciplined mind. They are known to be temptations for saint as well as sinner; for the wise man and fool. Practical statesmen do not regard the will-to-power of a strong man as the vestigial remnant of barbarism. All common-sense political wisdom seeks to harness and to restrain, to make use of, and to guard against, the power impulse. A common sense regulation of economic life does not treat the economic motive as a force which is about to be eliminated from human society. It knows that motive to be one facet of the power of self-interest, which must be harnessed, deflected, beguiled and transmuted in the interest of the commonweal but which can never be completely suppressed. . . .

The real self, in its unity and integrity, is involved in the evils, particularly the evils of self-seeking, which it commits. This self is always sufficiently emancipated of natural necessity, not to be compelled to follow the course dictated by self-interest. If it does so nevertheless, it is held culpable both in the court of public opinion and in the secret of its own heart. The self finds itself free; but, as Augustine suggested, not free to do good. The self seeks its own despite its freedom to envisage a wider good than its own interest. Furthermore it uses its freedom to extend the domain of its own interests. . . .

This human egotism does not belong to nature. The eighteenth-century rationalists were wrong in asserting that men sought their own, just as every animal seeks to preserve its existence. The human self is different from other creatures in two respects: 1) It is able by its freedom to transmute nature's survival impulse into more potent and more destructive, more subtle and more comprehensive forms of self-seeking than the one-dimensional survival impulse of nature. 2) It is able to envisage a larger good than its own preservation, to make some fitful responses to this more inclusive obligation and to feel itself guilty for its failure to make a more consistent response.

Every animal will run as fast as it can from a superior foe, a strategy which subjects human beings to the charge of cowardice. Naturalists may argue that human actions have been reduced to the level of "physical events" to which no praise or blame can be attached because they always have "sufficient antecedents." But the common sense of mankind has never accepted this ridiculous denial of a unique freedom in human life and of a consequent responsibility and guilt in human action. The life and literature of the ages is replete with condemnation of cowardice and self-seeking and of praise for acts of bravery and lives of selfless devotion. Even the deterministic Marxists, who assume that moral ideals are inevitably pretentious rationalizations of self-interest, are unable to carry their determinism to its logical conclusion; for their political propaganda abounds in invectives against the dishonesty of their foes. This invective could have meaning only upon the assumption that men might be honest, rather than dishonest, and might actually seek, rather than merely pretend to seek, the good of the commonwealth rather than their own advantage.

In a similar fashion a liberal idealist who ostensibly believes that the progress of mankind depends upon the extension of the scientific method, periodically censures his fellowmen for their laziness and dishonesty, and for their inclination to make compromises with outmoded authoritarianism. "All I know about the future of progress," declares John Dewey, "is that it depends upon man to say whether he wants it or not." Thus the responsible self (and the guilty self insofar as it always falls short of its highest responsibilities) peeps through even the most intricate and elaborate façades of modern thought.

The real situation is that the human self is strongly inclined to seek its own but that it has a sufficient dimension of transcendence over self to be unable to ascribe this inclination merely to natural necessity. On the other hand, when it strives for a wider good it surreptitiously introduces its own interests into this more inclusive value. This fault may be provisionally regarded as the inevitable consequence of a finite viewpoint. The self sees the larger structure of value from its own standpoint. Yet this provisional disavowal of moral culpability is never finally convincing. The self's ignorance is never invincible ignorance. It sees beyond itself sufficiently to know that its own interests are not identical with the wider good. If it claims such identity nevertheless, there is an element of moral perversity, and not mere ignorance in the claim. Thus the cynical attitude of all common sense judgments toward the pretensions of nations and individuals is justified by the facts. Common sense at least touches the periphery of the mystery of original sin which uncommon sense so easily dismisses. . . .

The simple facts which we have enumerated are so obvious, supported by so much evidence and sustained by so many judgments of common sense in contravention to the prevailing theories of our age, that one is forced to the conclusion that something more than an honest error has entered into modern miscalculations of human behaviour and historical destiny. . . .

The modern interpretation of human life and history was a highly plausible evasion of some very inconvenient and embarrassing facts about human nature. It was an evasion both of the dimension of responsibility in human nature and of the fact of guilt. It made man the judge of his world and of himself and seemed to free him from the scrutiny of a higher judgment. Above all it annulled and erased the indictment of guilt contained in that higher judgment. It refuted the embarrassing suspicion that man himself is the author of the historical evils which beset him. The whole structure of the modern interpretation of life and history was, in short, a very clever contrivance of human pride to obscure the weakness and the insecurity of man; of the human conscience to hide the sin into which men fall through their efforts to override their weakness and insecurity; and of human sloth to evade responsibility.

The monotonous reiteration of the eighteenth century and of the belated children of the eighteenth century in our own age that their primary concern is to establish and to guard the "dignity of man" has the quality of a peculiar irony, when these evasions are considered.

The more consistent naturalistic versions of our culture are involved in the absurdity of ostensibly guarding the dignity of man while they actually deny the reality of a responsible self, by reducing human behaviour to the dimension of "facts of nature" about which no moral judgments can be made since every human act is the consequence of some "sufficient cause." The less consistent naturalist and the idealist do not indeed exalt the dignity of the human mind; but they do not understand its involvement in finite conditions. Thus they promise a mastery of historical destiny which contradicts the permanent ambiguity of the human situation. And they construct confident "philosophies of history" as if man completely surveyed the stuff of history in his mind even as he mastered the forces of history by his power. Meanwhile man's involvement in the forces which he ostensibly masters periodically produces a shock of disillusionment in modern complacency. The vaunted master of historical destiny is subject to fits of despair when he finds himself tossed about among historical forces beyond the power of his will; and the proud interpreter of the meaning of history is periodically reduced to despair, wondering whether any truth can be known, since every truth known is known only from a special and peculiar historical locus.

Though sometimes the dignity of man is denied because the responsible self is annulled, and sometimes the dignity is exaggerated because the weakness of man is forgotten, an even more grievous error dogs all these modern calculations. The misery of man, the fact of his guilt is evaded. The fact that human power and freedom contain destructive, as well as creative, possibilities is not recognized. The responsibility of the self in the center and quintessence of its will and personality for the destructive side of human freedom is denied with particular vehemence. Even if the self is regarded as a responsible self, the idea that guilt accompanies responsibility is denied as a monstrous form of religious morbidity.

These evasions are much more serious than any of the modern rational miscalculations. They suggest that the human situation can not be understood in some simple system of rational intelligibility. Man in his strength and in his weakness is too ambiguous to understand himself, unless his rational analyses are rooted in a faith that he is comprehended from beyond the ambiguities of his own understanding. The patterns of meaning in his history culminate in a realm of meaning and mystery which, if too easily dissolved into rational intelligibility, lead to nonsense, particularly to the nonsense of contradiction. But above all there is the mystery of man's responsibility and of his guilt in failing to fulfill it. That the recalcitrance of the human heart should not be simply the lag of nature but a corruption of freedom and should not be overcome by increasing freedom: this is the mystery of original sin. . . .

THE CHRISTIAN VIEW OF LIFE AND HISTORY. The sovereignty of God establishes the general frame of meaning for life and history, according to Biblical faith. But the first specific content of the drama of history is furnished by the assertion of divine sovereignty against man's rebellious efforts to establish himself as the perverse center of existence. Biblical faith does not deny the fact of evil in history. On the contrary it discerns that men are capable of such bold and persistent defiance of the laws and structures of their existence that only the resource of the divine power and love is finally able to overcome this rebellion. The patterns of human existence are filled with obscurities and abysses of meaninglessness because of this possibility of evil in human life.

The obscurities and incoherences of life are, according to Biblical faith, primarily the consequence of human actions. The incoherences and confusions, usually defined as "natural" evil, are not the chief concern of the Christian faith. Natural evil represents the failure of nature's processes to conform perfectly to human ends. It is the consequence of man's ambiguous position in nature. As a creature of nature he is subject to necessities and contingencies, which may be completely irrelevant to the wider purposes, interests, and ambitions which he conceives and elaborates as creative spirit. The most vivid symbol of natural evil is death. Death is a simple fact in the dimension of nature; but it is an irrelevance and a threat of meaninglessness in the realm of history. Biblical faith is, however, only obliquely interested in the problem of natural evil. It does not regard death, as such, as an evil. "The sting of death," declares St. Paul, "is sin."

Nor does it regard moral evil as due to man's involvement in natural finiteness. On the contrary, moral or historical evil is the consequence of man's abortive effort to overcome his insecurity by his own power, to hide the finiteness of his intelligence by pretensions of omniscience and to seek for emancipation from his ambiguous position by his own resources. Sin is, in short, the consequence of man's inclination to usurp the prerogatives of God, to think more highly of himself than he ought to think, thus making destructive use of his freedom by not observing the limits to which a creaturely freedom is bound.

Man is at variance with God through this abortive effort to establish himself as his own Lord; and he is at variance with his fellowmen by the force of the same pride which brings him in conflict with God. The prophets of Israel seemed to sense this primary form of historical evil most immediately in its collective form. They felt that Israel was guilty of it, because it drew complacent conclusions from the fact of its special covenant with God. The great nations and empires which encircled Israel were guilty because they imagined that their power made them immortal and secure. The myth of the Fall of Adam universalizes, as well as individualizes, this theme of man's revolt against God. The influence of this myth upon the Christian imagination is not primarily due to any literalistic illusions of Christian orthodoxy. The myth accurately symbolizes the consistent Biblical diagnosis of moral and historical evil. Adam and, together with him, all men seek to overstep the bounds which are set by the Creator for man as creature. St. Paul's definition of sin is in perfect conformity with this theme, even when he makes no specific reference to the Fall. Man's sin, declares St. Paul, is that he "changes the glory of the uncorruptible God into an image of corruptible man" (*Romans* 1:23). If men fail to penetrate to the mystery of the divine, the fault lies, according to the Bible, not so much in the finiteness of their intelligence as in the "vanity" of their imagination. They are, declares St. Paul, "without excuse" in their ignorance of God. For "the invisible things of him from the creation of the world are clearly seen, being understood by the things that are made" (*Romans* 1:20). It is obvious, in other words, that the world is not self-derived. It points beyond itself to its Creator. The failure to recognize this fact is not the fault of the mind but of the person who usurps the central position in the scheme of things and thereby brings confusion into his own life and into the whole order of history. Biblical faith has always insisted upon the embarrassing truth that the corruption of evil is at the heart of the human personality. It is not the inertia of its natural impulses in opposition to the purer impulses of the mind. The fact that it is a corruption which has a universal dominion over all men, though it is not by nature but in freedom that men sin, is the "mystery" or "original sin," which will always be an offense to rationalists. But it has the merit of being true to the facts of human existence. A scientific age will seek, and also find, specific reasons and causes for the jealousy of children, or the power lusts in mature individuals, or the naive egotism of even the saintly individual, or the envies and hatreds which infect all human relations. The discovery of specific causes of specific forms of these evils has obscured and will continue to obscure the profounder truth, that all men, saints and sinners, the righteous and the unrighteous, are inclined to use the freedom to transcend time, history, and themselves in such a way as to make themselves the false center of existence. Thus the same freedom which gives human life a creative power, not possessed by the other creatures, also endows it with destructive possibilities not known in nature. The two-fold possibility of creativity and destruction in human freedom accounts for the growth of both good and evil through the extension of human powers. The failure to recognize this obvious fact in modern culture accounts for most of its errors in estimating the actual trends of history.

The tendency of modern culture to see only the creative possibilities of human freedom makes the Christian estimate of the human situation seem morbid by contrast. Is not Kierkegaard morbid, even Christians are inclined to ask, when he insists that "before God man is always in the wrong"? Does such an emphasis not obscure the creative aspects of human freedom? Is it not true that men are able by increasing freedom to envisage a larger world and to assume a responsible attitude toward a wider and wider circle of claims upon their conscience? Does the Christian faith do justice, for instance, to the fact that increasing freedom has set the commandment, "Thou shalt love thy neighbor as thyself," in a larger frame of reference than ever before in history? Is it not significant that we have reached a global situation in which we may destroy ourselves and each other if we fail to organize a new global "neighborhood" into a tenable brotherhood?

Such misgivings fail to recognize how intimately the dignity and the misery of man are related in the Christian conception. The dignity of man, which modern culture is ostensibly so anxious to guard and validate, is greater than the modern mind realizes. For it consists of a unique freedom which is able, not only to transcend the "laws" of nature or of reason to which classical and modern culture would bind it, but also to defy and outrage the very structure of man's existence. The dignity of man is therefore no proof of his virtue; nor is the misery of man a proof of his "bestiality." Both the destructive and the creative powers of man are unique because of the special quality of freedom which he possesses.

If the destructive, rather than the creative, possibilities of freedom seem unduly emphasized in Biblical thought, that is because in the ultimate instance (that is when men are not judging themselves but feel themselves under a divine judgment) they become conscious of the self's persistent self-centeredness. When they are judging themselves they are inclined to be impressed by the self's virtuous inclination to consider interests other than its own.

It is worth noting that the behaviour of a man or nation, viewed from the standpoint of a critical rival or observer is invariably assessed, not as the morally complacent self judges its own actions, but as the devout and contrite self judges it. The Christian interpretation of the human situation corresponds to what men and nations say about each other, even without Christian insights. But without Christian insights they bring even greater confusion into the affairs of men by assuming that only their rivals and competitors are guilty of the pride and lust for power which they behold. Only under the judgment of God do they recognize the universality of this human situation of sin and guilt.

The capacity and inclination of man to disturb the order and harmony of human life by placing himself, individually and collectively, perversely into the center of the whole drama of life gives the pattern of history a much greater complexity than is supposed in those interpretations which assume that man conforms naturally to whatever "laws" of life his mind discerns. The Biblical interpretation of the pattern of history must incorporate the provisional meaninglessness and obscurity which human defiance of God's laws introduces into the drama of the human story. The drama, in essence, is not so much a contest between good and evil forces in history as a contest between all men and God. In this contest God has resources of power and mercy, finally to overcome the human rebellion. He asserts His sovereignty partly by the power which places an ultimate limit upon human defiance and partly by a resource of love and mercy which alone is able to touch the source of the rebellion in the human heart. The divine sovereignty is always partly "hidden" and the meaning of life and history is partly obscure, not only because human defiance and moral evil seem to enjoy long periods of immunity, thus calling the divine justice and power in question; but also because the relation of the divine mercy to the divine justice is obscure.

The climax of the Biblical revelation of the divine sovereignty over history is in the self-disclosure of a divine love, which on the one hand is able to overcome the evil inclination to self-worship in the human heart and which on the other hand takes the evil of history into and upon itself. These two facets of the divine love establish the two most important aspects of the Biblical interpretation of history. On the one hand there is a possibility of the renewal of life and the destruction of evil, whenever men and nations see themselves as they truly are under a divine judgment, which is as merciful as it is terrible. On the other hand the life of each individual as well as the total human enterprise remains in contradiction to God; and the final resolution of this contradiction is by God's mercy. From the one standpoint human history is a series of new beginnings. These new beginnings are not the inevitable springtime which follows the death of winter in nature. Life does not arise from death, as death from life, in natural cycles. Life may be reborn, if, under the divine judgment and mercy, the old self or the old culture or civilization is shattered.

From the other standpoint human life and human history remain a permanent enigma which only the divine mercy can overcome. No human life has a logical or consistent conclusion within itself. It requires not only a "life everlasting" which it is unable to achieve of itself, but also the "forgiveness of sins" which it cannot earn itself. The total human enterprise is in the same case. Human powers and capacities may continue to develop indeterminately. But a "last judgment" stands at the end of all human achievements; and the "Anti-Christ" manifests himself at the end of history. This is the Biblical symbol of the inconclusive character of human history. Biblical faith is, in short, the tremendous assertion that in Biblical revelation, culminating in the revelation of Christ, man has made contact with the divine power, which is able to overcome not only the ambiguity in which all human life and history is involved but also the evils of history which are due to man's abortive efforts to overcome them himself by his own resources. . . .

The points of reference for the structure of the meaning of history in the Christian faith are obviously not found by an empirical analysis of the observable structures and coherences of history. They are "revelations," apprehended by faith, of the character and purposes of God. The experience of faith by which they are apprehended is an experience at the ultimate limits of human knowledge; and it requires a condition of repentance which is a possibility for the individual, but only indirectly for nations and collectives.

The character of these points of reference or these foundations for a structure of meaning make it quite clear that it is not possible to speak simply of a "Christian philosophy of history." Perhaps it is not possible to have any adequate "philosophy" of history at all because a philosophy will reduce the antinomies, obscurities and the variety of forms in history to a too simple form of intelligibility. Yet a Christian theology of history is not an arbitrary construct. It "makes sense" out of life and history.

That the final clue to the mystery of the divine power is found in the suffering love of a man on the Cross is not a proposition which follows logically from the observable facts of history. But there are no observable facts of history which can not be interpreted in its light. When so interpreted the confusions and catastrophes of history may become the source of the renewal of life.

That life in history is meaningful—though the historic growth of human power may sharpen rather than mitigate the struggle between good and evil, and may accentuate rather than modify the inclination of the human heart to idolatry—is also not a proposition which follows inevitably from an observation of the historical drama. The sense of meaning is derived from the conviction that no human rebellion can rise so high as to challenge the divine sovereignty essentially. While this confidence in the final source and end of human life is not a fruit of empirical observation, it is worth noting that the philosophies which are the fruit of empirical observation either drive men to despair by charting the growing antinomies of life or they prompt complacency by obscuring the obvious tragic aspects of life and history.

The final vision of the fulfillment of life and history in Christian eschatology transcends the canons of reason and common sense even more explicitly. Christian eschatology looks forward to an "end" of history in which the conditions of nature-history are transfigured but not annulled. This picture of the fulfillment of life involves the rational absurdity of an eternity which incorporates the conditions of time: individuality and particularity. But the alternative faith by which men live either: 1) envisions an eternity which annuls the whole of history and thereby denies the significance of human life in history; or 2) falsely reduces the whole dimension of history with its partial and fragmentary meanings to the level of nature; or 3) assumes that a progressive history ceases at some point to be a history in time and culminates in an incredible utopia where unconditioned good is realized amidst the contingencies of history.

The Christian philosophy of history is rational, therefore, only in the sense that it is possible to prove that alternatives to it fail to do justice to all aspects of human existence; and that the basic presuppositions of the Christian faith, though transcending reason, make it possible to give an account of life and history in which all facts and antinomies are comprehended.

SUGGESTED READINGS

Some of the great systems of philosophy have been theistic: Descartes' system depends on the existence of a benevolent and omnipotent deity (see his *Meditations,* III–VI), as does Leibniz's system, though in quite a different way (see his *Theodicy* and, of the writings assembled by P. P. Wiener in *Leibniz: Selections,* the "Discourse on Metaphysics," "Monadology" and "Principles of Nature and Grace"). Systems like these are not necessarily affiliated with any special religious sect. J. Guttmann, in *Philosophies of Judaism,* studies major philosophical attempts to work out a specifically Jewish view. There are innumerable works of and about Christian theology and philosophy. E. Gilson's *Spirit of Mediaeval Philosophy* gives an excellent survey of mediaeval attempts to work out a Christian doctrine philosophically; for a more advanced and philosophically more sophisticated study, see J. Weinberg, *Short History of Mediaeval Philosophy.* H. A. Wolfson gives several illustrations, in *Religious Philosophy,* of various ways in which religious thinkers attempting to deal simply with religious problems are led into philosophical investigations. His first essay, "The Philonic God of Revelation and His Latter-Day Deniers," suggests how Philo would have replied to criticisms of belief in God offered by Spinoza, Hume, and Mill. A. C. McGiffert has written a useful, if somewhat tedious, *History of Christian Thought.*

F. R. Tennant's *Philosophical Theology* is an excellent example of careful use of philosophical techniques to solve problems arising from religious belief. W. Temple's *Nature, Man, and God* has been quite influential. P. Tillich's important *Systematic Theology* makes difficult reading, but some indication of Tillich's views can be obtained from his *Dynamics of Faith.*

Critiques of Theism

When we think about religion, we usually have theism in mind—the doctrine that a transcendent God, the source of all good, created the world and guides its destiny. This concern with theism is natural enough, since it is by far the most prevalent form of religious belief in modern Western culture. However, even a passing acquaintance with other religions suffices to show that theism is by no means the only form in which man's religious experience is expressed and should warn us against identifying attacks upon theism with a more general rejection of all religion.

Not all critics of theism are irreligious. Some are convinced that another type of religious view, such as pantheism, more adequately expresses their experience. Others are critical of theism only in part: even though they do not credit its claims to truth, they believe it symbolizes and expresses significant social and personal values. Other critics are more hostile. Some of them believe that theism is simply false, and others hold not merely that it is false but also that it is socially harmful. Throughout this range of criticism, however, there is a point of common agreement: theism cannot be accepted as an adequate account of the nature of the world. As a description of the nature of reality, it is either intellectually confused or it is simply false.

The selection from AYER offers a succinct argument against theism. Theists claim that it is possible to give an adequate interpretation of the world only on the assumption that God exists. Ayer argues that this assumption is in no way helpful in explaining what it is supposed to explain.

SPINOZA would agree with Ayer that theism fails to offer an adequate explanation of what occurs in the world. In addition, he seeks to show how Theism has arisen out of man's tendency to view the world anthropomorphically. Spinoza's own position is that of pantheism. According to Spinoza, God and Nature are one, and Nature itself is the proper object of religious reverence.

DEWEY represents humanism. Humanists accept a naturalistic view of the world and reject both the theistic conception of a transcendent creator and sustainer of nature and the pantheistic conception of nature as the proper object of religious reverence. They find the essence of religion in a special dimension of experience, but this dimension does not coincide with those experiences usually called "religious." Wherever there is an affirmation of ideal ends and a dedication of the self to the achievement of those ends, Dewey would hold that a religious attitude is present. In the following selection, he defends this view and argues that a properly religious outlook may be independent both of supernaturalism and of commitment to any particular religious institution.

A Comment on Supernaturalism[*]

A L F R E D J U L E S A Y E R [1910–   ]. See page 616.

I think that there are three intellectual needs which the belief in a super-natural deity may be thought to serve. It offers an explanation of the world's existence and of its nature; an assurance that life is worth living; and an answer to the question how one ought to live. Considered logically, indeed, it fulfils none of these functions. It does not fulfil the first of them, because it is no explanation of anything merely to say that a god designed it; it would be an explanation only if there were some way of testing the deity's intentions independently of the actual course of events, for in that case the religious hypothesis would have some predictive power; but a hypothesis which is consistent with anything that happens, or could conceivably happen, is altogether vacuous. It does not fulfil the second because even if one's life did fit into some design, it would not on this hypothesis, be a design of one's own choosing. And the difficulty about making the purposes of the deity one's own is that one has no means of knowing what they are. Neither does the promise of an afterlife affect the argument; for if one does not find one's life worth living as it is there is no good reason to wish for it to be prolonged. It does not fulfil the third, because the theist has to rely on his own moral sense in order to decide what it is that his deity wishes him to do. God commands only what is good; but we have independently to know what is good in order to know what God commands. A revelation which runs counter to our morality is not accepted as genuine. Nevertheless, the religious hypothesis is thought to fulfil these functions, even though it does not.

[*] From Ayer: "Religion and the Intellectuals," published in *The Partisan Review*, XVII (1950), No. 3. Reprinted by permission of *The Partisan Review* and the author.

The Idea of Divine Purpose[*]

B A R U C H   S P I N O Z A   [1632–1677] was one of the greatest of modern philosophers. A Dutch Jew, excommunicated by his own community and alien to the Christian community, he led a quiet life of study, supporting himself as a maker of lenses. Word of his philosophic originality gradually spread, but his greatest work, *Ethics,* was not published until after his death. This work is the clearest and most rigorous exposition of a pantheistic metaphysical and religious position in all philosophic literature. The views of man's nature and of morality which it defends have had great influence on subsequent thought.

I have now explained the nature of God and its properties. I have shown that He necessarily exists; that He is one God; that from that necessity alone of His own nature He is and acts; that He is and in what way He is, the free cause of all things; that all things are in Him, and so depend upon Him that without Him they can neither be nor can be conceived; and, finally, that all things have been predetermined by Him, not indeed from freedom of will or from absolute good pleasure, but from His absolute nature or infinite power.

Moreover, wherever an opportunity was afforded, I have endeavoured to remove prejudices which might hinder the perception of the truth of what I have demonstrated; but because not a few still remain which have been and are now sufficient to prove a very great hindrance to the comprehension of the connection of things in the manner in which I have explained it, I have thought it worth while to call them up to be examined by reason. But all these prejudices which I here undertake to point out depend upon this solely: that it is commonly supposed that all things in nature, like men, work to some end; and indeed it is thought to be certain that God Himself directs all things to some sure end, for it is said that God has made all things for man, and man that he may worship God. This, therefore, I will first investigate by inquiring, firstly, why so many rest in this prejudice, and why all are so naturally inclined to embrace it? I shall then show its falsity, and, finally, the manner in which there have arisen from it prejudices concerning good and evil, merit and sin, praise and blame, order and disorder, beauty and deformity, and so forth. This, however, is not the place to deduce these things from the nature of the human mind. It will be sufficient if I here take

[*] From Spinoza: *Ethics,* Book I, Appendix. Translated by W. H. White.

as an axiom that which no one ought to dispute, namely, that man is born ignorant of the causes of things, and that he has a desire of which he is conscious, to seek that which is profitable to him. From this it follows, firstly, that he thinks himself free because he is conscious of his wishes and appetites, whilst at the same time he is ignorant of the causes by which he is led to wish and desire, not dreaming what they are; and, secondly, it follows that man does everything for an end, namely, for that which is profitable to him, which is what he seeks. Hence it happens that he attempts to discover merely the final causes of that which has happened; and when he has heard them he is satisfied, because there is no longer any cause for further uncertainty. But if he cannot hear from another what these final causes are, nothing remains but to turn himself and reflect upon the ends which usually determine him to the like actions, and thus by his own mind he necessarily judges that of another. Moreover, since he discovers, both within and without himself, a multitude of means which contribute not a little to the attainment of what is profitable to himself—for example, the eyes, which are useful for seeing, the teeth for mastication, plants and animals for nourishment, the sun for giving light, the sea for feeding fish, &c.—it comes to pass that all natural objects are considered as means for obtaining what is profitable. These too being evidently discovered and not created by man, hence he has a cause for believing that some other person exists, who has prepared them for man's use. For having considered them as means it was impossible to believe that they had created themselves, and so he was obliged to infer from the means which he was in the habit of providing for himself that some ruler or rulers of nature exist, endowed with human liberty, who have taken care of all things for him, and have made all things for his use. Since he never heard anything about the mind of these rulers, he was compelled to judge of it from his own, and hence he affirmed that the gods direct everything for his advantage, in order that he may be bound to them and hold them in the highest honour. This is the reason why each man has devised for himself, out of his own brain, a different mode of worshipping God, so that God might love him above others, and direct all nature to the service of his blind cupidity and insatiable avarice.

Thus has this prejudice been turned into a superstition and has driven deep roots into the mind—a prejudice which was the reason why every one has so eagerly tried to discover and explain the final causes of things. The attempt, however, to show that nature does nothing in vain (that is to say, nothing which is not profitable to man), seems to end in showing that nature, the gods, and man are alike mad.

Do but see, I pray, to what all this has led. Amidst so much in nature that is beneficial, not a few things must have been observed which are injurious, such as storms, earthquakes, diseases, and it was affirmed that these things happened either because the gods were angry because of wrongs which had been inflicted on them by man, or because of sins committed in the method of worshipping them; and although experience daily contradicted this, and showed by an infinity of examples that both the beneficial and the injurious were indiscriminately bestowed on the pious and the impious, the inveterate prejudices on this point have not therefore been abandoned. For it was much easier for a man to place these things aside with others of the use of which he was ignorant, and thus retain his present and inborn state of ignorance, than to destroy the whole superstructure and think out a new one. Hence it was looked upon as indisputable that the judgments of the gods far surpass our comprehension; and this opinion alone would have been sufficient to keep the human race in darkness to all eternity, if mathematics, which does not deal with ends, but with the essences and properties of forms, had not placed before us another rule of truth. In addition to mathematics, other causes also might be assigned, which it is superfluous here to enumerate, tending to make men reflect upon these universal prejudices, and leading them to a true knowledge of things.

I have thus sufficiently explained what I promised in the first place to explain. There will now be no need of many words to show that nature has set no end before herself, and that all final causes are nothing but human fictions. For I believe that this is sufficiently evident both from the foundations and causes of this prejudice, and from all those propositions in which I have shown that all things are begotten by a certain eternal necessity of nature and in absolute perfection. Thus much, nevertheless, I will add, that this doctrine concerning an end altogether overturns nature. For that which is in truth the cause it considers as the effect, and vice versa. . . . For by way of example, if a stone has fallen from some roof on somebody's head and killed him, they will demonstrate in this manner that the stone has fallen in order to kill the man. For if it did not fall for that purpose by the will of God, how could so many circumstances concur through chance (and a number often simultaneously do concur)? You will answer, perhaps, that the event happened because the wind blew and the man was passing that way. But, they will urge, why did the wind blow at that time, and why did the man pass that way precisely at the same moment? If you again reply that the wind rose then because the sea on the preceding day began to be stormy, the weather hitherto having been calm, and that the man had been invited by a friend, they will urge again—because there is no end of questioning—But why was the sea agitated? why was the man invited at that time? And so they will not cease from asking the causes of causes, until at last you fly to the will of God, the refuge for ignorance.

So, also, when they behold the structure of the human body, they are amazed; and because they are ignorant of the causes of such art, they conclude that the body was made not by mechanical but by a supernatural or divine art, and has been formed in such a way so that the one part may not injure the other. Hence it happens that the man who endeavours to find out the true causes of miracles, and who desires as a wise man to understand nature, and not to gape at it like a fool, is generally considered and proclaimed to be a heretic and impious by those whom the vulgar worship as the interpreters both of nature and gods. For these know that if ignorance be removed, amazed stupidity, the sole ground on which they rely in arguing or in defending their authority, is taken away also. But these things I leave and pass on to that which I determined to do in the third place.

After man has persuaded himself that all things which exist are made for him, he must in everything adjudge that to be of the greatest importance which is most useful to him, and he must esteem that to be of surpassing worth by which he is most beneficially affected. In this way he is compelled to form those notions by which he explains nature; such, for instance, as good, evil, order, confusion, heat, cold, beauty, and deformity, &c.; and because he supposes himself to be free, notions like those of praise and blame, sin and merit, have arisen. These latter I shall hereafter explain when I have treated of human nature; the former I will here briefly unfold.

It is to be observed that man has given the name good to everything which leads to health and worship of God; on the contrary, everything which does not lead thereto he calls evil. But because those who do not understand nature affirm nothing about things themselves, but only imagine them, and take the imagination to be understanding, they therefore, ignorant of things and their nature, firmly believe an order to be in things; for when things are so placed that, if they are represented to us through the senses, we can easily imagine them, and consequently easily remember them, we call them well arranged; but if they are not placed so that we can imagine and remember them, we call them badly arranged or confused. Moreover, since those things are more especially pleasing to us which we can easily imagine, men therefore prefer order to confusion, as if order were something in nature apart from our own imagination; and they say that God has created everything in order, and in this manner they ignorantly attribute imagination to God, unless they mean perhaps that God, out of consideration for the human imagination, has disposed things in the manner in which they can most easily be imagined. No hesitation either seems to be caused by the fact that an infinite number of things are discovered which far surpass our imagination, and very many which confound it through its weakness. But enough of this. The other notions which I have mentioned are nothing

but modes in which the imagination is affected in different ways, and nevertheless they are regarded by the ignorant as being specially attributes of
things, because, as we have remarked, men consider all things as made for
themselves, and call the nature of a thing good, evil, sound, putrid, or corrupt, just as they are affected by it. For example, if the motion by which the
nerves are affected by means of objects represented to the eye conduces to
well-being, the objects by which it is caused are called beautiful; while those
exciting a contrary motion are called deformed. Those things, too, which
stimulate the senses through the nostrils are called sweet-smelling or stink-
ing; those which act through the taste are called sweet or bitter, full-
flavoured or insipid; those which act through the touch, hard or soft, heavy
or light; those, lastly, which act through the ears are said to make a noise,
sound, or harmony, the last having caused men to lose their senses to such a
degree that they have believed that God even is delighted with it. Indeed,
philosophers may be found who have persuaded themselves that the celestial
motions beget a harmony. All these things sufficiently show that every one
judges things by the constitution of his brain, or rather accepts the affections
of his imagination in the place of things. It is not, therefore, to be wondered
at, as we may observe in passing, that all those controversies which we see
have arisen amongst men, so that at last scepticism has been the result. For
although human bodies agree in many things, they differ in more, and therefore that which to one person is good will appear to another evil, that which
to one is well arranged to another is confused, that which pleases one will
displease another, and so on in other cases which I pass by both because we
cannot notice them at length here, and because they are within the experience of every one. For every one has heard the expressions: So many heads,
so many ways of thinking; Every one is satisfied with his own way of thinking; Differences of brains are not less common than differences of taste,—all
which maxims show that men decide upon matters according to the constitution of their brains, and imagine rather than understand things. If men
understood things, they would, as mathematics proves, at least be all alike
convinced if they were not all alike attracted. We see, therefore, that all
those methods by which the common people are in the habit of explaining
nature are only different sorts of imaginations, and do not reveal the nature
of anything in itself, but only the constitution of the imagination; and because they have names as if they were entities existing apart from the imagination, I call them entities not of the reason but of the imagination. All
argument, therefore, urged against us based upon such notions can be easily
refuted. Many people, for instance, are accustomed to argue thus: If all
things have followed from the necessity of the most perfect nature of God,
how is it that so many imperfections have arisen in nature—corruption for

instance, of things till they stink; deformity, exciting disgust; confusion, evil, crime &c.? But, as I have just observed, all this is easily answered. For the perfection of things is to be judged by their nature and power alone; nor are they more or less perfect because they delight or offend the human senses, or because they are beneficial or prejudicial to human nature.

Religion *vs.* The Religious[*]

JOHN DEWEY [1859–1952] was the most influential American philosopher of the twentieth century. He was born and educated in Vermont, and took his Ph.D. at the newly founded Johns Hopkins University. While teaching at Michigan, Chicago, and Columbia, Dewey wrote extensively in the fields of psychology, philosophy, education, and public affairs. His political and social writings were widely read, and his educational theories had a profound influence on the progressive movement in American education. His more technical works represent a comprehensive application of Pragmatism to all of the major areas of philosophy.

Never before in history has mankind been so much of two minds, so divided into two camps, as it is today. Religions have traditionally been allied with ideas of the supernatural, and often have been based upon explicit beliefs about it. Today there are many who hold that nothing worthy of being called religious is possible apart from the supernatural. Those who hold this belief differ in many respects. . . . But they agree in one point: the necessity for a Supernatural Being and for an immortality that is beyond the power of nature.

The opposed group consists of those who think the advance of culture and science has completely discredited the supernatural and with it all religions that were allied with belief in it. But they go beyond this point. The extremists in this group believe that with elimination of the supernatural not only must historic religions be dismissed but with them everything of a religious nature. When historical knowledge has discredited the claims made for the supernatural character of the persons said to have founded historic religions; when the supernatural inspiration attributed to literatures held sacred has been riddled, and when anthropological and psychological knowledge has disclosed the all-too-human source from which religious beliefs and practices have sprung, everything religious must, they say, also go.

There is one idea held in common by these two opposite groups: identification of the religious with the supernatural. The question I shall raise in these chapters concerns the ground for and the consequences of this identification: its reasons and its value. In the discussion I shall develop another conception of the nature of the religious phase of experience, one that separates it from the supernatural and the things that have grown up about it. I shally try to show that these derivations are encumbrances and that what is genuinely religious will undergo an emancipation when it is relieved from them; that then, for the first time, the religious aspect of experience will be free to develop freely on its own account.

This view is exposed to attack from both the other camps. It goes contrary to traditional religions, including those that have the greatest hold upon the religiously minded today. The view announced will seem to them to cut the vital nerve of the religious element itself in taking away the basis upon which traditional religions and institutions have been founded. From the other side, the position I am taking seems like a timid halfway position, a concession and compromise unworthy of thought that is thoroughgoing. It is regarded as a view entertained from mere tender-mindedness, as an emotional hangover from childhood indoctrination, or even as a manifestation of a desire to avoid disapproval and curry favor.

The heart of my point, as far as I shall develop it in this first section, is that there is a difference between religion, *a* religion, and the religious; between anything that may be denoted by a noun substantive and the quality of experience that is designated by an adjective. It is not easy to find a definition of religion in the substantive sense that wins general acceptance. However, in the *Oxford Dictionary* I find the following: "Recognition on the part of man of some unseen higher power as having control of his destiny and as being entitled to obedience, reverence and worship."

This particular definition is less explicit in assertion of the supernatural character of the higher unseen power than are others that might be cited. It is, however, surcharged with implications having their source in ideas connected with the belief in the supernatural, characteristic of historic religions. Let us suppose that one familiar with the history of religions, including those called primitive, compares the definition with the variety of known facts and by means of the comparison sets out to determine just what the definition means. I think he will be struck by three facts that reduce the terms of the definition to such a low common denominator that little meaning is left.

He will note that the "unseen powers" referred to have been conceived in a multitude of incompatible ways. Eliminating the differences, nothing is left beyond the bare reference to something unseen and powerful. This has been conceived as the vague and undefined Mana of the Melanesians; the Kami of primitive Shintoism; the fetish of the Africans; spirits, having some human properties, that pervade natural places and animate natural forces; the ultimate and impersonal principle of Buddhism; the unmoved mover of Greek thought; the gods and semidivine heroes of the Greek and Roman Pantheons; the personal and loving Providence of Christianity, omnipotent, and limited by a corresponding evil power; the arbitrary Will of Moslemism; the supreme legislator and judge of deism. And these are but a few of the outstanding varieties of ways in which the invisible power has been conceived.

There is no greater similarity in the ways in which obedience and reverence have been expressed. There has been worship of animals, of ghosts, of ancestors, phallic worship, as well as of a Being of dread power and of love and wisdom. Reverence has been expressed in the human sacrifices of the Peruvians and Aztecs; the sexual orgies of some Oriental religions; exorcisms and ablutions; the offering of the humble and contrite mind of the Hebrew prophet, the elaborate rituals of the Greek and Roman Churches. Not even sacrifice has been uniform; it is highly sublimated in Protestant denominations and in Moslemism. Where it has existed it has taken all kinds of forms and been directed to a great variety of powers and spirits. It has been used for expiation, for propitiation and for buying special favors. There is no conceivable purpose for which rites have not been employed.

Finally, there is no discernible unity in the moral motivations appealed to and utilized. They have been as far apart as fear of lasting torture; hope of enduring bliss, in which sexual enjoyment has sometimes been a conspicuous element; mortification of the flesh and extreme asceticism; prostitution and chastity; wars to extirpate the unbeliever; persecution to convert or punish the unbeliever, and philanthropic zeal; servile acceptance of imposed dogma, along with brotherly love and aspiration for a reign of justice among men.

I have, of course, mentioned only a sparse number of the facts which fill volumes in any well-stocked library. It may be asked by those who do not like to look upon the darker side of the history of religions why the darker facts should be brought up. We all know that civilized man has a background of bestiality and superstition and that these elements are still with us. Indeed, have not some religions, including the most influential forms of Christianity, taught that the heart of man is totally corrupt? How could the course of religion in its entire sweep not be marked by practices that are shameful in their cruelty and lustfulness, and by beliefs that are degraded and intellectually incredible? What else than what we find could be expected, in the case of people having little knowledge and no secure method of knowing; with primitive institutions, and with so little control of natural forces that they lived in a constant state of fear?

I gladly admit that historic religions have been relative to the conditions of social culture in which peoples lived. Indeed, what I am concerned with is to press home the logic of this method of disposal of outgrown traits of past religions. Beliefs and practices in a religion that now prevails are by this logic relative to the present state of culture. If so much flexibility has obtained in the past regarding an unseen power, the way it affects human destiny, and the attitudes we are to take toward it, why should it be assumed that change in conception and action has now come to an end? The logic involved in getting rid of inconvenient aspects of past religions compels us to inquire how much in religions now accepted are survivals from outgrown cultures. It compels us to ask what conception of unseen powers and our relations to them would be consonant with the best achievements and aspirations of the present. It demands that in imagination we wipe the slate clean and start afresh by asking what would be the idea of the unseen, of the manner of its control over us and the ways in which reverence and obedience would be manifested, if whatever is basically religious in experience had the opportunity to express itself free from all historic encumbrances.

So we return to the elements of the definition that has been given. What boots it to accept, in defense of the universality of religion, a definition that applies equally to the most savage and degraded beliefs and practices that have related to unseen powers and to noble ideals of a religion having the greatest share of moral content? There are two points involved. One of them is that there is nothing left worth preserving in the notions of unseen powers, controlling human destiny to which obedience, reverence and worship are due, if we glide silently over the nature that has been attributed to the powers, the radically diverse ways in which they have been supposed to control human destiny, and in which submission and awe have been manifested. The other point is that when we begin to select, to choose, and say that some present ways of thinking about the unseen powers are better than others; that the reverence shown by a free and self-respecting human being is better than the servile obedience rendered to an arbitrary power by frightened men; that we should believe that control of human destiny is exercised by a wise and loving spirit rather than by madcap ghosts or sheer force—when I say, we begin to choose, we have entered upon a road that has not yet come to an end. We have reached a point that invites us to proceed farther.

For we are forced to acknowledge that concretely there is no such thing as religion in the singular. There is only a multitude of religions. "Religion" is a strictly collective term and the collection it stands for is not even of the kind illustrated in textbooks of logic. It has not the unity of a regiment or assembly but that of any miscellaneous aggregate. Attempts to prove the universality prove too much or too little. It is probable that religions have been universal in the sense that all the peoples we know anything about have had *a* religion. But the differences among them are so great and so shocking that any common element that can be extracted is meaningless. The idea that religion is universal proves too little in that the older apologists for Christianity seem to have been better advised than some modern ones in condemning every religion but one as an impostor, as at bottom some kind of demon worship or at any rate a superstitious figment. Choice among religions is imperative, and the necessity for choice leaves nothing of any force in the argument from universality. Morever, when once we enter upon the road of choice, there is at once presented a possibility not yet generally realized.

For the historic increase of the ethical and ideal content of religions suggests that the process of purification may be carried further. It indicates that further choice is imminent in which certain values and functions in experience may be selected. This possibility is what I had in mind in speaking of the difference between the religious and a religion. I am not proposing a religion, but rather the emancipation of elements and outlooks that may be called religious. For the moment we have a religion, whether that of the Sioux Indian or of Judaism or of Christianity, that moment the ideal factors in experience that may be called religious take on a load that is not inherent in them, a load of current beliefs and of institutional practices that are irrelevant to them.

I can illustrate what I mean by a common phenomenon in contemporary life. It is widely supposed that a person who does not accept any religion is thereby shown to be a non-religious person. Yet it is conceivable that the present depression in religion is closely connected with the fact that religions now prevent, because of their weight of historic encumbrances, the religious quality of experience from coming to consciousness and finding the expression that is appropriate to present conditions, intellectual and moral. I believe that such is the case. I believe that many persons are so repelled from what exists as a religion by its intellectual and moral implications, that they are not even aware of attitudes in themselves that if they came to fruition would be genuinely religious. I hope that this remark may help make clear what I mean by the distinction between "religion" as a noun substantive and "religious" as adjectival.

To be somewhat more explicit, a religion (and as I have just said there is no such thing as religion in general) always signifies a special body of beliefs and practices having some kind of institutional organization, loose or tight. In contrast, the adjective "religious" denotes nothing in the way of a specifiable entity, either institutional or as a system of beliefs. It does not denote anything to which one can specifically point as one can point to this and that historic religion or existing church. For it does not denote anything that can exist by itself or that can be organized into a particular and distinctive form of existence. It denotes attitudes that may be taken toward every object and every proposed end or ideal. . . .

Any activity pursued in behalf of an ideal end against obstacles and in spite of threats of personal loss because of conviction of its general and enduring value is religious in quality. Many a person, inquirer, artist, philanthropist, citizen, men and women in the humblest walks of life, have achieved, without presumption and without display, such unification of themselves and of their relations to the conditions of existence. It remains to extend their spirit and inspiration to ever wider numbers. If I have said anything about religions and religion that seems harsh, I have said those things because of a firm belief that the claim on the part of religions to possess a monopoly of ideals and of the supernatural means by which alone, it is alleged, they can be furthered, stands in the way of the realization of distinctively religious values inherent in natural experience. For that reason, if for no other, I should be sorry if any were misled by the frequency with which I have employed the adjective "religious" to conceive of what I have said as a disguised apology for what have passed as religions. The opposition between religious values as I conceive them and religions is not to be bridged. Just because the release of these values is so important, their identification with the creeds and cults of religions must be dissolved.

FAITH AND ITS OBJECT. All religions, as I pointed out in the preceding chapter, involve specific intellectual beliefs, and they attach—some greater, some less—importance to assent to these doctrines as true, true in the intellectual sense. They have literatures held especially sacred, containing historical material with which the validity of the religions is connected. They have developed a doctrinal apparatus it is incumbent upon "believers" (with varying degrees of strictness in different religions) to accept. They also insist that there is some special and isolated channel of access to the truths they hold.

No one will deny, I suppose, that the present crisis in religion is intimately bound up with these claims. The skepticism and agnosticism that are rife and that from the standpoint of the religionist are fatal to the religious spirit are directly bound up with the intellectual contents, historical, cosmological, ethical, and theological, asserted to be indispensable in everything religious. There is no need for me here to go with any minuteness into the causes that have generated doubt and disbelief, uncertainty and rejection, as to these contents. It is enough to point out that all the beliefs and ideas in question, whether having to do with historical and literary matters, or with astronomy, geology and biology, or with the creation and structure of the world and man, are connected with the supernatural, and that this connection is the factor that has brought doubt upon them; the factor that from the standpoint of historic and institutional religions is sapping the religious life itself.

The obvious and simple facts of the case are that some views about the origin and constitution of the world and man, some views about the course of human history and personages and incidents in that history, have become so interwoven with religion as to be identified with it. On the other hand, the growth of knowledge and of its methods and tests has been such as to make acceptance of these beliefs increasingly onerous and even impossible for large numbers of cultivated men and women. With such persons, the result is that the more these ideas are used as the basis and justification of a religion, the more dubious that religion becomes.

Protestant denominations have largely abandoned the idea that particular ecclesiastic sources can authoritatively determine cosmic, historic and theological beliefs. The more liberal among them have at least mitigated the older belief that individual hardness and corruption of heart are the causes of intellectual rejection of the intellectual apparatus of the Christian religion. But these denominations have also, with exceptions numerically insignificant, retained a certain indispensable minimum of intellectual content. They ascribe peculiar religious force to certain literary documents and certain historic personages. Even when they have greatly reduced the bulk of intellectual content to be accepted, they have insisted at least upon theism and the immortality of the individual.

It is no part of my intention to rehearse in any detail the weighty facts that collectively go by the name of the conflict of science and religion—a conflict that is not done away with by calling it a conflict of science with theology, as long as even a minimum of intellectual assent is prescribed as essential. The impact of astronomy not merely upon the older cosmogony of religion but upon elements of creeds dealing with historic events—witness the idea of ascent into heaven—is familiar. Geological discoveries have displaced creation myths which once bulked large. Biology has revolutionized conceptions of soul and mind which once occupied a central place in religious beliefs and ideas, and this science has made a profound impression upon ideas of sin, redemption, and immortality. Anthropology, history and literary criticism have furnished a radically different version of the historic events and personages upon which Christian religions have built. Psychology is already opening to us natural explanations of phenomena so extraordinary that once their supernatural origin was, so to say, the natural explanation.

The significant bearing for my purpose of all this is that new methods of inquiry and reflection have become for the educated man today the final arbiter of all questions of fact, existence, and intellectual assent. Nothing less than a revolution in the "seat of intellectual authority" has taken place. This revolution, rather than any particular aspect of its impact upon this and that religious belief, is the central thing. In this revolution, every defeat is a stimulus to renewed inquiry; every victory won is the open door to more discoveries, and every discovery is a new seed planted in the soil of intelligence, from which grow fresh plants with new fruits. The mind of man is being habituated to a new method and ideal: There is but one sure road of access to truth—the road of patient, coöperative inquiry operating by means of observation, experiment, record and controlled reflection.

The scope of the change is well illustrated by the fact that whenever a particular outpost is surrendered it is usually met by the remark from a liberal theologian that the particular doctrine or supposed historic or literary tenet surrendered was never, after all, an intrinsic part of religious belief, and that without it the true nature of religion stands out more clearly than before. Equally significant is the growing gulf between fundamentalists and liberals in the churches. What is not realized—although perhaps it is more definitely seen by fundamentalists than by liberals—is that the issue does not concern this and that piecemeal *item* of belief, but centers in the question of the method by which any and every item of intellectual belief is to be arrived at and justified.

The positive lesson is that religious qualities and values if they are real at all are not bound up with any single item of intellectual assent, not even that of the existence of the God of theism; and that, under existing conditions, the religious function in experience can be emancipated only through surrender of the whole notion of special truths that are religious by their own nature, together with the idea of peculiar avenues of access to such truths. For were we to admit that there is but one method for ascertaining fact and truth—that conveyed by the word "scientific" in its most general and generous sense—no discovery in any branch of knowledge and inquiry could then disturb the faith that is religious. I should describe this faith as the unification of the self through allegiance to inclusive ideal ends, which imagination presents to us and to which the human will responds as worthy of controlling our desires and choices.

The aims and ideals that move us are generated through imagination. But they are not made out of imaginary stuff. They are made out of the hard stuff of the world of physical and social experience. The locomotive did not exist before Stevenson, nor the telegraph before the time of Morse. But the conditions for their existence were there in physical material and energies and in human capacity. Imagination seized hold upon the idea of a rearrangement of existing things that would evolve new objects. The same thing is true of a painter, a musician, a poet, a philanthropist, a moral prophet. The new vision does not arise out of nothing, but emerges through seeing, in terms of possibilities, that is, of imagination, old things in new relations serving a new end which the new end aids in creating.

Moreover the process of creation is experimental and continuous. The artist, scientific man, or good citizen, depends upon what others have done before him and are doing around him. The sense of new values that become ends to be realized arises first in dim and uncertain form. As the values are dwelt upon and carried forward in action they grow in definiteness and coherence. Interaction between aim and existent conditions improves and tests the ideal; and conditions are at the same time modified. Ideals change as they are applied in existent conditions. The process endures and advances with the life of humanity. What one person and one group accomplish becomes the standing ground and starting point of those who succeed them. When the vital factors in this natural process are generally acknowledged in emotion, thought and action, the process will be both accelerated and purified through elimination of that irrelevant element that culminates in the idea of the supernatural. When the vital factors attain the religious force that has been drafted into supernatural religions, the resulting reinforcement will be incalculable.

These considerations may be applied to the idea of God, or, to avoid misleading conceptions, to the idea of the divine. This idea, as I have said, is one of ideal possibilities unified through imaginative realization and projection. But this idea of God, or of the divine, is also connected with all the natural forces and conditions—including man and human association—that promote the growth of the ideal and that further its realization. We are in the presence neither of ideals completely embodied in existence nor yet of ideals that are mere rootless ideals, fantasies, utopias. For there are forces in nature and society that generate and support the ideals. They are further unified by the action that gives them coherence and solidity. It is this *active* relation between ideal and actual to which I would give the name "God." I would not insist that the name *must* be given. There are those who hold that the associations of the term with the supernatural are so numerous and close that any use of the word "God" is sure to give rise to misconception and be taken as a concession to traditional ideas.

They may be correct in this view. But the facts to which I have referred are there, and they need to be brought out with all possible clearness and force. There exist concretely and experimentally goods—the values of art in all its forms, of knowledge, of effort and of rest after striving, of education and fellowship, of friendship and love, of growth in mind and body. These goods are there and yet they are relatively embryonic. Many persons are shut out from generous participation in them; there are forces at work that threaten and sap existent goods as well as prevent their expansion. A clear and intense conception of a union of ideal ends with actual conditions is capable of arousing steady emotion. It may be fed by every experience, no matter what its material.

In a distracted age, the need for such an idea is urgent. It can unify interests and energies now dispersed; it can direct action and generate the heat of emotion and the light of intelligence. Whether one gives the name "God" to this union, operative in thought and action, is a matter for individual decision. But the *function* of such a working union of the ideal and actual seems to me to be identical with the force that has in fact been attached to the conception of God in all the religions that have a spiritual content; and a clear idea of that function seems to me urgently needed at the present time. . . .

In any case, whatever the name, the meaning is selective. For it involves no miscellaneous worship of everything in general. It selects those factors in existence that generate and support our idea of good as an end to be striven for. It excludes a multitude of forces that at any given time are irrelevant to this function. Nature produces whatever gives reinforcement and direction but also what occasions discord and confusion. The "divine" is thus a term of human choice and aspiration. A humanistic religion, if it excludes our relation to nature, is pale and thin, as it is presumptuous, when it takes humanity as an object of worship. Matthew Arnold's conception of a "power not ourselves" is too narrow in its reference to operative and sustaining conditions. While it is selective, it is too narrow in its basis of selection—righteousness. The conception thus needs to be widened in two ways. The powers that generate and support the good as experienced and as ideal, work *within* as well as without. There seems to be a reminiscence of an external Jehovah in Arnold's statement. And the powers work to enforce other values and ideals than righteousness. Arnold's sense of an opposition between Hellenism and Hebraism resulted in exclusion of beauty, truth, and friendship from the list of the consequences toward which powers work within and without.

In the relation between nature and human ends and endeavors, recent science has broken down the older dualism. It has been engaged in this task for three centuries. But as long as the conceptions of science were strictly mechanical (mechanical in the sense of assuming separate things acting upon one another purely externally by push and pull), religious apologists had a standing ground in pointing out the differences between man and physical nature. The differences could be used for arguing that something supernatural had intervened in the case of man. The recent acclaim, however, by apologists for religion of the surrender by science of the classic type of mechanicalism seems ill-advised from their own point of view. For the change in the modern scientific view of nature simply brings man and nature nearer together. We are no longer compelled to choose between explaining away what is distinctive in man through reducing him to another form of a mechanical model and the doctrine that something literally supernatural marks him off from nature. The less mechanical—in its older sense—physical nature is found to be, the closer is man to nature.

In his fascinating book, *The Dawn of Conscience,* James Henry Breasted refers to Haeckel as saying that the question he would most wish to have answered is this: Is the universe friendly to man? The question is an ambiguous one. Friendly to man in what respect? With respect to ease and comfort, to material success, to egoistic ambitions? Or to his aspiration to inquire and discover, to invent and create, to build a more secure order for human existence? In whatever form the question be put, the answer cannot in all honesty be an unqualified and absolute one. Mr. Breasted's answer, as a historian, is that nature has been friendly to the emergence and development of conscience and character. Those who will have all or nothing cannot be satisfied with this answer. Emergence and growth are not enough for them. They want something more than growth accompanied by toil and pain. They want final achievement. Others who are less absolutist may be content to think that, morally speaking, growth is a higher value and ideal than is sheer attainment. They will remember also that growth has not been confined to conscience and character; that it extends also to discovery, learning and knowledge, to creation in the arts, to furtherance of ties that hold men together in mutual aid and affection. These persons at least will be satisfied with an intellectual view of the religious function that is based on continuing choice directed toward ideal ends.

For, I would remind readers in conclusion, it is the intellectual side of the religious attitude that I have been considering. I have suggested that the religious element in life has been hampered by conceptions of the supernatural that were imbedded in those cultures wherein man had little control over outer nature and little in the way of sure method of inquiry and test. The crisis today as to the intellectual content of religious belief has been caused by the change in the intellectual climate due to the increase of our knowledge and our means of understanding. I have tried to show that this change is not fatal to the religious values in our common experience, however adverse its impact may be upon historic religions. Rather, provided that the methods and results of intelligence at work are frankly adopted, the change is liberating.

It clarifies our ideals, rendering them less subject to illusion and fantasy. It relieves us of the incubus of thinking of them as fixed, as without power of growth. It discloses that they develop in coherence and pertinency with increase of natural intelligence. The change gives aspiration for natural knowledge a definitely religious character, since growth in understanding of nature is seen to be organically related to the formation of ideal ends. The same change enables man to select those elements in natural conditions that may be organized to support and extend the sway of ideals. All purpose is selective, and all intelligent action includes deliberate choice. In the degree in which we cease to depend upon belief in the supernatural, selection is enlightened and choice can be made in behalf of ideals whose inherent relations to conditions and consequences are understood. Were the naturalistic foundations and bearings of religion grasped, the religious element in life would emerge from the throes of the crisis in religion. Religion would then be found to have its natural place in every aspect of human experience that is concerned with estimate of possibilities, with emotional stir by possibilities as yet unrealized, and with all action in behalf of their realization. All that is significant in human experience falls within this frame.

SUGGESTED READINGS

John Stuart Mill's *Three Essays on Religion* carry on the Humean tradition of dispassionate scrutiny of religious doctrine. All three are important, though the third, "Theism," is specially relevant here. Sir L. Stephen, in "An Agnostic's Apology" (reprinted in a book by that name), helped to make popular a term coined by T. H. Huxley in *Science and the Christian Tradition*. These writers are concerned in large part with the problem of evil, which has always proven a difficulty for theists. It is discussed almost as frequently as, and often in connection with, the free will issue. See, for example, St. Augustine, *City of God*, Book XI, 16–18 and Book XII, 1–9. R. A. Tsanoff, *The Nature of Evil*, presents a survey of discussions of the problem, together with his own views. J. S. Whale, *The Christian Answer to the Problem of Evil*, and F. Petit, *The Problem of Evil*, are two recent attempts by religious writers to deal with the question.

J. M. E. McTaggart's *Some Dogmas of Religion* examines a number of widely held religious beliefs and concludes that there is no rational justification for holding them; Chapters 6–8 are most relevant to Theism. The book is clear, careful, and well worth serious study. McTaggart thought himself able to demonstrate the truth of human pre-existence and immortality, but he did not believe in any sort of personal god. For an outline of his metaphysical position, see "An Ontological Idealism," in *Philosophical Studies*.

J. M. Robertson's *Short History of Free Thought* discusses many criticisms of theism by atheists. B. Russell's views are available in several sources; see, for example, *Why I Am Not a Christian*. For a general survey of atheistic positions and arguments, see the article on "Atheism" in the *Encyclopedia of Philosophy*, edited by P. Edwards.

A Defense of Naturalism

Naturalism is not a specific philosophy; it is rather a principle of interpretation, common to a variety of different philosophical positions. According to this principle, every aspect of the world, including human experience, can and should be interpreted in terms of the methods of the sciences. As a result, all naturalists agree in denying the existence of a realm above or beyond nature and in rejecting attempts to interpret all of nature in terms of some entity not accessible to empirical investigation.

Some naturalists, in fact, reject any attempt to construct a more unified world-view than can be attained through applying the methods of science to a series of specific problems. According to these naturalists, all meaningful problems about nature or man are scientific problems and can be answered only by the application of scientific methods. In their opinion it is not legitimate for philosophy to offer unconfirmed hypotheses about the world as a whole. The task of philosophy ought to be confined to the analysis of the methods of science and to the clarification of concepts and issues that arise in the sciences and in daily life.

Other naturalists believe that the scope of philosophy need not be confined to analysis. They hold that philosophers may legitimately attempt to construct a comprehensive world view, but they insist that any comprehensive philosophic theory should be founded on, and compatible with, scientific knowledge. This form of naturalism goes beyond the merely methodological principle common to all naturalism—that the methods and results of science form our most reliable knowledge—because it seeks to construct a world view that systematically brings together the results of science into one unified whole.

The reading from NAGEL defines the basic theses of naturalism and considers their application to human life and history. In his defense of naturalism, Nagel is particularly concerned to guard against misunderstandings that might result from a too hasty interpretation of its central ideas. He then examines and rejects two lines of attack currently leveled against a naturalistic world view.

Naturalism Reconsidered[*]

ERNEST NAGEL [1901–   ] taught philosophy at Columbia University from 1931 until 1966, when he assumed the chair of philosophy at Rockefeller University. A leading spokesman for contemporary naturalism, he has written extensively on logic, the philosophy of science, and special problems in scientific method.

It is surely not the highest reach for a philosopher to be a combatant in the perennial wars between standardized "isms" which fill conventional handbooks of philosophy. Philosophy at its best is a critical commentary upon existence and upon our claims to have knowledge of it; and its mission is to help illuminate what is obscure in experience and its objects, rather than to profess creeds or to repeat the battle-cries of philosophical schools aiming at intellectual hegemony. The conception of philosophy as a struggle between competing systems is especially sterile when the "ism" defended or attacked covers as miscellaneous an assortment of not always congruous views as fly the banner of naturalism. The number of distinguishable doctrines for which the word "naturalism" has been a counter in the history of thought, is notorious. Even among contemporaries who proclaim themselves to be naturalists in philosophy, there are not only important differences in stress and perspective, but also in specific doctrines professed and in intellectual methods used to support commitments made. I am aware, therefore, that in taking naturalism as my subject this evening, I run the risk of becoming involved in futile polemics—a risk made graver by the fact that although the stated title of my address may have aroused different expectations, it is not my intention to recant and to confess past errors. I must explain why, notwithstanding the hazards of my theme, I have elected to discuss it.

The past quarter century has been for philosophy in many parts of the world a period of acute self-questioning, engendered in no small measure by developments in scientific and logical thought, and in part no doubt by fundamental changes in the social order. In any event, there has come about a general loss of confidence in the competence of philosophy to provide by

* From Nagel: "Naturalism Reconsidered," The Presidential Address to the American Philosophical Association, Eastern Division, 1954. From *Proceedings and Addresses of The American Philosophical Association*, XXVIII. Reprinted by permission of The American Philosophical Association, and the author.

way of a distinctive intellectual method a basic ground-plan of the cosmos, or for that matter to contribute to knowledge of any primary subject-matter except by becoming a specialized positive science and subjecting itself to the discipline of empirical inquiry. Although the abysses of human ignorance are undeniably profound, it has also become apparent that ignorance, like actual knowledge, is of many special and heterogeneous things; and we have come to think, like the fox and unlike the hedgehog of whom Mr. Isaiah Berlin has recently reminded us, that there are a great many things which are already known or remain to be discovered, but that there is no one "big thing" which, if known, would make everything else coherent and unlock the mystery of creation. In consequence, many of us have ceased to emulate the great system-builders in the history of philosophy. In partial imitation of the strategy of modern science, and in the hope of achieving responsibly held conclusions about matters concerning which we could acquire genuine competence, we have tended to become specialists in our professional activities. We have come to direct our best energies to the resolution of limited problems and puzzles that emerge in the analysis of scientific and ordinary discourse, in the evaluation of claims to knowledge, in the interpretation and validation of ethical and esthetic judgments, and in the assessment of types of human experience. I hope I shall not be regarded as offensive in stating my impression that the majority of the best minds among us have turned away from the conception of the philosopher as the spectator of all time and existence, and have concentrated on restricted but manageable questions, with almost deliberate unconcern for the bearing of their often minute investigations upon an inclusive view of nature and man.

Some of us, I know, are distressed by the widespread scepticism of the traditional claims for a *philosophia perennis,* and have dismissed as utterly trivial most if not all the products of various current forms of analytical philosophy. I do not share this distress, nor do I think the dismissal is uniformly perspicacious and warranted. For in my judgment, the scepticism which many deplore is well-founded. Even though a fair-sized portion of recent analytical literature seems inconsequential also to me, analytical philosophy in our own day is the continuation of a major philosophic tradition, and can count substantial feats of clarification among its assets. Concentration on limited and determinate problems has yielded valuable fruits, not least in the form of an increased and refreshing sensitivity to the demands of responsible discourse.

On the other hand, philosophers like other men conduct their lives within the framework of certain comprehensive if not always explicit assumptions about the world they inhabit. These assumptions color evaluations of major ideals and proposed policies. I also suspect that the directions taken by analyses of specific intellectual problems are frequently if subtly controlled by the expressed or tacit beliefs philosophers hold concerning the over-all nature of things, by their views on human destiny, and by their conceptions of the scope of human reason. But conversely, resolutions of special problems made plausible by recent philosophical analysis, as well as by the findings of various positive sciences, seem to me to support certain broad generalizations about the cosmos and to disconfirm others. It is clearly desirable that such basic intellectual commitments, which are at once the matrix and the outcome of inquiries into specific problems, be made as explicit as possible. A philospher who is a reflective man by profession, certainly owes it to himself to articulate, if only occasionally, what sort of world he thinks he inhabits, and to make clear to himself where approximately lies the center of his convictions.

The discharge of the important obligations which is mine this evening, seems to me an appropriate occasion for stating as simply and as succinctly as I can the substance of those intellectual commitments I like to call "naturalism." The label itself is of no importance, but I use it partly because of its historical associations, and partly because it is a reminder that the doctrines for which it is a name are neither new nor untried. With Santayana, I prefer not to accept in philosophic debate what I do not believe when I am not arguing; and naturalism as I construe it merely formulates what centuries of human experience have repeatedly confirmed. At any rate, naturalism seems to me a sound generalized account of the world encountered in practice and in critical reflection, and a just perspective upon the human scene. I wish to state briefly and hence with little supporting argument what I take to be its major tenets, and to defend it against some recent criticisms.

Claims to knowledge cannot ultimately be divorced from an evaluation of the intellectual methods used to support those claims. It is nevertheless unfortunate that in recent years naturalists in philosophy have so frequently permitted their allegiance to a dependable method of inquiry to obscure their substantive views on things in general. For it is the inclusive intellectual image of nature and man which naturalism supplies that sets it off from other comprehensive philosophies. In my conception of it, at any rate, naturalism embraces a generalized account of the cosmic scheme and of man's place in it, as well as a logic of inquiry.

I hasten to add, however, that naturalism does not offer a theory of nature in the sense that Newtonian mechanics, for example, provides a theory of motion. Naturalism does not, like the latter, specify a set of substantive principles with the help of which the detailed course of concrete happenings can be explained or understood. Moreover, the principles affirmed by naturalism are not proposed as competitors or underpinnings for any of the special theories which the positive sciences assert. Nor, finally, does naturalism offer its general view of nature and man as the product of some special philosophical mode of knowing. The account of things proposed by naturalism is a distillation from knowledge acquired in the usual way in daily encounters with the world or in specialized scientific inquiry. Naturalism articulates features of the world which, because they have become so obvious, are rarely mentioned in discussions of special subject-matter, but which distinguish our actual world from other conceivable worlds. The major affirmations of naturalism are accordingly meager in content; but the principles affirmed are nevertheless effective guides in responsible criticism and evaluation.

Two theses seem to me central to naturalism as I conceive it. The first is the existential and causal primacy of organized matter in the executive order of nature. This is the assumption that the occurrence of events, qualities and processes, and the characteristic behaviors of various individuals, are contingent on the organization of spatio-temporally located bodies, whose internal structures and external relations determine and limit the appearance and disappearance of everything that happens. That this is so, is one of the best-tested conclusions of experience. We are frequently ignorant of the special conditions under which things come into being or pass away; but we have also found repeatedly that when we look closely, we eventually ascertain at least the approximate and gross conditions under which events occur, and we discover that those conditions invariably consist of some more or less complex organization of material substances. Naturalism does not maintain that only what is material exists, since many things noted in experience, for example, modes of action, relations of meaning, dreams, joys, plans, aspirations, are not as such material bodies or organizations of material bodies. What naturalism does assert as a truth about nature is that though *forms* of behavior or *functions* of material systems are indefeasibly parts of nature, forms and functions are not themselves agents in their own realization or in the realization of anything else. In the conception of nature's processes which naturalism affirms, there is no place for the operation of disembodied forces, no place for an immaterial spirit directing the course of events, no place for the survival of personality after the corruption of the body which exhibits it.

The second major contention of naturalism is that the manifest plurality and variety of things, of their qualities and their functions, are an irreducible feature of the cosmos, not a deceptive appearance cloaking some more homogeneous "ultimate reality" or transempirical substance, and that the sequential orders in which events occur or the manifold relations of dependence in which things exist are *contingent* connections, not the embodiments of a fixed and unified pattern of logically necessary links. The existential primacy of organized matter does not make illusory either the relatively permanent or the comparatively transient characters and forms which special configurations of bodies may possess. In particular, although the continued existence of the human scene is precarious and is dependent on a balance of forces that doubtless will not endure indefinitely, and even though its distinctive traits are not pervasive throughout space, it is nonetheless as much a part of the "ultimate" furniture of the world, and is as genuine a sample of what "really" exists, as are atoms and stars. There undoubtedly occur integrated systems of bodies, such as biological organisms, which have the capacity because of their material organization to maintain themselves and the direction of their characteristic activities. But there is no positive evidence, and much negative evidence, for the supposition that all existential structures are teleological systems in this sense, or for the view that whatever occurs is a phase in a unitary, teleologically organized, and all-inclusive process or system. Modern physical cosmology does indeed supply some evidence for definite patterns of evolutionary development of stars, galactic systems, and even of the entire physical universe; and it is quite possible that the stage of cosmic evolution reached at any given time causally limits the types of things which can occur during that period. On the other hand, the patterns of change investigated in physical cosmogony are not patterns that are exhaustive of everything that happens; and nothing in these current physical speculations requires the conclusion that changes in one star or galaxy are related by inherent necessity to every action of biological organisms in some remote planet. Even admittedly teleological systems contain parts and processes which are causally irrelevant to some of the activities maintained by those systems; and the causal dependencies known to hold between the parts of any system, teleological or not, have never been successfully established as forms of logically necessary relations. In brief, if naturalism is true, irreducible variety and logical contingency are fundamental traits of the world we actually inhabit. The orders and connections of things are all accessible to rational inquiry; but these orders and connections are not all derivable by deductive methods from any set of premises that deductive reason can certify.

It is in this framework of general ideas that naturalism envisages the career and destiny of man. Naturalism views the emergence and the continuance of human society as dependent on physical and physiological conditions that have not always obtained, and that will not permanently endure. But it does not in consequence regard man and his works as intrusions into nature, any more than it construes as intrusions the presence of heavenly bodies or of terrestrial protozoa. The stars are no more foreign to the cosmos than are men, even if the conditions for the existence of both stars and men are realized only occasionally or only in a few regions. Indeed, the conception of human life as a war with nature, as a struggle with an implacable foe that has doomed man to extinction, is but an inverted theology, with a malicious Devil in the seat of Omnipotence. It is a conception that is immodest as well as anthropomorphic in the importance it imputes to man in the scheme of things.

On the other hand, the affirmation that nature is man's "home" as much as it is the "home" of anything else, and the denial that cosmic forces are *intent* on destroying the human scene, do not warrant the interpretation that every sector of nature is explicable in terms of traits known to characterize only human individuals and human actions. Man undoubtedly possesses characteristics which are shared by everything that exists; but he also manifests traits and capacities that appear to be distinctive of him. Is anything gained but confusion when all forms of dependence between things, whether animate or inanimate, and all types of behaviors they display, are subsumed under distinctions that have an identifiable content only in reference to the human psyche? Measured by the illumination they bring, there is nothing to differentiate the thesis that human traits are nothing but the properties of bides which can be formulated exclusively in the language of current physical theory, from the view that every change and every mode of operation, in whatever sector of the cosmos it may be encountered, is simply an illustration of some category pertinent to the description of human behavior.

Indeed, even some professed naturalists sometimes appear to promote the confusion when they make a fetish of continuity. Naturalists usually stress the emergence of novel forms in physical and biological evolution, thereby emphasizing the fact that human traits are not identical with the traits from which they emerge. Nevertheless, some distinguished contemporary naturalists also insist, occasionally with overtones of anxiety, that there is a "continuity" between the typically human on the one hand, and the physical and biological on the other. But is man's foothold in the scheme of things really made more secure by showing that his distinctive traits are in some sense "continuous" with features pervasive in nature, and would man's place in nature be less secure if such continuity did not obtain? The actual evidence for a continuity of development is conclusive in some instances of human traits, however it may be in others. But I sometimes suspect that the cardinal importance philosophers assign to the alleged universality of such continuity is a lingering survival of that ancient conception, according to which things are intelligible only when seen as teleological systems producing definite ends, so that nature itself is properly understood only when construed as the habitat of human society. In any event, a naturalism that is not provincial in its outlook will not accept the intellectual incorporation of man into nature at the price of reading into all the processes of the cosmos the passions, the strivings, the defeats and the glories of human life, and then exhibiting man as the most adequate, because most representative, expression of nature's inherent constitution. No, a mature naturalism seeks to understand what man is, not in terms of a discovered or postulated continuity between what is distinctive of him and what is pervasive in all things. Without denying that even the most distinctive human traits are dependent on things which are non-human, a mature naturalism attempts to assess man's nature in the light of *his* actions and achievements, *his* aspirations and capacities, *his* limitations and tragic failures, and *his* splendid works of ingenuity and imagination.

Human nature and history, in short, are *human* nature and history, not the history and nature of anything else, however much knowledge of other things contributes to a just appraisal of what man is. In particular, the adequacy of proposed ideals for human life must be judged, not in terms of their causes and origins, but in reference to how the pursuit and possible realization of ideals contribute to the organization and release of *human* energies. Men are animated by many springs of action, no one of which is intrinsically good or evil; and a moral ideal is the imagined satisfaction of some complex of impulses, desires, and needs. When ideals are handled responsibly, they therefore function as hypotheses for achieving a balanced exercise of human powers. Moral ideals are not self-certifying, any more than are the theories of the physical sciences; and evidence drawn from experienced satisfactions is required to validate them, however difficult may be the process of sifting and weighing the available data. Moral problems arise from a conflict of specific impulses and interests. They cannot, however, be effectively resolved by invoking standards derived from the study of non-human nature, or of what is allegedly beyond nature. If moral problems can be resolved at all, they can be resolved only in the light of specific human capacities, historical circumstances and acquired skills, and the opportunities (revealed by an imagination disciplined by knowledge) for altering the physical and social environment and for redirecting habitual behaviors. Moreover, since human virtues are in part the products of the society in which human powers are matured, a naturalistic moral theory is at the same time a critique of civilization, that is, a critique of the institutions that channel human energies, so as to exhibit the possibilities and limitations of various forms and arrangements of society for bringing enduring satisfactions to individual human careers.

These are the central tenets of what I take to be philosophical naturalism. They are tenets which are supported by compelling empirical evidence, rather than dicta based on dogmatic preference. In my view of it, naturalism does not dismiss every other differing conception of the scheme of things as logically impossible; and it does not rule out all alternatives to itself on *a priori* grounds. It is possible, I think, to conceive without logical inconsistency a world in which disembodied forces are dynamic agents, or in which whatever happens is a manifestation of an unfolding logical pattern. In such possible worlds it would be an error to be a naturalist. But philosophy is not identical with pure mathematics, and its ultimate concern is with the actual world, even though philosophy must take cognizance of the fact that the actual world contains creatures who can envisage possible worlds and who employ different logical procedures for deciding which hypothetical world is the actual one. It is partly for this reason that contemporary naturalists devote so much attention to methods of evaluating evidence. When naturalists give their allegiance to the method of intelligence commonly designated as the method of modern empirical science, they do so because that method appears to be the most assured way of achieving reliable knowledge.

As judged by that method, the evidence in my opinion is at present conclusive for the truth of naturalism, and it is tempting to suppose that no one familiar with the evidence can fail to acknowledge that philosophy. Indeed, some commentators there are who assert that all philosophies are at bottom only expressions in different idioms of the same conceptions about the nature of things, so that the strife of philosophic systems is mainly a conflict over essentially linguistic matters. Yet many thinkers for whom I have a profound respect explicitly reject naturalism, and their espousal of contrary views seem to me incompatible with the irenic claim that we really are in agreement on fundamentals.

Although I do not have the time this evening to consider systematically the criticisms currently made of naturalism, I do wish to examine briefly two repeatedly voiced objections which, if valid, would in my opinion seriously jeopardize the integrity and adequacy of naturalism as a philosophy. Stated summarily, the first objection is that in relying exclusively on the logico-empirical method of modern science for establishing cognitive claims, naturalists are in effect stacking the cards in their own favor, since thereby all alternative philosophies are antecedently disqualified. It is maintained, for example, that naturalism rejects any hypothesis about trans-empirical causes or time-transcending spiritual substances as factors in the order of things, not because such hypotheses are actually shown to be false, but simply because the logic of proof adopted dismisses as irrelevant any evidence which might establish them.

This criticism does not seem to me to have merit: the logico-empirical method of evaluating cognitive claims to which naturalists subscribe does not eliminate by fiat any hypothesis about existence for which evidence can be procured, that is, evidence that in the last resort can be obtained through sensory or introspective observation. Thus, anyone who asserts a hypothesis postulating a trans-empirical ground for all existence, presumably seeks to understand in terms of that ground the actual occurrences in nature, and to account thereby for what actually happens as distinct from what is merely imagined to happen. There must therefore be some connection between the postulated character of the hypothetical trans-empirical ground, and the empirically observable traits in the world around us; for otherwise the hypothesis is otiose, and not relevant to the spatio-temporal processes of nature. This does not mean, as some critics of naturalism suppose the latter to maintain, that the hypothetical trans-empirical ground must be characterized exclusively in terms of the observable properties of the world, any more than that the sub-microscopic particles and processes which current physical theory postulates must be logical constructions out of the observable traits of macroscopic objects. But it does mean that unless the hypothesis implies, even if only by a circuitous route, some statements about empirical data, it is not adequate to the task for which it is proposed. If naturalists reject hypotheses about trans-empirical substances, they do not do so arbitrarily. They reject such hypotheses either because their relevance to the going concerns of nature is not established, or because, though their relevance is not in question, the actual evidence does not support them.

Nor does naturalism dismiss as unimportant and without consideration experiences such as of the holy, of divine illumination, or of mystical ecstasy, experiences which are of the greatest moment in the lives of many men, and which are often taken to signify the presence and operation of some purely spiritual reality. Such experiences have dimensions of meaning for those who have undergone them, that are admittedly not on par with the import of more common experiences like those of physical hunger, general well-being, or feelings of remorse and guilt. Yet such experiences are nonetheless events among other events; and though they may be evidence for something, their sheer occurrence does not certify *what* they are evidence for, any more than the sheer occurrence of dreams, hopes, and delusions authenticates the actual existence of their ostensible objects. In particular, whether the experience labelled as an experience of divine illumination is evidence for the existence of a divinity, is a question to be settled by inquiry, not by dogmatic affirmations or denials. When naturalists refuse to acknowledge, merely on the strength of such experiences, the operation or presence of a divine power, they do so not because their commitment to a logical method prevents them from treating it seriously, but because independent inquiry fails to confirm it. Knowledge is knowledge, and cannot without confusion be identified with intuitive insight or with the vivid immediacy of profoundly moving experiences. Claims to knowledge must be capable of being tested; and the testing must be conducted by eventual reference to such evidence as counts in the responsible conduct of everyday affairs as well as of systematic inquiry in the sciences. Naturalists are therefore not engaged in question-begging when, through the use of the logic of scientific intelligence, they judge non-naturalistic accounts of the order of things to be unfounded.

There is, however, a further objection to naturalism, to the effect that in committing itself to the logic of scientific proof, it is quite analogous to religious belief in resting on unsupported and indemonstrable faith. For that logic allegedly involves assumptions like the uniformity of nature or similar principles which transcend experience, cannot be justified empirically, and yet provide the premises that constitute the ultimate warrant for the conclusions of empirical inquiry. But if naturalism is thus based on unprovable articles of faith, on what cogent grounds can it reject a different conception of the true order of governance of events which rests on a different faith?

I cannot here deal adequately with the complex issues raised by this objection. Its point is not satisfactorily turned by claiming, as some have done, that instead of being articles of faith, the alleged indemonstrable postulates of scientific method are simply rules of the scientific game which *define* what in that game is to be understood by the words "knowledge" and "evidence." As I see it, however, the objection has force only for those whose ideal of reason is demonstration, and who therefore refuse to dignify anything as genuine knowledge unless it is demonstrable from self-luminous and self-evident premises. But if, as I also think, that ideal is not universally appropriate, and if, furthermore, a *wholesale* justification for knowledge and its methods is an unreasonable demand and a misplaced effort, the objection appears as quite pointless. The warrant for a proposition about some specific inter-relations of events does not derive from a faith in the uniformity of nature or in other principles with a cosmic scope. The warrant derives exclusively from the specific evidence available for that proposition, and from the contingent historical fact that the special ways employed in obtaining and appraising the evidence have been generally effective in yielding reliable knowledge. Subsequent inquiry may show that we were mistaken in accepting a proposition on the evidence available earlier; and further inquiry may also reveal that a given inductive policy, despite a record of successful past performance, requires correction if not total rejection. Fortunately, however, we are not always mistaken in accepting various propositions or in employing certain inductive policies, even though we are unable to demonstrate that we shall never fall into error. Accordingly, though many of our hopes for the stability of beliefs in the face of fresh experience may turn out to be baseless, and though no guarantees can be given that our most assured claims to knowledge may not eventually need revision, in adopting scientific method as the instrument for evaluating claims to knowledge, naturalists are not subscribing to an indemonstrable faith.

The bitter years of cataclysmic wars and social upheavals through which our generation has been passing have also witnessed a general decline of earlier hopes in the possibilities of modern science for achieving a liberal and humane civilization. Indeed, as is well known, many men have become convinced that the progress and spread of science, and the consequent secularization of society, are the prime sources of our present ills; and a not inconsiderable number of thinkers have made widely popular various revived forms of older religious and irrationalistic philosophies as guides to human salvation. Moreover, since naturalists have not abandoned their firm adherence to the method of scientific intelligence, naturalism has been repeatedly charged with insensitivity toward spiritual values, with a shallow optimism toward science as an instrument for ennobling the human estate, and with a philistine blindness toward the ineradicable miseries of human existence. I want to conclude with a few brief comments on these allegations.

It is almost painful to have to make a point of the elementary fact that whatever may happen to be the range of special interests and sensibilities of individual naturalists, there is no incompatibility, whether logical or psychological, between maintaining that warranted knowledge is secured only through the use of a definite logical method, and recognizing that the world can be experienced in many other ways than by knowing it. It is a matter of record that outstanding exponents of naturalism, in our own time as well as in the past, have exhibited an unequaled and tender sensitivity to the esthetic and moral dimensions of human experience; and they have been not only movingly eloquent celebrants of the role of moral idealism and of intellectual and esthetic contemplation in human life, but also vigorous defenders of the distinctive character of these values against facile attempts to reduce them to something else.

It seems to me singularly inept, moreover, to indict naturalism as a philosophy without a sense for the tragic aspects of life. For unlike many worldviews, naturalism offers no cosmic consolation for the unmerited defeats and undeserved sufferings which all men experience in one form or another. It has never sought to conceal its view of human destiny as an episode between two oblivions. To be sure, naturalism is not a philosophy of despair. For one facet in its radical pluralism is the truth that a human good is nonetheless a good, despite its transitory existence. There doubtless are foolish optimists among those professing naturalism, though naturalism has no monopoly in this respect, and it is from other quarters that one usually receives glad tidings of a universal nostrum. But in any event, neither the pluralism so central to naturalism, nor its cultivation of scientific reason, is compatible with any dogmatic assumption to the effect that men can be liberated from *all* the sorrows and evils to which they are now heirs, through the eventual advances of science and the institution of appropriate physical and social innovations. Indeed, why suppose that a philosophy which is wedded to the use of the sober logic of scientific intelligence, should thereby be committed to the dogma that there are no irremediable evils? On the contrary, human reason is potent only against evils that are *remediable*. At the same time, since it is impossible to decide responsibly, *antecedent* to inquiry, *which* of the many human ills can be mitigated if not eradicated by extending the operations of scientific reason into human affairs, naturalism is not a philosophy of *general* renunciation, even though it recognizes that it is the better part of wisdom to be equally resigned to what, in the light of available evidence, cannot be avoided. Human reason is not an omnipotent instrument for the achievement of human goods; but it is the only instrument we do possess, and it is not a contemptible one. Although naturalism is acutely sensitive to the actual limitations of rational effort, those limitations do not warrant a romantic philosophy of general despair, and they do not blind naturalism to the possibilities implicit in the exercise of disciplined reason for realizing human excellence.

SUGGESTED READINGS

One of the chief tasks of a naturalistic view is to offer an account of religious experience and religious institutions which does not explain them in terms of any supernatural being. German scholars and philosophers during the nineteenth century did much work on this problem. L. Feuerbach's *Essence of Christianity* is a classic attempt to explain religion in terms of the projection of man's desires and fears onto the universe, and D. Strauss's *Life of Jesus* is one of the first attempts to write about Christ in purely secular historical terms. Marx and Engels are as much concerned with the institutional structure of Christianity as they are with its personal side; their opinions are conveniently collected in a volume entitled *Marx and Engels on Religion*. Freud is another pioneer in the scientific study of religion. In *Moses and Monotheism, Totem and Taboo*, and *The Future of an Illusion*, he applies the insights of psychoanalysis to various aspects of religion. More recently Erik H. Erikson has written a fascinating study on *Young Man*

Luther from a psychoanalytic point of view. Many recent theologians have used psychoanalytic concepts in interpreting and defending religious experience and religious belief. Particularly noteworthy in this connection is Paul Tillich's *The Courage to Be.*

For a set of short, sometimes difficult, usually illuminating, essays on the meaning of religious questions, the reader should see J. Wisdom, *Paradox and Discovery,* I–V.

E. A. Burtt's *Types of Religious Philosophy,* Chapters 5, 6, and 9, gives an elementary survey of various nonreligious world views that are sometimes held as substitutes for religious beliefs. Chapter 2 of J. Dewey's *Experience and Nature* presents some of his central views. B. Russell has stated his position with his usual vigor in *A Free Man's Worship.* Sartre's nonreligious existentialism is outlined in *Existentialism Is a Humanism.*

Any thorough study of Naturalism should include a careful reading of "Nature," the first of the *Three Essays on Religion* by J. S. Mill.